# Introduction

This book has been designed to help students focus on God's principles and Christian values and beliefs. Students are presented with stories about children facing problems and dilemmas common in everyday life. Following each story are questions and activities students can think about and answer/complete to help them further grow in God's love.

In each story, readers have the opportunity to respond to the characters and the choices they make, their behavior, or the situation presented in a variety of ways. Students are also directed to find and read specific Bible verses relating to each story and to consider what Jesus might say or do in the situation or what he would expect a Christian to say or do. Students will have opportunities to think about how they can apply what they have learned in their own daily lives to the situations.

The stories included incorporate such issues as telling the truth, making false accusations, gossiping, teasing, stealing, getting even, using bad language, prejudice, cheating, obeying one's parents, caring about others, and controlling one's emotions. Students will respond by practicing such valuable skills as predicting outcomes, thinking critically, making inferences, drawing conclusions, determining the cause and the effect of an action, and more as they answer questions and complete stimulating, challenging activities.

Also included on page 32 are situations the students can read and respond to to further increase their awareness of how Jesus would react and want them to react. It also helps the students set up journals to record their responses to these types of situations.

Parents and teachers alike can participate with students to further discuss the stories presented. Reading the selections, answering the questions, and completing the activities are an effective way for students to reinforce God's principles and Christian values.

GP275001 WWJD © Grace Publications

# I Didn't Take It

Mr. Alan thought he had put his grade book in the top drawer of his desk along with the tests he had corrected last night. That's where he always put it, but it wasn't there, nor was it in his briefcase.

"Boys and girls," began Mr. Alan, "my grade book isn't in my desk where I usually keep it. Did anyone happen to notice it?"

"I saw Josie at your desk when you were out in the hall talking to the principal. I bet she took it," blurted Bruce, the class tattletale. Bruce knew Josie didn't take it, but he thought it would be fun to get her into trouble.

Unfortunately, Josie was recently involved in another conflict, so Mr. Alan couldn't help but wonder.

"Were you at my desk, Josie?" asked Mr. Alan.

"Yes, but I was only using the big dictionary," she said.

"Did you happen to notice my grade book?" he asked.

"No," said Josie, "and I didn't take it, either. What would I want with your grade book?" Then she started to cry. "Really, Mr. Alan, you've gotta believe me! I'd never do anything like that!" Josie was, in fact, telling the truth.

By this time, Bruce was quietly laughing at all the commotion he had helped create.

1. Pretend you are Josie. Describe your feelings. Tell why you feel the way you do. _____

_____

_____

_____

# I Didn't Take It continued

2. If Jesus were to suddenly appear, what do you think he would say to Bruce about falsely accusing Josie of something he knows she didn't do?

_____

_____

3. Jesus was also a victim of false accusations. People knew he was innocent, but they lied anyway. They wanted to get rid of Jesus and his teachings. Read Mark 14:53–65 to find out how Jesus reacted to his accusers. Tell what surprised you most and why. _____

_____

_____

4. What does this story show you about Jesus and his relationship with God?

_____

5. If you had been Josie, how might you have responded more like Jesus?

_____

_____

The mystery of the missing grade book remained unsolved until Mr. Alan got home that afternoon. Mr. Alan found his grade book on the dining room table where he had been correcting the tests last night. It had gotten mixed in with yesterday's paper and the mail.

6. Imagine it's the next morning. What do you think Mr. Alan should say to Josie? What do you think Bruce should say to Josie?

GP275001 WWJD © Grace Publications

# But I Really Want It

Matt decided to finish his homework before talking to his mother about something really important to him.

"Look, Mom. Here's the ad I was telling you about. It's for Turbo Man, the newest and best computer game ever. Can I get it? All my friends are getting it. Oh, Mom, please. It's only 50 dollars. I've never wanted anything more than I want this computer game. I won't ever ask for another game after this."

Mrs. Jameson quietly said to Matt, "I'd like you to count all the computer games you have already." Matt counted 15.

"And how many of them do you actually play?" she asked.

"Maybe one or two," answered Matt, "but I really really want this one."

"Matt," began Mrs. Jameson, "you say that every time you want something new. Just look around your room at all the things you have and almost never use."

"But, Mom . . ."

1. Do you think Matt has good reasons for wanting the game? _____

   Why or why not? _____

   _____

   _____

3/12

# But I Really Want It continued

2. Matt appears to believe that happiness depends on getting the things he wants. Think about what usually happens after Matt gets something. What might Jesus say to Matt about possessions and happiness? Read Luke 12:13–21 to help you.

3. Is there a game, toy, or some other object you want as much as Matt seems to want Turbo Man? What is it? _____

   List all the reasons why you want it. _____

   _____

   _____

   _____

   _____

4. Think about what you want as you answer the questions below.

   - Is it something you must have to live?          _____

   - Will it help make you a better person?          _____

   - Will it bring you unending happiness?          _____

   - Will it bring you closer to God?          _____

5. Now try to consider what Jesus might say, the reasons why you want that toy, game, or item, and how you answered the four questions before you try to pressure your parents into buying it for you.

GP275001 WWJD © Grace Publications

# Have You Heard?

"Hey, Tara," said Hayley, "have you heard about Lindsay Anderson's parents?"

"No," answered Tara. "What about them?"

"Well," began Hayley, "Samantha told me that Mary Beth overheard Lindsay's mom telling Mrs. Larsen that she and her husband are going to be separated. I bet they're gonna get a divorce."

"Wow!" exclaimed Tara. "That's too bad. Maybe that's why Lindsay has been acting so weird the last few days."

"Yeah, you're right about that," said Hayley.

"Let's go talk to Meredith. She lives next door to Lindsay. Maybe she knows what's going on," said Tara.

Hayley and Tara rode their bikes to Meredith's house. Meredith was in the backyard. After greeting one another, Hayley said, "Hey, Meredith. We've got something to ask you."

"What?" asked Meredith.

"Well," began Hayley, "we heard that Lindsay's parents are getting a divorce. Is that true?"

Just then, Lindsay walked into the backyard, but the girls did not see or hear her.

"Hi, everybody," said Lindsay. "Is what true?"

1. Hayley, Tara, and Meredith looked at each other and then at Lindsay. How would you answer Lindsay, if you were Tara, Hayley, or Meredith?

_____

_____

_____

# Have You Heard? continued

2. Tara and Hayley are guilty of spreading the rumor they had heard about Lindsay's parents. Sometimes a rumor is completely false. Sometimes a rumor is only partially true and changes as one person tells another. By the time the rumor about Lindsay's parents reached Meredith, it had changed. How? _____

_____

3. Tara and Hayley told Lindsay about the rumor they had heard—and had helped to spread. If you were Lindsay, how would you feel about your friends and the rumor that they were spreading? Why?_____

_____

_____

Lindsay was upset at first.

"How could you?" cried Lindsay. "And why didn't you say something to me when you first heard the story? By the way, it isn't true. My parents are not getting a divorce."

"Oh," said Tara and Hayley. "We're glad about that. We're also sorry for gossiping."

"The truth is," said Lindsay, "that my dad has to go to Europe for six months, and we can't go with him. He's leaving this weekend, and the separation is going to be really hard on us."

4. The Bible is very clear about a person who is a gossip. *A perverse man stirs up dissension, and a gossip separates close friends.* (Proverbs 16:28) *A gossip betrays a confidence; so avoid a man who talks too much.* (Proverbs 20:19) Tell what you think Jesus would want you to do the next time you hear a bad rumor about someone.

_____

_____

_____

_____

GP275001 WWJD © Grace Publications

# Stop Teasing Me!

Calvin's little brother, Leonard, can be a big pest. At least that's what Calvin tells his friends. Wherever Calvin goes, Leonard wants to go, and whatever Calvin does, Leonard wants to do, too. Leonard thinks Calvin is pretty cool most of the time. Calvin loves his brother, too, but sometimes he just doesn't want him hanging around. That's when Calvin resorts to teasing.

"Whatcha doin', Calvin?" asked Leonard one morning.

"Looking at my car," answered Calvin.

"Can I see it, too?" asked Leonard.

Calvin held up the car and said, "See."

"Come on, Calvin," said Leonard, "please let me see it."

"See with your eyes and not with your hands," teased Calvin. He then held the car over Leonard's head, just out of his reach. Leonard began jumping up and down in an effort to grab the car.

After a minute or two, a very frustrated Leonard was in tears, yelling, "STOP TEASING ME, CALVIN!" Calvin did not stop.

Hearing all the commotion, Mr. Peters went upstairs to see what was going on. At first, the boys didn't notice their father standing there. Mr. Peters knocked on the open door to get their attention.

1. What do you think Mr. Peters said to his sons?

   Mr. Peters looked at his sons and said, " _____

   _____

   _____

   _____

   _____ . "

# Stop Teasing Me! continued

2. Think about your own family. If you have brothers or sisters, you probably get on each other's nerves from time to time. Just like Calvin, you probably like your privacy, too. Teasing, however, is not the best way to deal with a pesky brother or sister. How and why might teasing actually make a situation worse? _____

_____

_____

3. What do you think Jesus would have to say about teasing, especially when it goes too far? _____

_____

_____

4. Jesus wants us to be kind and considerate. Find and read the following verses in your Bible: Galatians 6:10, Ephesians 4:32, Colossians 3:12. Then write what the word *kindness* means to you.

_____

_____

5. Pretend you are Calvin. Knowing what Jesus expects, come up with a way to deal with Leonard when he wants to tag along and you don't want him to. Then complete the scenario below.

"But Calvin, I want to go skateboarding with you and your friends, too," said Leonard.

Calvin said, " _____

_____

_____

Then _____

_____

_____

_____

_____

_____

_____

GP275001 WWJD © Grace Publications

Name _____

# Getting Even

"I'VE HAD IT WITH YOU, MIKEY! YOU'RE GONNA GET IT NOW!" yelled Jason, but Mikey had already disappeared down the street. He looked back just long enough to laugh at his latest victim.

Jason was fuming. Mikey had grabbed his backpack and tossed it up in a tree. It landed between two branches just out of Jason's reach, so he had to climb the tree to get it down. Unfortunately, this also made him late for school.

1. How would you feel if Mikey had tossed your backpack into a tree?

   _____

   _____

"I'm gonna find a way to get even with Mikey once and for all," grumbled Jason to himself. "It's time for him to get a taste of his own medicine. He's done things like this to me and a lot of other kids once too often, and he always seems to get away with it, too. I'm really angry."

2. Do you think it is OK for Jason to be angry? Why or why not? _____

   _____

   _____

# Getting Even continued

All morning long, Jason could think of nothing else but getting even with Mikey. He came up with all kinds of ideas. Now all he needed was a chance. Then it happened. Jason was eating lunch in the cafeteria when he noticed Mikey heading toward his table. He was carrying a tray with a plate of spaghetti and meatballs, salad, a container of milk, and a big bowl of chocolate pudding. Mikey was so busy talking to one of his friends that he didn't notice Jason.

"How easy it would be to trip Mikey," thought Jason. "All I have to do is stick out my foot a little farther as he passes by my table. Then we'd get to see Mikey on the floor with his lunch all over him. Now wouldn't that be a wonderful sight?"

3. Do you think tripping Mikey is the best way for Jason to solve his problem? Why or why not? What could happen as a result of Jason's actions?

   _____

   _____

4. What do you think Jesus would do in this situation? Would he try to get even like Jason wants to do? Read Matthew 5:43–48 to find out what Jesus had to say about those we consider to be our enemies. Then list some ways to solve conflicts that are not violent and mean-spirited. The next time you have a conflict with someone like Mikey, test out one of your ideas to see if it works.

   _____

   _____

   _____

   _____

   _____

GP275001 WWJD © Grace Publications

# It's Only a Candy Bar

Mark stopped at the store on his way home from school. His mother wanted him to buy a loaf of bread. As he was deciding what kind to get, he glanced over toward the candy display. That's when he saw his friend Jake take a candy bar and put it in his pocket.

"I can't believe Jake is shoplifting," said Mark to himself.

Jake looked up in time to see his friend staring at him. "I wonder if Mark saw me take that candy bar," he thought.

Mark walked over to Jake and . . .

1. Jake probably knows that it's wrong to steal. It's one of the Ten Commandments. Pretend you are Mark. What are some things you could say to Jake or do? Complete the list below.

   • I can act like I didn't see him.

   • I can _____

   • I can _____

   • I can _____

2. Read over your list of choices. Check the one you think is best. Then explain why you think so. _____

   _____

   _____

   _____

3. Read the verses below.

   *My brothers, if one of you should wander from the truth and someone should bring him back, remember this: Whoever turns a sinner from the error of his way will save him from death and cover over a multitude of sins. (James 5:19–20)*

GP275001 WWJD © Grace Publications

# It's Only a Candy Bar continued

Suppose you remind Jake that stealing is wrong, but he refuses to listen to you. He says, "It's only a candy bar." Then the next time you are with him, he tries to get you to shoplift, too. Do you think you should continue to hang around with Jake? Why or why not? Tell what you would do.

_____

_____

_____

4. Do you think Jesus would agree with your decision? Find and read these Bible verses to help you: Proverbs 1:10–15, Proverbs 13:20, 2 Thessalonians 3:14–15. _____

_____

_____

5. Reread the story. Then write an ending for it.

Mark walked over to Jake and _____

_____

_____

_____

_____

_____

_____

# no @~%$#*!

Charlie was hammering the very last nail into the board when it happened. He looked away for an instant and accidentally smashed his thumb with the hammer.

"@~%$#*," yelled Charlie, as he rubbed his injured thumb. Suddenly realizing what he had said, Charlie looked around to see if there was anyone who had heard him swear.

"I'll be in big trouble if Mom or Dad heard me," he thought, "or our next door neighbor, Mr. Lambert, because he'll tell them. I know I'm not supposed to swear, but I don't think it makes a difference if no one hears me, does it?"

1. What do you think about swearing? Are there any situations when it is OK to swear—like when you smash your thumb? Why or why not? _____

   _____

   _____

2. Would Jesus agree with you? _____ Find and read Ephesians 4:29 in your Bible and you will have the correct answer.

3. If you truly believe that swearing is wrong and then you say a bad word, do you think it makes a difference if no one is around to hear you? Why or why not? _____

   _____

   _____

4. Reread the last sentence of the story. Charlie probably doesn't realize that although his parents and neighbor may not have heard him, God did. In fact, God knows everything we say, do, and think. If you have any doubts, find and read these verses in your Bible: Proverbs 5:21, Proverbs 20:11, Ecclesiastes 12:14, Philippians 4:8.

# no @~%$#*! continued

5. Suppose you could talk to Charlie. Knowing what you do, how would you answer his question? _____

_____

_____

6. Are there times when you want to use bad words, or swear? When? Complete this sentence: *Sometimes I feel like swearing when . . .*

_____

_____

7. Knowing that God doesn't want you—or any of us—to use bad language, what can you do, say, or think instead when you find yourself in an upsetting situation? List some of your ideas and then share them with your parents. You may want to ask for their suggestions and add them to your list. _____

_____

_____

_____

8. The next time you are tempted to use bad language, try one of your ideas instead to see if it works. Begin a journal of your experiences. In the meantime, complete the story below, keeping in mind what God expects of you.

It was the last inning. We had two outs with a runner on second base and a runner on third. Both had to score if we were to win, and it was now up to me. The count was two strikes and three balls. The pitcher threw the ball. It looked good, so I swung and missed. "Strike three. You're out," yelled the umpire. I wanted to scream every bad word I could think of, but instead, I _____

_____

_____

_____

_____

_____

GP275001 WWJD © Grace Publications

Name _____

# No Trespassing

"Hurry up, Jimmy," yelled Chad. "It's just around the bend. You're not gonna believe this road. It's the absolute best place in town to skate and skateboard. My friends and I come here all the time. Look. Greg and Jeff are already there."

Jimmy and Chad were rounding the bend. Jimmy saw Greg and Jeff. Then he saw a sign posted next to the road.

"Hey, Chad," said Jimmy. "Look at the sign. We can't skate here."

"No one pays attention to that sign," said Chad. "We always skate here. Besides, the people who own the property and this road are never here except on weekends, and today is only Thursday."

"Well, suppose they just happen to show up. What then?" asked Jimmy.

"Don't be such a worry wart!" said Chad. "Come on, let's skate!"

1. What do you think is the right thing to do in this situation? Explain your answer. _____

_____

_____

_____

2. Pretend you are Jimmy. You want to skate, but you don't want to skate on private property. Chad and his friends keep pressuring you. Do you think it would be easy for you to do the right thing in this situation? Why or why not? _____

_____

_____

# No Trespassing continued

3. Have your friends ever tempted you to do or try something that was wrong, dangerous, or unhealthy? Below are some things that you may be tempted to try or do by peers. What else can you think of to add to the list?

   smoking, disobeying one's parents, chewing tobacco, shoplifting, _____

   _____

   _____

4. As you may have already discovered, it's not always easy to stick to your values and do what is right. The next time someone tries to get you to do the wrong thing, use Jesus as your model. Read Matthew 4:1–11 to learn how he stood up to the devil when he was in the wilderness. Then follow these steps:

   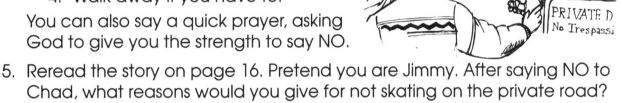

   1. Look the person in eye and say NO like you really mean it. You can give a reason if you want to.
   2. Suggest other things to do.
   3. Repeat yourself as often as you need to.
   4. Walk away if you have to.

   You can also say a quick prayer, asking God to give you the strength to say NO.

5. Reread the story on page 16. Pretend you are Jimmy. After saying NO to Chad, what reasons would you give for not skating on the private road?

   _____

   _____

6. What suggestions would you make to Chad, Greg, and Jeff? _____

   _____

   _____

7. Finish the prayer below.

   Dear God, _____

   _____

   _____

   _____

Name _____

# Please, Please, Please, Can I?

"See you tomorrow," said Lucy. "Don't forget that *Monster From the Sea* is on channel 9 tonight from 8 to 11 o'clock. My parents finally agreed to let me watch it. I told them it was for a homework assignment."

"Bye, Lucy," said Karen, "and thanks for reminding me. I forgot it was on."

Karen did all her homework, straightened up her room, and walked the dog without having to be reminded. She really wanted to see the movie. Karen waited to ask her mom about it until she was setting the table for dinner.

"Mom," said Karen, "there's a really cool movie on television tonight from 8 to 11 o'clock called *Monster From the Sea.* Can I stay up to watch it? Please, please, please, can I? My homework's done, and I even straightened up my room."

"What's the movie about?" asked Mrs. Betts.

"A gigantic prehistoric sea creature comes to the surface and attacks and eats everything it encounters," said Karen enthusiastically.

1. If you were Karen's mother, would you want her to watch *Monster From the Sea*? Why or why not? _____

_____

"I'm sorry, Karen," said Mrs. Betts, "but the answer is no."

"Why?" demanded Karen rather harshly.

"You know why, Karen," answered her mother calmly. "*Monster From the Sea* is just not the kind of movie I think you should be watching. Besides, 11 o'clock is two hours past your bedtime, and tomorrow is a school day."

"But, Mom," whined Karen, "all my friends are staying up to watch it."

"The answer is still no, Karen. We can do something else instead. In the meantime, please finish setting the table," said her mom.

Karen frowned, tossed the silverware on the table, and stomped off.

Name _____

# Please, Please . . . continued

2. How would you describe Karen's behavior? _____

_____

---

Karen was not about to give up. She waited for her father to get home.

"Hi, Dad," greeted Karen. "How was your day?"

"I had a great day," he said, "and how was yours?"

"It was fine, Dad," she said, "but it would be even better if you say I can watch a special movie tonight . . ."

---

3. Is Karen doing the right thing by now asking her father? Why or why not?

_____

_____

4. Look up the meaning of the word *honor* in the dictionary. Write the definition. Then read Ephesians 6:1–3.

   honor _____

5. As you can see, Karen failed to honor her mother's decision. Pretend you are Karen. Think about how you could have responded more respectfully to your mother and rewrite the conversation.

   "I'm sorry, Karen," said Mrs. Betts, "but the answer is no."

   Karen said, "_____

   _____

   _____

   _____

   _____

   _____."

6. Do you sometimes act like Karen? If you do, tell one thing you can do differently the next time your mom or dad says no. Then test it out.

   _____

   _____

   _____

GP275001 WWJD © Grace Publications

# She's Not Like Us . . .

"Have you seen the new girl yet?" asked Donna.

"No," answered Jenna and Becky. "Why?"

"You'll see," chimed in Dee Dee, laughing.

"I heard her name is Juhi," said Donna. "What kind of a name is that?"

"I don't know," said Chris.

"Shh," said Donna. "Here she comes." The girls stared at the new girl as she walked past them.

"Wow," laughed Jenna. "That's some outfit she's wearing."

"It sure is," said Donna. "Someone should tell her it's not Halloween yet."

"And what's that mark on her forehead?" asked Becky.

"Hey, Megan," said Chris. "What's wrong with you? You haven't said a word. Don't you agree that the new girl is weird?"

1. Pretend you are Megan and that Donna, Chris, Dee Dee, Jenna, and Becky are your friends. Write how you feel about the way your friends are behaving. _____

   _____

   _____

2. Reread the last paragraph. Then read John 4:4–26 in your Bible. It is about Jesus and a Samaritan woman. As you read, remember that Jesus' people despised the Samaritans. Then write how you would answer Chris' question in the last paragraph. _____

   _____

   _____

   _____

# She's Not Like Us . . . continued

3. Still pretending to be Megan, go up to Juhi a little later and talk to her. What do you say to her? What does she say to you? Think about how she must feel, knowing that people are talking about her. Write the conversation.

Megan: _____

Juhi: _____

_____

_____

_____

_____

_____

_____

4. Do you think outward differences are really important? How do you think Jesus would want you to behave the next time you encounter someone from a different culture or race, or someone who is handicapped, or someone who is less fortunate than you, for example? Write what you think Jesus would say.

GP275001 WWJD © Grace Publications

Name _____

# Show You Care

Logan was shocked to find out that there are families in his own town who are living out of their cars and in shelters because they lost their homes or can no longer afford to pay the rent. Until yesterday, he didn't even know there was a homeless shelter in his town. Logan once watched a television movie about a homeless family, but it was just a story with actors playing a role. Now it was real for Logan. He learned that Lewis, a boy in his own class, was living in the shelter downtown with his parents. This really upset him.

Logan mentioned his concerns to his friend Peter on the way home from school, but he wasn't much help. "My father says that the homeless are just a bunch of lazy people who don't want to work for a living. All they want is a handout."

"Well, I think your father is wrong," said Logan. "Lewis's father and mother both worked for the same company, but they were laid off along with many other workers. They just haven't been able to find new jobs yet. No matter what, I feel really bad for Lewis and his family and others just like them."

1. What do you think Jesus would want us to do about those who are in need? _____

_____

2. The Old Testament is very clear about what people were expected to do to help the needy in ancient times. Find and read these Bible verses: Exodus 23:10–11, Leviticus 25:35, Deuteronomy 15:11.

3. Jesus was very clear about what he expected, too. Read Matthew 6:25–34.

# Show You Care continued

4. Logan decided to find some way to help. He began by making a list of things he could do. Read his suggestions. Then add your own to the list he started.

- Organize a canned food drive.
- Take up a collection in the neighborhood.
- _____
- _____

5. Do you have things you no longer want or need that are still useful and in good condition? Make a list of these items. Then check with your parents to see if you can donate them to others who can use them.

_____   _____   _____

_____   _____   _____

_____   _____   _____

6. Is there a shelter in your community? Is there a soup kitchen? Does your church do anything to help the poor? Find out. Check the telephone directory. Ask your parents. Talk to your minister. Use the chart to record your findings.

| Name of Organization | Location | Telephone # | Services Offered |
|---|---|---|---|
|  |  |  |  |
|  |  |  |  |
|  |  |  |  |
|  |  |  |  |
|  |  |  |  |
|  |  |  |  |
|  |  |  |  |
|  |  |  |  |

Use everything you've learned to get involved in some way. Try to get your parents and the people in your neighborhood involved, too. Just remember what Jesus would have us do.

   GP275001 WWJD © Grace Publications

Name _____

# Tell Her I'm Not Home . . .

Brenda was watching her favorite television program when the telephone rang. Her brother, Greg, was the closest to the caller identification box so he checked to see who was on the line.

"It's Tanya," Greg said.

"I don't want to talk to her," said Brenda. "She's such a pest. Tell her I'm not home. Once she starts talking, she doesn't stop, and I don't want to miss my program. Besides, I'll see her at school tomorrow."

1. If you were Greg, would you tell Tanya that your sister isn't home? Why or why not?_____

   _____

2. Some people say it's OK to lie in certain situations. For example, they may not want to hurt a person's feelings or they don't think a person can handle the truth, so they tell a "little" lie. What do you think? Is it ever OK to lie, or should you always tell the truth, no matter what? _____

   _____

According to 1 Peter 2:22–23, Jesus never lied. Just as he always told the truth, Jesus expects us to do the same in every situation, too, but that doesn't mean we should be nasty or deliberately cruel, either. Sometimes we have to be tactful. That means we have to tell the truth in a nice way.

In the scene you just read, Brenda wanted Greg to lie to Tanya. Read on to see what happens.

"I'll get the phone, but I won't lie," Greg said to Brenda.

"OK, " said Brenda, "Then tell Tanya that . . ."

# Tell Her I'm . . . continued

3. Of the following things Tanya could say, which do you think Jesus would say is both truthful and tactful?

_____ . . . I don't want to talk to her because she's a real pest and I'm watching TV.

_____ . . . I'm doing something right now and can't come to the phone, but I'll talk to her tomorrow at school.

_____ . . . I'm not allowed to talk on the phone because I'm being punished.

4. Below are several other situations in which it is difficult to be as truthful as Jesus would want you to be. Try to be tactful when necessary as you write the truth.

• Your friend asks what you think of her new sweater. You really don't like it. In fact, you think it's kind of ugly. You don't want to lie to her, but you don't want to hurt her feelings, either, so you say,

"_____."

• Your brother asks if your parents bought him the skates he wants for his birthday. You don't want to give away the surprise, but you don't want to lie, either, so you say,

"_____."

• A stranger calls on the phone when you are home alone and asks to speak to your parents. You don't want to lie and say they are out, but you also know it's not safe to say you're home alone, so you say,

"_____."

• Your friend is painting a picture of his dog Boots. He asks how you like it. You try not to laugh because it doesn't look anything like Boots, except for the color of his fur. You don't want to lie, but you don't want to hurt his feelings, either, so you say,

"_____."

# The Quiz

"OK, boys and girls," said Mrs. Hunter, "if you don't have any more questions, you can put away your math books. I'm going to give you a quiz to see how much you've learned about measurement. You'll only need your pencil and a ruler."

Mrs. Hunter proceeded to distribute the quiz papers. She said, "You'll have 15 minutes to do the problems. There aren't any surprises on it. As always, there will be no talking or sharing of answers until after the quiz. In other words, no cheating, please."

Mandy was working on the next-to-the-last problem when she heard her best friend, Maggie, whisper, "Hey, Mandy, move your paper to the right so I can see your answers."

1. Mandy has to decide what to do. What do you think her options are? Make a list. Then write a possible consequence for each action. For example, if Mandy refuses to show Maggie her paper, Maggie might get angry with Mandy.

| Options | | Possible Consequences |
|---------|---|----------------------|
| _____ | → | _____ |
| _____ | → | _____ |
| _____ | → | _____ |
| _____ | → | _____ |

2. If you were Mandy, which option would you choose? Put a check next to your choice. Give a reason for your choice. _____

_____

_____

_____

_____

# The Quiz continued

Mandy decided not to show her quiz paper to Maggie. Later that morning, Maggie confronted her. "Some friend you are, Mandy! Why didn't you help me on the quiz?" asked Maggie.

"I didn't want to cheat!" answered Mandy.

"Well, friends are supposed to help friends, no matter what. Besides, it's not like it was a major test, Mandy," said Maggie. "It was just a dumb old quiz!"

3. Write what you would say to Maggie if you were Mandy.

   "Well, Maggie," began Mandy, "I_____

   _____

   _____._"

4. Maggie believes it's OK to cheat on little things like quizzes. Do you think Jesus would agree with Maggie? Read Luke 16:10 to find out. Then finish this sentence:

   Jesus wants us to be honest _____

   not just_____

   because when you lie or cheat, you are really hurting _____
   in the end.

5. Here's another situation to consider: Suppose you watched a TV program last night instead of finishing your homework. Then you were too tired to do it, so you never got it done. Which of the actions below do you think Jesus would have you do? Put a check next to your choice. Then give a reason for your choice on the back of this page.

   _____ Tell the teacher you didn't have
   enough time to finish it.

   _____ Copy a friend's homework on the bus.

   _____ Tell the teacher you watched TV and
   then ask to finish it during recess.

   _____ Tell the teacher you had to go
   somewhere with your parents last night.

   _____ Tell your teacher that you left it on the bus.

GP275001 WWJD © Grace Publications

# THUD! STOMP! SLAM! CRASH!

Martha and her brother, James, have been playing a game for the last hour. James has won four times already, and it looks like he's about to win again. Martha decides she has had enough.

"I don't want to play this dumb old game any more," explodes Martha suddenly, "especially with you." Martha throws the cards at her brother. Then she stands up—knocking her chair over with a great big thud. Martha stomps up the stairs to her room and slams the door behind her as hard as she can. The whole house seems to shake.

"I wonder what her problem is," mumbles James to himself.

1. Think about Martha's behavior. Which of the words below do you think best identifies her feelings or emotions? Put a check(s) next to your answer.

___ happiness    ___ sadness    ___ anger    ___ contentment

___ hatred    ___ jealousy    ___ love    ___ boredom

2. What might have caused Martha to have such feelings? _____
_____

3. What do you think of Martha's behavior? Was it appropriate for the situation? Why or why not? _____
_____

4. What are some possible consequences of Martha's behavior? _____
_____
_____

5. How else could she have expressed her feelings? _____
_____
_____

# THUD! STOMP! . . . continued

6. Read this statement: *Control your emotions instead of letting your emotions control you.* What do you think it means?_____

_____

Do you think Jesus would agree with the statement? _____
Why or why not? _____

_____

If you're not sure, find and read these Bible verses: Proverbs 16:32, Ephesians 4:26, James 1:19–20.

7. When you find yourself in a situation that makes you feel angry or upset, try to figure out why you feel that way. Then try to come up with a positive way to resolve it. Below is the first paragraph from the story on page 28. Rewrite the scene to show how Jesus would want Martha to deal with her angry feelings and resolve the situation.

   Martha and her brother, James, have been playing a game for the last hour. James has won four times already, and it looks like he's about to win again. Martha decides she has had enough.

   _____

   _____

   _____

   _____

   _____

   _____

   _____

8. Think about a time when you were angry and lost control of your emotions. Tell what you would do differently if you could relive the situation. _____

   _____

   _____

   _____

   _____

   _____

GP275001 WWJD © Grace Publications

Name _____

# What Am I Gonna Do now?

"Oh no!" moaned Max.

"What's wrong?" asked Luis.

"I just broke my brother's new truck," said Max. "He's gonna be really mad at me. He didn't want me playing with it in the first place. He made me promise I wouldn't do anything to break it. What am I gonna do now? He's gonna be home soon."

"Let me see it," said Luis. After examining the broken truck, Luis said, "You know, Max, I think we can fix this as good as new. Your brother will never know the difference. You won't even have to say a word to him about it."

1. How do you think Max feels at this moment? Why? _____

   _____

   _____

2. Think about Luis's suggestion. Do you think it's the best way for Max to handle his dilemma? Why or why not? _____

   _____

   _____

   _____

3. Here's another way to think about the situation: Suppose someone breaks something of yours and fixes it without saying anything to you. A week later, you find out it was broken. How would this make you feel? Why?

   _____

   _____

   _____

# What Am I . . . ? continued

4. In Matthew 7:12, Jesus said to his followers, *"So in everything, do to others what you would have them do to you . . ."* You also know that Jesus expects us to be truthful in all things.  When we tell someone the truth, we are showing respect for that person.

Now write yourself into the story. First, tell Luis what you think about his suggestion and why you think it's not the right thing to do. Then tell Max what you think is the right thing to do. Include a reason for your suggestion.

Interrupting Luis, I said, "I _____

_____

_____."

Then Max asked me, "Well, what do you think I should do?"

I said, " _____

_____

_____."

Max said, "Okay, I'll do it. I just hope you are right."

"Trust me," I said. "Telling the truth may not be the easiest thing to do at times, but it is the best thing to do in the end, even if it means that your brother is kind of mad at you at first."

5. Max's brother, Simon, came home a short time later. Write how you think the story will end.

"Simon," said Max, "I have to tell you something."

"What is it?" asked Simon.

Max began, "Well, I _____

_____

_____."

Simon said, " _____

_____

_____."

GP275001 WWJD © Grace Publications

Name _____

# Try This!

Below are some situations for you to consider. Can you think of any others? Add them to the list.

- You find a gold bracelet on the steps of the library. Can you keep it?

- Is it OK to watch a video at your friend's house if your parents wouldn't let you watch it at home?

- Is it wrong to keep a book that belongs to someone else if that person doesn't ask for it back?

- Is it OK to make copies of computer games and videos that your parents bought for you and give them to your friends?

- If you see your best friend cheating on a test, should you say something to him or her?

_____

_____

_____

_____

_____

_____

Try to answer the questions above. Here's how to get started. Think about what Jesus would do in each situation. If you aren't sure, try to find answers in your Bible. Think about the Ten Commandments and the Golden Rule. They can help you answer some of the questions. You can also talk with your parents, Sunday school teacher, and pastor for more help. You might even want to share the situations with your friends.

Here's something else to try. Begin a journal. Each time you solve a dilemma like the ones listed above, record it in your journal. Include the date, the dilemma, what you decided to do, and the outcome.

EMPIRES OF IDEAS

# Empires of Ideas

Creating *the* Modern University *from* Germany *to* America *to* China

WILLIAM C. KIRBY

THE BELKNAP PRESS OF HARVARD UNIVERSITY PRESS

*Cambridge, Massachusetts & London, England*

2022

First printing

*Library of Congress Cataloging-in-Publication Data*
Names: Kirby, William C., author.
Title: Empires of ideas : creating the modern university from Germany to America to
    China / William C. Kirby.
Description: Cambridge, Massachusetts : The Belknap Press of Harvard University Press,
    2022. | Includes bibliographical references and index.
Identifiers: LCCN 2021049001 | ISBN 9780674737716 (hardcover)
Subjects: LCSH: Universities and colleges—Germany—History. | Universities and
    colleges—United States—History. | Universities and colleges—China—History. |
    Education, Higher—Germany—History. | Education, Higher—United States—
    German influences. | Education, Higher—China—History.
Classification: LCC LA728 .K54 2022 | DDC 378.43—dc23/eng/20211129
LC record available at https://lccn.loc.gov/2021049001

# Contents

# Preface

子曰，學而時習之，不亦說乎？

The Master said: To study, and at due times to practice
what one has studied, is this not a pleasure?

This first line of the Confucian *Analects*, set down somewhere between the
fifth and third centuries BCE, captures better than any I know the challenges and rewards of the modern university. It reflects, too, my own path to
this book as a historian, teacher, and dean.

I have had the pleasure of learning and practicing in colleges and universities since I was eighteen. Studying as an undergraduate at Dartmouth and
Wellesley, and in Mainz, I learned to value an education in the liberal arts
and sciences, with an international dimension. In graduate studies in Berlin
and at Harvard, I sought to acquire the skills to apprentice as a professor. At
Washington University and at Harvard, I learned to practice what I had
studied, both as a scholar and as an official.

Along the way I learned gradually of the richness and complexity of our
world of universities from Europe to America to Asia. This book owes much
to the experience, collegiality, and assistance of individuals and institutions
on three continents.

At Washington University in St. Louis, a jewel among American universities, I could see how the good and principled leadership of William H.
Danforth and later Mark S. Wrighton could transform an institution in a
matter of decades while maintaining collegiate and clear governance. I owe

everything to my mentors there in the History Department and University College. Arriving at Harvard in the early 1990s, I had the opportunity of working under a remarkable dean, Jeremy R. Knowles, and a professor's president, the eloquently persuasive Neil L. Rudenstine, in what was, in retrospect, a golden decade for that university. In my own research abroad, in establishing international research partnerships, and in serving on advisory boards to Chinese and European universities, I came to appreciate the dynamism of China's resurgent universities and the impetus for renewal in Europe. From the institution-building of Chen Jining and Qiu Yong at Tsinghua University; Chen Jia'er, Wang Enge, and Hao Ping at Peking University; Victor Fung and Peter Mathieson at the University of Hong Kong; Susanne Weigelin-Schwiedrzik, first at Heidelberg and then Vienna; Marijk van den Wende, of Amsterdam University College and then Utrecht; and Mechthild Leutner and Peter-André Alt at Free University of Berlin, I learned a great deal. To these friends and colleagues, I am deeply grateful.

This book would not have been possible without the generous research funds received from Harvard Business School (HBS) during the tenure of Dean Nitin Nohria, who, like his predecessor Jay Light, gave unstinting support. My colleagues at the Harvard China Fund and the Harvard Center Shanghai, Julia Cai, Yi Wang, and Nancy Dai, provided critical logistical and research assistance.

The HBS case method has shaped this book, but my remarkable HBS research associates have helped to shape it further still. Joycelyn W. Eby provided extraordinary support for the American and Chinese sections, accompanied me on multiple interviews, and co-authored with me HBS cases on Berkeley, Tsinghua, and the University of Hong Kong that were early drafts of the final chapters. Yuanzhuo Wang co-authored the HBS case on Duke University and provided critical assistance in our research visit to Nanjing University. John McHugh and Joyce Kim did invaluable work in bringing the manuscript to completion, with their expertise on the Chinese and American scenes, respectively, and their deep commitment to the project. Mareike-Christin Bues helped to conceptualize the German cases, and Carolyn Taratko strengthened them greatly for the final submission. Noah Truwit assisted with post-submission updates and references. Ava Russell, my HBS faculty support specialist during the years this project was under way, kept us on budget and (somewhat) on time. Her successor, Alice Foster McCallum, reviewed the copyedited manuscript. For the assistance, advice, and support of these colleagues I could not be more grateful.

I have had the pleasure of working with two outstanding editors at Harvard University Press. Elizabeth Knoll originally signed me to the project and has given good counsel ever since. Andrew Kinney—a historian with deep knowledge of higher education—offered strong advice and edits of the entire manuscript, which he made shorter and better. Penelope Perkins, of Pen & Ink, gave every line of the manuscript a most rigorous editing and proofreading. Jenny Korte provided superb copyediting, Angela Piliouras oversaw final copyediting and typesetting, and Mary Mortensen prepared the index. I am indebted also to Joy de Menil, director of Belknap Publishing, and to two directors of Harvard University Press, Bill Sisler and George Andreou, who watched the project grow from idea to manuscript. I am most grateful for the comments and suggestions made by our two anonymous readers of this book.

A study such as this must rely on a wide variety of sources: published, archival, and oral. I am the beneficiary of the knowledge and assistance of archivists at Humboldt University; Free University of Berlin; Duke University; the University of California, Berkeley; Tsinghua University; Nanjing University; and the University of Hong Kong. For the remarkable access to materials past and present at Duke, I am especially grateful to University Librarian Deborah Jakubs and former provost Peter Lange.

I had the privilege of interviewing nearly one hundred leaders, past and present, of the institutions studied in the book. I was pleased, often amazed, by the candor with which these presidents, provosts, professors, and senior administrators addressed the issues confronting their universities. I cannot list them all here, but even a short list is a form of "who's who" of German, American, and Chinese higher education.

In Germany, I learned from the insights and experience of Presidents Heinrich Fink, Christoph Markschies, and Jan-Hendrik Olbertz of Humboldt University as well as their senior colleagues in administration and teaching such as Eva Inés Obergfell and Peter Frensch. I learned much from Heinz-Elmar Tenorth and the many colleagues who contributed to his magisterial history of the university's first two hundred years.

My research at Free University was made possible by the cooperation of President Alt, Vice President Klaus Mühlhahn, Herbert Grieshop, Matthias Dannenberg, Chancellor Andrea Bör, and the former chancellor, the incomparable Peter Lange. (One of two incomparable Peter Langes in this book.) I gained much from the advice of Hans Weiler and other members of Free University's International Advisory Committee, which advised the university on its strategy in Germany's Excellence Initiative.

At Harvard, of course, I had no shortage of colleagues to torment with interviews, former presidents Neil Rudenstine and Drew Faust, and future president Lawrence Bacow, chief among them. Former deans William Graham, Barry Bloom, and Venkatesh Narayanamurti, and former provost Steven Hyman gave unfiltered accounts of their tenures. Provost Alan Garber and Dean Frank Doyle addressed the challenges of engineering in a town where MIT resides, while Douglas Melton, leader of the Harvard Stem Cell Institute, looked farther west to identify Harvard's chief competitor.

At Berkeley, Chancellor Nicholas Dirks and his team shared with me the ambitions, tensions, and fiscal constraints that have marked Berkeley's recent history. Former chancellor Robert Birgeneau and future chancellor Carol Christ helped me grasp the university's distinctive culture, while former provost George Breslauer gave detailed context to Berkeley's endurance in the wake of the financial crisis of 2008. Another remarkable former provost, Judd King, graciously hosted me at Berkeley's Center for Studies in Higher Education. My fellow historians Wen-hsin Yeh and Sheldon Rothblatt, both great scholar-citizens of Berkeley, provided invaluable insight.

At Duke, the hospitality and openness of the entire institution followed the example set by President Richard Brodhead. Former president Nannerl Keohane provided important background. Provosts Peter Lange and Sally Kornbluth gave extensive interviews and provided access to a wealth of the university's planning documents. Executive Vice President James Roberts and Treasurer Tallman Trask III helped me unpack the financial picture, while Vice President Michael Merson set out Duke's international ambitions. To understand the ambitions and challenges of Duke Kunshan University in China, I am indebted to Blair Sheppard, Mary Brown Bullock, Haiyan Gao, Noah Pickus, Wendy Kuran, William Johnson, and, in particular, Nora Bynum. Kunshan Party Secretary Guan Aiguo and Vice Mayors Jin Naibing and Jin Ming provided important context on site in China.

At Tsinghua University I am grateful for the perspectives of Presidents Chen Jining and Qiu Yong; Party Secretary Chen Xu; Vice President Yang Bin; Deans Qian Yingyi, David Daokui Li, Xue Lan, and David Pan; and Professors Xie Zheping and Wang Hui. On Tsinghua's Schwarzman Scholars program, I learned firsthand from its founding trustee, Stephen A. Schwarzman, and its indefatigable CEO, Amy Stursberg. I thank friends and colleagues at Tsinghua's neighbor and rival, Peking University, for their broad perspective on Chinese higher education: Presidents Wan Enge and Lin Jianhua and Professors Jin Li and Yuan Ming, in particular.

My work at Nanjing University was aided by its remarkable modern historians Zhang Xianwen, Chen Qianping, and Jiang Liangqin, who provided deep background and arranged access to both archives and interviews. For their assistance I thank Party Secretaries Zhang Yibin and Hu Jinbo, Executive Vice Chancellor Yang Zhong, Vice President Wang Zhenlin, Professor He Chengzhou, and Professor Neil Kubler, the former co-director of the Hopkins-Nanjing Center.

Finally, I had the opportunity to research in Hong Kong at a time of comparative openness and much tension. I could not have pursued my work at the University of Hong Kong without the help of Presidents Peter Mathieson and Xiang Zhang, Provosts Roland Chin and Paul Tam, Pro-Vice Chancellors Amy Tsui and John Malpas, Deans Ian Holiday and Gabriel Leung, and Professors Xu Guoqi, Yang Rui, and (especially) John Carroll. Former and current council chairs Victor Fung and Arthur Li gave clarifying accounts of their tenures. On the promise and problems of the broader educational scene in Hong Kong, I learned directly from my colleagues on Hong Kong's University Grants Committee.

As always in a study such as this, only some of these archival and interview encounters will have made their way into the final book, but collectively they did a great deal to shape it.

I owe a particular debt of gratitude to Director Miaw-fen Lu and the Institute of Modern History of the Academia Sinica in Taiwan. I had the honor of presenting there an overview of this project as the 2017 Kuo Tingyee Memorial Lectures.[1]

One word on the romanization of Chinese names: I have used the standard *pinyin* romanization of the People's Republic of China, with the family name first, except when individuals were widely known or preferred to be known by another form.

An author whose work takes him so frequently abroad can succeed only with the help of a wonderful family at home. I am blessed by my son Ted, my daughter Elizabeth, my sister Katherine, and above all by my wife and fellow historian, Yvette Sheahan Kirby, whose patience is matched only by her experience in the world of universities. To her is this book dedicated.

# Introduction

## *The "World-Class" University*

W E LIVE in a world of universities. At least 30,000 institutions call themselves universities, some 1,400 of which are ranked in the *Times Higher Education World University Rankings*. Who is in the lead? By sheer numbers of higher education institutions, the answer may be India, with 1,043 universities and 42,343 colleges in 2020,[1] far outdistancing the United States with its nearly 4,000 degree-granting colleges and universities. China's Ministry of Education counted 3,012 higher education institutions in 2021. Israel has 63 and Palestine 25. North Korea has 3 by one assessment and 300 by another.[2] Even Greenland, Djibouti, and Monaco have 1 university, each.[3]

It is, of course, a world of rather different universities. There are Oxford and Cambridge—two of the world's oldest and still leading universities by any measure—and then there is the happily defunct and corrupt "Trump University," which like its namesake, is currently dethroned and out of business. And then there are the self-promoters of a different sort: the readers of this book will be able to name many institutions that once were "schools" or "colleges" that today recruit students as "universities." Sheldon Rothblatt, a distinguished historian of higher education, made this point in discussing "the history of the idea that a university derives its identity from an idea": throughout the centuries in which universities have existed, a "single idea of a university has never truly existed."[4] The offerings of some universities are capacious. Others are narrowly specialized. Universities in the former Soviet bloc were paragons of applied knowledge, their students graduating directly into preselected state enterprises. There are, as we shall see, rather different national systems of higher education, but not all are systematic. Universities may exist as form before there is function: think of the American neo-Gothic campuses that preceded the academic excellence later found in them.

The world of universities is not far removed from the world of power politics. Whom, after all, do universities serve? The individual? The community? The state? The Party? These are old questions of contemporary importance. The *Doktorvater* of all modern research universities, the University of Berlin, was founded to strengthen a defeated Prussian state, substituting the power of knowledge for lost land. Harvard, we will see, was a "state" university for much of its undistinguished first century, but it is now a famously private university with a strong sense of public purpose. The University of California, Berkeley, was, from its founding, a proud public university serving the state of California, but it is now increasingly a privately funded institution, still with the aspiration of serving a broad public. Tsinghua University was founded with a foreign policy mission: to bind the United States and China closer together by sending Tsinghua graduates to the United States. Today, Tsinghua is the recipient of American and other international talent as it climbs the ranks of the world's most admired institutions.

Yet the world of universities is singularly absent from many influential studies of power politics and of the rise and demise of nations. Paul Kennedy focuses on economic change and military conflict in his classic *Rise and Fall of the Great Powers*. David Landes, assessing *The Wealth and Poverty of Nations*, pays more attention to clocks and watches than to education in any form. In *Why Nations Fail*, Daron Acemoglu and James Robinson dig deep into the origins of power, prosperity, and poverty, but "education" is not to be found in the index. And my colleague Charles Maier, who is deeply knowledgeable about the state of higher education in general and at Harvard in particular, has little room for universities in his tour de force that looks at American ascendancy, *Among Empires*.[5] Yet in these analyses of the wealth and power among nations, at least Landes quotes one merchant banker from a Persian Gulf country at the height of the oil boom, pondering the nature of true wealth: *"Rich* is education . . . expertise . . . technology. *Rich* is knowing. We have money, yes. But we are not *rich*."[6]

"A rich country cannot have poor farmers." That was the lesson imparted to my Harvard Business School students by Dhanin Chearavanont, senior chairman of C. P. Group and leader of one of the world's most innovative agribusiness firms, when I taught a case about C. P.'s work in China. I believe it is also true that an enduring rich country cannot have, as a rule, poor universities. The capacity of a nation may be measured more precisely in gross domestic product or in military might, but if we cannot imagine equally precise calculations of the quality of higher education, it does not mean that it is unimportant.

The foremost global political and economic powers of the past three centuries have also been powerful leaders in scholarship and learning. In the seventeenth and eighteenth centuries, France dominated Europe more enduringly by the power of ideas than by its military prowess. In Asia the great Qing Empire, then at its height, defined what it meant to be learned and civilized in much of the East Asian world and was admired as such in Europe. In the nineteenth century, as first Britain, then France, and then Germany rose to be world powers, their power was accompanied by the global allure of their leading schools and universities. In Britain, elites from the British Empire (and later from the Commonwealth) would be educated at Cambridge or Oxford or at the many British-modeled institutions in the colonial world. The *grandes écoles* of France have not (until recently) been welcoming to international audiences, but they could be the educational venue of first choice for elites from *la France d'outre-mer*. German universities, by contrast, became the destination of choice for scholars the world around because they redefined what universities could be—and in an era of growing German national strength. And if American universities gained global prestige and increasing numbers of international students and scholars over the course of the twentieth century, this was closely tied to the ascent of the United States in an "American century." In 2022, as Chinese universities climb quickly in global rankings and attract more than a half-million international students to their campuses, this cannot easily be separated from China's return to a position of global power and influence.

This is not a book about geopolitics, but it is a book about the roles, historically and in prospect, of universities in a global context. This book is about the modern *research* university in three of its most powerful settings: Germany, the United States, and China. It is about the future of the university, in light of its past. I examine three leading global centers of higher education in the twenty-first century from a historian's perspective: I explore how they have grown, assess their greatest challenges today, and estimate which system (if any single one) is likely to set global standards in the twenty-first century.

German universities set in place the foundations of modern universities everywhere in the nineteenth century. American universities had enormous international influence by the end of the twentieth century. I pose a simple question: What, then, are the prospects for *Chinese* leadership in the twenty-first century? Simply to ask this question is to demand some level of comparative research on German, American, and Chinese universities.

In 2022 nearly every major ranking of global universities shows American institutions in leading positions. Yet we know this was not the case in 1922, and there is no reason to assume it will be true in 2122. American leadership in higher education—as in other areas—is today under great stress, particularly in its public universities but also in the realm of private research universities. Meanwhile, nowhere on earth have recent decades seen more revolutionary change in higher education than in the People's Republic of China. In 1977 Chinese universities were just reopening after the catastrophe of the Cultural Revolution. Today they are poised for positions of international leadership in research and education.

The rapid, recent growth of Chinese universities (with now more than forty million students enrolled) has outpaced the great postwar expansion in the United States or the growth of mass-enrollment universities in Europe in the 1970s and 1980s. Square acreage of universities in China has grown fivefold in the past two decades. And unlike the American expansion of the 1950s and the European growth of the 1970s, this growth has elements that are self-consciously elitist, with the aim of building a significant number of "world-class universities." The best of these are investing enormously in research, and the most innovative of these are also experimenting creatively with conceptions of "liberal education" that have both German and American antecedents.

My broader study, then, is an investigation, past and present, of three realms of higher education that have defined, or promise to define, excellence: those of Germany, the United States, and China over the past two centuries. I realize, of course, that there is often seemingly little "system" to the many varied institutions in Germany, the United States, and China. I have pursued this study not as a series of comprehensive, national studies, but through case studies of individual universities, from which we may draw lessons. Within the field of education, researchers have long used the case study to address "critical problems of practice" and to extend knowledge of the diversity of educational experiences.[7] In this book, each university, to be sure, is rooted in a larger system, but each has its own, distinctive narrative, its own character, and its own concerns. Each is its own drama, but with lessons, I hope, for a larger audience.

I have taught at Harvard University now for three decades, but in the last fifteen years also at Harvard Business School (HBS). I have seen how case studies and, in teaching, the case method, can illuminate the whole while focusing on the particular. Teaching an HBS case study has been described as "the art of managing uncertainty."[8] Our cases are primarily vehicles for teaching, with multiple possible outcomes: good stories that lead one to think about broader principles, not the other way around. The case studies in this book are not meant to build toward a single set of conclusions, but rather to enrich the readers' experience and lead them to contemplate, from multiple immersions into the lives of different universities, central themes common and distinct to the world's leading research universities.

For each university I will discuss, in the course of the narratives, factors that may make for excellence or decline: the leadership of presidents, chancellors, and rectors; the quality of faculty and students; and the capacity of financial resources, among others. I will pay particular attention to three interlocking phenomena that may be traced to the founding of the University of Berlin in 1810: The first is the concept of a university devoted to scientific research at the highest level—*Wissenschaft*, be it in philosophy or physics. The second is a commitment to foster a culture of education in the liberal arts and sciences that stresses, in its most basic sense, *Bildung* (the education of the whole person), as distinct from *Übung* (more practical training). In Chinese, this is the distinction between a broad-based education, or *jiaoyu*, and *xunlian*, a narrower, more repetitive schooling. In this combination, this idealized "German model" would remake American higher education from the second half of the nineteenth century to the present; and today it is this model (now often viewed as "American") that is becoming part of the system of higher education in contemporary China.

A third, and defining, aspiration of the *moderne Original*, as today's Humboldt University likes to describe itself, is in the realm of governance, specifically governance that accords the university the autonomy to make its own appointments and set its own priorities, insulated to a high degree from political winds. In the making or breaking of great global universities, perhaps no criterion is more important than the quality of governance.

For Germany our cases are the University of Berlin, the mother of all modern research universities, known over time also as Friedrich Wilhelm University and later Humboldt University; and Free University of

Berlin, founded with American foundation support at the onset of the Cold War.

In the United States, the cases are Harvard, which I know well from thirty years as a faculty member and, more intimately, as a department chair, center director, and dean of its Faculty of Arts and Sciences in the 1990s and early 2000s; the University of California, Berkeley, the once-premier public university in the United States, now undergoing painful transitions; and Duke University, a rapidly rising private university whose global ambitions outstrip those of either Harvard or Berkeley.

In China we focus on Tsinghua University, founded in 1911 as an American-funded preparatory school in the arts and sciences, now China's premier institution of science, engineering, and economics; Nanjing University, the former National Central University of China's Nationalist government, founded on the model of the University of Berlin; and the University of Hong Kong, a British imperial university that aspires to be "Asia's Global University."

## Disclosures

These universities are, of course, well known around the world, and they might be natural choices for any such book. I have chosen them also because I know them well from personal experience with each of them over the course of several decades. As a young scholar of German history, I studied in Berlin after college, receiving a German Academic Exchange Service fellowship to study at Free University of Berlin. Later, as a doctoral student and assistant professor in the field of modern Chinese history, I corresponded with and came to know well the outstanding cadre of sinologists at Humboldt University. Later still, I served on the International Advisory Board of Free University and studied the Berlin academic landscape more deeply. In the United States, apart from my time as a graduate student and (much later) a faculty member at Harvard, I served on multiple review committees for Berkeley, our peer and competitor in China studies and home to a leading Center for Higher Education Research, where I spent part of a semester as I began work on this book. I served as Senior Advisor on China for Duke University at its campus in Kunshan, China, and was frequently resident both in Durham and in Kunshan. I chaired the Academic Advisory Committee for the Schwarzman Scholars program at Tsinghua University and now sit on its board. I have visited Nanjing University and its nearby national archives of the pre-Communist era periodically since 1984. In Hong Kong, I served several terms on that city's University Grants Committee, which oversees its universities, and I was recently part of a major and controversial governance review of the University of Hong Kong.

So, I know these places well. That does not mean I study them uncritically. Above all, this book has emerged from my career as a historian—first of Germany and then of China—and as a practitioner of higher education, largely in the United States. As a young professor in my first position, at Washington University in St. Louis, I came to see how excellent leadership, strong but collegial governance, and a community of outstanding students and scholars could make a powerful difference in the life of an institution. When I accepted a deanship at Washington University, one of my doctoral advisers back at Harvard, John King Fairbank, wrote to me to say that he hoped it would prove "an early inoculation" from academic administration. That was not to be, and I have been fascinated with the making of academic excellence ever since.

Reasonable readers may wonder: How can a book on "the world of universities" leave out its oldest (Bologna); two of its most ancient, venerable, and still absolute best (Oxford and Cambridge); or the fast-growing and dynamic institutions that may be found in contemporary India? Of course, the excellence of Oxford and Cambridge long predated the rise of the research university in Germany. But it was only with the rise of the German model in the nineteenth century that Oxbridge scholars returning from Germany began to incorporate a research emphasis in their collegiate system.[9] Compared to China, India, with its vast, sprawling array of higher education institutions, does not have a robust arm of government to develop national higher education policy for quality assurance and funding.[10] Perhaps taking a page from China, only in 2020 did the Indian government launch an ambitious twenty-year plan to double its higher education capacity.[11]

In any event, no single book can do everything. Since my purpose is to explore both the leading sites and systems that clearly set global standards in the nineteenth, twentieth, and (possibly) twenty-first centuries, the choice of Germany, the United States, and China is compelling. The German, American, and Chinese universities studied in this book have all been, or aspire to be, global leaders. Throughout the book there will be references to how universities measure success and, in particular, how they have come to measure success against each other. This is the story of what we today call "rankings" or "league tables." It is the story of the quest for and measurement of leadership, the effort to be, or remain, world-class universities. So perhaps we should begin by investigating what it means to be "world class."

## Rankings and Reputations in Global Higher Education

Contemporary government leaders, academic administrators, parents, and students have been concerned with understanding and identifying world-class universities. As nations race to develop innovation-driven economies, they find themselves in a global competition to nurture, attract, and retain top talent. Universities are seen as a key means to accomplishing this goal.[12] Nowhere is this more apparent than in China, where the central government has poured funding into its most elite institutions with the explicit goal of achieving world-class status. University administrations took the goal very seriously as well. For example, the 2011–2015 development plan of Tsinghua University included the phrase "world-class university" twenty-seven times.[13]

But what does "world class" mean? Philip Altbach, an American expert who has written widely on international higher education, recognized: "Everyone wants a world-class university. No country feels it can do without one. The problem is that no one knows what a world-class university is, and no one has figured out how to get one."[14] Scholars and the media have long tried to classify and quantify what makes a university great. No clear agreement has emerged, but there are common threads. Assessments of the quality of universities have taken many forms, but one type in particular stands out for its longevity and popularity: ranking tables. Widely disseminated and quick to read, national and international ranking tables became one of the most popular ways to quantify "world-class" achievement. Today, everything from fine wine to hotels to dishwashers is given grades or ranks. Why not universities?

### *The American (Now Global) Obsession with Rankings*

Rankings began as an American pastime. One of the earliest examples of college rankings in the United States grew out of a more general project on the backgrounds of outstanding thinkers, led by psychologist James McKeen Cattell.[15] As part of a larger project on outstanding scholars, in 1910 Cattell compiled a list of the one thousand most distinguished "American Men of Science," fully ranked and grouped by deciles. He then aggregated information on where these men had attended school and worked, and he devel-

**Table I.1.** Top ten institutions by faculty (absolute) (0.5 faculty indicates an emeritus or part-time faculty member) (Source: James McKeen Cattell, ed., *American Men of Science: A Biographical Directory*, 2nd ed. [New York: The Science Press, 1910], 589.)

| Rank | Institution | Number of "Men of Science" faculty |
|------|-------------|-----------------------------------|
| 1 | Harvard | 79.5 |
| 2 | Columbia | 48 |
| 3 | Chicago | 47.5 |
| 4 | Yale | 38 |
| 5 | Cornell | 35 |
| 6 | Johns Hopkins | 33.5 |
| 7 | Wisconsin | 30 |
| 8 | Department of Agriculture | 28 |
| 9 | Geological Survey | 25.5 |
| 10 | MIT | 25 |

oped lists of institutions according to total number of distinguished faculty, total number of distinguished alumni, and ratio of distinguished faculty to the entire faculty body. Most important, one of his closing analyses listed the universities according to number of currently employed "Men of Science"—that is, faculty who did real research—weighted by each man's (and they were all men, then) individual ranking among his peers.

The importance of balancing the use of absolute and relative statistics was apparent from this first ranking: had Cattell ordered his chart according to the *ratio* of total number of faculty to number of "Men of Science," we would get a rather different outcome. For example, in 1910 Clark University—the Caltech of its day—was, pound for pound, far more distinguished in research than Harvard.

Cattell's work laid out the choices and trade-offs that have continued to confound ranking systems. Cattell's effort is an early example of one of the methodological pillars of rankings today: outcome-based analysis.[16] Outcome-based analyses judge universities on the basis of the various outputs and outcomes of their operations, such as famous alumni produced, prize-winning professors employed, or research papers published.

In 1924 chemist Raymond Hughes piloted a study that introduced the other pillar of modern ranking methodology: reputation-based analysis.[17] At the behest of the North Central Association of Schools and Colleges, he

**Table I.2.** Top ten institutions by faculty (relative) (Data source: James McKeen Cattell, ed., *American Men of Science: A Biographical Directory*, 2nd ed. [New York: The Science Press, 1910], 589.)

| Rank | Institution | Ratio of total faculty: "Men of Science" faculty |
|---|---|---|
| 1 | Clark | 2 |
| 2 | Johns Hopkins | 5.6 |
| 3 | Chicago | 6 |
| 4 | Stanford | 6.9 |
| 5 | Harvard | 7.8 |
| 6 | Bryn Mawr | 7.8 |
| 7 | Wesleyan | 8.5 |
| 8 | Case | 8.8 |
| 9 | Princeton | 9.8 |
| 10 | MIT | 10.1 |

surveyed faculty members at Miami University, asking them to rate twenty disciplines at thirty-six universities on a scale of one to five, and then aggregated these ratings into a comprehensive list. In the next iteration of his survey in 1934, Hughes surveyed respondents from a broader spread of universities, but he made aggregated results available only in alphabetical order, for his intention was not to determine a ranking. His work laid the foundation for a proliferation of reputation-based graduate program ranking systems in the 1950s and 1960s.

But it was not until 1983, with the first "America's Best Colleges" report by *U.S. News and World Report* (USNWR) that the general public gained access to and took interest in university rankings. *U.S. News and World Report* was a minor and failing newsweekly, outflanked by *Time* and *Newsweek*. It needed another mission, and it found one. "America's Best Colleges" began as a purely reputational survey and produced a ranking solely based on the opinions of university presidents. In response to criticism of its methodology, USNWR shifted its approach in 1988 to develop a ranking that was 25 percent reputational and 75 percent based on absolute data, including admissions and graduation rates, faculty performance, and so on. From then on, the USNWR ranking dominated the sphere of US university rankings at both the undergraduate and then graduate and professional levels, all now published annually.[18]

According to David S. Webster, "Just as democracy, according to Winston Churchill, is the worst form of government except for all the others, so quality rankings are the worst device for comparing the quality of American colleges and universities, except for all the others."[19] By the early 2000s, however, domestic US rankings were no longer the only ones that were debated. As faculty, students, jobs, and information became more globally mobile, universities found themselves in an increasingly internationalized marketplace. Globalization and the universal aspiration to world-class status led to a proliferation of ranking systems that compared institutions across national borders. This made a hard job even harder. It was difficult enough to try to objectively compare universities with a wide range of schools, specializations, and missions within even a single country like the United States.

But, despite the limitations of the rankings—and there are many—and the misgivings of university administrators and critics of higher education, who bemoan their ubiquity and their influence, the ranking systems did help establish a consensus for evaluation and comparison. Each system—*U.S. News and World Report,* the Shanghai Jiao Tong University Academic Ranking of World Universities (ARWU), *Times Higher Education World University Rankings,* and Quacquarelli Symonds (QS) World University Rankings—tended to place primary importance on the research produced at each university, perhaps the most easily quantifiable output. Outside the ranking systems, scholars and administrators established more nuanced definitions of greatness that incorporated abstract concepts such as academic freedom and institutional autonomy as well as measurable outputs such as faculty citations and prizes won by alumni. The common ground among the many definitions of "world class" lay in the consistent emphasis on excellence in three areas: faculty, students, and administration. More recently, and in China in particular, the definition of "world class" often also includes international and cultural exchange.

## Faculty

A faculty of the highest quality that produces plentiful research is key in almost every conception of "world class." As Henry Rosovsky, former dean of the Faculty of Arts and Sciences at Harvard, argued, the best schools "correctly assume that the quality of the faculty is the most important factor in maintaining their reputation and position. The best faculty attracts the finest students, produces the highest-quality research, gains the most outside support."[20] But what policies attract high-quality faculty members?

How do universities ensure that an exemplary scholar continues to produce research?

The most basic requirement for plentiful, high-quality research output from faculty is academic autonomy. The concepts of "freedom to teach" (*Lehrfreiheit*) and "freedom to learn" (*Lernfreiheit*) were central to the world's first research university, the University of Berlin. As the model of the research university spread and evolved in Europe and the United States, the value of academic freedom allowed professors, as experts in their fields, to pursue research in areas to the extent that their interests and resources allowed. This expanded freedom of research (never perfect to be sure) allowed universities to become centers of innovation and discovery. The protection of academic freedom was linked to an implicit social contract between the professoriat and society at large—those afforded the time and space to carry out research had a duty to share their findings with society and work toward the greater good.[21]

Of course, much is missing in the rankings game. Rankings rank only what can be measured. They privilege research publication in select (largely English-language) international journals. Criteria such as citation indexes may be critical to the field of economics but rather unhelpful in Celtic language studies. International rankings can focus on major research prizes, and universities glory in having on their faculty Nobel laureates, taking credit for work often done decades earlier at another university.

As a rule, rankings studiously ignore teaching, education, and curriculum, let alone mentoring or inspiration. Universities have to evaluate teaching on their own, and they do so unevenly. Few universities actively reward good teaching professionally or financially. In principle, outstanding teaching can connect cutting-edge faculty research with the nurturing of talented students. But even the best teaching and mentorship may be only vaguely represented in rankings by other measures, such as faculty-to-student ratios.

The centrality of faculty to the creation of world-class universities can be a financial and organizational burden for university administrations. Attracting the best faculty who are distinguished in research can mean entering a bidding war not unlike that in European football. Who would not want the Lionel Messi of the life sciences? Recruitment of the best requires outsized compensation, extraordinary resources, and facilities (often new), not to mention time *off* from teaching. Tenure systems, begun in part as a means to ensure academic autonomy, are now inextricably linked with competition among universities. To recruit or retain the very best in an international, competitive environment, universities have to offer lifelong tenure. Today, no national system of higher education is recruiting more vigorously across national borders than that of China. But China's Thousand Talents Program is but the latest example of a recruitment game long tested in the West.

## Students

Universities would not exist without students. The ability to attract top students and nurture exceptional and productive graduates (however these may be defined) is another key facet of a world-class university. A world-class university needs admissions mechanisms that allow it to recruit and admit students with the highest potential. Once admitted, students are exposed to new ideas and inspiring research. While the quality of faculty certainly affects the development of students, equally important is the quality of fellow students and, not the least, the nature of the curriculum.

In discussions of global excellence in universities, a curriculum based in the liberal arts (often in the form of general education requirements) is frequently cited as the central means to nurture students' future potential as citizens. The late president of the University of Iowa and Dartmouth College, James O. Freedman, one of the most articulate American advocates for an education in the liberal arts and sciences, stressed the public purpose of undergraduate education: "A liberal education seeks to strengthen students' capacities to deal with the world's and the nation's agendas, to expand their horizons, enrich their intellect, and deepen their spirit. It asks them to accept responsibility for their actions and for the welfare of others."[22] A 2013 report of the American Academy of Arts and Sciences, *The Heart of the Matter,* argued that an education in the humanities and social sciences was a national imperative for the United States, essential "1) to educate Americans in the knowledge, skills, and understanding they will need to thrive in a twenty-first-century democracy; 2) to foster a society that is innovative, competitive, and strong; and 3) to equip the nation for leadership in an interconnected world. These goals cannot be achieved by [natural] science alone."[23]

To be sure, exhortations to bolster the liberal arts are more than matched by academic hand-wringing about how their perceived virtues (e.g., teaching critical thinking, building character, educating for citizenship) are absent in practice.[24] Further, there is no consensus on how the liberal arts ought best be taught. As I recall from Harvard's own review of undergraduate education in the first decade of the 2000s, when, as dean, I commissioned sets of faculty and student essays on general education, there is no shortage of imaginative and quite divergent views on what an education in the liberal arts and sciences entails.[25]

Still, the idea remains powerful and global. In the early twenty-first century, European and Chinese universities began to emulate the practices of American liberal arts colleges, often in the form of elite honors colleges within research universities. Aspiring world-class universities sought ways to balance the holistic development of their students with the depth of their specialist knowledge.

## Governance

Universities commonly deemed "world class" may be said to have another distinguishing trait: they enjoy flexible and effective governance systems, largely insulated from political interference in their appointments and education, and with sufficient resources to implement their visions. This was the nineteenth-century Humboldtian vision, seldom realized perfectly anywhere. In the United States, most universities developed a governance system led by a president, at the top of an administrative hierarchy, and a board of trustees. Ideally this management structure allowed even publicly funded universities to (mostly) base decisions on the best interests of the institution, without being swept up in the political tides. But as the eminent scholar of American higher education Jonathan Cole, the former provost of Columbia University, argues, among the greatest threats faced by universities today is "government intrusion into the freedom of academic inquiry."[26]

Yet governments are essential to the lives and livelihoods of universities. Jamil Salmi, a leading scholar of international higher education, argues that in the current globalized world, "it is unlikely that a world-class university can be rapidly created without a favorable policy environment and direct public initiative and support."[27] A challenge for aspiring world-class universities today, as for German, American, and Chinese universities over the past two centuries, is to foster cooperative relationships with supportive, but not stifling, governments. Finding a relationship with the state that, as Goldilocks might say, is "just right," turns out not to be easy.

Regardless of political influences from outside the university, world-class universities also need effective systems of governance within their walls. For example, in most leading American universities, key budgeting or potentially contentious decisions are made by appointed deans, provosts, or other administrators rather than by faculty committees. German universities, by contrast, have traditions of elected deans and presidents, a process that Henry Rosovsky suggests "ensures that leadership is weak."[28] Chinese universities have experimented with every conceivable model over the last century, but today the growing role of the Communist Party in university administration brings the prospect of strong but perhaps not responsive leadership.

## Internationalization

While found in only three out of the four main ranking systems, international engagement is frequently cited as a criterion for world-class universities, especially in China. International engagement appears in many different ways on university campuses, including an internationally diverse faculty and student body, international academic exchange programs, and the founding of stand-alone or joint-venture international branch campuses. The current internationalization of universities has both responded to and led economic globalization, as universities compete to host a "global community of future leaders," as Tsinghua University claims for one of its flagship programs.[29] This, too, is not new: the leading universities studied in this book have each been the product of several centuries of academic internationalization.

## The Rule of Rankings

As discussions of world-class universities became an academic cottage industry in the twenty-first century, definitions of the term grew complex and, at times, contradictory. Chinese officials tended to emphasize contribution to the public good as a defining mark of a world-class university.[30] Others stressed the role of a university in innovation, while a few argued instead for the centrality of tradition.[31] It was unclear whether definitions would converge on a few key ideas or become more diverse over time.

Perhaps the debate over the meaning of "world class" was in part a reaction to the worship of rankings, which could drive universities to focus only on that which was ranked, rather than on a broad mission of academic exploration and discovery. Might not rankings—all of which measured past activity—in fact impede creativity in the building of new or renewed institutions? Yet the presidents, provosts, and deans around the world who ritually denounced the tyranny of rankings to their governing boards still did their best every day to rise in them.

And rankings do show, however imperfectly, the shifting tectonic plates of global leadership in higher education. Had rankings such as those issued by Shanghai Jiao Tong University (the ARWU ranking), read today by deans and presidents around the world, existed a century ago, German universities would still have held pride of place. Harvard University, which ranks very well at the present, would not have been in the top ten, perhaps not in the top twenty; it became a research university worthy of the name only in the late nineteenth century by emulating the practices of the University of Berlin. Today, at least according to the QS rankings, Peking University and Tsinghua University outperform *every* German university. Times change.

# CHAPTER ONE

# The University in Germany

## *A Historical Introduction*

A T THE center of Berlin, on the central avenue Unter den Linden, sits an armory, or *Zeughaus*, built by Frederick III, Elector of Brandenburg, in the late seventeenth and early eighteenth centuries. It became a military museum in 1875 under the unified Prussian-German Empire. In 1943 it was the site of a failed attempt to assassinate Adolf Hitler. Today it is home to the German Historical Museum.

Visitors entering the museum are introduced not to the story of "Germany," which as a political entity did not exist before 1870, but to the history of German-speaking peoples in a European context, whether under Prussian, Polish, Austrian, or French rule. Visitors progress through exhibits from late Roman times through to the Middle Ages. They experience the Reformation and the Thirty Years' War from alternative perspectives; dynastic rivalries between the Bourbons and the Habsburgs; the French Revolution and Napoleonic conquests; the abortive revolutions of 1848; Germany's unification and its defeat in World War I; the Weimar experiment; Hitler's rise, genocide, and Germany's demise in World War II. Then at 1949, the exhibit divides, and visitors must decide: to go left is to be greeted by a Trabant, the spunky socialist fiberglass auto, and to enter the German Democratic Republic; to go right is to be escorted by a Volkswagen bug to the Western world of the German Federal Republic. When visitors reach 1990, the exhibit, like Germany, reunites.

Like the path of German history, the story of German universities is not linear. As with the landscape traversed by the museum, some German-founded universities are no longer in the territory of any German-speaking state. The East Prussian University of Königsberg, for example, where Immanuel Kant taught and served as rector in the late eighteenth century, lies now in the Russian Federation, the site of a federal university recently renamed for Kant by Vladimir Putin. Today the University of Heidelberg calls itself "Germany's oldest university," but that is true only if one limits German geography to the present Federal Republic.[1] Scattered across the lands of the Holy Roman Empire, the medieval and early modern establishments that called themselves "universities" bore little resemblance to the research institutions that would transform the world of universities in the nineteenth century and beyond.

With papal blessing, Emperor Charles IV, who was also king of Bohemia, founded the University of Prague in 1348 to educate Bohemians, Bavarians, Poles, and Saxons, although it took the university more than a decade to produce its first graduate. His son-in-law, Rudolf IV, Duke of Austria, followed suit in 1365 with the University of Vienna. Divisions in Christianity fed the establishment of new institutions. The Western Schism of 1378 and ensuing confrontation led to the founding of the universities of Heidelberg (1386), Cologne (1388), and Erfurt (1392), as existing ecclesiastical institutions were enlarged into universities. A regional bishop typically administered the university, which was, in principle, subject only to the Emperor. After the establishment of universities in Greifswald in 1456 and Freiburg (Breisgau) in 1457, it was common practice to possess the "privileges" of the emperor, such as certain exemptions from taxation and military service, in addition to the one given by the pope. German universities had a public character from birth.

German universities grew in number, if not distinction, when the Protestant Reformation of the sixteenth century increased demand for institutions whose religious affiliations aligned with those of a sovereign: *cuius regio, eius religio* ("whose realm, his religion"). Before the Reformation, there were fifteen universities in German-speaking lands; by 1700 this number had doubled.

These were universally small institutions reliant on imperial, papal, or princely patronage. Enrollment and teaching positions fluctuated considerably; some universities came close to extinction. Enrollment at the best-regarded institutions ranged between one thousand and twelve hundred students, but the smallest universities had but eighty to one hundred attendees. Reputations rose and fell. No single university dominated the landscape. In the early fifteenth century, Erfurt and Cologne were among the largest and most eminent. A century later, Leipzig and Ingolstadt rose to prominence. Humanism and the Reformation gave Wittenberg and Leipzig, as well as Helmstedt, Frankfurt an der Oder, Jena, and Ingolstadt their days in the sun. During the Thirty Years' War, Königsberg, Rostock, and Cologne became comparatively large universities, with students fleeing war conflict zones and—in the best tradition of university students of any era—avoiding military conscription.

German universities in the eighteenth century trained men for professions, such as in medicine, the clergy, or (by studying law) the government. Universities were, in principle, the apogee of a variegated system of schools of highly uneven quality. Most of these served different segments of society for very specific functions. Cadet schools trained officers for the military, while seminaries graduated pastors. Aristocratic families sent young men to what we may call "knight schools"—the *Ritterakademien*—that became popular in the late sixteenth century as places to learn military and courtly manners. Sons of artisans and merchants studied at Latin schools for several years before learning a trade. These schools were not part of any systematic hierarchy, and, as a result, there was no single path to university. Whatever their type, these schools were mostly "ill-equipped, poorly run, and badly attended."[2]

The behavior of students did not enhance the reputation of universities. Eighteenth-century versions of *National Lampoon's Animal House* made universities infamous for intoxication and immorality—with brawling accompanied by swordplay (although the *Schmisse*, or dueling scar, would not become popular until the nineteenth century). The late-eighteenth century educational reformer Joachim Heinrich Campe asked rhetorically, "Do universities do more good than harm?" His answer was no. "The best young people are, if not destroyed completely, at least made wild at universities and return from them weakened in body and soul, lost to themselves and the world."[3]

Even—or perhaps especially—in the century of Enlightenment, German universities had a simply awful reputation. While in Paris and Oxford university life flourished, attracting scholars from across Europe, in Germany universities remained largely provincial. It was not a compliment when they were called "medieval." They were considered sites of rote learning, imparted to students by a professoriat reciting ancient texts and largely beholden to church and sovereign.[4] Professors lectured and (on occasion) published in Latin. Leading intellectuals largely made their reputations apart from university life. The great mathematician and philosopher Gottfried Wilhelm Leibniz thought of universities as monasteries with "sterile fancies."[5] He convinced the Elector of Brandenburg *not* to establish a new university, but to found instead (in 1700) a *Societät der Wissenschaften*, which became the Royal Prussian Academy of Sciences.

There were, however, attempts in the eighteenth century to reform the potential of German universities. The practical needs of the state with a growing bureaucracy, as well as early Enlightenment currents, gave impetus to rethinking the role of the university. The University of Halle was founded in 1694 by the same, reformist Elector of Brandenburg (Frederick III). It was built on the grounds of an existing *Ritterakademie*, to which were added faculties of theology and law. Early Enlightenment figures, like Christian Thomasius in Halle, sought to transform universities from places of orthodoxy and dogma and into havens for reflection and free speech well suited to the modern state. Thomasius began to lecture at Halle in the German vernacular, rather than in Latin. He brought together the medieval with the modern, in a curriculum that covered riding, fencing, and preparation for the Prussian civil service. Halle was also a business success, competing successfully for the offspring of the nobility (who paid higher fees than others) by combining an early modern "general education" with a contemporary legal education.[6]

Halle's early success (it would not last) inspired competition from the House of Hanover, now in union with Great Britain and a rival of Prussia. Founded in 1737 by George II of England and Elector of Hanover, the University of Göttingen foreshadowed in some ways the coming of the modern research university. It was nonsectarian; the state confirmed professorial appointments; it recruited talent from across German Europe by paying high salaries; it developed a strong *Philosophische Fakultät*, encompassing the arts and sciences; and, for eminently practical reasons, it brought together a superb law faculty. As a leading figure in Göttingen's rise, the Hanoverian official Gerlach Adolf von Münchhausen, noted, "That the legal faculty be filled with famous and excellent men is necessary above all, because that faculty must induce many rich and distinguished students to study in Göttingen."[7] Göttingen cultivated an enviable, internal esprit de corps. When in 1789 the Prussian minister Friedrich Gedike reported to King Frederick William II on the state of German universities, he wrote this about Göttingen: "Nowhere else have I found as much fondness for their university on the part of professors as here. They seem to take it as a foregone conclusion that their university is the best in Germany. They often speak of other universities with disdain or pity. It's as if they are all intoxicated with pride in the university's merits—partly real, partly alleged, and partly imagined." At least from a Prussian point of view, Göttingen was a scholarly paradise. Gedike found little of the "factionalization, envy, backbiting, and need to diminish one another's accomplishments" that was ubiquitous in other universities. "Or, at least, they are less apparent here."[8]

The University of Jena was another beacon of excellence. Located in the duchy of Saxe-Weimar, it reached its height in the second half of the eighteenth century under the Duke Karl August, who was Goethe's patron. It was a center of German idealism, where at different times the faculty included Fichte, Hegel, Schelling, and Schlegel. Even Schiller taught there briefly.

Yet the German university "system," to the degree one can describe it as such, still suffered from stasis and educated the privileged few at the turn of the nineteenth century. It remained polycentric, still (despite Göttingen's pretensions) with no single leading institution. It relied on princely patronage and the high tuition charged to noble and elite families, but its audience was shrinking, not growing. German universities outside Austria enrolled in toto, at most, nine thousand students in 1700. A century later, enrollments had fallen by at least one-third, to less than six thousand. Other estimates put the number as low as thirty-seven hundred in 1780.[9] To the degree that innovation had occurred at all, it was in the newer institutions of Halle and Göttingen, not in the large majority of institutions, where a lethargic and privileged professoriat defended its historical practices. In the view of educational reformers such as Campe, it was too late to reform: "To change the nature of the universities means to abolish them."[10] At the turn of the nineteenth century, the Prussian minister responsible for higher education proposed just that: the total elimination of the university as an institution.[11]

That this did not happen was in no small measure the result of the efforts generously attributed to a home-schooled man who never finished his university studies at Frankfurt an der Oder and Göttingen: Wilhelm von Humboldt. His story, and that of the University of Berlin, which he initiated in

1810 and which became the exemplar of the modern research university, is the subject of Chapter 2. Here we might simply set out several themes that endured from the pre-Humboldtian world of German universities to the world of universities today.

First, even after the ascendance of the University of Berlin over the course of the nineteenth century to a position of national and international eminence, German higher education remained decentralized, in the hands of the various political entities governing German-speaking lands. Despite several German unifications (1870, 1938, 1990) there would be no "national university." Today, it is still the individual states (*Länder*) of the Federal Republic that oversee German universities. Universities rose and fell in prestige and in competition one with another: if in the eighteenth century this was a competition for students, in the twenty-first century it is a race for recognition in an "Excellence Initiative."

Second, modern German universities inherited from their medieval and early modern ancestors certain traditions of institutional autonomy, initially as corporations, which set their own procedures of governance and were guarded jealously. Whereas in the eighteenth century this often fostered a defensive insularity and a stultifying pedantry, the self-regulating capacity of a renewed professoriat in the nineteenth century to set new standards of research and teaching would differentiate the German university from anything else. And disputes over internal governance would nearly bring German universities to their knees in the 1960s.

Third, from early modern times to nearly the present, governance meant the rule not just of professors, but of *Ordinarien,* of full professors. Nineteenth century reforms formally established the *Ordinarienuniversität,* or a university of chaired professors, as the norm. There were three basic ranks of faculty: the *Ordinarius,* or *ordentlicher* (full) *Professor,* who held a chair, or *Lehrstuhl;* what we might translate as associate professor, appropriately named *Extraordinarius,* or *außerordentlicher Professor,* whose only hope at a professorship was to be "called" to another university; and below that, the ranks of the *Privatdozent,* the learned scholar with a doctorate and a post-doctorate *Habilitation,* who was not formally a member of the faculty and was not a civil servant. This was (and is still today) no "tenure-track" system. Chaired professors ruled in their area of expertise; faculties were built around seminars or institutes, each headed by a chaired professor with an assemblage of academic help.[12] German universities created both a tradition of senior faculty rule and a class of permanently adjunct faculty.

Fourth, as a result, academic leadership of an institution seldom came from the top. A dean was seldom more than a coordinator of chairs. The rector, a chaired professor who nominally headed the university, was primus inter pares, representing the chairs externally. The rector was elected from among the chaired professors for a two-year term; and for the University of Berlin, it was a *nonrenewable* term until the 1930s. Only in the second half of the twentieth century was the position renamed "president." Presidents were officers who did not have to be professors nor members of the university, although normally they were.

Fifth, while professorial self-governance, an eventually rigorous appointment process, and generous funding of professorial chairs helped to make German universities extraordinary innovators in research in the nineteenth century, the absence of strong administrative leadership in the university meant that the states that funded German universities could, and at times would, have a decisive voice in determining their direction. Examples include the founding of the University of Berlin in 1810, its eminence in the natural sciences under the guidance of a strong Prussian minister in the late nineteenth century, and its Nazification in 1933.

Sixth, although German universities became global models in the nineteenth and early twentieth centuries, dissatisfaction with their limits spawned the growth of external research organizations. Just as Leibniz convinced the Elector of Brandenburg to found an Academy of Sciences in 1700, so two centuries later would Emperor William II establish the scientific societies that we today know as the Max Planck institutes—powerful engines of research but connected to German universities only along dotted lines. And in Communist East Germany, a revived Academy of Sciences (now on a Soviet model) competed with universities for funding and talent.

Finally, traditions of student independence and assertive behavior would endure as German universities matured in the nineteenth century and massified in the late twentieth. Dueling scars would be a badge of honor in German universities until the Nazis outlawed the practice in the 1930s. But it was political activism on the part of students that would repeatedly test institutions and governments. Nationalist student fraternities (*Burschenschaften*) would be banned in the era of Metternichian repression after 1819. Students would challenge the communization of the University of Berlin in 1948 and found their own, "free" university that same year. Twenty years later, students at Free University became poster children for the global left as they disrupted classes and sought to defenestrate professors.

These continuities matter, but they must not obscure the point. As Daniel Fallon has written in his study of *The German University*, the reinvention of the university in the nineteenth century was a radical act: "Perhaps the most remarkable fact about the widely admired German university of the nineteenth century is that it had no clear precedent." The idea of a *research* university was struck de novo.[3]

Contemplate the changing fate of German universities. By 1800 German universities were at once ancient and outmoded, ripe for abolition. A half-century later, the first president of the University of Michigan, Henry Philip Tappan, wrote: "The system of public instruction adopted by the State of Michigan is copied from the Prussian, acknowledged to be the most perfect in the world." By the late nineteenth century, the president of Clark University, then a leading institution of engineering and applied science in the United States, wrote: "The German University is today the freest spot on earth. . . . Nowhere has the passion to push on to the frontier of human knowledge been so general." Two world wars later, the former president of Harvard and the former American ambassador to West Germany, James B. Conant, was nostalgic as he called the German university "the best in the world—for the nineteenth century."[14]

Few would argue that German universities are the "best in the world" today. But they once were, and they are striving toward revival. In contemporary league tables, no matter what the ranking system, no German university enters the top twenty, and only a handful are listed in the top one hundred. The first ARWU ranking of 2003 prompted soul searching in Germany, as not a single German university was to be found among the top fifty.[15] It prompted, too, strategies for a return to "excellence."

As we shall see, in recent years German politicians and administrators have puzzled over how to claw their way back to the top, how to reignite dynamic research and recruit top international researchers. Europe-wide higher education reforms officially introduced in 1999 called the "Bologna Process" led German universities to streamline antiquated and idiosyncratic degree systems, making them more accessible to international students. The popular Erasmus program—a European Union–wide student exchange program—increased mobility and internationalization. Universities pooled resources to attract and retain talent. Three rounds of funding to reward distinctive, especially high-potential programming in the form of a nationwide "Excellence Initiative" propelled certain institutions forward, equipping them for research and teaching in the twenty-first century.

The best way to understand the rise, destruction, and revival of German higher education is to take a closer look at two universities. Although they are both located in the Prussian (now German) capital of Berlin, in many respects they are from two different worlds. Chapters 2 and 3 chart the histories of Humboldt University and Free University in Berlin. They provide case studies that allow a revealing look into the past and future of German higher education.

# CHAPTER TWO

# The Modern Original

## *The University of Berlin*

A s YOU enter the gates of today's Humboldt University, you pass the marble statues of the two men who became the university's namesakes. One was the scholar and statesman Wilhelm von Humboldt; the other, his great naturalist brother, Alexander. Located on Unter den Linden in the heart of Berlin, the main building once was home to the younger brother of Frederick the Great. Across the street from the university sits the Stadtschloß, the magnificent urban palace of the Hohenzollern monarchs that dates from the fifteenth century, was blown up by the Communists in the mid-twentieth century, and has now been reconstructed and reconceived in the twenty-first century as a cultural center at the heart of Germany's, and in some sense Europe's, capital.

Entering the university's *Hauptgebäude,* or main building, you find yourself in a grand foyer of red marble from East German mines. A grand staircase leads you to a landing with a large quotation in gold letters by one of the university's most famous alumni, Karl Marx. "Philosophers have only interpreted the world in various ways; the point, however, is to change it." The Communist regime had ordered the installation of Marx's epigrammatic eleventh thesis on Feuerbach in 1953, when the university was convulsed in change. Today, the stairs leading up to Marx's call to action are adorned with a satirical art installation. Each step forward warns: *"Vorsicht Stufe"* ("Beware of the step").

Arriving on the second level of the *Hauptgebäude,* the portraits of the university's twenty-nine Nobel laureates greet you. Among them are Fritz

**Figure 2.1.** Main building of Humboldt University. Beek100/Wikimedia Commons/CC BY-SA 3.0.

**Figure 2.2.** Karl Marx quote at Humboldt University. Photograph © William C. Kirby.

Haber, whose work made possible the production of reactive nitrogen, used in fertilizers; Theodor Mommsen, the renowned classical scholar, historian, and jurist; Robert Koch, who discovered the pathogens that cause infectious diseases; Otto Hahn, who conducted the first nuclear fission experiment; Max Planck, the founder of quantum theory; and, most famously, Albert Einstein.

From the red marble staircase, the way to the president's office leads down a long and wide corridor characteristic of eighteenth century neoclassical architecture. More impressive is the height of the ceilings, which makes it nearly impossible to cool the offices in summer or heat them in winter. Solitude and freedom, Wilhelm von Humboldt noted, were necessary to the proper functioning of the university. But in the case of Humboldt's recent leaders, solitude could feel more like isolation.

The University of Berlin was founded on the promise of change. As the world's first modern research university, it was a global model of innovation in research, teaching, and governance. In 2021, its president, Sabine Kunst, confronted the challenge of energizing an institution burdened by its history and enervated by a governance structure that has become belatedly (and perhaps too) democratic. After all, her predecessor declined his candidacy for a second term after failed attempts to change the university's leadership structure. Indeed, none of her predecessors since the fall of the Berlin Wall in 1989 completed more than a single term. Kunst came into office aware of the many challenges facing her: from a severely constrained financial situation, to the overdue professionalization of administration, to the pressure to be successful in the ongoing national "Excellence Initiative."

The experience of one of her recent predecessors, Christoph Markschies, was not promising. When greeting an international assembly of scholars (of which this author was one) to mark the two hundredth anniversary of the founding of the University at Berlin, Markschies noted that the university was home to "Humboldt's model." But what did that mean? Was it, he wondered, the "kind of university which developed into the Prussian State University in the middle of the nineteenth century . . . which was to be perverted by National Socialism and anti-Semitism, which finally degenerated at the hands of a petty bourgeoisie masquerading as Marxist"? In all these contexts, he noted, the university had been a model, "at first with worldwide recognition, then in the 'Großdeutsches Reich,' and finally, in East Germany."[1]

But what was the university today? In the two centuries that separated Humboldt from Markschies, the ambitions of the new university and its leadership had been repeatedly frustrated by political turmoil, restrictions on academic freedom, and cycles of financial hardship. In his welcoming address to this international conference on "Humboldt's Model," Markschies, in one of his final speeches as university president, told the assembled and astonished guests, "Today nobody anywhere in the world is prepared to take this university, which is financially and otherwise in the hands of one of the poorest States in the Federal Republic, as a model."[2]

## Founding the Modern Research University, 1810–1848

The University of Berlin, predecessor to the modern Humboldt University and to Free University of Berlin, was heir to multiple and mixed legacies. For its first century and more, it was literally and figuratively in the shadow of the palace, in the direct service of the Prussian-German state. It was home to the birth of modern scientific research in a university setting. It witnessed political battles for Germany's and the university's soul.

The University of Berlin was an upstart in comparison with venerable institutions such as Bologna (founded in 1088), Salamanca (1164), Oxford (1167), and Cambridge (1209). In German-speaking lands, Vienna (1365), Heidelberg (1386), Leipzig (1409), and Rostock (1419) all held pride of place. Yet Berlin would outdo them all by reimagining what a university could be. Within decades of its founding in 1810, the university developed into one of the world's leading institutions of higher education. It would lead Germany and eventually the world in creating a modern system of research-driven higher education.

In the beginning was Napoleon.[3] Two weeks after Napoleon and his army defeated Prussia at the battlefield outside Jena on October 14, 1806, French forces marched through the Brandenburg Gate, occupying and plundering Berlin. Remnant Prussian forces and King Frederick William III retreated to the East Prussian stronghold of Königsberg. The following year the Treaty of Tilsit brought a harsh peace. Prussia lost not only more than half of its territory but also its six universities west of the Elbe River. The French Revolution and Napoleon's conquests left Europe's university landscape devastated: in 1815, 60 of the 143 European universities that had existed before 1789 were closed. In the German states, 18 out of 34 universities were shuttered.[4] The University of Halle (established in 1694), Prussia's leading university at the time and a center of the eighteenth-century German Enlightenment, was among them. The French occupiers first turned the university into a military hospital; later its main building became a slaughterhouse. When a delegation of faculty from Halle visited King Frederick William III, he agreed to open a "general educational institution" (*allgemeine Lehranstalt*) in Berlin. "The state," the king reasoned, in a phrase seldom heard from political leaders, "must replace with intellectual strength what it has lost in physical strength."[5]

At the turn of the nineteenth century, Berlin was home to around 170,000 inhabitants and, despite being home to a vibrant, cosmopolitan community of intellectuals, doctors, lawyers, and artists, the city continued to suffer from a reputation as a garrison city. The Prussian capital could not rival Vienna in cultural terms. Furthermore, there was no university in the city. King Frederick William III's decision to establish new universities stimulated debate among educational reform thinkers such as Johann Gottlieb Fichte, Friedrich Schleiermacher, and Friedrich August Wolf. The critical move took place, however, when Friedrich Wilhelm Christian Karl Ferdinand Freiherr von Humboldt (Wilhelm von Humboldt) was appointed Director of the Section for Ecclesiastical Affairs and Education at the Ministry of the Interior in 1810.

**Figure 2.3.** Wilhelm von Humboldt, 1767–1835. Humboldt-Universität zu Berlin, Universitätsbibliothek.

Wilhelm von Humboldt was a man of letters of the German Enlighten-ment and a lifelong friend of Friedrich Schiller. He became a philosopher, linguist, philologist, diplomat, and, very briefly, a reformer of education. His work in each of these fields was notable, but he is known best for the sixteen months he spent in Berlin, in between diplomatic postings to the Vatican and Vienna. There he set out plans to reform all levels of public education: reshaping elementary schools to focus on individual growth and founding a new type of secondary school, the *Gymnasium*. And there he oversaw the founding of the University of Berlin. While his administrative commitment was limited in time, it was time well spent. The "Humboldtian" model largely shaped the world of modern universities.

What were German universities like before Humboldt? As we have seen, they were small, scattered, and largely undistinguished. There were but a few thousand students in *all* German universities by 1780. Many families could not afford the "idle time" for their sons.[6] The professoriat was paid poorly enough that most had second jobs or other income. Nepotism was rampant. As Charles McClelland notes, "Had the princely bureaucracies listened to whatever there was of public opinion in the late eighteenth century, they probably would have abolished the universities along with serfdom and other relics of the Middle Ages."[7]

Two institutions, Halle and Göttingen, sought to raise the quality of their faculty by being pioneers in recruiting "stars" from elsewhere and paying them more. Universities were largely preprofessional in training for medi-cine, theology, and law, the latter of which was a stepping-stone to gov-ernment service. By the end of the eighteenth century, many German states required some level of university education as a prerequisite to an of-ficial position.[8]

The idea that universities might serve and strengthen the state was thus not new, but with the founding of the University of Berlin this idea took a different form. Under the Stein-Hardenberg policies—named for the min-isters who oversaw them—Prussia began its transformation into a modern administrative state. Government finances and administration were ratio-nalized and gradually professionalized; municipalities were given powers of self-government, in part to create a broader interest in public affairs; the army was rebuilt; serfdom was abolished; Jews were "emancipated" from a wide range of discriminatory laws; and education was thoroughly reformed.

What was the role of the university in Prussia's renewal? Humboldt had already set to paper in 1792 (although not published) his theory of "The

Limits of State Action." Universities, Humboldt believed, would serve the state best *indirectly*. Just as his reforms of primary schools were designed to produce "well informed human beings and citizens" who could learn their vocations later, his vision of the university was one centered on the cultivation of individual capacities that, if allowed to develop freely, would best serve state and society.[9] His conception of *Bildung*, as the historian David Sorkin has argued, had both inward and civic dimensions: inward in the making of a learned, moral personality with "inner refinement"; civic in the engagement of educated men in society.[10]

Humboldt's conception of the new University of Berlin was part of a movement for "national education" (*Nationalerziehung*) led by the philosopher Johann Gottlieb Fichte, but one that should not be, in Humboldt's view, instrumentally nationalistic. Humboldt's reforms cut across social divides. He radically proposed that education should not be shaped by one's occupational or social standing, but that, "the lowest wage worker and the finest educated man must be equal in their dispositions (*Gemüt*)."[11] To achieve this, he recommended a common curriculum for all. Elementary schools would teach basic skills. High schools (*Gymnasien*) would teach not only *what* to learn but *how* to learn, and impart a degree of intellectual independence. There students would receive a "general education" (*allgemeine Menschenbildung*) in the classics, history, and mathematics.[12]

Humboldt spoke of the university as a community of teachers and students who would "devote themselves to science."[13] *Wissenschaft* incorporated learning, knowing, scholarship, and "science" in the broadest sense, including—especially—the humanities. The university would conduct scientific research at the highest level, emphasizing the transmission of knowledge to the next generation. Students would be selected on the basis of talent more than hereditary lineage; general education was offered to all on an equal basis. The university would foster a culture of liberal education that stressed education (in the sense of *Bildung*) as a progression of personal development distinct from practical training (*Übung*) in the professions.

Like other humanists of the day, Humboldt wanted to do away with what Schiller had called *Brotstudium* for careerist "bread students" seeking a moneymaking job. The aim was instead to foster the full self-development of a student's interests, capacities, and personality.[14] Humboldt convinced King Frederick William III to build on the liberal ideas of Friedrich Schleiermacher, who had petitioned the monarch to create a university, not to stress the practical, but "to stimulate the idea of science in the minds of the students, to encourage them to take account of the fundamental laws of science in all their thinking."[15]

Humboldt laid forth a new model for a university. It had three core principles. The first was the principle of the unity of research and teaching. It confirmed professors' responsibility to produce and disseminate original research for their teaching, which was quite new in 1810. At the same time, it introduced students to methods of research—for example, by supplementing lectures with small seminars and encouraging research-based study.

The second principle was the protection of academic freedom. Students were at liberty to pursue any curriculum of their choosing. Professors, in turn, had freedom of unrestricted inquiry in their teaching. *Lehrfreiheit,* the freedom to teach, and *Lernfreiheit,* the freedom to learn, became fundamentally intertwined principles. The state's role with regard to the university was to protect its freedom, not to impede it. To that end, Humboldt proposed that the university be financially independent, with its own endowment, making it a truly national institution at arm's length from the government.

The third principle was the centrality in the university of the *Philosophische Fakultät,* what in the United States today would be called the Faculty of Arts and Sciences. All students had to start their studies with arts and sciences and only then continue in specialized subjects. An education that would form creative individuals by the pursuit of knowledge would be, in time, the greatest contribution to the state that a university could make.[16]

These are principles echoed today in every college or university that professes to value the liberal arts and sciences. They would be difficult to achieve from the start.

When the university opened its doors for the winter semester of 1810, a commission led by Schleiermacher called fifty-three of Germany's most eminent scholars to Berlin. Humboldt understood that the selection of an outstanding faculty was, at the beginning and end of the day, "the crux of the matter."[17] These 53 men taught 256 students, largely, as Humboldt had intended, from non-aristocratic backgrounds. The first rector, the jurist Theodor Schmalz, was named in 1810, and he lasted but a year, having fought (and won) the first battle against censorship in the university.

Johann Gottlieb Fichte, the Idealist philosopher known best at the time for his patriotic *Reden an die deutsche Nation* at the height of the Napoleonic humiliation, became the first elected rector in July 1811. In his inaugural address to the university, he assured his audience of notables, professors, and students of the university's lofty goals in preserving the progress of humanity, and "that at no university in the world is academic freedom more secure and firmly in place as right here at this university."[18] He quickly came at odds with student groups, who—perhaps not surprisingly—were more interested in learning a profession and forging social ties than they were invested in the university's liberal curriculum.

Fichte, too, witnessed the university's first faculty controversy over student behavior. A Jewish student who had been challenged to a duel by a Christian student and member of a *Burschenschaft*, a nationalist student fraternity, declined and thereafter suffered public humiliation and ultimately an attack with a hunting whip in broad daylight.[19] The incident epitomized the way that rigid social customs among the student organizations terrorized perceived outsiders. Fichte resolved to make an example of the case. Yet his attempt to pursue the matter was prevented by the university senate. Instead, the affair was tried before a student "court of honor" with a severe punishment for the victim. As a result of this conflict and the ensuing bitterness, Fichte resolved to resign; he left office by February 1812.[20] The administrative half-life of the leaders of modern universities was, from the beginning, short.

The university grew and thrived, albeit in ways different than Humboldt had imagined. In its first decades it expanded by integrating existing institutions and infrastructure. The Charité, founded by Frederick the Great in 1726 as a "plague" hospital to treat the poor and infirm, became the Faculty of Medicine. A school of animal medicine became the Faculty of Veterinary Medicine. The royal library served as the university's first library.

To secure the university's independence, Humboldt suggested the university be provided with an endowment in the form of a large grant of royal land, but this plan was abandoned by his successors. Not only in finances, but also in governance, the university was intimately tied to the powers of the state. The state recruited students by limiting enrollment to graduates of the selective state-controlled *Gymnasien*. A state commission recruited and appointed the faculty. This relationship gave a monopoly to universities over the training of state officials and provided the state with academically trained civil servants. The close relationship between crown and gown was symbolized by the university's location at the very heart of Prussia's capital, surrounded by the Prussian Academy, the State Library, and the State Opera House. To house the university's central functions, the king donated the former palace of Prince Heinrich of Prussia—a gift from his brother Frederick the Great—to be the location of the university on Unter den Linden. In 1828 the university was renamed the Friedrich Wilhelm University in honor of its founding monarch, the formal name that it would retain until 1945.

*Bildung,* Humboldt believed, had the potential to "inoculate the Germans with the Greek spirit" and to "humanize the state."[21] But to realize that ideal he needed Prussian bureaucracy. Professors, after all, could not be counted on to run the university alone. "To direct a group of scholars," he wrote in a letter to his wife, "is not much better than to have a troop of comedians under you."[22] The appointment of professors was "the prerogative of the state . . . [for] the nature of the university is too closely tied to the vital interests of the state."[23] The accommodation of the two parties in this marriage required a constant process of negotiation between state control and liberal ideals.

The ideals of the new university would be tested severely in the era of restoration and reaction that followed the Napoleonic years. The Austrian statesman Klemens von Metternich dominated Central European politics from 1815 to 1848. He oversaw a constriction of academic discourse that began with the Carlsbad Decrees of 1819, enacted following the murder, by a radical student, of a Prussian diplomat and writer, August von Kotzebue. The decrees, enacted by the new German Confederation of states, aimed to limit liberal and nationalistic voices in the German-speaking world. Student organizations—the *Burschenschaften,* or fraternities—were restricted. Newspapers and periodicals were subject to state censorship. A state-selected "curator" was to be placed in each university—a kind of early nineteenth-century Party secretary. Although the decrees would not be repealed until the revolutions of 1848, their enforcement by the states of the loose and weak German Confederation (including Prussia) was uneven at best. In Göttingen, the "*Göttinger Sieben,*" seven professors (including the Brothers Grimm) who refused to swear loyalty to the new king after he moved to annul the kingdom's constitution, were removed from their university posts and became academic martyrs. In Berlin, the theologian Wilhelm de Wette was dismissed in 1819 for his liberal sympathies. But de Wette's ouster was protested by faculty of all political persuasions, and he soon found another post in Basel.

Even in an era of repression, most of the Humboldtian reforms endured in Berlin, and the Berlin model of a serious research university spread across Germany. It was already a famously serious place. Ludwig Feuerbach, later known best for Marx's "theses" on his work, was a student at Berlin in 1826 when he wrote, "Compared to this temple of work, the other universities appear like public houses."[24]

The university attracted an astonishing cadre of talent. The founding generation of Schleiermacher and Fichte was joined in the university's first decades by Georg Friedrich Wilhelm Hegel, the legal scholar Friedrich Carl von Savigny, the philosopher Arthur Schopenhauer, and the natural philosopher Friedrich von Schelling. Being a professor, in particular a full, or *ordentlicher Professor,* especially at Berlin, became a mark of singular social and cultural prestige. As Hegel wrote to a friend in 1816, a university post had become "an almost indispensable condition" for influence as a philosopher.[25]

The full professoriat, with a *Lehrstuhl,* or chair, was well funded but limited in numbers. They alone could not account for the "explosion of research and publication activities" in German universities in the nineteenth century.[26] For that—at Berlin and elsewhere—another innovation was critical: the growth of an academic underclass, what we would call today the "adjunct" faculty. Beyond the ranks of *ordentliche Professoren* grew a large cadre of *außerordentliche Professoren* and *Privatdozenten*—university teaching positions that brought with them prestige but little, if any, salary and no voting rights. This was a class of professors-in-waiting. In the university's 1816 statute, the *Habilitation* process, a procedure following the doctorate, which entitled the holder to hold lectures, was mentioned. Although this practice had existed before, over the course of the nineteenth and twentieth centuries it became formalized to a greater degree across German-speaking lands.[27] By the mid-nineteenth century across German universities, this distinguished adjunct faculty—increasingly composed of scholars with doctorates—well outnumbered the *Ordinarien.*[28]

The Revolution of 1848 took place in Berlin within earshot of the university: students and faculty must have heard the shooting on the Schloßplatz on March 18, which led to the promise, later betrayed, of a liberal democratic polity in Prussia and elsewhere in Germany. The university was not unaffected by the events of the following year, but neither was it a central actor. It was itself riven by disputes between the *Privatdozenten,* who sought their "corporate rights," and a conservative professoriat, which, together with the government, denied them.[29]

## Liberal Education in an Illiberal Polity, 1848–1909

One of the most important developments in the first half of the nineteenth century was the professionalization of university careers. Professors became state officials and, gradually, formed an elite that derived its status not from birthright, but from scholarship.[30] By the time of the convulsions of 1848, professors had become "notables," and as a group competed well in the elections of that democratic spring. Thus, the Frankfurt National Assembly—the first freely elected representative body for all of Germany, which aspired to a democratic unification of German states—became known as the "parliament of professors." Their efforts failed, but the constitution that parliament wrote would have an afterlife in that of the Weimar and Federal Republics. And the revolution's reversal did no apparent damage to the high prestige of German academics.[31]

The University of Berlin became part of the German nation-state that emerged in 1870. Members of the nation's ruling class spent their formative years in its lecture halls, training in disciplines such as political science or law, which were typical for the civil servants who administered the new nation-state. Much of the radical promise of the Humboldtian *Bildungs*-ideal gave way to cultivating and preserving a new ruling class. This also involved keeping certain people out. In 1878 Chancellor Otto von Bismarck passed anti-socialist legislation, which remained in effect until 1890. It banned socialists' meetings and newspapers, and deep prejudices and control over appointments effectively kept members of the Social Democratic Party (SPD) out of the higher ranks of the *Ordinarien*. Although party membership grew steadily over the late nineteenth and early twentieth centuries and was the largest in the Reichstag after 1912, before 1918 not a single Social Democrat could be found among the professors or teaching staff at German universities.[32] After passing a new law in 1898, the Prussian state permitted itself enhanced powers to remove instructors who were deemed politically unacceptable.[33]

With a strong administrative state, the university took on a more conservative role in cultivating the next generation of bureaucrats and advisors. Germany consolidated power on the world stage between 1870 and 1914 and became widely admired for its efficiency in technology and learning. Yet it retained elements of an illiberal political culture, with a complementary university structure, in which the fundamental decisions—not the least of which were war and peace—lay in a few hands. It was in the context of assertiveness abroad and conservatism at home that German universities became leaders.

In addition to their role in training the administrative and political class, in the last decades of the nineteenth century universities became subject to national education policies that stressed the importance of natural sciences and technology as instruments for national economic strength. German industrial enterprises and the military required scientific knowledge and results. By 1880 the number of students in the natural sciences in Berlin had grown rapidly, from 3 percent in 1867 to 18 percent in 1880.[34] And a second university was established in 1879 for this more applied purpose: the Royal Technical University (today the Technical University of Berlin). Like their Chinese counterparts a century later, a growing emphasis on technology and natural science made the Berlin universities engines for national industrial strength and military power. As Emperor William II declared at the onset of the twentieth century, with an unintended swipe at Humboldt, "The new century will be determined by the sciences, including technology, unlike the previous century determined by philosophy."[35]

In the rise of German science in the nineteenth and twentieth centuries, universities played a central, perhaps *the* central, role. They became the locus of scientific research and the beneficiaries of new levels of state support. *Bildung* was now linked directly to *Forschung*, a "research imperative" that prized originality and discovery across the arts and sciences.[36] The comparative amateurism of Humboldt's day gave way to an era of professional specialists that is with us still. No place was more central to all of this than Berlin. The University of Berlin produced groundbreaking discoveries in physics, chemistry, and medicine. Before the end of the First World War, approximately one-third of Nobel Prizes were awarded to German researchers. Around half of them (fourteen) were awarded to researchers associated with the University of Berlin. In the years before the onset of World War I, the University of Berlin received 15 percent of all Nobel Prizes.[37]

Many universities have been defined by their presidents or rectors. Not so the University of Berlin, where until 1933 rectors served, on average, a term of but one year, serving in a largely honorific capacity. Humboldt had "founded" the university not as rector but as a government official. When the university grew to be the academic crown jewel of a unified and industrializing Germany in the second half of the nineteenth century, the key figure was an official named Friedrich Althoff, who defined the university and much of Prussian higher education by what was later dubbed the "System

**Figure 2.4.** Left to right: Nobel Prize winners (all affiliated with the University of Berlin) Walther Nernst, Albert Einstein, Max Planck, Robert A. Millikan, and Max von Laue in the latter's apartment, around 1930. Nationaal Archief, Den Haag/Wikimedia Commons.

Althoff." Althoff was an associate professor of civil law at the University of Strasbourg who came to Prussia in 1882 to head the University Department of the Prussian Ministry for Education. He stayed in that position for a quarter century, a leader of the *Berufsbeamtentum*, the permanent civil service that stayed in place while ministers and rectors came and went. His aim was to concentrate excellence and specialization in a very few institutions. As a not-so-modest "czar" for Prussian universities, he pursued a strategic, unconventional *Wissenschaftspolitik*, in which he mobilized new funds for higher education, particularly for the University of Berlin. During his tenure, the number of institutes at the University of Berlin increased from thirty-eight to eighty-one. The university clinic Charité became a modern hospital, and the city's libraries coalesced into a network of specialized sites that co operated with each other, facilitating lending and acquisitions. And he himself recruited, retained, and reprimanded faculty, playing an extraordinary personal role in calling to Berlin Adolf von Harnack, Max Planck, Walther Nernst, Paul Ehrlich, Robert Koch, and Ferdinand von Richthofen, among others—sometimes ignoring the faculty's own recommendations. Althoff did not shy away from reminding faculty of their status as state employees and of his role in deciding their fates. Those who were not his favorites received no "call." Althoff's long dominance and his disregard for normal bureaucratic procedure diminished professorial self-governance, even as it made the university unparalleled in academic strength.[38]

While it remained a politically conservative institution, the University of Berlin took a mild step ahead on another front. In 1896 Prussia adapted its laws to accept women as guest auditors at universities. Prior to the new legislation, women needed a dispensation by the Minister of Education in Prussia to be accepted to audit lectures. Some lectures, like anatomy classes, remained exclusively for men. The University of Berlin had a comparatively high percentage of women auditing lectures, many of whom were Jewish women who had immigrated to Berlin from Russia. In 1899 Elsa Neumann obtained special approval from the Ministry of Education to receive a doctoral degree. She became the first woman to complete her doctoral studies in physics. Regular enrollment for women began only in 1908 and made up but 5 percent of the student body in that year. Yet one-third of the total number of women students in Germany were enrolled in Berlin.[39]

By the end of the nineteenth century, the University of Berlin was by some measure Germany's leading center of scholarship, outshining older venues such as Göttingen, Heidelberg, and Munich. It, without question, set the standards for research universities the world over. Berlin became a mecca for scholars and scientists and the center of a thriving academic community. It was the apex of a professorial career to receive a "call" to Berlin. Full professors in Berlin were therefore particularly old: in 1907 the average Berlin professor was almost sixty years old, whereas elsewhere in Prussia professors were, on average, six years younger.[40] Berlin offered not only prestige but good compensation. Then, as now, it paid to pay well. The average salaries in Berlin in 1905 and 1906 were 30 percent higher than academic salaries elsewhere in Prussia.[41]

Berlin—and by extension German universities as a whole—had become a model for the world. There were no comparable institutions in the United States, and access to British universities was severely restricted. An estimated nine thousand Americans had studied at German universities in the nineteenth century and were trained in the new scientific methods taught there. The reputation of the University of Berlin grew in tandem with that of Germany, which was at the height of what we today would call its "soft power." As Christopher Lasch has pointed out, for a generation of American progressives before 1914, Germany "stood for nothing if not progress."[42] For example, modeling itself after the University of Berlin, Johns Hopkins University established the first graduate school in the United States under the guidance of Daniel Coit Gilman in 1876. Most of its fifty-three faculty members had studied at German universities, and thirteen had received German doctorates.

## Beginning a Second Century, 1910–1932

The centenary of 1910 marked at once a high point and a decisive turn in the history of the university. The jubilee was marked by pomp and circumstance: Emperor William II and his empress attended the opening reception on October 11, 1910. It was a time of congratulatory myth-making: for the first time in a sustained way, the "Humboldtian ideals" that underlay the university's founding were celebrated and mythologized, often in unrecognizable form. And it was a time for reflection on what the university had become.[43]

The contrast with the fledgling institution of 1810 could not have been starker. The university had been founded in an era of defeat; its centenary was hailed in a triumphalist "culture of victory." At home and abroad, the university was "the most famous address in the world of research and learning."[44] Founded with the promise of autonomy from the state (and of an endowment to fund it), the university was now well supported, but exclusively by the state, and was inseparably part of the political culture of Wilhelmine Germany. In founding the university in the aftermath of military catastrophe, King Frederick William III aimed in 1810 to "replace with intellectual strength what it [the state] has lost in physical strength." Now the speeches in 1910 celebrated the university in martial metaphors: it was "Germany's first intellectual parade-ground." The Minister of Culture August von Trott zu Solz proclaimed it "an intellectual fortress for the protection of the Fatherland" and "the arsenal of its scientific weapons."[45] To these assertions there was no rejoinder, for at a university that had prized intellectual originality and witnessed firsthand the debates of the Napoleonic, Metternichian, and *Vormärz* eras, there now ruled a "graveyard peace" (*Friedhofsruhe*) in the realm of politics.[46]

Other developments of that anniversary year called into question founding concepts. While over the past century the university (as opposed to the court or academies of science) had cemented its status as the arbiter and home of the modern sciences, the founding of independent research institutions slowly shifted this balance. Again it was Althoff, sometimes described as the "Bismarck of German higher education," who before his death in 1908 had initiated the founding of the *Kaiser-Wilhelm-Gesellschaft* (KWG, later renamed the *Max-Planck-Gesellschaft*), which was inaugurated at the centenary. This society was an umbrella organization that housed the first independent graduate research institutions in Germany, with the central purpose to foster basic research in the natural sciences. They were joint ventures between industry and government, outside the walls of a university, albeit connected often by joint appointments. The KWG undid the universities' monopoly on research but manifested the state's support for German industry, so long as it helped to pay for it. A group of industrial enterprises, banks, and agricultural businesses provided the KWG with its initial funding. The state endowed the KWG with property in Berlin-Dahlem and created civil service posts for its directors. The establishment of twenty new KWG institutes between 1911 and 1933 forged a new, powerful alliance between the state, the economy, and science. For the University of Berlin, however, this development precipitated the search for a new identity. First, the university no longer held a monopoly on high-quality research in Berlin. Second, it now had to compete for leading faculty and public resources. Positions at the KWG institutes were particularly attractive to professors because they were institutes of advanced research, unencumbered by students.

In other words, in the centenary year in which the university celebrated an increasingly imaginary continuity with Humboldtian values, such as the unity of teaching and research, it began to turn in new directions. The centrality of the *Philosophische Fakultät*, in which research in the "pure" (not applied) sciences had been housed, was now diminished, for in addition to the establishment of the KWG, a new body of polytechnical schools emerged with the rank of university.[47]

Still, given Germany's rise, growing strength, and preeminence in higher education, the university seemed poised to lead in what promised to be the "German century." Students and professors reacted euphorically when the war broke out in 1914.

"War semesters are victorious semesters," the theologian Adolf Deißmann argued, with reference to the enormous support for the war effort at the university.[48] The departments of chemistry and physics were mobilized to support German forces. In 1915 a special unit led by the chemist Fritz Haber (winner of the Nobel Prize in Chemistry in 1918) worked to develop weaponized chlorine and other poisonous gases.

The Berlin professoriat before the war was overwhelmingly conservative, monarchist, and patriotic. As such it enjoyed influence and still a considerable degree of autonomy in the handling of its own affairs—within the limits of an illiberal polity, academic appointments in Wilhelmine Germany were based on merit, but also, implicitly, on *Gesinnung*, or ideology. The Berlin philosopher Friedrich Paulsen asserted that academic freedom remained "generally . . . a recognized and undisputed right at German universities," but within boundaries. Max Weber was harsher: "The 'freedom of science' exists in Germany within the limits of ecclesiastical and political acceptability. Outside these limits there is none."[49]

By the end of the war, 57 members of the faculty and 997 students had been killed. Yet for women, World War I presented new opportunities at the university. With young men at war, women finally received academic attention. By 1918, the beginning of the Weimar Republic, around 10 percent of the student body was female. By the end of the era of the Weimar Republic, this number grew slowly but steadily to around 20 percent.[50]

## Darkness: The University in the National Socialist Era, 1933–1945

Germany's descent from a nation of "poets and thinkers" (*Dichter und Denker*) to one of "judges and hangmen" (*Richter und Henker*)[51] came at the cost of its leadership in higher education. The impact of the Nazi regime that came to power in January 1933 became manifest on May 10 of that year, when the members of the German Student Union—among them many students from the University of Berlin—publicly piled and burned books from public libraries on the streets of Berlin's *Opernplatz*, the square opposite the university's main building. A crowd of seventy thousand, including students, professors, and members of the SA and SS—storm troopers for National Socialism—watched as thousands of volumes were torched.[52]

The university locked arms with the new regime. In the spring of 1933 student agitators spread pamphlets agitating for purges of "non-national" elements within the universities. The university rector at the time, Eduard Kohlrausch, found the agitators problematic. However, it was not the anti-Semitic content of their invective that he took issue with, but rather the agitators' choice of method of distributing pamphlets and posters at the university, including forcibly hanging a poster calling for "action against the un-German spirit" on campus.[53] Approval—whether tacit, or, as among the more opportunistic professors, more vocal—for the National Socialist's 1933 "Law for the Restoration of the Professional Civil Service," which expelled Jewish faculty, was the order of the day. Protests remained the exception, as many professors greeted the dismissal of Jewish colleagues as an opportunity for advancement and as a legitimate pursuit of national goals. Prominent faculty, including the agronomist Konrad Meyer and jurist Carl Schmitt, as well as anthropologist Eugen Fischer, who served as rector of the university between 1933 and 1935, enthusiastically contributed to National Socialist crimes and plans for domination and extermination.[54]

In short order the Nazi regime purged universities of non-Aryan and dissident members. Universities lost any capacity for self-government. The University of Berlin increasingly abandoned its own traditions of teaching and research. Scholarship serving truth for truth's sake was jettisoned for scholarship in service of the "Volk." The natural sciences as well as the departments of classics, theology, and literature were all affected and exploited by the dogma of "blood, soil, and race." Many German scholars eagerly embraced National Socialism and its ideology; more than a third of Berlin's faculty joined the Nazi Party. Perhaps one of the most extreme examples of the university's involvement in National Socialism was Konrad Meyer, professor of agriculture, who was named by Heinrich Himmler as the chief planner of the SS's infamous "*Generalplan Ost*," a plan to resettle occupied Poland with Germans while expelling, enslaving, and exterminating hundreds of thousands of Poles living in that area.

Nazi policies and the spread of anti-Semitism led to a sizeable intellectual migration to Britain and America. But beyond the famous names such as Albert Einstein, then of the Prussian Academy of Sciences, who was in the United States when Hitler came to power, there were many more who were denied asylum—for anti-Semitism was not a German monopoly in the 1930s.[55] One fortunate scholar was Hajo Holborn, a student at Berlin of the eminent historian Friedrich Meinecke. He was dismissed from his academic post in Berlin in 1933 and made his way to America, where he would become Sterling Professor of History at Yale and president of the American Historical Society. The architect Walter Gropius was another, having moved to Berlin from Dessau only to flee the city in 1934, making his way eventually to the United States, where he would chair the Department of Architecture at Harvard's Graduate School of Design and personally design the new Harvard Graduate Center. Not for the last time—as we shall see—the United States was a fortunate recipient of exiled intellectuals.

Resistance in the university to Nazi rule was limited. A famous exception was Dietrich Bonhoeffer, Protestant theologian and assistant professor at the University of Berlin. In the 1930s he helped organize the Confessing Church in opposition to the state church controlled by the Nazis. At the outbreak of World War II, he joined the resistance movement surrounding Admiral Wilhelm Canaris in the *Abwehr*, a military intelligence group that was intent on overthrowing and later assassinating Hitler. The Nazis hanged him naked during the last weeks of the war in the concentration camp Flossenbürg.

By the end of the war, various estimates put the loss of faculty across Germany at 40 percent of their prewar numbers. Although the statistics vary somewhat, it is clear that the war devastated the ranks of university faculty.[56] Berlin was hit particularly hard as 280 faculty members were forced to leave the university. The majority of these dismissals were for "racial" anti-Semitic reasons. As central Berlin became a target of Allied bombing in 1943 and 1944, the university operated at reduced capacity before ceasing to function altogether in October 1944.

## From Public University to SED University: Higher Education in a Socialist World Order, 1946–1989

In 1945 the University of Berlin, like most German universities, lay in ruins: 50 percent of the university's buildings were destroyed, including its main building and the medical department, Charité. Somehow the university library remained mostly intact. Berlin was divided among the victorious allies, and the university found itself in the Soviet sector. The Soviets decided to reopen the university only eight months after the war had ended.

At the ceremony celebrating the return of activity to the university, its leadership proudly declared that "the reopening is not only a matter of taking up the work and preserving received traditions, but it involves a total renewal of the external and, even more so, the internal character of the university."[57] Soviet authorities began a period of denazification, including purges among faculty and students, to distance themselves from the Nazi and militaristic past. The Soviet authorities viewed the professoriat with suspicion and held it partly responsible for the implementation of Nazi dictatorship and the preparation for war. As the university reopened, nearly 85 percent of its professors were dismissed on the grounds of their active collaboration with National Socialism.[58] Authorities feared the influence that accompanied these posts. The reorganization of the university in accordance with Soviet political principles followed soon after, aiming to transform students from bourgeois specialists to working socialists. The formal mission of educating the whole person—already long in retreat—was quickly replaced with creating a cadre of ideologically faithful socialists.

Soon social democratic, liberal, and conservative students, who had returned in small numbers after the fall of the Nazi regime, were suspended from the university, at times even arrested. In April 1948 a coalition of students, professors, and the American military governor in Berlin, General Lucius D. Clay, initiated a new university in the western sector of the city. This "Free University of Berlin," which we will encounter in detail in Chapter 3, was founded in the institutes of the old *Kaiser-Wilhelm-Gesellschaft* in Dahlem and claimed to be the true heir of the original university. Berlin was now two cities, housing two universities divided along the ideological lines of the Cold War, instantiating the increasing tensions between the Soviets and the West in the following decades.

On February 8, 1949, shortly after the foundation of Free University, the University of Berlin, which in 1946 had dropped "Friedrich Wilhelm" from its masthead, was renamed the "Humboldt University of Berlin" in honor of the Humboldt brothers. The reality, however, little reflected Humboldt's ideals of academic freedom and liberal education. The SED (Socialist Unity Party of Germany), the governing party of the German Democratic Republic (GDR), intended to create a socialist elite university, closely aligned with the party's ideology. These intentions affected the university's faculty. For example, the first five women in the university's history to take up full professorships were appointed in the immediate postwar years, but by 1948 all but one had left because of ever-tightening ideological controls.

Students took required classes in Marxism-Leninism and historical materialism, memorizing the new socialist catechism with the *Kadavergehorsamkeit* (the obedience of corpses) for which Prussia was once famous. Their summers involved obligatory labor service and duty. The university's leadership team was remodeled into a double structure of party and academic staff, the party having the final word in all essential decisions. Heinrich Fink, a theology professor who became the university's first president after reunification, recalled, "The president never decided anything without the party. The orders came from above."[59]

In the summer of 1961 the building of the Berlin Wall interrupted any contact between students and faculty and the West. The sixteen million inhabitants of the GDR were not allowed to travel and were held under strict police control. Between January and November 1961, 623 university members left the GDR, 379 of whom escaped secretly after the Wall was built.[60] The state security service ("Stasi") appointed a department with seventeen full-time members to supervise the university. The university in turn also participated actively in the GDR's surveillance system. For example, the university created a degree program in "Criminalistic," designed to be an unofficial entryway for a career with the Stasi. Beyond this there was no shortage of "IM," short for *inoffizielle Mitarbeiter,* or unofficial collaborators, at the university who collected and forwarded information on students and faculty to the Stasi. Between 1950 and 1989 an estimated 620,000 GDR citizens served as IM.[61] Faculty who dared to question the premises of the GDR regime or to advocate reforms were expelled.

Despite being walled off from the West, the university was not unaffected by the pivotal "year 1968," when political and societal debates in the West and in Poland, Yugoslavia, and Czechoslovakia sparked great interest. Many students entertained sympathies for the "Prague Spring" in 1968 and objected to its suppression. However, open opposition and demonstrative actions among students remained rare. Only eighteen students were subjected to disciplinary proceedings by the university.[62] Whether through fear or belief, students, faculty, and administration stayed loyal to the party line.[63]

Until the fall of the Wall in 1989, the university struggled with the effects of the scarcity of resources that was ubiquitous in the GDR. Overall, the university was characterized by academic stagnation, political control, and ideological paternalism. Nevertheless, outstanding research was still produced, particularly in medicine and the natural sciences. The university also looked across borders, establishing important exchange relationships with other institutions of higher education behind the Iron Curtain, and especially with the Soviet Union, as well as with socialist countries in Africa, Asia, and South America. As the largest university in the GDR, it still commanded international respect. Humboldt also opened up to students with worker family backgrounds and explicitly welcomed women. In 1989, 51.2 percent of the GDR's university students were female, one of the highest rates in the world.[64] Additionally, the university put more emphasis on the importance of teaching: the faculty-student ratio was around one-to-seven in 1989.[65] The university also established strong international research and exchange links with other universities in the "socialist brother countries" and gained distinctive strength in Russian/Soviet and Chinese studies.[66]

## Refounding Humboldt University in the Capital of a Reunited Germany, after 1990

The peaceful reunification of the two parts of Germany signified yet another turning point for Humboldt University and was, after the fascist and communist dictatorships, the third disruption it faced in the twentieth century. At first there was euphoria and then reality. As reform efforts from within failed, the university was redesigned by the initiative of the Senate of Berlin. Within a few years, the university was restructured and reorganized in a way that left little unchanged. The process resembled a new founding, except that the university continued its teaching and research operations throughout this phase.

As the first freely elected rector, or president, in the history of the University of Berlin, Heinrich Fink, recalled, "Everyone, from the lowest student to the university president, was in the spirit of Humboldt. You know the Humboldt spirit? Total science. And in the Humboldt spirit, without, and free from, ideology, we wanted to renew ourselves. We initiated a new program of study. We elected new committees. We had a newly elected, freely elected university president. . . . Then the West Berlin Senate said no, no, not like that. . . . You have too many professors and too many Marxists."[67]

Curricula were assessed and redefined, institutes and departments were merged and regrouped into three campuses, namely Campus Mitte, Campus Nord, and Campus Adlershof. Professors had to reapply for their positions and had to compete with colleagues from the West to keep their jobs. Former president Fink noted, "There was great tension above all among the staff, who suddenly found themselves being evaluated and who were not going to be [automatically] employed again."[68] To the purges of 1933 (against Jews and liberals) and 1945–1946 (against Nazi members, conservatives, and liberals) was now added the purge *nach der Wende* (literally, "after the turn") of 1989. Between 1990 and 1994, 477 professors were newly appointed. Among 2,755 employees in 1989, only 16.4 percent remained in the workforce by 1997.[69] Some viewed the evaluation of the faculty and academic employees as a necessary step for the decommunization of the university, while others called it an academic "colonization" from Western Germany, for the new appointees were almost entirely from the West.

At Humboldt University's archives are files of those dismissed in the 1990s. One was Roland Felber, the GDR's leading historian of modern China. He had studied in China at Peking University in the 1950s; received his doctorate at Leipzig; assumed the chair in Chinese history at Berlin in 1977; and was a widely respected scholar in Europe, North America, and Asia. Promoted to vice dean at Humboldt University in 1990, he was then interrogated and forced to fill out forms—loosely adapted from the denazification forms of the 1940s—on all that he had done under GDR rule. Did he work for the Stasi? (No.) Had he been paid by the Stasi? (No.) Was he a functionary of the SED? (No.) Was he a member of the SED? (Yes.) And so on. He was forced to reapply for his professorship only to be told that he had come in number two on the appointment list, to a much more junior scholar from Western Germany. Then, in 1993, he was summarily cashiered. His health broken, he was permitted to continue in a limited capacity until 2000.[70] Humboldt University has been undistinguished in this field ever since.

Berlin now housed three large universities: Humboldt University, Free University, and Technical University. Plans to form one large university in the capital of Germany—a national university—were quickly abandoned. Before 1990 the universities had been recipients of generous state funding from the competing East and West German governments. Now a united but poorer Berlin had to pay for them itself. With Free University (FU) in particular, a new phase of competition and collaboration began. In 1997–1998 the hospitals of Free University (Virchow Hospital) and Humboldt University (Charité) were merged to form the largest university hospital in Europe. At the same time, these two universities increasingly competed for resources and recognition from the Berlin Senate. Between 1995 and 2001 Berlin reduced its spending on higher education by 16.5 percent; between 1992 and 2000 grants for Humboldt University through the state of Berlin were cut by 14.5 percent.[71]

## Governance: From Authoritarianism to Anarchism

Slowly Humboldt University renewed itself, starting with its governance. The university metamorphosed from an SED-dominated university into a democratic, self-governed university. University laws very similar to those formed in the 1960s and 1970s in Western Germany were implemented, giving faculty and staff enormous agency, including the right to elect their leaders.

At the top was the president, a position that replaced that of the rector and was meant to give the university much stronger administrative leadership. Three vice presidents with designated areas of administration—the Vice President of Academic Affairs, the Vice President of Research, and the Vice President of Finance, Personnel, and Technical Matters—completed the Presidential Board. The members of this board were individually elected for five-year terms.[72] The Presidential Board governed the university in collaboration with three central administrative bodies: the Academic Senate, the Council, and the Board of Trustees.

The Academic Senate (AS) was entrusted with making decisions on myriad issues ranging from day-to-day matters to the university's strategic orientation. The AS was composed of twenty-five members with voting power who were elected for two-year terms. They represented four different constituencies of the university: academic employees, nonacademic employees, students, and professors. The first three of these subgroups each had four representatives, while professors were granted thirteen representatives, allowing the faculty a thin majority when acting unanimously. Ten additional groups held privileges to speak and make proposals during meetings of the AS.[73] The university's medical school, Charité, which operated in partnership with Free University, had a senate of its own.

The Council was, in principle, the university's highest governing body. In addition to the election of the Presidential Board, the Council was responsible for other fundamental decisions, such as enacting the university's constitution and electoral regulations, and debating the Presidential Board's annual report.[74] The Council had sixty-one members, elected for two years, consisting of the twenty-five members of the Academic Senate in addition to members from the same four subgroups that made up the AS. In toto, the Council comprised thirty-one professors, ten academic employees, ten nonacademic employees, and ten students. Elections for both the Academic Senate and the Council were held in one electoral process, in which all university members were both eligible and entitled to vote for members of their subgroups.

The Presidential Board reported to the Board of Trustees, consisting of nine voting members. The president and the Berlin senator responsible for universities were members ex officio.[75] The remaining seven members were elected by the Academic Senate.[76] The Board of Trustees advised the university in strategic questions and in decisions concerning public matters. It was also involved in electing the university president and vice presidents. The election or reelection to the Presidential Board required three steps. First, the Board of Trustees formed a search committee (with half of its eight members from the Council and the other half from the Board of Trustees) to identify candidates. Second, the search committee proposed candidates to the Council. Finally, the Council elected a candidate with an absolute majority vote.[77]

This ultrademocratic approach to governance was cherished by faculty, staff, and students and generally loathed by presidents because it often led to significant resistance to institutional changes.[78] As part of a renewed university with an altogether new professoriat after 1990, "Humboldtian" faculty identified strongly with their institution and its founding ideals.

The challenges in administration were greater given an unusual inheritance from German reunification in the 1990s. While the original professoriat was replaced by hundreds of professors from the West, the administrative staff, which in 2020, thirty years *nach der Wende* comprised around fifteen hundred people, remained basically intact and, given its voice in governance, self-perpetuating.[79] Differing values between a new faculty and an older bureaucracy entangled presidents, professors, and staff in endless battles.

A university with such a flat governance structure made decision-making often impossible. President Jan-Hendrik Olbertz stated at the end of his tenure, "The culture of democracy entails that elected officials are given a mandate, controlled of course [by university institutions]. This mandate is temporary and one has to legitimize [elected authority] with responsibility and results. It is however not possible to allow everybody the same right to vote on important questions; otherwise we would have no structure."[80]

But almost everybody *did* have a vote. Approval by the Academic Senate was essential for any major initiative. On the positive side, as Peter Frensch, Vice President for Research, noted, "Once you have a decision in the Academic Senate, then it is a done deal."[81] But from the president's office the view was different: Humboldt University was a place where "everybody takes part in decisions, but only a very small number of members of the university take part in responsibility."[82] And the most prestigious faculty members, as a rule, did not seek positions in the Academic Senate to "not get their hands dirty."[83]

Adding to leadership woes was the absence of a centralized budget and professional financial administration. The vice president for finance, personnel, and technical matters was not chosen by the president but elected from, and largely by, the faculty. During his presidency, Olbertz aimed to professionalize a cumbersome financial administration by installing—as was the norm in many German universities—a professional "chancellor" skilled in financial management in lieu of an academic vice president. Olbertz remarked, "I needed somebody at my side who is a professional in administration and who is a member of my team. But you are absolutely unable to create any reform in an encompassing way [in the current system]. That's why we are so behind on very important steps toward a modern administration.[84]

Before his presidency, Olbertz himself held the position of vice president for finance, personnel, and technical matters for six months, and he knew the challenges of a disconnected leadership corps. Olbertz wanted his own team. But after wrenching public debate, he failed to convince the Academic Senate of the need for change. When he declined to stand for reelection as president in 2016, he joined a distinguished list of his predecessors since 1990, not one of whom had completed a second term.

## Competing for Faculty

Humboldt University's bureaucratic silos perhaps contributed to making the university a place that was widely appreciated by the faculty for its individuality, creativity, collegiality, and freedom of thought. Olbertz, despite his frustration with the organization of his institution, considered this intellectual culture one of the university's main assets. "Sometimes," he stated, "I am afraid when I am looking for more structure and calculability that it is a danger for our intellectual atmosphere, our very high level of creativity, and openness to the interdisciplinarity. Would I kill this atmosphere by instituting a professional structure and administration?"[85] Overall, the university had great appeal to faculty members. A "call" to Berlin was not what it once was, but the reunified city itself was a big attraction. According to a high-ranking university administrator, the university was successful in hiring or retaining faculty in 70 to 80 percent of cases, an outstanding ratio illustrating its competitiveness vis-à-vis other German universities.[86]

Nevertheless, recruitment was not easy, given Berlin's budget constraints. This was true especially for international scholars. Professors were civil servants in Germany and their basic salaries were fixed by the states, not by the universities; salaries were not increased according to seniority. In 2020 Berlin's Senate granted a basic salary for full professors between €73,000 (US\$86,370) and €84,000 (around US\$99,380); junior professors earned a basic salary of around €56,000 (US\$66,200).[87] Beyond that, candidates could negotiate a bonus and other academic benefits (research assistants, research budgets), especially when the candidate had competing job offers. But salaries were hardly competitive internationally. Even within Germany, richer states had more generous compensation policies. With nine hours of teaching per week, the teaching requirements for faculty in Berlin were high compared to international standards.[88] The teaching load and the budget were tied in such a way that the number of teaching hours determined the number of students to be admitted; the admitted students in turn determined the size of the budget granted by Berlin's Senate. It was difficult for Humboldt University to hire international faculty at the height of their careers because the mandated retirement age in Berlin began at age sixty-five (and could only be extended to age sixty-eight).

In 2020 the faculty consisted of a total of 440 professors. Although nearly 20 percent of the positions were funded by external (third-party) sources in 2020, the rest were funded entirely (and inadequately) by the state.[89] The faculty was largely full professors, with the exception of fifty-one so-called junior professors. Junior professorships were created in Germany on a national level in 2002 to enable postdoctoral fellows to gain professorial appointments without being required to write the second dissertation, or *Habilitation*.[90]

Junior professors were initially appointed for three or four years, and, after an evaluation, their professorship could be extended to a total of six years. The creation of junior professorships was also an attempt to address the problem of underrepresentation of women in Germany's faculties by making the academic career path more flexible and hence more attractive. The demographic makeup of Humboldt University signaled the problem. While in 2020, 58 percent of the students were female, and over 50 percent of the academic employees that were not part of the professoriat were female, only 35 percent of Humboldt's professors (including junior professors) were women.[91] Still, compared to the German average of 24.7 percent (in 2018), the percentage at Humboldt was significantly higher.[92] In fact, in comparison with other German states, the state of Berlin had the highest percentage of female professors in 2018, while Bavaria had the lowest with around 20 percent.[93]

*Massification: The Student Body*

With 35,981 students (excluding about 8,200 students at Charité) enrolled, Humboldt University was one of the largest German universities in 2019–2020.[94] Since the mid-1990s student enrollment at Humboldt had grown five times as fast as faculty expansion,[95] and faster than the overall growth of students at Berlin universities.[96] Humboldt's students were enrolled in nine schools in a total of 172 degree programs. Women made up 57 percent of the student body, a number higher than the German average of 48 percent.[97] With 57 percent of students coming from local backgrounds (as of 2015 data), the university maintained the character of a regional state university.[98] Markschies described the difficulty of balancing access with excellence: "This is the consensus of a great coalition of old political parties in Germany: Every university should at the same time welcome all students of its local state and also satisfy the demands of being an elite university."[99]

Compared with their American and British counterparts, German universities were much less selective when it came to admission. In Berlin in particular, universities followed a strong egalitarian tradition. Nonselective admission policies were protected by Berlin's Senate, which also determined the total intake of students every year.[100] Similar to other German public universities, the only internal selection criterion at Humboldt was the so-called *Numerus Clausus* (NC). The NC is a classification policy based on final scores in the German *Abitur* examination. It is used at German universities to restrict admissions for sought-after areas of study by determining the lowest admitted grade. In 2014–2015, the acceptance rate in majors that had an NC, such as biology and economics, was around 15 percent.[101] Markschies described the problem: "In my farewell speech as president I addressed the mayor of Berlin and said to him, 'give us freedom to select our students and also the number of students.' He laughed at me, saying, 'never, ever, in my lifetime.'"[102]

*Reengaging the World*

The University of Berlin was once the place to which scholars from around the world flocked to learn what a university could be. In GDR times, it sent its own students abroad, mostly eastward, toward Moscow and the "socialist brother countries." Those ties atrophied (although they did not die entirely) with the fall of the Wall. By 2017 it had become attractive to new generations of international students, perhaps as much for Berlin as for the university. International enrollment at Humboldt University was 17.5 percent (the average at German universities was 12.3 percent).[103] With over two-thirds of international students hailing from European countries (41 percent from the European Union; 13 from the rest of Europe), Humboldt University's source of internationalization was primarily European. Asian students made up 14 percent of the international students, and North, Central, and South America together had a share of 28 percent of the international students.[104] Whereas Russian had been an international lingua franca for the university in GDR times, by 2020 the university offered thirty-three English-language degree programs.[105] In comparison with other German universities, Humboldt's faculty was also more international: 14 percent came from countries other than Germany, while the average for full-time academic employees and professors from outside Germany was around 7 percent.[106]

Within the context of the Bologna Process, Humboldt University, along with all other German higher education institutions, introduced a series of wide-ranging measures designed to reform the structure of the university in accordance with guidelines from the European Union. The Bologna Process officially began in 1999 with the signing of the Bologna Declaration and has been an ongoing series of ministerial conferences that aim to bring coherence and quality standardization of higher education across forty-eight European countries. Since 2003 this reform at Humboldt has aimed to establish internationally accepted degrees, improve the quality of courses of study, and enhance students' employability and mobility. Furthermore, the reform aspired to enhance the attractiveness of German institutions of higher education for students and young academics from abroad. Among the most debated reform measures was the introduction of a system of comprehensible and comparable degrees (with three-year bachelor's and two-year master's degree programs), which was a departure from the five-year bachelor's system in Germany.[107]

For Humboldt—a university that once set international standards—these Europe-wide efforts meant now adopting foreign models, such as the US baccalaureate. The Bologna Process aimed to make higher education in Europe a continental-wide enterprise, with mobility not only of students but also of faculty and staff, in part to compete with larger and more competitive systems of higher education in the United States and China.

But in the formal adoption of the baccalaureate, there was little interest in the educational values that have defined the bachelor of arts degree in many American colleges, which stressed, in the original spirit of Humboldt, a broad undergraduate education in the liberal arts and sciences. The "key competencies" for lifelong learning recommended by the European Parliament in 2006 quite appropriately include language learning; information and communication technologies; and math, science, and technology but not the humanities.

Humboldt University's own "International Agenda 2015" set out a modest strategy built around a limited series of international partnerships.[108] Before Humboldt launched this strategy, the first collaboration to support undergraduate, graduate student, and faculty exchanges was established with Princeton University in 2012. It supported research and teaching projects between the two institutions with a joint fund in the amount of €300,000 (US$390,000) per year. The academic partnership was complemented by a staff mobility program for administrative employees.[109] Other strategic partnerships were built with the National University of Singapore and Universidade de São Paulo.[110] Funded by money from the Excellence Initiative, a program called "KOSMOS" was designed to rebuild relations with the old Soviet bloc, inviting young academics from Eastern Europe and Russia to Humboldt University for limited periods.

## The Limits of Public Funding

Historically and today, universities in Germany are mainly public and funded by the public purse. There are a number of small private professional schools, but they enroll less than 5 percent of German students of university age. With its federal system, Germany's sixteen states are principally responsible for higher education. As a result, universities in poorer states (mostly former GDR states in Eastern Germany) receive less money than universities in wealthier states.

In the case of Humboldt University, the city-state of Berlin allocated an annual budget, which was supplemented by additional money from other, also mostly public, sources. In 2020 Humboldt University's total budget was just over US$520 million (or close to €461 million), including salaries for professors, who are civil servants in Germany. In 2016 third-party funds, mostly government money from the German Research Foundation, accounted for 28 percent of the university's budget.[111] Donations from the private sector were but a small source of additional funding for Humboldt and remained below 10 percent.[112] Humboldt had neither tradition nor capacity to gain financial support among alumni, who largely lacked a history of philanthropy. Potential industrial partners preferred to invest in the Technical University of Berlin.

Like most German universities, Humboldt was structurally underfunded. Therefore, when Germany's constitutional court overturned a 1976 law prohibiting tuition fees in 2005, many universities introduced annual charges (laws limited the fees to US$1,058 [or €1,000]). Berlin however, never introduced fees, and by 2014 all states had abolished fees in the wake of student protests and political pressure. For the most part, the states compensated the universities for the income lost when fees were abolished. But where fees were never levied, as in Berlin, compensation was never paid. In 2020 the total fees at Humboldt University were US$357 (or €316) per semester, including a public transport ticket for Berlin and Brandenburg whose value alone accounted for two-thirds of the fees. At different times since 1990, budget deficits forced the university to cut back on faculty and other staff members. In 1998 only 10 percent of midlevel academics who had been employed as of 1993 remained at the university.[113] In 2004 nearly eighty professorships (along with their academic employees, secretaries, and technical staff), constituting around 20 percent of the workforce, were axed for budgetary reasons.[114]

## Competing for Preeminence: The Excellence Initiative, 2005–2020

In the early 2000s policymakers in Germany were increasingly worried about the state of German universities, in particular their weak showing in international rankings, in spite of well-founded and often-voiced reservations against rankings in general among German policymakers and university administrators.[115] None of the German universities managed to enter the top twenty, and only a handful were listed in the top one hundred in influential global rankings such as the *Times Higher Education*, QS World University Rankings, and the Academic Ranking of World Universities.

At home, German universities faced increasing competition from nonuniversity research institutes, such as the Max Planck Society, the Leibniz Association, and the Helmholtz Association of German Research Centers. Many high-profile scientists found the independent institutes to be more attractive workplaces compared to universities: there was no teaching and more money. Perhaps even more problematic for Germany's universities was the "brain drain." Since the 1990s thousands of researchers had left Germany for other countries, mainly for the United States. This phenomenon is well illustrated by the fact that the four German Nobel Prize winners between 1998 and 2001 had transferred to American universities by the time their Nobel Prizes were awarded.[116]

The national Excellence Initiative (*Exzellenzinitiative*), begun in 2005, was an attempt to steer higher education in Germany in a new direction. In a period when public funding for universities decreased steadily in England and the United States, the tax-funded budget for higher education in Germany increased notably, even during the years after the 2008 financial crisis. Federal and state funding for higher education was US$19.5 (or €18.4) billion in 2005, rising more than 50 percent to US$30.5 (or €28.7) billion by 2015.[117] With the so-called Higher Education Pacts I and II, the federal government allocated US$8.5 (or €8) billion between 2007 and 2015 to the states to fund 425,000 student spots. Over its first twelve years, the Excellence Initiative allocated almost US$5 billion of funding, three-quarters of which was funded by the federal government and one-quarter by the sixteen states.[118]

German federal and state governments launched the initiative in 2005 to help a handful of German universities join the ranks of the global research elite. The German Research Foundation (*Deutsche Forschungsgemeinschaft*, or DFG), which together with the German Council of Science and Humanities (*Deutscher Wissenschaftsrat*) jointly ran the Excellence Initiative, defined the broader goal of the initiative as "mak[ing] Germany a more attractive research location, making it more internationally competitive, and focusing attention on the outstanding achievements of German universities and the German scientific community."[119] And indeed, the initiative did pay off for certain universities.

The Excellence Initiative's first funding round ran from 2006 to 2011. Competition for funding was divided into three lines: first, "graduate schools" to support young graduate researchers; second, "clusters of excellence" to promote collaborative projects within universities and with other scientific institutions (such as Max Planck institutes); and third, "institutional strategies" to provide promising research universities with extra funding on an institutional basis. In the first line of funding, the initiative sought to create more than fifty graduate schools for more integrated doctoral programs and enhanced research groups than could be found in the traditional disciplines or in a *Lehrstuhl* overseen by a single professor. The clusters of excellence promoted interdisciplinary cooperation across different realms of research.

Finally, the initiative aimed to bolster the long-term development of high-level research for German universities via the institutional strategies line of funding. To become a "University of Excellence" the applicant institution had to win at least one Cluster of Excellence and one Graduate School award. The institution also had to demonstrate a coherent overall strategy for building up its research profile. In the first round there were 319 proposals from 74 universities overall.[120]

In the first funding round, US\$2.5 billion was made available for a five-year period beginning in 2006, with, as noted, the federal government providing the lion's share and the states funding the rest. The money was, of course, an important motivator for Germany's underfinanced universities. Equally valuable was the galvanizing of German higher education institutions to rethink their priorities and to come up with strategies of world-class excellence.

Humboldt University was humiliated in the first round. But Humboldt's offspring, Free University, would now be known as a "University of Excellence," having established itself as a national leader in the humanities. Humboldt entered the second competition with trepidation, but it ultimately gained entry into the circle of elite universities, in part by partnering with Free University and the Max Planck institutes on a research cluster. For the university "and its institutional self-confidence this was very, very important," former President Olbertz recalled.[121]

For the third round of funding of the Excellence Initiative, the results of which were announced in 2019, there were only two, instead of the prior three lines of funding. One line was for clusters of excellence and the other was a new line called "universities of excellence," which encouraged institutions to apply jointly. Humboldt put all its eggs in a collaborative basket in a joint proposal for a "Berlin University Alliance" along with Free University, Charité, and the Technical University of Berlin. This joint strategy represented a resounding success, and the integrated research agenda received funding in both lines of funding.

Critics of the Excellence Initiative have pointed out that, compared to the funding of leading research institutions in other countries, the money distributed since the launch of the Excellence Initiative has had little significance in financial terms. The annual budget of the Excellence Initiative, around US\$530 (or €500) million, was distributed among ten to twelve universities. Had Humboldt University received the entire sum of annual nationwide funding of the initiative, its budget would have been but 17 percent of Stanford University's, but with Humboldt having around twice as many students.[122]

Yet this comparatively modest financial incentive made a big difference in attitudes. Even most critics conceded that the Excellence Initiative had changed Germany's higher education landscape. For the first time, German universities were spurred to compete for funding *and* to develop formal strategies to position themselves nationally and internationally. According to a recent study by the International Expert Commission on the Excellence Initiative ("Imboden report"), led by emeritus Professor Dieter Imboden of ETH Zurich, the initiative "succeeded in initiating a structural change at the universities."[123] Members of Humboldt University's leadership team, often stymied by the university's convoluted governance structure, described the initiative as a catalyst to set strategies. Olbertz recalled that the Excellence Initiative "brought enormous dynamism to the university."[124]

"Excellence" was measured, above all, by research. Indeed, data on citation impact of the eleven universities selected for institutional funding suggest that their research was cited more frequently than German universities in general. The proportion of papers from these eleven universities in the world's top 10 percent by citation grew from one-sixth in 2003 to nearly one-quarter in 2015. Yet data also showed that other universities less favored by the Excellence Initiative managed to keep pace when it came to highly cited papers.[125] These positive effects may also be partly explained by the general increase of research funding across Germany over the past decade. Still, even the top German universities ranked poorly against the world's leading institutions, and Humboldt University was no exception.

In the latest round of the Excellence Initiative competition in 2019, the Berlin partnership made great strides toward putting Humboldt University back on the map as part of a Berlin-wide academic "ecosystem."[126] The alliance strove to unite the research competencies of the institutions and to create networks of professional exchange and continuing education. The plan not only enabled the universities to compete nationally but also allowed them to act more nimbly on the international stage. In 2017, in the wake of Brexit, the Berlin universities partnered with Oxford to become its German counterpart for exchange and collaboration and to mitigate the effects of Britain's withdrawal from the EU on students and research.[127] As Humboldt President Sabine Kunst said, "Through collaboration with a top British university, we hope to put together a targeted collective strategy in order to circumvent any possible consequences of Brexit."[128] The alliance formalized a number of reciprocal visiting arrangements, cooperation with museums and libraries, and common research agendas, as well as set out plans for physical centers to be constructed in the near future to support intense collaboration and attract third-party funding. By making use of the city's existing institutional structures resulting from Berlin's patchwork history along with its reputation as an attractive place to live and conduct research, the alliance finally allowed Humboldt to put its best foot forward.

## Humboldt's Future, in the Light of its Past

At its bicentennial jubilee in 2010, as Humboldt University organized a conference to celebrate itself as "the modern original," the university could reflect on its past and contemplate its future. As a public university, its history was deeply intertwined with the history of Berlin. The university had outlasted five political regimes—the Kingdom of Prussia, the German Empire, the Weimar Republic, Nazi Germany, and the German Democratic Republic—to find itself in the Federal Republic of Germany, perhaps the only one truly receptive to the ideas of *Lehr- und Lernfreiheit* that had so animated Wilhelm von Humboldt. Through its tumultuous history, the university also showed an exceptional resilience.

For the first time since the early years in the history of the university, liberal education in the spirit of Humboldt was possible. But with democratization came also budget constraints and a nearly tenfold increase in the student body (today nearly thirty-six thousand). A student-faculty ratio of seven-to-one in GDR times was now fifteen-to-one.[129] If Nazism and Communism had suppressed any pretense of free and open inquiry at the university, the massification of the student body and the overwhelming obsession with research—as distinct from teaching and mentorship—in the era of the Excellence Initiative may ensure that Humboldtian ideals will be practiced as an exception rather than the rule in the classroom.

After nearly 180 years under authoritarian governance, Humboldt University embraced participatory democracy in its contemporary governance. An Academic Senate was composed of faculty, staff, and students who held veto power over major decisions of the university leadership. This is surely one reason for the extraordinarily short tenures of Humboldt's presidents. When President Sabine Kunst resigned in October 2021, less than a year into her second term, she was part of a lineage of post-1989 presidents for whom one term proved more than enough. After more than a century of

Prussian-German rule, twelve years of Nazism, and forty years of Communism, Humboldt University had become truly democratic in governance, and as a result also rudderless, until recently without clear academic direction and distinction, compared to the height of its glory. Physically surrounded by Berlin's great museums—including a new one in the rebuilt Hohenzollern Stadtschloß—Humboldt University is today a living museum of a university, striving to return to distinction. What is beyond doubt, however, is that the mother of all research universities was now but one among many, and by no means the most distinguished, even in Germany.

# CHAPTER THREE

# Truth, Justice, and Freedom in a Cold War World

## *Free University of Berlin*

O N JUNE 26, 1963, nearly two years after the erection of the Berlin Wall, John F. Kennedy flew to West Berlin. Before a cheering throng of 450,000, the American president delivered the most memorable speech of the Cold War. "All free men," he said as he closed his oration, "wherever they may live, are citizens of Berlin, and, therefore, as a free man, I take pride in the words '*Ich bin ein Berliner.*'"[1]

Hours later, Kennedy addressed twenty thousand faculty and students gathered on the campus of the Freie Universität Berlin (Free University, or FU). Receiving an honorary degree, he was "honored to become an instant graduate of this distinguished university." But was the word "free" not redundant? "The fact of the matter is," he argued, "that any university, if it is a university, is free." But not necessarily in Berlin. This was the challenge of those studying at Free University: "This school is not interested in turning out merely corporation lawyers or skilled accountants. What it is interested in . . . is in turning out citizens of the world . . . who are willing to commit their energies to the advancement of a free society. That is why you are here, and that is why this school was founded." Evoking Free University's motto of *veritas, iustitia, libertas,* Kennedy concluded, "The scholar, the teacher, the intellectual have a higher duty than any of the others, for society has trained you to think as well as to do. This community has committed itself to that objective, and you have a special obligation to think and to help forge the future of this city in terms of truth and justice and liberty."[2]

Humboldt could not have said it better. Twenty-six years after Kennedy's visit, the Berlin Wall fell, and the several parts of Berlin (and soon Germany)

**Figure 3.1.** John F. Kennedy speaking at Free University of Berlin, 1963.
Courtesy of Peter-André Alt.

were reunited. After another three decades, Free University found itself primus inter pares among Berlin universities and an exemplar of "excellence" in the Federal Republic. Yet its Cold War origins remained everywhere visible. The offices of the university president and leading administrators were housed in the building of the Allied Kommandatura—the governing body of immediate postwar Berlin—in Berlin-Dahlem, a Weimar-era edifice built in an aggressive modern style. In the corridor outside the president's office, pictures and documents of Kennedy's visit welcome visitors. Not far from the president's office sits the beautifully renovated Henry Ford Building, financed by the Ford Foundation and designed to be the *Hauptgebäude,* or main building, of the university to rival that of the original university in East Berlin. An imposing structure of two hundred thousand square feet, it is encased in glass and bathed in light, symbolizing the freedom, openness, and transparency that were founding hallmarks of Free University. The architect's client, the university denotes, was "democracy."[3]

More than fifty years after Kennedy's seismic speeches, President Peter-André Alt stepped out of his office in the old Kommandatura and reflected on the unexpected transformations of his university during his lifetime. By the time Alt assumed the presidency in 2010, FU, as it is colloquially called, had reinvented itself yet again as a modern, international university, rooted in the humanities in the Humboldtian tradition. In the twenty-first century, FU acquired national and international renown and was now one of eleven members of the "Excellence Initiative," a prestigious coalition of Germany's leading institutions of higher education. Under Alt's tenure, FU had outdone and outranked its more famous neighbor, named for Humboldt, in the east of the city. But this was a university that had experienced multiple moments of distinction and nearly as many near-death experiences. Alt knew his presidency was coming to a close, and that a colleague at FU, Günter Ziegler, would assume his role in July 2018. Reflecting on his eight years in the Kommandatura, Alt wondered, What would guarantee the future of modern Germany's most experimental university?

## "A Severely Tested Youth": Origin Stories, 1945–1948

Berlin, Germany's capital city, had been a focal point for Allied attacks during the Second World War. By the end of the war, the center of the city surrounding the Stadtschloß and the university was in rubble. Soon Berlin, like the rest of Germany, was divided into four sectors. The *Mitte* district, where most of the government ministries and the bulk of the university buildings were located, came under Soviet control. The rest of Berlin was then occupied by the three Western Allied powers: France, Great Britain, and the United States. The University of Berlin (today's Humboldt), located in the Soviet sector, was not subordinate to the Allied Kommandatura, the official governing body for the whole city, but came under Soviet control.

Berlin's unique situation—a city half-controlled by Western forces in the middle of the Soviet Occupation Zone of Germany—made it a natural focal point in the Cold War after 1947. The city was initially governed by a four-power Allied Control Council with a leadership that rotated monthly. However, as East-West relations deteriorated, the Soviets withdrew from the council and began governing their sector independently. The Control Council maintained the rotating leadership policy, although now involving only the three Western Allies.

The University of Berlin itself lay in ruins, with 90 percent of its buildings destroyed. Teaching had ceased altogether in 1944. Much of the faculty had emigrated, had been expelled, or were executed. Between 1933 and 1945 over a third of Berlin's faculty was forcibly removed from the university, representing one of the highest expulsion rates among German universities.

With Soviet permission, the University of Berlin reopened in January 1946. Five other universities in the Soviet sector also reopened at that time: Jena, Halle-Wittenberg, Leipzig, Greifswald, and Rostock. At all of these universities, the Soviets enforced a rigorous process of denazification, with the goal of eliminating the old fascist elites and "forming a generation capable of definitively establishing Communism."[4] All employees at every German university had to reapply for their positions. The University of Berlin subsequently employed only 120 of its 700 original professors and lecturers. The newly reestablished university admitted twenty-eight hundred students from more than nine thousand applicants.[5] When academic instruction resumed, professors and students had to prove that they were either victims of fascism or had ideologically distanced themselves from the Nazi regime. The surest way to do so was to join the Socialist Unity Party of Germany (SED), an amalgam of the former Social Democrats and Communists, although utterly dominated by the latter.

With the ultimate goal of forming a socialist "people's university," education in the Soviet sector was dominated by themes of class struggle. As in the Soviet Union—and later throughout the Soviet bloc, including China—

obligatory courses in all degree programs instructed students in Marxist-Leninist philosophy and political economy, à la Stalin. This system aimed to "proletarianize" universities and change the social makeup of the students and faculty. It also severely curbed academic freedom. It soon became apparent that the University of Berlin was intended by the Soviet leadership to be a training ground for future SED cadres. Admissions, and success, became tied to political orientation. In response, protests arose among a group of democratically inclined students who felt that the obligatory lectures offered little more than indoctrination in the tenets of Marxism-Leninism. Some voiced critiques against the role of the Soviets and the SED at the university and beyond.

Student activism led to rapid repression. In March 1947 Soviet police arrested Georg Wrazidlo, a medical student who was head of the student council, as he met with fellow students in Berlin's famous coffeehouse Café Kranzler. Two months later, five other students disappeared in a similar fashion. In a secret session, a Soviet court found Wrazidlo and several others guilty of "covert fascist activities." The students received prison sentences of between ten and twenty-five years. Wrazidlo had survived incarceration in Buchenwald under the Nazis. Now he found himself in a camp at Sachsenhausen under the Communists. He was forty when he was released from the camp in 1956.[6]

Yet dissident students who avoided arrest continued their resistance. A handful of particularly outspoken students, including Otto Hess, Joachim Schwarz, and Otto Stolz, declared, "Freedom, humanity and the rights of man are for us of inestimable worth, and we shall fight unrelentingly against anyone who attempts to infringe upon them. . . . This we wish to state quite openly: . . . we shall criticize anything that is worthy of criticism."[7]

By the end of 1947 the student activists were increasingly critical about the state of the university and its students. Hess wrote, "In Berlin the great majority of students obviously do not have the energy and courage anymore to represent their views, instead they allow themselves to be terrorized by a tiny minority without showing any resistance."[8] To these discouraged young reformers, it seemed more and more unlikely that it would be possible to change the old university. Because it was illegal under the occupation agreements to criticize Soviet authorities directly, dissidents could only seek to discredit the German SED authorities, while chronicling the demise of democratic institutions at universities in the Soviet zone. In a heavy-handed response, the central administration and the rector of the university expelled Stolz, Hess, and Schwarz in mid-April 1948 "because of publishing activities which act counter to the good manners and dignity of a student."[9]

Even though dozens of students had already received similar dismissals, having subsequently been placed under arrest or gone elsewhere to study, the latest expulsions electrified the dissident members of the student body. Immediately, different student groups organized a strike. On April 23, 1948, two thousand student protesters appeared at the Hotel Esplanade on Potsdamer Platz, located in the British sector in Western Berlin, only 150 feet away from the Soviet zone. There, students Erich Weber, from the University of Jena, and Otto Stolz announced an idea that was previously inconceivable: the establishment of a new university in the Western part of Berlin, one where students could study free of repression and ideological encroachment.

A young American journalist named Kendall Foss, who was on staff at the American-sponsored *Neue Zeitung*, had written about the events at the University of Berlin and witnessed the demonstration at the Esplanade. Impressed by Stolz's ardor, Foss offered to connect the students with the American authorities. Foss called on American General Lucius D. Clay, the American High Commissioner for Germany, and Herman Wells, the president of Indiana University, who had taken leave to be cultural adviser to the Allied Military Government. Wells hired Foss to serve as a special assistant to explore the establishment of a new university in the West: "Foss understood the situation and seemed to have the drive and competence."[10] A preparatory committee was formed, consisting of sympathetic German professors, politicians, and students seeking to establish a counter-university in Western Berlin. Foss and his committee submitted their findings to General Clay in May 1948. Foss was at pains to ensure it would not be an "American" university: "The committee believes that the project as it is developing will be (and should be) fundamentally German in its initiation and relation. U.S. participation can properly be confined to moral and material support of a worthy German idea."[11]

Seldom if ever has a university been started so quickly. At the urging of a now-enthusiastic General Clay, assisted by the German-American political scientist Carl J. Friedrich, who took leave from Harvard to serve as Clay's advisor, the preparatory committee concluded that a new university could start within six months and be up and running by autumn 1948. Recruitment of faculty was, to be sure, a challenge, but sixty of the sixty-six professors at the University of Berlin already lived in the West, and—in a bit of arrogance—it was felt that "a staff the equal of the present Berlin University could surely be found."[12] As the preparatory committee, now chaired by the governing mayor of Berlin, Ernst Reuter, began to take concrete steps, the students, too, planned for the establishment of the new university.

Across town, two-thirds of the student council of the University of Berlin had resigned their positions and formed their own preparatory committee. Their expectations in many ways defined the new university in both the immediate and distant future. As Otto Hess wrote in July 1948, "If a new university is to be more than merely an attempt to preserve honorable but outmoded traditions, then courage must be evident to go in new directions." Every generation had the right "to find its own way."[13]

Never has application to a new university been easier: students could apply by postcard, giving their academic history in the briefest form. University of Berlin students sat on the admissions committees in choosing the first cohort. By October 5,500 applications had yielded an inaugural class of 2,140.[14]

The appeal to raise support for the new university sought to place it in the tradition of the brothers Alexander and Wilhelm von Humboldt: "It is about the establishment of a free university, which serves truth for its own sake. Every student should know that this is a place where, in the spirit of true democracy, one's individuality can freely evolve and not become an object of one-sided propaganda."[15]

The original University of Berlin was founded by the king; Free University of Berlin was founded by students. At the least, without their combination of energy, idealism, and entrepreneurialism, no new university was conceivable in the Berlin of 1948. It followed, therefore, that the governing structure of the university entrusted students with a remarkable degree of influence. In what became known as the Berlin Model of university governance, students served as voting members of committees and on the highest authority of the university, its Board of Regents (*Kuratorium*). In direct contrast to what was, by 1949, called Humboldt University—and indeed to any German university—students ran "student affairs": they helped to set admissions criteria; they took part in student discipline; and they sat in the University Senate, where—for the first time in the history of German universities—students voted on professorial appointments. With this authority came responsibility, a significant workload, and, above all in the early years of FU, a sense of common purpose. As the constitution of the university stated, Free University would be "a community of scholars and teachers."[16]

The new university was distinguished also by establishing, partly on an American model, its own Board of Trustees, with authority to set budgets and major policies. Governing Mayor Ernst Reuter chaired the Board, but the structure argued for greater autonomy from the state than that enjoyed by any modern German university.

But even democracies need leaders, and before its inauguration, the university sought a "notable," a figure of eminence, to lead it. Edwin Redslob, a well-known art historian and early leader of the nascent faculty, argued that the new university had to be "built up from the top down," and its first rector should be a "celebrated personality." Celebrated personalities without compromised pasts were not easy to find in immediate postwar Berlin, but Ernst Reuter convinced the aging, ill, and increasingly deaf historian Friedrich Meinecke to assume the position. The octogenarian was widely regarded as the leading German historian alive. A man of centrist to moderate liberal politics, his work had contrasted the values of cosmopolitanism with those of the national state. The Nazis had dismissed him from his decades-long editorship of the *Historische Zeitschrift*, the world's most prestigious journal of historical research, in 1935. Meinecke took up the post on two conditions: that there be an executive vice rector (*Geschäftsführender Rektor*)—Edwin Redslob—to handle university administration and that Reuter get more electricity to Meinecke's apartment, so the old man could read.[17]

The *Gründungsfeier* inaugurating Free University took place on December 4, 1948. Bad weather and a bad cold kept Rector Meinecke home and in bed. Restricted transportation limited participation of rectors and academic leaders from other universities. Without facilities of its own, the university borrowed a public hall that was available on that date. But by all accounts the ceremony was unforgettable. Speaking from his home by RIAS (Radio in the American Sector), Meinecke began, "With joy I hear the voice of youth, and I welcome its call for a new university, for a true sanctuary of science (*Wissenschaft*) and its teaching." This was, he noted, "a new university rising directly from the passionate demands of a severely tested youth," and as "the oldest in the Faculty" and in a "grandfatherly relationship," he took "the outstretched hand of youth." He called for competition, not conflict, between Berlin's now two universities: "May the day come when we can be reunited."[18]

## Survival and Sustainability, 1949–1961

Lectures at FU had actually started in mid-November, before the *Gründungsfeier* was celebrated and just seven months after the three students had been expelled from the old university. Meinecke's hopes for the future notwithstanding, Berlin was now divided academically as it was politically. One day after the official ceremonies, elections for Berlin's municipal government were held in the Western sectors of Berlin, boycotted by the SED. But West Berlin had already become an isolated extension of the West.

The university was founded at the height of the Berlin blockade—the Soviet effort to make life in a separate, Allied-occupied West Berlin unsustainable. In response to Allied efforts to fuse the American, French, and British sectors of Western Germany into one political entity by initiating a new currency, the Soviets had blocked all ground access—railway, road, and canal—to the Western sectors of Berlin on June 26, 1948. The American and British air forces engaged in a massive logistical effort to supply the western part of the city through an audacious *Luftbrücke,* or "air bridge"—the Berlin Airlift.

The airlift was a heroic effort by the Americans, their allies, and the Berlin citizens who persevered through a winter of cold and dearth. The blockade lasted almost a year. With its extraordinary scale (270,000 flights to supply West Berlin for 11 months) and Allied solidarity (the French built a new airport in their sector in 90 days), the airlift made anything else seem possible, including the lightning founding of a new university.

Free University lacked everything from buildings to furniture to books; the medical faculty was short of basic equipment. The city of Berlin could provide moral and legal support, less so financial support. Among the Western occupation forces, only the United States actively supported the founding of the university. Free University quickly became a symbol of German-American friendship. The American occupying power subsidized the university during its first months of existence with earnings from newspapers issued in the American sector. In its founding months in 1948, Free University received approximately US$500,000 from the Americans.[19] They even carved out of the airlift shipments special allocations for Free University. This aid would grow significantly over time, as Berlin became a central battlefield in the global Cold War. From its founding through 1963, FU received US$5.7 million from the US government. The Ford Foundation, then in the heyday of its international engagement, awarded the university US$3.175 million, including the funds for Benjamin Franklin University Hospital and

**Figure 3.2.** Henry Ford Building. Times/Wikimedia Commons/CC BY-SA 3.0.

for the iconic Henry Ford Building that defined the early campus.[20] The early university was designed to have a residential campus in the American sense; this already distinguished it from other universities in Germany.

The university's location in Berlin-Dahlem spoke to its ambitions. In the beginning of the twentieth century, Dahlem had been chosen by Prussian authorities to become a "city of science." It was home to many scientific institutions, such as state archives and museums. Most famously, the *Kaiser-Wilhelm-Gesellschaft* (KWG), precursor of the Max Planck Society, was founded there in 1911 as a "German Oxford" (a rather strange metaphor given Berlin's dominance over Oxford in the sciences at that time). It was here in Dahlem, not in the downtown campus, that Nobel laureates Albert Einstein, Werner Heisenberg, and Max Planck made their names. After World War II these institutes belonged formally to Humboldt University. In 1949 the American authorities transferred the administration of these institutes to Free University, which (bizarrely, since legal ownership remained to be determined) paid rent to Humboldt University. But ultimately this was an appropriation of major facilities in the natural and medical sciences. Two years later, Humboldt University's faculty of veterinary medicine defected en masse to FU.

The 2,140 students enrolled in the inaugural class were taught in three faculties: the Philosophical Faculty, the Faculty of Law and Economics, and the Medical Faculty. The senior faculty of *ordentliche Professoren* numbered but forty-three, including the rector, deans, and "honorary professors" who lent their names to the enterprise. These were augmented by junior scholars and visiting faculty from American universities, including Stanford and Yale. In following years, the faculty grew by recruiting scholars disaffected with East German universities and, more gradually, as the university grew in size and reputation, from West German institutions. In the winter semester of 1948–1949, approximately 70 percent of the non-first-year students had studied at the University of Berlin downtown, and another 20 percent at other East German universities. Nine percent came from West German universities, joined by thirty international students.

The university grew steadily through the 1950s and 1960s to six thousand students in 1954, twelve thousand by 1960, and nearly fifteen thousand in 1968.[21] Budgets and faculty recruiting grew accordingly. With generous support from Bonn, Berlin, and the United States, the budget grew 30 percent annually between 1958 and 1968. By 1968 the university had 396 professors, offered 77 degrees, and housed 155 institutes.[22] It was a major university.

For its first decade, at least, FU retained much of the idealism and energy that had led to its founding. As intended in the Berlin Model, students played an important role in supportive governance, and—at a time before FU's reputation as a research university was established—faculty devoted their energies largely to undergraduate education. To the standard *Vorlesungen,* or lecture courses, was added the first tutorial system on an Anglo-American model. Begun as a form of remedial reentry point for students from East German universities, it gained a life of its own and external funding from the Ford Foundation. To this was added a program—equally innovative for a German university—of general education. In a system in which students were still admitted to study in a particular discipline or profession, general education borrowed from the recent American experience (e.g., at Harvard) to broaden the scope of inquiry toward contemporary social, political, and cultural affairs. And the new university reached out to the city that had given it life: its *Funk-Universität,* or radio university, began to broadcast basic courses for Berlin citizens as early as the summer of 1949—here again the first German university to do so. An in-person Evening University was added for the general public in 1952. The strong sense of collective resolve that had united students and faculty and the university with the city in 1948 endured—for a time.[23]

## Navigating the Global 1960s and After: Protest and Reform, 1962–1989

After its humble beginnings marked by economic austerity, Free University reached a status comparable to other West German institutions of higher learning by the early 1960s. While FU was widely known as a "reform" university, its West German peers resisted innovation and aimed for a "restoration" of German academic excellence of the pre-Nazi period.[24] As it recruited faculty and students now almost exclusively from West Germany, gradually, almost invisibly, FU was becoming part of a national system that was at once undynamic and unreformed.

Meanwhile, West Berlin was changing, gaining ever more of an original identity. The building of the Berlin Wall in 1961 made its western half, now surrounded with concrete barriers and watchtowers, even more of a Cold War island. It was deep in East Germany but deliberately distinct from the German Democratic Republic that encircled it. West Berlin was tied to the Federal Republic in the West, which bankrolled it substantially as a vibrant Western showcase, in comparison to the drab grayness (in Western eyes) *drüben,* "over there," in the East.

Once a great industrial city, Berlin grew to be an increasingly edgy cultural center, known for music and the arts and, increasingly, education. Independent-minded students who sought a university seemingly at the cutting edge, at the heart of global affairs, and in a city known for *Kinos und Kneipen* (movie houses and bars) chose Berlin. And for young men of draft age who studied in Berlin there was an additional incentive: residents of the former *Hauptstadt* were exempt from conscription into the West German *Bundeswehr,* since Berlin was not (yet) legally part of the Federal Republic. From a besieged Cold War city (which, in real terms, it still was), West Berlin became a cool, countercultural, subsidized alternative to Frankfurt, Hamburg, Stuttgart, and other materialist vanguards of the West German economic miracle.

President Kennedy's 1963 visit set the high water mark for pro-Western and pro-American sentiment in Berlin. His assassination later that year and American distraction toward Asia (Vietnam) seemed to dash hopes that the

Wall, and Berlin's division, would be short lived. Seeds of anti-American sentiment had been laid by FU students in the late 1950s protesting the proliferation of atomic weapons and the American rearmament of West Germany. Young Germans born after the war began to confront Germany's militarist past, spurred on by revisionist historians such as Fritz Fischer, whose 1961 book, *Griff nach der Weltmacht*, (published in English as *Germany's Aims in the First World War*) set out a powerful case for German war guilt in both world wars. Within two years of Kennedy's triumphal appearance, FU found itself facing a seemingly endless series of internal crises. A "free speech" movement akin to that at the University of California, Berkeley, challenged the right of administrators to approve external speakers. A junior faculty member accused the rector of proactive censorship in another case. Students gathered en masse to call for the rector's resignation. Within weeks, the historian James Tent has written, FU moved "from an apparently normally functioning urban university into a crisis-ridden institution whose very basis was being questioned."[25]

By 1966 the Berlin Model of faculty-student comity was on life support. Leftist students formed their own student groups that demanded *Mitbestimmung*, or full co-representation, as if they were a labor union in a major firm. With growing outrage over the American war in Vietnam, anti-American demonstrations (for example, against the Berlin visit of Vice President Hubert Humphrey in 1967) became numerous and turbulent. When in 1967 FU student Benno Ohnesorg was shot in the head by Berlin police while protesting the visit of the Shah of Iran, an American ally, on a state visit to Berlin, the outrage was universal, but the lessons drawn were generational. Fifteen thousand attended the services on FU campus in the Henry Ford Building for Ohnesorg, the first but not last victim of a cultural revolution at Free University.[26] The murder set off weeks of mass demonstrations in West Germany and radicalized the student movement. Ohnesorg's death also led to the resignation of the president of the police, the interior senator of Berlin, and the mayor of West Berlin, all of whom were forced to confront the brutality of the offending police officer. The officer himself was eventually acquitted, and subsequent investigations revealed that he and several witnesses had made false statements in an attempt to cover up the affair. The 2009 revelation that the officer in question was working as a Stasi-IM at the time further complicated the story, yet no evidence has been found that his intention in firing was to sow dissent in West Berlin.

**Figure 3.3.** Student sit-in on April 19–20, 1967, in the lobby of the Henry Ford Building. Courtesy of Bernard Larsson.

A university founded as a reaction to leftist extremism now found itself at the center of radical political movements that were spreading across the globe. In Paris, May 1968 saw the onset of student-led demonstrations that led to a general strike and nearly brought down the French government. In the United States, divisions over the Vietnam War roiled American campuses. In China, the Maoist Cultural Revolution disrupted and closed universities, while a loosely understood "Maoism" found favor among Western leftists. And in Berlin, a university that was the beneficiary of American largesse became a target for anti-American politics.

By the early 1970s the student movement had radicalized further and splintered into well-organized student groups, threatening the freedom of teaching and learning with agitprop techniques. The university became intensely politicized. The Academic Senate and the rector's office were periodically occupied by protesting students. Political graffiti adorned buildings old and new. In 1970 a part-time FU instructor, Ulrike Meinhof, masterminded the escape of a convicted political arsonist, Andreas Baader, and the consequent "Baader-Meinhof Gang" became synonymous with domestic terrorism. The nonfatal shooting of charismatic student movement leader Rudi Dutschke a year later brought matters to a boiling point.

All this gave rise to a movement for governance reform that would build on the original Berlin Model and take it further still, to incorporate (and ideally focus) student energies on the working of the university. An early advocate of what would become the new University Law of 1969 was the political scientist Alexander Schwan, who believed in *Mitbestimmung* and bringing students further into the running of the university. The new law did precisely that, institutionalizing radical student groups in university committees and programs. By 1971 Schwan had had enough and called the reformed law a mistake. The response by Maoist students was to attempt to defenestrate him—that is, to throw him out the window of his seminar in the Otto Suhr Institute, the home of political science at FU. Amid an intense physical struggle, Schwan was saved by a group of moderate students and by his wife, the young assistant professor Gesine Schwan.[27]

I was a student at Free University in 1972–1973, a postgraduate recipient of a DAAD (German Academic Exchange Service) grant and a *Luftbrückendankstipendium* (Airlift Thank-you Fellowship) from the city of Berlin. I was a student of history at the Friedrich Meinecke Institute, where I heard rumors of the near-defenestration of another scholar, Friedrich Zipfel, a historian of the Nazi era whose lectures I audited. In the winter semester the new Rostlaube building was opened, housing courses on history and political science. Before a single class could meet, its rusty exterior was covered in red and yellow political slogans. There I took a seminar on Marx in the Otto Suhr Institute. It was taught by Gesine Schwan, who would outlive her husband and all FU's disorder to become a major scholar and a political figure in Germany's Social Democratic Party. Schwan was then very early in her teaching career, and no seminar could have been more challenging. Among the fifteen or so students in our class, there were at least six different Communist parties or factions. Perhaps Marx has never been so thoroughly examined: from the vantage point of Maoists, of Stalinists, of Marxian anarchists, not to mention those who believed that little Albania practiced Marxism in its purist form. We the students read Marx collaboratively (more or less) in *Arbeitsgruppen,* or work groups, albeit usually in the friendly confines of a Berlin *Kneipe.* Because I was the only one among us who could cross the Wall as a citizen of an Allied power, I had the special task of buying our texts on the cheap in East Berlin. Schwan, whose every utterance in seminar was interrupted by one faction or the other, wins my vote for the Iron Cross in endurance and patience.

The university had reached the point of breakdown in the early 1970s. Berlin city officials lamented that the university's patent inability to govern itself meant that the state had to intervene. The Berlin Model of the university's early days was by then a distant memory, and revisions to the university law in 1974 and an altogether new legislation in 1978 restored the majority rule of the professoriat and strengthened the position of the president. These measures were carried further in the 1980s. As James Tent, whose political history of the first three decades of FU remains the standard account, wrote, "For a short time the Free University operated under a system so democratic as to excite the astonishment of any Communist-bloc nation or institution." The results were so polarizing as to invite an inevitable reaction. As political movements and university laws came and went, the original Free University of Berlin disappeared. Here again, Tent said, "The blunt fact was that no amount of tinkering with laws and constitutions could restore [what] had once made the Free University a unique institution for nearly a generation."[28]

Throughout this period, perhaps in an effort to coopt the university's radicalization, government spending on education increased, but curricula were altered to prepare students better for the job market, not for revolution. The revised Berlin University Law of 1978 focused not on the "whole person education" that had defined the founding years of both Berlin universities, but rather on "the needs of professional practice."[29] But the decade of turmoil at FU had made the university a less attractive place, perhaps especially to the practically minded. By the mid-1970s, the quality of the faculty and student body had decreased significantly. The number of students, however, increased dramatically. During the 1970s and 1980s the university—like many in Germany—became a mass university (*Massenuniversität*). Students came young and stayed late—in part because of the exemption from military service and because limits on time-to-degree were seldom enforced. Political pressures on the Berlin government led to ever-greater expansion. Since university budgets were determined in large measure by the number of students, there was a mutual incentive on the part of government and university to grow. And so the university bloated. The size of the student body rose from 15,778 in 1968 to 27,892 in 1973, to 61,198 in 1988, on the eve of the fall of the Berlin Wall.[30] Earlier concepts of small-group learning in tutorials and broader initiatives in general education atrophied.

In the 1980s, with a return to academic normalcy across the western world, moderating influences prevailed at FU. But as the university moved away from its politicized past, it grew undistinguished. It was now "a normal German university,"[31] but in an era when the global reputation of German universities was a distant memory. When state budgets inevitably became tight again, FU had to institute a hiring freeze; its medical clinic, Westend, closed. One compensating factor—and an auspicious sign for the future—was that the university began to attract third-party resources in Germany in a serious way. Between 1978 and 1985 the amount of independent support doubled to DM 56 million.[32] This enabled the university's Office of International Affairs to maintain the international programs that from its early days had defined FU as a university with special ties to America, and now beyond.

## *Nach der Wende:* Retrenchment, 1989–2000

With the fall of the Wall and the formal reunification of Germany eleven months later, the original raison d'être of Free University ceased to exist. FU and Humboldt University had begun minor areas of cooperation before 1989, but they would soon enter into a competitive struggle for survival.

Berlin was again to be the capital of a united Germany. It was inconceivable that Humboldt University, located in what again would be the real *Mitte* of Berlin, would cease to exist. Rather, as we have seen, immediate efforts were made to decommunize it and to give it more democratic governance. The question was, should Humboldt be *the* university in Berlin once more? And should a newly reunited country with a reunited capital not aspire further? German universities historically were funded by the states in which they were situated. Was it not time for a truly *national* university?

The answer was no. German reunification was going to be expensive enough, and there was neither the will nor the budget to build a national university. The newly unified Berlin was proud but broke. The West German funds that had subsidized West Berlin during the Cold War would be discontinued, and the city would have to fund higher education largely on its own, as Berlin became one of the sixteen states of Germany and one of the poorest.

The question then was this: Should Humboldt take over FU, and perhaps also the Technical University, to have one, huge, comprehensive university for Berlin in multiple parts of the city, with an elite core in the city center? The name Humboldt, after all, was world renowned, as was the legacy of the University of Berlin. The upstart FU had fewer claims to fame and had perhaps served its historic purpose. Berlin's Senator for Science Manfred Erhardt imagined a renewed, elite Humboldt whose influence would spread far beyond the city. The West German universities, he argued, were seen internationally as anything but a model, and the *Massenuniversitäten* of Free and Technical Universities had so many problems that it would take years of reform before they would enjoy a significant external reputation.[33]

That both Humboldt and FU survived, joined also by the Technical University, is testament to the power of inertia, of bureaucratic passive (and at times active) resistance on the part of the existing institutions; the absence of a vision of what a united university would look like; and, again, a lack of money. Ultimately, administrators and the Senate decided to keep both Humboldt and Free Universities in the hope that this would foster healthy intercollegiate competition, ultimately improving the teaching and research at both institutions.[34]

In the first years *nach der Wende*, after the fall of the Wall, a great number of students from the former East Germany sought to start or continue their studies at Free University. Enrollment increased and the number of students at FU exceeded sixty-two thousand. But as Berlin's budgetary realities hit home, and with fewer subsidies from the German federal government, the budget of FU was reduced considerably in the 1990s.

In 1988 FU had proposed to Berlin's Senate a structural plan that had envisaged a decade of university investment and stability in the 1990s.[35] That plan was now worthless. The Senate's 1993 University Structural Plan reduced funding for Berlin's universities by DM 1 billion (approximately US$600 million) over the next decade. The costs to FU were disproportionately great, for as Humboldt was being built back up, FU was seemingly drawn and quartered to help pay for it. The number of fully funded student seats at FU decreased by half: from nearly 40,000 in 1992, to 26,000 in 2001, and then to 21,000 in 2003. The number of professors in the same period declined even more radically: from approximately 700 (outside of medical fields) in 1990, to 440 in 1999, and to 368 in 2003.[36] Annually, between 1992 and 1999, the number of faculty departures far outweighed faculty appointments.

The cuts hit hardest at the core academic missions. The university could not downsize everywhere. Because nonacademic employees were largely permanent, with contracts that could not be nullified, many academic employees were laid off, while the nonacademic staff retained their positions in the university's bureaucracy. Beyond this, degree programs that were offered by both FU and Humboldt were subject to cutbacks. A number of smaller institutes were transferred from FU to Humboldt, including the institutes for library science, sports science, Scandinavian studies, and Slavic studies. The medical school, including the dental clinic and the pediatric clinic, was transferred to Humboldt University, leaving the future of the life sciences at FU in doubt. In 1996 the Berlin Senate reduced drastically the budget at both university libraries. In April 1996 and in the winter semester of 1997–1998, these cutbacks resulted in widespread student demonstrations and strikes. In an echo of the 1960s the offices of the FU president were once again occupied by students.

## Reinvention and Renewal in the Twenty-First Century

In the twenty-first century, Free University would have to reconceive itself yet again. The mass university had to shed students, faculty, and decades of accumulated fat and memory. That it would emerge a leaner, fitter, more competitive enterprise to compete with the resurrected Humboldt University—this no one could have imagined at the turn of the century.

Yet by 2017 the *Times Higher Education* ranked FU as one of the top five (out of more than one hundred) German research universities, and among the top twenty in the world in the humanities. And it had built on its early history of internationalization—being the product of a global Cold War—to be the leading German university in the realms of international studies and global partnerships. Spread across three modern campuses in Berlin, the university in 2020 had eleven academic units, now a joint medical school (Charité) with Humboldt University, as well as three international institutes that offered degrees in Eastern European, Latin American, and North American studies. In all, Free University offered some 180 bachelor's and master's degree programs as well as around 50 doctoral programs. It was known above all for its programs in the humanities and social sciences, but increasingly also for the natural and life sciences.

Free University made a remarkable comeback in the twenty-first century. How did it do it?

## Governance: The Capacity for Leadership

Part of the answer must lie in governance. Formally, many aspects of the governance of Free University today seem similar to the governance structures found at Humboldt and other German universities. Its Academic Senate (AS), led by the president, comprises twenty-five members, who are elected for two-year terms. The AS consists of four groups representing different interests at the university: thirteen professors and four representatives each from the student body, the academic staff, and the nonacademic staff. The professors hold an absolute majority, but only by one vote, and only if they voted unanimously. The AS passes resolutions on matters including university development and equipment plans and establishes basic principles applicable to instruction, studies, and research at the university. It confirms the number of students admitted each year. It is also involved in the establishment and elimination of courses of study and issues a position statement on the draft budget every year. Since FU is a public university, Berlin's Senate continues to function as an influential stakeholder. It negotiates the annual basic funding with Free University, and—more than the Academic Senate—determines the number of students admitted every year, since it is the Berlin Senate that pays for them.

As at Humboldt University, Free University is led by a president who serves for a term of four years and could be reelected. The president and the executive vice president are elected by a majority vote of the extended Academic Senate, which includes thirty-six additional members, on nomination by the same governing body. Together with the Academic Senate, the president proposes three additional vice presidents, who are responsible for different areas of administration and finance.

Compared with Humboldt University, the FU president has greater agency in choosing the FU leadership team. And perhaps because of the gravity of the crisis of the 1990s, the Academic Senate and university leadership work in comparative harmony. Unlike Humboldt University, where none of the presidents after 1989 served a full second term, the leadership at FU has much more continuity and de facto authority. The average presidential tenure in office is seven years. The president is part of an executive board, which also includes the chancellor, the executive vice president, and the vice presidents. It approves the draft budget and proposes structural and development plans. It also implements resolutions of the AS, such as the establishment and elimination of courses of study.

Of course, it is not just the positions but the people who hold them that matter. FU's history in the twenty-first century is testimony to the importance of continuity and quality of presidential leadership in a university. Despite, or more likely because of, FU's tumultuous experience in the past, presidents were accorded—and they asserted—more authority than was common for German universities. The legal scholar Johann Wilhelm Gerlach led the university from 1991 to 1999, resisting fiercely the attempted merger of FU with Humboldt University, encouraging student protests over budget cuts, and using court procedures to defend the university's institutional autonomy. Dieter Lenzen, a scholar of educational philosophy, was elected FU's sixth president in 2003, coming to office after having taught at Stanford, Columbia, and Tokyo, among other distinguished international universities. Lenzen's vision and drive led FU to build on its international strengths and to reform its administration, which led to its distinction in the first round of Excellence Initiative funding.[37] By all accounts a force of nature, Lenzen spearheaded FU's efforts in its first competition in the nationwide Excellence Initiative before leaving to preside over the University of Hamburg in 2010. And the distinguished scholar of German literature (eighteen monographs) Peter-André Alt led FU with a gentle disposition and iron backbone from 2010 until 2018, taking it to stunning success in the second and third rounds of Germany's Excellence competitions. He was succeeded by the internationally renowned mathematician Günter M. Ziegler, an MIT PhD who had founded the Berlin Mathematical School, a joint graduate program of the three major (including the Technical University) Berlin universities.

## The Iron Chancellor

Presidents are, or ought to be, central to the direction of any university. Equally important at FU was the role of professional administration. At Humboldt University, as we have seen, the *Berufsbeamtentum*, or professional civil service, was initially held over from GDR days. At FU, strength in administrative leadership was a key factor in the university's renewal.

Second to the role of the president at FU is the *Kanzler*. The *Kanzler* is chancellor—as in Britain's Chancellor of the Exchequer—and formally in charge of the budget. (It was the absence of this position at Humboldt University that would so frustrate its presidents.) At FU, the Board of Trustees elects the chancellor upon nomination of the president, and then the Berlin

Senate formally appoints the chancellor for a ten-year term. With responsibilities that have grown far beyond the budget, the chancellor plays a critical role at FU. The chancellor's term has outlasted that of any president, and the chancellor has had unique power and knowledge of the purse in times of dearth (such as the 1990s) or reinvestment (as in the 2010s).

The iron chancellor of the modern FU was Peter Lange. Peter Lange (pronounced *Lahn-ge,* and not to be confused with Peter Lange, the longtime provost of Duke, whom we shall meet in Chapter 7), began his association with FU in 1976 as a student of economics pedagogy and retired forty years later, having served as research associate and lecturer, then managing director for the Academic Senate, then as head of the presidential office for a decade, and, for his final fifteen years, as chancellor. Lange was the embodiment of administrative continuity in the turbulent and transformative quarter-century after the fall of the Wall. His coordination of FU's structural reform in the 1990s, his deft touch in working with the Berlin Senate, mastery of budgets and budgetary politics, and keen collaboration with a series of presidents all helped to ensure that as FU became smaller and leaner, it grasped the opportunity to become, pound-for-pound, much better. He contributed mightily to the raising of FU's profile domestically and internationally and above all to its successes in the Excellence Initiative. He also oversaw the development of the university's physical plant, as the client for Lord Norman Foster's Philological Library, which opened in 2005, and for the gracious complex completed in 2015 for the *Kleine Fächer,* or small departments, in the humanities and social sciences that were at the heart of FU's renewal—today the largest building on the campus.

Over his long tenure, Lange was the most enduringly powerful and least visible leader of the university. A student publication wrote in 2011 about its search for a "Phantom": "At the FU there rules an Invisible Man." Chancellor Peter Lange was among "the most influential" people, yet "hardly anyone on campus knows him."[38] Indeed, he would become widely and publicly feted only on retirement. President Peter-André Alt remarked at the retirement gathering for Lange in December 2015, when Lange's portrait was hung in the Henry Ford Building, that Lange was "the universalist" among chancellors. "What does this chancellor do?" Alt asked a large audience. "Almost everything. Budgets and personnel. Controls. Planning with academic departments on their goals. Coordination of centralized and decentralized processes. Construction and campus development. Energy and IT. Hiring of tenured faculty. Third-party funding. Research fit-outs. Li-

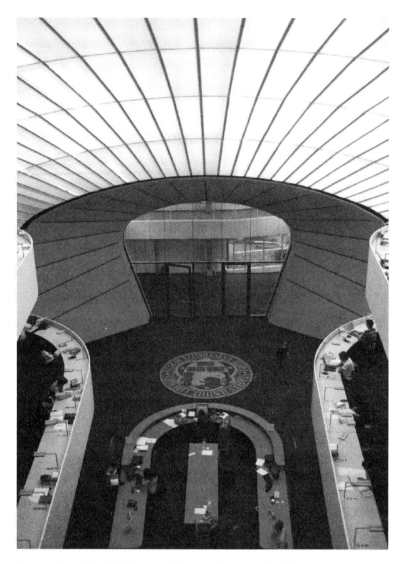

**Figure 3.4.** The Philological Library, designed by Norman Foster. senhormario/flickr/CC BY 2.0.

braries. Learning and teaching." Unlike other chancellors at German universities who focused solely on budgets, Lange "does it all. He takes on everything himself and is never haughty." Lange had "firm control" over the two thousand colleagues in the FU administration because "he knows what is to be done."[39]

When Lange retired, he was asked what he was most proud of: "The success of the Free University. To see a university, which in the reunited city [of Berlin] was repeatedly given no chance, develop so grandly after the painful cuts of the 1990s. This outcome is the result of a great many medium, large, and a few huge successes, all of which had to be pursued tirelessly—accompanied to be sure by setbacks. And as former chancellor I am naturally proud that we have succeeded in building one of the most modern and efficient university administrations in Germany."[40]

## Funding from the Outside

Lange and the presidents he served found success in an economy of scarcity, where priorities had to be set carefully. Berlin's fiscal crisis after the fall of the Wall led to vast cuts in state funding. The Berlin Senate shifted resources from FU and Technical University to Humboldt University, cutting FU's budget in half. Tuition fees could have served to compensate for the cutbacks in state funding, but even the contemplation of them in the 1990s led to massive student demonstrations at the Brandenburg Gate. In any event, the traditionally left-leaning Senate of Berlin was fundamentally against the idea of tuition, and it remained opposed even when tuition fees were first allowed by the German Supreme Court in 2005. By 2014 Germany's sixteen states had all abolished tuition charges for undergraduates. "In retrospect," President Alt would later lament, "we lost an opportunity to enhance our financial support and budget situations. We could have invested much more and done much more."[41] In 2020 student fees at FU were but US$340 per semester, two-thirds of which paid for a highly discounted public transit pass for greater Berlin.

To make things more difficult, German universities had a terrible record of raising money from private donors and industry. FU was no exception. As Alt analyzed the situation, "Since higher education is left to politics, there is no consciousness to support higher education. Private donors are a very small group when it comes to university funding. There has been a massive increase in private wealth. Maybe this will cause a change in the system, but this will need time, at least ten years from now." Private donations to FU totaled but US$1.1 million in 2016.[42]

The Senate of Berlin provided the main source of income for the university. In 2017 it designated a total of US$306 million. The funding was negotiated every three years in "university treaties" that were first established for all public universities in Berlin in 1997. Universities only received public funding under the condition that they complied with certain performance indicators, including the number of accepted students, faculty diversity, and internationalization. The university treaty gave FU planning stability, especially when it came to the appointment of new professors. Moreover, these funds were supplemented by salary and other support by partner institutions such as the Max Planck Society. Still, the funds provided by the Senate of Berlin were never sufficient for the university's expenses. FU's Structural Plan of 2015 described the funding situation as one of "forced structural overload."[43]

The federal government stepped in to provide additional public funding through its Higher Education Pact 2020. The initiative gave Free University additional funds, but only under the condition of increased enrollment. In 2017 these federal resources amounted to almost 12 percent of the university's total basic funding.

In recent years, Free University concentrated its efforts on raising *Drittmittel,* or third-party funds. Although the name "third-party funds" may suggest otherwise, these funds were largely public, taken from other sections of the federal education budget and the European Union. The difference between third-party funds and the general funds was that the universities had to compete for the third-party resources, which were linked to specific research projects. Between 1989 and 1995 third-party funds had doubled (from US$46 million to US$89 million) as state funding was slashed but were still ancillary to the regular state budget.[44] By 2017, however, third-party funds amounted to nearly 40 percent of the total funding of the university. The German Research Foundation (*Deutsche Forschungsgemeinschaft,* or DFG), found that FU was one of the strongest universities when it came to attracting third-party funds for research. In the reporting period 2014–2016, FU secured almost US$300 million in research funds from the DFG, ranking fifth among all German universities. In the humanities and social sciences, FU secured more third-party funds than any other German university.

Third-party funds made the university nationally competitive and internationally visible. They also created new pressures. The university was increasingly dependent on acquiring third-party funds, not the least because the funded projects were mostly short-term. Many research activities, especially new PhD programs, relied almost entirely on these resources and their prospect for renewal. That FU has attracted funding for new graduate degree programs is a vote of confidence in FU's judgment as to where academic fields are headed. The capacity to attract third-party funding became a major criterion for hiring decisions. It made the university at once more entrepreneurial (in seeking support) and more managerial (in using it). Full professors already had the task of running their *Lehrstuhl;* now they sought and managed sizeable external projects as well. And—as in leading research universities everywhere—third-party funds accentuated the already strong tendency to value research over teaching.

All that said, the necessary search for external support gave FU ever more of a start-up culture. And its early successes with DFG and other foundations proved to be preconditions for its performance in the most prestigious competition of all, the Excellence Initiative.

### A New Call to Berlin: Faculty and Students

Competitive success in any research university depends ultimately on the faculty. Through good times and bad, Free University's faculty has consisted of a dedicated body of scholars that produced world-renowned research. Since 1948 five Nobel laureates have taught at FU. The faculty also included seventeen Leibniz Prize winners, the highest endowed award in Germany; seven Max Planck research award winners; and fifteen members of the German National Academy of Sciences, Leopoldina, one of the oldest associations of scholars of natural science and medicine in Germany. For scholars and researchers of natural sciences, being elected a member of Leopoldina was considered one of the highest distinctions granted by any institution in Germany.

In the past decade, FU's faculty has experienced a surge. A "call" to Berlin—now to FU—was again a mark of great prestige. But beyond the "full" professoriat, whose numbers were limited by the Berlin Senate, several hundred new positions were created by other means. Between 2018 and 2022 FU planned to raise the percentage of academic personnel with permanent careers to 35 percent by adding a variety of new professorships and a tentative step toward a tenure-track path.[45] These include endowed professorships, Excellence Initiative professorships, joint professorships with other research institutions, and junior professorships. Junior professorships, a category established in 2002, are term-limited to six years, at which point scholars are expected to apply for professorships *elsewhere.* By 2020 their ranks had expanded to 96.

FU recruited well and retained well. Between 2000 and 2017 the average rate of success in retention negotiations was 82 percent.[46] In cases in which the university was not able to retain faculty members, the main area of contention was often salary. Compared to the other German states, the salaries for professors in Berlin had been relatively low (as indeed had been the cost of living). In 2016 the salary for a professor in Berlin was approximately 10 percent less than the highest paying German state, Baden-Württemberg.[47] Compared to the United States, the salaries at FU were especially low. Except for appointments of foreign professors, the average base salary for full professors at FU in 2017 was US\$107,000. For the highest rank (W3) professor, the average salary (including bonuses) was US\$144,000 in 2018.[48] Another issue was the high teaching load. Universities in Berlin required their professors to teach nine hours per week. As anywhere, faculty devised means to reduce those numbers, but the load was still comparatively high.[49]

In 2018 FU had 358 full professors, with forty-eight of them holding joint appointments, or "extraordinary professorships," with other higher education institutions in and around Berlin. In addition, there were 127 junior and other fixed-term professors, and 4,450 nonprofessorial staff members who supported teaching, research, and operations. The forty-eight so-called extraordinary professorships included, but were not limited to, the four major independent research institutions in Germany that were also publicly funded: the Max Planck Society, the Fraunhofer Society, the Helmholtz Association, and the Leibniz Association. Costs for the jointly appointed professors were distributed among the institutions. These partnerships intensified cooperation with nonuniversity institutions, particularly the Max Planck Society, that were nationally and internationally renowned for their research.

The teaching staff of 3,798 taught in 2018 some 33,000 undergraduate and master's level students and 4,000 doctoral candidates.[50] Faculty diversity was an issue: a faculty that was 63 percent male instructed an undergraduate population that was 59 percent female.[51] With 7,975 international students in 2018, about 13 percent of the undergraduate body and 26 percent of the master's students were from outside Germany.[52] Approximately 14 percent of the faculty was international.[53] In addition, approximately 600 international visiting scholars and scientists came to the university each year to serve in teaching and research roles.[54]

*Vanguard of Internationalization*

From its origin, a centrally distinguishing feature of Free University was its international profile. Internationalization would distinguish the university again in the twenty-first century.

Founded with American support, FU's first partnerships were naturally with American universities. But Free University had established connections with universities all over the world to remain academically relevant from its isolated position in West Berlin. While Humboldt University limited its international partnerships after World War II to universities in the "socialist brother countries," which became fewer after splits within the Soviet bloc, FU established partnerships with universities first in the West then, in the era of détente, with institutions in Eastern Europe, the Soviet Union, and China.

In 1968 FU established an exchange partnership with Leningrad State University (today's Saint Petersburg State University).[55] Partnerships with universities in Eastern Europe followed. In 1981 FU forged a partnership with Peking University, West Germany's first in China since the Communist takeover there. The following decades saw many more alliances, primarily with institutions in North America, Eastern Europe, and East Asia, most visibly in the humanities and social sciences.

By 2017 FU maintained more than 100 university-wide, bilateral partnerships and more than 330 university partnerships within the network of the Erasmus program, a European Union-sponsored exchange program that provides opportunities for students to gain study or work experience in a different European country and funds joint European degree programs. In addition, among the university's various departments and research institutes, more than fifty partner agreements with other higher education institutions had formed.

Of course, many universities boast a roster of international connections. It is easy for presidents to ink dozens of MOUs (memoranda of understanding) without much understanding of what, if anything, they may lead to. It is something else to maintain long-standing international alliances and to focus on the ones that make a difference. Over the past decade Free University has been active in all corners of the world, but also focused on six major strategic partnerships based on academic excellence, geographical diversity, and potential for future growth. In 2011 and 2012 FU initiated three strategic partnerships with the Hebrew University of Jerusalem, Peking

University, and Saint Petersburg State University. In 2014 the University of British Columbia and in 2016 the University of California, Berkeley, were added to the list of strategic partners. In 2017 they were joined by the University of Zurich. Partnership with Peking University led to the establishment of Germany's first Confucius Institute, which trains Chinese language teachers and hosts conferences and workshops (a number of which I have attended) as an extension of the university under the leadership of a distinguished FU sinologist, Mechthild Leutner.

A parallel focus of FU's internationalization strategy was the establishment of liaison offices across the globe. These offices aimed to increase FU's visibility outside of Germany, foster relationships with existing partnerships in the region, and serve as sites to recruit students and researchers for the university. By 2020 the international network of FU encompassed seven offices, the highest number for any university in Germany.[56] Given its historical ties with the United States, FU set up the first office in New York City in 2005 in cooperation with the Ludwig Maximilian University of Munich. This "German University Alliance," housed in an office facing the United Nations building in New York, sought to "build a bridge over the Atlantic and strengthen [FU's] international integration into the scientific community."[57] Offices in Brussels, Cairo, Moscow, New Delhi, Beijing, and Sao Paulo followed, each with a region-specific focus. These were modest, often shoestring, operations, but they planted FU's flag on five continents and lent credibility to the university's international ambitions. One result, according to the German Academic Exchange Service (DAAD) in 2016, was that FU received the most external funding of all German universities for international projects.

Free University was also by far the most popular destination in Germany for international students. A study published by the DAAD, *Wissenschaft Weltoffen 2019,* showed that FU also had the second highest number (761) of participants in the Erasmus program in Germany.[58] In 2016, 20 percent of FU's students came from foreign countries; this percentage was even higher for doctoral students (34 percent).[59] FU was a prized destination also for international research scholars. The Alexander von Humboldt Foundation (AvH) was one of the most prestigious sources of funding for international scholars, maintaining a worldwide network of more than 28,000 Humboldtians from all disciplines in more than 140 countries, including fifty-four Nobel Prize winners. Every year, the foundation enabled 2,000 researchers from around the world to conduct collaborative research in Germany. FU led all German universities as a destination, with 15 percent of Humboldtians landing there. Between 2014 and 2018 FU attracted 265 scholars for research stays longer than one month.[60]

In 2019 the European Commission launched the European Universities Initiative to strengthen strategic partnerships and increase the international competitiveness of European universities. This initiative included seventeen university alliances. FU was selected to be part of one of these alliances, the University Alliance Europa (UNA Europa), which was colloquially called the "University of the Future."[61] The goal was for universities within this alliance to focus their research and education on the interdisciplinary topics of European studies, data science and artificial intelligence, and cultural heritage to spur social innovation and internationalization.

In the twenty-first century, then, Free University was fast becoming an internationally networked university. It was about to be formally recognized as such.

## Creating a German "Ivy League": FU in the Excellence Initiative

Although Germany had been home to the world's best universities in the nineteenth and early twentieth centuries, that was a distant memory at the onset of the twenty-first century. Seldom did any German university appear in the top fifty of institutions ranked by the major university ranking systems. The limitations on funding, which came primarily from regional governments; the lack of revenue-generating tuition or academic philanthropy (as in the United States); and the outsourcing of prestigious research projects to institutions such as the Max Planck Society (research often involving university faculty but externally credited to the Max Planck institutes) all led to a massive underperformance in the research rankings of German universities. As we have seen, it was in response to this situation in 2005 that the federal and state governments, in cooperation with the German Council of Science and Humanities and the DFG, launched the Excellence Initiative, with the goal of selecting a small number of German universities to become internationally competitive higher education institutions.

With nine funded projects (some in collaboration with other universities), Free University was the most successful university during the first funding period. It was recognized as a "University of Excellence," building on its institutional strategy as an "International Network University." Developing this strategy entailed creating research alliances, promoting young researchers, and bolstering international collaboration through the creation of three centers: the Center for Research Strategy; the Dahlem Research School, which fostered an integrated cross-field set of doctoral programs for junior scholars; and the Center for International Collaboration. FU was awarded four clusters of excellence. Five graduate schools at FU also received funding. In addition, FU created two administrative bodies to oversee FU's Excellence Initiative efforts. One was the Excellence Council, an internal advisory board of twenty distinguished professors from across FU that advised the university's strategic research priorities within the Excellence Strategy. The other was the International Council, an external advisory body of twenty-one experts from twelve countries with international experience in university management and higher education policy.[62] (I served on the latter body from 2012 to 2018.)

In short, in the first round, following a university-wide, all-hands-on-deck planning effort overseen by President Lenzen and Chancellor Lange, FU vaulted to the top ranks of German universities. Lenzen's acumen channeled much of the funding into a robust administrative apparatus that equipped the university for competition in the twenty-first century while supporting its research agenda. In mid-2009 the federal and state governments decided to continue the Excellence Initiative for another five-year period from 2012 to 2017, now with more than US$3.5 billion in funding. In the second round, new proposals competed with prior applications for additional funding. Funding was awarded to forty-five graduate schools and forty-three clusters of excellence. President Alt now led FU to Excellence status once more. In June 2012 the "International Network University" Institutional Strategy was again funded. Three Excellence Clusters received further funding and two additional graduate schools were founded and funded. By 2012, under the umbrella of the Dahlem Research School, there were nine newly formed graduate schools.

We have seen that the first two rounds of the Excellence Initiative made dramatic changes to the university landscape in Germany, less because of the money itself (in the first two rounds FU's additional intake was less than US$300 million) than because of the spirit of academic entrepreneurship and ambition that the initiative encouraged. But when in fall 2018, the Excellence Initiative announced a third round, it encouraged less institutional risk-taking and seemed to promote consolidation across the higher education sector. There were two lines of funding: one again for clusters of excellence, and the other for a broader level of support for "universities of excellence," which would provide the institutions themselves with additional funding. For the first time, universities were encouraged to apply together in consortia under the universities of excellence funding line.

Given the long and complex history of the universities in Berlin, and the Berlin Senate's begrudging approval to maintain three institutions after 1989, it is not surprising that FU was strongly encouraged to apply in a consortium with its fellow Berlin institutions. Although in financial and reputational terms this was not obviously to the advantage of FU, it joined a Berlin University Alliance with Humboldt University, Technical University, and Charité Berlin University of Medicine (the reorganized Charité) in the Universities of Excellence funding competition through the strategy "Crossing Boundaries Towards an Integrated Research Environment."

The Excellence Initiative announced in July 2019 that the Berlin University Alliance would be one of thirteen German universities awarded Excellence status. The status came with a US$212 million award over a seven-year period for the alliance.[63] The consortium also won funding for four Excellence Clusters. Between the four institutions, there were over thirty international partnerships, liaison offices, and international campuses. As Alt reflected on FU's success in the Excellence Initiative, he called the strategic international partnerships one of "the most important elements of the general development of the university in this decade that may define the general progress of the institution."[64]

## Facing the Future

Despite the success of the third Excellence Initiative funding round, by investing in a more regional strategy through the Berlin University Alliance, there were questions to be raised. Was FU compromising its individual international efforts? Would the historically competitive dynamics between Humboldt and Free Universities limit their common success? Would the remarkable differences in administrative systems among the institutions that made up the Berlin University Alliance impede implementation of new research projects and hinder the transformation of these new projects into more sustainable, permanent structures? Would the Berlin Senate move toward an ever-greater integration or even consolidation of its universities?

By 2020 the Excellence Initiative had boosted research production and raised the international profile of German universities. The forty-five universities that received initiative funding received 76 percent of all third-party funds raised by German higher education institutions in 2012. Almost a quarter (23 percent) of academic staff in the graduate schools and clusters of excellence were recruited from outside Germany by 2015. German universities were beginning again to be a magnet for global talent.

When Free University of Berlin was founded in 1948, it envisioned itself as returning to the Humboldtian ideal of a university, providing a space to form and educate young people in an environment free of ideological commitments. The obstacles facing the university had primarily been political and economic, namely the institution's dependence on the support of Western Germany and the United States, as well as its struggle for funding, faculty, and recognition in devastated postwar Berlin.

During the first two decades of the twenty-first century, FU carved out a space for itself not just within the landscape of German higher education but also as a European institution. The 2016 Brexit referendum sent shockwaves through higher education, as students and researchers struggled to imagine a future of curtailed mobility. As the United Kingdom has sought to distance itself from the European project, Germany has stepped in and redoubled its commitment. This can be seen in its universities, and especially at FU, where Erasmus enrollments continue to increase yearly, making it among the most sought-after places to study and research, with new degree programs, many of which are offered in English and take advantage of the city's unique historical and cultural heritage. These rich offerings in higher education have in no small part contributed to Berlin's reputation as a truly European capital.

When President Alt left the university to become president of the German Rectors' Conference in 2018, Free University faced a different set of challenges. Over the previous decade, the institution had developed into a leading German university in one of Europe's most vibrant cities. Now it faced competition from other higher education institutions in Berlin, Germany, and overseas. And it faced the challenge of linking its destiny to those of the other Berlin universities.

Like his predecessor, President Günter M. Ziegler was an internal administrative appointment who had served as a faculty member in the Institute of Mathematics since 2011. Like Alt, he had a successful career in academia. Having established and run the Berlin Mathematical School, Ziegler also knew firsthand the challenge of cooperation in strengthening Berlin's higher education system. To that end, the latest Excellence Initiative / Strategy had not only provided additional university funding but also forced FU to re-align its own academic mission in a greater spirit of cooperation with Humboldt University and the Technical University. How that would affect the university's autonomy and development remained to be seen.

Protesting is a contemporary ritual in Berlin. But today, instead of the unruly student demonstrations of 1968 protesting against the inherent conservatism of universities or overseas entanglements, new solidarities have waxed and waned. From March 2019 young and old (but primarily young) Berliners congregated at open plazas as part of the global "Fridays for Future" climate strike, protesting the continued negligence of meaningful climate policy in Germany and all over the world. These gatherings also made their mark on FU. Free University was founded in political controversy and has at times (in the Cold War and in the leftist movements of the 1960s) been defined by it. Today, the topic of focus has become the environment, as the threat to the natural world seeps into the life of the university. In December 2019, over a year into Ziegler's presidency, FU declared a state of climate emergency.[65] The university announced it would aim to be climate neutral by 2025 and design curricula to center around topics of sustainability and climate protection. A new steering committee, comprising students, professors, and other university members, was formed to help plan the university's efforts to increase energy efficiency and expand the campus's renewable energy sources. This announcement built on FU's prior commitment toward sustainability efforts. Between 2001 and 2018 FU reduced its power and heat consumption by 25 percent and its carbon dioxide emissions by 75 percent. Reflecting on this announcement, Ziegler stated, "We as universities have a special responsibility. . . . Our task is not only to improve scientific knowledge and communicate this to society, but to also act in an exemplary way within our areas of responsibility."[66] This effort reflected Ziegler's view that universities should function as society's "living labs" (*Zukunftswerkstätten*) or dynamic environments that lead cutting-edge research and teaching to address society's most pressing issues.

I believe that John F. Kennedy would have agreed, for he asserted long ago that Free University of Berlin had a special mission. Its graduates were to be "citizens of the world" who had "a special obligation to think and to help forge the future."[67] Free University had for seven decades served as a "living lab" in the pursuit of *veritas, iustitia, libertas*. As the most experimental and international of German universities, it prepared to meet more challenges still.

# CHAPTER FOUR

# The Rise and Challenges of American Research Universities

TODAY, AMERICAN universities outrank their German counterparts in every global ranking system. And yet a century and a half ago the concept of the research university was completely foreign to the higher education institutions of the United States, including the ones that had deemed themselves universities in name. "During the nineteenth century German universities led the world in erudition and scientific investigation, and their great professors attracted many students from all parts of the world in quest of higher education. But times are altered." So declared Henry W. Diederich, U.S. Consul to Germany in an article in *Science* in 1904. He continued, "Despite all our imperfections one can not [*sic*] but admire the great upward strides which the American system of education, from the humble district school up, has been making during the last few decades."[1] The shifting tides of dominance in higher education were not just apparent on one side of the Atlantic. Speaking at the University Teachers' Day in Leipzig in 1909, the historian Karl Lamprecht warned his audience, "We are no longer atop the universities of the world. France and America have left us far behind."[2]

Time has demonstrated the prescience of Diederich and Lamprecht. How did this shift in the center of gravity in the research world happen? How did the trends that Diederich and Lamprecht observed at the turn of the twentieth century snowball into a broadly acknowledged American dominance in higher education over the course of the next century?

## The German Obsession and the Struggle for Greatness

By the early nineteenth century, higher education had a firmly established, if relatively small, presence in the United States. Nine colleges had been established prior to American independence in 1776. Cambridge and Oxford provided the original models for these colonial colleges. Even the charter establishing Harvard bore the phrase *pro modo Academiarum in Anglia* ("according to the manner of universities in England").[3] Yet, in each of these colonial colleges, the founders realized that differences in the physical and social environments of the American context precipitated unanticipated modifications to the English model.[4] By 1820 there were fifty-two American degree-granting institutions.[5]

The earliest higher education institutions were insular. As soon as Harvard had enough graduates from which to appoint presidents and professors, it looked no further than its own Yard for faculty.[6] By contrast, when establishing the University of Virginia in 1819, Thomas Jefferson's first instinct was to recruit talent from other American institutions, but, unable to poach faculty such as George Ticknor, who was at Harvard, he turned to recruitment of European professors.[7]

As the United States grew into its nationhood and engaged in its own right with European countries, there was an increasing awareness of the strengths of European, and particularly German, universities. In 1815 the Harvard Corporation, one of the governing boards of Harvard University, decided that before hiring Edward Everett as professor of Greek literature, they would send him and future Harvard professor George Ticknor to Germany for advanced study. Studying at Göttingen, Everett became the first American to earn a PhD at a German university, initiating a century-long pattern of top American scholars seeking their credentials at German institutions.

After studying at German universities, most scholars returned to the United States, bringing back with them conceptions of *Lehrfreiheit, Lernfreiheit,* and, above all, a commitment to *Wissenschaft* and the advancement of learning in all realms through research and discovery. Several generations of German-trained scholars transformed the American system from one in which generalist learned men educated students through recitations, lectures, and disputations to one in which specialist scholars furthered knowledge in their fields of interest through research while also training students in the latest developments in their disciplines.

In 1861 Yale University awarded the first American doctoral degrees, but it was not until 1876 that the first, true research university was founded in the United States. In 1873 six trustees of the estate of Baltimore financier Johns Hopkins reached out to three top leaders in higher education (Charles Eliot of Harvard, James Angell of the University of Michigan, and Andrew White of Cornell) for advice on how to use Hopkins's bequest of $7 million for a university. According to higher education historian Edwin Slosson, "With remarkable unanimity all three of these gentlemen answered that a university was a very different thing from the institutions over which they presided, and that Daniel C. Gilman [then the president of the University of California] should be president of it."[8] Under Gilman's leadership, Johns Hopkins University was established on a German model, with graduate seminars, doctoral programs, and a strong emphasis on research and the sciences that it has retained to this day.

Some leaders remained skeptical of the appropriateness of the German model in the United States—Harvard President Charles Eliot reportedly commented that the German model "would fit Harvard freshmen 'about as well as a barnyard would suit a whale.'"[9] Still, by the end of the century, most universities were inspired by the Johns Hopkins model (and staffed by Johns Hopkins alumni), and colleges around the country were transformed into universities by investing heavily in research-based graduate programs. The number of nonprofessional graduate schools grew from eight in 1850 to around four hundred in 1876 to over five thousand in 1910.[10]

American professors also began to make the German model their own. As one of the leading scholars of America higher education, Jonathan Cole, has noted, the laboratory of the famous developmental biologist Thomas Hunt Morgan established the "new standard in most academic disciplines" of a more democratic, less hierarchical lab environment in which graduate students worked closely with faculty members.[11] Edwin Slosson remarked upon the advantages and benefits of the emerging American model, or, as he called it, that "peculiar combination which has developed in the United States of instruction and research, graduate and undergraduate students, letters and technology."[12]

This shift in the nature of scholarship occurred in tandem with fundamental changes in the American economy and society that complemented and accelerated research and applied learning in American higher education. Industrialization, urbanization, and the further mechanization of agriculture resulted in higher demand for an educated workforce and citizenry. The need became great enough that the federal government, heretofore removed from higher education, made the development of new, public universities a priority when it passed the Morrill Act of 1862. This act donated federal lands in each state for the establishment of higher education institutions with a particular focus on agriculture and the mechanical arts. Many of the great American public universities, such as the universities of California and Wisconsin, and a few of the top private ones, such as Cornell and MIT, were founded (or significantly expanded) through the largess of the Morrill Act. The technical and scientific focus of the Morrill Act also promoted disciplines in the applied sciences and engineering against the backdrop of traditional liberal arts curricula.

Industrialization created a new class of American tycoons and a new culture of private philanthropy in support of higher education, particularly research universities. John D. Rockefeller referred to his gift establishing the University of Chicago in 1890 as "the best investment I ever made."[13] When Leland and Jane Stanford sought to establish an institution in memory of their son, they weighed the merits of different kinds of schools before founding Leland Stanford Jr. University in 1891.[14]

Even as the research capacity of American universities grew, undergraduate education remained a priority for many institutions. The broad liberal arts model of undergraduate education that had evolved in the colonial colleges had become an indelible part of higher education in America. Those institutions that chose to not emphasize their undergraduate education programs did so at their future peril. Johns Hopkins and Clark Universities, both known for their excellent German-style graduate research programs, watched their national reputations fall in the early twentieth century. Undergraduate education became an important driver of intellectual curiosity and a passion of the faculty.

In the less than three decades between the founding of Johns Hopkins and the observations of Diederich and Lamprecht, American universities gained a place on the global stage as exciting institutions that, in a manner that Humboldt would have admired, integrated teaching and research. It was the global political and institutional ramifications of the twentieth century's two world wars, however, that connected American research universities with an influx of international talent and expanded funding from government and industry, resources that in turn catapulted American research universities forward.

The Morrill Act provided federal government support for the establishment and expansion of universities, but it was the establishment of the National Research Council in 1916 that began to connect university research with government funding and priorities. The Council connected government resources and laboratories with university researchers and industrial production managers to create and manufacture new technology that supported the American effort in World War I.[15] Universities and the federal government found further partnership in programs such as the Student Army Training Corp, which trained students for the military on campus, both meeting the government's need for trained soldiers and, because they were given federal funding to run such programs, the universities' need for funding in the face of drastic enrollment drops. With the US entry into the war, enrollments at top universities dropped by as much as 40 percent. This early effort at federal government-university partnership laid the foundation for a much higher level of cooperation during the next world war.[16]

By the time the federal government again turned to university partnership to support the war effort in the 1940s, it found a university sector newly invigorated by the arrival of academic refugees from Europe in general and Germany in particular. As we have seen, the increasing militarization and then Nazification of German universities ended their status as global leaders and led to an exodus of talent, to the benefit of other countries, especially the United States. The numbers would have been larger still if not for the anti-immigrant and anti-Semitic attitudes in English-speaking countries. This influx of highly skilled humanists, social scientists, and, especially, scholars of the physical universe propelled American university research forward almost immediately, just as the federal government again began to turn to universities to support a new war effort.

## Postwar Booms

Following World War II, American higher education massified, as enrollment in higher education institutions in the United States surged from 1.5 million in 1940 to 2.4 million in 1950.[17] College and university enrollments reached 3.6 million in 1960, 8 million in 1970, and 11.6 million in 1980.[18] By 1980 the number of students attending college was eight times higher than it was before the beginning of World War II.[19] State universities in particular gave more students access to higher education, and there a cultural fascination with "collegiate life" grew.[20] Despite this expansion, higher education, particularly at the best research institutions, remained the province of a socially elite few. Harvard, Yale, and Princeton retained their esoteric admissions processes that heavily favored (white, Anglo-Saxon, Protestant) preparatory high school graduates.

The proponents of the Servicemen's Readjustment Act (commonly known as the GI Bill) estimated that only 8 to 10 percent of soldiers returning from service in World War II would take advantage of the act's education provision, which offered significant financial subsidies for discharged servicemen to pursue higher education. These estimates turned out to be incorrect. Instead, between the passing of the act in 1944 and 1950, 16 percent of eligible veterans (over two million out of fourteen million) took advantage of these provisions.[21] In 1947, at the height of veteran enrollment, veterans made up 49 percent of all students admitted to college.[22]

Students and professors were backed by new levels of government and industry support. Wartime cooperation between the academe and the government was managed by the Office of Scientific Research and Development (OSRD), established in 1941 by President Franklin D. Roosevelt and led by Vannevar Bush. As the end of the war drew near, Bush feared the end of government support for basic scientific research that had paid such dividends during the war.[23] In his 1947 manifesto, *Science: The Endless Frontier,* Bush argued that government, industry, and national economic development were dependent upon the basic research carried out in university labs and that such research should be supported (but not dictated) by a new government agency.[24] Following the Second World War, Bush argued for an academic declaration of independence from Germany: "We can no longer count on ravaged Europe as a source of fundamental knowledge. . . . We must pay increased attention to discovering this knowledge for ourselves."[25] This document precipitated the founding of the National Science Foundation—the American equivalent of the Kaiser Wilhelm / Max Planck Society—and the initiation of a new age of government-funded university research in peacetime.

Expanded engagement with the federal government meant not only new sources of funding but also increased oversight and efforts at control. The apex (or, if you will, nadir) of government intrusion into university campuses came during the McCarthy era, when universities across the country struggled with how to balance the anti-communist demands and political winds with principles of academic and institutional freedom that had been strengthened over the previous century of German influence. Concern over the relationship between the government and universities did not end with the downfall of Senator Joseph McCarthy but continued in a variety of forms. In his farewell address from the presidency of the United States in 1961, Dwight D. Eisenhower, who had served as Columbia University's president, warned against the growing strength of the military-industrial complex and the potential ramifications of the growing dependence of "the free university" on "Federal employment, project allocations, and the power of money."[26] The intense political activism on university campuses in the 1960s offered an even stronger critique of government intrusion in higher education. But government funding for and engagement with American higher education was now a permanent part of the academic landscape.

## A Hybrid System

The second half of the twentieth century saw the sustained rise—in terms of the size of individual institutions, the system overall, and general reputation—of the American research university. One of the great strengths of higher education in America is its institutional diversity.[27] The modern American research university was thus built upon a foundation of three diverse elements: an undergraduate liberal arts education in the tradition of the colonial colleges; participatory research evolved from the German tradition of the nineteenth century; and twentieth century engagement with government, industry, and private philanthropy.

As we look at American higher education from a global perspective in the twenty-first century, it is useful to clarify what American higher education is not. First, in spite of the common features listed previously, there is no American higher education *system*. There is no national university. Higher education institutions and policies differ from state to state, and each state may contain a diverse array of institutions—public and private, baccalaureate and doctoral, elite and massive. Many scholars have noted that this nonsystemized diversity has allowed American higher education to reach such a high level of quality, as institutions sought to maximize their comparative advantages in an open, competitive marketplace for the best faculty, students, and financial support.[28]

Yet, for all its lack of system, there are similarities that tie these diverse institutions together. "Universities tend to reflect, echo, and codify their national societies and culture," James Axtell has noted.[29] American ideals of democracy, equal opportunity, and individualism color American universities in various ways. More concretely, the competition among American universities has led to some basic structural similarities in governance, faculty policy, and finance.

## Governance

American universities tend to have similar overarching governance structures, although the relative power and influence of each of the bodies composing the structure vary greatly across institutions.[30] Typically, a board of trustees serves as the legal representative of the university. Trustees, who are often (particularly at private universities) alumni of the institution, are expected to bring their administrative and financial experience to bear in supporting (and monitoring) the work of the university president, whom they are also responsible for selecting.

University presidents are the apex of the academic leadership team, usually supported by a provost and a series of deans focused on different specific areas of academic and campus life. Former President of Harvard Derek Bok observed that administrative and fundraising duties increasingly dominate the time of university presidents, and, consequently, "presidents today tend to delegate most of the responsibility over academic affairs to provosts and deans."[31] American deans are faculty members, either chosen from existing faculty or recruited from other institutions for a specific decanal role. Unlike their European counterparts, American deans are not elected (or deposed) by their peers but generally serve for specific terms or at the pleasure of their university presidents.

The relative balances of power between the board and the president, between the president and the provost, and between the president and deans vary greatly across institutions. Differences in power structure are not clearly aligned with private versus public institutions. Harvard, for example, is (in)famously decentralized, with a large amount of money and power resting in the deans of its twelve schools, while relatively little is retained by the central administration. The central administration at Duke University, by contrast, maintains much more control, which it uses to guide the institution's strategic planning process. Balances of power among administrative bodies are functions of tradition and university cultures as well as of the personalities of individual leaders.

Beyond serving as a pool from which to draw deans and presidents, the faculty as a whole often plays a role in university governance through an academic senate or similar body. In general, this kind of collective faculty body has less power in the United States than analogous bodies do in European universities, where (as at Humboldt University) such a body would be charged with making key academic administrative appointments. Still, academic senates or meetings of faculty have proven able to influence decision making at key points in the history of many universities. As Bok noted, "as a practical matter, regardless of the formal organization, ultimate power resides with those who are most difficult to replace."[32] At elite research universities, which compete fiercely to gain and retain top professors, the faculty, when united, can prove extraordinarily powerful.

## Faculty

Faculty members at American research universities are protected not only by the power inherent in their importance to the university but also through "tenure" systems. This is a variant on the German *Lehrstuhl*, albeit typically with individually less prestige and resources, as the number of "full" professors in an American university is rather larger than at any German institution. American professors, even in state universities, are not *Beamten*, or permanent civil servants, in the German tradition. The tenure process, which essentially offers continuous employment to academics who have proven their worth through a series of rigorous reviews of their publications and (sometimes) teaching, was designed in principle to protect professors and guarantee their freedom to explore any topic they deem to have value. Most universities implement "up or out" tenure processes—denial of tenure for a candidate means not only that the candidate fails to move "up" into the company of tenured faculty but also that they will be sent "out" of the institution. The process not only stands as a significant hurdle to establishing a career in academia but also represents the high level of expected commitment to the faculty member from the university and vice versa.

There are two basic paths through which universities can improve the quality of their faculty. The first is through lateral hiring, or the recruiting of full tenured (and, often, star) professors from other universities. The second is through investing resources into the development of young, tenure-track faculty, ideally to reap the benefit of their subsequent scholarship.

The balance with which universities employ these two methods depends on institutional traditions and culture as well as available resources.

Another facet of the lives of university faculty in the United States is the sabbatical. Tenure-track and tenured faculty in research universities generally receive sabbaticals—regular, paid leaves of absences after six years of service so that the seventh might provide them with an opportunity to spend more time on research. The sabbatical system evolved out of the inadequacy of American-based advanced academic training in the early nineteenth century. Faculty (or potential future faculty) were granted study leaves to pursue advanced training in European (especially English and German) universities.[33] In 1880 Harvard University President Charles Eliot systematized sabbaticals for faculty for the first time, and by 1900 ten universities had adopted the practice. By 1920 at least fifty leading liberal arts colleges and universities, both public and private, had established sabbatical policies.[34] Now a common practice, the system is acknowledged to have a variety of benefits—both personal and institutional. Certainly few faculty members decline one.[35]

*Funding*

American universities, whether public or private, receive funding from a combination of sources, including earned revenue (tuition), government funding, and private philanthropy. The largest portion of federal funding for universities is allocated through Pell Grants, need-based financial aid awards offered by the federal government. In 2019, of the $75.6 billion in federal funding for higher education, Pell Grants accounted for nearly $30 billion. Federal research grants accounted for around one-third of total federal higher education spending ($24.6 billion).[36] Research funding is generally garnered through competitive grant processes and is given for specific research objectives. Both public and private universities receive federal funding. Additionally, public universities receive funding from their state governments. This state funding, in theory at least, allows public universities to charge lower tuition for local students.

Government support of research and higher education was one of the major factors enabling American research universities to reach such a prominent global position. Today that funding is in jeopardy. From 2010 to 2019 federal funding for research and development declined (in constant dollars) 28.9 percent.[37] State funding for public universities also decreased dramatically. In 2017, after adjusting for inflation, overall state funding for public two-year and four-year colleges was almost $9 billion below the 2008 level.[38] Currently, America's premier public research universities often receive less than 10 percent of their funding from the state.[39]

Government appropriations, of course, are not the only source of funding for American universities. Private philanthropy has played an important role in shaping the higher education landscape. According to the Council for Aid to Education, philanthropic giving to higher education totaled over $46.7 billion in 2018, the largest amount since the agency began collecting information in 1957.[40] This philanthropy was highly targeted. The increase in overall funds was driven by large gifts given to a small number of institutions—29 percent of philanthropic gifts were made to less than 1 percent of universities and colleges. Ten universities raised over $500 million each, and two, Stanford and Harvard, raised over $1 billion each.[41]

These impressive donations bolster already-substantial endowment coffers. Stanford and Harvard, for example, had endowments worth $27.7 and $40.9 billion, respectively, at the end of the 2019 fiscal year. The distribution of endowment funds across American universities and colleges has been skewed for quite some time. The 1990 National Association of College and University Business Officers Endowment Report showed that in that year, the top five university endowments (those of Harvard, Yale, the University of Texas system, Princeton, and Stanford) accounted for about 25 percent of the endowment value of all institutions surveyed. That remained true nearly thirty years later.[42] In short, the finances of American universities mirrored the country's growing disparities of wealth and income.

The change in magnitude of endowments at the highest end of the spectrum was significant. In 1990 the value of the top five US university endowments was equivalent to 0.26 percent of US gross domestic product. By 2019 this percentage had jumped to 0.72 percent.[43] Managers of these largest endowments moved increasing portions of their assets into alternative investment strategies: less liquid, high-risk, high-return vehicles, including private equity, hedge funds, venture capital, and energy and natural resources. This last category in particular began to draw protests from students in 2015 and after, as they advocated for divestment from fossil fuels.

Of course, the spectacular growth of university endowments in the 1990s and into the twenty-first century reflected the growth in value of the US stock market, and as much as universities benefited from market upswings, they were also vulnerable to its downturns. This was amply demonstrated in the financial crisis of 2008. Recovery from that crisis has proceeded in fits and starts. Through most of the 2010s low returns on investments drove down ten-year returns across American university endowments.[44] By 2020, however, university endowments' long-term average return had reached 8.4 percent on the back of a strong stock market performance.[45] But not everyone knew where to put their money: the richest university, Harvard, suffered from poor endowment returns in this period: in constant dollars its endowment was worth no more in 2020 than it had been in 2008.

Beyond reduced returns from endowments, American universities faced diminished funding from government (federal and state) in the first two decades of the twenty-first century. The primary remaining financial lever was tuition, which for decades had increased well in excess of inflation. With high scrutiny of diversity (both ethnic and socioeconomic), top universities increased tuition while also rapidly increasing student financial aid packages. Yet, the ability to provide such packages rested with elite institutions. In 2018 the fabulously wealthy businessman and former New York City mayor Michael Bloomberg gave a $1.8 billion gift to his alma mater, Johns Hopkins. In a *New York Times* op-ed, he explained that the main motivation for this gift was for financial aid for "qualified low- and middle-income students," because "there may be no better investment that we can make in the future of the American dream."[46] This was the largest donation given to an American university to date.[47]

There are growing questions about whether higher education can remain an effective vehicle for promoting social mobility and access to the "American dream." In the mid-twentieth century, higher education was seen as a public good, and society bore much of the cost through state taxes that supported public university budgets. By the 1980s the costs of financing higher education, even at public universities, were placed increasingly on students and their families, as higher education came to be seen as more of a "private good."[48]

## International Universities?

One of the enduring advantages of American research universities has been their welcoming of foreign scholars and students. In 1910 historian Edwin Slosson predicted that "greater and more influential than a State or a national university will be the international university of the future."[49] Today students from around the world seek out graduate and undergraduate education in the United States. In the 2018–2019 academic year 1,095,229 international students were enrolled in American higher education institutions, contributing $41 billion to the US economy, and supporting over 450,000 American jobs.[50] Still, the presence of these students, which enriched the diversity of perspective on campus and, often, institutional bottom lines, was not a given. As academic and other markets in their home countries became more promising for international students with advanced degrees (for example, for students from China), the capacity of American universities to attract and retain the top international scholars was diminished. These concerns were further heightened under the nativist administration of President Donald J. Trump, whose visa and other restrictions made the United States a distinctly less welcoming destination.

In the postwar period, American universities became leading centers of international and area studies. As we shall see, this emerged initially out of the need for wartime research under the government's Office of Strategic Services, a predecessor of the Central Intelligence Agency. The need remained during the Cold War era. In 1958 the US government authorized the National Defense Education Act (NDEA), which provided funding to foster expertise in international studies, area studies, and world cultures and languages. The impetus for this authorization was the government's own embarrassment that its ranks lacked broad or deep expertise on the many parts of the world in which the United States was now engaged. Expertise was particularly thin in the study of Cold War adversaries such as the Soviet Union and Maoist China. (Out of thirty-eight Soviet analysts in the Central Intelligence Agency in 1948, two-thirds spoke no Russian.[51]) Funding was given at the highest level to study the most "dangerous" parts of the world, hence the enduring strength in American universities of Russian and Chinese studies, compared to, say, South Asian studies. As the Cold War progressed, government leadership was matched by private groups, such as the Ford Foundation, which supported American-friendly institutions abroad (such as Free University of Berlin) and area studies at home. The international dimensions of the NDEA were reauthorized as part of the Higher Education Act of 1965, which is today responsible for funding National Resource Centers (NRCs) in universities across the United States. As of 2018 the U.S. Department of Education supported (albeit with diminishing dollars) over one hundred NRCs, across public and private higher education institutions, that seek to build knowledge capacity on the different regions of Asia, Russia and Eastern Europe, Latin America, and even such perilous places as Canada.[52]

US universities have also been increasing their physical presence abroad. Six US universities, including Northwestern and Cornell, established campuses in Qatar's government-supported "Education City," a large complex in which top universities receive facilities and funding in exchange for the establishment of programs on par with those at their home campuses.[53] At the start of the 2010s New York University opened campuses in Abu Dhabi and Shanghai. Duke University opened a campus in Kunshan, China, in 2013. Some universities partnered with universities in other countries to found centers focused on specific research areas, like the Tsinghua-Berkeley Shenzhen Institute, based in Shenzhen, China, which focused on fields that drew on both schools' strengths, including information technology, new energy, and precision medicine. Other universities, like Harvard, established research outposts to support the work of faculty and students abroad. Perhaps, as Slosson had predicted, the "international university" would indeed be the "university of the future."[54] At the very least, it seemed that every American university had to have an international strategy for the twenty-first century.

With global flows of faculty and students also came viruses. At the start of a new decade in 2020, with internationalization at a high point, a global pandemic set in. Emerging in Wuhan, China, COVID-19, an infectious disease that often caused severe respiratory illness, spread across the world. Beginning in March 2020 universities in the United States moved their classes online. Students' study abroad programs were cut short. Many international students returned home. As cities and states issued shelter-in-place advisories, many universities went completely online for the remainder of the spring 2020 semester. As the pandemic continued, all facets of the university were affected—including admissions, teaching, research, student and faculty mobility, and finances. While universities "reopened" in fall 2020, most did so from a distance, relying again on virtual learning. US institutions, which had been a magnet for international students, were looking at a much lower yield rate for incoming international students. Was the internationalization of American universities past its peak?

## American Exceptionalism?

Perhaps more than anything else, it was the diversity of the American experience in higher education—diversity of institutions, goals, thought, faculty, students, governance, funding sources, and more—that distinguished it from both its European ancestors and the many institutions around the world that seek to emulate its success. Historian David Labaree has argued that America's higher education success and its "unlikely ascendancy" resulted from five key traits: institutional autonomy, sensitivity to consumers, appeal to a broad array of constituencies, structural ambiguity, and organizational complexity.[55] These traits derived from dynamic market forces and an overall low dependence on the state and begot a "motley collection of 4,700 American colleges and universities."[56] Clark Kerr, who served as president of the University of California and as the first chancellor of the University of California, Berkeley, argued in his classic study, *The Uses of the University*, that there was a simpler explanation for the unlikely ascendance of American higher education. It came from the unique fusion of three models: (1) the English college, which focused on undergraduate liberal arts education; (2) the German research university, which emphasized research at the graduate level; and (3) the American land-grant college, which centered on vocational education and providing applied solutions to public problems.[57] The "modern American university" that emerged, he argued, "is not Oxford nor is it Berlin; it is a new type of institution in the world. As a new type of institution, it is not really private and it is not really public; it is neither entirely of the world nor entirely apart from it. It is unique."[58]

In Chapters 5 through 7, we will examine three unique American universities that reflect the diverse strengths and challenges of the American scene. Harvard University, the oldest higher education institution in America, was originally modeled after the English university and later remodeled on the German pattern. It is probably the best-known university on Earth today and is an example of enduring excellence in higher education. The University of California, Berkeley, a land-grant university, is the most highly regarded public university in the country. It is one of the world's top-ranked research universities and the crown jewel of the University of California system, which has been arguably the best system of public higher education in the world. Now, however, Berkeley faces the challenge of remaining a public university while depending on private funding. Finally, Duke University, with a strong research trajectory and an ambitious international agenda, is, I will argue, the fastest-rising research university in America, in part because it is the one that has planned most explicitly for its future.

These examples will, I hope, help to address this question: American universities came to lead the world in the second half of the twentieth century—but will they continue to do so into the twenty-first?

# CHAPTER FIVE

# Rising through Change and through Storm

## *Harvard University*

Fair Harvard! ~~thy sons to~~ <u>we join in</u> thy Jubilee throng,
And with blessings surrender thee o'er
By these Festival-rites, from the Age that is past,
To the Age that is waiting before.
O Relic and Type of our ancestors' worth,
That hast long kept their memory warm,
First flow'r of their wilderness! Star of their night!
Calm rising thro' change and thro' storm.
. . .
Let not moss-covered Error moor thee at its side,
As the world on Truth's current glides by,
Be the herald of Light, and the bearer of Love,
Till the ~~stock of the Puritans~~ the stars in the firmament die.

—Fair Harvard, *1836, by Samuel Gilman, class of 1811, original
lyrics and revisions, 1997, 2018*

## 1836

When *Fair Harvard* was composed by Reverend Gilman for the university's two hundredth anniversary in 1836, Harvard was an institution still firmly rooted in New England, of "Puritan stock." As it approached its four hundredth birthday in the twenty-first century, with a more inclusive anthem, its ambitions had become otherworldly—an institution of earthly fame and eternal life. That might have surprised Reverend Gilman and his twenty-fifth reunion classmates at Harvard's bicentennial in 1836.

Two years earlier, on a late May evening in 1834, Harvard undergraduates torched a recitation room and threw chairs out its window. In the continuing pandemonium, they set off firecrackers in the chapel and hanged an effigy of Josiah Quincy, the president of Harvard, from the Rebellion Tree in Harvard Yard. The riot was a culmination of Quincy's ironclad enforcement of discipline that was wildly unpopular with students. Quincy responded by expelling the entire sophomore class. Two hundred years after the university's founding, Harvard's class of 1836 was the smallest to graduate since 1809, with enrollments much lower than those of Yale, Princeton, and even Dartmouth.[1]

A former Congressman and six-term mayor of Boston, Josiah Quincy had been instated as president of Harvard in 1829. Drawing on Puritan sensibilities, Quincy's "heart's desire," noted by his son, "was to make the College a nursery of high-minded, high-principled, well-taught, well-conducted, well-bred gentlemen."[2] Undergraduates may have had misgivings about the steely president's obsession with order. Student "recitations" of an inherited, required, and utterly stultifying curriculum were graded daily on a scale of 1 to 8, and Quincy himself read students' report cards weekly. An ideal course, Quincy believed, was a "thorough drilling."[3] But Quincy did begin the process of offering "elective" classes for upperclassmen in the new fields that had begun to define German scholarship: history, chemistry, geology, and astronomy, among others. In later inaugurating the university's astronomical observatory, he created Harvard's first research unit. He became a defender of *Lehrfreiheit* on the part of the faculty and, slowly, grudgingly, partially, of *Lernfreiheit* on the part of undergraduates. It was in Quincy's tenure that the word *veritas* was formally added to the university's shield. Harvard was still a parochial place, but by its bicentennial, the university was poised to grow beyond its pioneering origins.

## 1936

For Harvard's bicentennial in 1836, only the presidents of other New England colleges were invited, and only one of them came. A century later, Harvard President James Bryant Conant welcomed presidents and representatives from 502 colleges, universities, and learned societies, along with the president of the United States, to its tercentenary. The ceremony was preceded by a two-week Conference of Arts and Sciences for scholars—including eleven Nobel Prize recipients—from across the globe. The emphasis was on the natural sciences (Conant was a distinguished chemist) and the growth of individual scientific disciplines. Specialization, Conant proclaimed, was the key to the advancement of scientific knowledge.[4]

When in 1936 Harvard, "the Mother of American Colleges," promised to be "a new center for the world's culture," according to the president of another American university, it had done so in large measure by adopting German models of scientific research in distinct disciplines. Yet 1936 was not a proud moment for the German academy, and only one German scholar attended. President Franklin D. Roosevelt declared that Harvard's and America's challenges were as much abroad as they were at home: "In this day of modern witch-burning, when freedom of thought has been exiled from the many lands which were once its home, it is the part of Harvard and America to stand for the freedom of the human mind and to carry the torch of truth."[5]

In the spirit of Roosevelt's internationalism, one representative from China's Peking University took part in the tercentenary and was granted an honorary degree. His name was Hu Shi. As a faculty member of Peking University after 1917, he became a leading figure in China's "New Culture" movement and an eloquent proponent of liberalism in China. Hu Shi's inscription on the marble stele that he presented to Harvard connected scholarly excellence with national strength: "It is by virtue of its culture that a nation arises, but truly it is due to learning that a culture flourishes." The stele graces Harvard Yard to this day.

With nearly one thousand Chinese alumni by 1936, Harvard was on its way to being more than a place of Puritan stock. Yet it was hardly inclusive. Not one of the eighty-six scholars invited to the tercentenary conference was a woman. The main ceremony was held on the High Holiday of Rosh Hashanah—befitting an era of institutional anti-Semitism—and was sternly Christian from invocation to benediction.[6]

In 1836 President Quincy had "adjourned" the assembly of alumni until "to meet again at this place" a century later.[7] In 1936, as the threat of a second world war loomed, the vice chancellor of Oxford doubted very much that, a century hence, another such celebration could take place.

**Figure 5.1.** Harvard
tercentenary stele.
Reproduced from *Notes on the
Harvard Tercentenary,* edited by
David T. W. McCord and
published by Harvard
University Press in 1936.

President Conant himself had his doubts. Would modern universities with their newfound wealth, giving faculty and students "facilities never before at the disposal of any body of scholars," retain "that popular admiration and respect which alone can guarantee their survival?" Would Harvard "escape the curse which has so often plagued large human enterprises well established by a significant history—the curse of complacent mediocrity?" "What," Conant wondered, "will be the role of the university, particularly the privately endowed university, when the four hundredth celebration draws near in the winter of 2036?"[8]

## 2036?

From Harvard's tercentenary to the present, the university achieved a reputation equal to, if not greater than, that of the University of Berlin in the nineteenth century. As it rose to national prominence in the twentieth century, universities across the United States vied to be the "Harvard of the South" (Duke, Vanderbilt, Rice), the "Harvard of the Midwest" (Michigan, Northwestern, Washington University), and the "Harvard of the West" (Stanford, once upon a time).[9]

Harvard's global reputation appears to have grown further, the greater the distance from Cambridge, Massachusetts. In China, for example, the State Administration for Industry and Trademark database recorded 375 attempts to register the name "Harvard" (*hafo*) as a trademark between 1997 and 2017. When Harvard established its Harvard Center Shanghai in 2010, it was initially told that it could open its doors, but it could not use the name "Harvard," for a "Harvard University" was already registered in the city. Today, the "Harvards" of China include an automobile (a best-selling SUV), a professional training center, a child-care center, a quick-service restaurant, a "Harvard Baby" disinfectant, and even a "Harvard Exam Sitters" company (*Hafo qiangshou*), which you pay to take your college entrance exams for you. They embrace, too, one of the world's best-selling books on higher education, *Harvard Girl Liu Yiting: A Character-Training Record* (*Hafo nühai Liu Yiting: suzhi peixun jishi*), which chronicles how tiger-parents Liu Weihua and Zhang Xinwu raised their daughter, Liu Yiting, to be disciplined and independent of mind. Yiting was accepted to Harvard in 1999. Published in 2000, this "how-to-get-into-Harvard manual" became an instant sensation and spawned an industry of copycats: *Cornell Girl, How We Got Our Child into Yale,* and (the least of these) *Our Dumb Little Son Goes to Cambridge.*[10]

Eighteen years short of Harvard's four hundredth anniversary, Harvard's president was not of an old Boston family like Josiah Quincy. Nor was he a descendent of early Massachusetts Bay settlers like James Bryant Conant. Lawrence S. Bacow was born in Detroit, Michigan, to an Auschwitz survivor mother and an Eastern European refugee father. He went on to attend the Massachusetts Institute of Technology as an undergraduate and Harvard, where he earned three graduate degrees (JD, MPP, and PhD). After graduate school, he taught at MIT for twenty-four years before becoming the institution's chair of faculty and then chancellor. He then served as the twelfth president of Tufts University for a decade. When on July 1, 2018,

Bacow began his tenure as Harvard's president, he arrived with more experience in academic leadership than any of his predecessors over the previous 382 years.

Harvard was both empowered and encumbered by its history. There was much to contemplate. Bacow inherited an institution more admired abroad than at home, in an era of public critique of American higher education; a university with an endowment so large that it begged to be taxed; and a formidable set of schools led by quasi-autonomous deans, several of whom controlled more resources than the president. He faced a daunting set of overlapping institutional priorities, including the growth of a new engineering school—this in a town where there was another institution rather more famous in that realm, one of several institutional rivals that now threatened the leadership of "America's University."[11] Harvard did not have the luxury of specialization. Its was the burden of doing more things, better, than anyone else.

When a global pandemic broke out during the second year of his presidency, Bacow's leadership was tested. The COVID-19 crisis was a watershed moment in higher education. On March 10, 2020, Bacow announced that all classes would move online. Following his announcement, many universities across the United States and across the world also closed their physical spaces.

For nearly four centuries, the decisions and actions of Harvard set the tone for American higher education, from President Henry Dunster's adoption of the abandoned British terms "freshman," "sophomore," "junior," and "senior" in 1640, to President Charles William Eliot's creation of an elective-based curriculum in 1886, to President James Bryant Conant's role in developing the SAT as a common admissions tool in the 1940s. Harvard had made big bets on bold ideas throughout its long history. But no institution stays on top by standing still. How would Harvard continue to lead the American higher education sector in the twenty-first century? Or would it?

## Foundations

The first British settlers of New England came from a society that had a long tradition of higher education, both for religious leaders and professionals in law and medicine. The ability to produce a supply of well-educated men to fill such roles in the newly established colony was of immediate concern to the settlers. When the Great and General Court of Massachusetts, whose forty-three members included six University of Cambridge alumni and one Trinity College, Dublin, alumnus and was led by the Oxford alumnus Governor Harry Vane, convened on October 28, 1636, they passed a legislative act to found a "scholae or colledge" in Newtowne, today's Cambridge.[12] Just what kind of men the institution would nurture, however, proved difficult to agree upon, and progress in establishing the institution was stymied by religious factionalism. Not until one year after the Court's original proclamation were they able to appoint the first "Overseers of the College," who quickly moved to recruit the recently immigrated Trinity College, Cambridge, and Dutch-educated Nathanial Eaton as the first master of the new college.

It was likely sometime during the summer of 1638, shortly after Eaton began teaching the first class of students, that he was visited by another recent immigrant, John Harvard, a graduate of Emmanuel College, Cambridge. Shortly thereafter, as John Harvard was dying of tuberculosis at the age of thirty, he dictated an oral will leaving his four-hundred-volume library and half of his estate to the new college. In what has turned out to be perhaps the best value in donor recognition of all time, the college was named Harvard in recognition of this gift in 1639.

Connecting John Harvard with the college was Eaton's greatest contribution to the school, but successful fundraisers are seldom remembered. Eaton was ousted from his position after just one year upon accusations of undue brutality against pupils and his wife's inadequate provision of beef and beer for the students. The young institution languished without a master for a year, before Henry Dunster, a thirty-year-old graduate of the University of Cambridge who had just landed in Boston, was assigned the new title of president on August 27, 1640.

Dunster sought to establish Harvard in the tradition of, and with legitimacy equal to, English institutions such as Eton College and the Oxbridge colleges: a residential setting for students and "masters," supported by endowment income.[13] Dunster focused on building Harvard's first student-scholar residences while initially serving as the primary instructor for all students. The curriculum he established, which remained largely in place until the early eighteenth century, was a further continuation of English tradition. It prescribed set courses in the Seven Liberal Arts and the Three Philosophies, reading of a classical canon, and the study of the so-called learned tongues, including Greek and Hebrew for reading of biblical texts.

The curriculum is a clue to the question, why was Harvard founded? It was not, as frequently has been asserted, simply to train preaching ministers. It *did* graduate ministers (some 50 percent of its seventeenth-century graduates), but its mission from the outset was the broader one of educating leaders in all professions for its New World. The tercentenary historian of Harvard, Samuel Eliot Morison, may have gone too far when he claimed that Harvard was founded to provide a broad "*liberal* education" for young gentlemen, but he was correct in writing that it was no divinity school.[14]

For that purpose, it began life as a public institution. Its founder was not John Harvard but the General Court of Massachusetts. It was supported in the seventeenth century by taxes and "contributions" from as far south as New Haven, at times levied in corn, and by the revenues of the Charlestown ferry that connected Cambridge to Boston, paid in wampumpeag (the currency of the Massachusetts Bay Colony). Other sources of early income included gifts (many from England), bequests, and student tuition, which was often paid in commodities such as beef, eggs, cheese, turnips, apples, and even boots and shoes, until the colony began to use its own form of currency. Even then, presidents could be well paid: it was reported in 1654 that Dunster had run the College for years on an average annual budget of £175, of which he retained £55 for his own salary.[15]

Dunster's tenure set many precedents. His assumed title of "president" would be handed down to the large majority of higher education institutions in the United States. More important, despite its legal and financial ties to the state, which supported Harvard into the nineteenth century, the College was both a public institution and an independent corporation. It was early on assumed that, like English colleges, Harvard would be run by its resident teachers. These being in short supply, a reorganized Board of Overseers was made a permanent institution by the General Court in 1642 to serve as an external board to run the College until the resident faculty could muster the strength. But when the College was formally chartered by the General Court in 1650, it formally established the "President and Fellows of Harvard College," also called the "Corporation," which owned the institution. The Corporation consisted of the president, the treasurer, and five fellows, who were initially teaching staff but later included outside community members. But in practice it would be overshadowed until the 1680s by the Board of Overseers, which continued to function. Thus Harvard's governance was complex and confusing right from the start.

In the first quarter of the eighteenth century, the role of the faculty in running the university was overshadowed by the growing role of the Corporation, with its Fellows acting as trustees, who were respected in the community in various fields but outside of the university. Governance by a president in conjunction with an external board has remained a characteristic common to most American higher education institutions.[16] As the president and Corporation governed the institution with considerable autonomy, the Overseers were placed in the advisory and subsidiary role they still occupy today. This structure of governance by external boards could at times buffer the College from the direct interference of the state. At the same time, it severely constrained the prospect of governance by faculty fellows that was at the heart of the English system. To this day, Harvard has no university-wide faculty body in a governance role.

Harvard was founded as a college with the pretense of a university. It was not called a "university" (except informally), but it appropriated the powers of one in order to grant its first bachelor's degrees in 1642. A final precedent set by Harvard in its early days was that a stand-alone college could function and give degrees that in England and Europe had historically been the prerogative of universities. (This right was formalized by the College's second charter of 1692, which gave the Corporation the right to "grant and admit to Academical Degrees, as in the Universities in England.")[17] The later explosive growth of liberal arts colleges in the United States—a truly distinctive element of American higher education—was one result. Another was the centrality of the undergraduate college, known as "Harvard College," within Harvard itself. As Harvard added professional and graduate schools in the eighteenth, nineteenth, and twentieth centuries, unlike many universities it did not subdivide undergraduate education by subject. For those studying literature, history, economics, engineering, or life sciences, there was a single admissions process to a single undergraduate college of liberal arts and sciences, taught by a single faculty, the Faculty of Arts and Sciences (FAS), which has been, and strives to remain, the center of the university.

Throughout the eighteenth and nineteenth centuries, Harvard strengthened its advanced offerings in professional disciplines, establishing the Medical School in 1782, formalizing the Divinity School in 1816, and adding the Law School in 1817. During this time, the school began to grow in both size and renown, but some outside New England saw it as a playground for the rich. Sixteen-year-old Benjamin Franklin, publishing under the pseudonym "Silence Dogood" in 1722, lambasted Harvard and, in particular "[the] extreme folly of those Parents, who, blind to their Children's Dulness, and insensible to the Solidarity of their Skulls, because they think their Purses can afford it, will needs send them to the Temple of Learning, where, for want of a suitable Genius, they learn little more than how to carry themselves handsomely, and enter a Room genteely (which might as well be acquired at a Dancing-School), and from whence they return, after abundance of trouble and Charges, as great Blockheads as ever, only more proud and self-conceited."[18]

## A German-English Hybrid

For nearly two hundred years, and despite the significant influence of traditional British educational structures on the establishment of Harvard, no Harvard faculty member had attended university in Europe. Harvard professors were born of Harvard men; no other qualification was desired. This changed in 1814, when future president Edward Everett was hired as professor of Greek literature, with the opportunity to spend the first two years of his salaried employment studying abroad in Europe. Everett wisely took advantage of this unprecedented opportunity, and, along with George Ticknor, Joseph Cogswell, and George Bancroft, all Harvard-affiliated scholars, studied at the University of Göttingen.[19]

The time spent in Europe profoundly influenced all four of these men. Ticknor, who while in Europe was appointed to a senior chair at Harvard, was particularly tenacious in the fight to remake education at Harvard based on the German model. The first hint of reform came in 1825, with the passage of a new regulation at Harvard that began to break up the hated recitation model by allowing students to attend and progress through classes according to ability.[20] Ticknor also advocated for improving the library as a tool of scholarship and brought foreign scholars into Harvard's faculty ranks. The increasing proportion of German-trained scholars helped to infuse Harvard with the German mentality of *Lernfreiheit* that had undergirded the growth and fame of the University of Berlin and other German universities as centers for research and discovery.[21]

Still, Harvard was then better known for its longevity than for outstanding academic achievement. Morison, the university historian, noted: "In the nineteenth century it was a saying that all a Harvard man had to do for his master's degree was to pay five dollars and stay out of jail."[22] Peer institutions like Yale, Princeton, Columbia, and Johns Hopkins were drawing in excellent scholars and leaders, while, spurred on by the Morrill Land-Grant Acts of 1862 and 1890, state universities in California, Wisconsin, and Michigan were also establishing themselves as centers for scholarship beyond the East Coast. In New England, meanwhile, the percentage of people attending college actually dropped between 1838 and 1869.[23] Harvard itself lacked strong direction. Between Josiah Quincy's retirement in 1845 and Charles Eliot's appointment in 1869, the university went through eight failed or acting presidencies, the longest of which was that of James Walker (1853–1860), who, according to Morison, was "stone deaf and totally devoid of aesthetic sense" yet founded Harvard's music curriculum.[24]

Harvard became a university worthy of the name under—and because of—the leadership of Charles William Eliot, without question "the greatest man in the history of Harvard."[25] His darkened portrait presides today over every meeting of the Faculty of Arts and Sciences, peering out from the wall behind the president's chair in the Faculty Room. At his inaugural address as president, on October 19, 1869, his remarks over the course of an hour and three-quarters were full of one-liners, some of which may be seen as offensive today, such as "The world knows next to nothing about the natural mental capacities of the female sex." He did not seek to ingratiate himself with the professoriat, noting that "very few Americans of eminent abilities are attracted to this profession," and (my favorite line as a dean) "[t]o see every day the evil fruit of a bad appointment must be the cruelest of official torments." Yet he noted that "the poverty of scholars is of inestimable worth in this money-getting nation." But his most telling statement, in retrospect, was this: "The inertia of a massive University is formidable. A good past is positively dangerous, if it makes us content with the present and so unprepared for the future."[26]

Eliot understood how far behind Harvard had fallen. Yale, not Harvard, had established the first graduate school in New England. Johns Hopkins was recruiting scholars from Germany. Where was Harvard? As Morison writes, "Harvard College was hidebound, the Harvard Law School senescent, the Medical School ineffective, and the [comparatively new] Lawrence Scientific School 'the resort of shirks and stragglers.'"[27]

Eliot was the consummate insider who took an outsider's view of things. He was the grandson of the donor who had endowed the Eliot professorship at Harvard; he was the son of a former university treasurer (and member of the Corporation); and he was first cousin to an Overseer who helped elect him president. He was also a former assistant professor of chemistry and mathematics, unloved by students and colleagues alike, and passed over for promotion. He sojourned to Europe and studied the academic landscape there, particularly in Germany. He returned in 1865 as professor of chemistry at the newly incorporated MIT and was elected a Harvard Overseer in 1868. When the Harvard presidency became open that same year, the man who was first offered the position declined. Eliot "was far from being everybody's second choice," but he was chosen when the alternatives to this middling chemist seemed worse.[28]

Eliot, who took the presidency at the age of thirty-five, wasted no time in establishing a vision for Harvard along the lines of the great universities that he had visited for two years in Europe. At his inauguration, he announced his intentions to improve academic standing across all disciplines, develop innovative pedagogical methods, recruit faculty from Europe, expand access to Harvard College for lower-income students, and generally update the practices of American universities, which he found to be "literally centuries behind the precept of the best thinkers upon education."[29]

Over his forty-year presidency, Eliot dominated Harvard. A professor of Greek history remarked that, having seen Eliot in action, he understood how Pericles held sway over Athenian assemblies.[30] In 1870 Eliot proclaimed in his commencement address, "We mean to build here, securely and slowly, a university in the largest sense."[31] He began by delegating some authority, appointing the first dean of the College faculty that year, and in 1890 he established the Faculty of Arts and Sciences. However, throughout his four decades as president, he alone made the final appointment and promotion decisions. With the founding of the Faculty of Arts and Sciences came Harvard's first, formal, academic departments, largely organized along the lines of German *Fachbereiche*.

His tenure saw the establishment of the Graduate School of Arts and Sciences in 1872, allowing students to receive advanced degrees in the sciences and humanities at Harvard for the first time. Building on Ticknor's reforms, Eliot further divided the faculty by subject and specialization. He also quickly expanded the College from 23 faculty members teaching 529 undergraduates in 1869 to 61 faculty members teaching 1,080 students in 1886. The graduation of Harvard's first African American student, Richard Theodore Greener (who transferred from Oberlin College), in 1870 and the beginning of the inclusion of women through the opening of the Harvard Annex (later Radcliffe College) in 1879 occurred during Eliot's tenure.

Despite Eliot's goal of increasing access for the less well off, between 1870 and 1890 the proportion of the entering freshman class that had graduated from public high schools declined from 38 percent to 23 percent. Moreover, membership in elitist social clubs and integration with Boston high society became an increasingly important part of student life.[32] Harvard was more elite than ever.

In undergraduate education, Eliot was democratic, gradually making the curriculum almost entirely elective. By 1885 Harvard had no undergraduate requirements save for English composition and either French or German. In short, he treated students as adults for the first time: "[A] well-instructed youth of eighteen can select for himself . . . a better course of study than any college faculty."[33] And they would be motivated to do so by the pursuit of "honors," as conferred by the faculty, a system of "seductive stimuli" for the "*élite* of brains and character" to find "self-fulfillment and social utility." Eventually even compulsory chapel was abolished, and, as Donald Fleming writes, "God had become an elective at Harvard."[34]

Innovations could be found in several forms. The growth of a research university demanded more books, which could hardly be contained in the existing setup of the College library. The answer was the bookstack: "the most flexible, compact, and accessible form of shelving books that had ever been known" as well as the creation of a "public card catalogue," for greater accessibility to the library.[35] Harvard's unquestioned leadership in university libraries dates from Eliot's time. So, too, did Harvard's eminence in football, even though Eliot despised the sport. He oversaw the building of Harvard Stadium (1903), witness to the first sustained wave of sports fanaticism in American colleges. From the curricular to the extracurricular, by the end of Eliot's presidency, Harvard itself had become the leading model of a comprehensive, distinctly American university.[36]

It was even famous internationally. In 1912 then president emeritus Eliot was approached by the government of the new Republic of China to dispatch an advisor to help write a constitution for the first republic in Asia. He sent Frank Goodnow, the first president of the American Political Science Association and later president of Johns Hopkins. In China, Goodnow's constitutional draft helped make China's strongman, Yuan Shikai, president for life. (Yuan's life was mercifully short, for he might well otherwise have become emperor.[37]) Such was Harvard's contribution to Chinese democracy.

By the time Eliot retired in May 1909, Harvard had become *Harvard*, a university as well as a college, with a national reputation and the largest,

**Figure 5.2.** Portrait of
Charles Eliot. Harvard
University Portrait Collection, Gift
by subscription from students and
various Harvard clubs to the
trustees of the Harvard Union,
1907, photo © President and
Fellows of Harvard College, H192.

most famous faculty in the land. Of the leading one thousand scientists in
the United States, one-quarter had studied at Harvard. Shortly before he
died in 1924, Eliot remarked, "The best is yet to come. Let us hail the
coming time."[38]

## Harvard's Long Twentieth Century

Harvard's rise to academic distinction was accompanied by a succession of
long-serving and impactful presidents: Charles Eliot for forty years, Abbott
Lawrence Lowell for twenty-four, James Conant for twenty, Nathan Pusey
for eighteen, Derek Bok for twenty, and Neil Rudenstine for ten (a long
tenure by the late twentieth century). Each put a distinctive stamp on the
place.

If Eliot was the architect of intellectual expansion at Harvard, his successor, Abbott Lawrence Lowell, led its physical remaking. If Eliot's foreign models for a modern university were to be found on the Continent, Lowell was an Anglophile. If Eliot let students liberally choose their courses, Lowell believed in structures and requirements. If Eliot was (for his time) open-minded on questions of faith and race, Lowell was (even for his time) a bigot.

In 1909 Lowell came to the helm of a Harvard with students divided, largely along socioeconomic lines, between private apartments and Harvard's own insufficient facilities. To promote cohesion among the student body and to transform the Harvard experience into something more akin to the Oxbridge model of colleges that blended study and student life, Lowell established new residences: first for freshmen, and then, toward the end of his presidency, for all upperclassmen in "the Houses," or residential colleges, made possible by the then-largest donation (and by a Yale graduate) in the university's history. To this was added an Oxbridge-style tutorial system.[39]

Lest his attempts to reform campus life be seen as progressive, Lowell was content to make this newly integrated academic-social campus scene available only to some. To him, the "stock of the Puritans" was a serious matter. Lowell tried to keep African American students out of the dormitories and established an unofficial cap on Jewish student enrollments.[40] In a letter to the father of a Black Harvard freshman, Lowell wrote, "I am sorry to have to tell you in the Freshman Halls, where residence is compulsory, we have felt from the beginning the necessity of not including colored men. . . . We have not thought it possible to compel men of different races to reside together."[41] Lowell sought to place a hard quota (12 percent) on Jewish freshmen, but the faculty rejected any formal quota. So an informal one took hold. During Lowell's tenure, the percentage of Jewish freshman at Harvard went from 27.6 percent in 1925 to less than 15 percent in 1933 when he retired.[42] As Lowell explained to a faculty colleague, "The summer hotel that is ruined by admitting Jews meets its fate, not because the Jews it admits are of bad character, but because they drive away the Gentiles."[43]

Of course, the most complete form of discrimination at Harvard took place against women. Radcliffe College was a distinct educational entity, even if the instructors were Harvard faculty. Radcliffe undergraduates could use Widener Library, the great temple of learning that opened in 1916, if they stayed confined to a small reading room. When Lamont Library was constructed after World War II as an undergraduate collection, it was off limits to women. Before Conant's time, only one of Harvard's graduate schools

(Education) admitted women, and it would have been out of business without them. The Law, Medical, and Business Schools "were all but unique" among their peers in excluding women.[44]

Lowell's focus on student life was accompanied by a rolling back of the curricular freedom beloved by Eliot. Lowell established a system of "Concentration and Distribution," which once again set the tone of higher education across America as almost all universities began to implement systems of majoring and minoring in certain subjects.[45]

With the curricular foundation set for another generation, it was Harvard's next president, James Bryant Conant, who propelled Harvard to the status of a research university of national and global stature, seeing Harvard's American peers more as Chicago, Hopkins, Columbia, and Berkeley, only one of which was part of the old Eastern academic world. From his inauguration in 1933, Conant focused on improving Harvard's profile as a research-driven institution: "If we have in each department of the university the most distinguished faculty which it is possible to obtain, we need have little worry about the future."[46] The problem was half of the Harvard faculty did not clear that bar in his view. Promotion reviews became more rigorous in an "up or out" tenure system. He similarly sought students from a wider range of means, talents, and geographies beyond the well-established Boston-New York axis. As the first Harvard president to espouse openly concepts of meritocracy in student admissions and the financial aid to support it, he founded the Harvard National Scholarships to "keep the way clear for the gifted youth of limited means."[47]

## University and Nation (I)

It was in Conant's tenure that Harvard—perhaps more than at any time since 1775, when sixteen hundred colonial troops were housed in Harvard Yard— came to be identified ever more closely with the American national mission. For Conant, meritocracy was linked to democracy and to some degree with what we might today call social justice. Unlike much of his alumni, he admired the administration of Franklin D. Roosevelt. Unlike some of his faculty, he was a staunch interventionist in the years before World War II.

Like their German counterparts when nationalist and patriotic spirit swept the University of Berlin in 1914, Harvard and its professoriat embraced war when it came in 1941. The day after Pearl Harbor, Conant gathered the student body to hear Roosevelt's "Day of Infamy" speech to Congress. Conant pledged Harvard's full resources toward the war effort. Soldiers—largely officers in training—again were housed on campus (some of their "temporary" dorms remain today).

Harvard faculty served the military effort in multiple ways. They developed advanced torpedoes for submarine warfare and the napalm used in the firebombing of enemy cities, and they assisted in creating the first atom bomb. They also provided intelligence. Numerous Harvard scholars joined the Office of Strategic Services (OSS), the precursor to the Central Intelligence Agency (CIA). William Langer, the doyen of diplomatic history in the United States, oversaw the OSS's research division.[48] Langer recruited an extraordinary cadre of young historians: the intellectual historian H. Stuart Hughes; historian of the Balkans Robert Lee Wolff; Crane Brinton, the iconic scholar of the French Revolution; John Clive, historian of Britain and its empire; John K. Fairbank, who would return from the war to lead Harvard's study of China; and the future dean of the Faculty of Arts and Sciences, Franklin Ford, whose OSS work focused on Germany. All would, in time, become senior faculty at Harvard. Their collective work at OSS, organized in regional departments, formed the foundation of postwar "area studies" at Harvard and across the United States, supported by the Department of Defense.

The enlarged relationship between university and nation was strengthened postwar by the influx of former soldiers attending college through the GI Bill. Harvard College enrollment increased from around thirty-five hundred before WWII to fifty-five hundred in 1946. Harvard had never been terribly selective in undergraduate admissions to that point, normally admitting two of every three applicants. Briefly, it had to choose one out of fifteen. That surge did not last, although it would return decades later. A more enduring legacy of the GI Bill was in the students. The large majority had always come from private schools, but by 1952, more than half of entering freshmen had attended public high schools, a trend that would not be reversed.[49]

Conant, like his predecessors, also left his mark on the undergraduate curriculum in a way designed to influence American education at large. In 1945 a stellar faculty committee, convened by Conant to review the undergraduate curriculum in light of a student body pulled from increasingly diverse secondary education backgrounds, published its final report: *General Education in a Free Society*. Known as the "Redbook," because of the color of its cover (it was, in fact, the faded purple that passes for Harvard "crimson"), the report laid out a comprehensive treatise on the roles of secondary and tertiary institutions in educating American citizens. Seeking for students what Conant called "a common . . . understanding of the society which they will possess in common," the Harvard undergraduate curriculum was re-formed once again such that one-fourth of the courses taken by an under-graduate were required to be newly created general education courses to pro-vide a broad, interdisciplinary foundation for learning *and citizenship*. "General Education" remains today in the DNA of a Harvard education.

While leading the way in undergraduate curriculum development, Har-vard was no pacesetter in its social policies. Harvard sustained its rich his-tory of discrimination. While the discriminatory, unofficial quotas limiting the enrollment of Jewish students had been abandoned by the 1950s, women were still not eligible to attend Harvard College or many of the Harvard professional schools. In 1960 only 4 out of 427 full professorships across the university were held by women.[50] During that decade, women attending Radcliffe were given permission to attend any class at Harvard, and in 1963 Radcliffe students were granted Harvard diplomas (although still signed by the Radcliffe president).[51] The proportion of African American students remained extremely low in the 1950s and 1960s, despite the lack of any particular policy barriers. Only later in the 1960s did the university more proactively seek diversity of ethnicity and gender in the student and fac-ulty body.

However conventional at home, Harvard's external reputation continued to grow, even in a more competitive postwar world, with its massive expan-sion of higher education. In a list of academic rankings of graduate schools cited by David Webster, a scholar of American higher education, not a single ranking between 1925 and 1982 placed Harvard lower than third-best in the nation.[52] Popular opinion abroad was no less supportive. A poll at the United States pavilion at the 1958 Brussels World's Fair asked where par-ticipants would like to send their son to college; over thirty-two thousand pavilion visitors responded "Harvard." "MIT" was the next most popular, with only half the number of responses.[53]

Harvard continued to grow in size and reputation in the second half of the twentieth century, albeit not without contention. As the College and fac-ulty expanded and slowly diversified, the larger professional schools grew in wealth and autonomy, and the undergraduates challenged authority. It was a measure of Harvard's insularity in previous presidential searches that the appointments of the non-Bostonian Nathan Marsh Pusey (1953–1971) and

Derek C. Bok (1971–1991), who did not attend Harvard College, could be seen as breaks with tradition.

## Money Matters: The Development State

"Harvard was always poor, strapped by a meager endowment," wrote Oscar Handlin of the university's first centuries.[54] No one could believe that after the presidency of Nathan Pusey. Plucked from comparative obscurity as the president of Lawrence College, a liberal arts college and music conservatory in Appleton, Wisconsin, Pusey became the prototype of the modern university president as fundraiser-in-chief. He deputed the administrative oversight of Harvard College and the Faculty of Arts and Sciences to the newly empowered dean of FAS, in this case, the formidable political scientist McGeorge Bundy.

In the postwar era, government—and especially foundation—grants (the American version of *Drittmittel*) grew in importance, but there Harvard was but one recipient among many. Large private gifts had come to Harvard before (for example, George F. Baker's single-handed funding of the new Harvard Business School campus in 1924), but a comprehensive "campaign" on the scale of the Program for Harvard College that was launched in 1957 had not been seen. Its goal of $82.4 million would be reached over four years, and it would set the stage for many repeat performances. Harvard alumni as a group were by no means among the most philanthropic of their peers. But the pockets of some Harvard alumni (the banker Thomas Lamont, AB 1892, for example—the namesake of Harvard's main undergraduate library) were deeper than others, and they partially emptied them when solicited.

That campaign and other gifts gave Harvard a newly modernist look: Le Corbusier's Center for the Visual Arts, Stubbins's Loeb Drama Center, Yamasaki's William James Hall, and Sert's Holyoke Center were among the thirty-three new buildings begun by Pusey. They nestled among the structures of the colonial and early federal campus, the late nineteenth century elegance of Richardson, and the early twentieth century obsession with neo-Georgian. The campaign was just the beginning of many more. Campaigns for the Business School, the Medical School, the Law School, and indeed every school of the university often competed for donations from the same group of donors. Thus began the combination of entrepreneurialism, competition, and bureaucratic Darwinism that has made Harvard fundraising so chaotic and so successful ever since. By 1964 the university's endowment had doubled in a decade and passed the magical mark of $1 billion.[55]

## University and Nation (II)

President John F. Kennedy (class of 1940) visited Harvard for the last time in October 1963, four months after his triumphal visit to Berlin and one month before his assassination. As in Berlin, where 1963 marked the height of pro-American sentiment at Free University, so at Harvard it was the high point of the university's relations with the US government. Dean of FAS McGeorge Bundy had become JFK's national security adviser; Arthur Schlesinger, Jr. (AB '38) became Kennedy's special assistant; David Bell (MA '41) was budget director; and Harvard Professors John Kenneth Galbraith and Edwin Reischauer (PhD '39) were ambassadors to India and Japan, respectively.

As at Free University, within four years Harvard was in political turmoil, generated in part by the muscular foreign policy that Kennedy had begun in Southeast Asia. Defense Secretary Robert S. McNamara (MBA 1939), on campus for a visit, escaped a confrontation with students via underground steam tunnels in 1966. Corporate recruiters tied to defense industries were barricaded in buildings the following year. Student demonstrations against the war, imperialism, racism, and simply against Harvard (as the incarnation of all these things with its CIA ties, officer-training programs, and corporate donors) multiplied, culminating in the student takeover, in the spring of 1969, of University Hall, the staid Bullfinch masterpiece at the center of Harvard Yard that housed the offices of the dean of the faculty.

Pusey had (mostly) defended the university against right-wing government intrusion at the height of the McCarthyite furor of the 1950s, and now he refused to yield to the left. The occupation of University Hall lasted less than 24 hours, with the 184 occupiers violently displaced by 400 state troopers and local police. And with that "Bust," as it was called, Harvard fell apart. FAS Dean Franklin Ford, who was among those evicted by students, suffered a stroke and later resigned. Pusey stayed on, but his presidency was over.

Amid the subsequent years of student strikes, faculty debates, and internal rebuilding, Harvard recalibrated its relationship with government, canceling the ROTC officers' training program on campus, forbidding government-classified research contracts and federal grants to support the salaries of tenured faculty, and limiting at least the outward appearance of too many ties to the CIA.

(Old habits die hard, however. When I was a doctoral student about to begin a Fulbright year in Taiwan in 1977, I was invited to meet with the director of the Office of Career Services. I was happy to do so, for I knew that upon return from my dissertation research, I would face a dismal academic job market, and I wanted to ask about opportunities in the "real world." The director surprised me, however, by asking if I might have some free time to do some ancillary research on Taiwan for an [unnamed] agency. At the time of my departure, the United States was withdrawing troops from Taiwan and contemplating diplomatic recognition of mainland China; anti-Americanism was growing in Nationalist government circles. There would be much to research. But I declined, politely, noting in passing that the last I looked, Taiwan was an island, and I was a poor swimmer. In retrospect, I should not have been surprised by the overture, for both of my mentors, Franklin Ford and John Fairbank, had served in the OSS during World War II. One of them must have thought this was a good idea.)

Derek Bok, who succeeded Pusey and served as president for the following two decades, sought to reengage the university with public affairs by building on Pusey's plans to remake a sleepy School of Public Administration into the Kennedy School of Government, now built on riverside land in modern structures, if clad in old-fashioned brick. It would prepare graduate students for public service and be a (less radical?) focal point for undergraduate engagement with the political world. It would also (re)train active public servants and serve as a way station for politicians on the way up, or (more commonly) on their loss of office. Led for most of Bok's tenure by a passionate dean, Graham Allison, the Kennedy School became what it still is today: a leading center for the study *and* practice of government.

Yet by the time he retired from the presidency in 1991, Bok lamented the enduring unmooring of the university from state and society. If in the 1950s "America and its universities were united in a common resolve to build a system of scientific research preeminent in the world and to expand our colleges to embrace . . . a much larger segment of the nation's youth," that understanding was long gone. He warned, in words that ring more strongly true today: "Unless society appreciates the contributions of its universities, it will continue to reduce them to the status of another interest group by gradually stripping away the protections and support they need to stay preeminent in the world."[56]

## A Golden Decade

Bok was succeeded by Neil Rudenstine, whose presidency during the 1990s was perhaps the most understated yet impactful of any decade in Harvard's modern history. A true intellectual, an erudite writer and speaker, gracious and curious, but with a backbone of steel gained from a decade of service as Princeton's provost, he was beloved by the faculty. His task was to prepare in a comparatively short time (he took office at age fifty-six—the oldest since President Walker on the eve of the Civil War) for a different, larger, yet more unified university, engaged in and far beyond the United States.

His challenges were formidable. Princeton was a highly centralized university, in which academic and budgetary authority was rooted in the president and provost. Harvard had no provost, and almost all of the spendable money was now in the hands of the deans. The "every tub on its own bottom" model of finance was designed to make the schools fiscally responsible. It made some of them also very rich. Rudenstine's challenge (not unlike that of Duke under Nannerl Keohane) was to gradually but steadily bring more resources to the center while not undoing the entrepreneurialism that underlay the schools' success. This he did by (1) taxation for infrastructure and (2) raising a then-ungodly amount of money.

Harvard was hardly poor, but it was not *that* much richer than its competitors. (Pound for pound, Princeton, with an endowment and student body then about the size of Harvard's Faculty of Arts and Sciences, was and remains the best endowed of all.) At the financial low point of the Bok years, endowment contributed but 18 percent of Harvard's revenues; today it contributes double that. But the 1990s was the decade when Harvard truly took off. Rudenstine's decade saw Harvard distance itself dramatically from other comprehensive research universities, as the Harvard endowment more than quadrupled from $4.7 billion in 1990 to $19.2 billion in 2000, supported by strong market conditions; the remarkable leadership of Jack Meyer, president and CEO of the Harvard Management Company (HMC), the entity founded in 1974 to manage Harvard's endowment; and an influx of largesse through "development," as fundraising was now called.

The University Campaign, led brilliantly by Rudenstine, was Harvard's first comprehensive university-wide fundraising effort. It was also Harvard's first—and, so far, last—endeavor at university-wide academic planning. It was linked to extensive processes of strategic planning in each school, while making room also for cross-university initiatives. Chaired by Rudenstine's close partner, Robert Stone, the Senior Fellow of the Corporation, the campaign raised $1 million a day and ended with $2.6 billion in gifts, exceeding its goal by half a billion.[57]

The Rudenstine years also witnessed a remarkable expansion of Harvard's physical footprint. The university had no place to grow in Cambridge. It rented land, for a time, in neighboring Watertown. For the longer haul, Harvard accelerated its purchase of land across the Charles River from Cambridge's Harvard Yard in the Allston neighborhood of Boston, home then only to the Business School and the athletic fields. On his rationale for this decision, Rudenstine recalled, "The idea was to think Harvard is going to need land over the next century, and we don't know exactly what will emerge, and so . . . we ought to leave a lot of land flexible to see what happened."[58] By 1997 Harvard had purchased 52.6 acres of land in Allston, bringing its total landholdings there to 192 acres (even while facing some discontent from the local community), compared with its 215 acres in Cambridge.[59] By 2017 the majority of Harvard's land holdings had shifted to Allston, where the university controlled 358 acres.[60]

The financial and physical expansion of the university during Rudenstine's tenure undergirded his overarching goal of increasing cooperation and integration (if not unification) across Harvard's many "tubs," which had grown increasingly autonomous over the Conant, Pusey, and Bok years. (In one reputed episode from 1994, the commanding and long-serving dean of Harvard Business School, John McArthur, engineered the merger of two Harvard-affiliated hospitals, Brigham and Women's, whose board he chaired, with Massachusetts General Hospital, leading to the creation of Partners Health-Care, of which he was a founding co-chair. McArthur apparently told the president of the university about the merger the night before its public announcement. The next year, HBS had a new dean.)

Rudenstine established the role of provost, the position he had filled at Princeton and from which he had been recruited to lead Harvard, to improve the capacity of a woefully understaffed central administration. He forged cross- and inter-disciplinary "inter-faculty initiatives" on the environment, health policy, ethics, and mind/brain/behavior. He drove (and led the fundraising for) major initiatives in international studies: the creation of the university-wide David Rockefeller Center for Latin American Studies and the Harvard University Asia Center. And he founded the Radcliffe Institute for Advanced Study as the successor to Radcliffe College and in the process recruited a future president.

In addition to using the carrot of new opportunities, Rudenstine used the stick of funding: deans were told to work together and critique each other's plans before they were accepted into the university-wide campaign.[61] Looking to fund expansion in Allston, he led the deans of Harvard's schools, who normally voted on nothing together, to endorse implementing an annual "tax" of 0.5 percent on each school's endowment.[62]

Rudenstine was clear-eyed about the idiosyncrasies of Harvard. He once compared for me the challenges of leading Princeton and Harvard. Princeton, he said, when it all worked well, was like conducting a symphony orchestra. Harvard, at its best, was a splendid collection of soloists. Yet he left the soloists with better instruments than he found them, and in a more collegial, prosperous, and expansive concert hall—all done in the most optimistic of spirits. Not bad for a decade's work. There is a reason Neil Rudenstine's lustrous portrait now sits over the main entrance to the Faculty Room in University Hall.

**Figure 5.3.** Portrait of Neil Rudenstine by Everett Raymond Kinstler. Harvard University Portrait Collection, Commissioned by the Faculty of Arts and Sciences, 2006, © Everett Raymond Kinstler Estate, H814.

## Early Twenty-First Century Trials

From Eliot through Rudenstine, Harvard had the good fortune of more than a century and a quarter of long-serving, impactful presidents. Between 2000 and 2006, by contrast, four individuals sat in the president's office in Massachusetts Hall. The governance structures of the university came under stress as its largest faculty voted "no confidence" in a president while the ancient Corporation—still composed, as in 1650, of its five "fellows," the treasurer, and the president—labored to give direction to a modern, decentralized, and disputatious university. Finances were mismanaged, and the (still largest in the word) university endowment lagged others in performance. Harvard's "new campus" across the Charles River remained desolate, with not a single academic building completed in its first quarter-century. And a university that had come to set national standards in teaching and research found itself with serious competition in an era of technological revolution and globalization. If by 2020 Harvard could still be primus inter pares in the world of universities, it was a measure of the power of its disparate schools and the capacity for renewal at the center.

When in October 2001 Lawrence Summers sat for his inauguration in the creaky, uncomfortable, three-legged "Holyoke Chair," a British relic from the sixteenth century, the former Harvard professor of economics and US Treasury secretary had a full agenda in mind for Harvard's twenty-first century. He would oversee, as Conant and Bok had in their tenures, a major reform in undergraduate education, seeking to ensure that Harvard College remained the heart of an expanding, decentralized, research university. He would maintain, as Conant had, a leadership position in the sciences. And he would build on Rudenstine's internationalist agenda to make Harvard more global still. In so doing, Harvard would expand physically and become more coherent internally. Altogether this was a compelling, indeed energizing, vision for Harvard's faculty and students (and was the central reason I, having served as chair of the history department and director of the Asia Center, agreed to be the dean of the Faculty of Arts and Sciences).

Four and a half years later, in February 2006, Summers announced his resignation. His would be the shortest Harvard presidency since that of Cornelius Conway Felton (1860–1862), who died in office. In some ways, the tensions of Summers's tenure were cultural in foundation. Summers was direct and plainspoken to a degree not experienced in a university still steeped in New England traditions of courtly nonconfrontation (at least in public).

After the "troubles" of the 1960s, meetings of the Faculty of Arts and Sciences had been constrained by rules of procedure meant to limit debate, and as a result had become somnambulant affairs. Not so in Summers's time. A faculty that had grown used to being reassured that it was the best in the world found itself confronted and challenged by a president/agitator who believed with the certainty of a modern economist that it could do better. Rudenstine could turn down a senior appointment yet leave a department chair feeling better having had the discussion with him. Summers could approve an offer of tenure and leave the nominating department bruised and insulted. In those days, the president and dean presided over some forty half-day tenure meetings per year, at which multiple faculty colleagues "testified"; so, the opportunities for discord were many.

Despite the tensions emanating from what was euphemistically called the president's "managerial style," Summers set important initiatives in motion during his short tenure. His ambitious plans for Allston, which included a five-hundred-thousand-square-foot science complex, new homes for the Schools of Public Health and Education, and new undergraduate houses promised a radical transformation of the campus. He pressed the deans of the separate schools to collaborate in hiring and doctoral education—with notable success in the historically siloed life sciences. He pushed hard to ensure that Harvard scientists would have a major role in the new Broad Institute, a biomedical and genomic research center that had emerged from MIT's Whitehead Institute. And, with most enduring impact, he worked with me as dean to earmark and raise funds to alter dramatically the scope of financial aid offered to Harvard College students. In 2004 we announced that Harvard would be cost-free for families with incomes below $40,000 (in 2020 that figure was $65,000), with much-reduced costs for those with family incomes up to $150,000. The message was simple: you did not need to be rich to go to Harvard. The message was well received, but the messenger was in increasing conflict on other matters—with the faculty (especially in FAS) and with multiple deans.

"A single spark can start a prairie fire," Mao Zedong once wrote. By the time that Summers, in the January of his fourth year as president, made his now-infamous comments on women in science, in which he speculated that the underrepresentation of female scientists may have been a result of "innate differences" between genders, the tinder at Harvard was very dry.[63] At the FAS faculty meeting on February 7, 2005, the reform of undergraduate education was the central, docketed item. It would not be passed for two more years, and then under an acting president. Instead the faculty erupted in a verbal assault on the president, the likes of which had not been seen even in the 1960s.

University Hall, designed in 1813 by Charles Bullfinch, the primary architect of the United States Capitol, is a neoclassical masterpiece of the early Federal period. The former chapel that dominates its second floor is today the Faculty Room, home to FAS faculty meetings. It is a room surrounded with history, dominated by portraits of Eliot, Lowell, Conant, and Bok (and today Rudenstine), but also spiced with images of lesser luminaries, such as the seventeenth-century wooden image of William Stoughton, an early donor and the only magistrate of the Salem witch trials never to repent.

The Faculty Room can seat two hundred people uncomfortably. Twice that number came in February 2005 to speak bitterness against the president, face to face. By tradition, the president chairs the FAS faculty meetings for, as the Philosophical Faculty in Humboldt's sense, FAS is at the center of the university. That same tradition exposes the president to any question that a colleague may wish to ask, or any statement. They were fast and furious in coming, and from the most senior faculty. The anthropologist Arthur Kleinman accused Summers of uttering "reckless and undigested words based in half-baked sociological prejudices." Theda Skocpol, the sociologist, wondered, "How do we want to proceed in addressing the pathologies of leadership that are undermining the honor, the competitive effectiveness, and the collegial governance of Harvard University?" The master of Lowell House, Diana Eck, asked how Summers would respond to "what is clearly a widening crisis of confidence in your fitness to lead our University?" Stephen Owen, a University Professor (Harvard's highest professorial rank), asked, "Mr. President, when did I cease being your colleague and start being your employee?" These were among the more restrained comments in a meeting that would be continued, in two further and larger sessions, for more than a month, before concluding at the largest venue available at Harvard for such a gathering: the Loeb Drama Center. On a stage that later that evening would host Christopher Marlowe's play, *Dido, Queen of Carthage*, about a woman's rule over a haven of civilization, the faculty passed a resolution—unprecedented in Harvard's history—of no confidence in the president.[64]

Although he would stay in office for another year, Summers's presidency effectively ended that afternoon. Initiatives ground to a halt. Allston planning was put on ice. The Harvard Corporation, that senior governing body which under Summers had become increasingly disengaged from the task of governance, came under intense critique. A year later, Derek Bok was back as interim president, and the search for new leadership for the twenty-first century resumed.

In turning to Drew Gilpin Faust, founding dean of the Radcliffe Institute, a chastened Corporation at once looked back to the Rudenstine era (Neil Rudenstine had recruited her, and Drew Faust shared his diplomatic skills) and looked forward to a leader who was creative and collaborative, compelling but not combative in argument. She preferred not to be known primarily as Harvard's first woman president: she was simply its twenty-eighth president. Harvard was by no means in the forefront of appointing women to presidencies: MIT, Princeton, and Penn had done so some years earlier. But at an old place still steeped in traditions of discrimination, Faust's appointment was widely celebrated.

Faust was barely in her third year as president when a major crisis of the twenty-first century unfolded. Just before the 2008 financial crisis, the Harvard endowment had reached a value of $36.9 billion. It would lose $10 billion in value in a matter of weeks. Seemingly overnight, 27.3 percent of the endowment was lost.[65] This was a performance lagging that of every peer.[66] What was worse, overnight $1.8 billion *in cash* of Harvard's everyday expenses disappeared.[67] Every university with an endowment saw a huge drop in value that autumn. Only Harvard managed to lose not only more than a quarter of its "savings account," that is, the endowment, *but also* most of its "checking account": the short-term reserves of every school.

This large-scale financial mismanagement tells us much about Harvard's governance and internal funding model. Each school is expected to be fiscally self-sufficient, but each school has a different funding model. Older schools (FAS and Divinity, for example) are heavily endowment-dependent. Younger ones (Education, Public Health) count heavily on tuition or external grants. The President's Office, by contrast, has neither tuition nor (much) endowment to count on, and so the center of the world's richest university is much poorer than any of Harvard's major schools. The funds from the President's Office rely on modest taxation of the individual schools and the investment of their annual, short-term reserves into a "central bank." When Summers was president, he sought (rightly, in my view) to enhance the Central Bank's financial capacity by investing those reserves, rather than simply holding them. By investing Harvard's cash holdings from its General Operating Account (GOA) into comparatively riskier instruments, alongside the endowment, he hoped to boost returns and bring more of the university's

**The majority of the funds that make up Harvard's endowment are restricted to specific programs, departments, or purposes**

**Figure 5.4.** FY 2019 Harvard endowment breakdown graph. Faculty of Arts and Sciences, Harvard University.

resources to the central administration. Had Summers remained as president, my guess is that he would have known when to get the university out of those investments. But two years after he left, there were few who had the memory or expertise to understand the potential risks that would cost the university nearly $2 billion in cash.[68] The Corporation, responsible for the university's finances, was uninformed and inattentive. The dean of the School of Public Health, for example, had nurtured a reserve of nearly $100 million. It was gone in a flash. The financial crisis led to the largest percentage financial decline in forty years for Harvard.[69] Larry Bacow, who joined the Corporation in 2011 and chaired its finance committee, recalled his surprise: "Harvard had zero capacity to plan, and not only that, the endowment was being managed completely independently from the operating budget. . . . When I got there, I couldn't believe what I saw."[70] Even as the economy improved, the effects of the Great Recession were long-lasting. Not until 2021 would the endowment be worth more, in real dollars, than it had been in 2008.

The sudden financial crisis left Harvard in a panicked scramble to make ends meet. Harvard had to rush out and borrow $2.5 billion at comparatively high interest rates, and annual interest expense alone grew to $265 million by 2010. Over the same period, the endowment distribution for annual operating expenses declined by $300 million. Early retirement incentive programs and layoffs were put in place, leading to more than eight hundred employees leaving in May 2009.[71] The Faculty of Arts and Sciences, which had begun a plan to expand its faculty, froze positions, and it has not grown since. Construction of an enormous life sciences complex in Allston was stopped and abandoned, even though the $400 million, four-story-deep foundation had already been poured, giving new meaning to the term "sunk cost." One major goal of Faust's tenure was creating more unity across Harvard's various schools, transforming them into "One Harvard." In the immediate wake of the financial crisis, however, it was *sauve qui peut*, as Harvard's schools were ever more consumed with self-reliance.

## Harvard in 2020

Despite an extraordinarily inauspicious start to the twenty-first century, the Harvard of 2020 remained one of the most highly regarded universities in the world. Many of its individual professional schools topped global rankings, while the university as a whole had been ranked the best university in the world by the Shanghai Academic Ranking of World Universities every year since the inception of that ranking system in 2003.

Harvard's over 371,000 living alumni could be found in 202 countries, helping to solidify its reputation around the world. However, it was Harvard's enduring ability to attract outstanding faculty and students—and ensure that somehow they learned, one from another—that kept it on or near the top.

### Faculty

Over time, the Harvard faculty has included fifty-two Nobel laureates and forty-four Pulitzer Prize winners. It was not always so. Through Lowell's presidency, Harvard's research reputation trailed that of Chicago and Columbia. Its most famous faculty were teaching, not research, stars, and long-term lecturers outnumbered tenured faculty. Conant, who believed that it was "mistaken philanthropy to keep a mediocre man in a university," inaugurated the tenure "clock" in 1939. The clock stopped at eight years, after which it was "up" to a tenured appointment or "out" of the university. In 1942 Conant also inaugurated the iconic Harvard way to review tenure cases: the ad hoc committee. Unlike most of its peer institutions, Harvard has no standing committee on appointments or promotions. Rather, for each tenure case, a separate committee consisting of scholars from outside Harvard (the majority of members) and from disparate departments within the university is assembled to review the case and advise the dean and the president, who has the final say, on the appointment.[72]

By the twenty-first century, the ad hoc committee was the final stage in a famously laborious sequence. Departments were permitted to "search" for a tenured appointment, be it an internal promotion or an external recruitment, and would send out "blind" letters asking colleagues from outside the university to review a list of names that did not indicate which was the preferred candidate. If, on receipt of the responses from these reviewers, the department voted in favor of promotion, all tenured department members then had to write confidential letters to the dean to say *why* they had voted the way they had. The dean would then review the case with his or her academic advisory group, and, if the dean approved, the case would go to the president and in time to the ad hoc interrogation, which would normally last at least three hours. Cumbersome and time consuming, the procedure ensured a high degree of external scrutiny even as it ensured that deans and presidents would remain current in their grasp of different academic disciplines. Above all (and especially when tenure was awarded only at the full professorial level after the 1960s), it ensured fewer "mistakes."

Harvard being Harvard, this ad hoc system was applied across the university in an ad hoc way. It was required for FAS and the smaller schools (e.g., Divinity and Education) and less stringently for the large and powerful professional Schools of Law, Business, and Medicine. But the need for presidential approval of any tenured appointment remained absolute.

Those were its strengths. Its weakness was to diminish mightily the prospect of promotion for "junior" faculty, as the untenured were called by their seniors. Judith Singer, the James Bryant Conant Professor of Education, noted that when she was hired at the Graduate School of Education in 1984, she was told, "Assume you will not get tenure."[73] From the 1970s to the early 2000s, an assistant professorship in the humanities and social sciences at Harvard was essentially a folding chair. The social and professional distance between the tenured faculty and the day laborers of assistant professors grew to be as great as could be found in any nineteenth-century German university. With recruitment of stars from the outside prized over the development of young talent at home, the best young scholars tended not to accept Harvard offers or to leave early, while the externally recruited tenured faculty in many fields were older, whiter, and more male than their counterparts at "tenure-track" universities. External recruits were on average ten years older than internal promotions, and their reputations were already well established. The risk was this: Had they already done their best work, elsewhere? They may have been known for explosive scholarship, but were they, as FAS Dean Jeremy Knowles worried in the 1990s, "extinct volcanoes"?

This appointment culture could limit a great department's capacity for self-renewal. Take the case of my own Department of History. In the third quarter of the twentieth century, Harvard's history department enjoyed a towering reputation. Its faculty (many of them having participated in OSS during the Second World War) were both learned and worldly. Its leadership in so many fields from American to European to Russian to Chinese history set the foundation for multiple regional research centers at Harvard. Yet it lacked the ambition of self-renewal, for who was good enough to join such a club? How could the current faculty be replaced? And so it missed dynamic revolutions in historical study, be they in the history of race, class, gender, or society. This was the kind of attitude that must have motivated Henry Rosovsky, surely the most accomplished dean ever to preside over the Faculty of Arts and Sciences (he served from 1973 to 1984 and again in 1990–1991) to place in his University Hall office that sober reckoning sometimes attributed to Charles de Gaulle: "The graveyards are full of indispensable men."

When I joined the History Department in 1992, it had 31 tenured colleagues, 1.5 of whom were female. (One was a joint appointment.) An external review committee had recently found History to be "a department in crisis." Appointments languished, for every senior scholar had a *liberum veto* on candidates in their field. When *The Harvard Crimson*, the undergraduate paper, published its *Confi Guide* to courses in 1993, the pages on the History Department opened with a large photo of the *Hindenburg* consumed in flames. American history, once the pride of the department, had withered to insignificance: no one had been tenured from within the department in American history since the Eisenhower administration. And great scholar-teachers, such as the twentieth-century political historian Alan Brinkley, had been let go. The *Crimson* still recommended the department to students, "You won't have to do much schoolwork. Most of the courses are work and grade guts." And so, they advised their fellow students, "You don't need to transfer to Yale, especially if you really don't care about the New Deal."[74]

Today a remarkably different, diverse, and talented department—44 percent female among its senior ranks—leads the study of history at Harvard. Assistant professors are hired only if they have the promise, with time and support, to be serious candidates for tenure. This turnabout was the result not of happenstance but of several department chairs, myself included, making old guards uncomfortable, recruiting new generations of leaders from without and within, all with the strong support of a president (Rudenstine) and dean (Knowles) who simply would not stand by and witness academic decay.

The lessons of the History Department's renewal formed the background for changes across FAS when I assumed the FAS deanship in 2002. Bizarre as it sounds, the formal procedures for promotion and tenure had never been made public. Department chairs had copies, and sometimes shared them with their untenured colleagues, but many younger colleagues simply had no clue. Procedures for a rigorous "tenure track" were drawn up, revised, and put online. Search processes across the multitude of FAS departments were monitored by University Hall. Tenure review letters were no longer "blind." Harvard began to focus more resources on the orientation, development, and retention of young faculty members. In other words, in its search for talent, Harvard was becoming a normal American university—albeit one with a higher degree of success in recruitment and retention.

Between 2004 and 2014 the number of tenured faculty grew by 22 percent, while tenure-track faculty shrank by 12 percent, which the Harvard Faculty Development and Diversity 2013–2014 Annual Report called "a result of all-time high internal promotion rates."[75] By 2010 a majority of university tenure appointments were made through internal promotion rather than external recruitment.[76]

Like the faculties of many top-tier universities in the United States, Harvard's was not known for its diversity. It was nearly three hundred years after the establishment of the university when in 1919 Alice Hamilton became the first woman to hold a faculty position at Harvard. In the Faculty of Arts and Sciences, there were no women until 1947, when a donor endowed a professorship *on the condition* that the holder of the chair be female. In 1985 just 45 out of 898 tenured faculty members across the university were female.[77] By 2020 this proportion had increased but remained well below gender parity levels—31 percent of Harvard faculty were female, up from 26 percent in 2004.[78]

Still, each department in FAS and each unit across the university retained elements of its individual culture, some of which were historically inimical to concepts of diversity. Economics was for years a "young boys' club." And Mathematics resisted the idea that colleagues may be promoted to tenure, nor did it hire female faculty from the outside. As a result, it has remained, until very recently, entirely male. (When President Drew Faust pronounced several years ago a *Verbot* on single-sex social organizations at Harvard—she was targeting the "Final Clubs," or fancy fraternities—I suggested she start with the Math Department.)

Some progress has been made in increasing the representation of minorities in the faculty. By 2019, 24 percent of Harvard faculty were members of minority groups, a 1 percent increase from 2004. This already-small group was disproportionately Asian (around 60 percent); Blacks, Latinx, and multiracial individuals made up just 10 percent of the faculty.

Despite the variability across schools and disciplines, in the first part of the twenty-first century an offer to teach at Harvard remained the most prestigious (if not always the most remunerative) offer a scholar might entertain. It was, still, the twenty-first century "call to Berlin." Negotiation of the terms of hiring a senior scholar (from within or outside) was, as anywhere, a courtship. But once the faculty member was hired, the courtship became a marriage. Harvard would co-invest in housing, helping scholars live in a pricey environment while incurring limited personal costs. It would invest in the education of faculty children by offering interest-free loans wherever they chose to study. These were both attractions and a set of golden handcuffs to retain faculty.

Of course, Harvard could and did lose faculty to peer institutions. After all, you don't want a faculty member that no one else wants. I recall that my last hours as dean, many time zones removed from Cambridge, were spent trying to dissuade a wonderful colleague from decamping to Stanford. I did not succeed, but Harvard's overall divorce rate remained remarkably low.

## Students: Admissions and Athletics

I used to tell my faculty colleagues when we were considering reform to undergraduate education, "You know, without the students, none of us would be here." That was surely true, for Harvard was founded as a teaching institution that grafted research onto its mission. It was never a rarefied institute of advanced study—a Max Planck, for example. And as a university, Harvard is defined as much by its students, and its alumni, as it is by its faculty.

One measure of the prestige of a university is how desperate people are to get into it. By this calculation Harvard remains the admissions gold standard for college students (and for business, law, and medical students). I have been asked in all corners of the world, "How do I (or my daughter or son) get into Harvard?" For this I have a ready answer: "Apply. If you don't apply, you really won't get in." But that counsel elides the point. *How does one get into Harvard?* One external view is by money. Several years ago, when I was at our Harvard Center Shanghai, three individuals came to see me to offer stunningly generous "donations" to Harvard, each at about $5 million. In each case, as I asked what prompted this admirable sense of philanthropy, it turned out that there was a family member in an admissions pool in one or another of Harvard's schools. And in each case, I thanked the would-be philanthropists for their generous spirit. Unfortunately, I informed them, we could not accept the funds because, I told them, "We would not want others to misunderstand your good intentions."

The reasons for the attempted bribery in Shanghai (but it could have been anywhere) were clear: admission to Harvard College had become insanely competitive in the early twenty-first century. The percentage of applicants admitted had fallen from around 10 percent in 2000 to less than 4 percent for the class of 2025. The College's yield of admitted students generally hovered around 80 percent, compared with yields of around 70 percent at Yale and Princeton.[79] Harvard's admissions statistics were almost perfectly matched by Stanford, which admitted 4.36 percent of applicants to its class of 2022 and reported an 82.4 percent yield rate.[80]

The increasing competitiveness of university admissions, especially in the most selective universities, has led prospective students and their parents to do whatever it takes to gain admission, even in unlawful ways. On March 12, 2019, US Attorney General Andrew Lelling announced the results of a national investigation internally nicknamed "Operation Varsity Blues." This criminal conspiracy entailed at least thirty-three parents paying a total of more than $25 million to William Rick Singer to bribe college admissions officials and provide fraudulent standardized testing scores. Many elite universities, including Stanford, Georgetown, and Yale, were implicated in this scandal. Although Harvard was not centrally involved in Operation Varsity Blues, it faced its own admissions scandal. That July, Harvard dismissed its fencing coach, Peter Brand, for a conflict of interest violation, in which his house was sold for nearly twice its estimated value to a parent of two fencers, one a Harvard undergraduate and the other an applicant to the College.[81]

Given the combined, intertwined pressures of admissions and athletics, it is almost a miracle that Harvard had not (yet) had a Varsity Blues-like scandal. For this, the university is indebted to the decades-long, principled partnership between Harvard's former athletic director, Robert Scalise, and its dean for admissions, William Fitzsimmons. Such people are rare in any institution. (Even the fencing scandal was avoidable. At Harvard, athletics, like admissions, reports to the dean of the Faculty of Arts and Sciences. When I was dean, I wanted to invest in new athletic facilities and make an older facility, the Malkin Athletic Center [MAC], into a student center. Among the complicated issues was the future of the fencing team, whose practices took a great deal of space in the MAC. Their relocation was not easy. I wondered openly if we actually needed a fencing team, but I learned quickly the risks of challenging college athletics, not the least in a sport where the students carry weapons.)

Athletics matter at Harvard far more than is widely known outside the university. Harvard has forty-two Division I intercollegiate National Collegiate Athletic Association (NCAA) sports, more than any college in the country, and so it has more varsity athletes than any college in the country. Harvard's athletes are *recruited* athletes. "Walk-ons" are a mythological species. Harvard's obsession with athletics began, as elsewhere in the United States, in the second half of the nineteenth century. Through the first quarter of the twentieth century, Harvard was a major player in big-time intercollegiate sports. Harvard football won nine national championships between 1890 and 1920, the last one capped off by crushing Oregon, 7–6, in the Rose Bowl. Harvard Stadium, built in 1903 as the first major reinforced concrete structure in the United States, is America's oldest stadium. Its physical layout, with stands coming right to the field, helped to determine the field size and rules of modern American football.

In more recent history, academics has taken precedence over athletics at Harvard, but sports still matter. The Ivy League, after all, is, in formal terms, simply an athletic conference. The number of championships that Harvard has held may have declined (save in squash and lightweight crew programs), but the number of sports, coaches, and recruited athletes is at an all-time high. In 2019 about twelve hundred undergraduates, nearly 20 percent of the student body, were intercollegiate athletes.[82] Their path to admission is easier: according to Harvard's Office of Institutional Research, athletes with high academic scores had an acceptance rate of 83 percent compared to 16 percent for non-athletes.[83] And while Ivy League schools officially give no "athletic scholarships," Harvard offers need-based scholarships to athletes that are ironclad: they remain intact even when an athlete is off the team.

Beyond athletes, of course, legacies—the offspring of alumni—also make up a significant proportion of the Harvard undergraduate population. The Harvard of 2020 may not be "your father's Harvard," but the class of 2022 was still 36.8 percent legacy students, about the same percentage as at Georgetown University.[84] Legacy admissions is another distinguishing feature of many elite American universities, with a much longer history of preferences than that of athletics. A 2013 analysis commissioned by the Office of Institutional Research demonstrated that legacy status granted applicants a forty-percentage-point advantage of being accepted over non-legacy applicants.[85] That is, children of alumni were six times more likely to be admitted than others.[86] Broadly speaking, admitted legacy students, like recruited athletes to Harvard, are academically competitive. But other great research universities, such as MIT, the California Institute of Technology, and Johns Hopkins, have shown that they can grow to greatness without any such preferences.

### Diversity

Not only was Harvard College increasingly selective, it was also becoming more diverse in ethnicity and socioeconomic status in the twenty-first century. For example, in 2013 Harvard launched the "Harvard College Connection," an admissions outreach program that sought to encourage low-income students to apply to Harvard and other elite schools while also increasing their understanding of opportunities for financial aid.[87] Over one-quarter of the class of 2023 identified as African American, Latinx, or Native American, with an additional 25.6 percent of the class identifying as Asian American.[88] Among all Harvard College students in 2019, 20 percent paid no tuition at all, under Harvard's financial aid policy that required no tuition contribution from families with a total income of less than $65,000.[89] For families with incomes above $65,000, expected contributions were calculated on a generous sliding scale—90 percent of students at Harvard would pay an equal amount or more for tuition at a state school.[90] In the 2017–2018 academic year, 16 percent of Harvard undergraduate students were Pell Grant recipients, compared with 16 percent at Yale, 19 percent at Princeton, and 16 percent at Stanford.[91] This was a sharp increase even from 2008, when only 6.5 percent of Harvard undergraduates received Pell Grants.[92]

Maintaining diversity was a highly political exercise. A 2014 lawsuit alleged that Harvard discriminated against Asian Americans by favoring Black and Latinx applicants. Two lower courts ruled in Harvard's favor. As of November 2021 the Supreme Court had yet to determine if it would hear the case.

## Curriculum

Students who put enormous effort into gaining admission to elite universities such as Harvard are, by and large, remarkably incurious about what it is they will learn once they get there. Perhaps that is because the curriculum keeps changing. In its modern history, Harvard College has often been at the cutting edge of undergraduate curriculum development, from Eliot's libertarian approach, to Lowell's more constrained program, to Conant's General Education of the 1940s, and the "Core Curriculum" inaugurated by Dean Henry Rosovsky in the 1970s. Each of these reforms made their mark in their day, and each became stale in time. They and their twenty-first century successors had several things in common, however. First was a grounding in some commonality in the undergraduate educational experience, but not a fully required curriculum, as in the "Great Books" approach of Columbia and Chicago. Second—this was and remains a distinguishing feature of Harvard—the teaching of "GenEd" or "Core" classes was not a burden to be assigned to the newest assistant professor but a privilege given to Harvard's leading faculty, who had to apply or be invited to teach in the program. This has been in the educational DNA of the place for at least a century, and it is one reason undergraduate education is still taken so seriously by the faculty.

I was stunned when, as dean, I began a review of undergraduate education and sought the participation of faculty colleagues. Of the one hundred colleagues I approached to assist with our review, only one turned me down. Those one hundred or so did not, of course, always agree with each other, but they were deeply committed to meeting the challenge of making a Harvard College education equal to that of the best small colleges in teaching and inspiration, while surpassing them by virtue of being at the heart of a great research university. These aspirations, articulated in multiple reports and faculty essays, had resonance well beyond Harvard. I recall the visit of the president of a major Chinese university. He wanted to study our soon-to-be-revamped Core Curriculum. When I told him we were getting rid of it, he changed his mind. Our subsequent reports on curricular reform were read at least as carefully in Beijing as they were in Boston.

Harvard's General Education program in 2020 is a product of accumulated history. It draws on the influence of Conant and the Redbook and his conviction that general education should address "that part of a student's whole education which looks first of all to his life as a responsible human being and citizen."[93] It agrees with Lowell's belief that the well-educated student should know "a little of everything and something well."[94] And it tips its hat to Eliot, who emphasized the power and importance of curricular choice in students' personal and professional development.

Curricular reviews certainly have their challenges. Bok once compared it to "moving a graveyard." And certainly there is no perfect curriculum for any given place or time. By far the most important thing, in my view—and here Harvard has succeeded in each iteration of undergraduate education—is to ensure that the current generation of faculty creates and owns the foundations of an undergraduate education. Great courses taught by imaginative teachers to welcoming undergraduates—these are much more important than any sets of rules, procedures, and categories. When in 2007 the FAS finally voted on the first iteration of curricular reform, it had debated long and hard (including with President Summers, who sought to shape it) for three years. When it finally passed with near unanimity, I was reminded of a major meeting in Chinese Communist Party history, which the minutes summarized: "The resolution passed unanimously, even though many Comrades were opposed." That has always been my best hope for a faculty meeting.

## Governance, Challenged

As the oldest university in the United States, Harvard had once set standards for university governance. It would ensure institutional autonomy by placing authority in independent boards. The Harvard Corporation and Board of Overseers performed that function since 1650. But as other American universities developed more sophisticated, responsive, and professional boards in the nineteenth and twentieth centuries, Harvard's remained untouched. The small Corporation, to which almost all power accrued, was self-contained and self-nominating. The Overseers became elegant wallpaper. This structure could work well enough as long as extraordinary people led the Corporation, such as the longtime Senior Fellow of the Corporation, Robert Stone, in the last quarter of the twentieth century. But for difficult times, as in the early 2000s, the seven-member Corporation was too remote, too uninformed, and simply too small to comprehend the challenges of governing a now massive and divided university. No major university or college in the country was governed by such a small body.

Shaken by the faculty revolt against Summers and then by the financial crisis of 2008, a besieged Corporation created a Governance Review Committee to undertake a review of its practices and responsibilities. The committee proposed and enacted a series of changes that pointed toward an increased emphasis on strategic planning and stronger coordination between the Corporation and the Board of Overseers. Most immediately, the seven-person Corporation was nearly doubled in size to include twelve members plus the president. Subcommittees, of a kind to be found in every other university's board of trustees, were established to focus on specific areas such as finance and facilities, to enable the body to more effectively evaluate projects. This was a welcome change.

The reorganized Corporation was to work even more closely with the second governing body, the Board of Overseers. The Board of Overseers comprised thirty members, elected by all Harvard degree holders for staggered, six-year terms, plus the president and treasurer of Harvard as ex officio members. In practice, the Corporation still ran the show, and the Overseers saw over the university from a considerable distance.

Both boards are managed by an Office of the Governing Boards, good people whose mission in life is to maintain the stability and secrecy of the work of the Governing Boards. My best analogy for the Office of the Governing Boards is that of the Japanese Imperial Household. Things *can* change, but change must come in imperceptible increments.

So, in formal governance terms, Harvard is an extraordinarily conservative institution, with a small governing center. Unlike most American universities, there is no university-wide body of faculty (e.g., academic senate) that can address university-wide issues. When the university has moved forward in recent decades, it has more often than not been at the impetus of its schools, all of which, in principle, report to the president and provost, but all of which have been, in fact, famously autonomous.

I have described earlier a history of Harvard as one of presidential reigns. And those do matter. But from the 1930s on, the role of Harvard's deans has been equally if not more important. Paul Buck, FAS dean under Conant, was the real author of the Redbook. McGeorge Bundy, Franklin Ford, and, especially, Henry Rosovsky left indelible marks on the Faculty of Arts and Sciences.

Take the case of Harvard Business School, one of the university's newer professional schools. HBS was founded amid a financial crisis in 1908 and able to celebrate its centenary in 2008 just in time for another. It has had many strong deans, but none more independent and more creatively idiosyncratic than its seventh, John McArthur, who served from 1979 to 1995. His leadership vaulted HBS to the top rank among management schools; he expanded its endowment sixfold; and he had an outsized influence on health care in the broader Boston metropolitan area. He also kept HBS healthily separate from the rest of the university: building its own gymnasium and even its own chapel! (For the latter act, he was summoned to report to the Corporation, one of only two occasions when he was asked to meet with his putative bosses.) His successors Kim Clark and Jay Light would make HBS the most international of Harvard's faculties. HBS's dean from 2010 to 2020, Nitin Nohria, was a leader in McArthur's mold, but he took the school from strength to strength not by isolating HBS across the moat of the Charles River, but by becoming, by some measure, the leading university citizen among all of Harvard's deans.

The story of Harvard's modern success, in short, is found not in the Corporation nor the Office of the Governing Boards, but above all in the deans and schools responsible for all the teaching and research, much of the fundraising, and nearly all the innovation to be found at Harvard.

That success can be measured also by the contributions of what one might call Harvard's *Berufsbeamtentum*, or permanent civil service. Executive and associate deans of FAS, HBS, and other large schools oversaw research, physical facilities, labs, and concert halls. And they kept to budgets. Names such as Laura Fisher and Angela Crispi will be known only to Harvard insiders, but they are the heart and the memory of the institution. The faculty at Harvard are generally excellent. The students are terrific. The professional staff is better still, including—especially—its unionized members.

*Funding*

Excellence costs money. Lots of money. Despite the financial mismanagement of 2008, Harvard remained rich by any conceivable standard. The total operating revenue for Harvard in the 2020–2021 fiscal year was $5.2 billion.[95]

The largest source of revenue was endowment income, which provided 39 percent of funds for the university overall, although this proportion ranged across the twelve schools and institutes from 80 percent and 72 percent at the Radcliffe Institute for Advanced Study and the Divinity School, respectively, to just 23 percent and 20 percent at the Business School and the T.H. Chan School of Public Health, respectively.[96] Other sources of operating revenue for the university included income from tuition and student fees (17 percent), sponsored support (18 percent), and gifts for current use (10 percent), with the remaining 16 percent from other sources. The largest category of Harvard's $5 billion reported operating expenses was salaries, wages, and employee benefits, which accounted for $2.7 billion, or approximately 54 percent of all expenses.[97] Although Harvard's financial reports were reported at a university-wide level, financial decisions were made by each school autonomously.

The value of Harvard's endowment in 2021 ($53.2 billion) was greater than the nominal GDP of one hundred countries. From 1974 to 2021 the endowment had garnered annualized returns of more than 11 percent.[98] The endowment was not a single entity, however, but rather a large collection of gifts accumulated over nearly four hundred years, often tied to specific or limited uses, many of which are constraining. And all the money in the world could not make a department strong.

Let me give you an example. The Department of Celtic Languages and Literatures is the best department of Celtic Studies in the United States. Indeed, it is the *only* such department in the United States. It exists today (and it is an excellent department) because its three senior professorships are all fully endowed chairs. But there is an existential scramble on the part of the department any time one of its senior chairs is open—so few are the potential candidates. As dean, I explored whether Celtic might not find more applicants were it part of our English Department. This was another fencing lesson, for I learned quickly enough why the Irish and the English need to be in different buildings.

## Harvard and the World

Harvard has always been an insular institution. Its first students came from somewhere else, and they did not want to go back. Even as international studies grew in strength and reputation in the twentieth century, the undergraduate experience was local, not global. Sustained by the mentality of "what place could possibly offer more than here?" for many years an extremely low proportion of Harvard undergraduate students studied abroad—for example, just 170 in the fall semester of 2000.[99] One can hardly blame those students who stayed home, for in order to study abroad, first they had to find the study abroad office, which was located in a windowless basement of the Office of Career Services. They then had to petition to withdraw both from their undergraduate House and from Harvard College. Then they had to write an essay to explain why studying abroad was not something you could do in Cambridge. If students had not graduated by the time these protracted steps were taken, they were likely to be given permission, although not promised academic credit for coursework elsewhere.

Old habits die hard, and Harvard undergraduates still stick close to home during the academic year. One result of the curricular reform of the early 2000s, however, was a broadening of international opportunities through some thirty Harvard Summer Schools abroad, robust global internship programs, and support of international public service and research. In that reform, undertaken when I was dean, we toyed with the idea of requiring an "international experience" of eight weeks or more for all undergraduates. Instead we made an international experience an "expectation," for students, leaving the rest to their sense of duty. About 80 percent have since been dutiful.

For the university as a whole, however, much of the world was terra incognita. In the early twenty-first century, American universities rushed to develop an "international strategy." Not Harvard. I recall that when I served as Duke University's Senior Advisor on China, Duke President Richard Brodhead asked each of his deans to report on the international strategy of a peer institution. The one tasked with talking about Harvard said, "This will be short, because as far as I can see there is none."

That was not entirely true, for there were as many international strategies as there were faculties and schools, just none for Harvard as a whole. Other universities took the lead. New York University set up fourteen Global Academic Centers and two full campuses, one each in Shanghai and Abu Dhabi. Duke established first a joint medical school with the National University of Singapore (NUS) and then a liberal arts campus in Kunshan, China. Both NYU and Duke had robust central offices, global programs, and strategies. Harvard did not create the position of vice provost for international affairs until 2005, and left it underresourced. Only when Yale University President Richard Levin announced in 2010 the establishment of Yale-NUS, a college of the liberal arts and sciences in Singapore, did Harvard convene an International Strategy Working Group to study—and reject—the idea of an international campus.[100]

It is worth noting that Harvard had established schools abroad in the past: the Harvard Medical School of China was in operation from 1911 to 1916; and the Harvard Business School played a role in the establishment of new business schools in Switzerland and France in the 1950s and 1960s. These efforts proved impermanent, but neither school was hurt by trying. Modern Harvard was more risk-averse.

In lieu of a campus, and under some alumni pressure to do something to match its peers (Faust wondered: "Are we missing something?"[101]), Harvard experimented with a new approach, a Harvard Global Institute (HGI), in 2015. This was an effort to focus on extending the research, not the teaching, mission of the university to different corners of the world. The idea was to bring together the decentralized schools and institutes of Harvard toward a single, signature global research program. But it relied entirely on external funding. Its first five years were funded by Wang Jianlin, the founder of the Dalian Wanda Group, a large Chinese real estate company.[102] The one major project funded was to investigate sustainability and climate change in China. HGI still awaits a second gift.

By 2020 Harvard had inadvertently committed to a different kind of international strategy that better fit its feudal structure. Individual schools had established their own presences in various locations—HBS, for example, had established a Global Initiative in 1996, which boasted eight research centers around the world by 2016. This decentralized approach was not without risk. But that risk was as much at home as abroad. Barry Bloom, the intrepid former dean of the Harvard School of Public Health (HSPH), prioritized international engagement. He increased dramatically the number of international students and put the school to work on tackling crises in global health. He successfully applied for a federal grant to have HSPH administer parts of the US President's Emergency Plan for AIDS Relief (PEPFAR), which largely operated in Africa—an effort that would in time make an enormous difference in the control of AIDS on that continent. He was far ahead of the university leadership, however. He recalled later the traumatic experience:

> I got called out of a meeting . . . into the president's office where I
> thought I was going to get a big hug for bagging the biggest grant in

the history of the university. Instead I got my ass torn out for putting the university at total risk at every level, financial, reputational. It reflected the lack of understanding of the assets of the university to make a difference in the world, and its lack of interest in doing so. I came to believe that Harvard is not a university, it's a brand. And everything that was done in the best interests of the university, in my view during that period, was to protect the brand.[103]

In time, after years of "bottom-up" internationalization initiatives across the schools, Harvard was now present, in one form or another, on at least five continents. By 2020 Harvard had twenty-two distinctive institutional centers and programs across the world. And it would take an increasingly vocal role in support of internationalization in the United States.

This was not the least because of the rapidly growing importance of international talent at Harvard. As of 2019 there were 791 international students at Harvard College, only about 12 percent of the undergraduate population.[104] But there were more than 10,000 international students and scholars from 155 countries across the university. Since the middle of the twentieth century, the university had grown in talent and research reputation in good measure because of its capacity to attract the best in talent irrespective of national background.

The COVID-19 crisis and the anti-immigrant policies of the Trump Administration challenged these connections. When in July 2020 the US government sought to bar international students from entering or remaining in the United States, it was Harvard's president, Larry Bacow, who took the courageous lead in criticizing a "cruel and reckless" policy that would affect Harvard students from 155 countries.[105] Harvard and MIT filed a lawsuit that was supported by over two hundred universities across the United States.[106] A week later, the US government backed down.

At home, then, as much as abroad, Harvard's future depended on deepened internationalization. As Mark Elliott, the university's vice provost of international affairs, stated, "Our future is at stake. American higher education is the undisputed global leader because of our ability to attract hardworking and creative students and scholars from all over the world to our institutions. . . . Without international students in our institutions of higher learning, contributing to academic discourse, furthering the research enterprise, and driving the growth of new businesses and industries, we are collectively much, much less well-off."[107]

The opportunities and risks of international engagement were nowhere clearer than in relations with China. For decades, Harvard had a symbiotic relationship with China. From educating the country's leaders to supporting the modernization of Chinese universities through capacity building and training academics, Harvard's reach and reputation has been great within Chinese higher education. For example, Ji Chaozhu, who served as a bridge between the two countries, was born in China and grew up primarily in the United States. He attended Harvard (and would have graduated in the class of 1952) until the Korean War broke out; he returned home in 1950 and attended Tsinghua University. He served as an interpreter for China's leaders, including Mao Zedong and Deng Xiaoping. He was an indispensable interlocutor during Henry A. Kissinger's 1971 secret visit to Beijing, which laid the foundation for President Richard Nixon to become the first American president to visit mainland China.

Harvard had established the Harvard Medical School of China in 1911 (it failed after a few years) and did not return in an institutional way for nearly a century when in 2010 the Harvard Center Shanghai (HCS) was established. This initiative, led by HBS Dean Jay Light and me as chair of the Harvard China Fund under the Provost's Office, established a platform upon which all parts of the university could further their engagement with China through teaching, research, conferences, and internships.[108] HBS—again the university citizen—was the "anchor tenant" for this and other global initiatives. The opening of HCS in 2010 capped off Harvard's most international decade so far, with the establishment of a record eight international centers, to be followed by ten more in the next decade.[109]

If, as Drew Faust declared at the launch of HCS, we were "in a world of universities without borders," where better to expand than China? By 2020 every school at Harvard had active research and related programs in China and programs at HCS. Well over one hundred faculty members visited annually, and over two hundred listed China as a place of serious research. Over four hundred undergraduates had participated in the Harvard China Summer Internship Program and hundreds more in the Harvard Beijing Academy for advanced Chinese language work. Back home, Harvard was now home to close to one thousand Chinese students and scores of visiting Chinese scholars across the university each year. Bottom-up internationalization at Harvard still fit the entrepreneurial spirit of its schools, but HCS was a hub that accelerated their engagement in the fastest growing sector of higher education in the world.

Beginning with Rudenstine, who in 1998 was the first sitting Harvard president to visit mainland China, every Harvard president since has visited to meet with the country's head of state and speak at its top universities. During a visit in 2002, accompanied by thirteen Harvard faculty, Summers spoke at Tsinghua University and announced a program that would train Chinese civil servants at Harvard's Kennedy School.[110] Faust met with President Xi Jinping and spoke at Tsinghua University on the importance of US and Chinese universities working together to address climate change in March 2015.[111] In the first year of his tenure in March 2019, Larry Bacow met with President Xi and gave a major address at Peking University, where he emphasized that universities were places "where the value of an idea is discussed and debated—not suppressed or silenced."[112]

Increased international engagement, especially in China, could also translate into tension. In January 2020 the FBI knocked on the door of Harvard professor Charles Lieber, the chair of the university's chemistry department, as part of a crackdown on alleged academic espionage, claiming that Lieber received substantial funds from China (in part to set up a lab there) and lied about it.[113]

Lieber's arrest came at a time when a nativist US administration sought to limit foreign ties on the part of universities. In February 2020 the US Education Department opened federal investigations into Harvard and Yale to see if the universities failed to report at least $375 million from countries including China, Russia, and Saudi Arabia.[114] Harvard had endured one "Red Scare" in the McCarthy era of the 1950s. It would now need to defend itself from another.

## Harvard Extended and Online

Harvard had extended the reach of its education at home for more than a century through the Harvard Extension School, offering courses in evenings and summers, and enrolling some fourteen thousand students in 2020—more than any other Harvard school. The Extension School was the first at Harvard to venture into online learning, setting a foundation for a larger effort.

Harvard was no first-mover in recognizing the potential of massive, open, online courses, but in 2012 it hitched itself to the bandwagon of MIT, a pioneer in the field, to establish edX, an online platform offering free courses to the general public on a technological platform developed by MIT.[115] Harvard, MIT, and partner institutions used the platform to offer courses to learners around the world under their own "institutionX" brands (for example, HarvardX). As a nonprofit institution, edX offered its courses for free, with an option for students to pay for a course completion certificate.

By 2019 more than ninety institutions around the world had developed over twenty-four hundred courses for the edX platform, with more than seventy million students enrolled. Faculty from 10 Harvard schools developed 140 courses. My own course, "ChinaX," created with my colleague and then-Vice Provost for Advances in Learning, Peter Bol, explores three thousand years of Chinese history, culture, economy, and society in ten mini-courses, and it has had more than a half million participants, including tens of thousands in China.

By 2016 edX was recognized as one of the "Big Three" players in online course offerings but was the only nonprofit among them. Its financial future seemed uncertain. Unlike the Extension School, which collected tuition and paid faculty well for their teaching, HarvardX had no significant income to distribute in its first years. The first faculty who taught in it did so essentially as volunteers. Even for the best citizens in the faculty, this was not a sustainable approach, which is why the Harvard Business School set up its own "HBX" (today, Harvard Business School Online), with a real business model. In online learning as in other realms, there would be no "One Harvard." In 2021 MIT and Harvard sold edX to a private tech startup, 2U, Inc., and for the first time began to outsource their educational offerings. For the Harvard faculty who participated in it, edX proved to be useful basic training when the world of universities went suddenly and completely online with the onset of COVID-19 in 2020.

## The Next Big Thing: Harvard and Engineering

By the twenty-first century, Harvard was known for excellence in multiple fields: literary and historical studies, political science and the history of science, economics and ecological science, stem cell research, and human evolution. Its big professional schools of law, business, and medicine seemed without peer. No one could say that about Harvard engineering, however. Yet making a mark in engineering was Harvard's big, multi-billion dollar bet for the twenty-first century. This was a huge bet, not the least because there already existed a world-class engineering institute in Cambridge, Massachusetts, and it was not Harvard.

Engineering and the applied sciences had always struggled to have a defined place within the academic structures at Harvard. Applied scientific disciplines first became a part of Harvard with the founding of the Lawrence Scientific School (LSS) in 1847, upon the receipt of the first (but not last) precedent-shattering donation for engineering at Harvard—$50,000 from prominent Massachusetts industrialist Abbott Lawrence, grandfather of Harvard's twenty-second president, Abbott Lawrence Lowell. Despite well-funded beginnings, LSS "never fulfilled the expectation of its founders," particularly after the establishment of neighboring MIT.[116] President Eliot, himself a former professor at MIT, recognized the inability of LSS to compete with MIT. He made multiple unsuccessful attempts to combine the two.[117] In 1905, after a long courtship, the union was favored by the corporations of both institutions, but the marriage was never consummated.

Instead, LSS was broken up into various programs that were scattered around Harvard in different ways, including a graduate-focused Harvard Engineering School, until 1949, when all levels of engineering and applied sciences education were brought together as the Division of Engineering and Applied Sciences (DEAS) under FAS. Despite a significant endowment, the division struggled in the more pure science-focused Harvard for the next fifty years. It was joined at the hip to FAS, for half of its faculty held joint appointments in the FAS physical science departments. Virginia Postrel, a columnist for *Bloomberg*, noted, "Harvard has never been the Harvard—or even the University of Pennsylvania—of engineering."[118] Harvard's most famous alumni in engineering and applied sciences founded great companies— Edwin Land (Polaroid), Morris Chang (Taiwan Semiconductor), Bill Gates (Microsoft), and Mark Zuckerberg (Facebook)—but they never bothered to complete their degrees.

The previously underappreciated role of DEAS within Harvard, however, began to change rapidly in the early twenty-first century. The demands of the modern job market, as well as competition from MIT and a quickly rising Stanford, made it clear that, in the words of former Harvard College dean and former interim dean of the School of Engineering and Applied Sciences (SEAS) Harry Lewis, "Harvard could not be a great university in the 21st century if it didn't have a great engineering school."[119] In 2007 Harvard announced that DEAS would officially become SEAS, still under the umbrella of FAS and maintaining its strong commitment to a liberal arts education. This, the founding dean of SEAS, Venkatesh "Venky" Narayanamurti, noted, would produce "Renaissance engineers."

Between 2007 and 2016 the profile of SEAS within Harvard continued to grow. The number of undergraduate concentrators, Harvard's term for "majors," in SEAS nearly tripled in just eight years, growing from 291 in 2008 to 887 in 2016.[120] In the 2013–2014 school year, the number of SEAS concentrators surpassed that of Arts and Humanities concentrators for the first time.[121] By 2019 SEAS concentrators made up 20 percent of Harvard College students.[122] In fall 2014, 12 percent of all students at Harvard College were enrolled in what the *Harvard Crimson* called "as much a campus cultural phenomenon as a class": SEAS's Introduction to Computer Science I (CS50).[123] The next year, CS50 lectures were live streamed to Yale, whose undergraduates could enroll in the course as Introduction to Computing and Programming. Students from both schools participated in joint activities like hackathons, and Yale students even came to the Harvard campus to attend professors' office hours.[124] CS50 became (by far) the most popular course among Harvard's online offerings.

For all this effort, in 2020 Harvard's engineering program was still ranked number twenty-five nationally, compared to the number one ranking of that other institution down the Charles River.[125] Harvard's School of Engineering and Applied Sciences was a small school, about the size of Caltech, but Caltech was the only small engineering school to rank among the leaders. For the rest, size mattered.

In 2015 John A. Paulson, the billionaire hedge fund manager and HBS graduate, made his historic gift of $400 million to endow what is now known as the Harvard John A. Paulson School of Engineering and Applied Sciences. In under ten years, SEAS found itself newly named and endowed, with a new dean, Frank Doyle—the first engineer to head engineering at Harvard—new professorships, a skyrocketing number of students, and a new engineering complex under construction in Allston.

## Can Harvard Lead?

For nearly four hundred years, Harvard had been at the forefront of higher education in America, spurred on by healthy rivalries with an increasing number of outstanding American universities. Harvard's global standing, however, was a relatively recent development. With concerted efforts by governments around the world to establish "world-class" universities, would Harvard be able to maintain its status as a global leader?

By the third decade of the twenty-first century, challenges seemed everywhere. With its extraordinary and unmatched libraries, Harvard had led in the information technology of the nineteenth and twentieth centuries. No university was remotely close. But the digitization of books and journals leveled the playing field, and Harvard was not (yet) cutting edge in the next age of information technology.

Its domestic rivals—Yale, Princeton, Stanford, and Duke among them—were all much more centralized institutions, capable of thinking of the future as whole universities. Some of them even *planned* for their future in regular and rigorous ways. Harvard, with its strong schools and weak center, lacked either the capacity or the appetite for strategic planning across the university.

The story of the Allston land is a case in point. When it was announced in 2013, in a decisive move by Provost Alan Garber, that the Engineering School would relocate to Allston in substantial measure, the idea was publicly opposed, in oral and written statements, by all the senior associate deans of the school.[126]

I recall a blizzard of prospective plans for the Allston Promised Land in my time as dean and after. They foresaw a cross-river campus integrated by new pathways and bridges—one designed to be expanded like the Ponte Vecchio in Florence, adorned by shops on either side. There were plans for new modes of transport: train tunnels, monorails, and even canals, absent gondolas. In the most radical concept, the landmass of Harvard would be brought together like a modern Pangaea by moving the Charles River.

None of this happened. External planning czars for Allston came and went and came again. By 2018 Harvard finally decided to outsource Allston. It created the Allston Land Company to oversee construction of a thirty-six-acre commercial "enterprise research campus" separate from the academic enterprises of the engineering and science departments.[127] The future could not and would not be planned by Harvard alone, but in a series of prospective private partnerships. Business partnerships now mattered in the world of universities. The *Times Higher Education World University Rankings* saw Harvard drop steadily from number one in 2011 down to number seven in 2020. A central reason for this drop was the ranking's factor of "Industry Income."[128]

Harvard's competition was no longer primarily with Ivy League schools or even with great research centers such as the University of Chicago and Johns Hopkins. It was with MIT, Caltech, Cambridge, and, especially, Stanford. Much of Stanford's success has been attributed to its entrepreneurial culture, leading to an illustrious alumni base including the founders of several Fortune 500 companies such as Google, Nike, and HP. Doug Melton, a University Professor and the former faculty dean of Eliot House, remarked:

> Stanford is far and away Harvard's challenge. If I had to place money on it, I would bet on Stanford. . . . I would say that Stanford has a couple of advantages which are significant. One is, despite what we say here, Stanford feels unbound by tradition. They really don't worry so much. You would never hear people there saying, "I wonder what the alumni would think" or "what the corporation would think." They just don't think like that. Our job is to build the future. We are not honoring the past. The second thing is, and I'm sorry to say this but it's a fact of American life, money matters. There is an enormous amount of wealth that has come out of Stanford itself and for other reasons that is now located on the West Coast.[129]

President Larry Bacow was, by contrast, an optimist: "Allston will be Greater Boston's next epicenter of research, discovery, and innovation. . . . Its work will have a long-lasting impact on the development of our campus—and the broader community—and spark and shape future enterprises that will change the world in ways that none of us could predict."[130] As former chancellor of MIT, Bacow knew how strengthening ties to industry could have strong benefits to a university. Kendall Square, the neighborhood encompassing MIT, was once known as a "dustbowl" with rundown parking lots and old factories.[131] Over the decades, the neighborhood became one of the world's leader centers of biotechnology and attracted an influx of tech companies, including tech giants Google, Facebook, and Microsoft, transforming into a vibrant innovation hub that collaborated with MIT.

Matching the success of Kendall Square (or for that matter Palo Alto) would not be easy. Much time had been lost. The photos below show Kendall Square and Allston in earlier decades, when both were desolate; and Kendall Square and Allston today, when one is a leading global center of innovation and the other is, well, pretty much the same as it was.

In November 2017 there was a "topping-off" ceremony for the last steel beam of the new engineering and science building in Allston to be put into place.[132] The crane rose to place the beam, a moment decades in the making. Then the crane broke. There would be no topping off. The new engineering building was scheduled to open in fall of 2020. However, in spring 2020

**Figure 5.5.** Kendall Square in 1966. "Transportation Systems Center Construction Site at Kendall Square, Looking East," ca. 1966; Records of the Research and Innovative Technology Administration [Transportation], 1965–2002, Record Group 467; National Archives and Records Administration at Boston.

**Figure 5.6.** Kendall Square present day. Les Vants Aerial Photos.

**Figure 5.7.** Allston in 1929. Aero Scenic Airviews Co./Boston Pictoral Archive/Boston Public Library/CC BY-NC-ND.

**Figure 5.8.** Allston present day. Courtesy of Steve Dunwell.

another delay emerged in the form of the COVID-19 global pandemic. The opening of the building was postponed again to August 2021.[133] Harvard may not have topped off, but with luck it had bottomed out in Allston.

As the oldest university in the United States, Harvard reflects as well as any institution the country of its origin. Born of immigrants, it remade its identity on these shores, while continuing to import the best ideas and people from abroad. It carries a belief, like so many Americans, of the virtues of limited government, and as a result it has the smallest and least intrusive central administration of any major American university and is undistinguished in central planning. Its faculties and schools enjoy what used to be called "states' rights," and they defend their autonomy and (the rich ones) their endowments with tenacity. It is a place, like the contemporary United States, of real income inequality across its schools, even as its students are recruited from every sector of American life. Like the United States, it has enviable resources, and it manages to exhaust almost all of them. It is a place of unmatched academic entrepreneurialism, in the future perhaps matched ever more directly with entrepreneurs from the world of commerce. It has survived a revolution, a civil war, and multiple periods of domestic unrest, and it has shown a remarkable capacity for self-renewal. As the historian of higher education David Labaree has written, "Everyone wants to be Harvard."[134] But can this systemically decentralized Harvard continue to be the "Harvard" of the twenty-first century? It will need to, somehow, if it is to continue to lead the world of universities.

# CHAPTER SIX

# Public Mission, Private Funding

## *The University of California, Berkeley*

> We stand at a crossroads. At stake is not our existence, per se, but the idea that society as a whole benefits when access to a world-class education is based on merit, not privilege or financial circumstances; that the private sector must not be allowed to become the sole repository of excellence; that research conducted in the public's interest is distinct from inquiry driven by the pursuit of profit; and that the deep commitment to making the world a better place that animates our campus is no accident.
>
> —*Nicholas Dirks, Former Chancellor of the University of California, Berkeley*

CAROL CHRIST, chancellor of the University of California, Berkeley, approached the podium to give the Chancellor's Installation Speech in 2017. Since first arriving on campus in 1970, Christ had watched Berkeley change over the decades and was intimately familiar with the history, culture, and legacy of America's premier public university. The following year would be Berkeley's sesquicentennial, or 150th anniversary. She wondered what the founders of the university envisioned in 1868 and asked what that meant for a twenty-first century university. In her remarks she paraphrased the former Berkeley chancellor and system president, Clark Kerr: "Universities can aim no higher than to be as British as possible in regard to undergraduate education, for universities like Oxford and Cambridge offered the model for residential liberal arts colleges; as German as possible in regard to graduate education and research, for Germany had developed the model of the research university; and as American as possible in regard to the public at large." This, she argued, was "Berkeley's founding synthesis, and one important to keep in mind as we begin our second one hundred and fifty years." She continued her speech by looking ahead, where she saw a more challenging landscape: "We stand, I believe, at a moment of transformation as great as any in Berkeley's history. Given the decline in state support, we must reimagine the financial model for the campus."[1]

Christ's predecessor, Nicholas Dirks, had begun to make headway on Berkeley's structural deficit before his resignation on June 1, 2017. He had announced plans that would reduce a $150 million deficit by $85 million by that summer.[2] Unfortunately, as difficult as were the budgetary issues confronting the university, even greater challenges loomed in Dirks's departing shadow. For many of the factors that had brought Berkeley distinction were now among its most intractable weaknesses.

At its heart, Berkeley was a public university dedicated to offering the citizens of California a world-class education. The 1960 Master Plan for Higher Education in California laid out a division of labor for the state's public institutions that for many years coordinated the efforts of the University of California (UC) and California State University (CSU) campuses, along with many California community colleges. Berkeley's identity as an engine of upward social mobility for the people of California remained deeply ingrained in the ethos of the university's community, long driving and inspiring the work of its members.

However, after a period of rapid growth and demographic shifts, California now looked very different than it had when the Master Plan was written. The state, its citizens, and the Berkeley community struggled to balance the Berkeley ideal of equitable access and the pursuit of excellence in the context of dramatic demographic shifts and ethnic diversity. More important, unlike in the era when the Master Plan was adopted, the state had— like so many US states—massively disinvested in public higher education: forty-four out of fifty US states spent less per student in 2017 than in 2008.[3] Berkeley, the state's flagship institution, received only 13 percent of its budget from the state in 2020, compared to 50 percent in 1990.[4] (From 1919 to 1968 the state had provided 95 percent of Berkeley's budget.[5]) Frequent student protests on campus and pronouncements from the Regents, the UC system's governing board, fought against tuition hikes, limiting the tools at the Berkeley administration's disposal to address diminishing state funding. Beyond funding, remarks by former California Governor Jerry Brown, disparaging Berkeley because "ordinary, normal students" were "getting frozen out," pointed toward a diminished state commitment to Berkeley as an exceptional institution.[6] Brown's successor, Governor Gavin Newsom, indicated early in his tenure that he saw value in UC, initially proposing an increase in funding for 2020–2021. But after the 2020 outbreak of COVID-19, he instead slashed higher education spending by 10 percent.[7] And yet, Berkeley faculty and students largely still operated under an assumption of entitlement to public funding, even in the face of years of evidence of declining support. The public mission that had made Berkeley so exceptional during the good times of state support now constrained its responses to, or even its acknowledgement of, reality during bad times.

The passion and dedication of the faculty to the governance of Berkeley was another long-standing institutional strength. But as growing financial constraints required increasingly tough decisions about resource allocation, Berkeley's model of faculty participation in governance, through highly democratic and equally inefficient mechanisms, often impeded the university's leadership and its capacity to move forward.

The legacy of Berkeley's mission and model remained renowned and a source of envy and emulation at public institutions in other states. Now, however, would the enduring squeeze on Berkeley's budget force its history of greatness to recede into myth? With Berkeley so long the gold standard of public higher education in America, the eyes of state university presidents across the country would be trained on its response to the challenge of what it meant to be a privately funded, public university in the United States.

## From Gold Rush to Gold Standard

The stories of both the University of California system and its Berkeley campus begin with the story of the College of California—a small academic outpost in the newly formed state of California. Higher education was so valued by the residents of what became California that discussions explored building a university even before achieving statehood. Initially, private institutions such as the College of California, founded by Yale alumni and incorporated in 1855, served citizens' demands for higher education.

Seven years later, in 1862, the US government passed the Morrill Act, which incentivized state governments to develop public higher education institutions by offering public lands to states that would use them to found (or fund) the establishment of colleges for agriculture and mechanics. A wave of new institutions—the so-called land-grant universities, such as Purdue and Cornell—were established in states across the country under the auspices of this act. Californians were eager to take advantage of the federal program and to build the public university they had long desired. However, recognizing the value of the foundation—both literal and figurative—built by the College of California, it was decided that, on the condition that the new institution would include a college of letters and science in addition to colleges of agriculture and mechanics, the land grant institution could be built on the campus of the College of California. On March 23, 1868, this new science and letters-land grant hybrid was christened the University of California.

Since 1868 UC—then one campus and now eleven—has been led by a president under the direction of a Board of Regents, a leadership structure codified in the California State Constitution, ratified on May 17, 1879. Today, the Board of Regents is composed of twenty-six members, including eighteen members appointed to twelve-year terms by the governor of California, one student representative, and seven ex officio members, including the governor, the lieutenant governor, the speaker of the assembly, the state superintendent of public instruction, the president and vice president of the alumni associations of the University of California, and the president of the university.[8] From its early years, the Board of Regents helped foster UC's inclusive and diverse demeanor, allowing women to attend beginning in 1870 and welcoming international students in the same period as well.

For the first decade of its existence, UC struggled to forge an identity acceptable to both the letters and science-oriented Yale descendants and the Morrill Act-inspired agriculture and mechanics faction.[9] At this key moment, UC was led by one of several particularly consequential presidents: Daniel Coit Gilman. Initially, Gilman was excited by the prospect of building UC. Comparing UC to German and New England models, he remarked, "It is not the University of Berlin nor of New Haven which we are to copy . . . but it is the University of this State. It must be adapted to this people, to their public and private schools, to their peculiar geographical position, to the requirements of their new society and their undeveloped resources."[10] Gilman served as UC president for only three years (1872–1875), during which he was often frustrated by political and financial difficulties and after which he left to become the founding president of Johns Hopkins University, where he established the first graduate university on the Berlin model.[11] Still, during his short tenure, he managed to overcome the disagreements about the nature of UC, and he moved it in the direction of a comprehensive academic institution.

Even as a young institution, UC struggled with its relationship to the state government. When California held its second constitutional convention in 1878, an important item of discussion was university-government relations. Thanks in part to the disenchantment of the convention's delegates with the state legislature and in part to the impassioned defense of institutional autonomy for universities by delegate Joseph Winans, the 1878 California constitution established the university as an autonomous institution that was "entirely independent of all political or sectarian influence, and kept free therefrom in the appointment of its regents and in the administration of its affairs."[12] UC's institutional independence was in principle so complete that it was sometimes referred to as the fourth branch of the California state government.

Asserting institutional autonomy is one thing. Exercising it as a public university that is funded by the state is quite another. UC began to flourish under the presidency of Benjamin Ide Wheeler, who served the university from 1899 to 1919. Wheeler's tenure established the UC president as a strong, central leader, as he gradually convinced the regents to cede decision-making rights on certain issues to the Office of the President (OP). By the end of Wheeler's tenure, the UC president was in charge of faculty hiring decisions as well as budgeting. This amount of power lay in stark contrast to the powers of Wheeler's immediate predecessor, Martin Kellogg, whose major victory in expanding presidential power had been gaining the right to hire, fire, and regulate janitors.[13]

Wheeler studied at several of the top higher education institutions in Germany and received a PhD from the University of Heidelberg. Like so many of his contemporaries, he was heavily influenced and inspired by the German model of a comprehensive research university. It was under Wheeler's tenure that UC began to develop multiple academic disciplines as well as a stronger orientation toward research. When Edwin Slosson observed the university for his 1910 volume, *Great American Universities,* he found that the conflict between the College of California's academic orientation and the Morrill Act's practical orientation had largely been resolved: "I know of no other university which cultivates both mechanics and metaphysics with such equal success, or which looks so far into space, and, at the same time, comes so close to the lives of the people."[14] Slosson also lauded UC for its egalitarian student body, composed of learners from a wide range of economic and ethnic backgrounds.

Wheeler's transformative tenure was not unlike that of Eliot at Harvard. And he was not without critics. Wheeler exercised so much power as president that when he retired, the Academic Senate carried out Berkeley's first faculty revolt, demanding that more power over academic and faculty affairs be placed in the hands of the faculty themselves, through the Academic Senate. This concerted effort during a power vacuum after Wheeler's retirement resulted in the strengthening of the powers of the UC Academic Senate to such an extent that, even in 2016, the Berkeley Division of the Academic Senate was still among the most influential governing bodies of any American university. The legacy of faculty involvement in and responsibility for academic decision-making became a lasting hallmark of the UC system and a central, distinguishing feature of Berkeley's governance.

## Master Planning and Insurgent Students

Just as the post-Wheeler faculty revolution was taking place, California's dramatic growth allowed the University of California to grow from its founding campus in Berkeley to be a multi-campus system spanning the state. With the discovery of oil in the southern part of the state at the turn of the twentieth century, the population, wealth, and influence of Southern California expanded; regents from Southern California pushed to upgrade local institutions to become part of UC. In 1919 the southern branch of UC (later, UCLA) was formally established in Los Angeles, based on the foundation of the Los Angeles Normal School. With the addition of a new campus, the UC governance structure remained largely unchanged. It was still led by the Board of Regents and a president, whose office remained housed on the UC Berkeley campus. The president remained the administrator in control of both institutions.

Throughout the early twentieth century, Berkeley continued to grow, even as California's educational resources were distributed across a broader and broader range of state higher education institutions. The student population of UC grew from 2,600 in 1899 to over 12,000 in 1919.[15] With 14,061 students in 1923, the University of California (all campuses) was the largest university in the United States and the world.[16] This rapid expansion in institutional size did not dilute the quality of Berkeley as an institution; rather, its reputation rose as it grew in size. From the first appearance of national ratings and rankings of US universities in 1906 to the global university rankings of 2019, Berkeley was consistently near the top of the league tables.

## Clark Kerr

By the end of the Second World War, Berkeley and its sister UC campuses were well established and well regarded. Still, the extraordinary postwar boom—both in the population of the state of California and in the number of students seeking admission to UC institutions—made it clear that California needed a higher education system that was larger still and better organized. Fortunately for California, UC had just the man for such a monumental logistical and intellectual challenge. Clark Kerr had received his doctorate from and spent much of his subsequent career at Berkeley. In 1952 when the Board of Regents recognized that it was increasingly untenable for all UC campuses to be managed by a single central administrator, they established chancellorships at Berkeley and UCLA to share in the administrative burden. Kerr became the inaugural chancellor at Berkeley. His key duties began with defining his newly created role in the context of a UC president who was reluctant to relinquish control. Kerr slowly re-centered administration and decision-making at the campus, rather than the UC, level. Kerr's experience as chancellor confirmed his understanding of the need for administrative flexibility and authority at local campuses, and it informed his subsequent role as president of UC from 1958 to 1967. He moved to make the campuses more independent against the influence of the center and the professoriat more independent from the campus administration by initiating UC's first "continuous tenure" system, which was adopted by the Regents in December 1958.[17] He later noted that the gradual decentralization of power to each of the campuses was one of the great successes of the system, because it allowed campuses to compete with one another and thus all achieve a higher standard, rather than elevating one or two campuses to an elite status and leaving the rest to founder. That said, Berkeley—later joined by UCLA—was the flagship of the system, and, as Nicolas Dirks would discover, Kerr's successors as system presidents would at times try to reverse the decentralization of authority.

Of Kerr's many contributions to Berkeley and higher education in California, the best known was his leading role in the development of the 1960 Master Plan for Higher Education in California. Under the Master Plan, any qualified student, defined as any student who graduated from a California high school, would have access to three tiers of higher education. The top one-eighth of high school graduates would be admitted to a UC campus, while the top one-third would be guaranteed admission into the California State College (today, State University, or CSU) system, and the remaining graduates would have places in community colleges. The UC and CSU universities would reserve a significant number of spots in their junior classes for transfer students from the community colleges. By contrast, when Harvard admitted one transfer student from a community college in 2019, it was national news.[18] The state government and the administrators of the relevant institutions united behind this plan, which for many years served the state of California as a powerful engine for social mobility even as the state itself went through significant demographic shifts, with an increasing proportion of the state's growing population made up of minorities (particularly Asian and Latinx), and widening income inequality.[19] It is not an overstatement to say that, under Kerr, California developed the leading system of public higher education in the world.

## Lernfreiheit, *California Style*

In the latter half of the twentieth century, more than any other university in the United States, Berkeley became synonymous with political activism and unrest. While Berkeley's best-known political struggle was the student-led Free Speech Movement, which began in 1964, political unrest stirred the campus as early as 1949, when the anti-communist sentiment that had been building on university campuses and in government halls across the country led UC President Robert Sproul and the Board of Regents to require faculty to sign a loyalty oath. Faculty response to this requirement was swift and contentious, and it became, in Kerr's words, "the greatest single confrontation between a university faculty and its board of trustees in American history."[20] Of the sixty-nine politically motivated faculty dismissals at US universities during the McCarthy era, thirty-one occurred at UC.[21] The conflict inaugurated an extended period of tense relations and mistrust between the university faculty and administration.

This storm was followed by the Free Speech Movement of 1964 and after, in which students won rights of free expression that were guaranteed in the United States Constitution but, until then, not permitted at Berkeley or on most American college campuses. This inaugurated years of intense campus politicization, which—as in Berlin, Boston, and Beijing—pitted students against university and state administration. Perhaps because Berkeley was so clearly in the forefront of the American student movement, the counter-revolution came sooner there. In 1966 the actor Ronald Reagan ran for governor of California on a platform of quelling the "student revolt at Berkeley."[22] His election brought to power a state government at odds with Kerr's leadership. In 1967 Kerr was fired from the UC presidency. Kerr was a man known for his wit and frankness. (He once famously quipped, "I find that the three major administrative problems on a campus are sex for the students, athletics for the alumni, and parking for the faculty.")[23] When he left office, he recalled, "The fact was that I had left the presidency of the university as I had entered it: 'fired with enthusiasm'; my own on the way in, that of certain others on my way out."[24]

Kerr was ousted, but Berkeley, and the higher education system of California that Kerr did so much to advance, continued to follow the trajectory of growth that he had established in the Master Plan. Growth continued even through increasingly uneven levels of financial and political support from California's governors and despite the growing number of UC campuses that further divided the pie of state funding and reduced Berkeley's special place in the UC system. Through it all, Berkeley remained an elite university. The biggest logistical, financial, and existential challenge, however, was yet to come.

## Struggles for Survival

By 2008 Berkeley had been through many financial ups and downs, but—as at Harvard, but more enduringly—none of these experiences compared to the 2008 financial crisis. The implosion of US financial markets not only wreaked havoc on Berkeley's endowment, which dropped over 20 percent from $2.9 billion in 2007 to $2.3 billion in 2009, and pension investments, but also had an even greater, deleterious impact on the state of California's budget.[25] Given recent trends in California legislation that had seen increased amounts of dedicated funding for earmarked purposes, the UC budget was one of the few areas in which government funds were not precommitted. Facing a state budget crisis, the legislature passed brutal cuts on to the universities; in 2008 the UC system had to decrease its budget by 20 percent.[26]

Although universities across the country confronted significantly reduced endowments and investment returns, few faced as severe a burden of funding loss as the UC campuses, which were hit both by the crash of their own investments and by the sudden elimination of much state funding. Berkeley found itself doing everything from cutting library hours and implementing faculty and staff furloughs to reducing new faculty positions by 90 percent to align expenses with a greatly diminished budget.[27] University departments around the country began to circle the Berkeley faculty, believing the time had finally come to poach academic stars from the institution.

Robert Birgeneau, Berkeley's chancellor from 2004 to 2013, did remarkably well in an impossible situation. He had to decide how to manage a world-class institution facing crises on almost every front. Former Executive Vice Chancellor and Provost George Breslauer recalled Birgeneau's fortitude: "He said he's never played defense in his life, and he didn't intend to come here and play defense. He told us, 'Go for it. We've got to come out of this with glory.'"[28]

Birgeneau and Breslauer approached their decimated budget strategically. Berkeley had never been as strong in financial management as, for example, Duke, because in the past it had not needed to. Even before the onset of the crisis, Birgeneau had taken groundbreaking steps toward the professionalization of financial management on the campus by hiring Nathan Brostrom, former J. P. Morgan Managing Director, as vice chancellor for administration in 2006.

Birgeneau also strengthened the financial holdings of the center of the university by directing funds received to endow a chair partially back to the center: 50 percent of the yield from chair endowments would return to the university budget in support of the chair faculty member's salary. This was a big symbolic step for Berkeley, where chairs had long been deemed the responsibility of the state to fund. While at other universities, such as Harvard, the income from an endowed chair would be returned entirely to the school administration, named chairs at Berkeley historically supported only the research, not the salary, of a professor.

Even the best financial management could not print money. Prior to the crisis, Breslauer had been responsible for allocating the Provost's office budget of about $45 million. Of this total budget, around $5 million served as a discretionary fund, which he used to support various projects across the university, such as new faculty positions. He recalled, "After the financial collapse of 2008, the fun was over." Determined to approach his budgeting strategically, Breslauer refrained from making uniform cuts across the campus. Rather, he evaluated all the units reporting to him using an extensive set of criteria, then stratified them into four tiers and made different kinds of cuts to each tier. Breslauer completed most of this process himself: "The crash was so severe and the cut from the state was so severe that . . . time just didn't seem to be on our side, and one thing I know about committees is that they take forever." Still, he focused on transparency and consultation, in the hope that, while painful, the cuts he proposed would have "credibility and legitimacy."[29]

By most accounts, Birgeneau's crisis management strategy, including professionalization of finance, strategic allocation of resources, and belated but concerted fundraising efforts through a capital campaign and pursuit of major grants and competitions, succeeded initially. At the worst point of the crisis, Berkeley lost fourteen faculty members in one year but quickly returned to its traditionally strong faculty retention rate and gradually found itself on steadier footing.[30]

It was with a spirit of optimism, then, that Birgeneau's successor, Nicholas Dirks, came to Berkeley in 2013. His was a distinguished record of scholarship and academic leadership; he had served as executive vice president for the arts and sciences and dean of the faculty at Columbia University. When he began his chancellorship, still in the aftermath of the global financial crisis of 2008, Berkeley was beginning to find firm enough footing to dedicate serious time and energy to thinking about its strategy for the future. The financial picture remained challenging, but Berkeley had endured. Dirks recalled, "There was a sense that the place had survived and now everybody could get back to work."[31]

Given freedom to set an agenda, Dirks focused on three strategic priorities: the undergraduate experience, interdisciplinary initiatives, and global partnerships. A team of administrators reviewed ways to enhance undergraduate life, not just in the classroom but also through stronger residential programs and campus activities. Interdisciplinary initiatives such as a data science initiative and the Social Science Matrix—an institute for cross-disciplinary social science research—promoted cooperation across departments and worked against departmental isolation. Global partnerships, as exemplified by a new Global Campus, would strengthen Berkeley's cooperation with institutions around the world. Yet, by his third year in office, Dirks found himself caught in an increasingly small space between an unsupportive governor, an active UC system president, and an engaged (and sometimes enraged) faculty.

## The Crisis of Berkeley's "New Normal"

Springtime was historically a time of protest on the Berkeley campus. The spring of 2016 would prove no exception. True, the university had survived the 2008 crisis and, with Dirks's appointment, appeared reinvigorated and ready to innovate. Berkeley was still home to 170 academic departments and programs housed in fourteen colleges and schools, attended by 27,000 undergraduate and 10,000 graduate students, led by 1,620 full-time faculty. But its state funding was now at just 57 percent of its 2007 level. Dirks launched a strategic planning initiative in February 2016 to finally confront what had become a permanent structural deficit. Dirks noted that "some of the changes we will undergo will be painful," but he concluded that these changes would in no way be "an abandonment of our commitment to a public mission." Rather, a transformed Berkeley would, he believed, embody "a fundamental defense of the concept of the public university, a concept that we must reinvent in order to preserve."[32]

But the optimistic tone of Dirks's announcement was at odds with an unpleasant reality: Berkeley was indeed playing defense. Moreover, the structural deficit Berkeley faced was not simply the result of the diminution of state spending. The deficit now approached $150 million as a result of the university's huge capital expenditures outside the academic realm. These included the rebuilding of California Memorial Stadium, home to Berkeley's football games. The complex relationship between athletics, fundraising, and funding was divisive on many American university campuses, and Berkeley was no exception.

California Memorial Stadium, built in 1922, is a wonderful, neoclassical structure. Unlike Harvard, Berkeley in the twenty-first century was still determined to play ball with the big guys and was a member of the PAC-12, one of the premier conferences in intercollegiate sports ("athletics for the alumni," as Clark Kerr said). The problem was that the stadium sat directly on top of the Hayward Fault, which made it susceptible to devastating earthquakes. The initial cost of retrofitting the stadium to make it safe was put at

$14 million. The budgeted cost in 2010 was $445 million, to be paid for in debt, initially to be financed by the selling of special seats—so good would "Cal football" be in a new stadium. But Cal football, despite producing great quarterbacks like Aaron Rodgers and Jared Goff, was never *that* good. The team was 1–11 in 2013, and it has lost as many games as it has won since the stadium's rebuilding. The seats didn't sell, and in 2012 the *Wall Street Journal* estimated that Berkeley's total financial obligation for the stadium would likely exceed $1 billion.[33] It was estimated that Berkeley would not even begin to pay off the principal on the loans associated with the stadium until 2032.[34] Fundraising and spending related to athletics were continued irritants between the faculty, which largely opposed them, and the administration.

But the stadium was now a sunk cost, and no state funds supported it. So strategic planning at Berkeley would have to include significant strategic cutting elsewhere. There was no other way. Dirks established Berkeley's first Office of Strategic Initiatives (OSI) to lead and coordinate this painful process.

Despite the efforts that began in Birgeneau's time, serious, cross-campus, strategic planning had never been Berkeley's practice or culture. Now it was an emergency measure. The process proved to be painful indeed, and

**Figure 6.1.** California Memorial Stadium. Kilfmuny/Wikimedia Commons/ CC BY-SA 4.0.

it reawakened faculty activists in the Academic Senate who continued to believe in the mission of Berkeley as a publicly funded institution (and the Senate's central role in guiding it) even in an era in which the state had effectively abdicated its role as funder. Never mind that the Academic Senate itself, with its long history of academic activism, was an enormous body which included every rank of faculty from instructors to professors emeriti (even retired colleagues could vote) and was in no position to undertake serious planning.

At the same time, another tempest arose. The overdue explosion against widespread sexual harassment that roiled tens of American campuses in 2015–2016 also led to strenuous conflict at Berkeley. The campus became embroiled in numerous harassment allegations, including several against prominent administrators and professors. In one case, when chemist Graham Fleming resigned from his position as vice chancellor for research after allegations of harassment were made by his assistant in April 2015, over one hundred faculty members signed a letter in support of Fleming and in critique of the investigatory process led by OP.[35] Fleming was subsequently appointed to a less conspicuous administrative role overseeing the development of global alliances for the Berkeley Global Campus. In March 2016, however, in an extraordinary step, UC President Janet Napolitano publicly overruled the chancellor and all but ordered Dirks to fire Fleming—who still enjoyed the support of his faculty colleagues—from his remaining administrative posts.[36]

Meanwhile, as Berkeley's administration began to move forward with the strategic planning process, faculty and staff anger grew over the perceived top-down nature of Dirks's initiatives. He had promised that his administration would avoid the lack of staff consultation that had led to faculty criticism of Birgeneau's crisis planning.[37] But "consultation" with the Academic Senate leadership, which advised the chancellor to keep discussion to small groups, would prove the death of Dirks's planning.

Suddenly other attacks against Dirks began. The construction of a $700,000 fence around the chancellor's residence on the Berkeley campus had begun in response to serious security concerns. Yet it drew widespread criticism, including a letter from the Academic Senate, for not being in keeping with Berkeley's open culture. But the house, sitting right at the edge of the campus, and thus an easy target for assault from inside or outside the university, was otherwise defenseless. Even this fence was more symbolic than secure; it would not keep out anyone who was determined to get in. The house had been subject to repeated, sometimes violent, demonstrations under Dirks's predecessors. During the tenure of former Chancellor Chang-

**Figure 6.2.** $700,000 fence around the chancellor's residence. Photograph © William C. Kirby.

Lin Tien, an armed woman forced her way into the residence and was shot and killed by police.[38] Still, Dirks, whose office in California Hall was at the center of the campus and a ten-minute walk from the residence, was pilloried for "fencing himself off" from Berkeley.

At the central level, Dirks's administrative team began to crumble in the face of public faculty attacks. In April 2016 Executive Vice Chancellor and Provost Claude Steele—the only senior executive whom Dirks had recruited from the outside—was criticized for his handling of another sexual harassment case. He announced his immediate resignation, followed days later by the announcement that Vice Provost of Strategic Academic and Facilities Planning Andrew Szeri would resign at the end of June 2016.[39]

Facing a furiously energized faculty with an increasingly thin administrative team reduced by resignations, retirements, and reshuffling, Dirks took to the podium at the spring meeting of the Academic Senate. "This has been a very deeply challenging year here at Berkeley," he began. "And I want to acknowledge that. I also want to assure you all, as members, as colleagues in the Academic Senate, that I've been hearing your concerns and I've been hearing your advice. . . . I appreciate the urgency with which you have offered both, and I am today resetting our strategic efforts in several fundamental dimensions."[40]

Dirks went on to announce a series of measures that diminished central power and strengthened faculty leadership, including the dissolution of his newly established Office of Strategic Initiatives, curtailment of the centralized Campus Shared Services program (a widely acknowledged failure begun under Birgeneau's administration), and an increased role for the Academic Senate in academic and financial planning.[41] He also announced plans for his office to be more directly involved with the handling of sexual harassment case findings.

Still, none of this academic politicking did anything to solve Berkeley's enduring financial and organizational challenges, nor did it save Dirks from being the convenient target of resentment in the community. Berkeley was broke. Dirks was willing to admit it. His unusual openness to discussing Berkeley's deficit and his willingness to put anything on the table had made him a lightning rod for discontent in an era of high faculty anxiety and insecurity. Dirks finally had had enough. On August 16, 2016, Chancellor Dirks notified UC President Napolitano that he intended to resign. In doing so, this Berkeley outsider honored one of Berkeley's oldest traditions: Daniel Gilman, the second UC president and one of Berkeley's most influential early leaders, also ended his term after just three years, "beset by financial difficulties and political harassment."[42] Dirks's two immediate predecessors, both, like him, recruited from the outside, had left office after some measure of faculty discontent as well.

## Governing Chaos and Disinvestment

Berkeley's ongoing Kulturkampf—not unlike that of the contemporary Humboldt University with its revolving-door presidencies—was rooted in part in its higher participatory governance structure. On the Berkeley campus itself, governance was shared between the senior administration, led by the chancellor, and Berkeley's uniquely strong Academic Senate. One faculty member noted, "The Academic Senate's role in everyday affairs is rather supreme . . . [it] has really total control of the curriculum and ninety-five percent control over all hiring, promotions, and advancements."[43] Formally a division of the UC Academic Senate, the Berkeley Academic Senate took its role "more seriously than [comparable institutions] anywhere else in the country."[44] Although the full Academic Senate was normally convened only a few times per year, forty Senate committees were organized by eight elected faculty members on (what else?) the Committee on Committees.

Of course, Berkeley was a campus within a larger university system, and thus the campus-level administrative structures made up only one of two tiers of governance, the other being the UC system-wide governance. The UC system had its Board of Regents, but unlike Harvard and Duke, the flag-ship Berkeley campus had no governing board of its own, limiting the chancellor's sources of advice and support. The president of the UC system was supposed to serve as the advocate for all the campuses vis-à-vis the state government. OP, therefore, was responsible for both negotiating with the state for funding and disbursing the funding to the ten campuses. The pres-ident also retained control over senior administrator compensation. If Dirks needed to recruit a new member for his administration, he first had to ne-gotiate the compensation offer with UC President Napolitano. Other impor-tant issues that fell under the mandate of OP included setting tuition and the ratio of in-state to out-of-state students. The state could therefore dic-tate the intake of students and limit Berkeley's capacity to charge them. Dirks noted, "You have to get approval from OP for many, many things that would seem to be within the discretion of any president of a private university."[45]

The work and success of the president of the UC system—and, by exten-sion, of Berkeley—were influenced also by the priorities of the governor of California. Breslauer recognized support from governors as one of the five main factors that historically had allowed Berkeley to achieve institutional eminence. He further argued that throughout the history of the state, with the famous exception of Reagan, governors chose to support Berkeley in dif-ficult times because of the persuasive leadership of the UC president.[46] After continued and nearly disastrous state disinvestment in the university, some hoped that the 2013 appointment of Napolitano, a former governor of Arizona, might help UC to have a stronger relationship with the governor. Napolitano and then-governor Jerry Brown began to work together closely, in what was referred to as "CO2," short for Committee of Two. One former administrator hoped that Napolitano could "stand up to [Governor Jerry Brown] and speak to him in his own terms and exercise power in a way that an academic in that position [would have trouble doing] unless you had a Clark Kerr."[47] (In August 2020 the former president of Ohio State Univer-sity, Michael V. Drake, succeeded Napolitano and became the UC's first Black president, giving California another leader with experience managing university-state relations elsewhere.)

Nonetheless, even as the state recovered from the Great Recession and re-filled its treasury, state support for UC showed only the most modest annual increases. Taking inflation and increased enrollment into account, state support had been halved over the past decades. During the 1990–1991 fiscal year, state funding for UC averaged $19,929 per student, or 78 percent of total education expenditures. From 2017–2018, state support was a mere $7,730 per student, or 37 percent of education expenditures.[48]

Gradual state disinvestment throughout the 1990s and early 2000s, followed by a steep drop in state funding in 2008, resulted in a University of California that was public in mission but not in primary funding. The passage of Proposition 30 in 2012, which approved increased personal income taxes to prevent cuts in the state education budget, indicated a potentially renewed interest of the California citizenry in funding education, and by 2013 Berkeley seemed headed toward more stable financial footing.[49]

The Berkeley 2013–2014 budget plan proposed revenues of about $2.35 billion and expenses of around $2.14 billion, with an additional $240 million in account fund balance transfers for debt service and capital investment.[50] The Berkeley administration had limited options to increase revenue—the Regents had committed to freezing student tuition (28 percent of Berkeley's revenue) in exchange for a slight increase in state support, which at that time provided 14 percent of revenue. Federal government contracts and grants, as well as other contracts and grants and nonoperating revenue, represented a further 32 percent of revenue that was not mutable by any action of Berkeley. Altogether, this meant that 73 percent of total revenue was constrained. If Berkeley were to need to cover increased costs—and it could expect regular, incremental increases in operating costs such as health care plan payments, facilities maintenance, and more—these would have to be financed through nongovernmental, nontuition sources of revenue, such as private philanthropy or corporate partnerships. "Time is not on our side," John Wilton, the Vice Chancellor of Administration and Finance, warned: in the absence of a concerted effort to shore up these revenue sources, Berkeley would face an unsustainable operating deficit.[51]

Berkeley began to explore new funding pathways. In a speech at the Times Higher Education World Academic Summit, Dirks expressed his commitment to increasing the engagement of the private sector in partnering with and funding public higher education institutions.[52] Berkeley already had a history of such partnerships, although they were often initially fraught with concern over how to maintain academic freedom in the face of corporate interests. The 2007 announcement of the Energy Biosciences Institute, a joint new energy technology research project between Berkeley, British Petroleum (BP), the University of Illinois at Urbana-Champaign, and Lawrence Berkeley National Laboratory, funded by an initial $500 million commitment from BP, initially drew fierce criticism from the faculty.[53] Similar controversy surrounded a partnership between Novartis and Berkeley's Department of Plant and Microbiology from 1998 to 2003.[54] Private sector partnerships were possible, but they were met routinely with skepticism on the part of vocal faculty members.

## A Nondevelopment State

Dirks had inherited an institution with a terrible record of private fundraising. None of the UC campuses, Berkeley in particular, had been prepared to wean themselves from the state as had other leading public universities, such as the University of Wisconsin or the University of Michigan, which in the early 1960s was the first public university to launch a large fundraising campaign. Within California, UCLA regularly outfundraised Berkeley, and both of these institutions fell far behind the University of Wisconsin-Madison, which raised an average of 31 percent more than Berkeley every year from 2008 to 2018.[55] While as a research university Berkeley regularly ranked among the top five universities in the world, it seldom was among the top twenty universities in the United States for fundraising. In reflecting on Berkeley's financial situation, Dirks stated, "I came to a university that was thirteen percent funded by the state. I'm not privatizing. *It has been privatized.*"[56]

The good news was how much room there was for improvement. After all, Berkeley was located in one of the wealthiest urban areas in the world. And while its alumni, like their alma mater, were known for their social consciousness, that had not stopped many of them from becoming enormously rich. A 2019 study ranked Berkeley's alumni base as the twelfth wealthiest of any university based on aggregate wealth of ultra-high net worth alumni, and a 2014 report found that Berkeley undergraduates had produced the eighth most billionaires among undergraduate alumni.[57] Based in the Bay Area, near the heart of Silicon Valley, Berkeley and its alumni were well placed to participate in the lucrative technology industry, and the alumni did so in droves. These statistics drive home that old adage about fundraising: Why do people give? Because they are *asked*. And if, as in Berkeley's case, you haven't asked, you haven't received.

Dirks therefore sought to enhance private giving, especially from alumni. In the 2016 academic year, Dirks led Berkeley to raise almost $480 million from nearly 100,000 gifts made by over 65,000 donors—new Berkeley records both for total amount raised and number of gifts. The new level of fundraising represented significant efforts to engage a wide variety of donors. Initiatives such as the "Big Give"—a 24-hour fundraising blitz timed to coincide with the "Big Game," that is, the annual football match between Berkeley and Stanford—appealed to a broad donor base. At the same time, Berkeley's fundraising operation also targeted larger gifts, recording a record number of gifts of over $1 million from 2015 to 2016.[58]

Dirks's successor, Chancellor Carol Christ, built on this momentum by publicly launching Berkeley's largest capital campaign ever in 2020. Begun quietly under Dirks in 2014, the "Light the Way" campaign's priorities included "expanding faculty and graduate student fellowships; improving the undergraduate experience; supporting multidisciplinary research initiatives aimed at solving the grand challenges of our time; and building better facilities for housing, athletics, and teaching and research."[59] Its launch event included the announcement of an anonymous $252 million gift, the largest in university history, toward the construction of a complex for Berkeley's Computing, Data Science, and Society division.[60] After the conclusion of the 2019–2020 fiscal year, Christ announced that Berkeley had raised $1.04 billion dollars, its most successful fundraising cycle ever.[61] But decades of overreliance on the state and neglect of its potentially philanthropic alumni meant that Berkeley was still playing catch-up. In 2019 Berkeley's combined endowment of private and public funds, worth $4.8 billion, was just a bit more than one-third of the University of Michigan's $12.4 billion endowment.

The Operational Excellence (OE) program was another effort to bridge Berkeley's funding gap. Launched under Birgeneau's chancellorship, the program focused on finding new ways to streamline administrative costs without sacrificing operational quality, with the ultimate goal of saving $75 million in operating costs annually. OE sought to meet this goal through projects like stronger campus-wide initiatives in budgeting and procurement, the creation of new online administrative tools to make important information accessible to students and faculty, and the centralization of administrative support. The OE program also included a Revenue Generation Program, through which OE program office staff worked with various campus units to launch revenue-generating projects that would also support academic goals.[62] The program, however, met with frosty faculty reception. Although John Wilton recognized the significant cost savings made through OE, faculty and staff remained suspicious of how the program determined layoffs.[63]

Wilton warned, "Expenses cannot be cut to balance the books without lasting impact on both the access to higher education and the standards achieved. The very metrics that we want to improve—time to degree, how many students graduate, debt levels, etc.—will worsen. Something has to happen on the revenue side as well as the cost side. There is no other real solution."[64] But neither state funding nor the aspirations of external fundraising had proven to be close to enough.

## Cultures of Excellence and Rebellion: Faculty and Students

Berkeley's long-term investment in faculty hiring meant that the campus had a dedicated body of scholars that produced world-renowned research. In 2021 Berkeley boasted a faculty that included ten active Nobel laureates, thirty-three MacArthur Fellows, one Fields Medal winner, four Pulitzer Prize winners, three A. M. Turing Award winners, 251 fellows of the American Academy of Arts and Sciences, and 144 members of the National Academy of Sciences.[65]

(A quick detour on parking: Clark Kerr had noted, rightly, that parking was an obsession with the faculty, and Berkeley was physically constrained in this area. How then to reward the most distinguished faculty? Berkeley has had twenty-two Nobel laureates among its faculty. Initially, Berkeley rewarded the Nobel winners with a new lab, or even a new building. That got expensive. Today, Nobel laureates receive neither a lab nor a building, but they do get their own dedicated parking spot on campus, marked with "NL." At this writing, it seems that there are many more "NL" parking spots on campus than there are Nobel laureates to use them, but perhaps that is just good marketing.)

A hallmark of Berkeley was the high level of faculty engagement and autonomy in driving the campus forward. Since 1919 the Academic Senate was responsible for the oversight and approval of faculty hiring, a process that involved input from many colleagues and which was taken very seriously. Dirks noted, "When [faculty] have a job search, they all read the work

**Figure 6.3.** Nobel laureate parking signs. Jose Camões Silva / flickr / CC BY 2.0.

together. They go to the job talks. It is really not just a collegial but a collective investment in trying to make these decisions."[66] Clark Kerr had credited many of the outstanding research achievements of Berkeley to the thorough and consultative hiring process administered by the Senate.[67]

Berkeley's hiring practices at the assistant professor level were among the most rigorous in the nation, perhaps in part because finances mitigated against the recruitment of external senior faculty. One result was that a large percentage of the faculty was promoted to tenure from within. Approximately 80 percent of assistant professors who joined Berkeley between 1985 and 2011 in the humanities, social sciences, physical sciences, engineering, technology, and mathematics ultimately achieved tenure.[68] Once they made it through the hiring process, faculty members were likely to remain at Berkeley. Berkeley faculty were notoriously difficult to lure away to work at other institutions, even when other institutions were able to offer significantly higher salaries. Birgeneau noted, "During the darkest days, our retention went up. . . . It was the best period for retention, when the largest number of our faculty had offers from private universities."[69] A senior administrator recalled:

[A professor] was making $150,000 base salary...Duke offered him $450,000 to leave Berkeley and come there....The dean brought him into my office, and we tried to talk sense to him. What we said to him was, "You have to understand there's no way we're going to even come close to what Duke is offering you... what number are you willing to settle for?" And I said, "Make sure it doesn't start with a three or a four." That's when he realized that if he was not careful about what he said, we might just let him go.[70]

Faculty and administrators at Berkeley could point to several reasons why the university was able to have such strong retaining power. First and foremost was the sense of camaraderie, equality, and responsibility among faculty members. Dirks found that faculty "wanted to stay here for reasons having to do with colleagues more than anything else . . . they find the depth and the kind of ethos of thought of their colleagues incomparable."[71] Unlike Harvard, with its historically huge social distance between senior faculty and everyone else, Berkeley made assistant professors colleagues.

Another reason was the dedication on the part of the faculty to Berkeley's public, social mission. Breslauer noted, "Some of [the faculty's desire to stay] comes from the sense and satisfaction about being a public university, and certainly an engine of upward mobility." Part of the appeal of this public mission was getting to work with students from a wide variety of socioeconomic backgrounds, including Berkeley's many first-generation college students and students from families with low incomes. Breslauer added, "When you ask most faculty, 'Why do you stay here?' they say, 'My colleagues, my students. I love them.'"[72]

This dedication could be a double-edged sword. Berkeley reaped the benefits of nurturing young scholars through the tenure process and maintaining their loyalty throughout their careers. This process produced faculty members who were proudly committed to Berkeley's culture but also inward looking. They could be suspicious of leaders hired from other institutions. As Dirks would discover, administrators who had not spent their careers at Berkeley were accused of "not really get[ting] what Berkeley is all about."[73]

While Berkeley excelled at retaining faculty, financial constraints had made hiring faculty difficult. From the early 1990s to 2018 the number of tenured faculty had stayed almost completely flat, falling to 1,133 in 2018 from 1,147 in 1993. During the same twenty-five-year period, the student population increased from just over 30,000 to 45,183.[74] The university increasingly relied on lower-ranked, non-tenured, non-tenure-track lecturers, whose numbers increased sevenfold from 54 in 1993 to 379 in 2018. At the same time, student demands for levels of service commensurate with the increasingly high tuition costs grew, as did political demands for regulatory compliance. University staff expanded to meet the demands of this changing environment—full-time administrative and managerial staff doubled from 306 in 1993 to 638 in 2011. By 2018 the staff in university management, business and financial operations, and office and administrative support occupations totaled nearly 3,000.[75] Thus, while the total number of tenured faculty had remained constant, they were becoming a smaller proportion of overall university employees. To some faculty, this seemed like a fundamental shift in the nature of the university.

Even the best faculty members have their limits. The faculty attacks on the university's leadership seem in retrospect less about their targets than a reflection of the combination of anger and insecurity that by 2010 had come to mark the faculty of America's premier public university. I noticed this firsthand when I chaired an external review committee of Berkeley's Institute of East Asian Studies. I had done this before, and with pleasure, because this institute, together with Harvard's Asia Center, was one of the two leading centers of East Asian studies in the United States and indeed in the world. It had a long and continuing history of distinguished faculty leadership. Like almost all such transregional operations, there were built-in tensions, as the study of each country reflected its status: thus China studies was overpopulated with faculty, compared to others, and under resourced, while Japanese studies was rich, but with few faculty members to spend its money on, and Korean studies was simply ignored until recently. Still, the institute was world renowned. With the enduring budget crisis after 2008, however, something seemed to snap.

When I visited in 2011–2012, in contrast to earlier visits, I found a faculty fatigued, fearful, and at the edge of civil war. Our report noted that we were at a time of "deep austerity and high anxiety across the Berkeley campus" that (and this was a big understatement) "tested the limits of collegiality" within the faculty. Our review of salaries showed how poorly paid were the excellent Berkeley faculty compared to their comrades elsewhere. And the esprit de corps that had once defined an underpaid but mission-driven faculty was gone. People were bitter and backbiting. They indulged in conspiracy theories ("there is money hidden away that *they* are not telling us about") both about the administration and their own colleagues. They believed the worst, not the best, about the motives of others. They believed things that were demonstrably not true. This, it struck me, was a great program and a great university, both in existential crisis.[76] My experience in the Institute of East Asian Studies can surely be multiplied many times across the campus over the past decade.

For a large and seemingly impersonal research university, it is refreshing to note that one of Berkeley's enduring strengths is its student body. The students at Berkeley have consistently stood out from their public university peers in terms of both excellence and diversity. Berkeley's overall graduation rate also stood out favorably compared with its public peers. By 2019 Berkeley undergraduates had a four-year graduation rate of 75.8 percent, up from 66 percent in 2008. This figure is comparable to the rate at the University of Michigan-Ann Arbor (79 percent), and well above that of the University of Wisconsin-Madison (62 percent) and the University of Texas-Austin (61 percent).[77] From 2012 to 2015 Berkeley had both the highest cumulative number of undergraduate program alumni receiving National Science Foundation (NSF) fellowships for graduate study as well as the highest number of graduate students on NSF fellowships.[78]

Earlier and better than any US private university, Berkeley demonstrated a strong commitment to helping a socioeconomically and ethnically diverse student community access its excellent undergraduate education. In 2018, 8,684 Berkeley undergraduates received Pell Grants, within throwing distance of all eight Ivy League institutions combined (11,001) and almost eight times as many as at local rival Stanford. These 8,684 students represented 28 percent of all Berkeley undergraduates, in comparison with the 1,133 Pell Grant recipients at Stanford who represented just 16 percent of that university's undergraduate population.[79] Berkeley was the first public university to have a comprehensive financial aid plan for middle-income students, as well as the first university, public or private, in the United States to offer comprehensive financial aid to undocumented students. In 2020, 23 percent of Berkeley freshmen were first-generation college students.[80] In 2019 underrepresented minorities made up 19.4 percent of the undergraduate population.[81] Berkeley even had a comprehensive support program for former foster children. In 2020 Christ also announced that Berkeley had committed to becoming a Hispanic-Serving Institution (HSI), a U.S. Department of Education designation, which meant that at least a quarter of its full-time enrolled students were Hispanic.[82]

Berkeley's students, like the Berkeley faculty, were distinguished also by what some called their "insurgent citizenship." It was students, after all, who had led the Free Speech Movement in the 1960s, and the student body remained vocal about various campus and social causes into the twenty-first century. Toward the end of the 1960s, Berkeley was home to some of the first nationwide protests that evolved into the establishment of ethnic studies departments across the United States. After the creation of the Third World Liberation Front (TWLF), a coalition of African American, Latin American, Asian American, and Native American students, at neighboring San Francisco State University in 1968, minority students at Berkeley created their own TWLF in early 1969.[83] The TWLF demanded the creation of a "Third World College" to create academic departments geared toward students of color. After ten weeks of strikes, the Academic Senate voted with a significant majority to establish an Ethnic Studies Department on the campus.[84] Berkeley's student activism reverberated across the country to Duke, where President Nannerl Keohane would later allude to the events at Berkeley as a precursor to the creation of Duke's Black Studies Department in 1969, and later its Latino/a and Asian American Studies programs.[85]

The call for shifts in curricula was not the only cause for student advocacy. A growing chorus of student protests against tuition hikes and budget cuts that began in 2009 culminated in a dramatic student "occupation" of Berkeley's Sproul Plaza in November 2011. Chancellor Birgeneau's handling of the incident recalled that of Nathan Pusey at Harvard, academic generations earlier. Birgeneau called on police, who used aggressive physical confrontation to break up the one-thousand-person demonstration, drawing even more protests and calls for his resignation.[86]

**Figure 6.4.** 2009 Sproul Plaza protest. Steve McConnell/UC Berkeley, © 2009 UC Regents.

Like their faculty mentors, the more politically active Berkeley students were deeply invested in the culture of their institution and their role in maintaining it. After years of student advocacy, several buildings were renamed because students alleged that their original namesakes perpetuated racist views. One notable building with a revoked name was Boalt Hall. Its nineteenth-century namesake, John Boalt, had called for the halt of Chinese immigration in the United States and espoused racist beliefs against Blacks and Native Americans. This was a big step because the term "Boalt Hall" had long been the de facto name of Berkeley's law school, and that was how it was known.

Dirks made improvement of the undergraduate experience one of the major goals for his chancellorship. The Chancellor's Undergraduate Initiative sought to create a more cohesive undergraduate experience across the university. The initiative had four major components: transforming the undergraduate program of the College of Letters and Science through a "College at Berkeley" liberal arts degree program; updating the undergraduate curriculum, particularly for first- and second-year students, to make it more cohesive and interdisciplinary; renewing physical spaces for the undergraduates; and developing a whole-student educational philosophy.[87] Dirks, from his background at Columbia with its strong commitment to the liberal arts and sciences, hoped to create an undergraduate program that would create a more shared curriculum, linking learning with Berkeley's research culture and integrating education with residential life.[88] All these efforts would stall in the crisis of Dirks's chancellorship.

Berkeley, like the other UC campuses, sought to maintain a level of ethnic diversity among its students that reflected that of the state of California's. This, however, was increasingly at odds with the mandate of the Master Plan, which required UC schools to first admit the top 12.5 percent of California's high school graduates, without reference to race or ethnicity. This became a greater challenge still when, in 1996, California voters approved Proposition 209, which effectively banned the use of affirmative action in public education. Demographic projections estimated that of California's college age cohort, almost half of the population would be Hispanic or Latinx by 2040.[89] Of undergraduates enrolled at Berkeley in 2019 only 11.5 percent identified as Hispanic or Latinx.[90] Berkeley faced difficult decisions about how to balance access and excellence in an equitable way.

The complexity of admissions decisions was compounded when out-of-state and international students were included. With in-state student tuition frozen by the Board of Regents, raising out-of-state tuition and increasing the proportion of out-of-state or international students was one of the few ways for Berkeley to increase tuition revenue. At the same time, the citizens of California were very sensitive to increases in admission of out-of-state and international students at a time when admissions at universities across the country were becoming increasingly competitive. Still, internationalization in higher education was a broader trend that Berkeley could not ignore.

## Cooperation and Competition Abroad and at Home

Berkeley had a long history of international engagement, from its early welcoming of international students to the establishment of the UC system-wide Education Abroad Program in 1962. Even the university's first philanthropic gift, from attorney and university regent Edward Tomkins in 1872, was for a professorship in "Oriental Languages and Literatures" to prepare students for expanded commerce between the United States and Asia. In a letter to his fellow regents of the university before establishing the professorship, Tomkins wrote that he felt "deeply the humiliation" of seeing students from East Asia who came to study in the United States "pass by us in almost daily procession to the other side of the continent, in search of that intellectual hospitality that we are not yet enlightened enough to extend to them."[91] Since then, Berkeley has maintained a strong commitment to international engagement at the individual and institutional level. In 2019, 1,555 students from ninety-four countries were admitted to Berkeley's freshman class.[92] Total international student enrollment at all levels more than doubled from 2005 to 2019.[93]

All that was good enough, but in an era when other American universities were establishing campuses (NYU, Duke) or centers (Harvard, Stanford, Chicago, Columbia) abroad—many of these in China—how could a cash-strapped state university with a mission to serve the residents of California compete? Dirks had a brilliant answer: he would build his international campus at home. One of his central projects was the planning of the Berkeley Global Campus in Richmond Bay, on prime, largely empty real estate along San Francisco Bay that was the university's to use. Announced by Dirks at a meeting of the Academic Senate on October 29, 2014, the campus was to provide a physical location for international partnerships between Berkeley and universities around the world. The first program to be established on the campus would be a graduate-level global citizenship curriculum. In Dirks's plans for the campus, this curriculum would be joined by a variety of other interdisciplinary, globally relevant teaching and research programs.[94] In October 2015 Dirks, joined by the leaders of the University of Cambridge and the National University of Singapore, announced a commitment to establish a global alliance between their three institutions, some of whose projects would be based on the new Richmond campus.[95]

These international initiatives represented a commitment to the trend of globalization and internationalization that was coming to dominate higher education, but at the same time, signified a departure from the export model that most universities had thus far employed to achieve "globalization." Berkeley's imported global campus would bring the world to California in a way that Dirks felt was better aligned with Berkeley's dual identity as a globally relevant, locally supported, public university.[96] And he believed (not wrongly) that many rising international universities would pay top dollar to co-locate research programs at Berkeley. For Berkeley itself, the initial investment would be minimal. Before his resignation, Dirks had neared completion of negotiations with several major international universities to co-locate research programs on the Global Campus.

But even a modest investment seemed too much to vocal faculty convinced that this was a diversion from the core and underfunded mission of the university. In the storm that was building in 2016, Dirks was forced to step back from his globalizing ambition. He was forced to say, "We are not investing," and repeat, "We are not investing any campus funds in the Richmond campus." With a faculty rebellion at home, an initiative that once had pride of place as a cornerstone in Dirks's vision for Berkeley and his chancellorship could no longer be a primary concern. By 2020 Berkeley's Richmond campus, in the absence of a compelling new vision, lay in a state of benign neglect.

But Dirks and his successor, Christ, recognized that in an increasingly globalized academic market, Berkeley needed to compete globally for talent and, as an institution that received 87 percent of its funding from nonstate sources, for resources.[97] While Berkeley still ranked very highly on every global higher education league table, rankings were lagging indicators. Universities that were not globally competitive in 2019 could quickly become so by successfully competing for key resources like talented faculty.

The global competition for talent was already beginning to affect young faculty recruitment; one particularly fierce competitor in this regard was

China. In the early twenty-first century, China introduced national government policies and funding schemes that supported international recruitment of outstanding university faculty, with a particular emphasis on encouraging Chinese scholars who had studied or begun their careers abroad to return to the Chinese mainland. Former chancellor Birgeneau told me that two of his students had chosen not to apply to entry-level faculty positions open in their fields at both Berkeley and MIT, choosing instead to return to top universities in China. "[China's talent recruitment] strategy is actually working. . . . A decade ago, there's no chance [these students] would've gone back to China."[98] Plentiful funding, immediate full professorships, and cultural and emotional arguments were just a few of the appealing factors drawing American-educated Chinese graduate students back to China. Tsinghua University alone boasted forty senior faculty members who had received their PhDs from Berkeley. Tsinghua had also been able to attract tenured faculty members from Berkeley to high-profile academic leadership positions: Qian Yingyi became dean of the Tsinghua School of Economics and Management after becoming a tenured professor at Berkeley, and Peng Kaiping, a tenured faculty member in the psychology department, served as the founding chair of Tsinghua's department of psychology.

At least one Berkeley school was entrepreneurial enough to venture out on its own with an international presence. With Dirks's blessing, the College of Engineering partnered with Tsinghua and the dynamic southern Chinese city of Shenzhen to build "TBSI," the Tsinghua-Berkeley Shenzhen Institute for research and education in engineering and the applied sciences. Shenzhen, home to several of the world's most dynamic companies (Tencent, Huawei), but without a well-known university of its own, footed the $220 million bill for construction. Tsinghua contributed $1 per year. And Berkeley, for whose faculty even that figure might have seemed too much, paid nothing.

## Competition Down the Road and Downstate

Some of Berkeley's fiercest competitors were also its closest neighbors. When Leland Stanford Junior University was founded just forty miles away from Berkeley in 1885, there was fear that the then-fledgling state would be unable to support two comprehensive research institutions. Instead, the founding and growth of Stanford has made the San Francisco Bay area the premiere bastion of academia west of the Mississippi River and helped establish a critical mass of scholars in the state. While Berkeley and Stanford remained rivals, their competition on the academic, as well as athletic, fields appeared to benefit both institutions. Like Harvard and Yale, or Tsinghua and Peking Universities, these two giants on either side of San Francisco Bay cooperated in almost nothing.

In its early days, UCLA was shrouded in a haze of Southern Californian angst over a perceived unequal distribution of state resources that purportedly favored Berkeley. There had been distinct growing pains as UCLA grew into an ever-stronger institution and gained more support from the state, but by 1960 UCLA had achieved prestige equal to that of Berkeley and received as much government support. Friendly competition between the two campuses spurred on their growth. Contentious relations between the state and UC, however, had the power to either strengthen or weaken this relationship. In 2020 many of the challenges that Berkeley faced—responding to state disinvestment, managing tuition levels, balancing ethnic diversity, determining out-of-state admissions—were faced also by UCLA, which, however, had been more nimble in fundraising and had built a larger endowment.

Berkeley contended not just with California-based institutions but also with many strong universities throughout the United States. Still, Berkeley was competitive with these institutions on several grounds, including overall academic excellence. In terms of national competition for faculty, Birgeneau recognized that Berkeley had a "huge competitive advantage" because of the appeal of its mission and role as a public university. "If [faculty] want to be at a public university, and they're of the caliber that they can get an offer from [the country's top universities], then it's going to be the elite private universities over there and one public [Berkeley] over here."[99] For California students, low in-state tuition ($14,312 in 2020–2021) remained a strong pull over elite private universities such as those in the Ivy League, which all had perceived costs of attendance (before financial aid) of more than $60,000 per year. The recruitment advantage of being a uniquely excellent public university was one reason for Berkeley to maintain its identity as a public institution even as state funding continued to decline as a percentage of revenue.

## The Postpandemic World

Shortly after Dirks declared Berkeley's "new normal" in 2016, Carol Christ was named the eleventh chancellor of Berkeley in March 2017, becoming the first woman to hold the position. She brought with her ample experience in higher education administration and was no stranger to the campus. A scholar of Victorian literature, Christ first came to Berkeley in 1970 as an assistant professor and became chair of the English department in 1985. For over three decades, she had served as a professor and an administrator, with roles ranging from dean to provost. In 2002 she left Berkeley to become the president of Smith College, where she stayed until 2013. She returned to Berkeley in 2015, where she held several leadership roles, including interim executive vice chancellor, before ultimately becoming chancellor. Her appointment was met with enthusiasm as she was a known and proven actor, an insider with outside experience, with a reputation for being community-oriented and consultative in her leadership style. Political science professor and the outgoing Academic Senate Chair Robert Powell said that faculty members appreciated Christ's leadership and called her style "consultative in a meaningful way."[100]

Yet the challenges that followed Dirks's departure did not leave with him. Immediate dilemmas included the budget deficit, new controversies surrounding the old topic of "free speech," and a student housing crisis. Christ reduced her inherited deficit to $56 million by June 2018.[101] Through the advocacy of students, alumni, and administrators, Governor Jerry Brown signed a 2018–2019 budget that included a $346.9 million funding increase, with $98.1 million as a permanent increase from the 2017–2018 budget and $25 million as one-time funding toward Berkeley's deficit. By September 2019 Berkeley reached a balanced budget and raised $1.2 billion in two consecutive, record-breaking fundraising years.[102] In response to sometimes-violent protests against right-wing activists, Christ also established a "Free-Speech Commission" and launched a "free speech year" to bring together students, faculty, and staff to engage in dialogue around what free speech meant for a university that had founded the Free Speech Movement.[103] Christ even took a stab at addressing Berkeley's university housing shortage. Out of all the schools in the UC system, Berkeley had the smallest housing capacity. Christ proposed nine new sites for expanded university housing, including one in Richmond where Dirks had planned to build the global campus.

Despite Christ's early successes, in the wake of sustained budget cuts and the steady loss of faculty members, Berkeley's position in university league tables declined. In the 2018 Quacquarelli Symonds survey, Berkeley slipped in eighty categories. In 2018 UCLA tied with Berkeley in the *U.S. News and World Report* rankings, making it the first time in almost twenty years that Berkeley was not the sole top public university in the United States.[104] Berkeley even was initially unranked in the 2019 edition of the USNWR because the university misreported the 2016 alumni giving rate, stating it was 11.6 percent instead of the true (and miserable) rate of 7.9 percent.[105] After rectifying this misreporting, Berkeley went back in the USNWR rankings, where its position dropped behind UCLA's in both 2019 and 2020.[106]

Dirks's term of "new normal" then took on new meaning in the 2019–2020 school year. COVID-19 sparked a global pandemic and brought on unexpected changes heralding an internationally felt "new normal." At Berkeley, this had profound implications for the university. After finally reaching a balanced budget, because of short-term revenue loss as well as deep and long-term cuts in state support, Berkeley again faced a projected budget deficit between $170 and $400 million.[107] Overall state budget cuts were also predicted to be as much as $53.4 billion over the next two years, which would further reduce state funding for the UC system.[108] In June 2020 Christ announced that Berkeley would have a hybrid fall semester, including small in-person classes; a "Semester in the Cloud," or online offerings for large survey courses; and staggered student arrivals along with restricted student housing of up to sixty-five hundred students.[109] To mitigate challenges brought on for California's public higher education systems, Governor Gavin Newsom organized a California Higher Education Recovery with Equity Taskforce in August 2020.[110] Former Provost Breslauer had believed that Berkeley's worst case scenario was if "the state doesn't come through, the competition gets wealthier and wealthier" leading the university "to get blown out of the water."[111] Would the COVID-19 pandemic prove his words prophetic?

A time of crisis had returned, and the toughest questions remained unanswered: What did it mean to be a "public" institution, when the vast majority of institutional funding came from private sources? What were Berkeley's obligations to the citizens, taxpayers, and children of the state of California, which no longer funded it in a sustainable fashion? Could Berkeley meet these regional expectations while remaining one of the best universities in the world? As Christ proclaimed, "This may be a perilous time, but so, too, is it a time of creative ferment and possibility."[112] How would the university's high-minded and vocal faculty, students, and staff respond to yet another crisis in an age of enduring austerity? Had one of Berkeley's historic strengths, faculty governance, made it impossible to face inevitably difficult choices? Had Berkeley—home to the Free Speech Movement, long traditions of academic autonomy, and insurgent citizenship—finally become both ungovernable and insolvent in the face of the multiple "new normals" bearing down on it?

# CHAPTER SEVEN

# Outrageous Ambitions

## *Duke University*

I N MAY 2017, nearly thirteen years after assuming Duke's presidency, Richard Brodhead found himself in the city of Kunshan, in Jiangsu Province of the People's Republic of China. He spoke to the Advisory Board of Duke Kunshan University (DKU), Duke's most ambitious international initiative, just weeks before he would step down as president. He recalled that when he assumed the presidency, he had spent his "whole adult life" at Yale, first as a student, then as a distinguished scholar of English literature, and then, for eleven years, as dean of Yale College. Many in New Haven could not imagine that he would abandon Yale for Duke. He was reminded of one student, who complained: "See, it was like Dean Brodhead was married to Yale—and now we learn he is leaving us for someone younger and more athletic."[1]

Duke was indeed younger and, in the early twenty-first century, considerably more athletic than the Ivy League schools it once measured itself against. Its famous men's basketball team had won five national championships—two during Brodhead's tenure—playing in Cameron Indoor Stadium, which Brodhead called "the boisterous home of Duke school spirit, where fans go crazy and foes wish they could just go home."[2] But it was Duke's academic athleticism—its relentless planning and its comparative lack of constraint in crossing intellectual and international boundaries—that made it an institution at once accomplished and aspiring, perhaps the most dynamic of American research universities.

Brodhead surveyed the stunningly modern DKU campus designed by Gensler & Associates and constructed by Kunshan, China's most entrepreneurial city.[3] Having just signed an agreement for the construction of the second phase of DKU's two-hundred-acre residential campus, Brodhead reflected on how far he and the university had come. Here he was, 18 hours (by air) from home, and 179 years removed from the founding of the institution that would become Duke University. Duke was establishing a liberal arts college, on American standards, in China—the first such Sino-American venture since the founding in 1919 of Yenching University, now the site of Peking University. Duke was investing academic capital aggressively into China, which was home to the fastest-growing system of higher education, in quality as well as quantity, in the world. China was home also to a major political crackdown on views deemed unorthodox by the ruling Chinese Communist Party.

As he left Kunshan at three hundred kilometers per hour by high-speed train back to Shanghai, and then by a familiar set of flights home to Durham, North Carolina, Brodhead thought about the legacy he would be leaving his successor, Vincent Price, who would assume office on July 1. DKU had been yet another daring move for Duke—perhaps the boldest yet of any American university in China—but it had not been without its challenges. Duke's Board of Trustees had called it a "one-hundred-year decision." Would it prove, for the new president, and for Duke, a mark of global leadership, distinguishing it from less determined American competitors? Or was it a risk too far, even for a university known, in the words of an earlier president, Terry Sanford, for "outrageous ambition"?[4] It was, in any event, one of the boldest ventures yet by a young university that less than a century ago was far removed from the forefront of higher education.

## Rural Origins and Homegrown Endowment

It was fitting that Duke would place its newest campus in what had been, until recent decades, a small city in the countryside outside Shanghai. By 2020 Duke University had become a leading private American research university with twelve schools, nearly sixteen thousand students, and over thirty-eight hundred faculty members spread over one thousand acres in Durham.[5] Its graduate and professional schools—in medicine, business, law, public policy, and the environment, among others—were regularly ranked among the top institutions in their fields. Its undergraduate college was among the most selective in the land, and its graduates were among the most highly regarded by employers.[6] But Duke traced its origins to Brown's Schoolhouse, a one-room school built by Methodist and Quaker families in rural North Carolina. Duke, Brodhead once said, was founded "in the hinterland of what was one of the South's least developed states. But no place is so poor that its people can't care about education, and no group is ever so deprived that it can't take steps to acquire this good."[7]

The school evolved into a normal school, training teachers, and then a small college that took the name Trinity College in 1859. It abandoned Trinity, North Carolina (the town was named for the college), in 1892 for the more urban and industrial setting of Durham. Overseeing the transition was an early Yale transplant, President John F. Crowell, who envisioned (what else?) a university on a German model that would be committed to research as well as teaching. Crowell was first disheartened by what he saw at Trinity, to the point he almost resigned and returned to the north. He began to put into motion reforms, including the development of the college's

**Figure 7.1.** Brown's Schoolhouse, 1892. David M. Rubenstein Rare Book & Manuscript Library, Duke University.

first general library. His plans were not only academic. He was a big proponent of athletics as a way to unify a student body that was divided across geographical and class lines and as a way to challenge the nearby state university at Chapel Hill.[8]

Late nineteenth-century Durham was a railway junction and the center of the American tobacco trade. North Carolina tobacco had become famous in the United States in the aftermath of the Civil War, when occupying Union troops became enamored of its sweet aroma. Washington Duke, a pioneer in the industry, was among those whose support lured Trinity College to Durham. His son, James Buchanan Duke, revolutionized the industry with the introduction of the cigarette-rolling machine. By the turn of the twentieth century, the Dukes' American Tobacco Company had a near monopoly of the American cigarette market and was well on its way, through alliance with British partners, to addicting a large part of the world to nicotine. The firm produced and sold some 55 billion cigarettes in China by 1930, establishing a male smoking culture there that endures to this day.[9]

In the 1890s Trinity College received support from Washington Duke and Julian S. Carr sufficient to construct a new campus at the site of today's East Campus to host the newly ambitious and now coeducational institution, where women, according to the terms of Washington Duke's gift, would be "on equal footing with men."[10] Recruiting faculty from the newly established graduate schools to the north, such as those of Johns Hopkins and Columbia, Trinity became in the early twentieth century a leading liberal arts college in the American south.[11]

The foundation of today's Duke University was laid under the long presidency of William Preston Few, who served from 1910 until his death in 1940. Then, as now, good fundraising took patience and fortitude. It was after at least a decade of pursuit that Few convinced James Buchanan Duke, who famously liked to "think big," to support Few's vision to build a "national" and "major" university, renamed in honor of Washington Duke.[12] Funded in 1924 with $40 million from a larger Duke endowment in support of education and health, Trinity was rebuilt in Georgian style in the 1920s to house the university's Women's College, while a spectacular neo-Gothic campus was conceived and constructed as the West Campus about a mile away.[13] Within a decade of Duke's gift, Trinity College had become Duke University, with a Graduate School, Divinity School, Medical School, and Nursing School, and with Schools of Engineering and Forestry soon to follow.

The locus and symbol of Duke's metamorphosis was the new West Campus, a refined design of a soaring chapel and flanking quadrangles, all in Collegiate Gothic, and all the design of the African American architect Julian Francis Abele of the Philadelphia firm of Horace Trumbauer. It is a telling story about the Duke University of those days that Abele, who designed for the university for a quarter-century, could not or would not visit North Carolina in that racist and segregationist age. The man who imagined modern Duke University's campus never set eyes on his creation.

In 1925, his last year of life, James B. Duke made another gift to the university: $4 million to establish the Duke School of Medicine, the School of Nursing, and Duke Hospital. His vision was then regional, hoping that Duke would become the greatest medical center between Baltimore and New Orleans. The medical campus and hospital were built just steps from West Campus.[14] Their physical proximity to the heart of Duke reflected the integral role they would come to play in the university life, operations, and aspirations. After opening in 1930, the nascent medical center quickly saw great success. By 1935 it entered the ranks of the nation's top twenty medical schools, according to the American Medical Association. Demand for the hospital's services grew rapidly, and a new hospital wing was added in 1940 to increase capacity.[15]

Duke's commitment to the public health of North Carolina continues today, bolstered in 1998 with the creation of the Duke University Health System (DUHS) that integrated Duke Regional Hospital with Raleigh Community Hospital and other nearby medical service providers to establish a single "academic health care system" for the region.[16] As we will see later, this regionally focused medical center was to become a first mover in Duke's ambitious internationalization with its 2005 partnership with the National University of Singapore to found Duke-NUS Medical School.

When the English novelist and philosopher Aldous Huxley visited North Carolina in 1937, he described traveling through forests "where one would never expect anything in particular to happen. And then, all of a sudden, something does happen. . . . There, astonishingly, is by far the largest Gothic building one has ever seen. . . . [T]his huge and fantastic structure which now houses a large university . . . is the most successful essay in neo-Gothic that I know."[17] In one architectural stroke, Duke was now the Collegiate Gothic equal of Princeton, the University of Chicago, and Washington University.

**Figure 7.2.** Aerial view of the Duke campus. Duke Today Staff.

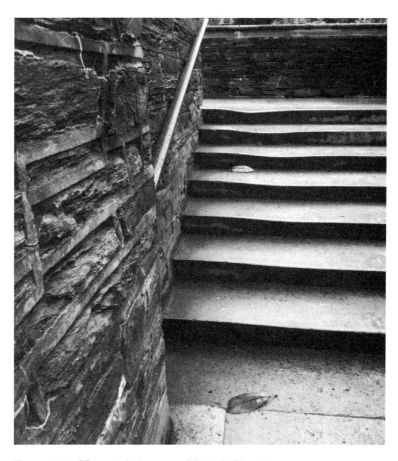

**Figure 7.3.** The scholarly steps of Duke's Chapel. Photograph © William C. Kirby.

There was no little pretense in its design—the stone stairs leading down from Duke Chapel were preternaturally worn, as if centuries of scholars had trod upon them. But as Duke's first comprehensive planning report noted in 1959, "The building of a magnificent plant was not itself an answer" to the question of what "the new University might become and achieve."[18] How, in short, would Duke create a university as good as its architecture?

## A Culture of Planning

Every university pretends to plan for its future. Some, like our Berlin universities, do so because the government mandates it in "treaties," or requires it in the context of the Excellence Initiative. Private American institutions such as Harvard do so mostly when launching fundraising campaigns: Why *should* we ask alumni for more funds? Individual schools in research universities necessarily plan for the next cycle of faculty appointments and capital projects, but very few institutions plan as a whole for long-term strategic direction. Duke was different. Even Duke's prologue to its 2006 *Making a Difference* strategic plan stated, "In many universities, strategic planning is an unromantic prospect, a bureaucratic exercise. . . . At Duke, strategic planning is exciting to undertake because it actually makes a difference." By the 1950s Duke already looked like a great university; it would need decades of serious planning to become one.

### Taking Stock, 1958–1964

Serious, university-wide academic planning began in the 1950s. In 1958 the Executive Committee of the Board of Trustees at Duke approved a "Statement of Procedure for Long-Range Planning" drafted by Vice President Paul M. Gross (the equivalent of provost at the time). President A. Hollis Edens posed three simple questions for the committee: Where was Duke lagging behind? What direction should Duke emphasize? What ought Duke to be in the future?[19] Gross's report forced Duke to decide: Would Duke aspire to be a research university on a national scale? The answer was yes, even if conflicted: As President Edens shared the report with the faculty, he noted that the (re)founders of Duke in the 1930s had "not set out to build a provincial university, though they were in sympathy with the need to render special service to the South."[20]

Duke's *First Progress Report* in 1959 provided a frank and, at times, brutal assessment of the university, its several schools, and the challenges ahead. The undergraduate college, it noted, was "in a strong position in the Southern region," but it fell "far short of the best national standards."[21] The Graduate School lacked "dynamic progress toward real educational leadership in the national and international sense."[22] Duke, with its four thousand largely southern, exclusively white undergraduate students, twelve hundred graduate and professional students of uneven quality, and eight hundred faculty members, was much more a reputable regional university in a segregated South than a contender for national distinction.[23] Duke did not desegregate until 1961, and it enrolled its first five undergraduate African American students in 1963.[24]

Duke was also well behind leading schools of the day in terms of financial resources. In 1958 direct instructional expenditures for the 5,612 full-time students at Duke totaled $4.9 million ($868 per student), compared to $24 million ($2,318 per student) for 10,536 students at Harvard.[25] Duke's endowment in 1960 stood at less than one-tenth of Harvard's: $60 million versus $625 million.[26]

The *Second Progress Report* and *Third Progress Report* on long-range planning in 1960 and 1961, respectively, continued to highlight the university's inadequacies. The *Second Progress Report,* in particular, called for improving Duke's undergraduate student body. Duke lagged behind its aspirational peers in SAT scores and other measures.[27] The report determined to raise the academic bar for admission in test scores, math, and foreign language preparation.

These three progress reports set the stage for the *Fifth Decade* report in 1964, which brought this six-year-long strategic planning process to a conclusion. Duke's fifth decade, it declared, would witness faculty recruitment and faculty salaries at a national scale, spending of at least $100 million (greater than the size of the endowment) on new facilities, and increased tuition to help pay for all this.[28] If Duke were to be a national university, it needed to start charging like one.

Only with this planning behind it did Duke engage in its *Fifth Decade* campaign, which raised $105 million by May 1971, the most by any school located in the American South at the time.[29] The funds raised supported twenty-four building projects that significantly expanded Duke's scientific research facilities, library, student housing, and recreational facilities.[30] It also created newly endowed professorships in chemistry, business administration, international affairs, and medicine to recruit a new generation of academic leaders.[31]

Not all of Duke's new recruits came without controversy. The Duke Lemur Center (DLC) was founded in 1966 by John Buettner-Janusch, a Yale anthropologist who relocated to Duke along with his lemurs, and Peter Klopfer, a Duke biologist.[32] Located on eighty acres of the Duke Forest, close to the main campus, this is an open-air primate facility to study and protect lemurs, the most endangered mammals on the planet. With some 230 lemurs from 14 species, the DLC today boasts the most diverse lemur population outside Madagascar.[33] The DLC was home to one of the world's most famous lemurs, Jovian, star of the PBS KIDS show *Zoboomafoo*.

Even the most charming recruitment story can have its dark side. After establishing the DLC, Buettner-Janusch left Duke in 1973 when NYU offered him a higher salary. While at NYU, he was convicted in 1980 of using his lab as a "drug factory" after federal agents found evidence of LSD and other drugs.[34] In 1987, a few years after his release from prison, he sent poisoned chocolates to the judge who convicted him and to a former Duke colleague.[35] The judge's wife ate the chocolates. She survived, and the lemurs were fine, too. Today the Duke Lemur Center draws over thirty-five thousand yearly patrons to this sanctuary for these magnetic mammals with hypnotic eyes.[36]

One lesson of the *Fifth Decade* campaign—that strong strategic planning could lead to successful capital campaigns—was not lost on Duke's subsequent leaders. However, future plans would also go well beyond outlining capital needs to defining Duke's ambitions.

## "Outrageous Ambitions" in the 1970s

When Duke unveiled its next strategic plan, eight years after its *Fifth Decade* report, it did so as a rapidly rising university under the leadership of a national political figure, Terry Sanford. In an address to the faculty on October 25, 1984, President Sanford proclaimed:

> This is not an Ivy League school. We are not of any flock or tribe. I quote from my inaugural speech: "I do not propose that we seek for ourselves a homogenized pattern of the half-dozen great private universities of the nation of which we are one, or that we try to 'catch up' or follow any university, no matter what its prestigious position. Simply

to do as some other university does, to teach as it teaches, to operate as it operates, to accept it as our model, would make our best success but a carbon copy. We strive to be Duke University, an institution seeking the highest scholarly attainment, and using to the fullest its own peculiar resources and creative capabilities."[37]

Like campuses from Berlin to Berkeley, Duke in the late 1960s was a site of protests in favor of civil rights and against the Vietnam War. President Douglas Knight was forced to resign in 1969 after African American students occupied the Allen Administration Building and tear gas was fired by police into a crowd of student onlookers.[38] Duke, like Harvard, Free University of Berlin, and, as we shall see, Tsinghua, found itself in the crosshairs of a generational revolution.

After Knight's departure, Terry Sanford, a progressive Democrat who supported desegregation and had doubled state spending for public schools while serving as governor of North Carolina from 1961 to 1965, was brought in by Duke's board to restore peace on campus and push the university forward as a national institution.[39] This ambition fitted an ambitious man. While president of Duke, Sanford would twice run for the presidency of the United States and eventually became a US senator after his departure from Duke. On his death, he would be entombed in the Duke University Chapel. During his tenure as president, he put Duke indelibly on the map.

Since its last strategic plan, much had improved. By 1972 undergraduates were now in the top 9 percent of all US college students as measured by average SAT scores, although Duke was still behind thirty-five to forty schools in terms of tested student quality.[40] Duke's professional schools were getting better fast. The Schools of Medicine and Law were now in the top ten nationally.[41] Duke's School of Business, founded in 1969, planned to expand its endowment fivefold to $5 million.[42]

Sanford's 1972 report aimed to push further and faster, with a key focus on undergraduate education. The rigor of the undergraduate curriculum was increased in the 1968–1969 academic year to help address "the lack of intellectual climate" at Duke and to engage students more directly in research.[43] Significant external resources were sought to improve financial aid and student diversity, with the aim that 10 percent of the undergraduate student body be minority students.[44]

In graduate education, because the majority of Duke's graduate school programs were already ranked in the top thirty nationally, the bar was raised to get most programs into the top twenty. To achieve this, the report called for the establishment of fifty new endowed professorships in addition to the forty-eight James B. Duke and other named professorships already in place.[45]

## Focused Excellence in the 1980s

Duke's rise since the 1950s had taken place in an era of largely continuous growth in the American economy. But in the aftermath of the stagflation of the late 1970s, Duke's 1980 plan, *Directions for Progress,* declared that Duke, like other private research universities, had to "plan for retrenchment, not growth."[46]

All of Duke's earlier plans had looked unsentimentally at existing programs, with an eye to reducing those that no longer showed promise. *Directions for Progress* went further to argue for substantial cuts.[47] Several programs improved their financial standing and survived the cuts. These included the School of Forestry and Environmental Studies as well as the Duke University Marine Lab which combined to form a new School of the Environment in 1991.[48]

*Directions for Progress* also proposed sweeping reforms in academic appointments to improve Duke's competitiveness, with stress on stricter tenure policy. Eighty percent of Duke's faculty outside of the Medical Center was tenured, a percentage that posed "significant risk of stagnation" for the university.[49] Tenured appointments were to be reserved for "leading scholars" who would be "excellent by every national standard." The university could no longer afford to "confuse conscientious service with potential greatness."[50]

When economic growth returned in the late 1980s, Duke's selective and aggressive hiring had paid off. The Academic Plan of 1987 confidently called on Duke to "carve out a distinctive niche in the top echelon of research universities" and create its own "peaks of excellence."[51] This had already begun in many areas. John Hope Franklin, a leading historian of the United States and of the African American experience, was awarded a James B. Duke professorship in 1982. Duke's Humanities Institute would be founded in his name and his honor in 1999. Joel Fleishman, a prominent law scholar, was recruited from Yale in 1971 to head the Institute of Policy Sciences and Public Affairs, which would evolve into today's Sanford School of Public Policy. Phillip Griffiths gave up an endowed chair at Harvard to become provost at Duke in 1984.[52] And to chair the English Department, Duke recruited in 1986 a bold academic entrepreneur and literary theorist, Stanley Fish, who was said to have taken "a respectable but staid Southern English department and transform[ed] it into the professional powerhouse of the day."[53]

The strategic planning efforts in the 1970s and 1980s were supported by two capital campaigns under Sanford, expanding research and student support, adding new facilities, and funding the recruitment of a national student body. The percentage of undergraduates from North Carolina and other Southeastern states decreased from 55 percent in 1958 to 35 percent in 1983; 48 percent of the students were now from the Northeast, and 15 percent were from the Midwest and Pacific coast.[54] The trend toward diversity intensified under Sanford's successor, Keith Brodie. The proportion of African American students at Duke increased from 4 percent in 1985 to 9 percent in 1993.[55] The percentage of undergraduates receiving financial aid at the school increased from 20 percent to 40 percent in the same period.[56] Fourteen percent of Duke undergrads received Pell Grants.[57]

### Coach K and Beyond

Also in the 1980s the roots for one of Duke's trademark programs were planted: the men's basketball team. From 1980 to 2022 Mike Krzyzewski served as head coach of this team, leading Duke to five national championships and twelve Final Fours by 2021. He holds the record for the most career wins in men's college basketball's most demanding division. Named after the coach, Krzyzewskiville, or K-ville, is an enduring Duke tradition that began in 1986 when students camped out in tents for days to get tickets to the annual game between the Duke "Blue Devils" and their blood rivals, the "Tar Heels" of the University of North Carolina, Chapel Hill. Now, K-ville has evolved into a phenomenon where students take turns camping out in tents to get tickets for basketball games anywhere from three to eight *weeks* before the game. Athletics, especially basketball, became a central part of Duke undergraduate culture. More students decide to study abroad during the fall semester than in the spring in order to be on campus for the basketball season in winter and spring. Athletics also brings in millions of dollars in revenue. For the 2018–2019 school year, Duke men's basketball brought in revenue of $35,489,891 and over $13 million in profit.[58]

It is difficult for an outsider to overstate the all-permeating and, I have to say, broadly positive impact of basketball on the Duke campus. As with football at Notre Dame, it is today part of a common culture among students, staff, faculty, and administration. I was on the Duke campus when the men's basketball team won the 2015 national championship. The next day, the 9,314 seats at Cameron Indoor Stadium were filled with students and fans from all corners of the university community to welcome home the team and its redoubtable coach.

When, several years earlier, I was invited to Duke to give an academic talk on China, I was hosted by Claire Conceison, a remarkable scholar and practitioner of Chinese drama and member of Duke's Asian/Pacific Studies Institute. (Today she is Professor of Chinese Culture and Theater Studies at MIT.) Claire taught a course at Duke called "Sports as Performance." It was very popular, I understood, with the basketball team. As I waited for her in her office in the hour before my lecture, one student after another dropped off their papers for her course. Each student was taller than the last. These were, by some measure, the tallest group of undergraduates I had ever set eyes on. As their papers piled up, I knew it would be wrong of me to take a look at them. In the end I could not resist and started reading. They were very good. I was impressed by the students, by Claire (who clearly drove them hard), and indirectly by Coach K, whose program has been untainted by academic scandal.

**Figure 7.4.** Coach K and the Duke 2015 National Champions men's basketball team. Duke Sports Information.

By 2019 student-athletes, or students on varsity sports teams, made up about 10 percent of the undergraduate student population—less than the percentage at Harvard (with fewer varsity sports), but more preprofessional in their aspirations in certain sports.[59] For sports was a tool for Duke's advancement as a university. Over the last three decades, no serious sports fan in the United States could credibly be unaware of Duke's extraordinary rise in basketball and, by extension, in other areas.

Yet, as elsewhere, there were dark suspicions about the prominence of athletics at Duke. In March 2006 charges of rape, kidnapping, and sexual offense allegations were raised by a Black student at North Carolina Central University, who worked as an exotic dancer on the side, and was hired to perform at an off-campus house party by the Duke men's lacrosse team over spring break.[60] The case drew national attention, and many believed that the culture of athletics had gotten out of hand. As the investigation progressed, the men's lacrosse team, which had been favored to be the national champions that year, was suspended. A year later, after contradictions from the accuser's story and mishandling of evidence by the Durham district attorney emerged, the three young men accused were declared innocent of all charges.[61] Yet the non-scandal scandal lingered in and beyond the university because so many believed it could have easily been true. In its time, the Duke lacrosse incident raised questions on the role of race, class, and elite sports within the nation's top universities—questions that have hardly gone away. Gone, however, is the house in which the incident was alleged to have occurred: it was torn down by the university as it had become a tourist attraction.

By the time Terry Sanford ended his transformative presidency (1969–1985), Duke was at once distinguished and differentiated in multiple areas of the academy. The size of the faculty had increased by 44 percent (in numbers from 984 to 1,424) from 1970 to 1985, but its perceived quality and interconnection had grown faster still. In a 1982 national ranking of biological sciences, Duke received third place, above both UC Berkeley and Harvard.[62] As a welcome external validation of Duke's rise, the university was ranked sixth among American universities by *U.S. News and World Report* in 1985, in the early days of the college-ranking business. Duke would remain in the top ten on the USNWR rankings of national universities every year save one between 1985 and 2020.[63]

Sanford said, in his final annual address to the faculty, "Everyone is seeking excellence, or claims to be. I sometimes think we have misused the word or weakened it by overuse. Excellence is not a brand of cheese. It is not even a place. It is more like a path or a guiding star. . . . It is a spirit; it is a determination; it is a set of personal and institutional values."[64]

## Shaping Duke's Future in the 1990s

Nannerl Keohane, president of Duke University from 1993 to 2004, described the Duke she inherited as a "flotilla" of schools. The strategic plans signaled directions and destinations to all ships in the flotilla, as Duke sought to rid itself of "Ivy envy" in competing with and surpassing other major research universities. Duke's admirals, commodores, and captains who followed the signals of the flagship received more resources.

But as Duke's professional schools became more distinguished and better funded, focusing the university's resources grew more challenging. When Keohane took office in 1993, she discovered that as president she had little more than $1 million in truly discretionary funds.[65] While the provost had more resources through his Common Fund and Academic Priorities Pool, these resources did not exceed $3.5 million per year.[66]

In 1992 *A Duke Plan: Positioning Duke for the 21st Century* was released. After Keohane's arrival in 1993, a new strategic plan, *Shaping Our Future*, was unveiled in 1994. In part to fund *Shaping Our Future*, a program of "Virtual Equity" was set up in 1994. Virtual Equity was an institutional reinvestment account (IRA) or an "internal bank," where Duke's different schools deposited their cash reserves to be invested by DUMAC, the Duke University Management Company, which managed Duke University's endowment. (The concept was similar to, but in time much better managed than, that of Harvard's Central Bank.) The schools were guaranteed a return equal to the thirty-day T-bill rate. When the generated returns exceeded 6 percent of the fund's liabilities, the funds were redirected to the central administration to fund strategic initiatives. By 2001 $60 million had accumulated, and future income was projected at $9 million annually.[67]

As before, after planning came campaigns: The Campaign for Duke, launched in 1996, raised $2.36 billion from 250,000 donors, making it at the time the fifth-largest single campaign in the history of American higher education.[68] Duke's endowment, which stood at approximately $700 million in 1994, increased to more than $3 billion by the end of 2003.[69] The success of the Campaign for Duke and the drafting of a new campus master plan (the first since the 1920s) just before the publication of *Shaping Our Future*, allowed the construction of more than forty buildings over the course of Keohane's tenure.[70]

## Controlled Chaos and Strategic Planning in Twenty-First Century Duke

Why was planning so successful at Duke? How did plans get traction and legitimacy? Reflecting on Duke's planning processes, Brodhead recalled, "Every unit participated in the planning exercise and there was high-level coordination of the themes that touched everybody. . . . When I read the Strategic Investment Plan, the way it identified funds by which to fund the plan—this was something I had never seen anywhere else." Duke's twenty-first century plans offer the best examples.

By the early twenty-first century, planning was in Duke's DNA. Success in planning was directly related to Duke's governance. While Duke's president was the "chief educational and administrative officer" of the university, the position of provost was a powerful "executive officer under the president responsible for all educational affairs and activities of the University," including strategic planning.[71] Just as Duke benefited from a series of long and successful presidencies, it was shaped also by its provosts. Peter Lange, who became provost in 1999 and remained in the position for fifteen years, stewarded the 2001 *Building on Excellence* and 2006 *Making a Difference* strategic plans.

If Free University of Berlin's Peter Lange was its Iron Chancellor, then Duke's Peter Lange was its Iron Provost. Both were strong forces of continuity and progress for their universities over the tenure of several presidencies. But while FU's Peter Lange played his formidable role noiselessly, largely outside the public eye, Duke's Peter Lange was omnipresent, with a hearty public presence and an energetic ambition to bring into alignment the stars of Duke's firmament. He had the (rare in these positions) capacity to see the big picture of university-wide development and the telling detail of trouble at the department level. The scope of the job of provost at Duke is officially quite simple and quite powerful: "The Provost is the chief academic officer of Duke University, responsible to the President for the University's teaching and research mission." The provost's office at Duke had much greater authority than that at Harvard, where it played a coordinating role, or at Berkeley, with its diminished resources and long tradition of student and faculty revolts. Reporting directly to the provost were Duke's eight schools (and their deans); its eleven interdisciplinary initiatives; six vice provosts over-seeing undergraduate education, academic affairs, finance, and more; and other offices such as those for admissions and research. As always in high-level administrative roles, other duties emerged. Once, in the midst of foot-ball season, Lange received an email stating that in a drumming class with thirteen students, seven were football players. A further concern was that the class had no syllabus. Knowing that the press was searching for instances like these in the wake of an academic fraud scandal at the neighboring University of North Carolina at Chapel Hill, Lange quickly took steps to meet with the relevant dean. In three days, the students were transferred to other classes and the potential crisis was mitigated. As Lange recalled, it was an "example of oversight." In taking on this role and serving for fifteen years, it surely helped that Duke's Peter Lange was a scholar of comparative politics. He became a compelling practitioner, too. Take, again, the case of planning.

Strategic planning under Lange took the form of democratic centralism (or "controlled chaos," in Lange's own words)—with goals set out by the lead-ership—yet with a fair amount of democracy. While individual schools submitted their planning documents to the center, Lange articulated stra-tegic themes that would help to define the overall university plan.[72] A steering committee for the plan facilitated dialogue between the provost's office, the deans, and faculty members, with the latter involved through the elected Ac-ademic Council—a strong, university-wide faculty body with power to ap-prove academic programs—and its subcommittees.

Proposals from schools and institutes were "graded" like student essays (A, B, C, etc.) based on the seriousness of their self-assessments, their vi-sion (or lack thereof), and the extent to which they aligned with the themes outlined by the provost.[73] Cross-school thematic working groups, where fac-ulty could provide input, were created in consultation with the deans of the several schools.[74]

Once the university-wide strategic plan was drafted, it faced formal re-view, first by the Academic Council and then by Duke's Board of Trustees, which had the final responsibility to review strategic plans.[75] For *Making a Difference,* the entire planning process from its beginning to approval by the Board of Trustees took two years.[76]

Lange provided the "control" in the "chaos" of feedback and participation from the broader campus community. Yet some level of "chaos" was indis-pensable to the planning process as it allowed new perspectives to be heard and incorporated, created support from multiple stakeholders, and ensured

217

that goals outlined by the plan reflected the realities of the schools' capabilities and interests. As Lange recalled, "Controlled chaos means that we [senior leadership] create the framework, the boxes that need to be filled. And it's going to be very hard for the planning process to add or change the boxes. But then it is up to the faculty, with our overview, to fill in the content of the boxes."[77] Provost Sally Kornbluth, who succeeded Lange, recalled that "part of the reason the previous plans looked so prescient is that they actually captured what was going on. You can't lead anybody anywhere without organic growth and a lot of faculty buy-in."[78]

## Building on Excellence with Deeper Pockets

A critical foundation of recent planning at Duke was its Strategic Investment Plan (SIP), which allowed the central administration to finance major initiatives for the university. Through the SIP and other means, resources were gradually gathered from the periphery and moved to the center of the university. Duke's leadership was fortunate in having among its ranks a second, long-serving administrator: its treasurer and executive vice president, Tallman Trask III, who served as the university's chief administrative and fiscal officer. Trask was responsible for an extraordinary range of activities, including the budget, finances, procurement, debt, campus planning, architecture, maintenance and construction, human resources, academic and administrative computing, and more. Gradually, steadily, but surely, Trask brought financial capacity to the center of the university. Trask had one iron-clad rule in managing Duke's complex finances for strategic purposes: "Never take from people money that they *know* they have."[79]

In May 2000 Duke's Board of Trustees approved a new spending rate and distribution structure for income from Duke University's endowment. The resulting change generated $45 million over a five-year period for strategic investments by the deans of Duke's different schools with the agreement of the provost.[80] Combined with another $10 million from other unassigned and unrestricted income sources and income from the Virtual Equity program created in 1994, a total of $160 million was placed at the disposal of Duke's president and provost between fiscal year (FY) 2000–2001 and FY 2004–2005 to fund strategic initiatives; this was a sharply higher figure than the approximately $4.5 million annually available in 1994 when *Shaping Our Future* was drafted.

Lange was charged with spending these funds well. He achieved this through the SIP created in *Building on Excellence*. Combined with school resources, the SIP amounted to $727 million in spending over the course of five years. Duke had already gained recognition as one of the top ten universities in the country; the strategic initiatives outlined in the plan were meant to help it become one "among the small number of institutions that define what is best in American higher education."[81] Above all, as Lange recalled, "We decided in 1999–2000 that Duke could not be the national university leader we aspired to be in the twenty-first century with the 'boutique' engineering school we had then."[82] This led to major strategic investments in engineering and in what would become, thanks to a lead gift by Ed Pratt, a Duke alumnus who was chairman and CEO of Pfizer, Duke's renamed and expanded Pratt School of Engineering.

Although central financial resources accounted for only 22 percent ($160 million) of the entire SIP, these central funds encouraged schools to follow the university's central priorities. "Only a small percentage of academic funding was in the strategic programs," reflected Brodhead, but "the strategic initiatives meant that the autonomous units had massive self-interest in collaborating to win the small margin."[83]

## Making a Difference in 2006

*Building on Excellence* was followed by *Making a Difference* in 2006. Duke's "enduring themes"—now central to the university's identity—were explicitly called out in *Making a Difference*. In addition to interdisciplinarity, internationalization, and diversity, new leitmotifs such as "knowledge in the service of society" were added to reinforce the plan to "make a difference."[84] *Building on Excellence* had emphasized science and engineering; *Making a Difference* now added "the centrality of the humanities and interpretative social sciences" as an enduring commitment. "Affordability and access" remained a central goal. Already offering need-blind admissions, Duke followed Harvard's lead by eliminating parental contributions for students from families making less than $60,000 per year and eliminating loans for families making less than $40,000 per year in the 2008–2009 academic year.[85] As with *Building on Excellence*, goals for *Making a Difference* were backed up by the SIP, with a planned $1.3 billion expenditure over the course of six to eight years.

But all of Duke's planning could not foresee the Great Recession that began in 2008. Implementation of the SIP was interrupted. In March 2009 Brodhead acknowledged in a letter to members of the Duke community that "the disappearance of short-term investment returns [had] removed a significant source of revenue for strategic initiatives."[86] Duke's endowment, which stood at $6.1 billion in June 2008, shrank by 20 percent, which was projected to decrease the university's operating budget by $100–125 million by 2012.[87]

To minimize damage, university leadership froze salaries for all Duke employees making more than $50,000 per year.[88] Hundreds of jobs were eliminated by voluntary retirement programs; tight controls were placed on vacancies and overtime.[89] Planning for construction continued but construction of new buildings was delayed.[90] In April 2009 Lange told the deans of Duke's various schools to review their school-level strategic plans to further prioritize scarce resources.[91] Thanks in part to these measures, the long-term trajectory of the university did not appear to be fundamentally affected. Duke's endowment, which had bottomed out at $4.4 billion in 2008–2009, returned to growth, passing the $7 billion mark in 2013–2014, and reaching $8.6 billion at the end of 2019. By July 2021, Duke's endowment stood at $12.7 billion.[92]

Duke managed its way through the crisis without a financial meltdown (or a liquidity crisis like Harvard) and with its sense of mission intact. Peter Lange drafted a letter to the faculty: "At times like this, it is sometimes useful to draw upon history. Duke was born and began to thrive in the midst of this country's deepest economic despair. Through skill, vision, hard work, and an entrepreneurial spirit, our university rapidly exceeded even the most optimistic expectation to assume a position of leadership in the nation and the world."[93]

Despite the financial crisis, the *Making a Difference* plan of 2006 still allowed university administrators to (as Brodhead put it) "build the architecture of the Duke Forward campaign [launched in 2012] on a very richly orchestrated consensus among the schools." The campaign reached its goal of $3.25 billion in July 2016, a year ahead of schedule.[94]

The newly enduring theme of "knowledge in the service of society" took root. Launched in 2007, DukeEngage allowed 4,800 Duke students to volunteer more than 1.6 million hours in six hundred community organizations in forty-six US cities and eighty-four countries by summer 2019.[95] The Sanford Institute for Public Policy was upgraded to a school in 2009, demonstrating commitment to using interdisciplinary approaches to address policy issues and provide service to society.

Together with interdisciplinarity and internationalization, civic engagement had become a part of Duke's signature branding. Noah Pickus, former Associate Provost and former Director of the Kenan Institute for Ethics at Duke, observed that "when you ask Duke students on their applications why they choose Duke, everyone always used to say, great school, basketball. Now in principle they say, great school, DukeEngage, civic engagement."[96]

## Planning Interdisciplinarity

Every university talks about "interdisciplinarity" as a key to academic innovation: How do we get colleagues from different fields to work together on common problems? How might the insights of disciplines as distinct as psychology and economics be focused? Or, simply, how can universities get around the sclerotic organizational rigidity of long-standing departments in which appointments are rooted? As a younger and hungrier institution, Duke saw interdisciplinarity as a differentiator. Major administrative changes were made in the 1990s to stimulate interdisciplinary programs. An Office of the Vice Provost for Interdisciplinary Studies (OVPIS) was created, and money followed. Interdisciplinary initiatives expanded in 2001 under *Building on Excellence,* with over $150 million of the $727 million Strategic Investment Plan devoted to distinctive programs such as the John Hope Franklin Humanities Institute, the Institute for Genome Sciences and Policy, and the Social Science Initiative.[97]

Duke's passion for the interdisciplinary accelerated under *Making a Difference.* The Duke Global Health Institute was founded with a big aim: to reduce health disparities in communities worldwide based on collaboration between medicine, economics, political science, and other fields.[98] Brodhead lured to Duke his old Yale colleague, Michael Merson, then Dean of Public Health at Yale's School of Medicine. Merson energized the new Duke effort, leading it to national prominence and, unusually, embedding its activities and (often joint) faculty appointments in nearly every school at Duke. Other initiatives and institutes launched between 2006 and 2016 spanned areas of brain science, health policy, energy, entrepreneurship, and big data.

Together these formed what became known as Duke's UICs, or "Signature University Institutes and Centers."

The UICs proved to be a magnet to attract talent to Duke. *Making a Difference* stressed the need for joint and "cluster" hiring of faculty drawn to interdisciplinary work of strategic importance at Duke.[99] The UICs offered centrally financed research funds and encouraged joint appointments across the university.[100] Joint appointments almost anywhere can sound better than they are, and younger faculty in particular worry about "falling between two stools" in multi-school appointments. To energize the effort, Provost Lange set up a Joint School-UIC Tenure/Tenure Track Faculty Hiring Program, which provided funds over a nine-year period for joint hiring of faculty appointed half-time in a UIC.[101] By 2018 there were a total of 104 joint faculty appointments across different schools and UICs at Duke.[102]

The UICs gave administrative support, physical space, and technical training and services to interdisciplinary efforts, by 2018 managing $33 million in internal and external faculty grants.[103] The Duke Center for Genomic and Computational Biology offered customized genetic sequencing for labs in biological sciences, biomedical engineering, and the School of Medicine.[104] The Social Science Research Institute sponsored workshops on quantitative methods in social sciences across multiple social science disciplines.[105] Being in competition with older and better endowed universities, the centralization of services across different schools and disciplines built serious economies of scale, enabling Duke, as Provost Sally Kornbluth explained, "to do more with less."[106]

Planned interdisciplinarity emerged as a major part of Duke's identity. In Brodhead's opinion, Duke had achieved "a deeper understanding that interdisciplinarity wasn't just a cool thing" but engendered "new forms of intelligence that are going to be needed to solve problems in a successor generation."[107] According to Lange, Duke's UICs became central to faculty recruitment and retention and "put a stamp on Duke as an interdisciplinary place," even for colleagues who were not associated with the institutes.[108] Haiyan Gao, a distinguished physicist, observed that while interdisciplinary research was "pretty fashionable" when she joined the faculty in 2002, after over a decade of investment, interdisciplinary research was "becoming a part of the Duke DNA" since most of the faculty she knew were involved, "consciously or subconsciously," in interdisciplinary research or teaching.[109] Kornbluth thought Duke's willingness to cross disciplinary boundaries had helped the school put together "combinations" that became "unique niches that other people later wish they had been in," which in turn helped Duke to "punch above its weight."[110]

But—to extend the boxing metaphor—what weight class was Duke in? Lange recalled that when he first joined the Duke faculty in 1981, "we still had a lot of Ivy envy. And I would say that one of the biggest changes in Duke over the last twenty years is that we don't have Ivy envy anymore. Really." It was, Lange felt, particularly in its interdisciplinary drive, beginning with the *Crossing Boundaries* plan, that Duke came to realize that "Our success is dependent on not being exactly like [those guys]. We have assets that allow us to be different than those northeast guys, and we need to employ those assets to be different, not similar." Even the undergraduates, with whom there was "a shitload of Ivy envy" twenty years ago, had come to realize that Duke was a compellingly singular place.[111]

## *Together Duke 2017*

Duke kicked off a new round of strategic planning in December 2014 under the leadership of Provost Kornbluth. The draft plan, which in 2017 was named *Together Duke: Advancing Excellence through Community,* recalled Duke's now "strong foundations" of interdisciplinarity, globalization, and knowledge in service of society.[112] The strategic plan had four goals, backed by an additional $132 million of centrally mobilized resources.

When university-wide strategic planning began at Duke in 1959, Duke was an all-white university in the American South, celebrating its regional excellence while becoming aware of the distance it had to go to achieve national prominence. In 2019, 57 percent of Duke's nearly sixteen thousand students were racial or ethnic minorities or were from another country. It was a top ten university in the United States, and it ranked among the top thirty universities in the world.[113]

In the flotilla of Duke's schools, the School of Medicine was ranked in the top fifteen in the United States in 2019 along with the School of Law.[114] The School of Nursing, which was phased out by the *Directions for Progress* plan in 1980, was reorganized and revived in 1985 to focus on graduate education and research. By 2019 it ranked number two for graduate nursing programs in the United States.[115] In 2019 USNWR ranked the Fuqua School of Business tenth best among business schools.[116] Thanks to the Nicholas School of the Environment, Duke was ranked sixth in the world for programs in environment and ecology.[117]

Duke was now unquestionably successful at home, with a growing international reputation. It determined now to make its mark abroad, particularly in Asia.

## Planning Internationalization

The first significant reference at Duke to internationalization occurred in the 1972 strategic plan. Duke was by then a national, American university, but only marginally global in reach or intent. It had some academic presence in international studies, the most successful being its (British) Commonwealth Studies and South Asia programs.[118] In the early 1970s only 1 percent of undergraduates studied abroad.[119] The foreign nationals studying at Duke consisted of less than 1 percent and 11 percent of the undergraduate and graduate student bodies, respectively.[120]

Only two decades later did active planning begin to internationalize Duke. In 1992 Peter Lange chaired a faculty committee urging Duke's internationalization abroad and on campus. In 1994 President Keohane appointed Lange as the first Vice Provost for Academic Affairs and International Education (later renamed to Vice President and Vice Provost for Global Affairs) to mobilize Duke's internationalization.[121] Lange's ambitions, reflected in Duke's 1994 *Shaping Our Future* strategic plan, called for Duke to become "a leading international university and be recognized as such."[122] *Shaping Our Future* asked Duke's leaders to "become visible bearers" of the university's commitment to internationalize and build its international reputation by actively establishing partnerships abroad.[123]

Internationalization gained traction in the schools. For example, in 1996 Duke's Fuqua School of Business launched a Global Executive MBA program, which allowed executives who lived anywhere in the world to obtain an MBA with courses on the internet coupled with "residencies" in multiple sites: Dubai, London, New Delhi, Shanghai, St. Petersburg, and Johannesburg, in addition to Durham itself.[124] A Cross Continent MBA program was launched in 2000 for early and mid-career professionals.[125]

By 2001 Duke had formed two hundred academic partnerships across the globe.[126] The *Building on Excellence* strategic plan called also for increasing the number of international students at Duke and encouraging Duke students to study in non-English-speaking countries.[127]

Internationalization accelerated when Brodhead became president in 2004 and was formalized as an enduring theme in the 2006 plan, *Making a Dif-*

*ference.* Under Brodhead, internationalization intersected with interdisciplinarity and civic engagement. DukeEngage and another program, Duke Immerse, allowed undergraduates to collaborate closely with faculty and conduct interdisciplinary research that was then tested in practice in sites around the world. In his 2011 address to faculty, Brodhead stated, "Intellectual work is increasingly done collaboratively, in partnerships not limited by physical location. The university that fails to build connectivity to a broad array of high-end partners will be the backwater of tomorrow." Duke students could now also study abroad with the forty-three programs administered by Duke; 47 percent of the class of 2020 students chose to do.[128]

In Durham, Duke's twelve international and area studies centers provided interdisciplinary teaching to students, as well as research expertise and linkages to different regions around the globe. Duke's interdisciplinary UICs sponsored their own international activities, with internationalization a central component of their strategic plans. In 2017 the Global Health Institute alone hosted 115 students in twenty-five countries around the world for field work.[129]

## Duke-NUS Medical School

It is one thing to internationalize at home; it is quite another to build campuses around the world. Along with New York University, Duke became a first mover among contemporary American universities in building a physical presence abroad. In 2005 Duke entered into an agreement with the National University of Singapore (NUS) with strong backing from the government of Singapore, which was determined to make Singapore the biomedical hub of Asia. This American-style graduate medical school was designed both to train physicians and to produce leaders in biomedical sciences for Singapore and beyond. The school's 26,000-square-meter Khoo Teck Puat Building was finished three years ahead of schedule and became operational in May 2009 under the name of Duke-NUS Graduate Medical School (Duke-NUS). The curriculum was modeled on that of Duke's School of Medicine, and Duke retained decision-making power on academic affairs. At the time, the CEO of DUHS, Victor Dzau, said, "The success of Duke-NUS is integral to the success of Duke Medicine's mission of transforming medicine and health to improve peoples' lives around the world."[130] Better health care for Americans now started in Singapore.

Duke-NUS was Duke's first permanent physical presence abroad and was an unqualified success. The project validated a main reason for making internationalization a strategic priority—the recruitment of talent. The access to Asian patients for clinical research in an American medical school setting and to unique understudied diseases in Southeast Asia proved attractive for many potential Duke faculty recruits. Duke expanded the reach of its faculty through its presence in Singapore and additional partnerships in Asia built through Duke-NUS.[131] The collaborative agreement between Duke and NUS was extended in 2010 and again in 2016. The success of Duke-NUS engendered further ambition—this time in China.

## Duke Kunshan University

The pioneering origins of Duke University can be traced to its founding in rural North Carolina. Its signature international venture would be found in a place once part of the Chinese countryside. Until the late twentieth century, Kunshan was more famous for its "hairy crabs," which could be found on every Shanghai plate in autumn, than it was for business, let alone for education. Kunshan had been a center of learning in the Ming (1368–1644) and Qing (1644–1912) dynasties. But in modern times, Kunshan had become a backwater, a forgotten town between the big industrial cities of Shanghai and Suzhou.

All that changed with China's "opening and reform" that began in 1979. Under the dynamic and business-savvy leadership of its local government, Kunshan became a center of foreign direct investment from Taiwan and Singapore, and a center of global electronics manufacturing. This self-starting city became a national model in China for rapid and sustainable development. It was the wealthiest small city in China by the 2010s.

By the time Kunshan approached Duke University in 2006–2007 to explore the possibility of building a joint-venture campus, its government, led by its energetic mayor and Party secretary, Guan Aiguo, imagined a future with Kunshan as the Silicon Valley of China, focused on education, research, and development. Eager to attract a renowned research university as a potential magnet for talent, Kunshan offered Duke free land and agreed to pay for the construction of a two-hundred-acre residential campus.[132] It has been estimated that if the first phase (one-third) of the campus had been built in Durham, it would have cost as much as $260 million.[133]

Guan Aiguo found his entrepreneurial partner in Blair Sheppard, the incoming dean of Duke's Fuqua School of Business. Sheppard had spearheaded the creation of Fuqua's Global Executive MBA and Cross Continent MBA programs. He was CEO of Duke Corporate Education (one of the leading executive education programs in the United States) when he was asked to lead Fuqua. A visionary and innovative dean, Sheppard planned a series of global campuses for Fuqua in order to offer truly international business education and to differentiate Fuqua among leading American business schools. He visited Kunshan in 2006 and 2007 and reached a framework agreement with lightning speed.

The faculty at Fuqua—ranked in the top ten American business schools—was not used to moving with lightning speed, and they resisted Sheppard's global vision. But Duke's leadership, Brodhead and Lange, embraced the challenge on behalf of the university. When a Cooperation Agreement was signed between Duke University and the government of Kunshan in 2010, Fuqua would still take part in the project, offering one of the several planned master's degrees, but Duke's vision was bolder still: to establish, in Kunshan, an undergraduate college in the arts and sciences at Duke's standards.

Partnering with Wuhan University, China's oldest comprehensive university, located in a city bearing the same name in China's central province of Hubei, Duke signed a "Cooperation Principles Statement" in January 2011. The project was now officially known as "Duke Kunshan University" (DKU), and "Kunshan Duke University" in Chinese translation. Duke's investment in the first phase of the DKU project was approximately $42.5 million, which included a $5.5 million initial investment and an estimated $37 million over six years to cover 52 percent of DKU's operating costs.[134] The City of Kunshan agreed to provide the land, the construction, and the other 48 percent of operating costs.[135]

Wuhan University was a fitting partner for China's most prestigious joint-venture university. Wuhan and the surrounding province of Hubei have long been leading centers of commerce, scholarship, and political leadership. It was the great reforming Governor-General Zhang Zhidong who founded in 1893—five years before Peking University was established—the "Self-Strengthening Institute" that would become Wuhan University. The Self-Strengthening Institute initially focused instrumentally on the study of those subjects that would bring about China's return to "wealth and power," primarily mathematics, science, and business, although not initially at the expense of China's educational tradition. Zhang's famous *Exhortation to Study*, published in 1898, argued that "Chinese learning" (education in the classics) had to remain the foundation, while "Western learning" was for "practical matters." By 1928, however, Wuhan University had become one of China's first comprehensive, national universities, with a distinguished and internationalized Faculty of Arts to match those in Law, Science, and Engineering. After 1949 the university was reordered on Soviet models and then became one of the national centers of strife and bloodshed during the Cultural Revolution. Today it is again a major comprehensive university, with a faculty of four thousand teaching a student body of thirty-four thousand undergraduates and twenty-one thousand graduate students and regularly ranked as fourth among Chinese universities. Duke's prospective partner in China had seen it all.

Duke's culture of strategic planning helped it launch DKU, which became a university-wide endeavor at Duke, mobilizing deans, vice presidents, and faculty, organized into multiple committees. The faculty-led Academic Council and Board of Trustees had final authority on curriculum and major commitments. In September 2012 Duke appointed Liu Jingnan and Mary Brown Bullock to serve as chancellor and executive vice chancellor, respectively, of DKU. Liu had been the president of Wuhan University from 2003 to 2008, and Bullock was the president of Agnes Scott College from 1995 to 2006. This combination of leaders from China and the United States, the former with a background in the engineering sciences and the latter in Chinese history and the liberal arts, represented the multifaceted goal of DKU to be a world-class, comprehensive university, rooted in the liberal arts, in one of the most commercial cities in China.[136]

To address concerns about intellectual freedom in China—where the ruling Communist Party was at once powerful and powerfully insecure—and to ensure Duke's control over a project that carried significant reputational risk for the university, DKU's final Joint Venture Agreement vested the "highest authority" at the school in an independent Board of Trustees on which Duke had full veto power. Senior administrators from Duke, including its provost, were ex-officio members. Internet access, which was censored by the infamous "Great Firewall" in China, would be unrestricted on DKU's campus through a virtual private network (VPN) with servers in Singapore.[137]

Duke had limited liability financially for DKU, except for the amount it agreed to contribute to its operations, and it had the right to withdraw its name from DKU should it feel necessary. An advisory board of distinguished global business leaders and retired Chinese officials was established to provide counsel, financial support, and political insulation.

A total of 137 students from eleven countries were enrolled in DKU's inaugural master's and undergraduate programs in 2014 when DKU opened. These were curtain-raisers for the larger enterprise of a four-year, liberal arts degree program that began in 2018.

## A Liberal Arts Education in China?

Duke had a long history of connection with China. In 1881 Charlie Soong, patriarch of one of modern China's most influential families, attended Trinity College as the school's first international student, returning to China as a missionary, during which time he lived in Kunshan for several years. Still, given the damage that China's universities had sustained during the first decades of the People's Republic, and especially during the Cultural Revolution, the challenges of introducing (or, more accurately, reintroducing) an education in the liberal arts in China could not be underestimated. By the early twenty-first century, however, the belief that a liberal arts education could be a driver in China of innovation and entrepreneurship (as was believed in America) was widely held among presidents of Chinese universities and, indeed, by the Communist Party Secretary and mayor of Kunshan.

For its part, Duke's faculty, which had been conducting research and teaching in China for decades, now had the opportunity of a lifetime: to create an entirely new undergraduate curriculum for a university as yet unencumbered by either full-time students or faculty. A Liberal Arts in China Committee (LACC) was formed in Durham in 2014. According to Professor Haiyan Gao, a member of the committee and Vice Chancellor for Academic Affairs at DKU, committee members spent two years researching global experiments in the liberal arts and sciences and visiting multiple Chinese universities.[138] Their final curriculum promoted integrative and international learning that (in the Duke tradition) de-emphasized disciplinary boundaries. It stressed an education of "rooted globalism," with the mission "to cultivate informed and engaged citizens who are knowledgeable about each other's histories, traditions of thought and affiliations, and skilled in navigating local, national, and global identities and commitments with an international perspective."[139] To stress Duke's responsibility for the graduates of its newest school, DKU students would receive a Duke University degree.

After two years of intense discussion over the scale of the operation, China's potential restrictions on academic freedom, and reputational risks for Duke, the Academic Council of Duke's faculty overwhelmingly approved the DKU curriculum in November 2016. The result of the vote was the fruit of assiduous outreach by Duke's leadership to convince its faculty to embrace a strategically important but "high risk, high reward" proposition for the school. Brodhead and Kornbluth met with representatives from every school and many more members of the university's various governance committees to answer any questions they had regarding Duke's plans in China. Testimonies by Duke's faculty members who had worked at DKU that they encountered only unimpeded freedom to engage in discussion of even controversial subjects on DKU's campus were also crucial in alleviating faculty concerns. At the Academic Council meeting in October 2016, Brodhead made perhaps the strongest argument: "China is a part of every issue involving global health, global environment, global economics, global security, global information security, and everything else. . . . A university that can't find a way to engage in China will be a university that is unable to give its students the kind of education that will help them understand the world they need to be actors in." The Board of Trustees approved the degree program unanimously the following month.[140]

This was, in my view (and I was, by this time, Duke's Senior Advisor on China), university governance at its best. Brodhead and Lange (and later Kornbluth) established multiple layers of faculty oversight committees both to gain advice and to make the faculty part of the creative process of DKU. Budgetary figures (and risks) were shared openly and fully. Debate was robust, especially in the elected Academic Council. There were, as diplomats say, full and frank exchanges of views within the Academic Council. Duke's Board of Trustees—a larger and much more professional governance body than the Harvard Corporation of the early twenty-first century—studied the multiple proposals for DKU in both committees and plenary sessions. (It may have helped that the board was led by G. Richard "Rick" Wagoner, Jr., the former chairman and CEO of General Motors, who had personally negotiated the joint ventures in China that saved GM as a company.) At the end of the day, the faculty voted overwhelmingly and the trustees unanimously for the full establishment of DKU.

The support DKU received from the Duke community ran in contrast to the establishment of the first joint Chinese-American university in the People's Republic of China: NYU Shanghai.[141] Headed by the former president of Cornell, Jeffrey Lehman, NYU Shanghai has been an extraordinary success. But while Duke led a determined and transparent campaign of consultation with faculty on the development of DKU, NYU faculty criticized President John Sexton of pushing through NYU's international campuses by fiat. Sexton eventually departed after faculty passed the fourth vote of no confidence in his leadership. (NYU's experience would still benefit Duke: the executive vice chancellor for DKU in 2021 was Alfred Bloom, the founding vice chancellor of NYU Abu Dhabi.)

Meanwhile, in Kunshan, DKU's first master's programs and research centers, established in 2014, had attracted talent and research funding to the city and had further raised its profile internationally. Upon Duke's approval of the undergraduate program, Kunshan agreed in May 2017 to fund a second, larger phase of construction. There would still be financial challenges for DKU's operating costs, which it would have to meet by tuition and other income.[142] Duke's contribution to DKU's operating costs was capped at $5 million per year,[143] plus an additional $1 million annually to fund research or educational projects for Duke faculty in Kunshan.[144]

Duke's determination to build Duke Kunshan University proved to be a compelling, but not an easy, investment. A spectacular campus, in a style at once local and global, was in place to welcome its first undergraduates in the liberal arts and sciences. The Jiangnan (lower Yangzi) region in which Kunshan is located is marked by "water towns," of which the old center of Kunshan is one. The DKU campus was designed with water at its center, organized around a large man-made lake, with buildings and residences connected by bridges and walkways. Clad both in glass and in the distinctive white stone of Jiangnan, its terraces and pavilions offer calming water views for classrooms and conferences. To be sure, not all of the construction went smoothly. Duke erred by not sending its own facilities people to oversee construction in the first years, with resultant problems of delay and redesign. Kunshan, after all, had never constructed a campus for a "world-class" university. And so, when the first undergraduate students arrived, they and the faculty were housed in a downtown Kunshan hotel. (That necessary experiment went very well, for I recall a senior Duke faculty member who taught in Kunshan that term telling me with enthusiasm, "Now I know that a university is not a set of buildings.") By August 2019, however, phase one of the

**Figure 7.5.** Academic Building on the Duke Kunshan University campus. Dove Feng/Wikimedia Commons/CC BY-SA 4.0.

campus, which comprised six buildings, including the university's Innovation Center, was complete.[145] Construction for phase two, which would add twenty-two additional buildings, was set to finish by 2022.

Now that we have built it, Brodhead wondered, would they come? How would DKU, like its ancestor in Durham, form a university as fine as its architecture?

## Into the Future

When Duke's latest strategic plan was approved by the Academic Council in May 2017, Richard Brodhead's term as president was coming to an end. In December 2016 Duke's Board of Trustees had elected Vincent Price as the tenth president of Duke University. Price, the provost and chief academic officer of the University of Pennsylvania since 2009, seemed ideally suited to lead Duke. He had academic appointments across Penn (as the Steven H. Chaffee Professor of Communication in the Annenberg School for Communication and Professor of Political Science in the School of Arts and Sciences), and he served as a trustee of the Wistar Institute, a nonprofit biomedical research institute, as well as on the executive planning group for University of Pennsylvania Health System. These positions left him prepared to oversee Duke University's own powerful health system.[146] As provost, Price also led Penn's global strategy, hiring the university's first Vice Provost for Global Initiatives and spearheading the creation of the Penn Wharton China Center in Beijing, which opened in 2015.[147] After Price became Duke's tenth president in 2017, he looked to the future, toward "Duke's Second Century" by outlining a strategic framework with five core areas: "empowering people, transforming education, building community, forging partnerships, and engaging our network."[148] He oversaw the launch of DKU's four-year undergraduate program in August 2018. That year, DKU welcomed an inaugural class of 266, larger than the planned-for 225 because of a particularly successful recruitment season. They hailed from 27 countries, with 175 coming from mainland China, 10 from Taiwan, 39 from the United States, and 42 from elsewhere. Former President Brodhead spoke at DKU's first undergraduate convocation, telling his audience that "the partnership [between Duke and Kunshan] has worked because the contributors share an essential attribute, a commitment to plan for the long term."[149]

In early 2020 Duke and its ambitious internationalization faced a new challenge. COVID-19 emerged first in Wuhan, home to DKU's Chinese university partner, Wuhan University, about five hundred miles from the DKU campus. As of August 2020 there had been nearly 90,000 confirmed cases and an official death toll of 4,715 in China, but because of the country's relative success (after an initial cover-up) in containing the virus, it was not in the top thirty countries globally in total number of infections.[150] China's initial virus outbreak forced DKU into emergency actions. As with other universities in China, DKU followed the Chinese Ministry of Education's direction to move classes online. Yet moving a whole liberal arts campus to a remote, online format set out a significant challenge during a time when DKU was recruiting its third class.[151] Then in May 2020, after China controlled the virus, DKU fully reopened and welcomed staff back to campus. After being closed for nearly a semester, this was a joyous occasion.[152] Meanwhile, across the world and especially in the United States, the virus spread like wildfire, eventually to the home campus.

Like many American universities, Duke in Durham attempted a hybrid reopening of campus in fall 2020. Only freshmen and sophomores, as well as select students requiring campus housing, were welcomed back into on-campus residences. Those on campus could attend courses in person, but

President Price noted that all students should expect to "complete much of their course work remotely."[153] As at other US universities, international students were unable to enter the United States during the pandemic, but here DKU gave Duke an advantage. Unlike Duke in Durham, DKU welcomed to campus all students who were in, or able to enter, China. DKU thus opened its doors to 160 stranded students from Duke and other US universities.[154] Duke students studying at DKU would receive full credit from classes there for their Duke degrees.[155] While many viewed DKU as a risk at first, a robust overseas physical presence, particularly in China—the top country of origin for Duke's international students—was now an obvious asset in a world where international travel and connectivity were no longer a given. In the autumn of 2020 the safest Duke campus for teaching and learning was not East or West Campus, but its watery *Far Eastern* campus at Kunshan, the only place in the world where all Duke instruction could be held in person and in one time zone.

In his inaugural address as president, Brodhead had marveled at Duke's enduring capacity of metamorphosis, that willingness to "remake itself in sometimes fairly drastic ways to the end of becoming better." In private discussions, Brodhead contrasted Duke with more established universities, such as the Yale he knew so well. In such places it was "very hard for the school to want to do anything except to continue to extend the things the school was excellent in doing." Theirs, he said, in a telling phrase, was the "inertia of excellence." Duke, by contrast (in the words of Nancy Andrews, Dean of the School of Medicine from 2007 to 2016), was "inspired by its traditions but not determined by them."[156]

The challenge for Brodhead's successor would be to continue with innovation rooted in relentless planning so that Duke would grow as a research and global university on its own terms. "My anxiety for Duke," Brodhead said, "has always been that it would enter a phase of complacency. That it would tell itself that it was reaching for the stars when it was actually only reaching for the nearest shiny thing."[157]

In 2020 Duke faced a trifecta of challenges: a public health crisis, another global recession, and rising US-China tensions. A university that had planned its way toward interdisciplinary innovation and internationalization faced the prospect of an era of deglobalization. Meanwhile, "inspection teams" from the Chinese Communist Party's disciplinary enforcement body were paying visits to leading Chinese universities seeking to root out "corruption" of the ideological sort. They had yet to visit DKU. Yet as several Duke colleagues had pointed out during the Academic Council's debate on the DKU curriculum, these political challenges were confirmation of how important it was for Duke to remain engaged and, indeed, to be a leader in China and there, as at home, to set global standards.[158] After all, building an institution that might one day serve as a model for teaching and learning for forty million students in the world's second-largest economy was nothing less than an outrageous ambition.

# CHAPTER EIGHT

# A Chinese Century?

## *The Revival and Rise of Chinese Universities*

I N  T H E  twenty-first century, it is China that has the greatest ambitions for higher education, and its rise has been truly staggering. In 1978, after a decade of mostly closed universities, Chinese universities enrolled approximately 860,000 students.[1] This number increased gradually until 2000, with enrollment of about seven million at that time. The government subsequently accelerated the pace of expansion, and by the year 2010, over thirty million students were enrolled in Chinese universities. In 2020 there were more than forty million students in Chinese institutions of higher learning.[2]

In 1998 Chinese colleges and universities graduated 830,000 students annually; by 2010 the number was 6 million.[3] In 2000 China had approximately half the number of university students as the United States; by 2020 it had more than twice the number.[4] In 2000 there were 1,041 colleges and universities in China.[5] A decade later there were more than twice as many: 2,358.[6] From 1999 to 2009 Chinese institutions of higher education hired nearly 900,000 new, full-time faculty members.[7]

For most of the history of the People's Republic, higher education was an opportunity afforded to the very few. Now China has moved toward mass higher education. The gross enrollment ratio (college participation rate) of eighteen- to twenty-two-year-olds was 3 percent in 1999; it was 30 percent in 2013.[8] By 2020 over 50 percent of young adults in this age cohort were enrolled in colleges or universities.[9]

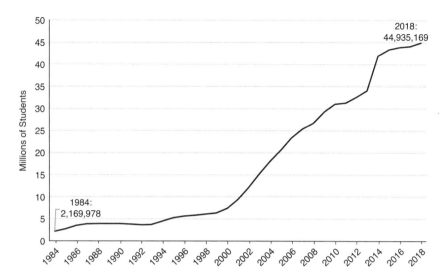

**Figure 8.1.** Tertiary education enrollment in China, 1984–2018 (in millions of students). Data source: UNESCO Institute for Statistics http://data.uis.unesco.org/#, accessed August 22, 2020.

This expansion of higher education is altogether new in its scope, but it is also a modern manifestation of centuries of dedication to advanced learning. To understand the Chinese higher education sector today, we must first look back at its foundations in imperial and Republican China.

## Legacies of Learning

China is home to the world's longest continuous civilization, with the longest continuing sets of philosophical and literary traditions. Before the introduction of Western-style higher education in the late nineteenth and early twentieth centuries, the study of these traditions defined not only what it meant to be a scholar but also what it meant to be powerful. Imperial China's civil service examination was the gateway to elite status. The educational system that prepared candidates for the test focused not on statecraft or tax collection but instead on what we would today call the humanities: the classics of Chinese civilization that set out principles of human behavior that servants of the state were to follow.

There has seldom been a higher academic ideal: good people embarking on the living study of great books in order to do good work in government for the benefit of society. As Song dynasty Emperor Zhenzong (968–1022) wrote, in his poem "Urge to Study," "When a man wishes to fulfill the ambition of his life/He only needs to diligently study the six classics by the window."[10] In imperial China, higher learning could transform one's destiny. The classical canon tested by the civil service examination was created during the Song era (960–1279) to include the Four Books (*Great Learning* and the *Doctrine of the Mean*—which were both originally from the *Book of Rites*—the Confucian *Analects* and *Mencius*) and the Five Classics (*Classic of Poetry, Book of Documents, Book of Rites, I Ching,* and the *Spring and Autumn Annals*).[11] The examination also required candidates to demonstrate knowledge of past and present government policies and the ability to write in good literary style.

Aspiring officials sat through tiers of examinations at the district, prefectural, provincial, and national levels. Candidates would enter the examination compounds with much ceremony, bringing with them only food, water, and their personal bucket for human waste. Test-takers would remain in their own examination cell until the multiday examination was complete; the only way out before a cannon shot signaled the end of the exam was as a corpse, thrown over the compound wall.

In navigating these brutal examinations, would-be scholar-officials rose through a system of local, provincial, and national examinations and preparatory institutions, at the pinnacle of which was the Imperial Academy (*taixue,* later known as *guozijian*) located in the capital of the empire.[12] Those who achieved high enough results on the examination could become members of the Hanlin Academy at the court and act as researchers, consultants to the emperor, and overseers of the examination system.[13] Complementing this formal, government-run system was an elite local system of academies, or *shuyuan,* run by scholars or academic societies. By late imperial times, *shuyuan* were increasingly associated with civil service examination preparation, but at times offered radical or differing interpretations of the body of literature found in the examinations.[14]

The civil service examination, like the imperial educational system that flowed from it, was the meritocratic bedrock upon which several of the world's greatest empires were built. It allowed—theoretically, at least—for social mobility in an otherwise hierarchical society, elevating only the truly educated into positions of power. Yet, as Benjamin Elman has shown, social mobility was never its purpose—a modest amount of it was instead an "unexpected consequence."[15] And there were practical limits to this system in more modern times: the absence of the study of mathematics, science, and practical affairs in the examinations did not mean that the empire was thereby better governed. Their absence arguably contributed to the empire's feeble capacity in the nineteenth century to respond to a militarized, industrialized, and otherwise energized West in a series of humiliations that would spell the end of a two-thousand-year-old imperial tradition. By the end of the nineteenth century, the system was admired more abroad than at home.

As Western powers encroached upon China in the nineteenth century, the Qing court attempted to modernize the civil service examination, broadening the tests to include subjects such as mathematics in 1887.[16] Some regional *shuyuan* began to offer courses in mathematics, Western languages, science, world geography, and world history by the 1890s.[17] At the same time, both the court and private citizens set up new modern training institutes to enable China to study and compete with the West. The empire fell in 1912, but the more important date in education is 1905, when the ancient examination system was abolished. It would be replaced by an emerging system of higher education that would educate several "new Chinas."

## Foreign Models for a Modern China

Taking the place of the examination system and the academies associated with it was a set of new colleges and universities on international models founded in late Qing and early Republican times. Theirs was the complex and often contradictory challenge that Wilhelm von Humboldt would have recognized: to bring global knowledge and international standards of higher education to China, while still serving the state and nation. The emergence of a Western-style university system in China began in Wuhan, a center of learning in imperial times, and the site of the founding of China's first modern university: the Self-Strengthening Institute (later Wuhan University) in 1893. Led by Governor-General Zhang Zhidong, its early, instrumentalist focus was toward the study of those subjects that would bring about China's return to "wealth and power," primarily mathematics, science, and business, although not at the expense of China's educational tradition.

What began in Wuhan soon spread throughout China, as a diverse crop of institutions sprouted up, heavily influenced by the higher education systems of Europe, Japan, and the United States. Public universities developed strong ties to foreign entities. Tsinghua University was founded in 1911 with

Boxer Indemnity funds returned by the United States. Tongji University in Shanghai grew into a private and then public university in the 1920s out of its origins as the German Medical School founded in 1907, and it has maintained its German connections to this day. Foreign influence was evident also in the universities and colleges established by various missionary groups, including St. John's University in Shanghai, founded by American Anglicans; Aurora University, founded by French Jesuits in Shanghai; and Yenching University, founded in Beijing by American Methodist Episcopalians and Congregationalists. Facing a mainland already dominated by foreign counterparts, the British raced to wield their educational influence by establishing the University of Hong Kong in 1911.

The influence of foreign models in reshaping education in China comes as no surprise, for modern Chinese history is inescapably international. During the eras of the First (1912), Second (1927), and Third (1949) Chinese Republics, each republic sought legitimacy in the form of one or another internationally authenticated "ism," from constitutionalism to communism. If the civil service examination had been a foundation of the Chinese empire's strength, international partnerships in higher education have energized modern China's century-plus long rise.

As international institutions introduced new models of higher education to China, returning Chinese scholars educated abroad helped them to flourish and endure. Faculty, deans, and presidents were recruited from the growing number of young Chinese studying internationally. The best early example of this trend was Cai Yuanpei, who served multiple terms as president of Peking University and studied in Germany and France from 1906 to 1910 and again from 1912 to 1916.

Prior to his European studies, Cai had passed the highest level (*jinshi*) of the imperial civil service examinations. Named in 1912 as the first Minister of Education of the new Republic, Cai issued an official opinion that universities should not simply serve government but should be granted institutional autonomy and be places for an "education with a worldview" (*shijieguan jiaoyu*), that is, an education with global perspective. Cai's reforms were deeply influenced by the German model of higher education. For instance, he believed in the separation of universities and technical schools, and he explicitly stressed the importance of *Bildung*, of broad, humanistic learning as the foundation of both teaching and scientific research (in the sense of *Wissenschaft*).[18]

When Cai Yuanpei assumed the presidency of Peking University in 1917, he introduced a broad range of international practices into Chinese higher education. He declared in his inaugural address: "People outside the university . . . observe that all who study here have it in their minds to become officials and get rich." Students, he said, should devote themselves to learning, not in narrow specializations but in the humanities and natural sciences. Cai's presidency saw the rapid growth of the humanities at "Beida," as Peking University became popularly called, and he phased out the business and engineering divisions. Cai famously stressed that:

> The modern principle of freedom of thought has already been publicly accepted, but the ability to make this happen rests solely with the university. The expression of thought by university teachers is not only free of restriction by religion or political parties but also free of constraints imposed by renowned scholars. . . . This is what makes a true institution of higher learning. . . . We must follow the general rule of freedom of thought and freedom of expression, and not allow any one branch of philosophy or any one tenet of religion to confine our minds.[19]

Cai recruited to the Peking University faculty the scholars Chen Duxiu and Li Dazhao, who would be instrumental in introducing Marxism to China. He recruited also China's leading proponent of liberalism, the philosopher Hu Shi, a student of John Dewey at Columbia, who had written, "For a country to lack a navy or an army is not a cause for shame; [but] a country without a university, a national library, museum, or art gallery, should be ashamed."[20] It was in the tradition of this intellectually vibrant and diverse Peking University that its students would play dramatic roles in challenging successive Chinese governments in the liberal and patriotic public demonstrations of 1919, 1935, and, eventually, 1989. Cai's presence is still felt today on the Beida campus, where a statue of his likeness stands not far from the liberal arts college named for him.

China's internationalization in higher education was at the center of the most transformative age in modern Chinese culture, the roughly ten years from 1915 to 1925, now known as the "May Fourth era." It was a cultural revolution more profound and enduring than the so-called Great Proletarian Cultural Revolution of Mao Zedong. The May Fourth Movement, unlike Mao's, focused on renewing Chinese society, rather than razing it. Its most famous moment occurred on May 4, 1919 (giving the era its name), when patriotic students protesting the Treaty of Versailles, which transferred Germany's territorial concession in China to Japan, rather than returning it to

China, poured out of the modern Red Building of Peking University to demonstrate at the nearby Forbidden City. Just a few thousand students took part, but they brought China's new universities to the forefront of Chinese political life.

In 1922 China's government sought to adopt what Ruth Hayhoe, a leading scholar of Chinese higher education, has called an "American ethos" in primary and secondary education.[21] Legislation broadened the definition of "university" to include not just institutions dedicated to theoretical studies but also those focused on professional or applied fields. This represented a shift from the German-influenced model, which drew a sharp distinction between universities and technical schools, toward a more inclusive American conception. The legislation also introduced the system of credits, which allowed students greater freedom to customize their studies. Reflecting the ambitions of the state, the legislation established a board of managers to make administrative decisions at universities, seeking to limit the role of professors in university governance.

This system-wide American influence was short-lived. As the Nationalist government consolidated power in Nanjing after 1927, it began also to exercise more centralized control over higher education.[22] In the 1930s it reorganized the higher education system according to recommendations from a League of Nations commission led by former Prussian Minister of Education C. H. Becker.[23] Reforms, made with the encouragement of the commission and heavily influenced by Prussian models, led to increased government control over a nationalized system of higher education. Political authorities favored more comprehensive universities in the 1920s, but the 1930s saw emphasis once again placed on science, mathematics, and engineering.[24]

Internationalization also took architectural form. In the twentieth century, the old examination compounds gave way to leafy campuses modeled after American and European universities. Tsinghua's campus reflects its American and (later) Soviet partners. National Central University in Nanjing channeled the University of Berlin. Alternatively, one can admire the *jingyuan* at Peking University, a lovely campus in Chinese style, built for its predecessor institution on that site, Yenching University—and designed by a New York architectural firm.

When war with Japan struck in the 1930s, Chinese universities chose to relocate and reimagine themselves during this period of tumult. As the Japanese army encroached upon Chinese borders and occupied urban centers, universities sought refuge in unoccupied areas. This movement began with the relocation of Dongbei University from Japanese-occupied Manchuria to Beijing in 1931, but it became larger in scale after 1937 when the Japanese army gained control of major cities such as Beijing and Shanghai. By 1938, 54 higher education institutions out of 114 had been damaged or destroyed by Japanese forces, and by 1941, in a heroic and patriotic migration across China, 77 institutions had relocated to temporary, safer locations.[25] At the apex of the wartime higher education system was the National Southwest Associated University (*Guoli xinan lianhe daxue*), a union of Tsinghua, Peking, and Nankai universities that remained a bastion of liberal thought and academic work despite its wartime surroundings. John Israel, an American historian who has written on *Lianda*, as it was called for short, argued that the chaotic political environment left universities free to flourish, much as they had under the less organized central governance of the 1920s.[26] This changed, however, as the war of resistance gave way to civil war and then to a new political regime, by which time most universities had returned to their original locations on China's eastern coast.

Before 1949 China had developed a vibrant and diverse, if small, system of higher education on international standards. Its leading scholars were internationally minded and often internationally educated. Its students were trained according to pedagogies and curricula broadly aligned with those at leading Western universities. In short, the intellectual and architectural foundations of every major Chinese university were international in origin.

## Restructuring and Destruction, 1949–1978

The Communist takeover prompted a sizeable flow of academic emigration from China's leading universities to Taiwan, Hong Kong, and, especially, the United States. After 1949 mainland Chinese universities ceased cooperation with Western partners but redirected their international efforts East: collaboration now took place with the Soviet Union and its East European allies, as Chinese higher education was restructured to support a planned economy on a Stalinist model. Management of higher education was centralized (as it had been under the Nationalists) under a national Ministry of Education, which initially recommended gradual reform. However, as the Soviet Union consolidated its influence in China in the early 1950s, the higher education system changed dramatically to emulate Soviet approaches. Institutions were reorganized to focus on specific tasks and subjects, often separating theoretical areas of study from related practical fields. In these sovietized institutions, there was a marked separation of teaching and research: universities were to be dedicated to the teaching and transmission of knowledge, while research activities were largely housed at separate academies that existed outside the higher education system.[27]

Throughout the 1950s and 1960s, the higher education system became at once ever more controlled and compartmentalized. In the 1950s Communist Party organs were established in every university to ensure ideological orthodoxy. Governance decisions were made within increasingly smaller units within university departments. Students entered into one of an expanding panorama of specializations (from 249 in 1953 to 627 in 1962 to over 1,000 in the 1980s), and they studied a uniform curriculum within their specialization. The goal of education was to serve the state and the Chinese Communist Party (CCP), not necessarily in that order; enrollment quotas for academic departments were decided according to the needs of national economic development plans, and universities were charged with political, not just academic, education.[28]

Mao Zedong's "Cultural Revolution," unleashed in 1966, nearly destroyed Chinese higher education.[29] From 1966 to 1969 enrollment of new students was stopped completely, intellectuals were persecuted, and several universities became political and military battlegrounds between competing Party factions. When reinstated in 1970, admissions were based on "mass recommendations" and political credentials, rather than the national college entrance examination (*gaokao*). Candidates were to be recommended by "the masses" (in practice by a "work unit," or place of employment), approved by leaders, and reviewed by the schools.[30] In principle, students were to be admitted in the first instance from the ranks of "workers, peasants, and soldiers," thereby upending the traditional structures of privilege. In practice, this system produced a cohort of university students with wildly divergent levels of academic preparation, while the lack of formal entrance exams favored the politically well connected.[31] Only with Mao's death and the ousting of his loyal "Gang of Four" in 1976 was the stage set for the restoration of China's universities, once again as part of a global world of universities.

## The Contemporary Chinese University System

Deng Xiaoping, who emerged as China's paramount leader in the post-Mao years, never attended university. But his father had studied at an early Chinese university, and, at the age of fifteen, Deng Xiaoping was shipped abroad to a work-study program in France, where he joined the Chinese Communist Party. He would later study briefly in Moscow. By the 1970s as a vice-premier having survived (barely) the Cultural Revolution, Deng was an early and vigorous supporter of reviving higher education. His beliefs that "scientific and technological development are the keys to modernization" and that "education is the basis of cultivating science and technology" were cited to justify reforms within higher education during a brief period of liberalization in the early 1970s.[32] Universities saw such statements as signs that higher education would soon be formally restored, and they began eliminating Cultural Revolution-era practices of their own accord by the mid-1970s.[33] The State Council affirmed this trajectory when it announced the *gaokao* would resume in October 1977.[34] The Party's recognition that China needed a new approach to national development after the catastrophe of Maoist rule underpinned the fast pace and wide scope of early reforms in higher education.

When universities reopened fully in 1978, the State Council moved swiftly to clear the wreckage of the Cultural Revolution. It established a long-lasting strategy of funneling extra resources into elite universities. It labeled eighty-eight universities as "key," with Peking, Tsinghua, and Fudan Universities selected as the top three institutions.[35] Key universities acted as the vanguards of the system, offering new degree programs, increasing their research, and garnering high levels of government funding. To supplement its own support for universities, the Chinese government sought foreign aid for this effort. In fact, the World Bank's first loan to the People's Republic of China (PRC) was $200 million to support the development of science and engineering departments at twenty-six universities in 1980.[36] A small number of elite institutions were run under the direct supervision of (and received more funding from) the central government, either through the Ministry of Education or another relevant department. Provincial and municipal governments were left to supervise and at least partially fund the remaining public colleges and universities.

During the 1980s the government experimented with a return to the principles guiding Chinese higher education in the early Republic, affording institutions greater intellectual autonomy and administrative control. Government leaders recognized that to develop growth-enhancing science and technology, Chinese intellectuals required space to set their own research agendas.[37] In 1982 constitutional reforms included legal protections for intellectual work, and the 1985 "Decision on Education Reform" went so far as to declare that "the key to restructuring higher education will lie in eliminating excessive government control over institutions of higher education."[38] That same year, government policy called for universities to become centers of both teaching and research, undoing the bifurcation of the Soviet model in the 1950s and 1960s. In brief, universities were deemed essential components in China's overall "opening and reform" agenda.

Yet during the early years of the reform era, Chinese higher education failed to meet the state's great expectations. Universities produced a glut of graduates who struggled to find jobs in China's still emerging economy.[39] Economic discontent combined with political protest in the huge and prolonged demonstrations—in which university students played a catalytic role—that took place in multiple cities in the spring of 1989, most famously in Beijing's Tiananmen Square. Deng Xiaoping's decision to crush the demonstrations by force led to the death of hundreds of students, the arrest and exile of thousands more, and enduring tensions between universities and the state. As a nationwide crackdown unfolded in the summer and autumn of 1989, the government reversed its position on political interference in academia. Deng Xiaoping now declared that "the biggest mistake of the decade was in education, particularly in regards to ideological and political education."[40] As in 1949 academic repression led to another wave of intellectual migration, largely to the United States and Europe. (One of my own doctoral students, the historian Wang Dan, had been a Peking University student leader of the Tiananmen protests. He served multiple prison terms in China before being exiled to continue his studies at Harvard. He came to us with stellar and proud recommendations from Peking University faculty. He remains active in the overseas movement for democratic reform in China.)

Tiananmen convinced Chinese political leaders that higher education should, first, be subservient to the Party and state and, second, serve China's developmental aspirations. In the early 1990s caps were placed on the growth of university enrollment to prevent the system from expanding further while officials debated how to proceed.[41] Soon, new restrictions were placed on teaching and research in the humanities and social sciences, reflecting the government's belief that these disciplines required greater ideological supervision. Yet higher education was again prioritized and liberalized when economic reforms restarted in 1992. And the system overall continued to grow. From 1999 to 2006 the total number of Chinese higher education institutions grew from 1,071 to 1,867.[42]

In 1993 the State Council announced that, throughout all levels of government, spending on universities should reach 4 percent of GNP by the year

2000. Actual expenditures on education hovered around 2.5 percent of GNP until 1997,[43] when an external shock, the Asian financial crisis, galvanized the government to increase infrastructure investment, including the construction of new university campuses, raising enrollment caps to fill these institutions. This was at once an investment in the future and a means of keeping unemployed young Chinese off the streets for an additional four years. From 2000 to 2003 the government's appropriations for higher education jumped by at least 20 percent each year and continued to increase by at least 10 percent annually until the financial crisis in 2008.[44]

Between 1998 and 2003 enrollment in Chinese universities tripled. In 1999 alone enrollment increased by 510,000 students.[45] The state-set target enrollment rate for the university-age population was raised from under 10 percent in 1998 to 15 percent by 2002. As China entered the new millennium, its universities were poised to play an even greater role in the country's economic and social development.

By the summer of 2020 there were 2,688 higher education institutions in China, including 1,265 four-year universities.[46] Of the four-year universities, 76 reported to the Ministry of Education; 38 to other central government,

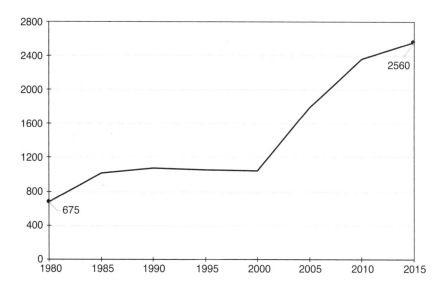

**Figure 8.2.** Total number of regular tertiary institutions in China, 1980–2015. Data source: China Statistical Yearbook 2018, http://www.stats.gov.cn /tjsj/ndsj/2018/indexeh.htm, accessed August 22, 2019.

CCP, or military organs; and 708 to provincial authorities.[47] Another 434 were classified as private institutions. Of these, over half (275) were so-called independent colleges, founded by public universities as a means to extend their outreach, enrollments, and, especially, income, for they could charge "private university" tuition rates.

Despite the fact that private ownership and administration of tertiary educational institutions were legalized only in 1982, the sector expanded rapidly, especially in the first two decades of the twenty-first century. Whereas private higher education institutions made up 6 percent of the higher education sector in 2002, by 2013 they accounted for over 30 percent of four-year institutions and 19.7 percent of student enrollment in higher education.[48] The number of four-year, degree-granting private institutions rose from 30 in 2007 to 423 in 2015, an increase of over 1,300 percent. One such institution can be found in the city of Xi'an, an ancient Chinese capital, where entrepreneurs worked with local officials to make that city China's capital of private higher education. Xi'an International University (*Xi'an waishi xueyuan*), founded in 1992 as an examination prep center, is now one of China's largest private universities, with a student body of thirty-four thousand. Its graduates enjoy better job placement rates than those of Peking or Tsinghua Universities. Unlike university presidents the world over, Xi'an's president, Huang Teng, does not worry about his tenure: he owns 55 percent of the university. President Huang has looked to establish branch campuses elsewhere in China and in North America.[49]

Large companies are also getting into the higher education game. Alibaba's Taobao unit launched "Taobao University" to train e-business owners, managers, salesmen, and professionals, and in time to extend business education to more than one million online students seeking the skills to start and sustain small- and medium-sized businesses. Taobao University made plans also to enroll some twenty thousand students "offline," that is, in person.[50]

Other forms of private institutions include new Sino-foreign joint-venture universities, which were established in China for the first time since the Communist revolution. Nine such institutions, whose foreign partners include universities from both the United States and the United Kingdom, have brought higher education and research centers beyond the plans of the Ministry of Education.[51] Modern British universities pioneered this movement, with the establishment in 2004 of the University of Nottingham Ningbo China, in partnership with a private Chinese education company. It offers liberal arts, engineering, and business education to eight thousand students in one of China's leading business cities. Its main structure is an architectural emulation of the elegant Trent Building on the Nottingham campus. The University of Liverpool partnered with Xi'an Jiaotong University to establish in 2008 a campus in the eastern industrial city of Suzhou, with a mission to "educate technical and managerial professionals with international perspectives and competitive capabilities."[52] In 2013 New York University established NYU Shanghai as a vertical university (that is, in a high-rise) as part of its global network and in partnership with one of China's most creative universities, East China Normal University. And, as we have seen, Duke University's two-hundred-acre residential campus in Kunshan, China's richest and most entrepreneurial town, located just west of Shanghai, opened its doors in 2014 as Duke Kunshan University.[53]

For all this expansion, land and capital have been made available by a variety of means. Land in China is owned by the state, specifically local governments, who have broad authority to expropriate it and to pay little in compensation to its historical inhabitants, often farmers. The result has been a quintupling in the acreage of Chinese universities since 2000. Old universities have built stunning new campuses. Zhejiang University, which was founded in 1897, houses its fifty thousand students across seven large campuses. Chongqing University, established in 1929, has opened beautifully landscaped new university grounds as part of an eight-university *daxuecheng*, or "university city." Until recently, higher education institutions had been concentrated in but a few areas, Beijing and the lower Yangzi region chief among them. Today cities and provinces never known for higher education compete to found, build, and expand colleges and universities—often within new science and technology zones—as part of their competitive strategies for growth, development, and prestige.

Unlike the growth of American universities in the 1950s and the extraordinary expansion of European institutions that began in the 1970s, the development of higher education in China has been elitist, focusing the majority of resources on a small subset of institutions favored by the state, as well as massive. The government-supervised higher education system was keen on tracking and comparing the performance of universities identified as nationally significant. The first university league tables, produced by the Chinese Academy of Management Sciences for publication in the state-run *Science and Technology Daily*, ranked the research performance in science, engineering, agriculture, and medical sciences of only eighty-six "key" universities.[54] Universities important enough to be measured for their contributions to key disciplines began to win rewards for subjecting themselves to such scrutiny in the 1990s. In 1995 the Ministry of Education launched "Project 211" to enhance the quality of about one hundred universities. It was followed in 1998 by "Project 985" to support thirty-nine elite universities, of which nine—China's so-called Ivy League—would be developed as "world-class" institutions (*guoji yiliu daxue*), defined as being "cradles" of high-level, creative researchers; frontiers of scientific research; forces of transformative research and innovation; and bridges for international exchange. To that end, Chinese central, provincial, and local governments, supplemented by university foundations and private philanthropy, have provided enormous revenues to the leading institutions, well outspending the (very significant) rewards given in recent European competitions, such as the Excellence Initiative in Germany.

In 2018, 44.94 million students were enrolled in some form of higher education institution in China.[55] The diversity, scale, and resources of the higher education landscape in China have left room for significant differentiation between its most and least elite institutions. Chinese universities have become deeply embedded in international networks of knowledge production and dissemination, seeking to emulate standards set by leaders in global higher education. At the same time, they remain shaped to at least an equal measure by national policies and priorities on university governance, funding, faculty, and students.

## Governance

In the post-Mao era, the government transferred an increasing amount of decision-making powers back to universities. In 1985 university presidents were given authority to make most decisions, save those of a political nature, which still fell under the jurisdiction of the university Party secretary.[56] The Higher Education Law of 1998 went further and specified seven areas in which higher education institutions had autonomy. These included both administrative areas, such as financial and property management, international structure, and personnel management, and academic programming decisions, including research and service, international exchange and cooperation, student admissions, teaching affairs, and the establishment of new specializations. In reality, most universities had to maintain close working relationships with the government, in what some have called a "state-supervised" model, in contrast with the "state-controlled" model of the pre-reform era.[57]

This changed with Xi Jinping's ascent to power. In 2014 the CCP reemphasized that public university governance in China occurred under "a system where the university president was responsible *under the leadership of the [university's] CCP Committee*" (italics added).[58] The university's Party secretary headed the university Party committee, while the president normally served as the first-ranked vice secretary. The rest of the committee would consist of other senior school administrators, including vice Party secretaries, vice presidents, and the secretary of the university's CCP discipline inspection commission, which was in charge of anti-corruption probes and, increasingly, "political discipline." The central role of the Party committee in decision-making, and the need for all Party members to "emulate" and "look to the [CCP leadership] core" has been reinforced in recent years in government departments, state-owned enterprises, and all public (and now even private) institutions, as well as universities.

The Party secretaries and presidents of the thirty-one most important Chinese universities (including Tsinghua and Peking) had administrative ranks equivalent to that of a government vice minister. Like all officials at or above vice minister rank in China, they were appointed to their roles by the Organization Department of the CCP Central Committee. With few exceptions, these leaders had to adhere to the mandatory retirement age of sixty-three for vice minister–ranked officials. Other senior leaders at these universities and the top leaders of other universities reporting to central government or Party organs were, in most cases, appointed by the Ministry of Education. Similarly, leaders of provincial universities were either appointed by the Organization Department of the province's CCP committee or its government's Department of Education, depending on their administrative ranks.

As of 2007 approximately one hundred universities (of which twenty were private) had formed boards of directors. However, unlike the boards of American universities, which often carry out governance or supervisory functions and are the legal representatives of universities, boards of public Chinese universities are limited in mandate and tend to focus on fundraising and building connections with industry. Chinese university presidents serve as the legal representatives of their institutions, and sometimes serve on boards. Overall board involvement in university affairs is minimal where Party committees are in charge.

Some private universities in China have taken governance boards more seriously. In 2015 several leading Chinese scholars planned a privately financed institution that could one day become China's Caltech. The result was Westlake University, located in the eastern city of Hangzhou and led by President Shi Yigong. Shi was elected by and responsible to a Board of Trustees chaired by Qian Yingyi, former dean of Tsinghua University's School of Economics and Management. The other nineteen members of the board included Nobel laureate and Caltech president emeritus David Baltimore, current and former leaders of leading Chinese universities, titans of industry and philanthropy, a representative of the Hangzhou city government, and the secretary of the university's Communist Party Committee. In private entrepreneurial universities such as Xi'an International University, boards may serve more as window dressing. As the president of one such institution once told me, "Yes, of course, we have a Board, but I make all the decisions."

## A Chinese Excellence Initiative

Growth in the higher education sector during the 1990s and the first decade of the 2000s was accompanied by the expansion and diversification of funding sources. By the end of this period, university funding came primarily from three sources: government, tuition fees, and commercial income.[59] As philanthropic efforts gained traction in China, donations became an increasingly important source of university income as well. By 2008, 108 higher education institutions had established fundraising foundations.[60]

Funding from various strata of government accounted for the largest portion of the budget of many universities, although this proportion was decreasing. Continuing patterns of funding established in the 1950s and 1960s and renewed in the post-Mao era, the government tended to funnel resources to a few select institutions in order to foster centers of excellence.[61] Funding for these elite universities came through two major government projects, the previously mentioned Project 211 and Project 985. Starting in 1995, Project 211 allocated approximately $2.2 billion to approximately one hundred top universities to support curricular and academic development within the disciplines as well as physical infrastructure. Universities applying for Project 211 funding submitted plans for how they would use the money to raise research and educational standards for consideration by the interministerial working group, which included leaders from the Ministry of Education (then the State Education Commission), the National Development and Reform Commission (then the State Planning Commission), and the Ministry of Finance. This working group assessed applications for Project 211 funding against the initiative's principles of "improving the level of national higher education, accelerating the development of the national economy, promoting the development of science and technology, enhancing comprehensive national strength and international competitiveness, and realizing high-level talent cultivation in China."[62]

Subsequently, the government launched Project 985 in 1998 at the centennial celebration of Peking University. Although structured similarly to Project 211, this project focused on allocating funding to a much smaller number of institutions—initially just two, later expanded to nine—but provided them with much larger sums. Both Tsinghua and Peking Universities, the original two universities chosen to participate, received a total of $225 million in the project's first three years. In 2003 the research labs at Project 985-funded universities received nearly half of the annual research funds for higher education despite their universities enrolling only 1 percent of the total students in higher education.[63] The initiative also gave birth to China's Ivy League equivalent, the "C9" group, which is composed of the nine universities that received early Project 985 funding.[64] The government has since expanded the project to provide funding for a total of thirty-nine universities. Between 2015 and 2017 funding under Project 211 and Project 985 was replaced by the Double First Class Universities Program, with "Double First Class" (DFC) standing for "first-class universities" and "first-class academic disciplines."

Universities' funding strategies were shaped also by the state's innovation and industrial policies. Since the higher education system's reestablishment, the state believed universities to be critical for fostering China's scientific and technological development. With the number of higher education institutions rapidly expanding at the start of the twenty-first century, the government experimented with new incentives for universities to focus their research on priority technologies. An early example was the State Council's 2001 announcement of a pilot for-profit enterprise program at Tsinghua and Peking Universities, which allowed them to operate revenue-generating companies that "further promote the industrialization of scientific and technological achievements in universities."[65] Municipal governments also began funding university-based research institutes that aligned with industrial policy priorities, one example being the Beijing-Tsinghua Industrial Development Institute in 1998. As China's industrial policy priorities evolved, so did the research programs universities were encouraged to contribute to. In 2015 the Ministry of Education advised universities that to solve "the poor employment prospects" of their graduates, they should focus on "innovation-driven development, Made in China 2025, Internet+, mass entrepreneurship and innovation, and the 'One Belt, One Road,' and other major national strategies to . . . truly enhance local universities to serve regional economic and social development."[66] As long as they agreed to incubate China's industrial policies, universities were promised greater latitude to develop new sources of income.

For universities outside the reach of these elite government projects, nongovernmental funding became increasingly important. In 1989 the state began to collect some tuition and fees from students, and from 1994, universities themselves were allowed to charge tuition, gaining a way to recoup costs for the first time. By 2001 tuition and fees covered over 50 percent of the total higher education expenditure, although elite universities still tended to have more diversified sources of income.[67] Facing the need for more funding and responding to the government's push to increase enrollment, many universities established affiliated "independent" colleges, as noted previously. These schools enjoyed lower prestige and higher tuition than their parent institutions. Generally, public universities charged the lowest tuition, while private, independent, and joint-venture institutions charged much higher fees.[68]

Support from provincial and local governments became increasingly important for Ministry of Education universities outside of Beijing. The "joint-building" or joint-funding of these universities with local governments became common in the late 1990s. Hoping to attract talent that could, in turn, attract high-tech companies and their investments, local governments launched ambitious projects to build new universities with both domestic and international partners. In 2011 the city of Shanghai partnered with the Chinese Academy of Sciences (CAS) to build ShanghaiTech University. The city spent over $700 million building ShanghaiTech's campus and contributed in part to an additional $3 billion to build surrounding key national laboratories, which were staffed and run with the help of CAS. The co-location of the university with key national laboratories was inspired by the example of the Lawrence Berkeley National Laboratory near the University of California, Berkeley. The teaching and research model at ShanghaiTech was inspired by Caltech. Shanghai municipality provided the land, the start-up funding for the university, and, as of 2018, 98 percent of the university's budget.[69]

## Faculty

The Ministry of Education set a goal in 2005 to raise the proportion of faculty members with graduate degrees to 80 percent of all faculty, with PhDs accounting for at least 30 percent.[70] This was an ambitious goal, for even among China's most elite institutions, the proportion of faculty with PhDs at that time was significantly lower than their American counterparts. At Tsinghua University in 2006, PhDs made up 62.7 percent of total faculty, while that year at Yale University, 91 percent held a doctorate. Still, Tsinghua's 62.7 percent represented a rapid increase from 1995, when only 15 percent of the faculty held doctorate degrees.[71]

To improve the diversity within and quality of institutions, the Ministry of Education also sought to break the tradition of "faculty inbreeding," through which faculty members completed their entire academic careers—from undergraduate student to senior faculty—at a single institution. The Ministry stipulated the goal that 70 percent or more of faculty should have completed at least one of their degrees at a different school or in a different department than the one in which they were employed. However, sample data collected by Beijing Normal University in 2009 showed that, although these efforts were starting to show progress, among the universities under the jurisdiction of the Ministry of Education, 57 percent of faculty could be classified as "inbred."[72]

Government policy supported the achievement of these quality improvement and diversification goals: in 2008 the central government launched the Thousand Talents Program, which attracted from overseas sixteen hundred scholars and entrepreneurs, mostly of Chinese descent. This success was followed by the Thousand Foreign Experts program in 2011. Both programs were designed to draw overseas research and innovation talent to China, with a particular focus on entrepreneurs and academics.[73]

Chinese university recruiting efforts overseas achieved highly publicized successes for recruiting both Chinese and non-Chinese scholars. Scholars were attracted to Chinese universities by supportive terms and unique opportunities. In 2007 the former President of Cornell University, Jeffrey Lehman, became the founding dean of the Peking University School of Transnational Law.[74] In 2012 he became vice chancellor of NYU Shanghai. In 2008 Tsinghua University convinced Professor Shi Yigong, then a prominent scientist at Princeton, to give up an endowed chair and turn down a $10 million grant from the Howard Hughes Medical Institute to take up the deanship of Tsinghua's School of Life Sciences.[75] As noted, Shi would later become president of Westlake University, showing Chinese higher education as a system attractive enough to recruit and retain international talent. The halls of top-tier Chinese universities were increasingly filled with scholars who had left tenured positions abroad to participate in the extraordinary growth—in quality as in quantity—of Chinese higher education.

## Admissions

Who gets into Chinese universities? As in the time of the imperial civil service examination, success in examination still determines the fate of students. One lone criterion—a high school student's score on the *gaokao*—largely dictates admission into university. Although the *gaokao* is officially titled the National Higher Education Entrance Examination, there have been significant regional differences in the test papers administered in various provinces. While from 1978 to 1987, the exam was standard across the nation, legislation in 1987 allowed each province to adjust the test according to local situations. Whereas each province's exams continued to cover similar subjects, by 2005 only sixteen out of China's thirty-one provinces used the national standard exam papers.[76] The examination usually comprised tests in Chinese, mathematics, and English as well as a set of three other subjects, either in the science track (physics, chemistry, and biology) or the humanities track (geography, history, and politics). The examination was infamous for its complexity, both in terms of the sheer depth of knowledge it required as well as the opacity of its questions.

In most regions, only students with an official residence permit (*hukou*) were allowed to sit for that region's test, despite the increasing number of migrant children who grow up and attend schools far away from their officially registered residences. Apart from the logistical and financial barriers associated with traveling to their (often rural) official residences for an exam, students faced a more fundamental obstacle: universities were allowed to determine regional admission quotas and set the lowest qualifying *gaokao* score for admission. This was ostensibly to give priority at each school to local students. However, since institutional quality varied greatly across the country, this gave distinct advantages to students who were born and raised in the big cities that house the country's flagship institutions. For example, Peking University and Tsinghua University are widely acknowledged to be the best universities in China. They are both located in Beijing. Data from 2013 showed that prospective students from Beijing were 30 times more likely to be accepted at Tsinghua than were *gaokao* takers from Guangdong.[77]

Reforms for this system were announced in late 2014. In the new system, students would be able to take examinations in a wider variety of subjects spread over multiple years of high school, rather than in a two-day national testing blitz.[78] The central government also planned for a greater level of standardization at the national level eventually. Finally, the government asked universities to incorporate other measures of performance beyond test scores to evaluate students' potential, while also moving to eliminate the often-exploited opportunities for students to score additional test points for extracurricular talents.

Still, public universities in China continued to admit students primarily on the basis of their test scores. Private colleges and universities, which were often considerably more expensive and less prestigious than the public institutions, mainly served students whose test scores did not reach the threshold for admittance to public universities. Independent colleges affiliated with public institutions did the same.

## *A Return to the Liberal Arts?*

As higher education institutions moved away from the Soviet-style specialization model and broadened their disciplinary offerings, institutions reconceived their undergraduate curricula. Chinese universities have long had general education (*tongshi jiaoyu*) programs of a certain sort, such as required classes (*bixiu ke*) in Marxism-Leninism-Mao Zedong Thought. And like required courses everywhere, students loathe and endure them. Over the past decade, however, mainland universities, together with those in Hong Kong and Taiwan, have competed to introduce general and liberal education programs that open opportunities for learning across the humanities and social sciences.

The idea of a "liberal education," that concept of German origin now with its deepest roots in North America, has begun to reestablish itself in Chinese thinking about the purpose of higher education as well. Just as many American educators believe (not wrongly) that young Chinese students are better educated in math and science than their American counterparts, many Chinese educators believe that it is the West, and particularly the Americans, who are "innovative" and "creative thinkers" while the Chinese people (despite all their ancient inventions and modern revolutions) remain "traditional," "rule bound," and "rote learners." For this, some blame the tortured path to university admission through the *gaokao*. How can students so completely focused on test scores to enter university possibly be innovators when they get there?

Leading American institutions claim to believe that for a truly liberal education, a study of the humanities is essential. Despite—or because of—a century-long obsession with engineering, this view is shared increasingly today in China's premier universities. Pacesetting Chinese universities believe that China's next generation of leaders should be broadly educated in the humanities and social sciences as well as in the sciences. In 2001 Peking University inaugurated the Yuanpei Program (now Yuanpei College) as part of a broad reform of undergraduate education to foster "a new generation of talented individuals with higher creativity as well as international competence so as to meet the needs of our present age." As we will see, Tsinghua University's School of Economics and Management, under the leadership of Dean Qian Yingyi, who received his doctorate at Harvard and held a professorship at UC Berkeley, has implemented one of the most imaginative programs in liberal arts and general education to be found in any Chinese university—and this in a professional school. Renmin University in Beijing, founded as the "People's University" on a Soviet model, now houses several of China's leading centers for classical studies and Chinese history.

## Internationalization

The early twenty-first century has been a time of expansion, outreach, and experimentation in Chinese higher education. These developments in China have promoted cooperation and competition across the realm of "Greater China": Hong Kong, Taiwan, and Singapore all compete with Beijing and Shanghai to be the educational center of the Chinese-speaking world.

While institutions internally sought out international best practices in undergraduate curriculum development, many also became increasingly intertwined in more explicit external partnerships with foreign institutions. Apart from the Sino-foreign universities discussed previously, the hugely successful China Europe International Business School, a joint venture with the European Union, ranks regularly as the top business school in China and among the top twenty-five worldwide.

Meanwhile, nearly every leading international university today believes that it needs to have a "China strategy" and to be somehow involved in the rapid growth of higher education in China. This has given rise to a healthy set of experiments and alternative models of engagement. Apart from formal campuses, Columbia University and the University of Chicago have opened an office and a center, respectively, in Beijing. Stanford University has built a courtyard center within the campus of Peking University. The Harvard Center Shanghai promotes research, student internships, conferences, and executive education in China.[79] Yet currently the Chinese government gives its international educational partners conflicting signals. New cooperative ventures in higher education are praised at the same time that the Ministry of Education terminated more than two hundred cooperative agreements, more than 20 percent of the total, with foreign universities.[80] Still, "Improving how Sino-foreign universities are run" was among the "China Education Modernization 2035" plan's top priorities.[81]

Internationalization is not a one-way street. The Ministry of Education reported that in 2018, over 1.5 million Chinese students were studying abroad.[82] Chinese students accounted for over 30 percent of foreign undergraduate students in the United States and composed the largest group of foreign students in countries as diverse as Finland, Italy, and South Korea.[83] Chinese institutions were internationalizing as well: in June 2015 Tsinghua University announced a partnership with the University of Washington and Microsoft to establish a graduate school for innovation in technology and has recently opened partnerships in Italy, Indonesia, and Chile.[84, 85] Peking University established a business school in Oxford. Xiamen University opened a $300 million campus in Malaysia in 2015, with plans for five thousand undergraduate and graduate students.[86] And Fudan University announced in 2021 its determination to open a campus in Hungary in 2024.[87] These are the first, and surely not last, examples of Chinese universities expanding beyond China's borders.

## World-Class Challenges

A little over forty years since the reestablishment of the college entrance examination, Chinese higher education had made great strides in expanding both quantity and quality of education. Long-term investments, such as those in faculty quality and state-of-the-art laboratories, were paying off: the academic reputation of Chinese universities, particularly top-tier institutions, was rising rapidly. In 2008 no Chinese university ranked above two hundredth place on Shanghai Jiao Tong University's Academic Ranking of World

Universities. By 2018 three were in the top one hundred. In 2021 Tsinghua and Peking Universities were ranked fifteenth and twenty-third, respectively, by the QS World University Rankings, the highest levels yet by Chinese universities in any international ranking. Tsinghua ranked above all but two of the American Ivy League schools.[88]

The Chinese government launched the Double First Class Universities Program in 2015 to boost further the standing of Chinese universities in the world. The program was built around a core group of forty-two leading Chinese universities considered either "well on their way" (Type A) or "have the potential" (Type B) to become world-leading universities. All of these forty-two universities were also part of either Project 211 or Project 985 or both. Ninety-five additional Chinese universities were selected as part of the program to become "first class in the world" in specific academic disciplines where they had existing strengths. Among the 110 academic disciplines being targeted, 36 percent were in engineering and technology fields where, by some measures, Chinese universities such as Tsinghua were already first class or even world leading.[89] Universities selected for the program that failed to perform well could be removed from the program and lose preferential funding.

Given the size and diversity of China's higher education sector, it is not surprising that there is a gulf between those who oversee Chinese universities (the central government and the Party-State at various levels) and those responsible for their day-to-day operation. "Education is the cornerstone of national rejuvenation," according to the preamble of China's 2010 National Plan for Medium and Long-Term Education Reform and Development.[90] From the central government's perspective, education takes as its goal the building of *national* strength, developing talent for the collective good, not primarily for individual merit. This viewpoint is in obvious tension with programs of general education at top Chinese universities that aim, like their American counterparts, also to liberate and educate the *individual* to be a critical thinker.

While the central government sees education as serving national strategies, making the best strategic use of the enormous funding now coming from all levels of government, the local and provincial officials who are the main funders of universities often have a shorter-term, more utilitarian viewpoint. They seek to spur economic growth, to enhance the job opportunities of people in their late teens and twenties, and to take advantage of the cheap credit offered by state banks for the expansion of higher education.

*Equity and Access*

If there is a "China model" for universities, it is not a particularly Communist one. As the historian Zhang Jishun, the former Party secretary of East China Normal University, has argued, just because enrollments have grown does not mean that access and equity have increased in equal measure. Take the case of tuition. There used to be none in Chinese universities. In 2020 a student majoring in the sciences, for example, would pay annual tuition of around $850 at Tsinghua University, a leading public university; $926 at Zhejiang University City College, an independent institution affiliated with the public Zhejiang University; $3,861 at the private Xi'an International University (although many times that in its preparatory programs); and $30,890 to attend NYU Shanghai.[91] While these figures are not high by American standards, the cost of attending a public university could easily exceed one-third of the disposable income of rural residents in China.[92] Tuition at private Chinese universities can be many times their annual income. This has led to a situation in which the poorest students, usually from rural areas, often end up at private universities, which are the most expensive, while wealthier and well-connected students from urban backgrounds have much better access to elite public institutions, which are among the least expensive.

We can see this in statistics of rural students attending Chinese universities. Nationwide, about 50 percent of university students hail from rural families (with a generous definition of what constitutes a rural family), but at the elite universities such as Peking and Tsinghua, only about 20 percent of the student body is made up of students from rural areas. In 2020 the higher education enrollment ratios in China's twelve most rural provinces were on average thirteen points lower than in China's eleven east coast provinces.[93] The Chinese government has now promised "universal higher education."[94] But for China's rural and poor, the army and public security bureaus offer better means of social mobility than do China's mass universities.

Finally, take the case of examinations and admissions. The *gaokao* persists, as did the old imperial examinations, because it has the appearance of rewarding merit and is one of the few national institutions that people believe is fair and honest. In principle, only the best, determined by competitive examination, are admitted. But the limitations of the *gaokao* have long been known, and elite universities are the leaders in setting patterns for alternative portals of entry through additional tests, interviews, "Olympic-style" prizes, and other mechanisms that privilege those of means and position who went to the best schools. The long-standing admissions quota system that favors local over out-of-province students contributes to inequality but also has proven difficult to reform. In May 2016 when the Ministry of Education attempted to increase the number of out-of-province student spots at certain universities, parents in four provinces garnered international media attention with their vocal protests.[95]

China's fifty-five officially recognized ethnic minority communities, which together compose about 8.5 percent of the PRC's population, have also faced barriers to full participation in higher education. But the share of minority enrollment in universities has grown significantly in the last decade, rising over 45 percent from 6.76 percent in 2010[96] to 9.86 percent in 2020.[97] The government has instituted affirmative action–style policies that give China's ethnic minorities a boost in university admissions, generally by lowering the *gaokao* score needed for a minority student to be accepted. At China's most elite universities, Tsinghua and Beida, this strategy seems to have worked, with ethnic minority students making up 9.7 percent of Tsinghua's 2020 freshmen class and about 12 percent of Beida's.[98] While minority representation in Chinese undergraduate programs has been enhanced, minorities represent only 5.47 percent of the postgraduate student body.[99]

## Politics

In 2013 the presidents from Fudan, Nanjing, and the rest of China's elite C9 institutions, along with the Association of American Universities and Australia's Group of Eight, cosigned the "Hefei Statement on the Ten Characteristics of Contemporary Research Universities."[100] The signers agreed that "the responsible exercise of academic freedom" is a tenet of contemporary university life.

These ideals have proven difficult to uphold. Perhaps the greatest challenges to the rise of Chinese universities lie in the realms of governance and politics. The hierarchical governance structures of Chinese universities leave many decisions to a very few people. Chinese universities are overseen by Party committees, and the university Party secretary normally outranks, and frequently outflanks, the president. A few extraordinary Party secretaries are key to their university's successes, but as a rule this system of parallel governance limits rather than enhances the flow of ideas. Few Party secretaries—like few presidents of American universities—look favorably upon the prospect of unbridled faculty governance. But the freedom of faculty to pursue ideas wherever they may lead is essential for sustained innovation. Where, after all, do the best ideas come from in universities? Deans and presidents everywhere must make decisions and set priorities. In practice, however, many of the best ideas—those that deans and presidents will be compelled to support on their intellectual merits—will come up from the mistakenly named "bottom": that is, from faculty at the top of their fields. Having an institutional structure to support this is rare anywhere, and in Chinese universities today it is rarer still. By any comparative measure of leading international universities, faculty in Chinese institutions have little role in governance.

It was not a good sign when China's Vice President (and President-designate) Xi Jinping visited China's leading universities in June 2012 to call for increased Party supervision of higher education. Indeed, the visit was a harbinger of the increasing emphasis on government control over the classroom under President Xi's tenure. A communiqué, known as Document 9, which was circulated among Party members in 2013 and later leaked to the media, enumerated seven forbidden topics of discussion, namely the promotion of Western constitutional democracy, "universal values," civil society, neoliberalism, Western (read: independent) journalism, historical nihilism, and, finally, any "Questioning Reform and Opening and the socialist nature of socialism with Chinese characteristics."[101] This weighty list was followed by Document 30, never made public, which called for stronger ideological control in higher education.

Taking the cue from the top, Minister of Education Yuan Guiren railed against the inclusion of "Western" values and ideas in Chinese university teaching. His pronouncements threatened a tightening of the academic freedom that had been expanding on university campuses. At a number of leading institutions, the Chinese Communist Party sought to reassert ideological discipline in the (still) required courses on Marxism-Leninism-Mao Zedong Thought as well as in other realms of the humanities and social sciences. At Peking University, the Party summarily dismissed President Wang Enge, a deeply respected scholar. As Peking University's assertive (now former) Party Secretary Zhu Shanlu wrote:

> We must grasp the right to the leadership, management, and discussion of ideological work tightly in our hands, and we can never put it to the side at any moment, or we will have committed an irrevocable and historic error. Universities are an important battleground for the production and confluence of ideology, and have an important role as leaders, models, and spreaders of ideas to all of society. Only by

firmly grasping the active authority of ideological work in universities will we be able to further strengthen the cohesiveness and appeal of the Party in high intellectual circles, and only then will we win over the youth and win the future.[102]

As a part of Xi Jinping's extensive anti-corruption campaign, "inspection teams" from the CCP's Central Discipline Inspection Commission were sent in 2017 across the country, including to leading universities. There they scrutinized university finances and the political loyalties of their leaders and faculty members. Heads of leading universities were accused of lax enforcement of ideological norms and inadequate work in strengthening Party organizations on campus. The inspection teams also warned that "clues" gathered during the inspection regarding individual disciplinary violations would be passed on to higher investigative organs.

On October 23, 2018, in meetings held on their individual campuses, representatives from the CCP's Central Organization Department announced a series of personnel changes at Peking and Nanjing Universities. Having reached the age of sixty-three, President Lin Jianhua of Peking University, it was announced, was suddenly going into retirement—the second Peking University president to be replaced in three years. He was succeeded by Peking University Party Secretary Hao Ping, who now served as vice Party secretary. Judge Qiu Shuiping became the university's new Party secretary and first in command. Qiu, a Peking University law graduate, spent his early career in local government in Beijing before serving as one of the city's top judicial and security officials, including briefly as the Party secretary of the city's State Security Bureau. Qiu was summoned back to Peking University from the position of president (chief judge) of the Shanxi Provincial High Court. This was not quite the equivalent of academic martial law, but close.

In November 2018 the Ministry of Education released "10 Guidelines for the Professional Behavior of Teachers in Colleges and Universities in the New Era," which underscored the Party's view that universities and their faculty must not cross political red lines. In President Xi Jinping's self-proclaimed "new era," professors were to meet "new and higher requirements . . . to implement the fundamental task of establishing morality." What were these requirements? At the top of the list were "no words and deeds that harm the authority of the Party Central Committee."[103]

Meanwhile the Party increased its authority over university governance. Between 2013 and 2017, 109 universities publicly published their institutional charters for the first time.[104] To varying degrees, these documents pledged that universities would adhere to the Party's leadership and follow its political prerogatives. In late 2019 three universities released revised charters further elevating the position of the Party in their institutions. Fudan University, one of China's most renowned institutions, removed references to academic independence and freedom of thought in favor of language supporting Party governance and patriotism.[105]

Challenges to Chinese universities' world-class aspirations came not just from within but also, and increasingly, from without. As the US-China economic clash over technology and innovation grew, Chinese universities and their international exchanges became caught in the crossfire. Cutting-edge research in engineering and the applied sciences relies on access to the latest software and hardware. The US government, particularly under the Trump administration, viewed Chinese universities' research in these areas as aiding the Party-State's military-civil fusion (MCF) strategy. Begun in 2015 MCF provided incentives for institutions throughout the Chinese economic and social landscape, including universities, to aid the People's Liberation Army in developing technology for military end uses.

To be sure, this policy is not unlike the many agreements between the U.S. Department of Defense and American institutions of higher education and private firms. Still, in May 2020 the Trump administration issued an executive order that would block the students, graduates, and affiliates of "Chinese entities that support China's MCF strategy" from entering the United States on certain visas often used to support academic and cultural exchanges.[106] Then in September the US government revoked over one thousand visas for Chinese students and researchers suspected of having ties to the Chinese military.[107] The US government also put, for the first time, two Chinese universities (Harbin Institute of Technology and Harbin Engineering University) on the U.S. Department of Commerce's "Entity List," which requires American firms to receive US government approval to sell their technology to targeted organizations.

## Cases

Let us turn now to three case studies of leading universities in greater China. At various points in time, all three have led in higher education in greater China and aim to lead again. First, I will examine Tsinghua, often referred to as China's MIT but which, in recent years, has become China's most globally competitive comprehensive university. Second, I present Nanjing University, the modern incarnation of the institution known during the Republican period as National Central University, itself modeled on the University of Berlin. Geographically and, at times, intellectually distant from the national government, Nanjing University is today a battleground in the Communist Party's campaign for control over higher education. Finally, we turn to the University of Hong Kong, which has the distinction of being the best university in the Chinese-speaking world that is not—at least not yet—under the direct leadership of the Chinese Communist Party.

All three of these institutions have legacies that span the history of modern higher education in China. All three have histories of partnership and cooperation with universities and experts outside of China's borders. Do these three have the potential to lead the world of higher education in the twenty-first century?

# CHAPTER NINE

# From Preparatory Academy to National Flagship

## *Tsinghua University*

O N SUNDAY, April 21, 2013, a crowd gathered at the Great Hall of the People on Tiananmen Square in central Beijing to inaugurate a new college at Tsinghua University. Letters from Chinese President Xi Jinping and US President Barack Obama were read aloud, followed by video testimonials from past and present American secretaries of state: Henry Kissinger, Colin Powell, and John Kerry. Together with Chinese Vice Premier Liu Yandong, who hosted the meeting, all identified the`founding of Schwarzman College at Tsinghua as a landmark in the history of US-China relations and in the ascent of Chinese universities. The vision of Tsinghua and of the new college's benefactor, the American businessman and philanthropist Stephen A. Schwarzman, was to build a residential college that would house and educate, in China, the global leaders of the twenty-first century. Schwarzman College and its resident Schwarzman Scholars program would match in ambition and endowment the Rhodes Scholarships at Oxford University, which for more than a century have been committed to educating those "with potential for leadership."[1]

The dynamic president of Tsinghua University, Chen Jining (a rising star who would go on to become China's Minister of Environmental Protection and then mayor of Beijing), noted that the new college and program were part of Tsinghua's long history of internationalization. But whereas the university once prepared Chinese citizens to study in the United States, Tsinghua was now to be the educational destination of top postgraduate students from America, Europe, Asia, and beyond. With the celebration of the new program,

Tsinghua, already at the apex of China's rapidly expanding domestic higher education system, was announcing its arrival onto the global higher education stage.

## Wars, Revolutions, and the Evolution of Tsinghua

Tsinghua University today is one of China's two leading universities and one of the world's elite schools in terms of admission. China and the world of Chinese higher education have come a long way since Tsinghua was founded in 1911, the *xinhai* year of the Xuantong Emperor (that is, the last year of the last emperor of the last imperial dynasty, which was overthrown in 1912). The history of Tsinghua mirrors the story of higher education in modern China.

Tsinghua, like the University of Berlin, was founded in the aftermath of catastrophic military defeat. In the summer of 1900 the ruling Qing Empress Dowager Cixi declared war on the world, or at least on Great Britain, the United States, Russia, Japan, France, Germany, Italy, Spain, Austria-Hungary, the Netherlands, and even Belgium, bowing to a powerful anti-foreign movement known as the Boxer Uprising. In the subsequent "Fifty-five Days in Peking," a small contingent of foreigners (led by Charlton Heston and Ava Gardner in the Hollywood version) held out in their legations in Beijing before an expeditionary force of eight nations came to their rescue. Just 20,000 foreign troops subdued an empire of 400 million. The subsequent peace brought with it a crushing indemnity ($10 billion in 2018 prices) to be paid over the next four decades.

The humiliation of the Qing Empire was complete, but in its final decade—the first decade of the twentieth century—it restarted a series of "self-strengthening" reforms, not least in education. Tsinghua, founded by the Qing court as *Tsinghua xuetang* (Tsinghua Academy), began as a preparatory school for students selected to study in the United States. At the urging of then-president of the University of Illinois, Edmund J. James, US President Theodore Roosevelt remitted a large portion of America's Boxer Indemnity funds for the education of Chinese in the United States and the establishment of Tsinghua. China, James wrote to Roosevelt, was on the edge of revolution. "The nation which succeeds in educating the young Chinese of the present generation," he wrote, "will reap the largest possible returns in moral, intellectual, and commercial influence."[2]

In its first decade, Tsinghua built up an American-style campus—its Jeffersonian Grand Auditorium inspired by the auditorium at Urbana-Champaign—to prepare its students for study in the United States. American-educated Chinese scholars led young scholars through an eight-year preparatory program that qualified them to transfer into American universities as juniors. Because Tsinghua's main patron was the United States government, the academy was governed not through the Ministry of Education but by the Ministry of Foreign Affairs, and the American Ambassador to China maintained an implicit power to approve presidential appointments and budget decisions for the academy.[3]

When Tsing Hua College (as it was formally known in English—we will simply call it Tsinghua here) opened its doors on April 29, 1911, its sixteen students could choose from ten available disciplines: philosophy, Chinese literature, world literature, arts and music, history and politics, math and astronomy, physics and chemistry, biology, geology and geography, and athletics and craftsmanship.[4] The curriculum also included linguistic and cultural preparation for the students' future studies in America. The student body quickly expanded, as did ambitions for the institution, which reflected an increasing demand across China for domestic higher education. By 1925 Tsinghua had transformed itself into a university of liberal arts and sciences and was home to China's leading Institute of Chinese Studies, the *Guoxueyuan*. Its famous "Four Tutors"—Liang Qichao, Wang Guowei, Chen Yinke, and Zhao Yuanren—added international and scientific dimensions to the study of Chinese language, literature, linguistics, and archaeology.

Tsinghua's influence went well beyond China. Its history department, founded in 1926, was chaired for its first decade by T. F. Tsiang (Jiang Tingfu), a recipient of an American liberal arts education at Oberlin and a doctoral degree from Columbia. Tsiang revolutionized the study of China's modern international relations. He would go on to a distinguished diplomatic career, serving as the Republic of China's ambassador to the United Nations from 1946 to 1966. My own mentor in Chinese history, John K. Fairbank, the pioneer of modern Chinese studies in the United States, learned his Chinese history from T. F. Tsiang at Tsinghua in the early 1930s. Tsinghua's influence on Harvard continued: the undergraduate course on Chinese history that Fairbank began teaching at Harvard in 1939 became central to Harvard's General Education programs for more than eighty years; my colleague Peter Bol and I teach a rather different version of it to this day.

**Figure 9.1.** John K. and Wilma Cannon Fairbank with Liang Sicheng and Lin Huiyin. Courtesy of Holly and Laura Fairbank.

## *National Tsing Hua University*

With the establishment of the Nationalist government led by Chiang Kai-shek in 1927, Tsinghua was renamed National Tsing Hua University under the jurisdiction of the Ministry of Education. The university comprised four schools—Arts, Law, Sciences, and Engineering—which were further divided into seventeen departments. The university offered strong training in the sciences as well as a broader education in liberal arts. In 1929 Tsinghua inaugurated its graduate school. After less than a quarter century, Tsinghua had already gained renown not just for the scope of its programs—by 1935 Tsinghua's ten graduate departments counted for one-third of the graduate departments across China—but also for the excellence of its graduates.[5]

The 1930s witnessed Tsinghua's first golden age. Tsinghua was unusual among the "national" universities of that era in that it was a fully residential (and, after 1929, co-educational) campus in the American style, yet in a historically Chinese and bucolic setting, located well outside the walls of old Beijing and some eleven miles from the city center. Students and faculty comingled in the blue cotton gowns of scholars. The campus grounds and its lakes were maintained almost as a private garden, where students could enjoy recreations such as fishing, ice skating, and romantic liaisons in its quieter quarters. Tsinghua, so well supported by the Boxer Indemnity fund, expanded its campus in style, with a stunning library, a gymnasium filled with imported equipment, an auditorium with the best Western musical instruments, and laboratories stocked with the latest scientific instruments—all of it, as Wen-hsin Yeh has shown, "shipped directly from the United States."[6]

By 1937 Tsinghua had become a research university in the arts and sciences.[7] Because of its Boxer Indemnity funding, Tsinghua was less beholden to government support than institutions such as Peking University or National Central University and therefore more resistant to attempts by the ruling Nationalist (Guomindang) party to exert ideological control over it.

This period of development ended suddenly in 1937 when the Tsinghua campus was occupied by Japanese troops. In 1938 many of its faculty and students marched with the Nationalist government to the interior, where Tsinghua—along with Peking and Nankai Universities—became part of Kunming-based National Southwest Associated University (*Guoli xinan lianhe daxue,* or *"Lianda"*) for the duration of the war. Despite the wartime atmosphere, this period has been recalled as a special moment in Chinese higher education, characterized by a relatively liberal academic environment and close cooperation between the country's top scholars, previously spread across three campuses. Some of Tsinghua's most famous and innovative alumni, such as Nobel laureate physicists C. N. Yang (Yang Zhenning) and C. T. Li (Li Zhendao), completed their studies during this time.[8] Tsinghua's president and the leader of *Lianda,* Mei Yiqi, is remembered still today for his advocacy of liberal education, institutional autonomy, and academic freedom even in the darkest moments of the war. For that he has earned the honor, by alumni who know this history, of being Tsinghua's "eternal president" (*Tsinghua daxue yongyuande xiaozhang*).

The university's return to its Beijing campus in 1946 would offer only a short respite before the onset of civil war and the Communist conquest of China. In December 1948 President Mei Yiqi left Beijing. In 1956 he became president of a renewed and distinguished National Tsing Hua University in Taiwan, leading one part of a divided Tsinghua in a divided China.

## Communist Tsinghua University

With the Communist victory on the Chinese mainland, Tsinghua's long-standing ties with the United States were severed, not to be resumed for three decades. The new People's Republic of China (PRC) forged a close alliance with the Soviet Union—the "socialist elder brother" that had founded the Chinese Communist Party in 1921. China's political system was reordered along Stalinist lines and retains still today an indelible Soviet DNA. China's universities, including Tsinghua, were rapidly sovietized. A new Tsinghua campus arose next to the original one. Its thirteen-story Main Building (*Zhulou*), a brutal Stalinist complex of three structures, now dominated the campus. Tsinghua in the 1950s looked less like Urbana-Champaign and more like Moscow State.

In 1952 Tsinghua became a polytechnic university to train engineers. The schools of sciences and humanities, agriculture, and law were all abolished, and their faculty members were scattered to other institutions, primarily Peking University. In return, faculty from the engineering schools of Peking and Yenching Universities were transferred to Tsinghua. Faculty who would not or could not work under the new regime either fled abroad or were purged at home. Tsinghua was now academically more on the model of the East German Humboldt University than any American university. Within the newly combined engineering schools, the curriculum was reorganized to eliminate the credit system and instead provide each student with a structured set of courses according to a specific major chosen upon admittance to the university, leading normally to a specific job in government or a state-owned enterprise, Soviet-style. Anxious to ensure its competitiveness despite losing many of its most famous scholars during the reorganization, the university developed new programs under the engineering umbrella. The number of majors available to students increased from twenty-two in 1952, just after the reorganization, to forty in 1966.

This reorganization positioned Tsinghua for leadership during the PRC's First Five-Year Plan (1953–1958), which was modeled on Soviet five-year plans. Tsinghua trained many of China's subsequent political and technocratic elites, but the relentless politicization of universities under Mao Zedong first weakened, and then nearly destroyed, Tsinghua. The breaking point at Tsinghua came in the summer of 1966, when the campus was a central political battleground in the political and ideological struggle between Mao Zedong, who was the Party and military chief, and Liu Shaoqi, China's president. An early political target was Jiang Nanxiang, who had served not only as president and Party secretary of Tsinghua since 1952 but also as Minister of Higher Education.[9] He was quickly denounced at the onset of the Cultural Revolution in June 1966, and the university government apparatus was entirely suspended by the work team sent to the campus by the central authorities under Mao Zedong. Small-scale clashes occurred on campus for two years before erupting into outright warfare.

China's 1960s were much more violent and bloody than those in Berlin, Boston, or Berkeley. In the "one-hundred-day war" on the Tsinghua campus in 1968, at least eighteen people were killed, thirty permanently disabled, and eleven hundred injured. After the army finally seized control, remaining students and academic staff were "sent down" for physical and ideological rehabilitation to rural farming areas, where more than one thousand of them suffered from schistosomiasis, a parasitic disease. Back on campus, in principle, only students who were workers, peasants, and soldiers were to be enrolled in a proletarianized Tsinghua. (Still there was room for some of the children of the elite, who were neither workers, nor peasants, nor soldiers. One of these was Xi Jinping, who graduated with a degree in chemical engineering in 1977. But even he still had to do farm work while a student.)[10]

The Cultural Revolution even destroyed Tsinghua's iconic gate, replaced for a time by a huge statue of Mao, which was in turn supplanted by a replica of the original gate in 1991. Tsinghua resumed full operation, and even then on a skeletal basis, only in 1978.[11]

**Figure 9.2.** Red Guards tearing down Tsinghua University's gate. Reproduced from https://xsg.tsinghua.edu.cn/info/1003/2288.htm.

## Tsinghua University Reborn

Like China, Tsinghua was revolutionized, traumatized, nearly paralyzed, and utterly immiserated during the first three decades of the People's Republic. It emerged from the Maoist years a shell of its former self. Over the subsequent decades, however, Tsinghua's resurgence was tied closely with that of the era of "reform and opening." Tsinghua became again in fact, if not in name, *national* Tsinghua University. The university received extraordinary government investment and rose rapidly to lead China in engineering, topping the country's first rankings table for "key" engineering universities in 1987.[12] Flush with government aid, Tsinghua built its faculty again and established a series of graduate and professional schools. In 1984 Zhu Rongji, who later served as premier, became the founding dean of the newly established School of Economics and Management, which has become the most selective school in the world for undergraduate admissions. Tsinghua's graduates came to dominate the Chinese leadership elite, counting among them Presidents Hu Jintao and Xi Jinping.[13]

Over the course of the past several decades, Tsinghua has reestablished itself as the comprehensive university it was in Republican China, and more. A School of Humanities and Social Sciences was established in 1993, and in 2012 it was divided into separate schools. Tsinghua's Law School was reestablished in 1995. In 1999 the former Central Academy of Arts and Design became part of Tsinghua, as did Peking Union Medical College in 2006. In November 2009 Tsinghua revived its famous Institute of Chinese Studies. The Tsinghua School of Economics and Management began to lead the university in reforming its general education curriculum. And at the university's one hundredth anniversary in 2011, a magnificent New Tsinghua Academy (*Xin Tsinghua xuetang*) was dedicated not to the fields of engineering, science, and technology, for which Tsinghua has been best known in recent decades, but to the performing arts.

President James of the University of Illinois was convinced, in 1907, that "[e]very great nation in the world will inevitably be drawn into more or less intimate relations" with a rapidly changing China.[14] He imagined a world where China learned from others, not the other way around. But he also conceived of a China that would rise because of its international educational alliances. Today an ever more academically diverse and internationally connected Tsinghua is without a doubt a leader in higher education in China, and, increasingly, in the global higher education market. Tsinghua was ranked fifteenth in the 2021 QS World University Rankings (two spots above Yale University), reflecting Tsinghua's rising research output as well as its increasingly high reputation in academic circles.[15]

By 2020 over 50,000 students studied at Tsinghua under the guidance of over 3,600 faculty members and 2,836 postdoctoral researchers organized into 21 schools. Tsinghua's over 16,000 undergraduate students chose from 82 majors, and studied in an environment that connected them closely with over 19,700 masters and over 17,200 doctoral students.[16]

Tsinghua now aimed to be "world class." While still focusing primarily on engineering and applied sciences, in broadening its offerings, Tsinghua acted on the belief of many scholars that a world-class university had to encompass a wide variety of disciplines.[17] It was not enough to be known (as Tsinghua was) as the "MIT of China" even though institutions in the United States such as the Massachusetts and California Institutes of Technology were regularly considered world-class institutions despite their narrower offerings. If anything, Tsinghua began to look more akin to Stanford, a comprehensive research university with particular strengths in engineering and applied science.

Tsinghua's decades-long pursuit of becoming a comprehensive, world-class university was rooted in long-term planning and shaped by the Chinese government's national development objectives. In 2003, when Tsinghua President Wang Dazhong articulated a "three nine-year, three-step" plan to transform Tsinghua into a comprehensive, world-class university by 2020, he noted that university planning for world-class status had begun in 1993 as a response to the 16th National Congress of the Communist Party of China's goal of "building a well-off society in an all-round way and accelerating socialist modernization."[18] Reconstituting Tsinghua into a truly comprehensive university was the primary objective of this world-class plan's first step in the three nine-year segments, from 1994 to 2002. In unveiling the second step (from 2003 to 2011), Wang identified "striving to be among the world's top universities" as the university's top priority. Tsinghua achieved this objective. By 2011 it ranked among the top one hundred universities in multiple international rankings, and within the top twenty in the *Times Higher Education* ranking of engineering programs.[19] According to Wang, the third step for Tsinghua would run from 2012 to 2020 and would focus on achieving world-class status across multiple disciplines.

Achieving comprehensive, world-class status by 2020 remained at the forefront of Tsinghua's strategic planning as the university entered what

Wang had viewed as its last "step" toward this goal. The 2011–2015 university development plan declared that this was the "key period in accelerating the development [of Tsinghua] as a world-class university." To this end, the administration outlined its many priorities for institutional reform, including everything from comprehensively strengthening academic disciplines to increasing international cooperation. The 2016–2020 development plan took on an even greater sense of mission and urgency, with its introduction declaring that "it is necessary . . . to ensure that [Tsinghua] reaches the level of world-class universities by 2020."[20]

On the face of it, Tsinghua's administration had kept its eye on the prize since first announcing its aim of becoming a world-class university. However, even as Tsinghua rose in global university rankings, navigating competing interest groups within the Tsinghua community and the Party-State proved to be a persistent challenge for university leadership. The 2016–2020 development plan's references to increasing Tsinghua's contributions to industrial policies such as military-civil fusion and Made in China 2025 underscored the Party-State's view of universities as vehicles to advance its own interests, which might not always align with fostering world-class practices at Tsinghua. The 2016–2020 plan acknowledged that obstacles to Tsinghua's institutional reform would persist long after 2020 by laying out goals for becoming "one of the world's top universities" by 2050.[21] As Tsinghua's self-imposed deadline of achieving world-class status by 2020 has now passed, what is the university's track record of adopting international best practices? And how has the Chinese political system shaped Tsinghua's successes and shortcomings?

## May a Thousand Talents Bloom

As we have seen, the recipe for a leading university requires at least three ingredients: an exceptional faculty; a talented student body; and means of governance that promote outstanding research and teaching, ideally unencumbered by political constraint. How has Tsinghua fared in these dimensions?

### Faculty

The 3,565 faculty members of Tsinghua are an illustrious group. As of 2019 among them numbered fifty-four members of the Chinese Academy of Sciences, forty members of the Chinese Academy of Engineering, and many other winners of accolades. They carry out a wide variety of research in Tsinghua's 447 research institutions, which in 2020 included many designated as "key" by the national and regional governments.[22] Since Tsinghua's founding, the university administration sought to enhance the quality of the faculty by recruiting foreign-trained Chinese scholars, and this tradition continued throughout the reform era. Qian Yingyi, Dean of the School of Economics and Management (SEM), for example, was recruited to lead SEM after terms on the faculties of Stanford University, the University of Maryland, and the University of California, Berkeley. As dean of one of the most competitive schools at Tsinghua, Qian implemented vast reforms within SEM, both in terms of curriculum—creating a mandatory, two-year, general education core curriculum for undergraduates and reorganizing the graduate programs— as well as in administration—establishing a tenure track and simplifying the salary system.

In its 2011–2015 development plan, the university administration acknowledged that "there was still a relatively large distance between the overall level of our faculty and that of the world's elite universities."[23] By many counts, however, that distance was closing fast. Whereas in 1995, only 15 percent of Tsinghua faculty held doctoral degrees, by 2006 this proportion had risen to 62.7 percent. By 2020, 91.02 percent of faculty at Tsinghua held doctoral degrees.[24] Yet the 2016–2020 plan noted that Tsinghua still faced a number of challenges in attracting "excellence," including competition for top faculty from "famous" universities outside China. Although Tsinghua aimed to become a world-class university by 2020, the university gave itself until 2050 to build a faculty with an "overall top level," a goal that Tsinghua hoped would coincide with becoming "one of the world's top universities." Older, less productive faculty would be phased (not forced) out with retirement.

Tsinghua also hoped that the government's Thousand Talents Program, announced in 2008, would aid the university's efforts to recruit world-class faculty. The program offered foreign-based scholars—mostly, but not exclusively, of Chinese origin—very generous financial packages to join Chinese universities. Tsinghua seized the opportunity. The 2011–2015 development plan noted that Tsinghua would "make full use of the Thousand Talents Program" in order to "recruit first-class international scholars."[25] By 2016 the university had recruited 111 senior scholars through the program.[26] By 2019 the Chinese government ceased to promote the program publicly, in response to US concerns that it "encourage[d] theft of intellectual property."[27] Indeed, it was Harvard chemistry professor Charles Lieber's participation in the Thousand Talents Program that led to his arrest in 2019. Tsinghua continued to attract scholars through the Thousand Talents Program, albeit at a slower pace. In 2018 nine new "talents" joined Tsinghua, whereas only four were recruited in 2019.[28] As Tsinghua competed with prestigious and well-funded global universities for talent, government financial support for the recruitment of "stars" remained an important resource for the university.

But Tsinghua was still burdened by its socialist past. Hindering Tsinghua's recruitment of high-quality faculty in an international job market were human resource policies that were relics of the planned economy in which an "iron rice bowl" of enduring employment was standard. After 1995 Tsinghua relied in principle on an "up or out" employment policy. An assistant professor (formerly, lecturer) had up to nine years—three three-year contracts—to receive a promotion to the associate professor level. An associate professorship implied entry into the tenure track, although there was no specific time frame at which an associate professor became a full professor. Full professors were expected to sign two more three-year contracts before ultimately being offered a non-time-specified contract, essentially giving them lifetime tenure. Faculty members tended to be promoted almost exclusively from within, competing against others within their department for promotion. Central planning by university administration determined quotas for each level of faculty in each school, leaving schools few means to affect the scope of their hiring processes.

Faculty salaries were calculated on a monthly basis. But the structure of the system made it difficult to recruit outstanding international researchers who were used to annual, rather than monthly, salary systems. When scholars recruited from abroad were eventually offered annual (and higher) salaries, this naturally created intradepartmental tensions.[29]

Nonetheless, SEM, as a kind of "special economic zone" of experimentation, phased in higher annual salaries for faculty members, as well as an international-standard tenure system. Its approach became part of Tsinghua's 2011–2015 overall development plan.[30] But not all schools at Tsinghua were so rich in funding and experimental in attitude. The university's 2016–2020 plan acknowledged that the salary models for faculty would be established "according to what is suitable for each department."[31]

In terms of credentials, Tsinghua valued hiring its own alumni, especially those who had done their undergraduate work at Tsinghua. But as Li Daokui, a renowned economist and the founding dean of the Schwarzman

Scholars program noted, "If a person does not have a foreign PhD, that person will face tremendous trouble at Tsinghua."[32] Tenure awards required ample publications in prestigious, international journals outside of China. Faculty with international doctorates had a clear advantage in the race to publish and achieve tenure, and their work would help Tsinghua in the international rankings with which it and its peers were so obsessed. At the same time, the international focus of these tenure policies had the potential to lure younger professors to focus on research topics that would be well received internationally rather than on issues most relevant to the Chinese scene. For an institution whose motto was "self-discipline and social commitment," this was a challenge.

## Students

That English-language translation of the university motto hardly captures Tsinghua's sense of special mission and status. The motto, *Ziqiang bu xi, hou de zai wu,* taken from the *Book of Changes,* calls for the superior person to "self-strengthen without cease" and "with great virtue to take charge of the world." Indeed, Tsinghua's most famous alumni in the PRC era have been those who took charge of the world, or a good part of it: Xi Jinping, president of China, former President Hu Jintao, and former Premier Zhu Rongji all graduated from engineering programs at Tsinghua. Tsinghua continues to draw many of China's most gifted students through one of the most competitive admissions processes in the world. The top humanities division *gaokao* scorers from twenty-eight of the thirty-two provincial-level administrative units on the Chinese mainland enrolled at Tsinghua in 2018. Top scorers in the science division from fourteen provincial administrative units chose to attend Tsinghua as well.[33] From my own lectures and seminars at Tsinghua, and from many visits, I can attest: Tsinghua students are second to none.

Tsinghua clearly attracts some of the best students in the world. But how are they educated once they walk through its iconic gate? Since the revival of Tsinghua as a comprehensive university, it has experimented with multiple approaches to new curricula and pedagogy. All of Tsinghua's schools have some general education requirements, including a nationally required political curriculum as well as university-based initiatives. All students are able to take advantage of freshman seminars, designed to foster more discussion-based and participatory learning. Students can also participate in the Student Research Training (SRT) program, working alongside faculty on specific projects to gain research experience. Tsinghua reports that over 60 percent of its undergraduates participate in more than one thousand SRT projects offered annually.[34] Gifted students who are interested in pursuing careers in academia can apply for the Tsinghua Xuetang Talents program, which offers high-level academic training in a variety of scientific and quantitative fields. Still, despite this growing emphasis on specialized educational opportunities, the average undergraduate class size at Tsinghua is fifty, and only 35.3 percent of undergraduate courses are taught by full professors.[35] With over sixteen thousand undergraduate students, developing a feasible educational program that promotes individualization and creativity is a significant challenge.

Not an institution to shy away from a challenge, in September 2014 Tsinghua built on its existing experience and launched a new undergraduate residential college experience combined with a more rigorous general education curriculum. Students at the new institution, Xinya College, were expected to earn twelve credits from a host of newly designed, seminar-style core courses that emphasized "Chinese and Western civilizations and the interconnectedness between different civilizations and cultures."[36] Students entered Xinya without having been divided into majors and spent their entire first year studying a variety of courses, including general education, before choosing a major in their second year.[37]

A key feature of the program was student life: Xinya students lived together in residential college style, as a multidisciplinary cohort. This was a departure from traditional campus life at Tsinghua, in which students were grouped together and assigned dormitories by discipline, leaving few opportunities for cross-disciplinary interactions within or outside the classroom. Within the Xinya residence, emphasis was placed on student life and activities outside the classroom as well. Students ran festivals and events and established various interest groups with their peers.

By the time this cross-school experiment was first piloted in 2014, those in charge of Xinya College were able to draw on the experience of the School of Economics and Management, which had led the way in curricular reform by instituting its own undergraduate general education requirement in 2009. Here again the figure of SEM Dean Qian Yingyi looms large.

Qian Yingyi is a remarkable man. He passed the college entrance exams the first year they were revived after the Cultural Revolution, when a decade's worth of candidates took the exams for a miniscule number of admission slots. He graduated from Tsinghua in mathematics and went on to receive his doctorate at Harvard in economics. Qian was professor of economics at Berkeley when he was recruited back to Tsinghua by former Premier Zhu Rongji, the founding dean of SEM. Qian then succeeded Zhu in this role, serving as dean of the School of Economics and Management from 2006 to 2018. A scholar who had published in all the leading journals of his field, Dean Qian authored multiple books on China's economic reform and, closest to his heart, on the early, pre-Communist, distinguished history of the social sciences at Tsinghua.[38]

The years of his deanship coincided with a great boom of the Chinese economy and of Tsinghua's reputation. SEM became the destination of choice not only for undergraduates but for executive education MBAs. SEM's parking lot would be filled every weekend with the private vehicles of China's new corporate elite, from Mercedes to Maseratis. Qian, by contrast, parked the only vehicle he owned: an old bicycle so rusty and tired that no one would steal it.

Qian's passion—so unusual for an age consumed with research rankings—was undergraduate education. He had studied the core and general education

**Figure 9.3.** Dean Qian Yingyi and his bicycle on Tsinghua's campus.
Photograph © William C. Kirby.

curricula at Harvard and other American universities, and I recall long discussions with him on the merits of each. He knew that university-wide reform of undergraduate education at Tsinghua would be a steep, uphill and, possibly, political battle, but he could start more quietly at SEM and set an example. He concluded, "Given . . . that Chinese students are strong in some aspects but very weak in terms of worldview, global vision, and critical thinking, at the very beginning, I realized that undergraduate curriculum is the most important thing to change." Guided by the goal of "training the mind to think," rather than merely helping students acquire knowledge, and working closely with his faculty, Qian built a curriculum of core classes that dominated most of the students' first two years in SEM. As Qian recalled, the general education program "integrated value formation, skills development and attainment of core knowledge of human civilizations, stressing the importance of nurturing curiosity, imagination, and critical thinking. . . . The new curriculum was geared to global needs of the future . . . and placed the development of students at the center of the design."[39]

The impact of this new curriculum was felt in many ways at SEM. One of the central components of the general education curriculum was a course called "Critical Thinking and Moral Reasoning." One day, Qian told me, he heard students say, "'Have you CTMR-ed?' They use this as a verb. I was struck! Because when a company's name becomes a verb, it's a tremendous achievement." While some students clearly warmed to the new curriculum, others were more skeptical. Many students worried that the lack of study in specialized subjects like finance and accounting during their first and second years would make them less competitive candidates for internships. Still, with quiet determination and a carefully cultivated personal legitimacy, Qian was able to successfully implement his envisioned curricular reforms. Each year, he reformed the requirements of a different degree until every program at SEM fit his vision.

*Governance: The Case of the School of Economics and Management*

Like all public universities in China, Tsinghua was governed by a president (Qiu Yong) who worked in coordination with the Chinese Communist Party Committee (led by Party Secretary Chen Xu). Su-Yan Pan, research assistant professor in the Faculty of Education at the University of Hong Kong, described the relationship between Tsinghua and the government as "semi-independent," wherein the university had "the power to protect itself from external intervention in certain areas, and [could] act upon its own initiative to respond to social needs within the framework of the government's policies."[40] Much like the University of Berlin in Wilhelmine times, Tsinghua's loyalty, or at least adherence, to the ruling system was assumed. As the alma mater of so many prominent Chinese political leaders, Tsinghua had greater autonomy than its more free-spirited neighbor in Beijing, Peking University, where the Party intervened early and often in controlling its leadership. While the university president and Party secretary's interests did not always align, Tsinghua's leadership and the central government were both determined to turn Tsinghua into a world-class university.

Administrative decision-making powers not reserved for the Party Committee were split between the university president and the dean of each individual school. Each school, and indeed each department, also had a Party Committee, but Tsinghua deans had considerable freedom within their fiefdoms, be it on matters of curriculum (as in SEM) or on the allocation of their budgets. The central university administration, on the other hand, maintained some control over each school by setting quotas for the hiring and promotion of professors.

Because salaries were paid out of SEM's budget, the school was able to implement its reforms without requiring more funds from the central university budget. However, this did not mean that the dean was free to take unilateral action. Rather, Qian went through a long, consultative process during which he worked closely with many faculty committees to establish the new salary system. He noted that while in most other countries, salary negotiations normally took place one-on-one between the dean and faculty member, this would be unacceptable in the Chinese context. Rather, the system was reformed so that salaries for each faculty member were reviewed, negotiated, and decided through anonymous vote by a seven-person salary committee.

The tenure system reform exemplified the relative governance roles of the university and individual schools. Changes to the hiring process required university approval as they would affect decisions that were previously under the jurisdiction of the central administration. This was not a case of the "shoot first and ask forgiveness later" strategy that defines so much private enterprise in China today. Innovative as it was, SEM had to keep the central administration well informed of its efforts.

Faculty without administrative roles played a limited role in university governance. The main vehicle for faculty engagement was the Faculty and Staff Representative Assembly, a body drawn from the whole university by school or department, and consisting of no less than 60 percent of faculty. Its meetings bore no resemblance to those of Harvard's Faculty of Arts and Sciences, not to mention Berkeley's Academic Senate. The Assembly, falling under the university's Party-led labor union (which was not a union formed by employees in the European or American sense), had extremely limited prerogatives. Its powers, as laid out in its charter, were at most consultative: listening to and issuing opinions on reports on the workings of the university and its administrators. The Assembly's regulations did not stipulate any mechanism by which these opinions had to be taken into account.[41]

Ultimately, governance issues at Tsinghua in general and at SEM were subject to political winds blowing eleven miles to the south, in the Chinese Communist Party's leadership compound in Zhongnanhai, in the shadow of the Qing Forbidden City. The tightening of censorship and academic control that marked the presidency of Xi Jinping after 2012 led to an enhanced role of the Party in university affairs and greater scrutiny of individual schools. For example, SEM, like all leading Chinese business schools, had a strong executive education program and robust income from it. But from one day to the next, it was announced that state-owned enterprises (SOEs) should not and could not pay the high levels of tuition charged for executive MBA programs. Worse, even if an SOE executive was but one credit from receiving the MBA, he or she had to withdraw from the program. Worse still, for SEM, it was required to refund the *entire tuition* received over many years of SOE executives in its programs.

The Party's Central Commission for Discipline Inspection (CCDI) investigated Tsinghua (as it did all leading universities) in 2017. The CCDI criticized the universities, including Tsinghua, declaring that their "implementation of ideological systems is not strong enough."[42] At Tsinghua, the CCDI sought evidence of corruption of either the monetary or ideological sort. They found none at SEM, but they did discover that Dean Qian's office was a few square meters larger than central regulations allowed. This was a common finding in Chinese university administrative offices, but unlike some of his peers, who hired carpenters to build fake walls to make their offices smaller, Qian simply turned his office into a seminar room (he had already used it as such), and moved across the hall to a space the size of a typical office cubicle.

## Tsinghua, Incorporated

In 2020 Tsinghua reported projected expenditures of over US$4.6 billion.[43] Of its total projected income in 2020, 39 percent came from university earned revenue, including student tuition and fees.[44] Tuition levels for undergraduate, MA, and PhD programs are set by the Ministry of Education. Undergraduate tuition varies by program, but in 2020 it was under US$1,000 per year, with the exception of the fine arts program, whose annual tuition was closer to US$1,500. Graduate program annual tuition fell in the US$1,200 to $1,500 range. Tuition for professional degree programs is proposed by the relevant school's administration and negotiated with the Ministry of Education.[45] At over $29,600, tuition for SEM's MBA program was significantly higher than that of other schools.[46] These state-set (or state-negotiated) tuition rates change, however, for international students. The 1,198 full-time international undergraduate students at Tsinghua in 2019 paid tuition of between $2,000 and $5,000.[47]

As one of the primary beneficiaries of Project 211 and Project 985, Tsinghua received extraordinary research and capital improvement funding from the government. However, university accounting of government funds was rather opaque. While an exact figure for the amount of government support Tsinghua receives is unknown, it is surely substantial. Yet senior administration members predicted that absolute support was likely to fall in the coming years as the government started to express more concern for regional equity in contrast with previous policies that funneled government support into a few, select institutions. In addition, the composition of the government funding Tsinghua receives is changing as the state's national development priorities evolve. One of the few areas of government funding for Tsinghua to grow in 2020 was outlays for its science and technology expenditures.

Expanding military-civil fusion research and teaching programs at Tsinghua is one emerging area receiving growing support from the Chinese government. MCF, a national strategy launched in 2015 by Xi Jinping to incentivize contributions to China's defense industrial base by nonmilitary actors, is used to justify "strategic cooperation and resource docking with the military" in Tsinghua's 2016–2020 plan.[48] Since the plan's release, Tsinghua launched new programs educating People's Liberation Army officers, opened laboratories researching MCF technologies, and invested in companies developing MCF-focused projects.[49]

Tsinghua's STEM initiatives have also benefited from incentives created by the government to support the "Made in China 2025" (MIC 2025) industrial policy. Released by the State Council in 2015, MIC 2025 laid out a blueprint for fostering globally competitive and increasingly self-sufficient Chinese industries in technologies such as semiconductors, automobiles, artificial intelligence, and telecommunication equipment.[50] Tsinghua jumped to signal its support for the policy.[51] Behind Tsinghua's early and eager support for MIC 2025 were expectations of immense, new state-backed financial support for higher education research, reported to exceed US$1.6 billion between 2016 and 2020, to be disbursed among all universities.[52] Moreover, the Ministry of Industry and Information Technology named university cooperation a "basic principle" for projects in application materials for MIC 2025 subsidies.[53] Since its release, Tsinghua has initiated a series of research centers and teaching programs in support of MIC 2025.[54]

Tsinghua's financial relationship with the state had both local and national elements. The Beijing municipal government opened applications for subsidies that would fund military-civil fusion projects in Tsinghua's home district of Haidian.[55] Tsinghua played a role in industrial policies in MIC 2025 plans ranging across the country, from Tianjin to Qinghai[56]—operations that continued well after the central government dropped official references to the plan.[57] In 2018 state media reported that since MIC 2025's release in 2015, Tsinghua had received eighty projects and US$288 million in government funding.[58] Although regular government funding for Tsinghua had declined as a proportion of the university's revenue, the rise of special industrial policy projects at Tsinghua suggests that, as an official *Drittmittel* funder in the German context, the state remained the central actor in the composition and allocation of Tsinghua's resources.

## Institutional Entrepreneurship

And yet Tsinghua has set out on its own to develop sources of funding beyond government research support and government-controlled tuition. Tsinghua encourages an institutional entrepreneurial culture that is more like Stanford or MIT than Harvard or Berkeley. The university takes stakes in commercial endeavors started at the Tsinghua University Science Park (TusPark), including Tsinghua Unigroup and Tsinghua Tongfang Co., Ltd. As university-based enterprises, both companies receive partial tax exemption.[59]

These companies and TusPark are all part of Tsinghua Holdings Co., Ltd., the investment arm of the university, which at the end of the 2019 financial year held over US$73 billion in assets and had 1,908 subsidiaries.[60] In 2019 *Fortune China* ranked it the 187th largest company based on operating income.[61]

But entrepreneurialism is not always rewarded in Xi Jinping's China. Attempts to diversify Tsinghua's income through commercial enterprises were complicated by the 2017 investigation by the Central Commission for Discipline Inspection into "Party leadership" at twenty-nine Chinese universities. In the CCDI's report on Tsinghua's conduct, the university was told explicitly to strengthen "the leadership of [Tsinghua's] Party committees over holding companies" and to restructure commercial enterprises to reduce investment levels and operational risks.[62] In May 2018 the government doubled down on this position, declaring that universities must institute "state capital management reform" in order to "focus on education."[63] State interference in Tsinghua's investment plans leaves uncertain the role of commercial endeavors in diversifying its income. If Tsinghua follows through on the state's mandate to divest itself of commercial assets, its budget would be ever more reliant on government funding, making Tsinghua more responsive to state interests in the future.

The university also seeks and receives private donations. Tsinghua is home to the People's Republic of China's first university endowment, the Tsinghua University Education Foundation (TUEF), governed by a twenty-five-person board of directors. Founded in 1994 with an initial balance of less than US$3 million, the fund grew to a total value of over US$1.4 billion by 2019 and had a reputation as one of the highest-performing university endowments in China.[64] In 2019 the investments of TUEF earned over US$150 million in investment income (roughly a 12.2 percent return).[65] Annual donations to TUEF have increased steadily; in 2018 the fund received about US$300 million in donations, around one-tenth of which was donated from outside China. Foreign donations proved hard to sustain year-on-year, falling 75 percent in 2019 to account for just 2 percent of total donations that year, while overall gifts to the endowment fell by only around 9 percent.[66] While a small endowment by American standards, TUEF was attempting to build a foundation in a short period for future growth. Following Tsinghua's model, there are now 623 Chinese university endowments. Tsinghua's remains the largest and most successful, earning nearly double the investment income of its closest competitor, Peking University, in 2020.[67]

Like Harvard and many American universities, however, central fundraising was but part of the story and by no means the largest one. Individual schools also housed their own fundraising teams. SEM was the first school at Tsinghua to begin running its own fundraising campaigns, with several other schools following its lead. TUEF played an active role in trying to get more schools to increase their fundraising capacity and form their own development offices.

SEM is again a case in point. Its Advisory Board is perhaps among the most distinguished, in business terms, and surely both the most powerful and the wealthiest, of any board of any part of any university anywhere in the world. Its membership is a Who's Who of Chinese political and Western business elites. Chaired by the former PRC premier and founding dean of SEM, Zhu Rongji, its 2018 Chinese leadership included Vice President Wang Qishan (Xi Jinping's closest supporter); Chen Jining, the former Tsinghua president and now mayor of Beijing; Yi Gang, governor of the People's Bank of China; Jack Ma of Alibaba; Robin Li of Baidu, and on and on. And the foreign members were no slouches, either: Mary Barra, head of General Motors; Lloyd Blankfein of Goldman Sachs; Tim Cook of Apple; Elon Musk of Tesla; Stephen Schwarzman of Blackstone; and the man who would do absolutely anything to have his company legalized in China, Mark Zuckerberg of Facebook. SEM, and its Advisory Board, was for foreign business leaders a privileged port of entry to China's political and business stratosphere.

Out of this came donations to SEM as well. Advisory Board member John Thornton, formerly of Goldman Sachs, established the John L. Thornton China Center both at Tsinghua and at the Brookings Institution in Washington. But some of the biggest fish at Tsinghua, as at most universities, were reserved for the central administration. While Dean Qian of SEM may have imagined what Stephen Schwarzman could do for his school, President Chen Jining had larger ambitions, and the new Schwarzman College at Tsinghua, supported by a half-billion dollar fundraising effort led by Schwarzman, would be Chen's signature program.

These donations, as well as profits from university-affiliated companies, were an important step toward financial flexibility for the university as a whole and for the individual schools because of the many limitations on other fundraising means. The Ministry of Education controlled the levels of tuition, and the government now forbade schools from taking out bank loans to complete capital projects. The mega-gifts from foreigners were a start. But as Qian noted, with the rapid increase in wealthy Chinese individuals, it was likely that private donations from within China would become a fast-growing source of university funding in the future.[68]

## Competition at Home and Abroad

Tsinghua has successfully reestablished itself as a leading comprehensive university in China, but it must confront many challenges before it can enduringly be considered among the world's leading universities. Tsinghua's comparative advantage in China, as Li Daokui says, has been the university's position "at the center of national politics, science, technology, development, and education."[69] However, as China's population has become more internationally mobile and aware, international universities are increasingly Tsinghua's stiffest competitors for high-performing Chinese students and top rankings. With one exception.

Tsinghua's fiercest competitor within China for government grants and international reputation may be found just across the street from its own gates. Founded in the center of the capital in 1898, Peking University (PKU) has long been one of China's flagship institutions. It took over the residential campus of Yenching University in 1952, forming with Tsinghua and other universities a cluster of higher education institutions in what is now northwestern Beijing. Yet the two institutions were intended to serve different purposes from their early history. As Li Daokui once explained to me, PKU's "tradition is to be critical of the government . . . far away from politics. . . . Tsinghua, on the other hand . . . it's close to politics. That's the difference."[70]

Like Tsinghua, PKU expanded in the reform era to once again become a comprehensive university, determined to rise to world-class status. Today, both universities have been primary recipients of Project 985 funding, and both compete for other state subsidies. In November 2015 China's State Council announced the "Double First Class" (DFC) program, a national project aimed at building world-leading "first-class universities" with "first-class academic disciplines."[71] In January 2017 Tsinghua was picked for 34 of the total 110 disciplines being considered, slightly behind PKU, which had 41.[72] Moreover, PKU's world-class ambitions led it to share many of the same ambitions as Tsinghua. PKU's Yenching Academy, for example, mirrored many aspects of Tsinghua's Schwarzman Scholars program. Like Tsinghua, PKU seeks to compete with the world's best universities. This pursuit has opened both universities up to new challenges.

With increased mobility and international awareness, growing numbers of high-performing Chinese students are choosing to attend top international universities, forgoing China's leading institutions. Many top-tier Chinese high schools offer special tracks designed to prepare students for international college admissions procedures, rather than the traditional *gaokao*. During the first decade of the twenty-first century, the number of Chinese students pursuing foreign higher education grew by over 20 percent each year, while the number of students taking the *gaokao* declined every year from 2008 to 2013.[73] In 2013, 686 students from mainland China studied at Harvard alone—representing the largest international cohort on that campus.[74] Since opening their doors to fee-paying mainland students in 2002, the well-regarded universities of Hong Kong have also competed with Tsinghua to recruit top students. While China's integration into the international system has transformed Tsinghua's institutional ambitions, the university's international competitors have, if only slightly, diminished one of Tsinghua's key strengths: its ability to recruit the elite of the elite among China's top students.

As Tsinghua gains the vast resources world-class comprehensive universities require, its individual programs must compete with specialized institutions devoted to world-leading status in a single field. While Tsinghua's joint executive MBA program between SEM and the Institut Européen d'Administration des Affaires (INSEAD), a leading European business school, was ranked first among all executive MBA programs in the world by the *Financial Times* in 2015, the full-time MBA program of SEM faced stiff competition from the China Europe International Business School (CEIBS), a joint venture between the Chinese government and the European Union, which ranked eleventh in the 2015 *Financial Times* ranking of full-time, global MBA programs.[75] CEIBS offered a targeted education with an international flavor to Chinese and foreign business students. The relatively small size and focused nature of CEIBS ran counter to Tsinghua's strategy of expansion of disciplines, but its clear results challenged the feasibility and desirability of Tsinghua's vision.

State support fueled Tsinghua's rise to the apex of the country's higher education system, but contributing to Beijing's research priorities for China's universities required Tsinghua to double down on its traditional strengths at the cost of improving in dramatic ways its performance in new or renewed fields. Tsinghua was, of course, among the forty-two universities China's DFC identified as "having the potential to develop into a world-class university."[76] These schools were chosen because of their leading positions in specific academic disciplines in China, and all were expected to build toward leading positions in their chosen fields in the world. Almost two-thirds of Tsinghua's chosen disciplines were in engineering, information technology, and the natural and physical sciences.[77] Government funding, which still makes up a significant portion of Tsinghua's budget, was disproportionately distributed to areas in which Tsinghua already excelled internationally.

For Qiu Yong, Tsinghua's president, the state's support of a discrete and focused number of disciplines limited his capacity to make Tsinghua become more than a world-leading university in any field but engineering. During meetings with university leaders and faculty, Qiu reminded them of the enormous influence Tsinghua once had in China in the humanities and social sciences, through figures such as the Four Tutors.[78] The educational philosophy of Tsinghua was to integrate the "shaping of values," the "cultivation of abilities," and the "transfer of knowledge" to create innovative talent for the country. To do this, he argued, students had to engage deeply across disciplines in the liberal arts and sciences to understand how the leading minds in different fields approached and solved problems. But ultimately the state's emphasis on and investments in Tsinghua's natural and applied sciences left the university's commitment to educating the "whole person" rather unbalanced.

And so, in recent years, Tsinghua has recommitted to raising its already excellent engineering disciplines, rather than the university's comprehensive standing, into leading positions in the world by 2030 and to being at the very top of their fields by 2050. Between 2015 and 2018, Tsinghua led the world in the number of publications in both engineering and physical science and mathematics and computer science. The research done by Tsinghua faculty was not only plentiful but also influential. Of the top 1 percent of the most frequently cited papers in the physical sciences and engineering, Tsinghua faculty authored the third most papers, lagging behind only MIT and Stanford in the same period.[79] Tsinghua was ranked first and ninth in the world in engineering by the 2021 *U.S. News and World Report* and QS subject rankings, respectively.

## Spirits Independent?

Surely it is not surprising that a country led by engineers (individuals with engineering educations or backgrounds have dominated China's leadership over the past two decades) would be less enamored with the promotion of the humanities and social sciences. And since 1949 the Chinese Party-State has concerned itself more with the control, censorship, and political mobilization of the humanities and social sciences than with their research excellence. After many oscillations, the political pressure ramped up again after 2012. The 2017 CCDI investigation into Tsinghua required that the university "strengthen political control over textbooks" and "expand supervision of teaching" to help resolve the "issue of lax controls over positions." Moreover, the investigation forced thirteen liberal arts departments to "add requirements for political standards . . . to teaching appointments . . . and [have] academic standards reflect the specific requirements of Chinese characteristics."[80] This political rubric for what was acceptable work in the humanities and social sciences made it difficult for Tsinghua to revive its institutional roots in the liberal arts through "vigorously promoting the 'new humanities,'" as had been called for in the 2016–2020 plan. Yet Tsinghua made it through the CCDI inspection relatively unscathed compared to other Chinese universities, as we will see in the case of Nanjing University.

To be sure, Chinese universities have rich experience in trying to delay, deflect, or ignore untoward state intrusion. They have seen it all before, and worse, in the Maoist years. Take the example of textbooks. A major course at Tsinghua used a leading international textbook on economic issues. The problem was that the textbook contained accurate information about the near-destruction of the Chinese economy under Mao's Great Leap Forward. What to do? Customs and postal censors (yes, there are censors everywhere) offered to allow the book to be used if a few pages were torn out. Fine, said a Tsinghua professor. But then some censor read further, and now it was clear that the book—which had been used at Tsinghua for a decade or more— could not enter the country at all. Miraculously, the international author of the textbook emailed the Tsinghua students a PDF of the book, as a gift. Everyone, except possibly the publisher, was then happy. The censors had done their job, for the physical book had not entered the country. The faculty members had done their job, for their text of choice could now be read. And the author had reached his intended audience. Philanthropy can have its academic virtues.

Tsinghua's participation in state-backed initiatives, such as the Thousand Talents Program, military-civil fusion, and Made in China 2025, presented political risks for the university's international reputation. Universities positioning themselves to receive financial and political support from their government would normally be unremarkable in any country. However, growing distrust of the Chinese government in certain Western countries, such as the United States and Australia, has put Tsinghua's contributions to state policy priorities under a microscope.[81] The Thousand Talents Program has helped Tsinghua recruit world-class scholars who may improve its research output, but, as previously mentioned, concerns about economic competition with China have led some foreign governments to view the initiative as a vehicle for "stealing" intellectual property, as articulated in a US congressional report on the program.[82] The rise of military-civil fusion projects at Tsinghua has led to growing concerns in foreign capitals that some research collaborations between Tsinghua and foreign scholars support the Chinese military.[83]

In my opinion, much of this concern is misplaced. As we have seen in earlier chapters, it is a mark of a great university to recruit and retain the best possible scholars and teachers. A "thousand talents" program would not have suited a Harvard, Berkeley, or Duke—but only because the numbers were too large. The leading American universities, like China's, have as their central mission the recruitment of the best possible faculty. When I expanded the Faculty of Arts and Sciences at Harvard by one hundred faculty members in the first years of this century, one might well have called it a "Hundred Talents Program." And, as we have seen from Harvard's history, the role of universities assisting national militaries is hardly unique to China. Perhaps there ought to be some limits, however. I recall when, in the 1990s, the Harvard Kennedy School hosted a program for colonels from China's People's Liberation Army to meet and study with their American counterparts. I still cringe when I recall a toast offered by the then-director of the Kennedy School program, Ambassador Robert Blackwill: "To the enduring cooperation between Harvard and the People's Liberation Army!" That was a bridge too far for me.

The most immediate challenge to Tsinghua's rise is not geopolitics; it is the resurgence of political repression within China, which has a direct effect on the university community. This is especially the case in the humanities and social sciences. In July 2018 Xu Zhangrun, a professor in Tsinghua's School of Law and one of the Top 10 Young Legal Scholars of China in 2005, published an open letter on the internet entitled, "Imminent Fears, Immediate Hopes."[84] It was a scathing critique of Xi Jinping's grasp for enduring powers by ending term limits for the country's president. Xu feared, not without reason, a return to a state where the Party's leadership demanded absolute political and ideological loyalty. The letter received enormous attention on both Chinese social media and in the international press. Then the reaction set in. It was reported in March 2019 that Professor Xu had been suspended from all his teaching and research positions at Tsinghua. Then in July 2020 Professor Xu was formally detained after having published a further series of essays brutally critical of Xi Jinping's government during the coronavirus pandemic.[85] In one of his last commentaries, published immediately before the convening of the National People's Congress, Xu wrote that "there should be an end to the persecution of university professors who dare to speak out," referring not to himself but to ten Wuhan University professors who had signed a letter demanding free speech protections following the death of Doctor Li Wenliang, a martyr and whistle-blower for China's cover-up of its coronavirus outbreak.[86]

Upon Professor Xu's release from detention six days after his arrest, he received notice from Tsinghua that he had been fired. To justify his position's termination, Tsinghua claimed Xu's essays had put him in violation of the "10 standards of professional conduct for teachers in tertiary institutes in the new era," a regulation published by the Ministry of Education in 2018, which made "words and deeds that harm the authority of the Party Central Committee or violate the Party's line" a fireable offense.[87] Yet despite the Tsinghua administration's decision to dismiss Xu, many within Tsinghua were sympathetic to his plight. Nearly six hundred from the Tsinghua community donated over US$14,000 to Xu, who had lost his salary along with his livelihood, but the professor declined their generosity, encouraging them to give instead to those "who are truly in need."[88] Yet, although Xu promised to bear any burden to continue his work, Tsinghua's administration, which I imagine did its best to protect him as long as possible, could no longer hold back the political forces that basically threw Xu out of the Chinese academy.

While scholars at Tsinghua are afforded many privileges because of their institution's prestige and personal connections to China's rulers, the case of Xu Zhangrun shows the real limits, human and intellectual, of Chinese higher education even at the country's university most committed to world-class standing. Tsinghua has risen on the back of its great access to state resources and officials, but it is also, perhaps in some ways uniquely, vulnerable to being caught in the crossfire of political debates.

Here we are reminded of the time, in the Republican era, when Tsinghua was home to four of the most famous scholars in the land. Liang Qichao, Wang Guowei, Chen Yinke, and Zhao Yuanren were all products of both classical and international learning. All were at home in Chinese culture while also cutting-edge scholars in the modern humanities and social sciences. And all were famous abroad as at home. After Wang Guowei ended his own life in 1927, his colleague Chen Yinke inscribed on a commemorative stele on campus in honor of Wang Guowei: "A spirit independent and a mind unfettered" (*Duli zhi jingshen, ziyou zhi sixiang*).

These ten characters are known to every Tsinghua scholar. Tsinghua's faculty—despite all the political turbulence and repression of recent decades—still venerates the virtues inscribed on Wang Guowei's commemorative stele. However, in April 2019, on the 108th anniversary of the founding of Tsinghua University, when Tsinghua faculty and alumni, including Professor Xu Zhangrun, sought to pay respect to Wang Guowei's stele, they found it walled off and "under repair." On the construction wall surrounding the monument, a sardonic poster reframed Chen Yinke's famous inscription: "Tsinghua at 108 years: A self-made barrier against any independent spirit; so thick that no mind remains unfettered." As Tsinghua sought to propel itself into the global elite, its capacity to recruit, support, and protect scholars of "spirits independent and minds unfettered" also seemed under repair.

## Abroad at Home: Internationalization at Tsinghua

Tsinghua was founded as a prep school for those looking to go abroad. As a university in Republican China, its faculty and students looked toward the United States. In the early People's Republic, they looked toward Moscow. During Mao's Cultural Revolution, Tsinghua faced inward and went nowhere. From the beginning of the reform era after 1979, Tsinghua was determined to be again part of the larger world of universities.

Weaving through contemporary Tsinghua's approach to excellence in faculty recruitment and research, student achievement, and administration was a renewed push toward internationalization. This had begun with the faculty. As Tsinghua sought to raise its profile on the international stage, it focused on recruiting overseas Chinese scholars, especially Tsinghua alumni, to return to China as distinguished faculty. Both Qian Yingyi and Li Daokui were part of this early wave of returnees. Among Chinese universities, this approach to recruitment was hardly unique to Tsinghua; however, Tsinghua carried the advantage of prestige, funding, and an alumni base both large and elite from which to recruit. For many scholars of Qian and Li's generation, the call to return and serve the motherland was difficult to ignore, particularly during the early twenty-first century, when government incentives and general funding for higher education made faculty positions extremely attractive. Once on board, faculty were expected to publish in international journals and with international coauthors, which would in turn contribute to higher research rankings for the university.

Students at Tsinghua also found themselves among an increasingly international cohort. Tsinghua hosted a total of 3,257 international students in 2019.[89] Nearly 2,000 Tsinghua undergraduate students participated in some form of international experience in 2017, with exchange programs with over 140 universities around the world that had signed official exchange agreements with Tsinghua.[90] The opening of the Schwarzman Scholars program at the newly built Schwarzman College courtyard within the Tsinghua campus in 2016 brought even more international graduate students, professors, and media attention to Tsinghua.

At an institutional level, Tsinghua actively pursued partnerships with universities outside of China as well. In 2014 it announced the opening of the Tsinghua-Berkeley Shenzhen Institute in Shenzhen in partnership with the University of California, Berkeley.[91] In 2015 Tsinghua became the first Chinese university to build major research facilities outside of China when it entered into a partnership with Microsoft and the University of Washington to form the Global Innovation Exchange, a Seattle-based graduate school for technology and innovation.[92]

Tsinghua's international partnerships increasingly extended to the developing world as well, in tandem with the Chinese government's international infrastructure program, the Belt and Road Initiative (BRI). Although infrastructure investments are the heart of the BRI, collaboration in education is also included in the plan to foster people-to-people ties and educate technical elites in countries receiving investments. A white paper released by the Ministry of Education in 2016 declared that "China is willing to work with countries along the route to expand humanities exchanges, strengthen personnel training, and jointly create a better future through education."[93] Tsinghua announced its intention to align with BRI priorities in its 2016–2020 development plan, noting that the university would "promote the 'Belt and Road'" and "make full use of countries" that joined the initiative.[94] Since then, Tsinghua has established a range of BRI offerings, from a BRI-focused think tank and annual forum to increasing enrollment from BRI countries and even a degree in public administration along the BRI.[95]

Tsinghua also engaged in international business. In 2015 Tsinghua Unigroup, a subsidiary of the Tsinghua University-owned Tsinghua Holdings, attempted a $23 billion acquisition of Micron, an American chip manufacturer, more than quadrupling the previous record deal value of a Chinese acquisition of an American company. The deal was blocked, however, by the US government because of alleged national security concerns.[96]

*A Special Education Zone: Schwarzman College*

The growing political pressures within China and an unpredictable international environment threatened to limit Tsinghua's internationalization at home and its rise globally. But there were new opportunities at home. Just as China's economic "opening up and reform" in the 1980s had begun with special economic zones such as Shenzhen, the first decades of the twentieth century saw a series of what might be deemed "special education zones" through Sino-foreign joint ventures, of which NYU Shanghai and Duke Kunshan University are the best known. Tsinghua created its own special zone, within the gates of the university.

Stephen A. Schwarzman, chairman and CEO of the Blackstone Group, a leading private equity firm, had strong business interests in China ever since China's sovereign wealth fund invested in Blackstone at the time of its initial public offering in 2007. He served on the Advisory Board of Tsinghua's School of Economics and Management. SEM Dean Qian Yingyi had hoped to approach Schwarzman, who as a philanthropist had given generously to the New York Public Library and other institutions, for a major gift. But presidents often steal a dean's best prospects, and President Chen Jining had larger ambitions still. He aimed to work with Schwarzman on a project that he hoped would transform Tsinghua and its place in the world.

After years of negotiation, planning, building, and recruiting both students and faculty, the result was Schwarzman College, an international, residential graduate school of global affairs, located on the Tsinghua campus, aimed at "the next generation of global leaders."

I became involved in this project in late 2011, when Steve Schwarzman came to my HBS office to ask my advice. At that point, Tsinghua's plans for his potential gift were still undefined, except that it was to be large. Very large. Schwarzman, too, had not clarified what he wished to do, save that he wanted it to be transformative, and above all he wanted it to promote the long-term development of Chinese-American relations—to bring the next generations of Chinese and American leaders together to learn with, and from, one another. In his own words, Schwarzman's aim was for students to "study under Chinese and Western professors who would help them find the links between cultures. Each cohort of scholars would be enriched by the experience. Then as they rose to positions of influence in different countries, they would understand each other and their ambitions. They would act out of friendship and reason, not with the kind of suspicions and mistrust that cause countries to stumble into the 'Thucydides trap.'"[97] Within a few months, my HBS colleague Warren McFarlan and I were advising Schwarzman on every aspect of a project that, by American academic standards, began to move with lightning speed.

It is no easy thing to start a new college, anywhere. A new college within a university is perhaps particularly challenging, for the energy and resources devoted to it inevitably come at some cost to existing schools and their deans, who have little to gain from it. But President Chen Jining—and then his successor, Qiu Yong—mobilized the schools and faculty of Tsinghua for this project, for they too believed it to be transformative for the university as a whole, bringing international students, faculty, and standards to the heart of the Tsinghua campus. Everything was up for definition and negotiation, except for the program's intended impact on Tsinghua, China, the United States, and the wider world. Even Schwarzman's Chinese name was given new character, as it were. Formerly, the name Schwarzman had simply been transliterated in Chinese. Chen Jining now gave him a real three-character Chinese name that meant something: *Su Shimin*, that is, Mr. Su, World Citizen.

Both Chen Jining and Schwarzman were men in a hurry. Chen and Tsinghua worked at "China speed," a phrase that conveys the remarkable speed with which things can be built in China today. (There is a bridge at Harvard across the Charles River that recently took six years to repair. A bridge of similar size in China was replaced in forty-eight hours.) But often enough "China speed" was no match for "Schwarzman speed," which moved the project forward at a breathtaking pace. By the end of 2012 fundamental agreement was reached on the nature and funding of the project; a global search for an architect was under way; I had formed and chaired a global Academic Advisory Council; Tsinghua had recruited a founding dean, the charismatic and prolific economist, Professor Li Daokui; and Schwarzman had pledged $100 million of his own funds while he undertook to raise almost all of the rest. Since few of his acquaintances can turn down Steve

Schwarzman, by 2020 pledges for the program's endowment stood at nearly $600 million.[98]

That level of funding would be needed to build and sustain the program that has become Schwarzman Scholars. The program planned a maximum of two hundred graduate students, for whom everything (tuition, fees, housing, meals, transportation) would be provided gratis. They would reside in a stunning new residential college that housed, in the Oxbridge model, students and (some) faculty, containing also case-study classrooms, an opulent auditorium, open meeting spaces, a gymnasium and, for good measure, a pub. (That was my idea.) In the tradition of early twentieth century Chinese campuses, an American architect, Robert A. Stern, was given the commission. He designed a thoroughly modern campus with Chinese characteristics, including Beijing-style brick and a courtyard.

Schwarzman College, as the physical complex is known, stood in lush contrast to any Tsinghua student residence, with its individual rooms, bathrooms, and suites. (It was built on the site of the public showers used by Tsinghua students whose dorms had none.) It boasted state-of-the-art filtration systems for air and water, protecting its inhabitants from Beijing's often noxious environment. It had its own, dedicated internet service that could transcend the Great Firewall of Chinese censorship. Its library had international newspapers, magazines, and scholarly books—as well as the bound Collected Speeches of Xi Jinping in ten languages.

**Figure 9.4.** Schwarzman College. Photograph © William C. Kirby.

Was this a new, academic kind of treaty port, with extraterritorial privileges? Certainly in part, although the extensive public programs of the college, featuring Chinese and international leaders from all fields, were open to the university community. Was it also a sign of the direction Tsinghua itself wished to head? Without question. Faced with the inevitable critique of the comparative opulence and openness of the new college, Chen Jining said bluntly that the new college could be a model for Tsinghua's future. (As Deng Xiaoping had said, in inaugurating the first Special Economic Zones decades earlier, it was no betrayal of Chinese socialism if some people got rich first.)

By 2020 the Schwarzman Scholars at Tsinghua University was an unquestioned success, even if temporarily displaced from Beijing by the global pandemic. With its fellowship competition modeled on that of the Rhodes Scholarships, it admitted students from the United States, the Chinese mainland, Hong Kong, Macao, and Taiwan in addition to scholars from a further seventy-four countries around the world. It rapidly became among the most selective of international graduate programs, admitting approximately 4 percent of applicants, and with an admissions yield of 94 percent. Its Masters of Global Affairs degree focuses on politics, business, and science, while immersing students in issues facing China and the world. It has so far been insulated from the growing political oversight of the Xi Jinping era. Led now by a distinguished scholar and administrator, Dean Xue Lan, its faculty includes a stellar list of Tsinghua and international scholars, teaching ambitious cohorts of young people who are told that they shall become "leaders prepared to deepen understanding between China and the rest of the world."

### Can Tsinghua Lead?

Within China, Tsinghua already leads in many areas. Tsinghua is China's top comprehensive university in the most prestigious international rankings. In discipline-specific rankings, Tsinghua is world-leading, or nipping at the heels of the world's best. Excellence in STEM has afforded it greater stability than other Chinese universities in its overall budget. Publicly funded science and technology expenditures at Tsinghua rose nearly 30 percent in 2020, while government outlays for Tsinghua's peers declined following the COVID-19 pandemic.[99] However, Tsinghua's reliance on the support of the political system that fueled its rise has not come without cost. Like the University of Berlin in Wilhelmine times, Tsinghua is part and parcel of a rising nation-state that is among global leaders in science and technology. It promotes liberal education and yet remains broadly illiberal in its national politics. Moreover, the state's enormous support for Tsinghua's STEM fields underscores a view that the university serves China's development priorities, not, primarily, the creation and dissemination of knowledge. Will a program such as Schwarzman Scholars suffice for Tsinghua to present itself to be a truly internationalized university in values as well as research?

We shall see. Meanwhile, Tsinghua, an institution founded to send Chinese students away for their education, now hosts proudly what it calls the Rhodes Scholarship for the twenty-first century. After all, why should the best and brightest of the world's young leaders go to Oxford—to a foggy, chilly, self-isolating island, in decline, off the coast of Europe—when they could come to Tsinghua in Beijing, the capital of a rising China? Cecil Rhodes had aimed to educate those with "the potential for leadership." Surely Tsinghua, too, has the potential for leadership.

# CHAPTER TEN

# The Burden of History

## *Nanjing University*

NANJING, OR Nanking, as it was long known in English, is China's "southern capital." At least, that is what the characters mean. Today, the city of Nanjing occupies an unclear position in China's political and economic hierarchies. With political power headquartered in Beijing, financial might at home in Shanghai, and trade and manufacturing centered in Guangdong, what is Nanjing but one of a growing number of wealthy, industrialized provincial capitals? Of course, that is no minor status: this metropolis of 8.5 million inhabitants is the capital of Jiangsu province, long one of China's commercial and intellectual centers, whose eighty million citizens enjoy one of China's highest standards of living. Certainly, Nanjing occupies a higher place in the hierarchy of Chinese cities than Durham, North Carolina, does in the hierarchy of American cities. But, today, Nanjing University confronts a challenge not unlike that once faced by Duke University: how to punch above its place.

The city of Nanjing, in east-central China on the banks of the great Yangzi River, was once at the absolute center, with a longer and more distinguished history than that of Beijing, which lies at the dusty northern frontier of the North China plain. Nanjing was the capital of multiple Chinese dynasties. Called Yingtian when capital of the Ming dynasty (1368–1644), it may have been the largest city in the world, with a half-million inhabitants in 1400. When the Ming established its "northern capital" in *Bei*jing, Yingtian became *Nan*jing, or the southern (and suddenly secondary) capital. In the Qing dynasty (1644–1912) the city was for a decade in the mid-nineteenth century called *Tian*jing, or the "heavenly capital" of the rebellious Taiping Heavenly Kingdom. When the Republic of China was established in 1912, Nanjing was initially named the capital. And it would be China's national capital, in fact, under the Nationalist regime from 1927 to 1949.

In modern times Nanjing has experienced both tragedy and hope. Massacres of its inhabitants occurred twice during the Taiping Rebellion of the mid-nineteenth century. Thirty thousand imperial troops were stabbed, burned, or drowned when the Taiping forces took the city in 1853. Eleven years later, when imperial troops retook the city, their commander, Zeng Guofan, reported that one hundred thousand rebels had perished. In 1911, when Nanjing fell in a bloody battle to revolutionary forces seeking to overthrow the Qing, the days of the last imperial dynasty were numbered. In 1937 the Japanese "rape of Nanjing" set new standards for military criminality. The seven-week-long mass execution of Chinese soldiers and the slaughter and rape of tens of thousands of civilians took place in contravention of all rules of modern warfare and in the full view of international observers.

Yet when it was China's capital after 1927, Nanjing had dreams of a return to glory. The city's boundaries were vastly expanded to house both the new National Government and an anticipated population of two million (in retrospect, a conservative estimate). Rail connections were to grow and a huge airport to be built. A new government district of nearly ten square kilometers was to be erected on the site just west of the old Ming palace, and south of the Ming tombs was to be an imposing mausoleum for the Nationalist founder, Sun Yat-sen. Located at the district's center would be a modern palace complex situated on a north-south axis, dominated at its northern end by a massive Nationalist Party headquarters, an international architectural marvel combining features of Beijing's Temple of Heaven and the U.S. Capitol in Washington, DC. Beyond all this, the city would be beautified. In Parisian style, trees would line the avenues and electric lights in the shape of Chinese lanterns would line the streets. A system of parkways and boulevards was conceived, dominated by the grand, six-lane Zhongshan Lu, or Sun Yat-sen Road. A "ring boulevard" was to encircle the new capital, but not, as later in Beijing, at the expense of the ancient city wall. Nanjing's great city wall would be retained, perhaps with the thought—times being what they were—that it might be needed. So Nanjing's ring road would run *on top* of the old wall, offering its motorists a parkway with a panorama of city, river, and suburbs.[1]

Not all of these things were built. A few were, however, and they serve today as reminders of what Nanjing was meant to be. Sun Yat-sen Boulevard is the main thoroughfare, leading through the city to Sun's stunning mausoleum. The city walls remain—among the best-preserved in China. And massive numbers of what locals called "French trees" (in fact a hybrid of American sycamore and Oriental plane) were planted. Seedlings imported from France would in time shade a Communist Nanjing.

## Inheritances

It was during these years of ambition and revival, before the establishment of the People's Republic of China, that Nanjing University's predecessors, institutions such as National Central University and the University of Nanking, were founded and flourished. Before they merged under the umbrella of Nanjing University, or Nanda, as it became known (distinguishing itself from Beida, or Peking University), each had developed a distinctive institutional culture closely connected with the international trends and models in higher education of their era.[2]

### National Central University: Berlin on the Yangzi

Nanjing University's primary predecessor, National Central University (NCU), was itself born out of a series of institutions established during the late Qing dynasty's reform movement. NCU's lineage may be first traced to Sanjiang Normal School, founded in 1902 at the urging of Zhang Zhidong, the reformist Governor General of Liangjiang (today's Jiangsu, Jiangxi, and Anhui provinces). Zhang believed the region needed a modern education system, basing Sanjiang on a Japanese model, which was itself inspired by Western models. The institution changed rapidly in its first two decades. In 1905, just a year after Sanjiang enrolled its first students, it was renamed Liangjiang Normal School, and an expanded curriculum was introduced offering students greater flexibility to specialize. The school was restructured again in 1914, this time as National Nanjing Higher Normal School, and the Japanese-inspired curriculum was replaced with one based on American and European models.[3] Behind this shift was school president Guo Bingwen, a major figure in this era of Chinese education. A recipient of a Boxer Indemnity Scholarship, he studied at the University (now College) of Wooster in Ohio, where he became committed to an education in the sciences and the humanities. Guo was one of the first Chinese nationals to receive a doctorate from an American institution, and he wrote his Columbia doctoral thesis on "The Chinese System of Public Education." As president, Guo introduced reforms based on practices in Euro-American higher education that were considered innovative to China, including offering elective courses and opening the school's doors to women. By 1920 he had transformed the school into a full university. Three years later it was given a name to fit its mission: National Southeast University, the leading institution at the center of the country.

National Southeast University was a major institution for its time. It employed over two hundred faculty and staff, enrolled sixteen hundred students, and housed twenty-seven departments within five schools. The university's curriculum began with a general education program before students declared academic majors and chose elective courses. The university was deeply engaged with the significant intellectual movements of Republican China. In response to the May Fourth Movement and the Peking University–led New Culture movement, which sharply critiqued China's cultural legacy, several scholars at National Southeast University sought to preserve China's "national essence" while infusing it with elements of Western culture. Their "Xueheng School," so named for the journal *Xueheng* (Critical Review), was led by a group of "aggressive, outspoken" young scholars trained at Harvard under Irving Babbitt, whose literary and political writings helped to define American conservative thought in the 1920s and 1930s.[4]

While it left an important mark on Nanda's historical foundations, National Southeast University lasted but four years before being again restructured in the aftermath of the Nationalist revolution of 1926–1927, which brought to power the Guomindang, or Nationalist Party, and the government it led.

The Nationalist government, established in 1927, desired a comprehensive, flagship, *national* university for its new capital, Nanjing. It sought a University of Berlin for its Berlin. It also sought a flagship *Party* university: the Nationalists were heirs to the permanent revolutionary, Sun Yat-sen, the first provisional president of the Chinese republic. Sun died in 1925, but his mission of Party-led national development became the political gospel for his Nationalist successors led by Chiang Kai-shek.

Chiang's rule would emphasize a commitment to political discipline and scientific/technological advancement, in equal measure. National Central University, born on May 16, 1928, of a merger of National Southeast University with eight other institutions, came to life under the direct sponsorship of the ruling party. This new university was then China's largest, with eight schools, 1,762 students, and 346 faculty members—far larger than Tsinghua University at the time. Although the structure of the curriculum stayed initially constant in the transition to National Central University, its content became subject to politicization. Students were required to study English and Sun Yat-sen's famous "Three People's Principles" (nationalism, socialism, democracy, in the short version) from the point of view of the ruling party and also pass military training and physical education courses.[5]

In a period of profound German influence on China's military, industrial, and educational development in the decade before the onset of China's war with Japan in 1937,[6] the presidency (1930–1932) of German-educated geologist Zhu Jiahua aimed to make National Central University China's national model. Higher education was to be "partified" (*danghua*), with an emphasis on alignment with the state's political priorities and a commitment to science. Chiang Kai-shek himself extolled the educational values of Prussia / Germany—values of "patriotism, discipline, honor, and order."[7] He even sent his son, Chiang Wei-kuo, to be a cadet at the Munich *Kriegsschule*, from which he participated in the German *Anschluß* with Austria in 1938. But students, even at National Central University, were more nationalist than Nationalist, and they protested vigorously Japan's recurrent incursions. The Japanese takeover of Manchuria in 1931 led to such student protests in Nanjing that Chiang Kai-shek temporarily suspended the university's operations. At Chiang's request, Luo Jialun gave up his presidency at Tsinghua to run and reform National Central University.

Having studied at the Universities of Berlin, Paris, and London, Luo was determined to make NCU an important player in China's cultural rejuvenation. He focused on recruiting outstanding faculty and raising the bar for full professorship (which did not endear him to the faculty). His second priority was to link the university's academic development to China's social and economic needs. For example, Luo Rong'an of MIT was recruited to build National Central University's mechanical engineering department, which produced China's first aeronautical engineers. Finally, Luo streamlined the university's administrative structure, reducing redundancy, improving efficiency, and cutting costs. The money saved was used to purchase books and remake the university's campus, which included building its iconic Brandenburg Gate in 1933 and auditorium in 1934, modeled after that of the University of Berlin. Luo's most ambitious plan, a new campus to ac-

**Figure 10.1.** The "Brandenburg Gate" of National Central University.
Wikimedia Commons.

commodate an additional ten thousand students, was permanently derailed by the Japanese invasion.

When Nanjing fell to the Japanese army in 1937, a Japanese-led Chinese "puppet" government, now in formal alliance with National Socialist Germany, operated its own National Central University on the site of the original institution. Jiang Zemin, future president of the People's Republic of China, attended this NCU from 1943 until shortly after the war ended in 1945. There, he became an active participant in anti-Japanese student protests. However, when the war ended and the Chinese government returned to Nanjing in 1945, the Nationalists refused to recognize the education given Jiang and others at the Japanese-run NCU. Jiang was forced to finish his education at Shanghai's Jiao Tong University, where he promptly joined the Communist Party.[8]

The Nationalist-led NCU reopened in Nanjing in 1946 as China's leading comprehensive university. Chiang Kai-shek had been named NCU president during World War II, when the university was relocated to China's southwest. He remained president emeritus after the war, but the university's recovery would be short-lived. Following the Communist military victory in the Chinese Civil War (1946–1949), the university was once again renamed, this time as National Nanjing University. Then, after an edict eliminated

"National" from all university names, the institution finally settled on a name that would last: Nanjing University.

## The University of Nanking

National Central University may be the most important ancestor of Nanjing University, but Nanda's lineage includes also leading Christian colleges, which were important actors in Chinese higher education during the late nineteenth and early twentieth centuries. They bequeathed to modern Nanda a strong commitment to teaching, which arguably remains stronger at Nanda than at other leading Chinese universities.

The University of Nanking (UNK), a direct predecessor of Nanda, was founded in 1910 as a merger of several institutions operated by American missionaries in Nanjing and was incorporated by the Regents of the University of the State of New York.[9] Why New York? The New York legislature worked to establish "benevolent, charitable, scientific and missionary societies" overseas, guide their development, and give academic recognition to the course work completed.[10]

These Christian aspirations for UNK were reflected in its academic offerings, specializing in disciplines often associated with missionary work in China, such as education, medicine, agronomy, and the humanities.[11] Its curriculum was influenced by American models, focusing on English language, interactive classroom pedagogies, and applied projects.[12] UNK's American ties were also the source of much of its funding, with the founding missionary board providing 65 percent of its budget. The university achieved some repute, ranking eleventh overall in a 1928 study of greater China's undergraduate programs by a University of California, Berkeley, scholar.[13] While UNK's foreign relationships diminished under the scrutiny of the Nationalist government, the institution continued to grow, having a student body of 675 and 214 faculty members divided into three schools and one Center for Research on Chinese Culture by 1934.[14] However, as with National Central University, war with Japan upended UNK's operations as it was moved to Chengdu from 1937 to 1946 by order of the Ministry of Education.

While UNK flourished again in Nanjing immediately after the war's end, the Chinese Civil War prevented it from finding permanent footing. In 1948 UNK had surpassed its prewar size, with 1,100 students and 150 faculty members. But its good fortune was short-lived. Only a year later, much of the Nationalist governing apparatus and many affiliated institutions fled to Taiwan as the conflict turned in the Communists' favor. UNK's administration chose to remain in Nanjing, a decision that cost the university its independence. In January 1951 UNK was forced by the new PRC's Ministry of Education to cut all ties with its American missionary funding sources and was restructured into the public National University of Nanking. Soon thereafter, it was merged with Ginling College, but the unified institution lasted less than a year before being hoovered up into the newly created Nanjing University.

## Ginling College

Nomenclature confusion abounds in the ancestral tree of Nanda. The Chinese name of the University of Nanking was *Jinling daxue,* or Jinling University ("Jinling" or "Ginling" being a historical name for Nanjing). Ginling *College* or, as it was also called in English, Ginling College for Women (*Jinling nüzi daxue*), had a different origin and represents another important branch in Nanda's ancestral tree. Founded in 1912 by five American missionary organizations in Nanjing, Ginling College was a women's liberal arts college modeled after the American "Seven Sisters" and was affiliated with UNK. American missionaries were inspired by the US Progressive Era, in which promoting educational opportunities for women had become a central cause.[15] Ginling was the first college in China to grant bachelors' degrees to women. The college's first president, Matilda C. Thurston, was an alumna of Mount Holyoke College, but Ginling built its strongest relationship with Smith College, with which it exchanged faculty and even received financial support through fundraising by Smith alumnae.[16] Wu Yifang, a PhD from the University of Michigan, served as Ginling's president from 1928 to 1951 and was China's first female college president. In 1937 an acting Ginling president, the American missionary Wilhelmina Vautrin, known as the "Goddess of Mercy," protected ten thousand women and children on the campus during the Nanking massacre.[17] As with many institutions of higher education, Ginling College dispersed during the Second World War but returned, eager to continue the school's mission, in 1946.[18] However, the college would remain independent only for another five years, before finding itself under the new umbrella of Nanjing University.

**Figure 10.2.** Students at Ginling College. Gamewell, Mary Louise Ninde, *New Life Currents in China*. Missionary Education Movement in the United States and Canada, 1919, page 194/Wikimedia Commons.

## Communist Nanda

With the Communist takeover of China in 1949, Nanjing was suddenly no longer the national capital. National Central University, Nanjing's and the country's most prestigious institution of higher learning, ceased to exist. Like Humboldt University in 1945 and again in the 1990s, it was purged of faculty and administrators deemed most loyal to the *ancien régime*. Once central in every respect and centrally funded, it was now decidedly provincial. Carrying with it the "original sin" of being *the* Nationalist university, the new Nanjing University that took the place of NCU was for decades refused the special resources devoted to institutions in the Northern Capital. Beida and Tsinghua became China's new "national" universities in fact, if not in name.[19] Moreover, the strong missionary connections of several of its ancestors ensured Communist Nanda was in for rough sledding from the start.

Nanda was not only de-Nationalized but reduced in size. It was quickly sovietized and reformed as a purely teaching university with no mandate to pursue new research. Stripped of its programs in engineering, education, and agriculture, Nanda was housed on former campuses of National Central University and Ginling College, and the curriculum focused on the basic sciences and humanities.[20] By 1956 Nanda was home to just ten departments, mainly in literature, languages, and basic math and science. The university lost 36 percent of its teaching faculty in the reorganization, although it retained renowned scholars in math and science, allowing it to retain a leading position in these fields.[21]

NCU, Ginling, and UNK had all had strong relations with Europe or America. Like all Chinese universities, Nanda was now constricted to the Soviet bloc for its international partners. It brought scholars from the "socialist brother countries" to Nanjing and sent Nanda affiliates to the Soviet Union and Eastern Europe, but it was never a leading actor in Sino-Soviet exchanges. Nanda's somnambulance lasted until 1963, when Kuang Yaming, a scholar of traditional Chinese culture and a biographer of Confucius, was appointed president. The ambitious and outspoken Kuang began his tenure during a brief period of political loosening in China, and he tried to make the most of it. He criticized the Soviet model of ultra-specialization. He opened new research institutes, hosted conferences, published academic journals, and sought to put Nanda again at the forefront of research universities in China. He developed ten-year plans to bring Nanda back from the scholarly wilderness. As it turned out, he only had three years.

Kuang Yaming—like every Chinese university president in the modern era—had to be alert to changing political winds. After Mao Zedong openly criticized university education as elitist and out of touch in 1964 and 1965, Kuang moved proactively in early 1966 to show Nanda's loyalty. He sent five hundred students and faculty in the humanities to the countryside for an extended period of "half-farming, half-study." They lived the Maoist ideal in principle. In fact, the working conditions were horrific, and they resented Nanda's engineers who remained home in Nanjing. When the Cultural Revolution broke out on Beijing campuses that summer, these rusticized and begrudged faculty and students led a political attack on Kuang, to which he responded by labeling them reactionaries and "rightists." Kuang was then bizarrely accused by radicals in Beijing of stifling "the student movement," and soon the man who was trying to do what he *thought* Mao wanted was accused by *People's Daily* of "anti-Party and anti-socialist crimes of suppressing the revolutionary mass movement and undermining the proletariat Cultural Revolution."[22]

President Kuang was unceremoniously deposed on June 1, 1966; a few weeks later he and his subordinates were hauled before a mass rally where they were beaten and then paraded around campus. The campus, like the city and indeed the country, descended into factional strife and chaos. Mass movements and struggles arose across Nanjing, while three different Nanda student groups played leading roles in the factional conflicts and lethal armed conflict that continued well into 1967. That same year, in the midst of all this, the university halted admissions and basically shut down. The next class was not enrolled until 1972, when admissions were limited in principle to workers, peasants, and soldiers and, as at Tsinghua, based on recommendations and class identities.[23] Nanda was a shell of its former self and a basket case of a university.

## Rebirth

In 1978, after twelve years of chaos and dysfunction, Nanda came back to life. Kuang Yaming was exhumed from his academic tomb to resume the presidency of the university. And he was ready to lead. He abandoned Soviet-era specializations in favor of a more open undergraduate curriculum with a credit system. China's central government established a national system of eighty-eight key universities, of which Nanda was one. With newfound support from the central and provincial governments, and with a newly tolerant perspective on education, Kuang seized the opportunity for higher education presented by China's reform and opening.[24]

Kuang quickly rehired talented scholars who had been purged from the academy during the anti-intellectual tumult of the Cultural Revolution. Because of Nanda's pre-1949 strength in the sciences, which he had enhanced during his first presidency, Kuang started with a strong, if now aging, base. In 1978 Nanda's scientific projects received fifty-four awards at China's National Science Convention, outshining all other Chinese universities. He further sought to retain and reward young talent by promoting junior faculty and by sending them abroad to attend international conferences. His reforms extended to Nanda's curriculum, which, for the first time in the Communist era, introduced an element of "general education," as each department was required to offer at least one "foundational course" open to nonmajors. Kuang himself taught a writing course required of all students. By 1981 Nanda was on the path to be again a comprehensive university when it reopened its graduate school, which then offered twenty-four doctoral programs and fifty-three master's degrees.

Nanda's academic and research culture in this era seemed to absorb Kuang's increasingly independent intellectual instincts. The university's humanities institute received national attention for the work of Hu Fuming, then an associate professor in the politics department. His 1978 essay, "Practice is the Sole Criterion of Truth," was a stunning and forceful renunciation of Maoist infallibility. He famously rebutted the doctrine, promoted by Mao's immediate successor as Party Chairman, Hua Guofeng, that "we must support whatever decisions made by . . . whatever instructions given by" the now-dead Mao Zedong. Hu Fuming's critique made waves nationwide, and it gave theoretical ballast to the return to power of Deng Xiaoping, who became China's paramount leader later that year. Nanda, for once, was now on the winning side of Chinese politics.

Nanda also led a revival of historical studies, a largely forbidden area in the Maoist period, save for the most ideological works. In Chinese historical tradition, every new ruling house writes the official history (*zhengshi*) of the previous dynasty. There are twenty-four such "standard histories" composed over two millennia, the last being the Ming history, completed in 1775.

In Republican China a *draft* Qing history was composed but never completed; after 1949, when the government of the Republic of China moved to Taiwan, competing Qing history projects continued on either side of the Taiwan Strait. The very act of composing an official history is meant to lend legitimacy to the new ruling house, and so the People's Republic was determined to write *its* history of the Republic, thereby consigning it to history. Most of the effort was centered in Nanjing, the old Nationalist capital. A Research Institute for the History of the Republic of China was established at Nanjing University under a courageous and astute historian, Zhang Xianwen, who would also chair its History Department and Institute for Historical Studies. Zhang led a groundbreaking effort beginning in the 1980s to write a defining history of the Republic on the basis of materials housed in the Republic's old *Guoshiguan,* or Academia Historica, which became the home of the PRC's Second Historical Archive, storing materials of the Republican era. Zhang's *Outline of the History of the Republic of China* was acclaimed for its objective analysis and use of primary sources on a topic that had been more the subject of propaganda than sober analysis on both sides of the Taiwan Strait.[25] (The topic was sensitive enough that the writer of its preface admitted that he had not read the book.)

Because of the work of Zhang Xianwen and his colleagues, Nanda became the center of historical research on twentieth-century China. I recall attending many workshops and conferences held by Professor Zhang and his colleagues in the 1980s. With his introduction, I also was among the first foreigners to be granted extensive access to the Nationalist-era documents in the Second Historical Archive. It was, in retrospect, a golden time for work in my field, even if the archives were not yet accustomed to international scholarly norms. (Behind the archivist's desk there was a large set of printed rules on the wall, including a prohibition against accurate footnotes: scholars could cite the full details of a document, but not name the archive; or they could name the archive but not the details. When I asked an archivist why this rule existed, she responded, "Well, then *everyone* would know!")

Zhang Xianwen and Nanda leveraged the attention received by his work on Republican China to establish serious academic exchanges with Taiwan—something illegal in the Maoist period—and even pursued fundraising from Taiwanese businesses.[26] In multiple dimensions, then, Nanda was asserting its leadership to study China's Republican past, when Nanjing and its universities were at the center.

## Internationalization

That historical context mattered when Nanda built on its pre-Communist history of international exchanges to reengage with the world in the post-Mao era. It hosted its first post-Cultural Revolution group of international students and scholars in 1979. That same year, Kuang Yaming led the first delegation of Chinese university presidents to the United States since the Communist revolution.[27] While in Maryland, he invited Professor Chih-Yung Chien of Johns Hopkins University, who was a friend of that university's president, Steven Muller, to spend three months in China lecturing at Nanda and other universities.[28] For his part, Muller was interested in opening a Hopkins campus in China, as its School of Advanced International Studies (SAIS) had done in Bologna, Italy. To Muller, even in 1979, "China was the future." Chien returned from his trip to China convinced that Nanjing—not as political as Beijing nor as commercial as Shanghai—was the ideal location for such a venture.

In 1981 Muller traveled to Nanjing to negotiate an agreement with Kuang, which was approved by the Ministry of Education. Construction began in 1984, and in 1986 Nanda opened the Hopkins-Nanjing Center for Chinese and American Studies (HNC) in partnership with Hopkins' SAIS.[29] The Hopkins-Nanjing Center was the first academic joint-venture institution between Chinese and American universities since the founding of the People's Republic. It remains to this day the most rigorous. It was designed as a demanding, joint, interdisciplinary master's degree program in both Chinese and American studies, with intense language requirements on both sides. For example, American applicants typically completed three to four years of college-level Chinese before matriculating. The Americans took classes mostly in Mandarin Chinese, while the Chinese students studied mostly in English. It was designed to serve as the premier gateway to China for aspiring US government officials, businesspeople, and academics and as an opportunity to build relationships between these Americans and their Chinese counterparts. To foster friendships among students of different backgrounds, each dorm room had one American and one Chinese occupant.

Teaching—a historically distinguishing strength of Nanda—was at the core of the Hopkins-Nanjing Center's reputation for academic excellence. From its onset, the student body was small (originally 100, now 170), as were the intensive classes in American and Chinese history, politics, and culture. The Center's pedagogical and intellectual openness was enhanced from the beginning by an open-stack and uncensored library, bountifully stocked with books and periodicals ordered by both partner universities, including academic and media materials otherwise banned in China. (This was, and remains, the only open-stack library I have seen in hundreds of visits to Chinese universities.) The Hopkins-Nanjing Center set the academic bar high for a joint-venture program. Followers, such as NYU Shanghai (in partnership with East China Normal University), Duke Kunshan University (with Wuhan University as its partner), and Schwarzman Scholars (at Tsinghua) would all emulate the standards of academic autonomy first set at HNC. Nanjing, China's national capital in the more internationalist era of Republican China, was back at the center and in the vanguard of China's reentry into global systems.

The success of the Hopkins-Nanjing experiment was not easily won. The political and bureaucratic cultures of SAIS, in Washington, DC, and Nanjing University were strikingly different, and the American codirectors tended to stay for comparatively short tenures. The macrotensions of US-China relations periodically complicated the microproblems of running a bicultural institution. Yet HNC would endure and thrive. It taught the first course anywhere in China on the Cultural Revolution, and it has maintained its early promise of academic autonomy ever since. When formal processes failed, there were other means of addressing problems. I recall visiting and speaking at the Center in 1987 as the guest of the American codirector, Leon Slawecki, a retired foreign service officer who had studied China's foreign relations from a distance and now up close. He knew China well. And he knew that to smooth any problem, a liberal sampling of *baijiu*, the potent white liquor of which the Nanjing region boasted many famous brands, was his most useful diplomatic tool. His apartment held a famous collection of more than two hundred different types of *baijiu*.

There were, to be sure, some unexpected and unhappy outcomes of Nanjing's renewed internationalism. Nanda and other Nanjing universities welcomed a large number of students from Africa in the 1980s, seeking to revive ties from the 1950s that had been cut off by the Cultural Revolution. At a time when admission spots in any Chinese university were still severely limited, there arose resentment against African scholars who were recruited with comparatively large stipends. Added to this was the envy and resentment by male Chinese students of male African students who dated Chinese women. A combination of political and sexual frustrations among Chinese students, plus anti-African racism and anti-foreignism, sparked an incident on Christmas Eve in 1988 on a nearby campus that in turn led to a brawl that led to large student demonstrations at the Nanjing railway station, threatening the African students who were trying to leave the city. (I was introduced to this story by a remarkable Harvard undergraduate, whose 1989 senior thesis, "Anti-Africanism in China," remains one of the best pieces of undergraduate writing I have read. I encouraged her to pursue a doctorate in history. She declined: she wanted to be an actress. Six years later Mira Sorvino won an Academy Award.)[30]

Even the nationwide demonstrations and crackdown of 1989, which played out with such tragic consequences in Tiananmen Square in Beijing, proved to only pause Nanda's push to reinvigorate itself on international standards. Student protests in Nanjing during the spring of that year, while passionate and well attended, were not as large or organized as those in Beijing, nor did they face the same degree of military suppression. This did not mean that 1989 posed no challenges. Some at Johns Hopkins University pushed President Muller to close the Hopkins-Nanjing Center. However, with the aid of Hopkins' SAIS China Studies chair, A. Doak Barnett, Muller convinced the trustees that staying in China, and especially the partnership with Nanda, was the right course, even through tumult and crisis.[31]

*Ambitions, Setbacks, and Renewal*

Nanda's ambition to return to the center of Chinese higher education and be again a leading comprehensive university continued after Kuang's second term as Nanda's president ended in 1982. His successor, the astrophysicist Qu Qinyue, was another remarkable and remarkably independent leader. Unusually for a PRC university president, he was not a Communist Party member. Even more unusually, he aimed to make Nanjing University a model of the integration of teaching and research. Nanda's curriculum was dispersed nationwide by the publication of hundreds of textbooks. Qu oversaw the revision of undergraduate and graduate education, established a School of Graduate Studies in 1984, and three years later established the first medical school in a Chinese university since the Communist takeover.[32]

Kuang, who remained influential after his presidency, lobbied the central government for support. However, when Deng Xiaoping announced five universities to receive special funding, Nanda was not among them.[33] Deng prioritized investments in Beijing's and Shanghai's top universities as the likeliest candidates to become China's "key" strategic universities.[34] Nanjing was again on the periphery. President Qu lobbied for resources as well, but he failed initially, with the central government increasing investments in fifteen universities but, again, not Nanda.[35] Only in 1993, when Nanda was named among the one hundred universities to receive funding through Project 211 and, in a greater boost to its standing, was later among the nine elite schools, eventually termed the "C9," selected for the second round of Project 985, could the university again aspire to national stature. Yet the national commitment remained small in financial terms. It fell to the Jiangsu provincial government to invest the funds needed to keep Nanda in the national conversation after 1999.[36]

Like Duke in North America, Nanda had to do more with less. It focused resources on faculty recruitment and talent development, the renovation of its central campus in Nanjing's ancient Gulou (Drum Tower) district, and building a new, "independent" campus in Pukou, on the north bank of the Yangzi River, allowing it to expand student enrollment and tuition revenue.

Given its comparatively small size and limited resources, Nanda consistently punched above its weight in research. According to Thomson Scientific's Science Citation Index (SCI), which is widely used in China and around the world to evaluate a university's research prowess in the sciences, Nanda boasted the highest total number of papers published in international scientific journals among all Chinese universities for six consecutive years from 1992 to 1998.[37] However, as competition for talent and resources increased with the rapid development of higher education in China, Nanda found that its academic needs consistently outpaced government outlays. Frustrated by the government's fiscal timidity, President Qu, in a move unprecedented at a Chinese university, resigned his position in 1997, explaining, "If the government does not change its lip service into taking real responsibility, it will be very difficult for the development of education to meet the needs of social change, and the morale of university leaders and faculty and education will be inevitably affected."[38]

## A Return to the Center? Massification and the Quest for Global Repute in the Twenty-First Century

In the twenty-first century, the financial gloves came off. Nanjing University rode the dramatic wave of expansion within Chinese higher education, growing far larger while finally regaining its position as one of China's top universities. In 2019 Nanda served 63,876 students across 31 schools and departments, including 13,129 undergraduates, 14,937 postgraduates, 6,996 doctoral students, and 3,205 foreign students. Although Nanda had capped undergraduate enrollment at around 13,000 since 2005, its graduate student population grew eightfold over a period of 25 years, from 2,409 in 1995 to over 20,000 in 2019.[39] International university rankings consistently placed Nanda sixth or seventh within China and in the top 100 to 150 institutions globally. This was a dramatic improvement over the start of this century, when Nanda did not place among the top three hundred international universities in 2004. A two-hundred place improvement within fifteen years would be cheered as a success by most university administrations, and it was at Nanda. But after President Xi Jinping named Nanda as among five universities on track to become "the first famous Chinese institutions of higher education" in 2014, developing Nanda into a world-class university became an inescapable, central tenet of its institutional strategy.

Nanda's thirteenth five-year plan, released in 2016, declared its intent to pursue a development model with "Chinese and world-class characteristics" with the goal of "maintaining a leading position at home while accelerating its pace toward becoming a world-class university."[40] The plan conceded, frankly, that this was "a tough time to join the ranks of world-class universities," but Nanda's leadership declared itself ready for the challenge. The following year, Nanda released its "Plan for Building a World-Class University," which foresaw Nanda jumping to the "forefront of world-class universities to realize the great rejuvenation of the Chinese nation."[41] The "great rejuvenation" was a catch phrase of President Xi's, to whose political agenda Nanda was now increasingly tied. Although Nanda was far from the only Chinese university to have set its sights high, it held a number of distinct institutional advantages.

## Teaching Your Way to the Top?

Building on Nanda's inherited traditions of independent intellectualism and the reforms of Presidents Kuang and Qu, the university sought to differentiate itself from national and international peers not only by advances in research but also, and indeed primarily, by focusing on cultivating talented students. "Talent training," according to Nanda's World-Class University plan, "is a foundational part of creating a world-class university."[42] But how does a university improve how talent is "trained"? For Nanda, the answer lay in the classroom.

This was an unusual strategy, in which Nanda sought to differentiate itself from other Chinese universities whose success was determined almost exclusively by research outcomes and where outstanding teaching was seldom rewarded. After all, why not distinguish yourself in teaching, which had long been in Nanda's DNA, especially as no one else is doing it? It is a competition you can win. In 2006 Nanda's small, teaching-intensive Kuang Yaming Honors School was founded to provide science students with an interdisciplinary education.[43] Reforms to university-wide general education followed in 2009. Students could now enter Nanda without having declared a major, as in an American college. Only after completing the general education sequence could students formally declare a major. Reforms to Nanda's general education requirements also included a focus on seminars and the formal evaluation of teaching. The emphasis on teaching and curricular quality echoed the work of Dean Qian Yingyi at Tsinghua. But Qian only had to convince his own unit of Tsinghua to adopt the program. Nanda sought to build a general education program that all students would share. In 2016 Nanda, with a bit of a numerical fetish, set the goal of creating ten courses recognized as world class, one hundred courses that were among the best in China, and one thousand courses that utilized modern, "individualized" pedagogies. So proud was Nanda's administration of its new curriculum that, in 2018, international educators were invited to attend class sessions and see for themselves the education on offer at Nanda.

Building on its signature program with Johns Hopkins, "promoting international exchanges and cooperation" remained a core tenet of Nanda's strategy to build "international resources, reputation, and support."[44] The university committed itself to establishing a new range of foreign exchanges with the strategic purpose of helping the university improve its talent training initiatives, strengthen its academic departments, and raise research standards. At their best, Nanda's internationalization strategies showed an openness to identifying and adopting the highest international standards of academic excellence. By 2020 Nanda boasted student, faculty, or academic exchanges with more than forty European institutions; eight in the UK; nine in Australia; forty across Asia; twenty in the United States; and two in Latin America.

By the end of the second decade of the twenty-first century, however, Nanda's internationalist, cosmopolitan academic culture—aspirationally "world class"—began to come under scrutiny at home. Beijing would remind Nanjing who, at the end of the day, was at the center, and who was in charge.

## Serving the State, Pursuing Rankings

Nanjing University's return to respectability in the post-Mao era was rooted in its history: its great inheritance from the Republican era in the liberal arts and sciences. But from the government's perspective, universities were, above all, vehicles for achieving national priorities—and priorities can change. This was as true of the Nationalists in the days of National Central University as it would be for the Communists in the era of reform. For Nanda, this led to a pivot to rebuild departments in engineering and applied sciences that it had lost during the restructuring of Chinese universities in the 1950s. Nanda had nearly merged with Southeast University, which was (re)created out of many of the applied departments lost to Nanda in the 1950s, but this plan was scrapped at least in part due to opposition from the Southeast University faculty.[45] (Even in China, faculty can make serious trouble for administrators.) Surging government funding for engineering became an opportunity for Nanda to realize these ambitions and climb higher in the league tables.

Nanda's thirteenth five-year plan in 2016 was brutally frank, somewhat like a Duke plan. It was noted that the university had not produced "many landmark achievements in response to major national strategic needs." To improve its standing, Nanda committed to being "guided by the major needs of national and regional economic and social development by integrating engineering disciplines and R&D resources."[46]

In now giving priority to applied disciplines, over 40 percent of Nanda's hiring opportunities were for scholars in STEM disciplines.[47] Scholars in STEM recruited through Nanda's "high-level talent" program were eligible to receive salary bonuses, start-up grants, housing stipends, and teams of research assistants.[48] With government funding opportunities in STEM fields proliferating, Nanda had set up the Research Fund Management Center in 2014 to manage grant opportunities, applications, and distributions from cultural, scientific, and military funding sources for the entire university. But while Nanda received accolades from the Jiangsu and Nanjing governments for its contributions to regional development, the university's national rankings in engineering, physics, chemistry, atmospheric sciences, and environmental science all fell in 2017. Success in these realms was a moving target. Worse yet, disciplines that Nanda saw as its strengths, such as foreign languages and literature, fell in the rankings as well. To succeed in the brutally competitive world of Chinese universities, Nanda concluded that it had to get bigger and richer, fast.

Unlike several leading Chinese universities, which had grown in scale and fortune by relentless mergers with regional institutions (for example, Zhejiang University with its seven campuses), Nanjing University was slow to reach its current scale. The one big merger it sought, with Southeast University, had foundered. Vice Secretary Yang Zhong sought to put Nanda in its best light when he explained, "We believe that world-class universities don't rely on scale. . . . The most important thing is to look at the level of quality of your human talent cultivation. A university's greatness isn't in its size, but rather in its way of thinking, in its innovation."[49] Still, Nanda aimed to grow in size and income. In 1998 it opened a new incarnation of Ginling College, officially Jinling College of Nanjing University (*Nanjing daxue jinling xueyuan*). This was a separate but affiliated school in partnership with the state-owned Jiangsu International Trust Corporation, Ltd. The trust provided RMB 100 million in funding, and the school was established with an independent organizational structure, legal status, campus, and budget system.[50] Whereas Nanda's standard undergraduate program was strong in basic research, Jinling College was built to bolster Nanda's "integration of industry, academia, and research" by focusing on attracting and training those talented in the applied disciples, such as engineering, business, and media.[51] The college was relocated to Nanda's Pukou campus in 2009, but enrollment was capped to control the quality of education. This hesitation to increase Nanda and its affiliate's size had an opportunity cost: stagnant revenue from tuition dollars just when the university needed more money with fewer strings attached. By 2020 Nanda seemed eager to square this circle. Jinling College would be moved again, this time to an entirely different city: Suzhou. This, Nanda hoped, would allow Jinling's applied disciplines greater opportunities to thrive in an industrial hub with an entrepreneurial city government.[52] As for Pukou, it would become home to a new center for executive education, another potential revenue generator, with a research and development innovation park to serve Nanjing's regional economy.[53]

This ancillary income aside, the most significant portion of Nanda's income came from government sources. As with other Chinese universities, and as we have seen with Tsinghua, Nanda does not publish a transparent accounting of income the university receives from government appropriations. However, using Nanda's disclosures of how much the university received directly from the Ministry of Finance as a baseline, it is clear that government funding plays by far the largest role in Nanda's budget. In 2019, of the university's projected income of US$1.2 billion, US$402.6 million, or about one-third of the total, came directly from the Ministry of Finance.[54] Yet with a significant portion of these outlays tied to the size of a university's enrollment, as long as the university capped enrollment, Nanda's options to increase state funding were limited largely to competing for subsidies tied to strategic initiatives. Nanda had a policy of limiting the number of new undergraduates each year to around three thousand.[55] Although Nanda's endowment had grown from just over US$34 million in 2009 to over $US163 million in 2017, the Nanda Education Foundation, which managed these funds, earned only around US$7 million from investments in 2017.[56]

University leadership hoped that Nanda's opening of a new campus in Nanjing's burgeoning Xianlin "University City," east of the city's center, in 2009 would help to sustain the university's growth for the next one hundred years. By 2012 Nanda Xianlin was Nanda's principal campus and home to the university's engineering and applied sciences departments, while basic science departments, such as mathematics and physics, and professional schools (business, law, and medicine) remained at Nanda's historic Gulou

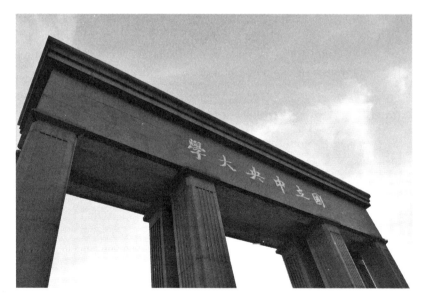

**Figure 10.3.** The new "Brandenburg Gate" commemorating National Central University at Nanjing University's Xianlin campus. zhongwenpan/ Pixabay.

**Figure 10.4.** Nanjing University's new Xianlin campus. Ozonefrance/Wikimedia Commons/CC BY-SA 3.0.

campus. The physical expansion and redistribution of Nanda split the university, quite literally, into the old and the new. Xianlin would be home to an RMB 5-billion science park to deepen enterprise-university partnerships, which could become a source of innovation and, ideally, revenue.

The Jiangsu provincial government and Nanjing's municipal authorities cheered the move and supported it financially. Nanda's alumni financed part of the project. Xianlin was the physical manifestation of Nanda's determination to rise through investment in policy and political priorities.

## Competition Abroad, Attacks at Home

In the twenty-first century, Nanda continued to innovate in its international partnerships. Nanda was chosen as one of the first two Chinese universities to host American students from the U.S. Department of Defense–funded Chinese Language Flagship program.[57] Managed by the National Security Education Program, the Language Flagship program was founded to create cohorts of Americans with advanced language proficiency in "critical languages"—those spoken in countries considered especially important to US national security.[58] When the Language Flagship rolled out an undergraduate program in 2006, Nanda partnered with Brigham Young University, with which it had held exchanges since the 1980s, to open one of two PRC-based Chinese Flagship Centers.[59] Annually thereafter, forty of the top American students from the twelve Chinese Flagship programs at US universities took a semester at Nanda.[60] Unlike the Hopkins-Nanjing Center, Chinese Flagship students enrolled directly at Nanda, choosing among the same courses (all taught in Chinese) as regular Nanda undergraduate and graduate students, a testament to Nanda's growing confidence in its curriculum. As the US-China relationship rose in importance in the twenty-first century, Nanda's early and eager engagement with US universities positioned it to capitalize on the growing American appetite for educational exchanges with China.

The advent of the "America First" administration of President Donald Trump in 2016 threw all this into doubt, as the US government criticized international education cooperation with China. Beginning with the National Defense Authorization Act of 2018, an annual piece of US legislation, universities that housed both Chinese Flagship programs and Confucius Institutes (Chinese language and cultural promotion ventures partially funded by the PRC's Ministry of Education) were required to close their Confucius Institutes to receive Flagship funding. To protect their Flagship programs, six US universities shuttered their Confucius Institutes.[61] There were also signs that the Flagship program was seeking to shift a growing proportion of its operations from mainland China to Taiwan, as US-China tensions rose under Trump. Since the program's start, there had always been two PRC-based Flagship centers, but in 2019 the second campus moved to National Taiwan University. All of this put Nanda, with its Chinese Republican ancestry, suddenly in uneasy and public competition with the Republic of China on Taiwan.[62]

Meanwhile, Nanda's premier international education program, the Hopkins-Nanjing Center, faced competitive pressures from China's most elite institutions. Tsinghua and Peking Universities had charted a different path to attract the world's top students. Unlike Hopkins-Nanjing, Tsinghua's Schwarzman College, announced in 2013, and Peking's Yenching Academy, announced in 2014, were independent ventures, not joint partnerships. Their core differentiators included the unmatched prestige of those institutions and a deep well of funding. Framed as merit scholarships, Schwarzman and Yenching courted comparisons to Oxford's Rhodes Scholarship, as we have seen. They sought to build endowments that rivaled that of the Rhodes. Indeed, the Schwarzman Scholars' $600 million endowment exceeded the Rhodes Trust's $390 million[63] and far exceeded the endowment of *all* of Nanjing University. The Hopkins-Nanjing Center, supported in part through the Johns Hopkins University School of Advanced International Studies, which had its own fiscal challenges, had no such financial firepower.

Schwarzman and Yenching had no Chinese language prerequisites, a central feature of Hopkins-Nanjing. This expanded their potential applicant pool dramatically. In the Schwarzman Scholarship's first year, more than three thousand students applied.[64] Numbers have continued to climb, reaching over forty-seven hundred in the 2019 admissions cycle.[65] Yenching Academy did not report the size of its applicant pool, but it enrolled around 125 students per year with a reported acceptance rate of 2.7 percent, indicating that it also received thousands of applications.[66] Successful admits to these new programs were, on average, of higher academic caliber than those admitted to Hopkins-Nanjing. Competitive applicants to Yenching had undergraduate grade point averages (GPAs) of 3.7 or higher, while the average GPA of a Schwarzman scholar was 3.8.[67] The middle 50 percent of undergraduate GPAs for Hopkins-Nanjing students ranged from 3.30 to 3.77 in 2019.[68] With Schwarzman and Yenching each enrolling more students than Hopkins-Nanjing annually, Nanda's mantle as China's premier provider of graduate-level instruction in Chinese studies to international students, and especially to Americans, seems to have been lost.

### The Party Strikes Back

The tensions inherent in building a "world-class" university that also met President Xi Jinping's definition of building one of "the first famous Chinese institutions of higher education," have become painfully apparent in recent years. In Nanda's 2016 five-year plan, achieving world-class status became formally tied to Xi's rhetoric of "realizing the Chinese dream."[69] Yet it was Nanda's inclusion on the list of twenty-nine Chinese universities scrutinized by the Party's Central Commission for Discipline Inspection (CCDI) in 2017 that led the Party and its politics to intrude in dramatic ways on Nanda's leadership and governance.

The CCDI launched its investigation into universities to ensure that the Party retained—or, more accurately in the case of Nanda, regained—its ideological and operational grip over higher education. Wang Qishan, secretary of the CCDI and a top aide to Xi Jinping, presided over the announcement of the investigation, which emphasized examining universities for the strictness of their "political discipline" as well as whether they were abiding by "the core role of the Party's leadership" and adhering to the Party's education policies.[70] CCDI inspectors were deployed to universities in mid-March to conduct their work until May of 2017.[71] President Xi himself took part in this inspection, underscoring the significance of the effort to his political agenda. While surveying the Chinese University of Political Science and Law on the eve of the anniversary of the May Fourth Movement, Xi stated that "university Party committees were responsible for managing both the Party and the schools themselves."[72]

Upon the inspection's conclusion, Nanda's Party Secretary Zhang Yibin and Executive Vice President Lu Jian convened an extraordinary meeting of faculty and staff to express the significance of the CCDI's findings to the future of the university. To fulfill the inspectors' wishes, Secretary Zhang told a packed auditorium that the university must focus on three areas: political consciousness, political discipline, and political responsibilities. Nothing about teaching. Nothing about research. Nothing about outreach. Executive Vice President Lu emphasized that addressing these areas was now Nanda's "biggest political task."[73]

The sense of urgency among these administrators was evident when the CCDI's findings were publicly circulated, revealing that Nanda had performed poorly during the exercise. Regarding the strength of Party leadership at Nanda, the CCDI inspection team concluded that "the outstanding problems . . . are objective, profound, and crucial" and that these results should serve as an "alarm bell" for Nanda.[74]

In short, Nanda, with its Nationalist and internationalist roots, needed "rectification." To address the CCDI's concern, Nanda created a "rectification task list" of over one hundred action items the university committed to implement. Reforms to the policies governing the diffusion of ideology throughout Nanda's staff and classrooms were given prominent treatment in the university's response.[75] Nanda's own "Inspection and Rectification Report," written by a taskforce made up of Nanda Party Committee members, stated that it had released new guidelines for ideological training and supervision with the hope that these would "clarify the content and form of theoretical learning at different levels for schools, departments, and Party members" to ensure the Party's ideology would receive "full coverage throughout learning" at Nanda. The "Inspection and Rectification Report" committed Nanda to release a "Plan for Building a World-Class University," which would "comprehensively implement the Party's education policy, adhere to the guidance for social schools, and strengthen the Party's leadership of the school."[76] In reorienting the role of the Party at Nanda, the university also began the process of limiting its world-class ambitions to be in alignment with those the Party would allow. The severity of the CCDI's criticisms, which all but indicted Nanda of subverting Party leadership of the university, and the sweeping "rectification tasks" now required, suggest that the inspection was another existential crisis for Nanda.

The CCDI inspection's admonishments of Nanda left it more sensitive to changing political winds in China than at any time since the Cultural Revolution. Following the enshrinement of Xi Jinping's "thought" in the Party's constitution in October 2017, Nanda's Party Committee convened a study session to promote greater understanding of these constitutional amendments so that the university would "be in line with the central government." Nanda's president, Chen Jun, also attended the meeting to express the required view that the university would "connect" these constitutional amendments to the "school's development."[77] Nanda's Party Committee then pressed for greater authority over the direction of reforms within the university. In April 2018 Nanda Party Secretary Zhang Yibin laid out the year's key tasks to an audience of Nanda Party members. All involved strengthening Party governance over Nanda, improving adherence to political rules, and not just "consolidating" but also "expanding" the university's response to the CCDI inspection.[78]

Could Nanda have resisted this onslaught? No. As a provincial university of Nationalist heritage, and without the political network of a Beijing-based Tsinghua, Nanda was more than vulnerable to the state's political pressures. Moreover, without a global reputation like that of Tsinghua, the Party could meddle in Nanda's affairs without worrying it would undermine a national treasure.

In December 2017, six months after the CCDI inspection's conclusion, the university released the "Plan for Building a World-Class University," broadly rewriting Nanda's institutional development priorities into closer alignment with the Party's political and economic agenda. If lip service to the "Chinese dream" in Nanda's thirteenth five-year plan might have been excused as pure rhetoric, the same could not be said of this new "world-class" plan. Unlike the plans of Kuang Yaming and Qu Qinyue in earlier decades, this was not an academic plan. It was an ideological call to arms. Now, Nanda's educational aim was to "guide Nanjing University through adherence to Marxism, fully implement the Party's education policy, [and] adhere to socialist governance of schools."[79] Following the Party Committee's constitution study session in November 2017, Xi Jinping Thought was named Nanda's "guiding ideology" in its world-class plan.

The politicization of Nanda's strategy harbored significant consequences for its efforts to pursue excellence in teaching and internationalization. By 2030 Nanda was committed to having "the core values of socialism fully integrated into the whole process of educating people." Teaching and research in the humanities and social sciences, the heart of the university's push to offer all students a broad-based and interdisciplinary general education, needed now to conform to "Chinese characteristics." Teachers and students, Nanda plans now stated, had to be "armed with the latest achievements of the Sinicization of Marxism so that they acted politically and ideologically."[80] While Nanda's general education website continued to state that the program prioritized "students' independent thinking and free development," the boundaries of intellectual independence at Nanda became increasingly limited.

All this had to have an effect on the university's internationalization. Nanda had cultivated partnerships with elite foreign universities to attract top students and scholars. But the arrival of President Xi's Belt and Road Initiative redirected some of Nanda's internationalization efforts toward partnerships with developing countries along the "New Silk Road." Nanda's revised world-class strategy stated that "Building the Belt and Road Initiative was an opportunity to focus on research and the development of academic disciplines on matters useful to the initiative."[81] The university established a Belt and Road research institute, held international symposia to generate ideas for the program, and received government scholarships for students from Belt and Road countries. But few believed that the international future of Nanjing University lay more in Lahore than in London or Los Angeles.

## Marx versus "Marxism"

The politicization of higher education spread to many other areas of university life at Nanda. The Party mandated an expanded study of Marxism, in contrast to (presumably other) "Western" values. The CCP had launched a major initiative in 2004 to generate more research on Marxism and produced a series of stultifying Party-approved textbooks that integrated "the new achievements realized by the Sinicization of Marxism," making them "relevant" to China under the CCP's rule.[82] Nanda's Philosophy Department, one of the top five in the country, actively participated in this project. The Nanda *Undergraduate Education Quality Report of 2017–2018* (published in December 2018) prioritized work to "perform political gate-keeping on philosophy and social science textbooks" and "strictly manage the use of original versions of textbooks published outside China" for the future so as to "not allow textbooks that propagate erroneous Western views to enter the classroom."[83]

Students at Nanda took the government at its word and began to read the original, fiery, revolutionary works of Marx. In the autumn of 2014 several enthusiastic students approached faculty members in Nanda's Philosophy Department to start a "Marxist Reading and Research Society" (MRRS). As students and government cadres alike had been officially encouraged (read: told) to study Marxism by Xi Jinping, faculty members agreed to support the students, and one of them sponsored the formal registration of their group on campus. Earlier that year, the Nanda Party Committee had released *Several Opinions on Strengthening and Improving the Construction of Teachers' Morality,* which endorsed an expanded role for Marxist ideology in how Nanda was to educate its student body. The "Opinions" named "promoting the core value of socialism into . . . students' minds" as one of the "main tasks" for the university's faculty.[84] But Nanda's students did not want to be restricted to book learning. To put what they learned in original Marxist texts into action, the students approached cleaning staff and workers in the school's kitchens to help with their work and donated items to improve their lives. The students also organized events around campus to encourage the study of Marx. For these activities, they were praised by the secretary of Nanda's Communist Youth League, the official CCP youth organ.[85]

In July 2018 students of the MRRS learned that workers at a Jasic Technology Company factory in Shenzhen were trying to form independent unions to fight for better wages and working conditions. When the workers' efforts were suppressed by the company with the help of local police, several Nanda students joined students from other leading universities in China, many belonging to similar Marxist study groups, to form a support group for the Shenzhen workers.[86] They protested in front of a local police station involved in the arrest of the labor organizers.[87] In late August riot police broke into the apartments of student activists and arrested them.[88] Many, including students from Nanda, were later released and allowed to return to their schools in September.[89]

When Nanda MRRS students returned to campus, they found they had to reregister their group with the school administration. Their longtime sponsor in the Department of Philosophy was initially reluctant to sponsor them again.[90] After long conversations, MRRS leaders agreed to some changes in their leadership and removed phrases like "paying attention to social realities, discussing current events, and focusing on social practice" from their registration material in exchange for support from their longtime sponsor. In agreeing to support the students again, the sponsoring professor admonished members of the MRRS to "read more books, organize fewer events."[91]

On September 9 several MRRS students met up with student activists from other schools and some Jasic workers at Mao Zedong's birthplace in Hunan to commemorate the anniversary of his death.[92] By mid-September, MRRS's registration material was returned by its sponsor, and the students were informed by the university that the group had to undergo additional evaluation. MRRS leaders then went on a frantic search for a new sponsor, knocking on the doors of every humanities and social science department at Nanda in September and October. In late September MRRS leaders submitted a petition to Nanda Party Secretary and renowned Marxist scholar Zhang Yibin, pleading for him to support the organization, as he had done during its founding. One faculty member in the School of Marxism and another in the School of Social and Behavioral Sciences finally agreed to help, but they backed out after meetings with more senior administrators. Throughout this period, MRRS students continued to organize activities on campus including their signature volunteer program to help cafeteria workers as well as protests against the administrative barriers to their registration as a student group. Some of the students were photographed and followed by plainclothes security agents during and after these events. The student leader of the MRRS was summoned and cornered by staff from the school's security office and police to "answer questions."[93]

On October 23, 2018, the ax fell. A university-wide meeting of faculty and administrators was held, announcing Party Secretary Zhang Yibin's (heretofore unknown) request to step down early from his leadership position and the appointment of Hu Jinbo as the new Party Secretary of Nanda. Zhang was highly praised by representatives of the CCP Central Organization Department, the Ministry of Education, the Jiangsu CCP Committee, the Jiangsu Department of Education, and President Lu Jian, and he was thanked for his service.[94]

Two days later, MRRS students submitted an open letter to the new Party Secretary, asking again for the support of the school leadership. The letter quoted a speech made by Xi Jinping at Peking University in May 2018, asking university faculty to "deepen student understanding of the theoretical and real-life meaning of Marxism, educate them to observe the world and analyze the world using Marxist principles so that they might fully realize the power of Marxist truth."[95] The students felt they were answering the call of the General Secretary, so why were they being mistreated?

The Party had successfully pressured Nanda's administration into ideological lockstep with its priorities, but the students—unexpectedly idealistic in China's reform-era material culture—proved a greater challenge. In 2018 Nanda's students were joined by comrades in Peking and Renmin Universities in organizing labor movements in Guangdong in the summer and protests on campus in the fall.[96] All three universities prided themselves on their strengths in the humanities and social sciences and had top-ranked philosophy departments in China. And in all three universities the students were punished severely, with some arrested, some expelled, and all disciplined in some form.[97] And all three universities saw sudden "retirements" or leadership shuffles of their presidents or senior members of their Party committees.[98] (Bizarrely, in a fit of American political correctness, when the Renmin University students were sanctioned, Cornell University's School of Industrial and Labor Relations suspended its research and exchange program with Renmin, utterly ignorant of how far that university had gone to try to support its students.[99])

## New Rules for a "New Era"

Xi Jinping has declared that China has entered a "new era," and that phrase may be found in political pronouncements at every level of Chinese society. For Nanda, it meant a new university charter. Chinese universities had begun publishing charters in 2013, shortly after Xi's ascendence to the role of paramount leader. Nanda's first charter, released in 2015, noted that it was "committed . . . to realizing the Chinese dream and great rejuvenation of the Chinese nation" in the document's second paragraph but did not state its commitment to the Party's ideological construction and to "fully implementing the Party's educational policies" until Article 6 of the charter.[100] This was clearly not enough. The revised charter of 2019 did not beat around the bush. The preamble's second paragraph was amended to open with,

"Facing the future, Nanjing University adheres to the overall leadership of the Party."[101] New powers and prominence for the Party were incorporated throughout the document. Fudan University in Shanghai, often considered one of China's top three institutions of higher education, also released a revised charter in which it removed a commitment to freedom of thought in the preamble, replacing it with a statement supporting "the leadership of the Chinese Communist Party, full implementation of the Party's educational policies, and adherence to the guiding role of Marxism and direction of socialism."[102] Across the country, new university charters were presented as a pledge of allegiance to the Party,

Nanda's new charter afforded the Party new roles in university governance. Article 22 included the Party Secretary among the school executives with the authority to convene special university leadership meetings to discuss pressing administrative matters and challenges at Nanda, a power previously reserved for the president. Nanda's joint Party and government committee would now not simply be charged with "reviewing" and "implementing" the university's development plans but instead specifically be tasked with "formulating work plans" that addressed the "Party's and country's lines, principles, and policies." Moreover, the charter enhanced the roles of those with Party and government leadership positions in Nanda's academic committee, the university's "highest academic body."[103]

In response to student unrest at Nanda in the previous year, the 2019 charter stressed the deepening of the Party's ideology in campus organizations. Article 14 in the latest revision included a commitment to "leading the school's ideological, political, and moral education work [and] maintaining the political stability and safety of campus."[104] However, a new clause was added in 2019 that pledged Nanda would "strengthen the theoretical study of Party members, insist on arming the mind with the Party's scientific theory, and . . . organize Party members to study the Party's line, principles, policies and resolutions."[105]

All these changes were not universally embraced by university communities. The deputy dean of the liberal arts school posted online that the revisions were an "evil act" that challenged the academy's ethical commitments.[106] Other universities saw campus unrest following the publication of the new charters. At Fudan, which had removed its charter's commitment to freedom of thought, students protested these changes in the university cafeteria by singing Fudan's anthem, which includes lyrics that reflected Humboldtian values. Two universities that had long promoted concepts of academic autonomy, East China Normal University and Wuhan University, the joint-venture partners of New York University and Duke University, respectively,[107] both maintained language supporting academic freedom in their charters. Asked about Nanda's charter revisions, a spokesperson for Johns Hopkins University, Nanda's joint-venture partner for the Hopkins-Nanjing Center, stated that the Center "was founded on the principle of academic freedom. . . . Any externally imposed limits or restraints on academic freedom in the classroom or on students' or faculty members' work would be wholly inconsistent with [these] principles."[108]

## What Now?

The pressures of expansion and politicization at Nanda placed into question whether the university, with its rich pre-Communist history and its remarkable recovery in the early reform period, could succeed in the contest for world-class standing in a highly politicized homeland. Nanjing, after all, had been the capital of the country. It was now a provincial capital: the capital of a rich province to be sure, but provincial nonetheless. The university that is now Nanda had once been China's National Central University, modeled on the University of Berlin. Its history and legacy enhanced its reputation, but in the twenty-first century it was again forced to kneel to the politics of the day.

Today's Nanda is rich with the seeds for excellence on an international scale. However, its fate has been strongly tied to the ambitions of two Party-States: that of the Nationalists before 1949 and that of the Communists ever since. As the case of Tsinghua University shows, some universities can both serve the Party-State and make their distinctive mark on higher education in China and internationally. But Nanda is perhaps not so well positioned. As it adheres to an increasingly rigid ideological regimen, it places in question the durability of the confident openness that defined its international profile when establishing its partnership with Johns Hopkins.

At the very least, the recent politicization of higher education has done the university no favors. Expanding the role of the Party's ideology in the classroom threatens to crowd out curriculum designed to foster the critical thinking skills that had been at the heart of Nanda's distinctive undergraduate education. Moreover, the press for ideological purity has fed student unrest, rather than nurturing stability. As US-China relations nose-dived in the eras of Trump and Xi, flagship exchange programs were threatened by the political crossfire. Pressure to expand its offerings in the applied disciplines has increased Nanda's appetite for resources that it already found hard to come by for existing programs. Nanda's efforts to so visibly align itself with the Party's priorities had yet to do it any good in domestic and international rankings. Once considered among the top three institutions within China, Nanda had fallen to sixth or seventh place, depending on which rankings table was consulted.

The COVID-19 pandemic underscored the precarious position Nanda found itself in. The economic hardship brought on by virus-induced lockdowns reduced the Chinese government's income and reserves, leading it to slash outlays for many budget items. Unlike Tsinghua, Nanda has not been immune from the government's call to "vigorously reduce" public expenditures in response to the pandemic.[109] For the 2020–2021 fiscal year, Nanda's public funding fell by 17.5 percent. The greater strain on Nanda and its future is revealed by the over 50 percent decline in Nanda's science and technology expenditures, funded by the government. Nanda's laboratories experienced a budget reduction of over 60 percent, and the university's expenditures on basic research, traditionally Nanda's strong suit, declined by 55 percent.[110] In short, Nanda's efforts to build out its science and technology offerings still have a long way to go before it can compete with China's top engineering universities. If acceding to state economic priorities pays so little in tough times, how resilient can Nanda's current institutional strategy be?

Hard choices face Nanjing University in the years ahead. Will its strategy of riding the wave of politicization in Chinese higher education begin to pay dividends? As hawkish perceptions of China and its universities proliferate in the United States, will the bilateral partnerships Nanda has relied on to build its international reputation in the United States and elsewhere become more fragile and fraught?

Unlike Duke University, which has been able to overcome its provincial geography to win national repute and status in the United States, Nanda currently lacks the room to innovate, experiment, and plan on its own terms in China. It had done so, remarkably, in the early years of China's reform and opening. That spirit seems suppressed, for now. Yet, as we have seen, Nanda has survived multiple revolutions and endures, if not as a leader, as one of the leading followers in Chinese higher education.

One of the strengths of both the German and American public universities is that they are, to be sure, state funded, but funded by different states: by the *Länder* in Germany and the fifty states of the sometimes United States.

Chinese universities, far flung and different in their origins and capacities, also have—or have had—the capacity for differentiation as great as that of the economies or cuisines of China's many regions and cultures. This was amply demonstrated by Nanjing University's accomplishments in the early reform era, led by truly courageous presidents. But the standardization and synchronizing of the academic and ideological universes under Xi Jinping appear to have called a sharp pause, if not a halt, to regional experimentation.

*Tian gao, Huangdi yuan.* "Heaven is high, and the emperor is far away." This old phrase, said to date from the Yuan dynasty, implies that the farther away you are from the capital, the greater your capacity to act. But today the emperor, or at least his "thought," is omnipresent, a presence in every provincial university—perhaps especially this one, with its roots in the previous dynasty. The sun may be setting on the prospects for the great and historical university in China's Southern Capital.

# CHAPTER ELEVEN

# Asia's Global University?

## *The University of Hong Kong*

X IANG ZHANG, the president of the University of Hong Kong (HKU), was told of the Occupy Central movement and its accompanying protests while interviewing for the position in 2017. Born in mainland China and educated both at home and in the United States, where he rose to be a chaired professor at UC Berkeley, Zhang embodied the aspirations of "Asia's Global University." At the time, Zhang recalled, "everybody said that the tensions were gone."[1] Indeed, when Zhang succeeded outgoing president Peter Mathieson in 2018, it appeared that the major protests had subsided in Hong Kong. In what was then a rare moment of calm in Hong Kong, Zhang arrived eager to build on Mathieson's work to internationalize HKU and improve its global standing. The strategic plan Mathieson had crafted, *Vision 2016–2025*, was "a good plan," Zhang said, but he added that the university needed "more concrete and executable steps."[2] Although Zhang was still working through how he would execute this vision, his ambitions for HKU were clear cut and sky high: "We want to be the next Harvard. We want to be the next Cambridge. In twenty or fifty years, we want to say that, yes, we can compete with Harvard in terms of faculty recruiting, or students, or alumni. That is what we will measure."[3] Yet as Zhang tried to unite HKU's many stakeholders around a substantive, long-term agenda for the university, political tensions—of a different sort than those at Nanjing University—were never far below the surface of HKU's campus and city.

For much of its history, HKU was Hong Kong's only university. Although HKU now competes against seven other higher education institutions in Hong Kong for government funding and support, by reputation it was the leading university in Hong Kong and, by accidents of history, the leading Chinese university that was *not* under the guidance of the Chinese Communist Party. Zhang believed that HKU needed to look outward in order to climb higher. Only through internationalization could HKU continue to thrive. He stated that "if you want to be a global university, a world-leading university, you have to look at global issues, important issues, not just the city's issues."[4]

Historically, HKU's unique value lay not only in its monopoly on higher education in Hong Kong but also in its role as a bridge between an inaccessible mainland China and the rest of the world. As mainland Chinese universities gained international reputations and partnerships, HKU's role as an intermediary between East and West came under threat. The *Vision 2016–2025* plan developed under Mathieson sought to leverage China's renewed global presence while competing with the growing influence of China's top universities. As an English-language institution at the crossroads of China and the wider world, HKU would be "Asia's Global University." Zhang believed that with strong leadership, HKU, located in China's Special Administrative Region of Hong Kong, could ride the wave of China's rise to improve its own standing: "HKU is always among the top three or four universities in Asia. We should not be happy with that, especially as the world order is undergoing transformation."[5]

To achieve this, HKU needed a period of peace and productivity. Yet only one year into President Zhang's tenure, Hong Kong witnessed the largest political protests in its history. HKU's greatest challenges seemed increasingly local. How could HKU deepen its ties with mainland universities at a time when millions were protesting the city's subservient relationship to mainland authorities? How could HKU maintain its position as a top institution linking East and West in an era of growing East-West tensions and in such a volatile metropolis?

## An Imperial Project

From its inception, HKU was an institution with many goals. It was intended to link Great Britain, its colonial overlord, with mainland China, while providing high-quality, local educational opportunities for the young men of the British colonies in Southeast Asia and strengthening the capacities of Hong Kong citizens. Its greatest early champion, Frederick Lugard, governor of Hong Kong from 1907 to 1912, envisioned HKU as a key establishment in and accomplishment of the British Empire.[6] Lugard wrote, "What England has done for India and Egypt in mitigation of famine . . . she can help China to do for herself."[7] A longtime diplomat, Lugard did not have extensive experience in the field of education, but he nonetheless believed in the economic and moral merit of establishing a local university.

The sense of competition among imperial powers was also an impetus for the founding of HKU. Already by 1905 newspapers warned that British influence in China was being surpassed by Japan, which was an early destination for Chinese students studying abroad.[8] The British eyed with envy the progress made by Americans, particularly American missionaries, in developing higher education in mainland China. The German establishment of Tongji University in Shanghai in 1907 and plans to develop a research university in Kiaochow (Qingdao) in 1908 further encouraged the British to develop an institution of their own. Indeed, it was the news of the founding of the German school that led Hormusjee Nowrojee Mody, a prominent Parsi merchant who became one of the most generous donors to HKU, to ask Governor Lugard and his wife, "[W]hy cannot we get ahead of them?"[9]

Vocal about the important role the university could play in empire building, Lugard was still unable to gather significant financial support from the British government. Most of the early funding for the university came from the private sector, although the government maintained a high level of involvement in administrative decisions. Mody was an early supporter, sponsoring the construction of HKU's iconic Main Building, with donations ultimately valued at HK$365,000 (approximately £36,500, or US$5.9 million in today's value).[10] More early support was received in May 1909, when the firm of John Swire & Sons announced the donation of £40,000 to the university endowment, which would be worth US$6.7 million in 2021.[11] These gifts initiated enough fundraising from individuals in Hong Kong, mainland China, and overseas Chinese communities in Australia, Malaya, and French Saigon[12] as well as the governments in Beijing and Guangdong—after their fears of a new university as a revolutionary hotbed were assuaged—to build the skeleton of a university just before the end of Lugard's tenure as governor of Hong Kong in 1912.

The first university to be founded in Hong Kong, HKU was preceded by a number of technical and ecclesiastical colleges. One, the Hong Kong

College of Medicine for Chinese, founded in 1887, became HKU's School of Medicine. When the university opened its doors to its first cohort of seventy-five students in the autumn of 1912,[13] it offered courses at its School of Medicine as well as its School of Engineering, joined by the School of the Arts in 1913. The University Ordinance of 1911 established HKU's tripartite governance structure of Court (for government and societal oversight), Council (for administrative matters), and Senate (for academic matters). While responsibilities and power of the three groups shifted over time and the Court grew increasingly ceremonial, the basic structure remained almost unchanged into the twenty-first century.

The ordinance also laid out a nondiscrimination policy, stating, "No distinction of race or nationality shall be permitted, and no test of religious

**Figure 11.1.** Hong Kong University Main Building, the oldest structure on HKU's main campus, 1912. *Growing with Hong Kong: The University and Its Graduates,* Hong Kong University Press, 2002/Wikimedia Commons.

belief or profession shall be imposed, in order to entitle any person to be admitted as a member, professor, reader, lecturer, teacher, or student of the University or to hold office therein or to graduate thereof or to hold any advantage or privilege thereof."[14] Initially, this ethos was applied much more readily to students than to faculty. Founders of HKU felt that having well-qualified, British lecturers was necessary to bolster the fledgling institution's reputation.[15] This preferential policy was challenged by some of the university administration in 1919 when HKU sought to fill the newly created position of the Chair of Pathology and was torn between a Senate-supported British candidate and the Council-supported Dr. Wang Chung Yik, a graduate of the Hong Kong College of Medicine and Edinburgh University. The withdrawal of the Senate-supported candidate led to the appointment of Dr. Wang, HKU's first ethnic Chinese academic.[16]

During its first decade, the university struggled to remain solvent. By 1919 the Colonial Government finally agreed to help pull HKU out of debt, but only with the expansion of government oversight of the university. Throughout the next few decades, up to and beyond World War II, the university continued to toe a delicate line with the government, gradually gaining more public financial support, but also subjecting itself to increasing government inquiries and reports.

The university's small initial budget limited its research agenda; it was ultimately the provision of sufficient resources—and donor preferences—that transformed HKU into a more research-oriented institution. In 1922 the Rockefeller Foundation, which supported medical education around the world and at several institutions in mainland China, endowed two chairs at the School of Medicine, followed by a third chair less than two years later. This funding allowed the medical school to expand its professoriat and gave the school a stronger research orientation. By 1929 endowment income accounted for 62 percent of HKU's operating funds.

The founding of HKU had been predicated on its ability to keep young men out of radical politics—by which was meant the politics of modern Chinese nationalism. As the Nationalist movement led by the Guomindang grew in power in southern China, it challenged the British colonial presence. A major test of politicization on campus came in 1925 when, following a shooting of Chinese protesters in the foreign concession of Guangzhou on the mainland, a general strike and boycott of British goods spread to Hong Kong. University administrators were relieved to discover that HKU students generally sided with the British, going so far as to step in as assistant caretakers at an insane asylum when workers went on strike.[17] Chinese staff members also supported British interests. From that point forward, there was growing acceptance by the colonial authorities of HKU students as loyal subjects of the British Empire.

By the 1930s HKU was financially stable, helped first by the Rockefeller Foundation, then by funds from the British Boxer Indemnity that were returned to the university in 1931.[18] Yet, it still lacked a role in the educational landscape of greater China. HKU had been founded in the same era when a wave of Western-style higher education institutions was being established in mainland China. By the 1930s mainland China offered a variety of excellent higher education opportunities, many of which were connected with institutions in America, Europe, or Japan. HKU had the tenuous position of offering a more expensive, less convenient education that still lacked the professional and social cache of a Western degree.[19]

In response to this questionable positioning, a commission of colonial government and business representatives was tasked in 1937 with examining the university's role in society and its future development. Their subsequent report drew the ire of many faculty for its suggestions—for example, that HKU faculty need not hold high-level research degrees—that threatened to relegate the university to second-class status. Heated debate over the report's recommendations raged in the HKU Senate as well as the colonial government. The HKU Senate issued a response stating that it was of the "unanimous opinion that research is a necessary and integral function of every university."[20]

Ultimately, Duncan Sloss, the newly appointed vice-chancellor of HKU, used the controversy over the 1937 report to broaden the sense of purpose of HKU and elevate its standards. After arguing for the need to make HKU "a University in the British sense" rather than "a much more modest institution, a superior technical college,"[21] Sloss arranged for the establishment of a committee to draft the *University Development Report* of 1939, which laid out an ambitious plan for improved recruitment of students from mainland China as well as reforms in curriculum and upgrades to the physical plant.[22]

## Defeat and Detention

Alas, Sloss built his strategy for growth when China was already two years into the war with Japan. Just two years later, in 1941, all plans came to an abrupt halt when Japan invaded Hong Kong.[23] When the Japanese invaded,

HKU faculty and students dispersed, and Japanese troops transformed the campus into an army base, requisitioning medical and scientific supplies and equipment for military use.

This was a time of unprecedented suffering. The Japanese ruled Hong Kong by martial law. Streets and buildings were renamed in Japanese. Food became scarce and scarcer still when rationing was implemented. Hong Kong suffered its first real famine. Later in the war, it also suffered sustained American bombing. Between deaths and deportations, Hong Kong's population dropped by more than half under Japanese occupation: from approximately 1.6 million in 1941 to little more than 600,000 in 1945. The colony was the site of numerous Japanese war crimes, including the execution of ten thousand civilians.

Many of the European faculty members spent the war in internment camps under desperate and often horrific conditions. Some quietly attempted to continue research and plan for the return of the university. Many others perished. HKU staff, students, and alumni who had the opportunity fled to Free China, that is, to the areas under Nationalist control during the war. Others continued their studies at the top mainland universities, such as National Central University in Japanese-occupied Nanjing. It was a time of uncertain identities and loyalties, as indeed would be the postwar years.

Duncan Sloss was held during the war in the Stanley Internment Camp, on the southern side of Hong Kong Island. After Hong Kong was liberated, and as Sloss prepared to return to London for rest and recuperation in September 1945, he noted in his farewell address to students the promise of a new age with China's survival and indeed victory in an eight-year-long war: "We shall work together to get a University going of which we can all be proud and which, turned toward a new China, shall be a perpetually open line of communication between China and England and equally between England and China. We base our efforts on a realisation of what China can do for Western civilization no less than what Western ideas and standards can do for China."[24]

*Postwar Traumas and Opportunities*

By the end of World War II, the buildings of HKU were in ruins, its supplies lacking, students scattered, and faculty largely gone. The government of Hong Kong, along with the remaining university administration, went through a period of soul-searching before deciding in 1948 to reopen the university.[25] This decision turned out to be a prescient one, as the landscape of higher education in greater China was soon to be rocked by the Communist victory in the Chinese Civil War and the founding of the People's Republic of China in 1949. Many mainland Chinese scholars fled to Hong Kong, while many local Hong Kong students who in the past would have gone to China for university studies found that path blocked.

The Communist conquest of China proved both a burden and a blessing for Hong Kong. Hong Kong was suddenly inundated with refugees from the mainland, at times at a rate of more than one hundred thousand per month, and its population swelled to more than two million in the early 1950s. It received both extraordinary entrepreneurial talent—business families fleeing Shanghai and other urban centers—and outstanding scholars. And, in much larger numbers, it received people simply fleeing communism, who needed help and education to make their way in a suddenly populous Hong Kong, economically cut off from its Chinese hinterland.

In the 1950s and 1960s HKU expanded as quickly as its limited finances and physical plant would allow to meet a rapidly growing Hong Kong's need for qualified professionals. In 1963 three postsecondary colleges combined to establish the second public university in Hong Kong, the Chinese University of Hong Kong (CUHK).[26] CUHK was born of émigré, anti-communist intellectuals from the mainland and of the desire to set up a comprehensive, Chinese-speaking university in the British colony. In 1965, responding to the growing complexity of the higher education sector, Hong Kong's Legislative Council established a University Grants Committee (UGC), along the British model, to coordinate tertiary education financing in the colony and to serve as the governing body between the government's Education Bureau and the individual campuses.

In the late 1960s, as the Cultural Revolution wreaked havoc on the social order in mainland China, protests spilled over the border to Hong Kong, which suffered the worst riots it would see until 2019. Unlike on the mainland, however, where university campuses became physical battlegrounds and education ground to a halt, HKU remained relatively apolitical. The HKU Students' Union declined to participate in demonstrations.[27] HKU students became more engaged politically in the 1970s, participating, for example, in the 1974 protests that led to the establishment of Chinese as an official language of the colony alongside English.[28]

## From Britain to China

By the Treaty of Nanjing (1842), Hong Kong Island, on which HKU is located, was ceded to Great Britain in perpetuity. But the physically largest part of modern Hong Kong, the New Territories, which became part of the colony in 1898 on a ninety-nine-year lease, and where much of Hong Kong's population (not to mention the Chinese University of Hong Kong) is located, was destined to return to China in 1997. Assuming the indivisibility of the colony, the 1984 Sino-British Joint Declaration confirmed the return of *all* of Hong Kong to Chinese sovereignty in 1997. That agreement, negotiated at the height of China's post-Mao promise of political reform, would be rudely followed in 1989 by the brutal military crackdown on student and other protestors in Beijing's Tiananmen Square, setting off a major crisis of confidence for the future of Hong Kong in general, and, on campus, for HKU.

China proposed a "One Country, Two Systems" framework for Hong Kong, promising that, even under PRC sovereignty, "laws currently in force in Hong Kong will remain basically unchanged" until 2047, fifty years following the handover.[29] Anxiety in Hong Kong was high, inspiring British colonial authorities to introduce major public sector investments in the 1990s, not the least in education. Public education enrollment at all levels expanded. From 1989 to 1994, higher education enrollment grew from less than 3 percent to 18 percent of graduating secondary school students. A major new institution, Hong Kong University of Science and Technology, was founded as Hong Kong's third university (and "Hong Kong's MIT") in 1991 under the dynamic leadership of its founding president, Chia-wei Woo, a Shanghai-born, American-educated academic leader. Soon thereafter, several colleges were promoted to university status to absorb the increase in enrollment.[30] As the primary body overseeing publicly funded universities, the UGC oversaw this expansion: it funded universities through block grants, allowing each university to maintain a high degree of academic and administrative autonomy. HKU would continue its role as Hong Kong's flagship university, but in a suddenly more crowded and competitive sector.

It is difficult to overstate the uncertainties gripping Hong Kong in the years preceding the handover. A half-million residents left the colony, and many others found second domiciles abroad. Having governed Hong Kong as a Crown Colony since 1842, the British introduced a series of democratic reforms, including an expanded franchise for elections to the Legislative Council. Even Hong Kong's most privileged residents harbored doubts. I recall a conversation in early 1997 with one of Hong Kong's "tycoons," as the local press labeled the leaders of the richest families. He told me he was leaving Hong Kong "because the communists are coming in." By "communists" he did not mean the Chinese Communist Party—with which he had a good relationship—but rather Hong Kong's Democratic Party, which had vowed to raise taxes on tycoons like him. (He did not leave.)

Anxieties were higher still at HKU. The 1990 "Basic Law" adopted by China's National People's Congress became Hong Kong's *de facto* constitution. It provided that "educational institutions of all kinds may retain their autonomy and enjoy academic freedom." But in the aftermath of the Tiananmen crisis and the subsequent crackdown on mainland universities, HKU's leadership was anxious about how its academic autonomy could be maintained in practice.[31] Several well-known scholars left Hong Kong for positions in Great Britain and Australia, although many ultimately returned to Hong Kong after the stability of the political and economic environment seemed ensured. In June 1997, shortly before Hong Kong's retrocession to China, HKU students attempted to display on campus the *Pillar of Shame*, a pro-democracy sculpture by Danish artist Jens Galschiot, in commemoration of the eighth anniversary of the Tiananmen Incident. Administrators initially refused to allow the display because of "safety concerns." The university was clearly wary of upsetting Beijing on the eve of Chinese President Jiang Zemin's greatest personal triumph: overseeing the return of Hong Kong and putting a final end to the last vestiges of colonial rule on Chinese territory. After students moved the statue on campus anyway, the university agreed to allow its display.[32] The incident foreshadowed what would become growing tensions as the university struggled to balance its role as a public institution under a complex governing system with its commitment to academic freedom and autonomy.

At the same time, Hong Kong's return to China offered new opportunities, new leadership, and new visions for HKU. Having been founded as the premier university in British colonial Asia, HKU's reach had shrunk with the diminution of Britain's empire, of which Hong Kong had been one of the last remnants. In the last years of British rule, facing an increasingly crowded local higher education sector, HKU had become a locally focused institution, concerned primarily with besting its local competitors and educating a student body almost entirely from Hong Kong.

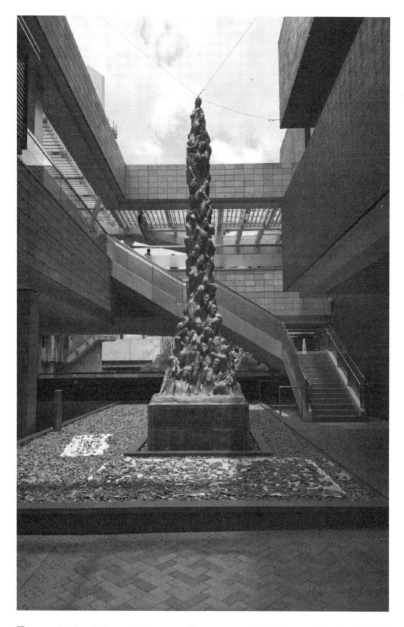

**Figure 11.2.** *Pillar of Shame*, on "permanent" display outside the HKU Student Union until 2021. Photograph © William C. Kirby.

This relatively narrow vision was challenged and then greatly broadened by new, local leadership with a global outlook. The prominent Hong Kong businessman and former Harvard Business School professor Victor Fung served as a transformative chairman of the HKU Council from 2003 to 2009. Fung had distinguished himself both in business and in public service. He and his brother, William, turned their family firm, Li & Fung, into the world's leader in supply-chain management. Victor Fung also chaired Hong Kong's Airport Authority and oversaw in the final years of British rule (and over intense Chinese opposition) the building of today's extraordinary Hong Kong International Airport, which has proven a key element in Hong Kong's post-handover prosperity. His desire to make Hong Kong a center of Asia's modern development extended to education. As council chair (broadly equivalent to chair of a university board of trustees), Fung spearheaded the re-envisioning of HKU as not just the flagship institution of higher education in Hong Kong but also a leading university in Asia and the world. This new vision was supported by a wide range of major reforms in university governance that promoted modern, streamlined administrative practices. Working closely with Vice Chancellor Lap-Chee Tsui and a reorganized and reinvigorated Council, Fung built faculty and student consensus around this new vision of the university and established the foundation for HKU's continued pursuit of global excellence in the twenty-first century.

## The University of Hong Kong in the Twenty-First Century

By 2019 HKU was in many ways still at the apex of eight publicly funded higher education institutions in Hong Kong. As the system's flagship English-language research institution, HKU offered internationally competitive teaching in all fields, as well as internationally competitive research in select areas.[33] HKU was home to over seventeen thousand undergraduate students and thirteen thousand graduate students. From its inception, HKU had sought to attract a regionally diverse population, but its capacity to attract mainland Chinese students was better served in the early twenty-first century than it was a century earlier. In the 2019–2020 school year, 23.5 percent of undergraduate students and 35.5 percent of students overall held mainland or international passports.[34]

HKU's diverse student population studied under an academic staff of nearly two thousand, grouped into ten faculties (its original faculties of Medicine, Engineering, and the Arts, plus Architecture, Business and Economics, Dentistry, Education, Law, Science, and Social Sciences) and a Graduate School.[35] Its programs in medicine, as well as the humanities, social sciences, and business and management, were among its strongest. Across all programs, the employment rate of graduates six months after graduation was 99.3 percent.

In his time as council chair, Victor Fung had determined that HKU should rise to be among the top twenty-five universities in the world. HKU, he argued, should not compare itself with the Chinese University of Hong Kong or the Hong Kong University of Science and Technology. It should vie with Berkeley, Stanford, Harvard, and others for global leadership. When, in 2007, the *Times Higher Education World University Rankings* placed HKU as number eighteen in the world—one position above the nineteenth-ranked Stanford University, HKU seemed on its way.[36]

That rise did not continue, however. Overall in 2019, HKU was ranked twenty-fifth in the world in the QS ranking, thirty-sixth in the *Times Higher Education World University Rankings,* and in the 101–150 bracket in the ARWU ranking. During his term as president, Peter Mathieson had not been overly concerned with this recent drop: "My attitude toward rankings is publicly expressed: I will never set institutional strategy in order to satisfy any particular league table."[37] The task of rising further—or even staying in its current positions—would be challenged by the vortex of local, national, and international politics that would consume the university in the second decade of the twenty-first century. First, however, HKU would attempt to reinvent its education in the liberal arts and sciences.

## Curricular Extension and Institutional Expansion

HKU had long been known for graduating those who would quickly find their way in the professions—medicine, law, and government in particular. As in Britain, students were admitted directly into departments for a three-year curriculum. HKU had never been known for liberal education in either the Humboldtian sense or in the American practice. In 2005 the UGC mandated the expansion of undergraduate education at Hong Kong's eight public universities from three to four years. The aim of this reform was to create space in the university curriculum for new general education curricula and to align Hong Kong's universities with the most prestigious global practices. After the reform, students in Hong Kong received six years (as opposed to seven) of secondary education (equivalent to junior and senior high school in the American system), and then, optionally, attended a four-year university program, earning the reform the moniker "3 + 3 + 4."

Planning for this large-scale change commenced immediately, and HKU began to implement some elements of its new general education program as early as 2009.[38] In 2012 HKU welcomed both its first cohort of students in its newly designed four-year program and its last cohort of three-year students. Arthur Li, the former Vice Chancellor of the Chinese University of Hong Kong and former Secretary for Education and Manpower in Hong Kong's government, who oversaw the four-year undergraduate curriculum change in Hong Kong, commented, "The British system was very good if you know what you want to do, right when you are a kid of 18 . . . but if you want more rounded individuals for the twenty-first century, where you have to have multi-tasking, where you have to have flexibility within your workforce, is it such a good thing that you make up your mind so early in life at that point in time?"[39]

The "3 + 3 + 4" plan energized HKU's faculty. After all, how often do you get to argue over what will be taught in a whole extra year in a university? After lengthy discussion and consultation, six Common Core classes introduced four Areas of Inquiry—Scientific and Technological Literacy; Humanities; Global Issues; and China: Culture, State, and Society.

Such a big rethinking of undergraduate education presented academic and financial challenges. HKU needed to recruit and fund a 20 percent increase in faculty positions. It seized the chance to recruit young faculty with a strong research orientation. Funding was more of a burden, as the government provided but 60 percent of the cost of the extra year. This led HKU irretrievably into the world of high-level fundraising.

The impact of such a fundamental change in undergraduate education reached into every department. Each program had to rethink its major requirements and create new course offerings. This proved less of a challenge for faculty members—by 2015 the Common Core already boasted 175 course offerings—than for the students, who, like students everywhere, were focused on their postgraduate careers. Vice President for Teaching and Learning Ian Holliday noted that, while program implementation had largely been successful, there was still a "mismatch of expectations," with students not understanding the reasoning behind a transition that asked them to delay courses in their major until later in their studies.[40]

Finally, there was the physical challenge of providing classroom and living space to many more students. While the physical campus of HKU, located on a rocky hill overlooking the sea on the western edge of Hong Kong Island, had long been circumscribed, the opening of a rapid transit station at the HKU campus in December 2014 eased transportation to the rest of Hong Kong and presented the possibility of housing students on other parts of the island. Advancements in engineering allowed HKU to expand over the reservoir abutting the campus on the west to establish the Centennial Campus. This expansion, part of the school's one hundredth anniversary celebration, included classroom space where the four-year undergraduate degree program would be centered.

A new institution, Centennial College (not located on the Centennial Campus), was an effort at a different kind of outreach: it offered four-year undergraduate degrees and became part of what was now known as the for-profit HKU Group, whose initiatives were primarily financed by student tuition payments, not government subsidies.

## Multicultural Environment

HKU had a long history as a diverse campus, and this remained true in the twenty-first century. Since Rayson Huang's appointment as the first ethnic Chinese vice chancellor in 1972, that position had been held by a mix of ethnic Chinese and British administrators.[41] The majority of the faculty remained international, although there had been an increase in the hiring of local scholars after 1997. Even with more balance overall, faculty members from Hong Kong, mainland China, and other countries had differing perceptions of and experiences at HKU. One Chinese faculty member noted the constant need to juggle two systems of behavior, the formal use of the Western system and the informal use of the Chinese one: "Most people will clearly feel the tensions between what I call the formal and informal systems. . . . In my life, I constantly need to adjust myself. In this situation I need to be Chinese, and in this situation, quickly, sometimes, and very dramatically, I need to be a Westerner."[42]

Academic freedom was one issue that could drive a wedge between Chinese and non-Chinese faculty members. The academic environment at HKU was very open; former Provost Roland Chin noted in 2015 that Chinese Communist Party communiqués limiting acceptable topics of discussion "don't apply now. You can argue that there's some self-restraint, but it's not apparent." But by 2047, he warned, "this might change." Thinking about potential future flashpoints at HKU, an American professor noted, "I guess there's the academic freedom issue, which I don't really see as much of an issue. Although, even there, there's a dividing line between foreigners and Chinese."[43] As the HKU campus became increasingly involved in politics, the division between "protected" foreign staff and the more vulnerable local or ethnic Chinese faculty had the potential to become more acute.

While there were inevitable tensions in a professoriat with deep cultural and ethnic divides, the cosmopolitan and international atmosphere of HKU remained one of its distinct strengths. Chin noted that, in recent years, other universities in Hong Kong had tended to become more Chinese and less international. HKU, on the other hand, had worked hard to retain its internationalism. In Chin's eyes, Hong Kong's institutional autonomy was very different from that of the higher education system on the mainland. "In addition, if a university is local and isolated, its value and influence to the world is small. The support from the society and the government would very much depend on the economic and political situation at that time. If it is international and connected, the society would value its existence and diversity."[44] The prolonged anti-government (and, implicitly, anti-Beijing) demonstrations of 2019 would test these assumptions.

One of the challenges that HKU faced in 2019 was how to address the antiquated personnel policies that limited its ability to recruit leading scholars. With the onset of formal government subsidies for HKU in 1952, the pay scales and retirement policies of professors were linked to those of civil servants. In the early 2000s salaries were delinked from the civil service pay scale, allowing HKU to make more competitive offers when recruiting faculty. While this improved HKU's recruiting power, the institution was still hampered by the civil service–influenced retirement age of sixty, which made it nearly impossible to recruit scholars at the height of their academic careers. In 2016 HKU ended its policy of granting rare, ad hoc exemptions to the mandatory retirement age, instead offering faculty turning sixty the option of applying for nontenured positions.[45]

Both the administration and departments with high ratios of teaching-oriented, older faculty, favored keeping the retirement age intact, so as to renew the faculty. Other departments, particularly those in fields like the humanities in which scholars tended to produce their best work later in their careers, were eager to change the policy to aid in recruiting. This was important in recruiting scholars from beyond Hong Kong, who made up nearly 60 percent of the professoriat. HKU could offer impressive salaries, research support, and generous housing allowances. (Where else could a new faculty colleague live inexpensively in a large flat with an ocean view?) But on retirement those benefits ceased, and HKU faculty who had not invested long before in Hong Kong real estate would find themselves competing to buy or rent property in the most expensive housing market on Earth. (In 2020 the average price for a residential property in Hong Kong was US$1.25 million.)

In 2018 members of the University Court, one of the university's governing boards, called on the university to "reconsider whether the current retirement policy at HKU is in line with the best interest of the university."[46] Discontent among the faculty rose as growing numbers applied for new contracts as they turned sixty. Faculty were concerned that nontenured contracts might offer lower pay and renewals subject to vague performance criteria. Some worried that political considerations affected which contracts were renewed, and for how long.[47] In response, HKU's administration held a townhall explaining the rationale for the policy but did not commit to its reform.[48] The retirement age remains unretired.

### "Fit for Purpose": Governance and Its Reform

Governance matters for every university, but among the universities of greater China, perhaps nowhere was it more important than at the University of Hong Kong. As the leading university not under the supervision of the Chinese Communist Party, if HKU were to realize its vision as "Asia's Global University," it would need to retain the traditions of academic autonomy and unfettered teaching and research inherited from the latter period of British rule.

HKU had a complex and archaic governance structure that was poorly suited to university-wide academic planning. But the need to set a strategy was palpable. In the transition years of the late 1990s Vice Chancellor Patrick Cheng had to create an ad hoc strategic advisory working group of senior academic staff to discuss the large issues facing the university, including its international and local positioning as well as how to maintain its leadership role. This laid the groundwork for a blue-ribbon commission of leading scholars and businessmen to develop HKU's first modern strategic plan in 2003.

How was the university structured? The university administration was led formally by the chancellor, the chief officer of the university, a position originally reserved for the colonial governor and now for the chief executive (CE) of Hong Kong. The CE served as chancellor at each of Hong Kong's eight public universities, largely in a ceremonial role. In reality, most administrative control at each university lay in the hands of its president (or vice chancellor). The president was "the principal academic and administrative officer of the University," supported by a provost, an executive vice president (administration) and a team of vice presidents, who together with the registrar and director of finance made up the senior management team and reported to the University Council.

The University Council was the chief governing body. It managed financial and human resources as well as strategic planning. The Council was composed of nonuniversity affiliates, HKU administrators, faculty, staff, and students who, by the turn of the twenty-first century, collectively numbered over fifty. This changed during the Council chairmanship of Victor Fung, who engaged a blue-ribbon panel of three experts—Neil Rudenstine, the recently retired president of Harvard; Andrew Li, a former chairman of the UGC and head of the Hong Kong Court of Final Appeal; and John Nyland, former president of the University of New South Wales—to review the governance and management structures of the university. The panel reported their recommendations in the 2003 *Fit for Purpose* report, which put forth seventeen recommendations for good governance, the majority of which focused on the role of the Council. The report recommended the transformation of the Council from its unwieldy, large number into a body of eighteen to twenty-four members, and it reaffirmed the Council as the "de facto supreme governing body of the University."[49] The panel also recommended changes to the membership of the reformed Council, which, under Fung, came to include a greater number of student representatives and, for the first time, included union representatives of senior and junior faculty, as well as of professional staff.

While the Council dealt primarily with administration, political matters, and budgeting, the Senate was responsible for academics and all matters related to education. As such, the Senate was heavily engaged in managing the shift from the three- to four-year curriculum. Its membership consisted of professors, deans, and several student representatives.[50] This body did provide a forum for debate of policy but did not enact any itself.

The third central administrative body was the University Court, which met once a year and served largely useless but charming ceremonial purposes. It was led by the chancellor with a membership of elected representatives from various political and educational bodies.[51]

One of the challenges Vice Chancellor Cheng addressed was the highly compartmentalized academic and financial structure of HKU. Traditionally, the key unit of management was the department, and HKU had over eighty departments, each one of which reported to the central administration. The departments and the schools in which they were organized had neither an organizational mandate nor any incentive to work together. Funding was disbursed to departments based on the number of undergraduates they taught, leading to redundancies in teaching as each department fought to maintain the highest possible student numbers. For example, the civil engineering department might hire a mathematics professor to teach that subject to its students, rather than working with the existing capacity of the mathematics department to meet students' needs.[52]

HKU faced a challenge common to many universities (recall our discussion of Duke): how to bring more resources from the periphery to the center. In a surely unpopular but effective way, Cheng established a new policy of "top-slicing." The majority of funding would continue to be disbursed as it had been in the past, but 10 to 15 percent would be held by the central administration to support strategic initiatives. In principle, this would incentivize departments to be less concerned about their individual numbers and to work together as schools and faculties to plan projects.[53]

The administrative capacity of HKU's schools was further strengthened by the reforms, several of American provenance, enacted during Victor Fung's Council chairmanship. Deans were henceforth appointed by the central administration based on an international search. Previously, deans had been (in the German style) elected by their colleagues, leaving them less accountable to the central administration and unlikely to implement significant but necessary changes that might upset their lifelong colleagues. This was but one of the seventeen administrative changes recommended in the *Fit for Purpose* report and approved for subsequent implementation. It was also under Fung's leadership that faculty and staff salaries were delinked from the civil service pay scale.[54]

HKU was not a young university, but it had never had a formal strategic plan. Fung and Vice Chancellor Lap-Chee Tsui spearheaded the creation of the 2003–2008 strategic plan that prioritized four areas: enhancing academic excellence, raising global presence and visibility, partnering with society and serving the community, and developing and supporting "the university family."[55] Bolstered by a modernized governance system with a streamlined Council, Fung visited each of the HKU faculties in person, meeting with senior faculty at each school and discussing their plans for external benchmarking. This was when Fung set the goal for HKU to make it into the top twenty-five of the *Times Higher Education World University Rankings*. Certainly even Fung did not expect the seemingly instantaneous results of 2007, when HKU jumped from thirty-third in the 2006 rankings to eighteenth.[56]

In 2016 Peter Mathieson launched *Vision 2016–2025,* a strategic plan that built on *Fit for Purpose* by doubling down on internationalization at all levels of university operations. *Vision 2016–2025* committed HKU to increasing opportunities for "learning experiences in mainland China and overseas."[57] HKU, whose identity had been that of a university *not* of mainland China, now experimented with ways to increase its engagement with the mainland, establishing an engineering research institute in Zhejiang and a teaching hospital in Shenzhen, the dynamic new city just to Hong Kong's north.[58]

Faculty and administrators broadly agreed on the lasting effects of the governance and management reforms laid out in *Fit for Purpose.* Feelings about HKU's strategic planning were rather more equivocal. Clearly, HKU's plans did not command the authority of Duke's, on that university's campus. One former senior administrator felt that long-term change had been achieved in the promotion of performance-based evaluation, noting, "The culture of the institution accepted the fact that it was appropriate to measure performance, it was appropriate to reward good performance." At the same time, he noted his amusement at "how [the strategic plans] were, I use the term 'shelved.' The plan was put on the shelf and life went on as normal."

## Funding

Whatever its goals, HKU was in a financially enviable position to realize them. The HKU Group—including HKU, Centennial College, and HKU School of Professional and Continuing Education—ended the 2019–2020 academic year with a budget surplus of over US$180 million. Its finance department attributed the surplus primarily to the block funding from the UGC and growing donations to HKU.[59] Funding for the university came from four major sources: government funds, tuition and fees, donations, and investment returns.

As one of the eight publicly funded higher education institutions in Hong Kong, a large part of HKU's operating budget came from the UGC, in the form of triennial block grants, allowing for stability and predictability in financial planning, as well as funding for specific capital projects, research initiatives, or other specific purposes. For example, in 2014 HKU received a new type of funding from the UGC specifically for internationalization and engagement of mainland China.

Tuition and fees were the second largest source of income for HKU. The university offered different tuition scales for local and foreign students. In 2019 one year of tuition for a local undergraduate student was around US$5,400, while all nonlocal students, including those from mainland China, paid nearly US$21,000 per year.[60] Attending Centennial College cost much more for local students (around US$11,300 per year) but less for international students (around US$15,200 per year).[61] In 2015 the university announced that self-financed programs like Centennial College brought in nearly 40 percent of the HKU Group's total tuition and fee income, despite being responsible for less than 15 percent of the group's total expenditures.[62]

Donations and investment returns made up most of the rest of HKU's revenue. Donations included funds dedicated to research, scholarships, and capital expansion. In addition to returns on invested endowment funds, the HKU Group also owned 20 percent stakes in leading firms in Hong Kong's growing medical services industry.[63] With its enviable budget surplus in 2019, HKU had progressed well beyond its financially strained early years. Looking to the future, however, HKU's financial situation appeared less certain. One professor recalled a conversation with a politically connected university administrator, who said, "We have no friends [in the government]. The left wing [i.e., pro-China] politicians hate universities in general because we're not patriotic enough. The democratic ones think we take too many mainland students."[64] High-level administrators expected that funding provided by the government would drop well below 50 percent of the university's operating budget in the future—to be sure an enviable number from the perspective of an American public university, such as Berkeley. To make up the difference, HKU planned to increase fundraising and development efforts. This was the task of Sabrina Lin, vice president of institutional advancement. She would have, even for Hong Kong, a high mountain to climb. One of her projects was to increase the percentage of alumni donors. In 2018 that consisted of just 2.5 percent of alumni.

## Hong Kong's Political Order and Disorder

Hong Kong's post-1997 political order, enshrined in the city's Basic Law approved by China's National People's Congress, enabled HKU's growth in the early twenty-first century. The "One Country, Two Systems" model provided Hong Kong's university system with academic freedoms not offered to mainland institutions. As HKU's leadership aspired to create "Asia's Global University," it assumed there would be continuity in both the generous funding and academic autonomy that were hallmarks of HKU under Hong Kong's post-handover polity. Yet it was not clear that Hong Kong's special status in greater China would survive. By 2017 Hong Kong's "high degree of autonomy" promised in the Basic Law had endured basically intact for two decades, but years of political contention and protests left it weakened in the eyes of Hong Kongers and mainland officials.

Hong Kong had an archaic and increasingly dysfunctional political system. Its "prince," or chief executive, was basically appointed by Beijing. The CE enjoyed significant authority but little legitimacy, and the tenure of each CE was rockier than that of the last. The parliament, or Legislative Council, had the trappings of democracy, and because its members were in part directly elected, it enjoyed legitimacy, but it had little real authority. Hong Kong had a strong professional civil service, with an historically independent court system and honest police force. These were stable elements in this volatile mix, although they too would be tested in the extreme in Hong Kong's recurrent crises.

Attempts at political reform in Hong Kong did not reverse rising displeasure among residents about the city's management. By 2013 over 50 percent of Hong Kong residents polled responded that they were dissatisfied with the pace of the city's political development, an increase from just 29 percent in 2007.[65] Support for the "One Country, Two Systems" model also began to crumble. While nearly three-quarters of the city's residents supported that concept in 2007, barely half of those polled in 2012 said they were confident in the system.[66] Beijing seemed to be racing against time to lay the groundwork for gradual political reforms in Hong Kong. Economic inequality was worsening, and demands not only for political reforms but also for a new political identity in Hong Kong were emerging.

Beijing's bid to maintain stability and public support in Hong Kong faced multiple obstacles. Although an influential indicator of quality of life in Hong Kong hit an all-time high in 2008, the trend has since been downward.[67]

Results released in 2012 showed the measure fell below its score for 2003.[68] Restricted voting rights for residents limited outlets for frustrated Hong Kongers. In circumscribing democratic rights, the mainland's cautious approach to political reforms in Hong Kong led Beijing both to exacerbate and be caught in the crossfire of the city's internal social divisions. Dissatisfaction with the mainland's management of Hong Kong's political development contributed to a rising proportion of residents identifying primarily as "Hong Kongers," instead of "Chinese."[69] Growing desire for strong "local," over national, identity heightened the political stakes of debates over democratic and legal reforms in Hong Kong and at HKU.

Since 1997 there had been a gradual increase in conflicts at HKU over engagement with China. In 2000 Vice Chancellor Patrick Cheng and his deputy stepped down amid accusations that they had pressured a university researcher to stop his opinion polling, which had showed declining support for the Beijing-picked chief executive.[70] Because the issue was framed by some as one of academic freedom, it put much academic and emotional stress on the university. In 2011, when Vice Chancellor Lap-Chee Tsui announced his decision to not seek a third term, many speculated that it was related to the accusations of overly harsh treatment of student protestors during the visit of Chinese Vice Premier Li Keqiang.[71] None of these incidents, however, compared to the scale and influence of Occupy Central.

## Occupy Central

Beijing had promised Hong Kong that the CE would in time be chosen by universal suffrage. But in 2014 Beijing proposed extending the electorate but limiting the candidates, which sparked intense resistance.

These developments had been followed closely by a group called Occupy Central with Love and Peace, led in part by HKU Faculty of Law associate professor Benny Tai. The group, along with many university and even high school students, launched a civil disobedience campaign in late September 2014, occupying some of Hong Kong's commercial center's busiest streets and demanding full universal suffrage. This movement was galvanized on September 28, 2014, when police used tear gas on demonstrators. This drew attention and sympathy to the demonstrators, whose ranks were ultimately swelled by citizens opposed to any police use of force. The movement, which came to be known as the Umbrella Movement, in reference to the umbrellas carried by protestors to protect themselves from tear gas, continued to occupy the streets of Hong Kong for seventy-nine days.[72] Ultimately, the election format endorsed by the National People's Congress was rejected by the Hong Kong Legislative Council—a dubious victory for the Occupy Central movement, as it left citizens of Hong Kong with no form of popular participation in the 2017 election.[73]

Occupy Central remained a divisive topic in Hong Kong with many fierce proponents and opponents. Because of the high-profile involvement of HKU faculty like Benny Tai (who was later sentenced to sixteen months in prison by a Hong Kong court for "conspiring to commit public nuisance") as well as heavy participation by HKU students, the university seemed inextricably tied to the extended but notably restrained protest movement.[74] (In all seventy-nine days of protest and dispersal, no students were injured.) Government relations with HKU became increasingly tense at a time when the central government of China was already tightening its ideological control over mainland universities, as we have seen at Tsinghua and Nanda.

An early indication of the deteriorating relationship between the Hong Kong and Chinese central governments, on the one hand, and HKU, on the other, was the controversy over Professor Johannes Chan. The public conflict over the delayed confirmation of Chan, a professor and former dean of HKU's Faculty of Law, as vice president of academic staffing and resources lent a concrete form to abstract fears of government interference in university affairs and called into question the role of Hong Kong's chief executive in university administration. In December 2014 a university selection committee nominated Chan for the vice president position, which had been vacant for five years.[75] HKU's Council then delayed responding to the nomination on grounds of waiting until HKU first filled the position of provost, and could then allow the new administrator to weigh in on the decision. It was widely suspected that the delay was due to Chan's connection with Occupy Central—Benny Tai had served as associate dean of the Faculty of Law from 2000 to 2008, overlapping with Chan's deanship for six years.

Seven months later, there was still no response to the selection committee's recommendation. In July 2015 a group of students stormed a meeting of the Council to protest the delay. More than one thousand HKU alumni and over three thousand others then signed an online petition condemning the actions of the students.[76] With the issue still unresolved on September 1, 2015, more than seven thousand HKU staff and alumni called on the Council to confirm Chan within thirty days.[77] On September 29, 2015, the Council voted twelve to eight against Chan's nomination.[78] Following the vote, one of the student representatives on the Council broke confidentiality and published his summary of the meeting. His report indicated that the vote had largely been split between the university-based members of the Council, who voted in favor of Chan's appointment, and the government-appointed members, who had carried the vote against.[79] University faculty and many members of the public believed that his rejection was attributable to political pressure from outside the university's walls.

This led to a constitutional crisis at HKU. How, in fact, was the university being governed? If a deanship approved by a university search committee and the president could be cast aside, what did that portend? This led in turn to scrutiny of the Council and the Chief Executive's right to appoint members, some of whom appeared to be his political allies. For historical reasons, across Hong Kong's universities, only at HKU was the CE entitled to appoint the chair and other members of the Council *without* consultation with the president. Tensions over this power of the CE came to a head with the 2015 appointment of Arthur Li, who was known for his strong leadership style, as Council chairman. Despite protests in 2016, Li's chairmanship was extended for three more years in 2018.[80]

## Governance, Reviewed but not Renewed

There was widespread belief that Chief Executive C. Y. Leung had become deeply engaged in HKU university politics, from the very public Johannes Chan affair to the (publicly invisible) selection of HKU honorary degree candidates. The chief executive's position of chancellor (as distinct from vice chancellor or president) had become largely honorific under his predecessors. But Leung took the title literally: he intervened early and often in university affairs.

Under enormous pressure from faculty, students, and staff to ensure the university's academic integrity, the University Council undertook its second major review of governance in the twenty-first century by establishing an independent Review Panel on University Governance in April 2016. Framed as a successor to 2003's *Fit for Purpose* and the 2009 follow-up report, the review panel put forth recommendations aimed to insulate HKU's governance and its academic autonomy from the *Sturm und Drang* of Hong Kong's incessantly contentious politics.

The story of this panel and its work tells us much about the present state of HKU and Hong Kong. It was chaired by Sir Malcolm Grant, chancellor of the University of York in the United Kingdom and the recent president and provost of University College London. A longtime and influential member of Hong Kong's University Grants Committee, Grant also chaired Britain's National Health Service. I was asked to join the review, for I, too, was a former, longtime member of UGC and had a strong commitment to Hong Kong's universities. Sir Malcolm and I were joined by a distinguished senior barrister in Hong Kong, Peter Van Tu Nguyen, former High Court judge of the Hong Kong Special Administrative Region.

Our review was commissioned by HKU's Council with broad terms of reference: to conduct an overall review of the governance structure of the university; to take into consideration other recent assessments (such as *Fit for Purpose*); to meet with all relevant constituencies; to review all ordinances and statutes as to their current appropriateness; and to make recommendations to enhance the university's governance.

We did all that, and more. We solicited confidential, written input from all university stakeholders, including faculty, students, and alumni, and received forty formal written submissions, many quite extensive, all kept confidential to the members of the review panel and its secretary. We held thirty-three meetings with different groups across the university, several in public settings, others in confidence. We indicated at the commencement of each meeting that we would operate under so-called Chatham House rules, meaning that views expressed to us might be quoted directly but would not be attributed to any individual. Our secretary prepared a summary of each meeting, in which speakers were identified only by the order of their speaking and not by name. We reviewed all recent agenda and minutes of the university's governing boards, including the Council.

Our committee met in a "safe" and quiet conference room to review what we had encountered and to make our recommendations. We had reason to assume that our deliberations would in fact be made in confidence, until we were prepared to make them public. But this was Hong Kong. There is good reason why Hong Kong is a frequent locus of John le Carré novels and James Bond films. Nothing stays secret in Hong Kong.

Our review panel made a lengthy report with thirty-five formal recommendations. Many of them were simple housekeeping: how to make things work more efficiently. But others sought to address the great crisis of confidence gripping HKU at the time. The most consequential recommendation was that the chancellorship, held in a hereditary fashion by the chief executive, become clearly honorary, with the chancellor delegating unusual and potentially political powers (such as unilaterally naming Council chairs and members) to the Council itself, and to do the same with other matters, such as the awarding of honorary degrees. Further, we saw distinct advantages of separating the chancellorship from the government, following the current norms in the United Kingdom, Australia, and other countries that had followed British practice.[81] The point was not to accuse the current chief executive of interference in university affairs, but—as he was about to step down—to relieve his successor of the burden of being perceived as acting with political motives toward the university.

We contemplated these recommendations, the three of us, over the course of an intensive week in our private, "sealed" room on the HKU campus. Early in our deliberations we had asked to speak with the chief executive, but his office sent us a curt reply that he had no time. However, before we had come to our (still confidential) conclusions, we were suddenly summoned to Government House to meet with him.

Our room, it seems, was neither sealed nor confidential; it had "ears." When we met with the CE, C. Y. Leung, he was brief on etiquette. He told us, before we had said scarcely a word, "I will never agree to what you are recommending. And Beijing won't allow it." (We had not yet finalized our recommendations.) We reminded him that, as chief executive, he already had very significant power, not the least of the purse, over Hong Kong's universities in general and HKU in particular. He seemed to agree, for he said, "You know, I do not need to be chancellor in order to interfere with the University of Hong Kong." But he was unrelenting in his refusal to accept recommendations that we had yet to set down on paper. He told us as we departed that this was an off-the-record conversation and, indeed, no staff were present. We agreed to keep it among ourselves—until we had dinner that night with Council Chair Arthur Li, who gave us chapter and verse about the "confidential" meeting we had just attended with the chief executive.

What came of all this? The views of the review panel members were reinforced by the brutal meeting with C. Y. Leung, and we agreed unanimously to the first draft of the report in September 2016, which was sent to Arthur Li and Peter Mathieson for their review. Then, however (and here one can only speculate), Nguyen, the only local member of our panel, must have been subject to great pressure, and he ceased all communication with Sir Malcolm and me. He very belatedly endorsed the report nearly in full, save for those recommendations related to the chief executive. For his part, Arthur

Li, the Council Chair, buried the report in Council until the following spring, when a new chief executive was in place, and then eviscerated its main points.

Eventually, the University Council adopted the majority of the review panel's multiple recommendations, but the most significant ones, aimed to improve the Council's transparency and autonomy, were rejected.[82] The rejected recommendations included those making the role of chancellor "largely honorary," with its powers delegated to the Council, including the rights to nominate members and select its chair.[83] After the new CE reappointed Arthur Li as council chair, over thirty student, staff, and alumni groups at HKU issued a joint statement demanding the Council remove the chancellor's powers to appoint members and select a chairman without public consultation.[84] As protests consumed Hong Kong again in the summer of 2019, the Council's ability to effectively govern HKU while protecting its institutional autonomy from political storms would be tested again.

### Anti-Extradition Bill Protests

In spring 2019 Hong Kong's government proposed legislation for allowing the CE to determine ad hoc extraditions of suspected criminals on Hong Kong territory to jurisdictions with which it lacked mutual extradition treaties.[85] The bill raised concerns in Hong Kong that it could be used by a pro-Beijing CE to arrest political dissidents and extradite them to mainland China for trial.[86] Responding to criticism, Hong Kong CE Carrie Lam, the successor to C. Y. Leung, introduced an amended bill she argued would limit the threat of its use for political ends and pushed for its swift passage.[87]

Amendments to the bill did not satisfy the public, and Lam's intention to press on sparked enormous protests in June, with many HKU students participating.[88] When Lam suspended the bill, HKU students were among those who declared they would continue to protest until its formal withdrawal.[89] The protests also led to tensions between local students, who largely supported the anti-extradition bill movement and mainland students, who supported Beijing. At an HKU forum held to discuss the protests, mainland students who voiced concerns were jeered.[90] HKU's attempts to convince students that the ongoing protests should not be allowed to affect campus learning were ignored, as student groups opened the academic year with a class boycott.[91] HKU's tradition of student activism had again drawn the university into Hong Kong's protest politics.

As anti-extradition bill demonstrations continued, protester demands expanded and violence grew, placing Hong Kong's political order in jeopardy. In September Lam announced the formal withdrawal of the extradition bill, but by then, protester demands had grown to encompass greater democratic rights and an investigation into police brutality.[92] HKU's student union encouraged their classmates to support these demands, and a survey revealed college-aged and college-educated participants were the protests' largest constituency.[93] The turn toward radical politics in protests coincided with growing violence at them. By the end of the summer, over two thousand protesters had been reported injured, and on the seventieth anniversary of the People's Republic of China, the first Hong Kong protester was shot by a police officer.[94] Although China doubled its paramilitary presence in Hong Kong, Chinese President Xi Jinping reportedly did not want to quell protests with military force.[95] Yet, as Hong Kong's municipal government struggled to end the demonstrations, Beijing's patience seemed to be running thin.

In October Xi threatened that "anyone attempting to split China in any part of the country will end in crushed bodies and shattered bones."[96] This poured oil on Hong Kong's fire, and more violent demonstrations ensued.

As student protesters grew fearful that a Beijing-condoned crackdown was imminent, universities became the protests' front line. In mid-November, clashes between protesters and police broke out on the campuses of HKU, the Chinese University of Hong Kong, and Hong Kong Polytechnic University (PolyU) as police sought entry to arrest student protesters.[97] Students and other demonstrators responded by attempting to barricade themselves inside their campuses. Police deployed tear gas in an attempt to disperse protesters and clear the areas, and protesters were reported to have responded with bows and arrows and even javelins to ward off the approaching officers.[98] The police siege of PolyU lasted twelve days and attracted global media attention. When police arrived in armored cars, protesters at PolyU targeted their vehicles with explosive petrol bombs.[99] This latest round of skirmishes set off the most significant crisis universities in Hong Kong had faced since the protests began. University facilities across Hong Kong, including HKU's, were significantly damaged.[100] Many mainland students were reported to have fled the city, and over a dozen foreign universities suspended study abroad programs in Hong Kong.[101] On November 14 the president of HKU announced that classes on the university's main campus were suspended for the rest of the semester.[102]

**Figure 11.3.** Protests in Hong Kong, June 16, 2019. Studio Incendo/Wikimedia Commons/CC BY 2.0.

367

With protests reaching a fever pitch in late fall 2019, Hong Kong's government needed a way to dissipate tensions. An opportunity for détente with the city's residents arrived with the November 24 District Council elections. District Council members represent city neighborhoods and do not wield significant political power. However, during a time of political tensions, the District Council's 117 seats on the 1,200-person Election Committee that selects the CE were symbolically important. Pro-democracy parties achieved a stunning victory in the November 24 election, winning 389 of 452 District Council seats with a record 71 percent voter turnout citywide.

CE Carrie Lam told pro-Beijing officials that the election results signaled "dissatisfaction with the government." Despite—or because of—the overwhelming unpopularity of its policies in Hong Kong, Beijing clamped down hard. In January 2020 Luo Huining, former Party Secretary of Shanxi province and before that of Qinghai province, was appointed director of the central government's Hong Kong Liaison Office. In Shanxi and Qinghai, Luo was known for using hardline tactics to bring corrupt officials and dissidents to heel.[103] The first Liaison Office director to have not previously held a Hong Kong-related position, Luo was known to be trusted by Beijing because of his diligent implementation of Xi Jinping's anti-corruption campaign.[104] Under Luo, the Liaison Office became more vocal in its efforts to secure the mainland's control over Hong Kong. In April 2020 the office stated for the first time that Article 22 of the Basic Law, which guaranteed noninterference by mainland departments in Hong Kong affairs did "not apply to the liaison office," undercutting both the legal stipulations and the spirit of the "One Country, Two Systems" policy.[105] Luo himself also urged the Legislative Council to pass controversial national security legislation to defend the city against "violent" protesters and "foreign influence."[106] A similar effort in 2003 had provoked what were then Hong Kong's largest protests posttransition.

The mainland government then moved unilaterally to introduce its own National Security Law for Hong Kong at the May 2020 meeting of the National People's Congress.[107] Beijing had wanted the long-delayed law finally pushed through after the previous year's protests consumed the city, but many expected pro-Beijing forces in the Legislative Council to lead the charge.[108] Instead, the National People's Congress passed a resolution committing the central government to draft legislation for Hong Kong that would ban secession, subversion of state power, foreign intervention, and terrorism as well.[109] This surprise decision sparked a swift backlash, with Hong Kong experiencing its first large protests since the coronavirus lockdown had begun in the winter of 2020.[110] Yet HKU Council chair Arthur Li spoke out in support of the forthcoming legislation and likened the previous year's protesters to a neo-Nazi group.[111] Even HKU's President Zhang tentatively backed the law before a draft had even been publicly released, signing a letter with four other Hong Kong university presidents stating, "We fully support 'One Country, Two Systems,' understand the need for national security legislation, and value the freedom of speech, of the press, of publication, of assembly, and other rights the Basic Law confers upon the people of Hong Kong."[112]

Beijing held the draft's text so close to the chest that not even CE Lam had seen it before the National People's Congress Standing Committee voted the bill into law in the dark of night on June 30.[113] The law was published at 11:00 p.m., Beijing time, the moment it went into force. Why would Beijing resort to such cloak-and-dagger legislating? The reason became clear as the world read the final law in full. Under the law, an expansive national security apparatus, afforded a long leash and reporting ultimately to Beijing, would be set up to pacify Hong Kong. A broad and vague list of offenses (ranging from "disrupting . . . the performance of duties" by the government to "provoking by unlawful means hatred among Hong Kong residents towards" their government) would be deemed national security crimes and carry up to a lifetime prison sentence. Hong Kong's education sector did not escape the law's reach. Under the national security law, "the Hong Kong Special Administrative Region shall promote national security education in schools and universities . . . to raise the awareness of Hong Kong residents of national security and of the obligation to abide by the law."[114] Whereas President Zhang announced his early support for the law prior to its release, neither he nor HKU made any public comment on the law in its wake.

Concerns about the future of academic freedom in Hong Kong gripped scholars at HKU and other universities in the city. The national security law's broad but vague language left HKU's faculty to debate the degree to which academic discussions could run afoul of the bill.[115] Some within HKU's administration, however, seemed to have already decided that constricting academic speech was now a legal requirement. The program director for the humanities and law faculty at HKU's School of Professional and Continuing Education wrote to staff that "[a]ny behavior in eliciting further discussion on sensitive issues MUST be avoided" and warned there would be "zero-tolerance against politics or personal political views brought into classrooms."[116] HKU responded to inquiries by stating that although this was not an official university policy, classrooms must be "politically neutral." To be sure, the frost settling over academic speech in Hong Kong's universities aligned with the interests of CE Lam, who had criticized universities for allowing "teaching materials" and "classroom teaching" to politicize higher education.[117] Yet it was still unknown whether these were warning shots designed to silence dissident academics and students, or if this uncertainty would give way to greater scrutiny and intrusions into Hong Kong's academic life. Would the universities of Hong Kong be pressed to align themselves with the rules and restrictions governing the mainland's universities?

The dismissal of dissident legal scholar Benny Tai in July 2020 by HKU's University Council was the first concrete signal that the passing of the National Security Law did indeed mark the beginning of a new, less free era for academic life in Hong Kong. Tai had been sentenced to sixteen months in prison in April 2019 for "conspiracy to commit public nuisance" because of his role in the 2014 Occupy Central protests.[118] At President Zhang's behest, HKU initiated an inquiry into Tai's behavior, which found that although his actions did meet the criteria for "misconduct," they fell short of the threshold for dismissal. The HKU Senate, composed mostly of faculty, ratified this recommendation, but it was Arthur Li's University Council, where many members were pro-establishment, that had the final say in the matter. In a vote of eighteen to two, the Council overturned the Senate's recommendations in favor of terminating Tai's employment at HKU. Three members, including President Zhang, declined to cast a ballot. Upon learning of the decision, Tai released a statement that it "marked the end of academic freedom in Hong Kong." Beijing's officers in Hong Kong could not contain their glee. The mainland's Hong Kong Liaison Office cheered HKU for holding Tai accountable for his "evil" actions.[119]

Although Arthur Li, HKU's Council chair, discounted concerns about the Benny Tai case, stating that Tai's sacking was "not a political decision," Hong Kong's government signaled that purging institutions of dissident faculty had become a priority.[120] Hong Kong's Secretary for Security, John Lee, stated that the city had "failed to do a good job with education" since the handover and that his first priority would be to "deal with schools" and their "bad apples" by depoliticizing the education sector.[121] Such an intervention seemed at odds with Article 137 of Hong Kong's Basic Law, which guaranteed academic freedom and autonomy for institutions, but the demands of national security seemed set to subordinate these and many other rights that had been promised to Hong Kong. Benny Tai, for his part, appealed the Council's decision to CE Lam, also HKU's chancellor, potentially forcing a direct and visible political intervention in his case even though, he acknowledged, the chances of Lam reversing the decision were virtually none.[122]

### Complacency and Competition

Amid all its political turmoil, HKU still had to focus on its place in an increasingly competitive local, regional, and global landscape for higher education. Mathieson had warned, "There's a real danger of complacency in what, in this part of the world, is a relatively old university. We can't say that because we're 104 years old and we had a good reputation in the past therefore that's fine and we just need to carry on doing what we're doing."[123] These sentiments were echoed by Arthur Li: "I think that will be our biggest enemy at Hong Kong University. It's the complacency. We have always been the top dog. We are good. We are wonderful, you know. There is self-congratulations and so on. And I think that has to be shaken up."[124] The rapid expansion of higher education in Hong Kong in the early 1990s gave students many more options for advanced study. While none of the universities that were established or expanded in recent years were as comprehensive as HKU, some, like the Hong Kong University of Science and Technology, were strong competitors in certain disciplines.

HKU found itself competing not just for human, but also for financial, resources. Government funding for public institutions was increasingly distributed through competitive, project-based grants from Hong Kong's Research Grants Council, stiffening the competition between local universities for faculty and the funding they might attract. HKU was positioned to do well in this competition, so long as it remained apolitical.

For many years, HKU had been the primary beneficiary of the largess of Hong Kong businesspeople, many of whom were not alumni but appreciated the university's contribution to society, particularly to health care and governance. "For sixty years or so, leaders in Hong Kong were all HKU graduates, and this will change," noted former Provost Roland Chin. "Ten . . .

twenty years from now, most of these people will retire, and then the younger generation [will come to power], and they are from [other universities]."[125] HKU was no longer the only respectable, local alma mater for mature professionals and could therefore expect to lose some of its dominance in private funding.

Meanwhile, as we have seen, the mainland Chinese government had begun a concerted effort to nurture world-class universities. Leading institutions such as Peking and Tsinghua Universities were armed with increased funding, more flexible faculty recruiting policies, and low tuition fees to attract the best students. For example, annual tuition for most undergraduate programs at Tsinghua for a mainland Chinese student would be no more than US$1,000. Even for students who would not be considered local at either Tsinghua or HKU, the tuition difference was striking. International undergraduates at Tsinghua could expect to pay annual tuition of around US$4,000 per year, less than 20 percent of the cost of a year of study at HKU.[126]

HKU's tradition of English instruction remained a major differentiating factor between it and the top mainland universities. However, programs like Tsinghua University's School of Economics and Management were beginning to incorporate more English-taught courses and degrees. Victor Fung also observed HKU's diminishing competitive advantage, "We are the only university in China that is taught completely in English. We are the only one. And I think that means something. And, I think the Tsinghuas are getting a lot of resources. I'm sure they will improve and improve and improve. They may exceed Hong Kong."[127] To be sure, before Occupy Central and other demonstrations, HKU had no problem attracting absolutely top students from the mainland who might otherwise have gone to Tsinghua or Beida. But over time, the steady rise of mainland universities, combined with Hong Kong's political instability, meant that HKU would have to work harder to attract mainland students and faculty in the future.

Competition for HKU was not limited to mainland China. In 2012 the National University of Singapore (NUS) overtook HKU in the *Times Higher Education World University Rankings* for the first time, becoming the second ranked institution in Asia after the University of Tokyo.[128] In subsequent years, HKU remained relegated to third place in Asia.[129] NUS in particular was increasingly known for its experimentation with internationalization, including its partnership with Yale University to develop a new liberal arts college, Yale NUS, and with Duke University to found the Duke-NUS

Medical School.[130] Moreover, whereas the Hong Kong government was committed to funding Hong Kong's eight higher education institutions equitably, the Singaporean government had prioritized a few, elite institutions, including NUS; in 2014 NUS received 60 percent more funding from the Singaporean government than HKU did from its government.[131]

Finally, HKU's position in international league tables was never far from the minds of its leaders. Although *Vision 2016–2025* and the *Report of the Review Panel on University Governance* may have helped HKU recover a bit in ratings, the university still lagged behind its peak performance following the release of *Fit for Purpose*. Strategic plans seemed less relevant in a period of deep unrest and anxiety. The media and the public jumped on any dip in the university's performance, and the university itself noted that rankings "are now a permanent part of the higher education landscape and cannot be disregarded in setting institutional strategies."[132] Peter Mathieson noted more general public awareness of international rankings but added that the public's chief interest in such rankings was still the relative position of Hong Kong's universities to each other. Victor Fung recalled a similar dynamic during the initial period of his Council tenure: "The University was beset by rivalry between HKU and Chinese U. This rivalry had no reference, however, to absolute standards of excellence. Should not these schools instead be benchmarked against the top universities in the world?"[133] In the world of higher education, there were competitors everywhere, but HKU, it seemed, had still to truly recognize those beyond Hong Kong's borders. The events of 2019–2020 had not made that task easier.

## Facing the Future

The University of Hong Kong was founded on the assumption that its students would steer clear of politics. When HKU was established, the obstacles to fulfilling its role as a flagship higher education institution had been primarily internal—disagreements over the balance of teaching and research, constant dearth of funding, and wavering political support for the institution from a distant ruling power. After 1997, with Hong Kong's return to China under "One Country, Two Systems," HKU sought to seize the opportunity of being arguably the leading university in greater China, with a governance structure unimpeded by Communist Party secretaries. Generously funded by Hong Kong's government and supported by an apolitical University Grants Committee, it faced unmatched opportunities. Under

Victor Fung's dynamic Council chairmanship, it sought to be in reality, as later it would be in slogan, "Asia's Global University," benchmarking itself against the best in the world. In its massive rethinking and expansion of undergraduate education, it showed itself capable of major change. In Peter Mathieson's *Vision 2016–2025* plan, it set out its ambition. On taking office, President Zhang sought to take HKU's globalizing goals further still: "A great university includes a number of dimensions. First, education and transmission of knowledge, as we do in the British system. Research degrees like in the German system. Third one, which the U.S. does, is research innovation. . . . I am also looking at the fourth dimension, societal impact, which U.S. universities talk about."[134] Since the beginning of the twenty-first century, HKU has committed itself to aiming high and charting paths to achieve its ambitions. This determination has helped the university remain upright even as its city was consumed with the politics of protest in the 2010s. Yet the seemingly permanent political crisis of Hong Kong threatened even the best laid plans.

By 2022 HKU faced a much different set of challenges. Not only did it have to compete with a host of excellent higher education institutions within Hong Kong—from whom it had not truly distanced itself—it faced also stiff competition from the increasingly internationalized universities of mainland China, Singapore, and the world. Provost Paul Tam had commented in 2015: "HKU is a global university, but it also has China as a hinterland, so we have to make the best use of our position to ensure that our research is relevant on the world stage and has world reputation, making use of the China factor, but also hoping to help China by bringing in the international aspect."[135] Just five years later, it was not China, but an embattled HKU that seemed isolated and in need of help.

Within the university, its governance issues had grown more acute. In late 2021, HKU withdrew recognition of its student union and ordered the removal of the *Pillar of Shame*, which for nearly a quarter-century had symbolized a commitment to freedom of speech.[136] HKU's Council had become a state-within-the-state, under a strong-willed chairman who at times acted like the former university president and government minister he had been, deeply compromising HKU's capacity for self-governance, let alone self-renewal.

President Xiang Zhang remained resolute. The University of Hong Kong, he told its faculty and students in late 2019, was "a citadel of freedom and knowledge, where we cherish civil and rational debate, and seek to find solutions with knowledge, wisdom, and imagination. I am here to support and promote a diverse and vibrant campus culture premised on openness, civility, and respect. . . . I know many of you are in pain, Hong Kong is in pain. It is time to think differently, to work on solutions and find ways forward together."[137]

# Conclusion

## *Lessons and Prospects*

THIS HAS been a book about the modern research
university in three of its most powerful settings—
Germany, the United States, and China—and in eight of its leading institutions. I posed a simple question: German universities set in place the foundations of modern universities everywhere in the nineteenth century; American universities had enormous international influence by the end of the twentieth century; what then are the prospects for Chinese leadership in the twenty-first century?

Before we address that final question, we must remember that none of these are static systems, frozen in place and time in earlier centuries. How might we assess, even briefly, the current trajectories of German and American higher education?

### A German Reawakening

Over the first two decades of the twenty-first century, German universities have witnessed gradual, consistent, and consequential changes that promise to reshape German higher education. First, the Excellence Initiative has introduced an enduring ethic of competition among leading institutions— places that *know* they are leading because they have been designated "Universities of Excellence." Second, the competition for "third party" funds (*Drittmittel*) has intensified greatly and is changing the landscape of German university funding. Third, a cluster of dynamic and innovative private universities has emerged, challenging the monopoly of state institutions not in numbers but in creativity.

The Excellence Initiative has shocked, energized, mobilized, and organized the modern German university since its announcement in 2005. The system as a whole had become complacent and comfortable with the egalitarian ethos that emerged from the turbulent 1960s and the massification of higher education in the 1970s and 1980s. Now, suddenly, excellence mattered again. It was a jolt when, in the very first set of Excellence awards announced in 2006, venerable Heidelberg was passed over in favor of its upstart neighbor, Karlsruhe, once a sleepy technical school. With strong leadership and Excellence funding, Karlsruhe University became the Karlsruhe Institute of Technology, or KIT, and the MIT at least of Baden-Württemberg. A leading center of nanotechnology, KIT ranked first among German universities in the physical sciences in 2020.[1] "People used to say elite was a dirty word," remarked Heidelberg's rector at the time, Peter Hommelhoff, but thanks to the Excellence Initiative, "the idea of elites is no longer a problem in Germany."[2]

Fifteen years later, it is clear that this nationwide competition and the resources that accompanied it have enabled German universities to attract and retain talent, expand and hone their research profiles, and become innovative, international hubs for research. The fact that the funding is not permanent is a further incentive to remain, in a formal sense, "excellent" or to find other sources of support. In short, the Excellence Initiative has made German universities academically entrepreneurial and, in many fields, newly competitive internationally. In 2017, as the second round of Excellence funding was drawing to a close, a lively debate about the future of the initiative and of German universities themselves took place in the political sphere and in the press. Among the solutions offered was the idea that the federal government establish several elite universities, leaving the others to be run by the states.[3] This would take a page out of the Chinese book, where extraordinary resources are given to Tsinghua and Peking Universities, leaving the rest to fight it out for recognition. But despite—or perhaps because of—the University of Berlin serving as a de facto national university in the nineteenth century, this revived vision did not materialize. Meanwhile, it seems likely that the Excellence funding, now under the title "Excellence Strategy" (*Exzellenzstrategie*), which commenced in 2019, will remain a central part of German higher education. Another opportunity for universities to receive funding under the Excellence Strategy will take place in 2026 and will bring new applicants into the mix. But, as the strategy aims to encourage competition, sustained or permanent funding for all selected clusters, graduate schools, and universities remains conditional on performance. This, in my view, is a very good thing.

The quasi-permanence of the Excellence Initiative funding reflects the directive planning of Germany's Federal Ministry of Education and Research for German universities, which had historically been funded by the individual states. Federal government investment in extra-university institutions has also increased dramatically, in some cases displacing universities as the centers of research excellence. Nonuniversity institutions with long histories, such as the Max Planck Society and the Leibniz Association, carry out research with an international pedigree, untethered to teaching responsibilities. In research published in leading journals in the natural sciences, Max Planck institutes ranked third in the world in 2020—trailing the Chinese Academy of Sciences and Harvard University.[4]

The perpetual competition for resources seems certain to remain a distinguishing feature of the German academy in the future. Third-party funding today increases a scholar's prospects of academic success and supports many of the most innovative projects. The German Research Foundation publishes a "Funding Atlas" (*Förderatlas*) that shows which institutions have received what funding for which projects across German universities, revealing the status of third-party funding as an overall measure of a university's quality.[5] This development has not met with universal praise: critics charge that tying universities to their ability to attract funding makes market-worthiness the distinguishing metric of the academy.[6] Still, the ability to attract external funding remains a significant—if not the most significant—factor in influencing a scholar and a university's standing. It shows no sign of fading.

Where external markets have truly entered the world of German universities is in the private sector. The largest and best-known research universities remain all public institutions. But in the first decades of the twenty-first century, a handful of private universities have sprouted, with specialized and distinguishing offerings. These private initiatives aim to bring to Germany international models of education, be it campus life or truly international degree programs. They are financed through nonprofit foundations (*Stiftungen*). The first of these, Jacobs University in Bremen, was founded in 1999 as the International University Bremen with the support of the University of Bremen, Rice University in the United States, and the City of Bremen and opened its doors to students in 2001. Located in a former Nazi barracks that was used for displaced persons after the war, the university aimed to bring the American campus experience to an international community of students in Bremen, a port city with historic global ties. In 2006, after years of financial trouble and wavering commitment of the city, the Jacobs Foundation rescued the university and took on a controlling stake. "We are small, innovative and agile," its ambitious young president, Katja Windt, told me in 2016. In 2021 the university offered fifteen degree programs in English ranging from BA to PhD, teaching a total of 1,500 students.

Not long after Jacobs was founded, two other private institutions appeared on the scene. In 2003 the Hertie School opened its doors near Humboldt University in Berlin. The school offered English language degree programs, targeting German and international students seeking professional training in public administration and governance. As of 2019, 687 students were enrolled as the school planned its move to a larger campus at the renovated Robert Koch Forum near the Reichstag, a complex of Wilhelmine buildings that were originally the home of the natural scientific and medical institutes of the University of Berlin.[7]

History is inescapable in Germany. The Hertie Foundation that funds the Hertie School stems from the retail chain that founded the modern department store in Germany. Its business was "aryanized" by the Nazis in 1933, the assets seized, and its owners forced into exile. A postwar settlement allowed Hertie stores to return across the West German (and West Berlin) landscape, and the philanthropic foundation was founded in the 1970s.

A different story can be found farther south. Around the same time that the Hertie School opened, on the shores of Lake Constance in the southern state of Baden-Württemberg, another private institution welcomed its first class of undergraduates. At Zeppelin University in Friedrichshafen, hand-picked cohorts of students arrive to study the intersections of business, technology, and culture in modern facilities. Its research focuses on globalization, cultural production, and the computational social sciences. The university is supported by the Zeppelin Foundation, whose funding was derived from the fortune of the airship company founded by Ferdinand Graf von Zeppelin at the beginning of the century. The *Graf Zeppelin II*, named for the late count, was a sister ship of the *Hindenburg* and the last of its kind. When the *Hindenburg* went down in flames in 1937, the company turned to making V-2 rockets to attack England during World War II. Not quite the Hertie story.

Zeppelin University (ZU) aims not to be rooted in the German past but to be "the university of the 21st century" that "bridges business, culture, and politics." Its curriculum stresses interdisciplinarity and innovation, encouraging students and faculty to work closely with businesses and entrepreneurs. Its selective admissions process distinguishes it from German state universities, as it requires a written application and interview. It emphasizes that old principle of the unity of teaching and research and small class size in its fourteen bachelor's and master's degree programs, as well as in its doctoral courses. Its program in economic sciences was ranked first (tied with Frankfurt) among German universities in 2020–2021.[8] Students spend their final "Humboldt Year" on a research project at one of its eighty-five international partner universities. Perhaps taking a swipe at the censorship at leading Chinese universities (remember the "seven forbidden topics" on Chinese campuses?), the first principle of ZU's mission statement is this: a university "has to be a place where every question is allowed." ZU's current president, Klaus Mühlhahn, a former vice president of Free University of Berlin, is a leading historian of modern China.[9]

The three institutions just discussed remain exceptions in German higher education. Their small size and comparatively large endowments allow them a degree of flexibility that eludes their public counterparts. In particular, the small size, English language degree programs, and campus environment offered by the undergraduate bachelor's programs at Jacobs and Zeppelin Universities have made them attractive destinations for German and international students and, perhaps, models for more established universities. In 2012 the University of Freiburg founded the first "university college" in Germany. Freiburg followed a model that has been brilliantly successful in the Netherlands, where, most notably, Amsterdam University College was founded as an elite college of the liberal arts and sciences in partnership with two major research universities.[10] University College Freiburg offers a four-year liberal arts program to undergraduates from across the world, paralleling in many ways the American small college experience but nested within a large research institution. The degree program is conducted in English, and the class size is kept deliberately small: annual intake averages eighty students per year.

In sum, between the Excellence Initiative, with its compelled competition and forced planning; the growing strength of research foundations and the scope of "third party" funding; and the educational start-up culture seen at Hertie, Jacobs, Zeppelin, and Freiburg, the German scene is more dynamic and imaginative than anyone could have predicted two decades ago. German universities were once purveyors of best practices in higher education. They are now among the keenest consumers of the lessons found in global university systems. They are taking the best of the Chinese model of state commitment and financial incentives, and, at the edges, of the American experience of the innovative possibilities of private universities.[11]

German universities may not again dominate the global stage, but they are, once again, centers of excellence and innovation.

## The United States: The Trials of Public Higher Education

From most external perspectives—and certainly from the viewpoint of Europe or Asia—American universities remain the envy of the world. Judging from the Academic Ranking of World Universities in 2021, eight of the ten leading universities in the world were American—and seventeen of the top twenty-five. The *Times Higher Education World University Rankings* is similarly generous (eight of the top ten, if only fifteen of the top twenty-five). Even the 2021 QS World University Rankings, historically tougher on the Americans, gives them half of the top ten and twenty-five slots.

Yet within the United States there is a broad and deep anxiety about the future of American higher education. A sizeable cottage industry of books has grown up bewailing the limits, failings, or demise of American universities. The former Harvard president, Derek Bok, has written about *Our Underachieving Colleges.* My learned colleague in Harvard's English Department, Jim Engell, worries about *Saving Higher Education in the Age of Money.* On a similar theme, Duke University's Charles Clotfelter has authored *Unequal Colleges in the Age of Disparity.* The former chancellor of the University of North Carolina, Holden Thorp, has written of the need to "rebuild the partnership between America and its colleges." James Shulman, then of the Mellon Foundation, collaborated with Princeton's former president, William G. Bowen, to study *The Game of Life* and how collegiate sports in the United States have warped educational values. The American Academy of Arts and Sciences, apart from worrying that the humanities are no longer *The Heart of the Matter,* warned about *The Perils of Complacency* in American science and engineering. Oxford's Simon Marginson, invited by Berkeley to give the Clark Kerr Lectures on the Role of Higher Education in Society, concluded that *The Dream is Over.* Others believe that the most important agenda for American education is now *Surpassing Shanghai.* American higher education has become a *Palace of Ashes,* according to another book, the subtitle of which is *China and the Decline of American Higher Education.*[12]

Critiques of access and inequality have become increasingly numerous and sharp. Anthony Abraham Jack describes how even lower-income students given scholarships to elite colleges remain *The Privileged Poor*. Elizabeth Armstrong and Laura Hamilton unmask the social and cultural effects of "Greek" and "party" life for students of lower socioeconomic backgrounds. Sara Goldrick-Rab calls the crisis of affordability and the United States's extraordinary number of dropouts a *Betrayal of the American Dream*. Tressie McMillan Cottom calls American for-profit colleges *Lower Ed* and highlights how they exacerbate inequalities. And Jennifer Hirsch and Shamus Khan, in *Sexual Citizens,* explore the pervasive nature of sexual assault on university campuses.[13]

The critique of leading institutions is a healthy part of American political life. And perhaps there is no market for books about what's right with American universities. But these books, collectively, serve as a powerful early warning system that the age of American ascendency and hubris may be coming to an end, in the world of universities as in other realms.

There is much to worry about in the very uneven state of private colleges and universities in the United States. Our two examples of Harvard and Duke, for all their challenges, should be among the least concerned. To be sure, Harvard, as a historically second-wave innovator and comparatively risk-averse, faces the danger of what Richard Brodhead called "the inertia of excellence." (Harvard has not absorbed the lesson of Duke's Peter Lange that "the greater your reputation, the greater your capacity to take risk.")[14] But it is truly in the realm of public higher education, which we explored in detail in the case of Berkeley, that the United States should be very worried indeed.

Six of the world's twenty-five leading universities in the ARWU tables are public American institutions. All but one of these six have come under severe financial pressure in the past several decades because of a common, nationwide phenomenon: the American disinvestment from public higher education.

We have seen some of the consequences of disinvestment at Berkeley, where a once proud and mission-driven campus devolved into turmoil and backbiting, driven in good measure by an enduring economy of scarcity. What is true at Berkeley is true, in some measure, across the University of California system.[15] The state of California made a commitment in 1911 to fund the UC system in proportion to its growth: as the state expanded and enrollments grew, so too would state support of higher education. Not anymore. The University of California has maintained the commitment in Clark Kerr's Master Plan to admit the top 12.5 percent of California high school graduates. But as enrollments grew from 166,500 in 1990 to 291,200 in 2020,[16] the state scaled back its commitment. Economic downturns in the early 1990s, in 2001, and, especially, in 2008, were each accompanied by cuts in public funding for the UC system. The state spent 18 percent of its budget on higher education in the mid-1970s, but only 12 percent in 2017. The UC itself received 8.1 percent of the state's general funds in 1996–1997; ten years later that figure was 2.5 percent.[17] In the year 2000 the state supported 24 percent of the UC operating budget. By 2014 that number had fallen to 10 percent, and it has fallen further since. In 1988 the state expended approximately $25,000 (in inflation-adjusted dollars) per UC and California State University student; by 2015 it was closer to $10,000. What the state no longer funds is paid for by higher tuition. In-state students at UC Berkeley paid $4,050 in 2000, a figure that had risen to $14,250 in 2019–2020. One could go on and on with such statistics, but they all tell the same story.[18]

California is always a first-mover. It has led in both the rise and decline of public higher education in the United States. What in 2009 Berkeley Chancellor Robert Birgeneau called California's "completely irresponsible disinvestment in the future of its public universities"[19] is now a national phenomenon. Across the country, state support for public colleges and universities (measured as funding per full-time student) declined 30 percent between 2000 and 2014. Whereas nationwide, state appropriations accounted for 32 percent of revenue per public university student in 2000, by 2016 it was but 18 percent. By 2020 state funding for public higher education nationwide remained 9 percent below pre-2008 levels (that is, before the Great Recession) and 18 percent below the level of 2001. In 2009 Birgeneau proposed that the US government pass "a 21st-century version of the Morrill Act" to reinvigorate flagship public universities with federal funds.[20] Nothing came of that. As one analyst of higher education funding noted in 2020, "With every recession, funding for higher ed has had steeper declines and shallower recoveries."[21] We shall see if this is true also for the economic recession induced by the COVID-19 pandemic. With rising tuition making up much of the shortfall, more students incurred debt: 54 percent of public university students graduated with some student loan debt in 2012–2013, with nearly 20 percent owing more than $20,000. Nearly 70 percent of American college graduates in 2019 (here counting both private and public institutions) took out student loans; their average debt was $29,900.[22] The growing debt and its consequences are particularly pronounced for less affluent students of color.[23]

In the financing of higher education, California was by no means the worst performer. By 2020 it was among seven states to return to pre-2008 levels of overall education appropriation per full-time equivalent student (albeit in current dollars). Another seven states were more than 30 percent below their pre-2008 levels of funding. The others were somewhere in between.[24] In short, that means that forty-three of the fifty American states had disinvested in public higher education since 2008.

Why is there so little public support for public universities? It is not hard to understand how leading American private universities can become lightning rods for public criticism. Harvard may be perceived as elite, aloof, and unfathomably rich. Why not tax its endowment? But why do not the citizens of Alabama take as much pride in their public University of Alabama as they do in the success of the Crimson Tide, the university football team? It is a mystery to me. Perhaps it is the result of a renewed American aversion to paying taxes for anything. Public institutions in the United States educate three-quarters of all American university students. They count among their ranks many of the world's leading universities. It is an ongoing tragedy when even the states most historically supportive of public higher education, such as California and Michigan, fail to reinvest in their extraordinary flagship institutions. As the *New York Times* columnist Bob Herbert wrote in 2009, "It will say a great deal about what kind of nation we've become if we let these most valuable assets slip into a period of decline."[25]

Make no mistake: the slow-motion defunding of US public higher education will have consequences also for the private schools, the Stanfords and the Harvards. If the public universities decline, so in time will the private ones, who compete with their public counterparts for the same faculty, graduate students, and senior administrators. There is no greater threat to the leading position of American higher education than America's growing parsimony in the support of public higher education. I had a premonitory shiver in 1991, when I was considering taking a senior leadership position at the University of Washington. I had been invited to a private dinner with the university's president, the late Bill Gerberding. The president was delayed in arriving, being held up in meetings with the legislature on the university's budget. I will never forget his arrival. He came in, wordlessly, and he ordered an enormous Scotch. Then he told me: "You know, Mr. Kirby, this is a much better university than the taxpayers of this state deserve."

# Lessons

Before we turn to the future, and the role of Chinese universities, let us think of what we have learned through our case studies on factors that may enhance, or retard, a university's quest to be among the best. For this we should first return to several of the founding principles of Humboldt.

First, we can be reassured that the primary and *new* mission assigned to universities by Humboldt and his successors—the pursuit of *Wissenschaft*, of knowledge pure and applied—has succeeded far beyond his or anyone of his generation's imagination. Ideas and inventions developed in universities have empowered nation-states, such as Germany, the United States, and China, in war and in peace, and the reach of university research has expanded fantastically (to the Moon? to Mars? to an exoplanet?). It is no accident that universities have been at the forefront of the medical, epidemiological, and public health research that has led to treatments, vaccines, and public health strategies for COVID-19 in the third decade of the twenty-first century.

Second, Humboldt's commitment to an education rooted in the arts and sciences—idealistic in his own time, when most university students pursued forms of professional education—has endured, surprisingly, across two centuries of the evolution of the research university. It became, and it remains, the foundation of American undergraduate education in most public and private universities. It has been re-imported into Germany, thanks in part to the Excellence Initiative and its high level of support for the humanities and social sciences; and because of the example next door, in the Netherlands, of university colleges of arts and sciences that have enrolled no small number of German students and which set the stage for experiments such as we have seen at Freiburg.

One of the more striking developments in elite Chinese higher education in the twenty-first century is the independent understanding that the general education of China's students—in the arts and humanities as well as the sciences and social sciences—will be as important as their specialized, professional training. "General education" (*tongshi jiaoyu* and other formulations) is now a cornerstone of curricular reform throughout the People's Republic, as well as in Hong Kong and Taiwan. Nanjing University's efforts are among the most ambitious, requiring all students to complete a shared general education curriculum before choosing their major.

Why are Chinese educational leaders, at least in the elite institutions, experimenting with general education in the arts and sciences? They believe that they need to do this in part because in China, as in the United States, as in Germany, all the pressures are in the opposite direction—on the part of students, who too single-mindedly pursue their careers, and on the part of faculty, whose careers and interests are ever more specialized—leading to a situation in which students and faculty interact on ever-more-narrow ground. It would be nice, as Henry Rosovsky once declared, if it were true that precisely what the faculty wanted to teach was exactly what the students needed to learn. But as Dean Rosovsky knew, that has never been the case, and it is the job of leading universities to ensure that our students learn broadly from the best faculty how to think, to reflect, to analyze, and to become the critical thinkers and problem-solvers of the next generation. For this, in my judgment, a study of the humanities remains essential. And—despite the increased pressures of political oversight on their campuses—this is a view shared broadly by the presidents of China's top universities. Perhaps this is because they know, better than anyone else, what life can be like in the absence of the humanities. For that is part of the tragedy of China's mid-century Maoism, which is deeply remembered, if not much talked about.

Third, governance matters, today as much as in any period. Humboldt's ideal of a university with the autonomy to govern itself, to make its own appointments, set its own curricula, and chart its future insulated from the politics of the day has never come to pass, not the least for universities founded by, and in some sense for, the state. (That would include every one of the universities chronicled in this book, except Duke.) Yet the broad degree of academic independence that characterized the University of Berlin in its first century, where professorial appointments were made largely on the basis of proven excellence or exceptional promise, would come to define how the "tenure-track" system would evolve in the United States and, in recent decades, again in China.

Beyond faculty appointments, there is no single or easy measure of good governance in universities. Harvard is the oldest of the institutions we have studied, with the oldest set of governing boards. Harvard's president, you will recall, is selected by, and is responsible to, not the Commonwealth of Massachusetts but the Harvard Corporation, a self-perpetuating body that consisted of but seven members from 1650 to 2010. This small and secretive structure worked well when it had outstanding leadership (for example, under Robert Stone, a Corporation member from 1975 to 2002). But a crisis of governance and confidence in both the president and the Corporation in 2005–2006 led in time to an expanded (thirteen members), more expert, less clubby board. It is still a remarkably small and private board for an enterprise with an annual budget of more than $5 billion and a community of some forty thousand students, faculty, and staff. Duke University, by contrast, has long had a larger board of trustees (thirty-five in 2021) from a range of professions and industries, and with multiple committees. It has been deeply and publicly engaged in the strategic planning that has come to define Duke.

"Not everything is improved by making it more democratic." This was Henry Rosovsky's first principle of university governance.[26] Surely the experiences of an ultra-democratic and increasingly ungovernable Berkeley would bear out this observation. So too, after the fall of the Berlin Wall, would the experience of the newly democratized Humboldt University, with its revolving-door rectorships and presidencies.

In these universities simplicity and clarity of governance would appear to trump complexity. The dual-governance structure of contemporary Chinese universities, with the Party secretary elevated above the president, and with Party secretaries in every major school alongside the deans, aims to keep universities aligned with Party priorities; but Chinese universities have grown in stature despite, not because of, the intrusion of Party oversight.

Fourth, leadership matters, not only at the presidential level but also at the next and the next levels down. Harvard had Charles Eliot and Berkeley had Clark Kerr, two individuals who profoundly altered the future of their institutions. One might add the name of Friedrich Althoff, who was never rector of the University of Berlin but who, as the de facto Minister of Culture in Prussia, did as much to shape it as an institution as anyone else. There is no shortage of books on presidential leadership in universities, usually written by former presidents—the successful ones presumably.[27] Much less is written about the individuals who run the universities day-to-day, with a long-term perspective on their future.

Free University would likely not be among the leading German universities today were it not for the extraordinary (and extraordinarily quiet) work of Peter Lange, who served the university for three decades, the last fifteen as *Kanzler,* or financial vice president. His cross-Atlantic namesake, Peter Lange of Duke, spearheaded Duke's internationalization as a faculty member and oversaw its academic and financial integration in his fifteen years as provost. In this work he partnered closely with another long-timer, Tallman Trask III, the executive vice president overseeing both administration and finances—a man who, like FU's Peter Lange, knew where the money was and how to get it, quietly.

Every great university has such individuals who do quietly transformative work outside the limelight of the presidency. At Berkeley, Provost George Breslauer kept the lights on and the university running at the depth of the financial collapse after 2009. At Harvard, Provost Harvey Fineberg, who established the position, and two long-term successors, Stephen Hyman and Alan Garber, have had the Sisyphean labor of knitting together a far-flung university of independent kingdoms that share little connective tissue. At Tsinghua, Dean Qian Yingyi was the transformative and long-term dean of the School of Economics and Management, where he experimented with general education reforms that would have an impact on the whole university. His former deputy dean, Yang Bin, has risen to be provost and vice president of Tsinghua and chairman of the Tsinghua University Education Foundation, the university's endowment. Yang Bin's real portfolio includes much more, including Tsinghua's international partnerships at home and abroad. He is provost, vice president, and minister of foreign affairs at Tsinghua, to name only his better-known responsibilities. His long, discrete, and powerfully effective service has made him one of the most trusted and influential voices in Chinese higher education. To this list I must add the name of Hao Ping. He is currently president of Peking University and formerly its Party secretary. Before that, and perhaps most consequentially, he was China's vice minister of education who oversaw—and gave critical support to—all the major joint-venture initiatives between Chinese and international universities: the University of Nottingham Ningbo; Xi'an Jiaotong-Liverpool University in Suzhou; New York University Shanghai; Duke Kunshan University; and Schwarzman College at Tsinghua University. It is not too much to say that Hao Ping is the Friedrich Althoff of the internationalization of Chinese higher education.

Leadership matters also at the board level. I have mentioned the tenure of Bob Stone on the Harvard Corporation, a man who was known, rightly, as "Mr. Harvard" over the course of three university presidencies. Rick Wagoner was a powerfully positive chair of the Duke board when Duke was establishing its campus in China, a place Wagoner knew well from his time as CEO of General Motors. Victor Fung, as chair of the Council of the University of Hong Kong, accomplished more in his tenure than did many presidents in theirs. Fung spearheaded the re-imagination of HKU as a leading university in Asia and the world. He reformed an archaic set of governance boards, making the council leaner and stronger. He reformed

HKU's appointment, promotion, and tenure processes. And, with his unique combination of intelligence, persistence, and personal modesty, he built a new consensus among faculty and students as to what HKU could be. It is sad that so much of his work has been undone by a successor.

Fifth, money matters (a lot), but success is measured in how you plan to use it. Harvard's great wealth allows it to do much more, and at a higher level, than any university on Earth. It maintains a culture of excellence in appointing faculty—the individuals who will be both the recipients and spenders of university funds. Its resources have allowed it to survive its own fiscal mismanagement in and around the recession of 2008. But uniquely among the universities we have encountered in this book, the management and use of Harvard's resources are still widely dispersed across individual schools, with broadly excellent but inevitably uneven leadership. The university still seems to lack the capacity or even the will to do deep, university-wide strategic planning—the kind of planning that has allowed Duke, in certain areas, to do more with much less. Planning has mattered critically, too, to FU's success in the Excellence Initiative. For without the detailed assessment of its own capacities and ambitions, FU could never have been competitive for, much less received, the financial and reputational rewards of being a "University of Excellence." There is wide adoption of strategic planning among Chinese universities, too. This has helped to realize their ambitions to rise in the rankings of global higher education. Yet what Chinese universities plan for, and what they can actually do, may depend on the priorities of the Chinese Party-State—sometimes to their detriment, as in the case Nanjing University.

Planning for higher education at the national level can make a difference. Just compare the roles of today's German Federal Ministry of Education and Research and the (more powerful) Chinese Ministry of Education with the absent or invisible U.S. Department of Education in the funding, promotion, and guidance of higher education.

Berkeley and our two Berlin universities are examples of how great universities can be brought nearly to their knees by financial crises; and of these three, FU stands out as the best managed. Our Chinese universities, by contrast, do not want for resources at present, however unevenly they may be distributed. Their resources and domestic rankings are almost preordained. For the foreseeable future China will have two "number one" universities; seven others content to be in the C9; and everyone else. For all of them, as

I suggested earlier, the test is not how good you are when the funds are flooding in; it is how you fare when they dry up. If history is any guide, that day will come, but we are not there yet.

## Can China Lead the World of Universities?

This is the question with which I began this research more than eight years ago. Then, the trajectory of Chinese higher education was unrelentingly upward, in values as in accomplishments. China's was an educational landscape of ambition, with a diversity of institutions. The PRC showed a willingness to take risks, for example by welcoming international partners to found new institutions in China. If, in the first half of the twentieth century, China could build one of the strongest small systems of higher education, how could it not succeed when it addressed the challenge of building at scale—China scale?

As Germany retools and revives its universities, and as America disinvests, at least from its public institutions, China has shown an unmatched ambition to build more of the best, "world-class" universities than anyone else. To this effort it has mobilized both state and private resources, and it has at hand more of the best human capital—Chinese scholars at home or in the diaspora—than any university system in the world.

Chinese universities continue to rise in the various rankings tables, and two of them, Tsinghua and Beida, will surely be among the world's top ten in short order. For their ascent is a factor both of their own growing excellence and the broader geopolitical rise of China.

The rise of China and its modern universities has been coterminous with periods of openness and internationalization. Germany, the United States, and the Soviet Union have at different times and places all played the role of partner. The very short period of Chinese "self-reliance" during Mao's Cultural Revolution was a near-death experience for Chinese universities. There is little question that Chinese universities will continue their international engagement, but in which direction?

### *A Chinese Model Along the New Silk Road?*

In 2021 Chinese universities remain open to the world, but they are also open to official redefinition. As we have seen, President Xi Jinping aspires to build Chinese universities that are singular and distinctive from their international partners: not China's Harvard, but China's Tsinghua, China's Nanda. And Chinese universities have been mobilized for a new national goal: China going abroad along the "New Silk Road" (NSR), presumably to provide Chinese models for higher education in Central Asia, Africa, and even Europe. The NSR metaphor invokes the legacy of land-based trading routes across Eurasia that, at specific points in history, connected East and Central Asian markets to those of the Middle East and Mediterranean. These were famously termed the *Seidenstraße*, or Silk Road, by the German explorer Ferdinand von Richthofen in 1877. In economic terms, the Silk Road has been as moribund in modern times as it was for large stretches of history. Yet President Xi Jinping's 2015 announcement that higher education cooperation was to be an important element of the NSR suggested that the initiative might make the "New Silk Road" a conduit for ideas.

What are the implications of the rise and internationalization of Chinese higher education for the NSR, otherwise known by the less metaphorical name, the "Belt and Road Initiative"? This ambitious concept of multilayered cooperation between China and over 130 Eurasian, African, and Latin American countries is predicated on Chinese institutions "going out" into the world to make their mark, be it in business, infrastructure, or education. By deploying the Silk Road metaphor and legacy to support the initiative, the NSR seems to redirect, at least rhetorically, the trajectory of Chinese higher education's historically Western-focused internationalization.

Chinese universities are expanding abroad, some along a generous interpretation of the Silk Road: Suzhou University in Laos took in its first students in 2012; the Yunnan University of Finance and Economics (YUFE) set up the YUFE Business School in Bangkok in 2014; and Xiamen University established its Malaysia campus in 2015. But larger efforts still have gone toward established centers of higher education. The Beijing Language and Culture University (BLCU) partnered with Japan's ISI Corporation to establish BLCU Tokyo College in 2015. In 2016 the first wholly owned Chinese tertiary institute in Australia, the Global Business College of Australia, welcomed its first class of students. In 2019 Beijing Normal University (BNU) and Cardiff University (CU) in Wales, agreed to build the BNU-CU Chinese College in Cardiff.[28] In 2020 the Peking University HSBC Business School opened the "first [completed] Chinese campus in the developed world," in Oxfordshire, England in a neo-Gothic and modern campus inherited from Britain's Open University.[29] As noted, Tsinghua University and the University of Washington, both partnering with Microsoft, founded a

391

dual-degree program known as the Global Innovation Exchange in 2015 and have completed the first Chinese university research facility in the United States. Its home is the new, one-hundred-thousand-square-foot Steve Ballmer Building, named for the Microsoft co-founder (and Harvard graduate). And in June 2021 Fudan University in Shanghai announced plans to construct its European campus in Budapest.

Chinese students, who have long "gone out" to seek education abroad (more than 700,000 in 2019), have largely flown over or by NSR countries to seek their education in North America, Australia, the United Kingdom, the European Union, or Japan. Students from NSR countries have indeed come to China to study in increasing numbers, and scientists from NSR countries have been recruited to newly established "Belt and Road" laboratories. But at the moment, this is a one-way road. Precious few Chinese find their way to graduate programs in Karachi or Almaty. Aiding China's rise as a destination for international students is the recent surge of nationalism in the United States and United Kingdom, long the top destinations for international students, which has led students to increasingly consider institutions in alternative locations. This development may "internationalize" Chinese universities in new ways. As of 2021 the rhetoric and propaganda of the NSR has outpaced the development of a coherent strategy on the Chinese side. Higher education cooperation along the New Silk Road can make Chinese universities more "international" in their posture, but the nature of such institutional exchanges may do little to aid Chinese universities' pursuit of "world-class status."[30] Just as Richthofen's *Seidenstraße* invented a history of Eurasian exchange that was less robust and coherent than his imagination of it, the implications of the NSR for the internationalization of Chinese education are likely to be less significant than many envision.

The point here is that leading Chinese universities have been, and see themselves as, a part of a web of elite global institutions, and today they measure themselves above all vis-à-vis their counterparts in Europe and North America. They may have ever more students from the New Silk Road countries, but they recruit their faculty from, and focus on building their premier research partnerships with, the leading "Western" universities. Today, the path toward global excellence of Chinese universities still lies clearly in cooperation and competition with European and American institutions.

So, is there a "Chinese model" for universities that may be exported, along the New Silk Road or anywhere else? Is there such a thing as "a university with Chinese characteristics"? The answer is basically no. What distinguishes leading Chinese universities today is how they have grown as part of an international system of higher education and research, now buttressed by enviable financial support from the Chinese state. Like the Americans, who developed universities of a high reputation by plagiarizing the norms of German and British institutions, Chinese universities have learned from other global leaders over the past century, be they European, American, or Soviet. In university governance, for example, the "Chinese model" of the role of Party secretaries is hardly a Chinese invention. One can find the same in every "socialist brother country," as we have seen with Humboldt University in East German times. This is not, in any event, a readily exportable model at present, unless your export market is North Korea.

This is not to say that Chinese universities partake in all of the trends of contemporary international universities. In the United States, along with accessibility, there is increasing focus on issues of diversity and inclusion, particularly regarding students of color. There is no evidence that these issues are front and center in China.[31] As we have seen, the idea of universities as political sites is actively resisted by Chinese authorities. This is doubly true at present, as the Chinese Communist Party renews its attempt to assimilate and "make Chinese" China's multiple ethnic and religious minorities.

## Can Chinese Universities Lead?

The greatest challenge confronting Chinese universities today is not the competition they face abroad but the obstruction they encounter at home. In many private conversations with Chinese educational leaders, past and present, I have asked this question: What is your greatest problem? The answer, invariably, is "the Party." The founding ideals of great institutions such as Peking University and Tsinghua University remain in tension with a powerful—and powerfully insecure—Chinese Communist Party, which limits debate in multiple realms of the humanities and social sciences, even as Chinese researchers become recognized as global leaders in the pure and applied sciences. There is enduring anxiety in the Party that universities can be—as they have been throughout modern Chinese history—powerful centers of dissent.

When the founder of China's first modern university, Governor-General Zhang Zhidong, wrote his *Exhortation to Study* in 1898, he stressed that "Chinese learning" (education in the classics) had to remain the foundation, while "Western learning" was for "practical matters." Chinese political leaders today continue to distinguish between "Chinese" and "Western" values. In Chinese government policy today, a new version of "Chinese learning" is often given official pride of place over "Western learning." At least in Zhang Zhidong's day, people knew what Chinese learning—a deep education in the classical canon—meant. Today, it is "socialism with Chinese characteristics" and the "guiding role of Marxism in ideology," according to the former Minister of Education, Yuan Guiren, who suggested that to arm themselves against "Western values," students should study the theories of President Xi Jinping.[32] Compared to the Four Books and Five Classics of the traditional canon, this is thin gruel indeed. As a system born of international influences and massively strengthened by Chinese government support, Chinese higher education faces an ideological tightening not seen since the Cultural Revolution.

At the end of the day, can "world-class" universities—however they are defined—exist in a politically illiberal system? In a country where there are "seven topics" that must never be broached? The answer is yes, if we recall the German university of the nineteenth century, where political orthodoxy was seldom questioned. Yet Wilhelmine Germany was no match for contemporary China in its control of political and historical narratives. Is there room today, for example, in the study of Chinese history, for a Chinese Mommsen or a Chinese Meinecke? Perhaps, but as Cai Yuanpei argued a century ago, only with a significant degree of autonomy within the walls of the university. German universities in the nineteenth century had many political pressures, but they valued traditions of institutional and intellectual freedom. China's universities today boast superb scholars and among the world's most talented students. China's university leaders have been among the best in the world. But in recent ideological campaigns, its students are forced to sit through required courses in Party ideology, and they learn a comic book version of the history of their own nation. Despite excellent new programs of general education, in the realm of politics and history the distance between what students have to learn in order to graduate, and what they know to be true, grows greater every year. In this environment, China's great universities—which have the responsibility to produce leaders for China and the world in the twenty-first century—face the prospect of graduating two kinds of students: cynics and opportunists. For these students know, as do the eminent scholars who teach them, that world-class universities are places where there is not a *single* topic that cannot be addressed, let alone seven.

But let us not end so pessimistically. No civilization has a longer or more enduringly successful record than China of educating, examining, and promoting talent to serve state and society. Over the course of the past 130 years, modern universities have propelled China to the first ranks in science and engineering, while—whenever political circumstances have permitted—also promoting the values of open inquiry that have marked the world's leading institutions of higher learning. After all, it was at a Chinese university (Peking University) that Marxism was introduced to China a century ago.

Chinese universities were founded in the late Qing dynasty, they flourished in the early Republic, and several became notable national institutions of international repute under the Nationalist government. They educated young Chinese leaders from the back country of Free China during World War II. They survived war, civil war, sovietization, and the Cultural Revolution. They have outlived an empire, several republics, and multiple incarnations of the People's Republic of China. They have seen political campaigns, such as the current ones, come and go. They must take the long view. So should we.

The most compelling statement of the principles and values of contemporary research universities was announced at the 2013 annual meeting of China's C9 universities in the city of Hefei, west of Nanjing, home to the University of Science and Technology of China. The statement, now known the world over at the "Hefei Statement on the Ten Characteristics of Contemporary Research Universities," was drawn up in concert with the Association of American Universities, the League of European Research Universities, and Australia's Group of Eight universities.[33] In its commitment to research integrity, academic freedom, and institutional autonomy, the Hefei Statement is a powerful, twenty-first-century articulation of Humboldtian values. For the leaders of Chinese universities in 2021, several of these principles may seem more aspirational than achieved, but they set out, accurately in my view, the shared ambitions of great universities the world over.

Can Chinese universities set global standards in the twenty-first century? Yes, of course. But not alone. Chinese universities have grown and flourished on international models and in partnership with the great institutions of Europe and North America. It is that company that they wish to keep, to compete in, and to lead.

# Notes

## Preface

1. William C. Kirby, *The World of Universities in the 21st Century: The 2017 Kuo Ting-yee Memorial Lectures* (Taipei: Institute of Modern History, Academia Sinica, 2019).

## Introduction

1. *All India Survey on Higher Education 2019-20* (New Delhi: Ministry of Education, 2020), 1.
2. See Wikipedia, "List of Universities in North Korea," https://en.wikipedia .org/wiki/List_of_universities_in_North_Korea.
3. For alternative numbers see "Countries Arranged by Number of Universities in Top Ranks," July 2021 edition, http://www.webometrics.info/en/distribution _by_country.
4. Sheldon Rothblatt, *The Modern University and its Discontents* (Cambridge: Cambridge University Press, 1997), 1.
5. Paul Kennedy, *Rise and Fall of the Great Powers: Economic Change and Military Conflict* (New York: Vintage Books, 1987); David Landes, *The Wealth and Poverty of Nations* (New York: Norton, 1998); Daron Acemoglu and James A. Robinson, *Why Nations Fail* (New York: Crown Business, 2012); Charles S. Maier, *Among Empires* (Cambridge, MA: Harvard University Press, 2006).
6. Landes, *Wealth and Poverty*, 409.
7. Sharan B. Merriam, *Case Study Research in Education: A Qualitative Approach* (San Francisco: Jossey-Bass Publishers, 1988), xiii. See also Robert E. Stake, *The Art of Case Study Research* (Thousand Oaks, CA: SAGE Publications, 1995).
8. See "Teaching by the Case Method," https://www.hbs.edu/teaching/case -method/Pages/default.aspx.

9. L. W. B. Brockliss, "The European University 1789–1850," in *University of Oxford*, VI, Part I, 131–133, cited in *A History of the University in Europe: Volume III, Universities in the Nineteenth and Early Twentieth Centuries (1800–1945)*, Walter Rüegg, ed. (Cambridge: Cambridge University Press, 2004), 11.

10. Phillip Altbach, foreword to *Indian Higher Education: Envisioning the Future* by Pawan Agarwal (Thousand Oaks, CA: SAGE Publications, 2009), xi–xii.

11. Arvind Panagariya, "Higher Education: A New Dawn—National Education Policy 2020 Offers Transformative Road Map for Colleges and Universities," *Times of India*, August 19, 2020, https://timesofindia.indiatimes.com/blogs/toi-edit-page/higher-education-a-new-dawn-national-education-policy-2020-offers-transformative-road-map-for-colleges-and-universities/, accessed March 9, 2020.

12. Jamil Salmi, *The Challenge of Establishing World-Class Universities* (Washington, DC: World Bank, 2009), 1–2.

13. Tsinghua University, *Qinghua daxue shiye fazhan shi er wu guihua gangyao* [Outline of Tsinghua University's Twelfth Five-Year Plan] (Beijing: Tsinghua University, 2011), http://www.tsinghua.edu.cn/publish/newthu/openness/attachments/fzgh/fzgh.htm, accessed October 2014. China's large-scale funding efforts began with the announcement of Project 211 in 1995, which ultimately provided increased funding for one hundred universities. The even more elite Project 985 was launched in 1998 and funneled billions of RMB to thirty-seven institutions, including 1.8 billion each to Peking University and Tsinghua University.

14. Philip G. Altbach, "Costs and Benefits of World-Class Universities," *Academe* 90 (2004): 21.

15. Luke Meyers and Jonathan Robe, *College Ranking: History, Criticism and Reform* (Washington, DC: Center for College Affordability and Productivity, 2009).

16. James McKeen Cattell, *American Men of Science: A Biographical Directory* (New York: Science Press, 1906).

17. Meyers and Robe, *College Ranking*.

18. Meyers and Robe, *College Ranking*, 17.

19. David S. Webster, *Academic Quality Rankings of American Colleges and Universities* (Springfield, IL: C. C. Thomas, 1986), 6.

20. Henry Rosovsky, *The University: An Owner's Manual* (New York: W. W. Norton, 1990), 33.

21. Justin Thorens, "Liberties, Freedom and Autonomy: A Few Reflections on Academia's Estate," *Higher Education Policy*, no. 19 (2006): 87–110, cited in Kai Ren and Jun Li, "Academic Freedom and University Autonomy: A Higher Education Policy Perspective," *Higher Education Policy*, no. 26 (2013): 509.

22. James O. Freedman, *Liberal Education and the Public Interest* (Iowa City: University of Iowa Press, 2003), xi.

23. *The Heart of the Matter: The Humanities and Social Sciences for a Vibrant, Competitive and Secure Nation* (Cambridge, MA: American Academy of Arts and Sciences, 2013), 6.

24. See Derek Bok, *Our Underachieving Colleges: A Candid Look at How Much Students Learn and Why They Should Be Learning More* (Princeton: Princeton University Press, 2006).

25. See *Essays on General Education in Harvard College* (Cambridge, MA: President and Fellows of Harvard College, 2004); *On the Purpose and Structure of a Harvard Education* (Cambridge, MA: President and Fellows of Harvard College, 2005).

26. Jonathan R. Cole, *The Great American University: Its Rise to Preeminence, Its Indispensable National Role, Why It Must Be Protected* (New York: Public Affairs, 2009), 8.

27. Jamil Salmi, *The Challenge of Establishing World-Class Universities*, 7.

28. Rosovsky, *The University: An Owner's Manual*, 34.

29. "Lead the Future," Schwarzman Scholars at Tsinghua University, https:// www.schwarzmanscholars.org, accessed November 28, 2021.

30. See, for example, Qinghua University Educational Research Institute's "Creating First-Class Universities: Combining National Determination with the University Spirit: Round-Up of an Academic Seminar on the Theory and Practice of Establishing First-Class Universities" in *Chinese Education and Society* 37, no. 6 (Nov/Dec 2004).

31. See, for example, the discussion by Jamil Salmi in *The Challenge of Establishing World-Class Universities*, 6–7.

## 1. The University in Germany

1. On universities in the contemporary Federal Republic see Christian Bode et al., eds., *Universitäten in Deutschland* (München: Prestel Verlag, 2015).

2. James J. Sheehan, *German History 1770–1866* (Oxford: Clarendon Press, 1989), 135.

3. Charles E. McClelland, *State, Society, and University in Germany 1700–1914* (Cambridge: Cambridge University Press, 1980), 78–79.

4. Daniel Fallon, *The German University: A Heroic Ideal in Conflict with the Modern World* (Boulder: Colorado Associated University Press, 1980), 6.

5. Fallon, *The German University*, 5.

6. McClelland, *State, Society, and University*, 34–35.

7. Quoted in McClelland, *State, Society, and University*, 43.

8. Friedrich Gedike, Report to King Friedrich Wilhelm II of Germany, reprinted with commentary in Louis Menand, Paul Reitter, and Chat Wellmon, eds., *The Rise of the Research University: A Sourcebook* (Chicago: University of Chicago Press, 2017), 14–15.

9. Alternative numbers come from McClelland, *State, Society, and University*, 28; Sheehan, *German History*, 137.

10. Quoted in McClelland, *State, Society, and University*, 79.

11. See McClelland, *State, Society, and University*, 28, 56, 63–64; Fallon, *The German University*, 8.
12. See Fallon, *The German University*, 32–34.
13. Fallon, *The German University*, 5.
14. All quoted in Fallon, *The German University*, 2–3.
15. See also William C. Kirby and Joycelyn W. Eby, "'World-Class' Universities: Rankings and Reputation in Global Higher Education," Case 316-065 (Boston: Harvard Business School, 2015).

## 2. The Modern Original

1. Christoph Markschies, "Words of Welcome by the President of Humboldt-Universität-zu-Berlin," Conference Program, *HU200: Humboldt's Model: The Future of Universities in the World of Research*, October 7–9, 2010, 6–7.
2. Markschies, "Words of Welcome," 7.
3. The famous first line of Thomas Nipperdey, *Deutsche Geschichte 1800–1866: Bürgerwelt und starker Staat* (München: C. H. Beck, 1983), 11.
4. See also Walter Rüegg, "Themes," in *A History of the University in Europe: Volume III, Universities in the Nineteenth and Early Twentieth Centuries (1800–1945)*, Walter Rüegg, ed. (Cambridge: Cambridge University Press, 2004), 3.
5. See also Max Lenz, *Geschichte der Königlichen Friedrich-Wilhelms-Universität zu Berlin. Erster Band: Gründung und Ausbau* (Halle: Verlag der Buchhandlung des Waisenhauses, 1910), 78.
6. James J. Sheehan, *German History, 1770–1876* (Oxford: Oxford University Press, 1989), 137.
7. Charles E. McClelland, *State, Society, and University in Germany, 1740–1914* (Cambridge: Cambridge University Press, 1980), 115.
8. Sheehan, *German History*, 137–141.
9. See Karl-Heinz Günther, "Profiles of Educators: Wilhelm von Humboldt (1767–1835)," *Prospects* 18, no. 1 (March 1988).
10. David Sorkin, "Wilhelm von Humboldt: The Theory and Practice of Self-Formation (Bildung), 1791–1810," *Journal of the History of Ideas* 44, no. 1 (1983): 55–73.
11. Wilhelm Humboldt, "Der Königsberger und der Litauische Schulplan (1809)," in *Wilhelm von Humboldts Gesammelte Schriften, Band 13*, A. Leitzmann, ed. (Berlin: B. Behr Verlag, 1920), 277.
12. Sorkin, "Wilhelm von Humboldt," 63.
13. McClelland, *State, Society, and University*, 125.
14. See also Brad S. Gregory, *The Unintended Reformation: How a Religious Revolution Secularized Society* (Cambridge, MA: Harvard University Press, 2012), 349.
15. Quoted in Walter Rüegg, "Themes," 5. See also Friedrich Schleiermacher, *Gelegentliche Gedanken über Universitäten im deutschen Sinn. Nebst einem Anhang über eine neu zu errichtende* (Berlin: In der Realschulbuchhandlung, 1808), 32–33.

16. See Daniel Fallon, *The German University: A Heroic Ideal in Conflict with the Modern World* (Boulder: Colorado Associated University Press, 1980), 29.
17. Quoted in Fallon, *The German University*, 19.
18. Johann Gottlieb Fichte, "Über die einzig mögliche Störung der akademische Freiheit: Eine Rede beim Antritte seines Rektorats an der Universität zu Berlin den 19ten Oktober 1811," (Berlin: L. W. Wittich, 1812).
19. Lenz, *Geschichte*, 410.
20. Ilka Thom and Kirsten Weining, *Mittendrin: Eine Universität macht Geschichte: Eine Ausstellung anlässlich des 200-jährigen Jubiläums der Humboldt-Universität zu Berlin* (Berlin: Akademie Verlag, 2010), 43.
21. Sheehan, *Germany History*, 365; Fallon, *The German University*, 25.
22. Fallon, *The German University*, 25–26.
23. Quoted in Fallon, *The German University*, 25.
24. Cited in David McLellan, *Karl Marx: A Biography* (London: Palgrave Macmillan, 2006), 15.
25. Sheehan, *German History*, 575.
26. McClelland, *State, Society, and University*, 164.
27. Sylvia Paletschek, *Die permanente Erfindung einer Tradition. Die Universität Tübingen im Kaiserreich und in der Weimarer Republik* (Stuttgart: Steiner, 2001), 234.
28. McClelland, *State, Society, and University*, 165–167.
29. Thom and Weining, *Mittendrin*, 53; Sheehan, *German History*, 666–668; see especially Heinz-Elmar Tenorth, "Universität im Protest und auf den Barrikaden—Studenten und Dozenten," in *Geschichte der Universität Unter den Linden: Gründung und Blütezeit der Universität zu Berlin, 1810-1918*, vol 1, Heinz-Elmar Tenorth, ed. (Berlin: Akademie Verlag, 2012), 381–424.
30. See also Fritz K. Ringer, *The Decline of the German Mandarins: The German Academic Community, 1890–1933* (Cambridge, MA: Harvard University Press, 1969), 5–6.
31. McClelland, *State, Society, and University*, 221–223.
32. Ringer, *The Decline of the German Mandarins*, 141–142.
33. Robert Proctor, *Value-Free Science? Purity and Power in Modern Knowledge* (Cambridge, MA: Harvard University Press, 1991), 106–107.
34. See also Hartmut Titze, *Datenhandbuch zur deutschen Bildungsgeschichte: Wachstum und Differenzierung der deutschen Universitäten 1830–1945* (Göttingen: Vandenhoeck & Ruprecht, 1995), 81.
35. Einweihung der Ruhmeshalle in Görlitz (29 November 1902). See Ernst Johann, *Reden des Kaisers: Ansprachen, Predigten und Trinksprüche Wilhelms II.* (München: Deutscher Taschenbuch Verlag, 1966), 107.
36. Sheehan, *German History*, 307–309.
37. Nobel Prize winners in the fields of chemistry, literature, medicine, and physics: https://www.hu-berlin.de/en/about/history/nobel-laureates.
38. See McClelland, *State, Society, and University*, 291–299; see also Proctor, *Value-Free Science*, 106.

39. See also Friedrich Lenz, *Beiträge zur Universitätsstatistik* (Halle: Verlag der Buchhandlung des Waisenhauses, 1912), 15; Titze, *Datenhandbuch,* 82.

40. See also Franz Eulenburg, *Der akademische Nachwuchs: Eine Untersuchung über die Lage und die Aufgaben der Extraordinarien und Privatdozenten* (Berlin: B. G. Teubner, 1908), 80–81. See also Ulrich von Lübtow, *Die Rechtsstellung der entpflichteten Professoren* (Berlin: Duncker & Humblot, 1967), 24–25.

41. In 1905–1906, the average salary in Berlin was 7,653 Mark; the average salary for all Prussian universities was 5,825 Mark. See also Lenz, *Beiträge,* 35, table X.

42. Christopher Lasch, *The American Liberals and the Russian Revolution* (New York: McGraw Hill, 1962), 26.

43. Max Lenz, *Geschichte der Königlichen Friedrichs-Wilhelms-Universität zu Berlin,* 5 vols. (Halle: Verlag der Buchhandlung des Waisenhauses, 1910). For the extraordinary volumes published for the bicentenary, see Heinz-Elmar Tenorth, ed., *Geschichte der Universität Unter den Linden,* 6 vols. (Berlin: Akademie Verlag, 2012).

44. Quotes from Charles E. McClelland, "Die Universität am Ende ihres ersten Jahrhunderts—Mythos Humboldt?" in Tenorth, *Geschichte,* vol. 1, 637, 641.

45. McClelland, "Die Universität," 640.

46. McClelland, "Die Universität," 651.

47. See McClelland, "Die Universität," 652–653.

48. Original quote: "Kriegssemester sind die gewonnenen Semester." Thom and Weining, *Mittendrin,* 68.

49. Both quoted in McClelland, *State, Society, and University,* 315.

50. See also Titze, *Datenhandbuch,* 82.

51. See Hans Kohn, *The Mind of Germany* (New York: Scribner's, 1960); Istvan Deak, *Weimar Germany's Left-Wing Intellectuals* (Berkeley: University of California Press, 1968), 44.

52. Censored authors included Erich-Maria Remarque, Stefan Zweig, Sigmund Freud, Erich Kästner, Heinrich Mann, Karl Marx, and Kurt Tucholsky.

53. Heinz-Elmar Tenorth, "Eduard Sprangers hochschulpolitischer Konflikt 1933. Politisches Handeln eines preußischen Gelehrten," *Zeitschrift für Pädogogik* 36 (1990): 573–596; United States Holocaust Memorial Museum, "Telegram Regarding the 'Action against the Un-German Spirit,'" https://perspectives.ushmm.org/item/telegram-regarding-the-action-against-the-un-german-spirit.

54. Jens Thiel, "Der Lehrkörper der Friedrich-Wilhelms-Universität im Nationalsozialismus," in *Geschichte: Der Berliner Universität zwischen den Weltkriegen, 1918–1945,* vol. 2, Tenorth, ed., 465–538.

55. See Lauren Leff, *Well Worth Saving: American Universities' Life-and-Death Decisions on Refugees from Nazi Europe* (New Haven, CT: Yale University Press, 2019).

56. Christian von Ferber, *Die Entwicklung des Lehrkörpers des deutschen Universitäten und Hochschulen, 1864–1954* (Göttingen: Vandenhoeck & Ruptrecht, 1956).

57. Cited in Carlo Jordan, *Kaderschmiede Humboldt-Universität zu Berlin: Aufbegehren, Säuberungen und Militarisierung, 1945–1989* (Berlin: Ch. Links Verlag, 2001), 20.

58. Jordan, *Kaderschmiede*, 14.

59. Author interview with Heinrich Fink, Berlin, October 9, 2015.

60. See also Ilko-Sascha Kowalczuk, "Die Humboldt-Universität zu Berlin und das Ministerium für Staatssicherheit," in *Geschichte: Sozialistisches Experiment und Erneuerung in der Demokratie—die Humboldt-Universität zu Berlin 1945–2010*, vol. 3, Tenorth, ed., 462.

61. "Inoffizieller Mitarbeiter (IM)" *MFS-Lexikon*, Bundesbeauftragte für die Unterlagen des Staatssicherheitsdienstes der ehemaligen Deutschen Demokratischen Republik, https://www.bstu.de/mfs-lexikon/detail/inoffizieller -mitarbeiter-im/.

62. See also Kowalczuk, "Die Humboldt-Universität zu Berlin," 466.

63. Stefanie Endlich, ed., *Gedenkstätte für die Opfer des Nationalsozialismus. Eine Dokumentation* (Berlin: Bundeszentral für politische Bildung, 2002), 111.

64. Hannelore Scholz, "A Free University—Free of Women? Women and Higher Education in Berlin since 1989," in *Berlin in Focus: Cultural Transformations in Germany*, Barbara Becker-Cantarino, ed. (Westport, CT: Praeger, 1996), 38.

65. See also Konrad H. Jarausch, "Umgestaltung von außen, Dezember 1990– März 1994," in *Geschichte*, vol. 3, Tenorth, ed., 653.

66. See Helmut Klein, ed., *Humboldt-Universität zu Berlin: Überblick 1810–1985* (Berlin: VEB Deutscher Verlag der Wissenschaften, 1985), 145–146.

67. Author interview with Heinrich Fink, October 9, 2015.

68. Author interview with Heinrich Fink, October 9, 2015.

69. See also Jarausch, "Umgestaltung," 646–647.

70. Personalabeilting, file of Prof. Dr. Roland Felber, 1983–2010, Universitätsarchiv der Humboldt-Universität zu Berlin.

71. See also Jarausch, "Umgestaltung," 660, 683.

72. Constitution of Humboldt University, §13 (1).

73. Constitution of Humboldt University, §4 (2).

74. Constitution of Humboldt University, §8.

75. Constitution of Humboldt University, §2 (1).

76. Constitution of Humboldt University, §2 (3).

77. Constitution of Humboldt University, §13 (2), (3).

78. Author interview with Christoph Markschies, Berlin, October 5, 2015.

79. Humboldt-Universität zu Berlin, Personenstatistik-Daten, 1995–2020, https://www2.hu-berlin.de/personalstatistik/components/personal/daten .php#.

80. Author interview with Jan-Hendrik Olbertz, Berlin, December 2, 2015.

81. Author interview with Peter Frensch, Berlin, January 10, 2017.
82. Author interview with Jan-Hendrik Olbertz, December 2, 2015.
83. Author interview with Christoph Markschies, October 5, 2015.
84. Author interview with Jan-Hendrik Olbertz, December 2, 2015.
85. Author interview with Jan-Hendrik Olbertz, December 2, 2015.
86. Author interview with Recardo Manzke, Berlin, January 10, 2017.
87. Öffentlicher-Dienst.info, "Besoldungstabelle Beamte Berlin 2016," http://
   oeffentlicher-dienst.info/c/t/rechner/beamte/be?id=beamte-berlin-2016
   &matrix=1.
88. Verordnung über die Lehrverpflichtung an Hochschulen (Lehrverpflicht-
   ungsverordnung - LVVO), March 27, 2001, §2, http://gesetze.berlin.de
   /jportal/;jsessionid=418B777FD7942163F6B45CEC000D0E46.jp26?quelle
   =jlink&query=LehrVPflV+BE&psml=bsbeprod.psml&max=true&aiz
   =true#jlr-LehrVPflVBEV2P5.
89. Humboldt-Universität zu Berlin, Personenstatistik-Daten, https://www2.hu
   -berlin.de/personalstatistik/components/personal/diagram.php.
90. Federal Ministry of Education and Research, "The Path to a Professorship,"
   https://www.research-in-germany.org/en/jobs-and-careers/info-for-postdocs
   -and-junior-researchers/career-paths/path-to-professorship.html.
91. Humboldt-Universität zu Berlin, Personenstatistik-Daten, https://www2.hu
   -berlin.de/personalstatistik/components/personal/daten.php.
92. The number had risen from 23 percent in 2015: Statisches Bundesamt,
   "Frauenanteil in Professorenschaft 2015 auf 23% gestiegen," https://www
   .destatis.de/DE/Presse/Pressemitteilungen/2016/07/PD16_245_213.html.
93. Statista, "Frauenanteil in der Professorenschaft in Deutschland im Jahr
   2020 nach Bundesländern," https://de.statista.com/statistik/daten/studie
   /197898/umfrage/frauenanteil-in-der-professorenschaft-nach-bundes
   laendern/.
94. Humboldt-Universität zu Berlin, "Daten und Zahlen zur Humboldt-
   Universität," https://www.hu-berlin.de/de/ueberblick/humboldt-universitaet
   -zu-berlin/daten-und-zahlen.
95. Humboldt-Universität zu Berlin, "Daten und Zahlen zur Humboldt-
   Universität," https://www2.hu-berlin.de/personalstatistik/components
   /personal/diagram.php; https://www.hu-berlin.de/de/ueberblick/humboldt
   -universitaet-zu-berlin/daten-und-zahlen.
96. Statista, "Number of students at universities in Berlin in Germany in the
   winter semesters from 1998/1999 to 2019/20," https://www-statista-com
   .ezp-prod1.hul.harvard.edu/statistics/1114450/students-number-universities
   -berlin-germany/.
97. Source for percentage of female students at Humboldt University (in 2016):
   https://www.hu-berlin.de/de/ueberblick/humboldt-universitaet-zu-berlin
   /daten-und-zahlen. Source for percentage of female students in Germany
   (in 2015): https://www.destatis.de/DE/ZahlenFakten/GesellschaftStaat
   /BildungForschungKultur/Hochschulen/Tabellen/FrauenanteileAkademisc
   heLaufbahn.html.

98. Humboldt-Universität zu Berlin, "Studierendenstatistik, Studierende nach Bundesland und Hochschulzugangsberechtigung," http://edoc.hu-berlin.de /browsing/series/index.php?l[2]=Einrichtungen&l[3]=Humboldt-Universit %C3%A4t%2C+Studierendenstatistik&c[3][corp_id]=27501&l[4]=Studiere nde+nach+Bundesland+der+Hochschulzugangsberechtigung+-&c[4][series _id]=41035&_=521a552fece06b8245430c05a864183b.
99. Author interview with Christoph Markschies, October 5, 2015.
100. See also Jan-Hendrik Olbertz, *Angelegenheit vier: Abschiedsworte des Präsidenten Christoph Markschies am 18. Oktober 2010,* 7.
101. Humboldt-Universität zu Berlin, "Studierendenstatistik, Bewerbungen und Einschreibungen im 1. Fachsemester in NC-Studienfächern im Akademischen Jahr 2016–17," http://edoc.hu-berlin.de/browsing/series/index.php ?l%5B2%5D=Einrichtungen&l%5B3%5D=Humboldt-Universit%C3%A4t %2C+Studierendenstatistik&c%5B3%5D%5Bcorp_id%5D=27501&_=383 6b3faa3c66a2336969e24a2857081.
102. Author interview with Christoph Markschies, October 5, 2015.
103. Source for percentage of international students at HU (in 2016): Studierendenstatistik, Anteile ausländischer und männlicher Studierender, http:// edoc.hu-berlin.de/browsing/series/index.php?l%5B2%5D=Einrichtungen &l%5B3%5D=Humboldt-Universit%C3%A4t%2C+Studierendenstatistik &c%5B3%5D%5Bcorp_id%5D=27501&_=3836b3faa3c66a2336969e24a28 57081; Source for percentage of international students in Germany (in 2015–16): https://de.statista.com/statistik/daten/studie/222/umfrage/anteil-auslaendischer -studenten-an-hochschulen/.
104. Numbers for 2016–17. Studierendenstatik, Ausländische Studierende in grundständigen und weiterführenden Studiengängen nach Herkunft und Fächern, https://edoc.hu-berlin.de/bitstream/handle/18452/18752/tab_15 _17_Auslaendische_Studierende_in_Programmstudien_nach_Herkunft _und_Faecher.pdf?sequence=1&isAllowed=y.
105. Humboldt-Universität zu Berlin, "Daten und Zahlen zur Humboldt-Universität 2019," https://www.hu-berlin.de/de/ueberblick/humboldt -universitaet-zu-berlin/daten-und-zahlen#personal.
106. Numbers for 2014. Calculated by Deutsches Zentrum für Hochschul- und Wissenschaftsforschung based on Statistisches Bundesamt, in Deutsches Zentrum für Hochschul- und Wissenschaftsforschung and Deutscher Akademischer Ausstauschdienst, eds., *Wissenschaft weltoffen kompakt 2016: Facts and Figures on the International Nature of Studies and Research in Germany,* fig. 24, 25.
107. "BMBF Initiatives in the Context of the Bologna Process," Federal Ministry of Education and Research (Germany), https://www.bmbf.de/bmbf/en/aca demia/the-bologna-process/initiatives/bmbf-initiatives-in-the-context-of-the -bologna-process.html; Stephan L. Thompson and Johannes Trunzer, "Did the Bologna Process Challenge the German Apprenticeship System? Evidence from a Natural Experiment," IZA Institute of Labor Economics, October 2020, https://www.econstor.eu/bitstream/10419/227333/1/dp13806.pdf.

108. See also International Agenda of the Presidential Committee of Humboldt-Universität zu Berlin, 2015.
109. Humboldt-Universität zu Berlin, Strategische Partnerschaften der HU-Berlin: "Princeton University," https://www.international.hu-berlin .de/de/internationales-profil/strategische-partnerschaften-der-hu-berlin /PU.
110. Source for Sao Paulo: https://www.international.hu-berlin.de/de/inter nationales-profil/partnerschaften/profilpartnerschaften/universidade-de -sao-paulo. Source for Singapore: https://www.international.hu-berlin.de /de/internationales-profil/partnerschaften/profilpartnerschaften/NUS.
111. Humboldt-Universität zu Berlin, "Daten und Zahlen zur Humboldt-Universität 2019," https://www.hu-berlin.de/de/ueberblick/humboldt -universitaet-zu-berlin/daten-und-zahlen#personal.
112. Author interview with Recardo Manzke, January 10, 2017.
113. Frank Bösch, *A History Shared and Divided: East and West Germany Since the 1970s* (New York: Berghahn Books, 2018), 419.
114. Katerina Selin, "Berlin's Humboldt University Plans Massive Job Cuts," December 19, 2016, https://www.wsws.org/en/articles/2016/12/19/humb-d19 .html, accessed January 2021; see also Manzke interview.
115. See William C. Kirby and Joycelyn W. Eby, "'World-Class' Universities: Rankings and Reputation in Global Higher Education," Case 316-065 (Boston: Harvard Business School, 2015).
116. Anja Krieger, "Equality or Excellence," *Nature,* 537 (2016): 12, http://www .nature.com/nature/journal/v537/n7618_supp/full/537S12a.html?WT.mc _id=TWT_OUTLOOK_SLE.
117. The number for 2015 is an estimate. https://de.statista.com/statistik/daten /studie/36284/umfrage/oeffentliche-ausgaben-fuer-hochschulen-nach -koerperschaftsgruppen/.
118. The first phase of the Excellence Initiative provided US$2 (or €1.9) billion of funding. The second phase allocated US$2.9 (or €2.7) billion.
119. Deutsche Forschungsgemeinschaft, "Excellence Initiative General Information," http://www.dfg.de/en/research_funding/programmes/excellence _initiative/general_information/index.html.
120. Deutsche Forschungsgemeinschaft, "Excellence Initiative at a Glance: The Programme by the German Federal and State Governments to Promote Top-level Research at Universities," 16, https://www.dfg.de/download/pdf /dfg_im_profil/geschaeftsstelle/publikationen/exin_broschuere_en.pdf.
121. Author interview with Jan-Hendrik Olbertz, December 2, 2015.
122. Stanford Facts 2016, http://facts.stanford.edu/pdf/StanfordFacts_2016.pdf. Number of students at Stanford in 2015 (page 9): 16,122; annual budget in 2015–16 (page 44): US$5.5 (or €5.02) billion. For Humboldt University: https://www.hu-berlin.de/de/ueberblick/humboldt-universitaet-zu-berlin /daten-und-zahlen. Number of students at HU in 2016: 32,553 (without Charité); annual budget in 2016: US$413 (or €397) million.

123. "Internationale Expertenkommission zur Evaluation der Exzellenzinitiative: Endbericht," (Jan. 2016), https://www.gwk-bonn.de/fileadmin/Redaktion /Dokumente/Papers/Imboden-Bericht-2016.pdf.

124. Stabsstelle Presse- und Öffentlichkeitsarbeit der Humboldt-Universität zu Berlin, ed. *Spuren der Exzellenzinitiative. Die Humboldt-Universität zu Berlin zieht Zwischenbilanz—The Excellence Initiative makes its mark—Humboldt-Universität reviews its successes and looks ahead* (2015) 14.

125. Findings by *Nature* based on an analysis of articles in Scopus database using Elsevier's SciVal tool, http://www.nature.com/news/germany-claims-success -for-elite-universities-drive-1.18312.

126. "Zusammenfassung des Antrags: Berlin University Alliance—Crossing Boundaries toward an Integrated Research Environment," Berlin University Alliance, Exzellenzstrategie, https://www.berlin-university-alliance.de /press/berlin-university-alliance-summary.pdf, accessed January 7, 2020.

127. "The Oxford / Berlin Research Partnership," *Berlin University Alliance—Our Goals*, https://www.berlin-universityalliance.de/en/commitments/international /oxford/index.html.

128. "Wide-ranging new research partnership with Berlin universities," *Oxford Sparks*, https://www.oxfordsparks.ox.ac.uk/content/wide-ranging-new -research-partnership-berlin-universities.

129. Jarausch, "Umgestaltung," 653.

## 3. Truth, Justice, and Freedom in a Cold War World

1. Remarks of President John F. Kennedy at the Rudolph Wilde Platz, Berlin, June 26, 1963, John F. Kennedy Presidential Library and Museum, Boston, https://www.jfklibrary.org/archives/other-resources/john-f-kennedy-speeches /berlin-w-germany-rudolph-wilde-platz-19630626.

2. Remarks of the President at Free University, West Berlin, Germany, June 26, 1963 (as delivered), https://www.jfklibrary.org/asset-viewer/archives/JFKPOF /045/JFKPOF-045-028.

3. "Henry Ford Building: Construction," Freie Universität Berlin, https://www .fu-berlin.de/en/sites/hfb/geschichte/bau/index.html.

4. Karol Kubicki and Siegward Lönnendonker. *Die Freie Universität Berlin 1948–2007: Von der Gründung bis zum Exzellenwettbewerb* (Göttingen, Germany: V&R Unipress, 2008), 14.

5. James Tent, *The Free University of Berlin: A Political History* (Indianapolis: Indiana University Press, 1988), 36.

6. Tent, *The Free University*, 65–66.

7. Tent, *The Free University*, 78.

8. Tent, *The Free University*, 81–82.

9. Tent, *The Free University*, 85.

10. Tent, *The Free University*, 95.

11. Tent, *The Free University*, 104.

12. Quoted in Tent, *The Free University*, 106.
13. Quoted in Tent, *The Free University*, 139.
14. Tent, *The Free University*, 141.
15. Taken from the appeal to found the Free University, July 23, 1948.
16. See Tent, *The Free University*, 160–164. Quote from 161.
17. Quote and background from Tent, *The Free University*, 154–155.
18. Full speeches in official booklet on the occasion: *Gründungsfeier der Freien Universität Berlin* (Berlin: Erich Blaschker, 1949); see also Tent, *The Free University*, 166–168.
19. Fritz von Bergmann, "Die Hilfe der USA für die Freie Universität Berlin," 189, in *Freie Universität Berlin 1948–1973: Hochschule im Umbruch, Teil III: Auf dem Weg in den Dissens (1957–1964)*, Universitätsarchiv der Freien Universität Berlin (hereafter, FU Archives).
20. Kubicki and Lönnendonker, *Die Freie Universität Berlin*, 50.
21. Der Präsident der Freien Universität Berlin, ed., *40 Jahre Freie Universität Berlin: Die Geschichte 1948–1988, Einblicke, Ausblicke* (Berlin: Zentrale Universitätsdruckerei der Freien Universität Berlin, 1988), 53.
22. Kubicki and Lönnendonker, *Die Freie Universität Berlin*, 50.
23. See Tent, *The Free University*, 219–220, 244–249.
24. See Tent, *The Free University*, 281–286.
25. Tent, *The Free University*, 303.
26. Tent, *The Free University*, 324–325.
27. Gerhard Göhler, "Politischer Wissenschaftler und Philosoph. Zum Tode von Alexander Schwan," in *Politische Vierteljahresschrift* 31 (1990), Heft 1, 97–100. On the Maoists see Anke Jaspers et al., eds., *Ein kleines rotes Buch. Über die 'Mao-Bibel' und die Bücher-Revolution der Sachzicherjahre* (Berlin: Matthes & Seitz, 2018).
28. See Tent, *The Free University*, 403–407. Quotes are from Tent, *The Free University*, 406–407.
29. Quoted in Tent, *The Free University*, 417.
30. *40 Jahre Freie Universität Berlin*, 53.
31. Tent, *The Free University*, 451.
32. Tent, *The Free University*, 446.
33. Freie Universität Berlin, *Fünfzig Jahre Freie Universität Berlin* (Berlin, 1998), 72.
34. Landeshochschulstrukturkommission Berlin, ed., *Stellungnahmen und Empfehlungen zu Struktur und Entwicklung der Berliner Hochschulen* (Berlin, 1992), 63.
35. "Empfehlungen zur Struktur der Freien Universität Berlin in den Neunziger Jahren" (April 1988), FU Archives.
36. Kubicki and Lönnendonker, *Die Freie Universität Berlin*, 141. Numbers used here are from "Zwischen Wende und Jahrtausendwende: Freie Universität Berlin, 1989–1999. Zahlen-Daten-Fakten," 3, FU Archives.
37. Author interview with Herbert Grieshop, Berlin, June 17, 2015.

38. "Der Unsichtbare Kanzler," *Furios. Studentisches Campusmagazin an der FU Berlin,* Jan. 24, 2011, https://furios-campus.de/2011/01/24/der-unsichtbare -kanzler/.

39. Peter-André Alt, "Rede anlässlich der Abschiedsfeier für den langjährigen Kanzler der Freien Universität Berlin, Peter Lange, am 18. Dezember 2015," full text in FU Berlin *Campus.Leben,* December 22, 2015, https://www.fu-berlin.de /campusleben/campus/2015/151222-abschied-peter-lange/index.html.

40. Interview with Peter Lange, *Berliner Tagespiegel,* Feb. 13, 2016.

41. Jon Marcus, "Germany Proves Tuition-Free College is Not a Silver Bullet for America's Education Woes," *Quartz,* October 18, 2016, https://qz.com /812200/is-free-college-possible-germany-shows-there-are-downsides-to -tuition-free-college/.

42. Information provided by Free University.

43. See also *Struktur- und Entwicklungsplan für die Freie Universität Berlin (Stand 2015),* https://www.fu-berlin.de/universitaet/media/strukturplan -2015.pdf.

44. Kubicki and Lönnendonker, *Die Freie Universität Berlin,* 142.

45. "Fortschreibung des Struktur- und Entwicklungsplans für die Freie Universität Berlin (Stand 2018)," https://www.fu-berlin.de/universitaet/media /strukturplan-2018.pdf.

46. Data provided by Free University.

47. Deutscher Hochschul Verband, "Grundgehälter und Besoldungsanpassungen," https://www.hochschulverband.de/fileadmin/redaktion/download /pdf/besoldungstabellen/grundgehaelter_w.pdf.

48. Information provided by FU. Data do not include medicine. "Der Besoldungsdurchschnitt für die Freie Universität Berlin ist für das Jahr 2017 durch amtliche Bekanntmachung auf monatlich."

49. *Times Higher Education World University Rankings,* "Free University Berlin," https://www.timeshighereducation.com/world-university-rankings/free -university-berlin.

50. "Leistungsbericht über das Jahr 2018" Professorinnen und Professoren: 559; Sonstige wiss. U. künstl. Beschäftigte: 2,286; Nebenberufliches Lehrpersonal: 953; 35. See https://www.berlin.de/sen/wissenschaft/service/leistungsberichte/.

51. Berlin University Alliance, vi, https://www.berlin-university-alliance.de /excellence-strategy/universities-of-excellence/berlin-university-alliance -proposal.pdf.

52. "Freie Universität Berlin," *U.S. News and World Report,* https://www.usnews .com/education/best-global-universities/freie-universitat-berlin-502084; Freie Universität Berlin, "Facts and Figures," https://www.fu-berlin.de/en /universitaet/leitbegriffe/zahlen/index.html.

53. "Freie Universität Berlin," *U.S. News and World Report,* https://www.usnews .com/education/best-global-universities/freie-universitat-berlin-502084; "Facts and Figures," Freie Universität Berlin, https://www.fu-berlin.de/en /universitaet/leitbegriffe/zahlen/index.html.

54. "Freie Universität Berlin," *U.S. News and World Report.*
55. Deutsche Wissenschafts- und Innovationshäuser (German Center for Research and Innovation), *Annual Report 2018,* 79, https://www.dwih -netzwerk.de/files/2019/08/DWIH-JB_2018_zweiseitig.pdf.
56. Deutscher Akademischer Austauschdienst, *Wissenschaft Weltoffen 2019: Daten und Fakten zur Internationalität vom Studium und Forschung in Deutschland* (Bielefeld: wvb Media, 2019), 136.
57. Kubicki and Lönnendonker, *Die Freie Universität Berlin,* 152.
58. *Wissenschaft Weltoffen 2019,* 82.
59. Data provided by Free University.
60. Alexander von Humboldt Foundation, *Annual Report 2018,* 127, https://www.humboldt-foundation.de/pls/web/docs/F634970970/jahresbericht _2018.pdf.
61. European Commission, UNA Europe, https://ec.europa.eu/education/sites /education/files/document-library-docs/european-universities-factsheet-una -europa.pdf.
62. "International Council," Freie Universität Berlin, https://www.fu-berlin.de /en/sites/inu/network-university/international-council/index.html.
63. "Decision in the German Excellence Strategy," Berlin University Alliance, https://www.berlin-university-alliance.de/en/news/items/20190719-decision -excellence-strategy.html.
64. Author interview with Peter-André Alt, Berlin, June 18, 2015.
65. "Freie Universität Declares State of Climate Emergency," Freie Universität Berlin, https://www.fu-berlin.de/en/presse/informationen/fup/2019/fup_19 _398-klimanotstand/index.html.
66. Ibid.
67. Remarks of the President at Free University, West Berlin, Germany, June 26, 1963 (as delivered), https://www.jfklibrary.org/asset-viewer/archives /JFKPOF/045/JFKPOF-045-028.

## 4. The Rise and Challenges of American Research Universities

1. Henry W. Diederich, "American and German Universities," *Science,* July 29, 1904, 157.
2. "German Universities Left Behind," *Literary Digest,* December 11, 1909, 1067.
3. John S. Brubacher and Willis Rudy, *Higher Education in Transition: A History of American Colleges and Universities* (New Brunswick, NJ: Transaction Publishers, 1997), 3; Samuel Eliot Morison, *The Founding of Harvard College* (Cambridge, MA: Harvard University Press, 1998), 127.
4. Brubacher and Rudy, *Higher Education in Transition,* 4.
5. Arthur M. Cohen, *The Shaping of American Higher Education: Emergence and Growth of the Contemporary System* (San Francisco: Jossey-Bass, 1998), 57.
6. Samuel Eliot Morison, *Three Centuries of Harvard* (Cambridge, MA: Harvard University Press, 1946), 224.

7. Philip Alexander Bruce, "History of the University of Virginia, 1819–1919: The Lengthened Shadow of One Man," vol. 1, 339–342, https://babel.hathitrust.org/cgi/pt?id=coo1.ark:/13960/t48p6m780;view=1up;seq=363;size=150.

8. Edwin Emery Slosson, *Great American Universities* (New York: MacMillan, 1910), 374.

9. Jonathan R. Cole, *The Great American University: Its Rise to Preeminence, Its Indispensable National Role, Why It Must Be Protected* (New York: Public Affairs, 2012), 22.

10. Slosson, *Great American Universities*, 375.

11. Cole, *The Great American University*, 26–27.

12. Slosson, *Great American Universities*, 383.

13. "A Brief History of the University of Chicago," University of Chicago, http://www-news.uchicago.edu/resources/brief-history.html.

14. "A History of Stanford," Stanford University, https://www.stanford.edu/about/history/.

15. Roger Geiger, *American Higher Education since World War II: A History* (Princeton, NJ: Princeton University Press, 2015), 426–427.

16. John R. Thelin, *A History of American Higher Education* (Baltimore, MD: Johns Hopkins University Press, 2011), 199–201.

17. David F. Labaree, *A Perfect Mess: The Unlikely Ascendancy of American Higher Education* (Chicago: The University of Chicago Press, 2017), 106.

18. Labaree, *A Perfect Mess*.

19. Ibid.

20. Geiger, *American Higher Education since World War II*.

21. Thelin, *A History of American Higher Education*, 263.

22. "History and Timeline," U.S. Department of Veterans Affairs, http://www.benefits.va.gov/gibill/history.asp.

23. "The Office of Scientific Research and Development (OSRD) Collection," Library of Congress, https://www.loc.gov/rr/scitech/trs/trsosrd.html.

24. National Science Foundation, "Science The Endless Frontier," A Report to the President by Vannevar Bush, Director of the Office of Scientific Research and Development, July 1945, https://www.nsf.gov/od/lpa/nsf50/vbush1945.htm.

25. National Science Foundation, "Science The Endless Frontier."

26. "Farewell Address," Dwight D. Eisenhower Library, https://www.eisenhowerlibrary.gov/research/online-documents/farewell-address.

27. Charles T. Clotfelter, introduction to *American Universities in a Global Market*, Charles T. Clotfelter, ed. (Chicago: University of Chicago Press, 2010).

28. See, for example, Clotfelter, *American Universities;* James Axtell, *Wisdom's Workshop: The Rise of the Modern University* (Princeton, NJ: Princeton University Press, 2016); or Hunter R. Rawlings, "The Lion in the Path," remarks at Princeton University Alumni Day, February 22, 2014, https://www

.princeton.edu/main/news/archive/S39/33/39I39/index.xml?section=topstories, accessed August 16, 2016.

29. Axtell, *Wisdom's Workshop*, 365.

30. Derek Bok, *Higher Education in America* (Princeton, NJ: Princeton University Press, 2013), 44–46.

31. Bok, *Higher Education in America*, 49.

32. Bok, *Higher Education in America*, 51.

33. Axtell, *Wisdom's Workshop*, 228.

34. Walter Crosby Eells, "The Origin and Early History of Sabbatical Leave," *AAUP Bulletin* 48, no. 3 (September 1962): 253–256.

35. Celina M. Sima, "The Role and Benefits of the Sabbatical Leave in Faculty Development and Satisfaction," *New Directions for Institutional Research* 2000, no. 105: 67–75.

36. "Federal and State Funding of Higher Education," Pew Trusts, June 11, 2015, http://www.pewtrusts.org/en/research-and-analysis/issue-briefs/2015 /06/federal-and-state-funding-of-higher-education.

37. "Historical Trends in Federal R&D," American Association for the Advancement of Science, https://www.aaas.org/programs/r-d-budget-and-policy /historical-trends-federal-rd.

38. Michael Mitchell, Michael Leachman, and Kathleen Masterson, "A Lost Decade in Higher Education Funding," Center on Budget and Policy Priorities, August 23, 2017, https://www.cbpp.org/research/state-budget-and-tax /a-lost-decade-in-higher-education-funding, accessed September 2019.

39. Labaree, *A Perfect Mess*, 7.

40. Melissa Korn, "Giving to Colleges Jumps 7.2% to Record $46.7 Billion," *Wall Street Journal*, February 11, 2019, https://www.wsj.com/articles/giving -to-colleges-jumps-7-2-to-record-46-7-billion-11549861260.

41. Council for Aid to Education, "Colleges and Universities Raise Record $40.30 Billion in 2015," press release, http://cae.org/images/uploads/pdf /VSE_2015_Press_Release.pdf, accessed August 17, 2016.

42. National Association of College and University Business Officers (NACUBO), "Endowment Study," (Boston: Cambridge Associates Inc., 1990), 23; "Number of U.S. Institutional Respondents to the 2019 NTSE, and Respondents' Total Endowment Market Value, by Endowment Size and Institution Type," NACUBO, https://www.nacubo.org/Research/2020 /Public-NTSE-Tables, accessed March 15, 2021.

43. "GDP data," World Bank, United States, https://data.worldbank.org /country/united-states, accessed March 15, 2021.

44. National Association of College and University Business Officers, "Educational Endowments' Investment Returns Decline Sharply to 2.4% in FY2015; 10-Year Returns Fall to 6.3%," *2015 NACUBO-Commonfund Study of Endowments*, http://www.nacubo.org/Documents/2015%20NCSE%20 Press%20Release%20%20FINAL.pdf.

45. "U.S. Educational Endowments Report 5.4 Percent Average Return in FY19," National Association of College and University Business Officers,

January 30, 2020, https://www.nacubo.org/Press-Releases/2020/US
-Educational-Endowments-Report-5-3-Percent-Average-Return-in-FY19.

46. Michael Bloomberg, "Michael Bloomberg: Why I'm Giving $1.8 Billion in
College Financial Aid," *New York Times*, November 18, 2018, https://www
.nytimes.com/2018/11/18/opinion/bloomberg-college-donation-financial
-aid.html.

47. Michael Bloomberg, "Why I'm Giving $1.8 Billion."

48. Phillip G. Altbach, *Global Perspectives on Higher Education* (Baltimore, MD:
Johns Hopkins University Press, 2016), 32.

49. Slosson, *Great American Universities*, 180.

50. "Number of International Students in the United States Hits All-Time
High," Institute for International Education, November 18, 2019, https://
www.iie.org/Why-IIE/Announcements/2019/11/Number-of-International
-Students-in-the-United-States-Hits-All-Time-High, accessed June 2020;
"NAFSA International Student Economic Value Tool," National Association
of International Educators, https://www.nafsa.org/policy-and-advocacy
/policy-resources/nafsa-international-student-economic-value-tool-v2, accessed
June 2020.

51. David Engerman, *Know Your Enemy: The Rise and Fall of America's Soviet
Experts* (New York: Oxford University Press, 2006); Mitchell L. Stevens,
Cynthia Miller-Idriss, and Seteney Shami, *Seeing the World: How US Universities Make Knowledge in a Global Era* (Princeton, NJ: Princeton University Press, 2018).

52. "Announcement: IFLE Awards Over $71 Million in FY 2018 Grants to
Strengthen International Studies, World Language Training, and Global
Experiences for Educators and Students," U.S. Department of Education,
https://www2.ed.gov/about/offices/list/ope/iegps/2018news.html.

53. Nick Anderson, "In Qatar's Education City, U.S. Colleges Are Building
an Academic Oasis," *Washington Post*, December 6, 2015, https://www
.washingtonpost.com/local/education/in-qatars-education-city-us-colleges
-are-building-an-academic-oasis/2015/12/06/6b538702-8e01-11e5-ae1f
-af46b7df8483_story.html.

54. Slosson, *Great American Universities*, 180.

55. Labaree, *A Perfect Mess*, 183–185.

56. Labaree, *A Perfect Mess*, 2.

57. Clark Kerr, *The Uses of the University* (Cambridge, MA: Harvard University
Press, 2001), 7–11; Labaree, *A Perfect Mess*, 13, 73.

58. Kerr, *The Uses of the University*, 1; Labaree, *A Perfect Mess*, 129.

## 5. Rising through Change and through Storm

1. Samuel Eliot Morison, *Three Centuries of Harvard* (Cambridge, MA: Harvard
University Press, 1946), 253.

2. Morison, *Three Centuries*, 251.

3. Quoted in Morison, *Three Centuries*, 260.

4. This section relies on the superb account of the tercentenary in Morton Keller and Phyllis Keller, *Making Harvard Modern: The Rise of America's University* (Oxford: Oxford University Press, 2001), 3–10.
5. Quoted in Keller and Keller, *Making Harvard Modern*, 8.
6. Keller and Keller, *Making Harvard Modern*, 4–5.
7. Morison, *Three Centuries*, 272.
8. Quoted in Keller and Keller, *Making Harvard Modern*, 10.
9. Gene I. Maeroff, "Harvard of the West Climbing in Ratings," *New York Times*, October 10, 1977, https://www.nytimes.com/1977/10/10/archives /harvard-of-the-west-climbing-in-ratings.html.
10. For a summary, see Eugenia V. Levenson, "Harvard Girl," *Harvard Magazine*, July-August 2002, https://harvardmagazine.com/2002/07/harvard-girl.html.
11. The phrase from the subtitle of Keller and Keller, *Making Harvard Modern*.
12. Morison, *Three Centuries*, 5.
13. See Bernard Bailyn, "Foundations," in *Glimpses of the Harvard Past*, Bernard Bailyn, Donald Fleming, Oscar Handlin, and Stephan Thernstrom (Cambridge, MA: Harvard University Press, 1986), 9.
14. Morison, *Three Centuries*, 22–24.
15. Morison, *Three Centuries*, 14–16.
16. Morison, *Three Centuries*, 69–71.
17. Bailyn, "Foundations," 11.
18. Bailyn, "Foundations," 61.
19. Bailyn, "Foundations," 224–226.
20. Bailyn, "Foundations," 232.
21. Bailyn, "Foundations," 254.
22. Bailyn, "Foundations," 35.
23. Bailyn, "Foundations," 324.
24. Morison, *Three Centuries*, 295.
25. Donald Fleming, "Eliot's New Broom," in Bailyn et al., *Glimpses*, 63.
26. All quotes from Fleming, "Eliot's New Broom," 62–63.
27. Morison, *Three Centuries*, 324.
28. Fleming, "Eliot's New Broom," 65.
29. Morison, *Three Centuries*, 330.
30. Fleming, "Eliot's New Broom," 65.
31. Records of the President of Harvard University, Charles W. Eliot, Addresses, Speeches, and Articles, 1869–1925, 1870 Harvard Commencement Address, Harvard University Archives.
32. Morison, *Three Centuries*, 421.
33. Quoted in Fleming, "Eliot's New Broom," 70.
34. Fleming, "Eliot's New Broom," 76.
35. Fleming, "Eliot's New Broom," 73.
36. Fleming, "Eliot's New Broom," 384.
37. See Ernest P. Young, *The Presidency of Yuan Shikai* (Ann Arbor: University of Michigan Press, 1977), 47–48, 172–176. Quote on 175.

38. Quoted in Richard Norton Smith, *The Harvard Century: The Making of a University to a Nation* (Cambridge, MA: Harvard University Press, 1986), 60.

39. John King Fairbank, *Chinabound: A Fifty-Year Memoir* (New York: Harper & Row, 1982), 155.

40. Keller and Keller, *Making Harvard Modern*, 14.

41. Stephen Steinberg, *The Ethnic Myth: Race, Ethnicity, and Class in America* (Boston: Beacon Press, 2001), 245.

42. Jerome Karabel, *The Chosen: The Hidden History of Admission and Exclusion at Harvard, Yale, and Princeton* (Boston: Houghton Mifflin, 2005), 126.

43. Karabel, *The Chosen*, 88; Steinberg, *The Ethnic Myth*, 245.

44. Keller and Keller, *Making Harvard Modern*, 51. See their subsection "No Women Allowed . . . ," 51–59.

45. Morison, *Three Centuries*, 446.

46. Keller and Keller, *Making Harvard Modern*, 23.

47. Keller and Keller, *Making Harvard Modern*, 24.

48. Keller and Keller, *Making Harvard Modern*, 163–164.

49. John T. Bethell, *Harvard Observed: An Illustrated History of the University in the Twentieth Century* (Cambridge, MA: Harvard University Press, 1998), 34.

50. Bethell, *Harvard Observed*, 278.

51. "It's Complicated: 375 Years of Women at Harvard," Radcliffe Institute for Advanced Study, Harvard University, https://www.radcliffe.harvard.edu /event/2012-its-complicated-exhibition.

52. David S. Webster, *Academic Quality Rankings of American Colleges and Universities* (Springfield, IL: Charles C. Thomas, 1986), 137–139.

53. Keller and Keller, *Making Harvard Modern*, xii.

54. Oscar Handlin, "Making Men of the Boys," in Bailyn et al., *Glimpses*, 48.

55. Bethell, *Harvard Observed*, 198–201; Keller and Keller, *Making Harvard Modern*, 178–183.

56. Quoted in Keller and Keller, *Making Harvard Modern*, 347–348.

57. Johanna Berkman, "Harvard's Hoard," *New York Times*, June 24, 2001, http://www.nytimes.com/2001/06/24/magazine/24HARVARD.html ?pagewanted=all; see also Keller and Keller, *Making Harvard Modern*, 372.

58. Author interview with Neil Rudenstine, New York City, August 26, 2016.

59. Sara Rimer, "Some Seeing Crimson at Harvard 'Land Grab,'" *New York Times*, June 17, 1997, http://www.nytimes.com/1997/06/17/us/some-seeing -crimson-at-harvard-land-grab.html.

60. Sarah Wu, "Lessons from Barry's Corner," *Harvard Crimson*, May 10, 2017, https://www.thecrimson.com/article/2017/5/10/barrys-corner-allston -feature/.

61. Steve Stecklow, "Management 101: Harvard's President, Too Slow to Delegate, Got Swamped in Detail—It's a Uniquely Tough Job, and Rudenstine's Style Made it Even Tougher, Will He Return After a Rest?," *Wall Street Journal*, December 1994.

62. Laura L. Krug, "Allston Tax Extended to 25 Years," *Harvard Crimson*, January 9, 2004, https://www.thecrimson.com/article/2004/1/9/allston-tax-extended-to-25-years/.

63. Daniel J. Hemel, "Summers' Comments on Women and Science Draw Ire," *Harvard Crimson*, January 14, 2005, https://www.thecrimson.com/article/2005/1/14/summers-comments-on-women-and-science/.

64. William C. Marra and Sara E. Polsky, "Lack of Confidence," *Harvard Crimson*, March 15, 2005, https://www.thecrimson.com/article/2005/3/15/lack-of-confidence-in-a-sharp/.

65. Geraldine Fabrikant, "Harvard and Yale Report Losses in Endowments," *New York Times*, September 10, 2009, https://www.nytimes.com/2009/09/11/business/11harvard.html.

66. "$11 Billion Less," *Harvard Magazine*, November-December 2009, http://harvardmagazine.com/2009/11/harvard-endowment-update.

67. Beth Healy, "Harvard Ignored Warnings about Investments," *Boston Globe*, November 29, 2009, http://archive.boston.com/news/local/massachusetts/articles/2009/11/29/harvard_ignored_warnings_about_investments/; Geraldine Fabrikant, "Harvard and Yale Report Losses in Endowments."

68. "Further Financial Fallout," *Harvard Magazine*, January-February 2010, https://harvardmagazine.com/2010/01/harvard-2009-financial-losses-grow.

69. Geraldine Fabrikant, "Harvard and Yale Report Losses in Endowments."

70. Author interview with Lawrence S. Bacow, Cambridge, MA, July 7, 2016.

71. "Looming Layoffs," *Harvard Magazine*, July-August 2009, https://harvardmagazine.com/2009/07/looming-layoffs.

72. Keller and Keller, *Making Harvard Modern*, 64–70; Conant quotation, 65.

73. "The New Tenure Track," *Harvard Magazine*, September-October 2010, http://harvardmagazine.com/2010/09/the-new-tenure-track.

74. *The 68th Annual Harvard Crimson Confidential Guide to Courses at Harvard* (1993), 133.

75. Harvard University Office of the Senior Vice Provost, *Faculty Development & Diversity Annual Report 2013–2014*, https://hwpi.harvard.edu/files/faculty-diversity/files/fdd_annual_report_2013-2014_hq.pdf.

76. "The New Tenure Track."

77. Colin Campbell, "The Harvard Factor," *New York Times Magazine*, July 20, 1986, http://www.nytimes.com/1986/07/20/magazine/the-harvard-factor.html?pagewanted=all.

78. *Faculty Development & Diversity Annual Report 2013–2014*; Julie Chung, "Women at Work," *Harvard Magazine*, March-April 2020, https://harvardmagazine.com/2020/03/jhj-undergraduate-women-at-work, accessed April 2020.

79. Noah J. Delwiche and Daphne C. Thompson, "Yield Remains Steady at 81 Percent for Class of 2019," *Harvard Crimson*, May 15, 2015, http://www.thecrimson.com/article/2015/5/15/class-2019-yield-81-percent/; Tyler Fog-

gatt, "Yield Drops, Diversity Increases for Class of 2019," *Yale Daily News*, September 3, 2015, http://yaledailynews.com/blog/2015/09/03/yield-drops -diversity-increases-for-class-of-2019/; "At 69.4 Percent, Class of 2019 Yield Highest Ever," *The Daily Princetonian*, May 8, 2015, http://www.dailyprinceto-nian.com/article/2015/05/at-69-4-percent-class-of-2019-yield-highest-ever.

80. Victor Xu, "Record 81.1 Percent Yield for Class of 2019," *The Stanford Daily*, June 9, 2015, http://www.stanforddaily.com/2015/06/09/de-vx-record-81-1 -percent-yield-rate-reported-for-class-of-2019/.

81. Susan Svrluga, "Harvard Fencing Coach Dismissed for Conflict-of-Interest Violation," *Washington Post*, July 10, 2019, https://www.washingtonpost.com /education/2019/07/10/harvard-fencing-coach-dismissed-conflict-of-interest -violation/.

82. Derek Thompson, "The Cult of Rich-Kid Sports," *The Atlantic*, October 2, 2019, https://www.theatlantic.com/ideas/archive/2019/10/harvard-univer sity-and-scandal-sports-recruitment/599248/.

83. William L. Wang, "Filings Show Athletes with High Academic Scores Have 83 Percent Acceptance Rate," *Harvard Crimson*, June 30, 2018, https://www.thecrimson.com/article/2018/6/30/athlete-admissions/.

84. "Meet the Class of 2022," *Harvard Crimson*, https://features.thecrimson .com/2018/freshman-survey/makeup/.

85. Max Larkin and Mayowa Aina, "Legacy Admissions Offer and Advan-tage—And Not Just at Schools Like Harvard," NPR, November 4, 2018, https://www.npr.org/2018/11/04/663629750/legacy-admissions-offer-an -advantage-and-not-just-at-schools-like-harvard.

86. Preston Cooper, "The Real Problem with Legacy Admissions," *Forbes*, Feb. 20, 2020.

87. Zohra D. Yaqhubi, "New Admissions Outreach Initiative Seeks to En-courage Low-Income College Applicants," *Harvard Crimson*, October 24, 2013, http://www.thecrimson.com/article/2013/10/24/financial-aid-office -connection/.

88. Camille G. Caldera, "83 Percent of Harvard College Admits Accept Spots in Class of 2023," *Harvard Crimson*, May 10, 2019, https://www.thecrimson .com/article/2019/5/10/class-of-2023-yield/, accessed October 2019.

89. "How Aid Works," Harvard College, https://college.harvard.edu/financial -aid/how-aid-works.

90. Ibid.

91. "Economic Diversity," *U.S. News and World Report*, https://www.usnews .com/best-colleges/rankings/national-universities/economic-diversity.

92. David Leonhardt, "How Elite Colleges Still Aren't Diverse," *New York Times*, March 29, 2011, https://economix.blogs.nytimes.com/2011/03/29 /how-elite-colleges-still-arent-diverse/.

93. *General Education in a Free Society* (Cambridge, MA: Harvard University Press, 1945), 51. As quoted in http://harvardmagazine.com/sites/default /files/GenEd.pdf.

94. See Morison, *Three Centuries*, 446. As cited in http://harvardmagazine.com /sites/default/files/GenEd.pdf.

95. "Financial Administration," Harvard University, https://finance.harvard.edu /financial-overview.

96. "Financial Report FY2021," Harvard University, https://finance.harvard .edu/files/fad/files/fy21_harvard_financial_report.pdf.

97. Ibid.

98. Harvard Management Company, *Annual Report 2021*, "Message from the CEO," October 2021, https://www.hmc.harvard.edu/wp-content/uploads /2021/10/FY21_HMC_Annual_Report.pdf.

99. Doug Gavel, "University Has a Cosmopolitan Flair," *Harvard Gazette*, November 16, 2000, https://news.harvard.edu/gazette/story/2000/11/harvard -gazette-university-has-a-cosmopolitan-flair/.

100. Michael C. George and Alyza J. Sebenius, "Between Harvard and Yale, a World of Difference," *Harvard Crimson*, May 24, 2012, http://www.thecrimson .com/article/2012/5/24/international-harvard-yale-singapore/?page=single.

101. John S. Rosenberg, "Going Global, Gradually," *Harvard Magazine*, November 24, 2015, https://www.harvardmagazine.com/2015/11/harvard-global-institute, accessed June 2020.

102. "About HGI," Harvard Global Institute, https://globalinstitute.harvard.edu /about-hgi, accessed June 2020.

103. Author interview with Barry Bloom, Cambridge, MA, May 25, 2016.

104. "Statistics," Harvard International Office, http://www.hio.harvard.edu /statistics.

105. United States District Court for the District of Massachusetts, "Civil Action No. 1:20-cv-11283," https://www.harvard.edu/sites/default/files /content/sevp_filing.pdf.

106. Camille G. Caldera and Michelle G. Kurilla, "Harvard Affiliates, Other Colleges and Universities File Amicus Briefs in Support of ICE Lawsuit," *Harvard Crimson*, July 12, 2020, https://www.thecrimson.com/article/2020 /7/13/harvard-mit-ice-lawsuit-amici/.

107. Nate Herpich, "The Conundrum for International Students," *Harvard Gazette*, July 31, 2020, https://news.harvard.edu/gazette/story/2020/07/harvard -addresses-the-challenges-for-international-students/.

108. Christine Heenan, "Harvard Center Shanghai Opens Its Doors," *Harvard Gazette*, March 20, 2010, http://news.harvard.edu/gazette/story/2010/03 /harvard-center-shanghai-opens-its-doors/.

109. "Harvard in the World," Harvard Worldwide, https://worldwide.harvard .edu/harvard-world, accessed September 2020.

110. "Summers Visits People's Republic of China," *Harvard Gazette*, May 16, 2002, https://news.harvard.edu/gazette/story/2002/05/summers-visits -peoples-republic-of-china/.

111. Theodore R. Delwiche, "In Beijing, Faust Talks Climate Change with Chinese President," *Harvard Crimson*, March 17, 2015, https://www.thecrimson .com/article/2015/3/17/faust-visits-chinese-president/.

112. Colleen Walsh, "In China, Bacow Emphasizes Common Values," *Harvard Gazette*, March 20, 2019, https://news.harvard.edu/gazette/story/2019/03/harvard-president-speaks-at-peking-university/.

113. Nidhi Subbaraman, "Harvard Chemistry Chief's Arrest over China Links Shocks Researchers," *Nature*, February 3, 2020, https://www.nature.com/articles/d41586-020-00291-2; James S. Bikales and Kevin R. Chen, "Former Chemistry Chair Lieber Indicted on Four Additional Felonies for Tax Offenses," *Harvard Crimson*, July 29, 2020, https://www.thecrimson.com/article/2020/7/29/lieber-tax-offenses-charges/.

114. Kate O'Keefe, "Education Department Investigating Harvard, Yale over Foreign Funding," *Wall Street Journal*, February 13, 2020, https://www.wsj.com/articles/education-department-investigating-harvard-yale-over-foreign-funding-11581539042; U.S. Department of Education, "U.S. Department of Education Launches Investigation into Foreign Gifts Reporting at Ivy League Universities," February 12, 2020, https://content.govdelivery.com/accounts/USED/bulletins/27b7801.

115. Meg P. Bernhard and Ignacio Sabate, "The Founders: The Evolution of edX at Harvard and MIT," *Harvard Crimson*, May 28, 2015, http://www.thecrimson.com/article/2015/5/28/the-founders/.

116. Morison, *Three Centuries,* 371.

117. Morison, *Three Centuries,* 371–372.

118. Virginia Postrel, "Harvard Gets Its Geek On: Can Big-Ticket Gifts Lift Harvard's Engineering Schools to the Top Ranks?," *Bloomberg,* June 18, 2015, http://www.bloombergview.com/articles/2015-06-18/harvard-gets-its-geek-on.

119. Postrel, "Harvard Gets Its Geek On."

120. Jonathan Shaw and John S. Rosenberg, "Engineering a School's Future," *Harvard Magazine*, January-February 2016, http://harvardmagazine.com/2015/12/engineering-a-school-s-future.

121. "Ballmer Boosts Harvard Computer Science," *Harvard Magazine*, November 13, 2014, http://harvardmagazine.com/2014/11/ballmer-boosts-harvard-computer-science-faculty.

122. "Frequently Asked Questions," Harvard John A. Paulson School of Engineering and Applied Sciences, https://www.seas.harvard.edu/prospective-students/prospective-undergraduate-students/frequently-asked-questions-faqs.

123. Meg P. Bernhard, "CS50 Logs Record-Breaking Enrollment Numbers," *Harvard Crimson*, September 11, 2014, http://www.thecrimson.com/article/2014/9/11/cs50-breaks-enrollment-records/?page=single; Melissa C. Rodman, "CS50's First Semester Winds Down at Yale," *Harvard Crimson*, December 16, 2015, http://www.thecrimson.com/article/2015/12/16/cs50-yale-end-semester/.

124. Melissa C. Rodman, "CS50's First Semester Winds Down at Yale."

125. "Best Undergraduate Engineering Programs Rankings 2020," *U.S. News and World Report,* https://www.usnews.com/best-colleges/rankings/engineering-doctorate.

126. "Allston: The Killer App," *Harvard Magazine*, February 5, 2013, https://harvardmagazine.com/2013/02/harvard-moving-engineering-school-to-allston-campus-0.

127. John S. Rosenberg, "Allston Land Company Leads Harvard Commercial Development," *Harvard Magazine*, November 29, 2018, https://www.harvardmagazine.com/2018/11/harvard-allston-land-development-company.

128. *Times Higher Education World University Rankings*, https://www.timeshighereducation.com/world-university-rankings/2020/world-ranking#!/page/0/length/25/sort_by/rank/sort_order/asc/cols/scores.

129. Author interview with Douglas A. Melton, Cambridge, MA, May 24, 2016.

130. John S. Rosenberg, "Allston Land Company Leads Harvard Commercial Development."

131. Jay London, "The Transformation of Kendall Square: The Past, Present, and Future of MIT's Neighborhood," *Slice of MIT*, October 7, 2015, https://alum.mit.edu/slice/transformation-kendall-square-past-present-and-future-mits-neighborhood; Andy Metzger, "Kendall Square: From Dustbowl of 1970s to Tech Hub of Today," *Wicked Local*, April 27, 2012, https://www.wickedlocal.com/article/20120427/News/304279870, accessed September 2020.

132. "Science and Engineering Complex Gets Final Beam," *Harvard Gazette*, November 29, 2017, https://news.harvard.edu/gazette/story/2017/11/final-beam-placed-in-harvards-science-and-engineering-complex/.

133. Brigid O'Rourke, "SEAS Moves Opening of Science and Engineering Complex to Spring Semester '21," *Harvard Gazette*, April 10, 2020, https://news.harvard.edu/gazette/story/2020/04/opening-of-new-science-and-engineering-complex-moves-to-spring-21/.

134. David F. Labaree, *A Perfect Mess: The Unlikely Ascendancy of American Higher Education* (Chicago: The University of Chicago Press, 2017), 13.

## 6. Public Mission, Private Funding

*Epigraph:* Nicholas Dirks, "Chancellor's Corner: Traditions of Excellence Worth Maintaining," *The Daily Californian*, February 6, 2015, http://www.dailycal.org/2015/02/06/chancellors-corner-traditions-excellence-worth-maintaining/, accessed December 7, 2015.

1. Will Kane, "Chancellor Christ Sworn in as 600 Graduate during Winter Ceremony," *UC Berkeley News*, December 17, 2017, https://news.berkeley.edu/2017/12/17/chancellor-christ-sworn-in-as-600-graduate-during-winter-ceremony/.

2. "Update on Campus Budget," University of California, Berkeley Office of the Chancellor, April 11, 2016, http://chancellor.berkeley.edu/update-campus-budget, accessed August 3, 2016; "Reducing UC Berkeley's Def-

icit," University of California, Berkeley Office of the Chancellor, http://chancellor.berkeley.edu/deficitreduction, accessed August 3, 2016.

3. Center on Budget and Policy Priorities, "A Lost Decade in Higher Education Funding: State Cuts Have Driven Up Tuition and Reduced Quality," August 23, 2017, https://www.cbpp.org/research/state-budget-and-tax/a-lost-decade-in-higher-education-funding.

4. "Budget 101," University of California, Berkeley Office of the Chief Financial Officer, https://cfo.berkeley.edu/budget-101.

5. "History," UC Berkeley Foundation, https://www.ucberkeleyfoundation.org/history-mission/.

6. Ry Rivard, "The New Normal at Berkeley," *Inside Higher Ed,* January 23, 2015, https://www.insidehighered.com/news/2015/01/23/gov-brown-says-normal-californians-cant-get-berkeley-problem-some-californians-blame, accessed December 7, 2015.

7. Michael Burke and Larry Gordon, "Newsom's proposed budget cuts to higher education force difficult choices ahead," EdSource, May 15, 2020, https://edsource.org/2020/newsoms-proposed-budget-cuts-to-higher-education-force-difficult-choices-ahead/631681; John Aubrey Douglass, "Why Does UC Berkeley Need $6 Billion?," UC Berkeley Blog, March 12, 2020, https://blogs.berkeley.edu/2020/03/12/why-does-uc-berkeley-need-6-billion/.

8. "An Act to Create and Organize the University of California," California State Assembly Bill No. 583, March 5, 1868, http://bancroft.berkeley.edu/CalHistory/charter.html, accessed August 18, 2016; "Bylaws," University of California Board of Regents, November 2015, http://regents.universityofcalifornia.edu/governance/bylaws/index.html, accessed August 18, 2016.

9. Patricia A. Pelfrey, *A Brief History of the University of California,* 2nd edition (Berkeley: University of California Press, 2004), 9.

10. Pelfrey, *A Brief History,* v.

11. Pelfrey, *A Brief History,* 11.

12. Pelfrey, *A Brief History,* 14–15.

13. Clark Kerr, *The Gold and the Blue: A Personal Memoir of the University of California, 1949–1967: Volume One: Academic Triumphs* (Berkeley: University of California Press, 2001), 39.

14. Edwin Emery Slosson, *Great American Universities* (New York: MacMillan, 1910), 149; Pelfrey, *A Brief History,* 22.

15. Pelfrey, *A Brief History,* 24.

16. Pelfrey, *A Brief History,* 28–29.

17. Kerr, *The Gold and the Blue: Academic Triumphs,* 140.

18. Jennifer Fenn Lefferts, "From Community College to Harvard," *Boston Globe,* May 23, 2019, https://www.bostonglobe.com/metro/globelocal/2019/05/22/from-community-college-harvard/ff9D4BQZYgsWTFpIo45NGO/story.html.

19. See Belinda Reyes, ed., *A Portrait of Race and Ethnicity in California: An Assessment of Social and Economic Well-Being* (Public Policy Institute of

California, 2001), http://www.ppic.org/content/pubs/report/R_201BRR
.pdf; Deborah Reed, Melissa Glenn Haber, and Laura Mameesh, "The Distribution of Income in California," (Public Policy Institute of California,
July 1996), http://www.ppic.org/content/pubs/report/R_796DRR.pdf, accessed
August 22, 2016.

20. Clark Kerr, *The Gold and the Blue: A Personal Memoir of the University of
California, 1949–1967: Volume Two: Political Turmoil* (Berkeley: University of
California Press, 2001), 28.

21. Kerr, *The Gold and the Blue: Political Turmoil,* 28.

22. Kerr, *The Gold and the Blue: Political Turmoil,* 288.

23. Quoted in "Education: View from the Bridge," *Time Magazine,* November 17,
1958.

24. Kerr, *The Gold and the Blue: Political Turmoil,* 309.

25. University of California Annual Endowment Report 2007, http://regents
.universityofcalifornia.edu/regmeet/mar08/i3attach.pdf, accessed August 18, 2016; University of California Annual Endowment Report 2009,
http://regents.universityofcalifornia.edu/regmeet/feb10/i6attach.pdf, accessed August 18, 2016.

26. Kevin O'Leary, "California's Crisis Hits Its Prized Universities," *Time
Magazine,* July 18, 2009, http://content.time.com/time/nation/article
/0,8599,1911455,00.html, accessed December 7, 2015.

27. Kevin O'Leary, "California's Crisis Hits its Prized Universities."

28. Author interview with George Breslauer, Berkeley, CA, April 28, 2015.

29. Author interview with George Breslauer, April 28, 2015.

30. Mac Taylor, *Faculty Recruitment and Retention at the University of California,*
Report of the Legislative Analyst's Office of California, December 13,
2012, http://www.lao.ca.gov/reports/2012/edu/uc-faculty/uc-faculty-121312
.pdf, accessed December 7, 2015.

31. Author interview with Nicholas Dirks, Berkeley, CA, May 3, 2015.

32. "Announcement of Comprehensive Planning and Analysis Process," UC
Berkeley Office of the Chancellor, February 10, 2016, http://chancellor
.berkeley.edu/announcement-comprehensive-planning-and-analysis-process,
accessed August 18, 2016.

33. Rachel Bachman, "Cal's Football-Stadium Gamble," *Wall Street Journal,*
April 18, 2012.

34. Nanette Asimov, "Cal Scrambling to Cover Stadium Bill," *SFGate,* June 16,
2013, http://www.sfgate.com/collegesports/article/Cal-scrambling-to-cover
-stadium-bill-4604221.php, accessed August 23, 2016.

35. Amy Jiang, "Campus Faculty Urge Review of Investigation into Allegations
Faced by Former Vice Chancellor," *The Daily Californian,* April 21, 2015,
https://www.dailycal.org/2015/04/20/uc-berkeley-faculty-sign-letter-review
-allegations-former-vice-chancellor-graham-fleming/, accessed September 2019.

36. Andrea Platten, "Napolitano Addresses Sexual Misconduct Cases, Orders
Graham Fleming Fired from New Post," *The Daily Californian,* March 13,

2016, https://www.dailycal.org/2016/03/12/graham-fleming-fired-from-role
-as-berkeley-global-campus-ambassador/, accessed September 2019.

37. UC Berkeley Public Affairs, "Berkeley's Budget Challenge: Reduce, Rethink, Restructure," *UC Berkeley News,* March 11, 2016, http://news.berkeley.edu /2016/03/11/berkeleys-budget-challenge/, accessed August 9, 2016.

38. Phillip Matier and Andrew Ross, "Fence and Its Costs Rising at UC Berkeley Chancellor's Home," *San Francisco Chronicle,* August 29, 2015, http://www.sfchronicle.com/bayarea/matier-ross/article/Fence-and-its-costs -rising-at-UC-Berkeley-6472768.php, accessed August 8, 2016.

39. Teresa Watanabe, "UC Berkeley Provost Resigns after Criticism of Handling of Sexual Harassment and Budget Issues," *Los Angeles Times,* April 15, 2016, http://www.latimes.com/local/lanow/la-me-ln-berkeley -provost-resigns-20160415-story.html, accessed August 3, 2016; Suhauna Hussain, "Andrew Szeri Resigns from Position as Vice Provost of Strategic Academic and Facilities Planning," *The Daily Californian,* June 19, 2016, http://www.dailycal.org/2016/06/19/andrew-szeri-resigns-position-vice -provost-strategic-academic-facilities-planning/, accessed August 8, 2016.

40. University of California, Berkeley Academic Senate Spring Division Meeting, audio recording, May 3, 2016, http://academic-senate.berkeley.edu /meetings/division/property-0-3, accessed August 9, 2016.

41. Nanette Asimov, "UC Berkeley Chancellor Faces Skeptical Academic Senate," *SFGate,* May 3, 2016, http://www.sfgate.com/news/article/UC-Berkeley -chancellor-faces-skeptical-Academic-7391798.php, accessed August 8, 2016.

42. Pelfrey, *A Brief History,* 11.

43. Author interview with Sheldon Rothblatt, Berkeley, CA, May 3, 2015.

44. Author interview with George Breslauer, April 28, 2015.

45. Author interview with Nicholas Dirks, May 3, 2015.

46. George Breslauer, "What Made Berkeley Great? The Sources of Berkeley's Sustained Academic Excellence," University of California, Berkeley Center for Studies in Higher Education Research & Occasional Paper Series: CSHE.3.11, January 2011.

47. Author interview with George Breslauer, April 28, 2015.

48. University of California, *Budget for Current Operations Report: Summary of the Budget Request As Presented to the Regents for Approval 2019–20,* 9, https://www.ucop.edu/operating-budget/_files/rbudget/2019-20-budget -summary.pdf, accessed September 2019.

49. Curan Mehra, "Prop. 20 Passes, Midyear UC Tuition Increase Avoided," *The Daily Californian,* November 6, 2012, http://www.dailycal.org/2012/11 /06/fate-of-prop-30-still-unclear/, accessed December 8, 2015.

50. *2013–2014 UC Berkeley Budget Plan,* http://cfo.berkeley.edu/sites/default /files/2013-14%20UC%20Berkeley%20Budget%20Plan%20-%20Final%20 %289-5-13%29.pdf, accessed December 7, 2015.

51. John Wilton, "Time Is Not on Our Side," Berkeley Administration and Finance, November 29, 2013, part 1, 5–6, http://vcaf.berkeley.edu/sites/default

/files/Time%20is%20not%20on%20our%20side%202%20%2011.29.13%20 FINAL.pdf, accessed December 7, 2015.

52. *Times Higher Education,* "THE World Academic Summit: Nicholas Dirks," YouTube video, 46:59, October 2, 2015, https://www.youtube.com/watch?v =3NkoyHAJiPY, accessed December 7, 2015; Nicholas Dirks, "The Future of World-Class Universities," *University World News,* no. 385 (October 2, 2015), http://www.universityworldnews.com/article.php?story=2015100100 4022774, accessed December 7, 2015.

53. "Energy Biosciences Institute: About EBI," 2015, Energy & Biosciences, http://www.energybiosciencesinstitute.org/content/energy-biosciences -institute, accessed December 7, 2015; Rick DelVecchio, "UC Faculty Critical of BP Deal," *SFGate,* March 9, 2007, http://www.sfgate.com/education /article/BERKELEY-UC-faculty-critical-of-BP-deal-2611643.php, accessed August 23, 2016.

54. Charles Burress, "Probe of Research Pact at Cal Released," *SFGate,* July 31, 2004, http://www.sfgate.com/bayarea/article/BERKELEY-Probe-of -research-pact-at-Cal-released-2737385.php, accessed August 23, 2016; Lawrence Busch et al., *External Review of the Collaborative Research Agreement between Novartis Agricultural Discovery Institute, Inc. and the Regents of the University of California* (East Lansing, MI: Institute for Food and Agricultural Standards, Michigan State University, 2004); Robert M. Price and Laurie Goldman, *The Novartis Agreement: An Appraisal,* UC Berkeley Administrative Review, October 4, 2004.

55. Data from the National Center for Education Statistics Integrated Postsecondary Education Data System, http://nces.ed.gov/ipeds/, accessed August 26, 2020.

56. Author interview with Nicholas Dirks, May 3, 2015.

57. "University Ultra High Net Worth Alumni Rankings 2019," Wealth-X, https://www.wealthx.com/wp-content/uploads/2019/08/University-Ultra -High-Net-Worth-Alumni-Rankings-2019.pdf; Chris Parr, "Top 20 Universities for Producing Billionaires," *Times Higher Education,* November 20, 2014, https://www.timeshighereducation.com/news/top-20-universities-for -producing-billionaires/2017097.article.

58. UC Berkeley Public Affairs, "Campus Sets New Records for Fundraising," *UC Berkeley News,* July 14, 2016, http://news.berkeley.edu/2016/07/14 /campus-sets-new-records-for-fundraising/, accessed August 18, 2016.

59. UC Berkeley, "Light the Way: The Campaign for Berkeley: FAQ," https:// light.berkeley.edu/o/about/, accessed September 2020.

60. UC Berkeley Public Affairs, "At Saturday Event, Berkeley Kicks off $6 Billion 'Light the Way' Campaign," *UC Berkeley News,* March 2, 2020, https:// news.berkeley.edu/2020/03/02/at-saturday-event-berkeley-kicks-off-6 -billion-light-the-way-campaign/.

61. UC Berkeley, "Light the Way: The Campaign for Berkeley."

62. "Berkeley Operational Excellence: About," http://oe.berkeley.edu/about, accessed December 7, 2015.

63. Logan Goldberg, "Campus Leaders Address 'Painful' Budget Cuts, Other Changes at Staff Forum," *The Daily Californian,* February 24, 2015, http://www.dailycal.org/2015/02/24/campus-leaders-address-painful -budget-cuts-changes-staff-forum/, accessed August 9, 2016; Curan Mehra and Jordan Bach-Lombardo, "Birgeneau Leaves Legacy of Complicated Commitment to Public Mission," *The Daily Californian,* May 3, 2013, http://www.dailycal.org/2013/05/03/birgeneau-leaves-legacy-of-complicated -commitment-to-public-mission/, accessed August 9, 2016.

64. Wilton, "Time Is Not on Our Side," part 1.

65. UC Berkeley Research, "Faculty Excellence," https://vcresearch.berkeley.edu /excellence/faculty-excellence, accessed March 16, 2021.

66. Author interview with Nicholas Dirks, May 3, 2015.

67. Kerr, *The Gold and the Blue: Academic Triumphs,* 8-9.

68. Marc Gould, "UCB Faculty Advancement Slides, 1985–2011 by Discipline," Office for Faculty Equity and Welfare, http://ofew.berkeley.edu/sites/default /files/ucb_faculty_advancement_slides_by_discipline_2011.pdf, accessed August 18, 2016.

69. Author interview with Robert Birgeneau, Berkeley, CA, May 3, 2015.

70. Confidential author interview, April 2015.

71. Author interview with Nicholas Dirks, May 3, 2015.

72. Author interview with George Breslauer, April 28, 2015.

73. Teresa Watanabe, "UC Berkeley Chancellor to Resign Following Wide-spread Criticism by Faculty," *Los Angeles Times,* August 16, 2016, http:// www.latimes.com/local/lanow/la-me-ln-uc-berkeley-chancellor-resign -20160816-snap-story.html, accessed August 18, 2016.

74. Data from the National Center for Education Statistics Integrated Post-secondary Education Data System, http://nces.ed.gov/ipeds/, accessed August 24, 2016.

75. National Center for Education Statistics, "UC Berkeley: Human Resources," https://nces.ed.gov/ipeds/datacenter/Facsimile.aspx?unitid=110635, accessed September 2020.

76. *Review of the Institute of East Asian Studies, University of California, Berkeley, 2011–2012,* submitted January 27, 2012.

77. "Best Colleges, 2020," *U.S. News and World Report,* 2019, http://colleges .usnews.rankingsandreviews.com/best-colleges/, accessed September 2019.

78. Wilton, "Time Is Not on Our Side," part 2, 2-3.

79. Wilton, "Time Is Not on Our Side," part 2, 2; U.S. Department of Education, "Distribution of Federal Pell Grant Program Funds by Institution," https://www2.ed.gov/finaid/prof/resources/data/pell-institution.html, accessed August 26, 2020; "Economic Diversity Among the Top 25," *U.S. News and World Report,* https://www.usnews.com/best-colleges/rankings

/national-universities/economic-diversity-among-top-ranked-schools, accessed August 26, 2020.

80. "By the Numbers," 2015, University of California, Berkeley, http://www.berkeley.edu/about/bythenumbers, accessed December 7, 2015.

81. "UC Berkeley Fall Enrollment Data," University of California, Berkeley Office of Planning and Analysis, https://opa.berkeley.edu/uc-berkeley-fall-enrollment-data, accessed August 26, 2020.

82. "A Semester Unlike Any Other," University of California, Berkeley Division of Equity and Inclusion, https://diversity.berkeley.edu/news/semester-unlike-any-other, accessed September 25, 2020.

83. See Gary Y. Okihiro's *Third World Studies: Theorizing Liberation* (Durham, NC: Duke University Press, 2016) for an in-depth history of the Third World Liberation Front.

84. The Berkeley Revolution, "The Third World Liberation Front," http://revolution.berkeley.edu/projects/twlf/.

85. Gino Nuzzolillo and Trey Walk, "You Should Take an Ethnic Studies Course," *The Chronicle,* January 15, 2019, https://www.dukechronicle.com/article/2019/01/duke-university-you-should-take-an-ethnic-studies-course.

86. Tyler Kingkade, "Occupy Cal Berkeley Protest Draws Thousands, As Two Years of Occupation Come Home," *Huffington Post,* November 10, 2011, http://www.huffingtonpost.com/2011/11/10/thousands-gather-for-occupy-cal-protest_n_1086963.html, accessed August 18, 2016; Amruta Trivedi, "Chancellor's Statement to ASUC Senate Cut Short by Calls for Resignation," *The Daily Californian,* December 8, 2011, http://www.dailycal.org/2011/12/07/chancellors-statement-to-asuc-senate-cut-short/, accessed August 18, 2016; Chloe Hunt and J. D. Morris, "Robert Birgeneau to Step Down as Chancellor of UC Berkeley," *The Daily Californian,* March 14, 2012, http://www.dailycal.org/2012/03/13/uc-berkeley-chancellor-robert-birgeneau-announces-he-will-step-down-at-years-end/, accessed August 18, 2016.

87. "The Berkeley Undergraduate Initiative Executive Summary," University of California, Berkeley Vice Chancellor for Undergraduate Education, March 30, 2016, http://vcue.berkeley.edu/sites/default/files/the_undergraduate_initiative-_executive_summary_final.pdf.

88. Interview with Nicholas Dirks, May 3, 2015.

89. "CA Demographics," University of California, https://www.universityofcalifornia.edu/infocenter/ca-demographics, accessed September 2020.

90. "UC Berkeley Fall Enrollment Data," University of California, Berkeley Office of Planning and Analysis, https://opa.berkeley.edu/uc-berkeley-fall-enrollment-data, accessed August 26, 2020.

91. Doris Sze Chun, "John Fryer, The First Agassiz Professor of Oriental Languages and Literature, Berkeley," *Chronicle of the University of California,* no. 7 (Fall 2005): 2, https://cshe.berkeley.edu/sites/default/files/chron7_excerpt_fryer.pdf.

92. "International Student Enrollment, Fall 2019," University of California, Berkeley International Office, https://internationaloffice.berkeley.edu/sites/default/files/student-stats2019.pdf.

93. "International Student Enrollment Data," Berkeley International Office, http://internationaloffice.berkeley.edu/students/current/enrollment_data.

94. Larry Gordon, "UC Berkeley Studies International Education Campus in Richmond," *Los Angeles Times*, February 24, 2015, http://www.latimes.com/local/education/la-me-uc-richmond-20150224-story.html#page=1, accessed December 7, 2015.

95. UC Berkeley Public Affairs, "Campus Launches Effort to Form New Global Alliance," *UC Berkeley News*, October 16, 2015, http://news.berkeley.edu/2015/10/16/campus-announces-new-global-alliance/, accessed December 7, 2015.

96. Larry Gordon, "UC Berkeley Studies International Education Campus"; Nicholas Dirks, "Open Letter to the Richmond Community from UC Berkeley Chancellor Nicholas Dirks: An Update on the Berkeley Global Campus," May 28, 2015, http://chancellor.berkeley.edu/sites/default/files/UCB-ChancellorDirksOpenLetterRichmond-BGCRB-5-28-15.pdf, accessed December 7, 2015.

97. Wilton, "Time Is Not on Our Side," part 1, 3.

98. Author interview with Robert Birgeneau, May 3, 2015.

99. Author interview with Robert Birgeneau, May 3, 2015.

100. Teresa Watanabe, "UC Berkeley's New Chancellor Brings Optimism—and a World Record—to an Embattled Campus," *The Baltimore Sun*, August 18, 2017, https://www.baltimoresun.com/la-me-uc-berkeley-new-chancellor-20170818-story.html, accessed May 2020.

101. Teresa Watanabe, "UC Berkeley's New Chancellor Brings Optimism."

102. Maxine Mouly and Olivia Buccieri, "Campus Officials Announce Elimination of $150M Deficit," *The Daily Californian*, September 26, 2019, https://www.dailycal.org/2019/09/24/campus-officials-announce-elimination-of-150-million-deficit/, accessed May 2020.

103. UC Berkeley Public Affairs, "Chancellor Christ: Free Speech Is Who We Are," *UC Berkeley News*, August 23, 2017, https://news.berkeley.edu/2017/08/23/chancellor-christ-free-speech-is-who-we-are/, accessed May 2020.

104. Yao Huang, "UC Berkeley Ranks Below UCLA as 2nd-Best Public School in US," *The Daily Californian*, September 13, 2018, https://www.dailycal.org/2018/09/13/uc-berkeley-ranks-below-ucla-as-2nd-best-public-school-in-us/, accessed May 2020.

105. Robert Morse, Matt Mason, and Eric Brooks, "Updates to 5 Schools' 2019 Best Colleges Rankings Data," *U.S. News and World Report*, July 25, 2019, https://www.usnews.com/education/blogs/college-rankings-blog/articles/2019-07-25/updates-to-5-schools-2019-best-colleges-rankings-data, accessed September 2019.

106. UC Berkeley Public Affairs, "UCLA, UC Berkeley Top Publics in *U.S. News* National Rankings," *UC Berkeley News*, September 2019, https://news

.berkeley.edu/2019/09/09/us-news-national-rankings2020/, accessed May 2020; Yao Huang, "UC Berkeley Ranks Below UCLA."

107. UC Berkeley Public Affairs, "In Online Conversation, Carol Christ Gives Budget, Campus Updates," *UC Berkeley News,* May 12, 2020, https://news .berkeley.edu/2020/05/12/in-online-conversation-carol-christ-gives-budget -campus-updates/, accessed May 2020.

108. UC Berkeley Public Affairs, "In Online Conversation, Carol Christ Gives Budget, Campus Updates."

109. "UC Berkeley Announces Plans for Fall Semester," *UC Berkeley News,* June 17, 2020, https://news.berkeley.edu/2020/06/17/uc-berkeley-announces -plans-for-fall-semester/, accessed June 2020.

110. Jessica Ruf, "California Creates Higher Ed Recovery Taskforce to Mitigate COVID-19 Impact," *Diverse Education,* August 10, 2020, https://diversee ducation.com/article/187160/.

111. Interview with George Breslauer, April 28, 2015.

112. "A Semester Unlike Any Other," University of California, Berkeley Division of Equity & Inclusion, https://diversity.berkeley.edu/news/semester-unlike -any-other, accessed September 2020.

## 7. Outrageous Ambitions

1. This story was first related in Brodhead's inaugural address, "More Day to Dawn," September 18, 2004, reprinted in Richard H. Brodhead, *Speaking of Duke: Leading the 21st Century University* (Durham, NC: Duke University Press, 2017), 19.

2. Brodhead, "Constructing Duke," Freshman Convocation, August 19, 2015, in Brodhead, *Speaking of Duke,* 220.

3. See William C. Kirby, Nora Bynum, Tracy Yuen Manty, and Erica M. Zendell, "Kunshan, Incorporated: The Making of China's Richest Town," Case 313–103 (Boston: Harvard Business School, 2013).

4. Terry Sanford, "Outrageous Ambitions," Address to the Annual Meeting of the Faculty, October 25, 1984, https://dukespace.lib.duke.edu/dspace /bitstream/handle/10161/91/outrageousambitions.pdf?sequence=1.

5. "Facts," Duke University, https://facts.duke.edu, accessed August 2020; "Quick Statistics about Duke University," Duke University Libraries, https://library.duke.edu/rubenstein/uarchives/history/articles/statistics, accessed September 2020.

6. "Global Companies Rank Universities," *New York Times,* October 25, 2012, https://archive.nytimes.com/www.nytimes.com/imagepages/2012/10/25 /world/asia/25iht-sreducemerging25-graphic.html.

7. Brodhead, "More Day to Dawn," in Brodhead, *Speaking of Duke,* 20.

8. On Crowell and the move to Durham, see Robert F. Durden, *The Dukes of Durham, 1865–1929* (Durham, NC: Duke University Press, 1975), 91–96. See also Crowell's memoirs: John Franklin Crowell, *Personal Collections of*

*Trinity College, North Carolina, 1887–1894* (Durham, NC: Duke University Press, 1939). The Duke University Archives hold Crowell's papers, including account books and grade books in the collection "John Franklin Crowell Records and Papers, 1883–1932."

9. See Robert F. Durden, *The Dukes of Durham*; on the British-American Tobacco Company's success in China see Sherman Cochran, *Big Business in China: Sino-foreign Rivalry in the Cigarette Industry* (Cambridge, MA: Harvard University Press, 1980).

10. "Washington Duke and the Education of Women," Duke University Libraries, https://library.duke.edu/rubenstein/uarchives/history/articles/washington-duke-women, accessed September 2019.

11. See Nora Campbell Chaffin, *Trinity College, 1839–1892: The Beginnings of Duke University* (Durham, NC: Duke University Press, 1950); Earl W. Porter, *Trinity and Duke, 1892–1924: Foundations of Duke University* (Durham, NC: Duke University Press, 1964).

12. See Robert F. Durden, *Bold Entrepreneur: A Life of James B. Duke* (Durham, NC: Carolina Academic Press, 2003), 155.

13. Robert F. Durden, *The Launching of Duke University: 1924–1949* (Durham, NC: Duke University Press, 2005), 26.

14. "Medical Center History—Overview," Duke University Medical Center Archives, https://archives.mc.duke.edu/history, accessed September 2020.

15. "History of Duke Hospital," Duke Department of Surgery, https://surgery.duke.edu/about-department/history, accessed September 2020.

16. "History of Duke Hospital," Duke Department of Surgery.

17. Cited in Tallman Trask III, foreword to *Duke University: An Architectural Tour* by Ken Friedlein and John Pearce (New York: Princeton Architectural Press, 2015), 11–12.

18. *First Progress Report*, Committee on Planning and Development at Duke University (June 1959), 5.

19. *First Progress Report*, Introductory Statement.

20. Quoted in Robert F. Durden, *Lasting Legacy to the Carolinas: The Duke Endowment, 1924–1994* (Durham, NC: Duke University Press, 1998), 149.

21. Durden, *Lasting Legacy*, 36.

22. Durden, *Lasting Legacy*, 36–37.

23. Durden, *Lasting Legacy*, 32; "Quick Statistics about Duke University," Duke University Library, https://library.duke.edu/rubenstein/uarchives/history/articles/statistics.

24. "Commemorating 50 Years of Black Students at Duke University," Duke University, https://spotlight.duke.edu/50years/.

25. *First Progress Report*, 36.

26. Richard H. Brodhead, "Coming through the Current Challenges," *Duke Today*, February 10, 2010, https://today.duke.edu/2010/02/rhbspeech.html.

27. *Long Range Planning at Duke University: Second Progress Report*, Duke University (1960), 19.

28. *The Fifth Decade,* Duke University (1964); *Duke University in the Decade Ahead (Third Progress Report),* Duke University Committee on Long Range Planning (1961).

29. "Profile of Duke University 1956–1976," Duke University (1976), 15.

30. "Profile of Duke University 1956–1976," 16–18.

31. "Profile of Duke University 1956–1976," 20.

32. "History and Mission," Duke Lemur Center, https://lemur.duke.edu/about/history-mission/.

33. "History and Mission," Duke Lemur Center.

34. John Markis, "From Lemurs to Poisoned Chocolate: The Tale of a Lemur Center Founder," *The Chronicle,* April 23, 2019, https://www.dukechronicle.com/article/2019/04/duke-university-from-lemurs-to-poisoned-chocolate-the-tale-of-a-lemur-center-founder-john-buettner-janusch.

35. Markis, "From Lemurs to Poisoned Chocolate."

36. "History and Mission," Duke Lemur Center.

37. Sanford, "Outrageous Ambitions."

38. Howard E. Covington and Marion A. Ellis, *Terry Sanford: Politics, Progress, & Outrageous Ambitions* (Durham, NC: Duke University Press, 1999), 368–369.

39. Covington and Ellis, *Terry Sanford,* 373; "Meet Terry Sanford," Duke Sanford School of Public Policy, https://sanford.duke.edu/about-us/inside-sanford/meet-terry-sanford.

40. "Summary Report of the University Planning Committee," Duke University (1972).

41. "Summary Report," Duke University (1972).

42. Ibid.

43. Ibid.

44. Terry Sanford, "A Time for Greatness at Duke: The Epoch Campaign," Duke University (1973), 21, https://ia600401.us.archive.org/24/items/timeforgreatness00duke/timeforgreatness00duke.pdf.

45. Sanford, "A Time for Greatness at Duke," 20.

46. *Directions for Progress: A Report to the Duke University Board of Trustees,* Duke University (1980), 1–2.

47. *Directions for Progress,* 2.

48. "History and Quick Facts," Duke Nicholas School of the Environment, https://nicholas.duke.edu/general/history-quick-facts.

49. *Directions for Progress,* 3.

50. *Directions for Progress,* 64.

51. "Academic Plan," Duke University (1987), 15–16.

52. Covington and Ellis, *Terry Sanford,* 421.

53. David Yaffe, "The Department That Fell to Earth: The Deflation of Duke English," http://Linguafranca.mirror.theinfo.org/9902/yaffe.html.

54. *Crossing Boundaries: Interdisciplinary Planning for the Nineties,* Duke University Self-Study (1988), 46.

55. Adam Beyer, "Remembering Keith Brodie: Community Mourns Passing of the Former Duke President," *The Chronicle*, December 6, 2016, http://www.dukechronicle.com/article/2016/12/remembering-keith-brodie-community-fathers-to-mourn-passing-of-the-former-duke-president.

56. Beyer, "Remembering Keith Brodie."

57. "Economic Diversity among the Top 25 National Universities," *U.S. News and World Report*, https://www.usnews.com/best-colleges/rankings/national-universities/economic-diversity-among-top-ranked-schools, accessed June 2020.

58. U.S. Department of Education, "Equity in Athletics Data Analysis," https://ope.ed.gov/athletics/#/, accessed June 2020.

59. Niharika Vattikonda, "Duke Athletics' Annual Equity Report Sheds Light on Spending, Coaching for Men's and Women's Teams," *The Chronicle*, April 10, 2019, https://www.dukechronicle.com/article/2019/04/duke-athletics-annual-equity-report-shows-differences-between-mens-and-womens-teams, accessed June 2020.

60. Burton Bollag, "Men's Lacrosse Team at Duke U. Forfeits Games Following Accusations of Rape at Party," *The Chronicle of Higher Education*, March 27, 2006, https://www.chronicle.com/article/Mens-Lacrosse-Team-at-Duke-U/117736, accessed June 2020.

61. Duff Wilson and David Barstow, "All Charges Dropped in Duke Case," *New York Times*, April 12, 2007, https://www.nytimes.com/2007/04/12/us/12duke.html, accessed June 2020.

62. David S. Webster, *Academic Quality Rankings of American Colleges and Universities* (Springfield, IL: Charles C. Thomas Publisher, 1986), 127, 131; citing David S. Webster, "America's Highest Ranked Graduate Schools, 1925–1982," *Change: The Magazine of Higher Education* 15, no. 4 (May–June 1983).

63. "U.S. News & World Report Historical University Rankings," data compiled by Andrew G. Reiter, https://sites.google.com/site/andyreiter/data.

64. Sanford, "Outrageous Ambitions."

65. *Shaping Our Future: A Young University Faces a New Century*, Duke University (1994), 6–8.

66. *Shaping Our Future*, Duke University (1994).

67. *Building on Excellence*, Duke University (2001), 160.

68. "$2 Billion and Counting," *Duke Magazine*, January-February 2003, https://alumni.duke.edu/magazine/articles/2-billion-and-counting.

69. "$2 Billion and Counting."

70. "Master Plan," Duke Facilities Management, https://facilities.duke.edu/campus/master-plan, accessed March 16, 2021.

71. "Bylaws of Duke University," Duke University Board of Trustees, https://trustees.duke.edu/governing-documents/bylaws-duke-university.

72. Author interview with Peter Lange, Durham, NC, April 13, 2015.

73. "Minutes of the Regular Meeting of the Academic Council: January 19, 2006," Duke University Academic Council, https://academiccouncil.duke.edu/sites/default/files/AC01-19-061.pdf, accessed June 2020.

74. Ibid.
75. "Bylaws of Duke University."
76. "Minutes of the Regular Meeting of the Academic Council: September 21, 2006," Duke University Academic Council, https://academiccouncil.duke .edu/sites/default/files/AC09-21-06P.pdf, accessed June 2020.
77. Author interview with Peter Lange, April 13, 2015.
78. Author interview with Sally Kornbluth, Durham, NC, April 10, 2015.
79. Author interview with Tallman Trask III, Durham, NC, April 15, 2015.
80. *Building on Excellence,* 160.
81. *Building on Excellence,* 177.
82. Author correspondence with Peter Lange, February 7, 2021.
83. Author interview with Richard Brodhead, Durham, NC, April 15, 2015.
84. "Minutes of the Regular Meeting of the Academic Council: September 21, 2006," Duke University Academic Council, https://academiccouncil.duke .edu/sites/default/files/AC09-21-06P.pdf, accessed June 2020.
85. "Duke's Financial Aid Initiative Raises $308.5 Million," *Duke Today,* January 26, 2009, https://today.duke.edu/2009/01/fai.html.
86. "In Letter to Staff, President Brodhead Outlines Duke's Response to Economic Downturn," *Duke Today,* March 1, 2009, https://today.duke.edu /2009/03/rhbletter.html.
87. "In Letter to Staff."
88. Ibid.
89. Ibid.
90. Ibid.
91. "Memo: Peter Lange Charges Deans to Review Strategic Plan," *Duke Today,* April 29, 2009, https://today.duke.edu/2009/04/stratmemo.html.
92. "Duke University's Endowment: 2015–16 Snapshot," Duke University (2016), https://dukeforward.duke.edu/downloads/Duke_Endowment-2016 _D.pdf; Jake Satisky, "University Endowment Rises to Record $8.6 Billion after 'Economic Headwinds,'" *The Chronicle,* September 28, 2019, https:// www.dukechronicle.com/article/2019/09/duke-university-endowment -record-board-of-trustees#:~:text=University%20endowment%20rises%20 to%20record%20%248.6%20billion%20after%20'economic%20headwinds; "Duke's Endowment Returns Nearly 56 Percent in Fiscal Year 2021," *The Chronicle,* October 15, 2021, https://www.dukechronicle.com/article/2021 /10/duke-university-endowment-gain-56-percent-dumac-how-used-financial -aid-faculty-pay-who-manages.
93. Draft of Peter Lange Letter to the Faculty, Duke University Archives, Office of the Provost, Common Archives, 2000–2007.
94. Rachel Chason, "How Brodhead Changed Duke," *The Chronicle,* April 12, 2017, http://www.dukechronicle.com/article/2017/04/how-brodhead -changed-duke.
95. "About DukeEngage," DukeEngage, https://dukeengage.duke.edu/about -dukeengage.

96. Author interview with Noah Pickus, Durham, NC, April 9, 2015.
97. *Building on Excellence,* 165.
98. "About Duke Global Health Institute," Duke Global Health Institute, https://globalhealth.duke.edu/about.
99. *Making a Difference,* Duke University (2006), 45–47.
100. "Interdisciplinarity at Duke: A Brief Inventory of Connections among Schools and University-Wide Institutes, Initiatives, and Centers," Duke OVPIS (2018), https://sites.duke.edu/interdisciplinary/files/2018/09/interdisciplinarity-at-duke-august2018-1.pdf, accessed September 2019.
101. "Interdisciplinarity at Duke."
102. Ibid.
103. Ibid.
104. Ibid.
105. Ibid.
106. Author interview with Sally Kornbluth, April 10, 2015.
107. Author interview with Richard Brodhead, April 15, 2015.
108. Author interview with Peter Lange, April 13, 2015.
109. Author interview with Haiyan Gao, Durham, NC, April 9, 2015.
110. Author interview with Sally Kornbluth, April 10, 2015.
111. Author interview with Peter Lange, April 13, 2015.
112. *Together Duke: Advancing Excellence through Community,* Duke University (April 2017).
113. *Times Higher Education World University Rankings,* 2017, https://www.timeshighereducation.com/world-university-rankings/2017/world-ranking#!/page/0/length/25/sort_by/rank/sort_order/asc/cols/stats; "QS World University Rankings 2016–2017," QS Top Universities (2017), https://www.topuniversities.com/university-rankings/world-university-rankings/2016; Duke University, Academic Ranking of World Universities, http://www.shanghairanking.com/World-University-Rankings/Duke-University.html.
114. "Best Medical Schools," USNWR Rankings 2019, https://www.usnews.com/best-graduate-schools/top-medical-schools/research-rankings; "Best Law Schools," USNWR Rankings 2019, https://www.usnews.com/best-graduate-schools/top-law-schools/law-rankings.
115. "Best Nursing Schools: Research," USNWR Rankings 2019, https://www.usnews.com/best-graduate-schools/top-nursing-schools/nur-rankings.
116. "Best Business Schools," USNWR Rankings 2019, https://www.usnews.com/best-graduate-schools/top-business-schools/mba-rankings.
117. "Duke Ranks as 6th Best Global University in Environment and Ecology," Duke Nicholas School of the Environment (2016) citing USNWR rankings, https://nicholas.duke.edu/about/news/duke-ranks-6th-best-global-university-environment-and-ecology.
118. *Summary Report of the University Planning Committee,* Duke University (1972), 95.

119. Ibid.

120. Ibid.

121. Lisa K. Childress, *The Twenty-first Century University: Developing Faculty Engagement in Internationalization* (Frankfurt, Germany: Peter Lang Publishing, 2009), 43–44.

122. *Shaping Our Future,* Duke University (1994), 26.

123. *Shaping Our Future,* Duke University (1994), 27.

124. "A Global Vision for Duke University," Duke University Global Priorities Committee (2013), Fuqua Global Executive MBA Program, http://www .fuqua.duke.edu/programs/duke_mba/global-executive/.

125. Fuqua Cross Continent MBA Program, http://www.fuqua.duke.edu /programs/duke_mba/cross_continent/.

126. *Building on Excellence,* 89–90.

127. *Building on Excellence,* 89–92.

128. "About," Duke Global Education Office, https://globaled.duke.edu/about, accessed September 2020.

129. *Duke Global Health Institute 2015–2016 Impact Report,* Duke Global Health Institute (2018), https://globalhealth.duke.edu/sites/default/files/files/dghi _annual-report-2017-2018_final-forweb.pdf.

130. "Duke University and National University of Singapore Advance to Second Phase of Medical School Partnership," November 30, 2010, Duke Health, https://corporate.dukehealth.org/news/duke-university-and-national-university -singapore-advance-second-phase-medical-school.

131. Author interview with Richard Brodhead, April 15, 2015.

132. "Duke-Kunshan Planning Guide," Duke University Office of the Provost and Office of Global Strategy and Programs (2011); Kirby et al., "Kunshan, Incorporated"; See my filmed interview with Party Secretary Guan Aiguo at my online course, ChinaX, Part 10, Section 49.6, "Kunshan Field Trip," https://www .edx.org/course/contemporary-china-the-peoples-republic-taiwan-and.

133. "Duke-Kunshan Planning Guide."

134. "Duke-Kunshan Planning Guide," 20.

135. "Duke-Kunshan Planning Guide," 19.

136. "Senior Leaders Appointed for Duke Kunshan University," *Duke Today,* September 20, 2012, http://today.duke.edu/2012/09/dkuexecs.

137. "Duke-Kunshan Planning Guide."

138. Author interview with Haiyan Gao, Kunshan, China, March 22, 2017.

139. "Undergraduate Curriculum: Liberal Arts in the 21st Century," Duke Kunshan University, https://dukekunshan.edu.cn/en/academics/undergraduate -curriculum.

140. "Trustees Approve Undergraduate Program for Duke Kunshan University," *Duke Today,* December 3, 2016, https://today.duke.edu/2016/12/trustees -approve-undergraduate-program-duke-kunshan-university.

141. New York University, "The Creation of NYU Shanghai," March 27, 2011, https://www.nyu.edu/about/leadership-university-administration/office-of -the-president-emeritus/communications/the-creation-of-nyu-shanghai.html.

142. Sally Kornbluth, "Memo to the Faculty from Provost Sally Kornbluth," March 16, 2016, https://provost.duke.edu/sites/all/files/Duke%20and%20 the%20Development%20of%20DKU%20rev%20Aug%202016%20.pdf, accessed June 2020.

143. Ibid.

144. Ibid.

145. Maria Morrison, "Duke Kunshan University Breaks Ground on 47-acre Expansion," *The Chronicle* August 19, 2019, https://www.dukechronicle.com /article/2019/08/duke-kunshan-university-breaks-down-phase-2-expansion -china, accessed May 2020.

146. "Vincent Price Named Duke University 10th President," *Duke Today*, December 2, 2016, https://today.duke.edu/2016/12/presannouncement.

147. Ibid.

148. Duke Strategic Framework, https://president.duke.edu/wp-content/uploads /2019/04/Duke-Will-Strategic-Framework.pdf, accessed October 2019.

149. Duke Kunshan University, "Duke Kunshan University Welcomes Its First Undergraduate Class," August 14, 2018, http://webcache.googleusercontent .com/search?q=cache:EqrvPB1A45cJ:https://dukekunshan.edu.cn/en/news /arrival-class-of-2022&hl=en&gl=us&strip=1&vwsrc=0.

150. Johns Hopkins University Coronavirus Resource Center, "COVID-19 Dashboard by the Center for Systems Science and Engineering (CSSE) at Johns Hopkins University," https://coronavirus.jhu.edu/map.html, accessed September 2020.

151. Nick Anderson, "China's Coronavirus Crisis Forces Duke Kunshan University to Teach Online," *Washington Post*, February 22, 2020, https://www .washingtonpost.com/local/education/chinas-coronavirus-crisis-forces-duke -kunshan-university-to-teach-online/2020/02/22/311349aa-5333-11ea-929a -64efa7482a77_story.html.

152. Duke Kunshan University, "Coronavirus: Updates on DKU's Response," May 14, 2020, https://dukekunshan.edu.cn/en/news/special-message-novel -coronavirus, accessed June 2020.

153. Matthew Griffin and Carter Forinash, "Duke Limits Fall Housing to First-years and Sophomores, Scaling Back Reopening Plans," *The Chronicle*, July 26, 2020, https://www.dukechronicle.com/article/2020/07/duke -university-email-fall-changes-housing-limited-first-years-sophomore -coronavirus.

154. "A Global Celebration for Duke Kunshan's Class of 2024," *Duke Today*, August 26, 2020, https://today.duke.edu/2020/08/global-celebration-duke -kunshan%E2%80%99s-class-2024.

155. Duke Office of Duke Kunshan University Relations, "Message to Duke '24 International Students: DKU Option for Fall 2020," https://dkurelations .duke.edu/students/duke-students-dku/message-duke-24-international -students-dku-option-fall-2020.

156. Author interview with Richard Brodhead, April 15, 2015.

157. Ibid.

158. "Minutes of the Meeting of the Academic Council: November 17, 2016," Duke University Academic Council, http://academiccouncil.duke.edu/sites /default/files/11-17-16%20minutes.pdf.

## 8. A Chinese Century?

1. Qi Wang and Nian Cai Liu, "Higher Education Research Institutes in Chinese Universities," *Studies in Higher Education* 39, no. 8 (September 2014): 1488–1498.
2. "Sustainable Development Goals: National Monitoring: Enrolment by Level of Education: Enrolment in Tertiary Education, All Programmes, Both Sexes (Number): China," UNESCO, http://data.uis.unesco.org/#, accessed January 19, 2021.
3. Andrew Jacobs, "China's Army of Graduates Struggles for Jobs," *New York Times,* December 11, 2010, https://www.nytimes.com/2010/12/12/world /asia/12beijing.html; Qinying He, Yao Men, and Lin Xu, "Composition Effect Matters: Decomposing the Gender Pay Gap in Chinese University Graduates," *Economic Research* (*Ekonomska Istraživanja*) 33, no. 1 (March 2020), https://www.tandfonline.com/doi/full/10.1080/1331677X.2020 .1734850.
4. "College Enrollment in the United States from 1965 to 2018 and Projections up to 2029 for Public and Private Colleges," Statista, November 5, 2020, https://www.statista.com/statistics/183995/us-college-enrollment-and -projections-in-public-and-private-institutions/.
5. National Bureau of Statistics, "China Statistical Yearbook 2001: Number of Institutions of Higher Education by Region and Type (2000)," China Statistics Press, http://www.stats.gov.cn/english/statisticaldata/yearlydata /YB2001e/ml/indexE.htm, accessed January 19, 2021.
6. Guojia tongji ju, "Zhongguo tongji nianjian 2011: gaodeng xuexiao shuliang (2010)" [National Bureau of Statistics, China Statistical Yearbook 2011: Number of Schools or Institutions of Higher Education (2010)], China Statistics Press, http://www.stats.gov.cn/tjsj/ndsj/2011/indexeh.htm, accessed January 19, 2021.
7. William C. Kirby, "The Chinese Century? The Challenges of Higher Education," *Daedalus* 143, no. 2 (Spring 2014): 145–156, https://www.jstor.org /stable/43297323.
8. UNESCO Institute for Statistics, "School Enrollment, Tertiary (% Gross)," World Bank, http://data.worldbank.org/indicator/SE.TER.ENRR/countries /CN-4E-XT?display=graph, accessed May 12, 2020.
9. For an overview of all these trends, see David A. Stanfield and Yukiko Shimmi, "Chinese Higher Education: Statistics and Trends," in *International Briefs for Higher Education Leaders,* no. 1 (2012): 5–7. On broad trends, see the annual *Zhongguo jiaoyu fazhan baogao* [Report on China's Economic Development], edition 21 sheji jiaoyu yanjiuyuan (Beijing: Shehui kexue

wenxian chubanshe, 2011); "Mao ruxue lu da 51.6% gaodeng jiaoyu geng pujile" [The Collegiate Gross Enrollment Rate is 51.6%, Higher Education Has Become More Popular], *Xinhua*, November 26, 2020, http://www .xinhuanet.com/local/2020-11/26/c_1126786875.htm.

10. Kai Yu, Andrea Lynn Stith, Li Liu, and Huizhong Chen, *Tertiary Education at a Glance: China* (Boston: Sense Publishers, 2012), 7.

11. See Ichisada Miyazaki, *China's Examination Hell: The Civil Service Exams of Imperial China*, trans. by Conrad Schirokauer (New Haven, CT: Yale University Press, 1976).

12. Ji Xianlin, as quoted in Hao Ping, *Peking University and the Origins of Higher Education in China* (Los Angeles: Bridge21 Publications, 2013), 384.

13. For a detailed presentation of the Hanlin Academy, see Adam Yuen-chung Lui, *The Hanlin Academy: Training Ground for the Ambitious 1644-1850*, (Hamden, CT: Archon Books, 1981).

14. Gu Ming-yuan, *Cultural Foundations of Chinese Education* (Leiden, Netherlands: Brill, 2014), 108-113.

15. Benjamin A. Elman, *Civil Examinations and Meritocracy in Late Imperial China* (Cambridge, MA: Harvard University Press, 2013).

16. Frank J. Swetz, "The Introduction of Mathematics in Higher Education in China, 1865-1887," *Historia Mathematica* 1 (2, 1974), 169.

17. Richard A. Hartnett, *The Saga of Chinese Higher Education from the Tongzhi Restoration to Tiananmen Square* (Lewiston, NY: Edwin Mellen, 1998), 7.

18. See Timothy B. Weston, *The Power of Position* (Berkeley: University of California Press, 2004), 81ff.

19. Cai Yuanpei, "Daxue jiaoyu" [University Education], in *Cai Yuanpei quanji* [Collected Works of Cai Yuanpei], vol. 5 (Beijing: Zhonghua shuju, 1988), 507-508.

20. Hu Shi, "Guoli daxue zhi zhongyao" [Important Features of National Universities], in *Hu Shi sanwen* [Hu Shi's Essays], Yao Peng and Fan Qiao, eds. (Beijing: Zhongguo guangbo dianshi chubanshe, 1992), 191-192.

21. See Ruth Hayhoe, *China's Universities 1895-1995: A Century of Cultural Conflict* (New York: Routledge, 1996), 47.

22. See Wen-Hsin Yeh, *The Alienated Academy: Culture and Politics in Republican China 1919-1937* (Cambridge, MA: Harvard University Press, 1990).

23. For a critical—and American—response, see Stephen Duggan, "A Critique of the Report of the League of Nations' Mission of Educational Experts to China," *Institute of International Education* 14, no. 3 (January 1933).

24. William C. Kirby, "The Internationalization of China: Foreign Relations at Home and Abroad in the Republican Era," *China Quarterly*, no. 150 (June 1997): 455.

25. "Recent Conditions of Chinese Universities, Colleges, and Libraries," *China Institute Bulletin* 3, no. 2 (November 1938): 51-62; John Israel, *Lianda: A Chinese University in War and Revolution* (Stanford: Stanford University Press, 1998), 15.

26. Israel, *Lianda: A Chinese University in War and Revolution*, 376.
27. Hayhoe, *China's Universities 1895–1995*, 78.
28. Robert Taylor, *Education and University Enrolment Policies in China, 1949–1971*, (Canberra: Australian National University Press, 1973).
29. See Andrew G. Walder, *Fractured Rebellion: The Beijing Red Guard Movement* (Cambridge, MA: Harvard University Press, 2009).
30. Joel Andreas, *Rise of the Red Engineers* (Stanford: Stanford University Press, 2009), 189.
31. Andreas, *Rise of the Red Engineers*, 210.
32. Chen Zhili, "Gaige kaifang ershinian de Zhongguo jiaoyu" [China's Education in the Past 20 Years of Reform and Opening Up], Zhonghua renmin gongheguo jiaoyubu [Ministry of Education of the People's Republic of China], http://www.moe.gov.cn/jyb_xwfb/xw_zt/moe_357/s3579/moe_90/tnull_3161.html, accessed May 12, 2020; Suzanne Pepper, *China's Education Reform in the 1980s* (Berkeley, CA: Institute of East Asian Studies), 69.
33. Pepper, *China's Education Reform in the 1980s*.
34. "Zhagen Zhongguo dadi fenjin qiangguo zhengcheng xin Zhongguo qishinian gaodeng jiaoyu gaige fazhan licheng" [Rooted in China's Land and March Towards a Powerful Country: The 70-Year History of Higher Education Reform and Development in New China], Zhonghua renmin gongheguo jiaoyubu [Ministry of Education of the People's Republic of China], http://www.moe.gov.cn/jyb_xwfb/s5147/201909/t20190924_400593.html, accessed May 12, 2020.
35. Wanhua Ma, "The Flagship University and China's Economic Reform," in *World Class Worldwide: Transforming Research Universities in Asia and Latin America*, P. G. Altbach and J. Bal, eds. (Baltimore, MD: Johns Hopkins University Press, 2007), 32.
36. Colin Norman, "China to Get $200 Million for University Expansion," *Science* 213, no. 4506 (1981): 420–421.
37. Martin King Whyte, "Deng Xiaoping," *China Quarterly*, no. 135 (September 1993): 515–535.
38. Ruth Hayhoe, "China's Universities and Western Academic Models," *Higher Education* 18, no. 1 (1989): 49–85.
39. Pepper, *China's Education Reform in the 1980s*.
40. Chen Zhili, "Gaige kaifang ershinian Zhongguo jiaoyu."
41. Ruth Hayhoe, "China's Universities since Tiananmen: A Critical Assessment," *China Quarterly*, no. 134 (June 1993): 291–309.
42. Guojia tongji ju, "Zhongguo tongji nianjian 2007: xuexiao shuliang (2006)" [National Bureau of Statistics, China Statistical Yearbook 2007: Number of Schools by Level and Type of School (2006)], China Statistics Press, http://www.stats.gov.cn/tjsj/ndsj/2007/indexeh.htm; National Bureau of Statistics, "Number of Institutions of Higher Education by Region and Type (1999)," http://www.stats.gov.cn/english/statisticaldata/yearlydata/YB2000e/T16E.htm, accessed January 19, 2021.

43. Li Lixu, "China's Higher Education Reform 1998–2003," *Asia Pacific Education Review* 5, no. 1 (2004): 14–22.

44. Xiaoyan Wang and Jian Liu, "China's Higher Education Expansion and the Task of Economic Revitalization," *Higher Education* 62, no. 2 (August 2011): 213–229."

45. Li Lixiu, "China's Higher Education Reform 1998–2003."

46. "Gaodeng jiaoyu xuexiao shuliang" [Number of Higher Education Schools (Institutions)], Zhonghua renmin gongheguo jiaoyubu [Ministry of Education of the People's Republic of China], http://www.moe.gov.cn/s78/A03 /moe_560/jytjsj_2019/qg/202006/t20200611_464789.html, accessed June 2020.

47. "2019 nian quanguo gaoxiao mingdan" [2019 National College List], Zhonghua renmin gongheguo jiaoyubu [Ministry of Education of the People's Republic of China], http://www.moe.gov.cn/jyb_xxgk/s5743/s5744 /201906/t20190617_386200.html, accessed August 2019.

48. Huiqing Jin, "China's Private Universities," *Science* 346, no. 6208 (2014): 40, http://www.sciencemag.org/content/346/6208/401.full, accessed August 13, 2015.

49. See William C. Kirby, Michael Shih-ta Chen, Keith Chi-ho Wong, and Tracy Manty, "Xi'an International University: The Growth of Private Universities in China," Case 309-074 (Boston: Harvard Business School, 2009).

50. Kirby, "The Chinese Century?"

51. "2019 nian quanquo gaoxiao mingdan."

52. "Vision and Mission," Xi'an Jiaotong-Liverpool University, https://www .xjtlu.edu.cn/en/about/overview/vision-and-mission.

53. William C. Kirby, Nora Bynum, Tracy Yuen Manty, and Erica M. Zendell, "Kunshan, Incorporated: The Making of China's Richest Town," Case 313–103 (Boston: Harvard Business School, 2013).

54. "Sanshinian qiande Zhongguo daxue paiming yilan, ni zenme kan? [What Do You Think of the Rankings of Chinese Universities 30 Years Ago?], *Sohu*, May 23, 2020, https://www.sohu.com/a/397252209_523175.

55. "Education: Enrolment by Level of Education: Enrolment in Tertiary Education, All Programmes, Both Sexes (Number)," UNESCO Institute for Statistics, http://data.uis.unesco.org/#, accessed May 12, 2020.

56. Hayhoe, *China's Universities 1895–1995*, 119.

57. Mei Li and Rui Yang, "Governance Reforms in Higher Education: A Study of Institutional Autonomy in China," in *Governance Reforms in Higher Education in Asia: A Study of Institutional Autonomy in Asian Countries*, N. V. Varghese and M. Martin, eds. (Paris: International Institute for Educational Planning, UNESCO, 2013), 70.

58. Zhongguo shehui kexue wang, "Zhong ban yinfa gaoxiao dangwei lingdao xia de xiaozhang fuze zhi shishi yijian" [Chinese Academy of Social Sciences, Opinion on the Implementation of the Principal Responsibility System under the Leadership of the University Party Committee], Oc-

tober 16, 2014, http://www.cssn.cn/zx/yw/201410/t20141016_1364866 .shtml, accessed August 2019.

59. Yao Li et al., "The Higher Educational Transformation of China and Its Global Implications," National Bureau of Economic Research, Working Paper 13849 (March 2008), 22–24.

60. Sun Yan, "Qinghua daxue jiaoyu jijinhui cheng licai gaoshou," [Tsinghua University Education Foundation Becomes a Master of Fundraising], *CNTV Online*, October 19, 2010, http://igongyi.cntv.cn/20101019/100856 .shtml, accessed October 2014.

61. Hayhoe, *China's Universities 1895–1995*, 95.

62. Zhonghua renmin gongheguo jiaoyubu, "211 gongcheng jianjie" [Ministry of Education of the People's Republic of China, Introduction to Project 211], https://web.archive.org/web/20121110220139/http://www.moe.edu.cn /publicfiles/business/htmlfiles/moe/moe_315/200409/3799.html, accessed March 3, 2021.

63. Yao Li et al., "The Higher Educational Transformation of China and Its Global Implications," 20.

64. Zhongguo xuewei yu yanjiusheng jiaoyu xinxi, "C9 lianmeng gaoxiao mingdan" [China Academic Degrees & Graduate Education Information, List of 'C9 Alliance' Universities], https://www.cdgdc.edu.cn/xwyyjsjyxx /xwsytjxx/yxmd/274942.shtml, accessed January 19, 2021.

65. Guowuyuan, "Guifan xiao ban qiye guanli tizhi zhongdian wenti de tongzhi" [State Council, Notice of Standardizing Issues of School-Run Enterprise Management System], November 1, 2001, http://www.gov.cn/zhengce /content/2012-12/14/content_5832.htm.

66. "Difang putong benke gaoxiao xiang yingyong xing zhuanbian de zhidao yijian" [Opinions on Guiding Some Local General Undergraduate Colleges and Universities to Transform into Application-Oriented Institutions], Zhonghua renmin gongheguo jiaoyubu [Ministry of Education of the People's Republic of China], October 23, 2015, http://www.moe.gov.cn /srcsite/A03/moe_1892/moe_630/201511/t20151113_218942.html.

67. Yao Li et al., "The Higher Educational Transformation of China and Its Global Implications," 19–21.

68. dxsbb.com [College Student's Essential Network], "2020 nian Qinghua daxue xuefei shi duoshao? Ge zhuanye shoufei biaozhun" [How Much Is the Tuition Fee of Tsinghua University in 2020? Fee Standards for Each Major], September 9, 2020, https://m.dxsbb.com/news/52163.html; Zhejiang daxue chengshi xueyuan, "Zhejiang daxue chengshi xueyuan 2020 nian xuefei shi duoshao? Shoufei biaozhun" [City College of Zhejiang University, How Much Is the Tuition Fee of City College of Zhejiang University in 2020? Fee Standards], January 14, 2020, https://www.szedu.com/data/r264225/; Daxuesheng bi bei wang, "Xi'an guoji daxue 2020 nian xue zafei shi duo-shao? Ge zhuanye shoufei biaozhun" [College Student's Essential Net, How Much Are Annual Tuition and Fees for Xi'an International University

in 2020? Fee Standards for Each Major], September 16, 2020, https://m
.dxsbb.com/news/56603.html; "Xuefei he jiangxuejin" [Tuition and Scholar-
ships], NYU Shanghai, https://shanghai.nyu.edu/cn/zsb/cost, accessed January 19, 2021.

69. Shanghai shi zhengfu, "2018 nian shanghai keji daxue yusuan an" [Shanghai
Municipal Government, ShanghaiTech Budget 2018], http://www.shanghai
.gov.cn/Attach/Attaches/201802/201802131116415044.pdf, accessed March
2019.

70. Sheng Yunlong, "Qinghua daxue jiaoshi xueli yu xue yuan jiegou de bianqia"
[Changes to Tsinghua University's Teaching Qualifications and Structure],
*Tsinghua daxue jiaoyu yanjiu* [Tsinghua Journal of Education] 29, no. 2
(April 2008): 92–98.

71. Ibid.

72. Lin Jie, "Zhong Mei liang guo daxue jiaoshi jinqin fanzhi zhi bijiao"
[Comparison of "Inbreeding" between Chinese and American University
Teachers], *Gaodeng jiaoyu yanjiu* [Higher Education Research] 30, no. 12
(December 2009): 39–51.

73. Guojia waiguo zhuanjia ju, "Gongzuo Zhongguo zhaopin waiguo zhuanjia
jihua: 1000 ren gao cengci waiguo zhuanjia rencai jihua" [State Administration of Foreign Expert Affairs, Work China Recruitment Program of
Foreign Experts: 1000 Talent Plan for High-Level Foreign Experts], http://
1000plan.safea.gov.cn/index.php?s=Cont&id=12742321, accessed August 28,
2015; Liz Gooch, "Chinese Universities Send Big Signals to Foreigners,"
*New York Times*, March 11, 2012, http://www.nytimes.com/2012/03/12/world
/asia/12iht-educlede12.html, accessed August 28, 2015.

74. Gooch, "Chinese Universities Send Big Signals to Foreigners."

75. Sharon LaFraniere, "Fighting Trend, China Is Luring Scientists Home,"
*New York Times*, January 6, 2010, http://www.nytimes.com/2010/01/07
/world/asia/07scholar.html, accessed August 28, 2015.

76. Kai Yu, *Diversification to a Degree: An Exploratory Study of Students' Experi-
ence at Four Higher Education Institutions in China* (Bern, Switzerland: Peter
Lang, 2010), 62, https://books.google.com/books?id=6VZHgCf3SEoC&pg
=PA62&lpg=PA62#v=onepage&q&f=false, accessed August 27, 2015.

77. Yiqun Fu, "Gaokao Statistics 2014," *TeaLeaf Nation*, https://docs.google
.com/spreadsheets/d/1XgT5uoO31m5gPnPXRpAQfc26LIlJHDCrhsl6a
sgm-WM/edit#gid=0, accessed August 28, 2015.

78. Kong Defang and Yao Chun, "China to Overhaul Exam, Enrollment
System by 2020," *People's Daily Online*, September 4, 2014, http://en.people
.cn/n/2014/0904/c90882-8778889.html, accessed August 28, 2015; Song
Rongrong, "Wo guo gaokao zhidu gaige shi da yaodian" [Ten key points
of China's college entrance examination system reform], *IFeng Talk*, September 4, 2014, http://edu.ifeng.com/a/20140904/40787450_0.shtml, accessed
August 28, 2015.

79. Kirby et al., "Kunshan, Incorporated."

80. "MOE closes 234 Chinese-Foreign Joint Education Institutions and Programs," Ministry of Education of the People's Republic of China, July 5, 2018, http://en.moe.gov.cn/News/Top_News/201807/t20180710_342467.html; Emily Feng, "China Closes a Fifth of Foreign University Partnerships," *Financial Times,* July 17, 2018, https://www.ft.com/content/794b77e8-8976-11e8-bf9e-8771d5404543.

81. "Jiaoyubu jiedu Zhongguo zhongyang, guowuyuan 'Zhongguo jiaoyu xiandaihua 2035' he 'shishi fang'an'" [Ministry of Education Statement on the 'China Education Modernization 2035' and 'Implementation Plan' of the Central Committee of the Communist Party of China and the State Council (with full text)], *Sohu,* February 24, 2019, https://www.sohu.com/a/297290631_473325.

82. "More Chinese Study Abroad in 2018," Ministry of Education of the People's Republic of China, March 28, 2009, http://en.moe.gov.cn/news/media_highlights/201904/t20190401_376249.html.

83. "Georgia on Their Minds," *The Economist,* February 21, 2015, https://www.economist.com/china/2015/02/19/georgia-on-their-minds, accessed August 28, 2015; Institute of International Education, "International Student Totals by Place of Origin," https://www.iie.org/Research-and-Insights/Open-Doors/Data/International-Students/Places-of-Origin, accessed May 12, 2020.

84. "The Unveiling Ceremony of the China-Italy Design Innovation Hub and the Tsinghua Arts and Design Institute in Milan," Tsinghua University, https://goglobal.tsinghua.edu.cn/en/news/news.en/lgR56myTb, accessed October 9, 2019.

85. "Ground-Breaking of the Tsinghua Southeast Asia Center in Indonesia," Tsinghua University, http://eng.pbcsf.tsinghua.edu.cn/portal/article/index/id/1421.html, accessed October 9, 2019.

86. Coco Liu, "Belt and Read: How China Is Exporting Education and Influence to Malaysia and Other Asean Countries," *South China Morning Post,* July 30, 2017, https://www.scmp.com/week-asia/politics/article/2097965/belt-road-and-books-how-chinas-trying-soft-power-outreach.

87. "Hungary Agrees to Open Chinese University Campus in Budapest by 2024," *Euronews,* February 5, 2021, https://www.euronews.com/2021/05/02/hungary-agrees-to-open-chinese-university-campus-in-budapest-by-2024.

88. *Times Higher Education World University Rankings,* 2020, https://www.timeshighereducation.co.uk/world-university-rankings/, accessed May 12, 2020; Academic Ranking of World Universities, "Academic Ranking of World Universities 2018," http://www.shanghairanking.com/ARWU2018.html, accessed January 19, 2021; QS Top Universities, "QS World University Rankings 2021," https://www.topuniversities.com/university-rankings/world-university-rankings/2021.

89. Calculated based on data from "Double First-Class University and Discipline List Policy Update," Australian Government, Department of Educa-

tion, Skills and Employment (December 14, 2017), https://international education.gov.au/International-network/china/PolicyUpdates-China/Pages /Double-First-Class-university-and-discipline-list-policy-update.aspx, accessed March 2018.

90. Zhonghua renmin gongheguo zhongyang zhengfu, "Guojia zhong chang qi jiaoyu gaige he fazhan guihua gangyao (2010–2020 nian)" [The Central Government of the People's Republic of China, Outline of the National Medium and Long-Term Education Reform and Development Plan (2010– 2020)], July 29, 2010, https://www.gov.cn/jrzg/2010-07/29/content_1667143 .htm.

91. dxsbb.com [College Student's Essential Network], "How Much Is the Tuition Fee of Tsinghua University in 2020? Fee Standards for Each Major," September 9, 2020, https://m.dxsbb.com/news/52163.html; City College of Zhejiang University, "How Much Is the Tuition Fee of City College of Zhejiang University in 2020? Fee Standards," January 14, 2020, https://www.szedu.com/data/r264225/, accessed January 19, 2021; College Student's Essential Network, "How Much Are Annual Tuition and Fees for Xi'an International University in 2020? Fee Standards for Each Major," September 16, 2020, https://m.dxsbb.com/news/56603.html, accessed January 19, 2021; "Tuition and Scholarships," NYU Shanghai, https://shanghai .nyu.edu/cn/zsb/cost, accessed January 19, 2021.

92. "Annual Per Capita Disposable Income of Rural and Urban Households in China 1990–2019," *Statista,* November 20, 2020, https://www.statista.com /statistics/259451/annual-per-capita-disposable-income-of-rural-and-urban -households-in-china/.

93. Zhongguo jiaoyu zai xian [China Education Online], June 9, 2020, https:// news.eol.cn/xueshu/202006/t20200609_1732373.shtml.

94. "Zhongguo gaodeng jiaoyu jinru pujihua shidai" [China's Higher Education Has Entered the Era of Popularization], *Xinhua,* October 13, 2020, http://www.xinhuanet.com/politics/2020-10/13/c_1126597896.htm.

95. Tom Mitchell, "China University Rule Change Sparks Protests in 4 Provinces," *Financial Times,* May 23, 2016, http://www.ft.com/intl/cms/s/0 /6a6c8b18-20be-11e6-aa98-db1e01fabc0c.html#axzz4AXbTFtYk, accessed June 3, 2016.

96. "Ge ji xuexiao shaoshu minzu xuesheng renshu" [Number of Minority Students in Schools of All Levels], Zhonghua renmin gongheguo jiaoyubu [Ministry of Education of the People's Republic of China], 2010, http:// www.moe.gov.cn/s78/A03/moe_560/s6200/201201/t20120117_129611 .html.

97. "Ge ji xuexiao shaoshu minzu xuesheng renshu" [Number of Minority Students in Schools of All Levels], Zhonghua renmin gonghequo jiaoyubu [Ministry of Education of the People's Republic of China], 2020, http://www.moe.gov .cn/s78/A03/moe_560/jytjsj_2019/qg/202006/t20200611_464796.html; "Zhonghua renmin gongheguo 2010 nian renkou pucha," Zhongguo tongji

chuban she [2010 Population Census of the People's Republic of China, China Statistics Press], http://www.stats.gov.cn/tjsj/pcsj/rkpc/6rp/indexch .htm.

98. Qinghua daxue, "2019–2020 xuenian benke jiaoyu zhiliang baogao" [Tsinghua University, 2019–2020 Academic Year Undergraduate Education Quality Report], December 2020, https://www.tsinghua.edu.cn/__local/C/24 /2D/B7896456DF4989A6A6CF192E2D1_515D4FF2_1B3A98.pdf; "939 suo gaozhong, 4,326 ren Beijing daxue 2020 nian luqu qingkuang ji shengyuan jiegou fenxi" [939 High Schools and 4,326 Students: A Structural Analysis of Peking University's 2020 Admissions Decisions and Accepted Students], September 2, 2020, http://m.mxzzzs.com/news/104886.html.

99. "Ge ji xuexiao shaoshu minzu xuesheng renshu," 2020.

100. Association of American Universities, "Hefei Statement on the Ten Characteristics of Contemporary Research Universities," https://www.aau.edu/sites /default/files/AAU%20Files/Education%20and%20Service/Hefei_statement .pdf.

101. "Document 9: A ChinaFile Translation," ChinaFile, November 8, 2013, https://www.chinafile.com/document-9-chinafile-translation.

102. Zhu Shanlu, "Yi peiyu he hongyang shehuizhuyi hexin jiazhiguan wei yinling zhashi zhua hao xin xingshi xia gaoxiao xuanchuan sixiang gongzuo" [Guided by the cultivation and promotion of core socialist values, begin incorporating propaganda and ideology into colleges and universities], *Zhongguo jiaoyu xinwen wang* [China Education News Online], Zhonghua renmin gongheguo jiaoyubu [Ministry of Education of the People's Republic of China], February 3, 2015, http://paper.jyb.cn /zgjyb/html/2015-02/03/content_430445.htm?div=-1, accessed September 10, 2015, trans. Joycelyn Eby.

103. "Xin shidai gaoxiao jiaoshi zhiye xingwei shi xiang zhunze" [Ten Guidelines on Professional Behavior of College Teachers in the New Era], *Zhongguo jiaoyu xinwen wang* [China Education News Online], Zhonghua renmin gongheguo jiaoyubu [Ministry of Education of the People's Republic of China], November 14, 2018, http://www.moe.gov.cn/srcsite/A10/s7002 /201811/t20181115_354921.html.

104. Emily Feng, "Chinese Universities Are Enshrining Communist Party Control in Their Charters," NPR, January 20, 2020, https://www.npr.org/2020 /01/20/796377204/chinese-universities-are-enshrining-communist-party -control-in-their-charters.

105. Philip Wen, "Demand for Absolute Loyalty to Beijing at Chinese Universities Triggers Dissent," *Wall Street Journal*, December 18, 2019, https://www .wsj.com/articles/demand-for-absolute-loyalty-to-beijing-at-chinese-univer sities-triggers-dissent-11576674047?mod=article_inline/.

106. White House, "President Donald J. Trump Is Protecting America from China's Efforts to Steal Technology and Intellectual Property," May 29, 2020, https://www.whitehouse.gov/briefings-statements/president-donald-j-trump -protecting-america-chinas-efforts-steal-technology-intellectual-property/.

107. Emily Feng, "As U.S. Revokes Chinese Students' Visas, Concerns Rise About Loss of Research Talent," NPR, September 23, 2020, https://www.npr.org/2020/09/23/915939365/critics-question-u-s-decision-to-revoke-chinese-students-visas.

## 9. From Preparatory Academy to National Flagship

1. Keith Bradscher, "$300 Million Scholarship for Study in China Signals a New Focus," *New York Times*, April 21, 2013; and "Oxford and the Rhodes Scholarship," http://www.rhodesscholar.org, accessed June 2013.

2. Edmund J. James, "Memorandum Concerning the Sending of an Educational Commission to China" (1907), cited in Mary Brown Bullock, "American Exchanges with China, Revisited," in *Educational Exchanges: Essays on the Sino-American Experiences*, Joyce K. Kallgren and Denis Fred Simon, eds. (Berkeley: Institute of East Asian Studies, 1987), 26.

3. Su-Yan Pan, *University Autonomy, the State, and Social Change in China* (Hong Kong: Hong Kong University Press, 2009), 71.

4. Qinghua daxue xiaoshi yanjiushe [Tsinghua University School History Research Office], *Qinghua daxue jiushinian* [Ninety Years of Tsinghua University] (Beijing: Tsinghua University, 2001), 9.

5. Yoshi S. Kuno, *Education Institutions in the Orient with Special Reference to Colleges and Universities in the United States, Part II* (Berkeley: University of California Press, 1928), 55–56.

6. See Wen-hsin Yeh, *The Alienated Academy: Culture and Politics in Republican China, 1919–1937* (Cambridge, MA: Harvard University Asia Center, 1990), 207–210, 224.

7. See Qian Yingyi and Li Qiang, eds., *Lao Qinghua de shehui kexue* [Social Sciences in Old Tsinghua] (Beijing: Qinghua daxue chubanshe, 2011).

8. See John Israel, *Lianda: A Chinese University in War and Revolution* (Stanford: Stanford University Press, 1998).

9. Israel, *Lianda*, 38.

10. See Andrew G. Walder, *Fractured Rebellion: The Beijing Red Guard Movement* (Cambridge, MA: Harvard University Press, 2009).

11. See Tang Shaojie, *Yi ye zhi qiu: Qinghua daxue 1968 nian "bai ri da wudou"* [A Single Leaf Heralds Autumn: Tsinghua University's 1968 "Hundred Days of Great Violence"] (Hong Kong: Zhongwen daxue chubanshe, 2003); and William Hinton, *Hundred Day War: The Cultural Revolution at Tsinghua University* (New York: Monthly Review Press, 1972).

12. "Sanshinian qian de Zhongguo daxue paiming yilan, ni zenme kan? [What Do You Think of the Rankings of Chinese Universities 30 Years Ago?], *Sohu*, May 23, 2020, https://www.sohu.com/a/397252209_523175.

13. See Cheng Li, *China's Leaders: The New Generation* (Lanham, MD: Rowman & Littlefield, 2001), 87–126.

14. James, "Memorandum Concerning the Sending of an Educational Commission to China."

15. QS Top Universities, "QS World University Rankings 2021," https://www
    .topuniversities.com/university-rankings/world-university-rankings/2021.

16. "Tongji shuju" [Statistical Data], Tsinghua University, https://www.tsinghua
    .edu.cn/xxgk/tjzl.htm.

17. Samuel Eliot Morison, *The Development of Harvard University Since the Inau-
    guration of President Eliot, 1869–1929* (Cambridge, MA: Harvard University
    Press, 1930), 329.

18. "Zhonggong Qinghua daxue weiyuanhui guanyu xunshi zhenggai qing-
    kuang" [Tsinghua University Committee of the Communist Party of China
    on the Inspection and Rectification], Tsinghua University, August 27, 2017,
    http://news.tsinghua.edu.cn/publish/thunews/11062/2017/201708270933
    52932836560/20170827093352932836560_.html.

19. "Tsinghua University," University Rankings, https://www.universityrankings
    .ch/results?ranking=Times&region=World&year=2011&q=Tsinghua
    +University, accessed May 12, 2020; *Times Higher Education World
    University Rankings*, "Tsinghua University," https://www.timeshighereducation
    .com/world-university-rankings/tsinghua-university, accessed May 12,
    2020.

20. Tsinghua University, "Shisanwu fazhan guihua gangyao" [Outline of Devel-
    opment Plan for the Thirteenth Five-Year Plan], July 2016, http://www.moe
    .gov.cn/s78/A08/gjs_left/s7187/zsgxgz_sswgh/201703/W0201703103325
    81867931.pdf.

21. Ibid.

22. "Keyan jigou" [Scientific Research Institutions], Tsinghua University,
    https://www.tsinghua.edu.cn/kxyj/kyjg1.htm, accessed January 19, 2020.

23. Tsinghua University, "Shisanwu fazhan guihua gangyao."

24. "Qinghua daxue 2019–2020 xuenian benke jiaoxue zhiliang baogao"
    [Tsinghua University 2019–2020 Academic Year Undergraduate Teaching
    Quality Report], Tsinghua University, http://tsinghua.edu.cn/jwc/info/1018
    /1072.htm; Sheng Yunlong, "Qinghua daxue jiaoshi xueli yu xueyuan jiegou
    de bianqian" [Changes to Tsinghua University's Teaching Qualifications and
    Structure], *Tsinghua Journal of Education* 29, no. 2 (April 2008): 92–98.

25. "Shi'erwu fazhan guihua gangyao" [Outline of the Development Plan for
    the Twelfth Five-Year Plan], December 2011, Tsinghua University,
    https://www.tsinghua.edu.cn/publish/newthu/openness/jbxx/fzgh.htm.

26. Tsinghua University, "Shisanwu fazhan guihua gangyao."

27. Yuan Yang and Nian Liu, "China Hushes Up Scheme to Recruit Overseas
    Scientists," *Financial Times,* January 9, 2019, https://www.ft.com/content
    /a06f414c-0e6e-11e9-a3aa-118c761d2745.

28. Quanguo gaoxiao sixiang zhengzhi gongzuo wang, "Qinghua Daxue" [Na-
    tional University Ideological and Political Work Net, Tsinghua University],
    October 28, 2019, http://www.sizhengwang.cn/zt/7102/2019scxmz/sfgx
    /2019/1028/2923.shtml.

29. Qian Yingyi, "Daxue renshi zhidu gaige: Yi Qinghua daxue jingji guanli
    xueyuan wei li" [Faculty Personnel System Reform: The Case of Tsinghua

University School of Economic and Management], *Qinghua daxue jiaoyu yanjiu* [Tsinghua Journal of Education] 34, no. 2 (April 2013): 1–8.

30. Tsinghua University, "Shisanwu fazhan guihua gangyao."

31. Ibid.

32. Author interview with David Daokui Li, Beijing, March 23, 2015.

33. "2018–2019 xuenian benke jiaoyu zhiliang baogao" [2018–2019 Academic Year Undergraduate Education Quality Report], December 2019, Tsinghua University, https://www.tsinghua.edu.cn/__local/D/51/C4/9C31C0CC9287 C56A7E246B71ED7_32475816_81794.pdf?e=.pdf.

34. "Shijian jiaoxue" [Practical Teaching], Tsinghua University, https://www .tsinghua.edu.cn/publish/newthu/newthu_cnt/education/edu-1-5.html, accessed May 12, 2020.

35. "2018–2019 xuenian jiaoshou benke kecheng zhan bi . . ." [The Proportion of Undergraduate Courses Taught by Professors in the 2018–2019 Academic Year . . .], Tsinghua University, https://www.tsinghua.edu.cn/xxgk/jxzlxx /zjbkkcdjs.htm, accessed January 19, 2021.

36. Li Cao, "The Significance and Practice of General Education in China: The Case of Tsinghua University," in *Experiences in Liberal Arts and Science Education from America, Europe, and Asia: A Dialogue across Continents,* William C. Kirby and Marijk van der Wende, eds. (New York: Palgrave, 2016).

37. "Qinghua daxue 2014–2015 xuenian benke jiaoxue zhiliang baogao" [Tsinghua University 2014–2015 Academic Year Undergraduate Teaching Quality Report], Tsinghua University, https://www.tsinghua.edu.cn/jwc /bkpy/zlbg.htm.

38. Qian Yingyi, *How Reform Worked in China: The Transition from Plan to Market* (Cambridge, MA: MIT Press, 2017); Qing and Li, *Lao Qinghua* [Old Tsinghua].

39. Tsinghua University School of Economics and Management 2013–2014, Tsinghua University brochure (Beijing, 2013), 41.

40. Pan, *University Autonomy,* 183.

41. "Qinghua daxue jiao zhigong daibiao dahui" [Tsinghua University Staff Congress], Tsinghua University, December 2012, http://www.tsinghua.edu .cn/publish/newthu/openness/jbxx/jzgdbdhgd.html.

42. Emily Feng, "China Universities Accused of Ideological Weakness," *Financial Times,* June 19, 2017, https://www.ft.com/content/88191d36-54b4-11e7 -9fed-c19e2700005f.

43. "Qinghua daxue 2019 nian bumen yusuan" [Tsinghua University 2019 Departmental Budgets], Tsinghua University, April 2019, https://www .tsinghua.edu.cn/publish/newthu/openness/cwzcjsfxx/cwyc_2019.htm.

44. "Qinghua daxue 2020 niandu yusuan" [Tsinghua University's Annual Budget 2020], Tsinghua University, https://www.tsinghua.edu.cn/publish /newthu/openness/newsml/cwyc_2020.htm.

45. dxsbb.com [College Student's Essential Network], "2020 nian Qinghua daxue xuefei shi duoshao? Ge zhuanye shoufei biaozhun" [How Much Is the

Tuition Fee of Tsinghua University in 2020? Fee Standards for Each Major], September 9, 2020, https://www.dxsbb.com/news/52163.html.

46. Tsinghua University SEM, "Feiyong he jiangxuejin" [Expenses and Scholarships], http://gmba.sem.tsinghua.edu.cn/content/page/expensesscholarship.html, accessed May 2020.

47. "Tongji shuju" [Statistical Data], Tsinghua University, https://www.tsinghua.edu.cn/publish/newthu/newthu_cnt/about/about-6.html, accessed May 12, 2020; College Student's Essential Network, "How Much Are the Tuition and Fees for Tsinghua University in 2020? Expenses for Each Major," September 9, 2020, https://www.dxsbb.com/news/52163.html.

48. Tsinghua University, "Shisanwu fazhan guihua gangyao."

49. Jun wang, "Qinghua daxue kaishe junmin ronghe gaoduan rencai zhuanxiu ban" [Military Net, Tsinghua University Launches Special Training Class on Military-Civilian Integration of High-End Talents], September 21, 2018, http://military.cnr.cn/zgjq/20180921/t20180921_524366936.html; Elsa B. Kania, "In Military-Civil Fusion, China Is Learning Lessons from the United States and Starting to Innovate," August 27, 2019, https://www.realcleardefense.com/articles/2019/08/27/in_military-civil_fusion_china_is_learning_lessons_from_the_united_states_and_starting_to_innovate_114699.html.

50. Guowuyuan, "Guowuyuan guanyu yinfa Zhongguo zhizao 2025 de tongzhi" [State Council, Notice of the State Council on Printing and Distributing Made in China 2025], May 8, 2015, http://www.gov.cn/zhengce/content/2015-05/19/content_9784.htm.

51. Tsinghua University, "Shisanwu fazhan guihua gangyao."

52. Kexue wang, "Zhongguo zhizao 2025 tian bai yi zijin 25 xiang renwu ruwei" [Science Net, Tens of Billions in Funds for 25 Shortlisted Tasks Available through Made in China 2025], October 12, 2017, http://news.sciencenet.cn/htmlnews/2017/10/390819.shtm.

53. Zhongguo qiche gongye xiehui, "Gongye he xinxi hua bu guanyu fabu 2017 nian gongye zhuanxing shengji (Zhongguo zhizao 2025) zijin (bumen yusuan) xiangmu zhinan de tongzhi" [China Association of Automobile Manufacturers, Notice of the Ministry of Industry and Information Technology on the Issuance of the 2017 Industrial Transformation and Upgrade (Made in China 2025) Funding (Departmental Budget) Project Guidelines], May 24, 2017, http://www.caam.org.cn/policySearch/con_5210981.html.

54. "Qinghua daxue shuju kexue yanjiu suo gongye da shuju yanjiu zhongxin chengli" [Tsinghua University Data Science Research Institute Industrial Big Data Research Center established], Tsinghua University, October 28, 2015, https://news.tsinghua.edu.cn/publish/thunews/9650/2015/2015102916041690987407/20151029160416909874073_.html; "Qinghua daxue 'Zhongguo zhizao 2025' yu 'shisanwu' Zhongguo zhizao qiye fazhan zhanlue di si qi gaoji yanxiu ban" [Tsinghua University's "Made in China 2025" and "Thirteenth Five-Year Plan" for Chinese Manufacturing Enter-

prises' Fourth Advanced Seminar], Tsinghua University, March 16, 2017, http://www.tsinghua-tj.org/news/3376.html; Tsinghua Shenzhen International Graduate School, "Xianjin zhizao xueyuan" [Faculty of Advanced Manufacturing], https://www.sigs.tsinghua.edu.cn/xjzzxb1/index.jhtml, accessed May 12, 2020.

55. Beijing shi haidian qu renmin zhengfu, "2018 Niandu haidian qu min ronghe zhuanti shenqing zhinan [Beijing Haidian District People's Government, 2018 Haidian District Military and Civil Integration Special Fund Application Guide], http://www.bjhd.gov.cn/ztzl2014/zxzt/Afour/sbzn/QYHXJZL /jmhz/201804/t20180417_1504152.htm, accessed May 12, 2020.

56. Qinghai sheng zhengfu, "Qinghai xing renmin zhengfu guanyu yinfa Zhongguo zhizao 2025 Qinghai xingdong fang'an de tongzhi" [Qinghai Provincial Government, Qinghai Provincial People's Government Notice on Printing and Distributing the Made in China 2025 Qinghai Action Plan], June 27, 2016, http://www.maqin.gov.cn/html/3142/241618.html, accessed May 12, 2020; *Tianjin ribao*, "Tianjin zhineng zhizao shuiping buduan tisheng," [Tianjin Daily, Tianjin's Smart Manufacturing Continues to Improve], May 8, 2018, http://www.gov.cn/xinwen/2018-05/08/content _5289067.htm.

57. Tom Holland, "Beijing's 'Made in China 2025' Plan Isn't Dead, It's Out of Control," *South China Morning Post,* April 8, 2019, https://www.scmp.com /week-asia/opinion/article/3004900/beijings-made-china-2025-plan-isnt -dead-its-out-control.

58. Xintangren dianshitai, "Fouren fangqi: Zhonggong guanmei pilu zhizao 2025 jingfei fenpei" [New Tang Dynasty Television, Disclaimer: the Chinese Communist Party's Official Media Disclosure of Funding Plan for Made in China 2025], November 13, 2018, https://www.ntdtv.com/gb/2018 /11/13/a1399033.html.

59. Wanhua Ma, "The Flagship University and China's Economic Reform" in *World Class Worldwide: Transforming Research Universities in Asia and Latin America,* Philip G. Altbach and Jorge Bal, eds. (Baltimore, MD: Johns Hopkins University Press, 2007), 39.

60. Zhang Di, "Qinghua konggu 'da shoushen': zichan die po wuqian yi gaige shangwei wancheng" [Tsinghua Holdings 'Slims Down': Assets Fall Below 500 Billion, Reform Has Not Been Completed], *Zhongguo jingying wang* [China Business Net], May 26, 2020, http://www.cb.com.cn/index/show/zj _m/cv/cv13487671267.

61. Tsinghua Holdings, "2019 caifu Zhongguo 500 qiang: Qinghua konggu lianxu liunian wen ju jisuanji hangye qian san" [2019 Fortune China's Top 500: Tsinghua Holdings Co., Ltd. Has Steadily Improved Its Ranking for Six Consecutive Years, Ranking Top 3 in the Computer Industry], July 15, 2019, https://www.thholding.com.cn/news/show/contentid/2847.html.

62. "Zhonggong Qinghua daxue jilu jiancha weiyuanhui" [Tsinghua University Committee of the Communist Party of China for Discipline and

Inspection], August 27, 2017, http://news.tsinghua.edu.cn/publish/thunews /11062/2017/20170827093352932836560/20170827093352932836560_.html.

63. "Xi Stresses Coordinated Efforts in Central, Local Institutional Reform," *Xinhua,* May 12, 2018, http://www.xinhuanet.com/english/2018-05/12/c _137172840.htm.

64. Yan Sun, "Qinghua daxue jiaoyu jijinhui cheng licai gaoshou" [Tsinghua University Education Foundation Becomes a Financial Expert], *CNTV On-line,* October 19, 2010, http://igongyi.cntv.cn/20101019/100856.shtml, ac-cessed October 2014; Qinghua daxue jiaoyu jijinhui, "Qinghua daxue jiaoyu jijin weiyuanhui 2018 nian gongzuo baogao" [Tsinghua University Educa-tion Fund Committee 2018 Work Report], March 25, 2019, http://www .tuef.tsinghua.edu.cn/sites/pdf/infomation/2018ndgzbg.pdf.

65. Tsinghua University Education Fund, "Qinghua daxue jiaoyu jijin weiyuanhui 2018 nian gongzuo baogao."

66. Ibid.

67. "Gaoxiao ju'e juanzeng bian shaole: hou yiqing shidai, gaoxiao yaoguo jin rizi? [Huge Donations to Colleges and Universities Have Decreased: In the Post-Epidemic Era, Do Colleges and Universities Have to Live a Tight Life?], *Sohu,* December 17, 2020, https://www.sohu.com/a/438929037_608848.

68. Author interview with Qian Yingyi, Beijing, March 23, 2015.

69. Author interview with David Daokui Li, March 23, 2015.

70. Ibid.

71. William C. Kirby, Joycelyn W. Eby, Yuanzhuo Wang, "Higher Education in China: Internationalization in Turbulent Times," Case 316-066 (Boston: Harvard Business School, 2019), 8.

72. Kirby, Eby, and Wang, "Higher Education in China," 22.

73. Zhongguo guojia tongji ju, "yanjiusheng he liuxue renyuan tongji" [National Bureau of Statistics of China, "Statistics on Postgraduates and Students Studying Abroad"], *China Statistical Yearbook 2019,* http://www.stats.gov.cn /tjsj/ndsj/2019/indexeh.htm; Gao Hongmei, Hu Yiwei, Zhao Hong, Zhao Lei, "Qi zhang tu zhu ni liaojie Zhongguo gaokao" [Seven Charts to Help You Understand China's Gaokao (National College Entrance Exam)], CGTN, June 8, 2018, https://news.cgtn.com/news/3d3d414f776b544f7745 7a6333566d54/share_p.html.

74. Alexis Lai, "Chinese Flock to Elite U.S. Schools," CNN, November 26, 2012, https://www.cnn.com/2012/11/25/world/asia/china-ivy-league -admission/index.html.

75. Laurent Ortmans, "What the 2015 Executive MBA Survey Reveals," *Fi-nancial Times,* October 18, 2015, https://www.ft.com/content/14c11226 -570e-11e5-9846-de406ccb37f2; "Global MBA Ranking 2015," *Financial Times,* http://rankings.ft.com/businessschoolrankings/global-mba-ranking -2015.

76. Australian Government, Department of Education, Skills and Employ-ment, "Double First-Class University and Discipline List Policy Update,"

December 14, 2017, https://internationaleducation.gov.au/International
-network/china/PolicyUpdates-China/Pages/Double-First-Class-university
-and-discipline-list-policy-update.aspx.

77. Kirby, Eby, and Wang, "Higher Education in China," 22.

78. "President Qiu Yong Visited the School of Humanities," Tsinghua University, April 1, 2015, https://news.tsinghua.edu.cn/info/1006/52325.htm.

79. CWTS Leiden Ranking, "CWTS Leiden Ranking 2020," https://www
.leidenranking.com/ranking/2020/list, accessed January 19, 2021.

80. "Zhonggong Qinghua daxue jilu jiancha weiyuanhui."

81. Kathrin Hille and Richard Waters, "Washington Unnerved by China's 'Military-Civil Fusion,'" *Financial Times,* November 8, 2018, https://www.ft
.com/content/8dcb534c-dbaf-11e8-9f04-38d397e6661c; Elsa B. Kania, "In Military-Civil Fusion, China Is Learning Lessons from the United States and Starting to Innovate."

82. Permanent Subcommittee on Investigations of the United States Senate, "Threats to the U.S. Research Enterprise: China's Talent Recruitment Plans," November 18, 2019, https://www.hsgac.senate.gov/imo/media/doc
/2019-11-18%20PSI%20Staff%20Report%20-%20China's%20Talent%20
Recruitment%20Plans.pdf.

83. U.S.-China Economic and Security Review Commission, *Technology, Trade, and Military-Civil Fusion: China's Pursuit of Artificial Intelligence, New Materials, and New Energy,* 116th Cong., 1st sess., 2019, https://www.uscc.gov
/sites/default/files/2019-10/June%207,%202019%20Hearing%20Transcript
.pdf.

84. Geremie R. Barmé, "Xu Zhangrun's Fears and Hopes, July 2018–July 2020," *China Heritage,* July 26, 2020, https://chinaheritage.net/journal/xu-zhangruns
-fears-hopes-july-2018-july-2020/.

85. Chris Buckley, "Seized by the Police, an Outspoken Chinese Professor Sees Fears Come True," *New York Times,* July 6, 2020, https://www.nytimes.com
/2020/07/06/world/asia/china-detains-xu-zhangrun-critic.html?smid=em
-share.

86. Geremie R. Barmé, "Remonstrating with Beijing—Xu Zhangrun's Advice to China's National People's Congress," *China Heritage,* May 21, 2020, http://chinaheritage.net/journal/remonstrating-with-beijing-xu-zhangruns
-advice-to-chinas-national-peoples-congress-21-may-2020/.

87. Josephine Ma and Guo Rui, "Chinese Professor Known for Challenging the Party Leadership Sacked by University," *South China Morning Post,* July 18, 2020, https://www.scmp.com/news/china/politics/article/3093769/chinese
-professor-known-challenging-party-leadership-sacked; Zhonghua renmin gongheguo jiaoyubu, "Jiaoyu bu yinfa xin shidai gaoxiao jiaoshi zhiye xingwei 'xin shidai zhong xiaoxue jiaoshi zhiye xingwei shi xiang zhidao yijian'" [Ministry of Education of the People's Republic of China, Ministry of Education on Printing and Distributing the Professional Behavior of College Teachers in the New Era: Ten Guidelines for the "Professional Behavior of

Primary and Secondary School Teachers in the New Era"], November 14, 2018, http://www.moe.gov.cn/srcsite/A10/s7002/201811/t20181115_354921 .html.

88. Geremie R. Barmé, "Responding to a Gesture of Support—Xu Zhangrun," *China Heritage,* July 19, 2020, http://chinaheritage.net/journal/responding -to-a-gesture-of-support-xu-zhangrun/.

89. "Tongji Shuju" [Statistical Data], Tsinghua University, https://www.tsinghua .edu.cn/xxgk/tjzl.htm.

90. "2018–2019 Academic Year Undergraduate Education Quality Report," Tsinghua University, December 2019, https://www.tsinghua.edu.cn/__local /D/51/C4/9C31C0CC9287C56A7E246B71ED7_32475816_81794.pdf?e= .pdf.

91. Karen Rhodes, "UC Berkeley and Tsinghua University Launch Research and Graduate Education Partnership," *Berkeley News,* September 6, 2014, http:// news.berkeley.edu/2014/09/06/uc-berkeley-and-tsinghua-university-launch -research-and-graduate-education-partnership/, accessed July 20, 2015.

92. Nick Wingfield, "University of Washington and Chinese University Unite to Form Technology Institute," *New York Times,* June 18, 2015, http://www .nytimes.com/2015/06/19/business/university-of-washington-and-chinese -university-unite-to-form-technology-institute.html, accessed July 20, 2015.

93. Zhonghua renmin gongheguo jiaoyubu, "Jiaoyubu guanyu yinfa tuijin gong jian yidai yilu jiaoyu xingdong fang'an de tongzhi" [Ministry of Education of the People's Republic of China, Notice of the Ministry of Education on Printing and Distributing the Education Action Plan for Promoting the Belt and Road Initiative], July 15, 2016, http://www.moe.gov.cn/srcsite/A20 /s7068/201608/t20160811_274679.html.

94. Tsinghua University, "Shisanwu fazhan guihua gangyao."

95. Beijing Net, "Qinghua daxue quanqiu gongtong fazhan yanjiuyuan ruxuan 'yidai yilu' yanjiu tese zhiku" [Tsinghua University Global Common Development Institute Selected as a Special Think-Tank for "Belt and Road" Research], November 18, 2019, https://www.yidianzixun.com/article/0Nob AQ9l?s; Tsinghua University, "Qinghua daxue juban di si jie 'yidai yilu' dawosi luntan" [Tsinghua University Holds the Fourth "Belt and Road" Davos Forum], January 23, 2020, http://news.tsinghua.edu.cn/publish/thunews /10303/2020/20200123162907289119592/20200123162907289119592_ .html; Tsinghua University, "Yidai yilu" guoji gonggong guanli shuoshi (IMPA-BRI) xiangmu 2020 nian zhoasheng jianzhang" [Belt and Road International Master of Public Administration (IMPA-BRI) project 2020 Admissions Guide], http://www.sppm.tsinghua.edu.cn/xwjy/IMPABRI/, accessed May 12, 2020.

96. Eva Dou, "Who is Tsinghua Unigroup, the Firm Preparing a $23 Billion Bid for Micron," *Wall Street Journal blog,* July 14, 2015, http://blogs.wsj.com /digits/2015/07/14/who-is-tsinghua-unigroup-the-firm-preparing-a-23 -billion-bid-for-micron/, accessed July 17, 2015; Paul Mozur and Quentin

Hardy, "Micron Technology Is Said to Be Takeover Target of Chinese Company," *New York Times,* July 14, 2015, http://www.nytimes.com/2015 /07/15/business/international/micron-technology-is-said-to-be-takeover -target-of-chinese-company.html, accessed July 17, 2015; John Kang, "Why China Wants U.S. Memory Chip Technology—And What Washington Is Doing About It," December 6, 2016, https://www.forbes.com/sites/johnkang /2016/12/06/china-beijing-u-s-washington-memory-chip-semiconductor -technology/#7fd7305a46f9.

97. Stephen A. Schwarzman, *What It Takes: Lessons in the Pursuit of Excellence* (New York: Avid Reader Press, 2019), 291.

98. Keith Bradsher, "$300 Million Scholarship for Study in China Signals a New Focus," *New York Times,* April 20, 2013, http://www.nytimes.com /2013/04/21/world/asia/us-financier-backs-china-scholarship-program .html, accessed July 20, 2015.

99. "Qinghua daxue 2020 nian bumen yusuan" [Tsinghua University 2020 Departmental Budget], Tsinghua University, July 2020, https://www.tsinghua .edu.cn/publish/newthu/openness/newsml/cwyc_2020.htm.

## 10. The Burden of History

1. William C. Kirby, "Engineers and the State in Modern China," in William P. Alford, Kenneth Winston, and William C. Kirby, eds., *Prospects for the Professions in China* (New York: Routledge, 2011), 286–287. Also see Charles D. Musgrove, *China's Contested Capital: Architecture, Ritual and Response in Nanjing* (Honolulu: University of Hawaii Press, 2013).

2. This section draws heavily on Wang Dezi, ed., *Nanjing daxueshi* [History of Nanjing University] (Nanjing: Nanjing daxue chubanshi, 1992) and Wang Dezi, Gong Fang, and Mao Rong, eds., *Nanjing daxue bainian shi* [One-Hundred Year History of Nanjing University] (Nanjing: Nanjing daxue chubanshi, 2002).

3. Wang, Gong, and Mao, *Nanjing daxue bainian shi,* 53.

4. Guy S. Alitto, *The Last Confucian: Liang Shu-ming and the Chinese Dilemma of Modernity* (Berkeley: University of California Press, 1979), 6–7; Laurence Schneider, "National Essence and the New Intelligentsia," in Charlotte Furth, ed., *The Limits of Change: Essays on Conservative Alternatives in Republican China* (Cambridge, MA: Harvard University Press, 1976), 58–75, *passim.* Description of Xueheng scholars from Schneider, 73.

5. Wang, *Nanjing daxueshi,* 134.

6. See William C. Kirby, *Germany and Republican China* (Stanford: Stanford University Press, 1984).

7. See Wen-hsin Yeh, *The Alienated Academy* (Cambridge, MA: Harvard University Asia Center, 1990), 179, and chap. 5, *passim.*

8. Robert Lawrence Kuhn, *The Man Who Changed China: The Life and Legacy of Jiang Zemin* (New York: Crown Publishers, 2004), 42.

9. See Augustus S. Downing, "Report on Higher Education for the School Year 1918-19," in *Sixteenth Annual Report of the Education Department: University of the State of New York, Volume III* (Albany: University of the State of New York and State Department of Education, 1919), 60-66, https://books.google.com/books?id=CdpJAQAAMAAJ&lpg=PA190&ots=jw3g2a YwjX&dq=new%20york%20state%20department%20of%20education%20 university%20of%20nanking&pg=PA62#v=onepage&q=nanking&f=false, accessed November 19, 2015.

10. Ibid, 63.

11. Wang, *Nanjing daxueshi,* 466-468.

12. Wang, *Nanjing daxueshi,* 476-477.

13. Yoshi S. Kuno, *Educational Institutions in the Orient with Special Reference to Colleges and Universities in the United States, Part II* (Berkeley: University of California, 1928); Wang Dezi, *Nanjing daxueshi,* 480.

14. Wang, *Nanjing daxueshi,* 498.

15. Mrs. Lawrence Thurston and Ruth M. Chester, *Ginling College* (New York: United Board for Christian Colleges in China, 1955), 2-3; Downing, "Report on Higher Education," 61-62, 71-74.

16. Ellen Widmer, "The Seven Sisters and China, 1900-1950," in *China's Christian Colleges: Cross-Cultural Connections, 1900-1950,* Daniel H. Bays and Ellen Widmer, eds. (Stanford: Stanford University Press, 2009), 88.

17. Hua Ling Hu, *American Goddess at the Rape of Nanking: The Courage of Minnie Vautrin* (Carbondale: Southern Illinois University Press, 2000).

18. Thurston and Chester, *Ginling College,* 135.

19. See Jun Li, Jing Lin, and Fang Gong, "Nanjing University: Redeeming the Past by Academic Merit," in Ruth Hayhoe, Jun Li, Jing Lin, and Qiang Zha, *Portraits of 21st Century Chinese Universities: In the Move to Mass Higher Education* (Dordrecht, NL: Springer, 2011), 135-136.

20. Widmer, "The Seven Sisters and China," 94.

21. Wang, Gong, and Mao, *Nanjing daxue bainian shi,* 305.

22. "Nanjing daxue jiu chu fan dang fan shehuizhuyi de fangeming fenzi Kuang Yaming. Jiangsu sheng wei jueding chexiao Kuang Yaming yiqie zhiwu, shoudao relie yonghu" [Nanjing University Uncovered Kuang Yaming as an Anti-Party and Anti-Socialist Counter-Revolutionary. The Jiangsu Provincial Party Committee's Decision to Remove Kuang Yaming from All Positions was Warmly Supported], *Renmin ribao* [People's Daily], June 16, 1966, http://www.morningsun.org/chinese/library/19660616.html.

23. A superb source on Nanda during the early stages of the Cultural Revolution is Dong Guoqian and Andrew G. Walder, "Factions in a Bureaucratic Setting: The Origins of Cultural Revolution Conflict in Nanjing," *The China Journal,* no. 65 (Jan. 2011), 1-25, esp. 11-18.

24. Li, Lin, and Fang, "Nanjing University," 137-138.

25. See Zhang Xianwen, *Zhonghua minguo shigang* [Outline History of the Republic of China] (Zhengshou: Henan renmin chubanshe, 1985).

26. Guido Samarani, "Studies on the History of Republican China in the PRC and the Nanjing Research Center," *Revue Bibliographique de Sinologie*, 14 (1996): 153–158.

27. Norton Wheeler, "Educational Exchange in Post-Mao U.S.-China Relations: The Hopkins-Nanjing Center," *The Journal of American-East Asian Relations* 17, no. 1 (2010): 56–88, http://www.jstor.org/stable/23613332.

28. Maria Blackburn, "Professor Chien, Diplomat," *Johns Hopkins Magazine*, June 10, 1986, https://pages.jh.edu/jhumag/0607web/chien.html.

29. Katie Pearce, "Trailblazing Chinese-American Grad Program Celebrates 30 Years in Nanjing," Johns Hopkins University, June 2016, http://hub.jhu.edu/2016/06/16/hopkins-nanjing-center-30th-anniversary, accessed October 2016.

30. Mira Sorvino, "Anti-Africanism in China: An Investigation into Chinese Attitudes toward Black Students in the PRC" (Undergraduate Honors Thesis, Department of East Asian Languages and Civilizations, Harvard College, December 1989).

31. Maria Blackburn, "Professor Chien, Diplomat."

32. Li, Lin, and Fang, "Nanjing University," 139–140.

33. "'211 gongcheng' he '985 gongcheng' yuan yu '835 jianyi'" ['Project 211' and 'Project 985' Originated from '835 Suggestions'], *Zhongguo Jiangsu wang* [Jiangsu Net], October 11, 2019, http://www.jiangsucc.com/5703-1.html.

34. Ibid.

35. "Dailing Nanjing daxue chengwei guonei dingjian gaoxiao de qian Nanda xiaozhang—Qu Qinyue [The President Who Led Nanjing University to Be at the Apex of Domestic Universities—Qu Qinyue], *Nanjing daxue xiaoyou wang* [Nanjing University Alumni Net], September 9, 2020, https://alumni.nju.edu.cn/8b/02/c21703a494338/pagem.htm.

36. *Nanjing daxue nianjian 1999* [Nanjing University 1999 Yearbook] (Nanjing: Nanjing daxue chubanshe, 2000), 10–21.

37. Naomi Ching, "Fame Is Fortune in Sino-science," *Nautilus*, September 19, 2013, https://nautil.us/issue/5/fame/fame-is-fortune-in-sino_science.

38. As quoted in Li, Lin, and Fang, "Nanjing University," 141.

39. Jun Li, et al., "Nanjing University," 142; Zhongguo tongji nianjian 2006 he 1991 [China Statistical Yearbook for 2006 and 1991], http://tongji.cnki.net/overseas/engnavi/YearBook.aspx?id=N2005120321&floor=1### and http://www.stats.gov.cn/tjsj/ndsj/2006/indexeh.htm; http://xiaoban.nju.edu.cn/687/list.htm.

40. Nanjing daxue, "Shisanwu fazhan guihua" [Nanjing University, 13th Five-Year Development Plan], July 2016, 12, http://webcache.googleusercontent.com/search?q=cache:udOp7NP9pk8J:fzghc.bnu.edu.cn/docs/2018112017 0123477926.pdf+&cd=1&hl=en&ct=clnk&gl=us.

41. Nanjing daxue, "Yiliu daxue jianshe guihua" [Nanjing University, World-Class University Development Plan], December 26, 2017, https://webcache.googleusercontent.com/search?q=cache:x7oX2S5vVtcJ:https://xkb.nju.edu

.cn/_upload/article/files/72/cf/56c3661c41d1b7bd0eceb2fd6d57/e27d8fad
-5d2d-4020-9b62-b1651aebea01.pdf+&cd=2&hl=en&ct=clnk&gl=us.

42. Ibid.

43. "School Profile," Kuang Yaming Honors School, Nanjing University,
https://dii.nju.edu.cn/kym_en.

44. Nanjing daxue, "Yiliu daxue jianshe guihua."

45. Li, Lin, and Fang, "Nanjing University," 152.

46. Nanjing daxue, "Shisanwu fazhan guihua."

47. Manhan Education, "Nanjing daxue 2019–2020 nian jiaoyan gangwei
rencai yinjin yu zhaopin jihua" [Nanjing University's 2019–2020 Teaching
and Research Post Talent Introduction and Recruitment Plan], *Zhihu*,
July 24, 2019, https://zhuanlan.zhihu.com/p/75070993.

48. Nanjing daxue xinwen wang, "Nanjing daxue qidong xin yi lun 'shandi
rencai zhichi jihua,' xuanba qingnian rencai ke xiangshou youdai" [Nanjing
University News Net, Nanjing University Has Launched a New Round of
"Mountain Talent Support Plan" and Selected Young Talents Can Enjoy
Preferential Treatment], Beijing Zhong Gong Education, May 15, 2018,
http://bj.offcn.com/html/2018/05/131161.html.

49. Author interview with Yang Zhong, Nanjing, March 30, 2015.

50. "History of NJU," Nanjing University School History Museum, https://web
.archive.org/web/20170504075303/http://museum.nju.edu.cn/univerhistory
/index_02.asp?column=01.

51. "Xuexiao jianjie" [School Profile], Nanjing University Jinling College,
https://www.jlxy.nju.edu.cn/xygk/xxjj.htm.

52. "Nanda jinling xueyuan xiaoyou xiao kule, san ben zhuan she wei 985
xiaoyuan chengwei Nanda xiaoyoule" [Alumni of Nanjing University's Jinling College Laughed and Cried as the Three Independent Colleges Were
Converted to a 985 Campus, and They Become Alumni of Nanjing Univer-
sity], Cunman Entertainment Network, July 19, 2020, http://www.cunman
.com/new/492725cfaef94e7a8f1795ef1c8f48f9.

53. "Nanjing daxue jinling xueyuan banqian hou pukou xiaoqu jiang bian cheng
zheyang" [After the Relocation of Nanjing University's Jinling College,
Pukou Campus Will Look Like This], 360 Kuai, May 14, 2019, https://www
.360kuai.com/pc/95688776f821940e5?cota=4&kuai_so=1&tj_url=so
_rec&sign=360_e39369d1.

54. "Nanjing daxue 2016 nian bumen yusuan" [Nanjing University 2016 Departmental Budget], Nanjing University, May 2016, http://xxgk.nju.edu.cn
/_upload/article/files/54/1a/20d4a9e8486997b264c51d78243f/9350f5b8
-ab18-4d53-a997-58dbbe667b6c.pdf.

55. "Nanjing daxue xiao shi" [Nanjing University School History], Nanjing University, https://web.archive.org/web/20160304030017/http://museum.nju.edu
.cn/univerhistory/index_02.asp?column=01; "Nanjing daxue benke jiaoxue
zhiliang baogao, 2013 niandu" [Nanjing University 2013 Undergraduate
Teaching Quality Annual Report], Nanjing University, http://xxgk.nju.edu.cn
/07/15/c199a1813/page.htm.

56. Nanjing daxue, "Nanjing daxue jiaoyu fazhan jijin hui gongzuo baogao, 2017 niandu" [Nanjing University, Nanjing University Education Development Foundation 2017 Annual Report], February 28, 2019, https://njuedf.nju.edu.cn/43/ae/c4443a279470/page.htm.

57. "The Flagship History," The Language Flagship, https://www.thelanguageflagship.org/content/flagship-history, accessed August 2020.

58. U.S. Department of Education, Office of Postsecondary Education, "Enhancing Foreign Language Proficiency in the United States" (Washington, DC, 2008), https://nsep.gov/sites/default/files/nsli-preliminary-results.pdf.

59. Joel Campbell, "BYU Trying to Recall Group from Nanjing," *Deseret News,* June 6, 1989, https://www.deseret.com/1989/6/6/18809954/byu-trying-to-recall-group-from-nanjing; The Nanjing Chinese Flagship Center, "About the Nanjing Chinese Flagship Center," https://chinesefs.byu.edu/, accessed August 2020.

60. William A. Stanton, "Arrival of Flagship in Taiwan Significant for US-Taiwan Relations," *Taiwan News,* October 13, 2019, https://www.taiwannews.com.tw/en/news/3794865.

61. Elizabeth Redden, "3 More Universities Close Confucius Institutes," *Inside Higher Ed,* May 1, 2019, https://www.insidehighered.com/quicktakes/2019/05/01/3-more-universities-close-confucius-institutes.

62. William A. Stanton, "Arrival of Flagship in Taiwan Significant for US-Taiwan Relations."

63. "Donors," Schwarzman Scholars, https://www.schwarzmanscholars.org/donors/, accessed August 2020.

64. "Schwarzman Scholars Announces Inaugural Class," Schwarzman Scholars, January 11, 2016, https://www.schwarzmanscholars.org/news-article/schwarzman-scholars-announces-inaugural-class/.

65. "Schwarzman Scholars Announces Class of 2021," Schwarzman Scholars, December 4, 2019, https://www.schwarzmanscholars.org/news-article/schwarzman-scholars-announces-class-of-2021/.

66. "Degrees of Danger," Week in China, August 30, 2019, https://www.weekinchina.com/2019/08/degrees-of-danger/; "FAQ," Yenching Academy of Peking University, https://yenchingacademy.pku.edu.cn/ADMISSIONS/Frequently_Asked_Questions.htm, accessed August 2020.

67. "Schwarzman Scholars: Global Leadership for the 21st Century," Schwarzman Scholars, December 2018, https://www.schwarzmanscholars.org/wp-content/uploads/2018/12/Schwarzman-Scholars-Brochure.pdf; "Fellowship Program Information Sheet –Yenching Scholarship," Smith College, https://www.smith.edu/fellowships/docs/1.YEN.2.001_Fellowship_Info_Sheet_Yenching.pdf, accessed August 2020.

68. "Class Profile: Hopkins-Nanjing Center," Johns Hopkins School of Advanced International Studies, https://sais.jhu.edu/hopkins-nanjing-center/class-profile-hopkins-nanjing-center, accessed August 2020.

69. Nanjing daxue, "Shisanwu fazhan guihua."

70. Shanghai Observer, "Zhongyang jiang dui Qinghua Beida deng 29 suo gaoxiao kaizhan xunshi. Wang Qishan: xunshi yao qizhixianming jiang zhengzhe" [The Central Government Will Conduct Special Inspections of 29 Universities, Including Tsinghua University and Peking University. Wang Qishan: The Inspections Must Take a Clear Stand and Speak to Politics], February 22, 2017, https://www.jfdaily.com/wx/detail.do?id=45466.

71. Emily Feng, "Ideological Purge Hits China Universities with Western Ties," *Financial Times*, April 24, 2017, https://www.ft.com/content/8a7552d8-1f68-11e7-a454-ab04428977f9.

72. "Xi Jinping zai Zhongguo zhengfa daxue kaocha" [Xi Jinping Inspects China University of Political Science and Law], *Xinhua*, May 3, 2017, http://www.xinhuanet.com//politics/2017-05/03/c_1120913310.htm.

73. Nanjing daxue zhonggong jiwei, "Nanjing daxue dangwei xunshi fankui qingkuang ji zhenggai luoshi gongzuo ganbu dahui zhaokai" [Nanjing University CCP Disciplinary Inspection Committee, Nanjing University Party Committee's Inspection Feedback and Rectification Implementation Work Cadre Meeting Held], *Nanjing daxue xinwen wang* [Nanjing University News Net], June 27, 2017, https://jwb.nju.edu.cn/29/01/c8317a207105/page.htm.

74. Zhonggong Nanjing daxue dangwei, "Nanjing daxue xunshi zhenggai tongbao: dui weiji zhongceng ganbu yi cha daodi" [Nanjing University Committee of the Communist Party of China, Nanjing University Inspection and Rectification Bulletin: A Thorough Investigation of Middle-Level Cadres Who Violate Discipline], *Sina News*, August 28, 2017, http://news.sina.com.cn/c/nd/2017-08-28/doc-ifykiurx2388342.shtml.

75. Ibid.

76. Ibid.

77. Nanjing daxue zhonggong jiwei, "Xiao dangwei zhongxin zu zhuanti xuexi xin dangzhang" [Nanjing University CCP Disciplinary Inspection Committee, The School Party Committee Leading Group Holds Special Meeting to Learn New Party Constitution], Nanjing daxue xinwen wang [Nanjing University News Net], November 2, 2017, https://jwb.nju.edu.cn/6f/85/c8317a225157/page.htm.

78. Nanjing daxue zhonggong jiwei, "Nanjing daxue xinwen 2018 nian quanmian cong yan zhi dang gongzuo huiyi" [Nanjing University CCP Disciplinary Inspection Committee, Nanjing University Holds the 2018 Comprehensive Party Governance Work Conference], Nanjing daxue xinwen wang [Nanjing University News Net], April 13, 2018, https://jwb.nju.edu.cn/eb/c1/c8317a256961/page.htm.

79. Nanjing daxue, "Yiliu daxue jianshe guihua."

80. Ibid.

81. Ibid.

82. "Makesi zhuyi lilun yanjiu yu jianshe xiangmu" [Marxist Theory Research and Construction Project"] *Zhongguo gongchandang xinwen* [Communist Party of China News], September 25, 2008, http://cpc.people.com.cn/GB

/134999/135000/8105941.html; "Zhonggong zhongyang guowuyuan yinfa guanyu jinyibu jiaqiang he gaijin daxuesheng sixiang zhengzhi jiaoyu de yijian" [The Central Committee of the Communist Party of China and the State Council Opinions on Further Strengthening and Improving the Ideological and Political Education of College Students], Zhonghua renmin gonghequo jiaoyubu [Ministry of Education of the People's Republic of China], October 14, 2004, http://www.moe.gov.cn/s78/A12/szs_lef/moe _1407/moe_1408/tnull_20566.html.

83. "Nanjing University 2017–2018 Undergraduate Education Quality Report," Nanjing University, December 20, 2018, https://xxgk.nju.edu.cn/e4/f7 /c15434a320759/page.htm, accessed August 2020.

84. Zhonggong Nanjing daxue weiyuanhui, "Nanjing daxue guanyu qieshi jiaqiang he gaijin shi de xuefeng jianshe de ruogan yijian" [Nanjing University Committee of the Communist Party of China, About Nanjing University: Several Opinions on Strengthening and Improving the Development of Teachers' Ethics and Style of Study], May 17, 2018, https://hr.nju.edu.cn/1d /cc/c12918a269772/pagem.htm.

85. Nanjing daxue Makesi zhuyi yuedu yanjiu she, "Nanda ma hui zhi Nanjing daxue dangwei shuji Hu Jinbo de gongkaixin" [Marxist Reading and Research Society, An Open Letter from a Nanjing University Club to the Secretary of the Nanjing University Party Committee Hu Jinbo], October 16, 2018, https://njured.wordpress.com/2018/10/16/.

86. Ran Ran, "Zhongguo zuoyi qingnian de chengzhang he guanfang de daya" [The Rise and Official Suppression of China's Left-Wing Youth], BBC News, December 28, 2018, https://www.bbc.com/zhongwen/simp/chinese -news-46616052.

87. "Shenzhen Jasic Workers' Rights Defense: Left-Wing Youth and Political Aspirations," BBC News, August 16, 2018, https://www.bbc.com/zhong wen/simp/chinese-news-45204596.

88. "Shenzhen jia shi weiquan: Shengyuan tuan chengyuan pilu bei jingfang dai zou guocheng" [Shenzhen Jasic Rights Defense: Members of the Support Group Disclose the Process of Being Taken Away by the Police], BBC News, August 29, 2018, https://www.bbc.com/zhongwen/simp/chinese -news-45341005.

89. Ran Ran, "Zhongguo zuoyi qingnian de chengzhang he guanfang de daya."

90. Nanjing daxue Makesi zhuyi yuedu yanjiu she, "Nanda ma hui zhi Nanjing daxue dangwei shuji Hu Jinbo de gongkaixin."

91. Nanjing daxue Makesi zhuyi yuedu yanjiu she, "Nanda Makesi zhuyi yuedu yanjiu hui julebu baoming shijian (09.12–11.05)" [Marxist Reading and Research Society of Nanjing University, Nanda's Marxist Reading and Research Society Club Registration Timeline (09.12–11.05)], November 2, 2018, https://njumarx.wordpress.com/2018/11/02/.

92. Voice of America, "Shenzhen jia shi weiquan huodong renshi zai zao jing-fang yanli zhenya" [Shenzhen Jasic Rights Activists Are Severely Suppressed

by the Police Again], November 11, 2018, https://www.voachinese.com/a
/China-Rounds-Up-Uni-Labor-Campaigners-20181111/4653698.html.

93. Nanjing daxue Makesi zhuyi yuedu yanjiu she, "Nanda Makesi zhuyi yuedu
yanjiu hui julebu baoming shijian (09.12–11.05)."

94. "Zhongong zhongyang ziyuan Hu Jinbo wei Nanjing shuji" [The Central
Committee of the Communist Party of China Appointed Hu Jinbo as Secretary of the Party Committee of Nanjing University], *Nanjing daxue
xiaoyou wang* [Nanjing University Alumni Net], October 23, 2018, https://
alumni.nju.edu.cn/90/17/c276a299031/pagem.htm; Yan Hongliang, "Zhang
Yibin xieren Nanda dangwei shuji: zhudong tichu cong lingdao gangwei tui
xia" [Zhang Yibin Stepped Down as Secretary of the Nanda Party Committee: Voluntarily Proposed to Retire from the Leadership Position], *Sina
News*, October 24, 2018, https://news.sina.com.cn/o/2018-10-24/doc
-ihmxrkzw0005437.shtml.

95. Nanjing daxue Makesi zhuyi yuedu yanjiu she, "Nanda ma hui zhi Nanjing
daxue dangwei shuji Hu Jinbo de gongkaixin."

96. Ran Ran, "Zhongguo zuoyi qingnian de chengzhang he guanfang de daya."

97. He Haiwei, "Zhongguo duo ming changdao gongren quanli de nianqing
huodong renshi shizong" [Several Young Activists Advocating for Workers'
Rights in China Have Disappeared], *New York Times* (Chinese Edition),
November 12, 2018, https://cn.nytimes.com/china/20181112/china-student
-activists/.

98. Wen Yuqing, Han Jie, and Luisetta Mudie, "China Replaces Head of Peking
University with Communist Party Chief," Radio Free Asia, November 25,
2018, https://www.rfa.org/english/news/china/university-party-102520
18143652.html; "Zhu Xinkai ren Zhongguo renmin daxue dangwei chan-
gwei, fu xiaozhang" [Zhu Xinkai Serves as a Member of the Standing Committee of the Party Committee and Vice President of Renmin University of
China], *Renmin ribao* [People's Daily], November 28, 2018, http://renshi
.people.com.cn/n1/2018/1128/c139617-30429118.html; "Qi Pengfei ren
Zhongguo renmin daxue dangwei fu shuji" [Qi Pengfei Is Appointed Deputy
Secretary of the Renmin University of China Party Committee], *Xinhua*,
June 27, 2019, http://www.xinhuanet.com/renshi/2019-06/27/c_1124678988
.htm; "Zhongong zhongyang ziyuan Hu Jinbo wei Nanjing shuji."

99. Javier C. Hernández, "Cornell Cuts Ties with Chinese School after Crackdown on Students," *New York Times*, October 29, 2018, https://www
.nytimes.com/2018/10/29/world/asia/cornell-university-renmin.html.

100. Beijing daxue jiaoyu fa yanjiu zhongxin, "Nanjing daxue zhangcheng" [Pe-
king University Research Center for Education Law, Charter of Nanjing
University], October 12, 2015, http://www.educationlaw.cn/plus/view.php
?aid=160.

101. "Jiaoyubu guanyu tongyi Fudan daxue zhangcheng tiaokuan xiugai de pifu"
[Reply of the Ministry of Education on Agreeing to the Revision of Some
Articles of Fudan University's Charter], Zhonghua renmin gongheguo

jiaoyubu [Ministry of Education of the People's Republic of China], December 5, 2019, http://www.moe.gov.cn/srcsite/A02/zfs_gdxxzc/201912/t20191216_412276.html.

102. Ibid.

103. Ibid.

104. Beijing daxue jiaoyu fa yanjiu zhongxin, "Nanjing daxue zhangcheng."

105. "Jiaoyubu guanyu tongyi Fudan daxue zhangcheng tiaokuan xiugai de pifu."

106. Philip Wen, "Delete 'Freedom' and Emphasize 'Loyalty': Chinese Colleges and Universities Revise Their Statutes, Raising Objections," *Wall Street Journal*, December 20, 2019, https://on.wsj.com/3qI9uE8.

107. Emily Feng, "Chinese Universities Are Enshrining Communist Party Control in Their Charters," NPR, January 20, 2020, https://www.npr.org/2020/01/20/796377204/chinese-universities-are-enshrining-communist-party-control-in-their-charters.

108. Douglas Belkin and Philip Wen, "American Colleges Watch for Changes at Chinese Universities," *Wall Street Journal*, December 27, 2019, https://www.wsj.com/articles/american-colleges-watch-for-changes-at-chinese-universities-11577474706.

109. "Jiaoyubu 2020 nian bumen yusuan" [Ministry of Education 2020 Departmental Budget], June 11, 2020, Ministry of Education of the People's Republic of China, http://www.moe.gov.cn/srcsite/A05/s7499/202006/t20200611_465019.html.

110. "Nanjing daxue 2020 nian bumen yusuan" [Nanjing University 2020 Departmental Budget], Nanjing University, July 3, 2020, https://xxgk.nju.edu.cn/63/fb/c15419a484347/page.htm.

## 11. Asia's Global University?

1. Author interview with Xiang Zhang, Hong Kong, October 15, 2019.

2. Ibid.

3. Ibid.

4. Ibid.

5. Ibid.

6. *London Gazette*, no. 28024, May 24, 1907, 3589, https://www.thegazette.co.uk/London/issue/28024/page/3589, accessed December 9, 2015; Peter Cunich, *A History of the University of Hong Kong, Volume 1: 1911–1945* (Hong Kong: Hong Kong University Press, 2012), 80.

7. From an article by Lugard published in the October 1910 issue of *The Nineteenth Century and After*, as quoted in Bernard Mellor, *Lugard in Hong Kong: Empires, Education and a Governor at Work, 1907–1912* (Hong Kong: Hong Kong University Press, 1992), 1–2.

8. Cunich, *A History of the University of Hong Kong*, 82.

9. Bert Becker, "The 'German Factor' in the Founding of the University of Hong Kong," in *An Impossible Dream: Hong Kong University from Foundation*

   *to Re-establishment, 1910–1950*, Lau Kit-Ching Chan and Peter Cunich, eds. (Oxford: Oxford University Press, 2002), 29.

10. Cunich, *A History of the University of Hong Kong*, 86.

11. Cunich, *A History of the University of Hong Kong*, 120.

12. Mellor, *Lugard in Hong Kong*, 3.

13. Cunich, *A History of the University of Hong Kong*, 185.

14. University of Hong Kong Calendar, 1955–1956. (Hong Kong: Cathay Press, 1955), 11.

15. Cunich, *A History of the University of Hong Kong*, 169.

16. Cunich, *A History of the University of Hong Kong*, 262.

17. Cunich, *A History of the University of Hong Kong*, 301.

18. Cunich, *A History of the University of Hong Kong*, 312.

19. Brian Harrison, "The Years of Growth," in *University of Hong Kong: The First 50 Years, 1911–1961*, Brian Harrison, ed. (Hong Kong: Cathay Press, 1963), 54–55.

20. Cunich, *A History of the University of Hong Kong*, 335.

21. Sloss, as quoted in Cunich, *A History of the University of Hong Kong*, 335.

22. Cunich, *A History of the University of Hong Kong*, 340.

23. Cunich, *A History of the University of Hong Kong*, 388–389.

24. As quoted in Cunich, *A History of the University of Hong Kong*, 433.

25. Francis Stock, "A New Beginning" in Harrison, *University of Hong Kong*, 86.

26. "Milestones through the Decades," Chinese University of Hong Kong, 2015, http://www.cuhk.edu.hk/ugallery/en/zone-a.html, accessed December 9, 2015.

27. *Faculty of Arts 100: A Century in Words and Images* (Hong Kong: University of Hong Kong Faculty of Arts, 2014), 100.

28. *Faculty of Arts 100*, 33.

29. Chinese Central Government, "Full Text of Sino-British Joint Declaration," Government of China, June 14, 2007, http://www.gov.cn/english/2007-06/14/content_649468.htm, accessed October 22, 2019.

30. Phoebe H. Stevenson, "Higher Education in Hong Kong: A Case Study of Universities Navigating through the Asian Economic Crisis" (dissertation, University of Pennsylvania, 2010), 14–15.

31. "The Basic Law of the Hong Kong Special Administrative Region of the People's Republic of China," Government of Hong Kong, accessed October 22, 2019, https://www.basiclaw.gov.hk/en/basiclawtext/images/basiclaw_full_text_en.pdf; "Wang Gungwu, Historian and Former Vice-Chancellor of the University of Hong Kong, Shares Life Memories and His Views on Hong Kong's Future," *South China Morning Post* video, September 7, 2019, https://www.scmp.com/video/hong-kong/3026052/wang-gungwu-historian-and-former-vice-chancellor-university-hong-kong.

32. "University Allows Display of Democracy Sculpture," *The Globe and Mail*, June 7, 1997, http://search.proquest.com.ezp-prod1.hul.harvard.edu/docview/1140556689?accountid=11311, accessed September 24, 2015.

33. University Grants Committee, *Hong Kong Higher Education: To Make a Difference, To Move with the Times,* January 2004, http://www.ugc.edu.hk/eng /doc/ugc/publication/report/policy_document_e.pdf, accessed December 9, 2015.

34. "Quick Stats," University of Hong Kong, http://www.cpao.hku.hk/qstats/, accessed October 28, 2015.

35. "Staff Profiles," Quick Stats, University of Hong Kong, https://www.cpao .hku.hk/qstats/staff-profiles, accessed November 2020.

36. Mimi Lau, "Global HKU is on Top of the World," *South China Morning Post,* November 10, 2007, http://www.scmp.com/article/615037/global-hku -top-world, accessed January 26, 2016.

37. Author interview with Peter Mathieson, Hong Kong, October 20, 2015.

38. University of Hong Kong Strategic Planning Unit, *University of Hong Kong Strategic 2009–2014 Development,* November 2009, 6, http://www .sppoweb.hku.hk/sdplan/eng/images/doc.pdf, accessed December 9, 2015.

39. Author interview with Arthur Li, Hong Kong, October 15, 2015.

40. Author interview with Ian Holliday, Hong Kong, May 12, 2015.

41. Rayson Huang, *A Lifetime in Academia* (Hong Kong: Hong Kong University Press, 2000), 102.

42. Author interview with anonymous source, Hong Kong, May 15, 2015.

43. Author interview with Roland Chin, Hong Kong, May 11, 2015.

44. Ibid.

45. "Terms for Re-appointment beyond Retirement Age," Human Resources of HKU, September 13, 2018, https://www.hr.hku.hk/news/internal_commu nication/announcement.php?id=428, accessed October 22, 2019.

46. Cindy Wan, "HKU court calls for review of retirement age," *The Standard,* December 18, 2018, http://www.thestandard.com.hk/section-news.php?id =203359&sid=11, accessed October 22, 2019.

47. Kris Cheng, "HKU grants 2-year contract extensions for liberal profs Johannes Chan and Petula Ho instead of 5," *Hong Kong Free Press,* August 10, 2018, https://www.hongkongfp.com/2018/08/10/hku-grants-2-year -contract-extensions-liberal-profs-johannes-chan-petula-ho-instead-5/, accessed October 22, 2019.

48. Karen Zhang, "HKU academic staff express discontent over retirement at 60 in forum with management and alumni," *South China Morning Post,* November 20, 2018, https://www.scmp.com/news/hong-kong/education/article /2174164/hku-academic-staff-express-discontent-retirement-60 forum, accessed October 22, 2019

49. *Fit for Purpose Report,* 2003, http://www.hku.hk/about/governance/purpose _report.html, accessed February 11, 2016.

50. "The Senate (Membership)," University of Hong Kong, 2015, http://www .hku.hk/about/governance/governance_structure/the-court/senate_member ship.html, accessed December 9, 2015.

51. "The Court (Membership)," University of Hong Kong, 2015, http://www
.hku.hk/about/governance/governance_structure/the-court/court_member
ship.html, accessed December 9, 2015.

52. Author interview with John Malpas, Hong Kong, May 12, 2015.

53. Ibid.

54. Ibid.

55. The University of Hong Kong—Strategic Development 2003–2008, "Transforming the University for the 21st Century," https://www.sppoweb.hku.hk
/sdplan/2003_08/english/fs-transform.htm.

56. The University of Hong Kong, "HKU Ranked 18th amongst the World's
Top 200 universities," https://www.hku.hk/press/news_detail_5651.html.

57. "Asia's Global University: The Next Decade: Our Vision for 2016–2025,"
The University of Hong Kong, https://www.sppoweb.hku.hk/vision2016
-2025/index.html.

58. "About ZIRI," Zhejiang Institute of Research and Innovation, http://www
.ziri.hku.hk/en/about.html; LKS Faculty of Medicine, The University of
Hong Kong, "The University of Hong Kong-Shenzhen Hospital," https://
fmpc.hku.hk/en/Clinical-Services/The-University-of-Hong-Kong
-Shenzhen-Hospital.

59. *University of Hong Kong Financial Report, 2018,* http://www.feo.hku.hk
/finance/information/annualreport/publications/2018/HTML/index.html
accessed October 21, 2019.

60. "Undergraduate Admissions," University of Hong Kong, 2019, https://aal
.hku.hk/admissions/international/admissions-information?page=en/fees
-and-scholarships and http://www.als.hku.hk/admission/mainland
/admission/overview#, accessed October 22, 2019.

61. "Centennial College," University of Hong Kong, 2019, https://www
.centennialcollege.hku.hk/en/faq, accessed October 22, 2019.

62. University of Hong Kong Financial Report, 2014, http://www.feo.hku.hk
/finance/information/annualreport.html?v=1449761272864, accessed December 10, 2015.

63. University of Hong Kong Financial Report, 2018, http://www.feo.hku.hk
/finance/information/annualreport/publications/2018/HTML/index.html,
accessed October 21, 2019.

64. Author interview with anonymous source, Hong Kong, May 15, 2015.

65. "People's Satisfaction with HKSARG's Pace of Democratic Development
(Half-Yearly Average)," HKU Public Opinion Programme, https://www
.hkupop.hku.hk/english/popexpress/sargperf/demo/halfyr/demo_halfyr
_chart.html, accessed January 2020.

66. "People's Lack of Confidence in HK's Future, People's Lack of Confidence
in China's Future and People's Lack of Confidence in 'One Country, Two
Systems,'" HKU Public Opinion Programme, accessed January 2020, https://
www.hkupop.hku.hk/english/popexpress/trust/conhkfuture/combine_no
/combine_no_halfyr_chart.html; "People's Confidence in HK's Future,

People's Confidence in China's Future and People's Confidence in 'One Country, Two Systems,'" HKU Public Opinion Programme, https://www.hkupop.hku.hk/english/popexpress/trust/conhkfuture/combine/combine_hfyear_chart.html, accessed January 2020.

67. "CUHK Hong Kong Quality of Life Index Reveals Continuous Improvement of Quality of Life for Hong Kong," CUHK Communications and Public Relations Office, https://www.cpr.cuhk.edu.hk/en/press_detail.php?id=487&t=cuhk-hong-kong-quality-of-life-index-reveals-continuous-improvement-of-quality-of-life-for-hong-kong, accessed January 2020.

68. "CUHK Hong Kong Quality of Life Index: Quality of Life in Hong Kong Declined," CUHK Communications and Public Relations Office, https://www.cpr.cuhk.edu.hk/en/press_detail.php?id=1351&t=cuhk-hong-kong-quality-of-life-index-quality-of-life-in-hong-kong-declined, accessed January 2020.

69. "Categorical Ethnic Identity (per poll)," HKU Public Opinion Programme, https://www.hkupop.hku.hk/english/popexpress/ethnic/eidentity/poll/eid_poll_chart.html, accessed January 2020.

70. "Hong Kong Controversy Strikes University Officials," *Wall Street Journal,* September 7, 2000, http://search.proquest.com.ezp-prod1.hul.harvard.edu/docview/398878047?accountid=11311, accessed December 9, 2015.

71. Peter So, "University Chief Vows Truth on Police Action," *South China Morning Post,* September 6, 2011, https://global.factiva.com/redir/default.aspx?P=sa&an=SCMCOM0020110906e7960000z&cat=a&ep=ASE, accessed December 10, 2015; Dennis Chong and Tanna Chong, "Tsui Denies He Was Forced to Quit University," *South China Morning Post,* October 27, 2011, https://global.factiva.com/redir/default.aspx?P=sa&an=SCMP000020111026e7ar0000p&cat=a&ep=ASE, accessed December 10, 2015.

72. Reuters, "Explainer: What Was Hong Kong's 'Occupy' Movement All About?," April 23, 2019, https://www.reuters.com/article/us-hongkong-politics-occupy-explainer/explainer-what-was-hong-kongs-occupy-movement-all-about-idUSKCN1S005M.

73. Hong Kong Special Administrative Region, "Decision of the Standing Committee of the National People's Congress on Issues Relating to the Selection of the Chief Executive of the Hong Kong Special Administrative Region by Universal Suffrage and on the Method for Forming the Legislative Council of the Hong Kong Special Administrative Region in the Year 2016," August 31, 2014, http://www.2017.gov.hk/filemanager/template/en/doc/20140831b.pdf.

74. Harry Ong, "What Is HKU's Murky Role in 'Occupy Central'?," *China Daily,* November 4, 2014, https://www.chinadaily.com.cn/hkedition/2014-11/04/content_18861375.htm.

75. Kris Cheng, "Explainer: The HKU Pro-Vice-Chancellor Debacle," *Hong Kong Free Press,* September 30, 2015, https://www.hongkongfp.com/2015

/09/30/explainer-hku-council-rejects-johannes-chan-appointment-to-pro
-vice-chancellor/, accessed December 10, 2015.

76. "Thousands Sign Petition against HKU Students," RTHK News, August 5, 2015, http://news.rthk.hk/rthk/en/component/k2/1203053-20150805.htm, accessed December 10, 2015.

77. RTHK, "7,000 HKU Alumni Favor Johannes Chan," *The Standard,* September 2, 2015, http://www.thestandard.com.hk/breaking_news_detail.asp ?id=66171&icid=3&d_str=, accessed December 10, 2015.

78. Michael Forsythe, "Vote at Hong Kong University Stirs Concern over Beijing's Influence," *New York Times,* September 30, 2015, http://www.nytimes .com/2015/10/01/world/asia/hong-kong-university-votes-against-promoting -johannes-chan.html, accessed December 10, 2015.

79. Billy Fung, "Zhuanzai: Feng Jing'en jiu yue ershijiu xiaoweihui huiyi zhi geren shengming quanwen" [Reprint: Billy Fung's Personal Recollection of the September 29 University Council Meeting], *Post 852,* September 29, 2015, http://www.post852.com/2015/09/29, accessed December 10, 2015.

80. Jeffie Lam, "More than 3,000 March against Arthur Li's Appointment as Chairman of HKU Governing Council," *South China Morning Post,* January 4, 2016, http://www.scmp.com/news/hong-kong/education-community /article/1897821/more-3000-march-against-arthur-lis-appointment, accessed February 11, 2016.

81. See *The Report of the Review Panel on University Governance* (University of Hong Kong, February 2017), http://www.gs.hku.hk/Grant_Report_and _Addendum.pdf, accessed October 22, 2019.

82. Working Party on the Recommendations of the Review Panel on University Governance, *Report of the Working Party* (University of Hong Kong, June 2017), http://www.gs.hku.hk/Report_of_Working_Party.pdf, accessed October 22, 2019.

83. *The Report of the Review Panel on University Governance.*

84. "HKU Groups Condemn Reappointment of Arthur Li," RTHK News, January 1, 2019, https://news.rthk.hk/rthk/en/component/k2/1435945-2019 0101.htm, accessed October 22, 2019.

85. *Fugitive Offenders and Mutual Legal Assistance in Criminal Matters Legislation (Amendment) Bill 2019* (Hong Kong Legislative Council, March 2019), https://www.legco.gov.hk/yr18-19/english/bills/b201903291.pdf, accessed October 22, 2019.

86. Fion Li and Carol Zhong, "Everything You Need to Know About the Extradition Bill Rocking Hong Kong," *Washington Post,* June 13, 2019, https://www.washingtonpost.com/business/everything-you-need-to-know -about-the-extradition-bill-rocking-hong-kong/2019/06/11/12a7907c-8c26 -11e9-b6f4-033356502dce_story.html, accessed October 22, 2019.

87. James Pomfret and Farah Master, "Hong Kong Pushes Bill Allowing Extraditions to China Despite Biggest Protest Since Handover," Reuters, June 9, 2019, https://www.reuters.com/article/us-hongkong-extradition/hong-kong

-pushes-bill-allowing-extraditions-to-china-despite-biggest-protest-since
-handover-idUSKCN1TB08W, accessed October 22, 2019.

88. "Hong Kong Protest: 'Nearly Two Million' Join Demonstration," BBC, June 17, 2019, https://www.bbc.com/news/world-asia-china-48656471, accessed October 17, 2019.

89. Hillary Leung, "Hong Kong University Students Reject Invitation to Meet City's Leader for Closed-Door Talks," *Time*, July 5, 2019, https://time.com /5620905/hong-kong-student-unions-reject-carrie-lam-meeting/, accessed October 22, 2019.

90. Alvin Lum, "University of Hong Kong President Zhang Xiang Calls for 'Every Corner of Society' to Mend Political Divide through Talking as City Gears up for More Marches," *South China Morning Post*, July 18, 2019, https://www.scmp.com/news/hong-kong/politics/article/3019223/university -hong-kong-president-zhang-xiang-calls-every, accessed October 22, 2019.

91. Yojana Sharma, "Students Defy University Warnings with Classes' Boycott," *University World News*, September 3, 2019, https://www.universityworldnews .com/post.php?story=20190903181638206, accessed October 22, 2019.

92. Center for Communication and Public Opinion Survey, "Onsite Survey Findings in Hong Kong's Anti-Extradition Bill Protests," Chinese University of Hong Kong, August 2019, http://www.com.cuhk.edu.hk/ccpos/en /pdf/ENG_antielab%20survey%20public%20report%20vf.pdf.

93. Ibid.

94. Li Xinxin, "Yuan Guoyong, "Fan xiuli shiwei chongtu shoushang renshu keneng yu 2000 ren" [Yuan Guoyong: The Number of Injured in the Anti-reform Demonstrations May Exceed 2,000], RTHK News, August 15, 2019, https://news.rthk.hk/rthk/ch/component/k2/1474890-20190815.htm, accessed October 22, 2019.

95. Greg Torode, James Pomfret, and David Lague, "China Quietly Doubles Troop Levels in Hong Kong, Envoy Says," Reuters, September 30, 2019, https://www.reuters.com/investigates/special-report/china-army-hongkong/, accessed October 22, 2019; Andrew J. Nathan, "How China Sees the Hong Kong Crisis," *Foreign Affairs*, September 30, 2019, https://www.foreign affairs.com/articles/china/2019-09-30/how-china-sees-hong-kong-crisis, accessed October 22, 2019.

96. Cannix Yau, Wendy Wu, and Gary Cheung, "Chinese President Xi Jinping Warns That Anyone Trying to Split Any Part of Country Will Be Crushed," *South China Morning Post*, October 13, 2019, https://www.scmp.com/news /hong-kong/politics/article/3032741/chinese-president xi-jinping-warns -anyone-trying-split-any, accessed October 22, 2019.

97. "Clashes Spread to Different Hong Kong Universities," RTHK, https:// news.rthk.hk/rthk/en/component/k2/1491306-20191111.htm, accessed January 2020.

98. Mary Hui, "Photos: Hong Kong Police and Students Are Fighting a War in One of the City's Top Universities," *Quartz*, https://qz.com/1746924/police

-students-battle-in-chinese-university-of-hong-kong/, accessed January 2020.

99. Wenxin Fan and Dan Strumpf, "Hong Kong's Harrowing University Siege Ends Not with a Bang but a Whimper," *Wall Street Journal,* https://www.wsj .com/articles/hong-kongs-harrowing-university-siege-ends-not-with-a-bang -but-a-whimper-11574942822, accessed January 2020.

100. Chan Ho-him, "Hong Kong Protests: City University Reveals Bill to Fix Vandalised Campus Will Run to Hundreds of Millions of Dollars," *South China Morning Post,* https://www.scmp.com/news/hong-kong/education /article/3040062/hong-kong-protests-city-university-reveals-bill-fix, ac-cessed January 2020.

101. Jinshan Hong, "Mainland Students Flee Hong Kong Campus Clash with China Aid," *Bloomberg,* https://www.bloomberg.com/news/articles/2019-11 -13/mainland-students-flee-hong-kong-campus-standoff-with-china-help, accessed January 2020; Theo Wayt, "U.S. Universities Suspend Hong Kong Study Programs amid Deadly Protests," NBC News, https://www.nbcnews .com/news/us-news/u-s-universities-suspend-hong-kong-study-programs -amid-deadly-n1084046, accessed January 2020.

102. "Teaching and Learning Arrangements for the Remainder of the Semester," The University of Hong Kong, https://www.hku.hk/press/press-releases /detail/20219.html, accessed January 2020.

103. Christian Shepherd and Sue Lin-Wong, "Luo Huining: Beijing's enforcer in Hong Kong," *Financial Times,* January 7, 2020, https://www.ft.com/content /c95614f6-3063-11ea-9703-eea0cae3f0de.

104. "Key Facts about New Head of China's Liaison Office in Hong Kong," Reuters, January 5, 2020, https://www.reuters.com/article/us-honkong -china-liaison-factbox/key-facts-about-new-head-of-chinas-liaison-office-in -hong-kong-idUSKBN1Z50AS; Natalie Lung, Iain Marlow, and Cathy Chan, "China's New Hong Kong Liaison Confident City Will Stabilize," Bloomberg, January 4, 2020, https://www.bloomberg.com/news/articles /2020-01-04/china-announces-new-top-liaison-official-for-hong-kong?sref =8JkQ65qI.

105. Natalie Wong, Gary Cheung, and Sum Lok-kei, "Beijing's Liaison Office Says It Has Right to Handle Hong Kong Affairs, as Provided by Constitu-tion and Basic Law," *South China Morning Post,* April 17, 2020, https://www .scmp.com/news/hong-kong/politics/article/3080506/beijings-liaison-office -says-it-has-right-handle-hong-kong.

106. Helen Davidson, "China's Top Official in Hong Kong Pushes for National Security Law," *The Guardian,* April 15, 2020, https://www.theguardian.com /world/2020/apr/15/china-official-hong-kong-luo-huining-pushes-national -security-law.

107. Anna Fifield, Tiffany Liang, Shibani Mahtani, and Timothy McLaughlin, "China to Impose Sweeping Security Law in Hong Kong, Heralding End of City's Autonomy," *Washington Post,* May 21, 2020, https://www.washingtonpost

.com/world/asia_pacific/china-signals-plan-to-take-full-control-of-hong-kong
-realigning-citys-status/2020/05/21/2c3850ee-9b48-11ea-ad79-eef7cd734641
_story.html; Keith Bradsher, "China Approves Plan to Rein in Hong Kong,
Defying Worldwide Outcry," *New York Times,* May 28, 2020, https://www
.nytimes.com/2020/05/28/world/asia/china-hong-kong-crackdown.html.

108. Chris Buckley, "China Vows Tougher Security in Hong Kong. Easier Said
Than Done," *New York Times,* November 6, 2019, https://www.nytimes.com
/2019/11/06/world/asia/hong-kong-protests-china-national-security.html.

109. Nectar Gan, "China Approves Controversial National Security Law for
Hong Kong," CNN, May 28, 2020, https://www.cnn.com/2020/05/28/asia
/china-npc-hk-security-law-intl-hnk/index.html.

110. James Griffiths and Helen Regan, "Hong Kong Protest over Proposed National Security Law Met with Tear Gas," May 24, 2020, https://www.cnn
.com/2020/05/24/asia/hong-kong-protest-national-security-law-intl-hnk
/index.html.

111. CGTN, "Arthur Li Voices Firm Opposition to External Interference in
HKSAR affairs," May 28, 2020, https://news.cgtn.com/news/2020-05-28
/Arthur-Li-voices-rejection-to-external-interference-in-HKSAR-affairs
-QR5cYpmMYo/index.html.

112. Wong Tsui-kai, "Hong Kong University Heads Release Statement Saying
They 'Understand' New National Security Law," *South China Morning Post,*
June 1, 2020, https://www.scmp.com/yp/discover/news/hong-kong/article
/3086981/hong-kong-university-heads-release-statement-saying-they.

113. Chris Buckley, "What China's New National Security Law Means for Hong
Kong," *New York Times,* June 28, 2020, https://www.nytimes.com/2020/06
/28/world/asia/china-hong-kong-national-security-law.html.

114. "English Translation of the Law of the People's Republic of China on Safe-
guarding National Security in the Hong Kong Special Administrative Region," July 1, 2020, *Xinhua,* http://webcache.googleusercontent.com/search
?q=cache:fTYutlWet2cJ:www.xinhuanet.com/english/2020-07/01/c
_139178753.htm+&cd=1&hl=en&ct=clnk&gl=us.

115. Chris Lau, "National Security Law: Hong Kong Academics Might Choose
Self-Censorship to Protect Themselves, Law Dean Warns," *South China
Morning Post,* July 15, 2020, https://www.scmp.com/news/hong-kong
/politics/article/3093337/national-security-law-hong-kong-academics-might
-choose-self.

116. Jerome Taylor and Su Xinqi, "Security Law: Hong Kong Scholars Fear for
Academic Freedom," *Hong Kong Free Press,* July 15, 2020, https://hongkong
fp.com/2020/07/15/security-law-hong-kong-scholars-fear-for-academic
-freedom/.

117. Kelly Ho, "Hong Kong's Carrie Lam Says Education Is 'Politised,' Blames
Media for 'Negative, Smearing' Coverage," *Hong Kong Free Press,* July 13,
2020, https://hongkongfp.com/2020/07/13/hong-kongs-carrie-lam-says
-education-is-politicised-blames-media-for-negative-smearing-coverage/.

118. Chan Ho-him, "University of Hong Kong Governing Council Sacks Legal Scholar Benny Tai over Convictions for Occupy Protests," *South China Morning Post,* July 28, 2020, https://www.scmp.com/news/hong-kong /politics/article/3095043/university-hong-kong-governing-council-sacks -legal-scholar.

119. Ibid.

120. Chan Ho-him, "University of Hong Kong's Governing Council Chief Defends Benny Tai Sacking, Rejects Allegations of Outside Interference in the Decision," *South China Morning Post,* July 31, 2020, https://www.scmp.com /news/hong-kong/politics/article/3095411/university-hong-kong-governing -council-chief-defends-benny.

121. "First Priority Is to Get Rid of 'Bad Apples' in Education: Hong Kong Security Chief," *Apple Daily,* July 30, 2020, https://hk.appledaily.com/us /20200730/XP6ZJSHFIONFE6G3UOZ7XNA27E/.

122. Chan Ho-him, "Sacked Legal Scholar Benny Tai to Challenge Hong Kong's Leader Carrie Lam over Dismissal," *South China Morning Post,* July 29, 2020, https://www.scmp.com/news/hong-kong/politics/article /3095120/sacked-legal-scholar-benny-tai-challenge-hong-kongs-leader.

123. Author interview with Peter Mathieson, October 20, 2015.

124. Author interview with Arthur Li, October 15, 2015.

125. Author interview with Roland Chin, May 11, 2015.

126. *Qinghua daxue jiaoyu shoufei hongshi* [Tsinghua University Tuition Fee Publication], Tsinghua University, http://www.tsinghua.edu.cn/publish /newthu/openness/cwzcjsfxx/sfxm.html, accessed December 10, 2015; University of Hong Kong, "Fees and Scholarships: Tuition Fee & Cost of Living Reference," University of Hong Kong International Undergraduate Admissions, 2019, http://www.aal.hku.hk/admissions/international /admissions-information?page=en/fees-and-scholarships, accessed October 22, 2019.

127. Author interview with Victor Fung, Hong Kong, October 21, 2015.

128. *Times Higher Education World University Rankings,* 2012–2013, https://www .timeshighereducation.com/world-university-rankings/2013/world-ranking#! /page/0/length/25/sort_by/rank/sort_order/asc/cols/undefined.

129. See *Times Higher Education World University Rankings,* https://www .timeshighereducation.com/world-university-rankings/2021/world-ranking#! /page/0/length/25/sort_by/rank/sort_order/asc/cols/stats.

130. Kelly Ng, "Yale-NUS and Duke-NUS Offer New Route for Liberal Arts Students to Become Doctors," *Today Online,* January 16, 2018, https://www .todayonline.com/singapore/yale-nus-and-duke-nus-offer-new-route-liberal -arts-students-become-doctors.

131. National University Singapore, "National University of Singapore and its Subsidiaries: Full Financial Statements for the Financial Year Ended 31 March 2014," https://www.nus.edu.sg/docs/default-source/annual-report /nus-financialreport-2014.pdf; University of Hong Kong, "An Extract from

the University's Annual Accounts 2013–2014," https://www4.hku.hk
/pubunit/review/2014/an_extract_2014.pdf.

132. University of Hong Kong Strategic Planning Unit, "University of Hong
Kong Strategic 2009–2014 Development," November 2009, 6, http://www
.sppoweb.hku.hk/sdplan/eng/images/doc.pdf, accessed December 9, 2015.

133. Author interview with Victor Fung, October 21, 2015.

134. Author interview with Xiang Zhang, October 15, 2019.

135. Author interview with Paul Tam, Hong Kong, May 15, 2015.

136. Shui-yin Sharon Yam and Alex Chow, "Hong Kong's Universities Have Fallen.
There May Be No Turning Back," *New York Times*, November 24, 2021.

137. "HKU President to Continue to Engage Students and University Members,"
The University of Hong Kong, https://www.hku.hk/press/press-release
/detail/20123.html, accessed January 2020.

## Conclusion

1. See "Nature Index—Physical Sciences Germany (1 August 2019–31
July 2020)," https://www.natureindex.com/institution-outputs/generate
/Physical%20Sciences/countries-Germany/academic/score, accessed
March 13, 2021.

2. Quoted in Mark Lander, "Seeking Quality, German Universities Scrap
Equality," *New York Times*, Oct. 20, 2006.

3. See Jürgen Kaube, "Überall Niveau. Schavans jüngster Einfall: Bundes-
universitäten," *FAZ* Nr. 39 v. (16.2.2011): 5. See also Ingo von Münch,
*Rechtspolitik und Rechtskultur* (Berlin: Berliner Wissenschafts-Verlag, 2011),
116–118.

4. "Nature Index," Wikipedia, last modified March 15, 2021, https://en.wikipedia
.org/wiki/Nature_Index.

5. German Research Foundation, *Funding Atlas 2018*, https://www.dfg.de/sites
/foerderatlas2018/index.html, accessed March 12, 2021. The atlas has been
published every three years since 1997.

6. See Alexander Mayer, *Universitäten im Wettbewerb: Deutschland von den
1980er Jahren bis zur Exzellenzinitiative* (Stuttgart: Franz Steiner Verlag,
2019).

7. See Hans N. Weiler, *Die Erfindung einer privaten Hochschule für öffenliches
Handeln* (Berlin: Hertie School of Governance, 2014).

8. See "ZU in the Current Rankings," https://www.zeppelin-university.com
/university/rankings.php, accessed March 12, 2021.

9. See Klaus Mühlhahn, *Making China Modern* (Cambridge, MA: Harvard
University Press, 2019).

10. See Marijk van der Wende and Belinda Stratton, *Amsterdam University
College: Liberal Arts and Sciences for the 21st Century: AUC's Experiences and
Achievements, 2009–2012* (Amsterdam: Amsterdam University College,
2012).

11. See Peter-André Alt, *Exzellent!? Zur Lage der deutschen Universität* (München: C. H. Beck, 2021).

12. Derek Bok, *Our Underachieving Colleges* (Princeton: Princeton University Press, 2006); James Engell and Anthony Dangerfield, *Saving Higher Education in the Age of Money* (Charlottesville: University of Virginia Press, 2005); Charles T. Clotfelter, *Unequal Colleges in the Age of Disparity* (Cambridge, MA: Harvard University Press, 2017); Holden Thorp and Buck Goldstein, *Our Higher Calling: Rebuilding the Partnership between America and Its Colleges and Universities* (Chapel Hill: University of North Carolina Press, 2018); James L. Shulman and William G. Bowen, *The Game of Life* (Princeton, NJ: Princeton University Press, 2001); *The Heart of the Matter: The Humanities and Social Sciences for a Vibrant, Competitive, and Secure Nation* (Cambridge, MA: American Academy of Arts and Sciences, 2013); *The Perils of Complacency: America at a Tipping Point in Science & Engineering* (Cambridge, MA: American Academy of Arts and Sciences, 2020); Simon Marginson, *The Dream Is Over: The Crisis of Clark Kerr's California Idea of Higher Education* (Berkeley: University of California Press, 2016); Mark S. Tucker, ed., *Surpassing Shanghai* (Cambridge, MA: Harvard Education Press, 2011); Mark S. Ferrara, *Palace of Ashes: China and the Decline of American Higher Education* (Baltimore, MD: Johns Hopkins University Press, 2015).

13. Anthony Abraham Jack, *The Privileged Poor: How Elite Colleges Are Failing Disadvantaged Students* (Cambridge, MA: Harvard University Press, 2019); Elizabeth A. Armstrong and Laura T. Hamilton, *Paying for the Party: How College Maintains Inequality* (Cambridge, MA: Harvard University Press, 2015); Sara Goldrick-Rab, *Paying the Price: College Costs, Financial Aid, and the Betrayal of the American Dream* (Chicago: University of Chicago Press, 2016); Tressie McMillan Cottom, *Lower Ed: The Troubling Rise of For-Profit Colleges in the New Economy* (New York: The New Press, 2017); Jennifer S. Hirsch and Shamus Khan, *Sexual Citizens: A Landmark Study of Sex, Power, and Assault on Campus* (New York: W. W. Norton & Company, 2020).

14. Author conversation with Peter Lange, July 2021.

15. Much of the discussion below is indebted to the superb report by John Douglass and Zachary Bleemer, *Approaching a Tipping Point? A History and Prospectus of Funding for the University of California* (Berkeley, CA: Center for Studies in Higher Education, 2018).

16. Report of the UC Office of the President, Jan. 21, 2020, https://www .universityofcalifornia.edu/press-room/uc-s-california-student-enrollment -climbs-fourth-straight-year, accessed March 14, 2021.

17. Yao Huang and Anna Ho, "2018 UC Accountability Report Shows High Enrollment Despite Low State Funding," August 8, 2018, https://www .dailycal.org/2018/08/08/2018-uc-accountability-report-shows-high -enrollment-despite-low-state-funding/, accessed March 14, 2021.

18. See Douglass and Bleemer, *Approaching a Tipping Point?*, 12–13, 21–23; UC Berkeley Office of Undergraduate Admissions, "Estimated Student Budget, 2019–2020," https://admissions.berkeley.edu/cost, accessed March 14, 2021.

19. Quoted in Bob Herbert, "Cracks in the Future," *New York Times*, October 3, 2009.

20. Robert J. Birgeneau and Frank D. Yeary, "Rescuing Our Public Universities," *Washington Post*, September 27. 2009.

21. Emma Whitford, "Public Higher Ed Funding Still Has Not Recovered from 2008 Recession," *Inside Higher Ed*, May 5, 2020, https://www.insidehighered.com/news/2020/05/05/public-higher-education-worse-spot-ever-heading-recession, accessed March 10, 2021. Quotation is of Sophia Laderman, a senior policy analyst at the State Higher Education Executive Officers Association.

22. American Academy of Arts and Sciences, *Public Research Universities. Recommitting to Lincoln's Vision: An Educational Compact for the 21st Century* (Cambridge, MA, 2016), 6–10; "A Look at the Shocking Student Loan Debt Statistics for 2021," Student Loan Hero, updated Jan. 27, 2021, https://studentloanhero.com/student-loan-debt-statistics/, accessed March 14, 2021.

23. Laura T. Hamilton and Kelly Nielsen, *Broke: The Racial Consequences of Underfunding Public Universities* (Chicago: University of Chicago Press, 2021).

24. State Higher Education Executive Officers Association, "State Higher Education Finance FY 2019 Report," April 2020, 10, https://shef.sheeo.org/wp-content/uploads/2020/04/SHEEO_SHEF_FY19_Report.pdf, accessed March 10, 2021.

25. Herbert, "Cracks in the Future."

26. Henry Rosovsky, *The University: An Owner's Manual* (New York: Norton, 1990), 262.

27. See William G. Bowen and Harold T. Shapiro, eds., *Universities and their Leadership* (Princeton, NJ: Princeton University Press, 1998), especially the chapters by Shapiro and Hanna Gray, 65–118; Scott Cowen, *Winnebagos on Wednesdays: How Visionary Leadership Can Transform Higher Education* (Princeton, NJ: Princeton University Press, 2018).

28. See Australian Government, Department of Education, Skills and Employment, "Chinese Universities Establishing Programs and Campuses in Foreign Countries," September 6, 2016, https://internationaleducation.gov.au/news/latest-news/Pages/Chinese-universities-establishing.aspx, accessed March 10, 2021.

29. See Peking University HSBC Business School website, https://uk.phbs.pku.edu.cn/index.php?m=content&c=index&a=lists&catid=21, accessed March 10, 2021.

30. See William C. Kirby, "The International Origins and Global Aspirations of Chinese Universities: Along the New Silk Road," in Marijk C. van der Wende, William C. Kirby, Nian Cai Liu, and Simon Marginson, eds., *China and Europe on the New Silk Road: Connecting Universities across Eurasia* (Oxford: Oxford University Press, 2020), 18–32.

31. Amy Binder and Kate Wood, *Becoming Right: How Campuses Shape Young Conservatives* (Princeton, NJ: Princeton University Press, 2014); Norimitsu Onishi, "Will American Ideas Tear France Apart? Some of Its Leaders Think So," *New York Times*, February 9, 2021, https://www.nytimes.com /2021/02/09/world/europe/france-threat-american-universities.html, accessed February 21, 2021; Norimitsu Onishi, "Heating Up Culture Wars, France To Scour Universities for Ideas That 'Corrupt Society,'" *New York Times*, February 18, 2021, https://www.nytimes.com/2021/02/18/world /europe/france-universities-culture-wars.html, accessed February 21, 2021.

32. "Education Minister Warns against 'Wrong Western Values,'" *Global Times*, February 3, 2015, https://www.globaltimes.cn/content/905557.shtml.

33. Association of American Universities, "Hefei Statement on the Ten Characteristics of Contemporary Research Universities," (2013) https://www.aau .edu/sites/default/files/AAU%20Files/Education%20and%20Service/Hefei _statement.pdf.

# Index

*Italic* page numbers refer to figures or tables.

# Intermediate Microeconomics

## With Calculus

## First Edition

# Intermediate Microeconomics

## With Calculus

### First Edition

## Hal R. Varian

Google and University of California at Berkeley

**W. W. Norton & Company • New York • London**

W. W. Norton & Company has been independent since its founding in 1923, when William Warder Norton and Mary D. Herter Norton first published lectures delivered at the People's Institute, the adult education division of New York City's Cooper Union. The firm soon expanded its program beyond the Institute, publishing books by celebrated academics from America and abroad. By mid-century, the two major pillars of Norton's publishing program—trade books and college texts—were firmly established. In the 1950s, the Norton family transferred control of the company to its employees, and today—with a staff of four hundred and a comparable number of trade, college, and professional titles published each year– W. W. Norton & Company stands as the largest and oldest publishing house owned wholly by its employees.

FIRST EDITION

Editor: Jack Repcheck
Senior project editor: Thom Foley
Production manager: Andy Ensor
Editorial assistant: Theresia Kowara
TEXnician: Hal Varian

ISBN 978-0-393-12398-2

W. W. Norton & Company, Inc., 500 Fifth Avenue, New York, N.Y. 10110
W. W. Norton & Company, Ltd., Castle House, 75/76 Wells Street, London W1T 3QT
www.wwnorton.com

1 2 3 4 5 6 7 8 9 0

To Carol

# CONTENTS

# 3 Preferences

# 4 Utility

# 5 Choice

# 6 Demand

# 7 Revealed Preference

# 8 Slutsky Equation

# 9 Buying and Selling

# 10 Intertemporal Choice

# 11 Asset Markets

# 12 Uncertainty

# 13 Risky Assets

# 14 Consumer's Surplus

# 15 Market Demand

# 16 Equilibrium

# 17 Measurement

# 18 Auctions

# 19 Technology

# 20 Profit Maximization

# 21 Cost Minimization

# 22 Cost Curves

# 23 Firm Supply

## 24 Industry Supply

## 25 Monopoly

## 26 Monopoly Behavior

## 27 Factor Markets

## 28 Oligopoly

## 29 Game Theory

## 30 Game Applications

## 31 Behavioral Economics

## 32 Exchange

## 33 Production

## 34 Welfare

## 35 Externalities

## 36 Information Technology

## 37 Public Goods

# 38 Asymmetric Information

# Mathematical Appendix

# Answers

# Index

# PREFACE

This book is my classic *Intermediate Microeconomics* text with the mathematical treatment that was previously in the chapter appendices incorporated into the body of the chapters. This makes the analysis flow somewhat better for those students who are comfortable with elementary calculus.

My aim in writing the original text was to present a treatment of the methods of microeconomics that would allow students to apply these tools on their own and not just passively absorb the predigested cases described in the text. I have found that the best way to do this is to emphasize the fundamental conceptual foundations of microeconomics and to provide concrete examples of their application rather than to attempt to provide an encyclopedia of terminology and anecdote.

The calculus treatment will, I hope, be helpful to students who have appropriate backgrounds. However, it should be remembered that one can go a long way with a few simple facts about linear demand functions and supply functions and some elementary algebra. It is perfectly possible to be analytical without being excessively mathematical.

The distinction is worth emphasizing. An analytical approach to economics is one that uses rigorous, logical reasoning. This does not necessarily require the use of advanced mathematical methods. The language of mathematics certainly helps to ensure a rigorous analysis and using it is undoubtedly the best way to proceed when possible, but it may not be appropriate for all students. This is why there are two versions of the text.

Calculus offers deeper ways to examine the same issues that one can also explore verbally and graphically. Many arguments are much simpler with a little mathematics, and all economics students should learn that. In many cases I've found that with a little motivation, and a few nice economic examples, students become quite enthusiastic about looking at things from an analytic perspective.

There are several other innovations in this text. First, the chapters are generally very short. I've tried to make most of them roughly "lecture size," so that they can be read in one sitting. I have followed the standard order of discussing first consumer theory and then producer theory, but I've spent a bit more time on consumer theory than is normally the case. This is not because I think that consumer theory is necessarily the most important part of microeconomics; rather, I have found that this is the material that students find the most mysterious, so I wanted to provide a more detailed treatment of it.

Second, I've tried to put in a lot of examples of how to use the theories described here. In most books, students look at a lot of diagrams of shifting curves, but they don't see much algebra, or much calculation of any sort for that matter. But it is the algebra that is used to solve problems in practice. Graphs can provide insight, but the real power of economic analysis comes in calculating quantitative answers to economic problems. Every economics student should be able to translate an economic story into an equation or a numerical example, but all too often the development of this skill is neglected. For this reason I have also provided a workbook that I feel is an integral accompaniment to this book. The workbook was written with my colleague Theodore Bergstrom, and we have put a lot of effort into generating interesting and instructive problems. We think that it provides an important aid to the student of microeconomics.

Third, I believe that the treatment of the topics in this book is more accurate than is usually the case in intermediate micro texts. It is true that I've sometimes chosen special cases to analyze when the general case is too difficult, but I've tried to be honest about that when I did it. In general, I've tried to spell out every step of each argument in detail. I believe that the discussion I've provided is not only more complete and more accurate than usual, but this attention to detail also makes the arguments easier to understand than the loose discussion presented in many other books.

## There Are Many Paths to Economic Enlightenment

There is more material in this book than can comfortably be taught in one semester, so it is worthwhile picking and choosing carefully the material that you want to study. If you start on page 1 and proceed through the chapters in order, you will run out of time long before you reach the end of the book. The modular structure of the book allows the instructor a great deal of freedom in choosing how to present the material, and I hope that more people will take advantage of this freedom. The following chart illustrates the chapter dependencies.

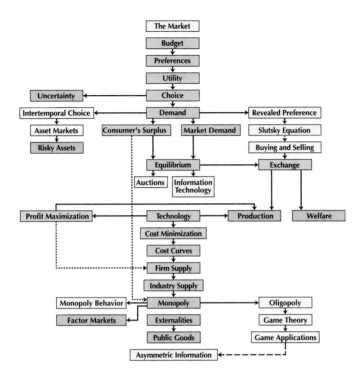

The darker colored chapters are "core" chapters—they should probably be covered in every intermediate microeconomics course. The lighter-colored chapters are "optional" chapters: I cover some but not all of these every semester. The gray chapters are chapters I usually don't cover in my course, but they could easily be covered in other courses. A solid line going from Chapter $A$ to Chapter $B$ means that Chapter $A$ should be read before chapter $B$. A broken line means that Chapter $B$ requires knowing some material in Chapter $A$, but doesn't depend on it in a significant way.

I generally cover consumer theory and markets and then proceed directly to producer theory. Another popular path is to do exchange right after consumer theory; many instructors prefer this route and I have gone to some trouble to make sure that this path is possible.

Some people like to do producer theory before consumer theory. This is possible with this text, but if you choose this path, you will need to supplement the textbook treatment. The material on isoquants, for example, assumes that the students have already seen indifference curves.

Much of the material on public goods, externalities, law, and information can be introduced earlier in the course. I've arranged the material so that it is quite easy to put it pretty much wherever you desire.

Similarly, the material on public goods can be introduced as an illustration of Edgeworth box analysis. Externalities can be introduced right after the discussion of cost curves, and topics from the information chapter can be introduced almost anywhere after students are familiar with the approach of economic analysis.

## Changes for this Edition

The text of the book is closely aligned with *Intermediate Microeconomics*. I have added a new chapter on measurement which describes some of the issues involved in estimating economic relationships. The idea is to introduce the student to some basic concepts from econometrics and try to bridge the theoretical treatment in the book with the practical problems encountered in practice.

I have offered some new examples drawn from Silicon Valley firms such as Apple, eBay, Google, Yahoo and others. I discuss topics such as the complementarity between the iPod and iTunes, the positive feedback associated with companies such as Facebook, and the ad auction models used by Google, Microsoft, and Yahoo. I believe that these are fresh and interesting examples of economics in action.

I've also added an extended discussion of mechanism design issues, including two-sided matching markets and the Vickrey-Clarke-Groves mechanisms. This field, which was once primarily theoretical in nature, has now taken on considerable practical importance.

## The Test Bank and Workbook

The workbook, *Workouts in Intermediate Microeconomics,* is an integral part of the course. It contains hundreds of fill-in-the-blank exercises that lead the students through the steps of actually applying the tools they have learned in the textbook. In addition to the exercises, *Workouts* contains a collection of short multiple-choice quizzes based on the workbook problems in each chapter. Answers to the quizzes are also included in *Workouts*. These quizzes give a quick way for the student to review the material he or she has learned by working the problems in the workbook.

But there is more ... instructors who have adopted *Workouts* for their course can make use of the *Test Bank* offered with the textbook. The *Test Bank* contains several alternative versions of each *Workouts* quiz. The questions in these quizzes use different numerical values but the same internal logic. They can be used to provide additional problems for students to practice, or quizzes to be taken in class. Grading is quick and reliable because the quizzes are multiple choice and can be graded electronically.

In our course, we tell the students to work through all the quiz questions for each chapter, either by themselves or with a study group. Then during the term we have a short in-class quiz every other week or so, using the alternative versions from the *Test Bank*. These are essentially the *Work-*

*outs* quizzes with different numbers. Hence, students who have done their homework find it easy to do well on the quizzes.

We firmly believe that you can't learn economics without working some problems. The quizzes provided in *Workouts* and in the *Test Bank* make the learning process much easier for both the student and the teacher.

A hard copy of the *Test Bank* is available from the publisher, as is the textbook's *Instructor's Manual*, which includes my teaching suggestions and lecture notes for each chapter of the textbook, and solutions to the exercises in *Workouts*.

A number of other useful ancillaries are also available with this textbook. These include a comprehensive set of PowerPoint slides, as well as the Norton Economic News Service, which alerts students to economic news related to specific material in the textbook. For information on these and other ancillaries, please visit the homepage for the book at `http://www.wwnorton.com/varian`.

## The Production of the Book

The entire book was typeset by the author using TEX, the wonderful typesetting system designed by Donald Knuth. I worked on a Linux system and using GNU `emacs` for editing, `rcs` for version control and the TEX Live system for processing. I used `makeindex` for the index, and Trevor Darrell's `psfig` software for inserting the diagrams.

The book design was by Nancy Dale Muldoon, with some modifications by Roy Tedoff and the author. Jack Repchek coordinated the whole effort in his capacity as editor.

## Acknowledgments

Several people contributed to this project. First, I must thank my editorial assistants for the first edition, John Miller and Debra Holt. John provided many comments, suggestions, and exercises based on early drafts of this text and made a significant contribution to the coherence of the final product. Debra did a careful proofreading and consistency check during the final stages and helped in preparing the index.

The following individuals provided me with many useful suggestions and comments during the preparation of the first edition: Ken Binmore (University of Michigan), Mark Bagnoli (Indiana University), Larry Chenault (Miami University), Jonathan Hoag (Bowling Green State University), Allen Jacobs (M.I.T.), John McMillan (University of California at San Diego), Hal White (University of California at San Diego), and Gary Yohe (Wesleyan University). In particular, I would like to thank Dr. Reiner Buchegger, who prepared the German translation, for his close reading of the first edition and for providing me with a detailed list of corrections. Other individuals to whom I owe thanks for suggestions prior to the first edition are Theodore Bergstrom, Jan Gerson, Oliver Landmann, Alasdair Smith, Barry Smith, and David Winch.

My editorial assistants for the second edition were Sharon Parrott and Angela Bills. They provided much useful assistance with the writing and editing. Robert M. Costrell (University of Massachusetts at Amherst), Ashley Lyman (University of Idaho), Daniel Schwallie (Case-Western Reserve), A. D. Slivinskie (Western Ontario), and Charles Plourde (York University) provided me with detailed comments and suggestions about how to improve the second edition.

In preparing the third edition I received useful comments from the following individuals: Doris Cheng (San Jose), Imre Csekó (Budapest), Gregory Hildebrandt (UCLA), Jamie Brown Kruse (Colorado), Richard Manning (Brigham Young), Janet Mitchell (Cornell), Charles Plourde (York University), Yeung-Nan Shieh (San Jose), and John Winder (Toronto). I especially want to thank Roger F. Miller (University of Wisconsin), and David Wildasin (Indiana) for their detailed comments, suggestions, and corrections.

The fifth edition benefited from comments by Kealoah Widdows (Wabash College), William Sims (Concordia University), Jennifer R. Reinganum (Vanderbilt University), and Paul D. Thistle (Western Michigan University).

I received comments that helped in preparation of the sixth edition from James S. Jordon (Pennsylvania State University), Brad Kamp (University of South Florida), Sten Nyberg (Stockholm University), Matthew R. Roelofs (Western Washington University), Maarten-Pieter Schinkel (University of Maastricht), and Arthur Walker (University of Northumbria).

The seventh edition received reviews by Irina Khindanova (Colorado School of Mines), Istvan Konya (Boston College), Shomu Banerjee (Georgia Tech), Andrew Helms (University of Georgia), Marc Melitz (Harvard University), Andrew Chatterjea (Cornell University), and Cheng-Zhong Qin (UC Santa Barbara).

Finally, I received helpful comments on the eighth edition from Kevin Balsam (Hunter College), Clive Belfield (Queens College, CUNY), Reiner Buchegger (Johannes Kepler University), Lars Metzger (Technische Universitaet Dortmund), Jeffrey Miron (Harvard University), Babu Nahata (University of Louisville), and Scott J. Savage (University of Colorado). I am particularly grateful to Carola Conces who provided research assistance in merging the calculus appendices with the chapter bodies.

Berkeley, California
January 2014

# CHAPTER **1**

# THE MARKET

The conventional first chapter of a microeconomics book is a discussion of the "scope and methods" of economics. Although this material can be very interesting, it hardly seems appropriate to *begin* your study of economics with such material. It is hard to appreciate such a discussion until you have seen some examples of economic analysis in action.

So instead, we will begin this book with an *example* of economic analysis. In this chapter we will examine a model of a particular market, the market for apartments. Along the way we will introduce several new ideas and tools of economics. Don't worry if it all goes by rather quickly. This chapter is meant only to provide a quick overview of how these ideas can be used. Later on we will study them in substantially more detail.

## 1.1 Constructing a Model

Economics proceeds by developing **models** of social phenomena. By a model we mean a simplified representation of reality. The emphasis here is on the word "simple." Think about how useless a map on a one-to-one scale would be. The same is true of an economic model that attempts to describe every aspect of reality. A model's power stems from the elimination of irrelevant detail, which allows the economist to focus on the essential features of the economic reality he or she is attempting to understand.

Here we are interested in what determines the price of apartments, so we want to have a simplified description of the apartment market. There is a certain art to choosing the right simplifications in building a model. In general we want to adopt the simplest model that is capable of describing the economic situation we are examining. We can then add complications one at a time, allowing the model to become more complex and, we hope, more realistic.

The particular example we want to consider is the market for apartments in a medium-size midwestern college town. In this town there are two sorts of apartments. There are some that are adjacent to the university, and others that are farther away. The adjacent apartments are generally considered to be more desirable by students, since they allow easier access to the university. The apartments that are farther away necessitate taking a bus, or a long, cold bicycle ride, so most students would prefer a nearby apartment ... if they can afford one.

We will think of the apartments as being located in two large rings surrounding the university. The adjacent apartments are in the inner ring, while the rest are located in the outer ring. We will focus exclusively on the market for apartments in the inner ring. The outer ring should be interpreted as where people can go who don't find one of the closer apartments. We'll suppose that there are many apartments available in the outer ring, and their price is fixed at some known level. We'll be concerned solely with the determination of the price of the inner-ring apartments and who gets to live there.

An economist would describe the distinction between the prices of the two kinds of apartments in this model by saying that the price of the outer-ring apartments is an **exogenous variable**, while the price of the inner-ring apartments is an **endogenous variable**. This means that the price of the outer-ring apartments is taken as determined by factors not discussed in this particular model, while the price of the inner-ring apartments is determined by forces described in the model.

The first simplification that we'll make in our model is that all apartments are identical in every respect except for location. Thus it will make sense to speak of "the price" of apartments, without worrying about whether the apartments have one bedroom, or two bedrooms, or whatever.

But what determines this price? What determines who will live in the inner-ring apartments and who will live farther out? What can be said about the desirability of different economic mechanisms for allocating apartments? What concepts can we use to judge the merit of different assignments of apartments to individuals? These are all questions that we want our model to address.

## 1.2 Optimization and Equilibrium

Whenever we try to explain the behavior of human beings we need to have a framework on which our analysis can be based. In much of economics we use a framework built on the following two simple principles.

**The optimization principle**: People try to choose the best patterns of consumption that they can afford.

**The equilibrium principle**: Prices adjust until the amount that people demand of something is equal to the amount that is supplied.

Let us consider these two principles. The first is *almost* tautological. If people are free to choose their actions, it is reasonable to assume that they try to choose things they want rather than things they don't want. Of course there are exceptions to this general principle, but they typically lie outside the domain of economic behavior.

The second notion is a bit more problematic. It is at least conceivable that at any given time peoples' demands and supplies are not compatible, and hence something must be changing. These changes may take a long time to work themselves out, and, even worse, they may induce other changes that might "destabilize" the whole system.

This kind of thing can happen ... but it usually doesn't. In the case of apartments, we typically see a fairly stable rental price from month to month. It is this *equilibrium* price that we are interested in, not in how the market gets to this equilibrium or how it might change over long periods of time.

It is worth observing that the definition used for equilibrium may be different in different models. In the case of the simple market we will examine in this chapter, the demand and supply equilibrium idea will be adequate for our needs. But in more general models we will need more general definitions of equilibrium. Typically, equilibrium will require that the economic agents' actions must be consistent with each other.

How do we use these two principles to determine the answers to the questions we raised above? It is time to introduce some economic concepts.

## 1.3 The Demand Curve

Suppose that we consider all of the possible renters of the apartments and ask each of them the maximum amount that he or she would be willing to pay to rent one of the apartments.

Let's start at the top. There must be someone who is willing to pay the highest price. Perhaps this person has a lot of money, perhaps he is very lazy and doesn't want to walk far ... or whatever. Suppose that this person is willing to pay $500 a month for an apartment.

If there is only one person who is willing to pay $500 a month to rent an apartment, then if the price for apartments were $500 a month, exactly one apartment would be rented—to the one person who was willing to pay that price.

Suppose that the next highest price that anyone is willing to pay is $490. Then if the market price were $499, there would still be only one apartment rented: the person who was *willing* to pay $500 would rent an apartment, but the person who was willing to pay $490 wouldn't. And so it goes. Only one apartment would be rented if the price were $498, $497, $496, and so on ... until we reach a price of $490. At that price, exactly two apartments would be rented: one to the $500 person and one to the $490 person.

Similarly, two apartments would be rented until we reach the maximum price that the person with the *third* highest price would be willing to pay, and so on.

Economists call a person's maximum willingness to pay for something that person's **reservation price**. The reservation price is the highest price that a given person will accept and still purchase the good. In other words, a person's reservation price is the price at which he or she is just indifferent between purchasing or not purchasing the good. In our example, if a person has a reservation price $p$ it means that he or she would be just indifferent between living in the inner ring and paying a price $p$ and living in the outer ring.

Thus the number of apartments that will be rented at a given price $p^*$ will just be the number of people who have a reservation price greater than or equal to $p^*$. For if the market price is $p^*$, then everyone who is willing to pay at least $p^*$ for an apartment will want an apartment in the inner ring, and everyone who is not willing to pay $p^*$ will choose to live in the outer ring.

We can plot these reservation prices in a diagram as in Figure 1.1. Here the price is depicted on the vertical axis and the number of people who are willing to pay that price or more is depicted on the horizontal axis.

Another way to view Figure 1.1 is to think of it as measuring how many people would want to rent apartments at any particular price. Such a curve is an example of a **demand curve**—a curve that relates the quantity demanded to price. When the market price is above $500, zero apartments will be rented. When the price is between $500 and $490, one apartment will be rented. When it is between $490 and the third highest reservation price, two apartments will be rented, and so on. The demand curve describes the quantity demanded at each of the possible prices.

The demand curve for apartments slopes down: as the price of apartments decreases more people will be willing to rent apartments. If there are many people and their reservation prices differ only slightly from person to

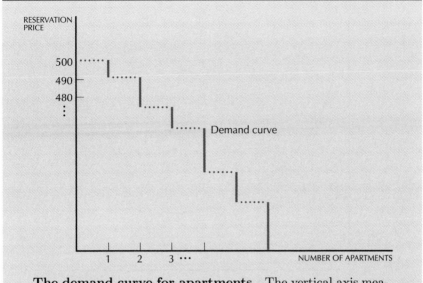

**The demand curve for apartments**. The vertical axis measures the market price and the horizontal axis measures how many apartments will be rented at each price.

Figure
1.1

person, it is reasonable to think of the demand curve as sloping smoothly downward, as in Figure 1.2. The curve in Figure 1.2 is what the demand curve in Figure 1.1 would look like if there were many people who want to rent the apartments. The "jumps" shown in Figure 1.1 are now so small relative to the size of the market that we can safely ignore them in drawing the market demand curve.

## 1.4 The Supply Curve

We now have a nice graphical representation of demand behavior, so let us turn to supply behavior. Here we have to think about the nature of the market we are examining. The situation we will consider is where there are many independent landlords who are each out to rent their apartments for the highest price the market will bear. We will refer to this as the case of a **competitive market**. Other sorts of market arrangements are certainly possible, and we will examine a few later.

For now, let's consider the case where there are many landlords who all operate independently. It is clear that if all landlords are trying to do the best they can and if the renters are fully informed about the prices the landlords charge, then the equilibrium price of all apartments in the inner ring must be the same. The argument is not difficult. Suppose instead that there is some high price, $p_h$, and some low price, $p_l$, being charged

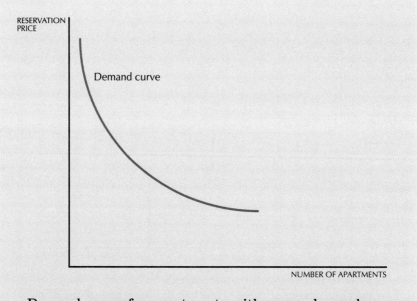

RESERVATION PRICE

Demand curve

NUMBER OF APARTMENTS

Figure
1.2

**Demand curve for apartments with many demanders.**
Because of the large number of demanders, the jumps between
prices will be small, and the demand curve will have the conventional smooth shape.

for apartments. The people who are renting their apartments for a high
price could go to a landlord renting for a low price and offer to pay a rent
somewhere between $p_h$ and $p_l$. A transaction at such a price would make
both the renter and the landlord better off. To the extent that all parties
are seeking to further their own interests and are aware of the alternative
prices being charged, a situation with different prices being charged for the
same good cannot persist in equilibrium.

But what will this single equilibrium price be? Let us try the method
that we used in our construction of the demand curve: we will pick a price
and ask how many apartments will be supplied at that price.

The answer depends to some degree on the time frame in which we are
examining the market. If we are considering a time frame of several years,
so that new construction can take place, the number of apartments will
certainly respond to the price that is charged. But in the "short run"—
within a given year, say—the number of apartments is more or less fixed.
If we consider only this short-run case, the supply of apartments will be
constant at some predetermined level.

The **supply curve** in this market is depicted in Figure 1.3 as a vertical
line. Whatever price is being charged, the same number of apartments will
be rented, namely, all the apartments that are available at that time.

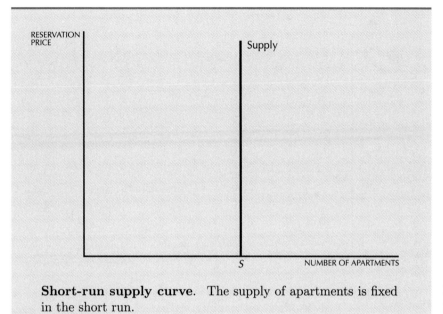

**Short-run supply curve.** The supply of apartments is fixed in the short run.

Figure 1.3

## 1.5 Market Equilibrium

We now have a way of representing the demand and the supply side of the apartment market. Let us put them together and ask what the equilibrium behavior of the market is. We do this by drawing both the demand and the supply curve on the same graph in Figure 1.4.

In this graph we have used $p^*$ to denote the price where the quantity of apartments demanded equals the quantity supplied. This is the **equilibrium price** of apartments. At this price, each consumer who is willing to pay at least $p^*$ is able to find an apartment to rent, and each landlord will be able to rent apartments at the going market price. Neither the consumers nor the landlords have any reason to change their behavior. This is why we refer to this as an *equilibrium:* no change in behavior will be observed.

To better understand this point, let us consider what would happen at a price other than $p^*$. For example, consider some price $p < p^*$ where demand is greater than supply. Can this price persist? At this price at least some of the landlords will have more renters than they can handle. There will be lines of people hoping to get an apartment at that price; there are more people who are willing to pay the price $p$ than there are apartments. Certainly some of the landlords would find it in their interest to raise the price of the apartments they are offering.

Similarly, suppose that the price of apartments is some $p$ greater than $p^*$.

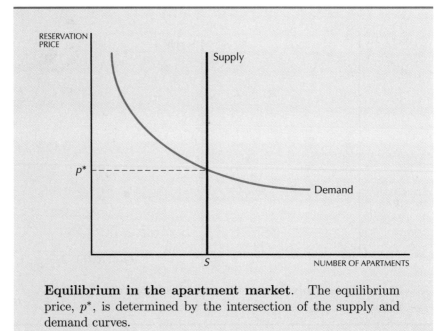

**Figure 1.4**

**Equilibrium in the apartment market.** The equilibrium price, $p^*$, is determined by the intersection of the supply and demand curves.

Then some of the apartments will be vacant: there are fewer people who are willing to pay $p$ than there are apartments. Some of the landlords are now in danger of getting no rent at all for their apartments. Thus they will have an incentive to lower their price in order to attract more renters.

If the price is above $p^*$ there are too few renters; if it is below $p^*$ there are too many renters. Only at the price of $p^*$ is the number of people who are willing to rent at that price equal to the number of apartments available for rent. Only at that price does demand equal supply.

At the price $p^*$ the landlords' and the renters' behaviors are compatible in the sense that the number of apartments demanded by the renters at $p^*$ is equal to the number of apartments supplied by the landlords. This is the equilibrium price in the market for apartments.

Once we've determined the market price for the inner-ring apartments, we can ask who ends up getting these apartments and who is exiled to the farther-away apartments. In our model there is a very simple answer to this question: in the market equilibrium everyone who is willing to pay $p^*$ or more gets an apartment in the inner ring, and everyone who is willing to pay less than $p^*$ gets one in the outer ring. The person who has a reservation price of $p^*$ is just indifferent between taking an apartment in the inner ring and taking one in the outer ring. The other people in the inner ring are getting their apartments at less than the maximum they would be willing to pay for them. Thus the assignment of apartments to renters is determined by how much they are willing to pay.

## 1.6 Comparative Statics

Now that we have an economic model of the apartment market, we can begin to use it to analyze the behavior of the equilibrium price. For example, we can ask how the price of apartments changes when various aspects of the market change. This kind of an exercise is known as **comparative statics**, because it involves comparing two "static" equilibria without worrying about how the market moves from one equilibrium to another.

The movement from one equilibrium to another can take a substantial amount of time, and questions about how such movement takes place can be very interesting and important. But we must walk before we can run, so we will ignore such dynamic questions for now. Comparative statics analysis is only concerned with comparing equilibria, and there will be enough questions to answer in this framework for the present.

Let's start with a simple case. Suppose that the supply of apartments is increased, as in Figure 1.5.

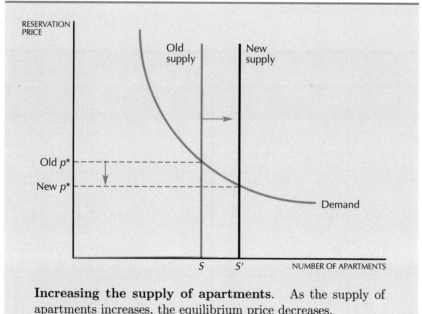

**Increasing the supply of apartments.** As the supply of apartments increases, the equilibrium price decreases.

Figure
1.5

It is easy to see in this diagram that the equilibrium price of apartments will fall. Similarly, if the supply of apartments were reduced the equilibrium price would rise.

Let's try a more complicated—and more interesting—example. Suppose that a developer decides to turn several of the apartments into condominiums. What will happen to the price of the remaining apartments?

Your first guess is probably that the price of apartments will go up, since the supply has been reduced. But this isn't necessarily right. It is true that the supply of apartments to rent has been reduced. But the *demand for apartments* has been reduced as well, since some of the people who were renting apartments may decide to purchase the new condominiums.

It is natural to assume that the condominium purchasers come from those who already live in the inner-ring apartments—those people who are willing to pay more than $p^*$ for an apartment. Suppose, for example, that the demanders with the 10 highest reservation prices decide to buy condos rather than rent apartments. Then the new demand curve is just the old demand curve with 10 fewer demanders at each price. Since there are also 10 fewer apartments to rent, the new equilibrium price is just what it was before, and exactly the same people end up living in the inner-ring apartments. This situation is depicted in Figure 1.6. Both the demand curve and the supply curve shift left by 10 apartments, and the equilibrium price remains unchanged.

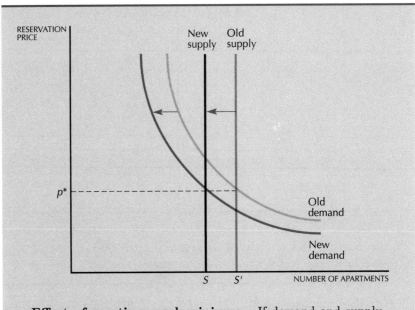

**Figure 1.6**

**Effect of creating condominiums.** If demand and supply both shift left by the same amount the equilibrium price is unchanged.

Most people find this result surprising. They tend to see just the reduction in the supply of apartments and don't think about the reduction in demand. The case we've considered is an extreme one: *all* of the condo purchasers were former apartment dwellers. But the other case—where none of the condo purchasers were apartment dwellers—is even more extreme.

The model, simple though it is, has led us to an important insight. If we want to determine how conversion to condominiums will affect the apartment market, we have to consider not only the effect on the supply of apartments but also the effect on the demand for apartments.

Let's consider another example of a surprising comparative statics analysis: the effect of an apartment tax. Suppose that the city council decides that there should be a tax on apartments of $50 a year. Thus each landlord will have to pay $50 a year to the city for each apartment that he owns. What will this do to the price of apartments?

Most people would think that at least some of the tax would get passed along to apartment renters. But, rather surprisingly, that is not the case. In fact, the equilibrium price of apartments will remain unchanged!

In order to verify this, we have to ask what happens to the demand curve and the supply curve. The supply curve doesn't change—there are just as many apartments after the tax as before the tax. And the demand curve doesn't change either, since the number of apartments that will be rented at each different price will be the same as well. If neither the demand curve nor the supply curve shifts, the price can't change as a result of the tax.

Here is a way to think about the effect of this tax. Before the tax is imposed, each landlord is charging the highest price that he can get that will keep his apartments occupied. The equilibrium price $p^*$ is the highest price that can be charged that is compatible with all of the apartments being rented. After the tax is imposed can the landlords raise their prices to compensate for the tax? The answer is no: if they could raise the price and keep their apartments occupied, they would have already done so. If they were charging the maximum price that the market could bear, the landlords couldn't raise their prices any more: none of the tax can get passed along to the renters. The landlords have to pay the entire amount of the tax.

This analysis depends on the assumption that the supply of apartments remains fixed. If the number of apartments can vary as the tax changes, then the price paid by the renters will typically change. We'll examine this kind of behavior later on, after we've built up some more powerful tools for analyzing such problems.

## 1.7 Other Ways to Allocate Apartments

In the previous section we described the equilibrium for apartments in a competitive market. But this is only one of many ways to allocate a resource; in this section we describe a few other ways. Some of these may sound rather strange, but each will illustrate an important economic point.

## The Discriminating Monopolist

First, let us consider a situation where there is one dominant landlord who owns all of the apartments. Or, alternatively, we could think of a number of individual landlords getting together and coordinating their actions to act as one. A situation where a market is dominated by a single seller of a product is known as a **monopoly**.

In renting the apartments the landlord could decide to auction them off one by one to the highest bidders. Since this means that different people would end up paying different prices for apartments, we will call this the case of the **discriminating monopolist**. Let us suppose for simplicity that the discriminating monopolist knows each person's reservation price for apartments. (This is not terribly realistic, but it will serve to illustrate an important point.)

This means that he would rent the first apartment to the fellow who would pay the most for it, in this case $500. The next apartment would go for $490 and so on as we moved down the demand curve. Each apartment would be rented to the person who was willing to pay the most for it.

Here is the interesting feature of the discriminating monopolist: *exactly the same people will get the apartments as in the case of the market solution,* namely, everyone who valued an apartment at more than $p^*$. The last person to rent an apartment pays the price $p^*$—the same as the equilibrium price in a competitive market. The discriminating monopolist's attempt to maximize his own profits leads to the same allocation of apartments as the supply and demand mechanism of the competitive market. The amount the people *pay* is different, but who gets the apartments is the same. It turns out that this is no accident, but we'll have to wait until later to explain the reason.

## The Ordinary Monopolist

We assumed that the discriminating monopolist was able to rent each apartment at a different price. But what if he were forced to rent all apartments at the same price? In this case the monopolist faces a tradeoff: if he chooses a low price he will rent more apartments, but he may end up making less money than if he sets a higher price.

Let us use $D(p)$ to represent the demand function—the number of apartments demanded at price $p$. Then if the monopolist sets a price $p$, he will rent $D(p)$ apartments and thus receive a revenue of $pD(p)$. The revenue that the monopolist receives can be thought of as the area of a box: the height of the box is the price $p$ and the width of the box is the number of apartments $D(p)$. The product of the height and the width—the area of the box—is the revenue the monopolist receives. This is the box depicted in Figure 1.7.

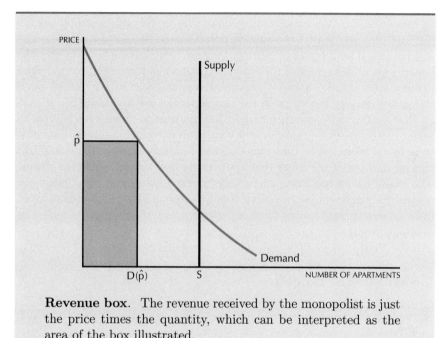

**Revenue box.** The revenue received by the monopolist is just the price times the quantity, which can be interpreted as the area of the box illustrated.

Figure 1.7

If the monopolist has no costs associated with renting an apartment, he would want to choose a price that has the largest associated revenue box. The largest revenue box in Figure 1.7 occurs at the price $\hat{p}$. In this case the monopolist will find it in his interest *not* to rent all of the apartments. In fact this will generally be the case for a monopolist. The monopolist will want to restrict the output available in order to maximize his profit. This means that the monopolist will generally want to charge a price that is higher than the equilibrium price in a competitive market, $p^*$. In the case of the ordinary monopolist, fewer apartments will be rented, and each apartment will be rented at a higher price than in the competitive market.

## Rent Control

A third and final case that we will discuss will be the case of rent control. Suppose that the city decides to impose a maximum rent that can be charged for apartments, say $p_{max}$. We suppose that the price $p_{max}$ is less than the equilibrium price in the competitive market, $p^*$. If this is so we would have a situation of **excess demand**: there are more people who are willing to rent apartments at $p_{max}$ than there are apartments available. Who will end up with the apartments?

The theory that we have described up until now doesn't have an answer to this question. We can describe what will happen when supply equals demand, but we don't have enough detail in the model to describe what will happen if supply doesn't equal demand. The answer to who gets the apartments under rent control depends on who has the most time to spend looking around, who knows the current tenants, and so on. All of these things are outside the scope of the simple model we've developed. It may be that exactly the same people get the apartments under rent control as under the competitive market. But that is an extremely unlikely outcome. It is much more likely that some of the formerly outer-ring people will end up in some of the inner-ring apartments and thus displace the people who would have been living there under the market system. So under rent control the same number of apartments will be rented at the rent-controlled price as were rented under the competitive price: they'll just be rented to different people.

## 1.8 Which Way Is Best?

We've now described four possible ways of allocating apartments to people:

- The competitive market.
- A discriminating monopolist.
- An ordinary monopolist.
- Rent control.

These are four different economic institutions for allocating apartments. Each method will result in different people getting apartments or in different prices being charged for apartments. We might well ask which economic institution is best. But first we have to define "best." What criteria might we use to compare these ways of allocating apartments?

One thing we can do is to look at the economic positions of the people involved. It is pretty obvious that the owners of the apartments end up with the most money if they can act as discriminating monopolists: this would generate the most revenues for the apartment owner(s). Similarly the rent-control solution is probably the worst situation for the apartment owners.

What about the renters? They are probably worse off on average in the case of a discriminating monopolist—most of them would be paying a higher price than they would under the other ways of allocating apartments.

Are the consumers better off in the case of rent control? Some of them are: the consumers *who end up getting the apartments* are better off than they would be under the market solution. But the ones who didn't get the apartments are *worse off* than they would be under the market solution.

What we need here is a way to look at the economic position of all the parties involved—all the renters *and* all the landlords. How can we examine the desirability of different ways to allocate apartments, taking everybody into account? What can be used as a criterion for a "good" way to allocate apartments taking into account *all* of the parties involved?

## 1.9 Pareto Efficiency

One useful criterion for comparing the outcomes of different economic institutions is a concept known as Pareto efficiency or economic efficiency.[1] We start with the following definition: if we can find a way to make some people better off without making anybody else worse off, we have a **Pareto improvement**. If an allocation allows for a Pareto improvement, it is called **Pareto inefficient**; if an allocation is such that no Pareto improvements are possible, it is called **Pareto efficient**.

A Pareto inefficient allocation has the undesirable feature that there is some way to make somebody better off without hurting anyone else. There may be other positive things about the allocation, but the fact that it is Pareto inefficient is certainly one strike against it. If there is a way to make someone better off without hurting anyone else, why not do it?

The idea of Pareto efficiency is an important one in economics and we will examine it in some detail later on. It has many subtle implications that we will have to investigate more slowly, but we can get an inkling of what is involved even now.

Here is a useful way to think about the idea of Pareto efficiency. Suppose that we assigned the renters to the inner- and outer-ring apartments randomly, but then allowed them to sublet their apartments to each other. Some people who really wanted to live close in might, through bad luck, end up with an outer-ring apartment. But then they could sublet an inner-ring apartment from someone who was assigned to such an apartment but who didn't value it as highly as the other person. If individuals were assigned randomly to apartments, there would generally be some who would want to trade apartments, if they were sufficiently compensated for doing so.

For example, suppose that person A is assigned an apartment in the inner ring that he feels is worth \$200, and that there is some person B in the outer ring who would be willing to pay \$300 for A's apartment. Then there is a

[1] Pareto efficiency is named after the nineteenth-century economist and sociologist Vilfredo Pareto (1848–1923) who was one of the first to examine the implications of this idea.

"gain from trade" if these two agents swap apartments and arrange a side payment from B to A of some amount of money between $200 and $300. The exact amount of the transaction isn't important. What is important is that the people who are willing to pay the most for the apartments get them—otherwise, there would be an incentive for someone who attached a low value to an inner-ring apartment to make a trade with someone who placed a high value on an inner-ring apartment.

Suppose that we think of all voluntary trades as being carried out so that all gains from trade are exhausted. The resulting allocation must be Pareto efficient. If not, there would be some trade that would make two people better off without hurting anyone else—but this would contradict the assumption that all voluntary trades had been carried out. An allocation in which all voluntary trades have been carried out is a Pareto efficient allocation.

## 1.10 Comparing Ways to Allocate Apartments

The trading process we've described above is so general that you wouldn't think that anything much could be said about its outcome. But there is one very interesting point that can be made. Let us ask who will end up with apartments in an allocation where all of the gains from trade have been exhausted.

To see the answer, just note that anyone who has an apartment in the inner ring must have a higher reservation price than anyone who has an apartment in the outer ring—otherwise, they could make a trade and make both people better off. Thus if there are $S$ apartments to be rented, then the $S$ people with the highest reservation prices end up getting apartments in the inner ring. This allocation is Pareto efficient—anything else is not, since any other assignment of apartments to people would allow for some trade that would make at least two of the people better off without hurting anyone else.

Let us try to apply this criterion of Pareto efficiency to the outcomes of the various resource allocation devices mentioned above. Let's start with the market mechanism. It is easy to see that the market mechanism assigns the people with the $S$ highest reservation prices to the inner ring—namely, those people who are willing to pay more than the equilibrium price, $p^*$, for their apartments. Thus there are no further gains from trade to be had once the apartments have been rented in a competitive market. The outcome of the competitive market is Pareto efficient.

What about the discriminating monopolist? Is that arrangement Pareto efficient? To answer this question, simply observe that the discriminating monopolist assigns apartments to exactly the same people who receive apartments in the competitive market. Under each system everyone who is willing to pay more than $p^*$ for an apartment gets an apartment. Thus the discriminating monopolist generates a Pareto efficient outcome as well.

Although both the competitive market and the discriminating monopolist generate Pareto efficient outcomes in the sense that there will be no further trades desired, they can result in quite different distributions of income. Certainly the consumers are much worse off under the discriminating monopolist than under the competitive market, and the landlord(s) are much better off. In general, Pareto efficiency doesn't have much to say about distribution of the gains from trade. It is only concerned with the *efficiency* of the trade: whether all of the possible trades have been made.

What about the ordinary monopolist who is constrained to charge just one price? It turns out that this situation is not Pareto efficient. All we have to do to verify this is to note that, since all the apartments will not in general be rented by the monopolist, he can increase his profits by renting an apartment to someone who doesn't have one at *any* positive price. There is some price at which both the monopolist and the renter must be better off. As long as the monopolist doesn't change the price that anybody else pays, the other renters are just as well off as they were before. Thus we have found a **Pareto improvement**—a way to make two parties better off without making anyone else worse off.

The final case is that of rent control. This also turns out not to be Pareto efficient. The argument here rests on the fact that an arbitrary assignment of renters to apartments will generally involve someone living in the inner ring (say Mr. In) who is willing to pay less for an apartment than someone living in the outer ring (say Ms. Out). Suppose that Mr. In's reservation price is $300 and Ms. Out's reservation price is $500.

We need to find a Pareto improvement—a way to make Mr. In and Ms. Out better off without hurting anyone else. But there is an easy way to do this: just let Mr. In sublet his apartment to Ms. Out. It is worth $500 to Ms. Out to live close to the university, but it is only worth $300 to Mr. In. If Ms. Out pays Mr. In $400, say, and trades apartments, they will both be better off: Ms. Out will get an apartment that she values at more than $400, and Mr. In will get $400 that he values more than an inner-ring apartment.

This example shows that the rent-controlled market will generally not result in a Pareto efficient allocation, since there will still be some trades that could be carried out after the market has operated. As long as some people get inner-ring apartments who value them less highly than people who don't get them, there will be gains to be had from trade.

## 1.11 Equilibrium in the Long Run

We have analyzed the equilibrium pricing of apartments in the **short run**—when there is a fixed supply of apartments. But in the **long run** the supply of apartments can change. Just as the demand curve measures the number of apartments that will be demanded at different prices, the supply curve measures the number of apartments that will be supplied at different prices.

The final determination of the market price for apartments will depend on the interaction of supply and demand.

And what is it that determines the supply behavior? In general, the number of new apartments that will be supplied by the private market will depend on how profitable it is to provide apartments, which depends, in part, on the price that landlords can charge for apartments. In order to analyze the behavior of the apartment market in the long run, we have to examine the behavior of suppliers as well as demanders, a task we will eventually undertake.

When supply is variable, we can ask questions not only about who gets the apartments, but about how many will be provided by various types of market institutions. Will a monopolist supply more or fewer apartments than a competitive market? Will rent control increase or decrease the equilibrium number of apartments? Which institutions will provide a Pareto efficient number of apartments? In order to answer these and similar questions we must develop more systematic and powerful tools for economic analysis.

## Summary

1. Economics proceeds by making models of social phenomena, which are simplified representations of reality.

2. In this task, economists are guided by the optimization principle, which states that people typically try to choose what's best for them, and by the equilibrium principle, which says that prices will adjust until demand and supply are equal.

3. The demand curve measures how much people wish to demand at each price, and the supply curve measures how much people wish to supply at each price. An equilibrium price is one where the amount demanded equals the amount supplied.

4. The study of how the equilibrium price and quantity change when the underlying conditions change is known as comparative statics.

5. An economic situation is Pareto efficient if there is no way to make some group of people better off without making some other group of people worse off. The concept of Pareto efficiency can be used to evaluate different ways of allocating resources.

# REVIEW QUESTIONS

1. Suppose that there were 25 people who had a reservation price of $500, and the 26th person had a reservation price of $200. What would the demand curve look like?

2. In the above example, what would the equilibrium price be if there were 24 apartments to rent? What if there were 26 apartments to rent? What if there were 25 apartments to rent?

3. If people have different reservation prices, why does the market demand curve slope down?

4. In the text we assumed that the condominium purchasers came from the inner-ring people—people who were already renting apartments. What would happen to the price of inner-ring apartments if all of the condominium purchasers were outer-ring people—the people who were not currently renting apartments in the inner ring?

5. Suppose now that the condominium purchasers were all inner-ring people, but that each condominium was constructed from two apartments. What would happen to the price of apartments?

6. What do you suppose the effect of a tax would be on the number of apartments that would be built in the long run?

7. Suppose the demand curve is $D(p) = 100 - 2p$. What price would the monopolist set if he had 60 apartments? How many would he rent? What price would he set if he had 40 apartments? How many would he rent?

8. If our model of rent control allowed for unrestricted subletting, who would end up getting apartments in the inner circle? Would the outcome be Pareto efficient?

# CHAPTER 2

# BUDGET CONSTRAINT

The economic theory of the consumer is very simple: economists assume that consumers choose the best bundle of goods they can afford. To give content to this theory, we have to describe more precisely what we mean by "best" and what we mean by "can afford." In this chapter we will examine how to describe what a consumer can afford; the next chapter will focus on the concept of how the consumer determines what is best. We will then be able to undertake a detailed study of the implications of this simple model of consumer behavior.

## 2.1 The Budget Constraint

We begin by examining the concept of the **budget constraint**. Suppose that there is some set of goods from which the consumer can choose. In real life there are many goods to consume, but for our purposes it is convenient to consider only the case of two goods, since we can then depict the consumer's choice behavior graphically.

We will indicate the consumer's **consumption bundle** by $(x_1, x_2)$. This is simply a list of two numbers that tells us how much the consumer is choosing to consume of good 1, $x_1$, and how much the consumer is choosing to consume of good 2, $x_2$. Sometimes it is convenient to denote the consumer's bundle by a single symbol like $X$, where $X$ is simply an abbreviation for the list of two numbers $(x_1, x_2)$.

We suppose that we can observe the prices of the two goods, $(p_1, p_2)$, and the amount of money the consumer has to spend, $m$. Then the budget constraint of the consumer can be written as

$$p_1 x_1 + p_2 x_2 \leq m. \tag{2.1}$$

Here $p_1 x_1$ is the amount of money the consumer is spending on good 1, and $p_2 x_2$ is the amount of money the consumer is spending on good 2. The budget constraint of the consumer requires that the amount of money spent on the two goods be no more than the total amount the consumer has to spend. The consumer's *affordable* consumption bundles are those that don't cost any more than $m$. We call this set of affordable consumption bundles at prices $(p_1, p_2)$ and income $m$ the **budget set** of the consumer.

## 2.2 Two Goods Are Often Enough

The two-good assumption is more general than you might think at first, since we can often interpret one of the goods as representing everything else the consumer might want to consume.

For example, if we are interested in studying a consumer's demand for milk, we might let $x_1$ measure his or her consumption of milk in quarts per month. We can then let $x_2$ stand for everything else the consumer might want to consume.

When we adopt this interpretation, it is convenient to think of good 2 as being the dollars that the consumer can use to spend on other goods. Under this interpretation the price of good 2 will automatically be 1, since the price of one dollar is one dollar. Thus the budget constraint will take the form

$$p_1 x_1 + x_2 \leq m. \tag{2.2}$$

This expression simply says that the amount of money spent on good 1, $p_1 x_1$, plus the amount of money spent on all other goods, $x_2$, must be no more than the total amount of money the consumer has to spend, $m$.

We say that good 2 represents a **composite good** that stands for everything else that the consumer might want to consume other than good 1. Such a composite good is invariably measured in dollars to be spent on goods other than good 1. As far as the algebraic form of the budget constraint is concerned, equation (2.2) is just a special case of the formula given in equation (2.1), with $p_2 = 1$, so everything that we have to say about the budget constraint in general will hold under the composite-good interpretation.

## 2.3 Properties of the Budget Set

The **budget line** is the set of bundles that cost exactly $m$:

$$p_1 x_1 + p_2 x_2 = m. \tag{2.3}$$

These are the bundles of goods that just exhaust the consumer's income.

The budget set is depicted in Figure 2.1. The heavy line is the budget line—the bundles that cost exactly $m$—and the bundles below this line are those that cost strictly less than $m$.

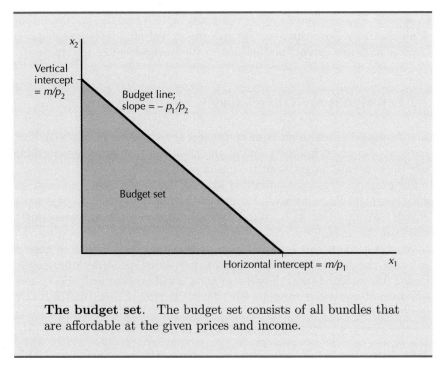

Figure
2.1    **The budget set.** The budget set consists of all bundles that are affordable at the given prices and income.

We can rearrange the budget line in equation (2.3) to give us the formula

$$x_2 = \frac{m}{p_2} - \frac{p_1}{p_2} x_1. \tag{2.4}$$

This is the formula for a straight line with a vertical intercept of $m/p_2$ and a slope of $-p_1/p_2$. The formula tells us how many units of good 2 the consumer needs to consume in order to just satisfy the budget constraint if she is consuming $x_1$ units of good 1.

Here is an easy way to draw a budget line given prices $(p_1, p_2)$ and income $m$. Just ask yourself how much of good 2 the consumer could buy if she spent all of her money on good 2. The answer is, of course, $m/p_2$. Then ask how much of good 1 the consumer could buy if she spent all of her money on good 1. The answer is $m/p_1$. Thus the horizontal and vertical intercepts measure how much the consumer could get if she spent all of her money on goods 1 and 2, respectively. In order to depict the budget line just plot these two points on the appropriate axes of the graph and connect them with a straight line.

The slope of the budget line has a nice economic interpretation. It measures the rate at which the market is willing to "substitute" good 1 for good 2. Suppose for example that the consumer is going to increase her consumption of good 1 by $dx_1$. How much will her consumption of good 2 have to change in order to satisfy her budget constraint? Let us use $dx_2$ to indicate her change in the consumption of good 2.

Now note that if she satisfies her budget constraint before and after making the change she must satisfy

$$p_1 x_1 + p_2 x_2 = m$$

and

$$p_1(x_1 + dx_1) + p_2(x_2 + dx_2) = m.$$

Subtracting the first equation from the second gives

$$p_1 dx_1 + p_2 dx_2 = 0.$$

This says that the total value of the change in her consumption must be zero. Solving for $dx_2/dx_1$, the rate at which good 2 can be substituted for good 1 while still satisfying the budget constraint, gives

$$\frac{dx_2}{dx_1} = -\frac{p_1}{p_2}.$$

This is just the slope of the budget line. The negative sign is there since $dx_1$ and $dx_2$ must always have opposite signs. If you consume more of good 1, you have to consume less of good 2 and vice versa if you continue to satisfy the budget constraint. Alternatively, we could have taken the implicit derivative of both sides of the budget constraint with respect to $x_1$ and obtained the same result.

Economists sometimes say that the slope of the budget line measures the **opportunity cost** of consuming good 1. In order to consume more of good 1 you have to give up some consumption of good 2. Giving up the opportunity to consume good 2 is the true economic cost of more good 1 consumption; and that cost is measured by the slope of the budget line.

## 2.4 How the Budget Line Changes

When prices and incomes change, the set of goods that a consumer can afford changes as well. How do these changes affect the budget set?

Let us first consider changes in income. It is easy to see from equation (2.4) that an increase in income will increase the vertical intercept and not affect the slope of the line. Thus an increase in income will result in a *parallel shift outward* of the budget line as in Figure 2.2. Similarly, a decrease in income will cause a parallel shift inward.

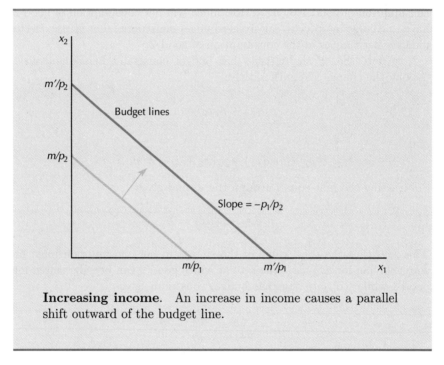

Figure
2.2

**Increasing income.** An increase in income causes a parallel shift outward of the budget line.

What about changes in prices? Let us first consider increasing price 1 while holding price 2 and income fixed. According to equation (2.4), increasing $p_1$ will not change the vertical intercept, but it will make the budget line steeper since $p_1/p_2$ will become larger.

Another way to see how the budget line changes is to use the trick described earlier for drawing the budget line. If you are spending all of your money on good 2, then increasing the price of good 1 doesn't change the maximum amount of good 2 you could buy—thus the vertical intercept of the budget line doesn't change. But if you are spending all of your money on good 1, and good 1 becomes more expensive, then your consumption of good 1 must decrease. Thus the horizontal intercept of the budget line must shift inward, resulting in the tilt depicted in Figure 2.3.

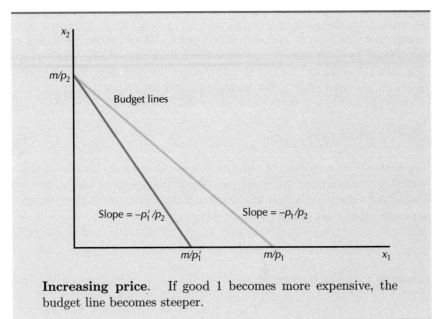

**Increasing price.** If good 1 becomes more expensive, the budget line becomes steeper.

Figure
2.3

What happens to the budget line when we change the prices of good 1 and good 2 at the same time? Suppose for example that we double the prices of both goods 1 and 2. In this case both the horizontal and vertical intercepts shift inward by a factor of one-half, and therefore the budget line shifts inward by one-half as well. Multiplying both prices by two is just like dividing income by 2.

We can also see this algebraically. Suppose our original budget line is

$$p_1 x_1 + p_2 x_2 = m.$$

Now suppose that both prices become $t$ times as large. Multiplying both prices by $t$ yields

$$t p_1 x_1 + t p_2 x_2 = m.$$

But this equation is the same as

$$p_1 x_1 + p_2 x_2 = \frac{m}{t}.$$

Thus multiplying both prices by a constant amount $t$ is just like dividing income by the same constant $t$. It follows that if we multiply both prices by $t$ *and* we multiply income by $t$, then the budget line won't change at all.

We can also consider price and income changes together. What happens if both prices go up and income goes down? Think about what happens to the horizontal and vertical intercepts. If $m$ decreases and $p_1$ and $p_2$ both increase, then the intercepts $m/p_1$ and $m/p_2$ must both decrease. This means that the budget line will shift inward. What about the slope of the budget line? If price 2 increases more than price 1, so that $-p_1/p_2$ decreases (in absolute value), then the budget line will be flatter; if price 2 increases less than price 1, the budget line will be steeper.

## 2.5 The Numeraire

The budget line is defined by two prices and one income, but one of these variables is redundant. We could peg one of the prices, or the income, to some fixed value, and adjust the other variables so as to describe exactly the same budget set. Thus the budget line

$$p_1 x_1 + p_2 x_2 = m$$

is exactly the same budget line as

$$\frac{p_1}{p_2} x_1 + x_2 = \frac{m}{p_2}$$

or

$$\frac{p_1}{m} x_1 + \frac{p_2}{m} x_2 = 1,$$

since the first budget line results from dividing everything by $p_2$, and the second budget line results from dividing everything by $m$. In the first case, we have pegged $p_2 = 1$, and in the second case, we have pegged $m = 1$. Pegging the price of one of the goods or income to 1 and adjusting the other price and income appropriately doesn't change the budget set at all.

When we set one of the prices to 1, as we did above, we often refer to that price as the **numeraire** price. The numeraire price is the price relative to which we are measuring the other price and income. It will occasionally be convenient to think of one of the goods as being a numeraire good, since there will then be one less price to worry about.

## 2.6 Taxes, Subsidies, and Rationing

Economic policy often uses tools that affect a consumer's budget constraint, such as taxes. For example, if the government imposes a **quantity tax**, this means that the consumer has to pay a certain amount to the government for each unit of the good he purchases. In the U.S., for example, we pay about 15 cents a gallon as a federal gasoline tax.

How does a quantity tax affect the budget line of a consumer? From the viewpoint of the consumer the tax is just like a higher price. Thus a quantity tax of $t$ dollars per unit of good 1 simply changes the price of good 1 from $p_1$ to $p_1 + t$. As we've seen above, this implies that the budget line must get steeper.

Another kind of tax is a **value** tax. As the name implies this is a tax on the value—the price—of a good, rather than the quantity purchased of a good. A value tax is usually expressed in percentage terms. Most states in the U.S. have sales taxes. If the sales tax is 6 percent, then a good that is priced at \$1 will actually sell for \$1.06. (Value taxes are also known as **ad valorem** taxes.)

If good 1 has a price of $p_1$ but is subject to a sales tax at rate $\tau$, then the actual price facing the consumer is $(1 + \tau)p_1$.[1] The consumer has to pay $p_1$ to the supplier and $\tau p_1$ to the government for each unit of the good so the total cost of the good to the consumer is $(1 + \tau)p_1$.

A **subsidy** is the opposite of a tax. In the case of a **quantity subsidy**, the government *gives* an amount to the consumer that depends on the amount of the good purchased. If, for example, the consumption of milk were subsidized, the government would pay some amount of money to each consumer of milk depending on the amount that consumer purchased. If the subsidy is $s$ dollars per unit of consumption of good 1, then from the viewpoint of the consumer, the price of good 1 would be $p_1 - s$. This would therefore make the budget line flatter.

Similarly an ad valorem subsidy is a subsidy based on the price of the good being subsidized. If the government gives you back \$1 for every \$2 you donate to charity, then your donations to charity are being subsidized at a rate of 50 percent. In general, if the price of good 1 is $p_1$ and good 1 is subject to an ad valorem subsidy at rate $\sigma$, then the actual price of good 1 facing the consumer is $(1 - \sigma)p_1$.[2]

You can see that taxes and subsidies affect prices in exactly the same way except for the algebraic sign: a tax increases the price to the consumer, and a subsidy decreases it.

Another kind of tax or subsidy that the government might use is a **lump-sum** tax or subsidy. In the case of a tax, this means that the government takes away some fixed amount of money, regardless of the individual's behavior. Thus a lump-sum tax means that the budget line of a consumer will shift inward because his money income has been reduced. Similarly, a lump-sum subsidy means that the budget line will shift outward. Quantity

---

[1]  The Greek letter $\tau$, tau, rhymes with "wow" in mathematical discourse, though modern Greeks pronounce it "taf."

[2]  The Greek letter $\sigma$ is pronounced "sig-ma."

taxes and value taxes tilt the budget line one way or the other depending on which good is being taxed, but a lump-sum tax shifts the budget line inward.

Governments also sometimes impose *rationing* constraints. This means that the level of consumption of some good is fixed to be no larger than some amount. For example, during World War II the U.S. government rationed certain foods like butter and meat.

Suppose, for example, that good 1 were rationed so that no more than $\overline{x}_1$ could be consumed by a given consumer. Then the budget set of the consumer would look like that depicted in Figure 2.4: it would be the old budget set with a piece lopped off. The lopped-off piece consists of all the consumption bundles that are affordable but have $x_1 > \overline{x}_1$.

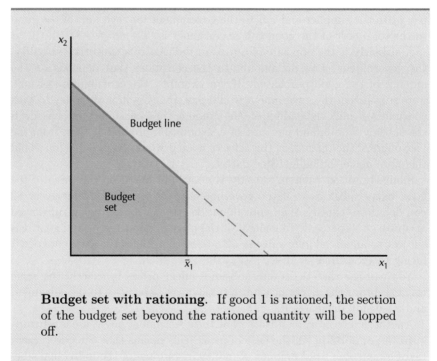

Figure
2.4

**Budget set with rationing.** If good 1 is rationed, the section of the budget set beyond the rationed quantity will be lopped off.

Sometimes taxes, subsidies, and rationing are combined. For example, we could consider a situation where a consumer could consume good 1 at a price of $p_1$ up to some level $\overline{x}_1$, and then had to pay a tax $t$ on all consumption in excess of $\overline{x}_1$. The budget set for this consumer is depicted in Figure 2.5. Here the budget line has a slope of $-p_1/p_2$ to the left of $\overline{x}_1$, and a slope of $-(p_1 + t)/p_2$ to the right of $\overline{x}_1$.

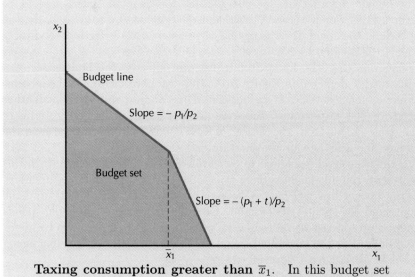

**Taxing consumption greater than $\bar{x}_1$.** In this budget set
the consumer must pay a tax only on the consumption of good
1 that is in excess of $\bar{x}_1$, so the budget line becomes steeper to
the right of $\bar{x}_1$.

Figure
2.5

## EXAMPLE: The Food Stamp Program

Since the Food Stamp Act of 1964 the U.S. federal government has provided
a subsidy on food for poor people. The details of this program have been
adjusted several times. Here we will describe the economic effects of one
of these adjustments.

Before 1979, households who met certain eligibility requirements were
allowed to purchase food stamps, which could then be used to purchase food
at retail outlets. In January 1975, for example, a family of four could receive
a maximum monthly allotment of $153 in food coupons by participating in
the program.

The price of these coupons to the household depended on the household
income. A family of four with an adjusted monthly income of $300 paid
$83 for the full monthly allotment of food stamps. If a family of four had
a monthly income of $100, the cost for the full monthly allotment would
have been $25.[3]

The pre-1979 Food Stamp program was an ad valorem subsidy on food.
The rate at which food was subsidized depended on the household income.

---

[3] These figures are taken from Kenneth Clarkson, *Food Stamps and Nutrition*, American Enterprise Institute, 1975.

The family of four that was charged $83 for their allotment paid $1 to receive $1.84 worth of food (1.84 equals 153 divided by 83). Similarly, the household that paid $25 was paying $1 to receive $6.12 worth of food (6.12 equals 153 divided by 25).

The way that the Food Stamp program affected the budget set of a household is depicted in Figure 2.6A. Here we have measured the amount of money spent on food on the horizontal axis and expenditures on all other goods on the vertical axis. Since we are measuring each good in terms of the money spent on it, the "price" of each good is automatically 1, and the budget line will therefore have a slope of $-1$.

If the household is allowed to buy $153 of food stamps for $25, then this represents roughly an 84 percent ($= 1 - 25/153$) subsidy of food purchases, so the budget line will have a slope of roughly $-.16$ ($= 25/153$) until the household has spent $153 on food. Each dollar that the household spends on food up to $153 would reduce its consumption of other goods by about 16 cents. After the household spends $153 on food, the budget line facing it would again have a slope of $-1$.

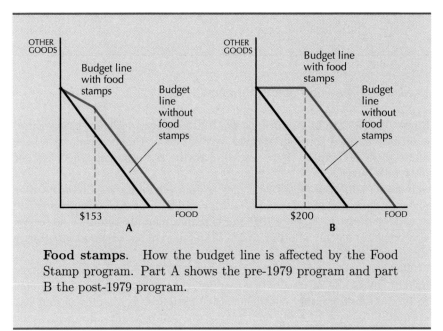

Figure 2.6

**Food stamps.** How the budget line is affected by the Food Stamp program. Part A shows the pre-1979 program and part B the post-1979 program.

These effects lead to the kind of "kink" depicted in Figure 2.6. Households with higher incomes had to pay more for their allotment of food stamps. Thus the slope of the budget line would become steeper as household income increased.

In 1979 the Food Stamp program was modified. Instead of requiring that households purchase food stamps, they are now simply given to qualified households. Figure 2.6B shows how this affects the budget set.

Suppose that a household now receives a grant of $200 of food stamps a month. Then this means that the household can consume $200 more food per month, regardless of how much it is spending on other goods, which implies that the budget line will shift to the right by $200. The slope will not change: $1 less spent on food would mean $1 more to spend on other things. But since the household cannot legally sell food stamps, the maximum amount that it can spend on other goods does not change. The Food Stamp program is effectively a lump-sum subsidy, except for the fact that the food stamps can't be sold.

## 2.7 Budget Line Changes

In the next chapter we will analyze how the consumer chooses an optimal consumption bundle from his or her budget set. But we can already state some observations here that follow from what we have learned about the movements of the budget line.

First, we can observe that since the budget set doesn't change when we multiply all prices and income by a positive number, the optimal choice of the consumer from the budget set can't change either. Without even analyzing the choice process itself, we have derived an important conclusion: a perfectly balanced inflation—one in which all prices and all incomes rise at the same rate—doesn't change anybody's budget set, and thus cannot change anybody's optimal choice.

Second, we can make some statements about how well-off the consumer can be at different prices and incomes. Suppose that the consumer's income increases and all prices remain the same. We know that this represents a parallel shift outward of the budget line. Thus every bundle the consumer was consuming at the lower income is also a possible choice at the higher income. But then the consumer must be at least as well-off at the higher income as at the lower income—since he or she has the same choices available as before plus some more. Similarly, if one price declines and all others stay the same, the consumer must be at least as well-off. This simple observation will be of considerable use later on.

## Summary

1. The budget set consists of all bundles of goods that the consumer can afford at given prices and income. We will typically assume that there are only two goods, but this assumption is more general than it seems.

2. The budget line is written as $p_1x_1 + p_2x_2 = m$. It has a slope of $-p_1/p_2$, a vertical intercept of $m/p_2$, and a horizontal intercept of $m/p_1$.

3. Increasing income shifts the budget line outward. Increasing the price of good 1 makes the budget line steeper. Increasing the price of good 2 makes the budget line flatter.

4. Taxes, subsidies, and rationing change the slope and position of the budget line by changing the prices paid by the consumer.

## REVIEW QUESTIONS

1. Originally the consumer faces the budget line $p_1 x_1 + p_2 x_2 = m$. Then the price of good 1 doubles, the price of good 2 becomes 8 times larger, and income becomes 4 times larger. Write down an equation for the new budget line in terms of the original prices and income.

2. What happens to the budget line if the price of good 2 increases, but the price of good 1 and income remain constant?

3. If the price of good 1 doubles and the price of good 2 triples, does the budget line become flatter or steeper?

4. What is the definition of a numeraire good?

5. Suppose that the government puts a tax of 15 cents a gallon on gasoline and then later decides to put a subsidy on gasoline at a rate of 7 cents a gallon. What net tax is this combination equivalent to?

6. Suppose that a budget equation is given by $p_1 x_1 + p_2 x_2 = m$. The government decides to impose a lump-sum tax of $u$, a quantity tax on good 1 of $t$, and a quantity subsidy on good 2 of $s$. What is the formula for the new budget line?

7. If the income of the consumer increases and one of the prices decreases at the same time, will the consumer necessarily be at least as well-off?

# CHAPTER 3

# PREFERENCES

We saw in Chapter 2 that the economic model of consumer behavior is very simple: people choose the best things they can afford. The last chapter was devoted to clarifying the meaning of "can afford," and this chapter will be devoted to clarifying the economic concept of "best things."

We call the objects of consumer choice **consumption bundles**. This is a complete list of the goods and services that are involved in the choice problem that we are investigating. The word "complete" deserves emphasis: when you analyze a consumer's choice problem, make sure that you include all of the appropriate goods in the definition of the consumption bundle.

If we are analyzing consumer choice at the broadest level, we would want not only a complete list of the goods that a consumer might consume, but also a description of when, where, and under what circumstances they would become available. After all, people care about how much food they will have tomorrow as well as how much food they have today. A raft in the middle of the Atlantic Ocean is very different from a raft in the middle of the Sahara Desert. And an umbrella when it is raining is quite a different good from an umbrella on a sunny day. It is often useful to think of the "same" good available in different locations or circumstances as a different good, since the consumer may value the good differently in those situations.

However, when we limit our attention to a simple choice problem, the relevant goods are usually pretty obvious. We'll often adopt the idea described earlier of using just two goods and calling one of them "all other goods" so that we can focus on the tradeoff between one good and everything else. In this way we can consider consumption choices involving many goods and still use two-dimensional diagrams.

So let us take our consumption bundle to consist of two goods, and let $x_1$ denote the amount of one good and $x_2$ the amount of the other. The complete consumption bundle is therefore denoted by $(x_1, x_2)$. As noted before, we will occasionally abbreviate this consumption bundle by $X$.

## 3.1 Consumer Preferences

We will suppose that given any two consumption bundles, $(x_1, x_2)$ and $(y_1, y_2)$, the consumer can rank them as to their desirability. That is, the consumer can determine that one of the consumption bundles is strictly better than the other, or decide that she is indifferent between the two bundles.

We will use the symbol $\succ$ to mean that one bundle is **strictly preferred** to another, so that $(x_1, x_2) \succ (y_1, y_2)$ should be interpreted as saying that the consumer **strictly prefers** $(x_1, x_2)$ to $(y_1, y_2)$, in the sense that she definitely wants the x-bundle rather than the y-bundle. This preference relation is meant to be an operational notion. If the consumer prefers one bundle to another, it means that he or she would choose one over the other, given the opportunity. Thus the idea of preference is based on the consumer's *behavior*. In order to tell whether one bundle is preferred to another, we see how the consumer behaves in choice situations involving the two bundles. If she always chooses $(x_1, x_2)$ when $(y_1, y_2)$ is available, then it is natural to say that this consumer prefers $(x_1, x_2)$ to $(y_1, y_2)$.

If the consumer is **indifferent** between two bundles of goods, we use the symbol $\sim$ and write $(x_1, x_2) \sim (y_1, y_2)$. Indifference means that the consumer would be just as satisfied, according to her own preferences, consuming the bundle $(x_1, x_2)$ as she would be consuming the other bundle, $(y_1, y_2)$.

If the consumer prefers or is indifferent between the two bundles we say that she **weakly prefers** $(x_1, x_2)$ to $(y_1, y_2)$ and write $(x_1, x_2) \succeq (y_1, y_2)$.

These relations of strict preference, weak preference, and indifference are not independent concepts; the relations are themselves related! For example, if $(x_1, x_2) \succeq (y_1, y_2)$ and $(y_1, y_2) \succeq (x_1, x_2)$ we can conclude that $(x_1, x_2) \sim (y_1, y_2)$. That is, if the consumer thinks that $(x_1, x_2)$ is at least as good as $(y_1, y_2)$ *and* that $(y_1, y_2)$ is at least as good as $(x_1, x_2)$, then the consumer must be indifferent between the two bundles of goods.

Similarly, if $(x_1, x_2) \succeq (y_1, y_2)$ but we know that it is *not* the case that $(x_1, x_2) \sim (y_1, y_2)$, we can conclude that we must have $(x_1, x_2) \succ (y_1, y_2)$. This just says that if the consumer thinks that $(x_1, x_2)$ is at least as good as $(y_1, y_2)$, and she is not indifferent between the two bundles, then it must be that she thinks that $(x_1, x_2)$ is strictly better than $(y_1, y_2)$.

## 3.2 Assumptions about Preferences

Economists usually make some assumptions about the "consistency" of consumers' preferences. For example, it seems unreasonable—not to say contradictory—to have a situation where $(x_1, x_2) \succ (y_1, y_2)$ and, at the same time, $(y_1, y_2) \succ (x_1, x_2)$. For this would mean that the consumer strictly prefers the x-bundle to the y-bundle ... and vice versa.

So we usually make some assumptions about how the preference relations work. Some of the assumptions about preferences are so fundamental that we can refer to them as "axioms" of consumer theory. Here are three such axioms about consumer preference.

**Complete**. We assume that any two bundles can be compared. That is, given any x-bundle and any y-bundle, we assume that $(x_1, x_2) \succeq (y_1, y_2)$, or $(y_1, y_2) \succeq (x_1, x_2)$, or both, in which case the consumer is indifferent between the two bundles.

**Reflexive**. We assume that any bundle is at least as good as itself: $(x_1, x_2) \succeq (x_1, x_2)$.

**Transitive**. If $(x_1, x_2) \succeq (y_1, y_2)$ and $(y_1, y_2) \succeq (z_1, z_2)$, then we assume that $(x_1, x_2) \succeq (z_1, z_2)$. In other words, if the consumer thinks that $X$ is at least as good as $Y$ and that $Y$ is at least as good as $Z$, then the consumer thinks that $X$ is at least as good as $Z$.

The first axiom, completeness, is hardly objectionable, at least for the kinds of choices economists generally examine. To say that any two bundles can be compared is simply to say that the consumer is able to make a choice between any two given bundles. One might imagine extreme situations involving life or death choices where ranking the alternatives might be difficult, or even impossible, but these choices are, for the most part, outside the domain of economic analysis.

The second axiom, reflexivity, is trivial. Any bundle is certainly at least as good as an identical bundle. Parents of small children may occasionally observe behavior that violates this assumption, but it seems plausible for most adult behavior.

The third axiom, transitivity, is more problematic. It isn't clear that transitivity of preferences is *necessarily* a property that preferences would have to have. The assumption that preferences are transitive doesn't seem compelling on grounds of pure logic alone. In fact it's not. Transitivity is a hypothesis about people's choice behavior, not a statement of pure logic. Whether it is a basic fact of logic or not isn't the point: it is whether or not it is a reasonably accurate description of how people behave that matters.

What would you think about a person who said that he preferred a bundle $X$ to $Y$, and preferred $Y$ to $Z$, but then also said that he preferred $Z$ to $X$? This would certainly be taken as evidence of peculiar behavior.

More importantly, how would this consumer behave if faced with choices among the three bundles $X$, $Y$, and $Z$? If we asked him to choose his most preferred bundle, he would have quite a problem, for whatever bundle he chose, there would always be one that was preferred to it. If we are to have a theory where people are making "best" choices, preferences must satisfy the transitivity axiom or something very much like it. If preferences were not transitive there could well be a set of bundles for which there is no best choice.

## 3.3 Indifference Curves

It turns out that the whole theory of consumer choice can be formulated in terms of preferences that satisfy the three axioms described above, plus a few more technical assumptions. However, we will find it convenient to describe preferences graphically by using a construction known as **indifference curves**.

Consider Figure 3.1 where we have illustrated two axes representing a consumer's consumption of goods 1 and 2. Let us pick a certain consumption bundle $(x_1, x_2)$ and shade in all of the consumption bundles that are weakly preferred to $(x_1, x_2)$. This is called the **weakly preferred set**. The bundles on the boundary of this set—the bundles for which the consumer is just indifferent to $(x_1, x_2)$—form the **indifference curve**.

We can draw an indifference curve through any consumption bundle we want. The indifference curve through a consumption bundle consists of all bundles of goods that leave the consumer indifferent to the given bundle.

One problem with using indifference curves to describe preferences is that they only show you the bundles that the consumer perceives as being indifferent to each other—they don't show you which bundles are better and which bundles are worse. It is sometimes useful to draw small arrows on the indifference curves to indicate the direction of the preferred bundles. We won't do this in every case, but we will do it in a few of the examples where confusion might arise.

If we make no further assumptions about preferences, indifference curves can take very peculiar shapes indeed. But even at this level of generality, we can state an important principle about indifference curves: *indifference curves representing distinct levels of preference cannot cross*. That is, the situation depicted in Figure 3.2 cannot occur.

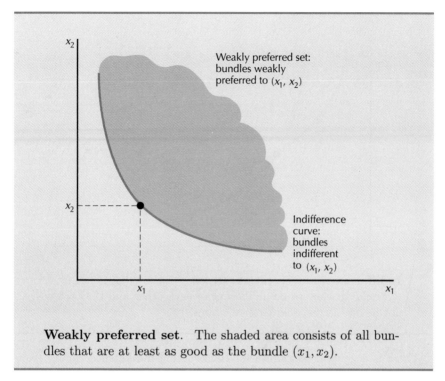

**Weakly preferred set**.  The shaded area consists of all bundles that are at least as good as the bundle $(x_1, x_2)$.

Figure
3.1

In order to prove this, let us choose three bundles of goods, $X$, $Y$, and $Z$, such that $X$ lies only on one indifference curve, $Y$ lies only on the other indifference curve, and $Z$ lies at the intersection of the indifference curves. By assumption the indifference curves represent distinct levels of preference, so one of the bundles, say $X$, is strictly preferred to the other bundle, $Y$. We know that $X \sim Z$ and $Z \sim Y$, and the axiom of transitivity therefore implies that $X \sim Y$. But this contradicts the assumption that $X \succ Y$. This contradiction establishes the result—indifference curves representing distinct levels of preference cannot cross.

What other properties do indifference curves have? In the abstract, the answer is: not many. Indifference curves are a way to describe preferences. Nearly any "reasonable" preferences that you can think of can be depicted by indifference curves. The trick is to learn what kinds of preferences give rise to what shapes of indifference curves.

## 3.4 Examples of Preferences

Let us try to relate preferences to indifference curves through some examples. We'll describe some preferences and then see what the indifference curves that represent them look like.

**Figure 3.2**

**Indifference curves cannot cross.** If they did, $X$, $Y$, and $Z$ would all have to be indifferent to each other and thus could not lie on distinct indifference curves.

There is a general procedure for constructing indifference curves given a "verbal" description of the preferences. First plop your pencil down on the graph at some consumption bundle $(x_1, x_2)$. Now think about giving a little more of good 1, $\Delta x_1$, to the consumer, moving him to $(x_1 + \Delta x_1, x_2)$. Now ask yourself how would you have to *change* the consumption of $x_2$ to make the consumer indifferent to the original consumption point? Call this change $\Delta x_2$. Ask yourself the question "For a given change in good 1, how does good 2 have to change to make the consumer just indifferent between $(x_1 + \Delta x_1, x_2 + \Delta x_2)$ and $(x_1, x_2)$?" Once you have determined this movement at one consumption bundle you have drawn a piece of the indifference curve. Now try it at another bundle, and so on, until you develop a clear picture of the overall shape of the indifference curves.

## Perfect Substitutes

Two goods are **perfect substitutes** if the consumer is willing to substitute one good for the other at a *constant* rate. The simplest case of perfect substitutes occurs when the consumer is willing to substitute the goods on a one-to-one basis.

Suppose, for example, that we are considering a choice between red pencils and blue pencils, and the consumer involved likes pencils, but doesn't care about color at all. Pick a consumption bundle, say $(10, 10)$. Then for this consumer, any other consumption bundle that has 20 pencils in it is just as good as $(10, 10)$. Mathematically speaking, any consumption bundle $(x_1, x_2)$ such that $x_1 + x_2 = 20$ will be on this consumer's indifference curve through $(10, 10)$. Thus the indifference curves for this consumer are all parallel straight lines with a slope of $-1$, as depicted in Figure 3.3. Bundles with more total pencils are preferred to bundles with fewer total pencils, so the direction of increasing preference is up and to the right, as illustrated in Figure 3.3.

How does this work in terms of general procedure for drawing indifference curves? If we are at $(10, 10)$, and we increase the amount of the first good by one unit to 11, how much do we have to change the second good to get back to the original indifference curve? The answer is clearly that we have to decrease the second good by 1 unit. Thus the indifference curve through $(10, 10)$ has a slope of $-1$. The same procedure can be carried out at any bundle of goods with the same results—in this case all the indifference curves have a constant slope of $-1$.

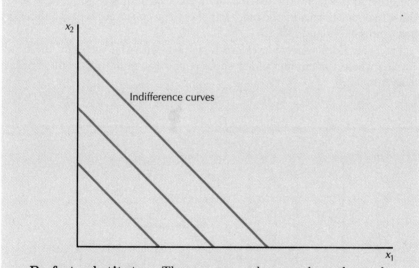

**Perfect substitutes.** The consumer only cares about the total number of pencils, not about their colors. Thus the indifference curves are straight lines with a slope of $-1$.

Figure 3.3

The important fact about perfect substitutes is that the indifference curves have a *constant* slope. Suppose, for example, that we graphed blue pencils on the vertical axis and *pairs* of red pencils on the horizontal axis. The indifference curves for these two goods would have a slope of $-2$, since the consumer would be willing to give up two blue pencils to get one more *pair* of red pencils.

In the textbook we'll primarily consider the case where goods are perfect substitutes on a one-for-one basis, and leave the treatment of the general case for the workbook.

## Perfect Complements

**Perfect complements** are goods that are always consumed together in fixed proportions. In some sense the goods "complement" each other. A nice example is that of right shoes and left shoes. The consumer likes shoes, but always wears right and left shoes together. Having only one out of a pair of shoes doesn't do the consumer a bit of good.

Let us draw the indifference curves for perfect complements. Suppose we pick the consumption bundle $(10, 10)$. Now add 1 more right shoe, so we have $(11, 10)$. By assumption this leaves the consumer indifferent to the original position: the extra shoe doesn't do him any good. The same thing happens if we add one more left shoe: the consumer is also indifferent between $(10, 11)$ and $(10, 10)$.

Thus the indifference curves are L-shaped, with the vertex of the L occurring where the number of left shoes equals the number of right shoes as in Figure 3.4.

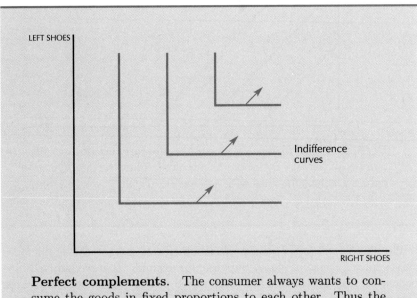

Figure
3.4

**Perfect complements**. The consumer always wants to consume the goods in fixed proportions to each other. Thus the indifference curves are L-shaped.

Increasing both the number of left shoes and the number of right shoes at the same time will move the consumer to a more preferred position, so the direction of increasing preference is again up and to the right, as illustrated in the diagram.

The important thing about perfect complements is that the consumer prefers to consume the goods in fixed proportions, not necessarily that the proportion is one-to-one. If a consumer always uses two teaspoons of sugar in her cup of tea, and doesn't use sugar for anything else, then the indifference curves will still be L-shaped. In this case the corners of the L will occur at (2 teaspoons sugar, 1 cup tea), (4 teaspoons sugar, 2 cups tea) and so on, rather than at (1 right shoe, 1 left shoe), (2 right shoes, 2 left shoes), and so on.

In the textbook we'll primarily consider the case where the goods are consumed in proportions of one-for-one and leave the treatment of the general case for the workbook.

## Bads

A **bad** is a commodity that the consumer doesn't like. For example, suppose that the commodities in question are now pepperoni and anchovies—and the consumer loves pepperoni but dislikes anchovies. But let us suppose there is some possible tradeoff between pepperoni and anchovies. That is, there would be some amount of pepperoni on a pizza that would compensate the consumer for having to consume a given amount of anchovies. How could we represent these preferences using indifference curves?

Pick a bundle $(x_1, x_2)$ consisting of some pepperoni and some anchovies. If we give the consumer more anchovies, what do we have to do with the pepperoni to keep him on the same indifference curve? Clearly, we have to give him some extra pepperoni to compensate him for having to put up with the anchovies. Thus this consumer must have indifference curves that slope up and to the right as depicted in Figure 3.5.

The direction of increasing preference is down and to the right—that is, toward the direction of decreased anchovy consumption and increased pepperoni consumption, just as the arrows in the diagram illustrate.

## Neutrals

A good is a **neutral good** if the consumer doesn't care about it one way or the other. What if a consumer is just neutral about anchovies?[1] In this case his indifference curves will be vertical lines as depicted in Figure 3.6.

---

[1] Is anybody neutral about anchovies?

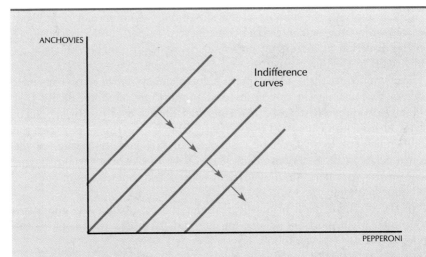

Figure
3.5

**Bads**. Here anchovies are a "bad," and pepperoni is a "good" for this consumer. Thus the indifference curves have a positive slope.

Figure
3.6

**A neutral good**. The consumer likes pepperoni but is neutral about anchovies, so the indifference curves are vertical lines.

He only cares about the amount of pepperoni he has and doesn't care at all about how many anchovies he has. The more pepperoni the better, but adding more anchovies doesn't affect him one way or the other.

## Satiation

We sometimes want to consider a situation involving **satiation**, where there is some overall best bundle for the consumer, and the "closer" he is to that best bundle, the better off he is in terms of his own preferences. For example, suppose that the consumer has some most preferred bundle of goods $(\overline{x}_1, \overline{x}_2)$, and the farther away he is from that bundle, the worse off he is. In this case we say that $(\overline{x}_1, \overline{x}_2)$ is a **satiation** point, or a **bliss** point. The indifference curves for the consumer look like those depicted in Figure 3.7. The best point is $(\overline{x}_1, \overline{x}_2)$ and points farther away from this bliss point lie on "lower" indifference curves.

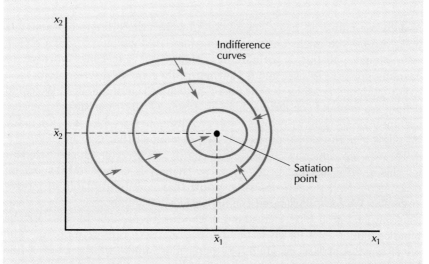

**Satiated preferences.**    The bundle $(\overline{x}_1, \overline{x}_2)$ is the satiation point or bliss point, and the indifference curves surround this point.

Figure
3.7

In this case the indifference curves have a negative slope when the consumer has "too little" or "too much" of both goods, and a positive slope when he has "too much" of one of the goods. When he has too much of one of the goods, it becomes a bad—reducing the consumption of the bad good moves him closer to his "bliss point." If he has too much of both goods, they both are bads, so reducing the consumption of each moves him closer to the bliss point.

Suppose, for example, that the two goods are chocolate cake and ice cream. There might well be some optimal amount of chocolate cake and ice cream that you would want to eat per week. Any less than that amount would make you worse off, but any more than that amount would also make you worse off.

If you think about it, most goods are like chocolate cake and ice cream in this respect—you can have too much of nearly anything. But people would generally not voluntarily *choose* to have too much of the goods they consume. Why would you choose to have more than you want of something? Thus the interesting region from the viewpoint of economic choice is where you have *less* than you want of most goods. The choices that people actually care about are choices of this sort, and these are the choices with which we will be concerned.

## Discrete Goods

Usually we think of measuring goods in units where fractional amounts make sense—you might on average consume 12.43 gallons of milk a month even though you buy it a quart at a time. But sometimes we want to examine preferences over goods that naturally come in discrete units.

For example, consider a consumer's demand for automobiles. We could define the demand for automobiles in terms of the time spent using an automobile, so that we would have a continuous variable, but for many purposes it is the actual number of cars demanded that is of interest.

There is no difficulty in using preferences to describe choice behavior for this kind of discrete good. Suppose that $x_2$ is money to be spent on other goods and $x_1$ is a **discrete good** that is only available in integer amounts. We have illustrated the appearance of indifference "curves" and a weakly preferred set for this kind of good in Figure 3.8. In this case the bundles indifferent to a given bundle will be a set of discrete points. The set of bundles at least as good as a particular bundle will be a set of line segments.

The choice of whether to emphasize the discrete nature of a good or not will depend on our application. If the consumer chooses only one or two units of the good during the time period of our analysis, recognizing the discrete nature of the choice may be important. But if the consumer is choosing 30 or 40 units of the good, then it will probably be convenient to think of this as a continuous good.

## 3.5 Well-Behaved Preferences

We've now seen some examples of indifference curves. As we've seen, many kinds of preferences, reasonable or unreasonable, can be described by these simple diagrams. But if we want to describe preferences in general, it will be convenient to focus on a few general shapes of indifference curves. In

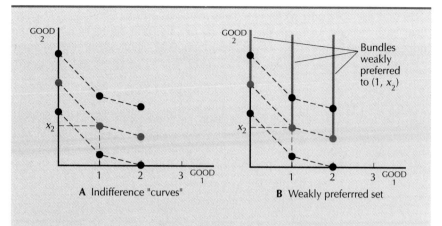

**A discrete good.** Here good 1 is only available in integer amounts. In panel A the dashed lines connect together the bundles that are indifferent, and in panel B the vertical lines represent bundles that are at least as good as the indicated bundle.

Figure
3.8

this section we will describe some more general assumptions that we will typically make about preferences and the implications of these assumptions for the shapes of the associated indifference curves. These assumptions are not the only possible ones; in some situations you might want to use different assumptions. But we will take them as the defining features for **well-behaved indifference curves**.

First we will typically assume that more is better, that is, that we are talking about *goods*, not bads. More precisely, if $(x_1, x_2)$ is a bundle of goods and $(y_1, y_2)$ is a bundle of goods with at least as much of both goods and more of one, then $(y_1, y_2) \succ (x_1, x_2)$. This assumption is sometimes called **monotonicity** of preferences. As we suggested in our discussion of satiation, more is better would probably only hold up to a point. Thus the assumption of monotonicity is saying only that we are going to examine situations *before* that point is reached—before any satiation sets in—while more *still is* better. Economics would not be a very interesting subject in a world where everyone was satiated in their consumption of every good.

What does monotonicity imply about the shape of indifference curves? It implies that they have a *negative* slope. Consider Figure 3.9. If we start at a bundle $(x_1, x_2)$ and move anywhere up and to the right, we must be moving to a preferred position. If we move down and to the left we must be moving to a worse position. So if we are moving to an *indifferent* position, we must be moving either left and up or right and down: the indifference curve must have a negative slope.

Second, we are going to assume that averages are preferred to extremes. That is, if we take two bundles of goods $(x_1, x_2)$ and $(y_1, y_2)$ on the same indifference curve and take a weighted average of the two bundles such as

$$\left(\frac{1}{2}x_1 + \frac{1}{2}y_1, \frac{1}{2}x_2 + \frac{1}{2}y_2\right),$$

then the average bundle will be at least as good as or strictly preferred to each of the two extreme bundles. This weighted-average bundle has the average amount of good 1 and the average amount of good 2 that is present in the two bundles. It therefore lies halfway along the straight line connecting the x–bundle and the y–bundle.

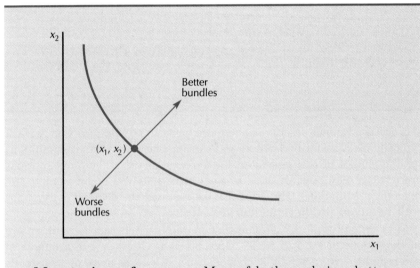

Figure
3.9

**Monotonic preferences.** More of both goods is a better bundle for this consumer; less of both goods represents a worse bundle.

Actually, we're going to assume this for any weight $t$ between 0 and 1, not just 1/2. Thus we are assuming that if $(x_1, x_2) \sim (y_1, y_2)$, then

$$(tx_1 + (1-t)y_1, tx_2 + (1-t)y_2) \succeq (x_1, x_2)$$

for any $t$ such that $0 \le t \le 1$. This weighted average of the two bundles gives a weight of $t$ to the x-bundle and a weight of $1-t$ to the y-bundle. Therefore, the distance from the x-bundle to the average bundle is just a fraction $t$ of the distance from the x-bundle to the y-bundle, along the straight line connecting the two bundles.

What does this assumption about preferences mean geometrically? It means that the set of bundles weakly preferred to $(x_1, x_2)$ is a **convex set**. For suppose that $(y_1, y_2)$ and $(x_1, x_2)$ are indifferent bundles. Then, if averages are preferred to extremes, all of the weighted averages of $(x_1, x_2)$ and $(y_1, y_2)$ are weakly preferred to $(x_1, x_2)$ and $(y_1, y_2)$. A convex set has the property that if you take *any* two points in the set and draw the line segment connecting those two points, that line segment lies entirely in the set.

Figure 3.10A depicts an example of convex preferences, while Figures 3.10B and 3.10C show two examples of nonconvex preferences. Figure 3.10C presents preferences that are so nonconvex that we might want to call them "concave preferences."

**Various kinds of preferences.** Panel A depicts convex preferences, panel B depicts nonconvex preferences, and panel C depicts "concave" preferences.

Figure 3.10

Can you think of preferences that are not convex? One possibility might be something like my preferences for ice cream and olives. I like ice cream and I like olives ... but I don't like to have them together! In considering my consumption in the next hour, I might be indifferent between consuming 8 ounces of ice cream and 2 ounces of olives, or 8 ounces of olives and 2 ounces of ice cream. But either one of these bundles would be better than consuming 5 ounces of each! These are the kind of preferences depicted in Figure 3.10C.

Why do we want to assume that well-behaved preferences are convex? Because, for the most part, goods are consumed together. The kinds of preferences depicted in Figures 3.10B and 3.10C imply that the consumer would prefer to specialize, at least to some degree, and to consume only one of the goods. However, the normal case is where the consumer would want to trade some of one good for the other and end up consuming some of each, rather than specializing in consuming only one of the two goods.

In fact, if we look at my preferences for *monthly* consumption of ice cream and olives, rather than at my immediate consumption, they would tend to look much more like Figure 3.10A than Figure 3.10C. Each month I would prefer having some ice cream and some olives—albeit at different times—to specializing in consuming either one for the entire month.

Finally, one extension of the assumption of convexity is the assumption of **strict convexity**. This means that the weighted average of two indifferent bundles is *strictly* preferred to the two extreme bundles. Convex preferences may have flat spots, while *strictly* convex preferences must have indifferences curves that are "rounded." The preferences for two goods that are perfect substitutes are convex, but not strictly convex.

## 3.6 The Marginal Rate of Substitution

We will often find it useful to refer to the slope of an indifference curve at a particular point. This idea is so useful that it even has a name: the slope of an indifference curve is known as the **marginal rate of substitution (MRS)**. The name comes from the fact that the MRS measures the rate at which the consumer is just willing to substitute one good for the other.

Suppose that we take a little of good 1, $\Delta x_1$, away from the consumer. Then we give him $\Delta x_2$, an amount that is just sufficient to put him back on his indifference curve, so that he is just as well off after this substitution of $x_2$ for $x_1$ as he was before. We think of the ratio $\Delta x_2 / \Delta x_1$ as being the *rate* at which the consumer is willing to substitute good 2 for good 1.

Now think of $\Delta x_1$ as being a very small change—a marginal change. When we imagine $\Delta x_1$ becoming infinitesimally small, we use the notation $dx_1$. Then the rate $dx_2 / dx_1$ measures the *marginal* rate of substitution of good 2 for good 1, or the slope of the indifference curve, as can be seen in Figure 3.11.

In economics, we commonly write about *marginal* changes, which you will learn to associate with slopes. The ratio defining the MRS will always describe the slope of the indifference curve: the rate at which the consumer is just willing to substitute a little more consumption of good 2 for a little less consumption of good 1.

One slightly confusing thing about the MRS is that it is typically a *negative* number. We've already seen that monotonic preferences imply that indifference curves must have a negative slope. Since the MRS is the numerical measure of the slope of an indifference curve, it will naturally be a negative number.

**The marginal rate of substitution (MRS).** The marginal
rate of substitution measures the slope of the indifference curve.

Figure
3.11

The marginal rate of substitution measures an interesting aspect of the
consumer's behavior. Suppose that the consumer has well-behaved preferences, that is, preferences that are monotonic and convex, and that he is
currently consuming some bundle $(x_1, x_2)$. We now will offer him a trade:
he can exchange good 1 for 2, or good 2 for 1, in any amount at a "rate of
exchange" of $E$.

That is, if the consumer gives up $dx_1$ units of good 1, he can get $E dx_1$
units of good 2 in exchange. Or, conversely, if he gives up $dx_2$ units of good
2, he can get $dx_2/E$ units of good 1. Geometrically, we are offering the
consumer an opportunity to move to any point along a line with slope $-E$
that passes through $(x_1, x_2)$, as depicted in Figure 3.12. Moving up and to
the left from $(x_1, x_2)$ involves exchanging good 1 for good 2, and moving
down and to the right involves exchanging good 2 for good 1. In either
movement, the exchange rate is $E$. Since exchange always involves giving
up one good in exchange for another, the exchange *rate* $E$ corresponds to
a *slope* of $-E$.

We can now ask what would the rate of exchange have to be in order for
the consumer to want to stay put at $(x_1, x_2)$? To answer this question, we
simply note that any time the exchange line *crosses* the indifference curve,
there will be some points on that line that are preferred to $(x_1, x_2)$—that
lie above the indifference curve. Thus, if there is to be no movement from

$(x_1, x_2)$, the exchange line must be tangent to the indifference curve. That is, the slope of the exchange line, $-E$, must be the slope of the indifference curve at $(x_1, x_2)$. At any other rate of exchange, the exchange line would cut the indifference curve and thus allow the consumer to move to a more preferred point.

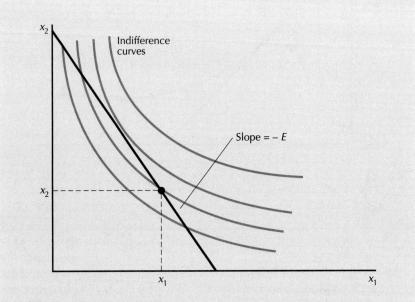

**Figure 3.12**

**Trading at an exchange rate.** Here we are allowing the consumer to trade the goods at an exchange rate $E$, which implies that the consumer can move along a line with slope $-E$.

Thus the slope of the indifference curve, the marginal rate of substitution, measures the rate at which the consumer is just on the margin of trading or not trading. At any rate of exchange other than the MRS, the consumer would want to trade one good for the other. But if the rate of exchange equals the MRS, the consumer wants to stay put.

## 3.7 Other Interpretations of the MRS

We have said that the MRS measures the rate at which the consumer is just on the margin of being willing to substitute good 1 for good 2. We could also say that the consumer is just on the margin of being willing to "pay" some of good 1 in order to buy some more of good 2. So sometimes you hear people say that the slope of the indifference curve measures the **marginal willingness to pay**.

If good 2 represents the consumption of "all other goods," and it is measured in dollars that you can spend on other goods, then the marginal-willingness-to-pay interpretation is very natural. The marginal rate of substitution of good 2 for good 1 is how many dollars you would just be willing to give up spending on other goods in order to consume a little bit more of good 1. Thus the MRS measures the marginal willingness to give up dollars in order to consume a small amount more of good 1. But giving up those dollars is just like paying dollars in order to consume a little more of good 1.

If you use the marginal-willingness-to-pay interpretation of the MRS, you should be careful to emphasize both the "marginal" and the "willingness" aspects. The MRS measures the amount of good 2 that one is *willing* to pay for a *marginal* amount of extra consumption of good 1. How much you actually *have* to pay for some given amount of extra consumption may be different than the amount you are willing to pay. How much you have to pay will depend on the price of the good in question. How much you are willing to pay doesn't depend on the price—it is determined by your preferences.

Similarly, how much you may be willing to pay for a large change in consumption may be different from how much you are willing to pay for a marginal change. How much you actually end up buying of a good will depend on your preferences for that good and the prices that you face. How much you would be willing to pay for a small amount extra of the good is a feature only of your preferences.

## 3.8 Behavior of the MRS

It is sometimes useful to describe the shapes of indifference curves by describing the behavior of the marginal rate of substitution. For example, the "perfect substitutes" indifference curves are characterized by the fact that the MRS is constant at $-1$. The "neutrals" case is characterized by the fact that the MRS is everywhere infinite. The preferences for "perfect complements" are characterized by the fact that the MRS is either zero or infinity, and nothing in between.

We've already pointed out that the assumption of monotonicity implies that indifference curves must have a negative slope, so the MRS always involves reducing the consumption of one good in order to get more of another for monotonic preferences.

The case of convex indifference curves exhibits yet another kind of behavior for the MRS. For strictly convex indifference curves, the MRS—the slope of the indifference curve—decreases (in absolute value) as we increase $x_1$. Thus the indifference curves exhibit a **diminishing marginal rate of**

**substitution**. This means that the amount of good 1 that the person is willing to give up for an additional amount of good 2 increases the amount of good 1 increases. Stated in this way, convexity of indifference curves seems very natural: it says that the more you have of one good, the more willing you are to give some of it up in exchange for the other good. (But remember the ice cream and olives example—for some pairs of goods this assumption might not hold!)

## Summary

1. Economists assume that a consumer can rank various consumption possibilities. The way in which the consumer ranks the consumption bundles describes the consumer's preferences.

2. Indifference curves can be used to depict different kinds of preferences.

3. Well-behaved preferences are monotonic (meaning more is better) and convex (meaning averages are preferred to extremes).

4. The marginal rate of substitution (MRS) measures the slope of the indifference curve. This can be interpreted as how much the consumer is willing to give up of good 2 to acquire more of good 1.

## REVIEW QUESTIONS

1. If we observe a consumer choosing $(x_1, x_2)$ when $(y_1, y_2)$ is available one time, are we justified in concluding that $(x_1, x_2) \succ (y_1, y_2)$?

2. Consider a group of people A, B, C and the relation "at least as tall as," as in "A is at least as tall as B." Is this relation transitive? Is it complete?

3. Take the same group of people and consider the relation "strictly taller than." Is this relation transitive? Is it reflexive? Is it complete?

4. A college football coach says that given any two linemen A and B, he always prefers the one who is bigger and faster. Is this preference relation transitive? Is it complete?

5. Can an indifference curve cross itself? For example, could Figure 3.2 depict a single indifference curve?

6. Could Figure 3.2 be a single indifference curve if preferences are monotonic?

7. If both pepperoni and anchovies are bads, will the indifference curve have a positive or a negative slope?

8. Explain why convex preferences means that "averages are preferred to extremes."

9. What is your marginal rate of substitution of $1 bills for $5 bills?

10. If good 1 is a "neutral," what is its marginal rate of substitution for good 2?

11. Think of some other goods for which your preferences might be concave.

# CHAPTER **4**

# UTILITY

In Victorian days, philosophers and economists talked blithely of "utility" as an indicator of a person's overall well-being. Utility was thought of as a numeric measure of a person's happiness. Given this idea, it was natural to think of consumers making choices so as to maximize their utility, that is, to make themselves as happy as possible.

The trouble is that these classical economists never really described how we were to measure utility. How are we supposed to quantify the "amount" of utility associated with different choices? Is one person's utility the same as another's? What would it mean to say that an extra candy bar would give me twice as much utility as an extra carrot? Does the concept of utility have any independent meaning other than its being what people maximize?

Because of these conceptual problems, economists have abandoned the old-fashioned view of utility as being a measure of happiness. Instead, the theory of consumer behavior has been reformulated entirely in terms of **consumer preferences**, and utility is seen only as a *way to describe preferences.*

Economists gradually came to recognize that all that mattered about utility as far as choice behavior was concerned was whether one bundle had a higher utility than another—how much higher didn't really matter.

Originally, preferences were defined in terms of utility: to say a bundle $(x_1, x_2)$ was preferred to a bundle $(y_1, y_2)$ meant that the x-bundle had a higher utility than the y-bundle. But now we tend to think of things the other way around. The *preferences* of the consumer are the fundamental description useful for analyzing choice, and utility is simply a way of describing preferences.

A **utility function** is a way of assigning a number to every possible consumption bundle such that more-preferred bundles get assigned larger numbers than less-preferred bundles. That is, a bundle $(x_1, x_2)$ is preferred to a bundle $(y_1, y_2)$ if and only if the utility of $(x_1, x_2)$ is larger than the utility of $(y_1, y_2)$: in symbols, $(x_1, x_2) \succ (y_1, y_2)$ if and only if $u(x_1, x_2) > u(y_1, y_2)$.

The only property of a utility assignment that is important is how it *orders* the bundles of goods. The magnitude of the utility function is only important insofar as it *ranks* the different consumption bundles; the size of the utility difference between any two consumption bundles doesn't matter. Because of this emphasis on ordering bundles of goods, this kind of utility is referred to as **ordinal utility**.

Consider for example Table 4.1, where we have illustrated several different ways of assigning utilities to three bundles of goods, all of which order the bundles in the same way. In this example, the consumer prefers A to B and B to C. All of the ways indicated are valid utility functions that describe the same preferences because they all have the property that A is assigned a higher number than B, which in turn is assigned a higher number than C.

**Different ways to assign utilities.**

Table
4.1

| Bundle | $U_1$ | $U_2$ | $U_3$ |
|--------|-------|-------|-------|
| A | 3 | 17 | −1 |
| B | 2 | 10 | −2 |
| C | 1 | .002 | −3 |

Since only the ranking of the bundles matters, there can be no unique way to assign utilities to bundles of goods. If we can find one way to assign utility numbers to bundles of goods, we can find an infinite number of ways to do it. If $u(x_1, x_2)$ represents a way to assign utility numbers to the bundles $(x_1, x_2)$, then multiplying $u(x_1, x_2)$ by 2 (or any other positive number) is just as good a way to assign utilities.

Multiplication by 2 is an example of a **monotonic transformation**. A monotonic transformation is a way of transforming one set of numbers into another set of numbers in a way that preserves the order of the numbers.

We typically represent a monotonic transformation by a function $f(u)$ that transforms each number $u$ into some other number $f(u)$, in a way that preserves the order of the numbers in the sense that $u_1 > u_2$ implies $f(u_1) > f(u_2)$. A monotonic transformation and a monotonic function are essentially the same thing.

Examples of monotonic transformations are multiplication by a positive number (e.g., $f(u) = 3u$), adding any number (e.g., $f(u) = u + 17$), raising $u$ to an odd power (e.g., $f(u) = u^3$), and so on.[1]

Provided that a monotonic function $f(u)$ is differentiable, its derivative $f'(u)$ is given by

$$f'(u) = \lim_{\hat{u} \to u} \frac{f(\hat{u}) - f(u)}{\hat{u} - u} > 0$$

For a monotonic transformation, $f(\hat{u}) - f(u)$ always has the same sign as $\hat{u} - u$. Thus a monotonic function always has a positive first derivative. This means that the graph of a monotonic function will always have a positive slope, as depicted in Figure 4.1A.

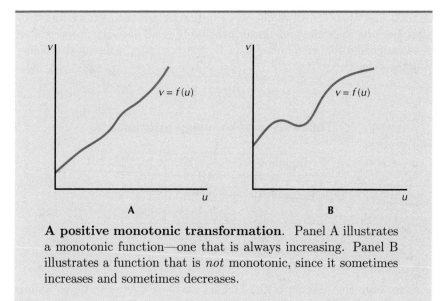

Figure 4.1

**A positive monotonic transformation.** Panel A illustrates a monotonic function—one that is always increasing. Panel B illustrates a function that is *not* monotonic, since it sometimes increases and sometimes decreases.

---

[1] What we are calling a "monotonic transformation" is, strictly speaking, called a "positive monotonic transformation," in order to distinguish it from a "negative monotonic transformation," which is one that *reverses* the order of the numbers. Monotonic transformations are sometimes called "monotonous transformations," which seems unfair, since they can actually be quite interesting.

If $f(u)$ is *any* monotonic transformation of a utility function that represents some particular preferences, then $f(u(x_1, x_2))$ is also a utility function that represents those same preferences.

Why? The argument is given in the following three statements:

1. To say that $u(x_1, x_2)$ represents some particular preferences means that $u(x_1, x_2) > u(y_1, y_2)$ if and only if $(x_1, x_2) \succ (y_1, y_2)$.
2. But if $f(u)$ is a monotonic transformation, then $u(x_1, x_2) > u(y_1, y_2)$ if and only if $f(u(x_1, x_2)) > f(u(y_1, y_2))$.
3. Therefore, $f(u(x_1, x_2)) > f(u(y_1, y_2))$ if and only if $(x_1, x_2) \succ (y_1, y_2)$, so the function $f(u)$ represents the preferences in the same way as the original utility function $u(x_1, x_2)$.

We summarize this discussion by stating the following principle: *a monotonic transformation of a utility function is a utility function that represents the same preferences as the original utility function.*

Geometrically, a utility function is a way to label indifference curves. Since every bundle on an indifference curve must have the same utility, a utility function is a way of assigning numbers to the different indifference curves in a way that higher indifference curves get assigned larger numbers. Seen from this point of view a monotonic transformation is just a relabeling of indifference curves. As long as indifference curves containing more-preferred bundles get a larger label than indifference curves containing less-preferred bundles, the labeling will represent the same preferences.

## 4.1 Cardinal Utility

There are some theories of utility that attach a significance to the magnitude of utility. These are known as **cardinal utility** theories. In a theory of cardinal utility, the size of the utility difference between two bundles of goods is supposed to have some sort of significance.

We know how to tell whether a given person prefers one bundle of goods to another: we simply offer him or her a choice between the two bundles and see which one is chosen. Thus we know how to assign an ordinal utility to the two bundles of goods: we just assign a higher utility to the chosen bundle than to the rejected bundle. Any assignment that does this will be a utility function. Thus we have an operational criterion for determining whether one bundle has a higher utility than another bundle for some individual.

But how do we tell if a person likes one bundle twice as much as another? How could you even tell if *you* like one bundle twice as much as another?

One could propose various definitions for this kind of assignment: I like one bundle twice as much as another if I am willing to pay twice as much for it. Or, I like one bundle twice as much as another if I am willing to run twice as far to get it, or to wait twice as long, or to gamble for it at twice the odds.

There is nothing wrong with any of these definitions; each one would give rise to a way of assigning utility levels in which the magnitude of the numbers assigned had some operational significance. But there isn't much right about them either. Although each of them is a possible interpretation of what it means to want one thing twice as much as another, none of them appears to be an especially compelling interpretation of that statement.

Even if we did find a way of assigning utility magnitudes that seemed to be especially compelling, what good would it do us in describing choice behavior? To tell whether one bundle or another will be chosen, we only have to know which is preferred—which has the larger utility. Knowing how much larger doesn't add anything to our description of choice. Since cardinal utility isn't needed to describe choice behavior and there is no compelling way to assign cardinal utilities anyway, we will stick with a purely ordinal utility framework.

## 4.2 Constructing a Utility Function

But are we assured that there is any way to assign ordinal utilities? Given a preference ordering can we always find a utility function that will order bundles of goods in the same way as those preferences? Is there a utility function that describes any reasonable preference ordering?

Not all kinds of preferences can be represented by a utility function. For example, suppose that someone had intransitive preferences so that $A \succ B \succ C \succ A$. Then a utility function for these preferences would have to consist of numbers $u(A)$, $u(B)$, and $u(C)$ such that $u(A) > u(B) > u(C) > u(A)$. But this is impossible.

However, if we rule out perverse cases like intransitive preferences, it turns out that we will typically be able to find a utility function to represent preferences. We will illustrate one construction here, and another one in Chapter 14.

Suppose that we are given an indifference map as in Figure 4.2. We know that a utility function is a way to label the indifference curves such that higher indifference curves get larger numbers. How can we do this?

One easy way is to draw the diagonal line illustrated and label each indifference curve with its distance from the origin measured along the line.

How do we know that this is a utility function? It is not hard to see that if preferences are monotonic then the line through the origin must intersect every indifference curve exactly once. Thus every bundle is getting a label, and those bundles on higher indifference curves are getting larger labels— and that's all it takes to be a utility function.

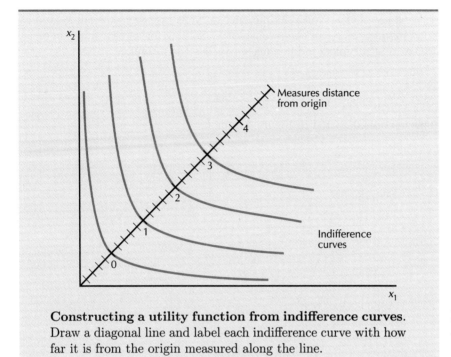

**Constructing a utility function from indifference curves.** Draw a diagonal line and label each indifference curve with how far it is from the origin measured along the line.

Figure 4.2

This gives us one way to find a labeling of indifference curves, at least as long as preferences are monotonic. This won't always be the most natural way in any given case, but at least it shows that the idea of an ordinal utility function is pretty general: nearly any kind of "reasonable" preferences can be represented by a utility function.

## 4.3 Some Examples of Utility Functions

In Chapter 3 we described some examples of preferences and the indifference curves that represented them. We can also represent these preferences by utility functions. If you are given a utility function, $u(x_1, x_2)$, it is relatively easy to draw the indifference curves: you just plot all the points $(x_1, x_2)$ such that $u(x_1, x_2)$ equals a constant. In mathematics, the set of all $(x_1, x_2)$ such that $u(x_1, x_2)$ equals a constant is called a **level set**. For each different value of the constant, you get a different indifference curve.

### EXAMPLE: Indifference Curves from Utility

Suppose that the utility function is given by: $u(x_1, x_2) = x_1 x_2$. What do the indifference curves look like?

We know that a typical indifference curve is just the set of all $x_1$ and $x_2$ such that $k = x_1 x_2$ for some constant $k$. Solving for $x_2$ as a function of $x_1$, we see that a typical indifference curve has the formula:

$$x_2 = \frac{k}{x_1}.$$

This curve is depicted in Figure 4.3 for $k = 1, 2, 3 \cdots$.

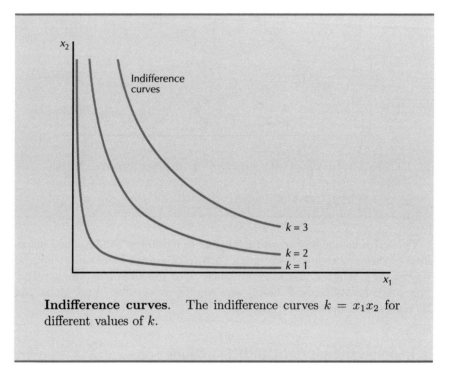

Figure
4.3   **Indifference curves.**   The indifference curves $k = x_1 x_2$ for different values of $k$.

Let's consider another example. Suppose that we were given a utility function $v(x_1, x_2) = x_1^2 x_2^2$. What do its indifference curves look like? By the standard rules of algebra we know that:

$$v(x_1, x_2) = x_1^2 x_2^2 = (x_1 x_2)^2 = u(x_1, x_2)^2.$$

Thus the utility function $v(x_1, x_2)$ is just the square of the utility function $u(x_1, x_2)$. Since $u(x_1, x_2)$ cannot be negative, it follows that $v(x_1, x_2)$ is a monotonic transformation of the previous utility function, $u(x_1, x_2)$. This means that the utility function $v(x_1, x_2) = x_1^2 x_2^2$ has to have exactly the same shaped indifference curves as those depicted in Figure 4.3. The labeling of the indifference curves will be different—the labels that were $1, 2, 3, \cdots$ will now be $1, 4, 9, \cdots$—but the set of bundles that has $v(x_1, x_2) =$

9 is exactly the same as the set of bundles that has $u(x_1, x_2) = 3$. Thus $v(x_1, x_2)$ describes exactly the same preferences as $u(x_1, x_2)$ since it *orders* all of the bundles in the same way.

Going the other direction—finding a utility function that represents some indifference curves—is somewhat more difficult. There are two ways to proceed. The first way is mathematical. Given the indifference curves, we want to find a function that is constant along each indifference curve and that assigns higher values to higher indifference curves.

The second way is a bit more intuitive. Given a description of the preferences, we try to think about what the consumer is trying to maximize—what combination of the goods describes the choice behavior of the consumer. This may seem a little vague at the moment, but it will be more meaningful after we discuss a few examples.

## Perfect Substitutes

Remember the red pencil and blue pencil example? All that mattered to the consumer was the total number of pencils. Thus it is natural to measure utility by the total number of pencils. Therefore we provisionally pick the utility function $u(x_1, x_2) = x_1 + x_2$. Does this work? Just ask two things: is this utility function constant along the indifference curves? Does it assign a higher label to more-preferred bundles? The answer to both questions is yes, so we have a utility function.

Of course, this isn't the only utility function that we could use. We could also use the *square* of the number of pencils. Thus the utility function $v(x_1, x_2) = (x_1 + x_2)^2 = x_1^2 + 2x_1x_2 + x_2^2$ will also represent the perfect-substitutes preferences, as would any other monotonic transformation of $u(x_1, x_2)$.

What if the consumer is willing to substitute good 1 for good 2 at a rate that is different from one-to-one? Suppose, for example, that the consumer would require *two* units of good 2 to compensate him for giving up one unit of good 1. This means that good 1 is *twice* as valuable to the consumer as good 2. The utility function therefore takes the form $u(x_1, x_2) = 2x_1 + x_2$. Note that this utility yields indifference curves with a slope of $-2$.

In general, preferences for perfect substitutes can be represented by a utility function of the form

$$u(x_1, x_2) = ax_1 + bx_2.$$

Here $a$ and $b$ are some positive numbers that measure the "value" of goods 1 and 2 to the consumer. Note that the slope of a typical indifference curve is given by $-a/b$.

## Perfect Complements

This is the left shoe–right shoe case. In these preferences the consumer only cares about the number of *pairs* of shoes he has, so it is natural to choose the number of pairs of shoes as the utility function. The number of complete pairs of shoes that you have is the *minimum* of the number of right shoes you have, $x_1$, and the number of left shoes you have, $x_2$. Thus the utility function for perfect complements takes the form $u(x_1, x_2) = \min\{x_1, x_2\}$.

To verify that this utility function actually works, pick a bundle of goods such as $(10, 10)$. If we add one more unit of good 1 we get $(11, 10)$, which should leave us on the same indifference curve. Does it? Yes, since $\min\{10, 10\} = \min\{11, 10\} = 10$.

So $u(x_1, x_2) = \min\{x_1, x_2\}$ is a possible utility function to describe perfect complements. As usual, any monotonic transformation would be suitable as well.

What about the case where the consumer wants to consume the goods in some proportion other than one-to-one? For example, what about the consumer who always uses 2 teaspoons of sugar with each cup of tea? If $x_1$ is the number of cups of tea available and $x_2$ is the number of teaspoons of sugar available, then the number of correctly sweetened cups of tea will be $\min\{x_1, \frac{1}{2}x_2\}$.

This is a little tricky so we should stop to think about it. If the number of cups of tea is greater than half the number of teaspoons of sugar, then we know that we won't be able to put 2 teaspoons of sugar in each cup. In this case, we will only end up with $\frac{1}{2}x_2$ correctly sweetened cups of tea. (Substitute some numbers in for $x_1$ and $x_2$ to convince yourself.)

Of course, any monotonic transformation of this utility function will describe the same preferences. For example, we might want to multiply by 2 to get rid of the fraction. This gives us the utility function $u(x_1, x_2) = \min\{2x_1, x_2\}$.

In general, a utility function that describes perfect-complement preferences is given by

$$u(x_1, x_2) = \min\{ax_1, bx_2\},$$

where $a$ and $b$ are positive numbers that indicate the proportions in which the goods are consumed.

## Quasilinear Preferences

Here's a shape of indifference curves that we haven't seen before. Suppose that a consumer has indifference curves that are vertical translates of one another, as in Figure 4.4. This means that all of the indifference curves are just vertically "shifted" versions of one indifference curve. It follows that the equation for an indifference curve takes the form $x_2 = k - v(x_1)$, where $k$ is a different constant for each indifference curve. This equation says that the height of each indifference curve is some function of $x_1$, $-v(x_1)$, plus a constant $k$. Higher values of $k$ give higher indifference curves. (The minus sign is only a convention; we'll see why it is convenient below.)

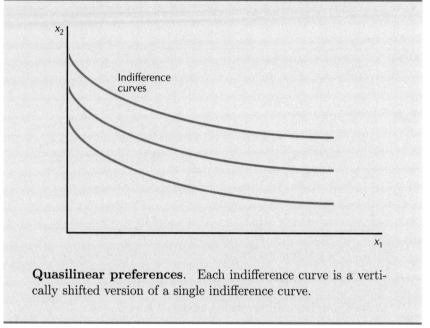

**Quasilinear preferences.** Each indifference curve is a vertically shifted version of a single indifference curve.

Figure 4.4

The natural way to label indifference curves here is with $k$—roughly speaking, the height of the indifference curve along the vertical axis. Solving for $k$ and setting it equal to utility, we have

$$u(x_1, x_2) = k = v(x_1) + x_2.$$

In this case the utility function is linear in good 2, but (possibly) nonlinear in good 1; hence the name **quasilinear utility**, meaning "partly linear" utility. Specific examples of quasilinear utility would be $u(x_1, x_2) = \sqrt{x_1} + x_2$, or $u(x_1, x_2) = \ln x_1 + x_2$. Quasilinear utility functions are not particularly realistic, but they are very easy to work with, as we'll see in several examples later on in the book.

## Cobb-Douglas Preferences

Another commonly used utility function is the **Cobb-Douglas** utility function

$$u(x_1, x_2) = x_1^c x_2^d,$$

where $c$ and $d$ are positive numbers that describe the preferences of the consumer.[2]

The Cobb-Douglas utility function will be useful in several examples. The preferences represented by the Cobb-Douglas utility function have the general shape depicted in Figure 4.5. In Figure 4.5A, we have illustrated the indifference curves for $c = 1/2$, $d = 1/2$. In Figure 4.5B, we have illustrated the indifference curves for $c = 1/5$, $d = 4/5$. Note how different values of the parameters $c$ and $d$ lead to different shapes of the indifference curves.

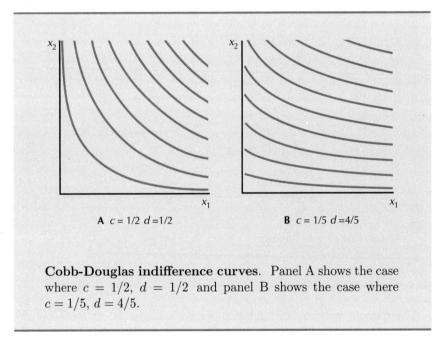

**A** $c = 1/2 \; d = 1/2$        **B** $c = 1/5 \; d = 4/5$

Figure
4.5

**Cobb-Douglas indifference curves.** Panel A shows the case where $c = 1/2$, $d = 1/2$ and panel B shows the case where $c = 1/5$, $d = 4/5$.

Cobb-Douglas indifference curves look just like the nice convex monotonic indifference curves that we referred to as "well-behaved indifference curves" in Chapter 3. Cobb-Douglas preferences are the standard example of indifference curves that look well-behaved, and in fact the formula describing them is about the simplest algebraic expression that generates well-behaved preferences. We'll find Cobb-Douglas preferences quite useful to present algebraic examples of the economic ideas we'll study later.

Of course a monotonic transformation of the Cobb-Douglas utility function will represent exactly the same preferences, and it is useful to see a couple of examples of these transformations.

---

[2] Paul Douglas was a twentieth-century economist at the University of Chicago who later became a U.S. senator. Charles Cobb was a mathematician at Amherst College. The Cobb-Douglas functional form was originally used to study production behavior.

First, if we take the natural log of utility, the product of the terms will become a sum so that we have

$$v(x_1, x_2) = \ln(x_1^c x_2^d) = c \ln x_1 + d \ln x_2.$$

The indifference curves for this utility function will look just like the ones for the first Cobb-Douglas function, since the logarithm is a monotonic transformation. (For a brief review of natural logarithms, see the Mathematical Appendix at the end of the book.)

For the second example, suppose that we start with the Cobb-Douglas form

$$v(x_1, x_2) = x_1^c x_2^d.$$

Then raising utility to the $1/(c+d)$ power, we have

$$x_1^{\frac{c}{c+d}} x_2^{\frac{d}{c+d}}.$$

Now define a new number

$$a = \frac{c}{c+d}.$$

We can now write our utility function as

$$v(x_1, x_2) = x_1^a x_2^{1-a}.$$

This means that we can always take a monotonic transformation of the Cobb-Douglas utility function that make the exponents sum to 1. This will turn out to have a useful interpretation later on.

The Cobb-Douglas utility function can be expressed in a variety of ways; you should learn to recognize them, as this family of preferences is very useful for examples.

## 4.4 Marginal Utility

Consider a consumer who is consuming some bundle of goods, $(x_1, x_2)$. How does this consumer's utility change as we give him or her a little more of good 1? This rate of change is called the **marginal utility** with respect to good 1. We write it as $MU_1$ and think of it as being a ratio that measures the rate of change in utility associated with a small change in the amount of good 1, holding the amount of good 2 fixed.

As elsewhere in economics, "marginal" just means a derivative. So the marginal utility of good 1 is just

$$MU_1 = \lim_{\Delta x_1 \to 0} \frac{u(x_1 + \Delta x_1, x_2) - u(x_1, x_2)}{\Delta x_1} = \frac{\partial u(x_1, x_2)}{\partial x_1}.$$

Note that we have used the *partial* derivative here, since the marginal utility of good 1 is computed holding good 2 constant.

This definition implies that to calculate the change in utility associated with a small change in consumption of good 1, we can just multiply the change in consumption by the marginal utility of the good:

$$dU = MU_1 dx_1.$$

The marginal utility with respect to good 2 is defined in a similar manner:

$$MU_2 = \lim_{\Delta x_2 \to 0} \frac{u(x_1, x_2 + \Delta x_2) - u(x_1, x_2)}{\Delta x_2} = \frac{\partial u(x_1, x_2)}{\partial x_2}.$$

Note that when we compute the marginal utility with respect to good 2 we keep the amount of good 1 constant. We can calculate the change in utility associated with a change in the consumption of good 2 by the formula

$$dU = MU_2 dx_2.$$

It is important to realize that the magnitude of marginal utility depends on the magnitude of utility. Thus it depends on the particular way that we choose to measure utility. If we multiplied utility by 2, then marginal utility would also be multiplied by 2. We would still have a perfectly valid utility function in that it would represent the same preferences, but it would just be scaled differently.

This means that marginal utility itself has no behavioral content. How can we calculate marginal utility from a consumer's choice behavior? We can't. Choice behavior only reveals information about the way a consumer *ranks* different bundles of goods. Marginal utility depends on the particular utility function that we use to reflect the preference ordering and its magnitude has no particular significance. However, it turns out that marginal utility can be used to calculate something that does have behavioral content, as we will see in the next section.

## 4.5 Marginal Utility and MRS

A utility function $u(x_1, x_2)$ can be used to measure the marginal rate of substitution (MRS) defined in Chapter 3. Recall that the MRS measures the slope of the indifference curve at a given bundle of goods; it can be interpreted as the rate at which a consumer is just willing to substitute a small amount of good 2 for good 1.

The algebraic sign of the MRS is negative: if you get more of good 1 you have to get *less* of good 2 in order to keep the same level of utility. However, it gets very tedious to keep track of that pesky minus sign, so economists often refer to the MRS by its absolute value—that is, as a positive number. We'll follow this convention as long as no confusion will result.

We can formally derive the MRS in two ways: first by using differentials, and second by using implicit functions.

For the first method, we consider making a change $(dx_1, dx_2)$ that keeps utility constant. So we want

$$du = \frac{\partial u(x_1, x_2)}{\partial x_1} dx_1 + \frac{\partial u(x_1, x_2)}{\partial x_2} dx_2 = 0.$$

The first term measures the increase in utility from the small change $dx_1$, and the second term measures the increase in utility from the small change $dx_2$. We want to pick these changes so that the total change in utility, $du$, is zero. Solving for $dx_2/dx_1$ gives us

$$\frac{dx_2}{dx_1} = -\frac{\partial u(x_1, x_2)/\partial x_1}{\partial u(x_1, x_2)/\partial x_2}.$$

As for the second method, we now think of the indifference curve as being described by a function $x_2(x_1)$. That is, for each value of $x_1$, the function $x_2(x_1)$ tells us how much $x_2$ we need to get on that specific indifference curve. Thus the function $x_2(x_1)$ has to satisfy the identity

$$u(x_1, x_2(x_1)) \equiv k,$$

where $k$ is the utility label of the indifference curve in question.

We can differentiate both sides of this identity with respect to $x_1$ to get

$$\frac{\partial u(x_1, x_2)}{\partial x_1} + \frac{\partial u(x_1, x_2)}{\partial x_2} \frac{\partial x_2(x_1)}{\partial x_1} = 0.$$

Notice that $x_1$ occurs in two places in this identity, so changing $x_1$ will change the function in two ways, and we have to take the derivative at each place that $x_1$ appears.

We then solve this equation for $\partial x_2(x_1)/\partial x_1$ to find

$$\frac{\partial x_2(x_1)}{\partial x_1} = -\frac{\partial u(x_1, x_2)/\partial x_1}{\partial u(x_1, x_2)/\partial x_2},$$

just as we had before.

The implicit function method is a little more rigorous, but the differential method is more direct, as long as you don't do something silly.

Suppose that we take a monotonic transformation of a utility function, say, $v(x_1, x_2) = f(u(x_1, x_2))$. Let's calculate the MRS for this utility function. Using the chain rule

$$\begin{aligned}
\text{MRS} &= -\frac{\partial v/\partial x_1}{\partial v/\partial x_2} = -\frac{\partial f/\partial u \; \partial u/\partial x_1}{\partial f/\partial u \; \partial u/\partial x_2} \\
&= -\frac{\partial u/\partial x_1}{\partial u/\partial x_2}
\end{aligned}$$

since the $\partial f / \partial u$ term cancels out from both the numerator and denominator. This shows that the MRS is independent of the utility representation.

This gives a useful way to recognize preferences that are represented by different utility functions: given two utility functions, just compute the marginal rates of substitution and see if they are the same. If they are, then the two utility functions have the same indifference curves. If the direction of increasing preference is the same for each utility function, then the underlying preferences must be the same.

Now here is the interesting thing about the MRS calculation: the MRS can be measured by observing a person's actual behavior—we find that rate of exchange where he or she is just willing to stay put, as described in Chapter 3.

The utility function, and therefore the marginal utility function, is not uniquely determined. Any monotonic transformation of a utility function leaves you with another equally valid utility function. Thus, if we multiply utility by 2, for example, the marginal utility is multiplied by 2. Thus the magnitude of the marginal utility function depends on the choice of utility function, which is arbitrary. It doesn't depend on behavior alone; instead it depends on the utility function that we use to describe behavior.

But the *ratio* of marginal utilities gives us an observable magnitude—namely the marginal rate of substitution. The ratio of marginal utilities is independent of the particular transformation of the utility function you choose to use. Look at what happens if you multiply utility by 2. The MRS becomes

$$\text{MRS} = -\frac{2MU_1}{2MU_2}.$$

The 2s just cancel out, so the MRS remains the same.

The same sort of thing occurs when we take any monotonic transformation of a utility function. Taking a monotonic transformation is just relabeling the indifference curves, and the calculation for the MRS described above is concerned with moving along a given indifference curve. Even though the marginal utilities are changed by monotonic transformations, the *ratio* of marginal utilities is independent of the particular way chosen to represent the preferences.

## EXAMPLE: Cobb-Douglas Preferences

The MRS for Cobb-Douglas preferences is easy to calculate by using the formula derived above.

If we choose the log representation where

$$u(x_1, x_2) = c \ln x_1 + d \ln x_2,$$

then we have

$$\begin{aligned}
\text{MRS} &= -\frac{\partial u(x_1, x_2)/\partial x_1}{\partial u(x_1, x_2)/\partial x_2} \\
&= -\frac{c/x_1}{d/x_2} \\
&= -\frac{c}{d}\frac{x_2}{x_1}.
\end{aligned}$$

Note that the MRS only depends on the ratio of the two parameters and the quantity of the two goods in this case.

What if we choose the exponent representation where

$$u(x_1, x_2) = x_1^c x_2^d?$$

Then we have

$$\begin{aligned}
\text{MRS} &= -\frac{\partial u(x_1, x_2)/\partial x_1}{\partial u(x_1, x_2)/\partial x_2} \\
&= -\frac{c x_1^{c-1} x_2^d}{d x_1^c x_2^{d-1}} \\
&= -\frac{c x_2}{d x_1},
\end{aligned}$$

which is the same as we had before. Of course you knew all along that a monotonic transformation couldn't change the marginal rate of substitution!

## 4.6 Utility for Commuting

Utility functions are basically ways of describing choice behavior: if a bundle of goods $X$ is chosen when a bundle of goods $Y$ is available, then $X$ must have a higher utility than $Y$. By examining choices consumers make we can estimate a utility function to describe their behavior.

This idea has been widely applied in the field of transportation economics to study consumers' commuting behavior. In most large cities commuters have a choice between taking public transit or driving to work. Each of these alternatives can be thought of as representing a bundle of different characteristics: travel time, waiting time, out-of-pocket costs, comfort, convenience, and so on. We could let $x_1$ be the amount of travel time involved in each kind of transportation, $x_2$ the amount of waiting time for each kind, and so on.

If $(x_1, x_2, \ldots, x_n)$ represents the values of $n$ different characteristics of driving, say, and $(y_1, y_2, \ldots, y_n)$ represents the values of taking the bus, we can consider a model where the consumer decides to drive or take the bus depending on whether he prefers one bundle of characteristics to the other.

More specifically, let us suppose that the average consumer's preferences for characteristics can be represented by a utility function of the form

$$U(x_1, x_2, \ldots, x_n) = \beta_1 x_1 + \beta_2 x_2 + \cdots + \beta_n x_n,$$

where the coefficients $\beta_1, \beta_2$, and so on are unknown parameters. Any monotonic transformation of this utility function would describe the choice behavior equally well, of course, but the linear form is especially easy to work with from a statistical point of view.

Suppose now that we observe a number of similar consumers making choices between driving and taking the bus based on the particular pattern of commute times, costs, and so on that they face. There are statistical techniques that can be used to find the values of the coefficients $\beta_i$ for $i = 1, \ldots, n$ that best fit the observed pattern of choices by a set of consumers. These statistical techniques give a way to estimate the utility function for different transportation modes.

One study reports a utility function that had the form[3]

$$U(TW, TT, C) = -0.147TW - 0.0411TT - 2.24C, \qquad (4.1)$$

where

$TW$ = total walking time to and from bus or car
$TT$ = total time of trip in minutes
$C$ = total cost of trip in dollars

The estimated utility function in the Domenich-McFadden book correctly described the choice between auto and bus transport for 93 percent of the households in their sample.

The coefficients on the variables in Equation (4.1) describe the weight that an average household places on the various characteristics of their commuting trips; that is, the marginal utility of each characteristic. The *ratio* of one coefficient to another measures the marginal rate of substitution between one characteristic and another. For example, the ratio of the marginal utility of walking time to the marginal utility of total time indicates that walking time is viewed as being roughly 3 times as onerous as travel time by the average consumer. In other words, the consumer would be willing to substitute 3 minutes of additional travel time to save 1 minute of walking time.

---

[3] See Thomas Domenich and Daniel McFadden, *Urban Travel Demand* (North-Holland Publishing Company, 1975). The estimation procedure in this book also incorporated various demographic characteristics of the households in addition to the purely economic variables described here. Daniel McFadden was awarded the Nobel Prize in economics in 2000 for his work in developing techniques to estimate models of this sort.

Similarly, the ratio of cost to travel time indicates the average consumer's tradeoff between these two variables. In this study, the average commuter valued a minute of commute time at $0.0411/2.24 = 0.0183$ dollars per minute, which is $1.10 per hour. For comparison, the hourly wage for the average commuter in 1967, the year of the study, was about $2.85 an hour.

Such estimated utility functions can be very valuable for determining whether or not it is worthwhile to make some change in the public transportation system. For example, in the above utility function one of the significant factors explaining mode choice is the time involved in taking the trip. The city transit authority can, at some cost, add more buses to reduce this travel time. But will the number of extra riders warrant the increased expense?

Given a utility function and a sample of consumers we can forecast which consumers will drive and which consumers will choose to take the bus. This will give us some idea as to whether the revenue will be sufficient to cover the extra cost.

Furthermore, we can use the marginal rate of substitution to estimate the *value* that each consumer places on the reduced travel time. We saw above that in the Domenich-McFadden study the average commuter in 1967 valued commute time at a rate of $1.10 per hour. Thus the commuter should be willing to pay about $0.37 to cut 20 minutes from his or her trip. This number gives us a measure of the dollar benefit of providing more timely bus service. This benefit must be compared to the cost of providing more timely bus service in order to determine if such provision is worthwhile. Having a quantitative measure of benefit will certainly be helpful in making a rational decision about transport policy.

## Summary

1. A utility function is simply a way to represent or summarize a preference ordering. The numerical magnitudes of utility levels have no intrinsic meaning.

2. Thus, given any one utility function, any monotonic transformation of it will represent the same preferences.

3. The marginal rate of substitution, MRS, can be calculated from the utility function via the formula MRS $= \Delta x_2/\Delta x_1 = -MU_1/MU_2$.

## REVIEW QUESTIONS

1. The text said that raising a number to an odd power was a monotonic transformation. What about raising a number to an even power? Is this a monotonic transformation? (Hint: consider the case $f(u) = u^2$.)

2. Which of the following are monotonic transformations? (1) $u = 2v - 13$; (2) $u = -1/v^2$; (3) $u = 1/v^2$; (4) $u = \ln v$; (5) $u = -e^{-v}$; (6) $u = v^2$; (7) $u = v^2$ for $v > 0$; (8) $u = v^2$ for $v < 0$.

3. We claimed in the text that if preferences were monotonic, then a diagonal line through the origin would intersect each indifference curve exactly once. Can you prove this rigorously? (Hint: what would happen if it intersected some indifference curve twice?)

4. What kind of preferences are represented by a utility function of the form $u(x_1, x_2) = \sqrt{x_1 + x_2}$? What about the utility function $v(x_1, x_2) = 13x_1 + 13x_2$?

5. What kind of preferences are represented by a utility function of the form $u(x_1, x_2) = x_1 + \sqrt{x_2}$? Is the utility function $v(x_1, x_2) = x_1^2 + 2x_1\sqrt{x_2} + x_2$ a monotonic transformation of $u(x_1, x_2)$?

6. Consider the utility function $u(x_1, x_2) = \sqrt{x_1 x_2}$. What kind of preferences does it represent? Is the function $v(x_1, x_2) = x_1^2 x_2$ a monotonic transformation of $u(x_1, x_2)$? Is the function $w(x_1, x_2) = x_1^2 x_2^2$ a monotonic transformation of $u(x_1, x_2)$?

7. Can you explain why taking a monotonic transformation of a utility function doesn't change the marginal rate of substitution?

# CHAPTER 5

# CHOICE

In this chapter we will put together the budget set and the theory of preferences in order to examine the optimal choice of consumers. We said earlier that the economic model of consumer choice is that people choose the best bundle they can afford. We can now rephrase this in terms that sound more professional by saying that "consumers choose the most preferred bundle from their budget sets."

## 5.1 Optimal Choice

A typical case is illustrated in Figure 5.1. Here we have drawn the budget set and several of the consumer's indifference curves on the same diagram. We want to find the bundle in the budget set that is on the highest indifference curve. Since preferences are well-behaved, so that more is preferred to less, we can restrict our attention to bundles of goods that lie *on* the budget line and not worry about those *beneath* the budget line.

Now simply start at the right-hand corner of the budget line and move to the left. As we move along the budget line we note that we are moving to higher and higher indifference curves. We stop when we get to the highest indifference curve that just touches the budget line. In the diagram, the bundle of goods that is associated with the highest indifference curve that just touches the budget line is labeled $(x_1^*, x_2^*)$.

The choice $(x_1^*, x_2^*)$ is an **optimal choice** for the consumer. The set of bundles that she prefers to $(x_1^*, x_2^*)$—the set of bundles *above* her indifference curve—doesn't intersect the bundles she can afford—the bundles *beneath* her budget line. Thus the bundle $(x_1^*, x_2^*)$ is the best bundle that the consumer can afford.

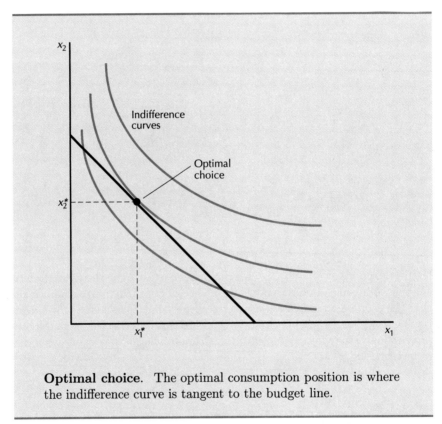

**Figure 5.1**

**Optimal choice.** The optimal consumption position is where the indifference curve is tangent to the budget line.

Note an important feature of this optimal bundle: at this choice, the indifference curve is *tangent* to the budget line. If you think about it a moment you'll see that this has to be the case: if the indifference curve weren't tangent, it would cross the budget line, and if it crossed the budget line, there would be some nearby point on the budget line that lies above the indifference curve—which means that we couldn't have started at an optimal bundle.

Does this tangency condition really *have* to hold at an optimal choice? Well, it doesn't hold in *all* cases, but it does hold for most interesting cases. What is always true is that at the optimal point the indifference curve can't cross the budget line. So when does "not crossing" imply tangent? Let's look at the exceptions first.

First, the indifference curve might not have a tangent line, as in Figure 5.2. Here the indifference curve has a kink at the optimal choice, and a tangent just isn't defined, since the mathematical definition of a tangent requires that there be a unique tangent line at each point. This case doesn't have much economic significance—it is more of a nuisance than anything else.

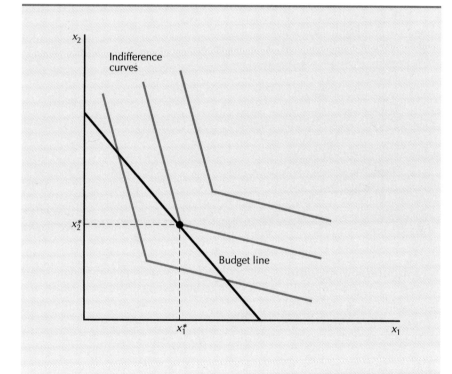

**Kinky tastes.** Here is an optimal consumption bundle where the indifference curve doesn't have a tangent.

Figure
5.2

The second exception is more interesting. Suppose that the optimal point occurs where the consumption of some good is zero as in Figure 5.3. Then the slope of the indifference curve and the slope of the budget line are different, but the indifference curve still doesn't *cross* the budget line.

We say that Figure 5.3 represents a **boundary optimum**, while a case like Figure 5.1 represents an **interior optimum**.

If we are willing to rule out "kinky tastes" we can forget about the example given in Figure 5.2.[1] And if we are willing to restrict ourselves only to *interior* optima, we can rule out the other example. If we have an interior optimum with smooth indifference curves, the slope of the indifference curve and the slope of the budget line must be the same ... because if they were different the indifference curve would cross the budget line, and we couldn't be at the optimal point.

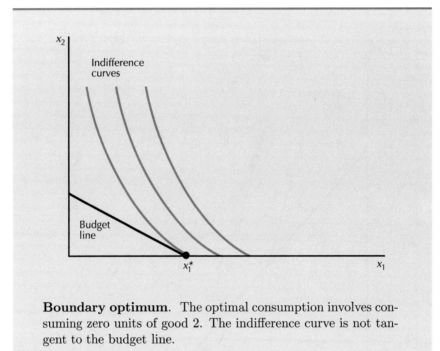

Figure 5.3

**Boundary optimum.** The optimal consumption involves consuming zero units of good 2. The indifference curve is not tangent to the budget line.

We've found a necessary condition that the optimal choice must satisfy. If the optimal choice involves consuming some of both goods—so that it is an interior optimum—then necessarily the indifference curve will be tangent to the budget line. But is the tangency condition a *sufficient* condition for a bundle to be optimal? If we find a bundle where the indifference curve is tangent to the budget line, can we be sure we have an optimal choice?

Look at Figure 5.4. Here we have three bundles where the tangency condition is satisfied, all of them interior, but only two of them are optimal.

[1] Otherwise, this book might get an R rating.

So in general, the tangency condition is only a necessary condition for optimality, not a sufficient condition.

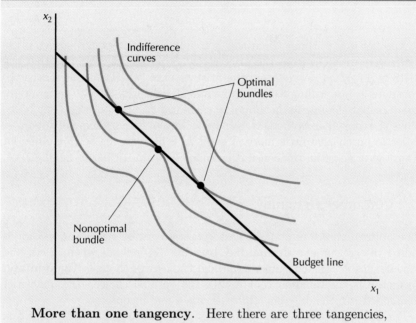

**More than one tangency.** Here there are three tangencies, but only two optimal points, so the tangency condition is necessary but not sufficient.

Figure 5.4

However, there is one important case where it is sufficient: the case of convex preferences. In the case of convex preferences, any point that satisfies the tangency condition must be an optimal point. This is clear geometrically: since convex indifference curves must curve away from the budget line, they can't bend back to touch it again.

Figure 5.4 also shows us that in general there may be more than one optimal bundle that satisfies the tangency condition. However, again convexity implies a restriction. If the indifference curves are *strictly* convex—they don't have any flat spots—then there will be only one optimal choice on each budget line. Although this can be shown mathematically, it is also quite plausible from looking at the figure.

The condition that the MRS must equal the slope of the budget line at an interior optimum is obvious graphically, but what does it mean economically? Recall that one of our interpretations of the MRS is that it is that rate of exchange at which the consumer is just willing to stay put. Well, the market is offering a rate of exchange to the consumer of $-p_1/p_2$—if you give up one unit of good 1, you can buy $p_1/p_2$ units of good 2. If the consumer is at a consumption bundle where he or she is willing to stay put, it must be one where the MRS is equal to this rate of exchange:

$$\text{MRS} = -\frac{p_1}{p_2}.$$

Another way to think about this is to imagine what would happen if the MRS were different from the price ratio. Suppose, for example, that the MRS is $\Delta x_2/\Delta x_1 = -1/2$ and the price ratio is $1/1$. Then this means the consumer is just willing to give up 2 units of good 1 in order to get 1 unit of good 2—but the market is willing to exchange them on a one-to-one basis. Thus the consumer would certainly be willing to give up some of good 1 in order to purchase a little more of good 2. Whenever the MRS is different from the price ratio, the consumer cannot be at his or her optimal choice.

## 5.2 Consumer Demand

The optimal choice of goods 1 and 2 at some set of prices and income is called the consumer's **demanded bundle**. In general when prices and income change, the consumer's optimal choice will change. The **demand function** is the function that relates the optimal choice—the quantities demanded—to the different values of prices and incomes.

We will write the demand functions as depending on both prices and income: $x_1(p_1, p_2, m)$ and $x_2(p_1, p_2, m)$. For each different set of prices and income, there will be a different combination of goods that is the optimal choice of the consumer. Different preferences will lead to different demand functions; we'll see some examples shortly. Our major goal in the next few chapters is to study the behavior of these demand functions—how the optimal choices change as prices and income change.

## 5.3 Some Examples

Let us apply the model of consumer choice we have developed to the examples of preferences described in Chapter 3. The basic procedure will be the same for each example: plot the indifference curves and budget line and find the point where the highest indifference curve touches the budget line.

### Perfect Substitutes

The case of perfect substitutes is illustrated in Figure 5.5. We have three possible cases. If $p_2 > p_1$, then the slope of the budget line is flatter than the slope of the indifference curves. In this case, the optimal bundle is where the consumer spends all of his or her money on good 1. If $p_1 > p_2$, then the consumer purchases only good 2. Finally, if $p_1 = p_2$, there is a whole range of optimal choices—any amount of goods 1 and 2 that satisfies the budget constraint is optimal in this case. Thus the demand function for good 1 will be

$$x_1 = \begin{cases} m/p_1 & \text{when } p_1 < p_2; \\ \text{any number between 0 and } m/p_1 & \text{when } p_1 = p_2; \\ 0 & \text{when } p_1 > p_2. \end{cases}$$

Are these results consistent with common sense? All they say is that if two goods are perfect substitutes, then a consumer will purchase the cheaper one. If both goods have the same price, then the consumer doesn't care which one he or she purchases.

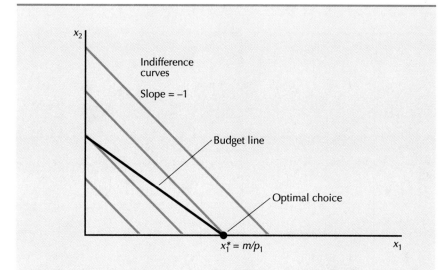

**Optimal choice with perfect substitutes.** If the goods are perfect substitutes, the optimal choice will usually be on the boundary.

Figure
5.5

## Perfect Complements

The case of perfect complements is illustrated in Figure 5.6. Note that the optimal choice must always lie on the diagonal, where the consumer is purchasing equal amounts of both goods, no matter what the prices are.

In terms of our example, this says that people with two feet buy shoes in pairs.[2]

Let us solve for the optimal choice algebraically. We know that this consumer is purchasing the same amount of good 1 and good 2, no matter what the prices. Let this amount be denoted by $x$. Then we have to satisfy the budget constraint

$$p_1 x + p_2 x = m.$$

Solving for $x$ gives us the optimal choices of goods 1 and 2:

$$x_1 = x_2 = x = \frac{m}{p_1 + p_2}.$$

The demand function for the optimal choice here is quite intuitive. Since the two goods are always consumed together, it is just as if the consumer were spending all of her money on a single good that had a price of $p_1 + p_2$.

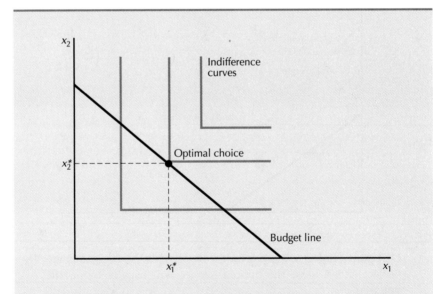

Figure
5.6

**Optimal choice with perfect complements.** If the goods are perfect complements, the quantities demanded will always lie on the diagonal since the optimal choice occurs where $x_1$ equals $x_2$.

---

[2] Don't worry, we'll get some more exciting results later on.

**Discrete goods.** In panel A the demand for good 1 is zero, while in panel B one unit will be demanded.

Figure
5.7

## Neutrals and Bads

In the case of a neutral good the consumer spends all of her money on the good she likes and doesn't purchase any of the neutral good. The same thing happens if one commodity is a bad. Thus, if commodity 1 is a good and commodity 2 is a bad, then the demand functions will be

$$x_1 = \frac{m}{p_1}$$
$$x_2 = 0.$$

## Discrete Goods

Suppose that good 1 is a discrete good that is available only in integer units, while good 2 is money to be spent on everything else. If the consumer chooses $1, 2, 3, \cdots$ units of good 1, she will implicitly choose the consumption bundles $(1, m - p_1)$, $(2, m - 2p_1)$, $(3, m - 3p_1)$, and so on. We can simply compare the utility of each of these bundles to see which has the highest utility.

Alternatively, we can use the indifference-curve analysis in Figure 5.7. As usual, the optimal bundle is the one on the highest indifference "curve." If the price of good 1 is very high, then the consumer will choose zero units of consumption; as the price decreases the consumer will find it optimal to consume 1 unit of the good. Typically, as the price decreases further the consumer will choose to consume more units of good 1.

## Concave Preferences

Consider the situation illustrated in Figure 5.8. Is $X$ the optimal choice? No! The optimal choice for these preferences is always going to be a boundary choice, like bundle $Z$. Think of what nonconvex preferences mean. If you have money to purchase ice cream and olives, and you don't like to consume them together, you'll spend all of your money on one or the other.

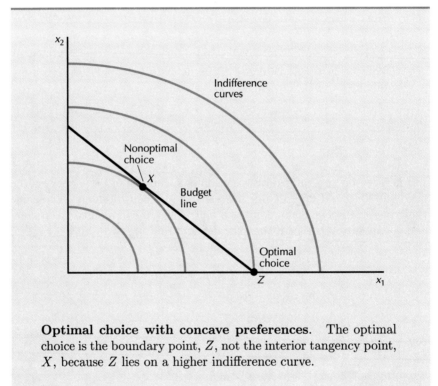

**Figure 5.8**  **Optimal choice with concave preferences.** The optimal choice is the boundary point, $Z$, not the interior tangency point, $X$, because $Z$ lies on a higher indifference curve.

## Solving the Preference Maximization Problem

It is very useful to be able to solve the preference-maximization problem and get algebraic examples of actual demand functions.

First, we will generally want to represent the consumer's preferences by a utility function, $u(x_1, x_2)$. We've seen in Chapter 4 that this is not a very restrictive assumption; most well-behaved preferences can be described by a utility function.

The first thing to observe is that we already *know* how to solve the optimal-choice problem. We just have to put together the facts that we learned in the last three chapters. We know from this chapter that an optimal choice $(x_1, x_2)$ must satisfy the condition

$$\text{MRS}(x_1, x_2) = -\frac{p_1}{p_2}, \tag{5.1}$$

and we saw in Chapter 4 that the MRS can be expressed as the negative of the ratio of derivatives of the utility function. Making this substitution and cancelling the minus signs, we have

$$\frac{\partial u(x_1, x_2)/\partial x_1}{\partial u(x_1, x_2)/\partial x_2} = \frac{p_1}{p_2}. \tag{5.2}$$

From Chapter 2 we know that the optimal choice must also satisfy the budget constraint

$$p_1 x_1 + p_2 x_2 = m. \tag{5.3}$$

This gives us two equations—the MRS condition and the budget constraint—and two unknowns, $x_1$ and $x_2$. All we have to do is to solve these two equations to find the optimal choices of $x_1$ and $x_2$ as a function of the prices and income. There are a number of ways to solve two equations in two unknowns. One way that always works, although it might not always be the simplest, is to solve the budget constraint for one of the choices, and then substitute that into the MRS condition.

Rewriting the budget constraint, we have

$$x_2 = \frac{m}{p_2} - \frac{p_1}{p_2} x_1 \tag{5.4}$$

and substituting this into equation (5.2) we get

$$\frac{\partial u(x_1, m/p_2 - (p_1/p_2)x_1)/\partial x_1}{\partial u(x_1, m/p_2 - (p_1/p_2)x_1)/\partial x_2} = \frac{p_1}{p_2}.$$

This rather formidable looking expression has only one unknown variable, $x_1$, and it can typically be solved for $x_1$ in terms of $(p_1, p_2, m)$. Then the budget constraint yields the solution for $x_2$ as a function of prices and income.

We can also derive the solution to the utility maximization problem in a more systematic way, using calculus conditions for maximization. To do this, we first pose the utility maximization problem as a constrained maximization problem:

$$\max_{x_1, x_2} u(x_1, x_2)$$

$$\text{such that } p_1 x_1 + p_2 x_2 = m.$$

This problem asks that we choose values of $x_1$ and $x_2$ that do two things: first, they have to satisfy the constraint, and second, they give a larger value for $u(x_1, x_2)$ than any other values of $x_1$ and $x_2$ that satisfy the constraint.

There are two useful ways to solve this kind of problem. The first way is simply to solve the constraint for one of the variables in terms of the other and then substitute it into the objective function.

For example, for any given value of $x_1$, the amount of $x_2$ that we need to satisfy the budget constraint is given by the linear function

$$x_2(x_1) = \frac{m}{p_2} - \frac{p_1}{p_2} x_1. \tag{5.5}$$

Now substitute $x_2(x_1)$ for $x_2$ in the utility function to get the *unconstrained* maximization problem

$$\max_{x_1} u(x_1, m/p_2 - (p_1/p_2)x_1).$$

This is an unconstrained maximization problem in $x_1$ alone, since we have used the function $x_2(x_1)$ to ensure that the value of $x_2$ will always satisfy the budget constraint, whatever the value of $x_1$ is.

We can solve this kind of problem just by differentiating with respect to $x_1$ and setting the result equal to zero in the usual way. This procedure will give us a first-order condition of the form

$$\frac{\partial u(x_1, x_2(x_1))}{\partial x_1} + \frac{\partial u(x_1, x_2(x_1))}{\partial x_2} \frac{dx_2}{dx_1} = 0. \tag{5.6}$$

Here the first term is the direct effect of how increasing $x_1$ increases utility. The second term consists of two parts: the rate of increase of utility as $x_2$ increases, $\partial u/\partial x_2$, times $dx_2/dx_1$, the rate of increase of $x_2$ as $x_1$ increases in order to continue to satisfy the budget equation. We can differentiate (5.5) to calculate this latter derivative

$$\frac{dx_2}{dx_1} = -\frac{p_1}{p_2}.$$

Substituting this into (5.6) gives us

$$\frac{\partial u(x_1^*, x_2^*)/\partial x_1}{\partial u(x_1^*, x_2^*)/\partial x_2} = \frac{p_1}{p_2},$$

which just says that the marginal rate of substitution between $x_1$ and $x_2$ must equal the price ratio at the optimal choice $(x_1^*, x_2^*)$. This is exactly the condition we derived above: the slope of the indifference curve must equal the slope of the budget line. Of course the optimal choice must also satisfy the budget constraint $p_1 x_1^* + p_2 x_2^* = m$, which again gives us two equations in two unknowns.

The second way that these problems can be solved is through the use of **Lagrange multipliers**. This method starts by defining an auxiliary function known as the *Lagrangian*:

$$L = u(x_1, x_2) - \lambda(p_1 x_1 + p_2 x_2 - m).$$

The new variable $\lambda$ is called a **Lagrange multiplier** since it is multiplied by the constraint.[3] Then Lagrange's theorem says that an optimal choice $(x_1^*, x_2^*)$ must satisfy the three first-order conditions

$$\frac{\partial L}{\partial x_1} = \frac{\partial u(x_1^*, x_2^*)}{\partial x_1} - \lambda p_1 = 0$$

$$\frac{\partial L}{\partial x_2} = \frac{\partial u(x_1^*, x_2^*)}{\partial x_2} - \lambda p_2 = 0$$

$$\frac{\partial L}{\partial \lambda} = p_1 x_1^* + p_2 x_2^* - m = 0.$$

There are several interesting things about these three equations. First, note that they are simply the derivatives of the Lagrangian with respect to $x_1$, $x_2$, and $\lambda$, each set equal to zero. The last derivative, with respect to $\lambda$, is just the budget constraint. Second, we now have three equations for the three unknowns, $x_1$, $x_2$, and $\lambda$. We have a hope of solving for $x_1$ and $x_2$ in terms of $p_1$, $p_2$, and $m$.

Lagrange's theorem is proved in any advanced calculus book. It is used quite extensively in advanced economics courses, but for our purposes we only need to know the statement of the theorem and how to use it.

In our particular case, it is worthwhile noting that if we divide the first condition by the second one, we get

$$\frac{\partial u(x_1^*, x_2^*)/\partial x_1}{\partial u(x_1^*, x_2^*)/\partial x_2} = \frac{p_1}{p_2},$$

which simply says the MRS must equal the price ratio, just as before. The budget constraint gives us the other equation, so we are back to two equations in two unknowns.

## Cobb-Douglas Preferences

In Chapter 4 we introduced the **Cobb-Douglas utility function**

$$u(x_1, x_2) = x_1^c x_2^d.$$

---

[3] The Greek letter $\lambda$ is pronounced "lamb-da."

Since utility functions are only defined up to a monotonic transformation, it is convenient to take logs of this expression and work with

$$\ln u(x_1, x_2) = c \ln x_1 + d \ln x_2.$$

Let's find the demand functions for $x_1$ and $x_2$ for the Cobb-Douglas utility function. The problem we want to solve is

$$\max_{x_1, x_2} c \ln x_1 + d \ln x_2$$

such that $p_1 x_1 + p_2 x_2 = m$.

There are at least three ways to solve this problem. One way is just to write down the MRS condition and the budget constraint. Using the expression for the MRS derived in Chapter 4, we have

$$\frac{cx_2}{dx_1} = \frac{p_1}{p_2}$$

$$p_1 x_1 + p_2 x_2 = m.$$

These are two equations in two unknowns that can be solved for the optimal choice of $x_1$ and $x_2$. One way to solve them is to substitute the second into the first to get

$$\frac{c(m/p_2 - x_1 p_1/p_2)}{dx_1} = \frac{p_1}{p_2}.$$

Cross multiplying gives

$$c(m - x_1 p_1) = d p_1 x_1.$$

Rearranging this equation gives

$$cm = (c + d)p_1 x_1$$

or

$$x_1 = \frac{c}{c + d} \frac{m}{p_1}.$$

This is the demand function for $x_1$. To find the demand function for $x_2$, substitute into the budget constraint to get

$$x_2 = \frac{m}{p_2} - \frac{p_1}{p_2} \frac{c}{c + d} \frac{m}{p_1}$$

$$= \frac{d}{c + d} \frac{m}{p_2}.$$

The second way is to substitute the budget constraint into the maximization problem at the beginning. If we do this, our problem becomes

$$\max_{x_1} c \ln x_1 + d \ln(m/p_2 - x_1 p_1/p_2).$$

The first-order condition for this problem is

$$\frac{c}{x_1} - d\frac{p_2}{m - p_1 x_1}\frac{p_1}{p_2} = 0.$$

A little algebra—which you should do!—gives us the solution

$$x_1 = \frac{c}{c+d}\frac{m}{p_1}.$$

Substitute this back into the budget constraint $x_2 = m/p_2 - x_1 p_1/p_2$ to get

$$x_2 = \frac{d}{c+d}\frac{m}{p_2}.$$

These are the demand functions for the two goods, which, happily, are the same as those derived earlier by the other method.

Now for Lagrange's method. Set up the Lagrangian

$$L = c\ln x_1 + d\ln x_2 - \lambda(p_1 x_1 + p_2 x_2 - m)$$

and differentiate to get the three first-order conditions

$$\frac{\partial L}{\partial x_1} = \frac{c}{x_1} - \lambda p_1 = 0$$

$$\frac{\partial L}{\partial x_2} = \frac{d}{x_2} - \lambda p_2 = 0$$

$$\frac{\partial L}{\partial \lambda} = p_1 x_1 + p_2 x_2 - m = 0.$$

Now the trick is to solve them! The best way to proceed is to first solve for $\lambda$ and then for $x_1$ and $x_2$. So we rearrange and cross multiply the first two equations to get

$$c = \lambda p_1 x_1$$
$$d = \lambda p_2 x_2.$$

These equations are just asking to be added together:

$$c + d = \lambda(p_1 x_1 + p_2 x_2) - \lambda m,$$

which gives us

$$\lambda = \frac{c+d}{m}.$$

Substitute this back into the first two equations and solve for $x_1$ and $x_2$ to get

$$x_1 = \frac{c}{c+d}\frac{m}{p_1}$$

$$x_2 = \frac{d}{c+d}\frac{m}{p_2},$$

just as before. The Cobb-Douglas preferences have a convenient property. Consider the fraction of his income that a Cobb-Douglas consumer spends on good 1. If he consumes $x_1$ units of good 1, this costs him $p_1 x_1$, so this represents a fraction $p_1 x_1 / m$ of total income. Substituting the demand function for $x_1$ we have

$$\frac{p_1 x_1}{m} = \frac{p_1}{m} \frac{c}{c+d} \frac{m}{p_1} = \frac{c}{c+d}.$$

Similarly the fraction of his income that the consumer spends on good 2 is $d/(c+d)$.

Thus the Cobb-Douglas consumer always spends a fixed fraction of his income on each good. The size of the fraction is determined by the exponent in the Cobb-Douglas function.

This is why it is often convenient to choose a representation of the Cobb-Douglas utility function in which the exponents sum to 1. If $u(x_1, x_2) = x_1^a x_2^{1-a}$, then we can immediately interpret $a$ as the fraction of income spent on good 1. For this reason we will usually write Cobb-Douglas preferences in this form. Because of the convenient properties of Cobb-Douglas preferences, they are often used in algebraic examples, so you should probably memorize the Cobb-Douglas demand functions.

## 5.4 Estimating Utility Functions

We've now seen several different forms for preferences and utility functions and have examined the kinds of demand behavior generated by these preferences. But in real life we usually have to work the other way around: we observe demand behavior, but our problem is to determine what kind of preferences generated the observed behavior.

For example, suppose that we observe a consumer's choices at several different prices and income levels. An example is depicted in Table 5.1. This is a table of the demand for two goods at the different levels of prices and incomes that prevailed in different years. We have also computed the share of income spent on each good in each year using the formulas $s_1 = p_1 x_1 / m$ and $s_2 = p_2 x_2 / m$.

For these data, the expenditure shares are relatively constant. There are small variations from observation to observation, but they probably aren't large enough to worry about. The average expenditure share for good 1 is about $1/4$, and the average income share for good 2 is about $3/4$. It appears that a utility function of the form $u(x_1, x_2) = x_1^{\frac{1}{4}} x_2^{\frac{3}{4}}$ seems to fit these data pretty well. That is, a utility function of this form would generate choice behavior that is pretty close to the observed choice behavior. For convenience we have calculated the utility associated with each observation using this estimated Cobb-Douglas utility function.

**Some data describing consumption behavior.**

Table 5.1

| Year | $p_1$ | $p_2$ | $m$ | $x_1$ | $x_2$ | $s_1$ | $s_2$ | Utility |
|------|-------|-------|-----|-------|-------|-------|-------|---------|
| 1 | 1 | 1 | 100 | 25 | 75 | .25 | .75 | 57.0 |
| 2 | 1 | 2 | 100 | 24 | 38 | .24 | .76 | 33.9 |
| 3 | 2 | 1 | 100 | 13 | 74 | .26 | .74 | 47.9 |
| 4 | 1 | 2 | 200 | 48 | 76 | .24 | .76 | 67.8 |
| 5 | 2 | 1 | 200 | 25 | 150 | .25 | .75 | 95.8 |
| 6 | 1 | 4 | 400 | 100 | 75 | .25 | .75 | 80.6 |
| 7 | 4 | 1 | 400 | 24 | 304 | .24 | .76 | 161.1 |

As far as we can tell from the observed behavior it appears as though the consumer is maximizing the function $u(x_1, x_2) = x_1^{\frac{1}{4}} x_2^{\frac{3}{4}}$. It may well be that further observations on the consumer's behavior would lead us to reject this hypothesis. But based on the data we have, the fit to the optimizing model is pretty good.

This has very important implications, since we can now use this "fitted" utility function to evaluate the impact of proposed policy changes. Suppose, for example, that the government was contemplating imposing a system of taxes that would result in this consumer facing prices $(2, 3)$ and having an income of 200. According to our estimates, the demanded bundle at these prices would be

$$x_1 = \frac{1}{4}\frac{200}{2} = 25$$

$$x_2 = \frac{3}{4}\frac{200}{3} = 50.$$

The estimated utility of this bundle is

$$u(x_1, x_2) = 25^{\frac{1}{4}} 50^{\frac{3}{4}} \approx 42.$$

This means that the new tax policy would make the consumer better off than he was in year 2, but worse off than he was in year 3. Thus we can use the observed choice behavior to value the implications of proposed policy changes on this consumer.

Since this is such an important idea in economics, let us review the logic one more time. Given some observations on choice behavior, we try to determine what, if anything, is being maximized. Once we have an estimate of what it is that is being maximized, we can use this both to predict choice behavior in new situations and to evaluate proposed changes in the economic environment.

Of course we have described a very simple situation. In reality, we normally don't have detailed data on individual consumption choices. But we often have data on groups of individuals—teenagers, middle-class households, elderly people, and so on. These groups may have different preferences for different goods that are reflected in their patterns of consumption expenditure. We can estimate a utility function that describes their consumption patterns and then use this estimated utility function to forecast demand and evaluate policy proposals.

In the simple example described above, it was apparent that income shares were relatively constant so that the Cobb-Douglas utility function would give us a pretty good fit. In other cases, a more complicated form for the utility function would be appropriate. The calculations may then become messier, and we may need to use a computer for the estimation, but the essential idea of the procedure is the same.

## 5.5 Implications of the MRS Condition

In the last section we examined the important idea that observation of demand behavior tells us important things about the underlying preferences of the consumers that generated that behavior. Given sufficient observations on consumer choices it will often be possible to estimate the utility function that generated those choices.

But even observing *one* consumer choice at one set of prices will allow us to make some kinds of useful inferences about how consumer utility will change when consumption changes. Let us see how this works.

In well-organized markets, it is typical that everyone faces roughly the same prices for goods. Take, for example, two goods like butter and milk. If everyone faces the same prices for butter and milk, and everyone is optimizing, and everyone is at an interior solution ... then everyone must have the same marginal rate of substitution for butter and milk.

This follows directly from the analysis given above. The market is offering everyone the same rate of exchange for butter and milk, and everyone is adjusting their consumption of the goods until their own "internal" marginal valuation of the two goods equals the market's "external" valuation of the two goods.

Now the interesting thing about this statement is that it is independent of income and tastes. People may value their *total* consumption of the two goods very differently. Some people may be consuming a lot of butter and a little milk, and some may be doing the reverse. Some wealthy people may be consuming a lot of milk and a lot of butter while other people may be consuming just a little of each good. But everyone who is consuming the two goods must have the same marginal rate of substitution. Everyone who is consuming the goods must agree on how much one is worth in terms of the other: how much of one they would be willing to sacrifice to get some more of the other.

The fact that price ratios measure marginal rates of substitution is very important, for it means that we have a way to value possible changes in consumption bundles. Suppose, for example, that the price of milk is $1 a quart and the price of butter is $2 a pound. Then the marginal rate of substitution for all people who consume milk and butter must be 2: they have to have 2 quarts of milk to compensate them for giving up 1 pound of butter. Or conversely, they have to have 1 pound of butter to make it worth their while to give up 2 quarts of milk. Hence everyone who is consuming both goods will value a marginal change in consumption in the same way.

Now suppose that an inventor discovers a new way of turning milk into butter: for every 3 quarts of milk poured into this machine, you get out 1 pound of butter, and no other useful byproducts. Question: is there a market for this device? Answer: the venture capitalists won't beat a path to his door, that's for sure. For everyone is already operating at a point where they are just willing to trade 2 quarts of milk for 1 pound of butter; why would they be willing to substitute 3 quarts of milk for 1 pound of butter? The answer is they wouldn't; this invention isn't worth anything.

But what would happen if he got it to run in reverse so he could dump in a pound of butter get out 3 quarts of milk? Is there a market for this device? Answer: yes! The market prices of milk and butter tell us that people are just barely willing to trade one pound of butter for 2 quarts of milk. So getting 3 quarts of milk for a pound of butter is a better deal than is currently being offered in the marketplace. Sign me up for a thousand shares! (And several pounds of butter.)

The market prices show that the first machine is unprofitable: it produces $2 of butter by using $3 of milk. The fact that it is unprofitable is just another way of saying that people value the inputs more than the outputs. The second machine produces $3 worth of milk by using only $2 worth of butter. This machine is profitable because people value the outputs more than the inputs.

The point is that, since prices measure the rate at which people are just willing to substitute one good for another, they can be used to value policy proposals that involve making changes in consumption. The fact that prices are not arbitrary numbers but reflect how people value things on the margin is one of the most fundamental and important ideas in economics.

If we observe one choice at one set of prices we get the MRS at one consumption point. If the prices change and we observe another choice we get another MRS. As we observe more and more choices we learn more and more about the shape of the underlying preferences that may have generated the observed choice behavior.

## 5.6 Choosing Taxes

Even the small bit of consumer theory we have discussed so far can be used to derive interesting and important conclusions. Here is a nice example describing a choice between two types of taxes. We saw that a **quantity**

**tax** is a tax on the amount consumed of a good, like a gasoline tax of 15 cents per gallon. An **income tax** is just a tax on income. If the government wants to raise a certain amount of revenue, is it better to raise it via a quantity tax or an income tax? Let's apply what we've learned to answer this question.

First we analyze the imposition of a quantity tax. Suppose that the original budget constraint is

$$p_1 x_1 + p_2 x_2 = m.$$

What is the budget constraint if we tax the consumption of good 1 at a rate of $t$? The answer is simple. From the viewpoint of the consumer it is just as if the price of good 1 has increased by an amount $t$. Thus the new budget constraint is

$$(p_1 + t)x_1 + p_2 x_2 = m. \tag{5.7}$$

Therefore a quantity tax on a good increases the price perceived by the consumer. Figure 5.9 gives an example of how that price change might affect demand. At this stage, we don't know for certain whether this tax will increase or decrease the consumption of good 1, although the presumption is that it will decrease it. Whichever is the case, we do know that the optimal choice, $(x_1^*, x_2^*)$, must satisfy the budget constraint

$$(p_1 + t)x_1^* + p_2 x_2^* = m. \tag{5.8}$$

The revenue raised by this tax is $R^* = tx_1^*$.

Let's now consider an income tax that raises the same amount of revenue. The form of this budget constraint would be

$$p_1 x_1 + p_2 x_2 = m - R^*$$

or, substituting for $R^*$,

$$p_1 x_1 + p_2 x_2 = m - tx_1^*.$$

Where does this budget line go in Figure 5.9?

It is easy to see that it has the same slope as the original budget line, $-p_1/p_2$, but the problem is to determine its location. As it turns out, the budget line with the income tax must pass through the point $(x_1^*, x_2^*)$. The way to check this is to plug $(x_1^*, x_2^*)$ into the income-tax budget constraint and see if it is satisfied.

Is it true that

$$p_1 x_1^* + p_2 x_2^* = m - tx_1^*?$$

Yes it is, since this is just a rearrangement of equation (5.8), which we know to be true.

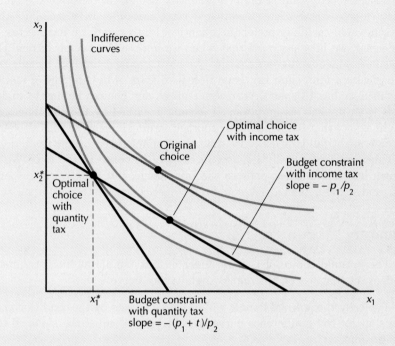

**Income tax versus a quantity tax.** Here we consider a quantity tax that raises revenue $R^*$ and an income tax that raises the same revenue. The consumer will be better off under the income tax, since he can choose a point on a higher indifference curve.

Figure
5.9

This establishes that $(x_1^*, x_2^*)$ lies on the income tax budget line: it is an *affordable* choice for the consumer. But is it an optimal choice? It is easy to see that the answer is no. At $(x_1^*, x_2^*)$ the MRS is $-(p_1 + t)/p_2$. But the income tax allows us to trade at a rate of exchange of $-p_1/p_2$. Thus the budget line cuts the indifference curve at $(x_1^*, x_2^*)$, which implies that there will be some point on the budget line that will be preferred to $(x_1^*, x_2^*)$.

Therefore the income tax is definitely superior to the quantity tax in the sense that you can raise the same amount of revenue from a consumer and still leave him or her better off under the income tax than under the quantity tax.

This is a nice result, and worth remembering, but it is also worthwhile understanding its limitations. First, it only applies to one consumer. The argument shows that for any given consumer there is an income tax that will raise as much money from that consumer as a quantity tax and leave him or her better off. But the amount of that income tax will typically differ from person to person. So a *uniform* income tax for all consumers is not necessarily better than a *uniform* quantity tax for all consumers. (Think about a case where some consumer doesn't consume any of good 1—this person would certainly prefer the quantity tax to a uniform income tax.)

Second, we have assumed that when we impose the tax on income the consumer's income doesn't change. We have assumed that the income tax is basically a lump sum tax—one that just changes the amount of money a consumer has to spend but doesn't affect any choices he has to make. This is an unlikely assumption. If income is earned by the consumer, we might expect that taxing it will discourage earning income, so that after-tax income might fall by even more than the amount taken by the tax.

Third, we have totally left out the supply response to the tax. We've shown how demand responds to the tax change, but supply will respond too, and a complete analysis would take those changes into account as well.

## Summary

1. The optimal choice of the consumer is that bundle in the consumer's budget set that lies on the highest indifference curve.

2. Typically the optimal bundle will be characterized by the condition that the slope of the indifference curve (the MRS) will equal the slope of the budget line.

3. If we observe several consumption choices it may be possible to estimate a utility function that would generate that sort of choice behavior. Such a utility function can be used to predict future choices and to estimate the utility to consumers of new economic policies.

4. If everyone faces the same prices for the two goods, then everyone will have the same marginal rate of substitution, and will thus be willing to trade off the two goods in the same way.

## REVIEW QUESTIONS

1. If two goods are perfect substitutes, what is the demand function for good 2?

2. Suppose that indifference curves are described by straight lines with a slope of $-b$. Given arbitrary prices and money income $p_1$, $p_2$, and $m$, what will the consumer's optimal choices look like?

3. Suppose that a consumer always consumes 2 spoons of sugar with each cup of coffee. If the price of sugar is $p_1$ per spoonful and the price of coffee is $p_2$ per cup and the consumer has $m$ dollars to spend on coffee and sugar, how much will he or she want to purchase?

4. Suppose that you have highly nonconvex preferences for ice cream and olives, like those given in the text, and that you face prices $p_1$, $p_2$ and have $m$ dollars to spend. List the choices for the optimal consumption bundles.

5. If a consumer has a utility function $u(x_1, x_2) = x_1 x_2^4$, what fraction of her income will she spend on good 2?

6. For what kind of preferences will the consumer be just as well-off facing a quantity tax as an income tax?

# CHAPTER **6**

# DEMAND

In the last chapter we presented the basic model of consumer choice: how maximizing utility subject to a budget constraint yields optimal choices. We saw that the optimal choices of the consumer depend on the consumer's income and the prices of the goods, and we worked a few examples to see what the optimal choices are for some simple kinds of preferences.

The consumer's **demand functions** give the optimal amounts of each of the goods as a function of the prices and income faced by the consumer. We write the demand functions as

$$x_1 = x_1(p_1, p_2, m)$$
$$x_2 = x_2(p_1, p_2, m).$$

The left-hand side of each equation stands for the quantity demanded. The right-hand side of each equation is the function that relates the prices and income to that quantity.

In this chapter we will examine how the demand for a good changes as prices and income change. Studying how a choice responds to changes in the economic environment is known as **comparative statics**, which we first described in Chapter 1. "Comparative" means that we want to compare two situations: before and after the change in the economic environment. "Statics" means that we are not concerned with any adjustment process that may be involved in moving from one choice to another; rather we will only examine the equilibrium choice.

In the case of the consumer, there are only two things in our model that affect the optimal choice: prices and income. The comparative statics questions in consumer theory therefore involve investigating how demand changes when prices and income change.

## 6.1 Normal and Inferior Goods

We start by considering how a consumer's demand for a good changes as his income changes. We want to know how the optimal choice at one income compares to the optimal choice at another level of income. During this exercise, we will hold the prices fixed and examine only the change in demand due to the income change.

We know how an increase in money income affects the budget line when prices are fixed—it shifts it outward in a parallel fashion. So how does this affect demand?

We would normally think that the demand for each good would increase when income increases, as shown in Figure 6.1. Economists, with a singular lack of imagination, call such goods **normal** goods. If good 1 is a normal good, then the demand for it increases when income increases, and decreases when income decreases. For a normal good the quantity demanded always changes in the same way as income changes:

$$\frac{dx_1}{dm} > 0.$$

If something is called normal, you can be sure that there must be a *possibility* of being abnormal. And indeed there is. Figure 6.2 presents an example of nice, well-behaved indifference curves where an increase of income results in a *reduction* in the consumption of one of the goods. Such a good is called an **inferior** good. This may be "abnormal," but when you think about it, inferior goods aren't all that unusual. There are many goods for which demand decreases as income increases; examples might include gruel, bologna, shacks, or nearly any kind of low-quality good.

Whether a good is inferior or not depends on the income level that we are examining. It might very well be that very poor people consume more bologna as their income increases. But after a point, the consumption of bologna would probably decline as income continued to increase. Since in real life the consumption of goods can increase or decrease when income increases, it is comforting to know that economic theory allows for both possibilities.

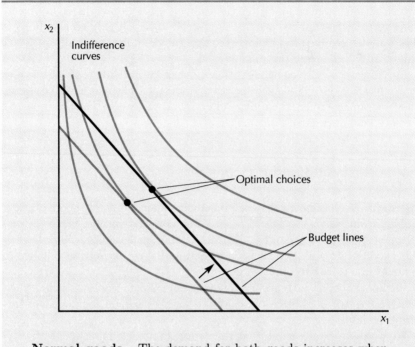

Figure
6.1
**Normal goods.** The demand for both goods increases when income increases, so both goods are normal goods.

## 6.2 Income Offer Curves and Engel Curves

We have seen that an increase in income corresponds to shifting the budget line outward in a parallel manner. We can connect together the demanded bundles that we get as we shift the budget line outward to construct the **income offer curve**. This curve illustrates the bundles of goods that are demanded at the different levels of income, as depicted in Figure 6.3A. The income offer curve is also known as the **income expansion path**. If both goods are normal goods, then the income expansion path will have a positive slope, as depicted in Figure 6.3A.

For each level of income, $m$, there will be some optimal choice for each of the goods. Let us focus on good 1 and consider the optimal choice at each set of prices and income, $x_1(p_1, p_2, m)$. This is simply the demand function for good 1. If we hold the prices of goods 1 and 2 fixed and look at how demand changes as we change income, we generate a curve known as the **Engel curve**. The Engel curve is a graph of the demand for one of the goods as a function of income, with all prices being held constant. For an example of an Engel curve, see Figure 6.3B.

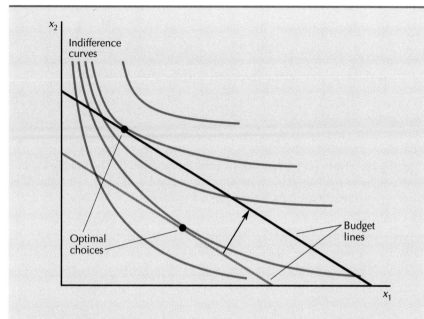

**An inferior good.** Good 1 is an inferior good, which means that the demand for it decreases when income increases.

Figure
6.2

**A** Income offer curve                    **B** Engel curve

**How demand changes as income changes.** The income of-fer curve (or income expansion path) shown in panel A depicts the optimal choice at different levels of income and constant prices. When we plot the optimal choice of good 1 against in-come, $m$, we get the Engel curve, depicted in panel B.

Figure
6.3

## 6.3 Some Examples

Let's consider some of the preferences that we examined in Chapter 5 and see what their income offer curves and Engel curves look like.

### Perfect Substitutes

The case of perfect substitutes is depicted in Figure 6.4. If $p_1 < p_2$, so that the consumer is specializing in consuming good 1, then if his income increases he will increase his consumption of good 1. Thus the income offer curve is the horizontal axis, as shown in Figure 6.4A.

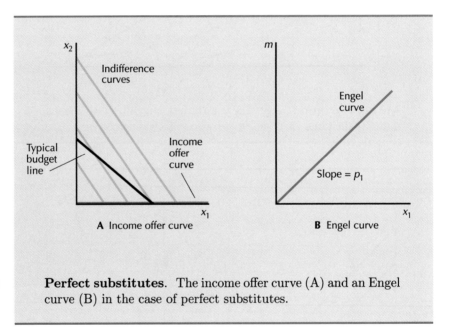

**A** Income offer curve        **B** Engel curve

Figure 6.4    **Perfect substitutes.** The income offer curve (A) and an Engel curve (B) in the case of perfect substitutes.

Since the demand for good 1 is $x_1 = m/p_1$ in this case, the Engel curve will be a straight line with a slope of $p_1$, as depicted in Figure 6.4B. (Since $m$ is on the vertical axis, and $x_1$ on the horizontal axis, we can write $m = p_1 x_1$, which makes it clear that the slope is $p_1$.)

### Perfect Complements

The demand behavior for perfect complements is shown in Figure 6.5. Since the consumer will always consume the same amount of each good, no matter what, the income offer curve is the diagonal line through the origin as depicted in Figure 6.5A. We have seen that the demand for good 1 is $x_1 = m/(p_1 + p_2)$, so the Engel curve is a straight line with a slope of $p_1 + p_2$ as shown in Figure 6.5B.

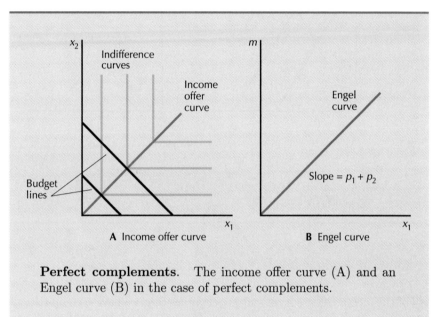

**A** Income offer curve    **B** Engel curve

**Perfect complements.** The income offer curve (A) and an Engel curve (B) in the case of perfect complements.

Figure 6.5

## Cobb-Douglas Preferences

For the case of Cobb-Douglas preferences it is easier to look at the algebraic form of the demand functions to see what the graphs will look like. If $u(x_1, x_2) = x_1^a x_2^{1-a}$, the Cobb-Douglas demand for good 1 has the form $x_1 = am/p_1$. For a fixed value of $p_1$, this is a *linear* function of $m$. Thus doubling $m$ will double demand, tripling $m$ will triple demand, and so on. In fact, multiplying $m$ by any positive number $t$ will just multiply demand by the same amount.

The demand for good 2 is $x_2 = (1-a)m/p_2$, and this is also clearly linear. The fact that the demand functions for both goods are linear functions of income means that the income expansion paths will be straight lines through the origin, as depicted in Figure 6.6A. The Engel curve for good 1 will be a straight line with a slope of $p_1/a$, as depicted in Figure 6.6B.

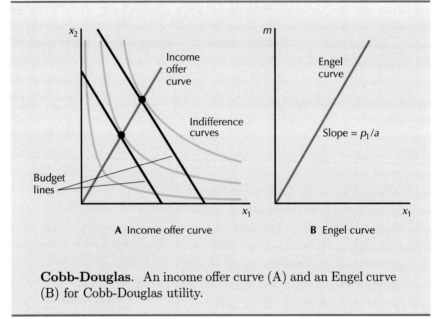

**A** Income offer curve    **B** Engel curve

Figure
6.6

**Cobb-Douglas.** An income offer curve (A) and an Engel curve
(B) for Cobb-Douglas utility.

## Homothetic Preferences

All of the income offer curves and Engel curves that we have seen up to now
have been straightforward—in fact they've been straight lines! This has
happened because our examples have been so simple. Real Engel curves do
not have to be straight lines. In general, when income goes up, the demand
for a good could increase more or less rapidly than income increases. If the
demand for a good goes up by a greater proportion than income, we say
that it is a **luxury good**, and if it goes up by a lesser proportion than
income we say that it is a **necessary good**.

The dividing line is the case where the demand for a good goes up by
the same proportion as income. This is what happened in the three cases
we examined above. What aspect of the consumer's preferences leads to
this behavior?

Suppose that the consumer's preferences only depend on the *ratio* of
good 1 to good 2. This means that if the consumer prefers $(x_1, x_2)$ to
$(y_1, y_2)$, then she automatically prefers $(2x_1, 2x_2)$ to $(2y_1, 2y_2)$, $(3x_1, 3x_2)$
to $(3y_1, 3y_2)$, and so on, since the ratio of good 1 to good 2 is the same for
all of these bundles. In fact, the consumer prefers $(tx_1, tx_2)$ to $(ty_1, ty_2)$ for
any positive value of $t$. Preferences that have this property are known as
**homothetic preferences**. It is not hard to show that the three examples
of preferences given above—perfect substitutes, perfect complements, and
Cobb-Douglas—are all homothetic preferences.

If the consumer has homothetic preferences, then the income offer curves are all straight lines through the origin, as shown in Figure 6.7. More specifically, if preferences are homothetic, it means that when income is scaled up or down by any amount $t > 0$, the demanded bundle scales up or down by the same amount. This can be established rigorously, but it is fairly clear from looking at the picture. If the indifference curve is tangent to the budget line at $(x_1^*, x_2^*)$, then the indifference curve through $(tx_1^*, tx_2^*)$ is tangent to the budget line that has $t$ times as much income and the same prices. This implies that the Engel curves are straight lines as well. If you double income, you just double the demand for each good.

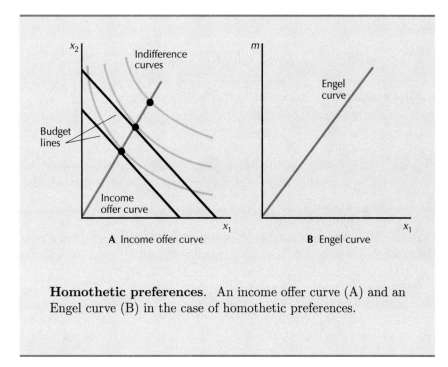

**Homothetic preferences.** An income offer curve (A) and an Engel curve (B) in the case of homothetic preferences.

Figure
6.7

Homothetic preferences are very convenient since the income effects are so simple. Unfortunately, homothetic preferences aren't very realistic for the same reason! But they will often be of use in our examples.

## Quasilinear Preferences

Another kind of preferences that generates a special form of income offer curves and Engel curves is the case of quasilinear preferences. Recall the definition of quasilinear preferences given in Chapter 4. This is the case where all indifference curves are parallel or "shifted" versions of one indifference curve as in Figure 6.8. These preferences can be represented by a utility function of the form

$$u(x_1, x_2) = v(x_1) + x_2.$$

The maximization problem for a utility function like this is

$$\max_{x_1, x_2} v(x_1) + x_2$$

$$\text{s.t. } p_1 x_1 + p_2 x_2 = m.$$

Solving the budget constraint for $x_2$ as a function of $x_1$ and substituting into the objective function, we have

$$\max_{x_1} v(x_1) + m/p_2 - p_1 x_1/p_2.$$

Differentiating gives us the first-order condition

$$v'(x_1^*) = \frac{p_1}{p_2}.$$

This demand function has the interesting feature that the demand for good 1 must be independent of income. The inverse demand curve is given by

$$p_1(x_1) = v'(x_1)p_2.$$

That is, the inverse demand function for good 1 is the derivative of the utility function times $p_2$. Once we have the demand function for good 1, the demand function for good 2 comes from the budget constraint.

We can also think of this feature in terms of budget lines. What happens if we shift the budget line outward? In this case, if an indifference curve is tangent to the budget line at a bundle $(x_1^*, x_2^*)$, then another indifference curve must also be tangent at $(x_1^*, x_2^* + k)$ for any constant $k$. Increasing income doesn't change the demand for good 1 at all, and all the extra income goes entirely to the consumption of good 2. If preferences are quasilinear, we sometimes say that there is a "zero income effect" for good 1. Thus the Engel curve for good 1 is a vertical line—as you change income, the demand for good 1 remains constant.

For example, let us calculate the demand functions for the utility function

$$u(x_1, x_2) = \ln x_1 + x_2.$$

Applying the first-order condition gives

$$\frac{1}{x_1} = \frac{p_1}{p_2},$$

so the direct demand function for good 1 is

$$x_1 = \frac{p_2}{p_1},$$

and the inverse demand function is

$$p_1(x_1) = \frac{p_2}{x_1}.$$

The direct demand function for good 2 comes from substituting $x_1 = p_2/p_1$ into the budget constraint:

$$x_2 = \frac{m}{p_2} - 1.$$

A warning is in order concerning these demand functions. Note that the demand for good 1 is independent of income in this example. This is a general feature of a quasilinear utility function—the demand for good 1 remains constant as income changes. However, this can only be true for some values of income. A demand function can't literally be independent of income for *all* values of income; after all, when income is zero, all demands are zero. It turns out that the quasilinear demand function derived above is only relevant when a positive amount of each good is being consumed.

In this example, when $m < p_2$, the optimal consumption of good 2 will be zero. As income increases the marginal utility of consumption of good 1 decreases. When $m = p_2$, the marginal utility from spending additional income on good 1 just equals the marginal utility from spending additional income on good 2. After that point, the consumer spends all additional income on good 2.

So a better way to write the demand for good 2 is:

$$x_2 = \begin{cases} 0 & \text{when } m \le p_2 \\ m/p_2 - 1 & \text{when } m > p_2 \end{cases}.$$

What would be a real-life situation where this kind of thing might occur? Suppose good 1 is pencils and good 2 is money to spend on other goods. Initially I may spend my income only on pencils, but when my income gets large enough, I stop buying additional pencils—all of my extra income is spent on other goods. Other examples of this sort might be salt or toothpaste. When we are examining a choice between all other goods and some single good that isn't a very large part of the consumer's budget, the quasilinear assumption may well be plausible, at least when the consumer's income is sufficiently large.

For more on the properties of quasilinear demand functions see Hal R. Varian, *Microeconomic Analysis,* 3rd ed. (New York: Norton, 1992).

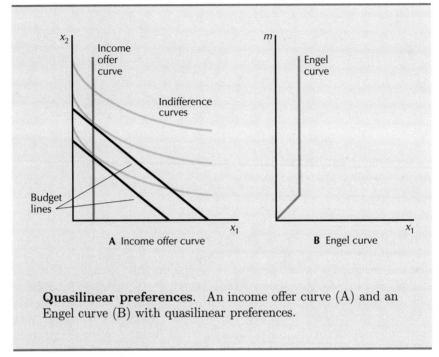

**A** Income offer curve  **B** Engel curve

Figure 6.8

**Quasilinear preferences.** An income offer curve (A) and an Engel curve (B) with quasilinear preferences.

## 6.4 Ordinary Goods and Giffen Goods

Let us now consider price changes. Suppose that we decrease the price of good 1 and hold the price of good 2 and money income fixed. Then what can happen to the quantity demanded of good 1? Intuition tells us that the quantity demanded of good 1 should increase when its price decreases. Indeed this is the ordinary case, as depicted in Figure 6.9.

When the price of good 1 decreases, the budget line becomes flatter. Or said another way, the vertical intercept is fixed and the horizontal intercept moves to the right. In Figure 6.9, the optimal choice of good 1 moves to the right as well: the quantity demanded of good 1 has increased. But we might wonder whether this always happens this way. Is it always the case that, no matter what kind of preferences the consumer has, the demand for a good must increase when its price goes down?

As it turns out, the answer is no. It is logically possible to find well-behaved preferences for which a decrease in the price of good 1 leads to a reduction in the demand for good 1. Such a good is called a **Giffen good**, after the nineteenth-century economist who first noted the possibility. An example is illustrated in Figure 6.10.

What is going on here in economic terms? What kind of preferences might give rise to the peculiar behavior depicted in Figure 6.10? Suppose that the two goods that you are consuming are gruel and milk and that

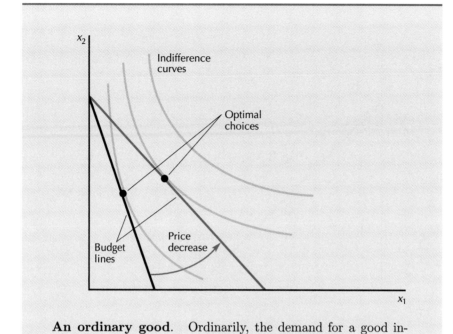

**An ordinary good**.  Ordinarily, the demand for a good in-       Figure
creases when its price decreases, as is the case here.              6.9

you are currently consuming 7 bowls of gruel and 7 cups of milk a week.
Now the price of gruel declines. If you consume the same 7 bowls of gruel
a week, you will have money left over with which you can purchase more
milk. In fact, with the extra money you have saved because of the lower
price of gruel, you may decide to consume even more milk and reduce your
consumption of gruel. The reduction in the price of gruel has freed up some
extra money to be spent on other things—but one thing you might want to
do with it is reduce your consumption of gruel! Thus the price change is to
some extent *like* an income change. Even though *money* income remains
constant, a change in the price of a good will change purchasing power,
and thereby change demand.

So the Giffen good is not implausible purely on logical grounds, although
Giffen goods are unlikely to be encountered in real-world behavior. Most
goods are ordinary goods—when their price increases, the demand for them
declines. We'll see why this is the ordinary situation a little later.

Incidentally, it is no accident that we used gruel as an example of both
an inferior good and a Giffen good. It turns out that there is an intimate
relationship between the two which we will explore in a later chapter.

But for now our exploration of consumer theory may leave you with
the impression that nearly anything can happen: if income increases the
demand for a good can go up or down, and if price increases the demand can

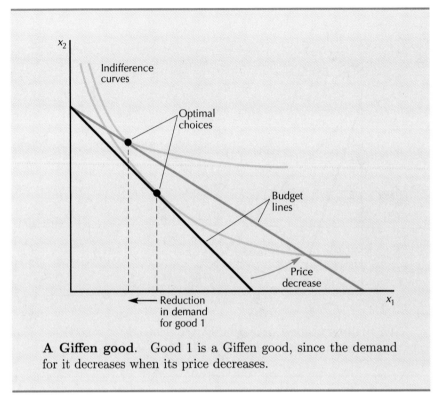

Figure
6.10

**A Giffen good.** Good 1 is a Giffen good, since the demand for it decreases when its price decreases.

go up or down. Is consumer theory compatible with *any* kind of behavior? Or are there some kinds of behavior that the economic model of consumer behavior rules out? It turns out that there *are* restrictions on behavior imposed by the maximizing model. But we'll have to wait until the next chapter to see what they are.

## 6.5 The Price Offer Curve and the Demand Curve

Suppose that we let the price of good 1 change while we hold $p_2$ and income fixed. Geometrically this involves pivoting the budget line. We can think of connecting together the optimal points to construct the **price offer curve** as illustrated in Figure 6.11A. This curve represents the bundles that would be demanded at different prices for good 1.

We can depict this same information in a different way. Again, hold the price of good 2 and money income fixed, and for each different value of $p_1$ plot the optimal level of consumption of good 1. The result is the **demand curve** depicted in Figure 6.11B. The demand curve is a plot of the demand function, $x_1(p_1, p_2, m)$, holding $p_2$ and $m$ fixed at some predetermined values.

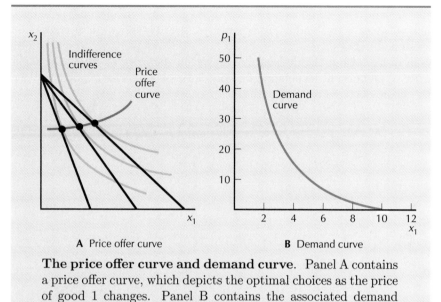

**A** Price offer curve                                    **B** Demand curve

**The price offer curve and demand curve.** Panel A contains
a price offer curve, which depicts the optimal choices as the price
of good 1 changes.  Panel B contains the associated demand
curve, which depicts a plot of the optimal choice of good 1 as a
function of its price.

Figure
6.11

Ordinarily, when the price of a good increases, the demand for that
good will decrease.  Thus the price and quantity of a good will move in
*opposite* directions, which means that the demand curve will typically have
a negative slope. In terms of rates of change, we would normally have

$$\frac{dx_1}{dp_1} < 0,$$

which simply says that demand curves usually have a negative slope.

However, we have also seen that in the case of Giffen goods, the demand
for a good may decrease when its price decreases. Thus it is possible, but
not likely, to have a demand curve with a positive slope.

## 6.6 Some Examples

Let's look at a few examples of demand curves, using the preferences that
we discussed in Chapter 3.

### Perfect Substitutes

The offer curve and demand curve for perfect substitutes—the red and blue
pencils example—are illustrated in Figure 6.12. As we saw in Chapter 5,

the demand for good 1 is zero when $p_1 > p_2$, any amount on the budget line when $p_1 = p_2$, and $m/p_1$ when $p_1 < p_2$. The offer curve traces out these possibilities.

In order to find the demand curve, we fix the price of good 2 at some price $p_2^*$ and graph the demand for good 1 versus the price of good 1 to get the shape depicted in Figure 6.12B.

**A** Price offer curve    **B** Demand curve

Figure
6.12

**Perfect substitutes.** Price offer curve (A) and demand curve (B) in the case of perfect substitutes.

## Perfect Complements

The case of perfect complements—the right and left shoes example—is depicted in Figure 6.13. We know that whatever the prices are, a consumer will demand the same amount of goods 1 and 2. Thus his offer curve will be a diagonal line as depicted in Figure 6.13A.

We saw in Chapter 5 that the demand for good 1 is given by

$$x_1 = \frac{m}{p_1 + p_2}.$$

If we fix $m$ and $p_2$ and plot the relationship between $x_1$ and $p_1$, we get the curve depicted in Figure 6.13B.

## A Discrete Good

Suppose that good 1 is a discrete good. If $p_1$ is very high then the consumer will strictly prefer to consume zero units; if $p_1$ is low enough the consumer

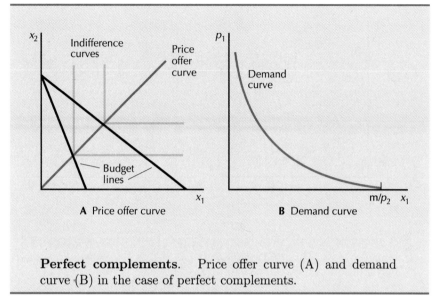

**Perfect complements.**    Price offer curve (A) and demand curve (B) in the case of perfect complements.

Figure
6.13

will strictly prefer to consume one unit. At some price $r_1$, the consumer will be indifferent between consuming good 1 or not consuming it. The price at which the consumer is just indifferent to consuming or not consuming the good is called the **reservation price**.[1] The indifference curves and demand curve are depicted in Figure 6.14.

It is clear from the diagram that the demand behavior can be described by a sequence of reservation prices at which the consumer is just willing to purchase another unit of the good. At a price of $r_1$ the consumer is willing to buy 1 unit of the good; if the price falls to $r_2$, he is willing to buy another unit, and so on.

These prices can be described in terms of the original utility function. For example, $r_1$ is the price where the consumer is just indifferent between consuming 0 or 1 unit of good 1, so it must satisfy the equation

$$u(0, m) = u(1, m - r_1).  \tag{6.1}$$

Similarly $r_2$ satisfies the equation

$$u(1, m - r_2) = u(2, m - 2r_2).  \tag{6.2}$$

---

[1] The term reservation price comes from auction markets. When someone wanted to sell something in an auction he would typically state a minimum price at which he was willing to sell the good. If the best price offered was below this stated price, the seller reserved the right to purchase the item himself. This price became known as the seller's reservation price and eventually came to be used to describe the price at which someone was just willing to buy or sell some item.

**A** Optimal bundles at different prices    **B** Demand curve

Figure
6.14

**A discrete good.** As the price of good 1 decreases there will
be some price, the reservation price, at which the consumer is
just indifferent between consuming good 1 or not consuming it.
As the price decreases further, more units of the discrete good
will be demanded.

The left-hand side of this equation is the utility from consuming one unit of
the good at a price of $r_2$. The right-hand side is the utility from consuming
two units of the good, each of which sells for $r_2$.

If the utility function is quasilinear, then the formulas describing the
reservation prices become somewhat simpler. If $u(x_1, x_2) = v(x_1) + x_2$,
and $v(0) = 0$, then we can write equation (6.1) as

$$v(0) + m = m = v(1) + m - r_1.$$

Since $v(0) = 0$, we can solve for $r_1$ to find

$$r_1 = v(1). \tag{6.3}$$

Similarly, we can write equation (6.2) as

$$v(1) + m - r_2 = v(2) + m - 2r_2.$$

Canceling terms and rearranging, this expression becomes

$$r_2 = v(2) - v(1).$$

Proceeding in this manner, the reservation price for the third unit of consumption is given by

$$r_3 = v(3) - v(2)$$

and so on.

In each case, the reservation price measures the increment in utility necessary to induce the consumer to choose an additional unit of the good. Loosely speaking, the reservation prices measure the marginal utilities associated with different levels of consumption of good 1. Our assumption of convex preferences implies that the sequence of reservation prices must decrease: $r_1 > r_2 > r_3 \cdots$.

Because of the special structure of the quasilinear utility function, the reservation prices do not depend on the amount of good 2 that the consumer has. This is certainly a special case, but it makes it very easy to describe demand behavior. Given any price $p$, we just find where it falls in the list of reservation prices. Suppose that $p$ falls between $r_6$ and $r_7$, for example. The fact that $r_6 > p$ means that the consumer is willing to give up $p$ dollars per unit bought to get 6 units of good 1, and the fact that $p > r_7$ means that the consumer is not willing to give up $p$ dollars per unit to get the seventh unit of good 1.

This argument is quite intuitive, but let's look at the math just to make sure that it is clear. Suppose that the consumer demands 6 units of good 1. We want to show that we must have $r_6 \geq p \geq r_7$.

If the consumer is maximizing utility, then we must have

$$v(6) + m - 6p \geq v(x_1) + m - px_1$$

for all possible choices of $x_1$. In particular, we must have that

$$v(6) + m - 6p \geq v(5) + m - 5p.$$

Rearranging this equation we have

$$r_6 = v(6) - v(5) \geq p,$$

which is half of what we wanted to show.

By the same logic,

$$v(6) + m - 6p \geq v(7) + m - 7p.$$

Rearranging this gives us

$$p \geq v(7) - v(6) = r_7,$$

which is the other half of the inequality we wanted to establish.

## 6.7 Substitutes and Complements

We have already used the terms substitutes and complements, but it is now appropriate to give a formal definition. Since we have seen *perfect* substitutes and *perfect* complements several times already, it seems reasonable to look at the imperfect case.

Let's think about substitutes first. We said that red pencils and blue pencils might be thought of as perfect substitutes, at least for someone who didn't care about color. But what about pencils and pens? This is a case of "imperfect" substitutes. That is, pens and pencils are, to some degree, a substitute for each other, although they aren't as perfect a substitute for each other as red pencils and blue pencils.

Similarly, we said that right shoes and left shoes were perfect complements. But what about a pair of shoes and a pair of socks? Right shoes and left shoes are nearly always consumed together, and shoes and socks are *usually* consumed together. Complementary goods are those like shoes and socks that tend to be consumed together, albeit not always.

Now that we've discussed the basic idea of complements and substitutes, we can give a precise economic definition. Recall that the demand function for good 1, say, will typically be a function of the price of both good 1 and good 2, so we write $x_1(p_1, p_2, m)$. We can ask how the demand for good 1 changes as the price of good 2 changes: does it go up or down?

If the demand for good 1 goes up when the price of good 2 goes up, then we say that good 1 is a **substitute** for good 2. In terms of rates of change, good 1 is a substitute for good 2 if

$$\frac{dx_1}{dp_2} > 0.$$

The idea is that when good 2 gets more expensive the consumer switches to consuming good 1: the consumer *substitutes* away from the more expensive good to the less expensive good.

On the other hand, if the demand for good 1 goes down when the price of good 2 goes up, we say that good 1 is a **complement** to good 2. This means that

$$\frac{dx_1}{dp_2} < 0.$$

Complements are goods that are consumed together, like coffee and sugar, so when the price of one good rises, the consumption of both goods will tend to decrease.

The cases of perfect substitutes and perfect complements illustrate these points nicely. Note that $dx_1/dp_2$ is positive (or zero) in the case of perfect substitutes, and that $dx_1/dp_2$ is negative in the case of perfect complements.

A couple of warnings are in order about these concepts. First, the two-good case is rather special when it comes to complements and substitutes. Since income is being held fixed, if you spend more money on good 1, you'll have to spend less on good 2. This puts some restrictions on the kinds of behavior that are possible. When there are more than two goods, these restrictions are not so much of a problem.

Second, although the definition of substitutes and complements in terms of consumer demand behavior seems sensible, there are some difficulties with the definitions in more general environments. For example, if we use the above definitions in a situation involving more than two goods, it is perfectly possible that good 1 may be a substitute for good 3, but good 3 may be a complement for good 1. Because of this peculiar feature, more advanced treatments typically use a somewhat different definition of substitutes and complements. The definitions given above describe concepts known as **gross substitutes** and **gross complements**; they will be sufficient for our needs.

## 6.8 The Inverse Demand Function

If we hold $p_2$ and $m$ fixed and plot $p_1$ against $x_1$ we get the **demand curve**. As suggested above, we typically think that the demand curve slopes downwards, so that higher prices lead to less demand, although the Giffen example shows that it could be otherwise.

As long as we do have a downward-sloping demand curve, as is usual, it is meaningful to speak of the **inverse demand function**. The inverse demand function is the demand function viewing price as a function of quantity. That is, for each level of demand for good 1, the inverse demand function measures what the price of good 1 would have to be in order for the consumer to choose that level of consumption. So the inverse demand function measures the same relationship as the direct demand function, but just from another point of view. Figure 6.15 depicts the inverse demand function—or the direct demand function, depending on your point of view.

Recall, for example, the Cobb-Douglas demand for good 1, $x_1 = am/p_1$. We could just as well write the relationship between price and quantity as $p_1 = am/x_1$. The first representation is the direct demand function; the second is the inverse demand function.

The inverse demand function has a useful economic interpretation. Recall that as long as both goods are being consumed in positive amounts, the optimal choice must satisfy the condition that the absolute value of the MRS equals the price ratio:

$$|\text{MRS}| = \frac{p_1}{p_2}.$$

This says that at the optimal level of demand for good 1, for example, we must have

$$p_1 = p_2|\text{MRS}|. \tag{6.4}$$

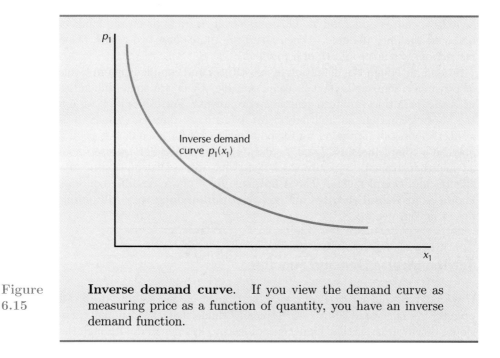

Figure
6.15

**Inverse demand curve.** If you view the demand curve as measuring price as a function of quantity, you have an inverse demand function.

Thus, at the optimal level of demand for good 1, the price of good 1 is proportional to the absolute value of the MRS between good 1 and good 2.

Suppose for simplicity that the price of good 2 is one. Then equation (6.4) tells us that at the optimal level of demand, the price of good 1 measures how much the consumer is willing to give up of good 2 in order to get a little more of good 1. In this case the inverse demand function is simply measuring the absolute value of the MRS. For any optimal level of $x_1$ the inverse demand function tells how much of good 2 the consumer would want to have to compensate him for a small reduction in the amount of good 1. Or, turning this around, the inverse demand function measures how much the consumer would be willing to sacrifice of good 2 to make him just indifferent to having a little more of good 1.

If we think of good 2 as being money to spend on other goods, then we can think of the MRS as being how many dollars the individual would be willing to give up to have a little more of good 1. We suggested earlier that in this case, we can think of the MRS as measuring the marginal willingness to pay. Since the price of good 1 is just the MRS in this case, this means that the price of good 1 itself is measuring the marginal willingness to pay.

At each quantity $x_1$, the inverse demand function measures how many dollars the consumer is willing to give up for a little more of good 1; or, said another way, how many dollars the consumer was willing to give up for the last unit purchased of good 1. For a small enough amount of good 1, they come down to the same thing.

Looked at in this way, the downward-sloping demand curve has a new meaning. When $x_1$ is very small, the consumer is willing to give up a lot of money—that is, a lot of other goods, to acquire a little bit more of good 1. As $x_1$ is larger, the consumer is willing to give up less money, on the margin, to acquire a little more of good 1. Thus the marginal willingness to pay, in the sense of the marginal willingness to sacrifice good 2 for good 1, is decreasing as we increase the consumption of good 1.

## Summary

1. The consumer's demand function for a good will in general depend on the prices of all goods and income.

2. A normal good is one for which the demand increases when income increases. An inferior good is one for which the demand decreases when income increases.

3. An ordinary good is one for which the demand decreases when its price increases. A Giffen good is one for which the demand increases when its price increases.

4. If the demand for good 1 increases when the price of good 2 increases, then good 1 is a substitute for good 2. If the demand for good 1 decreases in this situation, then it is a complement for good 2.

5. The inverse demand function measures the price at which a given quantity will be demanded. The height of the demand curve at a given level of consumption measures the marginal willingness to pay for an additional unit of the good at that consumption level.

## REVIEW QUESTIONS

1. If the consumer is consuming exactly two goods, and she is always spending all of her money, can both of them be inferior goods?

2. Show that perfect substitutes are an example of homothetic preferences.

3. Show that Cobb-Douglas preferences are homothetic preferences.

4. The income offer curve is to the Engel curve as the price offer curve is to ...?

5. If the preferences are concave will the consumer ever consume both of the goods together?

6. Are hamburgers and buns complements or substitutes?

7. What is the form of the inverse demand function for good 1 in the case of perfect complements?

8. True or false? If the demand function is $x_1 = -p_1$, then the inverse demand function is $x = -1/p_1$.

# CHAPTER 7

# REVEALED
# PREFERENCE

In Chapter 6 we saw how we can use information about the consumer's preferences and budget constraint to determine his or her demand. In this chapter we reverse this process and show how we can use information about the consumer's demand to discover information about his or her preferences. Up until now, we were thinking about what preferences could tell us about people's behavior. But in real life, preferences are not directly observable: we have to discover people's preferences from observing their behavior. In this chapter we'll develop some tools to do this.

When we talk of determining people's preferences from observing their behavior, we have to assume that the preferences will remain unchanged while we observe the behavior. Over very long time spans, this is not very reasonable. But for the monthly or quarterly time spans that economists usually deal with, it seems unlikely that a particular consumer's tastes would change radically. Thus we will adopt a maintained hypothesis that the consumer's preferences are stable over the time period for which we observe his or her choice behavior.

## 7.1 The Idea of Revealed Preference

Before we begin this investigation, let's adopt the convention that in this chapter, the underlying preferences—whatever they may be—are known to be strictly convex. Thus there will be a *unique* demanded bundle at each budget. This assumption is not necessary for the theory of revealed preference, but the exposition will be simpler with it.

Consider Figure 7.1, where we have depicted a consumer's demanded bundle, $(x_1, x_2)$, and another arbitrary bundle, $(y_1, y_2)$, that is beneath the consumer's budget line. Suppose that we are willing to postulate that this consumer is an optimizing consumer of the sort we have been studying. What can we say about the consumer's preferences between these two bundles of goods?

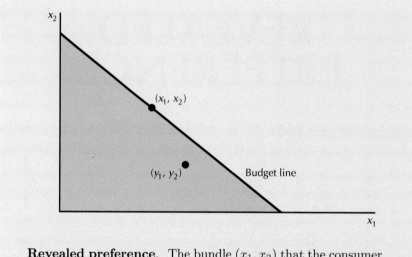

Figure
7.1

**Revealed preference.** The bundle $(x_1, x_2)$ that the consumer chooses is revealed preferred to the bundle $(y_1, y_2)$, a bundle that he could have chosen.

Well, the bundle $(y_1, y_2)$ is certainly an affordable purchase at the given budget—the consumer could have bought it if he or she wanted to, and would even have had money left over. Since $(x_1, x_2)$ is the *optimal* bundle, it must be better than anything else that the consumer could afford. Hence, in particular it must be better than $(y_1, y_2)$.

The same argument holds for any bundle on or underneath the budget line other than the demanded bundle. Since it *could* have been bought at the given budget but wasn't, then what *was* bought must be better. Here is where we use the assumption that there is a *unique* demanded bundle for each budget. If preferences are not strictly convex, so that indifference curves have flat spots, it may be that some bundles that are *on* the budget line might be just as good as the demanded bundle. This complication can be handled without too much difficulty, but it is easier to just assume it away.

In Figure 7.1 all of the bundles in the shaded area underneath the budget line are revealed worse than the demanded bundle $(x_1, x_2)$. This is because they could have been chosen, but were rejected in favor of $(x_1, x_2)$. We will now translate this geometric discussion of revealed preference into algebra.

Let $(x_1, x_2)$ be the bundle purchased at prices $(p_1, p_2)$ when the consumer has income $m$. What does it mean to say that $(y_1, y_2)$ is affordable at those prices and income? It simply means that $(y_1, y_2)$ satisfies the budget constraint

$$p_1 y_1 + p_2 y_2 \leq m.$$

Since $(x_1, x_2)$ is actually bought at the given budget, it must satisfy the budget constraint with equality

$$p_1 x_1 + p_2 x_2 = m.$$

Putting these two equations together, the fact that $(y_1, y_2)$ is affordable at the budget $(p_1, p_2, m)$ means that

$$p_1 x_1 + p_2 x_2 \geq p_1 y_1 + p_2 y_2.$$

If the above inequality is satisfied and $(y_1, y_2)$ is actually a different bundle from $(x_1, x_2)$, we say that $(x_1, x_2)$ is **directly revealed preferred** to $(y_1, y_2)$.

Note that the left-hand side of this inequality is the expenditure on the bundle that is *actually chosen* at prices $(p_1, p_2)$. Thus revealed preference is a relation that holds between the bundle that is actually demanded at some budget and the bundles that *could have been* demanded at that budget.

The term "revealed preference" is actually a bit misleading. It does not inherently have anything to do with preferences, although we've seen above that if the consumer is making optimal choices, the two ideas are closely related. Instead of saying "$X$ is revealed preferred to $Y$," it would be better to say "$X$ is chosen over $Y$." When we say that $X$ is revealed preferred to $Y$, all we are claiming is that $X$ is chosen when $Y$ could have been chosen; that is, that $p_1 x_1 + p_2 x_2 \geq p_1 y_1 + p_2 y_2$.

## 7.2 From Revealed Preference to Preference

We can summarize the above section very simply. It follows from our model of consumer behavior—that people are choosing the best things they can afford—that the choices they make are preferred to the choices that they could have made. Or, in the terminology of the last section, if $(x_1, x_2)$ is *directly revealed preferred* to $(y_1, y_2)$, then $(x_1, x_2)$ is in fact *preferred* to $(y_1, y_2)$. Let us state this principle more formally:

**The Principle of Revealed Preference.** *Let $(x_1, x_2)$ be the chosen bundle when prices are $(p_1, p_2)$, and let $(y_1, y_2)$ be some other bundle such that $p_1 x_1 + p_2 x_2 \geq p_1 y_1 + p_2 y_2$. Then if the consumer is choosing the most preferred bundle she can afford, we must have $(x_1, x_2) \succ (y_1, y_2)$.*

When you first encounter this principle, it may seem circular. If $X$ is revealed preferred to $Y$, doesn't that automatically mean that $X$ is preferred to $Y$? The answer is no. "Revealed preferred" just means that $X$ was chosen when $Y$ was affordable; "preference" means that the consumer ranks $X$ ahead of $Y$. If the consumer chooses the best bundles she can afford, then "revealed preference" implies "preference," but that is a consequence of the model of behavior, not the definitions of the terms.

This is why it would be better to say that one bundle is "chosen over" another, as suggested above. Then we would state the principle of revealed preference by saying: "If a bundle $X$ is chosen over a bundle $Y$, then $X$ must be preferred to $Y$." In this statement it is clear how the model of behavior allows us to use observed choices to infer something about the underlying preferences.

Whatever terminology you use, the essential point is clear: if we observe that one bundle is chosen when another one is affordable, then we have learned something about the preferences between the two bundles: namely, that the first is preferred to the second.

Now suppose that we happen to know that $(y_1, y_2)$ is a demanded bundle at prices $(q_1, q_2)$ and that $(y_1, y_2)$ is itself revealed preferred to some other bundle $(z_1, z_2)$. That is,

$$q_1 y_1 + q_2 y_2 \geq q_1 z_1 + q_2 z_2.$$

Then we know that $(x_1, x_2) \succ (y_1, y_2)$ and that $(y_1, y_2) \succ (z_1, z_2)$. From the transitivity assumption we can conclude that $(x_1, x_2) \succ (z_1, z_2)$.

This argument is illustrated in Figure 7.2. Revealed preference and transitivity tell us that $(x_1, x_2)$ must be better than $(z_1, z_2)$ for the consumer who made the illustrated choices.

It is natural to say that in this case $(x_1, x_2)$ is **indirectly revealed preferred** to $(z_1, z_2)$. Of course the "chain" of observed choices may be longer than just three: if bundle $A$ is directly revealed preferred to $B$, and $B$ to $C$, and $C$ to $D$, ... all the way to $M$, say, then bundle $A$ is still indirectly revealed preferred to $M$. The chain of direct comparisons can be of any length.

If a bundle is either directly or indirectly revealed preferred to another bundle, we will say that the first bundle is **revealed preferred** to the

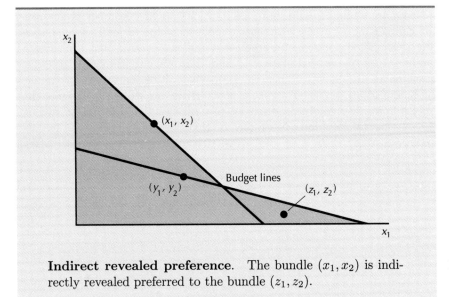

**Indirect revealed preference.**   The bundle $(x_1, x_2)$ is indirectly revealed preferred to the bundle $(z_1, z_2)$.

Figure
7.2

second.   The idea of revealed preference is simple, but it is surprisingly powerful.   Just looking at a consumer's choices can give us a lot of information about the underlying preferences.   Consider, for example, Figure 7.2.   Here we have several observations on demanded bundles at different budgets.   We can conclude from these observations that since $(x_1, x_2)$ is revealed preferred, either directly or indirectly, to all of the bundles in the shaded area, $(x_1, x_2)$ is in fact *preferred* to those bundles by the consumer who made these choices.   Another way to say this is to note that the true indifference curve through $(x_1, x_2)$, whatever it is, must lie above the shaded region.

## 7.3 Recovering Preferences

By observing choices made by the consumer, we can learn about his or her preferences.   As we observe more and more choices, we can get a better and better estimate of what the consumer's preferences are like.

Such information about preferences can be very important in making policy decisions.   Most economic policy involves trading off some goods for others: if we put a tax on shoes and subsidize clothing, we'll probably end up having more clothes and fewer shoes.   In order to evaluate the desirability of such a policy, it is important to have some idea of what consumer preferences between clothes and shoes look like.   By examining consumer choices, we can extract such information through the use of revealed preference and related techniques.

If we are willing to add more assumptions about consumer preferences, we can get more precise estimates about the shape of indifference curves. For example, suppose we observe two bundles $Y$ and $Z$ that are revealed preferred to $X$, as in Figure 7.3, and that we are willing to postulate preferences are convex. Then we know that all of the weighted averages of $Y$ and $Z$ are preferred to $X$ as well. If we are willing to assume that preferences are monotonic, then all the bundles that have more of both goods than $X$, $Y$, and $Z$—or any of their weighted averages—are also preferred to $X$.

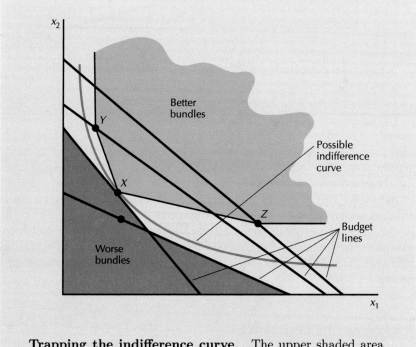

Figure
7.3

**Trapping the indifference curve.** The upper shaded area consists of bundles preferred to $X$, and the lower shaded area consists of bundles revealed worse than $X$. The indifference curve through $X$ must lie somewhere in the region between the two shaded areas.

The region labeled "Worse bundles" in Figure 7.3 consists of all the bundles to which $X$ is revealed preferred. That is, this region consists of all the bundles that cost less than $X$, along with all the bundles that cost less than bundles that cost less than $X$, and so on.

Thus, in Figure 7.3, we can conclude that all of the bundles in the upper shaded area are better than $X$, and that all of the bundles in the lower shaded area are worse than $X$, according to the preferences of the consumer who made the choices. The true indifference curve through $X$ must lie somewhere between the two shaded sets. We've managed to trap the indifference curve quite tightly simply by an intelligent application of the idea of revealed preference and a few simple assumptions about preferences.

## 7.4 The Weak Axiom of Revealed Preference

All of the above relies on the assumption that the consumer *has* preferences and that she is always choosing the best bundle of goods she can afford. If the consumer is not behaving this way, the "estimates" of the indifference curves that we constructed above have no meaning. The question naturally arises: how can we tell if the consumer is following the maximizing model? Or, to turn it around: what kind of observation would lead us to conclude that the consumer was *not* maximizing?

Consider the situation illustrated in Figure 7.4. Could both of these choices be generated by a maximizing consumer? According to the logic of revealed preference, Figure 7.4 allows us to conclude two things: (1) $(x_1, x_2)$ is preferred to $(y_1, y_2)$; and (2) $(y_1, y_2)$ is preferred to $(x_1, x_2)$. This is clearly absurd. In Figure 7.4 the consumer has apparently chosen $(x_1, x_2)$ when she could have chosen $(y_1, y_2)$, indicating that $(x_1, x_2)$ was preferred to $(y_1, y_2)$, but then she chose $(y_1, y_2)$ when she could have chosen $(x_1, x_2)$—indicating the opposite!

Clearly, this consumer cannot be a maximizing consumer. Either the consumer is not choosing the best bundle she can afford, or there is some other aspect of the choice problem that has changed that we have not observed. Perhaps the consumer's tastes or some other aspect of her economic environment have changed. In any event, a violation of this sort is not consistent with the model of consumer choice in an unchanged environment.

The theory of consumer choice implies that such observations will not occur. If the consumers are choosing the best things they can afford, then things that are affordable, but not chosen, must be worse than what is chosen. Economists have formulated this simple point in the following basic axiom of consumer theory

**Weak Axiom of Revealed Preference (WARP).** *If $(x_1, x_2)$ is directly revealed preferred to $(y_1, y_2)$, and the two bundles are not the same, then it cannot happen that $(y_1, y_2)$ is directly revealed preferred to $(x_1, x_2)$.*

In other words, if a bundle $(x_1, x_2)$ is purchased at prices $(p_1, p_2)$ and a different bundle $(y_1, y_2)$ is purchased at prices $(q_1, q_2)$, then if

$$p_1 x_1 + p_2 x_2 \geq p_1 y_1 + p_2 y_2,$$

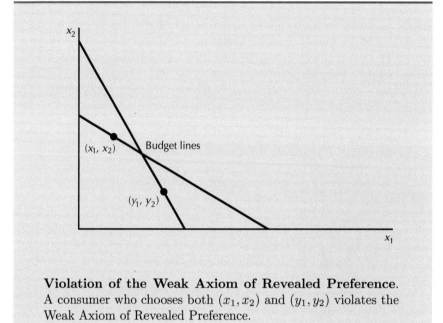

Figure
7.4

**Violation of the Weak Axiom of Revealed Preference.**
A consumer who chooses both $(x_1, x_2)$ and $(y_1, y_2)$ violates the
Weak Axiom of Revealed Preference.

it must *not* be the case that

$$q_1 y_1 + q_2 y_2 \geq q_1 x_1 + q_2 x_2.$$

In English: if the y-bundle is affordable when the x-bundle is purchased,
then when the y-bundle is purchased, the x-bundle must not be affordable.

The consumer in Figure 7.4 has *violated* WARP. Thus we know that this
consumer's behavior could not have been maximizing behavior.[1]

There is no set of indifference curves that could be drawn in Figure 7.4
that could make both bundles maximizing bundles. On the other hand,
the consumer in Figure 7.5 satisfies WARP. Here it is possible to find
indifference curves for which his behavior is optimal behavior. One possible
choice of indifference curves is illustrated.

Optional  ## 7.5 Checking WARP

It is important to understand that WARP is a condition that must be satisfied by a consumer who is always choosing the best things he or she can
afford. The Weak Axiom of Revealed Preference is a logical implication

---

[1] Could we say his behavior is WARPed? Well, we could, but not in polite company.

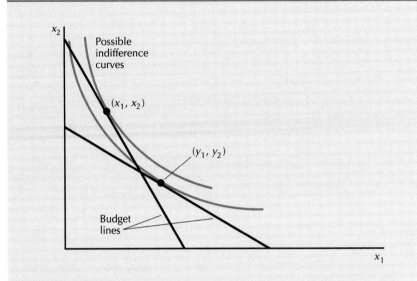

**Satisfying WARP.** Consumer choices that satisfy the Weak Axiom of Revealed Preference and some possible indifference curves.

Figure
7.5

of that model and can therefore be used to check whether or not a particular consumer, or an economic entity that we might want to model as a consumer, is consistent with our economic model.

Let's consider how we would go about systematically testing WARP in practice. Suppose that we observe several choices of bundles of goods at different prices. Let us use $(p_1^t, p_2^t)$ to denote the $t^{th}$ observation of prices and $(x_1^t, x_2^t)$ to denote the $t^{th}$ observation of choices. To use a specific example, let's take the data in Table 7.1.

**Some consumption data.**

Table
7.1

| Observation | $p_1$ | $p_2$ | $x_1$ | $x_2$ |
|:-----------:|:-----:|:-----:|:-----:|:-----:|
| 1 | 1 | 2 | 1 | 2 |
| 2 | 2 | 1 | 2 | 1 |
| 3 | 1 | 1 | 2 | 2 |

Given these data, we can compute how much it would cost the consumer to purchase each bundle of goods at each different set of prices, as we've done in Table 7.2. For example, the entry in row 3, column 1, measures how much money the consumer would have to spend at the third set of prices to purchase the first bundle of goods.

Table
7.2

**Cost of each bundle at each set of prices.**

Bundles

|        |   | 1  | 2  | 3 |
|--------|---|----|----|---|
|        | 1 | 5  | 4* | 6 |
| Prices | 2 | 4* | 5  | 6 |
|        | 3 | 3* | 3* | 4 |

The diagonal terms in Table 7.2 measure how much money the consumer is spending at each choice. The other entries in each row measure how much she would have spent if she had purchased a different bundle. Thus we can see whether bundle 3, say, is revealed preferred to bundle 1, by seeing if the entry in row 3, column 1 (how much the consumer would have to spend at the third set of prices to purchase the first bundle) is less than the entry in row 3, column 3 (how much the consumer actually spent at the third set of prices to purchase the third bundle). In this particular case, bundle 1 was affordable when bundle 3 was purchased, which means that bundle 3 is revealed preferred to bundle 1. Thus we put a star in row 3, column 1, of the table.

From a mathematical point of view, we simply put a star in the entry in row $s$, column $t$, if the number in that entry is less than the number in row $s$, column $s$.

We can use this table to check for violations of WARP. In this framework, a violation of WARP consists of two observations $t$ and $s$ such that row $t$, column $s$, contains a star *and* row $s$, column $t$, contains a star. For this would mean that the bundle purchased at $s$ is revealed preferred to the bundle purchased at $t$ and vice versa.

We can use a computer (or a research assistant) to check and see whether there are any pairs of observations like these in the observed choices. If there are, the choices are inconsistent with the economic theory of the consumer. Either the theory is wrong for this particular consumer, or something else has changed in the consumer's environment that we have not controlled for. Thus the Weak Axiom of Revealed Preference gives us an easily checkable condition for whether some observed choices are consistent with the economic theory of the consumer.

In Table 7.2, we observe that row 1, column 2, contains a star and row 2, column 1, contains a star. This means that observation 2 could have been chosen when the consumer actually chose observation 1 and vice versa. This is a violation of the Weak Axiom of Revealed Preference. We can conclude that the data depicted in Tables 7.1 and 7.2 could not be generated by a consumer with stable preferences who was always choosing the best things he or she could afford.

## 7.6 The Strong Axiom of Revealed Preference

The Weak Axiom of Revealed Preference described in the last section gives us an observable condition that must be satisfied by all optimizing consumers. But there is a stronger condition that is sometimes useful.

We have already noted that if a bundle of goods $X$ is revealed preferred to a bundle $Y$, and $Y$ is in turn revealed preferred to a bundle $Z$, then $X$ must in fact be preferred to $Z$. If the consumer has consistent preferences, then we should never observe a sequence of choices that would reveal that $Z$ was preferred to $X$.

The Weak Axiom of Revealed Preference requires that if $X$ is *directly* revealed preferred to $Y$, then we should never observe $Y$ being *directly* revealed preferred to $X$. The **Strong Axiom of Revealed Preference (SARP)** requires that the same sort of condition hold for *indirect* revealed preference. More formally, we have the following.

**Strong Axiom of Revealed Preference (SARP).** *If $(x_1, x_2)$ is revealed preferred to $(y_1, y_2)$ (either directly or indirectly) and $(y_1, y_2)$ is different from $(x_1, x_2)$, then $(y_1, y_2)$ cannot be directly or indirectly revealed preferred to $(x_1, x_2)$.*

It is clear that if the observed behavior is optimizing behavior then it must satisfy the SARP. For if the consumer is optimizing and $(x_1, x_2)$ is revealed preferred to $(y_1, y_2)$, either directly or indirectly, then we must have $(x_1, x_2) \succ (y_1, y_2)$. So having $(x_1, x_2)$ revealed preferred to $(y_1, y_2)$ *and* $(y_1, y_2)$ revealed preferred to $(x_1, x_2)$ would imply that $(x_1, x_2) \succ (y_1, y_2)$ *and* $(y_1, y_2) \succ (x_1, x_2)$, which is a contradiction. We can conclude that either the consumer must not be optimizing, or some other aspect of the consumer's environment—such as tastes, other prices, and so on—must have changed.

Roughly speaking, since the underlying preferences of the consumer must be transitive, it follows that the *revealed* preferences of the consumer must be transitive. Thus SARP is a *necessary* implication of optimizing behavior: if a consumer is always choosing the best things that he can afford, then his observed behavior must satisfy SARP. What is more surprising is that any behavior satisfying the Strong Axiom can be thought of as being generated by optimizing behavior in the following sense: if the observed choices satisfy SARP, we can always find nice, well-behaved preferences that *could have* generated the observed choices. In this sense SARP is a *sufficient* condition for optimizing behavior: if the observed choices satisfy SARP, then it is always possible to find preferences for which the observed behavior is optimizing behavior. The proof of this claim is unfortunately beyond the scope of this book, but appreciation of its importance is not.

What it means is that SARP gives us *all* of the restrictions on behavior imposed by the model of the optimizing consumer. For if the observed choices satisfy SARP, we can "construct" preferences that could have generated these choices. Thus SARP is both a necessary and a sufficient condition for observed choices to be compatible with the economic model of consumer choice.

Does this prove that the constructed preferences actually generated the observed choices? Of course not. As with any scientific statement, we can only show that observed behavior is not inconsistent with the statement. We can't prove that the economic model is correct; we can just determine the implications of that model and see if observed choices are consistent with those implications.

Optional    ## 7.7 How to Check SARP

Let us suppose that we have a table like Table 7.2 that has a star in row $t$ and column $s$ if observation $t$ is directly revealed preferred to observation $s$. How can we use this table to check SARP?

The easiest way is first to transform the table. An example is given in Table 7.3. This is a table just like Table 7.2, but it uses a different set of numbers. Here the stars indicate direct revealed preference. The star in parentheses will be explained below.

Table
7.3

**How to check SARP.**

|        |   | Bundles |     |     |
|--------|---|---------|-----|-----|
|        |   | 1       | 2   | 3   |
|        | 1 | 20      | 10* | 22(*) |
| Prices | 2 | 21      | 20  | 15* |
|        | 3 | 12      | 15  | 10  |

Now we systematically look through the entries of the table and see if there are any *chains* of observations that make some bundle indirectly revealed preferred to that one. For example, bundle 1 is directly revealed preferred to bundle 2 since there is a star in row 1, column 2. And bundle

2 is directly revealed preferred to bundle 3, since there is a star in row 2, column 3. Therefore bundle 1 is *indirectly* revealed preferred to bundle 3, and we indicate this by putting a star (in parentheses) in row 1, column 3.

In general, if we have many observations, we will have to look for chains of arbitrary length to see if one observation is indirectly revealed preferred to another. Although it may not be exactly obvious how to do this, it turns out that there are simple computer programs that can calculate the indirect revealed preference relation from the table describing the direct revealed preference relation. The computer can put a star in location $st$ of the table if observation $s$ is revealed preferred to observation $t$ by any chain of other observations.

Once we have done this calculation, we can easily test for SARP. We just see if there is a situation where there is a star in row $t$, column $s$, *and* also a star in row $s$, column $t$. If so, we have found a situation where observation $t$ is revealed preferred to observation $s$, either directly or indirectly, and, at the same time, observation $s$ is revealed preferred to observation $t$. This is a violation of the Strong Axiom of Revealed Preference.

On the other hand, if we do not find such violations, then we know that the observations we have are consistent with the economic theory of the consumer. These observations could have been made by an optimizing consumer with well-behaved preferences. Thus we have a completely operational test for whether or not a particular consumer is acting in a way consistent with economic theory.

This is important, since we can model several kinds of economic units as behaving like consumers. Think, for example, of a household consisting of several people. Will its consumption choices maximize "household utility"? If we have some data on household consumption choices, we can use the Strong Axiom of Revealed Preference to see. Another economic unit that we might think of as acting like a consumer is a nonprofit organization like a hospital or a university. Do universities maximize a utility function in making their economic choices? If we have a list of the economic choices that a university makes when faced with different prices, we can, in principle, answer this kind of question.

## 7.8 Index Numbers

Suppose we examine the consumption bundles of a consumer at two different times and we want to compare how consumption has changed from one time to the other. Let $b$ stand for the base period, and let $t$ be some other time. How does "average" consumption in year $t$ compare to consumption in the base period?

Suppose that at time $t$ prices are $(p_1^t, p_2^t)$ and that the consumer chooses $(x_1^t, x_2^t)$. In the base period $b$, the prices are $(p_1^b, p_2^b)$, and the consumer's choice is $(x_1^b, x_2^b)$. We want to ask how the "average" consumption of the consumer has changed.

If we let $w_1$ and $w_2$ be some "weights" that go into making an average, then we can look at the following kind of quantity index:

$$I_q = \frac{w_1 x_1^t + w_2 x_2^t}{w_1 x_1^b + w_2 x_2^b}.$$

If $I_q$ is greater than 1, we can say that the "average" consumption has gone up in the movement from $b$ to $t$; if $I_q$ is less than 1, we can say that the "average" consumption has gone down.

The question is, what do we use for the weights? A natural choice is to use the prices of the goods in question, since they measure in some sense the relative importance of the two goods. But there are two sets of prices here: which should we use?

If we use the base period prices for the weights, we have something called a **Laspeyres** index, and if we use the $t$ period prices, we have something called a **Paasche** index. Both of these indices answer the question of what has happened to "average" consumption, but they just use different weights in the averaging process.

Substituting the $t$ period prices for the weights, we see that the **Paasche quantity index** is given by

$$P_q = \frac{p_1^t x_1^t + p_2^t x_2^t}{p_1^t x_1^b + p_2^t x_2^b},$$

and substituting the $b$ period prices shows that the **Laspeyres quantity index** is given by

$$L_q = \frac{p_1^b x_1^t + p_2^b x_2^t}{p_1^b x_1^b + p_2^b x_2^b}.$$

It turns out that the magnitude of the Laspeyres and Paasche indices can tell us something quite interesting about the consumer's welfare. Suppose that we have a situation where the Paasche quantity index is greater than 1:

$$P_q = \frac{p_1^t x_1^t + p_2^t x_2^t}{p_1^t x_1^b + p_2^t x_2^b} > 1.$$

What can we conclude about how well-off the consumer is at time $t$ as compared to his situation at time $b$?

The answer is provided by revealed preference. Just cross multiply this inequality to give

$$p_1^t x_1^t + p_2^t x_2^t > p_1^t x_1^b + p_2^t x_2^b,$$

which immediately shows that the consumer must be better off at $t$ than at $b$, since he could have consumed the $b$ consumption bundle in the $t$ situation but chose not to do so.

What if the Paasche index is *less* than 1? Then we would have

$$p_1^t x_1^t + p_2^t x_2^t < p_1^t x_1^b + p_2^t x_2^b,$$

which says that when the consumer chose bundle $(x_1^t, x_2^t)$, bundle $(x_1^b, x_2^b)$ was not affordable. But that doesn't say anything about the consumer's ranking of the bundles. Just because something costs more than you can afford doesn't mean that you prefer it to what you're consuming now.

What about the Laspeyres index? It works in a similar way. Suppose that the Laspeyres index is *less* than 1:

$$L_q = \frac{p_1^b x_1^t + p_2^b x_2^t}{p_1^b x_1^b + p_2^b x_2^b} < 1.$$

Cross multiplying yields

$$p_1^b x_1^b + p_2^b x_2^b > p_1^b x_1^t + p_2^b x_2^t,$$

which says that $(x_1^b, x_2^b)$ is revealed preferred to $(x_1^t, x_2^t)$. Thus the consumer is better off at time $b$ than at time $t$.

## 7.9 Price Indices

Price indices work in much the same way. In general, a price index will be a weighted average of prices:

$$I_p = \frac{p_1^t w_1 + p_2^t w_2}{p_1^b w_1 + p_2^b w_2}.$$

In this case it is natural to choose the quantities as the weights for computing the averages. We get two different indices, depending on our choice of weights. If we choose the $t$ period quantities for weights, we get the **Paasche price index**:

$$P_p = \frac{p_1^t x_1^t + p_2^t x_2^t}{p_1^b x_1^t + p_2^b x_2^t},$$

and if we choose the base period quantities we get the **Laspeyres price index**:

$$L_p = \frac{p_1^t x_1^b + p_2^t x_2^b}{p_1^b x_1^b + p_2^b x_2^b}.$$

Suppose that the Paasche price index is less than 1; what does revealed preference have to say about the welfare situation of the consumer in periods $t$ and $b$?

Revealed preference doesn't say anything at all. The problem is that there are now different prices in the numerator and in the denominator of the fractions defining the indices, so the revealed preference comparison can't be made.

Let's define a new index of the change in total expenditure by

$$M = \frac{p_1^t x_1^t + p_2^t x_2^t}{p_1^b x_1^b + p_2^b x_2^b}.$$

This is the ratio of total expenditure in period $t$ to the total expenditure in period $b$.

Now suppose that you are told that the Paasche price index was greater than $M$. This means that

$$P_p = \frac{p_1^t x_1^t + p_2^t x_2^t}{p_1^b x_1^t + p_2^b x_2^t} > \frac{p_1^t x_1^t + p_2^t x_2^t}{p_1^b x_1^b + p_2^b x_2^b}.$$

Canceling the numerators from each side of this expression and cross multiplying, we have

$$p_1^b x_1^b + p_2^b x_2^b > p_1^b x_1^t + p_2^b x_2^t.$$

This statement says that the bundle chosen at year $b$ is revealed preferred to the bundle chosen at year $t$. This analysis implies that if the Paasche price index is greater than the expenditure index, then the consumer must be better off in year $b$ than in year $t$.

This is quite intuitive. After all, if prices rise by more than income rises in the movement from $b$ to $t$, we would expect that would tend to make the consumer worse off. The revealed preference analysis given above confirms this intuition.

A similar statement can be made for the Laspeyres price index. If the Laspeyres price index is less than $M$, then the consumer must be better off in year $t$ than in year $b$. Again, this simply confirms the intuitive idea that if prices rise less than income, the consumer would become better off. In the case of price indices, what matters is not whether the index is greater or less than 1, but whether it is greater or less than the expenditure index.

## EXAMPLE: Indexing Social Security Payments

Many elderly people have Social Security payments as their sole source of income. Because of this, there have been attempts to adjust Social Security payments in a way that will keep purchasing power constant even when prices change. Since the amount of payments will then depend on the movement of some price index or cost-of-living index, this kind of scheme is referred to as **indexing**.

One indexing proposal goes as follows. In some base year $b$, economists measure the average consumption bundle of senior citizens. In each subsequent year the Social Security system adjusts payments so that the "purchasing power" of the average senior citizen remains constant in the sense that the average Social Security recipient is just able to afford the consumption bundle available in year $b$, as depicted in Figure 7.6.

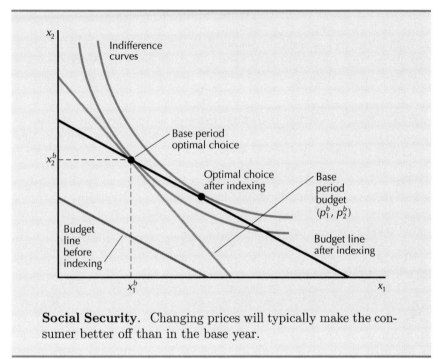

**Social Security.** Changing prices will typically make the consumer better off than in the base year.

Figure
7.6

One curious result of this indexing scheme is that the average senior citizen will almost always be better off than he or she was in the base year $b$. Suppose that year $b$ is chosen as the base year for the price index. Then the bundle $(x_1^b, x_2^b)$ is the optimal bundle at the prices $(p_1^b, p_2^b)$. This means that the budget line at prices $(p_1^b, p_2^b)$ must be tangent to the indifference curve through $(x_1^b, x_2^b)$.

Now suppose that prices change. To be specific, suppose that prices increase so that the budget line, in the absence of Social Security, would shift inward and tilt. The inward shift is due to the increase in prices; the tilt is due to the change in relative prices. The indexing program would then increase the Social Security payment so as to make the original bundle $(x_1^b, x_2^b)$ affordable at the new prices. But this means that the budget line would cut the indifference curve, and there would be some other bundle on the budget line that would be strictly preferred to $(x_1^b, x_2^b)$. Thus the consumer would typically be able to choose a better bundle than he or she chose in the base year.

## Summary

1. If one bundle is chosen when another could have been chosen, we say that the first bundle is revealed preferred to the second.

2. If the consumer is always choosing the most preferred bundles he or she can afford, this means that the chosen bundles must be preferred to the bundles that were affordable but weren't chosen.

3. Observing the choices of consumers can allow us to "recover" or estimate the preferences that lie behind those choices. The more choices we observe, the more precisely we can estimate the underlying preferences that generated those choices.

4. The Weak Axiom of Revealed Preference (WARP) and the Strong Axiom of Revealed Preference (SARP) are necessary conditions that consumer choices have to obey if they are to be consistent with the economic model of optimizing choice.

## REVIEW QUESTIONS

1. When prices are $(p_1, p_2) = (1, 2)$ a consumer demands $(x_1, x_2) = (1, 2)$, and when prices are $(q_1, q_2) = (2, 1)$ the consumer demands $(y_1, y_2) = (2, 1)$. Is this behavior consistent with the model of maximizing behavior?

2. When prices are $(p_1, p_2) = (2, 1)$ a consumer demands $(x_1, x_2) = (1, 2)$, and when prices are $(q_1, q_2) = (1, 2)$ the consumer demands $(y_1, y_2) = (2, 1)$. Is this behavior consistent with the model of maximizing behavior?

3. In the preceding exercise, which bundle is preferred by the consumer, the x-bundle or the y-bundle?

4. We saw that the Social Security adjustment for changing prices would typically make recipients at least as well-off as they were at the base year. What kind of price changes would leave them just as well-off, no matter what kind of preferences they had?

5. In the same framework as the above question, what kind of preferences would leave the consumer just as well-off as he was in the base year, for *all* price changes?

# CHAPTER **8**

# SLUTSKY EQUATION

Economists often are concerned with how a consumer's behavior changes in response to changes in the economic environment. The case we want to consider in this chapter is how a consumer's choice of a good responds to changes in its price. It is natural to think that when the price of a good rises the demand for it will fall. However, as we saw in Chapter 6 it is possible to construct examples where the optimal demand for a good *decreases* when its price falls. A good that has this property is called a **Giffen good**.

Giffen goods are pretty peculiar and are primarily a theoretical curiosity, but there are other situations where changes in prices might have "perverse" effects that, on reflection, turn out not to be so unreasonable. For example, we normally think that if people get a higher wage they will work more. But what if your wage went from $10 an hour to $1000 an hour? Would you really work more? Might you not decide to work fewer hours and use some of the money you've earned to do other things? What if your wage were $1,000,000 an hour? Wouldn't you work less?

For another example, think of what happens to your demand for apples when the price goes up. You would probably consume fewer apples. But how about a family who grew apples to sell? If the price of apples went up, their income might go up so much that they would feel that they could now afford to consume more of their own apples. For the consumers in this family, an increase in the price of apples might well lead to an increase in the consumption of apples.

What is going on here? How is it that changes in price can have these ambiguous effects on demand? In this chapter and the next we'll try to sort out these effects.

## 8.1 The Substitution Effect

When the price of a good changes, there are two sorts of effects: the rate at which you can exchange one good for another changes, and the total purchasing power of your income is altered. If, for example, good 1 becomes cheaper, it means that you have to give up less of good 2 to purchase good 1. The change in the price of good 1 has changed the rate at which the market allows you to "substitute" good 2 for good 1. The trade-off between the two goods that the market presents the consumer has changed.

At the same time, if good 1 becomes cheaper it means that your money income will buy more of good 1. The purchasing power of your money has gone up; although the number of dollars you have is the same, the amount that they will buy has increased.

The first part—the change in demand due to the change in the rate of exchange between the two goods—is called the **substitution effect**. The second effect—the change in demand due to having more purchasing power—is called the **income effect**. These are only rough definitions of the two effects. In order to give a more precise definition we have to consider the two effects in greater detail.

The way that we will do this is to break the price movement into two steps: first we will let the *relative* prices change and adjust money income so as to hold purchasing power constant, then we will let purchasing power adjust while holding the relative prices constant.

This is best explained by referring to Figure 8.1. Here we have a situation where the price of good 1 has declined. This means that the budget line rotates around the vertical intercept $m/p_2$ and becomes flatter. We can break this movement of the budget line up into two steps: first *pivot* the budget line around the *original* demanded bundle and then *shift* the pivoted line out to the *new* demanded bundle.

This "pivot-shift" operation gives us a convenient way to decompose the change in demand into two pieces. The first step—the pivot—is a movement where the slope of the budget line changes while its purchasing power stays constant, while the second step is a movement where the slope stays constant and the purchasing power changes. This decomposition is only a hypothetical construction—the consumer simply observes a change

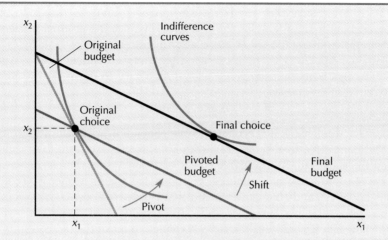

**Pivot and shift**. When the price of good 1 changes and income stays fixed, the budget line pivots around the vertical axis. We will view this adjustment as occurring in two stages: first pivot the budget line around the *original* choice, and then shift this line outward to the new demanded bundle.

Figure 8.1

in price and chooses a new bundle of goods in response. But in analyzing how the consumer's choice changes, it is useful to think of the budget line changing in two stages—first the pivot, then the shift.

What are the economic meanings of the pivoted and the shifted budget lines? Let us first consider the pivoted line. Here we have a budget line with the same slope and thus the same relative prices as the final budget line. However, the money income associated with this budget line is different, since the vertical intercept is different. Since the original consumption bundle $(x_1, x_2)$ lies on the pivoted budget line, that consumption bundle is just affordable. The purchasing power of the consumer has remained constant in the sense that the original bundle of goods is just affordable at the new pivoted line.

Let us calculate how much we have to adjust money income in order to keep the old bundle just affordable. Let $m'$ be the amount of money income that will just make the original consumption bundle affordable; this will be the amount of money income associated with the pivoted budget line. Since $(x_1, x_2)$ is affordable at both $(p_1, p_2, m)$ and $(p_1', p_2, m')$, we have

$$m' = p_1' x_1 + p_2 x_2$$
$$m = p_1 x_1 + p_2 x_2.$$

Subtracting the second equation from the first gives

$$m' - m = x_1 [p_1' - p_1].$$

This equation says that the change in money income necessary to make the old bundle affordable at the new prices is just the original amount of consumption of good 1 times the change in prices.

Letting $\Delta p_1 = p_1' - p_1$ represent the change in price 1, and $\Delta m = m' - m$ represent the change in income necessary to make the old bundle just affordable, we have

$$\Delta m = x_1 \Delta p_1. \tag{8.1}$$

Note that the change in income and the change in price will always move in the same direction: if the price goes up, then we have to raise income to keep the same bundle affordable.

Let's use some actual numbers. Suppose that the consumer is originally consuming 20 candy bars a week, and that candy bars cost 50 cents a piece. If the price of candy bars goes up by 10 cents—so that $\Delta p_1 = .60 - .50 = .10$—how much would income have to change to make the old consumption bundle affordable?

We can apply the formula given above. If the consumer had \$2.00 more income, he would just be able to consume the same number of candy bars, namely, 20. In terms of the formula:

$$\Delta m = \Delta p_1 \times x_1 = .10 \times 20 = \$2.00.$$

Now we have a formula for the pivoted budget line: it is just the budget line at the new price with income changed by $\Delta m$. Note that if the price of good 1 goes down, then the adjustment in income will be negative. When a price goes down, a consumer's purchasing power goes up, so we will have to decrease the consumer's income in order to keep purchasing power fixed. Similarly, when a price goes up, purchasing power goes down, so the change in income necessary to keep purchasing power constant must be positive.

Although $(x_1, x_2)$ is still affordable, it is not generally the optimal purchase at the pivoted budget line. In Figure 8.2 we have denoted the optimal purchase on the pivoted budget line by $Y$. This bundle of goods is the optimal bundle of goods when we change the price and then adjust dollar income so as to keep the old bundle of goods just affordable. The movement from $X$ to $Y$ is known as the **substitution effect**. It indicates how the consumer "substitutes" one good for the other when a price changes but purchasing power remains constant.

More precisely, the substitution effect, $\Delta x_1^s$, is the change in the demand for good 1 when the price of good 1 changes to $p_1'$ and, at the same time, money income changes to $m'$:

$$\Delta x_1^s = x_1(p_1', m') - x_1(p_1, m).$$

In order to determine the substitution effect, we must use the consumer's demand function to calculate the optimal choices at $(p_1', m')$ and $(p_1, m)$. The change in the demand for good 1 may be large or small, depending

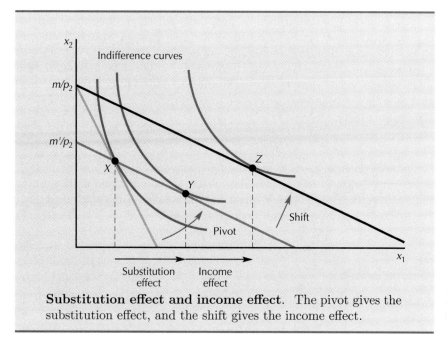

**Substitution effect and income effect.** The pivot gives the substitution effect, and the shift gives the income effect.

Figure
8.2

on the shape of the consumer's indifference curves. But given the demand function, it is easy to just plug in the numbers to calculate the substitution effect. (Of course the demand for good 1 may well depend on the price of good 2; but the price of good 2 is being held constant during this exercise, so we've left it out of the demand function so as not to clutter the notation.)

The substitution effect is sometimes called the change in **compensated demand**. The idea is that the consumer is being compensated for a price rise by having enough income given back to him to purchase his old bundle. Of course if the price goes down he is "compensated" by having money taken away from him. We'll generally stick with the "substitution" terminology, for consistency, but the "compensation" terminology is also widely used.

### EXAMPLE: Calculating the Substitution Effect

Suppose that the consumer has a demand function for milk of the form

$$x_1 = 10 + \frac{m}{10p_1}.$$

Originally his income is $120 per week and the price of milk is $3 per quart. Thus his demand for milk will be $10 + 120/(10 \times 3) = 14$ quarts per week.

Now suppose that the price of milk falls to $2 per quart. Then his demand at this new price will be $10 + 120/(10 \times 2) = 16$ quarts of milk per week. The *total* change in demand is $+2$ quarts a week.

In order to calculate the substitution effect, we must first calculate how much income would have to change in order to make the original consumption of milk just affordable when the price of milk is $2 a quart. We apply the formula (8.1):

$$\Delta m = x_1 \Delta p_1 = 14 \times (2 - 3) = -\$14.$$

Thus the level of income necessary to keep purchasing power constant is $m' = m + \Delta m = 120 - 14 = 106$. What is the consumer's demand for milk at the new price, $2 per quart, and this level of income? Just plug the numbers into the demand function to find

$$x_1(p_1', m') = x_1(2, 106) = 10 + \frac{106}{10 \times 2} = 15.3.$$

Thus the substitution effect is

$$\Delta x_1^s = x_1(2, 106) - x_1(3, 120) = 15.3 - 14 = 1.3.$$

## 8.2 The Income Effect

We turn now to the second stage of the price adjustment—the shift movement. This is also easy to interpret economically. We know that a parallel shift of the budget line is the movement that occurs when income changes while relative prices remain constant. Thus the second stage of the price adjustment is called the **income effect**. We simply change the consumer's income from $m'$ to $m$, keeping the prices constant at $(p_1', p_2)$. In Figure 8.2 this change moves us from the point $(y_1, y_2)$ to $(z_1, z_2)$. It is natural to call this last movement the income effect since all we are doing is changing income while keeping the prices fixed at the new prices.

More precisely, the income effect, $\Delta x_1^n$, is the change in the demand for good 1 when we change income from $m'$ to $m$, holding the price of good 1 fixed at $p_1'$:

$$\Delta x_1^n = x_1(p_1', m) - x_1(p_1', m').$$

We have already considered the income effect earlier in section 6.1. There we saw that the income effect can operate either way: it will tend to increase or decrease the demand for good 1 depending on whether we have a normal good or an inferior good.

When the price of a good decreases, we need to decrease income in order to keep purchasing power constant. If the good is a normal good, then this decrease in income will lead to a decrease in demand. If the good is an inferior good, then the decrease in income will lead to an increase in demand.

EXAMPLE: Calculating the Income Effect

In the example given earlier in this chapter we saw that

$$x_1(p_1', m) = x_1(2, 120) = 16$$
$$x_1(p_1', m') = x_1(2, 106) = 15.3.$$

Thus the income effect for this problem is

$$\Delta x_1^n = x_1(2, 120) - x_1(2, 106) = 16 - 15.3 = 0.7.$$

Since milk is a normal good for this consumer, the demand for milk increases when income increases.

## 8.3 Sign of the Substitution Effect

We have seen above that the income effect can be positive or negative, depending on whether the good is a normal good or an inferior good. What about the substitution effect? If the price of a good goes down, as in Figure 8.2, then the change in the demand for the good due to the substitution effect *must* be nonnegative. That is, if $p_1 > p_1'$, then we *must* have $x_1(p_1', m') \geq x_1(p_1, m)$, so that $\Delta x_1^s \geq 0$.

The proof of this goes as follows. Consider the points on the pivoted budget line in Figure 8.2 where the amount of good 1 consumed is less than at the bundle $X$. These bundles were all affordable at the old prices $(p_1, p_2)$ but they weren't purchased. Instead the bundle $X$ was purchased. If the consumer is always choosing the best bundle he can afford, then $X$ must be preferred to all of the bundles on the part of the pivoted line that lies inside the original budget set.

This means that the optimal choice on the pivoted budget line must not be one of the bundles that lies underneath the original budget line. The optimal choice on the pivoted line would have to be either $X$ or some point to the right of $X$. But this means that the new optimal choice must involve consuming at least as much of good 1 as originally, just as we wanted to show. In the case illustrated in Figure 8.2, the optimal choice at the pivoted budget line is the bundle $Y$, which certainly involves consuming more of good 1 than at the original consumption point, $X$.

The substitution effect always moves opposite to the price movement. We say that *the substitution effect is negative*, since the change in demand due to the substitution effect is opposite to the change in price: if the price increases, the demand for the good due to the substitution effect decreases.

## 8.4 The Total Change in Demand

The total change in demand, $\Delta x_1$, is the change in demand due to the change in price, holding income constant:

$$\Delta x_1 = x_1(p_1', m) - x_1(p_1, m).$$

We have seen above how this change can be broken up into two changes: the substitution effect and the income effect. In terms of the symbols defined above,

$$\Delta x_1 = \Delta x_1^s + \Delta x_1^n$$
$$x_1(p_1', m) - x_1(p_1, m) = [x_1(p_1', m') - x_1(p_1, m)]$$
$$+ [x_1(p_1', m) - x_1(p_1', m')].$$

In words this equation says that the total change in demand equals the substitution effect plus the income effect. This equation is called the **Slutsky identity**.[1] Note that it is an identity: it is true for all values of $p_1$, $p_1'$, $m$, and $m'$. The first and fourth terms on the right-hand side cancel out, so the right-hand side is *identically* equal to the left-hand side.

The content of the Slutsky identity is not just the algebraic identity—that is a mathematical triviality. The content comes in the interpretation of the two terms on the right-hand side: the substitution effect and the income effect. In particular, we can use what we know about the signs of the income and substitution effects to determine the sign of the total effect.

While the substitution effect must always be negative—opposite the change in the price—the income effect can go either way. Thus the total effect may be positive or negative. However, if we have a normal good, then the substitution effect and the income effect work in the same direction. An increase in price means that demand will go down due to the substitution effect. If the price goes up, it is like a decrease in income, which, for a normal good, means a decrease in demand. Both effects reinforce each other. In terms of our notation, the change in demand due to a price increase for a normal good means that

$$\Delta x_1 = \Delta x_1^s + \Delta x_1^n.$$
$$(-) \quad (-) \quad (-)$$

(The minus signs beneath each term indicate that each term in this expression is negative.)

---

[1] Named for Eugen Slutsky (1880–1948), a Russian economist who investigated demand theory.

Note carefully the sign on the income effect. Since we are considering a situation where the price rises, this implies a decrease in purchasing power—for a normal good this will imply a decrease in demand.

On the other hand, if we have an inferior good, it might happen that the income effect outweighs the substitution effect, so that the total change in demand associated with a price increase is actually positive. This would be a case where

$$\Delta x_1 = \Delta x_1^s + \Delta x_1^n.$$
$$(?) \quad (-) \quad (+)$$

If the second term on the right-hand side—the income effect—is large enough, the total change in demand could be positive. This would mean that an increase in price could result in an *increase* in demand. This is the perverse Giffen case described earlier: the increase in price has reduced the consumer's purchasing power so much that he has increased his consumption of the inferior good.

But the Slutsky identity shows that this kind of perverse effect can only occur for inferior goods: if a good is a normal good, then the income and substitution effects reinforce each other, so that the total change in demand is always in the "right" direction.

Thus a Giffen good must be an inferior good. But an inferior good is not necessarily a Giffen good: the income effect not only has to be of the "wrong" sign, it also has to be large enough to outweigh the "right" sign of the substitution effect. This is why Giffen goods are so rarely observed in real life: they would not only have to be inferior goods, but they would have to be *very* inferior.

This is illustrated graphically in Figure 8.3. Here we illustrate the usual pivot-shift operation to find the substitution effect and the income effect. In both cases, good 1 is an inferior good, and the income effect is therefore negative. In Figure 8.3A, the income effect is large enough to outweigh the substitution effect and produce a Giffen good. In Figure 8.3B, the income effect is smaller, and thus good 1 responds in the ordinary way to the change in its price.

## 8.5 Rates of Change

We have seen that the income and substitution effects can be described graphically as a combination of pivots and shifts, or they can be described algebraically in the Slutsky identity

$$\Delta x_1 = \Delta x_1^s + \Delta x_1^n,$$

which simply says that the total change in demand is the substitution effect plus the income effect. The Slutsky identity here is stated in terms

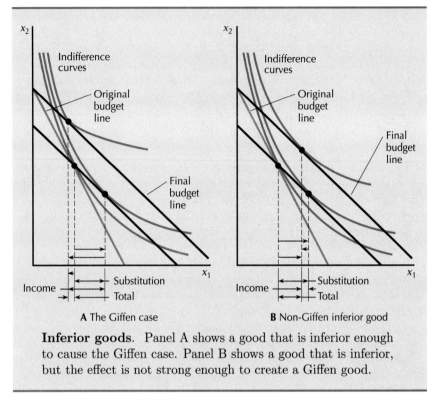

**A** The Giffen case      **B** Non-Giffen inferior good

Figure
8.3

**Inferior goods.** Panel A shows a good that is inferior enough
to cause the Giffen case. Panel B shows a good that is inferior,
but the effect is not strong enough to create a Giffen good.

of absolute changes, but it is more common to express it in terms of *rates*
of change.

When we express the Slutsky identity in terms of rates of change it turns
out to be convenient to define $\Delta x_1^m$ to be the *negative* of the income effect:

$$\Delta x_1^m = x_1(p_1', m') - x_1(p_1', m) = -\Delta x_1^n.$$

Given this definition, the Slutsky identity becomes

$$\Delta x_1 = \Delta x_1^s - \Delta x_1^m.$$

If we divide each side of the identity by $\Delta p_1$, we have

$$\frac{\Delta x_1}{\Delta p_1} = \frac{\Delta x_1^s}{\Delta p_1} - \frac{\Delta x_1^m}{\Delta p_1}. \tag{8.2}$$

The first term on the right-hand side is the rate of change of demand
when price changes and income is adjusted so as to keep the old bundle
affordable—the substitution effect. Let's work on the second term. Since
we have an income change in the numerator, it would be nice to get an
income change in the denominator.

Remember that the income change, $\Delta m$, and the price change, $\Delta p_1$, are related by the formula

$$\Delta m = x_1 \Delta p_1.$$

Solving for $\Delta p_1$ we find

$$\Delta p_1 = \frac{\Delta m}{x_1}.$$

Now substitute this expression into the last term in (8.2) to get our final formula:

$$\frac{\Delta x_1}{\Delta p_1} = \frac{\Delta x_1^s}{\Delta p_1} - \frac{\Delta x_1^m}{\Delta m} x_1.$$

This is the Slutsky identity in terms of rates of change. Note that this is true for any size price change $\Delta p_1$, so it is true for an infinitesimal price change $dp_1$. So we can write the equation in derivative form as

$$\frac{\partial x_1(p_1, p_2, \overline{m})}{\partial p_1} = \frac{\partial x_1^s(p_1, p_2, \overline{x}_1, \overline{x}_2)}{\partial p_1} + \frac{\partial x_1^n(p_1, p_2, \overline{m})}{\partial m} \overline{x}_1.$$

We can interpret each term as follows:

$$\frac{\Delta x_1}{\Delta p_1} = \frac{x_1(p_1', m) - x_1(p_1, m)}{\Delta p_1}$$

is the rate of change in demand as price changes, holding income fixed;

$$\frac{\Delta x_1^s}{\Delta p_1} = \frac{x_1(p_1', m') - x_1(p_1, m)}{\Delta p_1}$$

is the rate of change in demand as the price changes, adjusting income so as to keep the old bundle just affordable, that is, the substitution effect; and

$$\frac{\Delta x_1^m}{\Delta m} x_1 = \frac{x_1(p_1', m') - x_1(p_1', m)}{m' - m} x_1 \tag{8.3}$$

is the rate of change of demand holding prices fixed and adjusting income, that is, the income effect.

The income effect is itself composed of two pieces: how demand changes as income changes, times the original level of demand. When the price changes by $\Delta p_1$, the change in demand due to the income effect is

$$\Delta x_1^m = \frac{x_1(p_1', m') - x_1(p_1', m)}{\Delta m} x_1 \Delta p_1.$$

But this last term, $x_1 \Delta p_1$, is just the change in income necessary to keep the old bundle feasible. That is, $x_1 \Delta p_1 = \Delta m$, so the change in demand due to the income effect reduces to

$$\Delta x_1^m = \frac{x_1(p_1', m') - x_1(p_1', m)}{\Delta m} \Delta m,$$

just as we had before.

## 8.6 The Law of Demand

In Chapter 5 we voiced some concerns over the fact that consumer theory seemed to have no particular content: demand could go up or down when a price increased, and demand could go up or down when income increased. If a theory doesn't restrict observed behavior in *some* fashion it isn't much of a theory. A model that is consistent with all behavior has no real content.

However, we know that consumer theory does have some content—we've seen that choices generated by an optimizing consumer must satisfy the Strong Axiom of Revealed Preference. Furthermore, we've seen that any price change can be decomposed into two changes: a substitution effect that is sure to be negative—opposite the direction of the price change—and an income effect whose sign depends on whether the good is a normal good or an inferior good.

Although consumer theory doesn't restrict how demand changes when price changes or how demand changes when income changes, it does restrict how these two kinds of changes interact. In particular, we have the following.

**The Law of Demand.** *If the demand for a good increases when income increases, then the demand for that good must decrease when its price increases.*

This follows directly from the Slutsky equation: if the demand increases when income increases, we have a normal good. And if we have a normal good, then the substitution effect and the income effect reinforce each other, and an increase in price will unambiguously reduce demand.

## 8.7 Examples of Income and Substitution Effects

Let's now consider some examples of price changes for particular kinds of preferences and decompose the demand changes into the income and the substitution effects.

We start with the case of perfect complements. The Slutsky decomposition is illustrated in Figure 8.4. When we pivot the budget line around the chosen point, the optimal choice at the new budget line is the same as at the old one—this means that the substitution effect is zero. The change in demand is due entirely to the income effect.

What about the case of perfect substitutes, illustrated in Figure 8.5? Here when we tilt the budget line, the demand bundle jumps from the vertical axis to the horizontal axis. There is no shifting left to do! The entire change in demand is due to the substitution effect in this case.

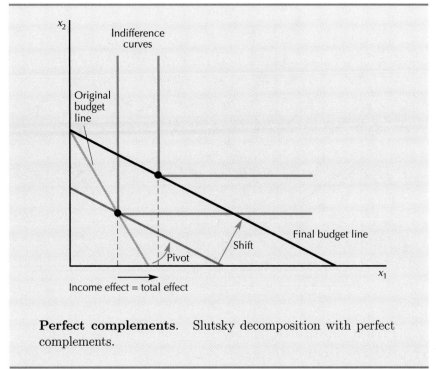

**Perfect complements.** Slutsky decomposition with perfect complements.

Figure
8.4

As a third example, let us consider the case of quasilinear preferences. This situation is somewhat peculiar. We have already seen that a shift in income causes no change in demand for good 1 when preferences are quasilinear. This means that the entire change in demand for good 1 is due to the substitution effect, and that the income effect is zero, as illustrated in Figure 8.6.

## EXAMPLE: Rebating a Tax

In 1974 the Organization of Petroleum Exporting Countries (OPEC) instituted an oil embargo against the United States. OPEC was able to stop oil shipments to U.S. ports for several weeks. The vulnerability of the United States to such disruptions was very disturbing to Congress and the president, and there were many plans proposed to reduce the United States's dependence on foreign oil.

One such plan involved increasing the gasoline tax. Increasing the cost of gasoline to the consumers would make them reduce their consumption of gasoline, and the reduced demand for gasoline would in turn reduce the demand for foreign oil.

But a straight increase in the tax on gasoline would hit consumers where it hurts—in the pocketbook—and by itself such a plan would be politically

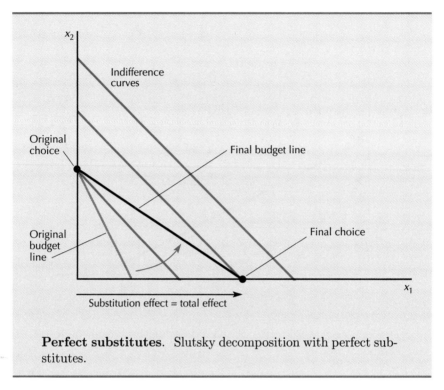

Figure
8.5
**Perfect substitutes.** Slutsky decomposition with perfect substitutes.

infeasible. So it was suggested that the revenues raised from consumers by this tax would be returned to the consumers in the form of direct money payments, or via the reduction of some other tax.

Critics of this proposal argued that paying the revenue raised by the tax back to the consumers would have no effect on demand since they could just use the rebated money to purchase more gasoline. What does economic analysis say about this plan?

Let us suppose, for simplicity, that the tax on gasoline would end up being passed along entirely to the consumers of gasoline so that the price of gasoline will go up by exactly the amount of the tax. (In general, only part of the tax would be passed along, but we will ignore that complication here.) Suppose that the tax would raise the price of gasoline from $p$ to $p' = p + t$, and that the average consumer would respond by reducing his demand from $x$ to $x'$. The average consumer is paying $t$ dollars more for gasoline, and he is consuming $x'$ gallons of gasoline after the tax is imposed, so the amount of revenue raised by the tax from the average consumer would be

$$R = tx' = (p' - p)x'.$$

Note that the revenue raised by the tax will depend on how much gasoline the consumer *ends up* consuming, $x'$, not how much he was initially

**Quasilinear preferences.** In the case of quasilinear preferences, the entire change in demand is due to the substitution
effect.

Figure
8.6

consuming, $x$.

If we let $y$ be the expenditure on all other goods and set its price to be
1, then the original budget constraint is

$$px + y = m,$$ (8.4)

and the budget constraint in the presence of the tax-rebate plan is

$$(p + t)x' + y' = m + tx'.$$ (8.5)

In budget constraint (8.5) the average consumer is choosing the left-hand
side variables—the consumption of each good—but the right-hand side—
his income and the rebate from the government—are taken as fixed. The
rebate depends on what all consumers do, not what the average consumer
does. In this case, the rebate turns out to be the taxes collected from the
average consumer—but that's because he is average, not because of any
causal connection.

If we cancel $tx'$ from each side of equation (8.5), we have

$$px' + y' = m.$$

Thus $(x', y')$ is a bundle that was affordable under the original budget
constraint and rejected in favor of $(x, y)$. Thus it must be that $(x, y)$

is preferred to $(x', y')$: the consumers are made worse off by this plan. Perhaps that is why it was never put into effect!

Using the Slutsky equation, the change in gas consumption will be given by

$$dx = \frac{\partial x}{\partial p} t + \frac{\partial x}{\partial m} tx.$$

The first term measures how demand responds to the price change times the amount of the price change—which gives us the price effect of the tax. The second terms tells us how demand responds to a change in income times the amount that income has changed—income has gone up by the amount of the tax revenues rebated to the consumer.

Now use Slutsky's equation to expand the first term on the right-hand side to get the substitution and income effects of the price change itself:

$$dx = \frac{\partial x^s}{\partial p} t - \frac{\partial x}{\partial m} tx + \frac{\partial x}{\partial m} tx = \frac{\partial x^s}{\partial p} t.$$

The income effect cancels out, and all that is left is the pure substitution effect. Imposing a small tax and rebating the revenues of the tax is just like imposing a price change and adjusting income so that the old consumption bundle is feasible—as long as the tax is small enough so that the derivative approximation is valid.

The equilibrium with a rebated tax is depicted in Figure 8.7. The tax makes good 1 more expensive, and the rebate increases money income. The original bundle is no longer affordable, and the consumer is definitely made worse off. The consumer's choice under the tax-rebate plan involves consuming less gasoline and more of "all other goods."

What can we say about the amount of consumption of gasoline? The average consumer could afford his old consumption of gasoline, but because of the tax, gasoline is now more expensive. In general, the consumer would choose to consume less of it.

## EXAMPLE: Voluntary Real Time Pricing

Electricity production suffers from an extreme capacity problem: it is relatively cheap to produce up to capacity, at which point it is, by definition, impossible to produce more. Building capacity is extremely expensive, so finding ways to reduce the use of electricity during periods of peak demand is very attractive from an economic point of view.

In states with warm climates, such as Georgia, roughly 30 percent of usage during periods of peak demand is due to air conditioning. Furthermore, it is relatively easy to forecast temperature one day ahead so that potential users will have time to adjust their demand by setting their air conditioning to a higher temperature, wearing light clothes, and so on.

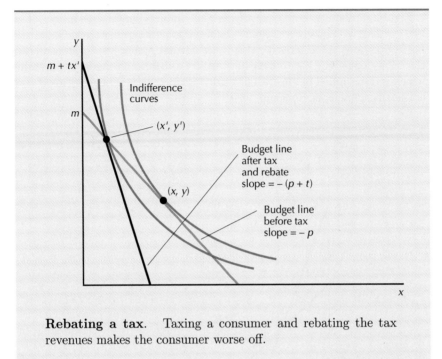

**Rebating a tax.**    Taxing a consumer and rebating the tax revenues makes the consumer worse off.

Figure
8.7

The challenge is to set up a pricing system so that those users who are able to cut back on their electricity use will have an incentive to reduce their consumption.

One way to accomplish this is through the use of Real Time Pricing (RTP). In a Real Time Pricing program, large industrial users are equipped with special meters that allow the price of electricity to vary from minute to minute, depending on signals sent from the electricity generating company. As the demand for electricity approaches capacity, the generating company increases the price so as to encourage users to cut back on their usage. The price schedule is determined as a function of the total demand for electricity.

Georgia Power Company claims that it runs the largest real time pricing program in the world. In 1999 it was able to reduce demand by 750 megawatts on high-price days by inducing some large customers to cut their demand by as much as 60 percent.

Georgia Power has devised several interesting variations on the basic real time pricing model. In one pricing plan, customers are assigned a baseline quantity, which represents their normal usage. When electricity is in short supply and the real time price increases, these users face a higher price for electricity use in excess of their baseline quantity. But they also receive a *rebate* if they can manage to cut their electricity use below their baseline amount.

Figure 8.8 shows how this affects the budget line of the users. The vertical axis is "money to spend on things other than electricity" and the horizontal axis is "electricity use." In normal times, users choose their electricity consumption to maximize utility subject to a budget constraint which is determined by the baseline price of electricity. The resulting choice is their baseline consumption.

OTHER GOODS

Consumption under RTP

RTP budget constraint

Baseline consumption

Baseline budget constraint

ELECTRICITY

Figure 8.8

**Voluntary real time pricing.** Users pay higher rates for additional electricity when the real time price rises, but they also get rebates at the same price if they cut back their use. This results in a pivot around the baseline use and tends to make the customers better off.

When the temperature rises, the real time price increases, making electricity more expensive. But this increase in price is a good thing for users who can cut back their consumption, since they receive a rebate based on the high real time price for every kilowatt of reduced usage. If usage stays at the baseline amount, then the user's bill will not change.

It is not hard to see that this pricing plan is a Slutsky pivot around the baseline consumption. Thus we can be confident that electricity usage will decline, and that users will be at least as well off at the real time price as at the baseline price. Indeed, the program has been quite popular, with over 1,600 voluntary participants.

## 8.8 Another Substitution Effect

The substitution effect is the name that economists give to the change in demand when prices change but a consumer's purchasing power is held constant, so that the original bundle remains affordable. At least this is *one* definition of the substitution effect. There is another definition that is also useful.

The definition we have studied above is called the **Slutsky substitution effect**. The definition we will describe in this section is called the **Hicks substitution effect**.[2]

Suppose that instead of pivoting the budget line around the original consumption bundle, we now *roll* the budget line around the indifference curve through the original consumption bundle, as depicted in Figure 8.9. In this way we present the consumer with a new budget line that has the same relative prices as the final budget line but has a different income. The purchasing power he has under this budget line will no longer be sufficient to purchase his original bundle of goods—but it will be sufficient to purchase a bundle that is just *indifferent* to his original bundle.

Thus the Hicks substitution effect keeps *utility* constant rather than keeping purchasing power constant. The Slutsky substitution effect gives the consumer just enough money to get back to his old level of consumption, while the Hicks substitution effect gives the consumer just enough money to get back to his old indifference curve. Despite this difference in definition, it turns out that the Hicks substitution effect must be negative—in the sense that it is in a direction opposite that of the price change—just like the Slutsky substitution effect.

The proof is again by revealed preference. Let $(x_1, x_2)$ be a demanded bundle at some prices $(p_1, p_2)$, and let $(y_1, y_2)$ be a demanded bundle at some other prices $(q_1, q_2)$. Suppose that income is such that the consumer is indifferent between $(x_1, x_2)$ and $(y_1, y_2)$. Since the consumer is indifferent between $(x_1, x_2)$ and $(y_1, y_2)$, neither bundle can be revealed preferred to the other.

Using the definition of revealed preference, this means that the following two inequalities are *not* true:

$$p_1 x_1 + p_2 x_2 > p_1 y_1 + p_2 y_2$$

$$q_1 y_1 + q_2 y_2 > q_1 x_1 + q_2 x_2.$$

It follows that these inequalities *are* true:

$$p_1 x_1 + p_2 x_2 \leq p_1 y_1 + p_2 y_2$$

---

[2] The concept is named for Sir John Hicks, an English recipient of the Nobel Prize in Economics.

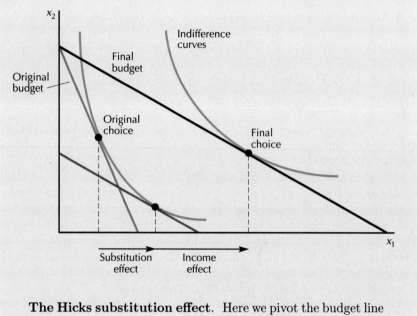

Figure
8.9

**The Hicks substitution effect.** Here we pivot the budget line around the indifference curve rather than around the original choice.

$$q_1 y_1 + q_2 y_2 \leq q_1 x_1 + q_2 x_2.$$

Adding these inequalities together and rearranging them we have

$$(q_1 - p_1)(y_1 - x_1) + (q_2 - p_2)(y_2 - x_2) \leq 0.$$

This is a general statement about how demands change when prices change if income is adjusted so as to keep the consumer on the same indifference curve. In the particular case we are concerned with, we are only changing the first price. Therefore $q_2 = p_2$, and we are left with

$$(q_1 - p_1)(y_1 - x_1) \leq 0.$$

This equation says that the change in the quantity demanded must have the opposite sign from that of the price change, which is what we wanted to show.

The total change in demand is still equal to the substitution effect plus the income effect—but now it is the Hicks substitution effect. Since the Hicks substitution effect is also negative, the Slutsky equation takes exactly the same form as we had earlier and has exactly the same interpretation. Both the Slutsky and Hicks definitions of the substitution effect have their place, and which is more useful depends on the problem at hand. It can be shown that for small changes in price, the two substitution effects are virtually identical.

## 8.9 Compensated Demand Curves

We have seen how the quantity demanded changes as a price changes in three different contexts: holding income fixed (the standard case), holding purchasing power fixed (the Slutsky substitution effect), and holding utility fixed (the Hicks substitution effect). We can draw the relationship between price and quantity demanded holding any of these three variables fixed. This gives rise to three different demand curves: the standard demand curve, the Slutsky demand curve, and the Hicks demand curve.

The analysis of this chapter shows that the Slutsky and Hicks demand curves are always downward sloping curves. Furthermore the ordinary demand curve is a downward sloping curve for normal goods. However, the Giffen analysis shows that it is theoretically possible that the ordinary demand curve may slope upwards for an inferior good.

The Hicksian demand curve—the one with utility held constant—is sometimes called the **compensated demand curve.** This terminology arises naturally if you think of constructing the Hicksian demand curve by adjusting income as the price changes so as to keep the consumer's utility constant. Hence the consumer is "compensated" for the price changes, and his utility is the same at every point on the Hicksian demand curve. This is in contrast to the situation with an ordinary demand curve. In this case the consumer is worse off facing higher prices than lower prices since his income is constant.

The compensated demand curve turns out to be very useful in advanced courses, especially in treatments of benefit-cost analysis. In this sort of analysis it is natural to ask what size payments are necessary to compensate consumers for some policy change. The magnitude of such payments gives a useful estimate of the cost of the policy change. However, actual calculation of compensated demand curves requires more mathematical machinery than we have developed in this text.

## Summary

1. When the price of a good decreases, there will be two effects on consumption. The change in relative prices makes the consumer want to consume more of the cheaper good. The increase in purchasing power due to the lower price may increase or decrease consumption, depending on whether the good is a normal good or an inferior good.

2. The change in demand due to the change in relative prices is called the substitution effect; the change due to the change in purchasing power is called the income effect.

3. The substitution effect is how demand changes when prices change and purchasing power is held constant, in the sense that the original bundle remains affordable. To hold real purchasing power constant, money income will have to change. The necessary change in money income is given by $\Delta m = x_1 \Delta p_1$.

4. The Slutsky equation says that the total change in demand is the sum of the substitution effect and the income effect.

5. The Law of Demand says that normal goods must have downward-sloping demand curves.

## REVIEW QUESTIONS

1. Suppose a consumer has preferences between two goods that are perfect substitutes. Can you change prices in such a way that the entire demand response is due to the income effect?

2. Suppose that preferences are concave. Is it still the case that the substitution effect is negative?

3. In the case of the gasoline tax, what would happen if the rebate to the consumers were based on their original consumption of gasoline, $x$, rather than on their final consumption of gasoline, $x'$?

4. In the case described in the preceding question, would the government be paying out more or less than it received in tax revenues?

5. In this case would the consumers be better off or worse off if the tax with rebate based on original consumption were in effect?

## APPENDIX

Let us derive the Slutsky equation using calculus. Consider the Slutsky definition of the substitution effect, in which the income is adjusted so as to give the consumer just enough to buy the original consumption bundle, which we will now denote by $(\bar{x}_1, \bar{x}_2)$. If the prices are $(p_1, p_2)$, then the consumer's actual choice with this adjustment will depend on $(p_1, p_2)$ and $(\bar{x}_1, \bar{x}_2)$. Let's call this relationship the **Slutsky demand function** for good 1, and write it as $x_1^s(p_1, p_2, \bar{x}_1, \bar{x}_2)$.

Suppose the original demanded bundle is $(\bar{x}_1, \bar{x}_2)$ at prices $(\bar{p}_1, \bar{p}_2)$ and income $\bar{m}$. The Slutsky demand function tells us what the consumer would demand facing some different prices $(p_1, p_2)$ and having income $p_1\bar{x}_1 + p_2\bar{x}_2$. Thus the Slutsky demand function at $(p_1, p_2, \bar{x}_1, \bar{x}_2)$ is the ordinary demand at $(p_1, p_2)$ and income $p_1\bar{x}_1 + p_2\bar{x}_2$. That is,

$$x_1^s(p_1, p_2, \bar{x}_1, \bar{x}_2) \equiv x_1(p_1, p_2, p_1\bar{x}_1 + p_2\bar{x}_2).$$

This equation says that the Slutsky demand at prices $(p_1, p_2)$ is that amount which the consumer would demand if he had enough income to purchase his original bundle of goods $(\overline{x}_1, \overline{x}_2)$. This is just the definition of the Slutsky demand function.

Differentiating this identity with respect to $p_1$, we have

$$\frac{\partial x_1^s(p_1, p_2, \overline{x}_1, \overline{x}_2)}{\partial p_1} = \frac{\partial x_1(p_1, p_2, \overline{m})}{\partial p_1} + \frac{\partial x_1(p_1, p_2, \overline{m})}{\partial m}\overline{x}_1.$$

Rearranging we have

$$\frac{\partial x_1(p_1, p_2, \overline{m})}{\partial p_1} = \frac{\partial x_1^s(p_1, p_2, \overline{x}_1, \overline{x}_2)}{\partial p_1} - \frac{\partial x_1(p_1, p_2, \overline{m})}{\partial m}\overline{x}_1.$$

Note the use of the chain rule in this calculation.

This is a derivative form of the Slutsky equation. It says that the total effect of a price change is composed of a substitution effect (where income is adjusted to keep the bundle $(\overline{x}_1, \overline{x}_2)$ feasible) and an income effect. We know from the text that the substitution effect is negative and that the sign of the income effect depends on whether the good in question is inferior or not. As you can see, this is just the form of the Slutsky equation considered in the text, except that we have replaced the $\Delta$'s with derivative signs.

What about the Hicks substitution effect? It is also possible to define a Slutsky equation for it. We let $x_1^h(p_1, p_2, \overline{u})$ be the Hicksian demand function, which measures how much the consumer demands of good 1 at prices $(p_1, p_2)$ if income is adjusted to keep the level of *utility* constant at the original level $\overline{u}$. It turns out that in this case the Slutsky equation takes the form

$$\frac{\partial x_1(p_1, p_2, m)}{\partial p_1} = \frac{\partial x_1^h(p_1, p_2, \overline{u})}{\partial p_1} - \frac{\partial x_1(p_1, p_2, m)}{\partial m}\overline{x}_1.$$

The proof of this equation hinges on the fact that

$$\frac{\partial x_1^h(p_1, p_2, \overline{u})}{\partial p_1} = \frac{\partial x_1^s(p_1, p_2, \overline{x}_1, \overline{x}_2)}{\partial p_1}$$

for infinitesimal changes in price. That is, for derivative size changes in price, the Slutsky substitution and the Hicks substitution effect are the same. The proof of this is not terribly difficult, but it involves some concepts that are beyond the scope of this book. A relatively simple proof is given in Hal R. Varian, *Microeconomic Analysis*, 3rd ed. (New York: Norton, 1992).

## EXAMPLE: Rebating a Small Tax

We can use the calculus version of the Slutsky equation to see how consumption choices would react to a small change in a tax when the tax revenues are rebated to the consumers.

Assume, as before, that the tax causes the price to rise by the full amount of the tax. Let $x$ be the amount of gasoline, $p$ its original price, and $t$ the amount of the tax. Then the change in consumption will be given by

$$dx = \frac{\partial x}{\partial p}t + \frac{\partial x}{\partial m}tx.$$

The first term measures how demand responds to the price change times the amount of the price change—which gives us the price effect of the tax. The second terms tells us how demand responds to a change in income times the amount that income has changed—income has gone up by the amount of the tax revenues rebated to the consumer.

Now use Slutsky's equation to expand the first term on the right-hand side to get the substitution and income effects of the price change itself:

$$dx = \frac{\partial x^s}{\partial p}t - \frac{\partial x}{\partial m}tx + \frac{\partial x}{\partial m}tx = \frac{\partial x^s}{\partial p}t.$$

The income effect cancels out, and all that is left is the pure substitution effect. Imposing a small tax and rebating the revenues of the tax is just like imposing a price change and adjusting income so that the old consumption bundle is feasible—as long as the tax is small enough so that the derivative approximation is valid.

# CHAPTER 9

# BUYING AND SELLING

In the simple model of the consumer that we considered in the preceding chapters, the income of the consumer was given. In reality people earn their income by selling things that they own: items that they have produced, assets that they have accumulated, or, most commonly, their own labor. In this chapter we will examine how the earlier model must be modified so as to describe this kind of behavior.

## 9.1 Net and Gross Demands

As before, we will limit ourselves to the two-good model. We now suppose that the consumer starts off with an **endowment** of the two goods, which we will denote by $(\omega_1, \omega_2)$.[1] This is how much of the two goods the consumer has *before* he enters the market. Think of a farmer who goes to market with $\omega_1$ units of carrots and $\omega_2$ units of potatoes. The farmer inspects the prices available at the market and decides how much he wants to buy and sell of the two goods.

---

[1] The Greek letter $\omega$, omega, is pronounced "o–may–gah."

Let us make a distinction here between the consumer's **gross demands** and his **net demands**. The gross demand for a good is the amount of the good that the consumer actually ends up consuming: how much of each of the goods he or she takes home from the market. The net demand for a good is the *difference* between what the consumer ends up with (the gross demand) and the initial endowment of goods. The net demand for a good is simply the amount that is bought or sold of the good.

If we let $(x_1, x_2)$ be the gross demands, then $(x_1 - \omega_1, x_2 - \omega_2)$ are the net demands. Note that while the gross demands are typically positive numbers, the net demands may be positive or negative. If the net demand for good 1 is negative, it means that the consumer wants to consume less of good 1 than she has; that is, she wants to *supply* good 1 to the market. A negative net demand is simply an amount supplied.

For purposes of economic analysis, the gross demands are the more important, since that is what the consumer is ultimately concerned with. But the net demands are what are actually exhibited in the market and thus are closer to what the layman means by demand or supply.

## 9.2 The Budget Constraint

The first thing we should do is to consider the form of the budget constraint. What constrains the consumer's final consumption? It must be that the value of the bundle of goods that she goes home with must be equal to the value of the bundle of goods that she came with. Or, algebraically:

$$p_1 x_1 + p_2 x_2 = p_1 \omega_1 + p_2 \omega_2.$$

We could just as well express this budget line in terms of net demands as

$$p_1(x_1 - \omega_1) + p_2(x_2 - \omega_2) = 0.$$

If $(x_1 - \omega_1)$ is positive we say that the consumer is a **net buyer** or **net demander** of good 1; if it is negative we say that she is a **net seller** or **net supplier**. Then the above equation says that the value of what the consumer buys must equal the value of what she sells, which seems sensible enough.

We could also express the budget line when the endowment is present in a form similar to the way we described it before. Now it takes two equations:

$$p_1 x_1 + p_2 x_2 = m$$
$$m = p_1 \omega_1 + p_2 \omega_2.$$

Once the prices are fixed, the value of the endowment, and hence the consumer's money income, is fixed.

What does the budget line look like graphically? When we fix the prices, money income is fixed, and we have a budget equation just like we had before. Thus the slope must be given by $-p_1/p_2$, just as before, so the only problem is to determine the location of the line.

The location of the line can be determined by the following simple observation: the endowment bundle is always on the budget line. That is, one value of $(x_1, x_2)$ that satisfies the budget line is $x_1 = \omega_1$ and $x_2 = \omega_2$. The endowment is always just affordable, since the amount you have to spend is precisely the value of the endowment.

Putting these facts together shows that the budget line has a slope of $-p_1/p_2$ and passes through the endowment point. This is depicted in Figure 9.1.

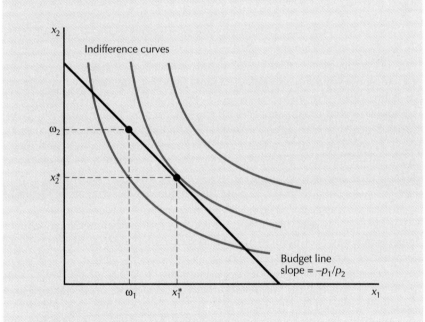

**The budget line.** The budget line passes through the endowment and has a slope of $-p_1/p_2$.

Figure 9.1

Given this budget constraint, the consumer can choose the optimal consumption bundle just as before. In Figure 9.1 we have shown an example of an optimal consumption bundle $(x_1^*, x_2^*)$. Just as before, it will satisfy the optimality condition that the marginal rate of substitution is equal to the price ratio.

In this particular case, $x_1^* > \omega_1$ and $x_2^* < \omega_2$, so the consumer is a net buyer of good 1 and a net seller of good 2. The net demands are simply the net amounts that the consumer buys or sells of the two goods. In general the consumer may decide to be either a buyer or a seller depending on the relative prices of the two goods.

## 9.3 Changing the Endowment

In our previous analysis of choice we examined how the optimal consumption changed as the money income changed while the prices remained fixed. We can do a similar analysis here by asking how the optimal consumption changes as the *endowment* changes while the prices remain fixed.

For example, suppose that the endowment changes from $(\omega_1, \omega_2)$ to some other value $(\omega_1', \omega_2')$ such that

$$p_1\omega_1 + p_2\omega_2 > p_1\omega_1' + p_2\omega_2'.$$

This inequality means that the new endowment $(\omega_1', \omega_2')$ is worth less than the old endowment—the money income that the consumer could achieve by selling her endowment is less.

This is depicted graphically in Figure 9.2A: the budget line shifts inward. Since this is exactly the same as a reduction in money income, we can conclude the same two things that we concluded in our examination of that case. First, the consumer is definitely worse off with the endowment $(\omega_1', \omega_2')$ than she was with the old endowment, since her consumption possibilities have been reduced. Second, her demand for each good will change according to whether that good is a normal good or an inferior good.

For example, if good 1 is a normal good and the consumer's endowment changes in a way that reduces its value, we can conclude that the consumer's demand for good 1 will decrease.

The case where the value of the endowment increases is depicted in Figure 9.2B. Following the above argument we conclude that if the budget line shifts outward in a parallel way, the consumer must be made better off. Algebraically, if the endowment changes from $(\omega_1, \omega_2)$ to $(\omega_1', \omega_2')$ and $p_1\omega_1 + p_2\omega_2 < p_1\omega_1' + p_2\omega_2'$, then the consumer's new budget set must contain her old budget set. This in turn implies that the optimal choice of the consumer with the new budget set must be preferred to the optimal choice given the old endowment.

It is worthwhile pondering this point a moment. In Chapter 7 we argued that just because a consumption bundle had a higher cost than another didn't mean that it would be preferred to the other bundle. But that only holds for a bundle that must be *consumed*. If a consumer can sell a bundle of goods on a free market at constant prices, then she will always prefer a higher-valued bundle to a lower-valued bundle, simply because a

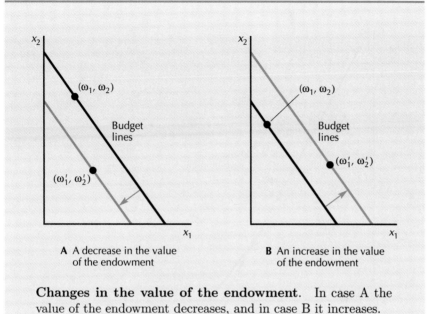

**A** A decrease in the value
of the endowment

**B** An increase in the value
of the endowment

**Changes in the value of the endowment.** In case A the
value of the endowment decreases, and in case B it increases.

Figure
9.2

higher-valued bundle gives her more income, and thus more consumption
possibilities. Therefore, an *endowment* that has a higher value will always
be preferred to an endowment with a lower value. This simple observation
will turn out to have some important implications later on.

There's one more case to consider: what happens if $p_1\omega_1 + p_2\omega_2 = p_1\omega_1' + p_2\omega_2'$? Then the budget set doesn't change at all: the consumer is just
as well-off with $(\omega_1, \omega_2)$ as with $(\omega_1', \omega_2')$, and her optimal choice should
be exactly the same. The endowment has just shifted along the original
budget line.

## 9.4 Price Changes

Earlier, when we examined how demand changed when price changed, we
conducted our investigation under the hypothesis that money income remained constant. Now, when money income is determined by the value
of the endowment, such a hypothesis is unreasonable: if the value of a
good you are selling changes, your money income will certainly change.
Thus in the case where the consumer has an endowment, changing prices
automatically implies changing income.

Let us first think about this geometrically. If the price of good 1 decreases, we know that the budget line becomes flatter. Since the endowment bundle is always affordable, this means that the budget line must
pivot around the endowment, as depicted in Figure 9.3.

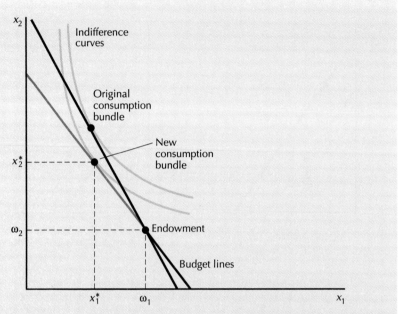

Figure
9.3

**Decreasing the price of good 1.** Lowering the price of good 1 makes the budget line pivot around the endowment. If the consumer remains a supplier she must be worse off.

In this case, the consumer is initially a seller of good 1 and remains a seller of good 1 even after the price has *declined*. What can we say about this consumer's welfare? In the case depicted, the consumer is on a lower indifference curve after the price change than before, but will this be true in general? The answer comes from applying the principle of revealed preference.

If the consumer remains a supplier, then her new consumption bundle must be on the colored part of the new budget line. But this part of the new budget line is inside the original budget set: all of these choices were open to the consumer before the price changed. Therefore, by revealed preference, all of these choices are worse than the original consumption bundle. We can therefore conclude that if the price of a good that a consumer is selling goes down, and the consumer decides to remain a seller, then the consumer's welfare must have declined.

What if the price of a good that the consumer is selling decreases and the consumer decides to switch to being a buyer of that good? In this case, the consumer may be better off or she may be worse off—there is no way to tell.

Let us now turn to the situation where the consumer is a net buyer of a good. In this case everything neatly turns around: if the consumer is a net buyer of a good, its price *increases*, and the consumer optimally decides to remain a buyer, then she must definitely be worse off. But if the price increase leads her to become a seller, it could go either way—she may be better off, or she may be worse off. These observations follow from a simple application of revealed preference just like the cases described above, but it is good practice for you to draw a graph just to make sure you understand how this works.

Revealed preference also allows us to make some interesting points about the decision of whether to remain a buyer or to become a seller when prices change. Suppose, as in Figure 9.4, that the consumer is a net buyer of good 1, and consider what happens if the price of good 1 *decreases*. Then the budget line becomes flatter as in Figure 9.4.

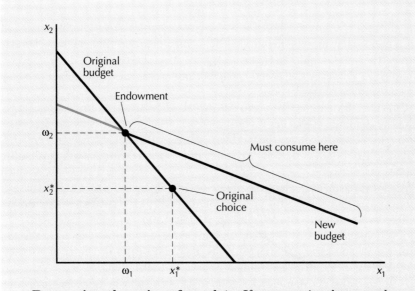

**Decreasing the price of good 1**. If a person is a buyer and the price of what she is buying decreases, she remains a buyer.

Figure 9.4

As usual we don't know for certain whether the consumer will buy more or less of good 1—it depends on her tastes. However, we can say something for sure: *the consumer will continue to be a net buyer of good 1—she will not switch to being a seller.*

How do we know this? Well, consider what would happen if the consumer did switch. Then she would be consuming somewhere on the colored part of the new budget line in Figure 9.4. But those consumption bundles were feasible for her when she faced the original budget line, and she rejected them in favor of $(x_1^*, x_2^*)$. So $(x_1^*, x_2^*)$ must be better than any of those points. And under the *new* budget line, $(x_1^*, x_2^*)$ is a feasible consumption bundle. So whatever she consumes under the new budget line, it must be better than $(x_1^*, x_2^*)$—and thus better than any points on the colored part of the new budget line. This implies that her consumption of $x_1$ must be to the right of her endowment point—that is, she must remain a net demander of good 1.

Again, this kind of observation applies equally well to a person who is a net seller of a good: if the price of what she is selling goes *up*, she will not switch to being a net buyer. We can't tell for sure if the consumer will consume more or less of the good she is selling—but we know that she will keep selling it if the price goes up.

## 9.5 Offer Curves and Demand Curves

Recall from Chapter 6 that price offer curves depict those combinations of both goods that may be demanded by a consumer and that demand curves depict the relationship between the price and the quantity demanded of some good. Exactly the same constructions work when the consumer has an endowment of both goods.

Consider, for example, Figure 9.5, which illustrates the price offer curve and the demand curve for a consumer. The offer curve will always pass through the endowment, because at some price the endowment will be a demanded bundle; that is, at some prices the consumer will optimally choose not to trade.

As we've seen, the consumer may decide to be a buyer of good 1 for some prices and a seller of good 1 for other prices. Thus the offer curve will generally pass to the left and to the right of the endowment point.

The demand curve illustrated in Figure 9.5B is the gross demand curve—it measures the total amount the consumer chooses to consume of good 1. We have illustrated the net demand curve in Figure 9.6.

Note that the net demand for good 1 will typically be negative for some prices. This will be when the price of good 1 becomes so high that the consumer chooses to become a seller of good 1. At some price the consumer switches between being a net demander to being a net supplier of good 1.

It is conventional to plot the supply curve in the positive orthant, although it actually makes more sense to think of supply as just a negative demand. We'll bow to tradition here and plot the net supply curve in the normal way—as a positive amount, as in Figure 9.6.

Algebraically the net demand for good 1, $d_1(p_1, p_2)$, is the difference between the gross demand $x_1(p_1, p_2)$ and the endowment of good 1, when this difference is positive; that is, when the consumer wants more of the good than he or she has:

$$d_1(p_1, p_2) = \begin{cases} x_1(p_1, p_2) - \omega_1 & \text{if this is positive;} \\ 0 & \text{otherwise.} \end{cases}$$

**The offer curve and the demand curve.** These are two ways of depicting the relationship between the demanded bundle and the prices when an endowment is present.

Figure
9.5

The net supply curve is the difference between how much the consumer has of good 1 and how much he or she wants when *this* difference is positive:

$$s_1(p_1, p_2) = \begin{cases} \omega_1 - x_1(p_1, p_2) & \text{if this is positive;} \\ 0 & \text{otherwise.} \end{cases}$$

Everything that we've established about the properties of demand behavior applies directly to the supply behavior of a consumer—because supply is just negative demand. If the *gross* demand curve is always downward sloping, then the net demand curve will be downward sloping and the supply curve will be upward sloping. Think about it: if an increase in the price makes the net demand more negative, then the net supply will be more positive.

## 9.6 The Slutsky Equation Revisited

The above applications of revealed preference are handy, but they don't really answer the main question: how does the demand for a good react to a change in its price? We saw in Chapter 8 that if money income was held constant, and the good was a normal good, then a reduction in its price must lead to an increase in demand.

The catch is the phrase "money income was held constant." The case we are examining here necessarily involves a change in money income, since the value of the endowment will necessarily change when a price changes.

Figure
9.6   **Gross demand, net demand, and net supply.** Using the
gross demand and net demand to depict the demand and supply
behavior.

In Chapter 8 we described the Slutsky equation that decomposed the
change in demand due to a price change into a substitution effect and an
income effect. The income effect was due to the change in purchasing power
when prices change. But now, purchasing power has two reasons to change
when a price changes. The first is the one involved in the definition of the
Slutsky equation: when a price falls, for example, you can buy just as much
of a good as you were consuming before and have some extra money left
over. Let us refer to this as the **ordinary income effect**. But the second
effect is new. When the price of a good changes, it changes the value of
your endowment and thus changes your money income. For example, if
you are a net supplier of a good, then a fall in its price will reduce your
money income directly since you won't be able to sell your endowment for
as much money as you could before. We will have the same effects that
we had before, plus an extra income effect from the influence of the prices
on the value of the endowment bundle. We'll call this the **endowment
income effect**.

In the earlier form of the Slutsky equation, the amount of money income
you had was fixed. Now we have to worry about how your money income
changes as the value of your endowment changes. Thus, when we calculate
the effect of a change in price on demand, the Slutsky equation will take
the form:

total change in demand = change due to substitution effect + change in demand due to ordinary income effect + change in demand due to endowment
income effect.

The first two effects are familiar. As before, let $\frac{\partial x_1}{\partial p_1}$ stand for the total rate of change in demand, with a subscript $s$ to stand for the substitution effect, and a subscript $m$ to stand for the ordinary income effect. Then we can substitute these terms into the above "verbal equation" to get the Slutsky equation in terms of rates of change:

$$\frac{\partial x_1}{\partial p_1} = \frac{\partial x_1^s}{\partial p_1} - x_1 \frac{\partial x_1^m}{\partial m} + \text{endowment income effect.} \qquad (9.1)$$

What will the last term look like? We'll derive an explicit expression below, but let us first think about what is involved. When the price of the endowment changes, money income will change, and this change in money income will induce a change in demand. Thus the endowment income effect will consist of two terms:

endowment income effect = change in demand when income changes
$\times$ the change in income when price changes. $\qquad (9.2)$

Let's look at the second effect first. Since income is defined to be

$$m = p_1 \omega_1 + p_2 \omega_2,$$

we have

$$\frac{\partial m}{\partial p_1} = \omega_1.$$

This tells us how money income changes when the price of good 1 changes: if you have 10 units of good 1 to sell, and its price goes up by \$1, your money income will go up by \$10.

The first term in equation (9.2) is just how demand changes when income changes. We already have an expression for this: it is $\frac{\partial x_1^m}{\partial m}$: the change in demand divided by the change in income. Thus the endowment income effect is given by

$$\text{endowment income effect} = \frac{\partial x_1^m}{\partial m} \frac{\partial m}{\partial p_1} = \frac{\partial x_1^m}{\partial m} \omega_1. \qquad (9 3)$$

Inserting equation (9.3) into equation (9.1) we get the final form of the Slutsky equation:

$$\frac{\partial x_1}{\partial p_1} = \frac{\partial x_1^s}{\partial p_1} + (\omega_1 - x_1) \frac{\partial x_1^m}{\partial m}.$$

The derivation of the Slutsky equation above contained one bit of hand waving. When we considered how changing the monetary value of the endowment affects demand, we said that it was equal to $\frac{\partial x_1^m}{\partial m}$. In our old version of the Slutsky equation this was the rate of change in demand when income changed so as to keep the original consumption bundle affordable. But that will not necessarily be equal to the rate of change of demand when the value of the endowment changes. Let's examine this point in a little more detail.

Let the price of good 1 change from $p_1$ to $p_1'$, and use $m''$ to denote the new money income at the price $p_1'$ due to the change in the value of the endowment. Suppose that the price of good 2 remains fixed so we can omit it as an argument of the demand function.

By definition of $m''$, we know that

$$m'' - m = \Delta p_1 \omega_1.$$

Note that it is identically true that

$$\frac{x_1(p_1', m'') - x_1(p_1, m)}{\Delta p_1} =$$

$$+ \frac{x_1(p_1', m') - x_1(p_1, m)}{\Delta p_1} \quad \text{(substitution effect)}$$

$$- \frac{x_1(p_1', m') - x_1(p_1', m)}{\Delta p_1} \quad \text{(ordinary income effect)}$$

$$+ \frac{x_1(p_1', m'') - x_1(p_1', m)}{\Delta p_1} \quad \text{(endowment income effect)}.$$

(Just cancel out identical terms with opposite signs on the right-hand side.)
By definition of the ordinary income effect,

$$\Delta p_1 = \frac{m' - m}{x_1}$$

and by definition of the endowment income effect,

$$\Delta p_1 = \frac{m'' - m}{\omega_1}.$$

Making these replacements gives us a Slutsky equation of the form

$$\frac{x_1(p_1', m'') - x_1(p_1, m)}{\Delta p_1} =$$

$$+ \frac{x_1(p_1', m') - x_1(p_1, m)}{\Delta p_1} \quad \text{(substitution effect)}$$

$$- \frac{x_1(p_1', m') - x_1(p_1', m)}{m' - m} x_1 \quad \text{(ordinary income effect)}$$

$$+ \frac{x_1(p_1', m'') - x_1(p_1', m)}{m'' - m} \omega_1 \quad \text{(endowment income effect)}.$$

Writing this in terms of $\Delta$s, we have

$$\frac{\Delta x_1}{\Delta p_1} = \frac{\Delta x_1^s}{\Delta p_1} - \frac{\Delta x_1^m}{\Delta m} x_1 + \frac{\Delta x_1^w}{\Delta m} \omega_1.$$

The only new term here is the last one. It tells how the demand for good 1 changes as income changes, times the *endowment* of good 1. This is precisely the endowment income effect.

Suppose that we are considering a very small price change, and thus a small associated income change. Then the fractions in the two income effects will be virtually the same, since the *rate* of change of good 1 when income changes from $m$ to $m'$ should be about the same as when income changes from $m$ to $m''$. For such small changes we can collect terms and write the last two terms—the income effects—as

$$\frac{\Delta x_1^m}{\Delta m}(\omega_1 - x_1),$$

which yields a Slutsky equation of the same form as that derived earlier:

$$\frac{\Delta x_1}{\Delta p_1} = \frac{\Delta x_1^s}{\Delta p_1} + (\omega_1 - x_1)\frac{\Delta x_1^m}{\Delta m}.$$

If we want to express the Slutsky equation in calculus terms, we can just take limits in this expression. Or, if you prefer, we can calculate the correct equation directly, just by taking partial derivatives. Let $x_1(p_1, m(p_1))$ be the demand function for good 1 where we hold price 2 fixed and recognize that money income depends on the price of good 1 via the relationship $m(p_1) = p_1\omega_1 + p_2\omega_2$. Then we can write

$$\frac{dx_1(p_1, m(p_1))}{dp_1} = \frac{\partial x_1(p_1, m)}{\partial p_1} + \frac{\partial x_1(p_1, m)}{\partial m}\frac{dm(p_1)}{dp_1}. \qquad (9.4)$$

By the definition of $m(p_1)$ we know how income changes when price changes:

$$\frac{\partial m(p_1)}{\partial p_1} = \omega_1, \qquad (9.5)$$

and by the Slutsky equation we know how demand changes when price changes, holding money income fixed:

$$\frac{\partial x_1(p_1, m)}{\partial p_1} = \frac{\partial x_1^s(p_1)}{\partial p_1} - \frac{\partial x(p_1, m)}{\partial m}x_1. \qquad (9.6)$$

Inserting equations (9.5) and (9.6) into equation (9.4) we have

$$\frac{dx_1(p_1, m(p_1))}{dp_1} = \frac{\partial x_1^s(p_1)}{\partial p_1} + \frac{\partial x(p_1, m)}{\partial m}(\omega_1 - x_1),$$

which is the form of the Slutsky equation that we want.

This equation can be used to answer the earlier question: how does the demand for a good react to a change in its price? We know that the sign of the substitution effect is always negative—opposite the direction of the change in price. Let us suppose that the good is a normal good, so that $\frac{\partial x_1^m}{\partial m} > 0$. Then the sign of the combined income effect depends on whether the person is a net demander or a net supplier of the good in question. If the person is a net demander of a normal good, and its price increases, then the consumer will necessarily buy less of it. If the consumer is a net supplier of a normal good, then the sign of the total effect is ambiguous: it depends on the magnitude of the (positive) combined income effect as compared to the magnitude of the (negative) substitution effect.

As before, each of these changes can be depicted graphically, although the graph gets rather messy. Refer to Figure 9.7, which depicts the Slutsky decomposition of a price change. The total change in the demand for good 1 is indicated by the movement from $A$ to $C$. This is the sum of three separate movements: the substitution effect, which is the movement from $A$ to $B$, and two income effects. The ordinary income effect, which is the movement from $B$ to $D$, is the change in demand *holding money income fixed*—that is, the same income effect that we examined in Chapter 8. But since the value of the endowment changes when prices change, there is now an extra income effect: because of the change in the value of the endowment, money income changes. This change in money income shifts the budget line back inward so that it passes through the endowment bundle. The change in demand from $D$ to $C$ measures this endowment income effect.

## 9.7 Use of the Slutsky Equation

Suppose that we have a consumer who sells apples and oranges that he grows on a few trees in his backyard, like the consumer we described at the beginning of Chapter 8. We said there that if the price of apples increased, then this consumer might actually consume more apples. Using the Slutsky equation derived in this chapter, it is not hard to see why. If we let $x_a$ stand for the consumer's demand for apples, and let $p_a$ be the price of apples, then we know that

$$\frac{\partial x_a}{\partial p_a} = \underset{(-)}{\frac{\partial x_a^s}{\partial p_a}} + \underset{(+)}{(\omega_a - x_a)} \underset{(+)}{\frac{\partial x_a^m}{\partial m}}.$$

This says that the total change in the demand for apples when the price of apples changes is the substitution effect plus the income effect. The substitution effect works in the right direction—increasing the price decreases the demand for apples. But if apples are a normal good for this consumer,

$x_2$

Endowment

Original
choice

Final choice

Indifference
curves

A       B C D                                    $x_1$

**The Slutsky equation revisited.**   Breaking up the effect
of the price change into the substitution effect $(A$ to $B)$, the
ordinary income effect $(B$ to $D)$, and the endowment income
effect $(D$ to $C)$.

Figure
9.7

the income effect works in the wrong direction. Since the consumer is a net
supplier of apples, the increase in the price of apples increases his money
income so much that he wants to consume more apples due to the income
effect. If the latter term is strong enough to outweigh the substitution
effect, we can easily get the "perverse" result.

## EXAMPLE: Calculating the Endowment Income Effect

Let's try a little numerical example. Suppose that a dairy farmer produces
40 quarts of milk a week. Initially the price of milk is $3 a quart. His
demand function for milk, for his own consumption, is

$$x_1 = 10 + \frac{m}{10p_1}.$$

Since he is producing 40 quarts at $3 a quart, his income is $120 a week.
His initial demand for milk is therefore $x_1 = 14$. Now suppose that the
price of milk changes to $2 a quart. His money income will then change to
$m' = 2 \times 40 = \$80$, and his demand will be $x_1' = 10 + 80/20 = 14$.

If his money income had remained fixed at $m = \$120$, he would have
purchased $x_1 = 10 + 120/10 \times 2 = 16$ quarts of milk at this price. Thus the

endowment income effect—the change in his demand due to the change in the value of his endowment—is $-2$. The substitution effect and the ordinary income effect for this problem were calculated in Chapter 8.

## 9.8 Labor Supply

Let us apply the idea of an endowment to analyzing a consumer's labor supply decision. The consumer can choose to work a lot and have relatively high consumption, or can choose to work a little and have a small consumption. The amount of consumption and labor will be determined by the interaction of the consumer's preferences and the budget constraint.

### The Budget Constraint

Let us suppose that the consumer initially has some money income $M$ that she receives whether she works or not. This might be income from investments or from relatives, for example. We call this amount the consumer's **nonlabor income**. (The consumer could have zero nonlabor income, but we want to allow for the possibility that it is positive.)

Let us use $C$ to indicate the amount of consumption the consumer has, and use $p$ to denote the price of consumption. Then letting $w$ be the wage rate, and $L$ the amount of labor supplied, we have the budget constraint:

$$pC = M + wL.$$

This says that the value of what the consumer consumes must be equal to her nonlabor income plus her labor income.

Let us try to compare the above formulation to the previous examples of budget constraints. The major difference is that we have something that the consumer is choosing—labor supply—on the right-hand side of the equation. We can easily transpose it to the left-hand side to get

$$pC - wL = M.$$

This is better, but we have a minus sign where we normally have a plus sign. How can we remedy this? Let us suppose that there is some maximum amount of labor supply possible—24 hours a day, 7 days a week, or whatever is compatible with the units of measurement we are using. Let $\overline{L}$ denote this amount of labor time. Then adding $w\overline{L}$ to each side and rearranging we have

$$pC + w(\overline{L} - L) = M + w\overline{L}.$$

Let us define $\overline{C} = M/p$, the amount of consumption that the consumer would have if she didn't work at all. That is, $\overline{C}$ is her endowment of consumption, so we write

$$pC + w(\overline{L} - L) = p\overline{C} + w\overline{L}.$$

Now we have an equation very much like those we've seen before. We have two choice variables on the left-hand side and two endowment variables on the right-hand side. The variable $\overline{L} - L$ can be interpreted as the amount of "leisure"—that is, time that isn't labor time. Let us use the variable $R$ (for relaxation!) to denote leisure, so that $R = \overline{L} - L$. Then the total amount of time you have available for leisure is $\overline{R} = \overline{L}$ and the budget constraint becomes

$$pC + wR = p\overline{C} + w\overline{R}.$$

The above equation is formally identical to the very first budget constraint that we wrote in this chapter. However, it has a much more interesting interpretation. It says that the value of a consumer's consumption plus her leisure has to equal the value of her endowment of consumption and her endowment of time, where her endowment of time is valued at her wage rate. The wage rate is not only the price of labor, it is also the price of *leisure*.

After all, if your wage rate is $10 an hour and you decide to consume an extra hour's leisure, how much does it cost you? The answer is that it costs you $10 in forgone income—that's the price of that extra hour's consumption of leisure. Economists sometimes say that the wage rate is the **opportunity cost** of leisure.

The right-hand side of this budget constraint is sometimes called the consumer's **full income** or **implicit income**. It measures the value of what the consumer owns—her endowment of consumption goods, if any, and her endowment of her own time. This is to be distinguished from the consumer's **measured income**, which is simply the income she receives from selling off some of her time.

The nice thing about this budget constraint is that it is just like the ones we've seen before. It passes through the endowment point $(\overline{L}, \overline{C})$ and has a slope of $-w/p$. The endowment would be what the consumer would get if she did not engage in market trade at all, and the slope of the budget line tells us the rate at which the market will exchange one good for another.

The optimal choice occurs where the marginal rate of substitution—the tradeoff between consumption and leisure—equals $w/p$, the **real wage**, as depicted in Figure 9.8. The value of the extra consumption to the consumer from working a little more has to be just equal to the value of the lost leisure that it takes to generate that consumption. The real wage is the amount of consumption that the consumer can purchase if she gives up an hour of leisure.

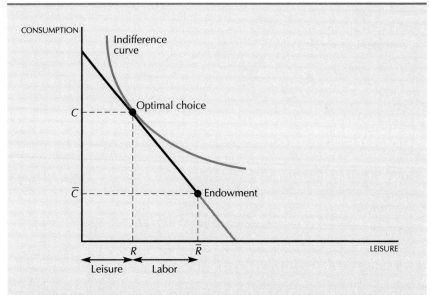

Figure
9.8

**Labor supply**. The optimal choice describes the demand for leisure measured from the origin to the right, and the supply of labor measured from the endowment to the left.

## 9.9 Comparative Statics of Labor Supply

First let us consider how a consumer's labor supply changes as money income changes with the price and wage held fixed. If you won the state lottery and got a big increase in nonlabor income, what would happen to your supply of labor? What would happen to your demand for leisure?

For most people, the supply of labor would drop when their money income increased. In other words, leisure is probably a normal good for most people: when their money income rises, people choose to consume more leisure. There seems to be a fair amount of evidence for this observation, so we will adopt it as a maintained hypothesis: we will assume that leisure is a normal good.

What does this imply about the response of the consumer's labor supply to changes in the wage rate? When the wage rate increases there are two effects: the return to working more increase and the cost of consuming leisure increases. By using the ideas of income and substitution effects and the Slutsky equation we can isolate these individual effects and analyze them.

When the wage rate increases, leisure becomes more expensive, which by itself leads people to want less of it (the substitution effect). Since leisure is a normal good, we would then predict that an increase in the wage rate would necessarily lead to a decrease in the demand for leisure—that is, an increase in the supply of labor. This follows from the Slutsky equation given in Chapter 8. A normal good must have a negatively sloped demand curve. If leisure is a normal good, then the supply curve of labor must be positively sloped.

But there is a problem with this analysis. First, at an intuitive level, it does not seem reasonable that increasing the wage would *always* result in an increased supply of labor. If my wage becomes very high, I might well "spend" the extra income in consuming leisure. How can we reconcile this apparently plausible behavior with the economic theory given above?

If the theory gives the wrong answer, it is probably because we've misapplied the theory. And indeed in this case we have. The Slutsky example described earlier gave the change in demand *holding money income constant*. But if the wage rate changes, then money income must change as well. The change in demand resulting from a change in money income is an extra income effect—the endowment income effect. It occurs on top of the ordinary income effect.

If we apply the *appropriate* version of the Slutsky equation given earlier in this chapter, we get the following expression:

$$\frac{\delta R}{\delta w} = \text{substitution effect} + (\overline{R} - R)\, \frac{\delta R}{\delta m}. \tag{9.7}$$
$$\phantom{\frac{\delta R}{\delta w} = } (-) \phantom{xxxxxx} (+) \phantom{xx} (+)$$

In this expression the substitution effect is definitely negative, as it always is, and $\delta R/\delta m$ is positive since we are assuming that leisure is a normal good. But $(\overline{R} - R)$ is positive as well, so the sign of the whole expression is ambiguous. Unlike the usual case of consumer demand, the demand for leisure will have an ambiguous sign, even if leisure is a normal good. As the wage rate increases, people may work more or less.

Why does this ambiguity arise? When the wage rate increases, the substitution effect says work more in order to substitute consumption for leisure. But when the wage rate increases, the value of the endowment goes up as well. This is just like extra income, which may very well be consumed in taking extra leisure. Which is the larger effect is an empirical matter and cannot be decided by theory alone. We have to look at people's actual labor supply decisions to determine which effect dominates.

The case where an increase in the wage rate results in a decrease in the supply of labor is represented by a **backward-bending labor supply curve**. The Slutsky equation tells us that this effect is more likely to occur the larger is $(\overline{R} - R)$, that is, the larger is the supply of labor. When $\overline{R} = R$, the consumer is consuming only leisure, so an increase in the wage will result in a pure substitution effect and thus an increase in the supply of labor. But as the labor supply increases, each increase in the wage gives the consumer additional income for all the hours he is working, so that after some point he may well decide to use this extra income to "purchase" additional leisure—that is, to *reduce* his supply of labor.

A backward-bending labor supply curve is depicted in Figure 9.9. When the wage rate is small, the substitution effect is larger than the income effect, and an increase in the wage will decrease the demand for leisure and hence increase the supply of labor. But for larger wage rates the income effect may outweigh the substitution effect, and an increase in the wage will *reduce* the supply of labor.

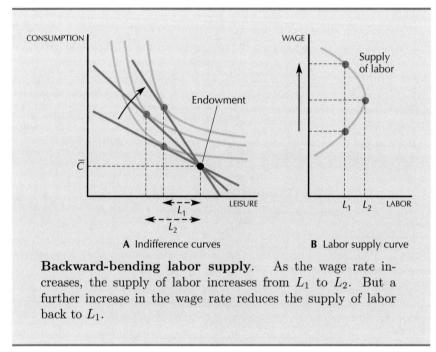

**A** Indifference curves  **B** Labor supply curve

Figure
9.9

**Backward-bending labor supply.**   As the wage rate increases, the supply of labor increases from $L_1$ to $L_2$. But a further increase in the wage rate reduces the supply of labor back to $L_1$.

## EXAMPLE: Overtime and the Supply of Labor

Consider a worker who has chosen to supply a certain amount of labor $L^* = \overline{R} - R^*$ when faced with the wage rate $w$ as depicted in Figure 9.10. Now suppose that the firm offers him a higher wage, $w' > w$, for extra time that he chooses to work. Such a payment is known as an **overtime wage**.

In terms of Figure 9.10, this means that the slope of the budget line will be steeper for labor supplied in excess of $L^*$. But then we know that the worker will optimally choose to supply more labor, by the usual sort of revealed preference argument: the choices involving working less than $L^*$ were available before the overtime was offered and were rejected.

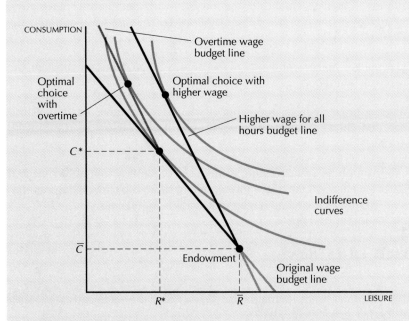

CONSUMPTION

Overtime wage
budget line

Optimal
choice
with
overtime

Optimal choice with
higher wage

Higher wage for all
hours budget line

$C^*$

Indifference
curves

$\bar{C}$

Endowment

Original wage
budget line

$R^*$                $\bar{R}$                LEISURE

**Overtime versus an ordinary wage increase.** An increase
in the overtime wage definitely increases the supply of labor,
while an increase in the straight wage could decrease the supply
of labor.

Figure
9.10

Note that we get an unambiguous increase in labor supply with an overtime wage, whereas just offering a higher wage for all hours worked has an
ambiguous effect—as discussed above, labor supply may increase or it may
decrease. The reason is that the response to an overtime wage is essentially
a pure substitution effect—the change in the optimal choice resulting from
*pivoting* the budget line around the chosen point. Overtime gives a higher
payment for the *extra* hours worked, whereas a straight increase in the wage
gives a higher payment for *all* hours worked. Thus a straight-wage increase
involves both a substitution and an income effect while an overtime-wage
increase results in a pure substitution effect. An example of this is shown in
Figure 9.10. There an increase in the straight wage results in a *decrease* in
labor supply, while an increase in the overtime wage results in an increase
in labor supply.

## Summary

1. Consumers earn income by selling their endowment of goods.

2. The gross demand for a good is the amount that the consumer ends up

consuming. The net demand for a good is the amount the consumer buys. Thus the net demand is the difference between the gross demand and the endowment.

3. The budget constraint has a slope of $-p_1/p_2$ and passes through the endowment bundle.

4. When a price changes, the value of what the consumer has to sell will change and thereby generate an additional income effect in the Slutsky equation.

5. Labor supply is an interesting example of the interaction of income and substitution effects. Due to the interaction of these two effects, the response of labor supply to a change in the wage rate is ambiguous.

## REVIEW QUESTIONS

1. If a consumer's net demands are $(5, -3)$ and her endowment is $(4, 4)$, what are her gross demands?

2. The prices are $(p_1, p_2) = (2, 3)$, and the consumer is currently consuming $(x_1, x_2) = (4, 4)$. There is a perfect market for the two goods in which they can be bought and sold costlessly. Will the consumer necessarily prefer consuming the bundle $(y_1, y_2) = (3, 5)$? Will she necessarily prefer having the bundle $(y_1, y_2)$?

3. The prices are $(p_1, p_2) = (2, 3)$, and the consumer is currently consuming $(x_1, x_2) = (4, 4)$. Now the prices change to $(q_1, q_2) = (2, 4)$. Could the consumer be better off under these new prices?

4. The U.S. currently imports about half of the petroleum that it uses. The rest of its needs are met by domestic production. Could the price of oil rise so much that the U.S. would be made better off?

5. Suppose that by some miracle the number of hours in the day increased from 24 to 30 hours (with luck this would happen shortly before exam week). How would this affect the budget constraint?

6. If leisure is an inferior good, what can you say about the slope of the labor supply curve?

# CHAPTER 10

# INTERTEMPORAL CHOICE

In this chapter we continue our examination of consumer behavior by considering the choices involved in saving and consuming over time. Choices of consumption over time are known as **intertemporal choices**.

## 10.1 The Budget Constraint

Let us imagine a consumer who chooses how much of some good to consume in each of two time periods. We will usually want to think of this good as being a composite good, as described in Chapter 2, but you can think of it as being a specific commodity if you wish. We denote the amount of consumption in each period by $(c_1, c_2)$ and suppose that the prices of consumption in each period are constant at 1. The amount of money the consumer will have in each period is denoted by $(m_1, m_2)$.

Suppose initially that the only way the consumer has of transferring money from period 1 to period 2 is by saving it without earning interest. Furthermore let us assume for the moment that he has no possibility of

Figure
10.1

**Budget constraint**. This is the budget constraint when the rate of interest is zero and no borrowing is allowed. The less the individual consumes in period 1, the more he can consume in period 2.

borrowing money, so that the most he can spend in period 1 is $m_1$. His budget constraint will then look like the one depicted in Figure 10.1.

We see that there will be two possible kinds of choices. The consumer could choose to consume at $(m_1, m_2)$, which means that he just consumes his income each period, or he can choose to consume less than his income during the first period. In this latter case, the consumer is saving some of his first-period consumption for a later date.

Now, let us allow the consumer to borrow and lend money at some interest rate $r$. Keeping the prices of consumption in each period at 1 for convenience, let us derive the budget constraint. Suppose first that the consumer decides to be a saver so his first period consumption, $c_1$, is less than his first-period income, $m_1$. In this case he will earn interest on the amount he saves, $m_1 - c_1$, at the interest rate $r$. The amount that he can consume next period is given by

$$c_2 = m_2 + (m_1 - c_1) + r(m_1 - c_1)$$
$$= m_2 + (1 + r)(m_1 - c_1). \qquad (10.1)$$

This says that the amount that the consumer can consume in period 2 is his income plus the amount he saved from period 1, plus the interest that he earned on his savings.

Now suppose that the consumer is a borrower so that his first-period consumption is greater than his first-period income. The consumer is a borrower if $c_1 > m_1$, and the interest he has to *pay* in the second period will be $r(c_1 - m_1)$. Of course, he also has to pay back the amount that he borrowed, $c_1 - m_1$. This means his budget constraint is given by

$$c_2 = m_2 - r(c_1 - m_1) - (c_1 - m_1)$$
$$= m_2 + (1 + r)(m_1 - c_1),$$

which is just what we had before. If $m_1 - c_1$ is positive, then the consumer earns interest on this savings; if $m_1 - c_1$ is negative, then the consumer pays interest on his borrowings.

If $c_1 = m_1$, then necessarily $c_2 = m_2$, and the consumer is neither a borrower nor a lender. We might say that this consumption position is the "Polonius point."[1]

We can rearrange the budget constraint for the consumer to get two alternative forms that are useful:

$$(1 + r)c_1 + c_2 = (1 + r)m_1 + m_2 \tag{10.2}$$

and

$$c_1 + \frac{c_2}{1 + r} = m_1 + \frac{m_2}{1 + r}. \tag{10.3}$$

Note that both equations have the form

$$p_1 x_1 + p_2 x_2 = p_1 m_1 + p_2 m_2.$$

In equation (10.2), $p_1 = 1 + r$ and $p_2 = 1$. In equation (10.3), $p_1 = 1$ and $p_2 = 1/(1 + r)$.

We say that equation (10.2) expresses the budget constraint in terms of **future value** and that equation (10.3) expresses the budget constraint in terms of **present value**. The reason for this terminology is that the first budget constraint makes the price of future consumption equal to 1, while the second budget constraint makes the price of present consumption equal to 1. The first budget constraint measures the period-1 price *relative* to the period-2 price, while the second equation does the reverse.

The geometric interpretation of present value and future value is given in Figure 10.2. The present value of an endowment of money in two periods is the amount of money in period 1 that would generate the same budget set as the endowment. This is just the horizontal intercept of the budget line, which gives the maximum amount of first-period consumption possible.

----

[1] "Neither a borrower, nor a lender be; For loan oft loses both itself and friend, And borrowing dulls the edge of husbandry." *Hamlet*, Act I, scene *iii*; Polonius giving advice to his son.

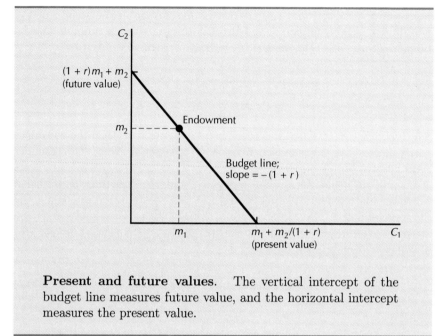

Figure
10.2

**Present and future values.** The vertical intercept of the budget line measures future value, and the horizontal intercept measures the present value.

Examining the budget constraint, this amount is $\bar{c}_1 = m_1 + m_2/(1+r)$, which is the present value of the endowment.

Similarly, the vertical intercept is the maximum amount of second-period consumption, which occurs when $c_1 = 0$. Again, from the budget constraint, we can solve for this amount $\bar{c}_2 = (1+r)m_1 + m_2$, the future value of the endowment.

The present-value form is the more important way to express the intertemporal budget constraint since it measures the future relative to the present, which is the way we naturally look at it.

It is easy from any of these equations to see the form of this budget constraint. The budget line passes through $(m_1, m_2)$, since that is always an *affordable* consumption pattern, and the budget line has a slope of $-(1+r)$.

## 10.2 Preferences for Consumption

Let us now consider the consumer's preferences, as represented by his indifference curves. The shape of the indifference curves indicates the consumer's tastes for consumption at different times. If we drew indifference curves with a constant slope of $-1$, for example, they would represent tastes of a consumer who didn't care whether he consumed today or tomorrow. His marginal rate of substitution between today and tomorrow is $-1$.

If we drew indifference curves for perfect complements, this would indicate that the consumer wanted to consume equal amounts today and tomorrow. Such a consumer would be unwilling to substitute consumption from one time period to the other, no matter what it might be worth to him to do so.

As usual, the intermediate case of well-behaved preferences is the more reasonable situation. The consumer is willing to substitute some amount of consumption today for consumption tomorrow, and how much he is willing to substitute depends on the particular pattern of consumption that he has.

Convexity of preferences is very natural in this context, since it says that the consumer would rather have an "average" amount of consumption each period rather than have a lot today and nothing tomorrow or vice versa.

## 10.3 Comparative Statics

Given a consumer's budget constraint and his preferences for consumption in each of the two periods, we can examine the optimal choice of consumption $(c_1, c_2)$. If the consumer chooses a point where $c_1 < m_1$, we will say that she is a **lender**, and if $c_1 > m_1$, we say that she is a **borrower**. In Figure 10.3A we have depicted a case where the consumer is a borrower, and in Figure 10.3B we have depicted a lender.

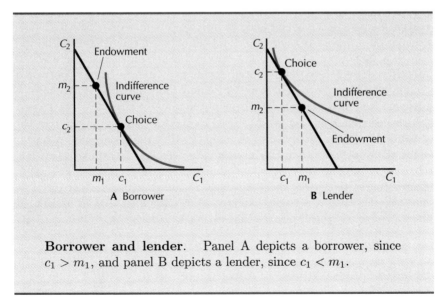

**Borrower and lender.**    Panel A depicts a borrower, since $c_1 > m_1$, and panel B depicts a lender, since $c_1 < m_1$.

Figure 10.3

Let us now consider how the consumer would react to a change in the interest rate. From equation (10.1) we see that increasing the rate of interest must tilt the budget line to a steeper position: for a given reduction in $c_1$ you will get more consumption in the second period if the interest rate is higher. Of course the endowment always remains affordable, so the tilt is really a pivot around the endowment.

We can also say something about how the choice of being a borrower or a lender changes as the interest rate changes. There are two cases, depending on whether the consumer is initially a borrower or initially a lender. Suppose first that he is a lender. Then it turns out that if the interest rate increases, the consumer must remain a lender.

This argument is illustrated in Figure 10.4. If the consumer is initially a lender, then his consumption bundle is to the left of the endowment point. Now let the interest rate increase. Is it possible that the consumer shifts to a new consumption point to the *right* of the endowment?

No, because that would violate the principle of revealed preference: choices to the right of the endowment point were available to the consumer when he faced the original budget set and were rejected in favor of the chosen point. Since the original optimal bundle is still available at the new budget line, the new optimal bundle must be a point *outside* the old budget set—which means it must be to the left of the endowment. The consumer must remain a lender when the interest rate increases.

There is a similar effect for borrowers: if the consumer is initially a borrower, and the interest rate declines, he or she will remain a borrower. (You might sketch a diagram similar to Figure 10.4 and see if you can spell out the argument.)

Thus if a person is a lender and the interest rate increases, he will remain a lender. If a person is a borrower and the interest rate decreases, he will remain a borrower. On the other hand, if a person is a lender and the interest rate decreases, he may well decide to switch to being a borrower; similarly, an increase in the interest rate may induce a borrower to become a lender. Revealed preference tells us nothing about these last two cases.

Revealed preference can also be used to make judgments about how the consumer's welfare changes as the interest rate changes. If the consumer is initially a borrower, and the interest rate rises, but he decides to remain a borrower, then he must be worse off at the new interest rate. This argument is illustrated in Figure 10.5; if the consumer remains a borrower, he must be operating at a point that was affordable under the old budget set but was rejected, which implies that he must be worse off.

## 10.4 The Slutsky Equation and Intertemporal Choice

The Slutsky equation can be used to decompose the change in demand due to an interest rate change into income effects and substitution effects, just

**If a person is a lender and the interest rate rises, he or she will remain a lender.** Increasing the interest rate pivots the budget line around the endowment to a steeper position; revealed preference implies that the new consumption bundle must lie to the left of the endowment.

Figure
10.4

as in Chapter 9. Suppose that the interest rate rises. What will be the effect on consumption in each period?

This is a case that is easier to analyze by using the future-value budget constraint, rather than the present-value constraint. In terms of the future-value budget constraint, raising the interest rate is just like raising the price of consumption today as compared to consumption tomorrow. Writing out the Slutsky equation we have

$$\frac{\delta c_1^t}{\delta p_1} = \frac{\delta c_1^s}{\delta p_1} + (m_1 - c_1) \frac{\delta c_1^m}{\delta m}.$$
$$(?) \quad\quad (-) \quad\quad\quad (?) \quad\quad (+)$$

The substitution effect, as always, works opposite the direction of price. In this case the price of period-1 consumption goes up, so the substitution effect says the consumer should consume less first period. This is the meaning of the minus sign under the substitution effect. Let's assume that consumption this period is a normal good, so that the very last term—how consumption changes as income changes—will be positive. So we put a plus sign under the last term. Now the sign of the whole expression will depend on the sign of $(m_1 - c_1)$. If the person is a borrower, this term will be negative and the whole expression will therefore unambiguously be

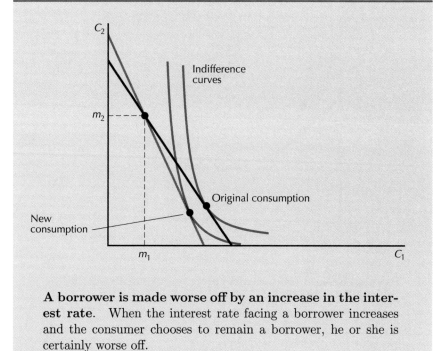

Figure
10.5
**A borrower is made worse off by an increase in the interest rate.** When the interest rate facing a borrower increases and the consumer chooses to remain a borrower, he or she is certainly worse off.

negative—for a borrower, an increase in the interest rate must lower today's consumption.

Why does this happen? When the interest rate rises, there is always a substitution effect towards consuming less today. For a borrower, an increase in the interest rate means that he will have to pay more interest tomorrow. This effect induces him to borrow less, and thus consume less, in the first period.

For a lender the effect is ambiguous. The total effect is the sum of a negative substitution effect and a positive income effect. From the viewpoint of a lender an increase in the interest rate may give him so much extra income that he will want to consume even more first period.

The effects of changing interest rates are not terribly mysterious. There is an income effect and a substitution effect as in any other price change. But without a tool like the Slutsky equation to separate out the various effects, the changes may be hard to disentangle. With such a tool, the sorting out of the effects is quite straightforward.

## 10.5 Inflation

The above analysis has all been conducted in terms of a general "consumption" good. Giving up $\delta c$ units of consumption today buys you $(1+r)\delta c$ units of consumption tomorrow. Implicit in this analysis is the assumption that the "price" of consumption doesn't change—there is no inflation or deflation.

However, the analysis is not hard to modify to deal with the case of inflation. Let us suppose that the consumption good now has a different price in each period. It is convenient to choose today's price of consumption as 1 and to let $p_2$ be the price of consumption tomorrow. It is also convenient to think of the endowment as being measured in units of the consumption goods as well, so that the monetary value of the endowment in period 2 is $p_2 m_2$. Then the amount of money the consumer can spend in the second period is given by

$$p_2 c_2 = p_2 m_2 + (1+r)(m_1 - c_1),$$

and the amount of consumption available second period is

$$c_2 = m_2 + \frac{1+r}{p_2}(m_1 - c_1).$$

Note that this equation is very similar to the equation given earlier—we just use $(1+r)/p_2$ rather than $1+r$.

Let us express this budget constraint in terms of the rate of inflation. The inflation rate, $\pi$, is just the rate at which prices grow. Recalling that $p_1 = 1$, we have

$$p_2 = 1 + \pi,$$

which gives us

$$c_2 = m_2 + \frac{1+r}{1+\pi}(m_1 - c_1).$$

Let's create a new variable $\rho$, the **real interest rate**, and define it by[2]

$$1 + \rho = \frac{1+r}{1+\pi}$$

so that the budget constraint becomes

$$c_2 = m_2 + (1+\rho)(m_1 - c_1).$$

One plus the real interest rate measures how much extra *consumption* you can get in period 2 if you give up some *consumption* in period 1. That is why it is called the *real* rate of interest: it tells you how much extra consumption you can get, not how many extra dollars you can get.

---

[2] The Greek letter $\rho$, rho, is pronounced "row."

The interest rate on dollars is called the **nominal** rate of interest. As we've seen above, the relationship between the two is given by

$$1 + \rho = \frac{1 + r}{1 + \pi}.$$

In order to get an explicit expression for $\rho$, we write this equation as

$$\rho = \frac{1 + r}{1 + \pi} - 1 = \frac{1 + r}{1 + \pi} - \frac{1 + \pi}{1 + \pi}$$
$$= \frac{r - \pi}{1 + \pi}.$$

This is an exact expression for the real interest rate, but it is common to use an approximation. If the inflation rate isn't too large, the denominator of the fraction will be only slightly larger than 1. Thus the real rate of interest will be approximately given by

$$\rho \approx r - \pi,$$

which says that the real rate of interest is just the nominal rate minus the rate of inflation. (The symbol $\approx$ means "approximately equal to.") This makes perfectly good sense: if the interest rate is 18 percent, but prices are rising at 10 percent, then the real interest rate—the extra consumption you can buy next period if you give up some consumption now—will be roughly 8 percent.

Of course, we are always looking into the future when making consumption plans. Typically, we know the nominal rate of interest for the next period, but the rate of inflation for next period is unknown. The real interest rate is usually taken to be the current interest rate minus the *expected* rate of inflation. To the extent that people have different estimates about what the next year's rate of inflation will be, they will have different estimates of the real interest rate. If inflation can be reasonably well forecast, these differences may not be too large.

## 10.6 Present Value: A Closer Look

Let us return now to the two forms of the budget constraint described earlier in section 10.1 in equations (10.2) and (10.3):

$$(1 + r)c_1 + c_2 = (1 + r)m_1 + m_2$$

and

$$c_1 + \frac{c_2}{1 + r} = m_1 + \frac{m_2}{1 + r}.$$

Consider just the right-hand sides of these two equations. We said that the first one expresses the value of the endowment in terms of future value and that the second one expresses it in terms of present value.

Let us examine the concept of future value first. If we can borrow and lend at an interest rate of $r$, what is the future equivalent of \$1 today? The answer is $(1+r)$ dollars. That is, \$1 today can be turned into $(1+r)$ dollars next period simply by lending it to the bank at an interest rate $r$. In other words, $(1+r)$ dollars next period is equivalent to \$1 today since that is how much you would have to pay next period to purchase—that is, borrow—\$1 today. The value $(1+r)$ is just the price of \$1 today, relative to \$1 next period. This can be easily seen from the first budget constraint: it is expressed in terms of future dollars—the second-period dollars have a price of 1, and first-period dollars are measured relative to them.

What about present value? This is just the reverse: everything is measured in terms of today's dollars. How much is a dollar next period worth in terms of a dollar today? The answer is $1/(1+r)$ dollars. This is because $1/(1+r)$ dollars can be turned into a dollar next period simply by saving it at the rate of interest $r$. The *present value* of a dollar to be delivered next period is $1/(1+r)$.

The concept of present value gives us another way to express the budget for a two-period consumption problem: a consumption plan is affordable if *the present value of consumption equals the present value of income.*

The idea of present value has an important implication that is closely related to a point made in Chapter 9: if the consumer can freely buy and sell goods at constant prices, then the consumer would always prefer a higher-valued endowment to a lower-valued one. In the case of intertemporal decisions, this principle implies that *if a consumer can freely borrow and lend at a constant interest rate, then the consumer would always prefer a pattern of income with a higher present value to a pattern with a lower present value.*

This is true for the same reason that the statement in Chapter 9 was true: an endowment with a higher value gives rise to a budget line that is farther out. The new budget set contains the old budget set, which means that the consumer would have all the consumption opportunities she had with the old budget set plus some more. Economists sometimes say that an endowment with a higher present value **dominates** one with a lower present value in the sense that the consumer can have larger consumption in *every* period by selling the endowment with the higher present value that she could get by selling the endowment with the lower present value.

Of course, if the present value of one endowment is higher than another, then the future value will be higher as well. However, it turns out that the present value is a more convenient way to measure the purchasing power of an endowment of money over time, and it is the measure to which we will devote the most attention.

## 10.7 Analyzing Present Value for Several Periods

Let us consider a three-period model. We suppose that we can borrow or lend money at an interest rate $r$ each period and that this interest rate will remain constant over the three periods. Thus the price of consumption in period 2 in terms of period-1 consumption will be $1/(1+r)$, just as before.

What will the price of period-3 consumption be? Well, if I invest \$1 today, it will grow into $(1+r)$ dollars next period; and if I leave this money invested, it will grow into $(1+r)^2$ dollars by the third period. Thus if I start with $1/(1+r)^2$ dollars today, I can turn this into \$1 in period 3. The price of period-3 consumption relative to period-1 consumption is therefore $1/(1+r)^2$. Each extra dollar's worth of consumption in period 3 costs me $1/(1+r)^2$ dollars today. This implies that the budget constraint will have the form

$$c_1 + \frac{c_2}{1+r} + \frac{c_3}{(1+r)^2} = m_1 + \frac{m_2}{1+r} + \frac{m_3}{(1+r)^2}.$$

This is just like the budget constraints we've seen before, where the price of period-$t$ consumption in terms of today's consumption is given by

$$p_t = \frac{1}{(1+r)^{t-1}}.$$

As before, moving to an endowment that has a higher present value at these prices will be preferred by any consumer, since such a change will necessarily shift the budget set farther out.

We have derived this budget constraint under the assumption of constant interest rates, but it is easy to generalize to the case of changing interest rates. Suppose, for example, that the interest earned on savings from period 1 to 2 is $r_1$, while savings from period 2 to 3 earn $r_2$. Then \$1 in period 1 will grow to $(1+r_1)(1+r_2)$ dollars in period 3. The present value of \$1 in period 3 is therefore $1/(1+r_1)(1+r_2)$. This implies that the correct form of the budget constraint is

$$c_1 + \frac{c_2}{1+r_1} + \frac{c_3}{(1+r_1)(1+r_2)} = m_1 + \frac{m_2}{1+r_1} + \frac{m_3}{(1+r_1)(1+r_2)}.$$

This expression is not so hard to deal with, but we will typically be content to examine the case of constant interest rates.

Table 10.1 contains some examples of the present value of \$1 $T$ years in the future at different interest rates. The notable fact about this table is how quickly the present value goes down for "reasonable" interest rates. For example, at an interest rate of 10 percent, the value of \$1 20 years from now is only 15 cents.

**The present value of \$1 $t$ years in the future.**

Table
10.1

| Rate | 1 | 2 | 5 | 10 | 15 | 20 | 25 | 30 |
|------|-----|-----|-----|-----|-----|-----|-----|-----|
| .05 | .95 | .91 | .78 | .61 | .48 | .37 | .30 | .23 |
| .10 | .91 | .83 | .62 | .39 | .24 | .15 | .09 | .06 |
| .15 | .87 | .76 | .50 | .25 | .12 | .06 | .03 | .02 |
| .20 | .83 | .69 | .40 | .16 | .06 | .03 | .01 | .00 |

## 10.8 Present Value in Continuous Time

Suppose that you invest \$1 in an asset yielding an interest rate $r$ where the interest is paid once a year. Then after $T$ years you will have $(1 + r)^T$ dollars. Suppose now that the interest is paid monthly. This means that the monthly interest rate will be $r/12$, and there will be $12T$ payments, so that after $T$ years you will have $(1 + r/12)^{12T}$ dollars. If the interest rate is paid daily, you will have $(1 + r/365)^{365T}$ and so on.

In general, if the interest is paid $n$ times a year, you will have $(1+r/n)^{nT}$ dollars after $T$ years. It is natural to ask how much money you will have if the interest is paid *continuously*. That is, we ask what is the limit of this expression as $n$ goes to infinity. It turns out that this is given by the following expression:

$$e^{rT} = \lim_{n \to \infty} (1 + r/n)^{nT},$$

where $e$ is $2.7183\ldots$, the base of natural logarithms. This is the formula used for continuous compounding.

## 10.9 Use of Present Value

Let us start by stating an important general principle: *present value is the only correct way to convert a stream of payments into today's dollars.* This principle follows directly from the definition of present value: the present value measures the value of a consumer's endowment of money. As long as the consumer can borrow and lend freely at a constant interest rate, an endowment with higher present value can always generate *more* consumption in every period than an endowment with lower present value. Regardless of your own tastes for consumption in different periods, you should always prefer a stream of money that has a higher present value to one with lower present value—since that always gives you more consumption possibilities in every period.

This argument is illustrated in Figure 10.6. In this figure, $(m'_1, m'_2)$ is a worse consumption bundle than the consumer's original endowment,

$(m_1, m_2)$, since it lies beneath the indifference curve through her endowment. Nevertheless, the consumer would prefer $(m'_1, m'_2)$ to $(m_1, m_2)$ if she is able to borrow and lend at the interest rate $r$. This is true because with the endowment $(m'_1, m'_2)$ she can afford to consume a bundle such as $(c_1, c_2)$, which is unambiguously better than her current consumption bundle.

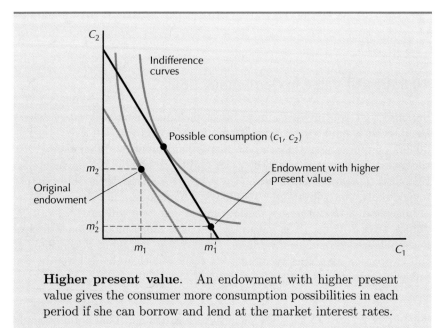

Figure
10.6

**Higher present value.** An endowment with higher present value gives the consumer more consumption possibilities in each period if she can borrow and lend at the market interest rates.

One very useful application of present value is in valuing the income streams offered by different kinds of investments. If you want to compare two different investments that yield different streams of payments to see which is better, you simply compute the two present values and choose the larger one. The investment with the larger present value always gives you more consumption possibilities.

Sometimes it is necessary to purchase an income stream by making a stream of payments over time. For example, one could purchase an apartment building by borrowing money from a bank and making mortgage payments over a number of years. Suppose that the income stream $(M_1, M_2)$ can be purchased by making a stream of payments $(P_1, P_2)$.

In this case we can evaluate the investment by comparing the present value of the income stream to the present value of the payment stream. If

$$M_1 + \frac{M_2}{1+r} > P_1 + \frac{P_2}{1+r}, \tag{10.4}$$

the present value of the income stream exceeds the present value of its cost, so this is a good investment—it will increase the present value of our endowment.

An equivalent way to value the investment is to use the idea of **net present value**. In order to calculate this number we calculate at the *net* cash flow in each period and then discount this stream back to the present. In this example, the net cash flow is $(M_1 - P_1, M_2 - P_2)$, and the net present value is

$$NPV = M_1 - P_1 + \frac{M_2 - P_2}{1 + r}.$$

Comparing this to equation (10.4) we see that the investment should be purchased if and only if the net present value is positive.

The net present value calculation is very convenient since it allows us to add all of the positive and negative cash flows together in each period and then discount the resulting stream of cash flows.

## EXAMPLE: Valuing a Stream of Payments

Suppose that we are considering two investments, A and B. Investment A pays $100 now and will also pay $200 next year. Investment B pays $0 now, and will generate $310 next year. Which is the better investment?

The answer depends on the interest rate. If the interest rate is zero, the answer is clear—just add up the payments. For if the interest rate is zero, then the present-value calculation boils down to summing up the payments.

If the interest rate is zero, the present value of investment A is

$$PV_A = 100 + 200 = 300,$$

and the present value of investment B is

$$PV_B = 0 + 310 = 310,$$

so B is the preferred investment.

But we get the opposite answer if the interest rate is high enough. Suppose, for example, that the interest rate is 20 percent. Then the present-value calculation becomes

$$PV_A = 100 + \frac{200}{1.20} = 266.67$$

$$PV_B = 0 + \frac{310}{1.20} = 258.33.$$

Now A is the better investment. The fact that A pays back more money earlier means that it will have a higher present value when the interest rate is large enough.

## EXAMPLE: The True Cost of a Credit Card

Borrowing money on a credit card is expensive: many companies quote yearly interest charges of 15 to 21 percent. However, because of the way these finance charges are computed, the true interest rate on credit card debt is much higher than this.

Suppose that a credit card owner charges a $2000 purchase on the first day of the month and that the finance charge is 1.5 percent a month. If the consumer pays the entire balance by the end of the month, he does not have to pay the finance charge. If the consumer pays none of the $2,000, he has to pay a finance charge of $2000 × .015 = $30 at the beginning of the next month.

What happens if the consumer pays $1,800 towards the $2000 balance on the last day of the month? In this case, the consumer has borrowed only $200, so the finance charge should be $3. However, many credit card companies charge the consumers much more than this. The reason is that many companies base their charges on the "average monthly balance," even if part of that balance is paid by the end of the month. In this example, the average monthly balance would be about $2000 (30 days of the $2000 balance and 1 day of the $200 balance). The finance charge would therefore be slightly less than $30, even though the consumer has only borrowed $200. Based on the actual amount of money borrowed, this is an interest rate of 15 percent a month!

## EXAMPLE: Extending Copyright

Article I, Section 8 of the U.S. Constitution enables Congress to grant patents and copyrights using this language: "To promote the Progress of Science and useful Arts, by securing for limited Times to Authors and Inventors the exclusive Right to their respective Writings and Discoveries."

But what does "limited Times" mean? The lifetime of a patent in the United States is fixed at 20 years; the lifetime for copyright is quite different.

The first copyright act, passed by Congress in 1790, offered a 14-year term along with a 14-year renewal. Subsequently, the copyright term was lengthened to 28 years in 1831, with a 28-year renewal option added in 1909. In 1962 the term became 47 years, and 67 years in 1978. In 1967 the term was defined as the life of the author plus 50 years, or 75 years for "works for hire." The 1998 Sonny Bono Copyright Term Extension Act lengthened this term to the life of the author plus 70 years for individuals and 75–95 years for works for hire.

It is questionable whether "the life of the author plus 70 years" should be considered a limited time. One might ask what *additional* incentive the 1998 extension creates for authors to create works?

Let us look at a simple example. Suppose that the interest rate is 7%. Then the increase in present value of extending the copyright term from 80 to 100 years is about 0.33% of the present value of the first 80 years. Those extra 20 years have almost no impact on the present value of the copyright at time of creation since they come so far in the future. Hence they likely provide miniscule incremental incentive to create the works in the first place.

Given this tiny increase in value from extending the copyright term why would it pay anybody to lobby for such a change? The answer is that the 1998 act extended the copyright term *retroactively* so that works that were near expiration were given a new lease on life.

For example, it has been widely claimed that Disney lobbied heavily for the copyright term extension, since the original Mickey Mouse film, *Steamboat Willie,* was about to go out of copyright.

Retroactive copyright extensions of this sort make no economic sense, since what matters for the authors are the incentives present at the time the work is created. If there were no such retroactive extension, it is unlikely that anyone would have bothered to ask for copyright extensions given the low economic value of the additional years of protection.

## 10.10 Bonds

**Securities** are financial instruments that promise certain patterns of payment schedules. There are many kinds of financial instruments because there are many kinds of payment schedules that people want. Financial markets give people the opportunity to trade different patterns of cash flows over time. These cash flows are typically used to finance consumption at some time or other.

The particular kind of security that we will examine here is a **bond**. Bonds are issued by governments and corporations. They are basically a way to borrow money. The borrower—the agent who issues the bond— promises to pay a fixed number of dollars $x$ (the **coupon**) each period until a certain date $T$ (the **maturity date**), at which point the borrower will pay an amount $F$ (the **face value**) to the holder of the bond.

Thus the payment stream of a bond looks like $(x, x, x, \ldots, F)$. If the interest rate is constant, the present discounted value of such a bond is easy to compute. It is given by

$$PV = \frac{x}{(1+r)} + \frac{x}{(1+r)^2} + \cdots + \frac{F}{(1+r)^T}.$$

Note that the present value of a bond will decline if the interest rate increases. Why is this? When the interest rate goes up the price now for $1 delivered in the future goes down. So the future payments of the bond will be worth less now.

There is a large and developed market for bonds. The market value of outstanding bonds will fluctuate as the interest rate fluctuates since the present value of the stream of payments represented by the bond will change.

An interesting special kind of a bond is a bond that makes payments forever. These are called **consols** or **perpetuities**. Suppose that we consider a consol that promises to pay $x$ a year forever. To compute the value of this consol we have to compute the infinite sum:

$$PV = \frac{x}{1+r} + \frac{x}{(1+r)^2} + \cdots .$$

The trick to computing this is to factor out $1/(1+r)$ to get

$$PV = \frac{1}{1+r} \left[ x + \frac{x}{(1+r)} + \frac{x}{(1+r)^2} + \cdots \right].$$

But the term in the brackets is just $x$ plus the present value! Substituting and solving for $PV$:

$$PV = \frac{1}{(1+r)} [x + PV]$$
$$= \frac{x}{r}.$$

This wasn't hard to do, but there is an easy way to get the answer right off. How much money, $V$, would you need at an interest rate $r$ to get $x$ dollars forever? Just write down the equation

$$Vr = x,$$

which says that the interest on $V$ must equal $x$. But then the value of such an investment is given by

$$V = \frac{x}{r}.$$

Thus it must be that the present value of a consol that promises to pay $x$ dollars forever must be given by $x/r$.

For a consol it is easy to see directly how increasing the interest rate reduces the value of a bond. Suppose, for example, that a consol is issued when the interest rate is 10 percent. Then if it promises to pay $10 a year forever, it will be worth $100 now—since $100 would generate $10 a year in interest income.

Now suppose that the interest rate goes up to 20 percent. The value of the consol must fall to $50, since it only takes $50 to earn $10 a year at a 20 percent interest rate.

The formula for the consol can be used to calculate an approximate value of a long-term bond. If the interest rate is 10 percent, for example, the value of $1 30 years from now is only 6 cents. For the size of interest rates we usually encounter, 30 years might as well be infinity.

## EXAMPLE: Installment Loans

Suppose that you borrow $1000 that you promise to pay back in 12 monthly installments of $100 each. What rate of interest are you paying?

At first glance it seems that your interest rate is 20 percent: you have borrowed $1000, and you are paying back $1200. But this analysis is incorrect. For you haven't really borrowed $1000 for an entire year. You have borrowed $1000 for a month, and then you pay back $100. Then you only have borrowed $900, and you owe only a month's interest on the $900. You borrow that for a month and then pay back another $100. And so on.

The stream of payments that we want to value is

$$(1000, -100, -100, \ldots, -100).$$

We can find the interest rate that makes the present value of this stream equal to zero by using a calculator or a computer. The actual interest rate that you are paying on the installment loan is about 35 percent!

## 10.11 Taxes

In the United States, interest payments are taxed as ordinary income. This means that you pay the same tax on interest income as on labor income. Suppose that your marginal tax bracket is $t$, so that each *extra* dollar of income, $\Delta m$, increases your tax liability by $t\Delta m$. Then if you invest $X$ dollars in an asset, you'll receive an interest payment of $rX$. But you'll also have to pay taxes of $trX$ on this income, which will leave you with only $(1-t)rX$ dollars of after-tax income. We call the rate $(1-t)r$ the **after-tax interest rate**.

What if you decide to borrow $X$ dollars, rather than lend them? Then you'll have to make an interest payment of $rX$. In the United States, some interest payments are tax deductible and some are not. For example, the interest payments for a mortgage are tax deductable, but interest payments on ordinary consumer loans are not. On the other hand, businesses can deduct most kinds of the interest payments that they make.

If a particular interest payment is tax deductible, you can subtract your interest payment from your other income and only pay taxes on what's left. Thus the $rX$ dollars you pay in interest will reduce your tax payments by $trX$. The total cost of the $X$ dollars you borrowed will be $rX - trX = (1-t)rX$.

Thus the after-tax interest rate is the same whether you are borrowing or lending, for people in the same tax bracket. The tax on saving will reduce the amount of money that people want to save, but the subsidy on borrowing will increase the amount of money that people want to borrow.

## EXAMPLE: Scholarships and Savings

Many students in the United States receive some form of financial aid to help defray college costs. The amount of financial aid a student receives depends on many factors, but one important factor is the family's ability to pay for college expenses. Most U.S. colleges and universities use a standard measure of ability to pay calculated by the College Entrance Examination Board (CEEB).

If a student wishes to apply for financial aid, his or her family must fill out a questionnaire describing their financial circumstances. The CEEB uses the information on the income and assets of the parents to construct a measure of "adjusted available income." The fraction of their adjusted available income that parents are expected to contribute varies between 22 and 47 percent, depending on income. In 1985, parents with a total before-tax income of around $35,000 dollars were expected to contribute about $7000 toward college expenses.

Each additional dollar of assets that the parents accumulate increases their expected contribution and decreases the amount of financial aid that their child can hope to receive. The formula used by the CEEB effectively imposes a tax on parents who save for their children's college education. Martin Feldstein, President of the National Bureau of Economic Research (NBER) and Professor of Economics at Harvard University, calculated the magnitude of this tax.[3]

Consider the situation of some parents contemplating saving an additional dollar just as their daughter enters college. At a 6 percent rate of interest, the future value of a dollar 4 years from now is $1.26. Since federal and state taxes must be paid on interest income, the dollar yields $1.19 in after-tax income in 4 years. However, since this additional dollar of savings increases the total assets of the parents, the amount of aid received by the daughter goes down during *each* of her four college years. The effect of this "education tax" is to reduce the future value of the dollar to only 87 cents after 4 years. This is equivalent to an income tax of 150 percent!

Feldstein also examined the savings behavior of a sample of middle-class households with pre-college children. He estimates that a household with income of $40,000 a year and two college-age children saves about 50 percent less than they would otherwise due to the combination of federal, state, and "education" taxes that they face.

## 10.12 Choice of the Interest Rate

---

[3] Martin Feldstein, "College Scholarship Rules and Private Savings," *American Economic Review*, 85, 3 (June 1995).

In the above discussion, we've talked about "the interest rate." In real life there are many interest rates: there are nominal rates, real rates, before-tax rates, after-tax rates, short-term rates, long-term rates, and so on. Which is the "right" rate to use in doing present-value analysis?

The way to answer this question is to think about the fundamentals. The idea of present discounted value arose because we wanted to be able to convert money at one point in time to an equivalent amount at another point in time. "The interest rate" is the return on an investment that allows us to transfer funds in this way.

If we want to apply this analysis when there are a variety of interest rates available, we need to ask which one has the properties most like the stream of payments we are trying to value. If the stream of payments is not taxed, we should use an after-tax interest rate. If the stream of payments will continue for 30 years, we should use a long-term interest rate. If the stream of payments is risky, we should use the interest rate on an investment with similar risk characteristics. (We'll have more to say later about what this last statement actually means.)

The interest rate measures the **opportunity cost** of funds—the value of alternative uses of your money. So every stream of payments should be compared to your best alternative that has similar characteristics in terms of tax treatment, risk, and liquidity.

## Summary

1. The budget constraint for intertemporal consumption can be expressed in terms of present value or future value.

2. The comparative statics results derived earlier for general choice problems can be applied to intertemporal consumption as well.

3. The real rate of interest measures the extra consumption that you can get in the future by giving up some consumption today.

4. A consumer who can borrow and lend at a constant interest rate should always prefer an endowment with a higher present value to one with a lower present value.

## REVIEW QUESTIONS

1. How much is $1 million to be delivered 20 years in the future worth today if the interest rate is 20 percent?

2. As the interest rate rises, does the intertemporal budget constraint become steeper or flatter?

3. Would the assumption that goods are perfect substitutes be valid in a study of intertemporal food purchases?

4. A consumer, who is initially a lender, remains a lender even after a decline in interest rates. Is this consumer better off or worse off after the change in interest rates? If the consumer becomes a borrower after the change is he better off or worse off?

5. What is the present value of $100 one year from now if the interest rate is 10%? What is the present value if the interest rate is 5%?

# CHAPTER 11

# ASSET MARKETS

**Assets** are goods that provide a flow of services over time. Assets can provide a flow of consumption services, like housing services, or can provide a flow of money that can be used to purchase consumption. Assets that provide a monetary flow are called **financial assets**.

The bonds that we discussed in the last chapter are examples of financial assets. The flow of services they provide is the flow of interest payments. Other sorts of financial assets such as corporate stock provide different patterns of cash flows. In this chapter we will examine the functioning of asset markets under conditions of complete certainty about the future flow of services provided by the asset.

## 11.1 Rates of Return

Under this admittedly extreme hypothesis, we have a simple principle relating asset rates of return: if there is no uncertainty about the cash flow provided by assets, then all assets have to have the same rate of return. The reason is obvious: if one asset had a higher rate of return than another, and both assets were otherwise identical, then no one would want to buy the asset with the lower rate of return. So in equilibrium, all assets that are actually held must pay the same rate of return.

Let us consider the process by which these rates of return adjust. Consider an asset A that has current price $p_0$ and is expected to have a price of $p_1$ tomorrow. Everyone is certain about what today's price of the asset is, and everyone is certain about what tomorrow's price will be. We suppose for simplicity that there are no dividends or other cash payments between periods 0 and 1. Suppose furthermore that there is another investment, B, that one can hold between periods 0 and 1 that will pay an interest rate of $r$. Now consider two possible investment plans: either invest one dollar in asset A and cash it in next period, or invest one dollar in asset B and earn interest of $r$ dollars over the period.

What are the values of these two investment plans at the end of the first period? We first ask how many units of the asset we must purchase to make a one dollar investment in it. Letting $x$ be this amount we have the equation

$$p_0 x = 1$$

or

$$x = \frac{1}{p_0}.$$

It follows that the future value of one dollar's worth of this asset next period will be

$$FV = p_1 x = \frac{p_1}{p_0}.$$

On the other hand, if we invest one dollar in asset B, we will have $1 + r$ dollars next period. If assets A and B are both held in equilibrium, then a dollar invested in either one of them must be worth the same amount second period. Thus we have an equilibrium condition:

$$1 + r = \frac{p_1}{p_0}.$$

What happens if this equality is not satisfied? Then there is a sure way to make money. For example, if

$$1 + r > \frac{p_1}{p_0},$$

people who own asset A can sell one unit for $p_0$ dollars in the first period and invest the money in asset B. Next period their investment in asset B will be worth $p_0(1 + r)$, which is greater than $p_1$ by the above equation. This will guarantee that second period they will have enough money to repurchase asset A, and be back where they started from, but now with extra money.

This kind of operation—buying some of one asset and selling some of another to realize a sure return—is known as **riskless arbitrage**, or **arbitrage** for short. As long as there are people around looking for "sure things" we would expect that well-functioning markets should quickly eliminate any opportunities for arbitrage. Therefore, another way to state our equilibrium condition is to say that in equilibrium *there should be no opportunities for arbitrage*. We'll refer to this as the **no arbitrage condition**.

But how does arbitrage actually work to eliminate the inequality? In the example given above, we argued that if $1 + r > p_1/p_0$, then anyone who held asset A would want to sell it first period, since they were guaranteed enough money to repurchase it second period. But who would they sell it to? Who would want to buy it? There would be plenty of people willing to supply asset A at $p_0$, but there wouldn't be anyone foolish enough to demand it at that price.

This means that supply would exceed demand and therefore the price will fall. How far will it fall? Just enough to satisfy the arbitrage condition: until $1 + r = p_1/p_0$.

## 11.2 Arbitrage and Present Value

We can rewrite the arbitrage condition in a useful way by cross multiplying to get

$$p_0 = \frac{p_1}{1 + r}.$$

This says that the current price of an asset must be its present value. Essentially we have converted the future-value comparison in the arbitrage condition to a present-value comparison. So if the no arbitrage condition is satisfied, then we are assured that assets must sell for their present values. Any deviation from present-value pricing leaves a sure way to make money.

## 11.3 Adjustments for Differences among Assets

The no arbitrage rule assumes that the asset services provided by the two assets are identical, except for the purely monetary difference. If the services provided by the assets have different characteristics, then we would want to adjust for those differences before we blandly assert that the two assets must have the same equilibrium rate of return.

For example, one asset might be easier to sell than the other. We sometimes express this by saying that one asset is more **liquid** than another. In this case, we might want to adjust the rate of return to take account of the difficulty involved in finding a buyer for the asset. Thus a house that is worth $100,000 is probably a less liquid asset than $100,000 in Treasury bills.

Similarly, one asset might be riskier than another. The rate of return on one asset may be guaranteed, while the rate of return on another asset may be highly risky. We'll examine ways to adjust for risk differences in Chapter 13.

Here we want to consider two other types of adjustment we might make. One is adjustment for assets that have some return in consumption value, and the other is for assets that have different tax characteristics.

## 11.4 Assets with Consumption Returns

Many assets pay off only in money. But there are other assets that pay off in terms of consumption as well. The prime example of this is housing. If you own a house that you live in, then you don't have to rent living quarters; thus part of the "return" to owning the house is the fact that you get to live in the house without paying rent. Or, put another way, you get to pay the rent for your house to yourself. This latter way of putting it sounds peculiar, but it contains an important insight.

It is true that you don't make an *explicit* rental payment to yourself for the privilege of living in your house, but it turns out to be fruitful to think of a homeowner as *implicitly* making such a payment. The **implicit rental rate** on your house is the rate at which you could rent a similar house. Or, equivalently, it is the rate at which you could rent your house to someone else on the open market. By choosing to "rent your house to yourself" you are forgoing the opportunity of earning rental payments from someone else, and thus incurring an opportunity cost.

Suppose that the implicit rental payment on your house would work out to $T$ dollars per year. Then part of the return to owning your house is the fact that it generates for you an implicit income of $T$ dollars per year—the money that you would otherwise have to pay to live in the same circumstances as you do now.

But that is not the entire return on your house. As real estate agents never tire of telling us, a house is also an *investment*. When you buy a house you pay a significant amount of money for it, and you might reasonably expect to earn a monetary return on this investment as well, through an increase in the value of your house. This increase in the value of an asset is known as **appreciation**.

Let us use $A$ to represent the expected appreciation in the dollar value of your house over a year. The total return to owning your house is the sum of the rental return, $T$, and the investment return, $A$. If your house initially cost $P$, then the *total* rate of return on your initial investment in housing is

$$h = \frac{T + A}{P}.$$

This total rate of return is composed of the consumption rate of return, $T/P$, and the investment rate of return, $A/P$.

Let us use $r$ to represent the rate of return on other financial assets. Then the total rate of return on housing should, in equilibrium, be equal to $r$:

$$r = \frac{T + A}{P}.$$

Think about it this way. At the beginning of the year, you can invest $P$ in a bank and earn $rP$ dollars, or you can invest $P$ dollars in a house and save $T$ dollars of rent and earn $A$ dollars by the end of the year. The total return from these two investments has to be the same. If $T + A < rP$ you would be better off investing your money in the bank and paying $T$ dollars in rent. You would then have $rP - T > A$ dollars at the end of the year. If $T + A > rP$, then housing would be the better choice. (Of course, this is ignoring the real estate agent's commission and other transactions costs associated with the purchase and sale.)

Since the total return should rise at the rate of interest, the financial rate of return $A/P$ will generally be less than the rate of interest. Thus in general, assets that pay off in consumption will in equilibrium have a lower financial rate of return than purely financial assets. This means that buying consumption goods such as houses, or paintings, or jewelry *solely* as a financial investment is probably not a good idea since the rate of return on these assets will probably be lower than the rate of return on purely financial assets, because part of the price of the asset reflects the consumption return that people receive from owning such assets. On the other hand, if you place a sufficiently high value on the consumption return on such assets, or you can generate rental income from the assets, it may well make sense to buy them. The *total* return on such assets may well make this a sensible choice.

## 11.5 Taxation of Asset Returns

The Internal Revenue Service distinguishes two kinds of asset returns for purposes of taxation. The first kind is the **dividend** or **interest** return. These are returns that are paid periodically—each year or each month—over the life of the asset. You pay taxes on interest and dividend income at your ordinary tax rate, the same rate that you pay on your labor income.

The second kind of returns are called **capital gains**. Capital gains occur when you sell an asset at a price higher than the price at which you bought it. Capital gains are taxed only when you actually sell the asset. Under the current tax law, capital gains are taxed at the same rate as ordinary income, but there are some proposals to tax them at a more favorable rate.

It is sometimes argued that taxing capital gains at the same rate as ordinary income is a "neutral" policy. However, this claim can be disputed for at least two reasons. The first reason is that the capital gains taxes are only paid when the asset is sold, while taxes on dividends or interest are paid every year. The fact that the capital gains taxes are deferred until time of sale makes the effective tax rate on capital gains *lower* than the tax rate on ordinary income.

A second reason that equal taxation of capital gains and ordinary income is not neutral is that the capital gains tax is based on the increase in the *dollar* value of an asset. If asset values are increasing just because of inflation, then a consumer may owe taxes on an asset whose *real* value hasn't changed. For example, suppose that a person buys an asset for $100 and 10 years later it is worth $200. Suppose that the general price level also doubles in this same ten-year period. Then the person would owe taxes on a $100 capital gain even though the purchasing power of his asset hadn't changed at all. This tends to make the tax on capital gains *higher* than that on ordinary income. Which of the two effects dominates is a controversial question.

In addition to the differential taxation of dividends and capital gains there are many other aspects of the tax law that treat asset returns differently. For example, in the United States, **municipal bonds**, bonds issued by cities or states, are not taxed by the Federal government. As we indicated earlier, the consumption return from owner-occupied housing is not taxed. Furthermore, in the United States even part of the capital gains from owner-occupied housing is not taxed.

The fact that different assets are taxed differently means that the arbitrage rule must adjust for the tax differences in comparing rates of return. Suppose that one asset pays a before-tax interest rate, $r_b$, and another asset pays a return that is tax exempt, $r_e$. Then if both assets are held by individuals who pay taxes on income at rate $t$, we must have

$$(1 - t)r_b = r_e.$$

That is, the after-tax return on each asset must be the same. Otherwise, individuals would not want to hold both assets—it would always pay them to switch exclusively to holding the asset that gave them the higher after-tax return. Of course, this discussion ignores other differences in the assets such as liquidity, risk, and so on.

## 11.6 Market Bubbles

Suppose you are contemplating buying a house that is absolutely certain to be worth $220,000 a year from now and that the current interest rate (reflecting your alternative investment opportunities) is 10%. A fair price for the house would be the present value, $200,000.

Now suppose that things aren't quite so certain: many people believe that the house will be worth $220,000 in a year, but there are no guarantees. We would expect that the house would sell for somewhat less than $200,000 due to the additional risk associated with purchase.

Suppose the year goes by and the house is worth $240,000, far more than anticipated. The house value went up by 20%, even though the prevailing interest rate was 10%. It may be that this experience will lead people to revise their view about how much the house will be worth in the future—who knows, maybe it will go up by 20% or even more next year.

If many people hold such beliefs, they can bid up the price of housing now—which may encourage others to make even more optimistic forecasts about the housing market. As in our discussion of price adjustment, assets that people expect to have a higher return than the rate of interest get pushed up in price. The higher price will tend to reduce current demand but it also may encourage people to expect an even higher return in the future.

The first effect—high prices reducing demand—tends to stablize prices. The second effect—high prices leading to an expectation of even higher prices in the future—tends to destabilize prices.

This is an example of an **asset bubble**. In a bubble, the price of an asset increases, for one reason or another, and this leads people to expect the price to go up even more in the future. But if they expect the asset price to rise significantly in the future, they will try to buy more today, pushing prices up even more rapidly.

Financial markets may be subject to such bubbles, particularly when the participants are inexperienced. For example, in 2000–01 we saw a dramatic run-up in the prices of technology stocks and in 2005–06 we saw a bubble in house prices in much of the United States and many other countries.

All bubbles eventually burst. Prices fall and some people are left holding assets that are worth much less than they paid for them.

The key to avoiding bubbles is to look at economic fundamentals. In the midst of the housing bubble in the United States, the ratio between the price of a house and the yearly rental rate on an identical house became far larger than historical norms. This gap presumably reflected buyers' expectations of future price increases.

Similarly, the ratio of median house prices to median income reached historical highs. Both of these were warning signs that the high prices were unsustainable.

"This time it's different" can be a very hazardous belief to hold, particularly when it comes to financial markets.

## 11.7 Applications

The fact that all riskless assets must earn the same return is obvious, but very important. It has surprisingly powerful implications for the functioning of asset markets.

## Depletable Resources

Let us study the market equilibrium for a depletable resource like oil. Consider a competitive oil market, with many suppliers, and suppose for simplicity that there are zero costs to extract oil from the ground. Then how will the price of oil change over time?

It turns out that the price of oil must rise at the rate of interest. To see this, simply note that oil in the ground is an asset like any other asset. If it is worthwhile for a producer to hold it from one period to the next, it must provide a return to him equivalent to the financial return he could get elsewhere. If we let $p_{t+1}$ and $p_t$ be the prices at times $t+1$ and $t$, then we have

$$p_{t+1} = (1+r)p_t$$

as our no arbitrage condition in the oil market.

The argument boils down to this simple idea: oil in the ground is like money in the bank. If money in the bank earns a rate of return of $r$, then oil in the ground must earn the same rate of return. If oil in the ground earned a higher return than money in the bank, then no one would take oil out of the ground, preferring to wait till later to extract it, thus pushing the current price of oil up. If oil in the ground earned a lower return than money in the bank, then the owners of oil wells would try to pump their oil out immediately in order to put the money in the bank, thereby depressing the current price of oil.

This argument tells us how the price of oil changes. But what determines the price level itself? The price level turns out to be determined by the demand for oil. Let us consider a very simple model of the demand side of the market.

Suppose that the demand for oil is constant at $D$ barrels a year and that there is a total world supply of $S$ barrels. Thus we have a total of $T = S/D$ years of oil left. When the oil has been depleted we will have to use an alternative technology, say liquefied coal, which can be produced at a constant cost of $C$ dollars per barrel. We suppose that liquefied coal is a perfect substitute for oil in all applications.

Now, $T$ years from now, when the oil is just being exhausted, how much must it sell for? Clearly it must sell for $C$ dollars a barrel, the price of its perfect substitute, liquefied coal. This means that the price today of a barrel of oil, $p_0$, must grow at the rate of interest $r$ over the next $T$ years to be equal to $C$. This gives us the equation

$$p_0(1+r)^T = C$$

or

$$p_0 = \frac{C}{(1+r)^T}.$$

This expression gives us the current price of oil as a function of the other variables in the problem. We can now ask interesting comparative statics questions. For example, what happens if there is an unforeseen new discovery of oil? This means that $T$, the number of years remaining of oil, will increase, and thus $(1 + r)^T$ will increase, thereby decreasing $p_0$. So an increase in the supply of oil will, not surprisingly, decrease its current price.

What if there is a technological breakthrough that decreases the value of $C$? Then the above equation shows that $p_0$ must decrease. The price of oil has to be equal to the price of its perfect substitute, liquefied coal, when liquefied coal is the only alternative.

## When to Cut a Forest

Suppose that the size of a forest—measured in terms of the lumber that you can get from it—is some function of time, $F(t)$. Suppose further that the price of lumber is constant and that the rate of growth of the tree starts high and gradually declines. If there is a competitive market for lumber, when should the forest be cut for timber?

Answer: when the rate of growth of the forest equals the interest rate. Before that, the forest is earning a higher rate of return than money in the bank, and after that point it is earning less than money in the bank. The optimal time to cut a forest is when its growth rate just equals the interest rate.

We can express this more formally by looking at the present value of cutting the forest at time $T$. This will be

$$PV = \frac{F(T)}{(1+r)^T}.$$

We want to find the choice of $T$ that maximizes the present value—that is, that makes the value of the forest as large as possible. If we choose a very small value of $T$, the rate of growth of the forest will exceed the interest rate, which means that the $PV$ would be increasing so it would pay to wait a little longer. On the other hand, if we consider a very large value of $T$, the forest would be growing more slowly than the interest rate, so the $PV$ would be decreasing. The choice of $T$ that maximizes present value occurs when the rate of growth of the forest just equals the interest rate.

This argument is illustrated in Figure 11.1. In Figure 11.1A we have plotted the *rate* of growth of the forest and the *rate* of growth of a dollar invested in a bank. If we want to have the largest amount of money at some unspecified point in the future, we should always invest our money in the asset with the highest return available at each point in time. When

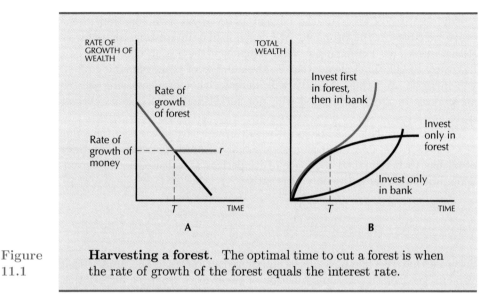

**Figure 11.1**

**Harvesting a forest.** The optimal time to cut a forest is when the rate of growth of the forest equals the interest rate.

the forest is young, it is the asset with the highest return. As it matures, its rate of growth declines, and eventually the bank offers a higher return.

The effect on total wealth is illustrated in Figure 11.1B. Before $T$ wealth grows most rapidly when invested in the forest. After $T$ it grows most rapidly when invested in the bank. Therefore, the optimal strategy is to invest in the forest up until time $T$, then harvest the forest, and invest the proceeds in the bank.

## EXAMPLE: Gasoline Prices during the Gulf War

In the Summer of 1990 Iraq invaded Kuwait. As a response to this, the United Nations imposed a blockade on oil imports from Iraq. Immediately after the blockade was announced the price of oil jumped up on world markets. At the same time price of gasoline at U.S. pumps increased significantly. This in turn led to cries of "war profiteering" and several segments about the oil industry on the evening news broadcasts.

Those who felt the price increase was unjustified argued that it would take at least 6 weeks for the new, higher-priced oil to wend its way across to the Atlantic and to be refined into gasoline. The oil companies, they argued, were making "excessive" profits by raising the price of gasoline that had already been produced using cheap oil.

Let's think about this argument as economists. Suppose that you own an asset—say gasoline in a storage tank—that is currently worth $1 a gallon. Six weeks from now, you know that it will be worth $1.50 a gallon. What price will you sell it for now? Certainly you would be foolish to sell it for much less than $1.50 a gallon—at any price much lower than that you would be better off letting the gasoline sit in the storage tank for 6 weeks. The same intertemporal arbitrage reasoning about extracting oil from the ground applies to gasoline in a storage tank. The (appropriate discounted) price of gasoline tomorrow has to equal the price of gasoline today if you want firms to supply gasoline today.

This makes perfect sense from a welfare point of view as well: if gasoline is going to be more expensive in the near future, doesn't it make sense to consume less of it today? The increased price of gasoline encourages immediate conservation measures and reflects the true scarcity price of gasoline.

Ironically, the same phenomenon occured two years later in Russia. During the transition to a market economy, Russian oil sold for about $3 a barrel at a time when the world price was about $19 a barrel. The oil producers anticipated that the price of oil would soon be allowed to rise—so they tried to hold back as much oil as possible from current production. As one Russian producer put it, "Have you seen anyone in New York selling one dollar for 10 cents?" The result was long lines in front of the gasoline pumps for Russian consumers.[1]

## 11.8 Financial Institutions

Asset markets allow people to change their pattern of consumption over time. Consider, for example, two people A and B who have different endowments of wealth. A might have $100 today and nothing tomorrow, while B might have $100 tomorrow and nothing today. It might well happen that each would rather have $50 today and $50 tomorrow. But they can reach this pattern of consumption simply by trading: A gives B $50 today, and B gives A $50 tomorrow.

In this particular case, the interest rate is zero: A lends B $50 and only gets $50 in return the next day. If people have convex preferences over consumption today and tomorrow, they would like to smooth their consumption over time, rather than consume everything in one period, even if the interest rate were zero.

We can repeat the same kind of story for other patterns of asset endowments. One individual might have an endowment that provides a steady stream of payments and prefer to have a lump sum, while another might have a lump sum and prefer a steady stream. For example, a twenty-year-old individual might want to have a lump sum of money now to buy a house, while a sixty-year-old might want to have a steady stream of money

---

[1] See Louis Uchitelle, "Russians Line Up for Gas as Refineries Sit on Cheap Oil," *New York Times,* July 12, 1992, page 4.

to finance his retirement. It is clear that both of these individuals could gain by trading their endowments with each other.

In a modern economy financial institutions exist to facilitate these trades. In the case described above, the sixty-year-old can put his lump sum of money in the bank, and the bank can then lend it to the twenty-year-old. The twenty-year-old then makes mortgage payments to the bank, which are, in turn, transferred to the sixty-year-old as interest payments. Of course, the bank takes its cut for arranging the trade, but if the banking industry is sufficiently competitive, this cut should end up pretty close to the actual costs of doing business.

Banks aren't the only kind of financial institution that allow one to reallocate consumption over time. Another important example is the stock market. Suppose that an entrepreneur starts a company that becomes successful. In order to start the company, the entrepreneur probably had some financial backers who put up money to help him get started—to pay the bills until the revenues started rolling in. Once the company has been established, the owners of the company have a claim to the profits that the company will generate in the future: they have a claim to a stream of payments.

But it may well be that they prefer a lump-sum reward for their efforts now. In this case, the owners can decide to sell the firm to other people via the stock market. They issue shares in the company that entitle the shareholders to a cut of the future profits of the firm in exchange for a lump-sum payment now. People who want to purchase part of the stream of profits of the firm pay the original owners for these shares. In this way, both sides of the market can reallocate their wealth over time.

There are a variety of other institutions and markets that help facilitate intertemporal trade. But what happens when the buyers and sellers aren't evenly matched? What happens if more people want to sell consumption tomorrow than want to buy it? Just as in any market, if the supply of something exceeds the demand, the price will fall. In this case, the price of consumption tomorrow will fall. We saw earlier that the price of consumption tomorrow was given by

$$p = \frac{1}{1+r},$$

so this means that the interest rate must rise. The increase in the interest rate induces people to save more and to demand less consumption now, and thus tends to equate demand and supply.

## Summary

1. In equilibrium, all assets with certain payoffs must earn the same rate of return. Otherwise there would be a riskless arbitrage opportunity.

2. The fact that all assets must earn the same return implies that all assets will sell for their present value.

3. If assets are taxed differently, or have different risk characteristics, then we must compare their after-tax rates of return or their risk-adjusted rates of return.

## REVIEW QUESTIONS

1. Suppose asset A can be sold for $11 next period. If assets similar to A are paying a rate of return of 10%, what must be asset A's current price?

2. A house, which you could rent for $10,000 a year and sell for $110,000 a year from now, can be purchased for $100,000. What is the rate of return on this house?

3. The payments of certain types of bonds (e.g., municipal bonds) are not taxable. If similar taxable bonds are paying 10% and everyone faces a marginal tax rate of 40%, what rate of return must the nontaxable bonds pay?

4. Suppose that a scarce resource, facing a constant demand, will be exhausted in 10 years. If an alternative resource will be available at a price of $40 and if the interest rate is 10%, what must the price of the scarce resource be today?

## APPENDIX

Suppose that you invest $1 in an asset yielding an interest rate $r$ where the interest is paid once a year. Then after $T$ years you will have $(1 + r)^T$ dollars. Suppose now that the interest is paid monthly. This means that the monthly interest rate will be $r/12$, and there will be $12T$ payments, so that after $T$ years you will have $(1+r/12)^{12T}$ dollars. If the interest rate is paid daily, you will have $(1 + r/365)^{365T}$ and so on.

In general, if the interest is paid $n$ times a year, you will have $(1 + r/n)^{nT}$ dollars after $T$ years. It is natural to ask how much money you will have if the interest is paid *continuously*. That is, we ask what is the limit of this expression as $n$ goes to infinity. It turns out that this is given by the following expression:

$$e^{rT} = \lim_{n \to \infty} (1 + r/n)^{nT},$$

where $e$ is 2.7183..., the base of natural logarithms.

This expression for continuous compounding is very convenient for calculations. For example, let us verify the claim in the text that the optimal time to harvest the forest is when the rate of growth of the forest equals the interest rate. Since the forest will be worth $F(T)$ at time $T$, the present value of the forest harvested at time $T$ is

$$V(T) = \frac{F(T)}{e^{rT}} = e^{-rT} F(T).$$

In order to maximize the present value, we differentiate this with respect to $T$ and set the resulting expression equal to zero. This yields

$$V'(T) = e^{-rT} F'(T) - r e^{-rT} F(T) = 0$$

or

$$F'(T) - r F(T) = 0.$$

This can be rearranged to establish the result:

$$r = \frac{F'(T)}{F(T)}.$$

This equation says that the optimal value of $T$ satisfies the condition that the rate of interest equals the rate of growth of the value of the forest.

# CHAPTER 12

# UNCERTAINTY

Uncertainty is a fact of life. People face risks every time they take a shower, walk across the street, or make an investment. But there are financial institutions such as insurance markets and the stock market that can mitigate at least some of these risks. We will study the functioning of these markets in the next chapter, but first we must study individual behavior with respect to choices involving uncertainty.

## 12.1 Contingent Consumption

Since we now know all about the standard theory of consumer choice, let's try to use what we know to understand choice under uncertainty. The first question to ask is what is the basic "thing" that is being chosen?

The consumer is presumably concerned with the **probability distribution** of getting different consumption bundles of goods. A probability distribution consists of a list of different outcomes—in this case, consumption bundles—and the probability associated with each outcome. When a consumer decides how much automobile insurance to buy or how much to invest in the stock market, he is in effect deciding on a pattern of probability distribution across different amounts of consumption.

For example, suppose that you have $100 now and that you are contemplating buying lottery ticket number 13. If number 13 is drawn in the lottery, the holder will be paid $200. This ticket costs, say, $5. The two outcomes that are of interest are the event that the ticket is drawn and the event that it isn't.

Your original endowment of wealth—the amount that you would have if you did not purchase the lottery ticket—is $100 if 13 is drawn, and $100 if it isn't drawn. But if you buy the lottery ticket for $5, you will have a wealth distribution consisting of $295 if the ticket is a winner, and $95 if it is not a winner. The original endowment of probabilities of wealth in different circumstances has been changed by the purchase of the lottery ticket. Let us examine this point in more detail.

In this discussion we'll restrict ourselves to examining monetary gambles for convenience of exposition. Of course, it is not money alone that matters; it is the consumption that money can buy that is the ultimate "good" being chosen. The same principles apply to gambles over goods, but restricting ourselves to monetary outcomes makes things simpler. Second, we will restrict ourselves to very simple situations where there are only a few possible outcomes. Again, this is only for reasons of simplicity.

Above we described the case of gambling in a lottery; here we'll consider the case of insurance. Suppose that an individual initially has $35,000 worth of assets, but there is a possibility that he may lose $10,000. For example, his car may be stolen, or a storm may damage his house. Suppose that the probability of this event happening is $p = .01$. Then the probability distribution the person is facing is a 1 percent probability of having $25,000 of assets, and a 99 percent probability of having $35,000.

Insurance offers a way to change this probability distribution. Suppose that there is an insurance contract that will pay the person $100 if the loss occurs in exchange for a $1 premium. Of course the premium must be paid whether or not the loss occurs. If the person decides to purchase $10,000 dollars of insurance, it will cost him $100. In this case he will have a 1 percent chance of having $34,900 ($35,000 of other assets − $10,000 loss + $10,000 payment from the insurance payment − $100 insurance premium) and a 99 percent chance of having $34,900 ($35,000 of assets − $100 insurance premium). Thus the consumer ends up with the same wealth no matter what happens. He is now fully insured against loss.

In general, if this person purchases $K$ dollars of insurance and has to pay a premium $\gamma K$, then he will face the gamble:[1]

probability .01 of getting $25,000 + K − \gamma K$

---

[1] The Greek letter $\gamma$, gamma, is pronounced "gam-ma."

and

probability .99 of getting $\$35,000 - \gamma K$.

What kind of insurance will this person choose? Well, that depends on his preferences. He might be very conservative and choose to purchase a lot of insurance, or he might like to take risks and not purchase any insurance at all. People have different preferences over probability distributions in the same way that they have different preferences over the consumption of ordinary goods.

In fact, one very fruitful way to look at decision making under uncertainty is just to think of the money available under different circumstances as different goods. A thousand dollars after a large loss has occurred may mean a very different thing from a thousand dollars when it hasn't. Of course, we don't have to apply this idea just to money: an ice cream cone if it happens to be hot and sunny tomorrow is a very different good from an ice cream cone if it is rainy and cold. In general, consumption goods will be of different value to a person depending upon the circumstances under which they become available.

Let us think of the different outcomes of some random event as being different **states of nature**. In the insurance example given above there were two states of nature: the loss occurs or it doesn't. But in general there could be many different states of nature. We can then think of a **contingent consumption plan** as being a specification of what will be consumed in each different state of nature—each different outcome of the random process. *Contingent* means depending on something not yet certain, so a contingent consumption plan means a plan that depends on the outcome of some event. In the case of insurance purchases, the contingent consumption was described by the terms of the insurance contract: how much money you would have if a loss occurred and how much you would have if it didn't. In the case of the rainy and sunny days, the contingent consumption would just be the *plan* of what would be consumed given the various outcomes of the weather.

People have preferences over different plans of consumption, just like they have preferences over actual consumption. It certainly might make you feel better now to know that you are fully insured. People make choices that reflect their preferences over consumption in different circumstances, and we can use the theory of choice that we have developed to analyze those choices.

If we think about a contingent consumption plan as being just an ordinary consumption bundle, we are right back in the framework described in the previous chapters. We can think of preferences as being defined over different consumption plans, with the "terms of trade" being given by the budget constraint. We can then model the consumer as choosing the best consumption plan he or she can afford, just as we have done all along.

Let's describe the insurance purchase in terms of the indifference-curve analysis we've been using. The two states of nature are the event that the loss occurs and the event that it doesn't. The contingent consumptions are the values of how much money you would have in each circumstance. We can plot this on a graph as in Figure 12.1.

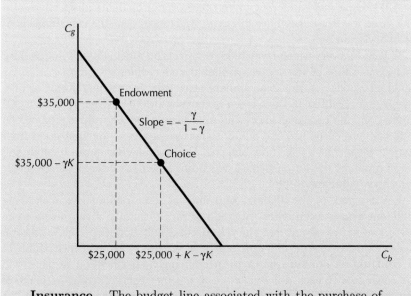

**Figure 12.1**

**Insurance.** The budget line associated with the purchase of insurance. The insurance premium $\gamma$ allows us to give up some consumption in the good outcome $(C_g)$ in order to have more consumption in the bad outcome $(C_b)$.

Your endowment of contingent consumption is \$25,000 in the "bad" state—if the loss occurs—and \$35,000 in the "good" state—if it doesn't occur. Insurance offers you a way to move away from this endowment point. If you purchase $K$ dollars' worth of insurance, you give up $\gamma K$ dollars of consumption possibilities in the good state in exchange for $K - \gamma K$ dollars of consumption possibilities in the bad state. Thus the consumption you lose in the good state, divided by the extra consumption you gain in the bad state, is

$$\frac{\delta C_g}{\delta C_b} = -\frac{\gamma K}{K - \gamma K} = -\frac{\gamma}{1 - \gamma}.$$

This is the slope of the budget line through your endowment. It is just as if the price of consumption in the good state is $1 - \gamma$ and the price in the bad state is $\gamma$.

We can draw in the indifference curves that a person might have for contingent consumption. Here again it is very natural for indifference curves to have a convex shape: this means that the person would rather have a constant amount of consumption in each state than a large amount in one state and a low amount in the other.

Given the indifference curves for consumption in each state of nature, we can look at the choice of how much insurance to purchase. As usual, this will be characterized by a tangency condition: the marginal rate of substitution between consumption in each state of nature should be equal to the price at which you can trade off consumption in those states.

Of course, once we have a model of optimal choice, we can apply all of the machinery developed in early chapters to its analysis. We can examine how the demand for insurance changes as the price of insurance changes, as the wealth of the consumer changes, and so on. The theory of consumer behavior is perfectly adequate to model behavior under uncertainty as well as certainty.

## EXAMPLE: Catastrophe Bonds

We have seen that insurance is a way to transfer wealth from good states of nature to bad states of nature. Of course there are two sides to these transactions: those who buy insurance and those who sell it. Here we focus on the sell side of insurance.

The sell side of the insurance market is divided into a retail component, which deals directly with end buyers, and a wholesale component, in which insurers sell risks to other parties. The wholesale part of the market is known as the **reinsurance market.**

Typically, the reinsurance market has relied on large investors such as pension funds to provide financial backing for risks. However, some reinsurers rely on large individual investors. Lloyd's of London, one of the most famous reinsurance consortia, generally uses private investors.

Recently, the reinsurance industry has been experimenting with **catastrophe bonds**, which, according to some, are a more flexible way to provide reinsurance. These bonds, generally sold to large institutions, have typically been tied to natural disasters, like earthquakes or hurricanes.

A financial intermediary, such as a reinsurance company or an investment bank, issues a bond tied to a particular insurable event, such as an earthquake involving, say, at least $500 million in insurance claims. If there is no earthquake, investors are paid a generous interest rate. But if the earthquake occurs and the claims exceed the amount specified in the bond, investors sacrifice their principal and interest.

Catastrophe bonds have some attractive features. They can spread risks widely and can be subdivided indefinitely, allowing each investor to bear only a small part of the risk. The money backing up the insurance is paid in advance, so there is no default risk to the insured.

From the economist's point of view, "cat bonds" are a form of **state contingent security**, that is, a security that pays off if and only if some particular event occurs. This concept was first introduced by Nobel laureate Kenneth J. Arrow in a paper published in 1952 and was long thought to be of only theoretical interest. But it turned out that all sorts of options and other derivatives could be best understood using contingent securities. Now Wall Street rocket scientists draw on this 60-year-old work when creating exotic new derivatives such as catastrophe bonds.

## 12.2 Utility Functions and Probabilities

If the consumer has reasonable preferences about consumption in different circumstances, then we will be able to use a utility function to describe these preferences, just as we have done in other contexts. However, the fact that we are considering choice under uncertainty does add a special structure to the choice problem. In general, how a person values consumption in one state as compared to another will depend on the *probability* that the state in question will actually occur. In other words, the rate at which I am willing to substitute consumption if it rains for consumption if it doesn't should have something to do with how likely I think it is to rain. The preferences for consumption in different states of nature will depend on the beliefs of the individual about how likely those states are.

For this reason, we will write the utility function as depending on the probabilities as well as on the consumption levels. Suppose that we are considering two mutually exclusive states such as rain and shine, loss or no loss, or whatever. Let $c_1$ and $c_2$ represent consumption in states 1 and 2, and let $\pi_1$ and $\pi_2$ be the probabilities that state 1 or state 2 actually occurs.

If the two states are mutually exclusive, so that only one of them can happen, then $\pi_2 = 1 - \pi_1$. But we'll generally write out both probabilities just to keep things looking symmetric.

Given this notation, we can write the utility function for consumption in states 1 and 2 as $u(c_1, c_2, \pi_1, \pi_2)$. This is the function that represents the individual's preference over consumption in each state.

## EXAMPLE: Some Examples of Utility Functions

We can use nearly any of the examples of utility functions that we've seen up until now in the context of choice under uncertainty. One nice example is the case of perfect substitutes. Here it is natural to weight each consumption by the probability that it will occur. This gives us a utility function of the form

$$u(c_1, c_2, \pi_1, \pi_2) = \pi_1 c_1 + \pi_2 c_2.$$

In the context of uncertainty, this kind of expression is known as the **expected value**. It is just the average level of consumption that you would get.

Another example of a utility function that might be used to examine choice under uncertainty is the Cobb–Douglas utility function:

$$u(c_1, c_2, \pi, 1 - \pi) = c_1^\pi c_2^{1-\pi}.$$

Here the utility attached to any combination of consumption bundles depends on the pattern of consumption in a nonlinear way.

As usual, we can take a monotonic transformation of utility and still represent the same preferences. It turns out that the logarithm of the Cobb-Douglas utility will be very convenient in what follows. This will give us a utility function of the form

$$\ln u(c_1, c_2, \pi_1, \pi_2) = \pi_1 \ln c_1 + \pi_2 \ln c_2.$$

## 12.3 Expected Utility

One particularly convenient form that the utility function might take is the following:

$$u(c_1, c_2, \pi_1, \pi_2) = \pi_1 v(c_1) + \pi_2 v(c_2).$$

This says that utility can be written as a weighted sum of some function of consumption in each state, $v(c_1)$ and $v(c_2)$, where the weights are given by the probabilities $\pi_1$ and $\pi_2$.

Two examples of this were given above. The perfect substitutes, or expected value utility function, had this form where $v(c) = c$. The Cobb Douglas didn't have this form originally, but when we expressed it in terms of logs, it had the linear form with $v(c) = \ln c$.

If one of the states is certain, so that $\pi_1 = 1$, say, then $v(c_1)$ is the utility of certain consumption in state 1. Similarly, if $\pi_2 = 1$, $v(c_2)$ is the utility of consumption in state 2. Thus the expression

$$\pi_1 v(c_1) + \pi_2 v(c_2)$$

represents the average utility, or the expected utility, of the pattern of consumption $(c_1, c_2)$.

For this reason, we refer to a utility function with the particular form described here as an **expected utility function**, or, sometimes, a **von Neumann-Morgenstern utility function**.[2]

When we say that a consumer's preferences can be represented by an expected utility function, or that the consumer's preferences have the expected utility property, we mean that we can choose a utility function that has the additive form described above. Of course we could also choose a different form; any monotonic transformation of an expected utility function is a utility function that describes the same preferences. But the additive form representation turns out to be especially convenient. If the consumer's preferences are described by $\pi_1 \ln c_1 + \pi_2 \ln c_2$ they will also be described by $c_1^{\pi_1} c_2^{\pi_2}$. But the latter representation does not have the expected utility property, while the former does.

On the other hand, the expected utility function can be subjected to some kinds of monotonic transformation and still have the expected utility property. We say that a function $v(u)$ is a **positive affine transformation** if it can be written in the form: $v(u) = au + b$ where $a > 0$. A positive affine transformation simply means multiplying by a positive number and adding a constant. It turns out that if you subject an expected utility function to a positive affine transformation, it not only represents the same preferences (this is obvious since an affine transformation is just a special kind of monotonic transformation) but it also still has the expected utility property.

Economists say that an expected utility function is "unique up to an affine transformation." This just means that you can apply an affine transformation to it and get another expected utility function that represents the same preferences. But any other kind of transformation will destroy the expected utility property.

## 12.4 Why Expected Utility Is Reasonable

The expected utility representation is a convenient one, but is it a reasonable one? Why would we think that preferences over uncertain choices would have the particular structure implied by the expected utility function? As it turns out there are compelling reasons why expected utility is a reasonable objective for choice problems in the face of uncertainty.

The fact that outcomes of the random choice are consumption goods that will be consumed in different circumstances means that ultimately *only one* of those outcomes is actually going to occur. Either your house

---

[2] John von Neumann was one of the major figures in mathematics in the twentieth century. He also contributed several important insights to physics, computer science, and economic theory. Oscar Morgenstern was an economist at Princeton who, along with von Neumann, helped to develop mathematical game theory.

will burn down or it won't; either it will be a rainy day or a sunny day. The way we have set up the choice problem means that only one of the many possible outcomes is going to occur, and hence only one of the contingent consumption plans will actually be realized.

This turns out to have a very interesting implication. Suppose you are considering purchasing fire insurance on your house for the coming year. In making this choice you will be concerned about wealth in three situations: your wealth now ($c_0$), your wealth if your house burns down ($c_1$), and your wealth if it doesn't ($c_2$). (Of course, what you really care about are your consumption possibilities in each outcome, but we are simply using wealth as a proxy for consumption here.) If $\pi_1$ is the probability that your house burns down and $\pi_2$ is the probability that it doesn't, then your preferences over these three different consumptions can generally be represented by a utility function $u(\pi_1, \pi_2, c_0, c_1, c_2)$.

Suppose that we are considering the tradeoff between wealth now and one of the possible outcomes—say, how much money we would be willing to sacrifice now to get a little more money if the house burns down. *Then this decision should be independent of how much consumption you will have in the other state of nature—how much wealth you will have if the house is not destroyed.* For the house will either burn down or it won't. If it happens to burn down, then the value of extra wealth shouldn't depend on how much wealth you would have if it *didn't* burn down. Bygones are bygones—so what *doesn't* happen shouldn't affect the value of consumption in the outcome that *does* happen.

Note that this is an *assumption* about an individual's preferences. It may be violated. When people are considering a choice between two things, the amount of a third thing they have typically matters. The choice between coffee and tea may well depend on how much cream you have. But this is because you consume coffee together with cream. If you considered a choice where you rolled a die and got either coffee, *or* tea, *or* cream, then the amount of cream that you might get shouldn't affect your preferences between coffee and tea. Why? Because you are either getting one thing or the other: if you end up with cream, the fact that you might have gotten either coffee or tea is irrelevant.

Thus in choice under uncertainty there is a natural kind of "independence" between the different outcomes because they must be consumed separately—in different states of nature. The choices that people plan to make in one state of nature should be independent from the choices that they plan to make in other states of nature. This assumption is known as the **independence assumption**. It turns out that this implies that the utility function for contingent consumption will take a very special structure: it has to be additive across the different contingent consumption bundles.

That is, if $c_1$, $c_2$, and $c_3$ are the consumptions in different states of nature, and $\pi_1$, $\pi_2$, and $\pi_3$ are the probabilities that these three different states of nature materialize, then if the independence assumption alluded to above is satisfied, the utility function must take the form

$$U(c_1, c_2, c_3) = \pi_1 u(c_1) + \pi_2 u(c_2) + \pi_3 u(c_3).$$

This is what we have called an expected utility function. Note that the expected utility function does indeed satisfy the property that the marginal rate of substitution between two goods is independent of how much there is of the third good. The marginal rate of substitution between goods 1 and 2, say, takes the form

$$\text{MRS}_{12} = -\frac{\partial U(c_1, c_2, c_3)/\partial c_1}{\partial U(c_1, c_2, c_3)/\partial c_2}$$
$$= -\frac{\pi_1 \delta u(c_1)/\delta c_1}{\pi_2 \delta u(c_2)/\delta c_2}.$$

This MRS depends only on how much you have of goods 1 and 2, not how much you have of good 3.

## 12.5 Risk Aversion

We claimed above that the expected utility function had some very convenient properties for analyzing choice under uncertainty. In this section we'll give an example of this.

Let's apply the expected utility framework to a simple choice problem. Suppose that a consumer currently has $10 of wealth and is contemplating a gamble that gives him a 50 percent probability of winning $5 and a 50 percent probability of losing $5. His wealth will therefore be random: he has a 50 percent probability of ending up with $5 and a 50 percent probability of ending up with $15. The *expected value* of his wealth is $10, and the expected utility is

$$\frac{1}{2} u(\$15) + \frac{1}{2} u(\$5).$$

This is depicted in Figure 12.2. The expected utility of wealth is the average of the two numbers $u(\$15)$ and $u(\$5)$, labeled $.5u(5) + .5u(15)$ in the graph. We have also depicted the utility of the expected value of wealth, which is labeled $u(\$10)$. Note that in this diagram the expected utility of wealth is less than the utility of the expected wealth. That is,

$$u\left(\frac{1}{2}15 + \frac{1}{2}5\right) = u(10) > \frac{1}{2}u(15) + \frac{1}{2}u(5).$$

**Risk aversion.**   For a risk-averse consumer the utility of the
expected value of wealth, $u(10)$, is greater than the expected
utility of wealth, $.5u(5) + .5u(15)$.

Figure
12.2

In this case we say that the consumer is **risk averse** since he prefers
to have the expected value of his wealth rather than face the gamble. Of
course, it could happen that the preferences of the consumer were such
that he prefers a a random distribution of wealth to its expected value, in
which case we say that the consumer is a **risk lover**. An example is given
in Figure 12.3.

Note the difference between Figures 12.2 and 12.3. The risk-averse consumer has a *concave* utility function—its slope gets flatter as wealth is increased. The risk-loving consumer has a *convex* utility function—its slope
gets steeper as wealth increases. Thus the curvature of the utility function
measures the consumer's attitude toward risk. A twice differentiable function is concave if its second derivative is negative, and convex if its second
derivative is positive. In general, the more concave the utility function,
the more risk averse the consumer will be, and the more convex the utility
function, the more risk loving the consumer will be.

The intermediate case is that of a linear utility function. The second
derivative of a linear function is zero. Here the consumer is **risk neutral**:
the expected utility of wealth is the utility of its expected value. In this
case the consumer doesn't care about the riskiness of his wealth at all—only
about its expected value.

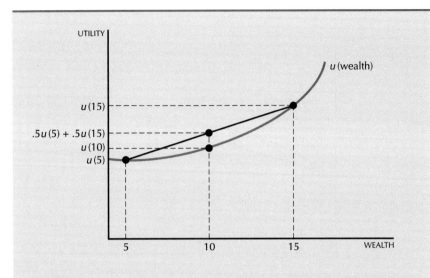

UTILITY

$u(15)$

$.5u(5) + .5u(15)$
$u(10)$
$u(5)$

5   10   15   WEALTH

$u\,(\text{wealth})$

Figure
12.3

**Risk loving.** For a risk-loving consumer the expected utility of wealth, $.5u(5) + .5u(15)$, is greater than the utility of the expected value of wealth, $u(10)$.

## EXAMPLE: The Demand for Insurance

Let's apply the expected utility structure to the demand for insurance that we considered earlier. Recall that in that example the person had a wealth of $35,000 and that he might incur a loss of $10,000. The probability of the loss was 1 percent, and it cost him $\gamma K$ to purchase $K$ dollars of insurance. By examining this choice problem using indifference curves we saw that the optimal choice of insurance was determined by the condition that the MRS between consumption in the two outcomes—loss or no loss—must be equal to $-\gamma/(1-\gamma)$. Let $\pi$ be the probability that the loss will occur, and $1 - \pi$ be the probability that it won't occur.

Let state 1 be the situation involving no loss, so that the person's wealth in that state is

$$c_1 = \$35,000 - \gamma K,$$

and let state 2 be the loss situation with wealth

$$c_2 = \$35,000 - \$10,000 + K - \gamma K.$$

Then the consumer's optimal choice of insurance is determined by the condition that his MRS between consumption in the two outcomes be equal to the price ratio:

$$\text{MRS} = -\frac{\pi \delta u(c_2)/\delta c_2}{(1-\pi)\delta u(c_1)/\delta c_1} = -\frac{\gamma}{1-\gamma}. \tag{12.1}$$

Now let us look at the insurance contract from the viewpoint of the insurance company. With probability $\pi$ they must pay out $K$, and with probability $(1-\pi)$ they pay out nothing. No matter what happens, they collect the premium $\gamma K$. Then the expected profit, $P$, of the insurance company is

$$P = \gamma K - \pi K - (1-\pi) \cdot 0 = \gamma K - \pi K.$$

Let us suppose that on the average the insurance company just breaks even on the contract. That is, they offer insurance at a "fair" rate, where "fair" means that the expected value of the insurance is just equal to its cost. Then we have

$$P = \gamma K - \pi K = 0,$$

which implies that $\gamma = \pi$.

Inserting this into equation (12.1) we have

$$\frac{\pi \delta u(c_2)/\delta c_2}{(1-\pi)\delta u(c_1)/\delta c_1} = \frac{\pi}{1-\pi}.$$

Canceling the $\pi$'s leaves us with the condition that the optimal amount of insurance must satisfy

$$\frac{\delta u(c_1)}{\delta c_1} = \frac{\delta u(c_2)}{\delta c_2}. \tag{12.2}$$

This equation says that the *marginal utility of an extra dollar of income if the loss occurs should be equal to the marginal utility of an extra dollar of income if the loss doesn't occur.*

Let us suppose that the consumer is risk averse, so that his marginal utility of money is declining as the amount of money he has increases. Then if $c_1 > c_2$, the marginal utility at $c_1$ would be less than the marginal utility at $c_2$, and vice versa. Furthermore, if the marginal utilities of income are equal at $c_1$ and $c_2$, as they are in equation (12.2), then we must have $c_1 = c_2$. Applying the formulas for $c_1$ and $c_2$, we find

$$35,000 - \gamma K = 25,000 + K - \gamma K,$$

which implies that $K = \$10,000$. This means that when given a chance to buy insurance at a "fair" premium, a risk-averse consumer will always choose to fully insure.

This happens because the utility of wealth in each state depends only on the total amount of wealth the consumer has in that state—and not what he *might* have in some other state—so that if the total amounts of wealth the consumer has in each state are equal, the marginal utilities of wealth must be equal as well.

To sum up: if the consumer is a risk-averse, expected utility maximizer and if he is offered fair insurance against a loss, then he will optimally choose to fully insure.

Let us examine a simple problem to demonstrate the principles of risk aversion and expected utility maximization. Suppose that the consumer has some wealth $w$ and is considering investing some amount $x$ in a risky asset. This asset could earn a return of $r_g$ in the "good" outcome, or it could earn a return of $r_b$ in the "bad" outcome. You should think of $r_g$ as being a positive return—the asset increases in value, and $r_b$ being a negative return—a decrease in asset value.

Thus the consumer's wealth in the good and bad outcomes will be

$$W_g = (w - x) + x(1 + r_g) = w + xr_g$$
$$W_b = (w - x) + x(1 + r_b) = w + xr_b.$$

Suppose that the good outcome occurs with probability $\pi$ and the bad outcome with probability $(1-\pi)$. Then the expected utility if the consumer decides to invest $x$ dollars is

$$EU(x) = \pi u(w + xr_g) + (1 - \pi)u(w + xr_b).$$

The consumer wants to choose $x$ so as to maximize this expression.

Differentiating with respect to $x$, we find the way in which utility changes as $x$ changes:

$$EU'(x) = \pi u'(w + xr_g)r_g + (1 - \pi)u'(w + xr_b)r_b. \qquad (12.3)$$

The second derivative of utility with respect to $x$ is

$$EU''(x) = \pi u''(w + xr_g)r_g^2 + (1 - \pi)u''(w + xr_b)r_b^2. \qquad (12.4)$$

If the consumer is risk averse his utility function will be concave, which implies that $u''(w) < 0$ for every level of wealth. Thus the second derivative of expected utility is unambiguously negative. Expected utility will be a concave function of $x$.

Consider the change in expected utility for the first dollar invested in the risky asset. This is just equation (12.3) with the derivative evaluated at $x = 0$:

$$EU'(0) = \pi u'(w)r_g + (1 - \pi)u'(w)r_b$$
$$= u'(w)[\pi r_g + (1 - \pi)r_b].$$

The expression inside the brackets is the **expected return** on the asset. If the expected return on the asset is negative, then expected utility must decrease when the first dollar is invested in the asset. But since the second derivative of expected utility is negative due to concavity, then utility must continue to decrease as additional dollars are invested.

Hence we have found that if the *expected value* of a gamble is negative, a risk averter will have the highest *expected utility* at $x^* = 0$: he will want no part of a losing proposition.

On the other hand, if the expected return on the asset is positive, then increasing $x$ from zero will increase expected utility. Thus he will always want to invest a little bit in the risky asset, no matter how risk averse he is.

Expected utility as a function of $x$ is illustrated in Figure 12.4. In Figure 12.4A the expected return is negative, and the optimal choice is $x^* = 0$. In Figure 12.4B the expected return is positive over some range, so the consumer wants to invest some positive amount $x^*$ in the risky asset.

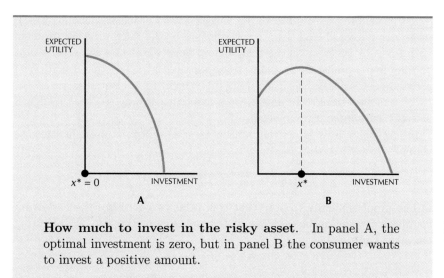

**How much to invest in the risky asset.** In panel A, the optimal investment is zero, but in panel B the consumer wants to invest a positive amount.

Figure
12.4

The optimal amount for the consumer to invest will be determined by the condition that the derivative of expected utility with respect to $x$ be equal to zero. Since the second derivative of utility is automatically negative due to concavity, this will be a global maximum.

Setting (12.3) equal to zero we have

$$EU'(x) = \pi u'(w + xr_g)r_g + (1 - \pi)u'(w + xr_b)r_b = 0. \qquad (12.5)$$

This equation determines the optimal choice of $x$ for the consumer in question.

## EXAMPLE: The Effect of Taxation on Investment in Risky Assets

How does the level of investment in a risky asset behave when you tax its return? If the individual pays taxes at rate $t$, then the after-tax returns will be $(1-t)r_g$ and $(1-t)r_b$. Thus the first-order condition determining his optimal investment, $x$, will be

$$EU'(x) = \pi u'(w+x(1-t)r_g)(1-t)r_g+(1-\pi)u'(w+x(1-t)r_b)(1-t)r_b = 0.$$

Canceling the $(1-t)$ terms, we have

$$EU'(x) = \pi u'(w + x(1-t)r_g)r_g + (1-\pi)u'(w + x(1-t)r_b)r_b = 0. \quad (12.6)$$

Let us denote the solution to the maximization problem without taxes— when $t = 0$—by $x^*$ and denote the solution to the maximization problem with taxes by $\hat{x}$. What is the relationship between $x^*$ and $\hat{x}$?

Your first impulse is probably to think that $x^* > \hat{x}$—that taxation of a risky asset will tend to discourage investment in it. But that turns out to be exactly wrong! Taxing a risky asset in the way we described will actually *encourage* investment in it!

In fact, there is an exact relation between $x^*$ and $\hat{x}$. It must be the case that

$$\hat{x} = \frac{x^*}{1-t}.$$

The proof is simply to note that this value of $\hat{x}$ satisfies the first-order condition for the optimal choice in the presence of the tax. Substituting this choice into equation (12.6) we have

$$EU'(\hat{x}) = \pi u'(w + \frac{x^*}{1-t}(1-t)r_g)r_g$$

$$+ (1-\pi)u'(w + \frac{x^*}{1-t}(1-t)r_b)r_b$$

$$= \pi u'(w + x^*r_g)r_g + (1-\pi)u'(w + x^*r_b)r_b = 0,$$

where the last equality follows from the fact that $x^*$ is the optimal solution when there is no tax.

What is going on here? How can imposing a tax increase the amount of investment in the risky asset? Here is what is happening. When the tax is imposed, the individual will have less of a gain in the good state, but he will also have *less of a loss in the bad state*. By scaling his original investment up by $1/(1-t)$ the consumer can reproduce the same *after-tax* returns that he had before the tax was put in place. The tax reduces his expected return, but it also reduces his risk: by increasing his investment the consumer can get exactly the same pattern of returns he had before and thus completely offset the effect of the tax. A tax on a risky investment represents a tax on the gain when the return is positive—but it represents a subsidy on the loss when the return is negative.

## 12.6 Diversification

Let us turn now to a different topic involving uncertainty—the benefits of diversification. Suppose that you are considering investing $100 in two different companies, one that makes sunglasses and one that makes raincoats. The long-range weather forecasters have told you that next summer is equally likely to be rainy or sunny. How should you invest your money?

Wouldn't it make sense to hedge your bets and put some money in each? By diversifying your holdings of the two investments, you can get a return on your investment that is more certain, and therefore more desirable if you are a risk-averse person.

Suppose, for example, that shares of the raincoat company and the sunglasses company currently sell for $10 apiece. If it is a rainy summer, the raincoat company will be worth $20 and the sunglasses company will be worth $5. If it is a sunny summer, the payoffs are reversed: the sunglasses company will be worth $20 and the raincoat company will be worth $5. If you invest your entire $100 in the sunglasses company, you are taking a gamble that has a 50 percent chance of giving you $200 and a 50 percent chance of giving you $50. The same magnitude of payoffs results if you invest all your money in the sunglasses company: in either case you have an expected payoff of $125.

But look what happens if you put half of your money in each. Then, if it is sunny you get $100 from the sunglasses investment and $25 from the raincoat investment. But if it is rainy, you get $100 from the raincoat investment and $25 from the sunglasses investment. Either way, you end up with $125 for sure. By diversifying your investment in the two companies, you have managed to reduce the overall risk of your investment, while keeping the expected payoff the same.

Diversification was quite easy in this example: the two assets were perfectly negatively correlated—when one went up, the other went down. Pairs of assets like this can be extremely valuable because they can reduce risk so dramatically. But, alas, they are also very hard to find. Most asset values move together: when GM stock is high, so is Ford stock, and so is Goodrich stock. But as long as asset price movements are not *perfectly* positively correlated, there will be some gains from diversification.

## 12.7 Risk Spreading

Let us return now to the example of insurance. There we considered the situation of an individual who had $35,000 and faced a .01 probability of a $10,000 loss. Suppose that there were 1000 such individuals. Then, on average, there would be 10 losses incurred, and thus $100,000 lost each year. Each of the 1000 people would face an *expected loss* of .01 times $10,000, or

$100 a year. Let us suppose that the probability that any person incurs a loss doesn't affect the probability that any of the others incur losses. That is, let us suppose that the risks are *independent*.

Then each individual will have an expected wealth of $.99 \times \$35,000 + .01 \times \$25,000 = \$34,900$. But each individual also bears a large amount of risk: each person has a 1 percent probability of losing $10,000.

Suppose that each consumer decides to *diversify* the risk that he or she faces. How can they do this? Answer: by selling some of their risk to other individuals. Suppose that the 1000 consumers decide to insure one another. If anybody incurs the $10,000 loss, each of the 1000 consumers will contribute $10 to that person. This way, the poor person whose house burns down is compensated for his loss, and the other consumers have the peace of mind that they will be compensated if that poor soul happens to be themselves! This is an example of **risk spreading**: each consumer spreads his risk over all of the other consumers and thereby reduces the amount of risk he bears.

Now on the average, 10 houses will burn down a year, so on the average, each of the 1000 individuals will be paying out $100 a year. But this is just on the average. Some years there might be 12 losses, and other years there might be 8 losses. The probability is very small that an individual would actually have to pay out more than $200, say, in any one year, but even so, the risk is there.

But there is even a way to diversify this risk. Suppose that the homeowners agree to pay $100 a year for certain, whether or not there are any losses. Then they can build up a cash reserve fund that can be used in those years when there are multiple fires. They are paying $100 a year for certain, and on average that money will be sufficient to compensate homeowners for fires.

As you can see, we now have something very much like a cooperative insurance company. We could add a few more features: the insurance company gets to invest its cash reserve fund and earn interest on its assets, and so on, but the essence of the insurance company is clearly present.

## 12.8 Role of the Stock Market

The stock market plays a role similar to that of the insurance market in that it allows for risk spreading. Recall from Chapter 11 that we argued that the stock market allowed the original owners of firms to convert their stream of returns over time to a lump sum. Well, the stock market also allows them to convert their risky position of having all their wealth tied up in one enterprise to a situation where they have a lump sum that they can invest in a variety of assets. The original owners of the firm have an incentive to issue shares in their company so that they can spread the risk of that single company over a large number of shareholders.

Similarly, the later shareholders of a company can use the stock market to reallocate their risks. If a company you hold shares in is adopting a policy that is too risky for your taste—or too conservative—you can sell those shares and purchase others.

In the case of insurance, an individual was able to reduce his risk to zero by purchasing insurance. For a flat fee of $100, the individual could purchase full insurance against the $10,000 loss. This was true because there was basically no risk in the aggregate: if the probability of the loss occurring was 1 percent, then on average 10 of the 1000 people would face a loss—we just didn't know which ones.

In the case of the stock market, there is risk in the aggregate. One year the stock market as a whole might do well, and another year it might do poorly. Somebody has to bear that kind of risk. The stock market offers a way to transfer risky investments from people who don't want to bear risk to people who are willing to bear risk.

Of course, few people outside of Las Vegas *like* to bear risk: most people are risk averse. Thus the stock market allows people to transfer risk from people who don't want to bear it to people who are willing to bear it if they are sufficiently compensated for it. We'll explore this idea further in the next chapter.

## Summary

1. Consumption in different states of nature can be viewed as consumption goods, and all the analysis of previous chapters can be applied to choice under uncertainty.

2. However, the utility function that summarizes choice behavior under uncertainty may have a special structure. In particular, if the utility function is linear in the probabilities, then the utility assigned to a gamble will just be the expected utility of the various outcomes.

3. The curvature of the expected utility function describes the consumer's attitudes toward risk. If it is concave, the consumer is a risk averter; and if it is convex, the consumer is a risk lover.

4. Financial institutions such as insurance markets and the stock market provide ways for consumers to diversify and spread risks.

## REVIEW QUESTIONS

1. How can one reach the consumption points to the left of the endowment in Figure 12.1?

2. Which of the following utility functions have the expected utility property? (a) $u(c_1, c_2, \pi_1, \pi_2) = a(\pi_1 c_1 + \pi_2 c_2)$, (b) $u(c_1, c_2, \pi_1, \pi_2) = \pi_1 c_1 + \pi_2 c_2^2$, (c) $u(c_1, c_2, \pi_1, \pi_2) = \pi_1 \ln c_1 + \pi_2 \ln c_2 + 17$.

3. A risk-averse individual is offered a choice between a gamble that pays $1000 with a probability of 25% and $100 with a probability of 75%, or a payment of $325. Which would he choose?

4. What if the payment was $320?

5. Draw a utility function that exhibits risk-loving behavior for small gambles and risk-averse behavior for larger gambles.

6. Why might a neighborhood group have a harder time self insuring for flood damage versus fire damage?

# CHAPTER **13**

# RISKY
# ASSETS

In the last chapter we examined a model of individual behavior under uncertainty and the role of two economic institutions for dealing with uncertainty: insurance markets and stock markets. In this chapter we will further explore how stock markets serve to allocate risk. In order to do this, it is convenient to consider a simplified model of behavior under uncertainty.

## 13.1 Mean-Variance Utility

In the last chapter we examined the expected utility model of choice under uncertainty. Another approach to choice under uncertainty is to describe the probability distributions that are the objects of choice by a few parameters and think of the utility function as being defined over those parameters. The most popular example of this approach is the **mean-variance model**. Instead of thinking that a consumer's preferences depend on the entire probability distribution of his wealth over every possible outcome, we suppose that his preferences can be well described by considering just a few summary statistics about the probability distribution of his wealth.

Let us suppose that a random variable $w$ takes on the values $w_s$ for $s = 1, \ldots, S$ with probability $\pi_s$. The **mean** of a probability distribution is simply its average value:

$$\mu_w = \sum_{s=1}^{S} \pi_s w_s.$$

This is the formula for an average: take each outcome $w_s$, weight it by the probability that it occurs, and sum it up over all outcomes.[1]

The **variance** of a probability distribution is the average value of $(w - \mu_w)^2$:

$$\sigma_w^2 = \sum_{s=1}^{S} \pi_s (w_s - \mu_w)^2.$$

The variance measures the "spread" of the distribution and is a reasonable measure of the riskiness involved. A closely related measure is the **standard deviation**, denoted by $\sigma_w$, which is the square root of the variance: $\sigma_w = \sqrt{\sigma_w^2}$.

The mean of a probability distribution measures its average value—what the distribution is centered around. The variance of the distribution measures the "spread" of the distribution—how spread out it is around the mean. See Figure 13.1 for a graphical depiction of probability distributions with different means and variances.

The mean-variance model assumes that the utility of a probability distribution that gives the investor wealth $w_s$ with a probability of $\pi_s$ can be expressed as a function of the mean and variance of that distribution, $u(\mu_w, \sigma_w^2)$. Or, if it is more convenient, the utility can be expressed as a function of the mean and standard deviation, $u(\mu_w, \sigma_w)$. Since both variance and standard deviation are measures of the riskiness of the wealth distribution, we can think of utility as depending on either one.

This model can be thought of as a simplification of the expected utility model described in the preceding chapter. If the choices that are being made can be completely characterized in terms of their mean and variance, then a utility function for mean and variance will be able to rank choices in the same way that an expected utility function will rank them. Furthermore, even if the probability distributions cannot be completely characterized by their means and variances, the mean-variance model may well serve as a reasonable approximation to the expected utility model.

We will make the natural assumption that a higher expected return is good, other things being equal, and that a higher variance is bad. This is simply another way to state the assumption that people are typically averse to risk.

---

[1] The Greek letter $\mu$, mu, is pronounced "mew." The Greek letter $\sigma$, sigma, is pronounced "sig-ma."

**Mean and variance.** The probability distribution depicted in panel A has a positive mean, while that depicted in panel B has a negative mean. The distribution in panel A is more "spread out" than the one in panel B, which means that it has a larger variance.

Figure
13.1

Let us use the mean-variance model to analyze a simple portfolio problem. Suppose that you can invest in two different assets. One of them, the **risk-free asset**, always pays a fixed rate of return, $r_f$. This would be something like a Treasury bill that pays a fixed rate of interest regardless of what happens.

The other asset is a **risky asset**. Think of this asset as being an investment in a large mutual fund that buys stocks. If the stock market does well, then your investment will do well. If the stock market does poorly, your investment will do poorly. Let $m_s$ be the return on this asset if state $s$ occurs, and let $\pi_s$ be the probability that state $s$ will occur. We'll use $r_m$ to denote the expected return of the risky asset and $\sigma_m$ to denote the standard deviation of its return.

Of course you don't have to choose one or the other of these assets; typically you'll be able to divide your wealth between the two. If you hold a fraction of your wealth $x$ in the risky asset, and a fraction $(1-x)$ in the risk-free asset, the expected return on your portfolio will be given by

$$r_x = \sum_{s=1}^{S}(xm_s + (1-x)r_f)\pi_s$$

$$= x\sum_{s=1}^{S}m_s\pi_s + (1-x)r_f\sum_{s=1}^{S}\pi_s.$$

Since $\sum \pi_s = 1$, we have

$$r_x = xr_m + (1-x)r_f.$$

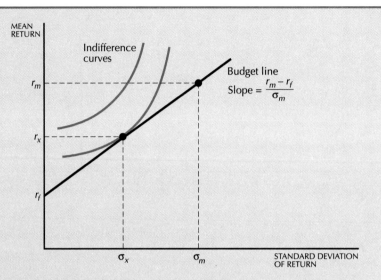

Figure
13.2
**Risk and return.** The budget line measures the cost of achieving a larger expected return in terms of the increased standard
deviation of the return. At the optimal choice the indifference
curve must be tangent to this budget line.

Thus the expected return on the portfolio is a weighted average of the two
expected returns.

The variance of your portfolio return will be given by

$$\sigma_x^2 = \sum_{s=1}^{S} (xm_s + (1-x)r_f - r_x)^2 \pi_s.$$

Substituting for $r_x$, this becomes

$$\sigma_x^2 = \sum_{s=1}^{S} (xm_s - xr_m)^2 \pi_s$$

$$= \sum_{s=1}^{S} x^2 (m_s - r_m)^2 \pi_s$$

$$= x^2 \sigma_m^2.$$

Thus the standard deviation of the portfolio return is given by

$$\sigma_x = \sqrt{x^2 \sigma_m^2} = x\sigma_m.$$

It is natural to assume that $r_m > r_f$, since a risk-averse investor would
never hold the risky asset if it had a lower expected return than the risk-
free asset. It follows that if you choose to devote a higher fraction of your
wealth to the risky asset, you will get a higher expected return, but you
will also incur higher risk. This is depicted in Figure 13.2.

If you set $x = 1$ you will put all of your money in the risky asset and you will have an expected return and standard deviation of $(r_m, \sigma_m)$. If you set $x = 0$ you will put all of your wealth in the sure asset and you have an expected return and standard deviation of $(r_f, 0)$. If you set $x$ somewhere between 0 and 1, you will end up somewhere in the middle of the line connecting these two points. This line gives us a budget line describing the market tradeoff between risk and return.

Since we are assuming that people's preferences depend only on the mean and variance of their wealth, we can draw indifference curves that illustrate an individual's preferences for risk and return. If people are risk averse, then a higher expected return makes them better off and a higher standard deviation makes them worse off. This means that standard deviation is a "bad." It follows that the indifference curves will have a positive slope, as shown in Figure 13.2.

At the optimal choice of risk and return the slope of the indifference curve has to equal the slope of the budget line in Figure 13.2. We might call this slope the **price of risk** since it measures how risk and return can be traded off in making portfolio choices. From inspection of Figure 13.2 the price of risk is given by

$$p = \frac{r_m - r_f}{\sigma_m}. \tag{13.1}$$

So our optimal portfolio choice between the sure and the risky asset could be characterized by saying that the marginal rate of substitution between risk and return must be equal to the price of risk:

$$\text{MRS} = -\frac{\partial U/\partial \sigma}{\partial U/\partial \mu} = \frac{r_m - r_f}{\sigma_m}. \tag{13.2}$$

Now suppose that there are many individuals who are choosing between these two assets. Each one of them has to have his marginal rate of substitution equal to the price of risk. Thus in equilibrium all of the individuals' MRSs will be equal: when people are given sufficient opportunities to trade risks, the equilibrium price of risk will be equal across individuals. Risk is like any other good in this respect.

We can use the ideas that we have developed in earlier chapters to examine how choices change as the parameters of the problem change. All of the framework of normal goods, inferior goods, revealed preference, and so on can be brought to bear on this model. For example, suppose that an individual is offered a choice of a new risky asset $y$ that has a mean return of $r_y$, say, and a standard deviation of $\sigma_y$, as illustrated in Figure 13.3.

If offered the choice between investing in $x$ and investing in $y$, which will the consumer choose? The original budget set and the new budget set are both depicted in Figure 13.3. Note that every choice of risk and return that was possible in the original budget set is possible with the new budget

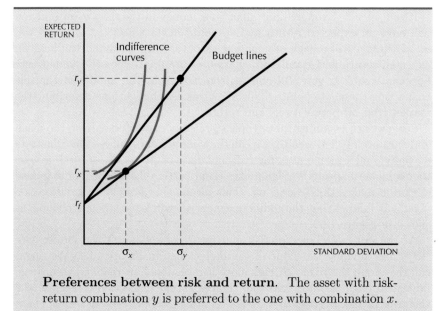

Figure
13.3 **Preferences between risk and return.** The asset with risk-return combination $y$ is preferred to the one with combination $x$.

set since the new budget set contains the old one. Thus investing in the asset $y$ and the risk-free asset is definitely better than investing in $x$ and the risk-free asset, since the consumer can choose a better final portfolio.

The fact that the consumer can choose how much of the risky asset he wants to hold is very important for this argument. If this were an "all or nothing" choice where the consumer was compelled to invest all of his money in either $x$ or $y$, we would get a very different outcome. In the example depicted in Figure 13.3, the consumer would prefer investing all of his money in $x$ to investing all of his money in $y$, since $x$ lies on a higher indifference curve than $y$. But if he can mix the risky asset with the risk-free asset, he would always prefer to mix with $y$ rather than to mix with $x$.

## 13.2 Measuring Risk

We have a model above that describes the price of risk ... but how do we measure the *amount* of risk in an asset? The first thing that you would probably think of is the standard deviation of an asset's return. After all, we are assuming that utility depends on the mean and variance of wealth, aren't we?

In the above example, where there is only one risky asset, that is exactly right: the amount of risk in the risky asset is its standard deviation. But if there are many risky assets, the standard deviation is not an appropriate measure for the amount of risk in an asset.

This is because a consumer's utility depends on the mean and variance of total wealth—not the mean and variance of any single asset that he might hold. What matters is how the returns of the various assets a consumer holds *interact* to create a mean and variance of his wealth. As in the rest of economics, it is the marginal impact of a given asset on total utility that determines its value, not the value of that asset held alone. Just as the value of an extra cup of coffee may depend on how much cream is available, the amount that someone would be willing to pay for an extra share of a risky asset will depend on how it interacts with other assets in his portfolio.

Suppose, for example, that you are considering purchasing two assets, and you know that there are only two possible outcomes that can happen. Asset A will be worth either $10 or −$5, and asset B will be worth either −$5 or $10. But when asset A is worth $10, asset B will be worth −$5 and vice versa. In other words the values of the two assets will be *negatively correlated:* when one has a large value, the other will have a small value.

Suppose that the two outcomes are equally likely, so that the average value of each asset will be $2.50. Then if you don't care about risk at all and you must hold one asset or the other, the most that you would be willing to pay for either one would be $2.50—the expected value of each asset. If you are averse to risk, you would be willing to pay even less than $2.50.

But what if you can hold both assets? Then if you hold one share of each asset, you will get $5 whichever outcome arises. Whenever one asset is worth $10, the other is worth −$5. Thus, if you can hold both assets, the amount that you would be willing to pay to purchase *both* assets would be $5.

This example shows in a vivid way that the value of an asset will depend in general on how it is correlated with other assets. Assets that move in opposite directions—that are negatively correlated with each other—are very valuable because they reduce overall risk. In general the value of an asset tends to depend much more on the correlation of its return with other assets than with its own variation. Thus the amount of risk in an asset depends on its correlation with other assets.

It is convenient to measure the risk in an asset relative to the risk in the stock market as a whole. We call the riskiness of a stock relative to the risk of the market the **beta** of a stock, and denote it by the Greek letter $\beta$. Thus, if $i$ represents some particular stock, we write $\beta_i$ for its riskiness relative to the market as a whole. Roughly speaking:

$$\beta_i = \frac{\text{how risky asset } i \text{ is}}{\text{how risky the stock market is}}.$$

If a stock has a beta of 1, then it is just as risky as the market as a whole;

when the market moves up by 10 percent, this stock will, on the average, move up by 10 percent. If a stock has a beta of less than 1, then when the market moves up by 10 percent, the stock will move up by less than 10 percent. The beta of a stock can be estimated by statistical methods to determine how sensitive the movements of one variable are relative to another, and there are many investment advisory services that can provide you with estimates of the beta of a stock.[2]

## 13.3 Counterparty Risk

Financial institutions loan money not just to individuals but to each other. There is always the chance that one party to a loan may fail to repay the loan, a risk known as **counterparty risk**.

To see how this works, imagine 3 banks, A, B, and C. Bank A owes B a billion dollars, Bank B owes C a billion dollars, and Bank C owes bank A a billion dollars. Now suppose that Bank A runs out of money and defaults on its loan. Bank B is now out a billion dollars and may not be able to pay C. Bank C, in turn, can't pay A, pushing A even further in the hole. This sort of effect is known as **financial contagion** or **systemic risk**. It is a very simplified version of what happened to U.S. financial institutions in the Fall of 2008.

What's the solution? One way to deal with this sort of problem is to have a "lender of last resort," which is typically a central bank, such as the U.S. Federal Reserve System. Bank A can go to the Federal Reserve and request an emergency loan of a billion dollars. It now pays off its loan from Bank B, which in turn pays Bank C, which in turn pays back Bank A. Bank A now has sufficient assets to pay back the loan from the central bank.

This is, of course, an overly simplified example. Initially, there was no net debt among the three banks. If they had gotten together to compare assets and liabilities, they would have certainly discovered that fact. However, when assets and liabilities span thousands of financial institutions, it may be difficult to determine net positions, which is why lenders of last resort may be necessary.

## 13.4 Equilibrium in a Market for Risky Assets

We are now in a position to state the equilibrium condition for a market with risky assets. Recall that in a market with only certain returns, we

---

[2] The Greek letter $\beta$, beta, is pronounced "bait-uh." For those of you who know some statistics, the beta of a stock is defined to be $\beta_i = \text{cov}(\tilde{r}_i, \tilde{r}_m)/\text{var}(\tilde{r}_m)$. That is, $\beta_i$ is the covariance of the return on the stock with the market return divided by the variance of the market return.

saw that all assets had to earn the same rate of return. Here we have a similar principle: all assets, after adjusting for risk, have to earn the same rate of return.

The catch is about adjusting for risk. How do we do that? The answer comes from the analysis of optimal choice given earlier. Recall that we considered the choice of an optimal portfolio that contained a riskless asset and a risky asset. The risky asset was interpreted as being a mutual fund—a diversified portfolio including many risky assets. In this section we'll suppose that this portfolio consists of *all* risky assets.

Then we can identify the expected return on this market portfolio of risky assets with the market expected return, $r_m$, and identify the standard deviation of the market return with the market risk, $\sigma_m$. The return on the safe asset is $r_f$, the risk-free return.

We saw in equation (13.1) that the price of risk, $p$, is given by

$$p = \frac{r_m - r_f}{\sigma_m}.$$

We said above that the amount of risk in a given asset $i$ relative to the total risk in the market is denoted by $\beta_i$. This means that to measure the *total* amount of risk in asset $i$, we have to multiply by the market risk, $\sigma_m$. Thus the total risk in asset $i$ is given by $\beta_i \sigma_m$.

What is the cost of this risk? Just multiply the total amount of risk, $\beta_i \sigma_m$, by the price of risk. This gives us the *risk adjustment:*

$$\text{risk adjustment} = \beta_i \sigma_m p$$
$$= \beta_i \sigma_m \frac{r_m - r_f}{\sigma_m}$$
$$= \beta_i (r_m - r_f).$$

Now we can state the equilibrium condition in markets for risky assets: in equilibrium all assets should have the same risk-adjusted rate of return. The logic is just like the logic used in Chapter 12: if one asset had a higher risk-adjusted rate of return than another, everyone would want to hold the asset with the higher risk-adjusted rate. Thus in equilibrium the risk-adjusted rates of return must be equalized.

If there are two assets $i$ and $j$ that have expected returns $r_i$ and $r_j$ and betas of $\beta_i$ and $\beta_j$, we must have the following equation satisfied in equilibrium:

$$r_i - \beta_i (r_m - r_f) = r_j - \beta_j (r_m - r_f).$$

This equation says that in equilibrium the risk-adjusted returns on the two assets must be the same—where the risk adjustment comes from multiplying the total risk of the asset by the price of risk.

Another way to express this condition is to note the following. The risk-free asset, by definition, must have $\beta_f = 0$. This is because it has zero risk,

EXPECTED
RETURN

$r_m$

Market line
(slope = $r_m - r_f$)

$r_f$

1

BETA

**Figure 13.4**

**The market line.** The market line depicts the combinations of expected return and beta for assets held in equilibrium.

and $\beta$ measures the amount of risk in an asset. Thus for any asset $i$ we must have

$$r_i - \beta_i(r_m - r_f) = r_f - \beta_f(r_m - r_f) = r_f.$$

Rearranging, this equation says

$$r_i = r_f + \beta_i(r_m - r_f)$$

or that the expected return on any asset must be the risk-free return plus the risk adjustment. This latter term reflects the extra return that people demand in order to bear the risk that the asset embodies. This equation is the main result of the **Capital Asset Pricing Model (CAPM)**, which has many uses in the study of financial markets.

## 13.5 How Returns Adjust

In studying asset markets under certainty, we showed how prices of assets adjust to equalize returns. Let's look at the same adjustment process here.

According to the model sketched out above, the expected return on any asset should be the risk-free return plus the risk premium:

$$r_i = r_f + \beta_i(r_m - r_f).$$

In Figure 13.4 we have illustrated this line in a graph with the different values of beta plotted along the horizontal axis and different expected returns on the vertical axis. According to our model, all assets that are held in equilibrium have to lie along this line. This line is called the **market line**.

What if some asset's expected return and beta didn't lie on the market line? What would happen?

The expected return on the asset is the expected change in its price divided by its current price:

$$r_i = \text{ expected value of } \frac{p_1 - p_0}{p_0}.$$

This is just like the definition we had before, with the addition of the word "expected." We have to include "expected" now since the price of the asset tomorrow is uncertain.

Suppose that you found an asset whose expected return, adjusted for risk, was higher than the risk-free rate:

$$r_i - \beta_i(r_m - r_f) > r_f.$$

Then this asset is a very good deal. It is giving a higher risk-adjusted return than the risk-free rate.

When people discover that this asset exists, they will want to buy it. They might want to keep it for themselves, or they might want to buy it and sell it to others, but since it is offering a better tradeoff between risk and return than existing assets, there is certainly a market for it.

But as people attempt to buy this asset they will bid up today's price: $p_0$ will rise. This means that the expected return $r_i = (p_1 - p_0)/p_0$ will fall. How far will it fall? Just enough to lower the expected rate of return back down to the market line.

Thus it is a good deal to buy an asset that lies above the market line. For when people discover that it has a higher return given its risk than assets they currently hold, they will bid up the price of that asset.

This is all dependent on the hypothesis that people agree about the amount of risk in various assets. If they disagree about the expected returns or the betas of different assets, the model becomes much more complicated.

## EXAMPLE: Value at Risk

It is sometimes of interest to determine the risk of a certain set of assets. For example, suppose that a bank holds a particular portfolio of stocks. It may want to estimate the probability that the portfolio will fall by more than a million dollars on a given day. If this probability is 5% then we say that the portfolio has a "one-day 5% **value at risk** of $1 million." Typically value at risk is computed for 1 day or 2 week periods, using loss probabilities of 1% or 5%.

The theoretical idea of VaR is attractive. All the challenges lie in figuring out ways to estimate it. But, as financial analyst Philippe Jorion has put it, "[T]he greatest benefit of VaR lies in the imposition of a structured methodology for critically thinking about risk. Institutions that go through the process of computing their VaR are forced to confront their exposure to financial risks and to set up a proper risk management function. Thus the process of getting to VaR may be as important as the number itself."

The VaR is determined entirely by the probability distribution of the value of the portfolio, and this depends on the correlation of the assets in the portfolio. Typically, assets are positively correlated, so they all move up or down at once. Even worse, the distribution of asset prices tends to have "fat tails" so that there may be a relatively high probability of an extreme price movement. Ideally, one would estimate VaR using a long history of price movements. In practice, this is difficult to do, particularly for new and exotic assets.

In the Fall of 2008 many financial institutions discovered that their VaR estimates were severely flawed since asset prices dropped much more than was anticipated. In part this was due to the fact that statistical estimates were based on very small samples that were gathered during a stable period of economic activity. The estimated values at risk understated the true risk of the assets in question.

## EXAMPLE: Ranking Mutual Funds

The Capital Asset Pricing Model can be used to compare different investments with respect to their risk and their return. One popular kind of investment is a mutual fund. These are large organizations that accept money from individual investors and use this money to buy and sell stocks of companies. The profits made by such investments are then paid out to the individual investors.

The advantage of a mutual fund is that you have professionals managing your money. The disadvantage is they charge you for managing it. These fees are usually not terribly large, however, and most small investors are probably well advised to use a mutual fund.

But how do you choose a mutual fund in which to invest? You want one with a high expected return of course, but you also probably want one with a minimum amount of risk. The question is, how much risk are you willing to tolerate to get that high expected return?

One thing that you might do is to look at the historical performance of various mutual funds and calculate the average yearly return and the beta—the amount of risk—of each mutual fund you are considering. Since we haven't discussed the precise definition of beta, you might find it hard to calculate. But there are books where you can look up the historical betas of mutual funds.

If you plotted the expected returns versus the betas, you would get a diagram similar to that depicted in Figure 13.5.[3]   Note that the mutual funds with high expected returns will generally have high risk. The high expected returns are there to compensate people for bearing risk.

One interesting thing you can do with the mutual fund diagram is to compare investing with professional managers to a very simple strategy like investing part of your money in an **index fund**. There are several indices of stock market activity like the Dow-Jones Industrial Average, or the Standard and Poor's Index, and so on. The indices are typically the average returns on a given day of a certain group of stocks. The Standard and Poor's Index, for example, is based on the average performance of 500 large stocks in the United States.

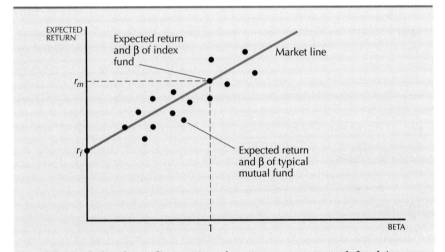

**Mutual funds.**   Comparing the returns on mutual fund investment to the market line.

Figure 13.5

An **index fund** is a mutual fund that holds the stocks that make up such an index. This means that you are guaranteed to get the average performance of the stocks in the index, virtually by definition. Since holding the average is not a very difficult thing to do—at least compared to trying to beat the average—index funds typically have low management fees. Since an index fund holds a very broad base of risky assets, it will have a beta

[3] See Michael Jensen, "The Performance of Mutual Funds in the Period 1945–1964," *Journal of Finance*, 23 (May 1968), 389–416, for a more detailed discussion of how to examine mutual fund performance using the tools we have sketched out in this chapter. Mark Grinblatt and Sheridan Titman have examined more recent data in "Mutual Fund Performance: An Analysis of Quarterly Portfolio Holdings," *The Journal of Business*, 62 (July 1989), 393–416.

that is very close to 1—it will be just as risky as the market as a whole, because the index fund holds nearly all the stocks in the market as a whole.

How does an index fund do as compared to the typical mutual fund? Remember the comparison has to be made with respect to both risk and return of the investment. One way to do this is to plot the expected return and beta of a Standard and Poor's Index fund, and draw the line connecting it to the risk-free rate, as in Figure 13.5. You can get any combination of risk and return on this line that you want just by deciding how much money you want to invest in the risk-free asset and how much you want to invest in the index fund.

Now let's count the number of mutual funds that plot below this line. These are mutual funds that offer risk and return combinations that are dominated by those available by the index fund/risk-free asset combinations. When this is done, it turns out that the vast majority of the risk-return combinations offered by mutual funds are below the line. The number of funds that plot above the line is no more than could be expected by chance alone.

But seen another way, this finding might not be too surprising. The stock market is an incredibly competitive environment. People are always trying to find undervalued stocks in order to purchase them. This means that on average, stocks are usually trading for what they're really worth. If that is the case, then betting the averages is a pretty reasonable strategy—since beating the averages is almost impossible.

## Summary

1. We can use the budget set and indifference curve apparatus developed earlier to examine the choice of how much money to invest in risky and riskless assets.

2. The marginal rate of substitution between risk and return will have to equal the slope of the budget line. This slope is known as the price of risk.

3. The amount of risk present in an asset depends to a large extent on its correlation with other assets. An asset that moves opposite the direction of other assets helps to reduce the overall risk of your portfolio.

4. The amount of risk in an asset relative to that of the market as a whole is called the **beta** of the asset.

5. The fundamental equilibrium condition in asset markets is that risk-adjusted returns have to be the same.

6. Counterparty risk, which is the risk that the other side of a transaction will not pay, can also be an important risk factor.

## REVIEW QUESTIONS

1. If the risk-free rate of return is 6%, and if a risky asset is available with a return of 9% and a standard deviation of 3%, what is the maximum rate of return you can achieve if you are willing to accept a standard deviation of 2%? What percentage of your wealth would have to be invested in the risky asset?

2. What is the price of risk in the above exercise?

3. If a stock has a $\beta$ of 1.5, the return on the market is 10%, and the risk-free rate of return is 5%, what expected rate of return should this stock offer according to the Capital Asset Pricing Model? If the expected value of the stock is $100, what price should the stock be selling for today?

# CHAPTER **14**

# CONSUMER'S SURPLUS

In the preceding chapters we have seen how to derive a consumer's demand function from the underlying preferences or utility function. But in practice we are usually concerned with the reverse problem—how to estimate preferences or utility from observed demand behavior.

We have already examined this problem in two other contexts. In Chapter 5 we showed how one could estimate the parameters of a utility function from observing demand behavior. In the Cobb-Douglas example used in that chapter, we were able to estimate a utility function that described the observed choice behavior simply by calculating the average expenditure share of each good. The resulting utility function could then be used to evaluate changes in consumption.

In Chapter 7 we described how to use revealed preference analysis to recover estimates of the underlying preferences that may have generated some observed choices. These estimated indifference curves can also be used to evaluate changes in consumption.

In this chapter we will consider some more approaches to the problem of estimating utility from observing demand behavior. Although some of the methods we will examine are less general than the two methods we examined previously, they will turn out to be useful in several applications that we will discuss later in the book.

We will start by reviewing a special case of demand behavior for which it is very easy to recover an estimate of utility. Later we will consider more general cases of preferences and demand behavior.

## 14.1 Demand for a Discrete Good

Let us start by reviewing demand for a discrete good with quasilinear utility, as described in Chapter 6. Suppose that the utility function takes the form $v(x) + y$ and that the x-good is only available in integer amounts. Let us think of the y-good as money to be spent on other goods and set its price to 1. Let $p$ be the price of the x-good.

We saw in Chapter 6 that in this case consumer behavior can be described in terms of the reservation prices, $r_1 = v(1) - v(0)$, $r_2 = v(2) - v(1)$, and so on. The relationship between reservation prices and demand was very simple: if $n$ units of the discrete good are demanded, then $r_n \geq p \geq r_{n+1}$.

To verify this, let's look at an example. Suppose that the consumer chooses to consume 6 units of the x-good when its price is $p$. Then the utility of consuming $(6, m - 6p)$ must be at least as large as the utility of consuming any other bundle $(x, m - px)$:

$$v(6) + m - 6p \geq v(x) + m - px. \tag{14.1}$$

In particular this inequality must hold for $x = 5$, which gives us

$$v(6) + m - 6p \geq v(5) + m - 5p.$$

Rearranging, we have $v(6) - v(5) = r_6 \geq p$.

Equation (14.1) must also hold for $x = 7$. This gives us

$$v(6) + m - 6p \geq v(7) + m - 7p,$$

which can be rearranged to yield

$$p \geq v(7) - v(6) = r_7.$$

This argument shows that if 6 units of the x-good is demanded, then the price of the x-good must lie between $r_6$ and $r_7$. In general, if $n$ units of the x-good are demanded at price $p$, then $r_n \geq p \geq r_{n+1}$, as we wanted to show. The list of reservation prices contains all the information necessary to describe the demand behavior. The graph of the reservation prices forms a "staircase" as shown in Figure 14.1. This staircase is precisely the demand curve for the discrete good.

## 14.2 Constructing Utility from Demand

We have just seen how to construct the demand curve given the reservation prices or the utility function. But we can also do the same operation in reverse. If we are given the demand curve, we can construct the utility function—at least in the special case of quasilinear utility.

At one level, this is just a trivial operation of arithmetic. The reservation prices are defined to be the difference in utility:

$$r_1 = v(1) - v(0)$$
$$r_2 = v(2) - v(1)$$
$$r_3 = v(3) - v(2)$$
$$\vdots$$

If we want to calculate $v(3)$, for example, we simply add up both sides of this list of equations to find

$$r_1 + r_2 + r_3 = v(3) - v(0).$$

It is convenient to set the utility from consuming zero units of the good equal to zero, so that $v(0) = 0$, and therefore $v(n)$ is just the sum of the first $n$ reservation prices.

This construction has a nice geometrical interpretation that is illustrated in Figure 14.1A. The utility from consuming $n$ units of the discrete good is just the area of the first $n$ bars which make up the demand function. This is true because the height of each bar is the reservation price associated with that level of demand and the width of each bar is 1. This area is sometimes called the **gross benefit** or the **gross consumer's surplus** associated with the consumption of the good.

Note that this is only the utility associated with the consumption of good 1. The final utility of consumption depends on the how much the consumer consumes of good 1 *and* good 2. If the consumer chooses $n$ units of the discrete good, then he will have $m - pn$ dollars left over to purchase other things. This leaves him with a total utility of

$$v(n) + m - pn.$$

This utility also has an interpretation as an area: we just take the area depicted in Figure 14.1A, subtract off the expenditure on the discrete good, and add $m$.

The term $v(n) - pn$ is called **consumer's surplus** or the **net consumer's surplus**. It measures the net benefits from consuming $n$ units of the discrete good: the utility $v(n)$ minus the reduction in the expenditure on consumption of the other good. The consumer's surplus is depicted in Figure 14.1B.

**Reservation prices and consumer's surplus.** The gross benefit in panel A is the area under the demand curve. This measures the utility from consuming the x-good. The consumer's surplus is depicted in panel B. It measures the utility from consuming both goods when the first good has to be purchased at a constant price $p$.

Figure
14.1

## 14.3 Other Interpretations of Consumer's Surplus

There are some other ways to think about consumer's surplus. Suppose that the price of the discrete good is $p$. Then the value that the consumer places on the first unit of consumption of that good is $r_1$, but he only has to pay $p$ for it. This gives him a "surplus" of $r_1 - p$ on the first unit of consumption. He values the second unit of consumption at $r_2$, but again he only has to pay $p$ for it. This gives him a surplus of $r_2 - p$ on that unit. If we add this up over all $n$ units the consumer chooses, we get his total consumer's surplus:

$$CS = r_1 - p + r_2 - p + \cdots + r_n - p = r_1 + \cdots + r_n - np.$$

Since the sum of the reservation prices just gives us the utility of consumption of good 1, we can also write this as

$$CS = v(n) - pn.$$

We can interpret consumer's surplus in yet another way. Suppose that a consumer is consuming $n$ units of the discrete good and paying $pn$ dollars to do so. How much money would he need to induce him to give up his entire consumption of this good? Let $R$ be the required amount of money. Then $R$ must satisfy the equation

$$v(0) + m + R = v(n) + m - pn.$$

Since $v(0) = 0$ by definition, this equation reduces to

$$R = v(n) - pn,$$

which is just consumer's surplus. Hence the consumer's surplus measures how much a consumer would need to be paid to give up his entire consumption of some good.

## 14.4 From Consumer's Surplus to Consumers' Surplus

Up until now we have been considering the case of a single consumer. If several consumers are involved we can add up each consumer's surplus across all the consumers to create an aggregate measure of the **consumers' surplus**. Note carefully the distinction between the two concepts: consumer's surplus refers to the surplus of a single consumer; consumers' surplus refers to the sum of the surpluses across a number of consumers.

Consumers' surplus serves as a convenient measure of the aggregate gains from trade, just as consumer's surplus serves as a measure of the individual gains from trade.

## 14.5 Approximating a Continuous Demand

We have seen that the area underneath the demand curve for a discrete good measures the utility of consumption of that good. We can extend this to the case of a good available in continuous quantities by approximating the continuous demand curve by a staircase demand curve. The area under the continuous demand curve is then approximately equal to the area under the staircase demand.

See Figure 14.2 for an example. In the Appendix to this chapter we show how to use calculus to calculate the exact area under a demand curve.

## 14.6 Quasilinear Utility

It is worth thinking about the role that quasilinear utility plays in this analysis. In general the price at which a consumer is willing to purchase

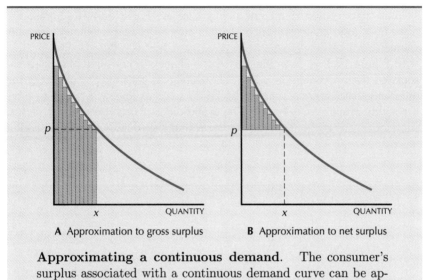

**Approximating a continuous demand.**   The consumer's surplus associated with a continuous demand curve can be approximated by the consumer's surplus associated with a discrete approximation to it.

Figure
14.2

some amount of good 1 will depend on how much money he has for consuming other goods. This means that in general the reservation prices for good 1 will depend on how much good 2 is being consumed.

But in the special case of quasilinear utility the reservation prices are independent of the amount of money the consumer has to spend on other goods. Economists say that with quasilinear utility there is "no income effect" since changes in income don't affect demand. This is what allows us to calculate utility in such a simple way. Using the area under the demand curve to measure utility will only be *exactly* correct when the utility function is quasilinear.

But it may often be a good approximation. If the demand for a good doesn't change very much when income changes, then the income effects won't matter very much, and the change in consumer's surplus will be a reasonable approximation to the change in the consumer's utility.[1]

## 14.7 Interpreting the Change in Consumer's Surplus

We are usually not terribly interested in the absolute level of consumer's surplus. We are generally more interested in the change in consumer's

---

[1]  Of course, the change in consumer's surplus is only one way to represent a change in utility—the change in the square root of consumer's surplus would be just as good. But it is standard to use consumer's surplus as a standard measure of utility.

surplus that results from some policy change. For example, suppose the price of a good changes from $p'$ to $p''$. How does the consumer's surplus change?

In Figure 14.3 we have illustrated the change in consumer's surplus associated with a change in price. The change in consumer's surplus is the difference between two roughly triangular regions and will therefore have a roughly trapezoidal shape. The trapezoid is further composed of two subregions, the rectangle indicated by $R$ and the roughly triangular region indicated by $T$.

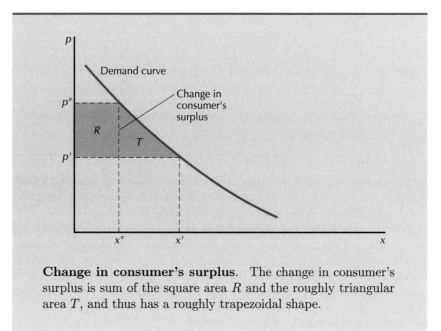

**Figure 14.3**

**Change in consumer's surplus.** The change in consumer's surplus is sum of the square area $R$ and the roughly triangular area $T$, and thus has a roughly trapezoidal shape.

The rectangle measures the loss in surplus due to the fact that the consumer is now paying more for all the units he continues to consume. After the price increases the consumer continues to consume $x''$ units of the good, and each unit of the good is now more expensive by $p'' - p'$. This means he has to spend $(p'' - p')x''$ more money than he did before just to consume $x''$ units of the good.

But this is not the entire welfare loss. Due to the increase in the price of the x-good, the consumer has decided to consume less of it than he was before. The triangle $T$ measures the value of the *lost* consumption of the x-good. The total loss to the consumer is the sum of these two effects: $R$ measures the loss from having to pay more for the units he continues to consume, and $T$ measures the loss from the reduced consumption.

## EXAMPLE: The Change in Consumer's Surplus

*Question:* Consider the linear demand curve $D(p) = 20 - 2p$. When the price changes from 2 to 3 what is the associated change in consumer's surplus?

*Answer:* When $p = 2$, $D(2) = 16$, and when $p = 3$, $D(3) = 14$. Thus we want to compute the area of a trapezoid with a height of 1 and bases of 14 and 16. This is equivalent to a rectangle with height 1 and base 14 (having an area of 14), plus a triangle of height 1 and base 2 (having an area of 1). The total area will therefore be 15.

## 14.8 Compensating and Equivalent Variation

The theory of consumer's surplus is very tidy in the case of quasilinear utility. Even if utility is not quasilinear, consumer's surplus may still be a reasonable measure of consumer's welfare in many applications. Usually the errors in measuring demand curves outweigh the approximation errors from using consumer's surplus.

But it may be that for some applications an approximation may not be good enough. In this section we'll outline a way to measure "utility changes" without using consumer's surplus. There are really two separate issues involved. The first has to do with how to estimate utility when we can observe a number of consumer choices. The second has to do with how we can measure utility in monetary units.

We've already investigated the estimation problem. We gave an example of how to estimate a Cobb-Douglas utility function in Chapter 6. In that example we noticed that expenditure shares were relatively constant and that we could use the average expenditure share as estimates of the Cobb-Douglas parameters. If the demand behavior didn't exhibit this particular feature, we would have to choose a more complicated utility function, but the principle would be just the same: if we have enough observations on demand behavior and that behavior is consistent with maximizing something, then we will generally be able to estimate the function that is being maximized.

Once we have an estimate of the utility function that describes some observed choice behavior we can use this function to evaluate the impact of proposed changes in prices and consumption levels. At the most fundamental level of analysis, this is the best we can hope for. All that matters are the consumer's preferences; any utility function that describes the consumer's preferences is as good as any other.

However, in some applications it may be convenient to use certain monetary measures of utility. For example, we could ask how much money we would have to give a consumer to compensate him for a change in his consumption patterns. A measure of this type essentially measures a change in utility, but it measures it in monetary units. What are convenient ways to do this?

Suppose that we consider the situation depicted in Figure 14.4. Here the consumer initially faces some prices $(p_1^*, 1)$ and consumes some bundle $(x_1^*, x_2^*)$. The price of good 1 then increases from $p_1^*$ to $\hat{p}_1$, and the consumer changes his consumption to $(\hat{x}_1, \hat{x}_2)$. How much does this price change hurt the consumer?

Figure 14.4

**The compensating and the equivalent variations.** Panel A shows the compensating variation (CV), and panel B shows the equivalent variation (EV).

One way to answer this question is to ask how much money we would have to give the consumer *after* the price change to make him just as well off as he was *before* the price change. In terms of the diagram, we ask how far up we would have to shift the new budget line to make it tangent to the indifference curve that passes through the original consumption point $(x_1^*, x_2^*)$. The change in income necessary to restore the consumer to his original indifference curve is called the **compensating variation** in income, since it is the change in income that will just compensate the consumer for the price change. The compensating variation measures how much extra money the government would have to give the consumer if it wanted to exactly compensate the consumer for the price change.

Another way to measure the impact of a price change in monetary terms is to ask how much money would have to be taken away from the consumer *before* the price change to leave him as well off as he would be *after* the price change. This is called the **equivalent variation** in income since it is the income change that is equivalent to the price change in terms of the change in utility. In Figure 14.4 we ask how far down we must shift the original budget line to just touch the indifference curve that passes through the new consumption bundle. The equivalent variation measures the maximum amount of income that the consumer would be willing to pay to avoid the price change.

In general the amount of money that the consumer would be willing to pay to avoid a price change would be different from the amount of money that the consumer would have to be paid to compensate him for a price change. After all, at different sets of prices a dollar is worth a different amount to a consumer since it will purchase different amounts of consumption.

In geometric terms, the compensating and equivalent variations are just two different ways to measure "how far apart" two indifference curves are. In each case we are measuring the distance between two indifference curves by seeing how far apart their tangent lines are. In general this measure of distance will depend on the slope of the tangent lines—that is, on the prices that we choose to determine the budget lines.

However, the compensating and equivalent variation are the same in one important case—the case of quasilinear utility. In this case the indifference curves are parallel, so the distance between any two indifference curves is the same no matter where it is measured, as depicted in Figure 14.5. In the case of quasilinear utility the compensating variation, the equivalent variation, and the change in consumer's surplus all give the same measure of the monetary value of a price change.

## EXAMPLE: Compensating and Equivalent Variations

Suppose that a consumer has a utility function $u(x_1, x_2) = x_1^{\frac{1}{2}} x_2^{\frac{1}{2}}$. He originally faces prices $(1, 1)$ and has income 100. Then the price of good 1 increases to 2. What are the compensating and equivalent variations?

We know that the demand functions for this Cobb-Douglas utility function are given by

$$x_1 = \frac{m}{2p_1}$$
$$x_2 = \frac{m}{2p_2}.$$

Using this formula, we see that the consumer's demands change from $(x_1^*, x_2^*) = (50, 50)$ to $(\hat{x}_1, \hat{x}_2) = (25, 50)$.

To calculate the compensating variation we ask how much money would be necessary at prices $(2,1)$ to make the consumer as well off as he was consuming the bundle $(50,50)$? If the prices were $(2,1)$ and the consumer

**Figure 14.5**

**Quasilinear preferences.** With quasilinear preferences, the distance between two indifference curves is independent of the slope of the budget lines.

had income $m$, we can substitute into the demand functions to find that the consumer would optimally choose the bundle $(m/4, m/2)$. Setting the utility of this bundle equal to the utility of the bundle $(50, 50)$ we have

$$\left(\frac{m}{4}\right)^{\frac{1}{2}} \left(\frac{m}{2}\right)^{\frac{1}{2}} = 50^{\frac{1}{2}} 50^{\frac{1}{2}}.$$

Solving for $m$ gives us

$$m = 100\sqrt{2} \approx 141.$$

Hence the consumer would need about $141 - 100 = \$41$ of additional money after the price change to make him as well off as he was before the price change.

In order to calculate the equivalent variation we ask how much money would be necessary at the prices $(1,1)$ to make the consumer as well off as he would be consuming the bundle $(25,50)$. Letting $m$ stand for this amount of money and following the same logic as before,

$$\left(\frac{m}{2}\right)^{\frac{1}{2}} \left(\frac{m}{2}\right)^{\frac{1}{2}} = 25^{\frac{1}{2}} 50^{\frac{1}{2}}.$$

Solving for $m$ gives us

$$m = 50\sqrt{2} \approx 70.$$

Thus if the consumer had an income of $70 at the original prices, he would be just as well off as he would be facing the new prices and having an income of $100. The equivalent variation in income is therefore about $100 - 70 = \$30$.

### EXAMPLE: Compensating and Equivalent Variation for Quasilinear Preferences

Suppose that the consumer has a quasilinear utility function $v(x_1) + x_2$. We know that in this case the demand for good 1 will depend only on the price of good 1, so we write it as $x_1(p_1)$. Suppose that the price changes from $p_1^*$ to $\hat{p}_1$. What are the compensating and equivalent variations?

At the price $p_1^*$, the consumer chooses $x_1^* = x_1(p_1^*)$ and has a utility of $v(x_1^*) + m - p_1^* x_1^*$. At the price $\hat{p}_1$, the consumer choose $\hat{x}_1 = x_1(\hat{p}_1)$ and has a utility of $v(\hat{x}_1) + m - \hat{p}_1 \hat{x}_1$.

Let $C$ be the compensating variation. This is the amount of extra money the consumer would need after the price change to make him as well off as he would be before the price change. Setting these utilities equal we have

$$v(\hat{x}_1) + m + C - \hat{p}_1 \hat{x}_1 = v(x_1^*) + m - p_1^* x_1^*.$$

Solving for $C$ we have

$$C = v(x_1^*) - v(\hat{x}_1) + \hat{p}_1 \hat{x}_1 - p_1^* x_1^*.$$

Let $E$ be the equivalent variation. This is the amount of money that you could take away from the consumer before the price change that would leave him with the same utility that he would have after the price change. Thus it satisfies the equation

$$v(x_1^*) + m - E - p_1^* x_1^* = v(\hat{x}_1) + m - \hat{p}_1 \hat{x}_1.$$

Solving for $E$, we have

$$E = v(x_1^*) - v(\hat{x}_1) + \hat{p}_1 \hat{x}_1 - p_1^* x_1^*.$$

Note that for the case of quasilinear utility the compensating and equivalent variation are the same. Furthermore, they are both equal to the change in (net) consumer's surplus:

$$\Delta CS = [v(x_1^*) - p_1^* x_1^*] - [v(\hat{x}_1) - \hat{p}_1 \hat{x}_1].$$

## 14.9 Producer's Surplus

The demand curve measures the amount that will be demanded at each price; the **supply curve** measures the amount that will be supplied at each price. Just as the area *under* the demand curve measures the surplus enjoyed by the demanders of a good, the area *above* the supply curve measures the surplus enjoyed by the suppliers of a good.

We've referred to the area under the demand curve as consumer's surplus. By analogy, the area above the supply curve is known as **producer's surplus**. The terms consumer's surplus and producer's surplus are somewhat misleading, since who is doing the consuming and who is doing the producing really doesn't matter. It would be better to use the terms "demander's surplus" and "supplier's surplus," but we'll bow to tradition and use the standard terminology.

Suppose that we have a supply curve for a good. This simply measures the amount of a good that will be supplied at each possible price. The good could be supplied by an individual who owns the good in question, or it could be supplied by a firm that produces the good. We'll take the latter interpretation so as to stick with the traditional terminology and depict the producer's supply curve in Figure 14.6. If the producer is able to sell $x^*$ units of her product in a market at a price $p^*$, what is the surplus she enjoys?

It is most convenient to conduct the analysis in terms of the producer's *inverse* supply curve, $p_s(x)$. This function measures what the price would have to be to get the producer to supply $x$ units of the good.

**Figure 14.6**

**Producer's surplus.** The net producer's surplus is the triangular area to the left of the supply curve in panel A, and the change in producer's surplus is the trapezoidal area in panel B.

Think about the inverse supply function for a discrete good. In this case the producer is willing to sell the first unit of the good at price $p_s(1)$, but she actually gets the market price $p^*$ for it. Similarly, she is willing to sell the second unit for $p_s(2)$, but she gets $p^*$ for it. Continuing in this way we see that the producer will be just willing to sell the last unit for $p_s(x^*) = p^*$.

The difference between the minimum amount she would be willing to sell the $x^*$ units for and the amount she actually sells the units for is the **net producer's surplus**. It is the triangular area depicted in Figure 14.6A.

Just as in the case of consumer's surplus, we can ask how producer's surplus changes when the price increases from $p'$ to $p''$. In general, the change in producer's surplus will be the difference between two triangular regions and will therefore generally have the roughly trapezoidal shape depicted in Figure 14.6B. As in the case of consumer's surplus, the roughly trapezoidal region will be composed of a rectangular region $R$ and a roughly triangular region $T$. The rectangle measures the gain from selling the units previously sold anyway at $p'$ at the higher price $p''$. The roughly triangular region measures the gain from selling the extra units at the price $p''$. This is analogous to the change in consumer's surplus considered earlier.

Although it is common to refer to this kind of change as an increase in producer's surplus, in a deeper sense it really represents an increase in consumer's surplus that accrues to the consumers who own the firm that generated the supply curve. Producer's surplus is closely related to the idea of profit, but we'll have to wait until we study firm behavior in more detail to spell out the relationship.

## 14.10 Benefit-Cost Analysis

We can use the consumer surplus apparatus we have developed to calculate the benefits and costs of various economic policies.

For example, let us examine the impact of a price ceiling. Consider the situation depicted in Figure 14.7. With no intervention, the price would be $p_0$ and the quantity sold would be $q_0$.

The authorities believe this price is too high and impose the price ceiling at $p_c$. This reduces the amount that suppliers are willing to supply to $q_c$ which, in turn, reduces their producer surplus to the shaded area in the diagram.

Now that there is only $q_c$ available for consumers, the question is who will get it?

One assumption is that the output will go to the consumers with the highest willingness to pay. Let $p_e$, the **effective price**, be the price that would induce consumers to demand $q_e$. If everyone who is willing to pay more than $p_e$ gets the good, then the producer surplus will be the shaded area in the diagram.

Note that the lost consumer and producer surplus is given by the trapezoidal area in the middle of the diagram. This is the difference between

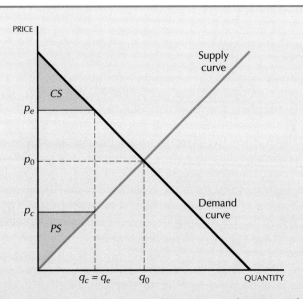

Figure
14.7

**A price ceiling.** The price ceiling at $p_c$ reduces supply to $q_e$. It reduces consumer surplus to $CS$ and producer surplus to $PS$. The effective price of the good, $p_e$, is the price that would clear the market. The diagram also shows what happens with rationing, in which case the price of a ration coupon would be $p_e - p_c$.

the consumer plus producer surplus in the competitive market and the difference in the market with the price ceiling.

Assuming that the quantity will go to consumers with the highest willingness to pay is overly optimistic in most situation. Hence, we we would generally expect that this trapezoidal area is a lower bound on the lost consumer plus producer surplus in the case of a price ceiling.

## Rationing

The diagram we have just examined can also be used to describe the social losses due to rationing. Instead of fixing a price ceiling of $p_c$, suppose that the authorities issue ration coupons that allow for only $q_c$ units to be purchased. In order to purchase one unit of the good, a consumer needs to pay $p_c$ to the seller and produce a ration coupon.

If the ration coupons are marketable, then they would sell for a price of $p_e - p_c$. This would make the the total price of the purchase equal to $p_e$, which is the price that clears the market for the good being sold.

## 14.11 Calculating Gains and Losses

If we have estimates of the market demand and supply curves for a good, it is not difficult in principle to calculate the loss in consumers' surplus due to changes in government policies. For example, suppose the government decides to change its tax treatment of some good. This will result in a change in the prices that consumers face and therefore a change in the amount of the good that they will choose to consume. We can calculate the consumers' surplus associated with different tax proposals and see which tax reforms generate the smallest loss.

This is often useful information for judging various methods of taxation, but it suffers from two defects. First, as we've indicated earlier, the consumer's surplus calculation is only valid for special forms of preferences—namely, preferences representable by a quasilinear utility function. We argued earlier that this kind of utility function may be a reasonable approximation for goods for which changes in income lead to small changes in demand, but for goods whose consumption is closely related to income, the use of consumer surplus may be inappropriate.

Second, the calculation of this loss effectively lumps together all the consumers and producers and generates an estimate of the "cost" of a social policy only for some mythical "representative consumer." In many cases it is desirable to know not only the average cost across the population, but who bears the costs. The political success or failure of policies often depends more on the *distribution* of gains and losses than on the average gain or loss.

Consumer's surplus may be easy to calculate, but we've seen that it is not that much more difficult to calculate the true compensating or equivalent variation associated with a price change. If we have estimates of the demand functions of each household—or at least the demand functions for a sample of representative households—we can calculate the impact of a policy change on each household in terms of the compensating or equivalent variation. Thus we will have a measure of the "benefits" or "costs" imposed on each household by the proposed policy change.

Mervyn King, an economist at the London School of Economics, has described a nice example of this approach to analyzing the implications of reforming the tax treatment of housing in Britain in his paper "Welfare Analysis of Tax Reforms Using Household Data," *Journal of Public Economics*, 21 (1983), 183–214.

King first examined the housing expenditures of 5,895 households and estimated a demand function that best described their purchases of housing services. Next, he used this demand function to determine a utility function for each household. Finally, he used the estimated utility function to calculate how much each household would gain or lose under certain changes in the taxation of housing in Britain. The measure that he used was similar to the equivalent variation described earlier in this chapter. The basic nature of the tax reform he studied was to eliminate tax concessions to owner-occupied housing and to raise rents in public housing. The revenues generated by these changes would be handed back to the households in the form of transfers proportional to household income.

King found that 4,888 of the 5,895 households would benefit from this kind of reform. More importantly he could identify explicitly those households that would have significant losses from the tax reform. King found, for example, that 94 percent of the highest income households gained from the reform, while only 58 percent of the lowest income households gained. This kind of information would allow special measures to be undertaken which might help in designing the tax reform in a way that could satisfy distributional objectives.

## Summary

1. In the case of a discrete good and quasilinear utility, the utility associated with the consumption of $n$ units of the discrete good is just the sum of the first $n$ reservation prices.

2. This sum is the gross benefit of consuming the good. If we subtract the amount spent on the purchase of the good, we get the consumer's surplus.

3. The change in consumer's surplus associated with a price change has a roughly trapezoidal shape. It can be interpreted as the change in utility associated with the price change.

4. In general, we can use the compensating variation and the equivalent variation in income to measure the monetary impact of a price change.

5. If utility is quasilinear, the compensating variation, the equivalent variation, and the change in consumer's surplus are all equal. Even if utility is not quasilinear, the change in consumer's surplus may serve as a good approximation of the impact of the price change on a consumer's utility.

6. In the case of supply behavior we can define a producer's surplus that measures the net benefits to the supplier from producing a given amount of output.

## REVIEW QUESTIONS

1. A good can be produced in a competitive industry at a cost of $10 per unit. There are 100 consumers are each willing to pay $12 each to consume

a single unit of the good (additional units have no value to them.) What is the equilibrium price and quantity sold? The government imposes a tax of $1 on the good. What is the deadweight loss of this tax?

2. Suppose that the demand curve is given by $D(p) = 10 - p$. What is the gross benefit from consuming 6 units of the good?

3. In the above example, if the price changes from 4 to 6, what is the change in consumer's surplus?

4. Suppose that a consumer is consuming 10 units of a discrete good and the price increases from $5 per unit to $6. However, after the price change the consumer continues to consume 10 units of the discrete good. What is the loss in the consumer's surplus from this price change?

## APPENDIX

Let's use some calculus to treat consumer's surplus rigorously. Start with the problem of maximizing quasilinear utility:

$$\max_{x,y} v(x) + y$$

such that $px + y = m$.

Substituting from the budget constraint we have

$$\max_{x} v(x) + m - px.$$

The first-order condition for this problem is

$$v'(x) = p.$$

This means that the inverse demand function $p(x)$ is defined by

$$p(x) = v'(x). \tag{14.2}$$

Note the analogy with the discrete-good framework described in the text: the price at which the consumer is just willing to consume $x$ units is equal to the marginal utility.

But since the inverse demand curve measures the derivative of utility, we can simply integrate under the inverse demand function to find the utility function.

Carrying out the integration we have:

$$v(x) = v(x) - v(0) = \int_0^x v'(t)\, dt = \int_0^x p(t)\, dt.$$

Hence utility associated with the consumption of the x-good is just the area under the demand curve.

Table
14.1

**Comparison of CV, CS, and EV.**

| $p_1$ | CV | CS | EV |
|---|---|---|---|
| 1 | 0.00 | 0.00 | 0.00 |
| 2 | 7.18 | 6.93 | 6.70 |
| 3 | 11.61 | 10.99 | 10.40 |
| 4 | 14.87 | 13.86 | 12.94 |
| 5 | 17.46 | 16.09 | 14.87 |

## EXAMPLE: A Few Demand Functions

Suppose that the demand function is linear, so that $x(p) = a - bp$. Then the change in consumer's surplus when the price moves from $p$ to $q$ is given by

$$\int_p^q (a - bt)\, dt = at - b\frac{t^2}{2}\Big]_p^q = a(q - p) - b\frac{q^2 - p^2}{2}.$$

Another commonly used demand function, which we examine in more detail in the next chapter, has the form $x(p) = Ap^\epsilon$, where $\epsilon < 0$ and $A$ is some positive constant. When the price changes from $p$ to $q$, the associated change in consumer's surplus is

$$\int_p^q At^\epsilon\, dt = A\frac{t^{\epsilon+1}}{\epsilon + 1}\Big]_p^q = A\frac{q^{\epsilon+1} - p^{\epsilon+1}}{\epsilon + 1},$$

for $\epsilon \neq -1$.

When $\epsilon = -1$, this demand function is $x(p) = A/p$, which is closely related to our old friend the Cobb-Douglas demand, $x(p) = am/p$. The change in consumer's surplus for the Cobb-Douglas demand is

$$\int_p^q \frac{am}{t}\, dt = am \ln t\Big]_p^q = am(\ln q - \ln p).$$

## EXAMPLE: CV, EV, and Consumer's Surplus

In the text we calculated the compensating and equivalent variations for the Cobb-Douglas utility function. In the preceding example we calculated the change in consumer's surplus for the Cobb-Douglas utility function. Here we compare these three monetary measures of the impact on utility of a price change.

Suppose that the price of good 1 changes from 1 to $2, 3 \ldots$ while the price of good 2 stays fixed at 1 and income stays fixed at 100. Table 14.1 shows the equivalent variation (EV), compensating variation (CV), and the change in consumer's surplus (CS) for the Cobb-Douglas utility function $u(x_1, x_2) = x_1^{\frac{1}{10}} x_2^{\frac{9}{10}}$.

Note that the change in consumer's surplus always lies between the CV and the EV and that the difference between the three numbers is relatively small. It is possible to show that both of these facts are true in reasonably general circumstances. See Robert Willig, "Consumer's Surplus without Apology," *American Economic Review*, 66 (1976), 589–597.

# CHAPTER 15

# MARKET DEMAND

We have seen in earlier chapters how to model individual consumer choice. Here we see how to add up individual choices to get total **market demand**. Once we have derived the market demand curve, we will examine some of its properties, such as the relationship between demand and revenue.

## 15.1 From Individual to Market Demand

Let us use $x_i^1(p_1, p_2, m_i)$ to represent consumer $i$'s demand function for good 1 and $x_i^2(p_1, p_2, m_i)$ for consumer $i$'s demand function for good 2. Suppose that there are $n$ consumers. Then the **market demand** for good 1, also called the **aggregate demand** for good 1, is the sum of these individual demands over all consumers:

$$X^1(p_1, p_2, m_1, \ldots, m_n) = \sum_{i=1}^{n} x_i^1(p_1, p_2, m_i).$$

The analogous equation holds for good 2.

Since each individual's demand for each good depends on prices and his or her money income, the aggregate demand will generally depend on prices and the *distribution* of incomes. However, it is sometimes convenient to think of the aggregate demand as the demand of some "representative consumer" who has an income that is just the sum of all individual incomes. The conditions under which this can be done are rather restrictive, and a complete discussion of this issue is beyond the scope of this book.

If we do make the representative consumer assumption, the aggregate demand function will have the form $X^1(p_1, p_2, M)$, where $M$ is the sum of the incomes of the individual consumers. Under this assumption, the aggregate demand in the economy is just like the demand of some individual who faces prices $(p_1, p_2)$ and has income $M$.

If we fix all the money incomes and the price of good 2, we can illustrate the relation between the aggregate demand for good 1 and its price, as in Figure 15.1. Note that this curve is drawn holding all other prices and incomes fixed. If these other prices and incomes change, the aggregate demand curve will shift.

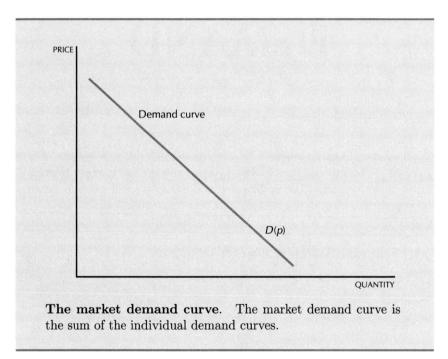

Figure 15.1

**The market demand curve.** The market demand curve is the sum of the individual demand curves.

For example, if goods 1 and 2 are substitutes, then we know that increasing the price of good 2 will tend to increase the demand for good 1 whatever its price. This means that increasing the price of good 2 will tend to shift the aggregate demand curve for good 1 outward. Similarly, if goods 1 and 2 are complements, increasing the price of good 2 will shift the aggregate demand curve for good 1 inward.

If good 1 is a normal good for an individual, then increasing that individual's money income, holding everything else fixed, would tend to increase that individual's demand, and therefore shift the aggregate demand curve outward. If we adopt the representative consumer model, and suppose that good 1 is a normal good for the representative consumer, then any economic change that increases aggregate income will increase the demand for good 1.

## 15.2 The Inverse Demand Function

We can look at the aggregate demand curve as giving us quantity as a function of price or as giving us price as a function of quantity. When we want to emphasize this latter view, we will sometimes refer to the **inverse demand function**, $P(X)$. This function measures what the market price for good 1 would have to be for $X$ units of it to be demanded.

We've seen earlier that the price of a good measures the marginal rate of substitution (MRS) between it and all other goods; that is, the price of a good represents the marginal willingness to pay for an extra unit of the good by anyone who is demanding that good. If all consumers are facing the same prices for goods, then all consumers will have the same marginal rate of substitution at their optimal choices. Thus the inverse demand function, $P(X)$, measures the marginal rate of substitution, or the marginal willingness to pay, of *every* consumer who is purchasing the good.

The geometric interpretation of this summing operation is pretty obvious. Note that we are summing the demand or supply curves *horizontally*: for any given price, we add up the individuals' quantities demanded, which, of course, are measured on the horizontal axis.

### EXAMPLE: Adding Up "Linear" Demand Curves

Suppose that one individual's demand curve is $D_1(p) = 20 - p$ and another individual's is $D_2(p) = 10 - 2p$. What is the market demand function? We have to be a little careful here about what we mean by "linear" demand functions. Since a negative amount of a good usually has no meaning, we *really* mean that the individual demand functions have the form

$$D_1(p) = \max\{20 - p, 0\}$$
$$D_2(p) = \max\{10 - 2p, 0\}.$$

What economists call "linear" demand curves actually aren't linear functions! The sum of the two demand curves looks like the curve depicted in Figure 15.2. Note the kink at $p = 5$.

Figure
15.2
**The sum of two "linear" demand curves.** Since the demand curves are only linear for positive quantities, there will typically be a kink in the market demand curve.

## 15.3 Discrete Goods

If a good is available only in discrete amounts, then we have seen that the demand for that good for a single consumer can be described in terms of the consumer's reservation prices. Here we examine the market demand for this kind of good. For simplicity, we will restrict ourselves to the case where the good will be available in units of zero or one.

In this case the demand of a consumer is completely described by his reservation price—the price at which he is just willing to purchase one unit. In Figure 15.3 we have depicted the demand curves for two consumers, A and B, and the market demand, which is the sum of these two demand curves. Note that the market demand curve in this case must "slope downward," since a decrease in the market price must increase the number of consumers who are willing to pay at least that price.

## 15.4 The Extensive and the Intensive Margin

In preceding chapters we have concentrated on consumer choice in which the consumer was consuming positive amounts of each good. When the price changes, the consumer decides to consume more or less of one good or the other, but still ends up consuming some of both goods. Economists sometimes say that this is an adjustment on the **intensive margin**.

In the reservation-price model, the consumers are deciding whether or not to enter the market for one of the goods. This is sometimes called an adjustment on the **extensive margin**. The slope of the aggregate demand curve will be affected by both sorts of decisions.

**Market demand for a discrete good.** The market demand
curve is the sum of the demand curves of all the consumers in
the market, here represented by the two consumers A and B.

Figure
15.3

We saw earlier that the adjustment on the intensive margin was in the
"right" direction for normal goods: when the price went up, the quantity
demanded went down. The adjustment on the extensive margin also works
in the "right" direction. Thus aggregate demand curves can generally be
expected to slope downward.

## 15.5 Elasticity

In Chapter 6 we saw how to derive a demand function from a consumer's
underlying preferences. It is often of interest to have a measure of how
"responsive" demand is to some change in price or income. Now the first
idea that springs to mind is to use the slope of a demand function as a
measure of responsiveness. After all, the definition of the slope of a demand
function is the change in quantity demanded divided by the change in price:

$$\text{slope of demand function} = \frac{\Delta q}{\Delta p},$$

and that certainly looks like a measure of responsiveness.

Well, it is a measure of responsiveness—but it presents some problems.
The most important one is that the slope of a demand function depends on
the units in which you measure price and quantity. If you measure demand
in gallons rather than in quarts, the slope becomes four times smaller.
Rather than specify units all the time, it is convenient to consider a unit-
free measure of responsiveness. Economists have chosen to use a measure
known as **elasticity**.

The **price elasticity of demand**, $\epsilon$, is defined to be the percent change
in quantity divided by the percent change in price.[1] A 10 percent increase

---

[1] The Greek letter $\epsilon$, epsilon, is pronounced "eps-i-lon."

in price is the same percentage increase whether the price is measured in American dollars or English pounds; thus measuring increases in percentage terms keeps the definition of elasticity unit-free.

In symbols the definition of elasticity is

$$\epsilon = \frac{\Delta q/q}{\Delta p/p}.$$

Rearranging this definition we have the more common expression:

$$\epsilon = \frac{p}{q} \frac{\Delta q}{\Delta p}.$$

Hence elasticity can be expressed as the ratio of price to quantity multiplied by the slope of the demand function. In the Appendix to this chapter we describe elasticity in terms of the derivative of the demand function. If you know calculus, the derivative formulation is the most convenient way to think about elasticity.

The sign of the elasticity of demand is generally negative, since demand curves invariably have a negative slope. However, it is tedious to keep referring to an elasticity of *minus* something-or-other, so it is common in verbal discussion to refer to elasticities of 2 or 3, rather than −2 or −3. We will try to keep the signs straight in the text by referring to the absolute value of elasticity, but you should be aware that verbal treatments tend to drop the minus sign.

Another problem with negative numbers arises when we compare magnitudes. Is an elasticity of −3 greater or less than an elasticity of −2? From an algebraic point of view −3 is smaller than −2, but economists tend to say that the demand with the elasticity of −3 is "more elastic" than the one with −2. In this book we will make comparisons in terms of absolute value so as to avoid this kind of ambiguity.

## EXAMPLE: The Elasticity of a Linear Demand Curve

Consider the linear demand curve, $q = a - bp$, depicted in Figure 15.4. The slope of this demand curve is a constant, $-b$. Plugging this into the formula for elasticity we have

$$\epsilon = \frac{-bp}{q} = \frac{-bp}{a - bp}.$$

When $p = 0$, the elasticity of demand is zero. When $q = 0$, the elasticity of demand is (negative) infinity. At what value of price is the elasticity of demand equal to −1?

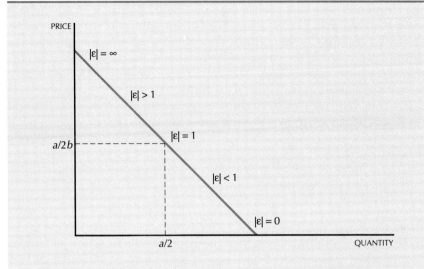

**The elasticity of a linear demand curve.**    Elasticity is    Figure
infinite at the vertical intercept, one halfway down the curve,    15.4
and zero at the horizontal intercept.

To find such a price, we write down the equation

$$\frac{-bp}{a - bp} = -1$$

and solve it for $p$. This gives

$$p = \frac{a}{2b},$$

which, as we see in Figure 15.4, is just halfway down the demand curve.

## 15.6 Elasticity and Demand

If a good has an elasticity of demand greater than 1 in absolute value we say
that it has an **elastic demand**. If the elasticity is less than 1 in absolute
value we say that it has an **inelastic demand**. And if it has an elasticity
of exactly $-1$, we say it has **unit elastic demand**.

An elastic demand curve is one for which the quantity demanded is very
responsive to price: if you increase the price by 1 percent, the quantity
demanded decreases by more than 1 percent. So think of elasticity as the
responsiveness of the quantity demanded to price, and it will be easy to
remember what elastic and inelastic mean.

In general the elasticity of demand for a good depends to a large extent
on how many close substitutes it has. Take an extreme case—our old friend,

the red pencils and blue pencils example. Suppose that everyone regards these goods as perfect substitutes. Then if some of each of them are bought, they must sell for the same price. Now think what would happen to the demand for red pencils if their price rose, and the price of blue pencils stayed constant. Clearly it would drop to zero—the demand for red pencils is very elastic since it has a perfect substitute.

If a good has many close substitutes, we would expect that its demand curve would be very responsive to its price changes. On the other hand, if there are few close substitutes for a good, it can exhibit a quite inelastic demand.

## 15.7 Elasticity and Revenue

**Revenue** is just the price of a good times the quantity sold of that good. If the price of a good increases, then the quantity sold decreases, so revenue may increase or decrease. Which way it goes obviously depends on how responsive demand is to the price change. If demand drops a lot when the price increases, then revenue will fall. If demand drops only a little when the price increases, then revenue will increase. This suggests that the direction of the change in revenue has something to do with the elasticity of demand.

Indeed, there is a very useful relationship between price elasticity and revenue change. The definition of revenue is

$$R = pq.$$

If we let the price change to $p + \Delta p$ and the quantity change to $q + \Delta q$, we have a new revenue of

$$R' = (p + \Delta p)(q + \Delta q)$$
$$= pq + q\Delta p + p\Delta q + \Delta p\Delta q.$$

Subtracting $R$ from $R'$ we have

$$\Delta R = q\Delta p + p\Delta q + \Delta p\Delta q.$$

For small values of $\Delta p$ and $\Delta q$, the last term can safely be neglected, leaving us with an expression for the change in revenue of the form

$$\Delta R = q\Delta p + p\Delta q.$$

That is, the change in revenue is roughly equal to the quantity times the change in price plus the original price times the change in quantity. If we want an expression for the rate of change of revenue per change in price, we just divide this expression by $\Delta p$ to get

$$\frac{\Delta R}{\Delta p} = q + p\frac{\Delta q}{\Delta p}.$$

This is treated geometrically in Figure 15.5. The revenue is just the area of the box: price times quantity. When the price increases, we add a rectangular area on the top of the box, which is approximately $q\Delta p$, but we subtract an area on the side of the box, which is approximately $p\Delta q$. For small changes, this is exactly the expression given above. (The leftover part, $\Delta p\Delta q$, is the little square in the corner of the box, which will be very small relative to the other magnitudes.)

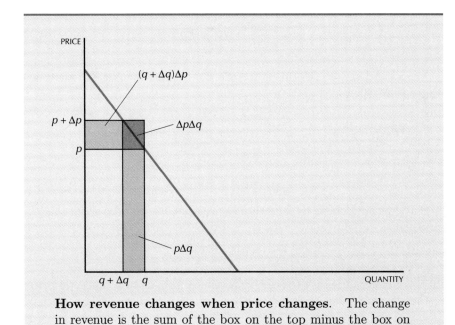

**How revenue changes when price changes.** The change in revenue is the sum of the box on the top minus the box on the side.

Figure 15.5

When will the net result of these two effects be positive? That is, when do we satisfy the following inequality:

$$\frac{\Delta R}{\Delta p} = p\frac{\Delta q}{\Delta p} + q(p) > 0?$$

Rearranging we have

$$\frac{p}{q}\frac{\Delta q}{\Delta p} > -1.$$

The left-hand side of this expression is $\epsilon(p)$, which is a negative number. Multiplying through by $-1$ reverses the direction of the inequality to give us:

$$|\epsilon(p)| < 1.$$

Thus revenue increases when price increases if the elasticity of demand is less than 1 in absolute value. Similarly, revenue decreases when price increases if the elasticity of demand is greater than 1 in absolute value.

Another way to see this is to write the revenue change as we did above:

$$\Delta R = p\Delta q + q\Delta p > 0$$

and rearrange this to get

$$-\frac{p}{q}\frac{\Delta q}{\Delta p} = |\epsilon(p)| < 1.$$

Yet a third way to see this is to take the formula for $\Delta R/\Delta p$ and rearrange it as follows:

$$\frac{\Delta R}{\Delta p} = q + p\frac{\Delta q}{\Delta p}$$
$$= q\left[1 + \frac{p}{q}\frac{\Delta q}{\Delta p}\right]$$
$$= q\left[1 + \epsilon(p)\right].$$

Since demand elasticity is naturally negative, we can also write this expression as

$$\frac{\Delta R}{\Delta p} = q\left[1 - |\epsilon(p)|\right].$$

In this formula it is easy to see how revenue responds to a change in price: if the absolute value of elasticity is greater than 1, then $\Delta R/\Delta p$ must be negative and vice versa.

The intuitive content of these mathematical facts is not hard to remember. If demand is very responsive to price—that is, it is very elastic—then an increase in price will reduce demand so much that revenue will fall. If demand is very unresponsive to price—it is very inelastic—then an increase in price will not change demand very much, and overall revenue will increase. The dividing line happens to be an elasticity of −1. At this point if the price increases by 1 percent, the quantity will decrease by 1 percent, so overall revenue doesn't change at all.

## EXAMPLE: Strikes and Profits

In 1979 the United Farm Workers called for a strike against lettuce growers in California. The strike was highly effective: the production of lettuce was cut almost in half. But the reduction in the supply of lettuce inevitably caused an increase in the price of lettuce. In fact, during the strike the price of lettuce rose by nearly 400 percent. Since production halved and prices quadrupled, the net result of was almost a *doubling* producer profits![2]

One might well ask why the producers eventually settled the strike. The answer involves short-run and long-run supply responses. Most of the lettuce consumed in U.S. during the winter months is grown in the Imperial Valley. When the supply of this lettuce was drastically reduced in one season, there wasn't time to replace it with lettuce from elsewhere so the market price of lettuce skyrocketed. If the strike had held for several seasons, lettuce could be planted in other regions. This increase in supply from other sources would tend reduce the price of lettuce back to its normal level, thereby reducing the profits of the Imperial Valley growers.

## 15.8 Constant Elasticity Demands

What kind of demand curve gives us a constant elasticity of demand? In a linear demand curve the elasticity of demand goes from zero to infinity, which is not exactly what you would call constant, so that's not the answer.

We can use the revenue calculation described above to get an example. We know that if the elasticity is 1 at price $p$, then the revenue will not change when the price changes by a small amount. So if the revenue remains constant for all changes in price, we must have a demand curve that has an elasticity of $-1$ everywhere.

But this is easy. We just want price and quantity to be related by the formula

$$pq = \overline{R},$$

which means that

$$q = \frac{\overline{R}}{p}$$

is the formula for a demand function with constant elasticity of $-1$. The graph of the function $q = \overline{R}/p$ is given in Figure 15.6. Note that price times quantity is constant along the demand curve.

The general formula for a demand with a constant elasticity of $\epsilon$ turns out to be

$$q = Ap^\epsilon,$$

where $A$ is an arbitrary positive constant and $\epsilon$, being an elasticity, will typically be negative. This formula will be useful in some examples later on.

A convenient way to express a constant elasticity demand curve is to take logarithms and write

$$\ln q = \ln A + \epsilon \ln p.$$

---

[2] See Colin Carter, et. al., "Agricultural Labor Strikes and Farmers' Incomes," *Economic Inquiry*, 25, 1987,121–133.

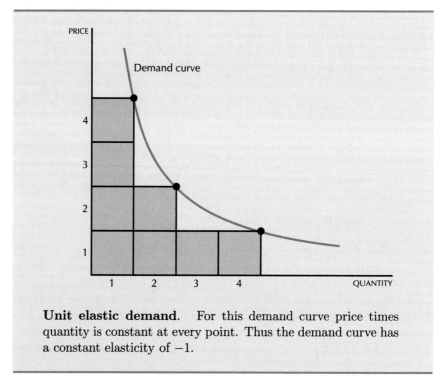

Figure
15.6

**Unit elastic demand.** For this demand curve price times quantity is constant at every point. Thus the demand curve has a constant elasticity of $-1$.

In this expression, the logarithm of $q$ depends in a linear way on the logarithm of $p$.

## 15.9 Elasticity and Marginal Revenue

In section 15.7 we examined how revenue changes when you change the price of a good, but it is often of interest to consider how revenue changes when you change the quantity of a good. This is especially useful when we are considering production decisions by firms.

We saw earlier that for small changes in price and quantity, the change in revenue is given by

$$\Delta R = p\Delta q + q\Delta p.$$

If we divide both sides of this expression by $\Delta q$, we get the expression for **marginal revenue**:

$$\text{MR} = \frac{\Delta R}{\Delta q} = p + q\frac{\Delta p}{\Delta q}.$$

There is a useful way to rearrange this formula. Note that we can also write this as

$$\frac{\Delta R}{\Delta q} = p\left[1 + \frac{q\Delta p}{p\Delta q}\right].$$

What is the second term inside the brackets? Nope, it's not elasticity, but you're close. It is the reciprocal of elasticity:

$$\frac{1}{\epsilon} = \frac{1}{\frac{p\Delta q}{q\Delta p}} = \frac{q\Delta p}{p\Delta q}.$$

Thus the expression for marginal revenue becomes

$$\frac{\Delta R}{\Delta q} = p(q)\left[1 + \frac{1}{\epsilon(q)}\right].$$

(Here we've written $p(q)$ and $\epsilon(q)$ to remind ourselves that both price and elasticity will typically depend on the level of output.)

When there is a danger of confusion due to the fact that elasticity is a negative number we will sometimes write this expression as

$$\frac{\Delta R}{\Delta q} = p(q)\left[1 - \frac{1}{|\epsilon(q)|}\right].$$

This means that if elasticity of demand is $-1$, then marginal revenue is zero—revenue doesn't change when you increase output. If demand is inelastic, then $|\epsilon|$ is less than 1, which means $1/|\epsilon|$ is greater than 1. Thus $1-1/|\epsilon|$ is negative, so that revenue will decrease when you increase output.

This is quite intuitive. If demand isn't very responsive to price, then you have to cut prices a lot to increase output: so revenue goes down. This is all completely consistent with the earlier discussion about how revenue changes as we change price, since an increase in quantity means a decrease in price and vice versa.

## EXAMPLE: Setting a Price

Suppose that you were in charge of setting a price for some product that you were producing and that you had a good estimate of the demand curve for that product. Let us suppose that your goal is to set a price that maximizes profits—revenue minus costs. Then you would never want to set it where the elasticity of demand was less than 1—you would never want to set a price where demand was inelastic.

Why? Consider what would happen if you raised your price. Then your revenues would increase—since demand was inelastic—and the quantity you were selling would decrease. But if the quantity sold decreases, then your production costs must also decrease, or at least, they can't increase. So your overall profit must rise, which shows that operating at an inelastic part of the demand curve cannot yield maximal profits.

## 15.10 Marginal Revenue Curves

We saw in the last section that marginal revenue is given by

$$\frac{\Delta R}{\Delta q} = p(q) + \frac{\Delta p(q)}{\Delta q} q$$

or

$$\frac{\Delta R}{\Delta q} = p(q) \left[ 1 - \frac{1}{|\epsilon(q)|} \right].$$

We will find it useful to plot these marginal revenue curves. First, note that when quantity is zero, marginal revenue is just equal to the price. For the first unit of the good sold, the extra revenue you get is just the price. But after that, the marginal revenue will be less than the price, since $\Delta p/\Delta q$ is negative.

Think about it. If you decide to sell one more unit of output, you will have to decrease the price. But this reduction in price reduces the revenue you receive on all the units of output that you were selling already. Thus the extra revenue you receive will be less than the price that you get for selling the extra unit.

Let's consider the special case of the linear (inverse) demand curve:

$$p(q) = a - bq.$$

Here it is easy to see that the slope of the inverse demand curve is constant:

$$\frac{\Delta p}{\Delta q} = -b.$$

Thus the formula for marginal revenue becomes

$$\begin{aligned}
\frac{\Delta R}{\Delta q} &= p(q) + \frac{\Delta p(q)}{\Delta q} q \\
&= p(q) - bq \\
&= a - bq - bq \\
&= a - 2bq.
\end{aligned}$$

This marginal revenue curve is depicted in Figure 15.7A. The marginal revenue curve has the same vertical intercept as the demand curve, but has twice the slope. Marginal revenue is negative when $q > a/2b$. The quantity $a/2b$ is the quantity at which the elasticity is equal to $-1$. At any larger

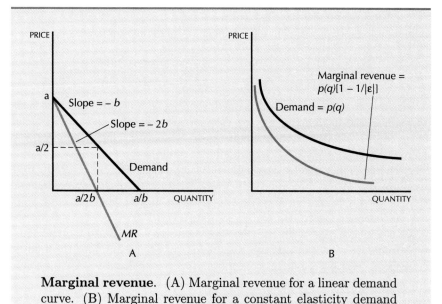

**Marginal revenue.** (A) Marginal revenue for a linear demand curve. (B) Marginal revenue for a constant elasticity demand curve.

Figure
15.7

quantity demand will be inelastic, which implies that marginal revenue is negative.

The constant elasticity demand curve provides another special case of the marginal revenue curve. (See Figure 15.7B.) If the elasticity of demand is constant at $\epsilon(q) = \epsilon$, then the marginal revenue curve will have the form

$$MR = p(q) \left[ 1 - \frac{1}{|\epsilon|} \right].$$

Since the term in brackets is constant, the marginal revenue curve is some constant fraction of the inverse demand curve. When $|\epsilon| = 1$, the marginal revenue curve is constant at zero. When $|\epsilon| > 1$, the marginal revenue curve lies below the inverse demand curve, as depicted. When $|\epsilon| < 1$, marginal revenue is negative.

## 15.11 Income Elasticity

Recall that the price elasticity of demand is defined as

$$\text{price elasticity of demand} = \frac{\% \text{ change in quantity demanded}}{\% \text{ change in price}}.$$

This gives us a unit-free measure of how the amount demanded responds to a change in price.

The **income elasticity of demand** is used to describe how the quantity demanded responds to a change in income; its definition is

$$\text{income elasticity of demand} = \frac{\%\ \text{change in quantity}}{\%\ \text{change in income}}.$$

Recall that a **normal good** is one for which an increase in income leads to an increase in demand; so for this sort of good the income elasticity of demand is positive. An **inferior good** is one for which an increase in income leads to a decrease in demand; for this sort of good, the income elasticity of demand is negative. Economists sometimes use the term **luxury goods**. These are goods that have an income elasticity of demand that is greater than 1: a 1 percent increase in income leads to *more* than a 1 percent increase in demand for a luxury good.

As a general rule of thumb, however, income elasticities tend to cluster around 1. We can see the reason for this by examining the budget constraint. Write the budget constraints for two different levels of income:

$$p_1 x_1' + p_2 x_2' = m'$$
$$p_1 x_1^0 + p_2 x_2^0 = m^0.$$

Subtract the second equation from the first and let $\Delta$ denote differences, as usual:

$$p_1\,\Delta x_1 + p_2\,\Delta x_2 = \Delta m.$$

Now multiply and divide price $i$ by $x_i/x_i$ and divide both sides by $m$:

$$\frac{p_1 x_1}{m}\frac{\Delta x_1}{x_1} + \frac{p_2 x_2}{m}\frac{\Delta x_2}{x_2} = \frac{\Delta m}{m}.$$

Finally, divide both sides by $\Delta m/m$, and use $s_i = p_i x_i/m$ to denote the **expenditure share** of good $i$. This gives us our final equation,

$$s_1\frac{\Delta x_1/x_1}{\Delta m/m} + s_2\frac{\Delta x_2/x_2}{\Delta m/m} = 1.$$

This equation says that the *weighted average of the income elasticities is 1*, where the weights are the expenditure shares. Luxury goods that have an income elasticity greater than 1 must be counterbalanced by goods that have an income elasticity less than 1, so that "on average" income elasticities are about 1.

## Summary

1. The market demand curve is simply the sum of the individual demand curves.

2. The reservation price measures the price at which a consumer is just indifferent between purchasing or not purchasing a good.

3. The demand function measures quantity demanded as a function of price. The inverse demand function measures price as a function of quantity. A given demand curve can be described in either way.

4. The elasticity of demand measures the responsiveness of the quantity demanded to price. It is formally defined as the percent change in quantity divided by the percent change in price.

5. If the absolute value of the elasticity of demand is less than 1 at some point, we say that demand is *inelastic* at that point. If the absolute value of elasticity is greater than 1 at some point, we say demand is *elastic* at that point. If the absolute value of the elasticity of demand at some point is exactly 1, we say that the demand has *unitary* elasticity at that point.

6. If demand is inelastic at some point, then an increase in quantity will result in a reduction in revenue. If demand is elastic, then an increase in quantity will result in an increase in revenue.

7. The marginal revenue is the extra revenue one gets from increasing the quantity sold. The formula relating marginal revenue and elasticity is $\text{MR} = p[1 + 1/\epsilon] = p[1 - 1/|\epsilon|]$.

8. If the inverse demand curve is a linear function $p(q) = a - bq$, then the marginal revenue is given by $\text{MR} = a - 2bq$.

9. Income elasticity measures the responsiveness of the quantity demanded to income. It is formally defined as the percent change in quantity divided by the percent change in income.

## REVIEW QUESTIONS

1. If the market demand curve is $D(p) = 100 - .5p$, what is the inverse demand curve?

2. An addict's demand function for a drug may be very inelastic, but the market demand function might be quite elastic. How can this be?

3. If $D(p) = 12 - 2p$, what price will maximize revenue?

4. Suppose that the demand curve for a good is given by $D(p) = 100/p$. What price will maximize revenue?

5. True or false? In a two good model if one good is an inferior good the other good must be a luxury good.

## APPENDIX

In terms of derivatives the price elasticity of demand is defined by

$$\epsilon = \frac{p}{q}\frac{dq}{dp}.$$

In the text we claimed that the formula for a constant elasticity demand curve was $q = Ap^\epsilon$. To verify that this is correct, we can just differentiate it with respect to price:

$$\frac{dq}{dp} = \epsilon Ap^{\epsilon-1}$$

and multiply by price over quantity:

$$\frac{p}{q}\frac{dq}{dp} = \frac{p}{Ap^\epsilon}\epsilon Ap^{\epsilon-1} = \epsilon.$$

Everything conveniently cancels, leaving us with $\epsilon$ as required.

A linear demand curve has the formula $q(p) = a - bp$. The elasticity of demand at a point $p$ is given by

$$\epsilon = \frac{p}{q}\frac{dq}{dp} = \frac{-bp}{a - bp}.$$

When $p$ is zero, the elasticity is zero. When $q$ is zero, the elasticity is infinite.

Revenue is given by $R(p) = pq(p)$. To see how revenue changes as $p$ changes we differentiate revenue with respect to $p$ to get

$$R'(p) = pq'(p) + q(p).$$

Suppose that revenue increases when $p$ increases. Then we have

$$R'(p) = p\frac{dq}{dp} + q(p) > 0.$$

Rearranging, we have

$$\epsilon = \frac{p}{q}\frac{dq}{dp} > -1.$$

Recalling that $dq/dp$ is negative and multiplying through by $-1$, we find

$$|\epsilon| < 1.$$

Hence if revenue increases when price increases, we must be at an inelastic part of the demand curve.

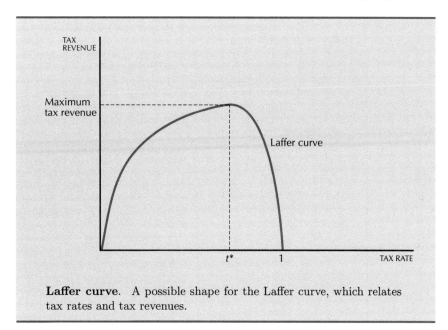

**Laffer curve.**   A possible shape for the Laffer curve, which relates tax rates and tax revenues.

Figure
15.8

### EXAMPLE: The Laffer Curve

In this section we'll consider some simple elasticity calculations that can be used to examine an issue of considerable policy interest, namely, how tax revenue changes when the tax rate changes.

Suppose that we graph tax revenue versus the tax rate. If the tax rate is zero, then tax revenues are zero; if the tax rate is 1, nobody will want to demand or supply the good in question, so the tax revenue is also zero. Thus revenue as a function of the tax rate must first increase and eventually decrease. (Of course, it can go up and down several times between zero and 1, but we'll ignore this possibility to keep things simple.) The curve that relates tax rates and tax revenues is known as the **Laffer curve**, depicted in Figure 15.8.

The interesting feature of the Laffer curve is that it suggests that when the tax rate is high enough, an increase in the tax rate will end up *reducing* the revenues collected. The reduction in the supply of the good due to the increase in the tax rate can be so large that tax revenue actually decreases. This is called the Laffer effect, after the economist who popularized this diagram in the early eighties. It has been said that the virtue of the Laffer curve is that you can explain it to a congressman in half an hour and he can talk about it for six months. Indeed, the Laffer curve figured prominently in the debate over the effect of the 1980 tax cuts. The catch in the above argument is the phrase "high enough." Just how high does the tax rate have to be for the Laffer effect to work?

To answer this question let's consider the following simple model of the labor market. Suppose that firms will demand zero labor if the wage is greater than $\overline{w}$ and an arbitrarily large amount of labor if the wage is exactly $\overline{w}$. This means that the demand curve for labor is flat at some wage $\overline{w}$. Suppose that the supply curve of labor, $S(w)$, has a conventional upward slope. The equilibrium in the labor market is depicted in Figure 15.9.

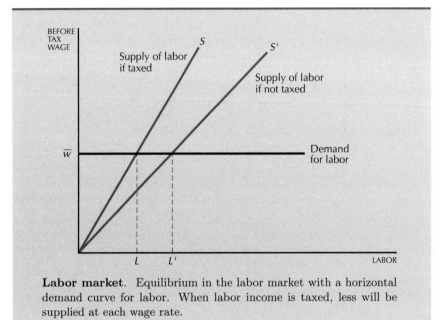

Figure
15.9

**Labor market.** Equilibrium in the labor market with a horizontal demand curve for labor. When labor income is taxed, less will be supplied at each wage rate.

If we put a tax on labor at the rate $t$, then if the firm pays $\overline{w}$, the worker only gets $w = (1 - t)\overline{w}$. Thus the supply curve of labor tilts to the left, and the amount of labor sold drops, as in Figure 15.9. The after-tax wage has gone down and this has discouraged the sale of labor. So far so good.

Tax revenue, $T$, is therefore given by the formula

$$T = t\overline{w}S(w),$$

where $w = (1 - t)\overline{w}$ and $S(w)$ is the supply of labor.

In order to see how tax revenue changes as we change the tax rate we differentiate this formula with respect to $t$ to find

$$\frac{dT}{dt} = \left[ -t\frac{dS(w)}{dw}\overline{w} + S(w) \right]\overline{w}. \qquad (15.1)$$

(Note the use of the chain rule and the fact that $dw/dt = -\overline{w}$.)

The Laffer effect occurs when revenues decline when $t$ increases—that is, when this expression is negative. Now this clearly means that the supply of labor is going to have to be quite elastic—it has to drop a lot when the tax increases. So let's try to see what values of elasticity will make this expression negative.

In order for equation (15.1) to be negative, we must have

$$-t\frac{dS(w)}{dw}\overline{w} + S(w) < 0.$$

Transposing yields

$$t\frac{dS(w)}{dw}\overline{w} > S(w),$$

and dividing both sides by $tS(w)$ gives

$$\frac{dS(w)}{dw}\frac{\overline{w}}{S(w)} > \frac{1}{t}.$$

Multiplying both sides by $(1-t)$ and using the fact that $w = (1-t)\overline{w}$ gives us

$$\frac{dS}{dw}\frac{w}{S} > \frac{1-t}{t}.$$

The left-hand side of this expression is the elasticity of labor supply. We have shown that the Laffer effect can only occur if the elasticity of labor supply is greater than $(1-t)/t$.

Let us take an extreme case and suppose that the tax rate on labor income is 50 percent. Then the Laffer effect can occur only when the elasticity of labor supply is greater than 1. This means that a 1 percent reduction in the wage would lead to more than a 1 percent reduction in the labor supply. This is a very large response.

Econometricians have often estimated labor-supply elasticities, and about the largest value anyone has ever found has been around 0.2. So the Laffer effect seems pretty unlikely for the kinds of tax rates that we have in the United States. However, in other countries, such as Sweden, tax rates go much higher, and there is some evidence that the Laffer phenomenon may have occurred.[3]

## EXAMPLE: Another Expression for Elasticity

Here is another expression for elasticity that is sometimes useful. It turns out that elasticity can also be expressed as

$$\frac{d\ln Q}{d\ln P}.$$

The proof involves repeated application of the chain rule. We start by noting that

$$\frac{d\ln Q}{d\ln P} = \frac{d\ln Q}{dQ}\frac{dQ}{d\ln P}$$

$$= \frac{1}{Q}\frac{dQ}{d\ln P}. \tag{15.2}$$

---

[3] See Charles E. Stuart, "Swedish Tax Rates, Labor Supply, and Tax Revenues," *Journal of Political Economy*, 89, 5 (October 1981), 1020–38.

We also note that

$$\frac{dQ}{dP} = \frac{dQ}{d \ln P} \frac{d \ln P}{dP}$$

$$= \frac{dQ}{d \ln P} \frac{1}{P},$$

which implies that

$$\frac{dQ}{d \ln P} = P \frac{dQ}{dP}.$$

Substituting this into equation (15.2), we have

$$\frac{d \ln Q}{d \ln P} = \frac{1}{Q} \frac{dQ}{dP} P = \epsilon,$$

which is what we wanted to establish.

Thus elasticity measures the slope of the demand curve plotted on log-log paper: how the log of the quantity changes as the log of the price changes.

# CHAPTER **16**

# EQUILIBRIUM

In preceding chapters we have seen how to construct individual demand curves by using information about preferences and prices. In Chapter 15 we added up these individual demand curves to construct market demand curves. In this chapter we will describe how to use these market demand curves to determine the equilibrium market price.

In Chapter 1 we said that there were two fundamental principles of microeconomic analysis. These were the optimization principle and the equilibrium principle. Up until now we have been studying examples of the optimization principle: what follows from the assumption that people choose their consumption optimally from their budget sets. In later chapters we will continue to use optimization analysis to study the profit-maximization behavior of firms. Finally, we combine the behavior of consumers and firms to study the equilibrium outcomes of their interaction in the market.

But before undertaking that study in detail it seems worthwhile at this point to give some examples of equilibrium analysis—how the prices adjust so as to make the demand and supply decisions of economic agents compatible. In order to do so, we will have to briefly consider the other side of the market—the supply side.

## 16.1 Supply

We have already seen a few examples of supply curves. In Chapter 1 we looked at a vertical supply curve for apartments. In Chapter 9 we considered situations where consumers would choose to be net suppliers or demanders of goods that they owned, and we analyzed labor-supply decisions.

In all of these cases the supply curve simply measured how much the consumer was willing to supply of a good at each possible market price. Indeed, this is the definition of the supply curve: for each $p$, we determine how much of the good will be supplied, $S(p)$. In the next few chapters we will discuss the supply behavior of firms. However, for many purposes, it is not really necessary to know where the supply curve or the demand curve comes from in terms of the optimizing behavior that generates the curves. For many problems the fact that there is a functional relationship between the price and the quantity that consumers want to demand or supply at that price is enough to highlight important insights.

## 16.2 Market Equilibrium

Suppose that we have a number of consumers of a good. Given their individual demand curves we can add them up to get a market demand curve. Similarly, if we have a number of independent suppliers of this good, we can add up their individual supply curves to get the **market supply curve**.

The individual demanders and suppliers are assumed to take prices as given—outside of their control—and simply determine their best response given those market prices. A market where each economic agent takes the market price as outside of his or her control is called a **competitive market.**

The usual justification for the competitive-market assumption is that each consumer or producer is a small part of the market as a whole and thus has a negligible effect on the market price. For example, each supplier of wheat takes the market price to be more or less independent of his actions when he determines how much wheat he wants to produce and supply to the market.

Although the market price may be independent of any *one* agent's actions in a competitive market, it is the actions of all the agents together that determine the market price. The **equilibrium price** of a good is that price where the supply of the good equals the demand. Geometrically, this is the price where the demand and the supply curves cross.

If we let $D(p)$ be the market demand curve and $S(p)$ the market supply curve, the equilibrium price is the price $p^*$ that solves the equation

$$D(p^*) = S(p^*).$$

The solution to this equation, $p^*$, is the price where market demand equals market supply.

Why should this be an equilibrium price? An economic equilibrium is a situation where all agents are choosing the best possible action for themselves and each person's behavior is consistent with that of the others. At any price other than an equilibrium price, some agents' behaviors would be infeasible, and there would therefore be a reason for their behavior to change. Thus a price that is not an equilibrium price cannot be expected to persist since at least some agents would have an incentive to change their behavior.

The demand and supply curves represent the optimal choices of the agents involved, and the fact that they are equal at some price $p^*$ indicates that the behaviors of the demanders and suppliers are compatible. At any price *other* than the price where demand equals supply these two conditions will *not* be met.

For example, suppose that we consider some price $p' < p^*$ where demand is greater than supply. Then some suppliers will realize that they can sell their goods at more than the going price $p'$ to the disappointed demanders. As more and more suppliers realize this, the market price will be pushed up to the point where demand and supply are equal.

Similarly if $p' > p^*$, so that demand is less than supply, then some suppliers will not be able to sell the amount that they expected to sell. The only way in which they will be able to sell more output will be to offer it at a lower price. But if all suppliers are selling the identical goods, and if some supplier offers to sell at a lower price, the other suppliers must match that price. Thus excess supply exerts a downward pressure on the market price. Only when the amount that people want to buy at a given price equals the amount that people want to sell at that price will the market be in equilibrium.

## 16.3 Two Special Cases

There are two special cases of market equilibrium that are worth mentioning since they come up fairly often. The first is the case of fixed supply. Here the amount supplied is some given number and is independent of price; that is, the supply curve is vertical. In this case the equilibrium *quantity* is determined entirely by the supply conditions and the equilibrium *price* is determined entirely by demand conditions.

The opposite case is the case where the supply curve is completely horizontal. If an industry has a perfectly horizontal supply curve, it means that the industry will supply any amount of a good at a constant price. In this situation the equilibrium *price* is determined by the supply conditions, while the equilibrium *quantity* is determined by the demand curve.

The two cases are depicted in Figure 16.1. In these two special cases the determination of price and quantity can be separated; but in the general case the equilibrium price and the equilibrium quantity are jointly determined by the demand and supply curves.

Figure
16.1

**Special cases of equilibrium.** Case A shows a vertical supply curve where the equilibrium price is determined solely by the demand curve. Case B depicts a horizontal supply curve where the equilibrium price is determined solely by the supply curve.

## 16.4 Inverse Demand and Supply Curves

We can look at market equilibrium in a slightly different way that is often useful. As indicated earlier, individual demand curves are normally viewed as giving the optimal quantities demanded as a function of the price charged. But we can also view them as inverse demand functions that measure the *price* that someone is willing to pay in order to acquire some given amount of a good. The same thing holds for supply curves. They can be viewed as measuring the quantity supplied as a function of the price. But we can also view them as measuring the *price* that must prevail in order to generate a given amount of supply.

These same constructions can be used with *market* demand and *market* supply curves, and the interpretations are just those given above. In this framework an equilibrium price is determined by finding that quantity at which the amount the demanders are willing to pay to consume that quantity is the same as the price that suppliers must receive in order to supply that quantity.

Thus, if we let $P_S(q)$ be the inverse supply function and $P_D(q)$ be the inverse demand function, equilibrium is determined by the condition

$$P_S(q^*) = P_D(q^*).$$

## EXAMPLE: Equilibrium with Linear Curves

Suppose that both the demand and the supply curves are linear:

$$D(p) = a - bp$$

$$S(p) = c + dp.$$

The coefficients $(a, b, c, d)$ are the parameters that determine the intercepts and slopes of these linear curves. The equilibrium price can be found by solving the following equation:

$$D(p) = a - bp = c + dp = S(p).$$

The answer is

$$p^* = \frac{a - c}{d + b}.$$

The equilibrium quantity demanded (and supplied) is

$$D(p^*) = a - bp^*$$
$$= a - b\frac{a - c}{b + d}$$
$$= \frac{ad + bc}{b + d}.$$

We can also solve this problem by using the inverse demand and supply curves. First we need to find the inverse demand curve. At what price is some quantity $q$ demanded? Simply substitute $q$ for $D(p)$ and solve for $p$. We have

$$q = a - bp,$$

so

$$P_D(q) = \frac{a - q}{b}.$$

In the same manner we find

$$P_S(q) = \frac{q - c}{d}.$$

Setting the demand price equal to the supply price and solving for the equilibrium quantity we have

$$P_D(q) = \frac{a - q}{b} = \frac{q - c}{d} = P_S(q)$$

$$q^* = \frac{ad + bc}{b + d}.$$

Note that this gives the same answer as in the original problem for both the equilibrium price and the equilibrium quantity.

## 16.5 Comparative Statics

After we have found an equilibrium by using the demand equals supply condition (or the demand price equals the supply price condition), we can see how it will change as the demand and supply curves change. For example, it is easy to see that if the demand curve shifts to the right in a parallel way—some fixed amount more is demanded at every price—the equilibrium price and quantity must both rise. On the other hand, if the supply curve shifts to the right, the equilibrium quantity rises, but the equilibrium price must fall.

What if both curves shift to the right? Then the quantity will definitely increase while the change in price is ambiguous—it could increase or it could decrease.

### EXAMPLE: Shifting Both Curves

*Question:* Consider the competitive market for apartments described in Chapter 1. Let the equilibrium price in that market be $p^*$ and the equilibrium quantity be $q^*$. Suppose that a developer converts $m$ of the apartments to condominiums, which are bought by the people who are currently living in the apartments. What happens to the equilibrium price?

*Answer:* The situation is depicted in Figure 16.2. The demand and supply curves both shift to the left by the *same* amount. Hence the price is unchanged and the quantity sold simply drops by $m$.

Algebraically the new equilibrium price is determined by

$$D(p) - m = S(p) - m,$$

which clearly has the same solution as the original demand equals supply condition.

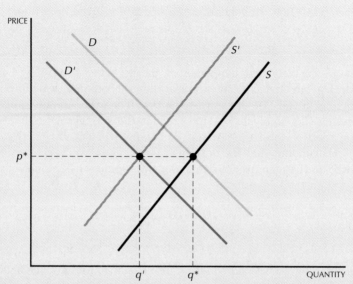

**Shifting both curves.** Both demand and supply curves shift to the left by the same amount, which implies the equilibrium price will remain unchanged.

Figure
16.2

## 16.6 Taxes

Describing a market before and after taxes are imposed presents a very nice exercise in comparative statics, as well as being of considerable interest in the conduct of economic policy. Let us see how it is done.

The fundamental thing to understand about taxes is that when a tax is present in a market, there are *two* prices of interest: the price the demander pays and the price the supplier gets. These two prices—the demand price and the supply price—differ by the amount of the tax.

There are several different kinds of taxes that one might impose. Two examples we will consider here are **quantity taxes** and **value** taxes (also called **ad valorem** taxes).

A quantity tax is a tax levied per unit of quantity bought or sold. Gasoline taxes are a good example of this. The gasoline tax is roughly 12 cents a gallon. If the demander is paying $P_D = \$1.50$ per gallon of gasoline, the supplier is getting $P_S = \$1.50 - .12 = \$1.38$ per gallon. In general, if $t$ is the amount of the quantity tax per unit sold, then

$$P_D = P_S + t.$$

A value tax is a tax expressed in percentage units. State sales taxes are the most common example of value taxes. If your state has a 5 percent sales tax, then when you pay $1.05 for something (including the tax), the supplier gets $1.00. In general, if the tax rate is given by $\tau$, then

$$P_D = (1+\tau)P_S.$$

Let us consider what happens in a market when a quantity tax is imposed. For our first case we suppose that the supplier is required to pay the tax, as in the case of the gasoline tax. Then the amount supplied will depend on the supply price—the amount the supplier actually gets after paying the tax—and the amount demanded will depend on the demand price—the amount that the demander pays. The amount that the supplier gets will be the amount the demander pays minus the amount of the tax. This gives us two equations:

$$D(P_D) = S(P_S)$$

$$P_S = P_D - t.$$

Substituting the second equation into the first, we have the equilibrium condition:

$$D(P_D) = S(P_D - t).$$

Alternatively we could also rearrange the second equation to get $P_D = P_S + t$ and then substitute to find

$$D(P_S + t) = S(P_S).$$

Either way is equally valid; which one you use will depends on convenience in a particular case.

Now suppose that instead of the supplier paying the tax, the demander has to pay the tax. Then we write

$$P_D - t = P_S,$$

which says that the amount paid by the demander minus the tax equals the price received by the supplier. Substituting this into the demand equals supply condition we find

$$D(P_D) = S(P_D - t).$$

Note that this is the same equation as in the case where the supplier pays the tax. As far as the equilibrium price facing the demanders and the suppliers is concerned, it really doesn't matter who is responsible for paying the tax—it just matters that the tax must be paid by someone.

This really isn't so mysterious. Think of the gasoline tax. There the tax is included in the posted price. But if the price were instead listed as the before-tax price and the gasoline tax were added on as a separate item to be paid by the demanders, then do you think that the amount of gasoline demanded would change? After all, the final price to the consumers would be the same whichever way the tax was charged. Insofar as the consumers can recognize the net cost to them of goods they purchase, it really doesn't matter which way the tax is levied.

There is an even simpler way to show this using the inverse demand and supply functions. The equilibrium quantity traded is that quantity $q^*$ such that the demand price at $q^*$ *minus the tax being paid* is just equal to the supply price at $q^*$. In symbols:

$$P_D(q^*) - t = P_S(q^*).$$

If the tax is being imposed on the suppliers, then the condition is that the supply price *plus the amount of the tax* must equal the demand price:

$$P_D(q^*) = P_S(q^*) + t.$$

But these are the same equations, so the same equilibrium prices and quantities must result.

Finally, we consider the geometry of the situation. This is most easily seen by using the inverse demand and supply curves discussed above. We want to find the quantity where the curve $P_D(q) - t$ crosses the curve $P_S(q)$. In order to locate this point we simply shift the demand curve down by $t$ and see where this shifted demand curve intersects the original supply curve. Alternatively we can find the quantity where $P_D(q)$ equals $P_S(q) + t$. To do this, we simply shift the supply curve up by the amount of the tax. Either way gives us the correct answer for the equilibrium quantity. The picture is given in Figure 16.3.

From this diagram we can easily see the qualitative effects of the tax. The quantity sold must decrease, the price paid by the demanders must go up, and the price received by the suppliers must go down.

Figure 16.4 depicts another way to determine the impact of a tax. Think about the definition of equilibrium in this market. We want to find a quantity $q^*$ such that when the supplier faces the price $p_s$ and the demander faces the price $p_d = p_s + t$, the quantity $q^*$ is demanded by the demander and supplied by the supplier. Let us represent the tax $t$ by a vertical line segment and slide it along the supply curve until it just touches the demand curve. That point is our equilibrium quantity!

## EXAMPLE: Taxation with Linear Demand and Supply

Suppose that the demand and supply curves are both linear. Then if we impose a tax in this market, the equilibrium is determined by the equations

$$a - bp_D = c + dp_S$$

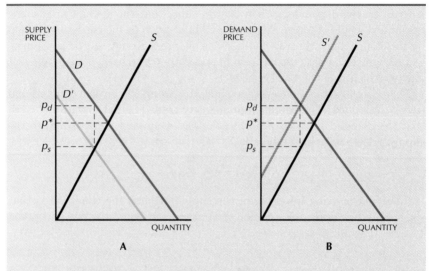

**Figure 16.3**

**The imposition of a tax.** In order to study the impact of a tax, we can either shift the demand curve down, as in panel A, or shift the supply curve up, as in panel B. The equilibrium prices paid by the demanders and received by the suppliers will be the same either way.

and

$$p_D = p_S + t.$$

Substituting from the second equation into the first, we have

$$a - b(p_S + t) = c + dp_S.$$

Solving for the equilibrium supply price, $p_S^*$, gives

$$p_S^* = \frac{a - c - bt}{d + b}.$$

The equilibrium demand price, $p_D^*$, is then given by $p_S^* + t$:

$$
\begin{aligned}
p_D^* &= \frac{a - c - bt}{d + b} + t \\
&= \frac{a - c + dt}{d + b}.
\end{aligned}
$$

Note that the price paid by the demander increases and the price received by the supplier decreases. The amount of the price change depends on the slope of the demand and supply curves.

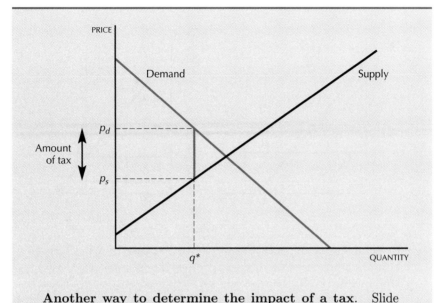

PRICE

Demand

Supply

$p_d$

Amount
of tax

$p_s$

$q^*$                                                    QUANTITY

**Another way to determine the impact of a tax.**  Slide   Figure
16.4
the line segment along the supply curve until it hits the demand
curve.

## 16.7 Passing Along a Tax

One often hears about how a tax on producers doesn't hurt profits, since
firms can simply pass along a tax to consumers. As we've seen above, a tax
really shouldn't be regarded as a tax on firms or on consumers. Rather,
taxes are on transactions *between* firms and consumers. In general, a tax
will both raise the price paid by consumers and lower the price received by
firms. How much of a tax gets passed along will therefore depend on the
characteristics of demand and supply.

This is easiest to see in the extreme cases: when we have a perfectly
horizontal supply curve or a perfectly vertical supply curve. These are also
known as the case of **perfectly elastic** and **perfectly inelastic** supply.

We've already encountered these two special cases earlier in this chapter.
If an industry has a horizontal supply curve, it means that the industry will
supply any amount desired of the good at some given price, and zero units
of the good at any lower price. In this case the price is entirely determined
by the supply curve and the quantity sold is determined by demand. If
an industry has a vertical supply curve, it means that the quantity of the
good is fixed. The equilibrium price of the good is determined entirely by
demand.

Let's consider the imposition of a tax in a market with a perfectly elastic
supply curve. As we've seen above, imposing a tax is just like shifting the

Figure
16.5

**Special cases of taxation.** (A) In the case of a perfectly
elastic supply curve the tax gets completely passed along to the
consumers. (B) In the case of a perfectly inelastic supply none
of the tax gets passed along.

supply curve up by the amount of the tax, as illustrated in Figure 16.5A.

In the case of a perfectly elastic supply curve it is easy to see that the
price to the consumers goes up by exactly the amount of the tax. The
supply price is exactly the same as it was before the tax, and the demanders
end up paying the entire tax. When you think about the meaning of the
horizontal supply curve, this is not hard to understand. The horizontal
supply curve means that the industry is willing to supply any amount of
the good at some particular price, $p^*$, and zero amount at any lower price.
Thus, if any amount of the good is going to be sold at all in equilibrium,
the suppliers must receive $p^*$ for selling it. This effectively determines the
equilibrium supply price, and the demand price is $p^* + t$.

The opposite case is illustrated in Figure 16.5B. If the supply curve is
vertical and we "shift the supply curve up," we don't change anything in
the diagram. The supply curve just slides along itself, and we still have
the same amount of the good supplied, with or without the tax. In this
case, the demanders determine the equilibrium price of the good, and they
are willing to pay a certain amount, $p^*$, for the supply of the good that is
available, tax or no tax. Thus they end up paying $p^*$, and the suppliers
end up receiving $p^* - t$. The entire amount of the tax is paid by the
suppliers.

This case often strikes people as paradoxical, but it really isn't. If the
suppliers could raise their prices after the tax is imposed and still sell their
entire fixed supply, they would have raised their prices before the tax was
imposed and made more money! If the demand curve doesn't move, then

the only way the price can increase is if the supply is reduced. If a policy doesn't change either supply or demand, it certainly can't affect price.

Now that we understand the special cases, we can examine the in-between case where the supply curve has an upward slope but is not perfectly vertical. In this situation, the amount of the tax that gets passed along will depend on the steepness of the supply curve relative to the demand curve. If the supply curve is nearly horizontal, nearly all of the tax gets passed along to the consumers, while if the supply curve is nearly vertical, almost none of the tax gets passed along. See Figure 16.6 for some examples.

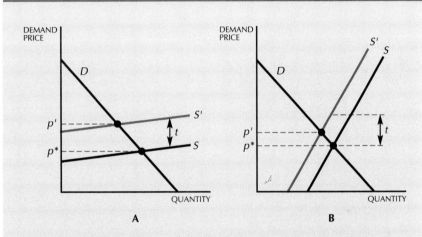

**Passing along a tax.** (A) If the supply curve is nearly horizontal, much of the tax can be passed along. (B) If it is nearly vertical, very little of the tax can be passed along.

Figure
16.6

## 16.8 The Deadweight Loss of a Tax

We've seen that taxing a good will typically increase the price paid by the demanders and decrease the price received by the suppliers. This certainly represents a cost to the demanders and suppliers, but from the economist's viewpoint, the real cost of the tax is that the output has been reduced.

The lost output is the social cost of the tax. Let us explore the social cost of a tax using the consumers' and producers' surplus tools developed in Chapter 14. We start with the diagram given in Figure 16.7. This depicts the equilibrium demand price and supply price after a tax, $t$, has been imposed.

Output has been decreased by this tax, and we can use the tools of consumers' and producers' surplus to value the social loss. The loss in consumers' surplus is given by the areas $A + B$, and the loss in producers' surplus is given in areas $C + D$. These are the same kind of losses that we examined in Chapter 14.

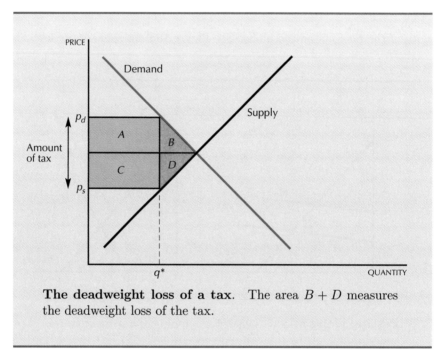

Figure
16.7

**The deadweight loss of a tax**. The area $B + D$ measures the deadweight loss of the tax.

Since we're after an expression for the social cost of the tax, it seems sensible to add the areas $A + B$ and $C + D$ to each other to get the total loss to the consumers and to the producers of the good in question. However, we've still left out one party—namely, the government.

The government *gains* revenue from the tax. And, of course, the consumers who benefit from the government services provided with these tax revenues also gain from the tax. We can't really say how much they gain until we know what the tax revenues will be spent on.

Let us make the assumption that the tax revenues will just be handed back to the consumers and the producers, or equivalently that the services provided by the government revenues will be just equal in value to the revenues spent on them.

Then the net benefit to the government is the area $A + C$—the total revenue from the tax. Since the loss of producers' and consumers' surpluses are net costs, and the tax revenue to the government is a net benefit, the total net cost of the tax is the algebraic sum of these areas: the loss in consumers' surplus, $-(A + B)$, the loss in producers' surplus, $-(C + D)$, and the gain in government revenue, $+(A + C)$.

The net result is the area $-(B + D)$. This area is known as the **deadweight loss** of the tax or the **excess burden** of the tax. This latter phrase is especially descriptive.

Recall the interpretation of the loss of consumers' surplus. It is how much the consumers would pay to avoid the tax. In terms of this diagram the consumers are willing to pay $A + B$ to avoid the tax. Similarly, the producers are willing to pay $C + D$ to avoid the tax. Together they are willing to pay $A + B + C + D$ to avoid a tax that raises $A + C$ dollars of revenue. The *excess burden* of the tax is therefore $B + D$.

What is the source of this excess burden? Basically it is the lost value to the consumers and producers due to the reduction in the sales of the good. You can't tax what isn't there.[1] So the government doesn't get any revenue on the reduction in sales of the good. From the viewpoint of society, it is a pure loss—a deadweight loss.

We could also derive the deadweight loss directly from its definition, by just measuring the social value of the lost output. Suppose that we start at the old equilibrium and start moving to the left. The first unit lost was one where the price that someone was willing to pay for it was just equal to the price that someone was willing to sell it for. Here there is hardly any social loss since this unit was the marginal unit that was sold.

Now move a little farther to the left. The demand price measures how much someone was willing to pay to receive the good, and the supply price measures the price at which someone was willing to supply the good. The difference is the lost value on that unit of the good. If we add this up over the units of the good that are not produced and consumed because of the presence of the tax, we get the deadweight loss.

## EXAMPLE: The Market for Loans

The amount of borrowing or lending in an economy is influenced to a large degree by the interest rate charged. The interest rate serves as a price in the market for loans.

We can let $D(r)$ be the demand for loans by borrowers and $S(r)$ be the supply of loans by lenders. The equilibrium interest rate, $r^*$, is then determined by the condition that demand equal supply:

$$D(r^*) = S(r^*). \tag{16.1}$$

Suppose we consider adding taxes to this model. What will happen to the equilibrium interest rate?

---

[1] At least the government hasn't figured out how to do this yet. But they're working on it.

In the U.S. economy individuals have to pay income tax on the interest they earn from lending money. If everyone is in the same tax bracket, $t$, the after-tax interest rate facing lenders will be $(1-t)r$. Thus the supply of loans, which depends on the after-tax interest rate, will be $S((1-t)r)$.

On the other hand, the Internal Revenue Service code allows many borrowers to deduct their interest charges, so if the borrowers are in the same tax bracket as the lenders, the after-tax interest rate they pay will be $(1-t)r$. Hence the demand for loans will be $D((1-t)r)$. The equation for interest rate determination with taxes present is then

$$D((1-t)r') = S((1-t)r').  \qquad (16.2)$$

Now observe that if $r^*$ solves equation (16.1), then $r^* = (1-t)r'$ must solve equation (16.2) so that

$$r^* = (1-t)r',$$

or

$$r' = \frac{r^*}{(1-t)}.$$

Thus the interest rate in the presence of the tax will be higher by $1/(1-t)$. The *after-tax* interest rate $(1-t)r'$ will be $r^*$, just as it was before the tax was imposed!

Figure 16.8 may make things clearer. Making interest income taxable will tilt the supply curve for loans up by a factor of $1/(1-t)$; but making interest payments tax deductible will also tilt the demand curve for loans up by $1/(1-t)$. The net result is that the market interest rate rises by precisely $1/(1-t)$.

Inverse demand and supply functions provide another way to look at this problem. Let $r_b(q)$ be the inverse demand function for borrowers. This tells us what the after-tax interest rate would have to be to induce people to borrow $q$. Similarly, let $r_l(q)$ be the inverse supply function for lenders. The equilibrium amount lent will then be determined by the condition

$$r_b(q^*) = r_l(q^*).  \qquad (16.3)$$

Now introduce taxes into the situation. To make things more interesting, we'll allow borrowers and lenders to be in different tax brackets, denoted by $t_b$ and $t_l$. If the market interest rate is $r$, then the after-tax rate facing borrowers will be $(1-t_b)r$, and the quantity they choose to borrow will be determined by the equation

$$(1-t_b)r = r_b(q),$$

or

$$r = \frac{r_b(q)}{1-t_b}.  \qquad (16.4)$$

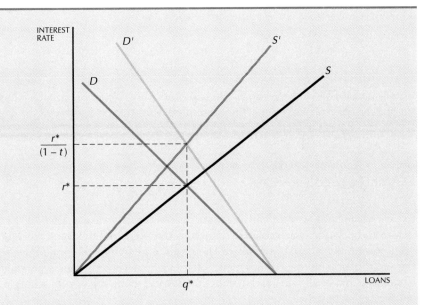

**Equilibrium in the loan market.** If borrowers and lenders are in the same tax bracket, the after-tax interest rate and the amount borrowed are unchanged.

Figure
16.8

Similarly, the after-tax rate facing lenders will be $(1-t_l)r$, and the amount they choose to lend will be determined by the equation

$$(1 - t_l)r = r_l(q)$$

or

$$r = \frac{r_l(q)}{1 - t_l}. \tag{16.5}$$

Combining equations (16.4) and (16.5) gives the equilibrium condition:

$$r = \frac{r_b(\hat{q})}{1 - t_b} = \frac{r_l(\hat{q})}{1 - t_l}. \tag{16.6}$$

From this equation it is easy to see that if borrowers and lenders are in the same tax bracket, so that $t_b = t_l$, then $\hat{q} = q^*$. What if they are in different tax brackets? It is not hard to see that the tax law is subsidizing borrowers and taxing lenders, but what is the net effect? If the borrowers face a higher price than the lenders, then the system is a net tax on borrowing, but if the borrowers face a lower price than the lenders, then it is a net subsidy. Rewriting the equilibrium condition, equation (16.6), we have

$$r_b(\hat{q}) = \frac{1 - t_b}{1 - t_l} r_l(\hat{q}).$$

Thus borrowers will face a higher price than lenders if

$$\frac{1 - t_b}{1 - t_l} > 1,$$

which means that $t_l > t_b$. So if the tax bracket of lenders is greater than the tax bracket of borrowers, the system is a net tax on borrowing, but if $t_l < t_b$, it is a net subsidy.

## EXAMPLE: Food Subsidies

In years when there were bad harvests in nineteenth-century England the rich would provide charitable assistance to the poor by buying up the harvest, consuming a fixed amount of the grain, and selling the remainder to the poor at half the price they paid for it. At first thought this seems like it would provide significant benefits to the poor, but on second thought, doubts begin to arise.

The only way that the poor can be made better off is if they end up consuming more grain. But there is a fixed amount of grain available after the harvest. So how can the poor be better off because of this policy?

As a matter of fact they are not; the poor end up paying exactly the same price for the grain with or without the policy. To see why, we will model the equilibrium with and without this program. Let $D(p)$ be the demand curve for the poor, $K$ the amount demanded by the rich, and $S$ the fixed amount supplied in a year with a bad harvest. By assumption the supply of grain and the demand by the rich are fixed. Without the charity provided by the rich, the equilibrium price is determined by total demand equals total supply:

$$D(p^*) + K = S.$$

With the program in place, the equilibrium price is determined by

$$D(\hat{p}/2) + K = S.$$

But now observe: if $p^*$ solves the first equation, then $\hat{p} = 2p^*$ solves the second equation. So when the rich offer to buy the grain and distribute it to the poor, the market price is simply bid up to twice the original price—and the poor pay the same price they did before!

When you think about it this isn't too surprising. If the demand of the rich is fixed and the supply of grain is fixed, then the amount that the poor can consume is fixed. Thus the equilibrium price facing the poor is determined entirely by their own demand curve; the equilibrium price will be the same, regardless of how the grain is provided to the poor.

## EXAMPLE: Subsidies in Iraq

Even subsidies that are put in place "for a good reason" can be extremely difficult to dislodge. Why? Because they create a political constituency that comes to rely on them. This is true in every country, but Iraq represents a particularly egregious case. As of 2005, fuel and food subsidies in Iraq consumed nearly one third of the government's budget.[2]

Almost all of the Iraqi government's budget comes from oil exports. There is very little refining capacity in the country, so Iraq imports gasoline at 30 to 35 cents a liter, which it then sells to the public at 1.5 cents. A substantial amount of this gasoline is sold on the black market and smuggled into Turkey, where gas is about one dollar a liter.

Food and fuel oil are also highly subsidized. Politicians are reluctant to remove these subsidies due to the politically unstable environment. When similar subsidies were removed in Yemen, there was rioting in the streets, with dozens of people dying. A World Bank study concluded that more than half of the GDP in Iraq was spent on subsidies. According to the finance minister, Ali Abdulameer Allawi, "They've reached the point where they've become insane. They distort the economy in a grotesque way, and create the worst incentives you can think of."

## 16.9 Pareto Efficiency

An economic situation is **Pareto efficient** if there is no way to make any person better off without hurting anybody else. Pareto efficiency is a desirable thing—if there is some way to make some group of people better off, why not do it?—but efficiency is not the only goal of economic policy. For example, efficiency has almost nothing to say about income distribution or economic justice.

However, efficiency is an important goal, and it is worth asking how well a competitive market does in achieving Pareto efficiency. A competitive market, or any economic mechanism, has to determine two things. First, how much is produced, and second, who gets it. A competitive market determines how much is produced based on how much people are willing to pay to purchase the good as compared to how much people must be paid to supply the good.

Consider Figure 16.9. At any amount of output less than the competitive amount $q^*$, there is someone who is willing to supply an extra unit of the

[2] James Glanz, "Despite Crushing Costs, Iraqi Cabinet Lets Big Subsidies Stand," *New York Times*, August 11, 2005.

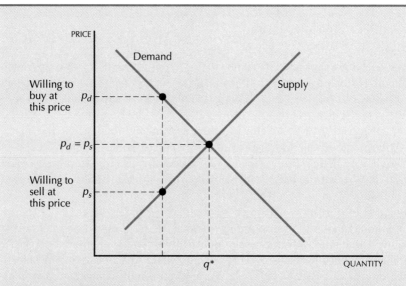

Figure
16.9

**Pareto efficiency.** The competitive market determines a Pareto efficient amount of output because at $q^*$ the price that someone is willing to pay to buy an extra unit of the good is equal to the price that someone must be paid to sell an extra unit of the good.

good at a price that is less than the price that someone is willing to pay for an extra unit of the good.

If the good were produced and exchanged between these two people at any price between the demand price and the supply price, they would both be made better off. Thus any amount less than the equilibrium amount cannot be Pareto efficient, since there will be at least two people who could be made better off.

Similarly, at any output larger than $q^*$, the amount someone would be willing to pay for an extra unit of the good is less than the price that it would take to get it supplied. Only at the market equilibrium $q^*$ would we have a Pareto efficient amount of output supplied—an amount such that the willingness to pay for an extra unit is just equal to the willingness to be paid to supply an extra unit.

Thus the competitive market produces a Pareto efficient amount of output. What about the way in which the good is allocated among the consumers? In a competitive market everyone pays the same price for a good— the marginal rate of substitution between the good and "all other goods" is equal to the price of the good. Everyone who is willing to pay this price is able to purchase the good, and everyone who is not willing to pay this price cannot purchase the good.

What would happen if there were an allocation of the good where the marginal rates of substitution between the good and "all other goods" were not the same? Then there must be at least two people who value a marginal unit of the good differently. Maybe one values a marginal unit at $5 and one values it at $4. Then if the one with the lower value sells a bit of the good to the one with the higher value at any price between $4 and $5, both people would be made better off. Thus any allocation with different marginal rates of substitution cannot be Pareto efficient.

## EXAMPLE: Waiting in Line

One commonly used way to allocate resources is by making people wait in line. We can analyze this mechanism for resource allocation using the same tools that we have developed for analyzing the market mechanism. Let us look at a concrete example: suppose that your university is going to distribute tickets to the championship basketball game. Each person who waits in line can get one ticket for free.

The cost of a ticket will then simply be the cost of waiting in line. People who want to see the basketball game very much will camp out outside the ticket office so as to be sure to get a ticket. People who don't care very much about the game may drop by a few minutes before the ticket window opens on the off chance that some tickets will be left. The willingness to pay for a ticket should no longer be measured in dollars but rather in waiting time, since tickets will be allocated according to willingness to wait.

Will waiting in line result in a Pareto efficient allocation of tickets? Ask yourself whether it is possible that someone who waited for a ticket might be willing to sell it to someone who didn't wait in line. Often this will be the case, simply because willingness to wait and willingness to pay differ across the population. If someone is willing to wait in line to buy a ticket and then sell it to someone else, allocating tickets by willingness to wait does not exhaust all the gains to trade—some people would generally still be willing to trade the tickets after the tickets have been allocated. Since waiting in line does not exhaust all of the gains from trade, it does not in general result in a Pareto efficient outcome.

If you allocate a good using a price set in dollars, then the dollars paid by the demanders provide benefits to the suppliers of the good. If you allocate a good using waiting time, the hours spent in line don't benefit anybody. The waiting time imposes a cost on the buyers of the good and provides no benefits at all to the suppliers. Waiting in line is a form of **deadweight loss**—the people who wait in line pay a "price" but no one else receives any benefits from the price they pay.

## Summary

1. The supply curve measures how much people will be willing to supply of some good at each price.

2. An equilibrium price is one where the quantity that people are willing to supply equals the quantity that people are willing to demand.

3. The study of how the equilibrium price and quantity change when the underlying demand and supply curves change is another example of comparative statics.

4. When a good is taxed, there will always be two prices: the price paid by the demanders and the price received by the suppliers. The difference between the two represents the amount of the tax.

5. How much of a tax gets passed along to consumers depends on the relative steepness of the demand and supply curves. If the supply curve is horizontal, all of the tax gets passed along to consumers; if the supply curve is vertical, none of the tax gets passed along.

6. The deadweight loss of a tax is the net loss in consumers' surplus plus producers' surplus that arises from imposing the tax. It measures the value of the output that is not sold due to the presence of the tax.

7. A situation is Pareto efficient if there is no way to make some group of people better off without making some other group worse off.

8. The Pareto efficient amount of output to supply in a single market is that amount where the demand and supply curves cross, since this is the only point where the amount that demanders are willing to pay for an extra unit of output equals the price at which suppliers are willing to supply an extra unit of output.

## REVIEW QUESTIONS

1. What is the effect of a subsidy in a market with a horizontal supply curve? With a vertical supply curve?

2. Suppose that the demand curve is vertical while the supply curve slopes upward. If a tax is imposed in this market who ends up paying it?

3. Suppose that all consumers view red pencils and blue pencils as perfect substitutes. Suppose that the supply curve for red pencils is upward sloping. Let the price of red pencils and blue pencils be $p_r$ and $p_b$. What would happen if the government put a tax only on red pencils?

4. The United States imports about half of its petroleum needs. Suppose that the rest of the oil producers are willing to supply as much oil as the United States wants at a constant price of $25 a barrel. What would happen to the price of domestic oil if a tax of $5 a barrel were placed on foreign oil?

5. Suppose that the supply curve is vertical. What is the deadweight loss of a tax in this market?

6. Consider the tax treatment of borrowing and lending described in the text. How much revenue does this tax system raise if borrowers and lenders are in the same tax bracket?

7. Does such a tax system raise a positive or negative amount of revenue when $t_l < t_b$?

# CHAPTER **17**

# MEASUREMENT

Up until now we have used simple algebraic expressions to describe utility functions, production functions, demand curves, supply curves, and so on. For actual applications we have to estimate these functions using statistical techniques. The study of how to do this effectively is known as **econometrics**.

When we analyze data we generally are concerned with the following questions.

**Summarize.** How can we describe the data succinctly? Example: how many cups of coffee are consumed per person per day?

**Estimate.** How can we estimate some unknown parameters? Example: what is the elasticity of demand for coffee?

**Test.** How can we determine whether an unknown parameter satisfies some restriction? Example: do men and women drink the same amount of coffee per day on average?

**Forecast.** How can we forecast what the price of coffee will be next year?

**Predict.** How can we predict what would happen to some variable of interest if something changes? Example: if the government imposed a 10% tax on coffee what would happen to consumption?

There are a variety of statistical techniques that can be used to answer such questions, which we will explore in this chapter. Our primary focus will be on estimation and prediction, but we will say a few words about the other topics.

## 17.1 Summarize data

The simplest way to summarize data is with a table. For example, Table 17.1 depicts data from an online survey of 1,000 consumers who were asked, "On average how many cups of coffee do you drink per day?" The table shows that about 45% of those who responded indicated that they drink zero cups of coffee per day. Closer inspection reveals that 16% averaged one cup a day and about the same number drank two cups per day.

**Coffee consumption from an online survey**

| 0 cups | 1 cup | 2 cups | 3 cups | 4+ cups |
|--------|-------|--------|--------|---------|
| 0.448  | 0.163 | 0.161  | 0.110  | 0.119   |

Table 17.1

This information can be presented in a more vivid way using a barplot (or barchart) as in Figure 17.1. In this chart it is clear that about the same fraction of respondents indicated they consumed 1 or 2 cups a day, and roughly the same number of respondents indicated they consumed 3 or 4+ cups per day.

We can also break down the information by category. The same survey reported gender of the respondents, so we could examine how reported coffee consumption varies across gender as in Table 17.2 or Figure 17.2. As before, a barplot summarizes the information in a way that is more readily understood. For example, it appears that a larger fraction of males than females report drinking 0 cups of coffee and that woman appear to drink more coffee than men overall.

It is often useful to compute various **summary statistics** based on the data. The **mean** number of cups of coffee consumed per day turns out to be 1.28. We can also compute **conditional means**, such as the average number of cups of coffee consumed by those who drink coffee, or the average number of cups of coffee consumed by males. Computing the conditional mean just involves computing an average over those consumers who satisfy

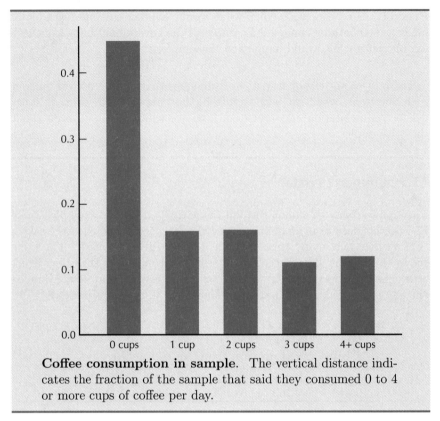

Figure
17.1

**Coffee consumption in sample.** The vertical distance indicates the fraction of the sample that said they consumed 0 to 4 or more cups of coffee per day.

the relevant condition (drink more than 0 cups per day, are males, and so on). In our sample, men drank 1.24 cups per day on average and women drank 1.39 cups per day.

Table
17.2

**Average coffee consumption by gender**

| Cups | Female | Male |
|------|--------|-------|
| 0 | 0.176 | 0.219 |
| 1 | 0.093 | 0.057 |
| 2 | 0.079 | 0.070 |
| 3 | 0.050 | 0.046 |
| 4+ | 0.057 | 0.052 |

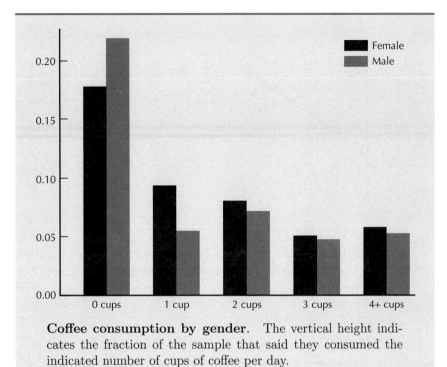

**Coffee consumption by gender.** The vertical height indicates the fraction of the sample that said they consumed the indicated number of cups of coffee per day.

Figure
17.2

## EXAMPLE: Simpson's paradox

Conditional means can sometimes behave in surprising ways. Suppose that we plot coffee consumption as a function of income among men and women. A hypothetical relationship might look like Figure 17.3. Note that consumption is increasing in income for both men and women, but that overall consumption is decreasing in income. This phenomenon is an example of **Simpson's paradox**.

Simpson's paradox is not uncommon in real life. Table 17.3 shows the application and admission statistics for men and women to graduate school at the University of California, Berkeley in Fall 1973.

**Applicants and admissions to UC Berkeley, Fall 1973**

Table
17.3

| Gender | Applicants | Admitted |
|--------|-----------|----------|
| Men | 8442 | 44% |
| Women | 4321 | 35% |

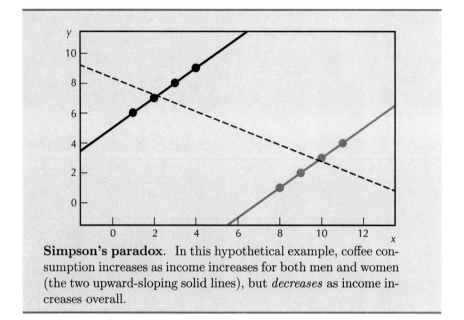

**Figure 17.3**

**Simpson's paradox.** In this hypothetical example, coffee consumption increases as income increases for both men and women (the two upward-sloping solid lines), but *decreases* as income increases overall.

It appears that men are more likely to have been admitted than were women. Is this an example of gender bias? Table 17.4 breaks the data down by department. In this table, it is easy to see that no department was significantly biased in favor of men; in fact, most departments had a small bias towards women.

**Table 17.4**

**Admission by department**

| Department | Men Applied | Men Admitted | Women Applied | Women Admitted |
|---|---|---|---|---|
| A | 825 | 62% | 108 | 82% |
| B | 560 | 63% | 25 | 68% |
| C | 325 | 37% | 593 | 34% |
| D | 417 | 33% | 375 | 35% |
| E | 191 | 28% | 393 | 24% |
| F | 272 | 6% | 341 | 7% |

A report concluded that the explanation for this apparent paradox was that women tended to apply to departments with low admission rates, while men tended to apply to departments with high admission rates. Even though there was no evidence of bias at a department level, the overall statistics gave an impression of bias.[1]

## 17.2 Test

In the previous section we saw that men drank 1.23 cups of coffee per day on average and women drank 1.39 cups per day on average. But this is just one particular sample of a thousand consumers. If we took a different sample, we would find different numbers. How confident can we be that the mean consumption of coffee by women exceeds the mean consumption of coffee by men in the entire population?

One way to answer this question is to pose it in the following way. Suppose that men and women actually drank the *same* amount of coffee per day. How likely would it be in a particular sample of 1,000 consumers to observe one group drinking $1.39 - 1.23 = 0.16$ cups more than the other?

In our sample, it turns out that with a few additional assumptions the probability that we would see a difference at least this large is about 9.6%. In other words, if men and women had the same average consumption in the population, we would see an estimated difference of this magnitude or larger in roughly 1 out of 10 samples. Even though our sample shows that coffee consumption is somewhat different between men and women, we can't be confident that this relationship holds for the population as a whole.

## 17.3 Estimating demand using experimental data

Suppose you work for a company that sells coffee beans via a website. Your coffee currently sells for $15 a pound, but you are contemplating cutting the price to $14. You hope that you will sell more coffee at the lower price, but how much more? Is it worth cutting your price to get more sales?

In this case it is natural to run an experiment to see how the demand for coffee changes when the price changes. For example, you could cut the price of the coffee for a few weeks and see how much additional coffee you sell. If your profit goes up, it might make sense to make the sale price permanent.

Another possibility would be to put the coffee on sale in just a few states or cities and see what happens in those locations. If we try this experiment, it is important to recognize that there are other factors that affect the demand for coffee than just the price. For example, the amount

---

[1] P. J. Bickel, E. A. Hammel and J. W. O'Connell (1975). "Sex Bias in Graduate Admissions: Data from Berkeley." *Science* 187 (4175): 398-404.

of coffee you sell in a given region during a given period could vary with the season of the year or with the weather.

Ideally, you would choose which cities are treated using some random method such as a coin flip. Such **randomized treatment** helps eliminate sources of systematic bias.

It would also be a good idea to think about ways you could control for these systematic effects. For example, you could compare the sales in the cities where you cut the price to sales in those cities where you kept the price constant. Or you could collect data on weather in the cities you examine and use statistical techniques to control for the observed variation in weather.

In the language of statistics, the cities where you reduce the price of coffee is your **treatment group** and the cities where you leave the price of coffee constant is your **control group**. Running the experiment is simply a small-scale version of the policy you are thinking about implementing—namely, cutting the price for everyone. If you make the experiment as much like the proposed policy as possible, then the experiment will probably give you a pretty good idea about what would happen if you scaled the experiment up to the entire country.

## 17.4 Effect of treatment

Another thing you could do to estimate how the demand for coffee would respond to a price cut is to send out coupons to a randomly chosen set of people and see how many people use these coupons to buy coffee.

The trouble with this procedure is that the people who redeem the coupons may be different from the population at large. It is likely that people who go to the trouble of using the coupons might be more price-sensitive on average than those who don't bother to use the coupons.

In the case of a coupon, some fraction of the population (the coupon users) are *choosing* to receive a lower price rather than simply facing a lower price for coffee. In general, those who *choose* to be treated are those who are more interested in the treatment and may be more likely to respond to it differently than the population as whole. So the impact of the treatment (the coupon) on those who choose to use it (the treated) could be quite different than the impact of a price cut for everyone.

On the other hand, sometimes you might be interested in the "effect of the treatment on the treated," as opposed to the effect of treatment on the population. For example, if the policy you had in mind was sending out coupons to the entire population, then an experiment that involved sending out coupons to a subset of the population would be an appropriate experiment.

The key issue is whether the consumers are making a choice of whether or not to be treated (that is, to get the lower price). Ideally, the experiment will mimic the proposed policy as closely as possible.

## 17.5 Estimating demand using observational data

Let us now consider a different situation. Suppose now you are interested in estimating how the *nationwide* demand for coffee in the United States changes as the price changes. In this case there is no obvious way to do an experiment. Since you don't have **experimental data**, you have to use **observational data**.

The statistical tool that economists use most commonly to address problems of this sort is called **regression**. A regression is simply a way to express conditional expectations. For example, a regression could describe the expected consumption of coffee by a randomly chosen consumer, conditional on the consumer being female. When we estimate a regression we are trying to describe the relationship between a variable of interest (in our case coffee consumption) and other characteristics, such as gender, income, age, price, and so on. There are many varieties of regression, but we will focus on the simplest form, which is called **ordinary least squares** or **OLS**.

So suppose we are given some data on prices and quantity sold of coffee at different time periods. How can we use this data to estimate a demand function?

It is important to think about the **data generation process**: how was this data produced? We can apply some of the theory developed in earlier chapters on consumer choice.

Think of a consumer as purchasing two things, coffee ($x_1$) and "all other goods" ($x_2$). Good 2 is sometimes referred to as a **composite commodity** or **quantity index**, as described in Chapter 7.

Denote the price of coffee by $p_1$, the price of "all other goods" by $p_2$, and the total expenditure by $m$. The utility maximization problem for a single consumer is

$$\max_{x_1, x_2} u(x_1, x_2)$$

such that $p_1 x_1 + p_2 x_2 = m$.

We can write the demand function for coffee as

$$x_1 = D(p_1, p_2, m).$$

As mentioned in section 2.4, we can multiply prices and income by any positive constant and demand stays the same. So let us multiply prices and income by $1/p_2$. This gives us

$$x_1 = D(p_1/p_2, 1, m/p_2).$$

This says the demand for coffee is a function of the price of coffee relative to the price of all other goods and income relative to the price of all other goods. In practice, we compute these numbers by using a price index, like the Consumer Price Index (CPI) or Personal Consumption Expenditure price index (PCEPI). (See the discussion in Chapter 7 on index numbers to see how these are constructed.)

Now we can add up demand across all consumers to get aggregate demand. In order to avoid additional notation, we will use the same notation as above to write $x = D(p, m)$, where $x$ is now the aggregate demand for coffee, $p$ is the price of coffee divided by the CPI, $m$ is total consumer expenditure divided by the CPI, and $D(p, m)$ is the aggregate demand function.

## Functional form

We now need to pick an algebraic formula for the demand function. There are three forms for demand functions commonly used in practice.

**Linear demand.** $x = c + bp + dm$.

**Log-linear demand.** $\log(x) = \log(c) + b\log(p) + d\log(m)$.

**Semi-log demand.** $\log(x) = c + bp + dm$.

The most popular form is log-linear demand, since it is easy to interpret the coefficients. As we have seen in Chapter 15, section 8, $b$ and $d$ measure the price and income elasticity of demand, respectively. (In these expressions, all logarithms are natural logarithms.)

## Statistical model

Of course, we would not expect our model to fit perfectly, so we need to add an **error term**, denoted by $e_t$. The error term measures the difference between our ideal specification of demand and the actual observed demand. It can be interpreted as the cumulative effect of all the omitted, unobserved variables that affect demand.

So our final specification of the data-generating process is

$$\log(x_t) = \log(c) + b\log(p_t) + d\log(m_t) + e_t,$$

where the error term is interpreted as the aggregate of all the other variables that might be correlated with coffee consumption.

Under certain conditions, ordinary least squares can be used to provide good estimates of the parameters $(b, c, d)$. The most important condition is that the price of coffee and total expenditure are not correlated with the error term.

It is not hard to see intuitively why this condition is necessary. The coefficient $b$ is supposed to measure how the demand for coffee changes as the price changes *holding everything else constant*. But if $p_t$ and $e_t$ are positively correlated in the data, then increases in $p_t$ will tend to be associated with increases in $e_t$ in our sample. So the observed change in $x_t$ will depend on both the change in $p_t$ *and* the change in $e_t$. In this case, we say that there is a **confounding effect**. We will get a poor estimate of how a change in price affects coffee consumption if other variables are changing systematically as the price of coffee changes.

The ideal way to ensure that the price of coffee is not correlated with the error term is to run an experiment. In this context that would mean choosing different prices of coffee and seeing how demand responds. However, as described above, **experimental data** of this sort would be difficult to collect for total coffee consumption. Often we are stuck with **observational data**.

Given what we know about the coffee market, is it likely that changes in the price of coffee would be correlated with factors that influence the demand for coffee? As it happens coffee beans are grown in dozens of countries and are sold on a world market. The supply of coffee beans varies significantly from year to year, with the important effects things such as weather, political events, changes in transportation costs, and so on.

From the point of view of a particular country, the price of coffee varies exogenously, since it depend on factors that primarily affect the supply of coffee, not the demand for coffee.

## Estimation

All that remains is to actually do the estimation. We can use a statistics package such as R or Stata to estimate the regression described above. The estimated price elasticity turns out to be $-0.077$, and the estimated income elasticity turns out to be 0.34. This says that a 1% increase in price results in a 0.77% drop in coffee consumption, so demand for coffee is pretty inelastic. It turns out that this estimate is rather imprecise, but it is the best we can do with the available data.

## 17.6 Identification

In estimating the demand for coffee, we argued that the world price of coffee was exogenous from the point of view of a specific country. In terms of supply and demand, we are saying that supply curve facing a single country is more or less flat at the equilibrium price. The price could shift from year to year, depending on weather and other factors, and the resulting equilibria would trace out the demand curve, as shown in Figure 17.4.

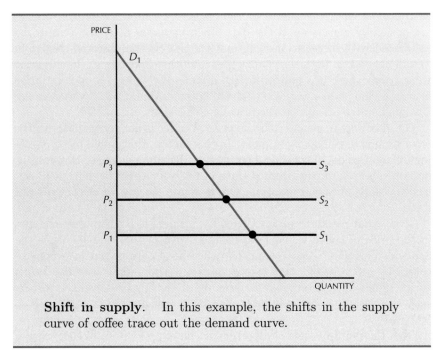

Figure
17.4

**Shift in supply.** In this example, the shifts in the supply curve of coffee trace out the demand curve.

But suppose we are interested in the *world* demand for coffee. In this case it is unreasonable to assume that the price is determined exogenously; rather it is determined by the interaction of supply and demand.

For example, we might think that the supply of coffee is more or less fixed in a given year but varies from year to year depending on the weather. In this case, the supply curve shifts, but the demand curve remains constant, and the observed prices and quantities would still lie along the demand function. So estimating demand as a function of price would still make sense.

The problematic case is where both supply and demand are shifting, as in Figure 17.5. In this case, it is impossible to estimate either curve. Generally you can estimate a demand function if there is something that shifts supply and not demand, and you can estimate a supply function if there is something that shifts demand but not supply. But if both curves shift in unknown ways, we can't identify what is driving price changes and quantity changes. This is known as the **identification problem**.

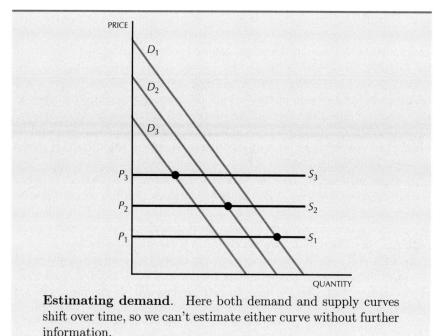

**Estimating demand.** Here both demand and supply curves shift over time, so we can't estimate either curve without further information.

Figure
17.5

## 17.7 What can go wrong?

Let us return to the simple demand estimation problem described earlier, but now consider a situation where the price of a product is set by the seller rather than the price being exogenously determined on world markets. To be specific, suppose a company called KoffeeTime makes a cold drink called Koffeetino. Over the years they have set the price according to market conditions. When the economic activity is slow, due to a recession, they see the sales of Koffeetino drop, so they quickly cut the price in response. When the economy is booming, they see the sales are high, so they raise the price.

This means that in the historical data we will see high prices associated with high sales and vice versa. The observed "demand curve" slopes up!

What is going on? We usually think that high prices cause consumers to purchase less. Here the drop in consumption is causing the prices to be cut. But what is causing the drop in consumption? The answer, in this case, is that income has dropped due to the "bad times." Income, in this case, is a **confounding variable** since it affects both the right-hand side and the left-hand side of the regression—both the price and the quantity.

For a *fixed* level of income, we would expect to see higher prices leading to less demand and lower prices leading to more demand for Koffeetino. If we add income to the regression (as theory tells us to do), then it is possible that we will get a meaningful estimate of price elasticity In econometric language, this is an example of **missing variable bias**: we failed to include an important variable in the regression and so we got a biased estimate of the effect.

But, in reality, there are always omitted variables—we can never have a complete list of everything that affects demand. For example, it may be that weather affects Koffeetino. In years with particularly cold temperatures sales fall and in warm years sales rise. The company may respond by raising or lowering price in response to the change in sales, leading to the same problem we had before.

As mentioned earlier, omitted variables that are not correlated with price are not much of a problem. But omitted variables that are correlated with price (confounding variables) can result in biased estimates. This will often be the case when the price is chosen, since the choice may depend on lots of things that the econometrician may not subsequently observe.

As it turns out, there are ways to address this problem that are covered in more advanced courses. Experiments are the gold standard, but sometimes observational data can be used to estimate causal effects even without explicit experiments.

## 17.8 Policy evaluation

A common reason to estimate the magnitude of some effect is that we are contemplating some policy change. Ideally, we would run an experiment on a small scale to estimate the impact of the proposed change. But, as we have seen, it is sometimes difficult or costly to run such an experiment.

Sometimes we can find a **natural experiment** that is similar to the ideal experiment we would run if we could. For example, in 2008 the State of Oregon ran a lottery among low-income adults to determine who would be allowed to apply for Medicare. A year after this lottery, the treatment group—those who were allowed to apply for Medicare—were substantially more likely to be covered by health insurance than those who weren't allowed to apply.[2]

The researchers were able to see how the treated group differed from the control group. In the first year of the study, it turned out that the treated group had higher health care utilization, lower out-of-pocket medical expenditures and medical debt, and better self-reported physical and mental health than the control group. One might reasonably expect that this would carry over to larger populations who were offered the chance to sign up for Medicare.

---

[2] Amy Finkelstein et. al., "The Oregon Health Insurance Experiment: Evidence from the First Year," http://economics.mit.edu/files/6796.

Of course, offering people the *opportunity* to sign up for Medicare is different from extending it to the entire population. In the first case, people still choose to apply and those who apply could be different from the entire population in relevant ways.

## EXAMPLE: Crime and police

It is important to distinguish correlation and causation. A classic example: if we observe more police in precincts with high crime rates, can we conclude that police cause crime? Of course not. A more likely explanation is that the causality runs the other direction: more police were assigned to high crime areas *because* they had high crime.

If we use statistical procedures to estimate the relationship between numbers of police and crime rates, we may well see a positive relationship (more police are associated with more crime). However, that says nothing about what would happen if we deliberately assigned more police to a given precinct.

In order to understand the *causal* impact of police on crime rates, we need to understand (1) how police were assigned to precincts in the historical data and (2) how the assignment of additional police to a given precinct changes crime rates.

Ideally we would use a controlled experiment to determine how the number of police affects crime rates. However, sometimes there might be a "natural experiment" that mimics such a random assignment. For example, the police department in Washington, DC, increases the number of police on the street during periods when there are security alerts concerning elevated risk of terrorist activity. Two economists examined the data on crime reports for these days and found that crime was substantially lower, particularly for auto theft.[3]

## Summary

1. Statistics can be used to summarize, estimate, test, and predict.

2. Omitted variable bias occurs when the analyst fails to include an important variable in the regression that is correlated with other variables. In this case the omitted variable is known as a confounding variable.

3. Observational data can only tell us about correlations, but we normally need experiments to determine causality.

---

[3] Jonathan Klick and Alexander Tababrok, "Using Terror Alert Levels to Estimate the Effect of Police on Crime," *Journal of Law and Economics* 48:1 (April 2005), 267–79.

4. However, in some cases there are natural experiments that can be useful in answering questions of interest.

5. It is important to distinguish between the effect of a policy that applies to the entire population and the effect of a policy that applies only to those who choose to participate.

6. In general, in evaluating a policy proposal, the experiment used should be as close as possible to the policy being considered.

## REVIEW QUESTIONS

1. When the *Titanic* sank in 1912, both male and female crew members had a higher survival rate than the third-class passengers. However, overall the third-class passengers had a higher survival rate than the crew. What do we call this phenomenon?

2. Suppose that you want to test the hypothesis that a coin has a probability of 1/2 of coming up heads when you flip it. You flip it 5 times and it comes up heads every time. How likely is it that you would see a pattern of 5 heads in a row if true probability of coming up heads is 1/2?

3. Suppose we estimate a demand function of the form $x = e^{c+bp}$, where $p$ is price, $x$ is the quantity consumed, and $b$ is a parameter. What is this functional form called?

# CHAPTER **18**

# AUCTIONS

Auctions are one of the oldest form of markets, dating back to at least 500 BC. Today, all sorts of commodities, from used computers to fresh flowers, are sold using auctions.

Economists became interested in auctions in the early 1970s when the OPEC oil cartel raised the price of oil. The U.S. Department of the Interior decided to hold auctions to sell the right to drill in coastal areas that were expected to contain vast amounts of oil. The government asked economists how to design these auctions, and private firms hired economists as consultants to help them design a bidding strategy. This effort prompted considerable research in auction design and strategy.

More recently, the Federal Communications Commission (FCC) decided to auction off parts of the radio spectrum for use by cellular phones, personal digital assistants, and other communication devices. Again, economists played a major role in the design of both the auctions and the strategies used by the bidders. These auctions were hailed as very successful public policy, resulting in revenues to the U.S. government of over twenty-three billion dollars to date.

Other countries have also used auctions for privatization projects. For example, Australia sold off several government-owned electricity plants, and New Zealand auctioned off parts of its state-owned telephone system.

Consumer-oriented auctions have also experienced something of a renaissance on the Internet. There are hundreds of auctions on the Internet, selling collectibles, computer equipment, travel services, and other items. OnSale claims to be the largest, reporting over forty-one million dollars worth of merchandise sold in 1997.

## 18.1 Classification of Auctions

The economic classification of auctions involves two considerations: first, what is the nature of the good that is being auctioned, and second, what are the rules of bidding? With respect to the nature of the good, economists distinguish between **private-value auctions** and **common-value auctions**.

In a private-value auction, each participant has a potentially different value for the good in question. A particular piece of art may be worth $500 to one collector, $200 to another, and $50 to yet another, depending on their taste. In a common-value auction, the good in question is worth essentially the same amount to every bidder, although the bidders may have different estimates of that common value. The auction for off-shore drilling rights described above had this characteristic: a given tract either had a certain amount of oil or not. Different oil companies may have had different estimates about how much oil was there, based on the outcomes of their geological surveys, but the oil had the same market value regardless of who won the auction.

We will spend most of the time in this chapter discussing private-value auctions, since they are the most familiar case. At the end of the chapter, we will describe some of the features of common-value auctions.

### Bidding Rules

The most prevalent form of bidding structure for an auction is the **English auction**. The auctioneer starts with a **reserve price**, which is the lowest price at which the seller of the good will part with it.[1] Bidders successively offer higher prices; generally each bid must exceed the previous bid by some minimal **bid increment**. When no participant is willing to increase the bid further, the item is awarded to the highest bidder.

Another form of auction is known as a **Dutch auction**, due to its use in the Netherlands for selling cheese and fresh flowers. In this case the auctioneer starts with a high price and gradually lowers it by steps until someone is willing to buy the item. In practice, the "auctioneer" is often

---

[1] See the footnote about "reservation price" in Chapter 6, which is essentially the same concept.

a mechanical device like a dial with a pointer which rotates to lower and lower values as the auction progresses. Dutch auctions can proceed very rapidly, which is one of their chief virtues.

Yet a third form of auctions is a **sealed-bid auction**. In this type of auction, each bidder writes down a bid on a slip of paper and seals it in an envelope. The envelopes are collected and opened, and the good is awarded to the person with the highest bid who then pays the auctioneer the amount that he or she bid. If there is a reserve price, and all bids are lower than the reserve price, then no one may receive the item.

Sealed-bid auctions are commonly used for construction work. The person who wants the construction work done requests bids from several contractors with the understanding that the job will be awarded to the contractor with the lowest bid.

Finally, we consider a variant on the sealed bid-auction that is known as the **philatelist auction** or **Vickrey auction**. The first name is due to the fact that this auction form was originally used by stamp collectors; the second name is in honor of William Vickrey, who received the 1996 Nobel prize for his pioneering work in analyzing auctions. The Vickrey auction is like the sealed-bid auction, with one critical difference: the good is awarded to the highest bidder, but at the *second-highest* price. In other words, the person who bids the most gets the good, but he or she only has to pay the bid made by the second-highest bidder. Though at first this sounds like a rather strange auction form, we will see below that it has some very nice properties.

## 18.2 Auction Design

Let us suppose that we have a single item to auction off and that there are $n$ bidders with (private) values $v_1, \ldots, v_n$. For simplicity, we assume that the values are all positive and that the seller has a zero value. Our goal is to choose an auction form to sell this item.

This is a special case of an **economic mechanism design** problem. In the case of the auction there are two natural goals that we might have in mind:

- **Pareto efficiency.** Design an auction that results in a Pareto efficient outcome.
- **Profit maximization.** Design an auction that yields the highest expected profit to the seller.

Profit maximization seems pretty straightforward, but what does Pareto efficiency mean in this context? It is not hard to see that Pareto efficiency requires that the good be assigned to the person with the highest value.

To see this, suppose that person 1 has the highest value and person 2 has some lower value for the good. If person 2 receives the good, then there is an easy way to make both 1 and 2 better off: transfer the good from person 2 to person 1 and have person 1 pay person 2 some price $p$ that lies between $v_1$ and $v_2$. This shows that assigning the good to anyone but the person who has the highest value cannot be Pareto efficient.

If the seller knows the values $v_1, \ldots, v_n$ the auction design problem is pretty trivial. In the case of profit maximization, the seller should just award the item to the person with the highest value and charge him or her that value. If the desired goal is Pareto efficiency, the person with the highest value should still get the good, but the price paid could be any amount between that person's value and zero, since the distribution of the surplus does not matter for Pareto efficiency.

The more interesting case is when the seller does not know the buyers' values. How can one achieve efficiency or profit maximization in this case?

First consider Pareto efficiency. It is not hard to see that an English auction achieves the desired outcome: the person with the highest value will end up with the good. It requires only a little more thought to determine the price that this person will pay: it will be the value of the *second-highest* bidder plus, perhaps, the minimal bid increment.

Think of a specific case where the highest value is, say $100, the second-highest value is $80, and the bid increment is, say, $5. Then the person with the $100 valuation would be willing to bid $85, while the person with the $80 value would not. Just as we claimed, the person with the highest valuation gets the good, at the second highest price (plus, perhaps, the bid increment). (We keep saying "perhaps" since if both players bid $80 there would be a tie and the exact outcome would depend on the rule used for tie-breaking.)

What about profit maximization? This case turns out to be more difficult to analyze since it depends on the *beliefs* that the seller has about the buyers' valuations. To see how this works, suppose that there are just two bidders either of whom could have a value of $10 or $100 for the item in question. Assume these two cases are equally likely, so that there are four equally probable arrangements for the values of bidders 1 and 2: (10,10), (10,100), (100,10), (100,100). Finally, suppose that the minimal bid increment is $1 and that ties are resolved by flipping a coin.

In this example, the winning bids in the four cases described above will be (10,11,11,100) and the bidder with the highest value will always get the good. The expected revenue to the seller is $33 = $\frac{1}{4}(10 + 11 + 11 + 100)$.

Can the seller do better than this? Yes, if he sets an appropriate reservation price. In this case, the profit-maximizing reservation price is $100. Three-quarters of the time, the seller will sell the item for this price, and one-quarter of the time there will be no winning bid. This yields an expected revenue of $75, much higher than the expected revenue yielded by the English auction with no reservation price.

Note that this policy is *not* Pareto efficient, since one-quarter of the time no one gets the good. This is analogous to the deadweight loss of monopoly and arises for exactly the same reason.

The addition of the reservation price is very important if you are interested in profit maximization. In 1990, the New Zealand government auctioned off some of the spectrum for use by radio, television, and cellular telephones, using a Vickrey auction. In one case, the winning bid was NZ$100,000, but the second-highest bid was only NZ$6! This auction may have led to a Pareto efficient outcome, but it was certainly not revenue maximizing!

We have seen that the English auction with a zero reservation price guarantees Pareto efficiency. What about the Dutch auction? The answer here is not necessarily. To see this, consider a case with two bidders who have values of $100 and $80. If the high-value person believes (erroneously!) that the second-highest value is $70, he or she would plan to wait until the auctioneer reached, say, $75 before bidding. But, by then, it would be too late—the person with the second-highest value would have already bought the good at $80. In general, there is no guarantee that the good will be awarded to the person with the highest valuation.

The same holds for the case of a sealed-bid auction. The optimal bid for each of the agents depends on their *beliefs* about the values of the other agents. If those beliefs are inaccurate, the good may easily end up being awarded to someone who does not have the highest valuation.[2]

Finally, we consider the Vickrey auction—the variant on the sealed-bid auction where the highest bidder gets the item, but only has to pay the second-highest price.

First we observe that *if* everyone bids their true value for the good in question, the item will end up being awarded to the person with the highest value, who will pay a price equal to that of the person with the second-highest value. This is essentially the same as the outcome of the English auction (up to the bid increment, which can be arbitrarily small).

But is it optimal to state your true value in a Vickrey auction? We saw that for the standard sealed-bid auction, this is not generally the case. But the Vickrey auction is different: the surprising answer is that it is always in each player's interest to write down his or her true value.

To see why, let us look at the special case of two bidders, who have values $v_1$ and $v_2$ and write down bids of $b_1$ and $b_2$. The expected payoff to bidder 1 is:

$$\text{Prob}(b_1 \geq b_2)[v_1 - b_2],$$

---

[2] On the other hand, if all players' beliefs are accurate, on average, and all bidders play optimally, the various auction forms described above turn out to yield the same allocation and the same expected price in equilibrium. For a detailed analysis, see P. Milgrom, "Auctions and Bidding: a Primer," *Journal of Economic Perspectives*, **3**(3), 1989, 3–22, and P. Klemperer, "Auction Theory: A Guide to the Literature," *Economic Surveys*, **13**(3), 1999, 227–286.

where "Prob" stands for "probability."

The first term in this expression is the probability that bidder 1 has the highest bid; the second term is the consumer surplus that bidder 1 enjoys if he wins. (If $b_1 < b_2$, then bidder 1 gets a surplus of 0, so there is no need to consider the term containing $\text{Prob}(b_1 \leq b_2)$.)

Suppose that $v_1 > b_2$. Then bidder 1 wants to make the probability of winning as large as possible, which he can do by setting $b_1 = v_1$. Suppose, on the other hand, that $v_1 < b_2$. Then bidder 1 wants to make the probability of winning as small as possible, which he can do by setting $b_1 = v_1$. In either case, an optimal strategy for bidder 1 is to set his bid equal to his true value! Honesty is the best policy ... at least in a Vickrey auction!

The interesting feature of the Vickrey auction is that it achieves essentially the same outcome as an English auction, but without the iteration. This is apparently why it was used by stamp collectors. They sold stamps at their conventions using English auctions and via their newsletters using sealed-bid auctions. Someone noticed that the sealed-bid auction would mimic the outcome of the English auctions if they used the second-highest bid rule. But it was left to Vickrey to conduct the full-fledged analysis of the philatelist auction and show that truth-telling was the optimal strategy and that the philatelist auction was equivalent to the English auction.

## EXAMPLE: Goethe's auction

In 1797 the German poet Johann Wolfgang von Goethe completed a poem that he wanted to offer to a publisher. He sent one of the possible publishers a letter that contained this passage:

> I am inclined to offer Mr. Vieweg from Berlin an epic poem, *Hermann and Dorothea,* which will have approximately 2000 hexameters ... Concerning the royalty we will proceed as follows: I will hand over to Mr. Counsel Böttiger a sealed note which contains my demand, and I wait for what Mr. Vieweg will suggest to offer for my work. If his offer is lower than my demand, then I take my note back, unopened, and the negotiation is broken. If, however, his offer is higher, then I will not ask for more than what is written in the note to be opened by Mr. Böttiger.

In essence this is a Vickrey auction. The publisher's dominant strategy is to name his true value, which will allow him to acquire the book only if Goethe's reserve price is less than his true value.

It was a great plan, but Goethe's lawyer, Böttiger, leaked the price in the sealed envelope, which was 1,000 thalers.[3] The publisher therefore bid the

---

[3] This refers to currency used at the time in Germany and is the ancestor of the term "dollars."

minimal amount and ended up making an estimated profit of 2,600 thalers.

Goethe was apparently suspicious that something was amiss, so the next time he wanted to sell a work, he set up a competitive auction involving 36 publishers and ended up doing much better.[4]

## 18.3 Other Auction Forms

The Vickrey auction was thought to be only of limited interest until online auctions became popular. The world's largest online auction house, eBay, claims to have almost 30 million registered users who, in 2000, traded $5 billion worth of merchandise.

Auctions run by eBay last for several days, or even weeks, and it is inconvenient for users to monitor the auction process continually. In order to avoid constant monitoring, eBay introduced an automated **bidding agent**, which they call a **proxy bidder**. Users tell their bidding agent the most they are willing to pay for an item and an initial bid. As the bidding progresses, the agent automatically increases a participant's bid by the minimal bid increment when necessary, as long as this doesn't raise the participant's bid over his or her maximum.

Essentially this is a Vickrey auction: each user reveals to their bidding agent the maximum price he or she is willing to pay. In theory, the participant who enters the highest bid will win the item but will only have to pay the second-highest bid (plus a minimal bid increment to break the tie.) According to the analysis in the text, each bidder has an incentive to reveal his or her true value for the item being sold.

In practice, bidder behavior is a bit different than that predicted by the Vickrey model. Often bidders wait until close to the end of the auction to enter their bids. This behavior appears to be for two distinct reasons: a reluctance to reveal interest too early in the game, and the hope to snatch up a bargain in an auction with few participants. Nevertheless, the bidding agent model seems to serve users very well. The Vickrey auction, which was once thought to be only of theoretical interest, is now the preferred method of bidding for the world's largest online auction house!

There are even more exotic auction designs in use. One peculiar example is the **escalation auction**. In this type of auction, the highest bidder wins the item, but the highest and the second-highest bidders *both* have to pay the amount they bid.

Suppose, for example, that you auction off 1 dollar to a number of bidders under the escalation auction rules. Typically a few people bid 10 or 15 cents, but eventually most of the bidders drop out. When the highest bid

---

[4] See the entire story in Benny Moldovanu and Manfred Tietzel, "Goethe's Second-Price Auction," *The Journal of Political Economy*, Vol. 106, No. 4 (Aug.1998), pp. 854–859.

approaches 1 dollar, the remaining bidders begin to catch on to the problem they face. If one has bid 90 cents, and the other 85 cents, the low bidder realizes that if he stays put, he will pay 85 cents and get nothing but, if he escalates to 95 cents, he will walk away with a nickel.

But once he has done this, the bidder who was at 90 cents can reason the same way. In fact, it is in her interest to bid *over* a dollar. If, for example, she bids $1.05 (and wins), she will lose only 5 cents rather than 90 cents! It's not uncommon to see the winning bid end up at $5 or $6.

A somewhat related auction is the **everyone pays auction**. Think of a crooked politician who announces that he will sell his vote under the following conditions: all the lobbyists contribute to his campaign, but he will vote for the appropriations favored by the highest contributor. This is essentially an auction where everyone pays but only the high bidder gets what she wants!

## EXAMPLE: Late Bidding on eBay

According to standard auction theory eBay's proxy bidder should induce people to bid their true value for an item. The highest bidder wins at (essentially) the second highest bid, just as in a Vickrey auction. But it doesn't work quite like that in practice. In many auctions, participants wait until virtually the last minute to place their bids. In one study, 37 percent of the auctions had bids in the last minute and 12 percent had bids in the last 10 seconds. Why do we see so many "late bids"?

There are at least two theories to explain this phenomenon. Patrick Bajari and Ali Hortaçsu, two auction experts, argue that for certain sorts of auctions, people don't want to bid early to avoid driving up the selling price. EBay typically displays the bidder identification and actual bids (not the maximum bids) for items being sold. If you are an expert on rare stamps, with a well-known eBay member name, you may want to hold back placing your bid so as not to reveal that you are interested in a particular stamp.

This explanation makes a lot of sense for collectibles such as stamps and coins, but late bidding also occurs in auctions for generic items, such as computer parts. Al Roth and Axel Ockenfels suggest that late bidding is a way to avoiding bidding wars.

Suppose that you and someone else are bidding for a Pez dispenser with a seller's reserve price of $2. It happens that you each value the dispenser at $10. If you both bid early, stating your true maximum value of $10, then even if the tie is resolved in your favor you end up paying $10—since that is also the other bidder's maximum value. You may "win" but you don't get any consumer surplus!

Alternatively, suppose that each of you waits until the auction is almost over and then bids $10 in the last possible seconds of the auction. (At eBay, this is called "sniping.") In this case, there's a good chance that one of the bids won't get through, so the winner ends up paying only the seller's reserve price of $2.

Bidding high at the last minute introduces some randomness into the outcome. One of the players gets a great deal and the other gets nothing. But that's not necessarily so bad: if they both bid early, one of the players ends up paying his full value and the other gets nothing.

In this analysis, the late bidding is a form of "implicit collusion." By waiting to bid, and allowing chance to play a role, bidders can end up doing substantially better on average than they do by bidding early.

## 18.4 Position Auctions

A **position auction** is a way to auction off positions, such as a position in a line or a position on a web page. The defining characteristic is that all players rank the positions in the same way, but they may value the positions differently. Everybody would agree that it is better to be in the front of the line than further back, but they could be willing to pay different amounts to be first in line.

One prominent example of a position auction is the auction used by search engine providers such as Google, Microsoft, and Yahoo to sell ads. In this case all advertisers agree that being in the top position is best, the second from the top position is second best, and so on. However, the advertisers are often selling different things, so the expected profit that they will get from a visitor to their web page will differ.

Here we describe a simplified version of these online ad auctions. Details differ across search engines, but the model below captures the general behavior.

We suppose that there are $s = 1, \ldots, S$ slots where ads can be displayed. Let $x_s$ denote the number of clicks that an ad can expect to receive in slot $s$. We assume that slots are ordered with respect to the number of clicks they are likely to receive, so $x_1 > x_2 > \cdots > x_S$.

Each of the advertisers has a value per click, which is related to the expected profit it can get from a visitor to its web site. Let $v_s$ be the value per click of the advertiser whose ad is shown in slot $s$.

Each advertiser states a bid, $b_s$, which is interpreted as the amount it is willing to pay for slot $s$. The best slot (slot 1) is awarded to the advertiser with the highest bid, the second-best slot (slot 2) is awarded to the advertiser with the second highest bid, and so on.

The price that an advertiser pays for a bid is determined by the bid of the advertiser below him. This is a variation on the Vickrey auction model described earlier and is sometimes known as a **generalized second price auction** or GSP.

In the GSP, advertiser 1 pays $b_2$ per click, advertiser 2 pays $b_3$ per click, and so on. The rationale for this arrangement is that if an advertiser paid the price it bid, it would have an incentive to cut its bid until it just beat the advertiser below it. By setting the payment of the advertiser in slot $s$ to be the bid of the advertiser in slot $s+1$, each advertiser ends up paying the minimum bid necessary to retain its position.

Putting these pieces together, we see that the profit of the advertiser in slot $s$ is $(v_s - b_{s+1})x_s$. This is just the value of the clicks minus the cost of the clicks that an advertiser receives.

What is the equilibrium of this auction? Extrapolating from the Vickrey auction, one might speculate that each advertiser should bid its true value. This is true if there is only one slot being auctioned, but is false in general.

## Two Bidders

Let us look at the case of 2 slots and 2 bidders. We assume that the high bidder gets $x_1$ clicks and pays the bid of the second highest bidder $b_2$. The second highest bidder gets slot 2 and pays a reserve price $r$.

Suppose your value is $v$ and you bid $b$. If $b > b_2$ you get a payoff of $(v - b_2)x_1$ and if $b \leq b_2$ you get a payoff of $(v - r)x_2$. Your expected payoff is then

$$\text{Prob}(b > b_2)(v - b_2)x_1 + [1 - \text{Prob}(b > b_2)](v - r)x_2.$$

We can rearrange your expected payoff to be

$$(v - r)x_2 + \text{Prob}(b > b_2)[v(x_1 - x_2) + rx_2 - b_2x_1] \qquad (18.1)$$

Note that when the term in the brackets is positive (i.e., you make a profit), you want the probability that $b > b_2$ to be as large as possible, and when the term is negative (you make a loss) you want the probability that $b > b_2$ to be as small as possible.

However, this can easily be arranged. Simply choose a bid according to this formula:

$$bx_1 = v(x_1 - x_2) + rx_2.$$

Now it is easy to check that when $b > b_2$, the bracketed term in expression (18.1) is positive and when $b \leq b_2$ the bracketed term in (18.1) is negative or zero. Hence this bid will win the auction exactly when you want to win and lose it exactly when you want to lose.

Note that this bidding rule is a dominant strategy: each bidder wants to bid according to this formula, regardless of what the other player bids. This means, of course, that the auction ends up putting the bidder with the highest value in first place.

It is also easy to interpret the bid. If there are two bidders and two slots, the second highest bidder will always get the second slot and end up paying $rx_2$. The contest is about the *extra* clicks that the highest bidder gets. The bidder who has the highest value will win those clicks, but that bidder only has to pay the minimum amount necessary to beat the second highest bidder.

We see that in this auction, you don't want to bid your true value per click, but you do want to bid an amount that reflects your true value of the *incremental clicks* you are getting.

## More Than Two Bidders

What happens if there are more than two bidders? In this case, there will typically not be a dominant strategy equilibrium, but there will be a equilibrium in prices. Let us look at a situation with 3 slots and 3 bidders.

The bidder in slot 3 pays a reservation price $r$. In equilibrium, the bidder won't want to move up to slot 2, so

$$(v_3 - r)x_3 \geq (v_3 - p_2)x_2$$

or

$$v_3(x_2 - x_3) \leq p_2 x_2 - r x_3.$$

This inequality says that if the bidder prefers position 3 to position 2, the value of the extra clicks it gets in position 2 must be less than the cost of those extra clicks.

This inequality gives us a bound on the cost of clicks in position 2:

$$p_2 x_2 \leq r x_3 + v_3(x_2 - x_3). \tag{18.2}$$

Applying the same argument to the bidder in position 2, we have

$$p_1 x_1 \leq p_2 x_2 + v_2(x_1 - x_2). \tag{18.3}$$

Substituting inequality (18.2) into inequality (18.3) we have

$$p_1 x_1 \leq r x_3 + v_3(x_2 - x_3) + v_2(x_1 - x_2). \tag{18.4}$$

The total revenue in the auction is $p_1 x_1 + p_2 x_2 + p_3 x_3$. Adding together inequality (18.2), inequality (18.3), and the revenue for slot 3 we have a lower bound on the total revenue in the auction

$$R_L \leq v_2(x_1 - x_2) + 2v_3(x_2 - x_3) + 3r x_3.$$

So far, we have looked at 3 bidders for 3 slots. What happens if there are 4 bidders for the 3 slots? In this case the reserve price is replaced by the value of the fourth bidder. The logic is that the fourth bidder is willing to buy any clicks that exceed its value, just as with the standard Vickrey auction. This gives us a revenue expression of

$$R_L \leq v_2(x_1 - x_2) + 2v_3(x_2 - x_3) + 3v_4x_3.$$

We note a few things about this expression. First, the competition in the search engine auction is about incremental clicks: how many clicks you get if you bid for a higher position. Second, the bigger the gap between clicks the larger the revenue. Third, when $v_4 > r$ the revenue will be larger. This simply says that competition tends to increase revenue.

## Quality Scores

In practice, the bids are multiplied by a **quality score** to get an auction ranking score. The ad with the highest bid times quality gets first position, the second-highest ranking ad gets the second position, and so on. Each ad pays the minimum price per click necessary to retain its position. If we let $q_s$ be the quality of the ad in slot $s$, the ads are ordered by $b_1q_1 > b_2q_s > b_3q_3 \cdots$ and so on.

The price that the ad in slot 1 pays is just enough to retain its position, so $p_1q_1 = b_2q_2$, or $p_1 = b_2q_2/q_1$. (There may be some rounding to break ties.)

There are several components of ad quality. However, the major component is typically the historical clickthrough rate that an ad gets. This means that ad rank is basically determined by

$$\frac{\text{cost}}{\text{clicks}} \times \frac{\text{clicks}}{\text{impressions}} = \frac{\text{cost}}{\text{impressions}}$$

Hence the ad that gets first place will be the one that is willing to pay the most per impression (i.e., ad view) rather than price per click.

When you think about it, this makes a lot of sense. Suppose one advertiser is willing to pay \$10 per click but is likely to get only 1 click in a day. Another advertiser is willing to pay \$1 per click will get 100 clicks in a day. Which ad should be shown in the most prominent position?

Ranking ads in this way also helps the users. If two ads have the same bid, then the one that users tend to click on more will get a higher position. Users can "vote with their clicks" for the ads that they find the most useful.

## 18.5 Should you advertise on your brand?

One question that sometimes arises in online ad auctions is whether advertisers should advertise on their own brand? This is particularly important for advertisers who have strong, well-known brands since they tend to be shown high up in the organic search results. Why should a well-known brand pay for ad clicks when it would get organic clicks anyway?

Let us examine this question using a little algebra. As above, we let $v$ be the value of a click (a visit to the website), which we will assume is the same for an organic click and an ad click. Let $x_a$ be the number of ad clicks, $x_{oa}$ be the number of organic clicks when an ad is present, and $x_{on}$ be the number of organic clicks when the ad is not present. Finally, let $c(x_a)$ be the cost of $x_a$ ad clicks.

If the website owner chooses to advertise, it has a profit of $vx_a + vx_{oa} - c(x_a)$. Note that advertiser gets both ad clicks and search results clicks, but only pays for the ad clicks. If the website owner chooses not to advertise, it gets $vx_{on}$. Putting these two expressions together, we see that the website owner will find it profitable to advertise when:

$$vx_a + vx_{oa} - c(x_a) > vx_{on},$$

where we have assumed the numerator is positive. Collecting terms, we see that the website owner will want to advertise when

$$v > \frac{c(x_a)}{x_a - (x_{on} - x_{oa})}.$$

The important piece of this expression is $x_{on} - x_{oa}$, which measures how the ad "cannibalizes" the organic clicks. If there is no cannibalization, so that $x_{on} = x_{oa}$, then the expression just reduces to "value greater than average cost." On the other hand, if there is a large amount of cannibalization, the value of a visitor would have to be high to overcome the reduction in organic clicks.

## 18.6 Auction revenue and number of bidders

It is interesting to see how the auction revenue changes as the number of bidders increases. Suppose that there is some distribution of values by the buyers, and we end up with a random draw of $n$ bidders for the auction, who have values $(v_1, \ldots, v_n)$. To keep things simple, suppose the reserve price is 0. If we have only one bidder, his value is $v_1$ and he gets the item for free. If we draw another bidder from the population, he has probability $1/2$ of having a larger bid than $v_1$ and the expected revenue is $\min(v_1, v_2)$. If we draw a third bidder, there is a $1/3$ probability that he has the maximum bid, and so it goes.

The general principle is that the expected revenue will keep increasing as the number of bidders increases, but it will do so at a slower rate. The expected revenue will be the expected value of the second-largest valuation in a sample of size $n$, a number known as the **second order statistic**. If we specify a particular distribution of values, we can see how this evolves as we add more participants to the auction.

Figure 18.1 depicts an example of what the expected revenue looks like if the values are distributed uniformly on the interval $[0, 1]$. As you can see, by the time there are 10 or so bidders, the expected value is pretty close to 1, illustrating that auctions are a pretty good way to generate revenue.

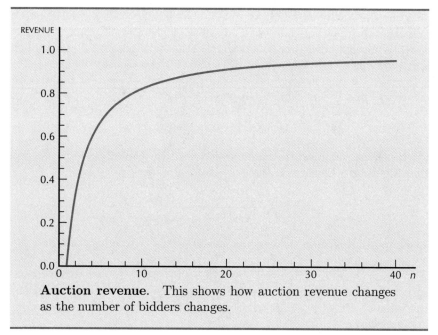

**Figure 18.1**

**Auction revenue.** This shows how auction revenue changes as the number of bidders changes.

## 18.7 Problems with Auctions

We've seen above that English auctions (or Vickrey auctions) have the desirable property of achieving Pareto efficient outcomes. This makes them attractive candidates for resource allocation mechanisms. In fact, most of the airwave auctions used by the FCC were variants on the English auction.

But English auctions are not perfect. They are still susceptible to collusion. The example of pooling in auction markets, described in Chapter 25, shows how antique dealers in Philadelphia colluded on their bidding strategies in auctions.

There are also various ways to manipulate the outcome of auctions. In the analysis described earlier, we assumed that a bid *committed* the bidder to pay. However, some auction designs allow bidders to drop out once the winning bids are revealed. Such an option allows for manipulation. For example, in 1993 the Australian government auctioned off licenses for satellite-television services using a standard sealed-bid auction. The winning bid for one of the licenses, A\$212 million, was made by a company called Ucom. Once the government announced Ucom had won, they proceeded to default on their bid, leaving the government to award the license to the second-highest bidder—which was also Ucom! They defaulted on this bid as well; four months later, after several more defaults, they paid A\$117 million for the license, which was A\$95 million less than their initial winning bid! The license ended up being awarded to the highest bidder at the second-highest price—but the poorly designed auction caused at least a year delay in bringing pay-TV to Australia.[5]

## EXAMPLE: Taking Bids Off the Wall

One common method for manipulating auctions is for the seller to take fictitious bids, a practice known as "taking bids off the wall." Such manipulation has found its way to online auctions as well, even where no walls are involved.

According to a recent news story,[6] a New York jeweler sold large quantities of diamonds, gold, and platinum jewelry online. Though the items were offered on eBay with no reserve price, the seller distributed spreadsheets to his employees which instructed them to place bids in order to increase the final sales price. According to the lawsuit, the employees placed over 232,000 bids in a one-year period, inflating the selling prices by 20% on average.

When confronted with the evidence, the jeweler agreed to pay a \$400,000 fine to settle the civil fraud complaint.

## 18.8 The Winner's Curse

We turn now to the examination of **common-value auctions**, where the good that is being awarded has the *same* value to all bidders. However, each of the bidders may have different estimates of that value. To emphasize this, let us write the (estimated) value of bidder $i$ as $v + \epsilon_i$ where $v$ is the

---

[5] See John McMillan, "Selling Spectrum Rights," *Journal of Economic Perspectives*, **8**(3), 145–152, for details of this story and how its lessons were incorporated into the design of the U.S. spectrum auction. This article also describes the New Zealand example mentioned earlier.

[6] Barnaby J. Feder, "Jeweler to Pay \$400,000 in Online Auction Fraud Settlement," *New York Times*, June 9, 2007.

true, common value and $\epsilon_i$ is the "error term" associated with bidder $i$'s estimate.

Let's examine a sealed-bid auction in this framework. What bid should bidder $i$ place? To develop some intuition, let's see what happens if each bidder bids their estimated value. In this case, the person with the highest value of $\epsilon_i$, $\epsilon_{max}$, gets the good. But as long as $\epsilon_{max} > 0$, this person is paying more than $v$, the true value of the good. This is the so-called **Winner's Curse**. If you win the auction, it is because you have overestimated the value of the good being sold. In other words, you have won only because you were too optimistic!

The *optimal* strategy in a common-value auction like this is to bid less than your estimated value—and the more bidders there are, the lower you want your own bid to be. Think about it: if you are the highest bidder out of five bidders you may be overly optimistic, but if you are the highest bidder out of twenty bidders you must be *super* optimistic. The more bidders there are, the more humble you should be about your own estimates of the "true value" of the good in question.

The Winner's Curse seemed to be operating in the FCC's May 1996 spectrum auction for personal communications services. The largest bidder in that auction, NextWave Personal Communications Inc., bid \$4.2 billion for sixty-three licenses, winning them all. However, in January 1998 the company filed for Chapter Eleven bankruptcy protection, after finding itself unable to pay its bills.

## 18.9 Stable Marriage Problem

There are many examples of **two-sided matching models** where consumers are matched up with each other. Men may be matched with women by a dating service or matchmaker, students may be matched with colleges, pledges may be matched with sororities, interns matched with hospitals, and so on.

What are good algorithms for making such matches? Do "stable" outcomes always exist? Here we examine a simple mechanism for making matches that are stable in a precisely defined sense.

Let us suppose that there are $n$ men and an equal number of women and we need to match them up as dancing partners. Each woman can rank the men according to her preferences and the same goes for the men. For simplicity, let us suppose that there are no ties in these rankings and that everyone would prefer to dance than to sit on the sidelines.

What is a good way to arrange for dancing partners? One attractive criterion is to find a way to produce a "stable" matching. The definition of stable, in this context, is that there is no couple that would prefer each other to their current partner. Said another way, if a man prefers another woman to his current partner, that woman wouldn't want him—she would prefer the partner she currently had.

Does a stable matching always exist? If so, how can one be found? The answer is that, contrary to the impression one would get from soap operas and romance novels, there always are stable matchings and they are relatively easy to construct.

The most famous algorithm, known as the **deferred acceptance algorithm**, goes like this.[7]

Step 1. Each man proposes to his most preferred woman.

Step 2. Each woman records the list of proposals she receives on her dance card.

Step 3. After all men have proposed to their most-preferred choice, each woman (gently) rejects all of the suitors except for her most preferred.

Step 4. The rejected suitors propose to the next woman on their lists.

Step 5. Continue to step 2 or terminate the algorithm when every woman has received an offer.

This algorithm always produce a stable matching. Suppose, to the contrary, that there is some man that prefers another woman to his present partner. Then he would have invited her to dance before his current partner. If she preferred him to her current partner, she would have rejected her current partner earlier in the process.

It turns out that this algorithm yields the best possible stable matching for the men in the sense that each man prefers the outcome of this matching process to any other stable matching. Of course, if we flipped the roles of men and women, we would find the woman-optimal stable matching.

Though the example described is slightly frivolous, processes like the deferred acceptance algorithm are used to match students to schools in Boston and New York, residents to hospitals nationwide, and even organ donors to recipients.

## 18.10 Mechanism Design

Auctions and the two-sided matching model that we have discussed in this chapter are examples of **economic mechanisms**. The idea of an economic

---

[7] Gale, David, and Lloyd Shapley [1962], "College Admissions and the Stability of Marriage," *American Mathematical Monthly,* 69, 9-15.

mechanism is to define a "game" or "market" that will yield some desired outcome.

For example, one might want to design a mechanism to sell a painting. A natural mechanism here would be an auction. But even with an auction, there are many design choices. Should it be designed to maximize efficiency (i.e., to ensure that the painting goes to the person who values it most highly) or should it be designed to maximize expected revenue for the seller, even if there is a risk that the painting may not be sold?

We've seen earlier that there are several different types of auctions, each with advantages and disadvantages. Which one is best in a particular circumstance?

Mechanism design is essentially the inverse of **game theory**. With game theory, we are given a description of the rules of the game and want to determine what the outcome will be. With mechanism design, we are given a description of the outcome that we want to reach and try to design a game that will reach it.[8]

Mechanism design is not limited to auctions or matching problems. It also includes **voting mechanisms** and **public goods** mechanisms, such as those described in Chapter 37, or **externality** mechanisms, such as those described in Chapter 35.

In a general mechanism, we think of a number of agents (i.e., consumers or firms) who each have some private information. In the case of an auction, this private information might be their value for the item being auctioned. In a problem involving firms, the private information might be their cost functions.

The agents report some message about their private information to the "center," which we might think of as an auctioneer. The center examines the messages and reports some outcome: who receives the item in question, what output firms should produce, how much various parties have to pay or be paid, and so on.

The major design decisions are 1) what sort of messages should be sent to the center and 2) what rule the center should use to determine the outcome. The constraints on the problem are the usual sort of resource constraints (i.e., there is only one item to be sold) and the constraints that the individuals will act in their own self-interest. This latter constraint is known as the **incentive compatibility constraint**.

There may be other constraints as well. For example, we may want the agents to participate voluntarily in the mechanism, which would require that they get at least as high a payoff from participating as not participating. We will ignore this constraint for simplicity.

To get a flavor of what mechanism design looks like, let us consider a simple problem of awarding an indivisible good to one of two different

---

[8] The 2007 Nobel Prize in Economics was awarded to Leo Hurwicz, Roger Myerson, and Eric Maskin for their contributions to economic mechanism design.

agents. Let $(x_1, x_2) = (1, 0)$ if agent 1 gets the good and $(x_1, x_2) = (0, 1)$ if agent 2 gets the good. Let $p$ be the price paid for the good.

We suppose that the message that each agent sends to the center is just a reported value for the good. This is known as a **direct revelation mechanism**. The center will then award the good to the agent with the highest reported value and charge that agent some price $p$.

What are the constraints on $p$? Suppose agent 1 has the highest value. Then his message to the center should be such that the payoff he gets in response to that message is at least as large as the payoff he would get if he sent the same message as agent 2 (who gets a zero payoff). This says

$$v_1 - p \geq 0.$$

By the same token, agent 2 must get at least as large a payoff from his message as he would get if he sent the message sent by agent 1 (which resulted in agent 1 getting the good). This says

$$0 \geq v_2 - p.$$

Putting these two conditions together, we have $v_1 \geq p \geq v_2$, which says that the price charged by the center must lie between the highest and second-highest value.

In order to determine which price the center must charge, we need to consider its objects and its information. If the center believes that the $v_1$ can be arbitrarily close to $v_2$ and it always wants to award the item to the highest bidder, then it has to set a price of $v_2$.

This is just the **Vickrey auction** described earlier, in which each party submits a bid and the item is awarded to the highest bidder at the second-highest bid. This is clearly an attractive mechanism for this particular problem.

## Summary

1. Auctions have been used for thousands of years to sell things.

2. If each bidder's value is independent of the other bidders, the auction is said to be a private-value auction. If the value of the item being sold is essentially the same for everyone, the auction is said to be a common-value auction.

3. Common auction forms are the English auction, the Dutch auction, the sealed-bid auction, and the Vickrey auction.

4. English auctions and Vickrey auctions have the desirable property that their outcomes are Pareto efficient.

5. Profit-maximizing auctions typically require a strategic choice of the reservation price.

6. Despite their advantages as market mechanisms, auctions are vulnerable to collusion and other forms of strategic behavior.

## REVIEW QUESTIONS

1. Consider an auction of antique quilts to collectors. Is this a private-value or a common-value auction?

2. Suppose that there are only two bidders with values of $8 and $10 for an item with a bid increment of $1. What should the reservation price be in a profit-maximizing English auction?

3. Suppose that we have two copies of *Intermediate Microeconomics* to sell to three (enthusiastic) students. How can we use a sealed-bid auction that will guarantee that the bidders with the two highest values get the books?

4. Consider the Ucom example in the text. Was the auction design efficient? Did it maximize profits?

5. A game theorist fills a jar with pennies and auctions it off on the first day of class using an English auction. Is this a private-value or a common-value auction? Do you think the winning bidder usually makes a profit?

# CHAPTER **19**

# TECHNOLOGY

In this chapter we begin our study of firm behavior. The first thing to do is to examine the constraints on a firm's behavior. When a firm makes choices it faces many constraints. These constraints are imposed by its customers, by its competitors, and by nature. In this chapter we're going to consider the latter source of constraints: nature. Nature imposes the constraint that there are only certain feasible ways to produce outputs from inputs: there are only certain kinds of technological choices that are possible. Here we will study how economists describe these technological constraints.

If you understand consumer theory, production theory will be very easy since the same tools are used. In fact, production theory is much simpler than consumption theory because the output of a production process is generally observable, whereas the "output" of consumption (utility) is not directly observable.

## 19.1 Inputs and Outputs

Inputs to production are called **factors of production**. Factors of production are often classified into broad categories such as land, labor, capital, and raw materials. It is pretty apparent what labor, land, and raw materials mean, but capital may be a new concept. **Capital goods** are those inputs to production that are themselves produced goods. Basically capital goods are machines of one sort or another: tractors, buildings, computers, or whatever.

Sometimes capital is used to describe the money used to start up or maintain a business. We will always use the term **financial capital** for this concept and use the term capital goods, or **physical capital**, for produced factors of production.

We will usually want to think of inputs and outputs as being measured in *flow* units: a certain amount of labor per week and a certain number of machine hours per week will produce a certain amount of output a week.

We won't find it necessary to use the classifications given above very often. Most of what we want to describe about technology can be done without reference to the *kind* of inputs and outputs involved—just with the amounts of inputs and outputs.

## 19.2 Describing Technological Constraints

Nature imposes **technological constraints** on firms: only certain combinations of inputs are feasible ways to produce a given amount of output, and the firm must limit itself to technologically feasible production plans.

The easiest way to describe feasible production plans is to list them. That is, we can list all combinations of inputs and outputs that are technologically feasible. The set of all combinations of inputs and outputs that comprise a technologically feasible way to produce is called a **production set.**

Suppose, for example, that we have only one input, measured by $x$, and one output, measured by $y$. Then a production set might have the shape indicated in Figure 19.1. To say that some point $(x, y)$ is in the production set is just to say that it is technologically possible to produce $y$ amount of output if you have $x$ amount of input. The production set shows the *possible* technological choices facing a firm.

As long as the inputs to the firm are costly it makes sense to limit ourselves to examining the *maximum possible output* for a given level of input. This is the boundary of the production set depicted in Figure 19.1. The function describing the boundary of this set is known as the **production function.** It measures the maximum possible output that you can get from a given amount of input.

Of course, the concept of a production function applies equally well if there are several inputs. If, for example, we consider the case of two inputs, the production function $f(x_1, x_2)$ would measure the maximum amount of output $y$ that we could get if we had $x_1$ units of factor 1 and $x_2$ units of factor 2.

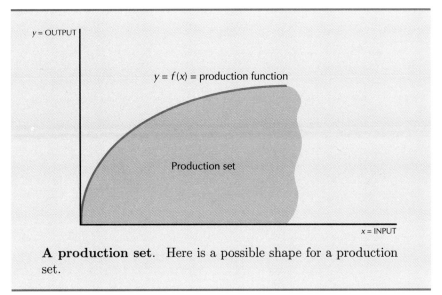

$y$ = OUTPUT

$y = f(x)$ = production function

Production set

$x$ = INPUT

**A production set.** Here is a possible shape for a production set.

Figure
19.1

In the two-input case there is a convenient way to depict production relations known as the **isoquant**. An isoquant is the set of all possible combinations of inputs 1 and 2 that are just sufficient to produce a given amount of output.

Isoquants are similar to indifference curves. As we've seen earlier, an indifference curve depicts the different consumption bundles that are just sufficient to produce a certain level of utility. But there is one important difference between indifference curves and isoquants. Isoquants are labeled with the amount of output they can produce, not with a utility level. Thus the labeling of isoquants is fixed by the technology and doesn't have the kind of arbitrary nature that the utility labeling has.

## 19.3 Examples of Technology

Since we already know a lot about indifference curves, it is easy to understand how isoquants work. Let's consider a few examples of technologies and their isoquants.

### Fixed Proportions

Suppose that we are producing holes and that the only way to get a hole is to use one man and one shovel. Extra shovels aren't worth anything, and neither are extra men. Thus the total number of holes that you can produce will be the minimum of the number of men and the number of shovels that you have. We write the production function as $f(x_1, x_2) = \min\{x_1, x_2\}$.

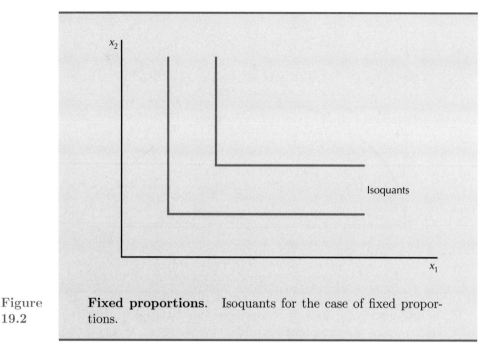

Isoquants

Figure
19.2        **Fixed proportions.**   Isoquants for the case of fixed proportions.

The isoquants look like those depicted in Figure 19.2. Note that these
isoquants are just like the case of perfect complements in consumer theory.

### Perfect Substitutes

Suppose now that we are producing homework and the inputs are red
pencils and blue pencils. The amount of homework produced depends only
on the total number of pencils, so we write the production function as
$f(x_1, x_2) = x_1 + x_2$. The resulting isoquants are just like the case of perfect
substitutes in consumer theory, as depicted in Figure 19.3.

### Cobb-Douglas

If the production function has the form $f(x_1, x_2) = Ax_1^a x_2^b$, then we say
that it is a **Cobb-Douglas production function**. This is just like the
functional form for Cobb-Douglas preferences that we studied earlier. The
numerical magnitude of the utility function was not important, so we set
$A = 1$ and usually set $a + b = 1$. But the magnitude of the production
function does matter so we have to allow these parameters to take arbitrary
values. The parameter $A$ measures, roughly speaking, the scale of production: how much output we would get if we used one unit of each input.
The parameters $a$ and $b$ measure how the amount of output responds to

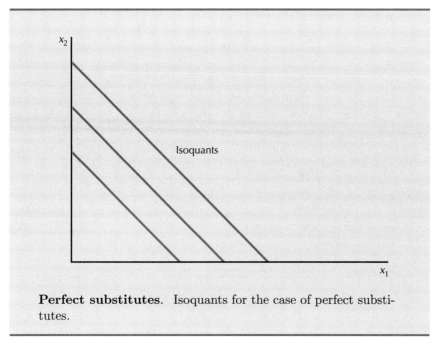

**Perfect substitutes.**  Isoquants for the case of perfect substitutes.                Figure
19.3

changes in the inputs. We'll examine their impact in more detail later on.
In some of the examples, we will choose to set $A = 1$ in order to simplify
the calculations.

The Cobb-Douglas isoquants have the same nice, well-behaved shape
that the Cobb-Douglas indifference curves have; as in the case of utility
functions, the Cobb-Douglas production function is about the simplest example of well-behaved isoquants.

## 19.4 Properties of Technology

As in the case of consumers, it is common to assume certain properties
about technology. First we will generally assume that technologies are
**monotonic**: if you increase the amount of at least one of the inputs, it
should be possible to produce at least as much output as you were producing originally. This is sometimes referred to as the property of **free
disposal**: if the firm can costlessly dispose of any inputs, having extra
inputs around can't hurt it.

Second, we will often assume that the technology is **convex**. This means
that if you have two ways to produce $y$ units of output, $(x_1, x_2)$ and $(z_1, z_2)$,
then their weighted average will produce *at least* $y$ units of output.

One argument for convex technologies goes as follows. Suppose that you
have a way to produce 1 unit of output using $a_1$ units of factor 1 and $a_2$

units of factor 2 and that you have another way to produce 1 unit of output using $b_1$ units of factor 1 and $b_2$ units of factor 2. We call these two ways to produce output **production techniques**.

Furthermore, let us suppose that you are free to scale the output up by arbitrary amounts so that $(100a_1, 100a_2)$ and $(100b_1, 100b_2)$ will produce 100 units of output. But now note that if you have $25a_1 + 75b_1$ units of factor 1 and $25a_2 + 75b_2$ units of factor 2 you can still produce 100 units of output: just produce 25 units of the output using the "a" technique and 75 units of the output using the "b" technique.

This is depicted in Figure 19.4. By choosing the level at which you operate each of the two activities, you can produce a given amount of output in a variety of different ways. In particular, every input combination along the line connecting $(100a_1, 100a_2)$ and $(100b_1, 100b_2)$ will be a feasible way to produce 100 units of output.

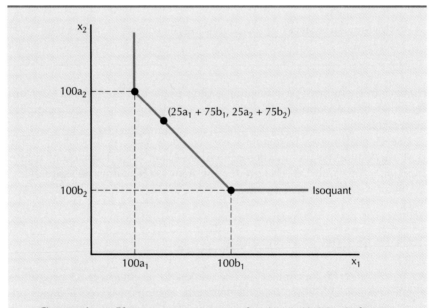

Figure
19.4

**Convexity**. If you can operate production activities independently, then weighted averages of production plans will also be feasible. Thus the isoquants will have a convex shape.

In this kind of technology, where you can scale the production process up and down easily and where separate production processes don't interfere with each other, convexity is a very natural assumption.

## 19.5 The Marginal Product

Suppose that we are operating at some point, $(x_1, x_2)$, and that we consider using a little bit more of factor 1 while keeping factor 2 fixed at the level $x_2$. How much more output will we get per additional unit of factor 1? This is described by the partial derivative of output with respect to factor 1:

$$\frac{\partial y}{\partial x_1} = \lim_{\Delta x_1 \to 0} \frac{f(x_1 + \Delta x_1, x_2) - f(x_1, x_2)}{\Delta x_1}.$$

We call this the **marginal product of factor 1**. The marginal product of factor 2 is defined in a similar way, and we denote them by $MP_1(x_1, x_2)$ and $MP_2(x_1, x_2)$, respectively.

Sometimes we will be a bit sloppy about the concept of marginal product and describe it as the extra output we get from having "one" more unit of factor 1. As long as "one" is small relative to the total amount of factor 1 that we are using, this will be satisfactory. But we should remember that a marginal product is a *rate*: the extra amount of output per unit of extra input.

The concept of marginal product is just like the concept of marginal utility that we described in our discussion of consumer theory, except for the ordinal nature of utility. Here, we are discussing physical output: the marginal product of a factor is a specific number, which can, in principle, be observed.

## 19.6 The Technical Rate of Substitution

Suppose that we are operating at some point $(x_1, x_2)$ and that we consider giving up a little bit of factor 1 and using just enough more of factor 2 to produce the same amount of output $y$. How much extra of factor 2, $\Delta x_2$, do we need if we are going to give up a little bit of factor 1, $\Delta x_1$? This is just the slope of the isoquant; we refer to it as the **technical rate of substitution (TRS)**, and denote it by $\text{TRS}(x_1, x_2)$.

The technical rate of substitution measures the tradeoff between two inputs in production. It measures the rate at which the firm will have to substitute one input for another in order to keep output constant.

To derive a formula for the TRS, we can use the same idea that we used to determine the slope of the indifference curve. Consider a change in our use of factors 1 and 2 that keeps output fixed. Then we have

$$\delta y = MP_1(x_1, x_2)\delta x_1 + MP_2(x_1, x_2)\delta x_2 = 0,$$

which we can solve to get

$$\text{TRS}(x_1, x_2) = \frac{\delta x_2}{\delta x_1} = -\frac{MP_1(x_1, x_2)}{MP_2(x_1, x_2)}.$$

Note the similarity with the definition of the marginal rate of substitution.

## 19.7 Diminishing Marginal Product

Suppose that we have certain amounts of factors 1 and 2 and we consider adding more of factor 1 while holding factor 2 fixed at a given level. What might happen to the marginal product of factor 1?

As long as we have a monotonic technology, we know that the total output will go up as we increase the amount of factor 1. But it is natural to expect that it will go up at a decreasing rate. Let's consider a specific example, the case of farming.

One man on one acre of land might produce 100 bushels of corn. If we add another man and keep the same amount of land, we might get 200 bushels of corn, so in this case the marginal product of an extra worker is 100. Now keep adding workers to this acre of land. Each worker may produce more output, but eventually the extra amount of corn produced by an extra worker will be less than 100 bushels. After 4 or 5 people are added the additional output per worker will drop to 90, 80, 70 ... or even fewer bushels of corn. If we get hundreds of workers crowded together on this one acre of land, an extra worker may even cause output to go down! As in the making of broth, extra cooks *can* make things worse.

Thus we would typically expect that the marginal product of a factor will diminish as we get more and more of that factor. This is called the **law of diminishing marginal product**. It isn't really a "law"; it's just a common feature of most kinds of production processes.

It is important to emphasize that the law of diminishing marginal product applies only when all *other* inputs are being held fixed. In the farming example, we considered changing only the labor input, holding the land and raw materials fixed.

## 19.8 Diminishing Technical Rate of Substitution

Another closely related assumption about technology is that of **diminishing technical rate of substitution**. This says that as we increase the amount of factor 1, and adjust factor 2 so as to stay on the same isoquant, the technical rate of substitution declines. Roughly speaking, the assumption of diminishing TRS means that the slope of an isoquant must decrease in absolute value as we move along the isoquant in the direction of increasing $x_1$, and it must increase as we move in the direction of increasing $x_2$. This means that the isoquants will have the same sort of convex shape that well-behaved indifference curves have.

The assumptions of a diminishing technical rate of substitution and diminishing marginal product are closely related but are not exactly the same. Diminishing marginal product is an assumption about how the marginal product changes as we increase the amount of one factor, *holding the other factor fixed.* Diminishing TRS is about how the *ratio* of the marginal products—the slope of the isoquant—changes as we increase the amount of one factor and *reduce the amount of the other factor so as to stay on the same isoquant.*

## 19.9 The Long Run and the Short Run

Let us return now to the original idea of a technology as being just a list of the feasible production plans. We may want to distinguish between the production plans that are *immediately* feasible and those that are *eventually* feasible.

In the **short run**, there will be some factors of production that are fixed at predetermined levels. Our farmer described above might only consider production plans that involve a fixed amount of land, if that is all he has access to. It may be true that if he had more land, he could produce more corn, but in the short run he is stuck with the amount of land that he has.

On the other hand, in the long run the farmer is free to purchase more land, or to sell some of the land he now owns. He can adjust the level of the land input so as to maximize his profits.

The economist's distinction between the long run and the short run is this: in the short run there is at least one factor of production that is fixed: a fixed amount of land, a fixed plant size, a fixed number of machines, or whatever. In the **long run**, *all* the factors of production can be varied.

There is no specific time interval implied here. What is the long run and what is the short run depends on what kinds of choices we are examining. In the short run at least some factors are fixed at given levels, but in the long run the amount used of these factors can be changed.

Let's suppose that factor 2, say, is fixed at $\bar{x}_2$ in the short run. Then the relevant production function for the short run is $f(x_1, \bar{x}_2)$. We can plot the functional relation between output and $x_1$ in a diagram like Figure 19.5.

Note that we have drawn the short-run production function as getting flatter and flatter as the amount of factor 1 increases. This is just the law of diminishing marginal product in action again. Of course, it can easily happen that there is an initial region of increasing marginal returns where the marginal product of factor 1 increases as we add more of it. In the case of the farmer adding labor, it might be that the first few workers added increase output more and more because they would be able to divide up jobs efficiently, and so on. But given the fixed amount of land, eventually the marginal product of labor will decline.

## 19.10 Returns to Scale

Now let's consider a different kind of experiment. Instead of increasing the amount of one input while holding the other input fixed, let's increase the

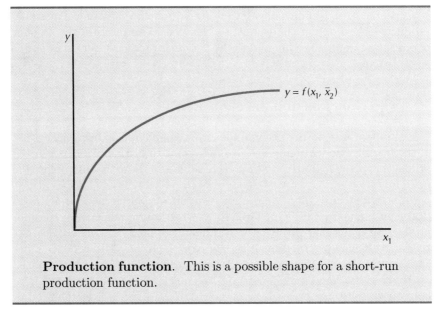

Figure
19.5

**Production function.** This is a possible shape for a short-run production function.

amount of *all* inputs to the production function. In other words, let's scale the amount of all inputs up by some constant factor: for example, use twice as much of both factor 1 and factor 2.

If we use twice as much of each input, how much output will we get? The most likely outcome is that we will get twice as much output. This is called the case of **constant returns to scale**. In terms of the production function, this means that two times as much of each input gives two times as much output. In the case of two inputs we can express this mathematically by

$$2f(x_1, x_2) = f(2x_1, 2x_2).$$

In general, if we scale all of the inputs up by some amount $t$, constant returns to scale implies that we should get $t$ times as much output:

$$tf(x_1, x_2) = f(tx_1, tx_2).$$

We say that this is the likely outcome for the following reason: it should typically be possible for the firm to *replicate* what it was doing before. If the firm has twice as much of each input, it can just set up two plants side by side and thereby get twice as much output. With three times as much of each input, it can set up three plants, and so on.

Note that it is perfectly possible for a technology to exhibit constant returns to scale and diminishing marginal product to each factor. **Returns to scale** describes what happens when you increase *all* inputs, while diminishing marginal product describes what happens when you increase *one* of the inputs and hold the others fixed.

Constant returns to scale is the most "natural" case because of the replication argument, but that isn't to say that other things might not happen. For example, it could happen that if we scale up both inputs by some factor $t$, we get *more* than $t$ times as much output. This is called the case of **increasing returns to scale**. Mathematically, increasing returns to scale means that

$$f(tx_1, tx_2) > tf(x_1, x_2).$$

for all $t > 1$.

What would be an example of a technology that had increasing returns to scale? One nice example is that of an oil pipeline. If we double the diameter of a pipe, we use twice as much materials, but the cross section of the pipe goes up by a factor of 4. Thus we will likely be able to pump more than twice as much oil through it.

(Of course, we can't push this example too far. If we keep doubling the diameter of the pipe, it will eventually collapse of its own weight. Increasing returns to scale usually just applies over some range of output.)

The other case to consider is that of **decreasing returns to scale**, where

$$f(tx_1, tx_2) < tf(x_1, x_2)$$

for all $t > 1$.

This case is somewhat peculiar. If we get less than twice as much output from having twice as much of each input, we must be doing something wrong. After all, we could just replicate what we were doing before!

The usual way in which diminishing returns to scale arises is because we forgot to account for some input. If we have twice as much of every input but one, we won't be able to exactly replicate what we were doing before, so there is no reason that we have to get twice as much output. Diminishing returns to scale is really a short-run phenomenon, with something being held fixed.

Of course, a technology can exhibit different kinds of returns to scale at different levels of production. It may well happen that for low levels of production, the technology exhibits increasing returns to scale—as you scale all the inputs by some small amount $t$, the output increases by *more* than $t$. Later on, for larger levels of output, increasing scale by $t$ may just increase output by the same factor $t$.

## EXAMPLE: Datacenters

Datacenters are large buildings that house thousands of computers used to perform tasks such as serving web pages. Internet companies such as Google, Yahoo, Microsoft, Amazon, and many others have built thousands of datacenters around the world.

A typical datacenter consists of hundreds of racks which hold computer motherboards that are similar to the motherboard in your desktop computer. Generally these systems are designed to be easily scalable so that the computational power of the data center can scale up or down just by adding or removing racks of computers.

The replication argument implies that the production function for computing services is effectively constant returns to scale: to double output, you simply double all inputs.

## EXAMPLE: Copy Exactly!

Intel operates dozens of "fab plants" that fabricate, assemble, sort, and test advanced computer chips. Chip fabrication is such a delicate process that Intel found it difficult to manage quality in a heterogeneous environment. Even minor variations in plant design, such as cleaning procedures or the length of cooling hoses, could have a large impact on the yield of the fab process.

In order to manage these very subtle effects, Intel moved to its Copy Exactly! process. According to Intel, the Copy Exactly directive is: "everything which might affect the process, or how it is run, is to be copied down to the finest detail, unless it is either physically impossible to do so, or there is an overwhelming competitive benefit to introducing a change."

This means that one Intel plant is very much like another, and deliberately so. As the replication argument suggests, the easiest way to scale up production at Intel is to replicate current operating procedures as closely as possible.

## Summary

1. The technological constraints of the firm are described by the production set, which depicts all the technologically feasible combinations of inputs and outputs, and by the production function, which gives the maximum amount of output associated with a given amount of the inputs.

2. Another way to describe the technological constraints facing a firm is through the use of isoquants—curves that indicate all the combinations of inputs capable of producing a given level of output.

3. We generally assume that isoquants are convex and monotonic, just like well–behaved preferences.

4. The marginal product measures the extra output per extra unit of an input, holding all other inputs fixed. We typically assume that the marginal product of an input diminishes as we use more and more of that input.

5. The technical rate of substitution (TRS) measures the slope of an iso-quant. We generally assume that the TRS diminishes as we move out along an isoquant—which is another way of saying that the isoquant has a convex shape.

6. In the short run some inputs are fixed, while in the long run all inputs are variable.

7. Returns to scale refers to the way that output changes as we change the *scale* of production. If we scale all inputs up by some amount $t$ and output goes up by the same factor, then we have constant returns to scale. If output scales up by more that $t$, we have increasing returns to scale; and if it scales up by less than $t$, we have decreasing returns to scale.

## REVIEW QUESTIONS

1. Consider the production function $f(x_1, x_2) = x_1^2 x_2^2$. Does this exhibit constant, increasing, or decreasing returns to scale?

2. Consider the production function $f(x_1, x_2) = 4x_1^{\frac{1}{2}} x_2^{\frac{1}{3}}$. Does this exhibit constant, increasing, or decreasing returns to scale?

3. The Cobb-Douglas production function is given by $f(x_1, x_2) = Ax_1^a x_2^b$. It turns out that the type of returns to scale of this function will depend on the magnitude of $a + b$. Which values of $a + b$ will be associated with the different kinds of returns to scale?

4. The technical rate of substitution between factors $x_2$ and $x_1$ is $-4$. If you desire to produce the same amount of output but cut your use of $x_1$ by 3 units, how many more units of $x_2$ will you need?

5. True or false? If the law of diminishing marginal product did not hold, the world's food supply could be grown in a flowerpot.

6. In a production process is it possible to have decreasing marginal product in an input and yet increasing returns to scale?

# CHAPTER 20

# PROFIT MAXIMIZATION

In the last chapter we discussed ways to describe the technological choices facing the firm. In this chapter we describe a model of how the firm chooses the amount to produce and the method of production to employ. The model we will use is the model of profit maximization: the firm chooses a production plan so as to maximize its profits.

In this chapter we will assume that the firm faces fixed prices for its inputs and outputs. We said earlier that economists call a market where the individual producers take the prices as outside their control a **competitive market**. So in this chapter we want to study the profit-maximization problem of a firm that faces competitive markets for the factors of production it uses and the output goods it produces.

## 20.1 Profits

**Profits** are defined as revenues minus cost. Suppose that the firm produces $n$ outputs $(y_1, \ldots, y_n)$ and uses $m$ inputs $(x_1, \ldots, x_m)$. Let the prices of the output goods be $(p_1, \ldots, p_n)$ and the prices of the inputs be $(w_1, \ldots, w_m)$.

The profits the firm receives, $\pi$, can be expressed as

$$\pi = \sum_{i=1}^{n} p_i y_i - \sum_{i=1}^{m} w_i x_i.$$

The first term is revenue, and the second term is cost.

In the expression for cost we should be sure to include *all* of the factors of production used by the firm, valued at their market price. Usually this is pretty obvious, but in cases where the firm is owned and operated by the same individual, it is possible to forget about some of the factors.

For example, if an individual works in his own firm, then his labor is an input and it should be counted as part of the costs. His wage rate is simply the market price of his labor—what he *would* be getting if he sold his labor on the open market. Similarly, if a farmer owns some land and uses it in his production, that land should be valued at its market value for purposes of computing the economic costs.

We have seen that economic costs like these are often referred to as **opportunity costs**. The name comes from the idea that if you are using your labor, for example, in one application, you forgo the opportunity of employing it elsewhere. Therefore those lost wages are part of the cost of production. Similarly with the land example: the farmer has the opportunity of renting his land to someone else, but he chooses to forgo that rental income in favor of renting it to himself. The lost rents are part of the opportunity cost of his production.

The economic definition of profit requires that we value all inputs and outputs at their opportunity cost. Profits as determined by accountants do not necessarily accurately measure economic profits, as they typically use historical costs—what a factor was purchased for originally—rather than economic costs—what a factor would cost if purchased now. There are many variations on the use of the term "profit," but we will always stick to the economic definition.

Another confusion that sometimes arises is due to getting time scales mixed up. We usually think of the factor inputs as being measured in terms of *flows*. So many labor hours per week and so many machine hours per week will produce so much output per week. Then the factor prices will be measured in units appropriate for the purchase of such flows. Wages are naturally expressed in terms of dollars per hour. The analog for machines would be the **rental rate**—the rate at which you can rent a machine for the given time period.

In many cases there isn't a very well-developed market for the rental of machines, since firms will typically buy their capital equipment. In this case, we have to compute the implicit rental rate by seeing how much it would cost to buy a machine at the beginning of the period and sell it at the end of the period.

## 20.2 The Organization of Firms

In a capitalist economy, firms are owned by individuals. Firms are only legal entities; ultimately it is the owners of firms who are responsible for the behavior of the firm, and it is the owners who reap the rewards or pay the costs of that behavior.

Generally speaking, firms can be organized as proprietorships, partnerships, or corporations. A **proprietorship** is a firm that is owned by a single individual. A **partnership** is owned by two or more individuals. A **corporation** is usually owned by several individuals as well, but under the law has an existence separate from that of its owners. Thus a partnership will last only as long as both partners are alive and agree to maintain its existence. A corporation can last longer than the lifetimes of any of its owners. For this reason, most large firms are organized as corporations.

The owners of each of these different types of firms may have different goals with respect to managing the operation of the firm. In a proprietorship or a partnership the owners of the firm usually take a direct role in actually managing the day-to-day operations of the firm, so they are in a position to carry out whatever objectives they have in operating the firm. Typically, the owners would be interested in maximizing the profits of their firm, but, if they have nonprofit goals, they can certainly indulge in these goals instead.

In a corporation, the owners of the corporation are often distinct from the managers of the corporation. Thus there is a separation of ownership and control. The owners of the corporation must define an objective for the managers to follow in their running of the firm, and then do their best to see that they actually pursue the goals the owners have in mind. Again, profit maximization is a common goal. As we'll see below, this goal, properly interpreted, is likely to lead the managers of the firm to choose actions that are in the interests of the owners of the firm.

## 20.3 Profits and Stock Market Value

Often the production process that a firm uses goes on for many periods. Inputs put in place at time $t$ pay off with a whole flow of services at later times. For example, a factory building erected by a firm could last for 50 or 100 years. In this case an input at one point in time helps to produce output at other times in the future.

In this case we have to value a flow of costs and a flow of revenues over time. As we've seen in Chapter 10, the appropriate way to do this is to use the concept of present value. When people can borrow and lend in financial markets, the interest rate can be used to define a natural price of consumption at different times. Firms have access to the same sorts of financial markets, and the interest rate can be used to value investment decisions in exactly the same way.

Consider a world of perfect certainty where a firm's flow of future profits is publicly known. Then the present value of those profits would be the **present value of the firm**. It would be how much someone would be willing to pay to purchase the firm.

As we indicated above, most large firms are organized as corporations, which means that they are jointly owned by a number of individuals. The corporation issues stock certificates to represent ownership of shares in the corporation. At certain times the corporation issues dividends on these shares, which represent a share of the profits of the firm. The shares of ownership in the corporation are bought and sold in the **stock market**. The price of a share represents the present value of the stream of dividends that people expect to receive from the corporation. The total stock market value of a firm represents the present value of the stream of profits that the firm is expected to generate. Thus the objective of the firm—maximizing the present value of the stream of profits the firm generates—could also be described as the goal of maximizing stock market value. In a world of certainty, these two goals are the same thing.

The owners of the firm will generally want the firm to choose production plans that maximize the stock market value of the firm, since that will make the value of the shares they hold as large as possible. We saw in Chapter 10 that whatever an individual's tastes for consumption at different times, he or she will always prefer an endowment with a higher present value to one with a lower present value. By maximizing stock market value, a firm makes its shareholders' budget sets as large as possible, and thereby acts in the best interests of all of its shareholders.

If there is uncertainty about a firm's stream of profits, then instructing managers to maximize profits has no meaning. Should they maximize expected profits? Should they maximize the expected utility of profits? What attitude toward risky investments should the managers have? It is difficult to assign a meaning to profit maximization when there is uncertainty present. However, in a world of uncertainty, maximizing *stock market value* still has meaning. If the managers of a firm attempt to make the value of the firm's shares as large as possible then they make the firm's owners—the shareholders—as well-off as possible. Thus maximizing stock market value gives a well-defined objective function to the firm in nearly all economic environments.

Despite these remarks about time and uncertainty, we will generally limit ourselves to the examination of much simpler profit-maximization problems, namely, those in which there is a single, certain output and a single period of time. This simple story still generates significant insights and builds the proper intuition to study more general models of firm behavior. Most of the ideas that we will examine carry over in a natural way to these more general models.

## 20.4 The Boundaries of the Firm

One question that constantly confronts managers of firms is whether to "make or buy." That is, should a firm make something internally or buy it from an external supplier? The question is broader than it sounds, as it can refer not only to physical goods, but also services of one sort or another. Indeed, in the broadest interpretation, "make or buy" applies to almost every decision a firm makes.

Should a company provide its own cafeteria? Janitorial services? Photocopying services? Travel assistance? Obviously, many factors enter into such decisions. One important consideration is size. A small mom-and-pop video store with 12 employees is probably not going to provide a cafeteria. But it might outsource janitorial services, depending on cost, capabilities, and staffing.

Even a large organization, which could easily afford to operate food services, may or may not choose to do so, depending on availability of alternatives. Employees of an organization located in a big city have access to many places to eat; if the organization is located in a remote area, choices may be fewer.

One critical issue is whether the goods or services in question are externally provided by a monopoly or by a competitive market. By and large, managers prefer to buy goods and services on a competitive market, if they are available. The second-best choice is dealing with an internal monopolist. The worse choice of all, in terms of price and quality of service, is dealing with an external monopolist.

Think about photocopying services. The ideal situation is to have dozens of competitive providers vying for your business; that way you will get cheap prices and high-quality service. If your school is large, or in an urban area, there may be many photocopying services vying for your business. On the other hand, small rural schools may have less choice and often higher prices.

The same is true of businesses. A highly competitive environment gives lots of choices to users. By comparison, an internal photocopying division may be less attractive. Even if prices are low, the service could be sluggish. But the least attractive option is surely to have to submit to a single external provider. An internal monopoly provider may have bad service, but at least the money stays inside the firm.

As technology changes, what is typically inside the firm changes. Forty years ago, firms managed many services themselves. Now they tend to outsource as much as possible. Food service, photocopying service, and janitorial services are often provided by external organizations that specialize in such activities. Such specialization often allows these companies to provide higher quality and less expensive services to the organizations that use their services.

## 20.5 Fixed and Variable Factors

In a given time period, it may be very difficult to adjust some of the inputs. Typically a firm may have contractual obligations to employ certain inputs at certain levels. An example of this would be a lease on a building, where the firm is legally obligated to purchase a certain amount of space over the period under examination. We refer to a factor of production that is in a fixed amount for the firm as a **fixed factor**. If a factor can be used in different amounts, we refer to it as a **variable factor**.

As we saw in Chapter 19, the short run is defined as that period of time in which there are some fixed factors—factors that can only be used in fixed amounts. In the long run, on the other hand, the firm is free to vary all of the factors of production: all factors are variable factors.

There is no rigid boundary between the short run and the long run. The exact time period involved depends on the problem under examination. The important thing is that some of the factors of production are fixed in the short run and variable in the long run. Since all factors are variable in the long run, a firm is always free to decide to use zero inputs and produce zero output—that is, to go out of business. Thus the least profits a firm can make in the long run are zero profits.

In the short run, the firm is obligated to employ some factors, even if it decides to produce zero output. Therefore it is perfectly possible that the firm could make *negative* profits in the short run.

By definition, fixed factors are factors of production that must be paid for even if the firm decides to produce zero output: if a firm has a long-term lease on a building, it must make its lease payments each period whether or not it decides to produce anything that period. But there is another category of factors that only need to be paid for if the firm decides to produce a positive amount of output. One example is electricity used for lighting. If the firm produces zero output, it doesn't have to provide any lighting; but if it produces any positive amount of output, it has to purchase a fixed amount of electricity to use for lighting.

Factors such as these are called **quasi-fixed factors**. They are factors of production that must be used in a fixed amount, independent of the output of the firm, as long as the output is positive. The distinction between fixed factors and quasi-fixed factors is sometimes useful in analyzing the economic behavior of the firm.

## 20.6 Short-Run Profit Maximization

Let's consider the short-run profit-maximization problem when input 2 is fixed at some level $\bar{x}_2$. Let $f(x_1, x_2)$ be the production function for the firm, let $p$ be the price of output, and let $w_1$ and $w_2$ be the prices of the two inputs. Then the profit-maximization problem facing the firm can be written as

$$\max_{x_1} pf(x_1, \bar{x}_2) - w_1 x_1 - w_2 \bar{x}_2.$$

The condition for the optimal choice of factor 1 is not difficult to determine.

If $x_1^*$ is the profit-maximizing choice of factor 1, then the output price times the marginal product of factor 1 should equal the price of factor 1. In symbols,

$$pMP_1(x_1^*, \bar{x}_2) = w_1.$$

In other words, the *value of the marginal product of a factor should equal its price*.

This rule comes from the first-order condition for the maximization problem:

$$p\frac{\partial f(x_1^*, \bar{x}_2)}{\partial x_1} - w_1 = 0$$

In order to understand this rule, think about the decision to employ a little more of factor 1. As you add a little more of it, $\delta x_1$, you produce $\delta y = MP_1 \delta x_1$ more output that is worth $pMP_1 \delta x_1$. But this marginal output costs $w_1 \delta x_1$ to produce. If the value of marginal product exceeds its cost, then profits can be increased by *increasing* input 1. If the value of marginal product is less than its cost, then profits can be increased by *decreasing* the level of input 1.

If the profits of the firm are as large as possible, then profits should not increase when we increase or decrease input 1. This means that at a profit-maximizing choice of inputs and outputs, the value of the marginal product, $pMP_1(x_1^*, \bar{x}_2)$, should equal the factor price, $w_1$.

We can derive the same condition graphically. Consider Figure 20.1. The curved line represents the production function holding factor 2 fixed at $\bar{x}_2$. Using $y$ to denote the output of the firm, profits are given by

$$\pi = py - w_1 x_1 - w_2 \bar{x}_2.$$

This expression can be solved for $y$ to express output as a function of $x_1$:

$$y = \frac{\pi}{p} + \frac{w_2}{p}\bar{x}_2 + \frac{w_1}{p}x_1. \tag{20.1}$$

This equation describes **isoprofit lines**. These are just all combinations of the input goods and the output good that give a constant level of profit, $\pi$. As $\pi$ varies we get a family of parallel straight lines each with a slope of $w_1/p$ and each having a vertical intercept of $\pi/p + w_2\bar{x}_2/p$, which measures the profits plus the fixed costs of the firm.

**Profit maximization.** The firm chooses the input and output combination that lies on the highest isoprofit line. In this case the profit-maximizing point is $(x_1^*, y^*)$.

Figure
20.1

The fixed costs are fixed, so the only thing that really varies as we move from one isoprofit line to another is the level of profits. Thus higher levels of profit will be associated with isoprofit lines with higher vertical intercepts.

The profit-maximization problem is then to find the point on the production function that has the highest associated isoprofit line. Such a point is illustrated in Figure 20.1. As usual it is characterized by a tangency condition: the slope of the production function should equal the slope of the isoprofit line. Since the slope of the production function is the marginal product, and the slope of the isoprofit line is $w_1/p$, this condition can also be written as

$$MP_1 = \frac{w_1}{p},$$

which is equivalent to the condition we derived above.

## 20.7 Comparative Statics

We can use the geometry depicted in Figure 20.1 to analyze how a firm's choice of inputs and outputs varies as the prices of inputs and outputs vary. This gives us one way to analyze the **comparative statics** of firm behavior.

For example: how does the optimal choice of factor 1 vary as we vary its factor price $w_1$? Referring to equation (20.1), which defines the isoprofit line, we see that increasing $w_1$ will make the isoprofit line steeper, as shown in Figure 20.2A. When the isoprofit line is steeper, the tangency must occur further to the left. Thus the optimal level of factor 1 must decrease. This simply means that as the price of factor 1 increases, the demand for factor 1 must decrease: factor demand curves must slope downward.

We can also derive this result using calculus. Suppose for simplicity that there is only one input to production so we can write the profit maximization problem as

$$\max_x pf(x) - wx.$$

The first- and second-order conditions for maximization are

$$pf'(x^*) = w$$

and

$$f''(x^*) \leq 0.$$

The factor demand function $x(w)$ must satisfy these conditions for all values of $w$, so we have the identity

$$f'(x(w)) \equiv w.$$

Differentiating both sides of this identity using the chain rule we have

$$f''(x(w))x'(w) \equiv 1.$$

As long as $f''(x)$ is *strictly* negative, it follows that $x'(w)$ is negative: factor demand curves must slope downward.

In calculus terms, we want to examine the partial derivative of $x_1^*$ with respect to $w_1$. We have defined $x_1^*$ implicitly by $\dfrac{\partial f(x_1^*, \bar{x}_2)}{\partial x_1} = \dfrac{w_1}{p}$. Implicitly differentiating both sides with respect to $w_1$ (and using the chain rule) gives:

$$\frac{\partial^2 f(x_1^*, \bar{x}_2)}{\partial^2 x_1^*} \frac{\partial x_1^*}{\partial w_1} = \frac{1}{p}.$$

Solving for $\dfrac{\partial x_1^*}{\partial w_1}$, and keeping in mind that $p > 0$ and $\dfrac{\partial^2 f(x_1^*, \bar{x}_2)}{\partial^2 x_1^*} < 0$, yields

$$\frac{\partial x_1^*}{\partial w_1} = \frac{1}{p \frac{\partial^2 f(x_1^*, \bar{x}_2)}{\partial^2 x_1^*}} < 0.$$

Similarly, if the output price decreases the isoprofit line must become steeper, as shown in Figure 20.2B. By the same argument as given in the last paragraph the profit-maximizing choice of factor 1 will decrease. If the amount of factor 1 decreases and the level of factor 2 is fixed in the short run by assumption, then the supply of output must decrease. This gives us

**Comparative statics.** Panel A shows that increasing $w_1$ will reduce the demand for factor 1. Panel B shows that increasing the price of output will increase the demand for factor 1 and therefore increase the supply of output.

Figure
20.2

another comparative statics result: a reduction in the output price must decrease the supply of output. In other words, the supply function must slope upwards.

Finally, we can ask what will happen if the price of factor 2 changes? Because this is a short-run analysis, changing the price of factor 2 will not change the firm's choice of factor 2—in the short run, the level of factor 2 is fixed at $\bar{x}_2$. Changing the price of factor 2 has no effect on the *slope* of the isoprofit line. Thus the optimal choice of factor 1 will not change, nor will the supply of output. All that changes are the profits that the firm makes.

## 20.8 Profit Maximization in the Long Run

In the long run the firm is free to choose the level of all inputs. Thus the long-run profit-maximization problem can be posed as

$$\max_{x_1, x_2} pf(x_1, x_2) - w_1 x_1 - w_2 x_2.$$

This is basically the same as the short-run problem described above, but now both factors are free to vary.

The condition describing the optimal choices is essentially the same as before, but now we have to apply it to *each* factor. Before we saw that the value of the marginal product of factor 1 must be equal to its price, whatever the level of factor 2. The same sort of condition must now hold for *each* factor choice. There are two first-order conditions, one for each factor:

$$p\frac{\partial f(x_1^*, x_2^*)}{\partial x_1} - w_1 = 0$$

$$p\frac{\partial f(x_1^*, x_2^*)}{\partial x_2} - w_2 = 0.$$

The first-order conditions imply:

$$pMP_1(x_1^*, x_2^*) = w_1$$

$$pMP_2(x_1^*, x_2^*) = w_2.$$

If the firm has made the optimal choices of factors 1 and 2, the value of the marginal product of each factor should equal its price. At the optimal choice, the firm's profits cannot increase by changing the level of either input.

The argument is the same as used for the short-run profit-maximizing decisions. If the value of the marginal product of factor 1, for example, exceeded the price of factor 1, then using a little more of factor 1 would produce $MP_1$ more output, which would sell for $pMP_1$ dollars. If the value of this output exceeds the cost of the factor used to produce it, it clearly pays to expand the use of this factor.

These two conditions give us two equations in two unknowns, $x_1^*$ and $x_2^*$. If we know how the marginal products behave as a function of $x_1$ and $x_2$, we will be able to solve for the optimal choice of each factor as a function of the prices. The resulting equations are known as the **factor demand curves**.

## EXAMPLE: Profit Maximization with Cobb-Douglas Production

Let's see how profit-maximizing behavior looks using the Cobb-Douglas production function.

Suppose the Cobb-Douglas function is given by $f(x_1, x_2) = x_1^a x_2^b$. Then the two first-order conditions become

$$pax_1^{a-1}x_2^b - w_1 = 0$$
$$pbx_1^a x_2^{b-1} - w_2 = 0.$$

Multiply the first equation by $x_1$ and the second equation by $x_2$ to get

$$pax_1^a x_2^b - w_1 x_1 = 0$$
$$pbx_1^a x_2^b - w_2 x_2 = 0.$$

Using $y = x_1^a x_2^b$ to denote the level of output of this firm we can rewrite these expressions as

$$pay = w_1 x_1$$
$$pby = w_2 x_2.$$

Solving for $x_1$ and $x_2$ we have

$$x_1^* = \frac{apy}{w_1}$$

$$x_2^* = \frac{bpy}{w_2}.$$

This gives us the demands for the two factors as a function of the optimal output choice. But we still have to solve for the optimal choice of output. Inserting the optimal factor demands into the Cobb-Douglas production function, we have the expression

$$\left(\frac{pay}{w_1}\right)^a \left(\frac{pby}{w_2}\right)^b = y.$$

Factoring out the $y$ gives

$$\left(\frac{pa}{w_1}\right)^a \left(\frac{pb}{w_2}\right)^b y^{a+b} = y.$$

Or

$$y = \left(\frac{pa}{w_1}\right)^{\frac{a}{1-a-b}} \left(\frac{pb}{w_2}\right)^{\frac{b}{1-a-b}}.$$

This gives us the supply function of the Cobb-Douglas firm. Along with the factor demand functions derived above it gives us a complete solution to the profit-maximization problem.

Note that when the firm exhibits constant returns to scale—when $a+b = 1$—this supply function is not well defined. As long as the output and input prices are consistent with zero profits, a firm with a Cobb-Douglas technology is indifferent about its level of supply.

## 20.9 Inverse Factor Demand Curves

The **factor demand curves** of a firm measure the relationship between the price of a factor and the profit-maximizing choice of that factor. We saw above how to find the profit-maximizing choices: for any prices, $(p, w_1, w_2)$, we just find those factor demands, $(x_1^*, x_2^*)$, such that the value of the marginal product of each factor equals its price.

The **inverse factor demand curve** measures the same relationship, but from a different point of view. It measures what the factor prices must be for some given quantity of inputs to be demanded. Given the optimal choice of factor 2, we can draw the relationship between the optimal choice of factor 1 and its price in a diagram like that depicted in Figure 20.3. This is simply a graph of the equation

$$pMP_1(x_1, x_2^*) = w_1.$$

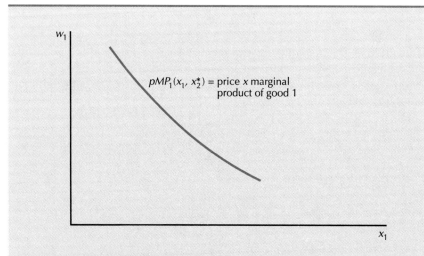

Figure
20.3

**The inverse factor demand curve.** This measures what the price of factor 1 must be to get $x_1$ units demanded if the level of the other factor is held fixed at $x_2^*$.

This curve will be downward sloping by the assumption of diminishing marginal product. For any level of $x_1$, this curve depicts what the factor price must be in order to induce the firm to demand that level of $x_1$, holding factor 2 fixed at $x_2^*$.

## 20.10 Profit Maximization and Returns to Scale

There is an important relationship between competitive profit maximization and returns to scale. Suppose that a firm has chosen a long-run profit-maximizing output $y^* = f(x_1^*, x_2^*)$, which it is producing using input levels $(x_1^*, x_2^*)$.

Then its profits are given by

$$\pi^* = py^* - w_1 x_1^* - w_2 x_2^*.$$

Suppose that this firm's production function exhibits constant returns to scale and that it is making positive profits in equilibrium. Then consider what would happen if it doubled the level of its input usage. According to the constant returns to scale hypothesis, it would double its output level. What would happen to profits?

It is not hard to see that its profits would also double. But this contradicts the assumption that its original choice was profit maximizing! We derived this contradiction by assuming that the original profit level was positive; if the original level of profits were zero there would be no problem: two times zero is still zero.

This argument shows that the only reasonable long-run level of profits for a competitive firm that has constant returns to scale at all levels of output is a zero level of profits. (Of course if a firm has negative profits in the long run, it should go out of business.)

Most people find this to be a surprising statement. Firms are out to maximize profits aren't they? How can it be that they can only get zero profits in the long run?

Think about what would happen to a firm that did try to expand indefinitely. Three things might occur. First, the firm could get so large that it could not really operate effectively. This is just saying that the firm *really* doesn't have constant returns to scale at all levels of output. Eventually, due to coordination problems, it might enter a region of decreasing returns to scale.

Second, the firm might get so large that it would totally dominate the market for its product. In this case there is no reason for it to behave competitively—to take the price of output as given. Instead, it would make sense for such a firm to try to use its size to influence the market price. The model of competitive profit maximization would no longer be a sensible way for the firm to behave, since it would effectively have no competitors. We'll investigate more appropriate models of firm behavior in this situation when we discuss monopoly.

Third, if one firm can make positive profits with a constant returns to scale technology, so can any other firm with access to the same technology. If one firm wants to expand its output, so would other firms. But if all firms expand their outputs, this will certainly push down the price of output and lower the profits of all the firms in the industry.

## 20.11 Revealed Profitability

When a profit-maximizing firm makes its choice of inputs and outputs it reveals two things: first, that the inputs and outputs used represent a *feasible* production plan, and second, that these choices are more profitable than other feasible choices that the firm could have made. Let us examine these points in more detail.

Suppose that we observe two choices that the firm makes at two different sets of prices. At time $t$, it faces prices $(p^t, w_1^t, w_2^t)$ and makes choices $(y^t, x_1^t, x_2^t)$. At time $s$, it faces prices $(p^s, w_1^s, w_2^s)$ and makes choices $(y^s, x_1^s, x_2^s)$. If the production function of the firm hasn't changed between times $s$ and $t$ and if the firm is a profit maximizer, then we must have

$$p^t y^t - w_1^t x_1^t - w_2^t x_2^t \geq p^t y^s - w_1^t x_1^s - w_2^t x_2^s \tag{20.2}$$

and

$$p^s y^s - w_1^s x_1^s - w_2^s x_2^s \geq p^s y^t - w_1^s x_1^t - w_2^s x_2^t. \tag{20.3}$$

That is, the profits that the firm achieved facing the $t$ period prices must be larger than if they used the $s$ period plan and vice versa. If either of these inequalities were violated, the firm could not have been a profit-maximizing firm (with an unchanging technology).

Thus if we ever observe two time periods where these inequalities are violated we would know that the firm was not maximizing profits in at least one of the two periods. The satisfaction of these inequalities is virtually an axiom of profit-maximizing behavior, so it might be referred to as the **Weak Axiom of Profit Maximization (WAPM)**.

If the firm's choices satisfy WAPM, we can derive a useful comparative statics statement about the behavior of factor demands and output supplies when prices change. Transpose the two sides of equation (20.3) to get

$$-p^s y^t + w_1^s x_1^t + w_2^s x_1^t \geq -p^s y^s + w_1^s x_1^s + w_2^s x_2^s \tag{20.4}$$

and add equation (20.4) to equation (20.2) to get

$$(p^t - p^s)y^t - (w_1^t - w_1^s)x_1^t - (w_2^t - w_2^s)x_2^t$$

$$\geq (p^t - p^s)y^s - (w_1^t - w_1^s)x_1^s - (w_2^t - w_2^s)x_2^s. \tag{20.5}$$

Now rearrange this equation to yield

$$(p^t - p^s)(y^t - y^s) - (w_1^t - w_1^s)(x_1^t - x_1^s) - (w_2^t - w_2^s)(x_2^t - x_2^s) \geq 0. \tag{20.6}$$

Finally define the change in prices, $\Delta p = (p^t - p^s)$, the change in output, $\Delta y = (y^t - y^s)$, and so on to find

$$\Delta p \Delta y - \Delta w_1 \Delta x_1 - \Delta w_2 \Delta x_2 \geq 0. \tag{20.7}$$

This equation is our final result. It says that the change in the price of output times the change in output minus the change in each factor price times the change in that factor must be nonnegative. This equation comes solely from the definition of profit maximization. Yet it contains all of the comparative statics results about profit-maximizing choices!

For example, suppose that we consider a situation where the price of output changes, but the price of each factor stays constant. If $\Delta w_1 = \Delta w_2 = 0$, then equation (20.7) reduces to

$$\Delta p \Delta y \geq 0.$$

Thus if the price of output goes up, so that $\Delta p > 0$, then the change in output must be nonnegative as well, $\Delta y \geq 0$. This says that the profit-maximizing supply curve of a competitive firm must have a positive (or at least a zero) slope.

Similarly, if the price of output and of factor 2 remain constant, equation (20.7) becomes

$$-\Delta w_1 \Delta x_1 \geq 0,$$

which is to say

$$\Delta w_1 \Delta x_1 \leq 0.$$

These inequalities can be used to obtain results about derivatives. For example,

$$\frac{\partial y}{\partial p} = \lim_{\Delta p \to 0} \frac{y(p^s + \Delta p) - y(p^s)}{\Delta p} = \lim_{\Delta p \to 0} \frac{\Delta y}{\Delta p} \geq 0.$$

Likewise,

$$\frac{\partial w_1}{\partial x_1} \leq 0.$$

Thus if the price of factor 1 goes up, so that $\Delta w_1 > 0$, then equation (20.7) implies that the demand for factor 1 will go down (or at worst stay the same), so that $\Delta x_1 \leq 0$. This means that the factor demand curve must be a decreasing function of the factor price: factor demand curves have a negative slope.

The simple inequality in WAPM, and its implication in equation (20.7), give us strong observable restrictions about how a firm will behave. It is natural to ask whether these are all of the restrictions that the model of profit maximization imposes on firm behavior. Said another way, if we observe a firm's choices, and these choices satisfy WAPM, can we construct an estimate of the technology for which the observed choices are profit-maximizing choices? It turns out that the answer is yes. Figure 20.4 shows how to construct such a technology.

In order to illustrate the argument graphically, we suppose that there is one input and one output. Suppose that we are given an observed choice in period $t$ and in period $s$, which we indicate by $(p^t, w_1^t, y^t, x_1^t)$ and $(p^s, w_1^s, y^s, x_1^s)$. In each period we can calculate the profits $\pi_s$ and $\pi_t$ and plot all the combinations of $y$ and $x_1$ that yield these profits.

That is, we plot the two isoprofit lines

$$\pi_t = p^t y - w_1^t x_1$$

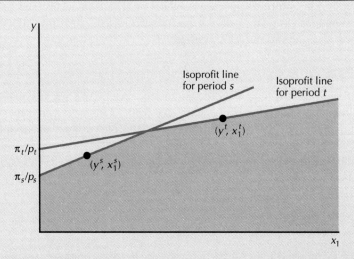

Figure
20.4   **Construction of a possible technology.** If the observed
choices are maximal profit choices at each set of prices, then we
can estimate the shape of the technology that generated those
choices by using the isoprofit lines.

and
$$\pi_s = p^s y - w_1^s x_1.$$

The points above the isoprofit line for period $t$ have higher profits than
$\pi_t$ at period $t$ prices, and the points above the isoprofit line for period $s$
have higher profits than $\pi_s$ at period $s$ prices. WAPM requires that the
choice in period $t$ must lie below the period $s$ isoprofit line and that the
choice in period $s$ must lie below the period $t$ isoprofit line.

If this condition is satisfied, it is not hard to generate a technology for
which $(y^t, x_1^t)$ and $(y^s, x_1^s)$ are profit-maximizing choices. Just take the
shaded area beneath the two lines. These are all of the choices that yield
lower profits than the observed choices at both sets of prices.

The proof that this technology will generate the observed choices as
profit-maximizing choices is clear geometrically. At the prices $(p^t, w_1^t)$, the
choice $(y^t, x_1^t)$ is on the highest isoprofit line possible, and the same goes
for the period $s$ choice.

Thus, when the observed choices satisfy WAPM, we can "reconstruct"
an estimate of a technology that might have generated the observations.
In this sense, any observed choices consistent with WAPM could be profit-
maximizing choices. As we observe more choices that the firm makes, we get
a tighter estimate of the production function, as illustrated in Figure 20.5.

This estimate of the production function can be used to forecast firm
behavior in other environments or for other uses in economic analysis.

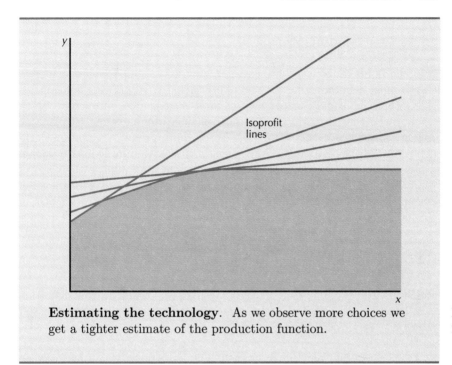

**Estimating the technology**.  As we observe more choices we get a tighter estimate of the production function.

Figure
20.5

## EXAMPLE: How Do Farmers React to Price Supports?

The U.S. government currently spends between \$40 and \$60 billion a year in aid to farmers.  A large fraction of this amount is used to subsidize the production of various products including milk, wheat, corn, soybeans, and cotton. Occasionally, attempts are made to reduce or eliminate these subsidies.  The effect of elimination of these subsidies would be to reduce the price of the product received by the farmers.

Farmers sometimes argue that eliminating the subsidies to milk, for example, would not reduce the total supply of milk, since dairy farmers would choose to *increase* their herds and their supply of milk so as to keep their standard of living constant.

If farmers are behaving so as to maximize profits, this is impossible. As we've seen above, the logic of profit maximization *requires* that a decrease in the price of an output leads to a reduction in its supply: if $\Delta p$ is negative, then $\Delta y$ must be negative as well.

It is certainly possible that small family farms have goals other than simple maximization of profits, but larger "agribusiness" farms are more likely to be profit maximizers. Thus the perverse response to the elimination of subsidies alluded to above could only occur on a limited scale, if at all.

## 20.12 Cost Minimization

If a firm is maximizing profits and if it chooses to supply some output $y$, then it must be minimizing the cost of producing $y$. If this were not so, then there would be some cheaper way of producing $y$ units of output, which would mean that the firm was not maximizing profits in the first place.

   This simple observation turns out to be quite useful in examining firm behavior. It turns out to be convenient to break the profit-maximization problem into two stages: first we figure out how to minimize the costs of producing any desired level of output $y$, then we figure out which level of output is indeed a profit-maximizing level of output. We begin this task in the next chapter.

## Summary

1. Profits are the difference between revenues and costs. In this definition it is important that all costs be measured using the appropriate market prices.

2. Fixed factors are factors whose amount is independent of the level of output; variable factors are factors whose amount used changes as the level of output changes.

3. In the short run, some factors must be used in predetermined amounts. In the long run, all factors are free to vary.

4. If the firm is maximizing profits, then the value of the marginal product of each factor that it is free to vary must equal its factor price.

5. The logic of profit maximization implies that the supply function of a competitive firm must be an increasing function of the price of output and that each factor demand function must be a decreasing function of its price.

6. If a competitive firm exhibits constant returns to scale, then its long-run maximum profits must be zero.

## REVIEW QUESTIONS

1. In the short run, if the price of the fixed factor is increased, what will happen to profits?

2. If a firm had everywhere increasing returns to scale, what would happen to its profits if prices remained fixed and if it doubled its scale of operation?

3. If a firm had decreasing returns to scale at all levels of output and it divided up into two equal-size smaller firms, what would happen to its overall profits?

4. A gardener exclaims: "For only $1 in seeds I've grown over $20 in produce!" Besides the fact that most of the produce is in the form of zucchini, what other observations would a cynical economist make about this situation?

5. Is maximizing a firm's profits always identical to maximizing the firm's stock market value?

6. If $pMP_1 > w_1$, then should the firm increase or decrease the amount of factor 1 in order to increase profits?

7. Suppose a firm is maximizing profits in the short run with variable factor $x_1$ and fixed factor $x_2$. If the price of $x_2$ goes down, what happens to the firm's use of $x_1$? What happens to the firm's level of profits?

8. A profit-maximizing competitive firm that is making positive profits in long-run equilibrium (may/may not) have a technology with constant returns to scale.

# CHAPTER **21**

# COST
# MINIMIZATION

Our goal is to study the behavior of profit-maximizing firms in both competitive and noncompetitive market environments. In the last chapter we began our investigation of profit-maximizing behavior in a competitive environment by examining the profit-maximization problem directly.

However, some important insights can be gained through a more indirect approach. Our strategy will be to break up the profit-maximization problem into two pieces. First, we will look at the problem of how to minimize the costs of producing any given level of output, and then we will look at how to choose the most profitable level of output. In this chapter we'll look at the first step—minimizing the costs of producing a given level of output.

## 21.1 Cost Minimization

Suppose that we have two factors of production that have prices $w_1$ and $w_2$, and that we want to figure out the cheapest way to produce a given level of output, $y$. If we let $x_1$ and $x_2$ measure the amounts used of the two factors and let $f(x_1, x_2)$ be the production function for the firm, we can write this problem as

$$\min_{x_1, x_2} w_1 x_1 + w_2 x_2$$

such that $f(x_1, x_2) = y$.

The same warnings apply as in the preceding chapter concerning this sort of analysis: make sure that you have included *all* costs of production in the calculation of costs, and make sure that everything is being measured on a compatible time scale.

The solution to this cost-minimization problem—the minimum costs necessary to achieve the desired level of output—will depend on $w_1$, $w_2$, and $y$, so we write it as $c(w_1, w_2, y)$. This function is known as the **cost function** and will be of considerable interest to us. The cost function $c(w_1, w_2, y)$ measures the minimal costs of producing $y$ units of output when factor prices are $(w_1, w_2)$.

In order to understand the solution to this problem, let us depict the costs and the technological constraints facing the firm on the same diagram. The isoquants give us the technological constraints—all the combinations of $x_1$ and $x_2$ that can produce $y$.

Suppose that we want to plot all the combinations of inputs that have some given level of cost, $C$. We can write this as

$$w_1 x_1 + w_2 x_2 = C,$$

which can be rearranged to give

$$x_2 = \frac{C}{w_2} - \frac{w_1}{w_2} x_1.$$

It is easy to see that this is a straight line with a slope of $-w_1/w_2$ and a vertical intercept of $C/w_2$. As we let the number $C$ vary we get a whole family of **isocost lines**. Every point on an isocost curve has the same cost, $C$, and higher isocost lines are associated with higher costs.

Thus our cost-minimization problem can be rephrased as: find the point on the isoquant that has the lowest possible isocost line associated with it. Such a point is illustrated in Figure 21.1.

Note that if the optimal solution involves using some of each factor, and if the isoquant is a nice smooth curve, then the cost-minimizing point will be characterized by a tangency condition: the slope of the isoquant must be equal to the slope of the isocost curve. Or, using the terminology of Chapter 19, the *technical rate of substitution must equal the factor price ratio:*

$$-\frac{MP_1(x_1^*, x_2^*)}{MP_2(x_1^*, x_2^*)} = \text{TRS}(x_1^*, x_2^*) = -\frac{w_1}{w_2}. \tag{21.1}$$

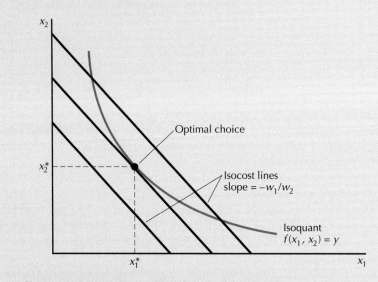

$x_2$

$x_2^*$

Optimal choice

Isocost lines
slope $= -w_1/w_2$

Isoquant
$f(x_1, x_2) = y$

$x_1^*$

$x_1$

Figure
21.1

**Cost minimization.** The choice of factors that minimize production costs can be determined by finding the point on the isoquant that has the lowest associated isocost curve.

(If we have a boundary solution where one of the two factors isn't used, this tangency condition need not be met. Similarly, if the production function has "kinks," the tangency condition has no meaning. These exceptions are just like the situation with the consumer, so we won't emphasize these cases in this chapter.)

The algebra that lies behind equation (21.1) is not difficult. Consider any change in the pattern of production $(\delta x_1, \delta x_2)$ that keeps output constant. Such a change must satisfy

$$MP_1(x_1^*, x_2^*)\delta x_1 + MP_2(x_1^*, x_2^*)\delta x_2 = 0. \tag{21.2}$$

Note that $\delta x_1$ and $\delta x_2$ must be of opposite signs; if you increase the amount used of factor 1 you must decrease the amount used of factor 2 in order to keep output constant.

If we are at the cost minimum, then this change cannot lower costs, so we have

$$w_1\delta x_1 + w_2\delta x_2 \geq 0. \tag{21.3}$$

Now consider the change $(-\delta x_1, -\delta x_2)$. This also produces a constant level of output, and it too cannot lower costs. This implies that

$$-w_1\delta x_1 - w_2\delta x_2 \geq 0. \tag{21.4}$$

Putting expressions (21.3) and (21.4) together gives us

$$w_1 \delta x_1 + w_2 \delta x_2 = 0. \tag{21.5}$$

Solving equations (21.2) and (21.5) for $\delta x_2 / \delta x_1$ gives

$$\frac{\delta x_2}{\delta x_1} = -\frac{w_1}{w_2} = -\frac{MP_1(x_1^*, x_2^*)}{MP_2(x_1^*, x_2^*)},$$

which is just the condition for cost minimization derived above by a geometric argument.

Let us study the cost-minimization problem using the optimization techniques introduced in Chapter 5. The problem is a constrained-minimization problem of the form

$$\min_{x_1, x_2} w_1 x_1 + w_2 x_2$$

such that $f(x_1, x_2) = y$.

Recall that we had several techniques to solve this kind of problem. One way was to substitute the constraint into the objective function. This can still be used when we have a specific functional form for $f(x_1, x_2)$, but isn't much use in the general case.

The second method was the method of Lagrange multipliers and that works fine. To apply this method we set up the Lagrangian

$$L = w_1 x_1 + w_2 x_2 - \lambda(f(x_1, x_2) - y)$$

and differentiate with respect to $x_1$, $x_2$ and $\lambda$. This gives us the first-order conditions:

$$w_1 - \lambda \frac{\partial f(x_1, x_2)}{\partial x_1} = 0$$

$$w_2 - \lambda \frac{\partial f(x_1, x_2)}{\partial x_2} = 0$$

$$f(x_1, x_2) - y = 0.$$

The last condition is simply the constraint. We can rearrange the first two equations and divide the first equation by the second equation to get

$$\frac{w_1}{w_2} = \frac{\partial f(x_1, x_2)/\partial x_1}{\partial f(x_1, x_2)/\partial x_2}.$$

Note that this is the same condition that we derived earlier: the technical rate of substitution must equal the factor price ratio.

Note that Figure 21.1 bears a certain resemblance to the solution to the consumer-choice problem depicted earlier. Although the solutions look the same, they really aren't the same kind of problem. In the consumer problem, the straight line was the budget constraint, and the consumer moved along the budget constraint to find the most-preferred position. In the producer problem, the isoquant is the technological constraint and the producer moves along the isoquant to find the optimal position.

The choices of inputs that yield minimal costs for the firm will in general depend on the input prices and the level of output that the firm wants to produce, so we write these choices as $x_1(w_1, w_2, y)$ and $x_2(w_1, w_2, y)$. These are called the **conditional factor demand functions**, or **derived factor demands**. They measure the relationship between the prices and output and the optimal factor choice of the firm, *conditional* on the firm producing a given level of output, $y$.

Note carefully the difference between the *conditional* factor demands and the profit-maximizing factor demands discussed in the last chapter. The conditional factor demands give the cost-minimizing choices for a given *level* of output; the profit-maximizing factor demands give the profit-maximizing choices for a given *price* of output.

Conditional factor demands are usually not directly observed; they are a hypothetical construct. They answer the question of how much of each factor *would* the firm use if it wanted to produce a given level of output in the cheapest way. However, the conditional factor demands are useful as a way of separating the problem of determining the optimal level of output from the problem of determining the most cost-effective method of production.

## EXAMPLE: Minimizing Costs for Specific Technologies

Suppose that we consider a technology where the factors are perfect complements, so that $f(x_1, x_2) = \min\{x_1, x_2\}$. Then if we want to produce $y$ units of output, we clearly need $y$ units of $x_1$ and $y$ units of $x_2$. Thus the minimal costs of production will be

$$c(w_1, w_2, y) = w_1 y + w_2 y = (w_1 + w_2)y.$$

What about the perfect substitutes technology, $f(x_1, x_2) = x_1 + x_2$? Since goods 1 and 2 are perfect substitutes in production it is clear that the firm will use whichever is cheaper. Thus the minimum cost of producing $y$ units of output will be $w_1 y$ or $w_2 y$, whichever is less. In other words:

$$c(w_1, w_2, y) = \min\{w_1 y, w_2 y\} = \min\{w_1, w_2\}y.$$

Finally, we consider the Cobb-Douglas technology, which is described by the formula $f(x_1, x_2) = x_1^a x_2^b$. In this case we can use calculus techniques to show that the cost function will have the form

$$c(w_1, w_2, y) = K w_1^{\frac{a}{a+b}} w_2^{\frac{b}{a+b}} y^{\frac{1}{a+b}},$$

where $K$ is a constant that depends on $a$ and $b$.

The cost-minimization problem is then

$$\min_{x_1, x_2} w_1 x_1 + w_2 x_2$$

such that $x_1^a x_2^b = y$.

Here we have a specific functional form, and we can solve it using either the substitution method or the Lagrangian method. The substitution method would involve first solving the constraint for $x_2$ as a function of $x_1$:

$$x_2 = \left(y x_1^{-a}\right)^{1/b}$$

and then substituting this into the objective function to get the unconstrained minimization problem

$$\min_{x_1} w_1 x_1 + w_2 \left(y x_1^{-a}\right)^{1/b}.$$

We could now differentiate with respect to $x_1$ and set resulting derivative equal to zero, as usual. The resulting equation can be solved to get $x_1$ as a function of $w_1$, $w_2$, and $y$, to get the conditional factor demand for $x_1$. This isn't hard to do, but the algebra is messy, so we won't write down the details.

We will, however, solve the Lagrangian problem. The three first-order conditions are

$$w_1 = \lambda a x_1^{a-1} x_2^b$$
$$w_2 = \lambda b x_1^a x_2^{b-1}$$
$$y = x_1^a x_2^b.$$

Multiply the first equation by $x_1$ and the second equation by $x_2$ to get

$$w_1 x_1 = \lambda a x_1^a x_2^b = \lambda a y$$

$$w_2 x_2 = \lambda b x_1^a x_2^b = \lambda b y,$$

so that

$$x_1 = \lambda \frac{ay}{w_1} \tag{21.6}$$

$$x_2 = \lambda \frac{by}{w_2}. \tag{21.7}$$

Now we use the third equation to solve for $\lambda$. Substituting the solutions for $x_1$ and $x_2$ into the third first-order condition, we have

$$\left(\frac{\lambda a y}{w_1}\right)^a \left(\frac{\lambda b y}{w_2}\right)^b = y.$$

We can solve this equation for $\lambda$ to get the rather formidable expression

$$\lambda = (a^{-a}b^{-b}w_1^a w_2^b y^{1-a-b})^{\frac{1}{a+b}},$$

which, along with equations (21.6) and (21.7), gives us our final solutions for $x_1$ and $x_2$. These factor demand functions will take the form

$$x_1(w_1, w_2, y) = \left(\frac{a}{b}\right)^{\frac{b}{a+b}} w_1^{\frac{-b}{a+b}} w_2^{\frac{b}{a+b}} y^{\frac{1}{a+b}}$$

$$x_2(w_1, w_2, y) = \left(\frac{a}{b}\right)^{-\frac{a}{a+b}} w_1^{\frac{a}{a+b}} w_2^{\frac{-a}{a+b}} y^{\frac{1}{a+b}}.$$

The cost function can be found by writing down the costs when the firm makes the cost-minimizing choices. That is,

$$c(w_1, w_2, y) = w_1 x_1(w_1, w_2, y) + w_2 x_2(w_1, w_2, y).$$

Some tedious algebra shows that

$$c(w_1, w_2, y) = \left[\left(\frac{a}{b}\right)^{\frac{b}{a+b}} + \left(\frac{a}{b}\right)^{\frac{-a}{a+b}}\right] w_1^{\frac{a}{a+b}} w_2^{\frac{b}{a+b}} y^{\frac{1}{a+b}}.$$

(Don't worry, this formula won't be on the final exam. It is presented only to demonstrate how to get an explicit solution to the cost-minimization problem by applying the method of Lagrange multipliers.)

Note that costs will increase more than, equal to, or less than linearly with output as $a + b$ is less than, equal to, or greater than 1. This makes sense since the Cobb-Douglas technology exhibits decreasing, constant, or increasing returns to scale depending on the value of $a + b$.

## 21.2 Revealed Cost Minimization

The assumption that the firm chooses factors to minimize the cost of producing output will have implications for how the observed choices change as factor prices change.

Suppose that we observe two sets of prices, $(w_1^t, w_2^t)$ and $(w_1^s, w_2^s)$, and the associated choices of the firm, $(x_1^t, x_2^t)$ and $(x_1^s, x_2^s)$. Suppose that each of these choices produces the same output level $y$. Then if each choice is a cost-minimizing choice at its associated prices, we must have

$$w_1^t x_1^t + w_2^t x_2^t \leq w_1^t x_1^s + w_2^t x_2^s$$

and

$$w_1^s x_1^s + w_2^s x_2^s \leq w_1^s x_1^t + w_2^s x_2^t.$$

If the firm is always choosing the cost-minimizing way to produce $y$ units of output, then its choices at times $t$ and $s$ must satisfy these inequalities. We will refer to these inequalities as the **Weak Axiom of Cost Minimization (WACM)**.

Write the second equation as

$$-w_1^s x_1^t - w_2^s x_2^t \leq -w_1^s x_1^s - w_2^s x_2^s$$

and add it to the first equation to get

$$(w_1^t - w_1^s)x_1^t + (w_2^t - w_2^s)x_2^t \leq (w_1^t - w_1^s)x_1^s + (w_2^t - w_2^s)x_2^s,$$

which can be rearranged to give us

$$(w_1^t - w_1^s)(x_1^t - x_1^s) + (w_2^t - w_2^s)(x_2^t - x_2^s) \leq 0.$$

Using the delta notation to depict the *changes* in the factor demands and factor prices, we have

$$\Delta w_1 \Delta x_1 + \Delta w_2 \Delta x_2 \leq 0.$$

This equation follows solely from the assumption of cost-minimizing behavior. It implies restrictions on how the firm's behavior can change when input prices change and output remains constant.

For example, if the price of the first factor increases and the price of the second factor stays constant, then $\Delta w_2 = 0$, so the inequality becomes

$$\Delta w_1 \Delta x_1 \leq 0.$$

If the price of factor 1 increases, then this inequality implies that the demand for factor 1 must decrease; thus the conditional factor demand functions must slope down.

What can we say about how the minimal costs change as we change the parameters of the problem? It is easy to see that costs must increase if either factor price increases: if one good becomes more expensive and the other stays the same, the minimal costs cannot go down and in general will increase. Similarly, if the firm chooses to produce more output and factor prices remain constant, the firm's costs will have to increase.

## 21.3 Returns to Scale and the Cost Function

In Chapter 19 we discussed the idea of returns to scale for the production function. Recall that a technology is said to have increasing, decreasing, or constant returns to scale as $f(tx_1, tx_2)$ is greater, less than, or equal to $tf(x_1, x_2)$ for all $t > 1$. It turns out that there is a nice relation between the kind of returns to scale exhibited by the production function and the behavior of the cost function.

Suppose first that we have the natural case of constant returns to scale. Imagine that we have solved the cost-minimization problem to produce 1 unit of output, so that we know the **unit cost function**, $c(w_1, w_2, 1)$. Now what is the cheapest way to produce $y$ units of output? Simple: we just use $y$ times as much of every input as we were using to produce 1 unit of output. This would mean that the minimal cost to produce $y$ units of output would just be $c(w_1, w_2, 1)y$. In the case of constant returns to scale, the cost function is linear in output.

What if we have increasing returns to scale? In this case it turns out that costs increase less than linearly in output. If the firm decides to produce twice as much output, it can do so at *less* than twice the cost, as long as the factor prices remain fixed. This is a natural implication of the idea of increasing returns to scale: if the firm doubles its inputs, it will more than double its output. Thus if it wants to produce double the output, it will be able to do so by using less than twice as much of every input.

But using twice as much of every input will exactly double costs. So using less than twice as much of every input will make costs go up by less than twice as much: this is just saying that the cost function will increase less than linearly with respect to output.

Similarly, if the technology exhibits decreasing returns to scale, the cost function will increase more than linearly with respect to output. If output doubles, costs will more than double.

These facts can be expressed in terms of the behavior of the **average cost function**. The average cost function is simply the cost *per unit* to produce $y$ units of output:

$$AC(y) = \frac{c(w_1, w_2, y)}{y}.$$

If the technology exhibits constant returns to scale, then we saw above that the cost function had the form $c(w_1, w_2, y) = c(w_1, w_2, 1)y$. This means that the average cost function will be

$$AC(w_1, w_2, y) = \frac{c(w_1, w_2, 1)y}{y} = c(w_1, w_2, 1).$$

That is, the cost per unit of output will be constant no matter what level of output the firm wants to produce.

If the technology exhibits increasing returns to scale, then the costs will increase less than linearly with respect to output, so the average costs will be declining in output: as output increases, the average costs of production will tend to fall.

Similarly, if the technology exhibits decreasing returns to scale, then average costs will rise as output increases.

As we saw earlier, a given technology can have *regions* of increasing, constant, or decreasing returns to scale—output can increase more rapidly, equally rapidly, or less rapidly than the scale of operation of the firm at different levels of production. Similarly, the cost function can increase less rapidly, equally rapidly, or more rapidly than output at different levels of production. This implies that the average cost function may decrease, remain constant, or increase over different levels of output. In the next chapter we will explore these possibilities in more detail.

From now on we will be most concerned with the behavior of the cost function with respect to the output variable. For the most part we will regard the factor prices as being fixed at some predetermined levels and only think of costs as depending on the output choice of the firm. Thus for the remainder of the book we will write the cost function as a function of output alone: $c(y)$.

## 21.4 Long-Run and Short-Run Costs

The cost function is defined as the minimum cost of achieving a given level of output. Often it is important to distinguish the minimum costs if the firm is allowed to adjust all of its factors of production from the minimum costs if the firm is only allowed to adjust some of its factors.

We have defined the short run to be a time period where some of the factors of production must be used in a fixed amount. In the long run, all factors are free to vary. The **short-run cost function** is defined as the minimum cost to produce a given level of output, only adjusting the variable factors of production. The **long-run cost function** gives the minimum cost of producing a given level of output, adjusting *all* of the factors of production.

Suppose that in the short run factor 2 is fixed at some predetermined level $\bar{x}_2$, but in the long run it is free to vary. Then the short-run cost function is defined by

$$c_s(y, \bar{x}_2) = \min_{x_1} w_1 x_1 + w_2 \bar{x}_2$$

such that $f(x_1, \bar{x}_2) = y$.

Note that in general the minimum cost to produce $y$ units of output in the short run will depend on the amount and cost of the fixed factor that is available.

In the case of two factors, this minimization problem is easy to solve: we just find the smallest amount of $x_1$ such that $f(x_1, \bar{x}_2) = y$. However, if there are many factors of production that are variable in the short run the cost-minimization problem will involve more elaborate calculation.

The short-run factor demand function for factor 1 is the amount of factor 1 that minimizes costs. In general it will depend on the factor prices and on the levels of the fixed factors as well, so we write the short-run factor demands as

$$x_1 = x_1^s(w_1, w_2, \overline{x}_2, y)$$
$$x_2 = \overline{x}_2.$$

These equations just say, for example, that if the building size is fixed in the short run, then the number of workers that a firm wants to hire at any given set of prices and output choice will typically depend on the size of the building.

Note that by definition of the short-run cost function

$$c_s(y, \overline{x}_2) = w_1 x_1^s(w_1, w_2, \overline{x}_2, y) + w_2 \overline{x}_2.$$

This just says that the minimum cost of producing output $y$ is the cost associated with using the cost-minimizing choice of inputs. This is true by definition but turns out to be useful nevertheless.

The long-run cost function in this example is defined by

$$c(y) = \min_{x_1, x_2} w_1 x_1 + w_2 x_2$$

such that $f(x_1, x_2) = y.$

Here both factors are free to vary. Long-run costs depend only on the level of output that the firm wants to produce along with factor prices. We write the long-run cost function as $c(y)$, and write the long-run factor demands as

$$x_1 = x_1(w_1, w_2, y)$$
$$x_2 = x_2(w_1, w_2, y).$$

We can also write the long-run cost function as

$$c(y) = w_1 x_1(w_1, w_2, y) + w_2 x_2(w_1, w_2, y).$$

Just as before, this simply says that the minimum costs are the costs that the firm gets by using the cost-minimizing choice of factors.

There is an interesting relation between the short-run and the long-run cost functions that we will use in the next chapter. For simplicity, let us suppose that factor prices are fixed at some predetermined levels and write the long-run factor demands as

$$x_1 = x_1(y)$$
$$x_2 = x_2(y).$$

Then the long-run cost function can also be written as

$$c(y) = c_s(y, x_2(y)).$$

To see why this is true, just think about what it means. The equation says that the minimum costs when all factors are variable is just the minimum cost when factor 2 is fixed *at the level that minimizes long-run costs*. It follows that the long-run demand for the variable factor—the cost-minimizing choice—is given by

$$x_1(w_1, w_2, y) = x_1^s(w_1, w_2, x_2(y), y).$$

This equation says that the cost-minimizing amount of the variable factor in the long run is that amount that the firm would choose in the short run—if it happened to have the long-run cost-minimizing amount of the fixed factor.

## 21.5 Fixed and Quasi-Fixed Costs

In Chapter 20 we made the distinction between fixed factors and quasi-fixed factors. Fixed factors are factors that must receive payment whether or not any output is produced. Quasi-fixed factors must be paid only if the firm decides to produce a positive amount of output.

It is natural to define fixed costs and quasi-fixed costs in a similar manner. **Fixed costs** are costs associated with the fixed factors: they are independent of the level of output, and, in particular, they must be paid whether or not the firm produces output. **Quasi-fixed costs** are costs that are also independent of the level of output, but only need to be paid if the firm produces a positive amount of output.

There are no fixed costs in the long run, by definition. However, there may easily be quasi-fixed costs in the long run. If it is necessary to spend a fixed amount of money before any output at all can be produced, then quasi-fixed costs will be present.

## 21.6 Sunk Costs

Sunk costs are another kind of fixed costs. The concept is best explained by example. Suppose that you have decided to lease an office for a year. The monthly rent that you have committed to pay is a fixed cost, since you are obligated to pay it regardless of the amount of output you produce. Now suppose that you decide to refurbish the office by painting it and buying furniture. The cost for paint is a fixed cost, but it is also a **sunk cost** since it is a payment that is made and cannot be recovered. The cost of buying the furniture, on the other hand, is not entirely sunk, since you can resell the furniture when you are done with it. It's only the *difference* between the cost of new and used furniture that is sunk.

To spell this out in more detail, suppose that you borrow $20,000 at the beginning of the year at, say, 10 percent interest. You sign a lease to rent an office and pay $12,000 in advance rent for next year. You spend $6,000 on office furniture and $2,000 to paint the office. At the end of the year you pay back the $20,000 loan plus the $2,000 interest payment and sell the used office furniture for $5,000.

Your total sunk costs consist of the $12,000 rent, the $2,000 of interest, the $2,000 of paint, but only $1,000 for the furniture, since $5,000 of the orginal furniture expenditure is recoverable.

The difference between sunk costs and recoverable costs can be quite significant. A $100,000 expenditure to purchase five light trucks sounds like a lot of money, but if they can later be sold on the used truck market for $80,000, the actual sunk cost is only $20,000. A $100,000 expenditure on a custom-made press for stamping out gizmos that has a zero resale value is quite different; in this case the entire expenditure is sunk.

The best way to keep these issues straight is to make sure to treat all expenditures on a flow basis: how much does it cost to do business for a year? That way, one is less likely to forget the resale value of capital equipment and more likely to keep the distinction between sunk costs and recoverable costs clear.

## Summary

1. The cost function, $c(w_1, w_2, y)$, measures the minimum costs of producing a given level of output at given factor prices.

2. Cost-minimizing behavior imposes observable restrictions on choices that firms make. In particular, conditional factor demand functions will be negatively sloped.

3. There is an intimate relationship between the returns to scale exhibited by the technology and the behavior of the cost function. *Increasing* returns to scale implies *decreasing* average cost, *decreasing* returns to scale implies *increasing* average cost, and *constant* returns to scale implies *constant* average cost.

4. Sunk costs are costs that are not recoverable.

## REVIEW QUESTIONS

1. Prove that a profit-maximizing firm will always minimize costs.

2. If a firm is producing where $MP_1/w_1 > MP_2/w_2$, what can it do to reduce costs but maintain the same output?

3. Suppose that a cost-minimizing firm uses two inputs that are perfect substitutes. If the two inputs are priced the same, what do the conditional factor demands look like for the inputs?

4. The price of paper used by a cost-minimizing firm increases. The firm responds to this price change by changing its demand for certain inputs, but it keeps its output constant. What happens to the firm's use of paper?

5. If a firm uses $n$ inputs ($n > 2$), what inequality does the theory of revealed cost minimization imply about changes in factor prices ($\Delta w_i$) and the changes in factor demands ($\Delta x_i$) for a given level of output?

# CHAPTER 22

# COST CURVES

In the last chapter we described the cost-minimizing behavior of a firm. Here we continue that investigation through the use of an important geometric construction, the **cost curve**. Cost curves can be used to depict graphically the cost function of a firm and are important in studying the determination of optimal output choices.

## 22.1 Average Costs

Consider the cost function described in the last chapter. This is the function $c(w_1, w_2, y)$ that gives the minimum cost of producing output level $y$ when factor prices are $(w_1, w_2)$. In the rest of this chapter we will take the factor prices to be fixed so that we can write cost as a function of $y$ alone, $c(y)$.

Some of the costs of the firm are independent of the level of output of the firm. As we've seen in Chapter 21, these are the fixed costs. Fixed costs are the costs that must be paid regardless of what level of output the firm produces. For example, the firm might have mortgage payments that are required no matter what its level of output.

Other costs change when output changes: these are the variable costs. The total costs of the firm can always be written as the sum of the variable costs, $c_v(y)$, and the fixed costs, $F$:

$$c(y) = c_v(y) + F.$$

The **average cost function** measures the cost per unit of output. The **average variable cost function** measures the variable costs per unit of output, and the **average fixed cost function** measures the fixed costs per unit output. By the above equation:

$$AC(y) = \frac{c(y)}{y} = \frac{c_v(y)}{y} + \frac{F}{y} = AVC(y) + AFC(y)$$

where $AVC(y)$ stands for average variable costs and $AFC(y)$ stands for average fixed costs. What do these functions look like? The easiest one is certainly the average fixed cost function: when $y = 0$ it is infinite, and as $y$ increases the average fixed cost decreases toward zero. This is depicted in Figure 22.1A.

**Construction of the average cost curve.** (A) The average fixed costs decrease as output is increased. (B) The average variable costs eventually increase as output is increased. (C) The combination of these two effects produces a U-shaped average cost curve.

Figure
22.1

Consider the variable cost function. Start at a zero level of output and consider producing one unit. Then the average variable costs at $y = 1$ is just the variable cost of producing this one unit. Now increase the level of production to 2 units. We would expect that, at worst, variable costs would double, so that average variable costs would remain constant. If we can organize production in a more efficient way as the scale of output is increased, the average variable costs might even decrease initially. But eventually we would expect the average variable costs to rise. Why? If fixed factors are present, they will eventually constrain the production process.

For example, suppose that the fixed costs are due to the rent or mortgage payments on a building of fixed size. Then as production increases, average variable costs—the per-unit production costs—may remain constant for a while. But as the capacity of the building is reached, these costs will rise sharply, producing an average variable cost curve of the form depicted in Figure 22.1B.

The average cost curve is the sum of these two curves; thus it will have the U-shape indicated in Figure 22.1C. The initial decline in average costs is due to the decline in average fixed costs; the eventual increase in average costs is due to the increase in average variable costs. The combination of these two effects yields the U-shape depicted in the diagram.

## 22.2 Marginal Costs

There is one more cost curve of interest: the **marginal cost curve**. The marginal cost curve measures the *change* in costs for a given change in output. That is, at any given level of output $y$, we can ask how costs will change if we change output by some amount $\delta y$:

$$MC(y) = \frac{\delta c(y)}{\delta y} = \frac{c(y + \delta y) - c(y)}{\delta y}.$$

We could just as well write the definition of marginal costs in terms of the variable cost function:

$$MC(y) = \frac{\delta c_v(y)}{\delta y} = \frac{c_v(y + \delta y) - c_v(y)}{\delta y}.$$

This is equivalent to the first definition, since $c(y) = c_v(y) + F$ and the fixed costs, $F$, don't change as $y$ changes.

Often we think of $\delta y$ as being one unit of output, so that marginal cost indicates the change in our costs if we consider producing one more discrete unit of output. If we are thinking of the production of a discrete good, then marginal cost of producing $y$ units of output is just $c(y) - c(y - 1)$. This is often a convenient way to think about marginal cost, but is sometimes misleading. Remember, marginal cost measures a *rate of change*: the change in costs divided by a change in output. If the change in output is a single unit, then marginal cost looks like a simple change in costs, but it is really a rate of change as we increase the output by one unit. If the produced good need not be discrete, we can think of $dy$ as being infinitesimally small, so that marginal cost function is the derivative of the cost function or variable cost function with respect to output.

How can we put this marginal cost curve on the diagram presented above? First we note the following. The variable costs are zero when zero units of output are produced, by definition. Thus for the first small amount of output produced,

$$\lim_{y \to 0} MC(y) = \lim_{y \to 0} \frac{c_v(y) + F - c_v(0) - F}{y} = \lim_{y \to 0} \frac{c_v(y)}{y} = \lim_{y \to 0} AVC(y).$$

Thus the marginal cost approaches the average variable cost as output approaches zero.

Now suppose that we are producing in a range of output where *average* variable costs are decreasing. Then it must be that the *marginal* costs are less than the average variable costs in this range. For the way that you push an average down is to add in numbers that are less than the average.

Think about a sequence of numbers representing average costs at different levels of output. If the average is decreasing, it must be that the cost of each additional unit produced is less than average up to that point. To make the average go down, you have to be adding additional units that are less than the average.

To see this formally, if the average variable costs are decreasing, this means that

$$\frac{d}{dy} \frac{c_v(y)}{y} < 0.$$

Using the quotient rule for derivatives,

$$\frac{d}{dy} \frac{c_v(y)}{y} = \frac{yc_v'(y) - c_v(y)}{y^2} > 0.$$

Since $y^2$ is positive, this means

$$yc_v'(y) > c_v(y),$$

or

$$c_v'(y) > \frac{c_v(y)}{y},$$

which means that marginal cost is greater than average variable cost.

Similarly, if we are in a region where average variable costs are rising, then it must be the case that the marginal costs are greater than the average variable costs—it is the higher marginal costs that are pushing the average up.

Thus we know that the marginal cost curve must lie below the average variable cost curve to the left of its minimum point and above it to the right. This implies that the marginal cost curve must intersect the average variable cost curve at its minimum point.

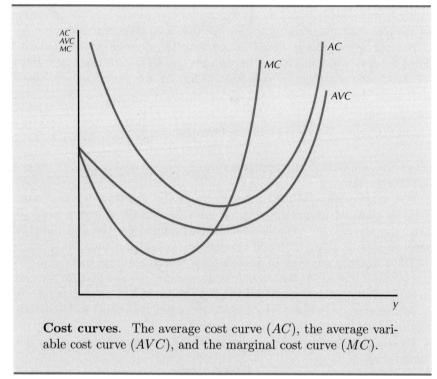

Figure
22.2
**Cost curves.** The average cost curve ($AC$), the average variable cost curve ($AVC$), and the marginal cost curve ($MC$).

Exactly the same kind of argument applies for the average cost curve. If average costs are falling, then marginal costs must be less than the average costs and if average costs are rising the marginal costs must be larger than the average costs. These observations allow us to draw in the marginal cost curve as in Figure 22.2.

To review the important points:

- The average variable cost curve may initially slope down but need not. However, it will eventually rise, as long as there are fixed factors that constrain production.

- The average cost curve will initially fall due to declining fixed costs but then rise due to the increasing average variable costs.

- The marginal cost and average variable cost are the same at the first small unit of output.

- The marginal cost curve passes through the minimum point of both the average variable cost and the average cost curves.

## 22.3 Marginal Costs and Variable Costs

There are also some other relationships between the various curves. Here is one that is not so obvious: it turns out that the area beneath the marginal cost curve up to $y$ gives us the variable cost of producing $y$ units of output. Why is that?

The marginal cost curve measures the cost of producing each additional unit of output. If we add up the cost of producing each unit of output we will get the total costs of production—except for fixed costs.

This argument can be made rigorous in the case where the output good is produced in discrete amounts. First, we note that

$$c_v(y) = [c_v(y) - c_v(y-1)] + [c_v(y-1) - c_v(y-2)] +$$
$$\cdots + [c_v(1) - c_v(0)].$$

This is true since $c_v(0) = 0$ and all the middle terms cancel out; that is, the second term cancels the third term, the fourth term cancels the fifth term, and so on. But each term in this sum is the marginal cost at a different level of output:

$$c_v(y) = MC(y-1) + MC(y-2) + \cdots + MC(0).$$

Thus each term in the sum represents the area of a rectangle with height $MC(y)$ and base of 1. Summing up all these rectangles gives us the area under the marginal cost curve as depicted in Figure 22.3.

When the output good is not produced in discrete amounts, the relationship can be derived from the fundamental theorem of calculus. Since

$$MC(y) = \frac{dc_v(y)}{dy},$$

we know that the area under the marginal cost curve is

$$c_v(y) = \int_0^y \frac{dc_v(x)}{dx} \, dx = c_v(y) - c_v(0) = c_v(y).$$

## EXAMPLE: Specific Cost Curves

Let's consider the cost function $c(y) = y^2 + 1$. We have the following derived cost curves:

- variable costs: $c_v(y) = y^2$

- fixed costs: $c_f(y) = 1$

- average variable costs: $AVC(y) = y^2/y = y$

Figure
22.3
**Marginal cost and variable costs.** The area under the
marginal cost curve gives the variable costs.

- average fixed costs: $AFC(y) = 1/y$

- average costs: $AC(y) = \dfrac{y^2 + 1}{y} = y + \dfrac{1}{y}$

- marginal costs: $MC(y) = c'(y) = 2y$

What do these cost curves look like? The easiest way to draw them is
first to draw the average variable cost curve, which is a straight line with
slope 1. Then it is also simple to draw the marginal cost curve, which is a
straight line with slope 2.

The average cost curve reaches its minimum where average cost equals
marginal cost, which says

$$y + \frac{1}{y} = 2y,$$

which can be solved to give $y_{\min} = 1$. The average cost at $y = 1$ is 2, which
is also the marginal cost. The final picture is given in Figure 22.4.


## EXAMPLE: Marginal Cost Curves for Two Plants

Suppose that you have two plants that have two different cost functions,
$c_1(y_1)$ and $c_2(y_2)$. You want to produce $y$ units of output in the cheapest
way. In general, you will want to produce some amount of output in each
plant. The question is, how much should you produce in each plant?

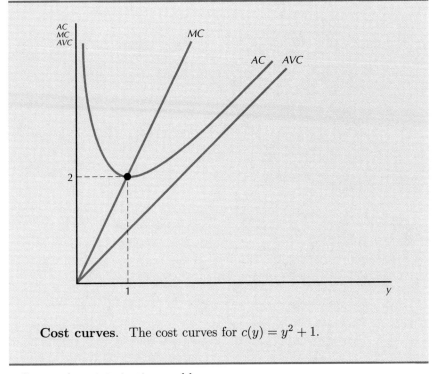

**Cost curves.** The cost curves for $c(y) = y^2 + 1$.

Figure
22.4

Set up the minimization problem:

$$\min_{y_1, y_2} c_1(y_1) + c_2(y_2)$$

such that $y_1 + y_2 = y$.

Now how do you solve it? It turns out that at the optimal division of output between the two plants we must have the marginal cost of producing output at plant 1 equal to the marginal cost of producing output at plant 2. In order to prove this, suppose the marginal costs were not equal; then it would pay to shift a small amount of output from the plant with higher marginal costs to the plant with lower marginal costs. If the output division is optimal, then switching output from one plant to the other can't lower costs.

Let $c(y)$ be the cost function that gives the cheapest way to produce $y$ units of output—that is, the cost of producing $y$ units of output given that you have divided output in the best way between the two plants. The marginal cost of producing an extra unit of output must be the same no matter which plant you produce it in.

We depict the two marginal cost curves, $MC_1(y_1)$ and $MC_2(y_2)$, in Figure 22.5. The marginal cost curve for the two plants taken together is just the horizontal sum of the two marginal cost curves, as depicted in Figure 22.5C.

Figure
22.5

**Marginal costs for a firm with two plants.** The overall marginal cost curve on the right is the horizontal sum of the marginal cost curves for the two plants shown on the left.

For any fixed level of marginal costs, say $c$, we will produce $y_1^*$ and $y_2^*$ such that $MC_1(y_1^*) = MC(y_2^*) = c$, and we will thus have $y_1^* + y_2^*$ units of output produced. Thus the amount of output produced at any marginal cost $c$ is just the sum of the outputs where the marginal cost of plant 1 equals $c$ and the marginal cost of plant 2 equals $c$: the horizontal sum of the marginal cost curves.

## 22.4 Cost Curves for Online Auctions

We explored an auction model of search engine advertising in Chapter 18. Recall the setup. When a user enters a query into a search engine, the query is matched with keywords chosen by advertisers. Those advertisers whose keywords match the query are entered into an auction. The highest bidder gets the most prominent position, the second-highest bidder gets the second most prominent position and so on. The more prominent the position, the more clicks the ad tends to get, other things (such as ad quality) being equal.

In the auction examined earlier, it was assumed that each advertiser could choose a separate bid for each keyword. In practice, an advertiser chooses a single bid that is used in all auctions in which they participate. The fact that prices are determined by an auction is not all that important from an advertiser's point of view. What matters is the relationship between the number of clicks the ad gets, $x$, and the cost of those clicks, $c(x)$.

This is just our old friend the total cost function. Once an advertiser knows the cost function, it can determine how many clicks it wants to buy. Letting $v$ represent the value of a click, the profit maximization problem is

$$\max_x vx - c(x).$$

As we have seen, the optimal solution entails setting value equal to marginal cost. Once the advertiser determines the profit-maximizing number of clicks, it can choose a bid that will yield that many clicks.

This process is shown in Figure 22.6, which is a standard plot of average cost and marginal cost, with the addition of a new line illustrating the bid.

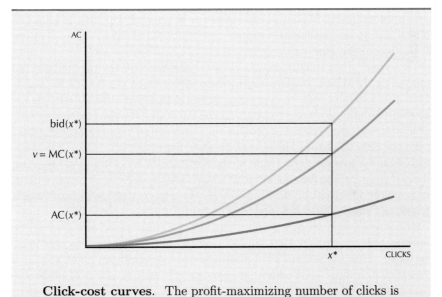

**Click-cost curves.** The profit-maximizing number of clicks is where value equals marginal cost, which determines the appropriate bid and average cost per click.

Figure 22.6

How does the advertising discover its cost curve? One answer is that the advertiser can experiment with different bids and record the resulting number of clicks and cost. Or, the search engine can provide an estimate of the cost function by using the information from the auctions.

Suppose, for example, we want to estimate what would happen if an advertiser increases its bid per click from 50 cents to 80 cents. The search engine can look at each auction in which the advertiser participates to how its position changes and how many new clicks it could be expected to receive in the new position.

## 22.5 Long-Run Costs

In the above analysis, we have regarded the firm's fixed costs as being the costs that involve payments to factors that it is unable to adjust in the short run. In the long run a firm can choose the level of its "fixed" factors—they are no longer fixed.

Of course, there may still be quasi-fixed factors in the long run. That is, it may be a feature of the technology that some costs have to be paid to produce any positive level of output. But in the long run there are no fixed costs, in the sense that it is always possible to produce zero units of output at zero costs—that is, it is always possible to go out of business. If quasi-fixed factors are present in the long run, then the average cost curve will tend to have a U-shape, just as in the short run. But in the long run it will always be possible to produce zero units of output at a zero cost, by definition of the long run.

Of course, what constitutes the long run depends on the problem we are analyzing. If we are considering the fixed factor to be the size of the plant, then the long run will be how long it would take the firm to change the size of its plant. If we are considering the fixed factor to be the contractual obligations to pay salaries, then the long run would be how long it would take the firm to change the size of its work force.

Just to be specific, let's think of the fixed factor as being plant size and denote it by $k$. The firm's short-run cost function, given that it has a plant of $k$ square feet, will be denoted by $c_s(y, k)$, where the $s$ subscript stands for "short run." (Here $k$ is playing the role of $\bar{x}_2$ in Chapter 21.)

For any given level of output, there will be some plant size that is the optimal size to produce that level of output. Let us denote this plant size by $k(y)$. This is the firm's conditional factor demand for plant size as a function of output. (Of course, it also depends on the prices of plant size and other factors of production, but we have suppressed these arguments.) Then, as we've seen in Chapter 21, the long-run cost function of the firm will be given by $c_s(y, k(y))$. This is the total cost of producing an output level $y$, given that the firm is allowed to adjust its plant size optimally. The long-run cost function of the firm is just the short-run cost function evaluated at the optimal choice of the fixed factors:

$$c(y) = c_s(y, k(y)).$$

Let us see how this looks graphically. Pick some level of output $y^*$, and let $k^* = k(y^*)$ be the optimal plant size for that level of output. The short-run cost function for a plant of size $k^*$ will be given by $c_s(y, k^*)$, and the long-run cost function will be given by $c(y) = c_s(y, k(y))$, just as above.

Now, note the important fact that the short-run cost to produce output $y$ must always be at least as large as the long-run cost to produce $y$. Why?

In the short run the firm has a fixed plant size, while in the long run the firm is free to adjust its plant size. Since one of its long-run choices is always to choose the plant size $k^*$, its optimal choice to produce $y$ units of output must have costs at least as small as $c(y, k^*)$. This means that the firm must be able to do at least as well by adjusting plant size as by having it fixed. Thus

$$c(y) \leq c_s(y, k^*)$$

for all levels of $y$.

In fact, at one particular level of $y$, namely $y^*$, we know that

$$c(y^*) = c_s(y^*, k^*).$$

Why? Because at $y^*$ the *optimal* choice of plant size is $k^*$. So at $y^*$, the long-run costs and the short-run costs are the same.

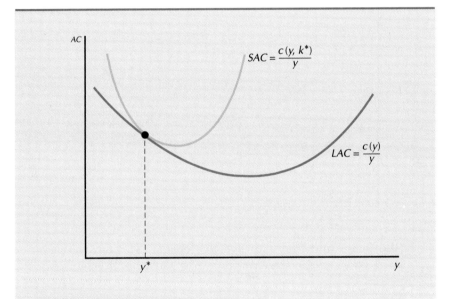

**Short-run and long-run average costs.** The short-run average cost curve must be tangent to the long-run average cost curve.

Figure
22.7

If the short-run cost is always greater than the long-run cost and they are equal at one level of output, then this means that the short-run and the long-run average costs have the same property: $AC(y) \leq AC_s(y, k^*)$ and $AC(y^*) = AC_s(y^*, k^*)$. This implies that the short-run average cost curve always lies above the long-run average cost curve and that they touch at one point, $y^*$. Thus the long-run average cost curve ($LAC$) and the short-run average cost curve ($SAC$) must be tangent at that point, as depicted in Figure 22.7.

We can do the same sort of construction for levels of output other than $y^*$. Suppose we pick outputs $y_1, y_2, \ldots, y_n$ and accompanying plant sizes $k_1 = k(y_1), k_2 = k(y_2), \ldots, k_n = k(y_n)$. Then we get a picture like that in Figure 22.8. We summarize Figure 22.8 by saying that the long-run average cost curve is the **lower envelope** of the short-run average cost curves.

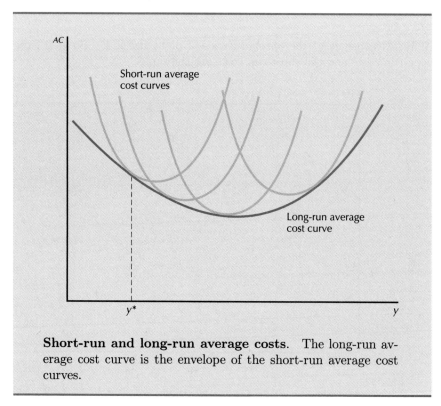

**Figure 22.8**

**Short-run and long-run average costs.** The long-run average cost curve is the envelope of the short-run average cost curves.

## 22.6 Discrete Levels of Plant Size

In the above discussion we have implicitly assumed that we can choose a continuous number of different plant sizes. Thus each different level of output has a unique optimal plant size associated with it. But we can also consider what happens if there are only a few different levels of plant size to choose from.

Suppose, for example, that we have four different choices, $k_1$, $k_2$, $k_3$, and $k_4$. We have depicted the four different average cost curves associated with these plant sizes in Figure 22.9.

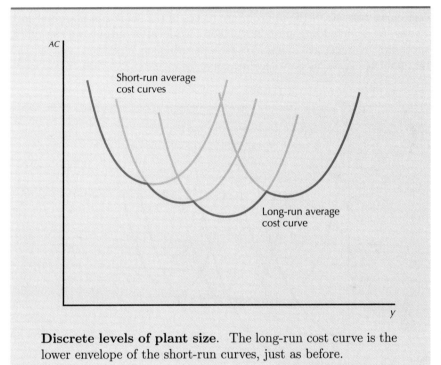

**Discrete levels of plant size.** The long-run cost curve is the lower envelope of the short-run curves, just as before.

Figure
22.9

How can we construct the long-run average cost curve? Well, remember the long-run average cost curve is the cost curve you get by adjusting $k$ optimally. In this case that isn't hard to do: since there are only four different plant sizes, we just see which one has the lowest costs associated with it and pick that plant size. That is, for any level of output $y$, we just choose the plant size that gives us the minimum cost of producing that output level.

Thus the long-run average cost curve will be the lower envelope of the short-run average costs, as depicted in Figure 22.9. Note that this figure has qualitatively the same implications as Figure 22.8: the short-run average costs always are at least as large as the long-run average costs, and they are the same at the level of output where the long-run demand for the fixed factor equals the amount of the fixed factor that you have.

## 22.7 Long-Run Marginal Costs

We've seen in the last section that the long-run average cost curve is the lower envelope of the short-run average cost curves. What are the implications of this for marginal costs? Let's first consider the case where there are discrete levels of plant size. In this situation the long-run marginal cost curve consists of the appropriate pieces of the short-run marginal cost curves, as depicted in Figure 22.10. For each level of output, we see which short-run average cost curve we are operating on and then look at the marginal cost associated with that curve.

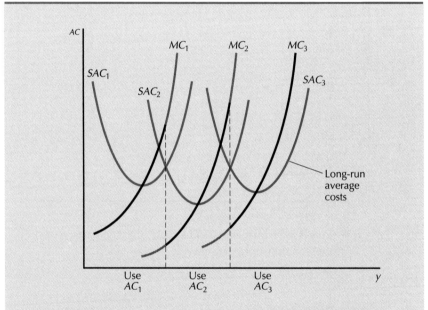

**Figure 22.10**

**Long-run marginal costs.** When there are discrete levels of the fixed factor, the firm will choose the amount of the fixed factor to minimize average costs. Thus the long-run marginal cost curve will consist of the various segments of the short-run marginal cost curves associated with each different level of the fixed factor.

This has to hold true no matter how many different plant sizes there are, so the picture for the continuous case looks like Figure 22.11. The long-run marginal cost at any output level $y$ has to equal the short-run marginal cost associated with the optimal level of plant size to produce $y$.

The discussion of long-run and short-run marginal cost curves is all pretty clear geometrically, but what does it mean economically? The intuition is simple. The marginal cost of production is just the change in cost that arises from changing output. In the short run we have to keep plant size (or whatever) fixed, while in the long run we are free to adjust it. So the long-run marginal cost will consist of two pieces: how costs change holding plant size fixed plus how costs change when plant size adjusts. But if the plant size is chosen optimally, this last term has to be zero! Thus the long-run and the short-run marginal costs have to be the same.

The mathematical proof involves the chain rule. By definition:

$$c(y) \equiv c_s(y, k(y)).$$

Differentiating with respect to $y$ gives

$$\frac{dc(y)}{dy} = \frac{\partial c_s(y, k)}{\partial y} + \frac{\partial c_s(y, k)}{\partial k} \frac{\partial k(y)}{\partial y}.$$

If we evaluate this at a specific level of output $y^*$ and its associated optimal plant size $k^* = k(y^*)$, we know that

$$\frac{\partial c_s(y^*, k^*)}{\partial k} = 0$$

because that is the necessary first-order condition for $k^*$ to be the cost-minimizing plant size at $y^*$. Thus the second term in the expression cancels out and all that we have left is the short-run marginal cost:

$$\frac{dc(y^*)}{dy} = \frac{\partial c_s(y^*, k^*)}{\partial y}.$$

## Summary

1. Average costs are composed of average variable costs plus average fixed costs. Average fixed costs always decline with output, while average variable costs tend to increase. The net result is a U-shaped average cost curve.

2. The marginal cost curve lies below the average cost curve when average costs are decreasing, and above when they are increasing. Thus marginal costs must equal average costs at the point of minimum average costs.

3. The area under the marginal cost curve measures the variable costs.

4. The long-run average cost curve is the lower envelope of the short-run average cost curves.

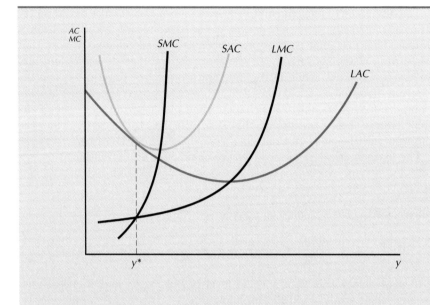

Figure
22.11
**Long-run marginal costs.** The relationship between the long-run and the short-run marginal costs with continuous levels of the fixed factor.

## REVIEW QUESTIONS

1. Which of the following are true? (1) Average fixed costs never increase with output; (2) average total costs are always greater than or equal to average variable costs; (3) average cost can never rise while marginal costs are declining.

2. A firm produces identical outputs at two different plants. If the marginal cost at the first plant exceeds the marginal cost at the second plant, how can the firm reduce costs and maintain the same level of output?

3. True or false? In the long run a firm always operates at the minimum level of average costs for the optimally sized plant to produce a given amount of output.

# CHAPTER 23

# FIRM SUPPLY

In this chapter we will see how to derive the supply curve of a competitive firm from its cost function using the model of profit maximization. The first thing we have to do is to describe the market environment in which the firm operates.

## 23.1 Market Environments

Every firm faces two important decisions: choosing how much it should produce and choosing what price it should set. If there were no constraints on a profit-maximizing firm, it would set an arbitrarily high price and produce an arbitrarily large amount of output. But no firm exists in such an unconstrained environment. In general, the firm faces two sorts of constraints on its actions.

First, it faces the **technological constraints** summarized by the production function. There are only certain feasible combinations of inputs and outputs, and even the most profit-hungry firm has to respect the realities of the physical world. We have already discussed how we can summarize the technological constraints, and we've seen how the technological constraints lead to the **economic constraints** summarized by the cost function.

But now we bring in a new constraint—or at least an old constraint from a different perspective. This is the **market constraint**. A firm can produce whatever is physically feasible, and it can set whatever price it wants ... but it can only sell as much as people are willing to buy.

If it sets a certain price $p$ it will sell a certain amount of output $x$. We call the relationship between the price a firm sets and the amount that it sells the **demand curve facing the firm**.

If there were only one firm in the market, the demand curve facing the firm would be very simple to describe: it is just the market demand curve described in earlier chapters on consumer behavior. For the market demand curve measures how much of the good people want to buy at each price. Thus the demand curve summarizes the market constraints facing a firm that has a market all to itself.

But if there are other firms in the market, the constraints facing an individual firm will be different. In this case, the firm has to guess how the *other* firms in the market will behave when it chooses its price and output.

This is not an easy problem to solve, either for firms or for economists. There are a lot of different possibilities, and we will try to examine them in a systematic way. We'll use the term **market environment** to describe the ways that firms respond to each other when they make their pricing and output decisions.

In this chapter we'll examine the simplest market environment, that of **pure competition**. This is a good comparison point for many other environments, and it is of considerable interest in its own right. First let's give the economist's definition of pure competition, and then we'll try to justify it.

## 23.2 Pure Competition

To a lay person, "competition" has the connotation of intense rivalry. That's why students are often surprised that the economist's definition of competition seems so passive: we say that a market is **purely competitive** if each firm assumes that the market price is independent of its own level of output. Thus, in a competitive market, each firm only has to worry about how much output it wants to produce. Whatever it produces can only be sold at one price: the going market price.

In what sort of environment might this be a reasonable assumption for a firm to make? Well, suppose that we have an industry composed of many firms that produce an identical product, and that each firm is a small part of the market. A good example would be the market for wheat. There are thousands of wheat farmers in the United States, and even the largest of them produces only an infinitesimal fraction of the total supply. It is reasonable in this case for any one firm in the industry to take the market price as being predetermined. A wheat farmer doesn't have to worry about what price to set for his wheat—if he wants to sell any at all, he has to sell it at the market price. He is a **price taker**: the price is given as far as he is concerned; all he has to worry about is how much to produce.

This kind of situation—an identical product and many small firms—is a classic example of a situation where price-taking behavior is sensible. But it is not the only case where price-taking behavior is possible. Even if there are only a few firms in the market, they may still treat the market price as being outside their control.

Think of a case where there is a fixed supply of a perishable good: say fresh fish or cut flowers in a marketplace. Even if there are only 3 or 4 firms in the market, each firm may have to take the *other* firms' prices as given. If the customers in the market only buy at the lowest price, then the lowest price being offered is the market price. If one of the other firms wants to sell anything at all, it will have to sell at the market price. So in this sort of situation competitive behavior—taking the market price as outside of your control—seems plausible as well.

We can describe the relationship between price and quantity perceived by a competitive firm in terms of a diagram as in Figure 23.1. As you can see, this demand curve is very simple. A competitive firm believes that it will sell nothing if it charges a price higher than the market price. If it sells at the market price, it can sell whatever amount it wants, and if it sells below the market price, it will get the entire market demand at that price.

As usual we can think of this kind of demand curve in two ways. If we think of quantity as a function of price, this curve says that you can sell any amount you want at or below the market price. If we think of price as a function of quantity, it says that no matter how much you sell, the market price will be independent of your sales.

(Of course, this doesn't have to be true for literally *any* amount. Price has to be independent of your output for any amount you might consider selling. In the case of the cut-flower seller, the price has to be independent of how much she sells for any amount up to her stock on hand—the maximum that she could consider selling.)

It is important to understand the difference between the "demand curve facing a firm" and the "market demand curve." The market demand curve measures the relationship between the market price and the total amount of output sold. The demand curve facing a firm measures the relationship between the market price and the output of *that particular firm*.

The market demand curve depends on consumers' behavior. The demand curve facing a firm not only depends on consumers' behavior but it also depends on the behavior of the other firms. The usual justification for the competitive model is that when there are many small firms in the market, each one faces a demand curve that is essentially flat. But even if there are only two firms in the market, and one insists on charging a fixed price no matter what, then the other firm in the market will face a competitive demand curve like the one depicted in Figure 23.1. Thus the competitive model may hold in a wider variety of circumstances than is apparent at first glance.

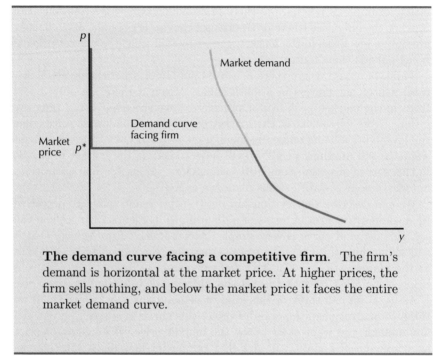

Figure 23.1

**The demand curve facing a competitive firm.** The firm's demand is horizontal at the market price. At higher prices, the firm sells nothing, and below the market price it faces the entire market demand curve.

## 23.3 The Supply Decision of a Competitive Firm

Let us use the facts we have discovered about cost curves to figure out the supply curve of a competitive firm. By definition a competitive firm ignores its influence on the market price. Thus the maximization problem facing a competitive firm is

$$\max_{y} py - c(y).$$

This just says that the competitive firm wants to maximize its profits: the difference between its revenue, $py$, and its costs, $c(y)$.

What level of output will a competitive firm choose to produce? Answer: it will operate where marginal revenue equals marginal cost—where the extra revenue gained by one more unit of output just equals the extra cost of producing another unit. If this condition did not hold, the firm could always increase its profits by changing its level of output.

The firm's profit-maximization problem is a constrained maximization problem:

$$\max_{y} \; py - c(y)$$

such that $y \geq 0$.

The necessary conditions for the optimal supply, $y^*$, are the first-order condition

$$p - c'(y^*) = 0$$

and the second-order condition

$$-c''(y^*) \leq 0.$$

The first-order condition says price equals marginal cost, and the second-order condition says that the marginal cost must be increasing. Of course this is presuming that $y^* > 0$. If price is less than average variable cost at $y^*$, it will pay the firm to produce a zero level of output. To determine the supply curve of a competitive firm, we must find all the points where the first- and second-order conditions are satisfied and compare them to each other—and to $y = 0$—and pick the one with the largest profits. That's the profit-maximizing supply.

In the case of a competitive firm, the first-order condition tells us that marginal revenue is simply the price.

Thus a competitive firm will choose a level of output $y$ where the marginal cost that it faces at $y$ is just equal to the market price. In symbols:

$$p = MC(y).$$

Thus the marginal cost curve of a competitive firm is precisely its supply curve. Or put another way, the market price is precisely marginal cost—as long as each firm is producing at its profit-maximizing level.

## 23.4 An Exception

Keep in mind that price equals marginal cost is a *necessary* condition for profit maximization. It is not in general a *sufficient* condition. Just because we find a point where price equals marginal cost doesn't mean that we've found the maximum profit point. But if we find the maximum profit point, we know that price must equal marginal cost.

Figure
23.2
**Marginal cost and supply.** Although there are two levels of output where price equals marginal cost, the profit-maximizing quantity supplied can lie only on the upward-sloping part of the marginal cost curve.

There may several levels of output where price equals marginal cost, such as the case depicted in Figure 23.2. Here there are two levels of output where price equals marginal cost. Which one will the firm choose?

It is not hard to see the answer. Consider the first intersection, where the marginal cost curve is sloping down. Now if we increase output a little bit here, the costs of each additional unit of output will decrease. That's what it means to say that the marginal cost curve is decreasing. But the market price will stay the same. Thus profits must definitely go up. This is where the second-order condition comes into play.

So we can rule out levels of output where the marginal cost curve slopes downward. At those points an increase in output must always increase profits. The supply curve of a competitive firm must lie along the upward-sloping part of the marginal cost curve. This means that the supply curve itself must always be upward sloping. The "Giffen good" phenomenon cannot arise for supply curves.

## 23.5 Another Exception

In addition to checking for solutions to the first- and second-order conditions, we need to consider the profits of the firm if it decides not to produce anything. After all it could be that the best thing for a firm to do is to produce zero output. Since it is always possible to produce a zero level of output, we have to compare our candidate for profit maximization with the choice of doing nothing at all.

If a firm produces zero output it still has to pay its fixed costs, $F$. Thus the profits from producing zero units of output are just $-F$. The profits from producing a level of output $y$ are $py - c_v(y) - F$. The firm is better off going out of business when

$$-F > py - c_v(y) - F,$$

that is, when the "profits" from producing nothing, and just paying the fixed costs, exceed the profits from producing where price equals marginal cost. Rearranging this equation gives us the **shutdown condition**:

$$AVC(y) = \frac{c_v(y)}{y} > p.$$

If average variable costs are greater than $p$, the firm would be better off producing zero units of output. This makes good sense, since it says that the revenues from selling the output $y$ don't even cover the *variable* costs of production, $c_v(y)$. In this case the firm might as well go out of business. If it produces nothing it will lose its fixed costs, but it would lose even more if it continued to produce.

This discussion indicates that only the portions of the marginal cost curve that lie above the average variable cost curve are possible points on the supply curve. If a point where price equals marginal cost is beneath the average variable cost curve, the firm would optimally choose to produce zero units of output.

We now have a picture for the supply curve like that in Figure 23.3. The competitive firm produces along the part of the marginal cost curve that is upward sloping and lies above the average variable cost curve.

## EXAMPLE: Pricing Operating Systems

A computer requires an operating system in order to run, and most hardware manufacturers sell their computers with the operating systems already installed. In the early 1980s several operating system producers were fighting for supremacy in the IBM-PC-compatible microcomputer market. The common practice at that time was for the producer of the operating system to charge the computer manufacturer for each copy of the operating system that was *installed* on a microcomputer that it sold.

Microsoft Corporation offered an alternative plan in which the charge to the manufacturer was based on the number of microcomputers that were

Figure
23.3

**Average variable cost and supply**. The supply curve is the upward-sloping part of the marginal cost curve that lies above the average variable cost curve. The firm will not operate on those points on the marginal cost curve below the average cost curve since it could have greater profits (less losses) by shutting down.

*built* by the manufacturer. Microsoft set their licensing fee low enough that this plan was attractive to the producers.

Note the clever nature of Microsoft's pricing strategy: once the contract with a manufacturer was signed, the marginal cost of installing MS-DOS on an already-built computer was zero. Installing a competing operating system, on the other hand, could cost $50 to $100. The hardware manufacturer (and ultimately the user) paid Microsoft for the operating system, but the structure of the pricing contract made MS-DOS very attractive relative to the competition. As a result, Microsoft ended up being the default operating system installed on microcomputers and achieved a market penetration of over 90 percent.

## 23.6 The Inverse Supply Function

We have seen that the supply curve of a competitive firm is determined by the condition that price equals marginal cost. As before we can express this relation between price and output in two ways: we can either think of output as a function of price, as we usually do, or we can think of the

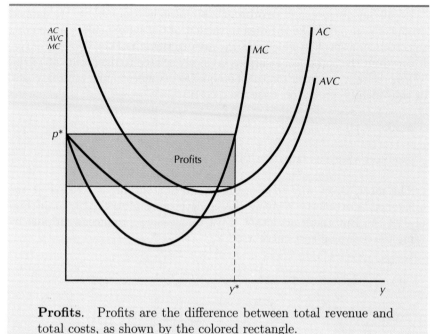

**Profits.**   Profits are the difference between total revenue and total costs, as shown by the colored rectangle.

Figure
23.4

"inverse supply function" that gives price as a function of output. There is a certain insight to be gained by looking at it in the latter way. Since price equals marginal cost at each point on the supply curve, the market price must be a measure of marginal cost for every firm operating in the industry. A firm that produces a lot of output and a firm that produces only a little output must have the *same marginal cost,* if they are both maximizing profits. The total cost of production of each firm can be very different, but the marginal cost of production must be the same.

The equation $p = MC(y)$ gives us the inverse supply function: price as a function of output. This way of expressing the supply curve can be very useful.

## 23.7 Profits and Producer's Surplus

Given the market price we can now compute the optimal operating position for the firm from the condition that $p = MC(y)$. Given the optimal operating position we can compute the profits of the firm. In Figure 23.4 the area of the box is just $p^*y^*$, or total revenue. The area $y^*AC(y^*)$ is total costs since

$$yAC(y) = y\frac{c(y)}{y} = c(y).$$

Profits are simply the difference between these two areas.

Recall our discussion of **producer's surplus** in Chapter 14. We defined producer's surplus to be the area to the left of the supply curve, in analogy to consumer's surplus, which was the area to the left of the demand curve. It turns out that producer's surplus is closely related to the profits of a firm. More precisely, producer's surplus is equal to revenues minus variable costs, or equivalently, profits plus the fixed costs:

$$\text{profits} = py - c_v(y) - F$$

$$\text{producer's surplus} = py - c_v(y).$$

The most direct way to measure producer's surplus is to look at the difference between the revenue box and the box $y^* AVC(y^*)$, as in Figure 23.5A. But there are other ways to measure producer's surplus by using the marginal cost curve itself.

**A** Revenue −variable costs

**B** Area above *MC* curve

**C** Area to the left of the supply curve

Figure 23.5

**Producer's surplus.** Three equivalent ways to measure producer's surplus. Panel A depicts a box measuring revenue minus variable cost. Panel B depicts the area above the marginal cost curve. Panel C uses the box up until output $z$ (area $R$) and then uses the area above the marginal cost curve (area $T$).

We know from Chapter 22 that the area under the marginal cost curve measures the total variable costs. This is true because the area under the marginal cost curve is the cost of producing the first unit plus the cost of producing the second unit, and so on. So to get producer's surplus, we can subtract the area under the marginal cost curve from the revenue box and get the area depicted in Figure 23.5B.

Finally, we can combine the two ways of measuring producer's surplus. Use the "box" definition up to the point where marginal cost equals average variable cost, and then use the area above the marginal cost curve, as shown in Figure 23.5C. This latter way is the most convenient for most applications since it is just the area to the left of the supply curve. Note that this is consistent with definition of producer's surplus given in Chapter 14.

We are seldom interested in the *total* amount of producer's surplus; more often it is the *change* in producer's surplus that is of interest. The change in producer's surplus when the firm moves from output $y^*$ to output $y'$ will generally be a trapezoidal shaped region like that depicted in Figure 23.6.

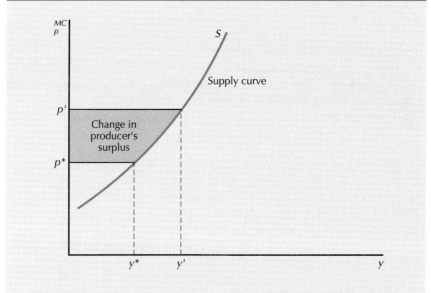

**The change in producer's surplus.**  Since the supply curve coincides with the upward-sloping part of the marginal cost curve, the change in producer's surplus will typically have a roughly trapezoidal shape.

Figure
23.6

Note that the change in producer's surplus in moving from $y^*$ to $y'$ is

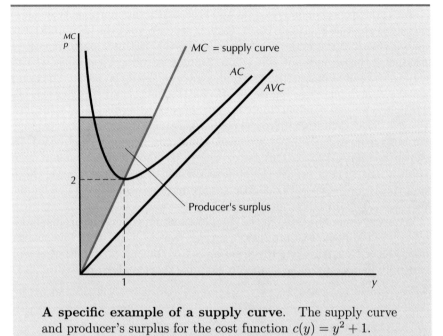

Figure
23.7

**A specific example of a supply curve.** The supply curve
and producer's surplus for the cost function $c(y) = y^2 + 1$.

just the change in profits in moving from $y^*$ to $y'$, since by definition the
fixed costs don't change. Thus we can measure the impact on profits of
a change in output from the information contained in the marginal cost
curve, without having to refer to the average cost curve at all.

## EXAMPLE: The Supply Curve for a Specific Cost Function

What does the supply curve look like for the example given in the last
chapter where $c(y) = y^2 + 1$? In that example the marginal cost curve
was always above the average variable cost curve, and it always sloped
upward. So "price equals marginal costs" gives us the supply curve directly.
Substituting $2y$ for marginal cost we get the formula

$$p = 2y.$$

This gives us the inverse supply curve, or price as a function of output.
Solving for output as a function of price we have

$$S(p) = y = \frac{p}{2}$$

as our formula for the supply curve. This is depicted in Figure 23.7.

If we substitute this supply function into the definition of profits, we can calculate the maximum profits for each price $p$. Performing the calculation we have:

$$\pi(p) = py - c(y)$$

$$= p\frac{p}{2} - \left(\frac{p}{2}\right)^2 - 1$$

$$= \frac{p^2}{4} - 1.$$

How do the maximum profits relate to producer's surplus? In Figure 23.7 we see that producer's surplus—the area to the left of the supply curve between a price of zero and a price of $p$—will be a triangle with a base of $y = p/2$ and a height of $p$. The area of this triangle is

$$A = \left(\frac{1}{2}\right)\left(\frac{p}{2}\right)p = \frac{p^2}{4}.$$

Comparing this with the profits expression, we see that producer's surplus equals profits plus fixed costs, as claimed.

## 23.8 The Long-Run Supply Curve of a Firm

The long-run supply function for the firm measures how much the firm would optimally produce when it is allowed to adjust plant size (or whatever factors are fixed in the short run). That is, the long-run supply curve will be given by

$$p = MC_l(y) = MC(y, k(y)).$$

The short-run supply curve is given by price equals marginal cost at some fixed level of $k$:

$$p = MC(y, k).$$

Note the difference between the two expressions. The short-run supply curve involves the marginal cost of output holding $k$ fixed at a given level of output, while the long-run supply curve involves the marginal cost of output when you adjust $k$ optimally.

Now, we know something about the relationship between short-run and long-run marginal costs: the short-run and the long-run marginal costs co-incide at the level of output $y^*$ where the fixed factor choice associated with the short-run marginal cost is the optimal choice, $k^*$. Thus the short-run and the long-run supply curves of the firm coincide at $y^*$, as in Figure 23.8.

In the short run the firm has some factors in fixed supply; in the long run these factors are variable. Thus, when the price of output changes, the

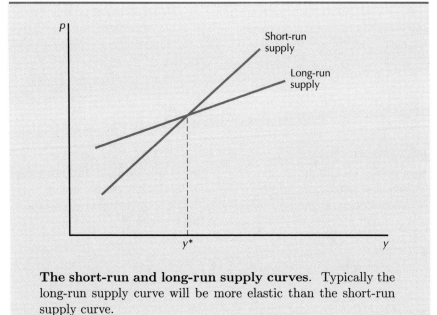

Figure
23.8

**The short-run and long-run supply curves.** Typically the long-run supply curve will be more elastic than the short-run supply curve.

firm has more choices to adjust in the long run than in the short run. This suggests that the long-run supply curve will be more responsive to price—more elastic—than the short-run supply curve, as illustrated in Figure 23.8.

What else can we say about the long-run supply curve? The long run is defined to be that time period in which the firm is free to adjust all of its inputs. One choice that the firm has is the choice of whether to remain in business. Since in the long run the firm can always get zero profits by going out of business, the profits that the firm makes in long-run equilibrium have to be at least zero:

$$py - c(y) \geq 0,$$

which means

$$p \geq \frac{c(y)}{y}.$$

This says that in the long run price has to be at least as large as average cost. Thus the relevant part of the long-run supply curve is the upward-sloping part of the marginal cost curve that lies above the long-run average cost curve, as depicted in Figure 23.9.

This is completely consistent with the short-run story. In the long run all costs are variable costs, so the short-run condition of having price above average variable cost is equivalent to the long-run condition of having price above average cost.

**The long-run supply curve.** The long-run supply curve will
be the upward-sloping part of the long-run marginal cost curve
that lies above the average cost curve.

Figure
23.9

## 23.9 Long-Run Constant Average Costs

One particular case of interest occurs when the long-run technology of the
firm exhibits constant returns to scale. Here the long-run supply curve will
be the long-run marginal cost curve, which, in the case of constant average
cost, coincides with the long-run average cost curve. Thus we have the
situation depicted in Figure 23.10, where the long-run supply curve is a
horizontal line at $c_{min}$, the level of constant average cost.

This supply curve means that the firm is willing to supply any amount of
output at $p = c_{min}$, an arbitrarily large amount of output at $p > c_{min}$, and
zero output at $p < c_{min}$. When we think about the replication argument
for constant returns to scale this makes perfect sense. Constant returns
to scale implies that if you can produce 1 unit for $c_{min}$ dollars, you can
produce $n$ units for $nc_{min}$ dollars. Therefore you will be willing to supply
any amount of output at a price equal to $c_{min}$, and an arbitrarily large
amount of output at any price greater than $c_{min}$.

On the other hand, if $p < c_{min}$, so that you cannot break even supplying even one unit of output, you will certainly not be able to break even
supplying $n$ units of output. Hence, for any price less than $c_{min}$, you will
want to supply zero units of output.

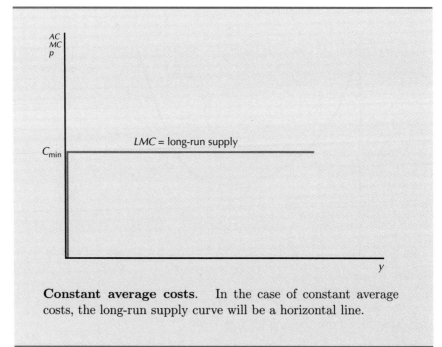

Figure
23.10

**Constant average costs.** In the case of constant average costs, the long-run supply curve will be a horizontal line.

## Summary

1. The relationship between the price a firm charges and the output that it sells is known as the demand curve facing the firm. By definition, a competitive firm faces a horizontal demand curve whose height is determined by the market price—the price charged by the other firms in the market.

2. The (short-run) supply curve of a competitive firm is that portion of its (short-run) marginal cost curve that is upward sloping and lies above the average variable cost curve.

3. The change in producer's surplus when the market price changes from $p_1$ to $p_2$ is the area to the left of the marginal cost curve between $p_1$ and $p_2$. It also measures the firm's change in profits.

4. The long-run supply curve of a firm is that portion of its long-run marginal cost curve that is upward sloping and that lies above its long-run average cost curve.

## REVIEW QUESTIONS

1. A firm has a cost function given by $c(y) = 10y^2 + 1000$. What is its supply curve?

2. A firm has a cost function given by $c(y) = 10y^2 + 1000$. At what output is average cost minimized?

3. If the supply curve is given by $S(p) = 100 + 20p$, what is the formula for the inverse supply curve?

4. A firm has a supply function given by $S(p) = 4p$. Its fixed costs are 100. If the price changes from 10 to 20, what is the change in its profits?

5. If the long-run cost function is $c(y) = y^2 + 1$, what is the long-run supply curve of the firm?

6. Classify each of the following as either technological or market constraints: the price of inputs, the number of other firms in the market, the quantity of output produced, and the ability to produce more given the current input levels.

7. What is the major assumption that characterizes a purely competitive market?

8. In a purely competitive market a firm's marginal revenue is always equal to what? A profit-maximizing firm in such a market will operate at what level of output?

9. If average variable costs exceed the market price, what level of output should the firm produce? What if there are no fixed costs?

10. Is it ever better for a perfectly competitive firm to produce output even though it is losing money? If so, when?

11. In a perfectly competitive market what is the relationship between the market price and the cost of production for all firms in the industry?

# CHAPTER 24

# INDUSTRY SUPPLY

We have seen how to derive a firm's supply curve from its marginal cost curve. But in a competitive market there will typically be many firms, so the supply curve the industry presents to the market will be the sum of the supplies of all the individual firms. In this chapter we will investigate the **industry supply curve**.

## 24.1 Short-Run Industry Supply

We begin by studying an industry with a fixed number of firms, $n$. We let $S_i(p)$ be the supply curve of firm $i$, so that the **industry supply curve**, or the **market supply curve** is

$$S(p) = \sum_{i=1}^{n} S_i(p),$$

which is the sum of the individual supply curves. Geometrically we take the sum of the quantities supplied by each firm at each price, which gives us a *horizontal* sum of supply curves, as in Figure 24.1.

**The industry supply curve.** The industry supply curve $(S_1 + S_2)$ is the sum of the individual supply curves ($S_1$ and $S_2$).

Figure
24.1

## 24.2 Industry Equilibrium in the Short Run

In order to find the industry equilibrium we take this market supply curve and find the intersection with the market demand curve. This gives us an equilibrium price, $p^*$.

Given this equilibrium price, we can go back to look at the individual firms and examine their output levels and profits. A typical configuration with three firms, A, B, and C, is illustrated in Figure 24.2. In this example, firm A is operating at a price and output combination that lies on its average cost curve. This means that

$$p = \frac{c(y)}{y}.$$

Cross multiplying and rearranging, we have

$$py - c(y) = 0.$$

Thus firm A is making zero profits.

Firm B is operating at a point where price is greater than average cost: $p > c(y)/y$, which means it is making a profit in this short-run equilibrium.

Firm **A**          Firm **B**          Firm **C**

**Figure 24.2**

**Short-run equilibrium.**  An example of a short-run equilibrium with three firms. Firm A is making zero profits, firm B is making positive profits, and firm C is making negative profits, that is, making a loss.

Firm C is operating where price is less than average cost, so it is making negative profits, that is, making a loss.

In general, combinations of price and output that lie above the average cost curve represent positive profits, and combinations that lie below represent negative profits. Even if a firm is making negative profits, it will still be better for it to stay in business in the short run if the price and output combination lie above the average *variable* cost curve. For in this case, it will make less of a loss by remaining in business than by producing a zero level of output.

## 24.3 Industry Equilibrium in the Long Run

In the long run, firms are able to adjust their fixed factors. They can choose the plant size, or the capital equipment, or whatever to maximize their long-run profits. This just means that they will move from their short-run to their long-run cost curves, and this adds no new analytical difficulties: we simply use the long-run supply curves as determined by the long-run marginal cost curve.

However, there is an additional long-run effect that may occur. If a firm is making losses in the long run, there is no reason to stay in the industry, so we would expect to see such a firm *exit* the industry, since by exiting from the industry, the firm could reduce its losses to zero. This is just another way of saying that the only relevant part of a firm's supply curve in the long run is that part that lies *on or above* the average cost curve—since these are locations that correspond to nonnegative profits.

Similarly, if a firm is making profits we would expect *entry* to occur. After all, the cost curve is supposed to include the cost of all factors necessary to produce output, measured at their market price (i.e., their opportunity cost). If a firm is making profits in the long run it means that *anybody* can go to market, acquire those factors, and produce the same amount of output at the same cost.

In most competitive industries there are no restrictions against new firms entering the industry; in this case we say the industry exhibits **free entry**. However, in some industries there are **barriers to entry**, such as licenses or legal restrictions on how many firms can be in the industry. For example, regulations on the sales of alcohol in many states prevent free entry to the retail liquor industry.

The two long-run effects—acquiring different fixed factors and the entry and exit phenomena—are closely related. An existing firm in an industry can decide to acquire a new plant or store and produce more output. Or a new firm may enter the industry by acquiring a new plant and producing output. The only difference is in who owns the new production facilities.

Of course as more firms enter the industry—and firms that are losing money exit the industry—the total amount produced will change and lead to a change in the market price. This in turn will affect profits and the incentives to exit and enter. What will the final equilibrium look like in an industry with free entry?

Let's examine a case where all firms have identical long-run cost functions, say, $c(y)$. Given the cost function we can compute the level of output where average costs are minimized, which we denote by $y^*$. We let $p^* = c(y^*)/y^*$ be the minimum value of average cost. This cost is significant because it is the lowest price that could be charged in the market and still allow firms to break even.

We can now graph the industry supply curves for each different number of firms that can be in the market. Figure 24.3 illustrates the industry supply curves if there are $1, \ldots, 4$ firms in the market. (We are using 4 firms only for purposes of an example; in reality, one would expect there to be many more firms in a competitive industry.) Note that since all firms have the same supply curve, the total amount supplied if 2 firms are in the market is just twice as much as when 1 firm is the market, the supply when 3 firms are in the market is just three times as much, and so on.

Now add two more lines to the diagram: a horizontal line at $p^*$, the minimum price consistent with nonnegative profits, and the market demand curve. Consider the intersections of the demand curve and the supply curves for $n = 1, 2, \ldots$ firms. If firms enter the industry when positive profits are being made, then the relevant intersection is the *lowest price consistent with nonnegative profits*. This is denoted by $p'$ in Figure 24.3, and it happens to occur when there are three firms in the market. If one

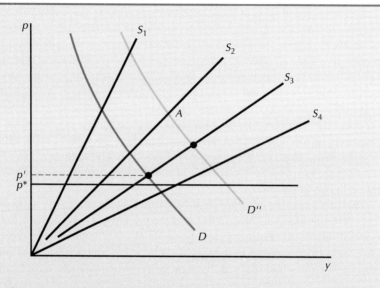

Figure
24.3    **Industry supply curves with free entry.** Supply curves for
$1, \ldots, 4$ firms. The equilibrium price, $p'$, occurs at the lowest
possible intersection of demand and supply such that $p' \geq p^*$.

more firm enters the market, profits are pushed to be negative. In this
case, the maximum number of competitive firms this industry can support
is three.

## 24.4 The Long-Run Supply Curve

The construction given in the last section—draw the industry supply curves
for each possible number of firms that could be in the market and then look
for the largest number of firms consistent with nonnegative profits—is perfectly rigorous and easy to apply. However, there is a useful approximation
that usually gives something very close to the right answer.

Let's see if there is some way to construct *one* industry supply curve out
of the $n$ curves we have above. The first thing to note is that we can rule
out all of the points on the supply curve that are below $p^*$, since those can
never be long-run operating positions. But we can also rule out some of
the points on the supply curves *above* $p^*$.

We typically assume that the market demand curve is downward sloping. The steepest possible demand curve is therefore a vertical line. This
implies that points like $A$ in Figure 24.3 would never be observed—for any
downward-sloping demand curve that passed through A would also have
to intersect a supply curve associated with a larger number of firms, as

shown by the hypothetical demand curve $D''$ passing through the point $A$ in Figure 24.3.

Thus we can eliminate a portion of each supply curve from being a possible long-run equilibrium position. Every point on the one-firm supply curve that lies to the right of the intersection of the two-firm supply curve and the line determined by $p^*$ cannot be consistent with long-run equilibrium. Similarly, every point on the two-firm supply curve that lies to the right of the intersection of the three-firm supply curve with the $p^*$ line cannot be consistent with long-run equilibrium ... and every point on the $n$-firm supply curve that lies to the right of the intersection of the $n + 1$-firm supply curve with the $p^*$ line cannot be consistent with equilibrium.

The parts of the supply curves on which the long-run equilibrium can actually occur are indicated by the black line segments in Figure 24.4. The $n^{th}$ black line segment shows all the combinations of prices and industry output that are consistent with having $n$ firms in long-run equilibrium. Note that these line segments get flatter and flatter as we consider larger and larger levels of industry output, involving more and more firms in the industry.

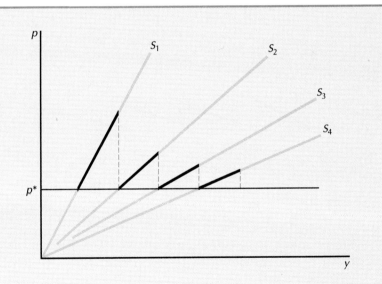

**The long-run supply curve.**    We can eliminate portions of the supply curves that can never be intersections with a downward-sloping market demand curve in the long run, such as the points on each supply curve to the right of the dotted lines.

Figure
24.4

Why do these curves get flatter? Think about it. If there is one firm in the market and the price goes up by $\delta p$, it will produce, say, $\delta y$ more output. If there are $n$ firms in the market and the price goes up by $\delta p$, *each* firm will produce $\delta y$ more output, so we will get $n\delta y$ more output in total. This means that the supply curve will be getting flatter and flatter as there are more and more firms in the market, since the supply of output will be more and more sensitive to price.

By the time we get a reasonable number of firms in the market, the slope of the supply curve will be very flat indeed. Flat enough so that it is reasonable to take it as having a slope of zero—that is, as taking the long-run industry supply curve to be a flat line at price equals minimum average cost. This will be a poor approximation if there are only a few firms in the industry in the long run. But the assumption that a small number of firms behave competitively will also probably be a poor approximation! If there are a reasonable number of firms in the long run, the equilibrium price cannot get far from minimum average cost. This is depicted in Figure 24.5.

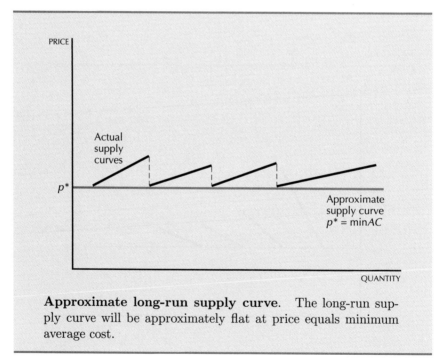

Figure
24.5

**Approximate long-run supply curve.** The long-run supply curve will be approximately flat at price equals minimum average cost.

This result has the important implication that in a competitive industry with free entry, profits cannot get very far from zero. If there are significant levels of profits in an industry with free entry, it will induce other firms to enter that industry and thereby push profits toward zero.

Remember, the correct calculation of economic costs involves measuring all factors of production at their market prices. As long as *all* factors are being measured and properly priced, a firm earning positive profits can be exactly duplicated by anyone. Anyone can go to the open market and purchase the factors of production necessary to produce the same output in the same way as the firm in question.

In an industry with free entry and exit, the long-run average cost curve should be essentially flat at a price equal to the minimum average cost. This is just the kind of long-run supply curve that a single firm with constant returns to scale would have. This is no accident. We argued that constant returns to scale was a reasonable assumption since a firm could always replicate what it was doing before. But another firm could replicate it as well! Expanding output by building a duplicate plant is just like a new firm entering the market with duplicate production facilities. Thus the long-run supply curve of a competitive industry with free entry will look like the long-run supply curve of a firm with constant returns to scale: a flat line at price equals minimum average cost.

## EXAMPLE: Taxation in the Long Run and in the Short Run

Consider an industry that has free entry and exit. Suppose that initially it is in a long-run equilibrium with a fixed number of firms, and zero profits, as depicted in Figure 24.6. In the short run, with a fixed number of firms, the supply curve of the industry is upward sloping, while in the long run, with a variable number of firms, the supply curve is flat at price equals minimum average cost.

What happens when we put a tax on this industry? We use the geometric analysis discussed in Chapter 16: in order to find the new price paid by the demanders, we shift the supply curve up by the amount of the tax.

In general, the consumers will face a higher price and the producers will receive a lower price after the tax is imposed. But the producers were just breaking even before the tax was imposed; thus they must be losing money at any lower price. These economic losses will encourage some firms to leave the industry. Thus the supply of output will be reduced, and the price to the consumers will rise even further.

In the long run, the industry will supply along the horizontal long-run supply curve. In order to supply along this curve, the firms will have to receive a price equal to the minimum average cost—just what they were receiving before the tax was imposed. Thus the price to the consumers will have to rise by the entire amount of the tax.

In Figure 24.6, the equilibrium is initially at $P_D = P_S$. Then the tax is imposed, shifting the short-run supply curve up by the amount of the tax, and the equilibrium price paid by the demanders increases to $P'_D$. The

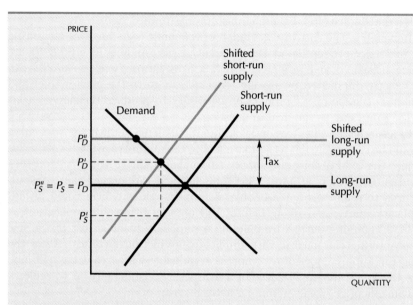

**Figure 24.6**

**Taxation in the short run and long run.** In the short run, with a fixed number of firms, the industry supply curve will have an upward slope, so that part of the tax falls on the consumers and part on the firms. In the long run, the industry supply curve will be horizontal so all of the tax falls on the consumers.

equilibrium price received by the suppliers falls to $P'_S = P'_D - t$. But this is only in the short run—when there are a fixed number of firms in the industry. Because of free entry and exit, the *long-run* supply curve in the industry is horizontal at $P_D = P_S = $ minimum average cost. Hence, in the long run, shifting up the supply curve implies that the entire amount of the tax gets passed along to the consumers.

To sum up: in an industry with free entry, a tax will initially raise the price to the consumers by less than the amount of the tax, since some of the incidence of the tax will fall on the producers. But in the long run the tax will induce firms to exit from the industry, thereby reducing supply, so that consumers will eventually end up paying the entire burden of the tax.

## 24.5 The Meaning of Zero Profits

In an industry with free entry, profits will be driven to zero by new entrants: whenever profits are positive, there will be an incentive for a new firm to come in to acquire some of those profits. When profits are zero it doesn't mean that the industry disappears; it just means that it stops growing, since there is no longer an inducement to enter.

In a long-run equilibrium with zero profits, all of the factors of production are being paid their market price—the same market price that these factors could earn elsewhere. The owner of the firm, for example, is still collecting a payment for her labor time, or for the amount of money she invested in the firm, or for whatever she contributes to the operation of the firm. The same goes for all other factors of production. The firm is still making money—it is just that all the money that it makes is being paid out to purchase the inputs that it uses. Each factor of production is earning the same amount in this industry that it could earn elsewhere, so there are no extra rewards—no pure profits—to attract new factors of production to this industry. But there is nothing to cause them to leave either. Industries in long-run equilibrium with zero profits are mature industries; they're not likely to appear as the cover story in *Business Week*, but they form the backbone of the economy.

Remember, economic profits are defined using the market prices of all factors of production. The market prices measure the opportunity cost of those factors—what they could earn elsewhere. Any amount of money earned in excess of the payments to the factors of production is a pure economic profit. But whenever someone finds a pure economic profit, other people will try to enter the industry and acquire some of that profit for themselves. It is this attempt to capture economic profits that eventually drives them to zero in a competitive industry with free entry.

In some quarters, the profit motive is regarded with some disdain. But when you think about it purely on economic grounds, profits are providing exactly the right signals as far as resource allocation is concerned. If a firm is making positive profits, it means that people value the output of the firm more highly than they value the inputs. Doesn't it make sense to have more firms producing that kind of output?

## 24.6 Fixed Factors and Economic Rent

If there is free entry, profits are driven to zero in the long run. But not every industry has free entry. In some industries the number of firms in the industry is fixed.

A common reason for this is that there are some factors of production that are available in fixed supply. We said that in the long run the fixed factors could be bought or sold by an individual firm. But there are some factors that are fixed for the *economy as a whole* even in the long run.

The most obvious example of this is in resource-extraction industries: oil in the ground is a necessary input to the oil-extraction industry, and there is only so much oil around to be extracted. A similar statement could be made for coal, gas, precious metals, or any other such resource.

Agriculture gives another example. There is only a certain amount of land that is suitable for agriculture.

A more exotic example of such a fixed factor is talent. There are only a certain number of people who possess the necessary level of talent to be professional athletes or entertainers. There may be "free entry" into such fields—but only for those who are good enough to get in!

There are other cases where the fixed factor is fixed not by nature, but by law. In many industries it is necessary to have a license or permit, and the number of these permits may be fixed by law. The taxicab industry in many cities is regulated in this way. Liquor licenses are another example.

If there are restrictions such as the above on the number of firms in the industry, so that firms cannot enter the industry freely, it may appear that it is possible to have an industry with positive profits in the long run, with no economic forces to drive those profits to zero.

This appearance is wrong. There is an economic force that pushes profits to zero. If a firm is operating at a point where its profits appear to be positive in the long run, it is probably because we are not appropriately measuring the market value of whatever it is that is preventing entry.

Here it is important to remember the economic definition of costs: we should value each factor of production at its *market price*—its opportunity cost. If it appears that a farmer is making positive profits after we have subtracted his costs of production, it is probably because we have forgotten to subtract the cost of his land.

Suppose that we manage to value all of the inputs to farming except for the land cost, and we end up with $\pi$ dollars per year for profits. How much would the land be worth on a free market? How much would someone pay to rent that land for a year?

The answer is: they would be willing to rent it for $\pi$ dollars per year, the "profits" that it brings in. You wouldn't even have to know anything about farming to rent this land and earn $\pi$ dollars—after all, we valued the farmer's labor at its market price as well, and that means that you can hire a farmer and still make $\pi$ dollars of profit. So the market value of that land—its competitive rent—is just $\pi$. The economic profits to farming are zero.

Note that the rental rate determined by this procedure may have nothing whatsoever to do with the historical cost of the farm. What matters is not what you bought it for, but what you can sell it for—that's what determines opportunity cost.

Whenever there is some fixed factor that is preventing entry into an industry, there will be an equilibrium rental rate for that factor. Even with fixed factors, you can always enter an industry by buying out the position of a firm that is currently in the industry. Every firm in the industry has the option of selling out—and the opportunity cost of not doing so is a cost of production that it has to consider.

Thus in one sense it is always the *possibility* of entry that drives profits to zero. After all, there are two ways to enter an industry: you can form a new firm, or you can buy out an existing firm that is currently in the industry. If a new firm can buy everything necessary to produce in an industry and still make a profit, it will do so. But if there are some factors that are in fixed supply, then competition for those factors among potential entrants will bid the prices of these factors up to a point where the profit disappears.

## EXAMPLE: Taxi Licenses in New York City

In 1986, licenses to operate New York City cabs sold for about $100,000. Yet in 1986 taxicab drivers made only about $400 for a 50-hour week; this translated into less than an $8 hourly wage. The New York Taxi and Limosine Commission argued that this wage was too low to attract skilled drivers and that taxi fares should be raised in order to attract better drivers.

An economist would argue that allowing the fares to increase would have virtually no effect on the take-home pay of the drivers; all that would happen is that the value of the taxicab license would increase. We can see why by examining the commission's figures for the costs of operating a taxi. In 1986, the lease rate was $55 for a day shift and $65 for a night shift. The driver who leased the taxi paid for the gasoline and netted about $80 a day in income.

But note how much the owner of the taxicab license made. Assuming that the cab could be rented for two shifts for 320 days a year, the lease income comes to $38,400. Insurance, depreciation, maintenance, and so on amounted to about $21,100 a year; this leaves a net profit of $17,300 per year. Since the license cost about $100,000, this indicates a total return of about 17 percent.

An increase in the rate that taxis were allowed to charge would be reflected directly in the value of the license. A fare increase that brought in an extra $10,000 a year would result in a license's value increasing by about $60,000. The wage rate for the cab drivers—which is set in the labor market—would not be affected by such a change.

By 2011, licenses were selling for above a million dollars. The owner of such a license can make net revenue of about $50,000 to $75,000 per year, which is a return of 5 to 7.5 percent. The purchaser of the license could have invested the million dollars in alternative ways–for example, buying stocks or bonds. Thus, there is an opportunity cost to using the funds to purchase the license. [1]

## 24.7 Economic Rent

---

[1] Figures are taken from an unsigned editorial in the *New York Times,* August 17, 1986, and from Felix Salmon, "Why taxi medallions cost $1 million", *Reuters,* October 21, 2011.

The examples in the last section are instances of **economic rent**. Economic rent is defined as those payments to a factor of production that are in excess of the minimum payment necessary to have that factor supplied.

Consider, for example, the case of oil discussed earlier. In order to produce oil you need some labor, some machinery, and, most importantly, some oil in the ground! Suppose that it costs $1 a barrel to pump oil out of the ground from an existing well. Then any price in excess of $1 a barrel will induce firms to supply oil from existing wells. But the actual price of oil is much higher than $1 a barrel. People want oil for various reasons, and they are willing to pay more than its cost of production to get it. The excess of the price of oil over its cost of production is economic rent.

Why don't firms enter this industry? Well, they try. But there is only a certain amount of oil available. Oil will sell for more than its cost of production because of the limited supply.

Now consider taxicab licenses. Viewed as pieces of paper, these cost almost nothing to produce. But in New York City a taxicab license can sell for $1,000,000! Why don't people enter this industry and produce more taxicab licenses? The reason is that entry is illegal—the supply of taxicab licenses is controlled by the city.

Farmland is yet another example of economic rent. In the aggregate, the total amount of land is fixed. There would be just as much land supplied at zero dollars an acre as at $1000 an acre. Thus in the aggregate, the payments to land constitute economic rent.

From the viewpoint of the economy as a whole, it is the price of agricultural products that determines the value of agricultural land. But from the viewpoint of the individual farmer, the value of his land is a cost of production that enters into the pricing of his product.

This is depicted in Figure 24.7. Here $AVC$ represents the average cost curve for all factors of production *excluding* land costs. (We are assuming that land is the only fixed factor.) If the price of the crop grown on this land is $p^*$, then the "profits" attributable to the land are measured by the area of the box: these are the economic rents. This is how much the land would rent for in a competitive market—whatever it took to drive the profits to zero.

The average cost curve *including* the value of the land is labeled $AC$. If we measure the value of the land correctly, the economic profits to operating the farm will be exactly zero. Since the equilibrium rent for the land will be whatever it takes to drive profits to zero, we have

$$p^*y^* - c_v(y^*) - \text{rent} = 0$$

or

$$\text{rent} = p^*y^* - c_v(y^*). \tag{24.1}$$

This is precisely what we referred to as producer's surplus earlier. Indeed, it is the same concept, simply viewed in a different light. Thus we can also

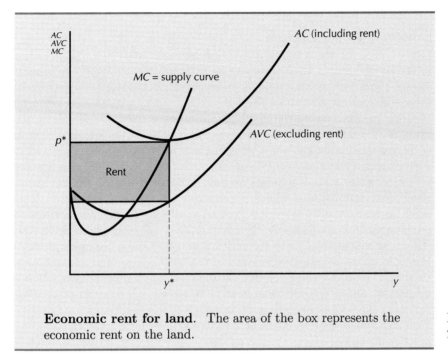

**Economic rent for land.** The area of the box represents the economic rent on the land.

Figure
24.7

measure rent by taking the area to the left of the marginal cost curve, as we saw earlier.

Given the definition of rent in equation (24.1), it is now easy to see the truth of what we said earlier: it is the equilibrium price that determines rent, not the reverse. The firm supplies along its marginal cost curve— which is independent of the expenditures on the fixed factors. The rent will adjust to drive profits to zero.

## 24.8 Rental Rates and Prices

Since we are measuring output in flow units—so much output per unit of time, we should be careful to measure profits and rents in dollars per unit of time. Thus in the above discussion we talked about the rent per year for land or for a taxicab license.

If the land or the license is to be sold outright rather than rented, the equilibrium price would be the present value of the stream of rental payments. This is a simple consequence of the usual argument that assets generating a stream of payments should sell for their present values in a competitive market.

## EXAMPLE: Liquor Licenses

In the United States, each state sets its own policy with respect to sales of alcohol. Some states have a liquor monopoly; other states issue licenses to those who wish to sell alcohol. In some cases, licenses are issued on payment of a fee; in other cases, the number of licenses is fixed. In Michigan, for example, the number of licenses for sales of beer and wine for consumption on premises is limited to one for every 1,500 residents.

After each Federal census, a state liquor control board allocates licenses to communities whose populations have grown. (Licenses are not taken away from communities whose populations have fallen, however.) This artificial scarcity of licenses has created a vibrant market for licenses to serve liquor in many fast-growing communities. For example, in 1983 Ann Arbor, Michigan, had sixty-six existing liquor licenses. Six new licenses were allowed to be issued as a result of the 1980 census, and 33 applicants lined up to lobby for these licenses. At the time, the market value of a liquor license was about $80,000. The local newspaper ran a story asserting that "demand exceeds supply for liquor licenses." It was hardly surprising to the local economists that giving away an $80,000 asset for a zero price resulted in excess demand!

There have been many proposals to relax the liquor control laws in Michigan by allowing the state to issue new licenses. However, these proposals have never been enacted into law due to the opposition of various political groups. Some of these groups are opposed to the consumption of alcohol on grounds of public health or religion. Others have somewhat different motives. For example, one of the most vociferous opponents of relaxed liquor laws is the Michigan Licensed Beverage Association, a group that represents the sellers of alcoholic beverages in Michigan. Though at first glance it appears paradoxical that this group would oppose liberalization of the liquor laws, a little reflection indicates a possible reason: issuing more liquor licenses would undoubtably lower the resale value of *existing* licenses—imposing significant capital losses on current holders of such licenses.

## 24.9 The Politics of Rent

Often economic rent exists because of legal restrictions on entry into the industry. We mentioned two examples above: taxicab licenses and liquor licenses. In each of these cases the number of licenses is fixed by law, thus restricting entry to the industry and creating economic rents.

Suppose that the New York City government wants to increase the number of operating taxicabs. What will happen to the market value of the existing taxicab licenses? Obviously they will fall in value. This reduction in value hits the industry right in the pocketbook, and it is sure to create a lobbying force to oppose any such move.

The federal government also artificially restricts output of some products in such a way as to create a rent. For example, the federal government has declared that tobacco can only be grown on certain lands. The value of this land is then determined by the demand for tobacco products. Any attempt to eliminate this licensing system has to contend with a serious lobby. Once the government creates artificial scarcity, it is very hard to eliminate it. The beneficiaries of the artificial scarcity—the people who have acquired the right to operate in the industry—will vigorously oppose any attempts to enlarge the industry.

The incumbents in an industry in which entry is legally restricted may well devote considerable resources to maintaining their favored position. Lobbying expenses, lawyers' fees, public relations costs, and so on can be substantial. From the viewpoint of society these kinds of expenses represent pure social waste. They aren't true costs of production; they don't lead to any *more* output being produced. Lobbying and public relations efforts just determine who gets the money associated with existing output.

Efforts directed at keeping or acquiring claims to factors in fixed supplies are sometimes referred to as **rent seeking**. From the viewpoint of society they represent a pure deadweight loss since they don't create any more output, they just change the market value of existing factors of production.

## EXAMPLE: Farming the Government

There is only one good thing to say about the U.S. program of farm subsidies: it produces a never-ending source of examples for economics textbooks. Every new reform of the farm program brings new problems. "If you want to find the holes in a program, just toss them out to farmers. No one is more innovative in finding ways to use them," says Terry Bar, the vice president of the National Council of Farm Cooperatives.[2]

Up until 1996 the basic structure of farm subsidies in the U.S. involved price supports: the Federal government guaranteed a support price for a crop and would make up the difference if the price fell below the support price. In order to qualify for this program, a farmer had to agree not to farm a certain fraction of his land.

By the very nature of this plan, most of the benefits accrued to the large farmers. According to one calculation, 13 percent of the direct Federal subsidies were going to the 1 percent of the farmers who had sales over $500,000 a year. The Food Security Act of 1985 significantly restricted the payments to large farmers. As a result, the farmers broke up their holdings

---

[2] Quoted in William Robbins, "Limits on Subsidies to Big Farms Go Awry, Sending Costs Climbing," *New York Times,* June 15, 1987, A1.

by leasing the land to local investors. The investors would acquire parcels large enough to take advantage of the subsidies, but too small to run into the restrictions aimed at large farmers. Once the land was acquired the investor would register it with a government program that would pay the investor *not* to plant the land. This practice became known as "farming the government."

According to one study, the restriction on payments to the large farmers in the 1985 farm act resulted in the creation of 31,000 new applicants for farm subsidies. The cost of these subsidies was in the neighborhood of $2.3 billion.

Note that the ostensible goal of the program—restricting the amount of government subsidies paid to large farmers—has not been achieved. When the large farmers rent their land to small farmers, the market price of the rents depends on the generosity of the Federal subsidies. The higher the subsidies, the higher the equilibrium rent the large farmers receive. The benefits from the subsidy program still falls on those who initially own the land, since it is ultimately the value of what the land can earn—either from growing crops or farming the government—that determines its market value.

The Farm Act of 1996 promised a phaseout of most agricultural subsidies by 2002. However, the 1998 federal budget restored over 6 billion dollars of federal farm subsidies, illustrating once again how hard it is to reconcile politics and economics.

## 24.10 Energy Policy

We end this chapter with an extended example that uses some of the concepts we have developed.

In 1974 the Organization of Petroleum Exporting Countries (OPEC) levied a significant increase in the price of oil. Countries that had no domestically produced petroleum had little choice about energy policy—the price of oil and goods produced using oil had to rise.

At that time the United States produced about half of its domestic oil consumption, and Congress felt that it was unfair that the domestic producers should receive "windfall profits" from an uncontrolled increase in price. (The term windfall profits refers to an increase in profits due to some outside event, as opposed to an increase in profits due to production decisions.) Consequently, Congress devised a bizarre plan to attempt to hold down the price of products that used oil. The most prominent of these products is gasoline, so we will analyze the effect of the program for that market.

## Two-Tiered Oil Pricing

The policy adopted by Congress was known as "two-tiered" oil pricing, and it went something like this. Imported oil would sell for whatever its market price was, but domestic oil—oil produced from wells that were in place before 1974—would sell for its old price: the price that it sold for before OPEC. Roughly speaking, we'll say that imported oil sold for about $15 a barrel, while domestic oil sold for around $5. The idea was that the average price of oil would then be about $10 a barrel and this would help hold down the price of gasoline.

Could such a scheme work? Let's think about it from the viewpoint of the gasoline producers. What would the supply curve of gasoline look like? In order to answer this question we have to ask what the marginal cost curve for gasoline looked like.

What would you do if you were a gasoline refiner? Obviously you would try to use the cheap domestic oil first. Only after you had exhausted your supplies of domestic oil would you turn to the more expensive imported oil. Thus the aggregate marginal cost curve—the industry supply curve—for gasoline would have to look something like that depicted in Figure 24.8. The curve takes a jump at the point where the U.S. production of domestic oil is exhausted and the imported oil begins to be used. Before that point, the domestic price of oil measures the relevant factor price for producing gasoline. After that point, it is the price of foreign oil that is the relevant factor price.

Figure 24.8 depicts the supply curve for gasoline if all oil were to sell for the world price of $15 a barrel, and if all oil were to sell for the domestic price of $5 a barrel. If domestic oil actually sells for $5 a barrel and foreign oil sells for $15 a barrel, then the supply curve for gasoline will coincide with the $5-a-barrel supply curve until the cheaper domestic oil is used up, and then coincide with the $15-a-barrel supply curve.

Now let's find the intersection of this supply curve with the market demand curve to find the equilibrium price in Figure 24.8. The diagram reveals an interesting fact: the price of gasoline is exactly the same in the two-tiered system as it would be if all oil sold at the price of foreign oil! The price of gasoline is determined by the *marginal* cost of production, and the *marginal* cost is determined by the cost of the imported oil.

If you think about it a minute, this makes perfectly good sense. The gasoline companies will sell their product at the price the market will bear. Just because you were lucky enough to get some cheap oil doesn't mean you won't sell your gasoline for the same price that other firms are selling theirs for.

Suppose for the moment that all oil did sell for one price, and that equilibrium was reached at the price $p^*$. Then the government comes along and lowers the price of the first 100 barrels of oil that each refiner used.

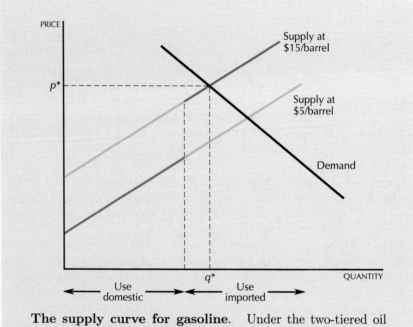

Figure
24.8 **The supply curve for gasoline.** Under the two-tiered oil pricing policy, the supply curve of gasoline would be discontinuous, jumping from the lower supply curve to the upper supply curve when the cheaper oil was exhausted.

Will this affect their supply decision? No way—in order to affect supply you have to change the incentives at the margin. The only way to get a lower price of gasoline is to increase the supply, which means that you have to make the marginal cost of oil cheaper.

The two-tiered oil pricing policy was simply a transfer from the domestic oil producers to the domestic oil refiners. The domestic producers got $10 less for their oil than they would have otherwise, and the profits they would have gotten went to the gasoline refiners. It had no effect on the supply of gasoline, and thus it could have no effect on the price of gasoline.

## Price Controls

The economic forces inherent in this argument didn't take long to make themselves felt. The Department of Energy soon realized that it couldn't allow market forces to determine the price of gasoline under the two-tiered system—since market forces alone would imply one price of gasoline, which would be the same price that would prevail in the absence of the two-tiered system.

So they instituted price controls on gasoline. Each refiner was required to charge a price for gasoline that was based on the costs of producing the gasoline—which in turn was primarily determined by the cost of the oil that the refiner was able to purchase.

The availability of cheap domestic oil varied with location. In Texas the refiners were close to the major source of production and thus were able to purchase large supplies of cheap oil. Due to the price controls, the price of Texas gasoline was relatively cheap. In New England, virtually all oil had to be imported, and thus the price of gasoline in New England was quite high.

When you have different prices for the same product, it is natural for firms to try to sell at the higher price. Again, the Department of Energy had to intervene to prevent the uncontrolled shipping of gasoline from low-price regions to high-price regions. The result of this intervention was the famous gasoline shortages of the mid-seventies. Periodically, the supply of gasoline in a region of the country would dry up, and there would be little available at any price. The free market system of supplying petroleum products had never exhibited such behavior; the shortages were entirely due to the two-tiered oil pricing system coupled with price controls.

Economists pointed this out at the time, but it didn't have much effect on policy. What did have an effect was lobbying by the gasoline refiners. Much of the domestic oil was sold on long-term contracts, and some refiners were able to buy a lot of it, while others could only buy the expensive foreign oil. Naturally they objected that this was unfair, so Congress figured out another scheme to allocate the cheap domestic oil more equitably.

## The Entitlement Program

This program was known as the "entitlement program," and it went something like this. Each time a refiner bought a barrel of expensive foreign oil he got a coupon that allowed him to buy a certain amount of cheap domestic oil. The amount that the refiner was allowed to buy depended on supply conditions, but let's say that it was one for one: each barrel of foreign oil that he bought for $15 allowed him to buy one barrel of domestic oil for $5.

What did this do to the marginal price of oil? Now the marginal price of oil was just a weighted average of the domestic price and the foreign price of oil; in the one-for-one case described above, the price would be $10. The effect on the supply curve of gasoline is depicted in Figure 24.9.

The marginal cost of oil was reduced all right, and that meant that the price of gasoline was reduced as well. But look who is paying for it: the domestic oil producers! The United States was buying foreign oil that cost $15 a barrel in real dollars and pretending that it only cost $10. The domestic oil producers were required to sell their oil for less than the

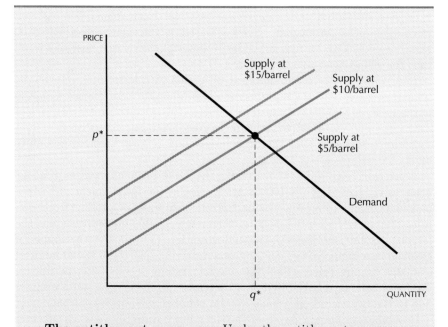

Figure
24.9

**The entitlement program.** Under the entitlement program the supply curve of gasoline would lie between the supply curve if all oil were provided at the imported price and the supply curve if all oil were provided at the domestic price.

market price on the world oil market. We were subsidizing the importation of foreign oil and forcing the domestic oil producers to pay the subsidy!

Eventually this program was abandoned as well, and the U.S. imposed a tax on the domestic production of oil so that the U.S. oil producers wouldn't reap windfall profits due to OPEC's action. Of course, such a tax discouraged production of domestic oil, and thereby increases the price of gasoline, but this was apparently acceptable to Congress at the time.

## 24.11 Carbon Tax Versus Cap and Trade

Motivated by concerns about global warming, several climatologists have urged governments to institute policies to reduce carbon emissions. Two of these reduction policies are particularly interesting from an economic point of view: **carbon taxes** and **cap and trade**.

A carbon tax imposes a tax on carbon emissions, while a cap and trade system grants licenses to emit carbon that can be traded on an organized market. To see how these systems compare, let us examine a simple model.

## Optimal Production of Emissions

We begin by examining the problem of producing a target amount of emissions in the least costly way. Suppose that there are two firms that have current levels of carbon emissions denoted by $(\overline{x}_1, \overline{x}_2)$. Firm $i$ can reduce its level of emissions by $x_i$ at a cost of $c_i(x_i)$. Figure 24.10 shows a possible shape for this cost function.

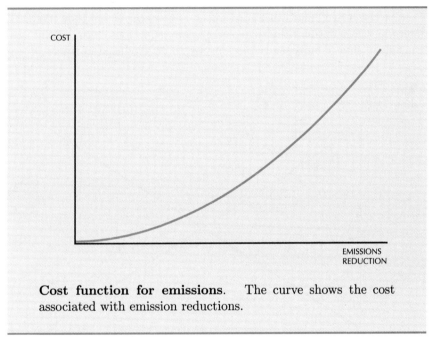

**Cost function for emissions.** The curve shows the cost associated with emission reductions.

Figure 24.10

The goal is to reduce emissions by some target amount, $T$, in the least costly way. This minimization problem can be written as

$$\min_{x_1, x_2} c_1(x_1) + c_2(x_2)$$

such that $x_1 + x_2 = T$.

If it knew the cost functions, the government could, in principle, solve this optimization problem and assign a specific amount of emission reductions to each firm. However, this is impractical if there are thousands of carbon emitters. The challenge is to find a decentralized, market-based way of achieving the optimal solution.

Let us examine the structure of the optimization problem. It is clear that at the optimal solution the marginal cost of reducing emissions must be the same for each firm. Otherwise it would pay to increase emissions in the firm with the lower marginal cost and decrease emissions in the firm with the higher marginal cost. This would keep the total output at the target level while reducing costs.

Hence we have a simple principle: at the optimal solution, the marginal cost of emissions reduction should be the same for every firm. In the two-firm case we are examining, we can find this optimal point using a simple diagram. Let $MC_1(x_1)$ be the marginal cost of reducing emissions by $x_1$ for firm 1 and write the marginal cost of emission-reduction for firm 2 as a function of firm 1's output: $MC_2(T - x_1)$, assuming the target is met. We plot these two curves in Figure 24.11. The point where they intersect determines the optimal division of emission reductions between the two firms given that $T$ emission reductions are to be produced in total.

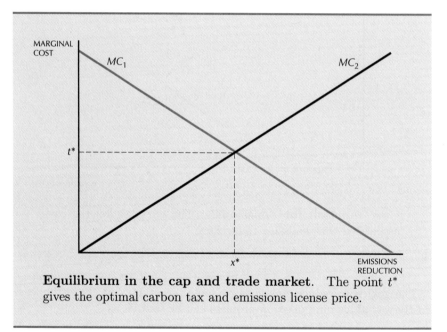

**Figure 24.11**

**Equilibrium in the cap and trade market.** The point $t^*$ gives the optimal carbon tax and emissions license price.

## A Carbon Tax

Instead of solving for the cost-minimizing solution directly, let us instead consider a decentralized solution using a carbon tax. In this framework, the government sets a tax rate $t$ that it charges for carbon emissions.

If firm 1 starts with $\overline{x}_1$ and reduces its emissions by $x_1$, then it ends up with $\overline{x}_1 - x_1$ emissions. If it pays $t$ per unit emitted, its carbon tax bill would be $t(\overline{x}_1 - x_1)$.

Faced with this tax, firm 1 would want to choose that level of emission reductions that minimized its total cost of operation: the cost of reducing emissions plus the cost of paying the carbon tax on the emissions that remain. This leads to the cost minimization problem

$$\min_{x_1} c_1(x_1) + t(\overline{x}_1 - x_1).$$

Clearly the firm will want to reduce emissions up to the point where the marginal cost of further reductions just equals the carbon tax, i.e., where $t = MC_1(x_1)$.

If the carbon tax is set to be the rate $t^*$, as determined in Figure 24.11, then the total amount of carbon emissions will be the targeted amount, $T$. Thus the carbon tax gives a decentralized way to achieve the optimal outcome.

## Cap and Trade

Suppose, alternatively that there is no carbon tax, but that the government issues tradable **emissions licenses**. Each license allows the firm that holds it to produce a certain amount of carbon emissions. The government chooses the number of emissions licenses to achieve the target reduction.

We imagine a market in these licenses so each firm can buy a license to emit $x$ units of carbon at a price of $p$ per unit. The cost to firm 1 of reducing its emissions by $x_1$ is $c_1(x_1) + p(\overline{x}_1 - x_1)$. Clearly the firm will want to operate where the price of an emissions license equals the marginal cost, $p = MC_1(x_1)$. That is, it will choose the level of emissions at the point where the cost of reducing carbon emissions by one unit would just equal the cost saved by not having to purchase a license.

Hence the marginal cost curve gives us the supply of emissions as a function of the price. The equilibrium price is the price where the total supply of emissions equals the target amount $T$. The associated price is the same as the optimal carbon tax rate $t^*$ in Figure 24.11.

The question that remains is how to distribute the licenses. One way would be to have the government sell the licenses to firms. This is essentially the same as the carbon tax system. The government could pick a price and sell however many licenses are demanded at that price. Alternatively, it could pick a target level of emissions and auction off permits, letting the firms themselves determine a price. This is one type of "cap and trade" system. Both of these policies should lead to essentially the same market-clearing price.

Another possibility would be for the government to hand out the licenses to the firms according to some formula. This formula could be based on a variety of criteria, but presumably an important reason to award these valuable permits would be building political support for the program. Permits might be handed out based on objective criteria, such as which firms have the most employees, or they might be handed out based on which firms have donated the most to some political causes.

From the economic point of view, it doesn't matter whether the government owns the licenses and sells them to the firms (which is basically a carbon tax system) or whether the firms are given the licenses and sell them to each other (which is basically cap and trade).

If a cap and trade system is created, firms will find it attractive to invest in ways to acquire the emission permits. For example, they would want to lobby Congress for such licenses. These lobbying expenditures should be counted as part of the cost of the system, as described in our earlier discussion of **rent seeking**. Of course, the carbon tax system would also be subject to similar lobbying. Firms would undoubtedly seek special carbon tax exemptions for one reason or another, but it has been argued that the carbon tax system is less susceptible to political manipulation than a cap and trade system.

## Summary

1. The short-run supply curve of an industry is just the horizontal sum of the supply curves of the individual firms in that industry.

2. The long-run supply curve of an industry must take into account the exit and entry of firms in the industry.

3. If there is free entry and exit, then the long-run equilibrium will involve the maximum number of firms consistent with nonnegative profits. This means that the long-run supply curve will be essentially horizontal at a price equal to the minimum average cost.

4. If there are forces preventing the entry of firms into a profitable industry, the factors that prevent entry will earn economic rents. The rent earned is determined by the price of the output of the industry.

## REVIEW QUESTIONS

1. If $S_1(p) = p-10$ and $S_2(p) = p-15$, then at what price does the industry supply curve have a kink in it?

2. In the short run the demand for cigarettes is totally inelastic. In the long run, suppose that it is perfectly elastic. What is the impact of a cigarette tax on the price that consumers pay in the short run and in the long run?

3. True or false? Convenience stores near the campus have high prices because they have to pay high rents.

4. True or false?  In long-run industry equilibrium no firm will be losing money.

5. According to the model presented in this chapter, what determines the amount of entry or exit a given industry experiences?

6. The model of entry presented in this chapter implies that the more firms in a given industry, the (steeper, flatter) is the long-run industry supply curve.

7. A New York City cab operator appears to be making positive profits in the long run after carefully accounting for the operating and labor costs. Does this violate the competitive model? Why or why not?

# CHAPTER 25

# MONOPOLY

In the preceding chapters we have analyzed the behavior of a competitive industry, a market structure that is most likely when there are a large number of small firms. In this chapter we turn to the opposite extreme and consider an industry structure when there is only *one* firm in the industry—a **monopoly**.

When there is only one firm in a market, that firm is very unlikely to take the market price as given. Instead, a monopoly would recognize its influence over the market price and choose that level of price and output that maximized its overall profits.

Of course, it can't choose price and output independently; for any given price, the monopoly will be able to sell only what the market will bear. If it chooses a high price, it will be able to sell only a small quantity. The demand behavior of the consumers will constrain the monopolist's choice of price and quantity.

We can view the monopolist as choosing the price and letting the consumers choose how much they wish to buy at that price, or we can think of the monopolist as choosing the quantity, and letting the consumers decide what price they will pay for that quantity. The first approach is probably more natural, but the second turns out to be analytically more convenient. Of course, both approaches are equivalent when done correctly.

## 25.1 Maximizing Profits

We begin by studying the monopolist's profit-maximization problem. Let us use $p(y)$ to denote the market inverse demand curve and $c(y)$ to denote the cost function. Let $r(y) = p(y)y$ denote the revenue function of the monopolist. The monopolist's profit-maximization problem then takes the form

$$\max_{y} \ r(y) - c(y).$$

The optimality condition for this problem is straightforward: at the optimal choice of output we must have marginal revenue equal to marginal cost. If marginal revenue were less than marginal cost it would pay the firm to decrease output, since the savings in cost would more than make up for the loss in revenue. If the marginal revenue were greater than the marginal cost, it would pay the firm to increase output. The only point where the firm has no incentive to change output is where marginal revenue equals marginal cost.

The first-order condition for this problem is simply

$$r'(y) - c'(y) = 0,$$

which implies that marginal revenue should equal marginal cost at the optimal choice of output, or

$$MR = MC.$$

The same $MR = MC$ condition has to hold in the case of a competitive firm; in that case, marginal revenue is equal to the price and the condition reduces to price equals marginal cost.

In the case of a monopolist, the marginal revenue term is slightly more complicated. If the monopolist decides to increase its output by $\delta y$, there are two effects on revenues. First it sells more output and receives a revenue of $p\delta y$ from that. But second, the monopolist pushes the price down by $\delta p$ and it gets this lower price on *all* the output it has been selling.

Thus the total effect on revenues of changing output by $\delta y$ will be

$$\delta r = p\delta y + y\delta p,$$

so that the change in revenue divided by the change in output—the marginal revenue—is

$$\frac{\delta r}{\delta y} = p + \frac{\delta p}{\delta y}y.$$

Equivalently, differentiating the definition of the revenue function gives $r'(y) = p(y) + p'(y)y$, and substituting this into the monopolist's first-order condition yields the alternative form

$$p(y) + p'(y)y = c'(y).$$

The second-order condition for the monopolist's profit-maximization problem is

$$r''(y) - c''(y) \leq 0.$$

This implies that

$$c''(y) \geq r''(y)$$

or that the slope of the marginal cost curve exceeds the slope of the marginal revenue curve.

(This is exactly the same derivation we went through in our discussion of marginal revenue in Chapter 15. You might want to review that material before proceeding.)

Another way to think about this is to think of the monopolist as choosing its output and price simultaneously—recognizing, of course, the constraint imposed by the demand curve. If the monopolist wants to sell more output it has to lower its price. But this lower price will mean a lower price for all of the units it is selling, not just the new units. Hence the term $y\delta p$.

In the competitive case, a firm that could lower its price below the price charged by other firms would immediately capture the entire market from its competitors. But in the monopolistic case, the monopoly already has the entire market; when it lowers its price, it has to take into account the effect of the price reduction on all the units it sells.

Following the discussion in Chapter 15, we can also express marginal revenue in terms of elasticity via the formula

$$MR(y) = p(y) \left[ 1 + \frac{1}{\epsilon(y)} \right]$$

and write the "marginal revenue equals marginal costs" optimality condition as

$$p(y) \left[ 1 + \frac{1}{\epsilon(y)} \right] = MC(y). \tag{25.1}$$

Since elasticity is naturally negative, we could also write this expression as

$$p(y) \left[ 1 - \frac{1}{|\epsilon(y)|} \right] = MC(y).$$

From these equations it is easy to see the connection with the competitive case: in the competitive case, the firm faces a flat demand curve—an infinitely elastic demand curve. This means that $1/|\epsilon| = 1/\infty = 0$, so the appropriate version of this equation for a competitive firm is simply price equals marginal cost.

Note that a monopolist will never choose to operate where the demand curve is *inelastic*. For if $|\epsilon| < 1$, then $1/|\epsilon| > 1$, and the marginal revenue is negative, so it can't possibly equal marginal cost. The meaning of this becomes clear when we think of what is implied by an inelastic demand curve: if $|\epsilon| < 1$, then reducing output will increase revenues, and reducing output must reduce total cost, so profits will necessarily increase. Thus any point where $|\epsilon| < 1$ cannot be a profit maximum for a monopolist, since it could increase its profits by producing less output. It follows that a point that yields maximum profits can only occur where $|\epsilon| \geq 1$.

## 25.2 Linear Demand Curve and Monopoly

Suppose that the monopolist faces a linear demand curve

$$p(y) = a - by.$$

Then the revenue function is

$$r(y) = p(y)y = ay - by^2,$$

and the marginal revenue function is

$$MR(y) = a - 2by.$$

(This follows from the formula given at the end of Chapter 15. It is easy to derive using simple calculus. If you don't know calculus, just memorize the formula, since we will use it quite a bit.)

Note that the marginal revenue function has the same vertical intercept, $a$, as the demand curve, but it is twice as steep. This gives us an easy way to draw the marginal revenue curve. We know that the vertical intercept is $a$. To get the horizontal intercept, just take half of the horizontal intercept of the demand curve. Then connect the two intercepts with a straight line. We have illustrated the demand curve and the marginal revenue curve in Figure 25.1.

The optimal output, $y^*$, is where the marginal revenue curve intersects the marginal cost curve. The monopolist will then charge the maximum price it can get at this output, $p(y^*)$. This gives the monopolist a revenue of $p(y^*)y^*$ from which we subtract the total cost $c(y^*) = AC(y^*)y^*$, leaving a profit area as illustrated.

## 25.3 Markup Pricing

We can use the elasticity formula for the monopolist to express its optimal pricing policy in another way. Rearranging equation (25.1) we have

$$p(y) = \frac{MC(y^*)}{1 - 1/|\epsilon(y)|}. \tag{25.2}$$

**Figure 25.1**

**Monopoly with a linear demand curve.** The monopolist's profit-maximizing output occurs where marginal revenue equals marginal cost.

This formulation indicates that the market price is a markup over marginal cost, where the amount of the markup depends on the elasticity of demand. The markup is given by

$$\frac{1}{1 - 1/|\epsilon(y)|}.$$

Since the monopolist always operates where the demand curve is elastic, we are assured that $|\epsilon| > 1$, and thus the markup is greater than 1.

In the case of a constant-elasticity demand curve, this formula is especially simple since $\epsilon(y)$ is a constant. A monopolist who faces a constant-elasticity demand curve will charge a price that is a *constant* markup on marginal cost. This is illustrated in Figure 25.2. The curve labeled $MC/(1 - 1/|\epsilon|)$ is a constant fraction higher than the marginal cost curve; the optimal level of output occurs where $p = MC/(1 - 1/|\epsilon|)$.

## EXAMPLE: The Impact of Taxes on a Monopolist

Let us consider a firm with constant marginal costs and ask what happens to the price charged when a quantity tax is imposed. Clearly the marginal costs go up by the amount of the tax, but what happens to the market price?

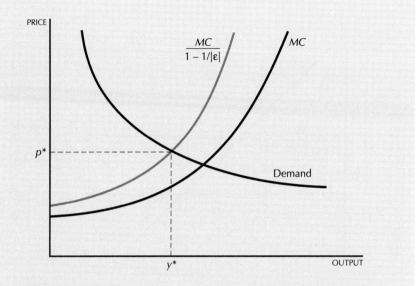

**Monopoly with constant elasticity demand.** To locate the profit-maximizing output level we find the output level where the curve $MC/(1 - 1/|\epsilon|)$ crosses the demand curve.

Figure
25.2

Let's first consider the case of a linear demand curve, as depicted in Figure 25.3. When the marginal cost curve, $MC$, shifts up by the amount of the tax to $MC+t$, the intersection of marginal revenue and marginal cost moves to the left. Since the demand curve is half as steep as the marginal revenue curve, the price goes up by half the amount of the tax.

This is easy to see algebraically. The marginal revenue equals marginal cost plus the tax condition is

$$a - 2by = c + t.$$

Solving for $y$ yields

$$y = \frac{a - c - t}{2b}.$$

Thus the change in output is given by

$$\frac{\delta y}{\delta t} = -\frac{1}{2b}.$$

The demand curve is

$$p(y) = a - by,$$

so price will change by $-b$ times the change in output:

$$\frac{\delta p}{\delta t} = -b \times -\frac{1}{2b} = \frac{1}{2}.$$

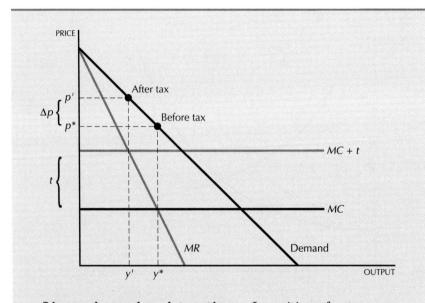

PRICE

$p'$

$\Delta p$ {

$p^*$

After tax

Before tax

MC + t

t {

MC

MR

Demand

$y'$   $y^*$

OUTPUT

Figure
25.3

**Linear demand and taxation.**   Imposition of a tax on a
monopolist facing a linear demand. Note that the price will rise
by half the amount of the tax.

In this calculation the factor $1/2$ occurs because of the assumptions of
the linear demand curve and constant marginal costs. Together these assumptions imply that the price rises by less than the tax increase. Is this
likely to be true in general?

The answer is no—in general a tax may increase the price by more or
less than the amount of the tax. For an easy example, consider the case of
a monopolist facing a constant-elasticity demand curve. Then we have

$$p = \frac{c + t}{1 - 1/|\epsilon|},$$

so that

$$\frac{\delta p}{\delta t} = \frac{1}{1 - 1/|\epsilon|},$$

which is certainly bigger than 1. In this case, the monopolist passes on
*more* than the amount of the tax.

Another kind of tax that we might consider is the case of a profits tax.
In this case the monopolist is required to pay some fraction $\tau$ of its profits
to the government. The maximization problem that it faces is then

$$\max_y \ (1 - \tau)[p(y)y - c(y)].$$

But the value of $y$ that maximizes profits will also maximize $(1 - \tau)$ times profits. Thus a pure profits tax will have no effect on a monopolist's choice of output.

## 25.4 Inefficiency of Monopoly

A competitive industry operates at a point where price equals marginal cost. A monopolized industry operates where price is greater than marginal cost. Thus in general the price will be higher and the output lower if a firm behaves monopolistically rather than competitively. For this reason, consumers will typically be worse off in an industry organized as a monopoly than in one organized competitively.

But, by the same token, the firm will be better off! Counting both the firm and the consumer, it is not clear whether competition or monopoly will be a "better" arrangement. It appears that one must make a value judgment about the relative welfare of consumers and the owners of firms. However, we will see that one can argue against monopoly on grounds of efficiency alone.

Consider a monopoly situation, as depicted in Figure 25.4. Suppose that we could somehow costlessly force this firm to behave as a competitor and take the market price as being set exogenously. Then we would have $(p_c, y_c)$ for the competitive price and output. Alternatively, if the firm recognized its influence on the market price and chose its level of output so as to maximize profits, we would see the monopoly price and output $(p_m, y_m)$.

Recall that an economic arrangement is Pareto efficient if there is no way to make anyone better off without making somebody else worse off. Is the monopoly level of output Pareto efficient?

Remember the definition of the inverse demand curve. At each level of output, $p(y)$ measures how much people are willing to pay for an additional unit of the good. Since $p(y)$ is greater than $MC(y)$ for all the output levels between $y_m$ and $y_c$, there is a whole range of output where people are willing to pay more for a unit of output than it costs to produce it. Clearly there is a potential for Pareto improvement here!

For example, consider the situation at the monopoly level of output $y_m$. Since $p(y_m) > MC(y_m)$ we know that there is someone who is willing to pay more for an extra unit of output than it costs to produce that extra unit. Suppose that the firm produces this extra output and sells it to this person at any price $p$ where $p(y_m) > p > MC(y_m)$. Then this consumer is made better off because he or she was just willing to pay $p(y_m)$ for that unit of consumption, and it was sold for $p < p(y_m)$. Similarly, it cost the monopolist $MC(y_m)$ to produce that extra unit of output and it sold it for $p > MC(y_m)$. All the other units of output are being sold for the same price as before, so nothing has changed there. But in the sale of the extra unit of output, each side of the market gets some extra surplus—each side

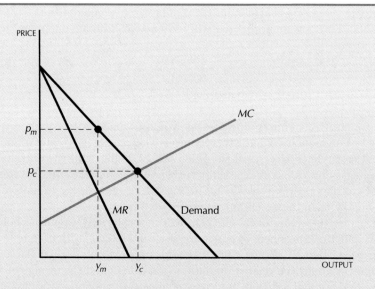

Figure
25.4

**Inefficiency of monopoly**. A monopolist produces less than the competitive amount of output and is therefore Pareto inefficient.

of the market is made better off and no one else is made worse off. We have found a Pareto improvement.

It is worthwhile considering the reason for this inefficiency. The efficient level of output is when the willingness to pay for an extra unit of output just equals the cost of producing this extra unit. A competitive firm makes this comparison. But a monopolist also looks at the effect of increasing output on the revenue received from the **inframarginal** units, and these inframarginal units have nothing to do with efficiency. A monopolist would always be ready to sell an additional unit at a lower price than it is currently charging if it did not have to lower the price of all the other inframarginal units that it is currently selling.

## 25.5 Deadweight Loss of Monopoly

Now that we know that a monopoly is inefficient, we might want to know just how inefficient it is. Is there a way to measure the total loss in efficiency due to a monopoly? We know how to measure the loss to the consumers from having to pay $p_m$ rather than $p_c$—we just look at the change in consumers' surplus. Similarly, for the firm we know how to measure the gain in profits from charging $p_m$ rather than $p_c$—we just use the change in producer's surplus.

The most natural way to combine these two numbers is to treat the firm—or, more properly, the owners of the firm—and the consumers of the firm's output symmetrically and add together the profits of the firm and the consumers' surplus. The change in the profits of the firm—the change in producer's surplus—measures how much the owners would be willing to pay to get the higher price under monopoly, and the change in consumers' surplus measures how much the consumers would have to be paid to compensate them for the higher price. Thus the difference between these two numbers should give a sensible measure of the net benefit or cost of the monopoly.

The changes in the producer's and consumers' surplus from a movement from monopolistic to competitive output are illustrated in Figure 25.5. The monopolist's surplus goes down by $A$ due to the lower price on the units he was already selling. It goes up by $C$ due to the profits on the extra units it is now selling.

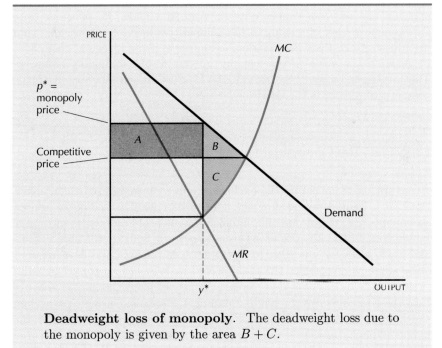

**Deadweight loss of monopoly.** The deadweight loss due to the monopoly is given by the area $B + C$.

Figure
25.5

The consumers' surplus goes up by $A$, since the consumers are now getting all the units they were buying before at a cheaper price; and it goes up by $B$, since they get some surplus on the extra units that are being sold. The area $A$ is just a transfer from the monopolist to the consumer;

one side of the market is made better off and one side is made worse off, but the total surplus doesn't change. The area $B + C$ represents a true increase in surplus—this area measures the value that the consumers and the producers place on the extra output that has been produced.

The area $B + C$ is known as the **deadweight loss** due to the monopoly. It provides a measure of how much worse off people are paying the monopoly price than paying the competitive price. The deadweight loss due to monopoly, like the deadweight loss due to a tax, measures the value of the lost output by valuing each unit of lost output at the price that people are willing to pay for that unit.

To see that the deadweight loss measures the value of the lost output, think about starting at the monopoly point and providing one additinal unit of output. The value of that marginal unit of output is the market price. The cost of producing the additional unit of output is the marginal cost. Thus the "social value" of producing an extra unit will be simply the price minus the marginal cost. Now consider the value of the next unit of output; again its social value will be the gap between price and marginal cost at that level of output. And so it goes. As we move from the monopoly level of output to the competitive level of output, we "sum up" the distances between the demand curve and the marginal cost curve to generate the value of the lost output due to the monopoly behavior. The total area between the two curves from the monopoly output to the competitive output is the deadweight loss.

## EXAMPLE: The Optimal Life of a Patent

A **patent** offers inventors the exclusive right to benefit from their inventions for a limited period of time. Thus a patent offers a kind of limited monopoly. The reason for offering such patent protection is to encourage innovation. In the absence of a patent system, it is likely that individuals and firms would be unwilling to invest much in research and development, since any new discoveries that they would make could be copied by competitors.

In the United States the life of a patent is 17 years. During that period, the holders of the patent have a monopoly on the invention; after the patent expires, anyone is free to utilize the technology described in the patent. The longer the life of a patent, the more gains can be accrued by the inventors, and thus the more incentive they have to invest in research and development. However, the longer the monopoly is allowed to exist, the more deadweight loss will be generated. The benefit from a long patent life is that it encourages innovation; the cost is that it encourages monopoly. The "optimal" patent life is the period that balances these two conflicting effects.

The problem of determining the optimal patent life has been examined by William Nordhaus of Yale University.[1] As Nordhaus indicates, the problem is very complex and there are many unknown relationships involved. Nevertheless, some simple calculations can give some insight as to whether the current patent life is wildly out of line with the estimated benefits and costs described above.

Nordhaus found that for "run-of-the-mill" inventions, a patent life of 17 years was roughly 90 percent efficient—meaning that it achieved 90 percent of the maximum possible consumers' surplus. On the basis of these figures, it does not seem like there is a compelling reason to make drastic changes in the patent system.

## EXAMPLE: Patent Thickets

The intellectual property protection offered by patents provides incentives to innovate, but this right can be abused. Some observers have argued that the extensions of intellectual property rights to business processes, software, and other domains has resulted in lower patent quality.

One might think of patents as having three dimensions: length, width, and height. The "length" is the time that the patent protection applies. The "width" is how broadly the claims in the patent are interpreted. The "height" is the standard of novelty applied in determining whether the patent really represents a new idea. Unfortunately, only the length is easily quantified. The other aspects of patent quality, breadth, and novelty, can be quite subjective.

Since it has become so easy to acquire patents in recent years, many firms have invested in acquiring patent portfolios on nearly every aspect of their business. Any company that wants to enter a business and compete with an incumbent who owns a broad range of patents may find itself encumbered in a **patent thicket**.

Even firms that are already well established find it important to invest in acquiring a patent portfolio. In 2004, Microsoft paid $440 million to InterTrust Technology to license a portfolio of patents related to computer security, and signed a 10-year pact with Sun Microsystems in which it paid $900 million to resolve patent issues. During 2003–04, Microsoft was granted over 1,000 patents.

Why the emphasis on patent portfolios? For large companies like Microsoft, their primary value is to be used as bargaining chips in cross-license agreements.

The patent thickets that each company sets up operate like the nuclear missiles held by the U.S. and USSR during the Cold War. Each had enough

---

[1] William Nordhaus, *Invention, Growth, and Welfare* (Cambridge, Mass.: M.I.T. Press, 1969).

missiles pointed at the other to create "mutually assured destruction" in the case that one side attacked. Hence, neither side could risk an attack.

It's the same issue with patent thickets. If IBM tries to sue HP for patent infringement, HP would pull out a collection of its own patents and countersue IBM for infringement in some other technology. Even companies that don't particularly want to patent aspects of their business are forced to do so in order to acquire the ammunition necessary for defense against other suits.

The "nuclear bomb" option in patent thickets is a "preliminary injunction." In certain circumstances, a judge might compel a company to stop selling an item that may be infringing on someone else's patent. This can be exceedingly costly. In 1986, Kodak had to completely shut down its instant photography business due to a court-ordered injunction. Eventually Kodak had to pay a billion-dollar judgment for patent infringement.

An injunction to stop production can be a huge threat, but it has no force against companies that don't produce anything. InterTrust, for example, didn't sell any products—all of its income came from licensing patents. Hence, it could threaten to sue other companies for patent infringement without much worry about the threat of countersuits.

### EXAMPLE: Managing the Supply of Potatoes

Everyone is familiar with the Organization of Petroleum Exporting Countries (OPEC), the international oil cartel that attempts to influence the price of oil by setting production quota. Normally, coordinating production to push up prices is illegal in the United States, but there are some industries that are exempt from antitrust rules.

A notable example is agricultural producers. The 1922 Capper-Volstead Act specifically exempts farmers from federal antitrust rules. The result has been the creation of a number of "agricultural marketing boards" that attempt to voluntarily regulate the supply of agricultural products.

For example, the United Potato Growers of America, formed in March 2005, has signed up potato farmers that represent over 60% of the potato acreage in the United States. In 2005 it claimed to reduce production of potatoes by 6.8 million sacks of potatoes, each weighing about 100 pounds a piece. According to the *Wall Street Journal* this is equivalent to about 1.3 billion orders of french fries.[2]

## 25.6 Natural Monopoly

---

[2] Timothy W. Martin, "This Spud's Not for You," *Wall Street Journal*, September 26, 2009.

We have seen earlier that the Pareto efficient amount of output in an industry occurs where price equals marginal cost. A monopolist produces where marginal revenue equals marginal cost and thus produces too little output. It would seem that regulating a monopoly to eliminate the inefficiency is pretty easy—all the regulator has to do is to set price equal to marginal cost, and profit maximization will do the rest. Unfortunately, this analysis leaves out one important aspect of the problem: it may be that the monopolist would make negative profits at such a price.

An example of this is shown in Figure 25.6. Here the minimum point of the average cost curve is to the right of the demand curve, and the intersection of demand and marginal cost lies underneath the average cost curve. Even though the level of output $y_{MC}$ is efficient, it is not profitable. If a regulator set this level of output, the monopolist would prefer to go out of business.

**A natural monopoly.** If a natural monopolist operates where price equals marginal cost, then it will produce an efficient level of output, $y_{MC}$, but it will be unable to cover its costs. If it is required to produce an output where price equals average cost, $y_{AC}$, then it will cover its costs, but will produce too little output relative to the efficient amount.

Figure
25.6

This kind of situation often arises with public utilities. Think of a gas company, for example. Here the technology involves very large fixed costs—

creating and maintaining the gas delivery pipes—and a very small marginal cost to providing extra units of gas—once the pipe is laid, it costs very little to pump more gas down the pipe. Similarly, a local telephone company involves very large fixed costs for providing the wires and switching network, while the marginal costs of an extra unit of telephone service is very low. When there are large fixed costs and small marginal costs, you can easily get the kind of situation described in Figure 25.6. Such a situation is referred to as a **natural monopoly**.

If allowing a natural monopolist to set the monopoly price is undesirable due to the Pareto inefficiency, and forcing the natural monopoly to produce at the competitive price is infeasible due to negative profits, what is left? For the most part natural monopolies are regulated or operated by governments. Different countries have adopted different approaches. In some countries the telephone service is provided by the government and in others it is provided by private firms that are regulated by the government. Both of these approaches have their advantages and disadvantages.

For example, let us consider the case of government regulation of a natural monopoly. If the regulated firm is to require no subsidy, it must make nonnegative profits, which means it must operate on or above the average cost curve. If it is to provide service to all who are willing to pay for it, it must also operate on the demand curve. Thus the natural operating position for a regulated firm is a point like $(p_{AC}, y_{AC})$ in Figure 25.6. Here the firm is selling its product at the average cost of production, so it covers its costs, but it is producing too little output relative to the efficient level of output.

This solution is often adopted as a reasonable pricing policy for a natural monopolist. Government regulators set the prices that the public utility is allowed to charge. Ideally these prices are supposed to be prices that just allow the firm to break even—produce at a point where price equals average costs.

The problem facing the regulators is to determine just what the true costs of the firm are. Usually there is a public utility commission that investigates the costs of the monopoly in an attempt to determine the true average cost and then sets a price that will cover costs. (Of course, one of these costs is the payment that the firm has to make to its shareholders and other creditors in exchange for the money they have loaned to the firm.)

In the United States these regulatory boards operate at the state and local level. Typically electricity, natural gas, and telephone service operate in this way. Other natural monopolies like cable TV are usually regulated at the local level.

The other solution to the problem of natural monopoly is to let the government operate it. The ideal solution here in this case is to operate the service at price equals marginal cost and provide a lump-sum subsidy to keep the firm in operation. This is often the practice for local public transportation systems such as buses and subways. The lump-sum subsidies may not reflect inefficient operation *per se* but rather, simply reflect the large fixed costs associated with such public utilities.

Then again, the subsidies may just represent inefficiency! The problem with government-run monopolies is that it is almost as difficult to measure their costs as it is to measure the costs of regulated public utilities. Government regulatory commissions that oversee the operations of public utilities often subject them to probing hearings to require them to justify cost data whereas an internal government bureaucracy may escape such intense scrutiny. The government bureaucrats who run such government monopolies may turn out to be less accountable to the public than those who run the regulated monopolies.

## 25.7 What Causes Monopolies?

Given information on costs and demand, when would we predict that an industry would be competitive and when would we predict that it would be monopolized? In general the answer depends on the relationship between the average cost curve and the demand curve. The crucial factor is the size of the **minimum efficient scale (MES)**, the level of output that minimizes average cost, relative to the size of demand.

Consider Figure 25.7 where we have illustrated the average cost curves and the market demand curves for two goods. In the first case there is room in the market for many firms, each charging a price close to $p^*$ and each operating at a relatively small scale. In the second market, only one firm can make positive profits. We would expect that the first market might well operate as a competitive market and that the second would operate as a monopolist.

Thus the shape of the average cost curve, which in turn is determined by the underlying technology, is one important aspect that determines whether a market will operate competitively or monopolistically. If the minimum efficient scale of production—the level of output that minimizes average costs—is small relative to the size of the market, we might expect that competitive conditions will prevail.

Note that this is a *relative* statement: what matters is the scale relative to the market size. We can't do too much about the minimum efficient scale— that is determined by the technology. But economic policy can influence the size of the market. If a country chooses nonrestrictive foreign-trade policies, so that domestic firms face foreign competition, then the domestic firms' ability to influence prices will be much less. Conversely, if a country adopts restrictive trade policies, so that the size of the market is limited only to that country, then monopolistic practices are more likely to take hold.

Figure
25.7
**Demand relative to minimum efficient scale.** (A) If demand is large relative to the minimum efficient scale, a competitive market is likely to result. (B) If it is small, a monopolistic industry structure is possible.

If monopolies arise because the minimum efficient scale is large relative to the size of the market, and it is infeasible to increase the size of the market, then the industry is a candidate for regulation or other sorts of government intervention. Of course such regulation and intervention are costly too. Regulatory boards cost money, and the efforts of the firm to satisfy the regulatory boards can be quite expensive. From society's point of view, the question should be whether the deadweight loss of the monopoly exceeds the costs of regulation.

A second reason why monopoly might occur is that several different firms in an industry might be able to collude and restrict output in order to raise prices and thereby increase their profits. When firms collude in this way and attempt to reduce output and increase price, we say the industry is organized as a **cartel**.

Cartels are illegal. The Antitrust Division of the Justice Department and the Bureau of Competition of the Federal Trade Commission are charged with searching for evidence of noncompetitive behavior on the part of firms. If the government can establish that a group of firms attempted to restrict output or engaged in certain other anticompetitive practices, the firms in question can be forced to pay heavy fines.

On the other hand, an industry may have one dominant firm purely by historical accident. If one firm is first to enter some market, it may have enough of a cost advantage to be able to discourage other firms from entering the industry. Suppose, for example, that there are very large "tooling-up" costs to entering an industry. Then the incumbent—the firm already in the industry—may under certain conditions be able to convince potential entrants that it will cut its prices drastically if they attempt to enter the industry. By preventing entry in this manner, a firm can eventually dominate a market. We will study an example of pricing to prevent entry in Chapter 29.

## EXAMPLE: Diamonds Are Forever

The De Beers diamond cartel was formed by Sir Ernest Oppenheimer, a South African mine operator, in 1930. It has since grown into one of the world's most successful cartels. De Beers handles over 80% of the world's yearly production of diamonds and has managed to maintain this near-monopoly for several decades. Over the years, De Beers has developed several mechanism to maintain control of the diamond market.

First, it maintains considerable stocks of diamonds of all types. If a producer attempts to sell outside the cartel, De Beers can quickly flood the market with the same type of diamond, thereby punishing the defector from the cartel. Second, large producers' quotas are based on the *proportion* of total sales. When the market is weak, everyone's production quota is reduced proportionally, thereby automatically increasing scarcity and raising prices.

Third, De Beers is involved at both the mining and wholesaling levels of diamond production. In the wholesale market diamonds are sold to cutters in boxes of assorted diamonds: buyers take a whole box or nothing—they cannot choose individual stones. If the market is weak for a certain size of diamond, De Beers can reduce the number of those diamonds offered in the boxes, thereby making them more scarce.

Finally, De Beers can influence the direction of final demand for diamonds by the $110 million a year it spends on advertising. Again, this advertising can be adjusted to encourage demand for the types and sizes of diamonds that are in relatively scarce supply.[3]

## EXAMPLE: Pooling in Auction Markets

Adam Smith once said "People of the same trade seldom meet together, even for merriment and diversion, but the conversation ends in a conspiracy against the public, or in some contrivance to raise prices." Bidding pools in auctions provide an illustrative example of Smith's observation. In 1988 the Justice Department charged 12 Philadelphia antique dealers

---

[3] A short description of the diamond market can be found in "The cartel lives to face another threat," *The Economist*, January 10, 1987, 58–60. A more detailed description can be found in Edward J. Epstein, *Cartel* (New York: Putnam, 1978).

with antitrust violations for their participation in this particular kind of "conspiracy against the public."[4]

The dealers were accused of participating in "bidding rings," or "pools," at antique furniture auctions. The members of a pool would appoint one member to bid on certain items. If this bidder succeeded in acquiring an item, the participating dealers would then hold a subsequent private auction, called a "knockout," in which the members of the pool bid among themselves for the item. This practice allowed the members of the pool to acquire the items at much lower prices than would have prevailed if they had bid separately; in many cases the prices in the knockout auctions were 50 to 100 percent greater than the prices paid to the original sellers of the goods.

The dealers were surprised by the Justice Department suit; they considered pooling a common business practice in their trade and did not think it was illegal. They thought of the pools as a tradition of cooperation among themselves; being invited to join a pool was considered a "mark of distinction." According to one dealer, "The day I was allowed to go into the pool was a banner day. If you weren't in the pool, you weren't considered much of a dealer." The dealers were so naive that they kept careful records of their payments in the knockout auctions, which were later used by the Justice Department in the suits against the dealers.

The Justice Department argued "if they are joining together to hold down the price [received by the seller] that is illegal." The Justice Department view prevailed over that of the dealers: 11 of the 12 dealers pleaded guilty and settled the matter with fines of $1,000 to $50,000 and probation. The dealer who held out for a jury trial was found guilty and sentenced to 30 days of house arrest and a fine of $30,000.

### EXAMPLE: Price Fixing in Computer Memory Markets

DRAM chips are the "dynamic random access memory" chips that go in your computer. They are pretty much an undifferentiated commodity product and the market for DRAMs is (usually) highly competitive. However, there are allegations that several DRAM producers conspired to fix prices and charge computer makers a higher price than would have obtained under purely competitive conditions. Apple Computer, Compaq, Dell, Gateway, HP, and IBM were apparently affected by this conspiracy.

The Department of Justice started investigating these allegations in 2002. In September 2004, Infineon, a German DRAM manufacturer, pleaded guilty to charges of price fixing, and agreed to pay a $160 million fine.

---

[4] See Meg Cox, "At Many Auctions, Illegal Bidding Thrives As a Longtime Practice Among Dealers," *Wall Street Journal*, February 19, 1988, which served as the source for this example.

This was the third largest criminal fine ever imposed by the Department of Justice's antitrust division.

According to the court documents, Infineon was charged with "Participating in meetings, conversations, and communications with competitors to discuss the prices of DRAM to be sold to certain customers; Agreeing to price levels of DRAM to be sold to certain customers; Exchanging information on sales of DRAM to certain customers, for the purpose of monitoring and enforcing the agreed-upon prices."

Subsequently, four executives at Infineon were sentenced to prison terms and had to pay hefty fines. The antitrust authorities take price fixing very seriously, and the consequences to companies and individuals that engage in such activities can be severe.

## Summary

1. When there is only a single firm in an industry, we say that it is a monopoly.

2. A monopolist operates at a point where marginal revenue equals marginal cost. Hence a monopolist charges a price that is a markup on marginal cost, where the size of the markup depends on the elasticity of demand.

3. Since a monopolist charges a price in excess of marginal cost, it will produce an inefficient amount of output. The size of the inefficiency can be measured by the deadweight loss—the net loss of consumers' and the producer's surplus.

4. A natural monopoly occurs when a firm cannot operate at an efficient level of output without losing money. Many public utilities are natural monopolies of this sort and are therefore regulated by the government.

5. Whether an industry is competitive or monopolized depends in part on the nature of technology. If the minimum efficient scale is large relative to demand, then the market is likely to be monopolized. But if the minimum efficient scale is small relative to demand, there is room for many firms in the industry, and there is a hope for a competitive market structure.

## REVIEW QUESTIONS

1. The market demand curve for heroin is said to be highly inelastic. Heroin supply is also said to be monopolized by the Mafia, which we assume to be interested in maximizing profits. Are these two statements consistent?

2. The monopolist faces a demand curve given by $D(p) = 100 - 2p$. Its cost function is $c(y) = 2y$. What is its optimal level of output and price?

3. The monopolist faces a demand curve given by $D(p) = 10p^{-3}$. Its cost function is $c(y) = 2y$. What is its optimal level of output and price?

4. If $D(p) = 100/p$ and $c(y) = y^2$, what is the optimal level of output of the monopolist? (Be careful.)

5. A monopolist is operating at an output level where $|\epsilon| = 3$. The government imposes a quantity tax of \$6 per unit of output. If the demand curve facing the monopolist is linear, how much does the price rise?

6. What is the answer to the above question if the demand curve facing the monopolist has constant elasticity?

7. If the demand curve facing the monopolist has a constant elasticity of 2, then what will be the monopolist's markup on marginal cost?

8. The government is considering subsidizing the marginal costs of the monopolist described in the question above. What level of subsidy should the government choose if it wants the monopolist to produce the socially optimal amount of output?

9. Show mathematically that a monopolist always sets its price above marginal cost.

10. True or false? Imposing a quantity tax on a monopolist will always cause the market price to increase by the amount of the tax.

11. What problems face a regulatory agency attempting to force a monopolist to charge the perfectly competitive price?

12. What kinds of economic and technological conditions are conducive to the formation of monopolies?

# CHAPTER 26

# MONOPOLY BEHAVIOR

In a competitive market there are typically several firms selling an identical product. Any attempt by one of the firms to sell its product at more than the market price leads consumers to desert the high-priced firm in favor of its competitors. In a monopolized market there is only one firm selling a given product. When a monopolist raises its price it loses some, but not all, of its customers.

In reality most industries are somewhere in between these two extremes. If a gas station in a small town raises the price at which it sells gasoline and it loses most of its customers, it is reasonable to think that this firm must behave as a competitive firm. If a restaurant in the same town raises its price and loses only a few of its customers, then it is reasonable to think that this restaurant has some degree of monopoly power.

If a firm has some degree of monopoly power it has more options open to it than a firm in a perfectly competitive industry. For example, it can use more complicated pricing and marketing strategies than a firm in a competitive industry. Or it can try to differentiate its product from the products sold by its competitors to enhance its market power even further. In this chapter we will examine how firms can enhance and exploit their market power.

## 26.1 Price Discrimination

We have argued earlier that a monopoly operates at an inefficient level of output since it restricts output to a point where people are willing to pay more for extra output than it costs to produce it. The monopolist doesn't want to produce this *extra* output, because it would force down the price that it would be able to get for *all* of its output.

But if the monopolist could sell different units of output at different prices, then we have another story. Selling different units of output at different prices is called **price discrimination**. Economists generally consider the following three kinds of price discrimination:

**First-degree price discrimination** means that the monopolist sells different units of output for different prices *and* these prices may differ from person to person. This is sometimes known as the case of **perfect price discrimination**.

**Second-degree price discrimination** means that the monopolist sells different units of output for different prices, but every individual who buys the same amount of the good pays the same price. Thus prices differ across the units of the good, but not across people. The most common example of this is bulk discounts.

**Third-degree price discrimination** occurs when the monopolist sells output to different people for different prices, but every unit of output sold to a given person sells for the same price. This is the most common form of price discrimination, and examples include senior citizens' discounts, student discounts, and so on.

Let us look at each of these to see what economics can say about how price discrimination works.

## 26.2 First-Degree Price Discrimination

Under **first-degree price discrimination**, or **perfect price discrimination**, each unit of the good is sold to the individual who values it most highly, at the maximum price that this individual is willing to pay for it.

Consider Figure 26.1, which illustrates two consumers' demand curves for a good. Think of a reservation price model for demand where the individuals choose integer amounts of the goods and each step in the demand curve represents a change in the willingness to pay for additional units of the good. We have also illustrated (constant) marginal cost curves for the good.

A producer who is able to perfectly price discriminate will sell each unit of the good at the highest price it will command, that is, at each consumer's reservation price. Since each unit is sold to each consumer at his or her reservation price for that unit, there is no consumers' surplus generated in

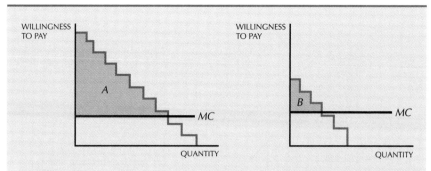

**First-degree price discrimination**.  Here are two consumers'
demand curves for a good along with the constant marginal cost
curve.  The producer sells each unit of the good at the maximum
price it will command, which yields it the maximum possible
profit.

Figure
26.1

this market; all the surplus goes to the producer. In Figure 26.1 the colored
areas indicate the *producer's surplus* accruing to the monopolist. In an ordinary competitive market setting these areas would represent *consumers'
surplus*, but in the case of perfect price discrimination, the monopolist is
able to appropriate this surplus for itself.

Since the producer gets all the surplus in the market, it wants to make
sure that the surplus is as large as possible. Put another way, the producer's
goal is to maximize its profits (producer's surplus) subject to the constraint
that the consumers are just willing to purchase the good.  This means
that the outcome will be Pareto efficient, since there will be no way to
make both the consumers and the producer better off: the producer's profit
can't be increased, since it is already the maximal possible profit, and the
consumers' surplus can't be increased without reducing the profit of the
producer.

If we move to the smooth demand curve approximation, as in Figure 26.2,
we see that a perfectly price-discriminating monopolist must produce at an
output level where price equals marginal cost: if price were greater than
marginal cost, that would mean that there is someone who is willing to pay
more than it costs to produce an extra unit of output. So why not produce
that extra unit and sell it to that person at his or her reservation price,
and thus increase profits?

Just as in the case of a competitive market, the sum of producer's and
consumers' surpluses is maximized. However, in the case of perfect price
discrimination the producer ends up getting *all* the surplus generated in
the market!

We have interpreted first-degree price discrimination as selling each unit
at the maximum price it will command. But we could also think of it as
selling a fixed amount of the good at a "take it or leave it" price. In the

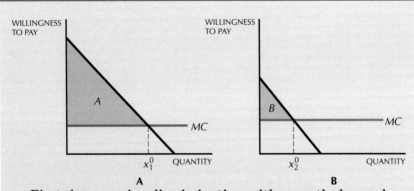

Figure 26.2

**First-degree price discrimination with smooth demand curves.** Here are two consumers' smoothed demand curves for a good along with the constant marginal cost curve. Here the producer maximizes profits by producing where price equals marginal cost, just as in the case of a competitive market.

case illustrated in Figure 26.2, the monopolist would offer to sell $x_1^0$ units of the good to person 1 at a price equal to the area under person 1's demand curve and offer to sell $x_2^0$ units of the good to person 2 at a price equal to the area under person 2's demand curve $B$. As before, each person would end up with zero consumer's surplus, and the entire surplus of $A + B$ would end up in the hands of the monopolist.

Perfect price discrimination is an idealized concept—as the word "perfect" might suggest—but it is interesting theoretically since it gives us an example of a resource allocation mechanism other than a competitive market that achieves Pareto efficiency. There are very few real-life examples of perfect price discrimination. The closest example would be something like a small-town doctor who charges his patients different prices, based on their ability to pay.

## EXAMPLE: First-degree Price Discrimination in Practice

As mentioned earlier, first-degree price discrimination is primarily a theoretical concept. It's hard to find real-world examples in which every individual is charged a different price. One possible example would be cases where prices are set by bargaining, as in automobile sales or in antique markets. However, these are not ideal examples.

In 2005, Southwest Airlines introduced a system called Ding that attempts something rather close to first-degree price discrimination.[1] The

---

[1] See Christopher Elliott, "Your Very Own Personal Air Fare," *New York Times,* August 9, 2005.

system uses the Internet in a clever way. The user installs a program on her computer (or iPhone) and the airline sends special fare offers to the user periodically. The fares are announced with a "ding" sound, hence the system name. According to one analyst, the fares offered by Ding were about 30 percent lower than comparable fares.

One might also use such a system to offer higher fares. However, that possibility seems unlikely given the intensely competitive nature of the airline industry. It's easy to switch back to standard ways of buying tickets if prices start creeping up. As of 2012, Ding is still around.

## 26.3 Second-Degree Price Discrimination

**Second-degree price discrimination** is also known as the case of **non-linear pricing**, since it means that the price per unit of output is not constant but depends on how much you buy. This form of price discrimination is commonly used by public utilities; for example, the price per unit of electricity often depends on how much is bought. In other industries bulk discounts for large purchases are sometimes available.

Let us consider the case depicted earlier in Figure 26.2. We saw that the monopolist would *like* to sell an amount $x_1^0$ to person 1 at price $A+$ cost and an amount $x_2^0$ to person 2 at price $B+$ cost. To set the right prices, the monopolist has to *know* the demand curves of the consumers; that is, the monopolist has to know the exact willingness to pay of each person. Even if the monopolist knows something about the statistical distribution of willingness to pay—for example, that college students are willing to pay less than yuppies for movie tickets—it might be hard to tell a yuppie from a college student when they are standing in line at the ticket booth.

Similarly, an airline ticket agent may know that business travelers are willing to pay more than tourists for their airplane tickets, but it is often difficult to tell whether a particular person is a business traveler or a tourist. If switching from a grey flannel suit to Bermuda shorts would save $500 on travel expenses, corporate dress codes could change quickly!

The problem with the first-degree price discrimination example depicted in Figure 26.2 is that person 1—the high-willingess-to-pay person—can *pretend* to be person 2, the low-willingess-to-pay person. The seller may have no effective way to tell them apart.

One way to get around this problem is to offer two different price-quantity packages in the market. One package will be targeted toward the high-demand person, the other package toward the low-demand person. It can often happen that the monopolist can construct price-quantity packages that will induce the consumers to choose the package meant for them; in economics jargon, the monopolist constructs price-quantity packages that give the consumers an incentive to **self select**.

In order to see how this works, Figure 26.3 illustrates the same kind of demand curves used in Figure 26.2, but now laid on top of each other. We've also set marginal cost equal to zero in this diagram to keep the argument simple.

Figure 26.3

**Second-degree price discrimination.** These are the demand curves of two consumers; the producer has zero marginal cost by assumption. Panel A illustrates the self-selection problem. Panel B shows what happens if the monopolist reduces the output targeted for consumer 1, and panel C illustrates the profit-maximizing solution.

As before, the monopolist would like to offer $x_1^0$ at price $A$ and to offer $x_2^0$ at price $A + B + C$. This would capture all the surplus for the monopolist and generate the most possible profit. Unfortunately for the monopolist, these price-quantity combinations are not compatible with self-selection. The high-demand consumer would find it optimal to choose the quantity $x_1^0$ and pay price $A$; this would leave him with a surplus equal to area $B$, which is better than the zero surplus he would get if he chose $x_2^0$.

One thing the monopolist can do is to offer $x_2^0$ at a price of $A+C$. In this case the high-demand consumer finds it optimal to choose $x_2^0$ and receive a gross surplus of $A + B + C$. He pays the monopolist $A + C$, which yields a net surplus of $B$ for consumer 2—just what he would get if he chose $x_1^0$. This generally yields more profit to the monopolist than it would get by offering only one price-quantity combination.

But the story doesn't end here. There's yet a further thing the monopolist can do to increase profits. Suppose that instead of offering $x_1^0$ at price $A$ to the low-demand consumer, the monopolist offers a bit less than that at a price slightly less than $A$. This reduces the monopolist's profits on person 1 by the small colored triangle illustrated in Figure 26.3B. But note that since person 1's package is now less attractive to person 2, the monopolist can now charge *more* to person 2 for $x_2^0$! By reducing $x_1^0$, the monopolist makes area $A$ a little smaller (by the dark triangle) but makes area $C$ bigger (by the triangle plus the light trapezoid area). The net result is that the monopolist's profits increase.

Continuing in this way, the monopolist will want to reduce the amount offered to person 1 up to the point where the profit lost on person 1 due to a further reduction in output just equals the profit gained on person 2. At this point, illustrated in Figure 26.3C, the marginal benefits and costs of quantity reduction just balance. Person 1 chooses $x_1^m$ and is charged $A$; person 2 chooses $x_2^0$ and is charged $A + C + D$. Person 1 ends up with a zero surplus and person 2 ends up with a surplus of $B$—just what he would get if he chose to consume $x_1^m$.

In practice, the monopolist often encourages this self-selection not by adjusting the *quantity* of the good, as in this example, but rather by adjusting the *quality* of the good. The quantities in the model just examined can be re-interpreted as qualities, and everything works as before. In general, the monopolist will want to reduce the quality offered to the low end of its market so as not to cannibalize sales at the high end. Without the high-end consumers, the low-end consumers would be offered higher quality, but they would still end up with zero surplus. Without the low-end consumers, the high-end consumers would have zero surplus, so it is beneficial to the high-end consumers to have the low-end consumers present. This is because the monopolist has to cut the price to the high-end consumers to discourage them from choosing the product targeted to the low-end consumers.

## EXAMPLE: Price Discrimination in Airfares

The airline industry has been very successful at price discrimination (although industry representatives prefer to use the term "yield management.") The model described above applies reasonably well to the problem faced by airlines: there are essentially two types of consumers, business travelers and individual travelers, who generally have quite different willingnesses to pay. Although there are several competing airlines in the U.S. market, it is quite common to see only one or two airlines serving specific city pairs. This gives the airlines considerable freedom in setting prices.

We have seen that the optimal pricing policy for a monopolist dealing with two groups of consumers is to sell to the high-willingness-to-pay market at a high price and offer a reduced-quality product to the market with the lower willingness to pay. The point of the reduced-quality product is to dissuade those with a high willingness to pay from purchasing the lower priced good.

The way the airlines implement this is to offer an "unrestricted fare" for business travel and a "restricted fare" for non-business travel. The restricted fare often requires advanced purchase, a Saturday-night stayover, or other such impositions. The point of these impositions, of course, is to be able to discriminate between the high-demand business travelers and the more price sensitive individual travelers. By offering a "degraded" product—the restricted fares—the airlines can charge the customers who require flexible travel arrangements considerably more for their tickets.

Such arrangements may well be socially useful; without the ability to price discriminate, a firm may decide that it is optimal to sell *only* to the high-demand markets.

Another way that airlines price discriminate is with first-class and coach-class travel. First-class travelers pay substantially more for their tickets, but they receive an enhanced level of service: more space, better food, and more attention. Coach-class travelers, on the other hand, receive a lower level of service on all these dimensions. This sort of quality discrimination has been a feature of transportation services for hundreds of years. Witness, for example, this commentary on railroad pricing by Emile Dupuit, a nineteenth century French economist:

It is not because of the few thousand francs which would have to be spent to put a roof over the third-class carriage or to upholster the third-class seats that some company or other has open carriages with wooden benches ... What the company is trying to do is prevent the passengers who can pay the second-class fare from traveling third class; it hits the poor, not because it wants to hurt them, but to frighten the rich ... And it is again for the same reason that the companies, having proved almost cruel to the third-class passengers and mean to the second-class ones, become lavish in dealing with first-class customers. Having refused the poor what is necessary, they give the rich what is superfluous.[2]

The next time you fly coach class, perhaps it will be of some solace to know that rail travel in nineteenth century France was even more uncomfortable!

## EXAMPLE: Prescription Drug Prices

A month's supply of the antidepressant Zoloft sells for $29.74 in Austria, $32.91 in Luxembourg, $40.97 in Mexico, and $64.67 in the United States. Why the difference? Drug makers, like other firms, charge what the market

---

[2] Translation by R. B. Ekelund in "Price Discrimination and Product Differentiation in Economic Theory: An Early Analysis," *Quarterly Journal of Economics*, 84 (1970), 268–78.

will bear. Poorer countries can't pay as much as richer ones, so drug prices tend to be lower.

But that's not the whole story. Bargaining power also differs dramatically from country to country. Canada, which has a national health plan, often has lower drug prices than the United States, where there is no centralized provider of health care.

It has been proposed that drug companies be forced to charge a single price worldwide. Leaving aside the thorny question of enforcement, we might well ask what the consequences of such a policy would be. Would the world overall end up with lower prices or higher prices?

The answer depends on the relative size of the market. A drug for malaria would find most of its demand in poor countries. If forced to charge a single price, drug companies would likely sell such a drug at a low price. But a drug for diseases that afflicted those in wealthy countries would likely sell for a high price, making it too expensive for those in poorer areas.

Typically, moving from price discrimination to a single-price regime will raise some prices and lower others, making some people better off and some people worse off. In some cases, a product may not be supplied at all to some markets if a seller is forced to apply uniform pricing.

## 26.4 Third-Degree Price Discrimination

Recall that this means that the monopolist sells to different people at different prices, but every unit of the good sold to a given group is sold at the same price. Third-degree price discrimination is the most common form of price discrimination. Examples of this might be student discounts at the movies, or senior citizens' discounts at the drugstore. How does the monopolist determine the optimal prices to charge in each market?

Let us suppose that the monopolist is able to identify two groups of people and can sell an item to each group at a different price. We suppose that the consumers in each market are not able to resell the good. Let us use $p_1(y_1)$ and $p_2(y_2)$ to denote the inverse demand curves of groups 1 and 2, respectively, and let $c(y_1 + y_2)$ be the cost of producing output. Then the profit-maximization problem facing the monopolist is

$$\max_{y_1, y_2} \; p_1(y_1)y_1 + p_2(y_2)y_2 - c(y_1 + y_2).$$

The optimal solution must have

$$MR_1(y_1) = MC(y_1 + y_2)$$

$$MR_2(y_2) = MC(y_1 + y_2).$$

That is, the marginal cost of producing an extra unit of output must be equal to the marginal revenue in *each* market. If the marginal revenue in market 1 exceeded marginal cost, it would pay to expand output in market 1, and similarly for market 2. Since marginal cost is the same in each market, this means of course that marginal revenue in each market must also be the same. Thus a good should bring the same increase in revenue whether it is sold in market 1 or in market 2.

We can use the standard elasticity formula for marginal revenue and write the profit-maximization conditions as

$$p_1(y_1) \left[ 1 - \frac{1}{|\epsilon_1(y_1)|} \right] = MC(y_1 + y_2)$$

$$p_2(y_2) \left[ 1 - \frac{1}{|\epsilon_2(y_2)|} \right] = MC(y_1 + y_2),$$

where $\epsilon_1(y_1)$ and $\epsilon_2(y_2)$ represent the elasticities of demand in the respective markets, evaluated at the profit-maximizing choices of output.

Now note the following. If $p_1 > p_2$, then we must have

$$1 - \frac{1}{|\epsilon_1(y_1)|} < 1 - \frac{1}{|\epsilon_2(y_2)|},$$

which in turn implies that

$$\frac{1}{|\epsilon_1(y_1)|} > \frac{1}{|\epsilon_2(y_2)|}.$$

This means that

$$|\epsilon_2(y_2)| > |\epsilon_1(y_1)|.$$

Thus the market with the higher price must have the lower elasticity of demand. Upon reflection, this is quite sensible. An elastic demand is a price-sensitive demand. A firm that price discriminates will therefore set a low price for the price-sensitive group and a high price for the group that is relatively price insensitive. In this way it maximizes its overall profits.

We suggested that senior citizens' discounts and student discounts were good examples of third-degree price discrimination. Now we can see why they have discounts. It is likely that students and senior citizens are more sensitive to price than the average consumer and thus have more elastic demands for the relevant region of prices. Therefore a profit-maximizing firm will price discriminate in their favor.

## EXAMPLE: Linear Demand Curves

Let us consider a problem where the firm faces two markets with linear demand curves, $x_1 = a - bp_1$ and $x_2 = c - dp_2$. Suppose for simplicity that marginal costs are zero. If the firm is allowed to price discriminate, it will produce where marginal revenue equals zero in each market—at a price and output combination that is halfway down each demand curve, with outputs $x_1^* = a/2$ and $x_2^* = c/2$ and prices $p_1^* = a/2b$ and $p_2^* = c/2d$.

Suppose that the firm were forced to sell in both markets at the same price. Then it would face a demand curve of $x = (a + c) - (b + d)p$ and would produce halfway down this demand curve, resulting in an output of $x^* = (a + c)/2$ and price of $p^* = (a + c)/2(b + d)$. Note that the total output is the same whether or not price discrimination is allowed. (This is a special feature of the linear demand curve and does not hold in general.)

However, there is an important exception to this statement. We have assumed that when the monopolist chooses the optimal single price it will sell a positive amount of output in each market. It may very well happen that at the profit-maximizing price, the monopolist will sell output to only one of the markets, as illustrated in Figure 26.4.

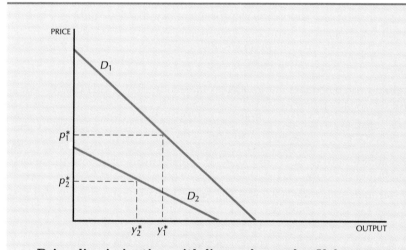

**Price discrimination with linear demands.** If the monopolist can charge only one price, it will charge $p_1^*$, and sell only to market 1. But if price discrimination is allowed, it will also sell at price $p_2^*$ to market 2.

Figure
26.4

Here we have two linear demand curves; since marginal cost is assumed to be zero, the monopolist will want to operate at a point where the elasticity of demand is $-1$, which we know to be halfway down the market demand curve. Thus the price $p_1^*$ is a profit-maximizing price—lowering the price any further would reduce revenues in market 1. If the demand in market 2 is very small, the monopolist may not want to lower its price any further in order to sell to this market: it will end up selling only to the larger market.

In this case, allowing price discrimination will unambiguously increase total output, since the monopolist will find it in its interest to sell to both markets if it can charge a different price in each one.

## EXAMPLE: Calculating Optimal Price Discrimination

Suppose that a monopolist faces two markets with demand curves given by

$$D_1(p_1) = 100 - p_1$$
$$D_2(p_2) = 100 - 2p_2.$$

Assume that the monopolist's marginal cost is constant at $20 a unit. If it can price discriminate, what price should it charge in each market in order to maximize profits? What if it can't price discriminate? Then what price should it charge?

To solve the price-discrimination problem, we first calculate the inverse demand functions:

$$p_1(y_1) = 100 - y_1$$
$$p_2(y_2) = 50 - y_2/2.$$

Marginal revenue equals marginal cost in each market yields the two equations:

$$100 - 2y_1 = 20$$
$$50 - y_2 = 20.$$

Solving we have $y_1^* = 40$ and $y_2^* = 30$. Substituting back into the inverse demand functions gives us the prices $p_1^* = 60$ and $p_2^* = 35$.

If the monopolist must charge the same price in each market, we first calculate the total demand:

$$D(p) = D_1(p_1) + D_2(p_2) = 200 - 3p.$$

The inverse demand curve is

$$p(y) = \frac{200}{3} - \frac{y}{3}.$$

Marginal revenue equals marginal cost gives us

$$\frac{200}{3} - \frac{2}{3}y = 20,$$

which can be solved to give $y^* = 70$ and $p^* = 43\frac{1}{3}$.

In accord with the discussion in the previous section, it is important to check that this price generates non-negative demands in each market. However, it is easily checked that this is the case.

## EXAMPLE: Price Discrimination in Academic Journals

Most written scholarly communication takes place in academic journals. These journals are sold by subscription to libraries and to individual scholars. It is very common to see different subscription prices being charged to libraries and individuals. In general, we would expect that the demand by libraries would be much more inelastic than demand by individuals, and, just as economic analysis would predict, the prices for library subscriptions are typically much higher than the prices for individual subscriptions. Often library subscriptions are 2 to 3 times more expensive than subscriptions to individuals.

More recently, some publishers have begun to price discriminate by geography. During 1984, when the U.S. dollar was at an all-time high as compared to the English pound, many British publishers began to charge different prices to U.S. subscribers than to European subscribers. It would be expected that the U.S. demand would be more inelastic. Since the dollar price of British journals was rather low due to the exchange rate, a 10 percent increase in the U.S. price would result in a smaller percentage drop in demand than a similar increase in the British price. Thus, on grounds of profit maximization, it made sense for the British publishers to raise the prices of their journals to the group with the lower elasticity of demand—the U.S. subscribers. According to a 1984 study, North American libraries were charged an average of 67 percent more for their journals than U.K. libraries, and 34 percent more than anyone else in the world.[3]

Further evidence for price discrimination can be found by examining the pattern of price increases. According to a study by the University of Michigan Library, "... publishers have carefully considered their new pricing strategy. There seems to be a direct correlation ... between patterns of library usage and the magnitude of the pricing differential. The greater the use, the larger the differential."[4]

By 1986 the exchange rate had turned in favor of the pound, and the dollar prices of the British journals had increased significantly. Along with the price increase came some serious resistance to the higher prices. The concluding sentences of the Michigan report are illustrative: "One expects that a vendor with a monopoly on a product will charge according to demand. What the campus as a customer must determine is whether it will continue to pay up to 114% more than its British counterparts for the identical product."

---

[3] Hamaker, C. and Astle, D., "Recent Pricing Patterns in British Journal Publishing," *Library Acquisitions: Practice and Theory*, 8, 4 (Spring 1984), 225–32.

[4] The study was conducted by Robert Houbeck for the University of Michigan Library, and published in Vol. 2, No. 1 of the *University Library Update*, April 1986.

## 26.5 Bundling

Firms often choose to sell goods in **bundles**: packages of related goods offered for sale together. A noteworthy example is a bundle of software, sometimes known as a "software suite." Such a bundle might consist of several different software tools—a word processor, a spreadsheet, and a presentation tool—that are sold together in one set. Another example is a magazine: this consists of a bundle of articles that could, in principle, be sold separately. Similarly, magazines are often sold via subscription—which is just a way of bundling separate issues together.

Bundling can be due to cost savings: it is often less expensive to sell several articles stapled together than it is to sell each of them separately. Or it may be due to complementarities among the goods involved: software programs sold in bundles often work together more effectively than off-the-shelf programs.

But there can also be reasons involving consumer behavior. Let's consider a simple example. Suppose that there are two classes of consumers and two different software programs, a word processor and a spreadsheet. Type A consumers are willing to pay $120 for the word processor and $100 for the spreadsheet. Type B consumers have the opposite preferences: they are willing to pay $120 for the spreadsheet and $100 for the word processor. This information is summarized in Table 26.1.

Table
26.1

**Willingness to pay for software components.**

| Type of consumer | Word processor | Spreadsheet |
| --- | --- | --- |
| Type A consumers | 120 | 100 |
| Type B consumers | 100 | 120 |

Suppose that you are selling these products. For simplicity, let us assume that the marginal cost is negligible so that you only want to maximize revenue. Furthermore, make the conservative assumption that the willingess to pay for the bundle consisting of the word processor and the spreadsheet is just the sum of the willingesses to pay for each component.

Now consider the profits from two different marketing policies. First, suppose that you sell each item separately. The revenue maximizing policy is to set a price of $100 for each piece of software. If you do this, you will sell two copies of the word processor and two copies of the spreadsheet, and receive a total revenue of $400.

But what if you bundle the items together? In this case, you could sell *each* bundle for $220, and receive a net revenue of $440. The bundling strategy is clearly more attractive!

What is going on in this example? Recall that when you sell an item to several different people, the price is determined by the purchaser who has the *lowest* willingess to pay. The more diverse the valuations of the individuals, the lower the price you have to charge to sell a given number of items. In this case bundling the word processor and the spreadsheet reduces the dispersion of willingess to pay—allowing the monopolist to set a higher price for the bundle of goods.

### EXAMPLE: Software Suites

Microsoft and other software manufacturers have taken to bundling much of their applications software. For example, the "Microsoft Office Home and Student" package, which contains Microsoft Excel, Word, Powerpoint, and OneNote, costs $150. Excel, Word, and PowerPoint each cost $140 and OneNote costs $80 if sold separately, so purchasing the four programs unbundled would cost $500, more than three times the price of the bundle! (If you think that's expensive, in 1993 the bundle cost $750 and the separate components sold for a total of $1,730!)

Software suites fit the bundling model well. Tastes for software are often very heterogeneous. Some people use a word processor every day and use a spreadsheet only occasionally. Other people have the reverse pattern of software use. If you wish to sell a spreadsheet to a large number of users, you have to sell it at a price that will be attractive to an occasional user. Similarly with the word processor: it is the willingness to pay of the *marginal* user that sets the market price. By bundling the two products together, the dispersion of willingnesses to pay is reduced and total profits can increase.

This is not to say that bundling is the whole story in software suites; other phenomena are also at work. The individual components of the suites are guaranteed to work well together; they are complementary goods in this respect. Furthermore, the success of a piece of software tends to depend strongly on how many people use it, and bundling software helps to build market share. We will investigate this phenomenon of **network externalities** in Chapter 36.

### 26.6 Two-Part Tariffs

Consider the pricing problem facing the owners of an amusement park. They can set one price for tickets to get into the park and another price for the rides. How should they set these two prices if they want to maximize profits? Note that the demand for access and the demand for rides are interrelated: the price that people are willing to pay to get into the park will depend on the price that they have to pay for the rides. This kind of two-part pricing scheme is known as a **two-part tariff**.[5]

Other applications of two-part tariffs abound: Polaroid sells its camera for one price and its film for another. People who are deciding whether or not to purchase the camera presumably consider the price of the film. A company that makes razor blades sells the razor for one price and the blades for another—again the price they set for the blades influences the demand for razors and vice versa.

Let us consider how to solve this pricing problem in the context of the original example: the so-called Disneyland Dilemma. As usual we will make some simplifying assumptions. First, we assume that there is only one kind of ride in Disneyland. Second, we assume that people only desire to go to Disneyland for the rides. Finally, we assume that everyone has the same tastes for rides.

In Figure 26.5 we have depicted the demand curve and the (constant) marginal cost curve for rides. As usual the demand curve slopes down—if Disney sets a high price for each ride, fewer rides will be taken. Suppose that they set a price of $p^*$, as in Figure 26.5, that leads to a demand for $x^*$ rides. How much will they be able to charge for admission to the park, given that the rides cost $p^*$?

The total willingness to pay for $x^*$ rides is measured by the consumers' surplus. Hence the most that the owners of the park can charge for admission is the area labeled "consumer's surplus" in Figure 26.5. The total profits to the monopolist is this area plus the profit on the rides, $(p^* - MC)x^*$.

It is not hard to see that total profits are maximized when price equals marginal cost: we've seen before that this price gives the largest possible consumer plus producer surplus. Since the monopolist gets to charge people their consumers' surplus, setting price equal to marginal cost and the entry fee to the resulting consumer's surplus is the profit-maximizing policy.

Indeed, this is the policy that Disneyland, and most other amusement parks follow. There is one price for admission, but then the attractions inside are free. It appears that the marginal cost of the rides is less than the transactions cost of collecting a separate payment for them.

## 26.7 Monopolistic Competition

We have described a monopolistic industry as being one in which there is a single large producer. But we've been somewhat vague about exactly what comprises an industry. One definition of an industry is that it consists of

---

[5] See the classic article by Walter Oi, "A Disneyland Dilemma: Two-Part Tariffs for a Mickey Mouse Monopoly," *Quarterly Journal of Economics*, 85 (1971), 77–96.

**Disneyland Dilemma.** If the owners of the park set a price of $p^*$, then $x^*$ rides will be demanded. The consumers' surplus measures the price that they can charge for admission to the park. The total profits of the firm are maximized when the owners set price equal to marginal cost.

Figure
26.5

all firms that produce a given product. But then what do we mean by product? After all, there is only one firm that produces Coca-Cola—does that mean that this firm is a monopolist?

Clearly the answer is no. The Coca-Cola firm still has to compete with other producers of soft drinks. We should really think of an industry as being the set of firms that produce products that are viewed as close substitutes by consumers. Each firm in the industry can produce a unique product—a unique brand name, say—but consumers view each of the brands as being substitutes to some degree.

Even though a firm may have a legal monopoly on its trademarks, and brand names, so that other firms can't produce *exactly* the same product, it is usually possible for other firms to produce *similar* products. From the viewpoint of a given firm, the production decisions of its competitors will be a very important consideration in deciding exactly how much it will produce and what price it can charge.

Thus the demand curve facing a firm will usually depend on the output decisions and the prices charged by other firms that produce similar products. The slope of the demand curve facing the firm will depend on how similar the other firms' products are. If a large number of the firms in the industry produce *identical* products, then the demand curve facing any one of them will be essentially flat. Each firm must sell its product for whatever price the other firms are charging. Any firm that tried to raise its price above the prices of the other firms selling identical products would soon lose all of its customers.

On the other hand, if one firm has the exclusive rights to sell a particular product, then it may be able to raise its price without losing all of its customers. Some, but not all, of its customers may switch to competitors' products. Just how many customers switch depends on how similar the customers think the products are—that is, on the elasticity of the demand curve facing the firm.

If a firm is making a profit selling a product in an industry, and other firms are not allowed to perfectly reproduce that product, they still may find it profitable to enter that industry and produce a similar but distinctive product. Economists refer to this phenomenon as **product differentiation**—each firm attempts to differentiate its product from the other firms in the industry. The more successful it is at differentiating its product from other firms selling similar products, the more monopoly power it has—that is, the less elastic is the demand curve for the product. For example, consider the soft drink industry. In this industry there are a number of firms producing similar, but not identical products. Each product has its following of consumers, and so has some degree of market power.

An industry structure such as that described above shares elements of both competition and monopoly; it is therefore referred to as **monopolistic competition**. The industry structure is monopolistic in that each firm faces a downward-sloping demand curve for its product. It therefore has some market power in the sense that it can set its own price, rather than passively accept the market price as does a competitive firm. On the other hand the firms must compete for customers in terms of both price and the kinds of products they sell. Furthermore, there are no restrictions against new firms entering into a monopolistically competitive industry. In these aspects the industry is like a competitive industry.

Monopolistic competition is probably the most prevalent form of industry structure. Unfortunately, it is also the most difficult form to analyze. The extreme cases of pure monopoly and pure competition are much simpler and can often be used as first approximations to more elaborate models of monopolistic competition. In a detailed model of a monopolistically competitive industry, much depends on the specific details of the products and technology, as well as on the nature of the strategic choices available to firms. It is unreasonable to model a monopolistically competitive industry in the abstract, as we have done with the simpler cases of pure competition and pure monopoly. Rather, the institutional details of the particular industry under consideration must be examined. We will describe some methods that economists use to analyze strategic choice in the next two chapters, but a detailed study of monopolistic competition will have to wait for more advanced courses.

We can, however, describe an interesting feature of the free entry aspect of monopolistic competition. As more and more firms enter the industry for a particular kind of product, how would we expect the demand curve of an incumbent firm to change? First, we would expect the demand curve to shift inward since we would expect that at each price, it would sell fewer units of output as more firms enter the industry. Second, we would expect that the demand curve facing a given firm would become more elastic as more firms produced more and more similar products. Thus entry into an industry by new firms with similar products will tend to shift the demand curves facing existing firms to the left and make them flatter.

If firms continue to enter the industry as long as they expect to make a profit, equilibrium must satisfy the following three conditions:

1. Each firm is selling at a price and output combination on its demand curve.

2. Each firm is maximizing its profits, given the demand curve facing it.

3. Entry has forced the profits of each firm down to zero.

These facts imply a very particular geometrical relationship between the demand curve and the average cost curve: the demand curve and the average cost curve must be tangent to each other.

The argument is illustrated in Figure 26.6. Fact 1 says that the output and price combination must be somewhere on the demand curve, and fact 3 says that the output and price combination must also be on the average cost curve. Thus the operating position of the firm must be at a point that lies on both curves. Could the demand curve cross the average cost curve? No, because then there would be some point on the demand curve above the average cost curve—but this would be a point yielding *positive* profits.[6] And by fact 2, the zero profit point is a profit maximum.

Another way to see this is to examine what would happen if the firm depicted in Figure 26.6 charged any price other than the break-even price. At any other price, higher or lower, the firm would lose money, while at the break-even price, the firm makes zero profits. Thus the break-even price is the profit-maximizing price.

There are two worthwhile observations about the monopolistically competitive equilibrium. First, although profits are zero, the situation is still Pareto inefficient. Profits have nothing to do with the efficiency question: when price is greater than marginal cost, there is an efficiency argument for expanding output.

Second, it is clear that firms will typically be operating to the left of the level of output where average cost is minimized. This has sometimes

---

[6] If $p > c(y)/y$, then simple algebra shows that $py - c(y) > 0$.

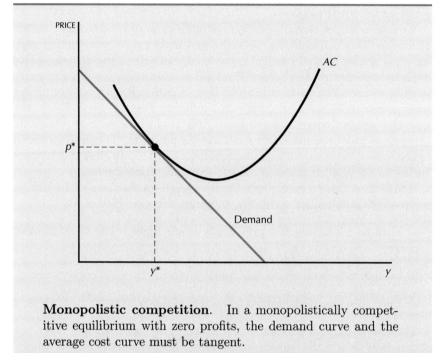

**Figure 26.6**

**Monopolistic competition.** In a monopolistically competitive equilibrium with zero profits, the demand curve and the average cost curve must be tangent.

been interpreted as saying that in monopolistic competition there is "excess capacity." If there were fewer firms, each could operate at a more efficient scale of operation, which would be better for consumers. However, if there were fewer firms there would also be less product variety, and this would tend to make consumers worse off. Which of these effects dominates is a difficult question to answer.

## 26.8 A Location Model of Product Differentiation

In Atlantic City there is a boardwalk that stretches along the beach. Some ice cream vendors with pushcarts want to sell ice cream on the boardwalk. If one vendor is going to be given the concession to sell ice cream on the boardwalk, where should he locate?[7]

Suppose that consumers are distributed evenly along the beach. From a social point of view, it makes sense to locate the ice cream vendor so that the total distance walked by all the consumers is minimized. It is not hard to see that this optimal location is halfway along the boardwalk.

---

[7] The discussion here is based on the classic model of Harold Hotelling, "Stability in Competition," *Economic Journal*, March 1929.

Now suppose that two ice cream vendors are allowed. Suppose that we fix the price that they are able to charge for their ice cream and just ask where they should locate in order to minimize the total distance walked. If each consumer walks to the ice cream vendor nearest him, we should put one vendor a quarter of the way along the boardwalk and one vendor three-quarters of the way along the boardwalk. The consumer halfway along the boardwalk will be indifferent between the two ice cream vendors; each has a market share of one-half of the consumers. (See Figure 26.7A.)

But do the ice cream vendors have an incentive to stay in these locations? Put yourself in the position of vendor $L$. If you move a little bit to the right, you will steal some of the other vendor's customers and you won't lose any of your own. By moving to the right, you will still be the closest vendor to all the customers to your left and you will still be closer to the customers on your right. You will therefore increase your market share and your profits.

**Competition in location.** Panel A shows the socially optimal location pattern; $L$ locates one-quarter of the way along the line and $R$ locates three-quarters of the way along. But each vendor will find it in its private interest to move toward the middle. The only equilibrium location is for both vendors to be in the middle, as shown in Panel B.

Figure 26.7

But vendor $R$ can reason the same way—by moving to the left, he will steal some of the other vendor's customers and not lose any of his own! This shows that the socially optimal location patterns are not an equilibrium. The only equilibrium is for both vendors to sell in the middle of the boardwalk, as shown in Figure 26.7B. In this case, competition for customers has resulted in an *inefficient* location pattern.

The boardwalk model can serve as a metaphor for other sorts of product-differentiation problems. Instead of the boardwalk, think of the choice of music varieties by two radio stations. At one extreme we have classical music and at the other we have heavy metal rock. Each listener chooses the station that appeals more to his tastes. If the classical station plays music that is a bit more toward the middle of the taste spectrum, it won't lose the classical clients, but it will gain a few of the middlebrow listeners. If the rock station moves a bit toward the middle, it won't lose any of its rock lovers but will get a few of the middlebrow listeners. In equilibrium, both stations play the same sort of music and the people with more extreme tastes are unhappy with both of them!

## 26.9 Product Differentiation

The boardwalk model suggest that monopolistic competition will result in too little product differentiation: each firm will want to make its product similar to that of the other firm in order to steal the other firm's customers. Indeed, we can think of markets in which there is too much imitation relative to what seems to be optimal.

However, it doesn't always work this way. Suppose that the boardwalk is *very* long. Then each ice cream vendor would be perfectly happy sitting near each end of the boardwalk. If their market areas don't overlap, nothing is to be gained from moving closer to the middle of the boardwalk. In this case, neither monopolist has an incentive to imitate the other, and the products are about as different as they can get.

It is possible to produce models of monopolistic competition where there is *excessive* product differentiation. In such models, each firm attempts to make consumers think that its product is different from the products of its competitors so as to create some degree of market power. If the firms succeed in convincing the consumers that their product has no close substitutes, they will be able to charge a higher price for it than they would otherwise be able to do.

This leads each producer to invest heavily in creating a distinctive brand identity. Laundry soap, for example, is a pretty standardized commodity. Yet manufacturers invest huge amounts of money in advertisements that claim cleaner clothes, better smell, a better marriage, and and a generally happier life if you choose their brand rather than a competitor's. This "product positioning" is much like the ice cream vendors locating far away from each other in order to avoid head-to-head competition.

There are critics who have argued that such excessive investment in product positioning is wasteful. Perhaps this is true in some cases, but then again, "excessive variety" may simply be a consequence of encouraging firms to provide consumers with a variety of products from which to choose.

## 26.10 More Vendors

We have shown that if there are two vendors whose market areas overlap, and each seller sells the same price, they will both end up located at the "middle" of the boardwalk. What happens if there are more than two vendors who compete in their location?

The next easiest case is that of three vendors. This case gives rise to a rather peculiar outcome: there may be *no* equilibrium location pattern! To see this, look at Figure 26.8. If there are three vendors located on the boardwalk, there must be one located between the other two. As before, it pays each of the "outside" vendors to move towards the middle vendor since they can steal some of its customers without losing any of their own. But if they get *too* close to the other vendor, it pays it to jump immediately to the right of its right-hand competitor or immediately to the left of its left-hand competitor to steal *its* market. No matter what the location pattern, it pays someone to move!

**No equilibrium.** There is no pure strategy equilibrium in the Hotelling model with 3 firms since for any configuration, at least one firm wants to change location.

Figure
26.8

Luckily, this "perverse" result only holds in the case of three competitors. If there are four or more competitors, an equilibrium location pattern will generally emerge.

## Summary

1. There will typically be an incentive for a monopolist to engage in price discrimination of some sort.

2. Perfect price discrimination involves charging each customer a different take-it-or-leave-it price. This will result in an efficient level of output.

3. If a firm can charge different prices in two different markets, it will tend to charge the lower price in the market with the more elastic demand.

4. If a firm can set a two-part tariff, and consumers are identical, then it will generally want to set price equal to marginal cost and make all of its profits from the entry fee.

5. The industry structure known as monopolistic competition refers to a situation in which there is product differentiation, so each firm has some degree of monopoly power, but there is also free entry so that profits are driven to zero.

6. Monopolistic competition can result in too much or too little product differentiation in general.

## REVIEW QUESTIONS

1. Will a monopoly ever provide a Pareto efficient level of output on its own?

2. Suppose that a monopolist sells to two groups that have constant elasticity demand curves, with elasticity $\epsilon_1$ and $\epsilon_2$. The marginal cost of production is constant at $c$. What price is charged to each group?

3. Suppose that the amusement park owner can practice perfect first-degree price discrimination by charging a different price for each ride. Assume that all rides have zero marginal cost and all consumers have the same tastes. Will the monopolist do better charging for rides and setting a zero price for admission, or better by charging for admission and setting a zero price for rides?

4. Disneyland also offers a discount on admissions to residents of Southern California. (You show them your zip code at the gate.) What kind of price discrimination is this? What does this imply about the elasticity of demand for Disney attractions by Southern Californians?

# CHAPTER **27**

# FACTOR MARKETS

In our examination of factor demands in Chapter 20 we only considered the case of a firm that faced a competitive output market and a competitive factor market. Now that we have studied monopoly behavior, we can examine some alternative specifications of factor demand behavior. For example, what happens to factor demands if a firm behaves as a monopolist in its output market? Or what happens to factor demands if a firm is the sole demander for the use of some factors? We investigate these questions and some related questions in this chapter.

## 27.1 Monopoly in the Output Market

When a firm determines its profit-maximizing demand for a factor, it will always want to choose a quantity such that the marginal revenue from hiring a little more of that factor just equals the marginal cost of doing so. This follows from the standard logic: if the marginal revenue of some action didn't equal the marginal cost of that action, then it would pay for the firm to change the action.

This general rule takes various special forms depending on our assumptions about the environment in which the firm operates. For example, suppose that the firm has a monopoly for its output. For simplicity we will suppose that there is only one factor of production and write the production function as $y = f(x)$. The revenue that the firm receives depends on its production of output so we write $R(y) = p(y)y$, where $p(y)$ is the inverse demand function. Let us see how a marginal increase in the amount of the input affects the revenues of the firm.

Suppose that we increase the amount of the input an infinitesimally small amount, $\delta x$. This will result in a small increase in output, $\delta y$. The ratio of the increase in output to the increase in the input is the **marginal product** of the factor:

$$MP_x = \frac{\delta y}{\delta x} = f'(x). \tag{27.1}$$

This increase in output will cause revenue to change. The change in revenue is called the **marginal revenue**.

$$MR_y = \frac{\delta R}{\delta y} = p(y) + p'(y)y. \tag{27.2}$$

The effect on revenue due to the marginal increase in the input is called the **marginal revenue product**. We can calculate marginal revenue product by using the chain rule. Let $y = f(x)$ be the production function and $p(y)$ be the inverse demand function. Revenue as a function of the factor employment is just

$$R(x) = p(f(x))f(x).$$

Differentiating this expression with respect to $x$ we have

$$\frac{dR(x)}{dx} = p(y)f'(x) + f(x)p'(y)f'(x)$$
$$= [p(y) + p'(y)y]f'(x)$$
$$= MR_y \times MP_x.$$

We can use our standard expression for marginal revenue to write this as

$$MRP_x = \left[p(y) + \frac{\delta p}{\delta y}y\right]MP_x$$
$$= p(y)\left[1 + \frac{1}{\epsilon}\right]MP_x$$
$$= p(y)\left[1 - \frac{1}{|\epsilon|}\right]MP_x.$$

The first expression is the usual expression for marginal revenue. The second and third expressions use the elasticity form of marginal revenue, which was discussed in Chapter 15.

Now it is easy to see how this generalizes the competitive case we examined earlier in Chapter 20. The elasticity of the demand curve facing an individual firm in a competitive market is infinite; consequently the marginal revenue for a competitive firm is just equal to price. Hence the "marginal revenue product" of an input for a firm in a competitive market is just the **value of the marginal product** of that input, $pMP_x$.

How does the marginal revenue product (in the case of a monopoly) compare to the value of the marginal product? Since the demand curve has a negative slope, we see that the marginal revenue product will always be less than the value of the marginal product:

$$MRP_x = p\left[1 - \frac{1}{|\epsilon|}\right]MP_x \leq pMP_x.$$

As long as the demand function is not perfectly elastic, the $MRP_x$ will be strictly less than $pMP_x$. This means that at any level of employment of the factor, the marginal value of an additional unit is less for a monopolist than for a competitive firm. In the rest of this section we will assume that we are dealing with this case—the case where the monopolist actually has some monopoly power.

At first encounter this statement seems paradoxical since a monopolist makes higher profits than a competitive firm. In this sense the total factor input is "worth more" to a monopolist than to a competitive firm.

The resolution of this "paradox" is to note the difference between total value and marginal value. The total amount employed of the factor is indeed worth more to the monopolist than to the competitive firm since the monopolist will make more profits from the factor than the competitive firm. However, at a *given* level of output an increase in the employment of the factor will increase output and *reduce* the price that a monopolist is able to charge. But an increase in a competitive firm's output will not change the price it can charge. Thus on the margin, a small *increase* in the employment of the factor is worth less to the monopolist than to the competitive firm.

Since increases in the factor employment are worth less to a monopolist than to a competitive firm on the margin in the short run, it makes sense that the monopolist would usually want to employ less of the input. Indeed this is generally true: the monopolist increases its profits by reducing its output, and so it will usually hire lower amounts of inputs than a competitive firm.

In order to determine how much of the factor a firm employs, we have to compare the marginal revenue of an additional unit of the factor to the marginal cost of hiring that factor. Let us assume that the firm operates in a competitive factor market, so that it can hire as much of the factor as it wants at a constant price of $w$. In this case, the competitive firm wants to hire $x_c$ units of the factor, where

$$pMP(x_c) = w.$$

The monopolist, on the other hand, wants to hire $x_m$ units of the factor, where

$$MRP(x_m) = w.$$

We have illustrated this in Figure 27.1. Since $MRP(x) < pMP(x)$, the point where $MRP(x_m) = w$ will always be to the left of the point where $pMP(x_c) = w$. Hence the monopolist will hire less than the competitive firm.

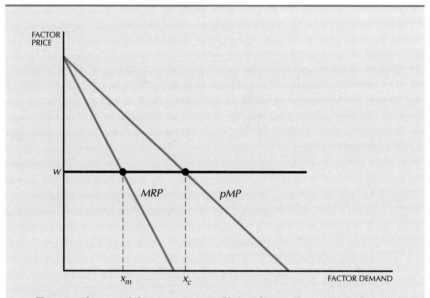

Figure 27.1

**Factor demand by a monopolist.** Since the marginal revenue product curve (MRP) lies beneath the curve measuring the value of the marginal product (pMP), the factor demand by a monopolist must be less than the factor demand by the same firm if it behaves competitively.

## 27.2 Monopsony

In a monopoly there is a single seller of a commodity. In a **monopsony** there is a single buyer. The analysis of a monopsonist is similar to that of a monopolist. For simplicity, we suppose that the buyer produces output that will be sold in a competitive market.

As above, we will suppose that the firm produces output using a single factor according to the production function $y = f(x)$. However, unlike the discussion above, we suppose that the firm dominates the factor market in which it operates and recognizes the amount of the factor that it demands will influence the price that it has to pay for this factor.

We summarize this relationship by the (inverse) supply curve $w(x)$. The interpretation of this function is that if the firm wants to hire $x$ units of the factor it must pay a price of $w(x)$. We assume that $w(x)$ is an increasing function: the more of the x-factor the firm wants to employ, the higher must be the factor price it offers.

A firm in a competitive factor market by definition faces a flat factor supply curve: it can hire as much as it wants at the going factor price. A monopsonist faces an upward-sloping factor supply curve: the more it wants to hire, the higher a factor price it must offer. A firm in a competitive factor market is a **price taker**. A monopsonist is a **price maker**.

The profit-maximization problem facing the monopsonist is

$$\max_{x}\ pf(x) - w(x)x.$$

Taking the first order condition with respect to $x$, we have

$$pf'(x) = w(x) + w'(x)x.$$

This condition tells us that the marginal revenue from hiring an extra unit of the factor should equal the marginal cost of that unit. Since we have assumed a competitive output market the marginal revenue is simply $pMP_x = pf'(x)$, the left hand side of the equation.

The right hand side is the marginal cost. The interpretation of this expression is similar to the interpretation of the marginal revenue expression: when the firm increases its employment of the factor it has to pay $w\delta x$ more in payment to the factor. But the increased demand for the factor will push the factor price up by $\delta w$, and the firm has to pay this higher price on all of the units it was previously employing.

We can also write the marginal cost of hiring additional units of the factor as

$$MC_x = w\left[1 + \frac{x}{w}\frac{\delta w}{\delta x}\right]$$
$$= w\left[1 + \frac{1}{\eta}\right]$$

where $\eta$ is the *supply* elasticity of the factor. Since supply curves typically slope upward, $\eta$ will be a positive number. If the supply curve is *perfectly elastic*, so that $\eta$ is infinite, this reduces to the case of a firm facing a competitive factor market. Note the similarity of these observations with the analogous case of a monopolist.

Let's analyze the case of a monopsonist facing a linear supply curve for the factor. The inverse supply curve has the form

$$w(x) = a + bx,$$

so that total costs have the form

$$C(x) = w(x)x = ax + bx^2,$$

and thus the marginal cost of an additional unit of the input is

$$MC_x(x) = a + 2bx.$$

The construction of the monopsony solution is given in Figure 27.2. We find the position where the value of the marginal product equals marginal cost to determine $x^*$ and then see what the factor price must be at that point.

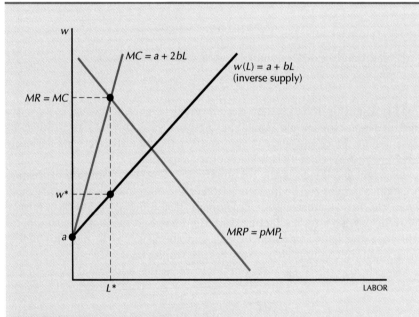

**Figure 27.2**

**Monopsony.** The firm operates where the marginal revenue from hiring an extra unit of the factor equals the marginal cost of that extra unit.

Since the marginal cost of hiring an extra unit of the factor exceeds the factor price, the factor price will be lower than if the firm had faced a competitive factor market. Too little of the factor will be hired relative to the competitive market. Just as in the case of the monopoly, a monopsonist operates at a Pareto inefficient point. But the inefficiency now lies in the factor market rather than in the output market.

## EXAMPLE: The Minimum Wage

Suppose that the labor market is competitive and that the government sets a minimum wage that is higher than the prevailing equilibrium wage. Since demand equals supply at the equilibrium wage, the supply of labor will exceed the demand for labor at the higher minimum wage. This is depicted in Figure 27.3A.

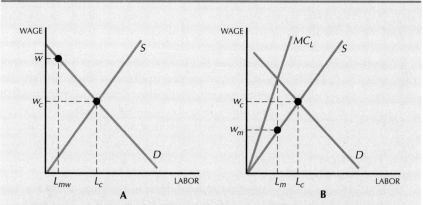

**Minimum wage.** Panel A shows the effect of a minimum wage in a competitive labor market. At the competitive wage, $w_c$, employment would be $L_c$. At the minimum wage, $\overline{w}$, employment is only $L_{mw}$. Panel B shows the effect of a minimum wage in a monopsonized labor market. Under monopsony, the wage is $w_m$ and employment is $L_m$, which is less than the employment in the competitive labor market. If the minimum wage is set to $w_c$, employment will increase to $L_c$.

Figure 27.3

Things are very different if the labor market is dominated by a monopsonist. In this case, it is possible that imposing a minimum wage may actually *increase* employment. This is depicted in Figure 27.3B. If the government sets the minimum wage equal to the wage that would prevail in a competitive market, the "monopsonist" now perceives that it can hire workers at a constant wage of $w_c$. Since the wage rate it faces is now independent of how many workers it hires, it will hire until the value of the marginal product equals $w_c$. That is, it will hire just as many workers as if it faced a competitive labor market.

Setting a wage floor for a monopsonist is just like setting a price ceiling for a monopolist; each policy makes the firm behave as though it faced a competitive market.

## 27.3 Upstream and Downstream Monopolies

We have now examined two cases involving imperfect competition and factor markets: the case of a firm with a monopoly in the output market but facing a competitive factor market, and the case of a firm with a competitive output market that faces a monopolized factor market. Other variations are possible. The firm could face a monopoly seller in its factor market for example. Or it could face a monopsony buyer in its output market. It doesn't make much sense to plod through each possible case; they quickly become repetitive. However, we will examine one interesting market structure in which a monopoly produces output that is used as a factor of production by another monopolist.

Suppose then that one monopolist produces output $x$ at a constant marginal cost of $c$. We call this monopolist the **upstream monopolist**. It sells the x-factor to another monopolist, the **downstream monopolist** at a price of $k$. The downstream monopolist uses the x-factor to produce output $y$ according to the production function $y = f(x)$. This output is then sold in a monopolist market in which the inverse demand curve is $p(y)$. For purposes of this example, we consider a linear inverse demand curve $p(y) = a - by$.

To make things simple, think of the production function as just being $y = x$, so that for each unit of the x-input, the monopolist can produce one unit of the y-output. We further suppose that the downstream monopolist has no costs of production other than the unit price $k$ that it must pay to the upstream monopolist.

In order to see how this market works, start with the downstream monopolist. Its profit-maximization problem is

$$\max_y \ p(y)y - ky = \max_y \ [a - by]y - ky.$$

Setting marginal revenue equal to marginal cost, we have

$$a - 2by = k,$$

which implies that

$$y = \frac{a - k}{2b}.$$

Since the monopolist demands one unit of the x-input for each y-output that it produces, this expression also determines the factor demand function

$$x = \frac{a - k}{2b}. \tag{27.3}$$

This function tells us the relationship between the factor price $k$ and the amount of the factor that the downstream monopolist will demand.

Turn now to the problem of the upstream monopolist. Presumably it understands this process and can determine how much of the $x$-good it will sell if it sets various prices $k$; this is simply the factor demand function given in equation (27.3). The upstream monopolist wants to choose $x$ to maximize its profit.

We can determine this level easily enough. Solving equation (27.3) for $k$ as a function of $x$ we have

$$k = a - 2bx.$$

The marginal revenue associated with this factor demand function is

$$MR = a - 4bx.$$

Setting marginal revenue equal to marginal cost we have

$$a - 4bx = c,$$

or

$$x = \frac{a - c}{4b}.$$

Since the production function is simply $y = x$, this also gives us the total amount of the final product that is produced:

$$y = \frac{a - c}{4b}. \tag{27.4}$$

It is of interest to compare this to the amount that would be produced by a single integrated monopolist. Suppose that the upstream and the downstream firms merged so that we had one monopolist who faced an output inverse demand function $p = a - by$ and faced a constant marginal cost of $c$ per unit produced. The marginal revenue equals marginal cost equation is

$$a - 2by = c,$$

which implies that the profit-maximizing output is

$$y = \frac{a - c}{2b}. \tag{27.5}$$

Comparing equation (27.4) to equation (27.5) we see that the integrated monopolist produces *twice* as much output as the nonintegrated monopolists.

This is depicted in Figure 27.4. The final demand curve facing the downstream monopolist $p(y)$, and the marginal revenue curve associated with this demand function is itself the demand function facing the upstream monopolist. The marginal revenue curve associated with this demand function

Figure
27.4

**Upstream and downstream monopoly.** The downstream
monopolist faces the (inverse) demand curve $p(y)$. The marginal revenue associated with this demand curve is $MR_D(y)$.
This in turn is the demand curve facing the upstream monopolist, and the associated marginal revenue curve is $MR_U(y)$.
The integrated monopolist produces at $y_i^*$; the nonintegrated
monopolist produces at $y_m^*$.

is therefore *four* times as steep as the final demand curve—which is why
the output in this market is half what it would be in the integrated market.

Of course the fact that the final marginal revenue curve is exactly four
times as steep is particular to the linear demand case. However, it is not
hard to see that an integrated monopolist will always produce more than an
upstream-downstream pair of monopolists. In the latter case the upstream
monopolist raises its price above its marginal cost and then the downstream
monopolist raises its price above this already marked-up cost. There is a
**double markup**. The price is not only too high from a social point of view,
it is too high from the viewpoint of maximizing total monopoly profits! If
the two monopolists merged, price would go down and profits would go up.

## Summary

1. A profit-maximizing firm always wants to set the marginal revenue of
each action it takes equal to the marginal cost of that action.

2. In the case of a monopolist, the marginal revenue associated with an

increase in the employment of a factor is called the marginal revenue product.

3. For a monopolist, the marginal revenue product will always be smaller than the value of the marginal product due to the fact that the marginal revenue from increasing output is always less than price.

4. Just as a monopoly consists of a market with a single seller, a monopsony consists of a market with a single buyer.

5. For a monopsonist the marginal cost curve associated with a factor will be steeper than the supply curve of that factor.

6. Hence a monopsonist will hire an inefficiently small amount of the factor of production.

7. If an upstream monopolist sells a factor to a downstream monopolist, then the final price of output will be too high due to the double markup phenomenon.

## REVIEW QUESTIONS

1. We saw that a monopolist never produced where the demand for output was inelastic. Will a monopsonist produce where a factor is inelastically supplied?

2. In our example of the minimum wage, what would happen if the labor market was dominated by a monopsonist and the government set a wage that was above the competitive wage?

3. In our examination of the upstream and downstream monopolists we derived expressions for the total output produced. What are the appropriate expressions for the equilibrium prices, $p$ and $k$?

# CHAPTER **28**

# OLIGOPOLY

We have now investigated two important forms of market structure: pure competition, where there are typically many small competitors, and pure monopoly, where there is only one large firm in the market. However, much of the world lies between these two extremes. Often there are a number of competitors in the market, but not so many as to regard each of them as having a negligible effect on price. This is the situation known as **oligopoly**.

The model of monopolistic competition described in Chapter 25 is a special form of oligopoly that emphasizes issues of product differentiation and entry. However, the models of oligopoly that we will study in this chapter are more concerned with the strategic interactions that arise in an industry with a small number of firms.

There are several models that are relevant since there are several different ways for firms to behave in an oligopolistic environment. It is unreasonable to expect one grand model since many different behavior patterns can be observed in the real world. What we want is a guide to some of the possible patterns of behavior and some indication of what factors might be important in deciding when the various models are applicable.

For simplicity, we will usually restrict ourselves to the case of two firms; this is called a situation of **duopoly**. The duopoly case allows us to capture many of the important features of firms engaged in strategic interaction without the notational complications involved in models with a larger number of firms. Also, we will limit ourselves to investigation of cases in which each firm is producing an identical product. This allows us to avoid the problems of product differentiation and focus only on strategic interactions.

## 28.1 Choosing a Strategy

If there are two firms in the market and they are producing a homogeneous product, then there are four variables of interest: the price that each firm charges and the quantities that each firm produces.

When one firm decides about its choices for prices and quantities it may already know the choices made by the other firm. If one firm gets to set its price before the other firm, we call it the **price leader** and the other firm the **price follower**. Similarly, one firm may get to choose its quantity first, in which case it is a **quantity leader** and the other is a **quantity follower**. The strategic interactions in these cases form a **sequential game**.[1]

On the other hand, it may be that when one firm makes its choices it doesn't know the choices made by the other firm. In this case, it has to guess about the other firm's choice in order to make a sensible decision itself. This is a **simultaneous game**. Again there are two possibilities: the firms could each simultaneously choose prices or each simultaneously choose quantities.

This classification scheme gives us four possibilities: quantity leadership, price leadership, simultaneous quantity setting, and simultaneous price setting. Each of these types of interaction gives rise to a different set of strategic issues.

There is also another possible form of interaction that we will examine. Instead of the firms competing against each other in one form or another they may be able to **collude**. In this case the two firms can jointly agree to set prices and quantities that maximize the sum of their profits. This sort of collusion is called a **cooperative game**.

### EXAMPLE: Pricing Matching

It is common to see advertisements where the vendor offers to "meet or beat" any price. These are generally considered to be a sign of intensely

---

[1] We will examine game theory in more detail in the next chapter, but it seems appropriate to introduce these specific examples here.

competitive market. However, such offers can also be used as a way to dampen competition.

Suppose there are two tire stores, East Side Tires and West Side Tires, that are advertising the same brand tire for $50.

If East Side Tires cuts its advertised price to $45 while the West Side price stays at $50, we would expect that some of those customers on the west side of town would be willing to travel a few extra minutes in order to save $5. East Side Tires would then sell more tires at a lower price. If the increase in sales was large enough to overcome the price reduction, its profits would increase.

That, in a nutshell, is the basic logic of competition: if customers are sufficiently sensitive to price, then a seller that cuts its price enjoys a surge in sales and an increase in profit.

But instead of actually cutting its price, suppose instead that West Side Tires continued to charge $50 but added a promise to match any lower price. What happens now if East Side cuts its advertised price?

In this case, those who find West Side Tires more convenient can just bring in the East Side ad and get the discounted price. Then, East Side Tires attracts no new customers from its price cut. In fact, it loses revenue since it sells essentially the same number of tires at a lower price.

The moral: a vendor that offers a low-price guarantee takes away much of its competitors' motivation for cutting prices.

## 28.2 Quantity Leadership

In the case of quantity leadership, one firm makes a choice before the other firm. This is sometimes called the **Stackelberg model** in honor of the first economist who systematically studied leader-follower interactions.[2]

The Stackelberg model is often used to describe industries in which there is a dominant firm, or a natural leader. For example, IBM is often considered to be a dominant firm in the computer industry. A commonly observed pattern of behavior is for smaller firms in the computer industry to wait for IBM's announcements of new products and then adjust their own product decisions accordingly. In this case we might want to model the computer industry with IBM playing the role of a Stackelberg leader, and the other firms in the industry being Stackelberg followers.

Let us turn now to the details of the theoretical model. Suppose that firm 1 is the leader and that it chooses to produce a quantity $y_1$. Firm 2 responds by choosing a quantity $y_2$. Each firm knows that the equilibrium price in the market depends on the total output produced. We use the

---

[2] Heinrich von Stackelberg was a German economist who published his influential work on market organization, *Marktform und Gleichgewicht*, in 1934.

inverse demand function $p(Y)$ to indicate the equilibrium price as a function of industry output, $Y = y_1 + y_2$.

What output should the leader choose to maximize its profits? The answer depends on how the leader thinks that the follower will react to its choice. Presumably the leader should expect that the follower will attempt to maximize profits as well, given the choice made by the leader. In order for the leader to make a sensible decision about its own production, it has to consider the follower's profit-maximization problem.

## The Follower's Problem

We assume that the follower wants to maximize its profits

$$\max_{y_2} \ p(y_1 + y_2)y_2 - c_2(y_2).$$

The follower's profit depends on the output choice of the leader, but from the viewpoint of the follower the leader's output is predetermined—the production by the leader has already been made, and the follower simply views it as a constant.

The follower wants to choose an output level such that marginal revenue equals marginal cost:

$$MR_2 = p(y_1 + y_2) + \frac{\delta p}{\delta y_2}y_2 = MC_2.$$

The marginal revenue has the usual interpretation. When the follower increases its output, it increases its revenue by selling more output at the market price. But it also pushes the price down by $\Delta p$, and this lowers its profits on all the units that were previously sold at the higher price.

The important thing to observe is that the profit-maximizing choice of the follower will depend on the choice made by the leader. We write this relationship as

$$y_2 = f_2(y_1).$$

The function $f_2(y_1)$ tells us the profit-maximizing output of the follower as a function of the leader's choice. This function is called the **reaction function** since it tells us how the follower will react to the leader's choice of output.

Let's derive a reaction curve in the simple case of linear demand. In this case the (inverse) demand function takes the form $p(y_1+y_2) = a-b(y_1+y_2)$. For convenience we'll take costs to be zero.

Then the profit function for firm 2 is

$$\pi_2(y_1, y_2) = [a - b(y_1 + y_2)]y_2$$

or

$$\pi_2(y_1, y_2) = ay_2 - by_1y_2 - by_2^2.$$

We can use this expression to draw the **isoprofit lines** in Figure 28.1. These are lines depicting those combinations of $y_1$ and $y_2$ that yield a constant level of profit to firm 2. That is, the isoprofit lines are comprised of all points $(y_1, y_2)$ that satisfy equations of the form

$$ay_2 - by_1y_2 - by_2^2 = \overline{\pi}_2.$$

Note that profits to firm 2 will increase as we move to isoprofit lines that are further to the left. This is true since if we fix the output of firm 2 at some level, firm 2's profits will increase as firm 1's output decreases. Firm 2 will make its maximum possible profits when it is a monopolist; that is, when firm 1 chooses to produce zero units of output.

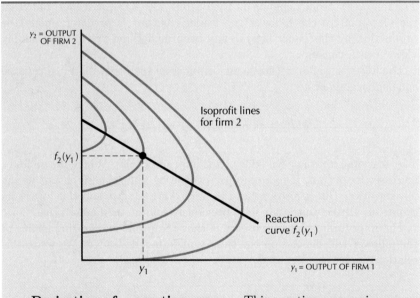

Figure 28.1

**Derivation of a reaction curve.** This reaction curve gives the profit-maximizing output for the follower, firm 2, for each output choice of the leader, firm 1. For each choice of $y_1$ the follower chooses the output level $f_2(y_1)$ associated with the isoprofit line farthest to the left.

For each possible choice of firm 1's output, firm 2 wants to choose its own output to make its profits as large as possible. This means that for each choice of $y_1$, firm 2 will pick the value of $y_2$ that puts it on the isoprofit line furthest to the left, as illustrated in Figure 28.1. This point will satisfy the usual sort of tangency condition: the slope of the isoprofit line must be vertical at the optimal choice. The locus of these tangencies describes firm 2's reaction curve, $f_2(y_1)$.

To see this result algebraically, we take the derivative of the profit function for firm 2 with respect to $y_2$ to obtain an expression for marginal revenue.

$$MR_2(y_1, y_2) = a - by_1 - 2by_2.$$

Setting the marginal revenue equal to marginal cost, which is zero in this example, we have

$$a - by_1 - 2by_2 = 0,$$

which we can solve to derive firm 2's reaction curve:

$$y_2 = \frac{a - by_1}{2b}.$$

This reaction curve is the straight line depicted in Figure 28.1.

## The Leader's Problem

We have now examined how the follower will choose its output *given* the choice of the leader. We turn now to the leader's profit-maximization problem.

Presumably, the leader is also aware that its actions influence the output choice of the follower. This relationship is summarized by the reaction function $f_2(y_1)$. Hence when making its output choice it should recognize the influence that it exerts on the follower.

The profit-maximization problem for the leader therefore becomes

$$\max_{y_1} p(y_1 + y_2)y_1 - c_1(y_1)$$

$$\text{such that } y_2 = f_2(y_1).$$

Substituting the second equation into the first gives us

$$\max_{y_1} p[y_1 + f_2(y_1)]y_1 - c_1(y_1).$$

Note that the leader recognizes that when it chooses output $y_1$, the total output produced will be $y_1 + f_2(y_1)$: its own output *plus* the output produced by the follower.

When the leader contemplates changing its output it has to recognize the influence it exerts on the follower. In general, we can solve the leader's maximization problem using our typical first-order condition strategy. To simplify things, let's examine this in the context of the linear demand curve described above. There we saw that the reaction function was given by

$$f_2(y_1) = y_2 = \frac{a - by_1}{2b}. \tag{28.1}$$

Since we've assumed that marginal costs are zero, the leader's profits are

$$\pi_1(y_1, y_2) = p(y_1 + y_2)y_1 = ay_1 - by_1^2 - by_1y_2. \tag{28.2}$$

But the output of the follower, $y_2$, will depend on the leader's choice via the reaction function $y_2 = f_2(y_1)$.

Substituting from equation (28.1) into equation (28.2) we have

$$\pi_1(y_1, y_2) = ay_1 - by_1^2 - by_1 f_2(y_1)$$

$$= ay_1 - by_1^2 - by_1 \frac{a - by_1}{2b}.$$

Simplifying this expression gives us

$$\pi_1(y_1, y_2) = \frac{a}{2}y_1 - \frac{b}{2}y_1^2.$$

The marginal revenue for this function is

$$MR = \frac{a}{2} - by_1.$$

Setting this equal to marginal cost, which is zero in this example, and solving for $y_1$ gives us

$$y_1^* = \frac{a}{2b}.$$

In order to find the follower's output, we simply substitute $y_1^*$ into the reaction function,

$$y_2^* = \frac{a - by_1^*}{2b}$$

$$= \frac{a}{4b}.$$

These two equations give a total industry output of $y_1^* + y_2^* = 3a/4b$.

The Stackelberg solution can also be illustrated graphically using the isoprofit curves depicted in Figure 28.2. (This figure also illustrates the Cournot equilibrium which will be described in section 28.5.) Here we have illustrated the reaction curves for both firms and the isoprofit curves for firm 1. The isoprofit curves for firm 1 have the same general shape as the isoprofit curves for firm 2; they are simply rotated 90 degrees. Higher profits for firm 1 are associated with isoprofit curves that are lower down since firm 1's profits will increase as firm 2's output decreases.

Firm 2 is behaving as a follower, which means that it will choose an output along its reaction curve, $f_2(y_1)$. Thus firm 1 wants to choose an output combination on the reaction curve that gives it the highest possible profits. But the highest possible profits means picking that point on the reaction curve that touches the *lowest* isoprofit line, as illustrated in Figure 28.2. It follows by the usual logic of maximization that the reaction curve must be tangent to the isoprofit curve at this point.

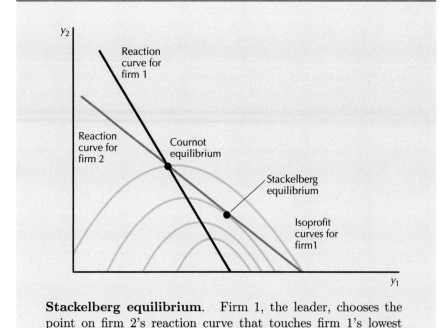

**Stackelberg equilibrium.**   Firm 1, the leader, chooses the
point on firm 2's reaction curve that touches firm 1's lowest
possible isoprofit line, thus yielding the highest possible profits
for firm 1.

Figure
28.2

## 28.3 Price Leadership

Instead of setting quantity, the leader may instead set price. In order to
make a sensible decision about how to set its price, the leader must forecast
how the follower will behave. Accordingly, we must first investigate the
profit-maximization problem facing the follower.

The first thing we observe is that in equilibrium the follower must always
set the same price as the leader. This follows from our assumption that the
two firms are selling identical products. If one charged a different price from
the other, all of the consumers would prefer the producer with the lower
price, and we couldn't have an equilibrium with both firms producing.

Suppose that the leader has set a price $p$. We will suppose that the
follower takes this price as given and chooses its profit-maximizing output.
This is essentially the same as the competitive behavior we investigated
earlier. In the competitive model, each firm takes the price as being outside
of its control because it is such a small part of the market; in the price-
leadership model, the follower takes the price as being outside of its control
since it has already been set by the leader.

The follower wants to maximize profits:

$$\max_{y_2} \ py_2 - c_2(y_2).$$

This leads to the familiar condition that the follower will want to choose an output level where price equals marginal cost. This determines a supply curve for the follower, $S(p)$, which we have illustrated in Figure 28.3.

Figure
28.3

**Price leader.** The demand curve facing the leader is the market demand curve minus the follower's supply curve. The leader equates marginal revenue and marginal cost to find the optimal quantity to supply, $y_L^*$. The total amount supplied to the market is $y_T^*$ and the equilibrium price is $p^*$.

Turn now to the problem facing the leader. It realizes that if it sets a price $p$, the follower will supply $S(p)$. That means that the amount of output the leader will sell will be $R(p) = D(p) - S(p)$. This is called the **residual demand curve** facing the leader.

Suppose that the leader has a constant marginal cost of production $c$. Then the profits that it achieves for any price $p$ are given by:

$$\pi_1(p) = (p - c)[D(p) - S(p)] = (p - c)R(p).$$

In order to maximize profits the leader wants to choose a price and output combination where marginal revenue equals marginal cost. However, the marginal revenue should be the marginal revenue for the *residual* demand curve—the curve that actually measures how much output it will be able to sell at each given price. In Figure 28.3 the residual demand curve is linear; therefore the marginal revenue curve associated with it will have the same vertical intercept and be twice as steep.

Let's look at a simple algebraic example. Suppose that the inverse demand curve is $D(p) = a - bp$. The follower has a cost function $c_2(y_2) = y_2^2/2$, and the leader has a cost function $c_1(y_1) = cy_1$.

For any price $p$ the follower wants to operate where price equals marginal cost. If the cost function is $c_2(y_2) = y_2^2/2$, it can be shown that the marginal cost curve is $MC_2(y_2) = y_2$. Setting price equal to marginal cost gives us

$$p = y_2.$$

Solving for the follower's supply curve gives $y_2 = S(p) = p$.

The demand curve facing the leader—the residual demand curve—is

$$R(p) = D(p) - S(p) = a - bp - p = a - (b+1)p.$$

From now on this is just like an ordinary monopoly problem. Solving for $p$ as a function of the leader's output $y_1$, we have

$$p = \frac{a}{b+1} - \frac{1}{b+1}y_1. \qquad (28.3)$$

This is the inverse demand function facing the leader. The associated marginal revenue curve has the same intercept and is twice as steep. This means that it is given by

$$MR_1 = \frac{a}{b+1} - \frac{2}{b+1}y_1.$$

Setting marginal revenue equal to marginal cost gives us the equation

$$MR_1 = \frac{a}{b+1} - \frac{2}{b+1}y_1 = c = MC_1.$$

Solving for the leader's profit-maximizing output, we have

$$y_1^* = \frac{a - c(b+1)}{2}.$$

We could go on and substitute this into equation (28.3) to get the equilibrium price, but the equation is not particularly interesting.

## 28.4 Comparing Price Leadership and Quantity Leadership

We've seen how to calculate the equilibrium price and output in the case of quantity leadership and price leadership. Each model determines a different equilibrium price and output combination; each model is appropriate in different circumstances.

One way to think about quantity setting is to think of the firm as making a capacity choice. When a firm sets a quantity it is in effect determining how much it is able to supply to the market. If one firm is able to make an investment in capacity first, then it is naturally modeled as a quantity leader.

On the other hand, suppose that we look at a market where capacity choices are not important but one of the firms distributes a catalog of prices. It is natural to think of this firm as a price setter. Its rivals may then take the catalog price as given and make their own pricing and supply decision accordingly.

Whether the price-leadership or the quantity-leadership model is appropriate is not a question that can be answered on the basis of pure theory. We have to look at how the firms actually make their decisions in order to choose the most appropriate model.

## 28.5 Simultaneous Quantity Setting

One difficulty with the leader-follower model is that it is necessarily asymmetric: one firm is able to make its decision before the other firm. In some situations this is unreasonable. For example, suppose that two firms are *simultaneously* trying to decide what quantity to produce. Here each firm has to forecast what the other firm's output will be in order to make a sensible decision itself.

In this section we will examine a one-period model in which each firm has to forecast the other firm's output choice. Given its forecast, each firm then chooses a profit-maximizing output for itself. We then seek an equilibrium in forecasts—a situation where each firm finds its beliefs about the other firm to be confirmed. This model is known as the **Cournot model**, after the nineteenth-century French mathematician who first examined its implications.[3]

We begin by assuming that firm 1 expects that firm 2 will produce $y_2^e$ units of output. (The e stands for *expected* output.) If firm 1 decides to produce $y_1$ units of output, it expects that the total output produced will

---

[3] Augustin Cournot (pronounced "core-no") was born in 1801. His book, *Researches into the Mathematical Principles of the Theory of Wealth*, was published in 1838.

be $Y = y_1 + y_2^e$, and output will yield a market price of $p(Y) = p(y_1 + y_2^e)$. The profit-maximization problem of firm 1 is then

$$\max_{y_1} p(y_1 + y_2^e)y_1 - c(y_1).$$

For any given belief about the output of firm 2, $y_2^e$, there will be some optimal choice of output for firm 1, $y_1$. Let us write this functional relationship between the *expected output* of firm 2 and the *optimal choice* of firm 1 as

$$y_1 = f_1(y_2^e).$$

This function is simply the reaction function that we investigated earlier in this chapter. In our original treatment the reaction function gave the follower's output as a function of the leader's choice. Here the reaction function gives one firm's optimal choice as a function of its *beliefs* about the other firm's choice. Although the interpretation of the reaction function is different in the two cases, the mathematical definition is exactly the same.

Similarly, we can derive firm 2's reaction curve:

$$y_2 = f_2(y_1^e),$$

which gives firm 2's optimal choice of output for a given expectation about firm 1's output, $y_1^e$.

Now, recall that each firm is choosing its output level *assuming* that the other firm's output will be at $y_1^e$ or $y_2^e$. For arbitrary values of $y_1^e$ and $y_2^e$ this won't happen—in general firm 1's *optimal* level of output, $y_1$, will be different from what firm 2 *expects* the output to be, $y_1^e$.

Let us seek an output combination $(y_1^*, y_2^*)$ such that the optimal output level for firm 1, assuming firm 2 produces $y_2^*$, is $y_1^*$ and the optimal output level for firm 2, assuming that firm 1 stays at $y_1^*$, is $y_2^*$. In other words, the output choices $(y_1^*, y_2^*)$ satisfy

$$y_1^* = f_1(y_2^*)$$

$$y_2^* = f_2(y_1^*).$$

Such a combination of output levels is known as a **Cournot equilibrium**. In a Cournot equilibrium, each firm is maximizing its profits, given its beliefs about the other firm's output choice, and, furthermore, those beliefs are confirmed in equilibrium: each firm optimally chooses to produce the amount of output that the other firm expects it to produce. In a Cournot equilibrium neither firm will find it profitable to change its output once it discovers the choice actually made by the other firm.

An example of a Cournot equilibrium is given in Figure 28.2. The Cournot equilibrium is simply the pair of outputs at which the two reaction curves cross. At such a point, each firm is producing a profit-maximizing level of output given the output choice of the other firm.

## 28.6 An Example of Cournot Equilibrium

Recall the case of the linear demand function and zero marginal costs that
we investigated earlier. We saw that in this case the reaction function for
firm 2 took the form

$$y_2 = \frac{a - by_1^e}{2b}.$$

Since in this example firm 1 is exactly the same as firm 2, its reaction
curve has the same form:

$$y_1 = \frac{a - by_2^e}{2b}.$$

Figure 28.4 depicts this pair of reaction curves. The intersection of the
two lines gives us the Cournot equilibrium. At this point each firm's choice
is the profit-maximizing choice, given its beliefs about the other firm's behavior, and each firm's beliefs about the other firm's behavior are confirmed
by its *actual* behavior.

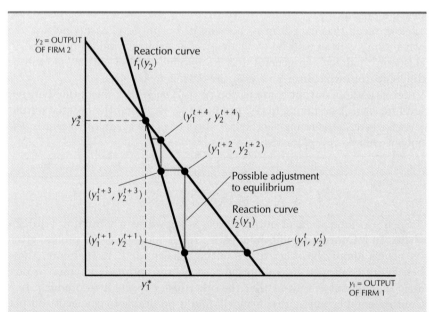

Figure
28.4

**Cournot equilibrium.** Each firm is maximizing its profits,
given its beliefs about the other firm's output decision. The
Cournot equilibrium is at $(y_1^*, y_2^*)$, where the two reaction curves
cross.

In order to calculate the Cournot equilibrium algebraically, we look for the point $(y_1, y_2)$ where each firm is doing what the other firm expects it to do. We set $y_1 = y_1^e$ and $y_2 = y_2^e$, which gives us the following two equations in two unknowns:

$$y_1 = \frac{a - by_2}{2b}$$

$$y_2 = \frac{a - by_1}{2b}.$$

In this example, both firms are identical, so each will produce the same level of output in equilibrium. Hence we can substitute $y_1 = y_2$ into one of the above equations to get

$$y_1 = \frac{a - by_1}{2b}.$$

Solving for $y_1^*$, we get

$$y_1^* = \frac{a}{3b}.$$

Since the two firms are identical, this implies that

$$y_2^* = \frac{a}{3b}$$

as well, and the total industry output is

$$y_1^* + y_2^* = \frac{2a}{3b}.$$

## 28.7 Adjustment to Equilibrium

We can use Figure 28.4 to describe a process of adjustment to equilibrium. Suppose that at time $t$ the firms are producing outputs $(y_1^t, y_2^t)$, which are not necessarily equilibrium outputs. If firm 1 expects that firm 2 is going to continue to keep its output at $y_2^t$, then next period firm 1 would want to choose the profit-maximizing output given that expectation, namely $f_1(y_2^t)$. Thus firm 1's choice in period $t + 1$ will be given by

$$y_1^{t+1} = f_1(y_2^t).$$

Firm 2 can reason the same way, so firm 2's choice next period will be

$$y_2^{t+1} = f_2(y_1^t).$$

These equations describe how each firm adjusts its output in the face of the other firm's choice. Figure 28.4 illustrates the movement of the outputs of the firms implied by this behavior. Here is the way to interpret the diagram. Start with some operating point $(y_1^t, y_2^t)$. Given firm 2's level of output, firm 1 optimally chooses to produce $y_1^{t+1} = f_1(y_2^t)$ next period. We find this point in the diagram by moving horizontally to the left until we hit firm 1's reaction curve.

If firm 2 expects firm 1 to continue to produce $y_1^{t+1}$, its optimal response is to produce $y_2^{t+1}$. We find this point by moving vertically upward until we hit firm 2's reaction function. We continue to move along the "staircase" to determine the sequence of output choices of the two firms. In the example illustrated, this adjustment process converges to the Cournot equilibrium. We say that in this case the Cournot equilibrium is a **stable equilibrium**.

Despite the intuitive appeal of this adjustment process, it does present some difficulties. Each firm is assuming that the other's output will be fixed from one period to the next, but as it turns out, both firms keep changing their output. Only in equilibrium is one firm's expectation about the other firm's output choice actually satisfied. For this reason, we will generally ignore the question of how the equilibrium is reached and focus only on the issue of how the firms behave in the equilibrium.

## 28.8 Many Firms in Cournot Equilibrium

Suppose now that we have several firms involved in a Cournot equilibrium, not just two. In this case we suppose that each firm has an expectation about the output choices of the other firms in the industry and seek to describe the equilibrium output.

Suppose that there are $n$ firms and let $Y = y_1 + \cdots + y_n$ be the total industry output. Then the "marginal revenue equals marginal cost condition" for firm $i$ is

$$p(Y) + \frac{\delta p}{\delta Y} y_i = MC(y_i).$$

If we factor out $P(Y)$ and multiply the second term by $Y/Y$, we can write this equation as

$$p(Y) \left[ 1 + \frac{\delta p}{\delta Y} \frac{Y}{p(Y)} \frac{y_i}{Y} \right] = MC(y_i).$$

Using the definition of elasticity of the aggregate demand curve and letting $s_i = y_i/Y$ be firm $i$'s share of total market output, this reduces to

$$p(Y) \left[ 1 - \frac{s_i}{|\epsilon(Y)|} \right] = MC(y_i). \tag{28.4}$$

We can also write this expression as

$$p(Y) \left[ 1 - \frac{1}{|\epsilon(Y)|/s_i} \right] = MC(y_i).$$

This looks just like the expression for the monopolist except for the $s_i$ term. We can think of $|\epsilon(Y)|/s_i$ as being the elasticity of the demand curve facing the firm: the smaller the market share of the firm, the more elastic the demand curve it faces.

If its market share is 1—the firm is a monopolist—the demand curve facing the firm is the market demand curve, so the condition just reduces to that of the monopolist. If the firm is a very small part of a large market, its market share is effectively zero, and the demand curve facing the firm is effectively flat. Thus the condition reduces to that of the pure competitor: price equals marginal cost.

This is one justification for the competitive model described in Chapter 23. If there are a large number of firms, then each firm's influence on the market price is negligible, and the Cournot equilibrium is effectively the same as pure competition.

## 28.9 Simultaneous Price Setting

In the Cournot model described above we have assumed that firms were choosing their quantities and letting the market determine the price. Another approach is to think of firms as setting their prices and letting the market determine the quantity sold. This model is known as **Bertrand competition.**[4]

When a firm chooses its price, it has to forecast the price set by the other firm in the industry. Just as in the case of Cournot equilibrium we want to find a pair of prices such that each price is a profit-maximizing choice given the choice made by the other firm.

What does a Bertrand equilibrium look like? When firms are selling identical products, as we have been assuming, the Bertrand equilibrium has a very simple structure indeed. It turns out to be the competitive equilibrium, where price equals marginal cost!

First we note that price can never be less than marginal cost since then either firm would increase its profits by producing less. So let us consider the case where price is greater than marginal cost. Suppose that both firms are selling output at some price $\hat{p}$ greater than marginal cost. Consider the position of firm 1. If it lowers its price by any small amount $\epsilon$ and if the other firm keeps its price fixed at $\hat{p}$, all of the consumers will prefer to purchase from firm 1. By cutting its price by an arbitrarily small amount, it can steal all of the customers from firm 2.

If firm 1 really believes that firm 2 will charge a price $\hat{p}$ that is greater than marginal cost, it will always pay firm 1 to cut its price to $\hat{p} - \epsilon$. But firm 2 can reason the same way! Thus any price higher than marginal

---

[4]  Joseph Bertrand, also a French mathematician, presented his model in a review of Cournot's work.

cost cannot be an equilibrium; the only equilibrium is the competitive equilibrium.

This result seems paradoxical when you first encounter it: how can we get a competitive price if there are only two firms in the market? If we think of the Bertrand model as a model of competitive bidding it makes more sense. Suppose that one firm "bids" for the consumers' business by quoting a price above marginal cost. Then the other firm can always make a profit by undercutting this price with a lower price. It follows that the only price that each firm cannot rationally expect to be undercut is a price equal to marginal cost.

It is often observed that competitive bidding among firms that are unable to collude can result in prices that are much lower than can be achieved by other means. This phenomenon is simply an example of the logic of Bertrand competition.

## 28.10 Collusion

In the models we have examined up until now the firms have operated independently. But if the firms collude so as to jointly determine their output, these models are not very reasonable. If collusion is possible, the firms would do better to choose the output that maximizes total industry profits and then divide up the profits among themselves. When firms get together and attempt to set prices and outputs so as to maximize total industry profits, they are known as a **cartel**. As we saw in Chapter 25, a cartel is simply a group of firms that jointly collude to behave like a single monopolist and maximize the sum of their profits.

Thus the profit-maximization problem facing the two firms is to choose their outputs $y_1$ and $y_2$ so as to maximize total industry profits:

$$\max_{y_1, y_2} \ p(y_1 + y_2)[y_1 + y_2] - c_1(y_1) - c_2(y_2).$$

This will have the optimality conditions

$$p(y_1^* + y_2^*) + \frac{\delta p}{\delta Y}[y_1^* + y_2^*] = MC_1(y_1^*)$$

$$p(y_1^* + y_2^*) + \frac{\delta p}{\delta Y}[y_1^* + y_2^*] = MC_2(y_2^*).$$

The interpretation of these conditions is interesting. When firm 1 considers expanding its output by $\delta y_1$, it will contemplate the usual two effects: the extra profits from selling more output and the reduction in profits from forcing the price down. But in the second effect, it now takes into account the effect of the lower price on both its own output and the output of the other firm. This is because it is now interested in maximizing total industry profits, not just its own profits.

The optimality conditions imply that the marginal revenue of an extra unit of output must be the same no matter where it is produced. It follows that $MC_1(y_1^*) = MC_2(y_2^*)$, so that the two marginal costs will be equal in equilibrium. If one firm has a cost advantage, so that its marginal cost curve always lies below that of the other firm, then it will necessarily produce more output in equilibrium in the cartel solution.

The problem with agreeing to join a cartel in real life is that there is always a temptation to cheat. Suppose, for example, that the two firms are operating at the outputs that maximize industry profits $(y_1^*, y_2^*)$ and firm 1 considers producing a little more output, $\delta y_1$. The marginal profits accruing to firm 1 will be

$$\frac{\partial \pi_1}{\partial y_1} = p(y_1^* + y_2^*) + \frac{\delta p}{\delta Y}y_1^* - MC_1(y_1^*). \tag{28.5}$$

We saw earlier that the optimality condition for the cartel solution is

$$p(y_1^* + y_2^*) + \frac{\delta p}{\delta Y}y_1^* + \frac{\delta p}{\delta Y}y_2^* - MC_1(y_1^*) = 0.$$

Rearranging this equation gives us

$$p(y_1^* + y_2^*) + \frac{\delta p}{\delta Y}y_1^* - MC_1(y_1^*) = -\frac{\delta p}{\delta Y}y_2^* > 0. \tag{28.6}$$

The last inequality follows since $\delta p/\delta Y$ is negative, since the market demand curve has a negative slope.

Inspecting equations (28.5) and (28.6) we see that

$$\frac{\partial \pi_1}{\partial y_1} > 0.$$

Thus, if firm 1 believes that firm 2 will keep its output fixed, then it will believe that it can increase profits by increasing its own production. In the cartel solution, the firms act together to restrict output so as not to "spoil" the market. They recognize the effect on joint profits from producing more output in either firm. But if each firm believes that the other firm will stick to its output quota, then each firm will be tempted to increase its own profits by unilaterally expanding its output. At the output levels that maximize joint profits, it will always be profitable for each firm to unilaterally increase its output—if each firm expects that the other firm will keep its output fixed.

The situation is even worse than that. If firm 1 believes that firm 2 will keep its output fixed, then it will find it profitable to increase its own output. But if it thinks that firm 2 will increase its output, then firm 1 would want increase its output first and make its profits while it can!

Thus, in order to maintain an effective cartel, the firms need a way to detect and punish cheating. If they have no way to observe each other's output, the temptation to cheat may break the cartel. We'll return to this point a little later.

To make sure that we understand the cartel solution, let's calculate it for the case of zero marginal costs and the linear demand curve we used in the Cournot case.

The aggregate profit function will be

$$\pi(y_1, y_2) = [a - b(y_1 + y_2)](y_1 + y_2) = a(y_1 + y_2) - b(y_1 + y_2)^2,$$

so the marginal revenue equals marginal cost conditions will be

$$a - 2b(y_1^* + y_2^*) = 0,$$

which implies that

$$y_1^* + y_2^* = \frac{a}{2b}.$$

Since marginal costs are zero, the division of output between the two firms doesn't matter. All that is determined is the total level of industry output.

This solution is shown in Figure 28.5. Here we have illustrated the isoprofit curves for each of the firms and have highlighted the locus of common tangents. Why is this line of interest? Since the cartel is trying to maximize total industry profits, it follows that the marginal profits from having either firm produce more output must be the same—otherwise it would pay to have the more profitable firm produce more output. This in turn implies that the slopes of the isoprofit curves must be the same for each firm; that is, that the isoprofit curves must be tangent to each other. Hence the output combinations that maximize total industry profits—the cartel solution—are those that lie along the line illustrated in Figure 28.5.

Figure 28.5 also illustrates the temptation to cheat that is present at the cartel solution. Consider, for example, the point where the two firms split the market equally. Think about what would happen if firm 1 believed that firm 2 would keep its output constant. If firm 1 increased its output and firm 2 kept constant output, then firm 1 would move to a lower isoprofit curve—which means that firm 1 would increase its profits. This is exactly the story told in the algebra above. If one firm thinks that the other's output will remain constant, it will be tempted to increase its own output and thereby make higher profits.

## 28.11 Punishment Strategies

We have seen that a cartel is fundamentally unstable in the sense that it is always in the interest of each of the firms to increase their production

**A cartel**. If industry profits are maximized, then the marginal profit from producing more output in either firm must be the same. This implies that the isoprofit curves must be tangent to one another at the profit-maximizing levels of output.

Figure
28.5

above that which maximizes aggregate profit. If the cartel is to operate successfully, some way must be found to "stabilize" the behavior. One way to do this is for firms to threaten to punish each other for cheating on the cartel agreement. In this section, we investigate the size of punishments necessary to stabilize a cartel.

Consider a duopoly composed of two identical firms. If each firm produces half the monopoly amount of output, total profits will be maximized and each firm will get a payoff of, say, $\pi_m$. In an effort to make this outcome stable, one firm announces to the other: "If you stay at the production level that maximizes joint industry projects, fine. But if I discover you cheating by producing more than this amount, I will punish you by producing the Cournot level of output forever." This is known as a **punishment strategy**.

When will this sort of threat be adequate to stabilize the cartel? We have to look at the benefits and costs of cheating as compared to those of cooperating. Suppose that cheating occurs, and the punishment is carried out. Since the optimal response to Cournot behavior is Cournot behavior (by definition), this results in each firm receiving a per-period profit of, say, $\pi_c$. Of course, the Cournot payoff, $\pi_c$ is less than the cartel payoff, $\pi_m$.

Let us suppose that the two firms are each producing at the collusive, monopoly level of production. Put yourself in the place of one of the firms trying to decide whether to continue to produce at your quota. If you produce more output, deviating from your quota, you make profit $\pi_d$, where $\pi_d > \pi_m$. This is the standard temptation facing a cartel member described above: if each firm restricts output and pushes the price up, then each firm has an incentive to capitalize on the high price by increasing its production.

But this isn't the end of the story because of the punishment for cheating. By producing at the cartel amount, each firm gets a steady stream of payments of $\pi_m$. The present value of this stream starting today is given by

$$\text{Present value of cartel behavior} = \pi_m + \frac{\pi_m}{r}.$$

If the firm produces more than the cartel amount, it gets a one-time benefit of profits $\pi_d$, but then has to live with the breakup of the cartel and the reversion to Cournot behavior:

$$\text{Present value of cheating} = \pi_d + \frac{\pi_c}{r}.$$

When will the present value of remaining at the cartel output be greater than the present value of cheating on the cartel agreement? Obviously when

$$\pi_m + \frac{\pi_m}{r} > \pi_d + \frac{\pi_c}{r},$$

which can also be written as

$$r < \frac{\pi_m - \pi_c}{\pi_d - \pi_m}.$$

Note that the numerator of this fraction is positive, since the monopoly profits are larger than the Cournot profits, and the denominator is positive, since deviation is even more profitable than sticking with the monopoly quota.

The inequality says that as long as the interest rate is sufficiently small, so that the prospect of future punishment is sufficiently important, it will pay the firms to stick to their quotas.

The weakness of this model is that the threat to revert to Cournot behavior forever is not very believable. One firm certainly may believe that the other will punish it for deviating, but "forever" is a long time. A more realistic model would consider shorter periods of retaliation, but the analysis then becomes much more complex. In the next chapter, we discuss some models of "repeated games" that illustrate some of the possible behaviors.

## EXAMPLE: Price Matching and Competition

We have seen that there is always a temptation for each member of a cartel to produce more than its quota. In order to maintain a successful cartel, some way must be found to police members' behavior by some form of punishment for deviations from the joint profit-maximizing output. In particular this means that firms must be able to keep track of the prices and production levels of the other firms in the cartel.

One easy way to acquire information about what the other firms in your industry are charging is to use your customers to spy on the other firms. It is common to see retail firms announce that they will "beat any price." In some cases, such an offer may indicate a highly competitive retail environment. But in other cases, this same policy can be used to gather information about other firms' prices in order to maintain a cartel.

Suppose, for example, that two firms agree, either explicitly or implicitly to sell a certain model of refrigerator for $700. How can either of the stores be sure that the other firm isn't cheating on their agreement and selling the refrigerator for $675? One way is to offer to beat any price a customer can find. That way, the customers report any attempts to cheat on the collusive arrangement.

## EXAMPLE: Voluntary Export Restraints

During the 1980s, the Japanese automobile companies agreed to a "voluntary export restraint (VER)." This meant that they would "voluntarily" reduce the exports of their automobiles to the United States. The typical U.S. consumer thought that this was a great victory for U.S. trade negotiators.

But if you think about this for a minute, things look quite different. In our examination of oligopoly we have seen that the problem facing firms in an industry is how to *restrict* output in order to support higher prices and discourage competition. As we've seen, there will always be a temptation to cheat on production agreements; every cartel must find a way to detect and prevent this cheating. It is especially convenient for the firms if a third party, such as the government, can serve this role. This is exactly the role that the U.S. government played for the Japanese auto makers!

According to one estimate Japanese imported cars were about $2500 more expensive in 1984 than they would have been without the VERs. Furthermore, the higher prices of imported cars allowed American producers to sell their automobiles at about $1000 more than they would have otherwise.[5]

Due to these higher prices the U.S. consumers paid about $10 billion more for Japanese cars in 1985–86 than they would have otherwise. This money has gone directly into the pockets of the Japanese automobile producers. Much of this additional profit appears to have been invested in

---

[5] Robert Crandall, "Import Quotas and the Automobile Industry: the Costs of Protectionism," *The Brookings Review,* Summer, 1984.

increasing productive capabilities, which allowed the Japanese auto producers to reduce the cost of producing new cars in subsequent years. The VERs did succeed in saving American jobs; however, it appears that the cost per job saved was about $160,000 per year.

If the goal of the VER policy was simply to increase the health of the American automobile industry, there was a much simpler way to do this: just impose a $2500 tariff on each imported Japanese car. This way the revenues due to the restriction of trade would accrue to the U.S. government rather than to the Japanese automobile industry. Rather than send $10 billion abroad during 1985–86, the U.S. government could have spent the money on projects designed to increase the long-term health of the U.S. auto industry.

## 28.12 Comparison of the Solutions

We have now examined several models of duopoly behavior: quantity leadership (Stackelberg), price leadership, simultaneous quantity setting (Cournot), simultaneous price setting (Bertrand), and the collusive solution. How do they compare?

In general, collusion results in the smallest industry output and the highest price. Bertrand equilibrium—the competitive equilibrium—gives us the highest output and the lowest price. The other models give results that are in between these two extremes.

A variety of other models are possible. For example, we could look at a model with differentiated products where the two goods produced were not perfect substitutes for each other. Or we could look at a model where the firms make a sequence of choices over time. In this framework, the choices that one firm makes at one time can influence the choices that the other firm makes later on.

We have also assumed that each firm knows the demand function and the cost functions of the other firms in the industry. In reality these functions are never known for sure. Each firm needs to estimate the demand and cost conditions facing its rivals when it makes its own decisions. All of these phenomena have been modeled by economists, but the models become much more complex.

## Summary

1. An oligopoly is characterized by a market with a few firms that recognize their strategic interdependence. There are several possible ways for oligopolies to behave depending on the exact nature of their interaction.

2. In the quantity-leader (Stackelberg) model one firm leads by setting its output, and the other firm follows. When the leader chooses an output, it will take into account how the follower will respond.

3. In the price-leader model, one firm sets its price, and the other firm chooses how much it wants to supply at that price. Again the leader has to take into account the behavior of the follower when it makes its decision.

4. In the Cournot model, each firm chooses its output so as to maximize its profits given its beliefs about the other firm's choice. In equilibrium each firm finds that its expectation about the other firm's choice is confirmed.

5. A Cournot equilibrium in which each firm has a small market share implies that price will be very close to marginal cost—that is, the industry will be nearly competitive.

6. In the Bertrand model each firm chooses its price given its beliefs about the price that the other firm will choose. The only equilibrium price is the competitive equilibrium.

7. A cartel consists of a number of firms colluding to restrict output and to maximize industry profit. A cartel will typically be unstable in the sense that each firm will be tempted to sell more than its agreed upon output if it believes that the other firms will not respond.

## REVIEW QUESTIONS

1. Suppose that we have two firms that face a linear demand curve $p(Y) = a - bY$ and have constant marginal costs, $c$, for each firm. Solve for the Cournot equilibrium output.

2. Consider a cartel in which each firm has identical and constant marginal costs. If the cartel maximizes total industry profits, what does this imply about the division of output between the firms?

3. Can the leader ever get a lower profit in a Stackelberg equilibrium than he would get in the Cournot equilibrium?

4. Suppose there are $n$ identical firms in a Cournot equilibrium. Show that the absolute value of the elasticity of the market demand curve must be greater than $1/n$. (Hint: in the case of a monopolist, $n = 1$, and this simply says that a monopolist operates at an elastic part of the demand curve. Apply the logic that we used to establish that fact to this problem.)

5. Draw a set of reaction curves that result in an unstable equilibrium.

6. Do oligopolies produce an efficient level of output?

# CHAPTER **29**

# GAME
# THEORY

The previous chapter on oligopoly theory presented the classical economic theory of strategic interaction among firms. But that is really just the tip of the iceberg. Economic agents can interact strategically in a variety of ways, and many of these have been studied by using the apparatus of **game theory**. Game theory is concerned with the general analysis of strategic interaction. It can be used to study parlor games, political negotiation, and economic behavior. In this chapter we will briefly explore this fascinating subject to give you a flavor of how it works and how it can be used to study economic behavior in oligopolistic markets.

## 29.1 The Payoff Matrix of a Game

Strategic interaction can involve many players and many strategies, but we'll limit ourselves to two-person games with a finite number of strategies. This will allow us to depict the game easily in a **payoff matrix**. It is simplest to examine this in the context of a specific example.

Suppose that two people are playing a simple game. Person A will write one of two words on a piece of paper, "top" or "bottom." Simultaneously, person B will independently write "left" or "right" on a piece of paper. After they do this, the papers will be examined and they will each get the payoff depicted in Table 29.1. If A says top and B says left, then we examine the top left-hand corner of the matrix. In this matrix the payoff to A is the first entry in the box, 1, and the payoff to B is the second entry, 2. Similarly, if A says bottom and B says right, then A will get a payoff of 1 and B will get a payoff of 0.

Person A has two strategies: he can choose top or he can choose bottom. These strategies could represent economic choices like "raise price" or "lower price." Or they could represent political choices like "declare war" or "don't declare war." The payoff matrix of a game simply depicts the payoffs to each player for each combination of strategies that are chosen.

What will be the outcome of this sort of game? The game depicted in Table 29.1 has a very simple solution. From the viewpoint of person A, it is always better for him to say bottom since his payoffs from that choice (2 or 1) are always greater than their corresponding entries in top (1 or 0). Similarly, it is always better for B to say left since 2 and 1 dominate 1 and 0. Thus we would expect that the equilibrium strategy is for A to play bottom and B to play left.

In this case, we have a **dominant strategy**. There is one optimal choice of strategy for each player no matter what the other player does. Whichever choice B makes, player A will get a higher payoff if he plays bottom, so it makes sense for A to play bottom. And whichever choice A makes, B will get a higher payoff if he plays left. Hence, these choices dominate the alternatives, and we have an equilibrium in dominant strategies.

Table
29.1

**A payoff matrix of a game.**

|  |  | Player B | |
|---|---|---|---|
|  |  | Left | Right |
| Player A | Top | 1, 2 | 0, 1 |
|  | Bottom | 2, 1 | 1, 0 |

If there is a dominant strategy for each player in some game, then we would predict that it would be the equilibrium outcome of the game. For a dominant strategy is a strategy that is best no matter what the other player does. In this example, we would expect an equilibrium outcome in which A plays bottom, receiving an equilibrium payoff of 2, and B plays left, receiving an equilibrium payoff of 1.

## 29.2 Nash Equilibrium

Dominant strategy equilibria are nice when they happen, but they don't happen all that often. For example, the game depicted in Table 29.2 doesn't have a dominant strategy equilibrium. Here when B chooses left the payoffs to A are 2 or 0. When B chooses right, the payoffs to A are 0 or 1. This means that when B chooses left, A would want to choose top; and when B chooses right, A would want to choose bottom. Thus A's optimal choice depends on what he thinks B will do.

**A Nash equilibrium.**

Table 29.2

|  |  | Player B | |
| --- | --- | --- | --- |
|  |  | Left | Right |
| **Player A** | Top | 2, 1 | 0, 0 |
|  | Bottom | 0, 0 | 1, 2 |

However, perhaps the dominant strategy equilibrium is too demanding. Rather than require that A's choice be optimal for *all* choices of B, we can just require that it be optimal for the *optimal* choices of B. For if B is a well-informed intelligent player, he will only want to choose optimal strategies. (Although, what is optimal for B will depend on A's choice as well!)

We will say that a pair of strategies is a **Nash equilibrium** if A's choice is optimal, given B's choice, *and* B's choice is optimal given A's choice.[1] Remember that neither person knows what the other person will do when he has to make his own choice of strategy. But each person may have

---

[1] John Nash is an American mathematician who formulated this fundamental concept of game theory in 1951. In 1994 he received the Nobel Prize in economics, along with two other game theory pioneers, John Harsanyi and Reinhard Selten. The 2002 film *A Beautiful Mind* is loosely based on John Nash's life; it won the Academy Award for best movie.

some expectation about what the other person's choice will be. A Nash equilibrium can be interpreted as a pair of expectations about each person's choice such that, when the other person's choice is revealed, neither individual wants to change his behavior.

In the case of Table 29.2, the strategy (top, left) is a Nash equilibrium. To prove this note that if A chooses top, then the best thing for B to do is to choose left, since the payoff to B from choosing left is 1 and from choosing right is 0. And if B chooses left, then the best thing for A to do is to choose top since then A will get a payoff of 2 rather than of 0.

Thus if A chooses top, the optimal choice for B is to choose left; and if B chooses left, then the optimal choice for A is top. So we have a Nash equilibrium: each person is making the optimal choice, *given* the other person's choice.

The Nash equilibrium is a generalization of the Cournot equilibrium described in the last chapter. There the choices were output levels, and each firm chose its output level taking the other firm's choice as being fixed. Each firm was supposed to do the best for itself, assuming that the other firm continued to produce the output level it had chosen—that is, it continued to play the strategy it had chosen. A Cournot equilibrium occurs when each firm is maximizing profits given the other firm's behavior; this is precisely the definition of a Nash equilibrium.

The Nash equilibrium notion has a certain logic. Unfortunately, it also has some problems. First, a game may have more than one Nash equilibrium. In fact, in Table 29.2 the choices (bottom, right) also comprise a Nash equilibrium. You can either verify this by the kind of argument used above, or just note that the structure of the game is symmetric: B's payoffs are the same in one outcome as A's payoffs are in the other, so that our proof that (top, left) is an equilibrium is also a proof that (bottom, right) is an equilibrium.

The second problem with the concept of a Nash equilibrium is that there are games that have no Nash equilibrium of the sort we have been describing at all. Consider, for example, the case depicted in Table 29.3. Here a Nash equilibrium of the sort we have been examining does not exist. If player A plays top, then player B wants to play left. But if player B plays left, then player A wants bottom. Similarly, if player A plays bottom, then player B will play right. But if player B plays right, then player A will play top.

## 29.3 Mixed Strategies

However, if we enlarge our definition of strategies, we can find a new sort of Nash equilibrium for this game. We have been thinking of each agent as choosing a strategy once and for all. That is, each agent is making one choice and sticking to it. This is called a **pure strategy**.

**A game with no Nash equilibrium (in pure strategies).**    Table 29.3

|  |  | Player B | |
|---|---|---|---|
|  |  | Left | Right |
| **Player A** | Top | 0, 0 | 0, −1 |
|  | Bottom | 1, 0 | −1, 3 |

Another way to think about it is to allow the agents to *randomize* their strategies—to assign a probability to each choice and to play their choices according to those probabilities. For example, A might choose to play top 50 percent of the time and bottom 50 percent of the time, while B might choose to play left 50 percent of the time and right 50 percent of the time. This kind of strategy is called a **mixed strategy**.

If A and B follow the mixed strategies given above, of playing each of their choices half the time, then they will have a probability of 1/4 of ending up in each of the four cells in the payoff matrix. Thus the average payoff to A will be 0, and the average payoff to B will be 1/2.

A Nash equilibrium in mixed strategies refers to an equilibrium in which each agent chooses the optimal frequency with which to play his strategies given the frequency choices of the other agent.

It can be shown that for the sort of games we are analyzing in this chapter, there will always exist a Nash equilibrium in mixed strategies. Because a Nash equilibrium in mixed strategies always exists, and because the concept has a certain inherent plausibility, it is a very popular equilibrium notion in analyzing game behavior. In the example in Table 29.3 it can be shown that if player A plays top with probability 3/4 and bottom with probability 1/4, and player B plays left with probability 1/2 and right with probability 1/2, this will constitute a Nash equilibrium.

## EXAMPLE: Rock Paper Scissors

But enough of this theory. Let's look at an example that really matters: the well-known pastime of "rock paper scissors." In this game, each player simultaneously chooses to display a fist (rock), a palm (paper), or his first two fingers (scissors). The rules: rock breaks scissors, scissors cuts paper, paper wraps rock.

Throughout history, countless hours have been spent in playing this game. There is even a professional society, the RPS Society, that promotes the game. It offers both a web site and a movie documenting the 2003 championships in Toronto.

Of course, game theorists recognize that the equilibrium strategy in rock paper scissors is to randomly choose one of the three outcomes. But humans are not necessarily so good at choosing totally random outcomes. If you can predict your opponent's choices to some degree, you can have an edge in making your own choices.

According to the somewhat tongue-in-cheek account of Jennifer 8. Lee, psychology is paramount.[2] In her article she writes that "most people have a go-to throw, reflective of their character, when they are caught off guard. Paper, considered a refined, even passive, throw, is apparently favored by literary types and journalists."

What is the go-to throw of economists, I wonder? Perhaps it is scissors, since we like to cut to the essential forces at work in human behavior. Should you play rock against an economist, then? Perhaps, but I wouldn't rely on it ...

## 29.4 The Prisoner's Dilemma

Another problem with the Nash equilibrium of a game is that it does not necessarily lead to Pareto efficient outcomes. Consider, for example, the game depicted in Table 29.4. This game is known as the **prisoner's dilemma**. The original discussion of the game considered a situation where two prisoners who were partners in a crime were being questioned in separate rooms. Each prisoner had a choice of confessing to the crime, and thereby implicating the other, or denying that he had participated in the crime. If only one prisoner confessed, then he would go free, and the authorities would throw the book at the other prisoner, requiring him to spend 6 months in prison. If both prisoners denied being involved, then both would be held for 1 month on a technicality, and if both prisoners confessed they would both be held for 3 months. The payoff matrix for this game is given in Table 29.4. The entries in each cell in the matrix represent the utility that each of the agents assigns to the various prison terms, which for simplicity we take to be the negative of the length of their prison terms.

Put yourself in the position of player A. If player B decides to deny committing the crime, then you are certainly better off confessing, since then you'll get off free. Similarly, if player B confesses, then you'll be better off confessing, since then you get a sentence of 3 months rather than a sentence of 6 months. Thus *whatever* player B does, player A is better off confessing.

---

[2] Yes, "8" really is her middle name. "Rock, Paper, Scissors: High Drama in the Tournament Ring" was published in the *New York Times* on September 5, 2004.

**The prisoner's dilemma.**

Table
29.4

|  |  | Player B | |
|---|---|---|---|
|  |  | Confess | Deny |
| **Player A** | Confess | −3, −3 | 0, −6 |
|  | Deny | −6, 0 | −1, −1 |

The same thing goes for player B—he is better off confessing as well. Thus the unique Nash equilibrium for this game is for both players to confess. In fact, both players confessing is not only a Nash equilibrium, it is a dominant strategy equilibrium, since each player has the same optimal choice independent of the other player.

But if they could both just hang tight, they would each be better off! If they both could be sure the other would hold out, and both could agree to hold out themselves, they would each get a payoff of −1, which would make each of them better off. The strategy (deny, deny) is Pareto efficient—there is no other strategy choice that makes both players better off—while the strategy (confess, confess) is Pareto inefficient.

The problem is that there is no way for the two prisoners to coordinate their actions. If each could trust the other, then they could both be made better off.

The prisoner's dilemma applies to a wide range of economic and political phenomena. Consider, for example, the problem of arms control. Interpret the strategy of "confess" as "deploy a new missile" and the strategy of "deny" as "don't deploy." Note that the payoffs are reasonable. If my opponent deploys his missile, I certainly want to deploy, even though the best strategy for both of us is to agree not to deploy. But if there is no way to make a binding agreement, we each end up deploying the missile and are both made worse off.

Another good example is the problem of cheating in a cartel. Now interpret confess as "produce more than your quota of output" and interpret deny as "stick to the original quota." If you think the other firm is going to stick to its quota, it will pay you to produce more than your own quota. And if you think that the other firm will overproduce, then you might as well, too!

The prisoner's dilemma has provoked a lot of controversy as to what is the "correct" way to play the game—or, more precisely, what is a reasonable way to play the game. The answer seems to depend on whether you are playing a one–shot game or whether the game is to be repeated an indefinite number of times.

If the game is going to be played just one time, the strategy of defecting—in this example, confessing—seems to be a reasonable one. After all, whatever the other fellow does, you are better off, and you have no way of influencing the other person's behavior.

## 29.5 Repeated Games

In the preceding section, the players met only once and played the prisoner's dilemma game a single time. However, the situation is different if the game is to be played repeatedly by the same players. In this case there are new strategic possibilities open to each player. If the other player chooses to defect on one round, then you can choose to defect on the next round. Thus your opponent can be "punished" for "bad" behavior. In a repeated game, each player has the opportunity to establish a reputation for cooperation, and thereby encourage the other player to do the same.

Whether this kind of strategy will be viable depends on whether the game is going to be played a *fixed* number of times or an *indefinite* number of times.

Let us consider the first case, where both players know that the game is going to be played 10 times, say. What will the outcome be? Suppose we consider round 10. This is the last time the game will be played, by assumption. In this case, it seems likely that each player will choose the dominant strategy equilibrium, and defect. After all, playing the game for the last time is just like playing it once, so we should expect the same outcome.

Now consider what will happen on round 9. We have just concluded that each player will defect on round 10. So why cooperate on round 9? If you cooperate, the other player might as well defect now and exploit your good nature. Each player can reason the same way, and thus each will defect.

Now consider round 8. If the other person is going to defect on round 9 ... and so it goes. If the game has a known, fixed number of rounds, then each player will defect on every round. If there is no way to enforce cooperation on the last round, there will be no way to enforce cooperation on the next to the last round, and so on.

Players cooperate because they hope that cooperation will induce further cooperation in the future. But this requires that there will always be the possibility of future play. Since there is no possibility of future play in the last round, no one will cooperate then. But then why should anyone cooperate on the next to the last round? Or the one before that? And so it goes—the cooperative solution "unravels" from the end in a prisoner's dilemma with a known, fixed number of plays.

But if the game is going to be repeated an indefinite number of times, then you *do* have a way of influencing your opponent's behavior: if he refuses to cooperate this time, you can refuse to cooperate next time. As long as both parties care enough about future payoffs, the threat of non-cooperation in the future may be sufficient to convince people to play the Pareto efficient strategy.

This has been demonstrated in a convincing way in a series of experiments run by Robert Axelrod.[3] He asked dozens of experts on game theory to submit their favorite strategies for the prisoner's dilemma and then ran a "tournament" on a computer to pit these strategies against each other. Every strategy was played against every other strategy on the computer, and the computer kept track of the total payoffs.

The winning strategy—the one with the highest overall payoff—turned out to be the simplest strategy. It is called "tit for tat" and goes like this. On the first round, you cooperate—play the "deny" strategy. On every round thereafter, if your opponent cooperated on the previous round, you cooperate. If your opponent defected on the previous round, you defect. In other words, do whatever the other player did in the last round.

The tit-for-tat strategy does very well because it offers an immediate punishment for defection. It is also a forgiving strategy: it punishes the other player only once for each defection. If he falls into line and starts to cooperate, then tit for tat will reward the other player with cooperation. It appears to be a remarkably good mechanism for achieving the efficient outcome in a prisoner's dilemma that will be played an indefinite number of times.

## 29.6 Enforcing a Cartel

In Chapter 28 we discussed the behavior of duopolists playing a price-setting game. We argued there that if each duopolist could choose his price, then the equilibrium outcome would be the competitive equilibrium. If each firm thought that the other firm would keep its price fixed, then each firm would find it profitable to undercut the other. The only place where this would not be true was if each firm were charging the lowest possible price, which in the case we examined was a price of zero, since the marginal costs were zero. In the terminology of this chapter, each firm charging a zero price is a Nash equilibrium in pricing strategies—what we called a Bertrand equilibrium in Chapter 28.

The payoff matrix for the duopoly game in pricing strategies has the same structure as the prisoner's dilemma. If each firm charges a high price, then they both get large profits. This is the situation where they are both cooperating to maintain the monopoly outcome. But if one firm is charging

---

[3] Robert Axelrod is a political scientist from the University of Michigan. For an extended discussion, see his book *The Evolution of Cooperation* (New York: Basic Books, 1984).

a high price, then it will pay the other firm to cut its price a little, capture the other fellow's market, and thereby get even higher profits. But if both firms cut their prices, they both end up making lower profits. Whatever price the other fellow is charging, it will always pay you to shave your price a little bit. The Nash equilibrium occurs when each fellow is charging the lowest possible price.

However, if the game is repeated an indefinite number of times, there may be other possible outcomes. Suppose that you decide to play tit for tat. If the other fellow cuts his price this week, you will cut yours next week. If each player knows that the other player is playing tit for tat, then each player would be fearful of cutting his price and starting a price war. The threat implicit in tit for tat may allow the firms to maintain high prices.

Real-life cartels sometimes appear to employ tit-for-tat strategies. For example, the Joint Executive Committee was a famous cartel that set the price of railroad freight in the United States in the late 1800s. The formation of this cartel preceded antitrust regulation in the United States, and at the time was perfectly legal.[4]

The cartel determined what market share each railroad could have of the freight shipped. Each firm set its rates individually, and the JEC kept track of how much freight each firm shipped. However, there were several occasions during 1881, 1884, and 1885 where some members of the cartel thought that other member firms were cutting rates so as to increase their market share, despite their agreement. During these periods, there were often price wars. When one firm tried to cheat, all firms would cut their prices so as to "punish" the defectors. This kind of tit-for-tat strategy was apparently able to support the cartel arrangement for some time.

## EXAMPLE: Tit for Tat in Airline Pricing

Airline pricing provides an interesting example of tit-for-tat behavior. Airlines often offer special promotional fares of one sort or another; many observers of the airline industry claim that these promotions can be used to signal competitors to refrain from cutting prices on key routes.

A senior director of marketing for a major U.S. airline described a case in which Northwest lowered fares on night flights from Minneapolis to various West Coast cities in an effort to fill empty seats. Continental Airlines interpreted this as an attempt to gain market share at its expense and responded by cutting *all* its Minneapolis fares to Northwest's night-fare

---

[4] For a detailed analysis, see Robert Porter, "A Study of Cartel Stability: the Joint Executive Committee, 1880–1886," *The Bell Journal of Economics*, 14, 2 (Autumn 1983), 301–25.

level. However, the Continental fare cuts were set to expire one or two days after they were introduced.

Northwest interpreted this as a signal from Continental that it was not serious about competing in this market, but simply wanted Northwest to retract its night-fare cuts. But Northwest decided to send a message of its own to Continental: it instituted a set of cheap fares to the West Coast for its flights departing from Houston, Continental's home base! Northwest thereby signaled that it felt its cuts were justified, while Continental's response was inappropriate.

All these fare cuts had very short expiration dates; this feature seems to indicate that they were meant more as messages to the competition than as bids for larger market share. As the analyst explained, fares that an airline doesn't want to offer "should almost always have an expiration date on them in the hopes that the competition will eventually wake up and match."

The implicit rules of competition in duopoly airline markets seem to be the following: if the other firm keeps its prices high, I will maintain my high prices; but if the other firm cuts its prices, I will play tit for tat and cut my prices in response. In other words, both firms "live by the Golden Rule": do unto others as you would have them do unto you. This threat of retaliation then serves to keep all prices high.[5]

## 29.7 Sequential Games

Up until now we have been thinking about games in which both players act simultaneously. But in many situations one player gets to move first, and the other player responds. An example of this is the Stackelberg model described in Chapter 28, where one player is a leader and the other player is a follower.

Let's describe a game like this. In the first round, player A gets to choose top or bottom. Player B gets to observe the first player's choice and then chooses left or right. The payoffs are illustrated in a game matrix in Table 29.5.

Note that when the game is presented in this form it has two Nash equilibria: (top, left) and (bottom, right). However, we'll show below that one of these equilibria isn't really reasonable. The payoff matrix hides the fact that one player gets to know what the other player has chosen before he makes his choice. In this case it is more useful to consider a diagram that illustrates the asymmetric nature of the game.

Figure 29.1 is a picture of the game in **extensive form**—a way to represent the game that shows the time pattern of the choices. First, player A

---

[5] Facts taken from A. Nomani, "Fare Warning: How Airlines Trade Price Plans," *Wall Street Journal*, October 9, 1990, B1.

Table
29.5

**The payoff matrix of a sequential game.**

|  |  | Player B | |
|---|---|---|---|
|  |  | Left | Right |
| Player A | Top | 1, 9 | 1, 9 |
|  | Bottom | 0, 0 | 2, 1 |

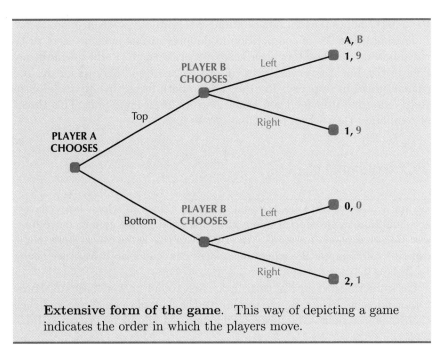

Figure
29.1

**Extensive form of the game.** This way of depicting a game indicates the order in which the players move.

has to choose top or bottom, and then player B has to choose left or right. But when B makes his choice, he will know what A has done.

The way to analyze this game is to go to the end and work backward. Suppose that player A has already made his choice and we are sitting in one branch of the game tree. If player A has chosen top, then it doesn't matter what player B does, and the payoff is (1,9). If player A has chosen bottom, then the sensible thing for player B to do is to choose right, and the payoff is (2,1).

Now think about player A's initial choice. If he chooses top, the outcome will be (1,9) and thus he will get a payoff of 1. But if he chooses bottom, he gets a payoff of 2. So the sensible thing for him to do is to choose bottom. Thus the equilibrium choices in the game will be (bottom, right), so that the payoff to player A will be 2 and to player B will be 1.

The strategies (top, left) are not a reasonable equilibrium in this sequential game. That is, they are not an equilibrium given the order in which the players actually get to make their choices. It is true that if player A chooses top, player B could choose left—but it would be silly for player A to ever choose top!

From player B's point of view this is rather unfortunate, since he ends up with a payoff of 1 rather than 9! What might he do about it?

Well, he can *threaten* to play left if player A plays bottom. If player A thought that player B would actually carry out this threat, he would be well advised to play top. For top gives him 1, while bottom—if player B carries out his threat—will only give him 0.

But is this threat credible? After all, once player A makes his choice, that's it. Player B can get either 0 or 1, and he might as well get 1. Unless player B can somehow convince player A that he will really carry out his threat—even when it hurts him to do so—he will just have to settle for the lower payoff.

Player B's problem is that once player A has made his choice, player A expects player B to do the rational thing. Player B would be better off if he could *commit* himself to play left if player A plays bottom.

One way for B to make such a commitment is to allow someone else to make his choices. For example, B might hire a lawyer and instruct him to play left if A plays bottom. If A is aware of these instructions, the situation is radically different from his point of view. If he knows about B's instructions to his lawyer, then he knows that if he plays bottom he will end up with a payoff of 0. So the sensible thing for him to do is to play top. In this case B has done better for himself by *limiting* his choices.

## 29.8 A Game of Entry Deterrence

In our examination of oligopoly we took the number of firms in the industry as fixed. But in many situations, entry is possible. Of course, it is in the interest of the firms in the industry to try to prevent such entry. Since they are already in the industry, they get to move first and thus have an advantage in choosing ways to keep their opponents out.

Suppose, for example, that we consider a monopolist who is facing a threat of entry by another firm. The entrant decides whether or not to come into the market, and then the incumbent decides whether or not to cut its price in response. If the entrant decides to stay out, it gets a payoff of 1 and the incumbent gets a payoff of 9.

If the entrant decides to come in, then its payoff depends on whether the incumbent fights—by competing vigorously—or not. If the incumbent fights, then we suppose that both players end up with 0. On the other hand, if the incumbent decides not to fight, we suppose that the entrant gets 2 and the incumbent gets 1. See Figure 29.2.

Note that this is exactly the structure of the sequential game we studied earlier, and thus it has a structure identical to that depicted in Figure 29.1. The incumbent is player B, while the potential entrant is player A. The top strategy is to stay out, and the bottom strategy is to enter. The left strategy is to fight and the right strategy is not to fight. As we've seen in this game, the equilibrium outcome is for the potential entrant to enter and the incumbent *not* to fight.

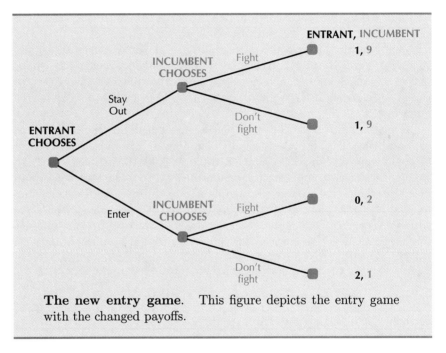

Figure 29.2    **The new entry game.** This figure depicts the entry game with the changed payoffs.

The incumbent's problem is that he cannot precommit himself to fighting if the other firm enters. If the other firm enters, the damage is done and the rational thing for the incumbent to do is to live and let live. Insofar as the potential entrant recognizes this, he will correctly view any threats to fight as empty.

But suppose that the incumbent can purchase some extra production capacity that will allow him to produce more output at his current marginal cost. Of course, if he remains a monopolist, he won't want to actually use this capacity since he is already producing the profit-maximizing monopoly output.

But, if the other firm enters, the incumbent will now be able to produce so much output that he may well be able to compete much more successfully against the new entrant. By investing in the extra capacity, he will lower his costs of fighting if the other firm tries to enter. Let us assume that if he purchases the extra capacity and if he chooses to fight, he will make a profit of 2. This changes the game tree to the form depicted in .

Now, because of the increased capacity, the threat of fighting is credible. If the potential entrant comes into the market, the incumbent will get a payoff of 2 if he fights and 1 if he doesn't; thus the incumbent will rationally choose to fight. The entrant will therefore get a payoff of 0 if he enters, and if he stays out he will get a payoff of 1. The sensible thing for the potential entrant to do is to stay out.

But this means that the incumbent will remain a monopolist and never have to use his extra capacity! Despite this, it is worthwhile for the monopolist to invest in the extra capacity in order to make credible the *threat* of fighting if a new firm tries to enter the market. By investing in "excess" capacity, the monopolist has signaled to the potential entrant that he will be able to successfully defend his market.

## Summary

1. A game can be described by indicating the payoffs to each of the players for each configuration of strategic choices they make.

2. A dominant strategy equilibrium is a set of choices for which each player's choices are optimal *regardless* of what the other players choose.

3. A Nash equilibrium is a set of choices for which each player's choice is optimal, given the choices of the other players.

4. The prisoner's dilemma is a particular game in which the Pareto efficient outcome is strategically dominated by an inefficient outcome.

5. If a prisoner's dilemma is repeated an indefinite number of times, then it is possible that the Pareto efficient outcome may result from rational play.

6. In a sequential game, the time pattern of choices is important. In these games, it can often be advantageous to find a way to precommit to a particular line of play.

## REVIEW QUESTIONS

1. Consider the tit-for-tat strategy in the repeated prisoner's dilemma. Suppose that one player makes a mistake and defects when he meant to cooperate. If both players continue to play tit for tat after that, what happens?

2. Are dominant strategy equilibria always Nash equilibria? Are Nash equilibria always dominant strategy equilibria?

3. Suppose your opponent is *not* playing her Nash equilibrium strategy. Should you play your Nash equilibrium strategy?

4. We know that the single-shot prisoner's dilemma game results in a dominant Nash equilibrium strategy that is Pareto inefficient. Suppose we allow the two prisoners to retaliate after their respective prison terms. Formally, what aspect of the game would this affect? Could a Pareto efficient outcome result?

5. What is the dominant Nash equilibrium strategy for the repeated prisoner's dilemma game when both players know that the game will end after one million repetitions? If you were going to run an experiment with human players for such a scenario, would you predict that players would use this strategy?

6. Suppose that player B rather than player A gets to move first in the sequential game described in this chapter. Draw the extensive form of the new game. What is the equilibrium for this game? Does player B prefer to move first or second?

# CHAPTER 30

# GAME APPLICATIONS

In the last chapter we described a number of important concepts in game theory and illustrated them using a few examples. In this chapter we examine four important issues in game theory—cooperation, competition, coexistence, and commitment—and see how they work in various strategic interactions.

In order to do this, we first develop an important analytic tool, **best response curves**, which can be used to solve for equilibria in games.

## 30.1 Best Response Curves

Consider a two-person game, and put yourself in the position of one of the players. For any choice the other player can make, your **best response** is the choice that maximizes your payoff. If there are several choices that maximize your payoff, then your best response will be the set of all such choices.

For example, consider the game depicted in Table 30.1, which we used to illustrate the concept of a Nash equilibrium. If the column player chooses left, row's best response is to choose top; if column chooses right, then

Table
30.1

**A simple game**

|  |  | Column | |
|---|---|---|---|
|  |  | Left | Right |
| Row | Top | 2, 1 | 0, 0 |
|  | Bottom | 0, 0 | 1, 2 |

row's best response is to choose bottom. Similarly, the best responses for column are to play left in response to top and to play right in response to bottom.

We can write this out in a little table:

| Column's choice: | Left | Right |
|---|---|---|
| Row's best response: | Top | Bottom |

| Row's choice: | Top | Bottom |
|---|---|---|
| Column's best response: | Left | Right |

Notice that if column thinks that row will play top, then column will want to play left, *and* if row thinks that column will play left, row will want to play top. So the pair of choices (top, left) are mutually consistent in the sense that each player is making an optimal response to the other player's choice.

Consider a general two-person game in which row has choices $r_1, \ldots, r_R$ and column has choices $c_1, \ldots, c_C$. For each choice $r$ that row makes, let $b_c(r)$ be a best response for column, and for each choice $c$ that column makes, let $b_r(c)$ be a best response for row. Then a **Nash equilibrium** is a pair of strategies $(r^*, c^*)$ such that

$$c^* = b_c(r^*)$$
$$r^* = b_r(c^*).$$

The concept of Nash equilibrium formalizes the idea of "mutual consistency." If row expects column to play left, then row will choose to play top, and if column expects row to play top, column will want to play left. So it is the *beliefs* and the *actions* of the players that are mutually consistent in a Nash equilibrium.

Note that in some cases one of the players may be indifferent among several best responses. This is why we only require that $c^*$ be *one* of column's best responses, and $r^*$ be *one* of row's best responses. If there is a unique best response for each choice then the best response *curves* can be represented as best response *functions*.

This way of looking at the concept of a Nash equilibrium makes it clear that it is simply a generalization of the Cournot equilibrium described in Chapter 27. In the Cournot case, the choice variable is the amount of output produced, which is a continuous variable. The Cournot equilibrium has the property that each firm is choosing its profit-maximizing output, given the choice of the other firm.

The Bertrand equilibrium, also described in Chapter 27, is a Nash equilibrium in pricing strategies. Each firm chooses the price that maximizes its profit, given the choice that it thinks the other firm will make.

These examples show how the best response curve generalizes the earlier models, and allows for a relatively simple way to solve for Nash equilibrium. These properties make best response curves a very helpful tool to solve for an equilibrium of a game.

## 30.2 Mixed Strategies

Let us use best response functions to analyze the game shown in Table 30.2.

**Solving for Nash equilibrium.**

Table 30.2

|  |  | Ms. Column | |
| --- | --- | --- | --- |
|  |  | Left | Right |
| Mr. Row | Top | 2, 1 | 0, 0 |
|  | Bottom | 0, 0 | 1, 2 |

We are interested in looking for mixed strategy equilibria as well as pure strategy equilibria, so we let $r$ be the probability that row plays top, and $(1 - r)$ the probability that he plays bottom. Similarly, let $c$ be the probability that column plays left, and $(1-c)$ the probability that she plays right. The pure strategies occur when $r$ and $c$ equal 0 or 1.

Let us calculate row's expected payoff if he chooses probability $r$ of playing top and column chooses probability $c$ of playing left. Look at the following array

| Combination | Probability | Payoff to Row |
|---|---|---|
| Top, Left | $rc$ | 2 |
| Bottom, Left | $(1-r)c$ | 0 |
| Top, Right | $r(1-c)$ | 0 |
| Bottom, Right | $(1-r)(1-c)$ | 1 |

To calculate the expected payoff to row, we weight row's payoffs in the third column by the probability that they occur, given in the second column, and add these up. The answer is

$$\text{Row's payoff} = 2rc + (1-r)(1-c),$$

which we can multiply out to be

$$\text{Row's payoff} = 2rc + 1 - r - c + rc.$$

Now suppose that row contemplates increasing $r$ by $\Delta r$. How will his payoff change?

$$\Delta \text{payoff to row} = 2c\,\Delta r - \Delta r + c\,\Delta r$$
$$= (3c - 1)\Delta r.$$

This expression will be positive when $3c > 1$ and negative when $3c < 1$. Hence, row will want to increase $r$ whenever $c > 1/3$, decrease $r$ when $c < 1/3$, and be happy with any value of $0 \leq r \leq 1$ when $c = 1/3$.

Similarly, the payoff to column is given by

$$\text{Column's payoff} = cr + 2(1-c)(1-r).$$

Column's payoff will change when $c$ changes by $\Delta c$ according to

$$\Delta \text{ payoff to column} = r\,\Delta c + 2r\,\Delta c - 2\Delta c$$
$$= (3r - 2)\Delta c.$$

Hence column will want to increase $c$ whenever $r > 2/3$, decrease $c$ when $r < 2/3$, and be happy with any value of $0 \leq c \leq 1$ when $r = 2/3$.

We can use this information to plot the best response curves. Start with row. If column choses $c = 0$, row will want to make $r$ as small as possible, so $r = 0$ is the best response to $c = 0$. This choice will continue to be the best response up until $c = 1/3$, at which point *any* value of $r$ between 0 and 1 is a best response. For all $c > 1/3$, the best response row can make is $r = 1$.

These curves are depicted in Figure 30.1. It is easy to see that they cross in three places: $(0,0)$, $(2/3, 1/3)$, and $(1,1)$, which correspond to the three Nash equilibria of this game. Two of these strategies are pure strategies, and one is a mixed strategy.

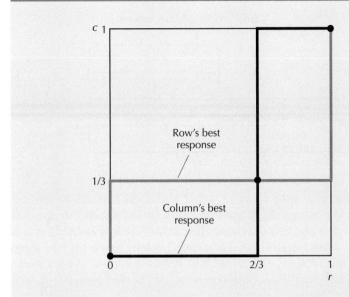

**Best response curves.** The two curves depict the best response of row and column to each other's choices. The intersections of the curves are Nash equilibria. In this case there are
three equilibria, two with pure strategies and one with mixed
strategies.

Figure
30.1

## 30.3 Games of Coordination

Armed with the tools of the last section we can examine our first class of
games, **coordination games**. These are games where the payoffs to the
players are highest when they can coordinate their strategies. The problem,
in practice, is to develop mechanisms that enable this coordination.

### Battle of the Sexes

The classic example of a coordination game is the so-called battle of the
sexes. In this game, a boy and a girl want to meet at a movie but haven't
had a chance to arrange which one. Alas, they forgot their cell phones,
so they have no way to coordinate their meeting and have to guess which
movie the other will want to attend.

The boy wants to see the latest action flick, while the girl would rather
go to an art film, but they would both rather go to the same movie than
not meet up at all. Payoffs consistent with these preferences are shown in

Table
30.3

**The battle of the sexes.**

|  |  | Girl | |
|---|---|---|---|
|  |  | Action | Art |
| **Boy** | Action | 2, 1 | 0, 0 |
|  | Art | 0, 0 | 1, 2 |

Table 30.3. Note the defining feature of coordination games: the payoffs are higher when the players coordinate their actions than when they don't.

What are the Nash equilibria of this game? Luckily, this is just the game we used in the last section to illustrate best response curves. We saw there that there are three equilibria: both choose action, both choose art, or each chooses his or her preferred choice with probability 2/3.

Since all of these are possible equilibria, it is hard to say what will happen from this description alone. Generally, we would look to considerations outside the formal description of the game to resolve the problem. For example, suppose that the art film was a closer destination for one of the two players. Then both players might reasonably suppose that would be the equilibrium choice.

When players have good reasons to believe that one of the equilibria is more "natural" than the others, it is called a **focal point** of the game.

## Prisoner's Dilemma

The prisoner's dilemma, which we discussed extensively in the last chapter, is also a coordination game. Recall the story: two prisoners can either confess, thereby implicating the other, or deny committing a crime. The payoffs are shown in Table 30.4.

The striking feature of the prisoner's dilemma is that confessing is a dominant strategy, even though coordination (both choose deny) is far superior in terms of the total payoff. Coordination would allow the prisoners to choose the best payoff, but the problem is that there is no easy way to make it happen in a single-shot game.

One way out of the prisoner's dilemma is to enlarge the game by adding new choices. We saw in the last chapter that an indefinitely repeated prisoner's dilemma game could achieve the cooperative outcome via strategies like tit for tat, in which players rewarded cooperation and punished lack of cooperation through their future actions. The extra strategic consideration

**The prisoner's dilemma.**

Table
30.4

|         |         | Player B | |
|---------|---------|----------|---------|
|         |         | Confess  | Deny    |
| **Player A** | Confess | $-3, -3$ | $0, -6$ |
|         | Deny    | $-6, 0$  | $-1, -1$ |

here is that refusing to cooperate today may result in extended punishment later on.

Another way to "solve" the prisoner's dilemma is to add the possibility of contracting. For example, both players could sign a contract saying that they will stick with the cooperative strategy. If either of them reneges on the contract, he or she will have to pay a fine or be punished in some way. Contracts are very helpful in achieving all sorts of outcomes, but they rely on the existence of a legal system that will enforce such contracts. This makes sense for business negotiations but is not an appropriate assumption in other contexts, such as military games or international negotiations.

## Assurance Games

Consider the U.S.-U.S.S.R. arms race of the 1950s in which each country could build nuclear missiles or refrain from building them. The payoffs to these strategies might look like those shown in Table 30.5. The best outcome for both parties is to refrain from building the missiles, giving a payoff of (4, 4). But if one refrains while the other builds, the payoff will be 3 to the builder and 1 to the refrainer. The payoff if they both build missile sites is (2, 2).

It is not hard to see that there are two pure strategy Nash equilibria, (refrain, refrain) and (build, build). However, (refrain, refrain) is better for both parties. The trouble is, neither party knows which choice the other will make. Before committing to refrain, each party wants some *assurance* that the other will refrain.

One way to achieve this assurance is for one of the players to move first, by opening itself to inspection, say. Note that this can be unilateral, at least as long as one believes the payoffs in the game. If one player announces that it is refraining from deploying nuclear missiles and gives the other player sufficient evidence of its choice, it can rest assured that the other player will also refrain.

Table 30.5

**An arms race.**

| | U.S.S.R. | |
| | Refrain | Build |
|---|---|---|
| **U.S.** Refrain | 4, 4 | 1, 3 |
| **U.S.** Build | 3, 1 | 2, 2 |

## Chicken

Our last coordination game is based on an automobile game popularized in the movies. Two teenagers start at opposite ends of the street and drive in a straight line toward each other. The first to swerve loses face; if neither swerves, they both crash into each other. Some possible payoffs are shown in Table 30.6.

There are two pure strategy Nash equilibria, (row swerves, column doesn't) and (column swerves, row doesn't). Column prefers the first equilibrium and row the second, but each equilibrium is better than a crash. Note the difference between this and the assurance game; there, both players were better off doing the same thing (building or refraining) than doing different things. Here, both players are worse off doing the same thing (driving straight or swerving) than if they did different things.

Each player knows that if he can commit himself to driving straight, the other will chicken out. But of course, each player also knows that it would be crazy to crash into each other. So how can one of the players enforce his preferred equilibrium?

One important strategy is commitment. Suppose that row ostentatiously fastened a steering wheel lock on his car before starting out. Column, recognizing that row now has no choice but to go straight, would choose to swerve. Of course if both players put on a lock, the outcome would be disastrous!

## How to Coordinate

If you are a player in a coordination game, you may want to get the other player to cooperate at an equilibrium that you both like (the assurance game), cooperate at an equilibrium one of you likes (battle of the sexes), play something other than the equilibrium strategy (the prisoner's dilemma), or make a choice leading to your preferred outcome (chicken).

In the assurance game, the battle of the sexes, and chicken, this can be accomplished by one player's moving first, and committing herself to a particular choice. The other player can then observe the choice and respond accordingly. In the prisoner's dilemma, this strategy doesn't work: if one player chooses not to confess, it is in the other's interest to do so. Instead of sequential moves, repetition and contracting are major ways to "solve" the prisoner's dilemma.

**Chicken.**

Table 30.6

|  |  | Column | |
|---|---|---|---|
|  |  | Swerve | Straight |
| **Row** | Swerve | 0, 0 | −1, 1 |
|  | Straight | 1, −1 | −2, −2 |

## 30.4 Games of Competition

The opposite pole from cooperation is competition. This is the famous case of **zero-sum games**, so called because the payoff to one player is equal to the losses of the other.

Most sports are effectively zero-sum games: a point awarded to one team is equivalent to a point subtracted from the other team. Competition is fierce in such games because the players' interests are diametrically opposed.

Let us illustrate a zero-sum game by looking at soccer, known as football in most of the world. Row is kicking a penalty shot and column is defending. Row can kick to the left or kick to the right; column can favor one side and defend to the left or defend to the right in order to deflect the kick.

We will express the payoffs to these strategies in terms of expected points. Obviously row will be more successful if column jumps the wrong way. On the other hand, the game may not be perfectly symmetric since row may be better at kicking in one direction than another and column may be better at defending one direction or the other.

Let us assume that row will score 80 percent of the time if he kicks to the left and column jumps to the right but only 50 percent of the time if column jumps to the left. If row kicks to the right, we will assume that he succeeds 90 percent of the time if column jumps to the left but 20 percent

Table 30.7

**Penalty point in soccer.**

|  |  | Column | |
| --- | --- | --- | --- |
|  |  | Defend left | Defend right |
| Row | Kick left | 50, –50 | 80, –80 |
|  | Kick right | 90, –90 | 20, –20 |

of the time if column jumps to the right. These payoffs are illustrated in Table 30.7.

Note that the payoffs in each entry sum to zero, indicating that the players have diametrically opposed goals. Row wants to maximize his expected payoff, and column wants to maximize her expected payoff—which means she wants to minimize row's payoff.

Obviously, if column knows which way row will kick she will have a tremendous advantage. Row, recognizing this, will therefore try to keep column guessing. In particular, he will kick sometimes to his strong side and sometimes to his weak side. That is, he will pursue a **mixed strategy**.

If row kicks left with probability $p$, he will get an expected payoff of $50p + 90(1 - p)$ when column jumps left and $80p + 20(1 - p)$ when column jumps right. Row wants to make this expected payoff as big as possible, and column wants to make it as small as possible.

For example, suppose that row chooses to kick left half the time. If column jumps left, row will have an expected payoff of $50 \times 1/2 + 90 \times 1/2 = 70$, and if column jumps right, row will have an expected payoff of $80 \times 1/2 + 20 \times 1/2 = 50$.

Column, of course, can carry through this same reasoning. If column believes that row will kick to the left half the time, then column will want to jump to the right, since this is the choice that minimizes row's expected payoff (thereby maximizing column's expected payoff).

Figure 30.2 shows row's expected payoffs for different choices of $p$. This simply involves graphing the two functions $50p + 90(1-p)$ and $80p + 20(1-p)$. Since these two expressions are linear functions of $p$, the graphs are straight lines.

Row recognizes that column will always try to minimize his expected payoff. Thus, for any $p$, the best payoff he can hope for is the *minimum* of the payoffs given by the two strategies. We've illustrated this by the colored line in Figure 30.2.

Where does the maximum of these minimum payoffs occur? Obviously, it occurs at the peak of the colored line, or, equivalently, where the two

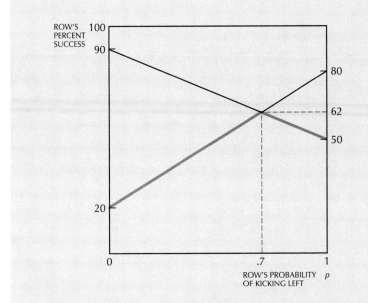

**Row's strategy.** The two curves show row's expected payoff as a function of $p$, the probability that he kicks to the left. Whatever $p$ he chooses, column will try to minimize row's payoff.

Figure 30.2

lines intersect. We can calculate this value algebraically by solving

$$50p + 90(1-p) = 80p + 20(1-p)$$

for $p$. You should verify that the solution is $p = .7$.

Hence, if row kicks to the left 70 percent of the time and column responds optimally, row will have an expected payoff of $50 \times .7 + 90 \times .3 = 62$.

What about column? We can perform a similar analysis for her choices. Suppose column decides to jump to the left with probability $q$ and jump to the right with probability $(1-q)$. Then row's expected payoff will be $50q + 80(1-q)$ if column jumps to the left and $90q + 20(1-q)$ if column jumps to the right. For each $q$, column will want to *minimize* row's payoff. But column recognizes that row wants to *maximize* this same payoff.

Hence, if column chooses to jump to the left with probability $1/2$, she recognizes that row will get an expected payoff of $50 \times 1/2 + 80 \times 1/2 = 65$ if row kicks left and $90 \times 1/2 + 20 \times 1/2 = 55$ if row kicks right. In this case row will, of course, choose to kick left.

We can plot the two payoffs in Figure 30.3, which is analogous to the previous diagram. From column's viewpoint, it is the maximum of the two lines that is relevant, since this reflects row's optimal choice for each choice of $q$. Hence, the diagram depicts these lines in color. Just as before we can find the best $q$ for column—the point where row's maximum payoff is minimized. This occurs where

$$50q + 80(1 - q) = 90q + 20(1 - q),$$

which implies $q = .6$.

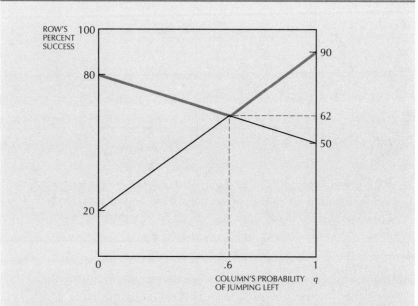

**Figure 30.3**

**Column's strategy.** The two lines show row's expected payoff as a function of $q$, the probability that column jumps to the left. Whatever $q$ column chooses, row will try to maximize his own payoff.

We have now calculated the equilibrium strategies for each of the two players. Row should kick to the left with probability .7, and column should jump to the left with probability .6. These values were chosen so that row's payoffs and column's payoffs will be the same, whatever the other player does, since we found the values by equating the payoffs from the two strategies the opposing player could choose.

So when row chooses .7, column is indifferent between jumping left and jumping right, or, for that matter jumping left with any probability $q$. In particular, column is perfectly happy jumping left with probability .6.

Similarly, if column jumps left with probability .6, then row is indifferent between kicking left and kicking right, or any mixture of the two. In

particular, he is happy to kick left with probability .7. Hence these choices
are a Nash equilibrium: each player is optimizing, given the choices of the
other.

In equilibrium row scores 62 percent of the time and fails to score 38
percent of the time. This is the best he can do, if the other player responds
optimally.

What if column responds nonoptimally? Can row do better? To answer
this question, we can use the best response curves introduced at the beginning of this chapter. We have already seen that when $p$ is less than .7,
column will want to jump left, and when $p$ is greater than .7, column will
want to jump right. Similarly when $q$ is less than .6, row will want to kick
left, and when $q$ is greater than .6, row will want to kick right.

Figure 30.4 depicts these best response curves. Note that they intersect
at the point where $p = .7$ and $q = .6$. The nice thing about the best
response curves is that they tell each player what to do for every choice
the other player makes, optimal or not. The only choice that is an optimal
response to an optimal choice is where the two curves cross—the Nash
equilibrium.

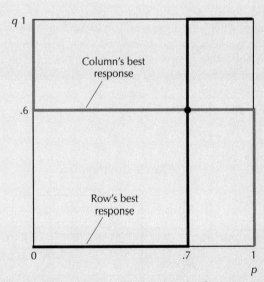

**Best response curves.** These are the best response curves
for row and column, as a function of $p$, the probability that row
kicks to the left, and $q$, the probability that column jumps to
the left.

Figure
30.4

## 30.5 Games of Coexistence

We have interpreted mixed strategies as randomization by the players. In the penalty kick game, if row's strategy is to play left with probability .7 and right with probability .3, then we think that row will "mix it up" and play left 70 percent of the time and right 30 percent of the time.

But there is another interpretation. Suppose that kickers and goalies are matched up at random and that 70 percent of the kickers always kick left and 30 percent always kick right. Then, from the goalie's point of view, it is just like facing a single player who randomizes with those probabilities.

This isn't all that compelling as a story for soccer games, but it is a reasonable story for animal behavior. The idea is that various kinds of behavior are genetically programmed and that evolution selects the mixtures of the population that are stable with respect to evolutionary forces. In recent years, biologists have come to regard game theory as an indispensible tool to study animal behavior.

The most famous game of animal interaction is the **hawk-dove game**. This doesn't refer to a game between hawks and doves (which would have a pretty predictable outcome) but rather to a game involving a single species that exhibits two kinds of behavior.

Think of a wild dog. When two wild dogs come across a piece of food, they have to decide whether to fight or to share. Fighting is the hawkish strategy: one will win and one will lose. Sharing is a dovish strategy: it works well when the other player is also dovish, but if the other player is hawkish, the offer to share is rejected and the dovish player will get nothing.

A possible set of payoffs is given in Table 30.8.

Table
30.8

**Hawk-dove game.**

|  |  | Column | |
|---|---|---|---|
|  |  | Hawk | Dove |
| Row | Hawk | −2, −2 | 4, 0 |
|  | Dove | 0, 4 | 2, 2 |

If both wild dogs play dove, they end up with (2, 2). If one plays hawk and the other plays dove, the hawkish player wins everything. But if both play hawk, each dog will be seriously injured.

It obviously can't be an equilibrium if everyone plays hawk, since if some dog played dove, it would end up with 0 rather than $-2$. And if all dogs played dove, it would pay someone to deviate and play hawk. So there will have to be some mixture of hawk types and dove types in equilibrium. What sort of mixture should we expect?

Suppose that the fraction playing hawk is $p$. Then a hawk will meet another hawk with probability $p$ and meet a dove with probability $1 - p$. The expected payoff to the hawk type will be

$$H = -2p + 4(1 - p).$$

The expected payoff to the dove type will be

$$D = 2(1 - p).$$

Suppose that the type that has the higher payoff reproduces more rapidly, passing its tendency to play hawk or dove on to its offspring. So if $H > D$, we would see the fraction of hawk types in the population increase, and if $H < D$, we would expect to see the number of dove types increase.

The only way the population can be in equilibrium is if the payoffs to each type are the same. This requires

$$H = -2p + 4(1 - p) = 2(1 - p) = D,$$

which solves for $p = 1/2$.

We have found that a 50-50 mixture of doves and hawks is an equilibrium. Is it stable, in some sense? We plot the payoffs to hawk and dove as a function of $p$, the fraction of the population playing hawk in Figure 30.5. Note that when $p > 1/2$, the payoff to playing hawk is less than that of playing dove, so we would expect to see the doves reproduce more rapidly, moving us back to the equilibrium 50-50 ratio. Similarly, when $p < 1/2$, the payoff to hawk is greater than the payoff to dove, leading the hawks to reproduce more rapidly.

This argument shows that not only is $p = 1/2$ an equilibrium but it is also stable under evolutionary forces. Considerations of this sort lead to a concept known as an **evolutionarily stable strategy** or an **ESS**.[1] Remarkably, an ESS turns out to be a Nash equilibrium, even though it was derived from quite different considerations.

The Nash equilibrium concept was designed to deal with calculating, rational individuals, each of whom is trying to devise a strategy appropriate for the best strategy the other player might choose. The ESS was designed to model animal behavior under evolutionary forces, where strategies that had greater fitness payoffs would reproduce more rapidly. But the ESS equilibria are also Nash equilibria, giving another argument for why this particular concept in game theory is so compelling.

---

[1] See John Maynard Smith, *Evolution and the Theory of Games*, (Cambridge University Press, 1982).

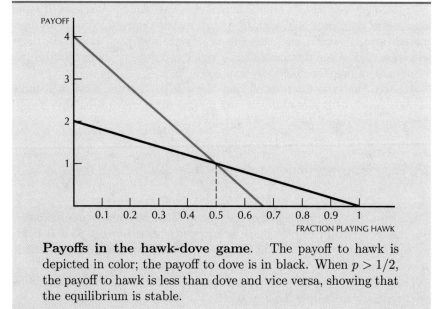

Figure
30.5

**Payoffs in the hawk-dove game.** The payoff to hawk is depicted in color; the payoff to dove is in black. When $p > 1/2$, the payoff to hawk is less than dove and vice versa, showing that the equilibrium is stable.

## 30.6 Games of Commitment

The previous examples involving games of cooperation and competition have been concerned with games with **simultaneous moves**. Each player had to make his or her choice without knowing what the other player was choosing (or had chosen). Indeed, games of coordination or competition can be quite trivial if one player knows the other's choices.

In this section we turn our attention to games with **sequential moves**. An important strategic issue that arises in such games is **commitment**. To see how this works, look back at the game of chicken described earlier in this chapter. We saw there that if one player could force himself to choose straight, the other player would optimally choose to swerve. In the assurance game, the outcome would be better for both players if one of them moved first.

Note that this committed choice must be both irreversible and observable by the other player. Irreversibility is part of what it means to be committed, while observability is crucial if the other player is going to be persuaded to change his or her behavior.

### The Frog and the Scorpion

We begin with the fable of the frog and the scorpion. They were standing on the bank of the river, trying to figure out a way across. "I know," said

the scorpion "I will climb on your back and you can swim across the river."
The frog said, "But what if you sting me with your stinger?" The scorpion
said, "Why would I do that? Then we would both die."

The frog found this convincing, so the scorpion climbed on his back and
they started across the river. Halfway across, at the deepest point, the
scorpion stung the frog. Writhing in pain, the frog cried out, "Why did
you do that? Now we are both doomed!" "Alas," said the scorpion, as he
sank into the river, "it is my nature."

Let's look at the frog and the scorpion from the viewpoint of game theory.
Figure 30.6 depicts a sequential game with payoffs consistent with the story.
Start at the bottom of the game tree. If the frog refuses the scorpion,
both get nothing. Looking up one line, we see that if the frog carries the
scorpion, he receives utility 5, for doing a good deed, and the scorpion
receives a payoff of 3, for getting across the river. In line where the frog
is stung, he receives a payoff of $-10$, and the scorpion gets a payoff of 5,
representing the satisfaction from fulfilling his natural instincts.

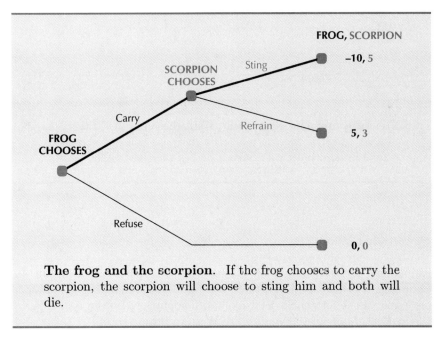

**The frog and the scorpion.** If the frog chooses to carry the
scorpion, the scorpion will choose to sting him and both will
die.

Figure
30.6

It is best to start with the final move of the game: the scorpion's choice
of sting or refrain. Stinging has a higher payoff to the scorpion because
"it is his nature" to sting. Hence the frog should rationally choose to
refuse to carry the scorpion. Unfortunately, the frog didn't understand
the scorpion's payoffs; apparently, he thought that the scorpion's payoffs

looked something like those in Figure 30.7. Alas, this mistake was fatal for the frog.

A smart frog would figure out some way to make the scorpion commit to not stinging. He could, for example, tie his tail. Or he could hire a hit frog, who would retaliate against the scorpion's family. Whatever the strategy, the critical thing for the frog to do is to change the payoffs to the scorpion by making stinging more costly or refraining more rewarding.

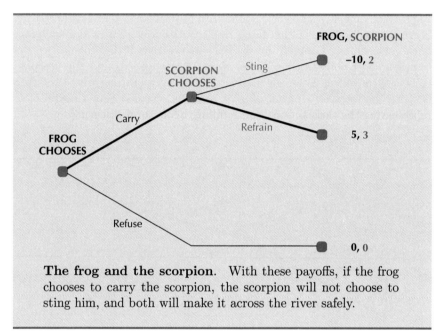

Figure 30.7

**The frog and the scorpion.** With these payoffs, if the frog chooses to carry the scorpion, the scorpion will not choose to sting him, and both will make it across the river safely.

## The Kindly Kidnapper

Kidnapping for ransom is a big business in some parts of the world. In Columbia, it is estimated that there are over 2,000 kidnappings for ransom per year. In the former Soviet Union, kidnappings rose from 5 in 1992 to 105 in 1999. Many of the victims are Western businesspeople.

Some countries, such as Italy, have laws against paying ransom. The reasoning is that if the victim's family or employers can commit themselves not to pay ransom, then the kidnappers will have no motive to abduct the victim in the first place.

The problem is, of course, once a kidnapping has taken place, a victim's family will prefer to pay the kidnappers, even if it is illegal to do so. Hence penalties for paying ransom may not be effective as a commitment device.

Suppose some kidnappers abduct a hostage and then discover that they can't get paid. Should they release the hostage? The hostage, of course, promises not to reveal the identity of the kidnappers. But will he keep this promise? Once he is released, he has no incentive to do so—and every incentive to try to punish the kidnappers. Even if the kidnappers want to let the hostage go, they can't do so for fear of being identified.

Figure 30.8 depicts some possible payoffs. The kidnapper would feel bad about killing the hostage, receiving a payoff of $-3$. Of course, the hostage would feel even worse, receiving a payoff of $-10$. If the hostage is released, and refrains from identifying the kidnapper, the hostage gets a payoff of 3 and the kidnapper gets a payoff of 5. But if the hostage does identify the kidnapper, he gets a payoff of 5, leaving the kidnapper with a payoff of $-5$.

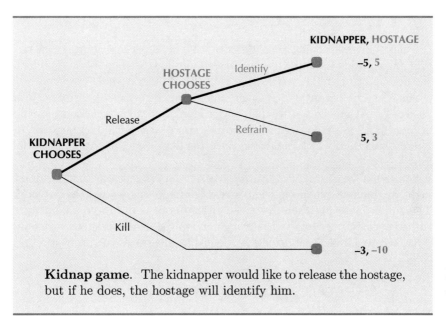

**Kidnap game**. The kidnapper would like to release the hostage, but if he does, the hostage will identify him.

Figure 30.8

Now it is the hostage who has the commitment problem: how can he convince the kidnappers that he won't renege on his promise and reveal their identity?

The hostage needs to figure out a way to change the payoffs of the game. In particular, he needs to find a way to impose a cost on himself if he identifies the kidnappers.

Thomas Schelling, an economist at the University of Maryland who has worked extensively on strategic analysis in dynamic games, suggests that the hostage might have the kidnappers photograph him in some embarrassing act and leave them with the photos. This effectively changes the payoffs from his subsequently revealing the identity of the kidnappers, since they then have the option of revealing the embarrassing photograph.

This sort of strategy is known as an "exchange of hostages." In the Middle Ages, when two kings wanted to ensure a contract wouldn't be broken, they would exchange hostages such as family members. If either king broke the agreement, the hostages would be sacrificed. Neither wanted to sacrifice their family members, so each king would have an incentive to respect the terms of their contract.

In the case of the kidnapping, the embarrassing photo would impose costs on the hostage if it were released, thereby ensuring that he will stick to his agreement not to reveal the identity of the kidnappers.

### When Strength Is Weakness

Our next example comes from the world of animal psychology. It turns out that pigs quickly establish dominance-subordinateness relations, in which the dominant pig tends to boss the subordinate pig around.

Some psychologists put two pigs, one dominant, one subordinate, in a long pen.[2] At one end of the pen was a lever that would release a portion of food to a trough located at the other end of the pen. The question of interest was this: which pig would push the lever and which would eat the food?

Somewhat surprisingly the outcome of the experiment was that the dominant pig pressed the lever, while the subordinate pig waited for the food. The subordinate pig then ate most of the food, while the dominant pig rushed as fast as it could to the trough end of the pen, ending up with only a few scraps. Table 30.9 depicts a game that illustrates the problem.

Table
30.9

**Pigs pressing levers.**

| | | Dominant Pig | |
| --- | --- | --- | --- |
| | | Don't press lever | Press lever |
| Subordinate Pig | Don't press lever | 0, 0 | 4, 1 |
| | Press lever | 0, 5 | 2, 3 |

---

[2] The original reference is Baldwin and Meese, "Social Behavior in Pigs Studied by Means of Operant Conditioning," (*Animal Behavior,* (1979)). I draw on the description of John Maynard Smith, *Evolution and the Theory of Games* (Cambridge University Press, 1982).

The subordinate pig compares a payoff of $(0, 4)$ to $(0, 2)$ and concludes, sensibly enough, that pressing the lever is dominated by not pressing it. Given that the subordinate pig doesn't press the lever, the dominant pig has no choice but to do so.

If the dominant pig could refrain from eating all the food and reward the subordinate pig for pressing the lever, it could achieve a better outcome. The problem is that pigs have no contracts, and the dominant pig can't help being a hog!

As in the case of the kindly kidnapper, the dominant pig has a commitment problem. If he could only commit to not eating all the food, he would end up much better off.

## Savings and Social Security

Commitment problems aren't limited to the animal world. They also show up in economic policy.

Saving for retirement is an interesting and timely example. Everyone gives lip service to the fact that saving is a good idea. Unfortunately, few people actually do it. Part of the reason for the reluctance to save is that individuals recognize that society won't let them starve, so there is a good chance they will be bailed out later on.

To formulate this in a game between the generations, let's consider two strategies for the older generation: save or squander. The younger generation likewise has two strategies: support their elders or save for their own retirement. A possible game matrix is shown in Table 30.10.

**Intergenerational conflict over savings.**

Table 30.10

|  |  | Younger Generation | |
|---|---|---|---|
|  |  | Support | Refrain |
| Older Generation | Save | 2, −1 | 1, 0 |
|  | Squander | 3, −1 | −2, −2 |

If the older generation saves and the younger generation also supports them, the old folks end up with a utility level of 2 and the young folks end up with −1. If the older generation squanders and the younger generation supports them, the elders end up with a utility of 3 and the young folks end up with −1.

If the younger generation refrains from providing support to their elders and the older generation saves, the old folks get 1 and the young folks get 0. Finally, if the old folks squander and the young folks neglect them, each ends up with utility of $-2$, the old folks from starving and the young folks from having to watch.

It is not hard to see that there are two Nash equilibria in this game. If the old folks choose to save, then the young folks will choose optimally to neglect them. But if the old folks choose to squander, then it is optimal for the younger generation to support them. And of course, given that the younger generation will support their elders, it is optimal for their elders to squander!

However, this analysis ignores the time structure of the game: one of the (few) advantages of being old is that you get to move first. If we draw out the game tree, the payoffs become those in Figure 30.9.

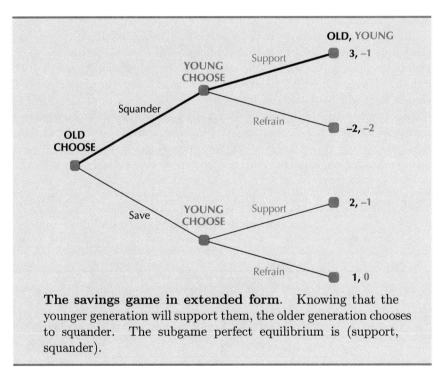

Figure 30.9    **The savings game in extended form.** Knowing that the younger generation will support them, the older generation chooses to squander. The subgame perfect equilibrium is (support, squander).

If the oldsters save, the youngsters will choose to neglect them, so the oldsters end up with a payoff of 1. If the oldsters squander, they know that the youngsters won't be able to bear watching them starve, so the oldsters end up with a payoff of 3. Hence the sensible thing for the oldsters to do is to squander, knowing they will be bailed out later on.

Of course, most developed countries now have a program like the U.S. Social Security program that forces each generation to save for retirement.

## EXAMPLE: Dynamic inefficiency of price discrimination

Recall the definition of first-degree price discrimination: the seller prices the good so that it extracts the entire consumer surplus from the buyer. We argued in Chapter 14 that this was efficient since all valuable trades were carried out.

Despite this, there are cases where first-degree price discrimination can lead to inefficiency. Suppose an salesman is such a good bargainer that he can extract the entire consumer surplus from each customer—he is an expert at first-degree price discrimination. But here's the problem: if everyone knows that he can extract all the consumer surplus, why would they ever want to buy something from him? At best, they would just break even.

This is a bit like the example of the dominant pig in the previous section. The dominant pig ended up in a worse position because it could not commit to sharing. Well, people are (usually) more intelligent than pigs, so they realize that if they want some repeat business they should make sure their customers get some surplus out of the transaction.

To do this it is necessary to find a way to commit to offering a good deal to the customers, perhaps by offering a coupon that can be used after the negotiation has taken place or by having a posted price that is available to everyone.

## Hold Up

Consider the following strategic interaction. You hire a contractor to build a warehouse. After the plans are approved and the construction is almost done, you realize that the color is bad, so you ask the contractor to change the paint, which involves a trivial expense. The contractor comes back and says: "That change order will be $1500, please."

You recognize that it will cost you at least that much to delay completion until you can find a painter, and you really do want the new color, so, muttering under your breath, you pay the cost. Congratulations, you have been held up!

Of course, contractors are not the only party at fault in this sort of game. The clients can "hold up" their payment as well, causing lots of grief for the contractor.

The game tree for the hold-up problem is depicted in Figure 30.10. We suppose that the value the owner places on having the new paint is $1500 and that the actual cost of painting is $200. Starting at the top of leaves of the tree, if the contractor charges $1500, it will realize a profit of $1300, and the client gets a net utility of zero.

If the client looks for another painter, it will cost him $200 to pay the painter and, say, $1400 in lost time. He gets the color he wants which is worth $1500, buy has to pay $1600 in direct costs and delay costs, leaving him with a net loss of $100.

If the contractor charges the client the actual cost of $200, he breaks even and the client gets a $1500 value for $200, leaving him with a net payoff of $1300.

As can be seen, the optimal choice for the contractor is to extort the payment, and the optimal choice for the customer is to give in. But a sensible client will recognize that change orders will occur in any project. Because of this, the client will be reluctant to hire contractors with a reputation for extortion which is, of course, bad for the contractor.

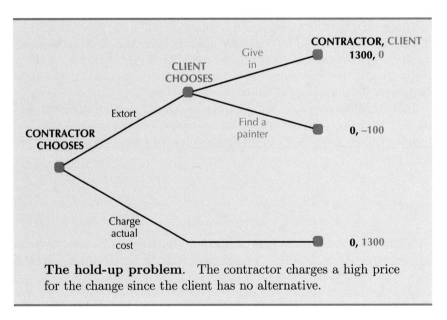

Figure 30.10 **The hold-up problem.** The contractor charges a high price for the change since the client has no alternative.

How do firms solve the hold-up problem? The basic answer is contracts. Normally, contractors negotiate a contract specifying what kinds of change orders are appropriate and how their costs will be determined. Sometimes there are even arbitration or other dispute resolution procedures built into the contracts. A lot of time, energy, and money goes into writing contracts just to make certain that hold up won't occur.

But contracts aren't the only solution. Another way to solve the problem is through commitment. For example, the contractor might post a bond guaranteeing timely completion of the project. Again, there will generally be some objectively specified terms about what constitutes completion.

Another important factor is reputation. Obviously, a contractor who persistently tries to extort his customers will get a bad reputation. He won't be hired again by this customer, and he certainly won't get good recommendations. This reputation effect can be examined in a repeated game context in which hold up today will cost the contractor in the future.

## 30.7 Bargaining

The classical bargaining problem is divide the dollar. Two players have a dollar that they want to divide between them. How do they do it?

The problem, as stated, has no answer since there is too little information to construct a reasonable model. The challenge in modeling bargaining is to find some other dimensions on which the players can negotiate.

One solution, the **Nash bargaining model**, takes an axiomatic approach by specifying certain properties that a reasonable bargaining solution should have and then proving that there is only one outcome that satisfies these axioms.

The outcome ends up depending on how risk averse the players are and what will happen if no bargain is made. Unfortunately, a full treatment of this model is beyond the scope of this book.

An alternative approach, the **Rubinstein bargaining model**, looks at a sequence of choices and then solves for the subgame perfect equilibrium. Luckily the basic insight of this model is easy to illustrate in simple cases.

Two players, Alice and Bob, have \$1 to divide between them. They agree to spend at most three days negotiating over the division. The first day, Alice will make an offer, Bob either accepts or comes back with a counteroffer the next day, and on the third day Alice gets to make one final offer. If they cannot reach an agreement in three days, both players get zero.

We assume Alice and Bob differ in their degree of impatience: Alice discounts payoffs in the future at a rate of $\alpha$ per day, and Bob discounts payoffs at a rate of $\beta$ per day. Finally, we assume that if a player is indifferent between two offers, he will accept the one that is most preferred by his opponent. This idea is that the opponent could offer some arbitrarily small amount that would make the player strictly prefer one choice and that this assumption allows us to approximate such an "arbitrarily small amount" by zero. It turns out that there is a unique subgame perfect equilibrium of this bargaining game.

We start our analysis at the end of the game, right before the last day. At this point Alice can make a take-it-or-leave-it offer to Bob. Clearly, the optimal thing for Alice to do at this point is to offer Bob the smallest possible amount that he would accept, which, by assumption, is zero. So if the game actually lasts three days, Alice would get $1 and Bob would get zero (i.e., an arbitrarily small amount).

Now go back to the previous move, when Bob gets to propose a division. At this point Bob should realize that Alice can guarantee herself $1 on the next move by simply rejecting his offer. A dollar next period is worth $\alpha$ to Alice this period, so any offer less than $\alpha$ would be sure to be rejected. Bob certainly prefers $1 - \alpha$ now to zero next period, so he should rationally offer $\alpha$ to Alice, which Alice will then accept. So if the game ends on the second move, Alice gets $\alpha$ and Bob gets $1 - \alpha$.

Now move to the first day. At this point Alice gets to make the offer and she realizes that Bob can get $1 - \alpha$ if he simply waits until the second day. Hence Alice must offer a payoff that has at least this present value to Bob in order to avoid delay. Thus she offers $\beta(1 - \alpha)$ to Bob. Bob finds this (just) acceptable and the game ends. The final outcome is that the game ends on the first move with Alice receiving $1 - \beta(1 - \alpha)$ and Bob receiving $\beta(1 - \alpha)$.

The first panel in Figure 30.11 illustrates this process for the case where $\alpha = \beta < 1$. The outermost diagonal line shows the possible payoff patterns on the first day, namely, all payoffs of the form $x_A + x_B = 1$. The next diagonal line moving toward the origin shows the present value of the payoffs if the game ends in the second period: $x_A + x_B = \alpha$. The diagonal line closest to the origin shows the present value of the payoffs if the game ends in the third period; the equation for this line is $x_A + x_B = \alpha^2$. The right-angled path depicts the minimum acceptable divisions each period, leading up to the final subgame perfect equilibrium. The second panel in Figure 30.11 shows how the same process might look with more stages in the negotiation.

It is natural to let the horizon go to infinity and ask what happens in the infinite game. It turns out that the subgame perfect equilibrium division is

$$\text{Payoff to Alice} = \frac{1 - \beta}{1 - \alpha\beta}$$

$$\text{Payoff to Bob} = \frac{\beta(1 - \alpha)}{1 - \alpha\beta}.$$

Note that if $\alpha = 1$ and $\beta < 1$, then Alice receives the entire payoff.

## The Ultimatum Game

The Rubinstein bargaining model is so elegant that economists rushed to test it in the laboratory. They found, alas, that elegance does not imply accuracy. Naive subjects (i.e., noneconomics majors) aren't very good at looking ahead more than one or two steps, if that.

In addition, there are other factors that cause problems. To see this, let us examine a one-step version of the bargaining model described above.

**A bargaining game.** The heavy line connects together the equilibrium outcomes in the subgames. The point on the line that is furthest out is the subgame perfect equilibrium.

Figure
30.11

Alice and Bob still have \$1 to divide between them. Alice proposes a division, and, if Bob agrees, the game ends. The question is, what should Alice say?

According to the theory, she should propose something like 99 cents for Alice, 1 cent for Bob. Bob, figuring that 1 cent is better than nothing, accepts, and Alice goes home happy that she studied economics.

Unfortunately, it doesn't work out like that. A more likely outcome is that Bob, disgusted by the paltry 1 cent, says "No way," and Alice ends up with nothing. Alice, recognizing this possibility, will tend to sweeten the offer. In actual experiments, the average offer for U.S. undergraduates is about 45 cents, and this offer tends to be accepted most of the time.

The offering players are behaving rationally, in the sense that the 45 cent offer is pretty close to maximizing the expected payoff, given the observed frequency of rejection. It is the receiving players who behave differently than the theory predicts, since they reject small offers, even though this makes them worse off.

There are many proposed explanations for this. One view is that too small an offer violates **social norms** of behavior. Indeed, economists have found quite significant cross-cultural differences in behavior in ultimatum games. Another, not inconsistent view, is that receivers get some utility payoff from hurting the offerers, in retaliation for the small offer. After all, if all you are losing is a penny, the satisfaction of striking back at the other player is pretty attractive by comparison. We will the ultimatum game in more detail in the next chapter.

## Summary

1. A player's best response function gives the optimal choice for him as a function of the choices the other player(s) might make.

2. A Nash equilibrium in a two-person game is a pair of strategies, one for each player, each of which is a best response to the other.

3. A mixed strategy Nash equilibrium involves randomizing among several strategies.

4. Common games of coordination are the battle of the sexes, where both players want to do the same thing rather than different things; the prisoner's dilemma, where the dominant strategy ends up hurting both players; the assurance game, where both players want to cooperate as long as they think the other will cooperate; and chicken, where players want to avoid doing the same thing.

5. A two-person zero-sum game is one where the payoffs to one player are the negative of the payoffs to the other.

6. Evolutionary games are concerned with outcomes that are stable under population reproduction.

7. In sequential games, players move in turn. Each player therefore has to reason about what the other will do in response to his or her choices.

8. In many sequential games, commitment is an important issue. Finding ways to force commitment to play particular strategies can be important.

## REVIEW QUESTIONS

1. In a two-person Nash equilibrium, each player is making a best response to what? In a dominant strategy equilibrium, each player is making a best response to what?

2. Look at the best responses for row and column in the section on mixed strategies. Do these give rise to best response functions?

3. If both players make the same choice in a coordination game, all will be well.

4. The text claims that row scores 62 percent of the time in equilibrium. Where does this number come from?

5. A contractor says that he intends to "low-ball the bid and make up for it on change orders." What does he mean?

# CHAPTER 31

# BEHAVIORAL ECONOMICS

The economic model of consumer choice that we have studied is simple and elegant, and is a reasonable starting place for many sorts of analysis. However, it is most definitely not the whole story, and in many cases a deeper model of consumer behavior is necessary to accurately describe choice behavior.

The field of **behavioral economics** is devoted to studying how consumers actually make choices. It uses some of the insights from psychology to develop predictions about choices people will make and many of these predictions are at odds with the conventional economic model of "rational" consumers.

In this chapter we will look at some of the most important phenomena that have been identified by behavioral economists, and contrast the predictions of these behavioral theories with those presented earlier in this book.[1]

---

[1] In writing this chapter, I have found Colin F. Camerer, George Loewenstein, and Matthew Rabin's book *Advances in Behavioral Economics,* Princeton University Press, 2003, to be very useful, particularly the introductory survey by Camerer and Loewenstein. Other works will be noted as the relevant topics are discussed.

## 31.1 Framing Effects in Consumer Choice

In the basic model of consumer behavior, the choices were described in the abstract: red pencils or blue pencils, hamburgers and french fries, and so on. However, in real life, people are strongly affected by how choices are presented to them or **framed**.

A faded pair of jeans in a thrift shop may be perceived very differently than the same jeans sold in an exclusive store. The decision to buy a stock may feel quite different than the decision to sell a stock, even if both transactions end up with the same portfolio. A store might sell dozens of copies of a book priced at $29.95, whereas the same book priced at $29.00 would have substantially fewer sales.

These are all examples of **framing effects**, and they are clearly a powerful force in choice behavior. Indeed, much of marketing practice is based on understanding and utilizing such biases in consumer choice.

### The Disease Dilemma

Framing effects are particularly common in choices involving uncertainty. For example, consider the following decision problem:[2]

A serious disease threatens 600 people. You are offered a choice between two treatments, A and B, which will yield the following outcomes.

**Treatment A.** Saving 200 lives for certain.

**Treatment B.** A 1/3 chance of saving 600 lives and a 2/3 chance of saving no one.

Which would you choose? Now consider the choices between these treatments.

**Treatment C.** Having 400 people die for certain.

**Treatment D.** A 2/3 chance of 600 people dying and a 1/3 chance of no one dying.

Now which treatment would you choose?

---

[2] A. Tversky and D. Kahneman, 1981, "The framing of decisions and the psychology of choice," *Science,* 211, 453–458.

In the **positive framing** comparison—which describes how many people will live—most individuals choose A over B, but in the **negative framing** comparison most people choose D over C even though the outcomes in A-C and B-D are exactly the same. Apparently, framing the question positively (in terms of lives saved) makes a treatment much more attractive than framing the choice negatively (in terms of lives lost).

Even expert decisions makers can fall into this trap. When psychologists tried this question on a group of physicians, 72 percent of them chose the safe treatment A over the risky treatment B. But when the question was framed negatively, only 22 percent chose the risky treatment C while 72 percent chose the safe treatment.

Though few of us are faced with life-or-death decisions, there are similar examples for more mundane choices, such as buying or selling stocks. A rational choice of an investment portfolio would, ideally, depend on an assessment of the possible outcomes of the investments rather than how one acquired those investments.

For example, suppose that you are given 100 shares of stock in Concrete-Blocks.com (whose slogan is "We give away the blocks, you pay for packing and shipping"). You might be reluctant to sell shares you received as a gift despite the fact that you would never consider buying them yourself.

People are often reluctant to sell losing stocks, thinking that they will "come back." Maybe they will, maybe they won't. But ultimately you shouldn't let history determine your investment portfolio—the right question to ask is whether you have the portfolio choices today that you want.

## Anchoring Effects

The hypothetical ConcreteBlocks.com example described above is related to the so-called **anchoring effect.** The idea here is that people's choices can be influenced by completely spurious information. In a classic study the experimenter spun a wheel of fortune and pointed out the number that came up to a subject.[3] The subject was then asked whether the number of African countries in the United Nations was greater or less than the number on the wheel of fortune.

After they responded, the subjects were asked for their best guess about how many African countries were in the United Nations. Even though the number shown on the wheel of fortune was obviously random, it exerted a significant influence on the subjects' reported guesses.

In a similar experimental design, MBA students were given an expensive bottle of wine and then asked if they would pay an amount for that bottle equal to the last two digits of their Social Security number. For example,

---

[3] D. Kahneman and A. Tversky, 1974, "Judgment under uncertainty: Heuristics and biases," *Science*, 185: 1124–1131.

if the last two digits were 29, the question was "Would you pay $29 for this bottle of wine?"

After answering that question, the students were asked what the maximum amount is that they *were* willing to pay for the wine. Their answers to this latter question were strongly influenced by the price determined by the last two digits of their Social Security number. For example, those with Social Security digits of 50 or under were willing to pay $11.62 on average, while those with digits in the upper half of the distribution were willing to pay $19.95 on average.

Again, these choices seem like mere laboratory games. However, there are very serious economic decisions that can also be influenced by minor variations in the way the choice is framed.

Consider, for example, choices of pension plans.[4]

Some economists looked at data from three employers that offered automatic enrollment in 401(k) plans. Employees could opt out, but they had to make an explicit choice to do so. The economists found that the participation rate in these programs with automatic enrollment was spectacularly high, with over 85 percent of workers accepting the default choice of enrolling in the 401(k) plans.

That's the good news. The bad news is that almost all of these workers also chose the default investment, typically a money market fund with very low returns and a low monthly contribution. Presumably, the employers made the default investment highly conservative to eliminate downside risk and possible employee lawsuits.

In subsequent work, these economists examined the experience at a company where there was no default choice of pension plan: within a month of starting work, employees were required to choose either to enroll in the 401(k) plan or to postpone enrollment.

By eliminating the standard default choices of non-enrollment, and of enrollment in a fund that had low rates of return, this "active decision" approach raised participation rates from 35 percent to 70 percent for newly hired employees. Moreover, employees who enrolled in the 401(k) plan overwhelmingly chose high savings rates.

As this example illustrates, careful design of human resources benefits programs can make a striking difference in which programs are chosen, potentially having a large effect on consumer savings behavior.

## Bracketing

People often have trouble understanding their own behavior, finding it too difficult to predict what they will actually choose in different circumstances.

---

[4] James Choi, David Laibson, Brigitte Madrian, and Andrew Metrick, "For Better or for Worse: Default Effects and 401(k) Savings Behavior," NBER working paper, W8651, 2001.

For example, a marketing professor gave students a choice of six different snacks that they could consume in each of three successive weeks during class.[5] (You should be so lucky!) In one treatment, the students had to choose the snacks in advance; in the other treatment, they chose the snacks on each day then immediately consumed them.

When the students had to choose in advance, they chose a much more diverse set of snacks. In fact, 64 percent chose a different snack each week in this treatment compared to only 9 percent in the other group. When faced with making the choices all at once, people apparently preferred variety to exclusivity. But when it came down to actually choosing, they made the choice with which they were most comfortable. We are all creatures of habit, even in our choice of snacks.

## Too Much Choice

Conventional theory argues that more choice is better. However, this claim ignores the costs of making choices. In affluent countries, consumers can easily become overwhelmed with choices, making it difficult for them to arrive at a decision.

In one experiment, two marketing researchers set up sampling booths for jam in a supermarket.[6] One booth offered 24 flavors and one offered only 6. More people stopped at the larger display, but substantially more people actually bought jam at the smaller display. More choice seemed to be attractive to shoppers, but the profusion of choices in the larger display appeared to make it more difficult for the shoppers to reach a decision.

Two experts in behavioral finance wondered whether the same problem with "excessive choice" showed up in investor decisions. They found that people who designed their own retirement portfolios tended to be just as happy with the average portfolio chosen by their co-workers as they were with their own choice. Having the flexibility to construct their own retirement portfolios didn't seem to make investors feel better off.[7]

## Constructed Preferences

How are we to interpret these examples? Psychologists and behavioral economists argue that preferences are not a guide to choice; rather, preferences are "discovered" in part through the experiences of choice.

---

[5] I. Simonson, 1990, "The effect of purchase quantity and timing on variety-seeking behavior," *Journal of Marketing Research*, 17: 150–164.

[6] Sheena S. Iyengar and Mark R. Lepper, "When choice is demotivating: can one desire too much of a good thing?" *Journal of Personality and Social Psychology*, 2000.

[7] Shlomo Benartzi and Richard Thaler, "How Much Is Investor Autonomy Worth?" UCLA working paper, 2001.

Imagine watching someone in the supermarket picking up a tomato, putting it down, then picking it up again. Do they want it or not? Is the price-quality combination offered acceptable? When you watch such behavior, you are seeing someone who is "on the margin" in terms of making the choice. They are, in the psychologists' interpretation, *discovering* their preferences.

Conventional theory treats preferences as preexisting. In this view, preferences *explain* behavior. Psychologists instead think of preferences as being constructed—people develop or create preferences through the act of choosing and consuming.

It seems likely that the psychological model is a better description of what actually happens. However, the two viewpoints are not entirely incompatible. As we have seen, once preferences have been discovered, albeit by some mysterious process, they tend to become built-in to choices. Choices, once made, tend to anchor decisions. If you tried to buy that tomato from that consumer once they have finally decided to choose it, you would likely have to pay more than it cost them.

## 31.2 Uncertainty

Ordinary choice is complicated enough, but choice under uncertainty tends to be particularly tricky. We've already seen that people's decisions may depend on how choice alternatives are phrased. But there are many other biases in behavior in this domain.

## Law of Small Numbers

If you have taken a course in statistics, you might be familiar with the Law of Large Numbers. This is a mathematical principle that says (roughly) that the average of a large sample from a population tends to be close to the mean of that population.

The Law of Small Numbers is a psychological statement that says that people tend to be overly influenced by small samples, particularly if they experience them themselves.[8]

Consider the following question:[9]

---

[8] The term originated with A. Tversky and D. Kahneman, 1971, "Belief in the law of small numbers," *Psychological Bulletin*, 76, 2: 105–110. Much of the following discussion is based on a working paper by Matthew Rabin of the University of California at Berkeley entitled "Inference by Believers in the Law of Small Numbers."

[9] A. Tversky and D. Kahneman, 1982, "Judgments of and by Representativeness," in *Judgment under Uncertainty: Heuristics and Biases,* D. Kahneman, P. Slovic, and A. Tversky, Cambridge University Press, 84–98.

"A certain town is served by two hospitals. In the larger hospital about 45 babies are born each day, and in the smaller hospital about 15 babies are born each day. As you know, about 50 percent of all babies are boys. However, the exact percentage varies from day to day. Sometimes it may be higher than 50 percent, sometimes lower. For a period of 1 year, each hospital recorded the days on which more than 60 percent of the babies born were boys. Which hospital do you think recorded more such days?"

In a survey of college students, 22 percent of the subjects said that they thought that it was more likely that the larger hospital recorded more such days, while 56 percent said that they thought the number of days would be about the same. Only 22 percent correctly said that the smaller hospital would report more days.

If the correct account seems peculiar to you, suppose the smaller hospital recorded 2 births per day and the larger hospital 100 births per day. Roughly 25 percent of the time the smaller hospital would have 100 percent male births, while this would be very rare for the large hospital.

It appears that people expect samples to look like the distribution from which they are drawn. Or, saying this another way, people underestimate the actual magnitude of the fluctuations in a sample.

A related issue is that people find it difficult to recognize randomness. In one experiment, subjects were asked to write down a series of 150 "random" coin tosses. About 15 percent of the sequences they produced had heads or tails three times in a row, but this pattern would occur randomly about 25 percent of the time. Only 3 percent of the subjects' sequences had 4 heads or 4 tails in a row, while probability theory says that this should occur about 12 percent of the time.

This has important implications for game theory, for example. We saw that in many cases people should try to randomize their strategy choices so as to keep their opponents guessing. But, as the psychological literature shows, people aren't very good at randomizing. On the other hand, people aren't very good at detecting non-random behavior either, at least without some training in statistics. The point of mixed strategy equilibria is not that choices are *mathematically* unpredictable, but rather that they should be unpredictable by the players in the game.

Some economic researchers studied final and semi-final tennis matches at Wimbledon.[10] Ideally, tennis players should switch their serves from side to side so that their opponent can't guess which side the serve is coming from. However, even very accomplished players can't do this quite as well as one might expect. According to the authors:

"Our tests indicate that the tennis players are not quite playing ran-

---

[10] M. Walker and J. Wooders, 1999, "Minimax Play at Wimbledon," University of Arizona working paper.

domly: they switch their serves from left to right and vice versa somewhat too often to be consistent with random play. This is consistent with extensive experimental research in psychology and economics which indicates that people who are attempting to behave truly randomly tend to "switch too often."

## Asset Integration and Loss Aversion

In our study of expected utility we made an implicit assumption that what individuals cared about was the total amount of wealth that they ended up with in various outcomes. This is known as the **asset integration hypothesis**.

Even though most people would accept this as a reasonable thing to do, it is hard to put into practice (even for economists). In general, people tend to avoid too many small risks and accept too many large risks.

Suppose that you make $100,000 a year and that you are offered a coin flip. If heads comes up you get $14 and if tails comes up you lose $10. This bet has an expected value of $12 and has a minuscule effect on your total income in a given year. Unless you have moral scruples about gambling, this would be a very attractive bet and you should almost certainly take it. However, a surprisingly large number of people won't take such a bet.

This **excess risk aversion** shows up in insurance markets where people tend to over-insure themselves against various small events. For example, people buy insurance against loosing their cell phone, even though they can often replace it at quite a low cost. People also buy auto insurance with deductibles that are much too low to make economic sense.

In general, when making insurance decisions you should look at the "house odds." If cell phone insurance costs you $3 a month, or $36 a year, and a new cell phone costs $180, then the house odds are 36/180, or 20 percent. The cell phone insurance would pay off in expected value only if you have more than a 20 percent chance of losing your phone or if it would be an extreme financial hardship to replace it.

It appears that people aren't really **risk averse** as much as they are **loss averse**. That is, people put seemingly excessive weight on the status quo—where they start—as opposed to where they end up.

In an experiment that has been replicated many times, two researchers gave half of the subjects in a group coffee mugs.[11] They asked this group to report the lowest price at which they would sell the mugs. Then they asked the group that didn't have mugs the highest price at which they would buy a mug. Since the groups were chosen randomly, the buying and selling prices should be about equal. However, in the experiment, the median

---

[11]  D. Kahneman, J. L. Kitsch, and R. Thaler, 1990, "Experimental tests of the endowment effect and the Coase theorem," *Journal of Political Economy*, 98, 1325–1348.

selling price was $5.79 and the median buying price was $2.25, a substantial difference. Apparently, the subjects with coffee mugs were more reluctant to part with them than subjects without mugs. Their preferences seemed to be influenced by their endowment, contrary to standard consumer theory.

A similar effect shows up in what is known as the **sunk cost fallacy**. Once you have bought something, the amount you paid is "sunk," or no longer recoverable. So future behavior should not be influenced by sunk costs.

But, alas, real people tend to care about how much they paid for something. Researchers have found that the price at which owners listed condominiums in Boston was highly correlated with the buying price.[12] As pointed out earlier, owners of stock are very reluctant to realize losses, even when it would be advantageous for tax reasons.

The fact that ordinary people are subject to the sunk cost fallacy is interesting, but perhaps it is even more interesting that professionals are less susceptible to this problem. For example, the authors of the condominium example mentioned above found that individuals who bought condos for investment purposes were less likely to be influenced by sunk costs than individuals who lived in the condos.

Similarly, financial advisers are seldom reluctant to realize losses, particularly when there is a tax advantage to do so. It appears that one reason to hire professional advisers is to draw on their dispassionate analysis of decisions.

## 31.3 Time

Just as behavior involving uncertainty is subject to various forms of anomalous behavior, behavior involving time has its own set of anomalies.

### Discounting

Consider, for example, time discounting. A standard model in economics, **exponential discounting**, posits that people discount the future at a constant fraction. If $u(c)$ is the utility of consumption today, then the utility of consumption $t$ years in the future looks like $\delta^t u(c)$, where $\delta < 1$.

This is a mathematically convenient specification, but there are other forms of discounting that seem to fit the data better.

One economist auctioned off bonds that paid off at various times in the future and found that people valued payment at future times less than the

---

[12] David Genesove and Christopher Mayer, 2001, "Loss aversion and seller behavior: Evidence from the housing market," *Quarterly Journal of Economics*, 116, 4, 1233–1260.

exponential discounting theory would predict. An alternative theory, called **hyperbolic discounting**, suggests that the discount factor does not take the form $\delta^t$ but rather takes the form $1/(1+kt)$.

One particularly attractive feature of exponential discounting is that behavior is "time consistent." Think about a person with a three-period planning horizon with utility function of the form

$$u(c_1) + \delta u(c_2) + \delta^2 u(c_3).$$

The marginal rate of substitution between periods 1 and 2 is

$$MRS_{12} = \frac{\delta MU(c_2)}{MU(c_1)},$$

while the MRS between periods 2 and 3 is

$$MRS_{23} = \frac{\delta^2 MU(c_3)}{\delta MU(c_2)} = \frac{\delta MU(c_3)}{MU(c_2)}.$$

This last expression shows that the rate at which the individual is willing to substitute consumption in period 2 for consumption in period 3 is the *same* whether viewed from the perspective of period 1 or of period 2. This is not true for hyperbolic discounting. An individual with hyperbolic discounting discounts the long-term future more heavily than he discounts the short-term future.

Such a person will exhibit **time inconsistency:** he may make a plan today about his future behavior, but when the future arrives he will want to do something different. Think of a couple who decide to spend $5,000 on a trip to Europe rather than save their money. They rationalize their decision on the grounds that they will start saving *next* summer. But when next summer arrives, they decide to spend their money on a cruise.

## Self-control

A closely related issue to the time consistency problem is the problem of **self-control**. Almost everyone faces this issue to some degree. We might vow to count our calories and eat less while standing on the bathroom scale, but our resolve can easily vanish when we sit down to a nice meal. Rational people are apparently slim and healthy, unlike the rest of us.

One important question is whether people are aware of their own difficulties with self-control. If I know that I have a tendency to procrastinate, perhaps I should realize that when an important task comes along I should do it right away. Or if I have a tendency to overcommit myself, perhaps I should learn to say no more often.

But there is the other possibility. If I know that I am likely to yield to the temptation to have another desert tomorrow, I may as well have another desert today. The flesh is weak, but the spirit may be weak too.

One way to deal with self-control is to find ways to commit yourself to future actions. That is, you can try to find a way to make it more costly to deviate from the desired action in the future. For example, people who make a public pronouncement about their future behavior might be less likely to deviate from their intended behavior. There are pills for alcoholics that make them violently sick if they drink alcohol. There are also **commitment devices** for dieters: someone who has his stomach stapled will be less likely to overeat.

Contracts between individuals are there to ensure that people carry out their future intentions—even when it might not be attractive for them to do so due to changed conditions. In a similar way, people can hire others to impose costs on them if they deviate from intended actions, making, in effect, a contract with themselves. Dieting spas, exercise instructors, and tutors are forms of "purchased self-control."

## EXAMPLE: Overconfidence

An interesting variation on self-control is the phenomenon of **overconfidence.** Two financial economists, Brad Barber and Terrance Odean, studied the performance of 66,465 households with discount brokerage accounts. During the period they studied, households that traded infrequently received an 18 percent return on their investments, while the return for the households that traded most actively was 11.3 percent.

One of the most important factors that apparently influenced this excessive trading was gender: the men traded a lot more than women. Psychologists commonly find that men tend to have excessive confidence in their own abilities, while women, for the most part, tend to be more realistic. Psychologists refer to men's behavior as self-serving attribution bias. Basically, men (or at least some men) tend to think their successes are a result of their own skill, rather than dumb luck, and so become overconfident.

This overconfidence can have financial repercussions. In the sample of brokerage accounts, men traded 45 percent more than women. This excessive trading resulted in the average return to men that was a full percentage point lower than the return to women. As Barber and Odean put it, "trading can be hazardous to your wealth."

## 31.4 Strategic Interaction and Social Norms

A particularly interesting set of psychological, or perhaps sociological, behaviors arise in strategic interaction. We have studied game theory, which attempts to predict how rational players should interact. But there is also a subject known as **behavioral game theory** that examines how actual people interact. Indeed, there are systematic and strong deviations from the pure theory.

## Ultimatum Game

Consider the **ultimatum game**, which was discussed briefly in the last chapter. As you will recall, this is a game with two players, the proposer and the responder. The proposer is given $10 and asked to propose a division between himself and the responder. The responder is then shown the division and asked whether or not he wishes to accept it. If he accepts, the division is carried out; if he refuses the division, both people walk away with nothing.

Let's first think about how fully rational players might act. Once the responder sees the division, he has a dominant strategy: accept the money as long as he gets anything at all. After all, suppose I offer you the choice between 10 cents and nothing. Wouldn't you rather have 10 cents than nothing at all?

Given that a rational responder will choose any amount, the divider should choose the minimal amount to give him—say, a penny. So the outcome predicted by game theory is an extreme split: the divider will end up with almost everything.

This isn't the way things turn out when the game is actually played. In fact, responders tend to reject offers that they perceive as unfair. Offers that give the responder less than 30 percent of the amount to be divided are rejected more than 50 percent of the time.

Of course, if the divider recognizes that the responder will reject "unfair" offers, the divider will rationally want to make a division that is closer to equal. The average division tends to be about 45 percent to the responder and 55 percent to the divider, with about 16 percent of the offers being rejected.

There has been a considerable amount of literature examining how the characteristics of the players affect the outcome of the game. One example is gender differences: it appears that men tend to receive more favorable divisions, particularly when the divisions are made by women.

Cultural differences can also be important. It appears that some cultures value fairness more than others, inducing people to reject offers that are perceived as unfair.[13] Interestingly enough, the offered amounts don't vary much from region to region and culture to culture, while there are

---

[13] See Swee-Hoon Chuah, Robert Hoffman, Martin Jones, and Geoffrey Williams, "Do Cultures Clash? Evidence from Cross-National Ultimatum Game Experiments," Nottingham University Business School working paper.

systematic differences in the divisions that are acceptable. The size of the pie is also important. If the size of the pie is $10, you might be reluctant to accept $1. But if the size of the pie is $1,000, would you be willing to reject $100? Apparently, responders do find it difficult to turn down larger amounts of money.

Another variation is in the design of the game. In one variant, the so-called **strategy method**, the responders are asked to name the minimal division that they will accept *before* seeing the amount they are offered. The proposers are aware that the decision will be made in advance but, of course, don't know what the minimum acceptable division is. This experimental design tends to increase the amounts that the proposers offer; that is, it tends to make the divisions more equal.

## Fairness

One effect at work in the ultimatum game seems to be a concern for fairness. Most people seem to have a natural bias towards equal (or at least not too unequal) division. This is not simply an individual phenomenon, but a social phenomenon. People will enforce **fairness norms** even when it is not directly in their interest to do so.

Consider, for example, **punishment games**, which are a generalization of ultimatum games with a third party who observes the choices made by the proposer/divider. The third party can choose, at some cost to himself, to deduct some of the proposer's profits.[14]

Experimenters have found that around 60 percent of these third-party observers will actually punish those who make unfair divisions. There seems to be something in the human makeup—whether innate or learned—that finds unfair behavior objectionable.

Indeed, there are differences across cultures with respect to social norms for fairness; individuals in some societies seem to value it highly, while in other societies fairness is less strongly valued. However, the urge to punish those who are unfair is widely felt. It has been suggested that a predilection towards "fair" outcomes is part of human nature, perhaps because individuals that behaved fairly towards each other had higher chances of surviving and reproducing.

## 31.5 Assessment of Behavioral Economics

Psychologists, marketers, and behavioral economists have amassed a variety of examples showing how the basic theory of economic choice is wrong, or, at least, incomplete.

---

[14] See Ernst Fehr and Urs Fischbacher, 2004, "Third-party punishment and social norms," *Evolution and Human Behavior*, 25, 63–87.

Some of these examples appear to be "optical illusions." For example, the fact that framing a choice problem differently can affect decisions is similar to the fact that human judgment of sizes and distances can be affected by how figures are drawn. If people took the time to consider the choices carefully—applying a measuring stick of dispassionate reasoning—they would reach the right conclusion.

Though it is undoubtedly true that people don't behave completely in accord with the simplest theories of economic behavior, one still might respond that no theory is 100 percent correct. Psychologists have also documented that people don't really understand simple principles of physics. Example: If you tie a weight to the end of a rope, swing it around your head in a circle and then let go, which way will the weight fly?

Many people say that the weight will fly radially outward rather than the correct response that the weight will move tangentially to the circle.[15] Of course, people have lived in the physical world their entire lives. If they occasionally misunderstand how it works, we shouldn't be too surprised when people misunderstand the economic world.

Apparently our intuitive understanding of physics is good enough for everyday life, and even the demands of amateur and professional sports: a baseball player may not be able to describe how a ball will travel, despite the fact that he can throw it well. Similarly, one might argue that people tend to be pretty good at the sorts of day-to-day decisions they are forced to make, even if they aren't very good at abstract reasoning about them.

Another reaction to behavioral anomalies is that markets tend to reward rational behavior, while punishing irrationality. Even if many participants do not behave rationally, those who *do* behave sensibly will have the biggest effect on prices and outcomes. There is likely some truth to this view as well. Recall the example that real estate investors seemed to be less influenced by sunk costs than ordinary individuals.

In addition, you can hire experts to help you make better decisions. Diet consultants and financial advisers can offer objective advice about how to eat and how to invest. If you are worried about being too fair, you can always hire a tough negotiator.

Returning to the optical illusion example, the reason that we use rulers and yardsticks is that we learn not to trust our own eyes. Similarly, in making important decisions it is prudent to consult the views of objective experts.

---

[15] See M. McCloskey, 1983, "Intuitive Physics," *Scientific American*, April, 114–123.

## Summary

1. Behavioral economics is concerned with how consumers make choices in reality.

2. In many cases, actual consumer behavior is different from that predicted by the simple model of the rational consumer.

3. Consumers make different choices depending on how a problem is framed or presented.

4. Too many choices may be overwhelming and make it difficult to make a decision.

5. Choice behavior can be particularly problematic in choices involving uncertainty.

6. Consumers seem to have a preference for "fair" divisions and will punish those who behave unfairly, even if harms themselves.

## REVIEW QUESTIONS

1. Subjects are allowed to buy tickets in a lottery. One group is told that they have a 55 percent chance of winning, the other group is told that they have a 45 percent chance of not winning. Which group is more likely to buy lottery tickets? What is the name for this effect?

2. Mary plans the entire week's meals for her family, while Fred shops each day. Which is likely to produce more varied meals? What is this effect called?

3. You are the human resources director for a medium-size company and are trying to decide how many mutual funds to offer in your employees' pension plan. Would it be better to offer 10 choices or 50 choices?

4. What is the probability that a fair coin will come up heads three times in a row when tossed?

5. John decides that he will save $5 this week and $10 next week. But when next week arrives, he decides to save only $8. What is the term used to describe this sort of inconsistent behavior?

# CHAPTER 32

# EXCHANGE

Up until now we have generally considered the market for a single good in isolation. We have viewed the demand and supply functions for a good as depending on its price alone, disregarding the prices of other goods. But in general the prices of other goods *will* affect people's demands and supplies for a particular good. Certainly the prices of substitutes and complements for a good will influence the demand for it, and, more subtly, the prices of goods that people sell will affect the amount of income they have and thereby influence how much of other goods they will be able to buy.

Up until now we have been ignoring the effect of these other prices on the market equilibrium. When we discussed the equilibrium conditions in a particular market, we only looked at part of the problem: how demand and supply were affected by the price of the particular good we were examining. This is called **partial equilibrium** analysis.

In this chapter we will begin our study of **general equilibrium** analysis: how demand and supply conditions interact in several markets to determine the prices of many goods. As you might suspect, this is a complex problem, and we will have to adopt several simplifications in order to deal with it.

First, we will limit our discussion to the behavior of competitive markets, so that each consumer or producer will take prices as given and optimize accordingly. The study of general equilibrium with imperfect competition is very interesting but too difficult to examine at this point.

Second, we will adopt our usual simplifying assumption of looking at the smallest number of goods and consumers that we possibly can. In this case, it turns out that many interesting phenomena can be depicted using only two goods and two consumers. All of the aspects of general equilibrium analysis that we will discuss can be generalized to arbitrary numbers of consumers and goods, but the exposition is simpler with two of each.

Third, we will look at the general equilibrium problem in two stages. We will start with an economy where people have fixed endowments of goods and examine how they might trade these goods among themselves; no production will be involved. This case is naturally known as the case of **pure exchange**. Once we have a clear understanding of pure exchange markets we will examine production behavior in the general equilibrium model.

## 32.1 The Edgeworth Box

There is a convenient graphical tool known as the **Edgeworth box** that can be used to analyze the exchange of two goods between two people.[1] The Edgeworth box allows us to depict the endowments and preferences of two individuals in one convenient diagram, which can be used to study various outcomes of the trading process. In order to understand the construction of an Edgeworth box it is necessary to examine the indifference curves and the endowments of the people involved.

Let us call the two people involved A and B and the two goods involved 1 and 2. We will denote A's consumption bundle by $X_A = (x_A^1, x_A^2)$, where $x_A^1$ represents A's consumption of good 1 and $x_A^2$ represents A's consumption of good 2. Then B's consumption bundle is denoted by $X_B = (x_B^1, x_B^2)$. A *pair* of consumption bundles, $X_A$ and $X_B$, is called an **allocation**. An allocation is a **feasible allocation** if the total amount of each good consumed is equal to the total amount available:

$$x_A^1 + x_B^1 = \omega_A^1 + \omega_B^1$$

$$x_A^2 + x_B^2 = \omega_A^2 + \omega_B^2.$$

A particular feasible allocation that is of interest is the **initial endowment allocation**, $(\omega_A^1, \omega_A^2)$ and $(\omega_B^1, \omega_B^2)$. This is the allocation that the consumers start with. It consists of the amount of each good that consumers bring to the market. They will exchange some of these goods with each other in the course of trade to end up at a **final allocation**.

---

[1]  The Edgeworth box is named in honor of Francis Ysidro Edgeworth (1845–1926), an English economist who was one of the first to use this analytical tool.

The Edgeworth box shown in Figure 32.1 can be used to illustrate these concepts graphically. We first use a standard consumer theory diagram to illustrate the endowment and preferences of consumer A. We can also mark off on these axes the *total* amount of each good in the economy— the amount that A has plus the amount that B has of each good. Since we will only be interested in feasible allocations of goods between the two consumers, we can draw a box that contains the set of possible bundles of the two goods that A can hold.

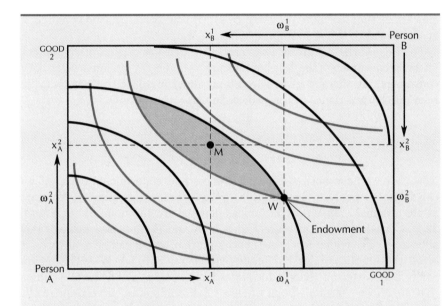

**An Edgeworth box.**    The width of the box measures the total amount of good 1 in the economy and the height measures the total amount of good 2. Person A's consumption choices are measured from the lower left-hand corner while person B's choices are measured from the upper right.

Figure
32.1

Note that the bundles in this box also indicate the amount of the goods that B can hold. If there are 10 units of good 1 and 20 units of good 2, then if A holds (7,12), B must be holding (3,8). We can depict how much A holds of good 1 by the distance along the horizontal axis from the origin in the lower left-hand corner of the box and the amount B holds of good 1 by measuring the distance along the horizontal axis from the upper right-hand corner. Similarly, distances along the vertical axes give the amounts of good 2 that A and B hold. Thus the points in this box give us both the bundles that A can hold and the bundles that B can hold—just measured from different origins. The points in the Edgeworth box can represent all feasible allocations in this simple economy.

We can depict A's indifference curves in the usual manner, but B's indifference curves take a somewhat different form. To construct them we take a standard diagram for B's indifference curves, turn it upside down, and "overlay" it on the Edgeworth box. This gives us B's indifference curves on the diagram. If we start at A's origin in the lower left-hand corner and move up and to the right, we will be moving to allocations that are more preferred by A. As we move down and to the left we will be moving to allocations that are more preferred by B. (If you rotate your book and look at the diagram, this discussion may seem clearer.)

The Edgeworth box allows us to depict the possible consumption bundles for both consumers—the feasible allocations—and the preferences of both consumers. It thereby gives a complete description of the economically relevant characteristics of the two consumers.

## 32.2 Trade

Now that we have both sets of preferences and endowments depicted we can begin to analyze the question of how trade takes place. We start at the original endowment of goods, denoted by the point $W$ in Figure 32.1. Consider the indifference curves of A and B that pass through this allocation. The region where A is better off than at her endowment consists of all the bundles above her indifference curve through $W$. The region where B is better off than at his endowment consists of all the allocations that are above—from his point of view—*his* indifference curve through $W$. (This is *below* his indifference curve from *our* point of view . . . unless you've still got your book upside down.)

Where is the region of the box where A and B are *both* made better off? Clearly it is in the intersection of these two regions. This is the lens-shaped region illustrated in Figure 32.1. Presumably in the course of their negotiations the two people involved will find some mutually advantageous trade—some trade that will move them to some point inside the lens-shaped area such as the point $M$ in Figure 32.1.

The particular movement to $M$ depicted in Figure 32.1 involves person A giving up $|x_A^1 - \omega_A^1|$ units of good 1 and acquiring in exchange $|x_A^2 - \omega_A^2|$ units of good 2. This means that B acquires $|x_B^1 - \omega_B^1|$ units of good 1 and gives up $|x_B^2 - \omega_B^2|$ units of good 2.

There is nothing particularly special about the allocation $M$. Any allocation inside the lens-shaped region would be possible—for every allocation of goods in this region is an allocation that makes each consumer better off than he or she was at the original endowment. We only need to suppose that the consumers trade to *some* point in this region.

Now we can repeat the same analysis at the point $M$. We can draw the two indifference curves through $M$, construct a new lens-shaped "region of mutual advantage," and imagine the traders moving to some new point $N$ in this region. And so it goes ... the trade will continue until there are no more trades that are preferred by both parties. What does such a position look like?

## 32.3 Pareto Efficient Allocations

The answer is given in Figure 32.2. At the point $M$ in this diagram the set of points above A's indifference curve doesn't intersect the set of points above B's indifference curve. The region where A is made better off is disjoint from the region where B is made better off. This means that any movement that makes one of the parties better off necessarily makes the other party worse off. Thus there are no exchanges that are advantageous for both parties. There are no mutually improving trades at such an allocation.

An allocation such as this is known as a **Pareto efficient** allocation. The idea of Pareto efficiency is a very important concept in economics that arises in various guises.

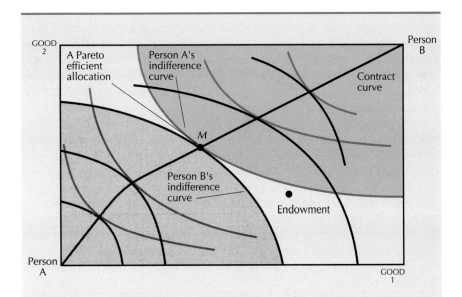

**A Pareto efficient allocation.** At a Pareto efficient alloca-     Figure
tion such as $M$, each person is on his highest possible indiffer-     32.2
ence curve, given the indifference curve of the other person. The
line connecting such points is known as the contract curve.

A Pareto efficient allocation can be described as an allocation where:

1. There is no way to make all the people involved better off; or

2. there is no way to make some individual better off without making someone else worse off; or

3. all of the gains from trade have been exhausted; or

4. there are no mutually advantageous trades to be made, and so on.

Indeed we have mentioned the concept of Pareto efficiency several times already in the context of a single market: we spoke of the Pareto efficient level of output in a single market as being that amount of output where the marginal willingness to buy equaled the marginal willingness to sell. At any level of output where these two numbers differed, there would be a way to make both sides of the market better off by carrying out a trade. In this chapter we will examine more deeply the idea of Pareto efficiency involving many goods and many traders.

Note the following simple geometry of Pareto efficient allocations: the indifference curves of the two agents must be tangent at any Pareto efficient allocation in the interior of the box. It is easy to see why. If the two indifference curves are not tangent at an allocation in the interior of the box, then they must cross. But if they cross, then there must be some mutually advantageous trade—so that point cannot be Pareto efficient. (It is possible to have Pareto efficient allocations on the sides of the box—where one consumer has zero consumption of some good—in which the indifference curves are not tangent. These boundary cases are not important for the current discussion.)

From the tangency condition it is easy to see that there are a lot of Pareto efficient allocations in the Edgeworth box. In fact, given any indifference curve for person A, for example, there is an easy way to find a Pareto efficient allocation. Simply move along A's indifference curve until you find the point that is the best point for B. This will be a Pareto efficient point, and thus both indifference curves must be tangent at this point.

The set of *all* Pareto efficient points in the Edgeworth box is known as the **Pareto set**, or the **contract curve**. The latter name comes from the idea that all "final contracts" for trade must lie on the Pareto set—otherwise they wouldn't be final because there would be some improvement that could be made!

In a typical case the contract curve will stretch from A's origin to B's origin across the Edgeworth box, as shown in Figure 32.2. If we start at A's origin, A has none of either good and B holds everything. This is Pareto efficient since the only way A can be made better off is to take something away from B. As we move up the contract curve A is getting more and more well-off until we finally get to B's origin.

The Pareto set describes all the possible outcomes of mutually advantageous trade from starting anywhere in the box. If we are given the starting point—the initial endowments for each consumer—we can look at the subset of the Pareto set that each consumer prefers to his initial endowment. This is simply the subset of the Pareto set that lies in the lens-shaped region depicted in Figure 32.1. The allocations in this lens-shaped region are the possible outcomes of mutual trade starting from the particular initial endowment depicted in that diagram. But the Pareto set itself doesn't depend on the initial endowment, except insofar as the endowment determines the total amounts of both goods that are available and thereby determines the dimensions of the box.

Let us examine the calculus conditions describing Pareto efficient allocations. By definition, a Pareto efficient allocation makes each agent as well-off as possible, given the utility of the other agent. So let us pick $\bar{u}$ as the utility level for agent B, say, and see how we can make agent A as well-off as possible.

The maximization problem is

$$\max_{x_A^1, x_A^2, x_B^1, x_B^2} u_A(x_A^1, x_A^2)$$

such that $u_B(x_B^1, x_B^2) = \bar{u}$

$$x_A^1 + x_B^1 = \omega^1$$

$$x_A^2 + x_B^2 = \omega^2.$$

Here $\omega^1 = \omega_A^1 + \omega_B^1$ is the total amount of good 1 available and $\omega^2 = \omega_A^2 + \omega_B^2$ is the total amount of good 2 available. This maximization problem asks us to find the allocation $(x_A^1, x_A^2, x_B^1, x_B^2)$ that makes person A's utility as large as possible, given a fixed level for person B's utility, and given that the total amount of each good used is equal to the amount available.

We can write the Lagrangian for this problem as

$$L = u_A(x_A^1, x_A^2) - \lambda(u_B(x_B^1, x_B^2) - \bar{u})$$
$$- \mu_1(x_A^1 + x_B^1 - \omega^1) - \mu_2(x_A^2 + x_B^2 - \omega^2).$$

Here $\lambda$ is the Lagrange multiplier on the utility constraint, and the $\mu$'s are the Lagrange multipliers on the resource constraints. When we differentiate with respect to each of the goods, we have four first-order conditions that must hold at the optimal solution:

$$\frac{\partial L}{\partial x_A^1} = \frac{\partial u_A}{\partial x_A^1} - \mu_1 = 0$$

$$\frac{\partial L}{\partial x_A^2} = \frac{\partial u_A}{\partial x_A^2} - \mu_2 = 0$$

$$\frac{\partial L}{\partial x_B^1} = -\lambda\frac{\partial u_B}{\partial x_B^1} - \mu_1 = 0$$

$$\frac{\partial L}{\partial x_B^2} = -\lambda\frac{\partial u_B}{\partial x_B^2} - \mu_2 = 0.$$

If we divide the first equation by the second, and the third equation by the fourth, we have

$$MRS_A = \frac{\partial u_A/\partial x_A^1}{\partial u_A/\partial x_A^2} = \frac{\mu_1}{\mu_2} \tag{32.1}$$

$$MRS_B = \frac{\partial u_B/\partial x_B^1}{\partial u_B/\partial x_B^2} = \frac{\mu_1}{\mu_2}. \tag{32.2}$$

The interpretation of these conditions is: at a Pareto efficient allocation, the marginal rates of substitution between the two goods must be the same. Otherwise, there would be some trade that would make each consumer better off.

Let us recall the conditions that must hold for optimal choice by consumers. If consumer A is maximizing utility subject to her budget constraint and consumer B is maximizing utility subject to his budget constraint, and both consumers face the same prices for goods 1 and 2, we must have

$$\frac{\partial u_A/\partial x_A^1}{\partial u_A/\partial x_A^2} = \frac{p_1}{p_2} \tag{32.3}$$

$$\frac{\partial u_B/\partial x_B^1}{\partial u_B/\partial x_B^2} = \frac{p_1}{p_2}. \tag{32.4}$$

Note the similarity with the efficiency conditions. The Lagrange multipliers in the efficiency conditions, $\mu_1$ and $\mu_2$, are just like the prices $p_1$ and $p_2$ in the consumer choice conditions. In fact the Lagrange multipliers in this kind of problem are sometimes known as **shadow prices** or **efficiency prices**.

Every Pareto efficient allocation has to satisfy conditions like those in equations (32.1) and (32.2). The conditions describing Pareto efficiency and the conditions describing individual maximization in a market environment are virtually the same.

## 32.4 Market Trade

The equilibrium of the trading process described above—the set of Pareto efficient allocations—is very important, but it still leaves a lot of ambiguity about where the agents end up. The reason is that the trading process we have described is very general. Essentially we have only assumed that the two parties will move to *some* allocation where they are both made better off.

If we have a *particular* trading process, we will have a more precise description of equilibrium. Let's try to describe a trading process that mimics the outcome of a competitive market.

Suppose that we have a third party who is willing to act as an "auctioneer" for the two agents A and B. The auctioneer chooses a price for good 1 and a price for good 2 and presents these prices to the agents A and B. Each agent then sees how much his or her endowment is worth at the prices $(p_1, p_2)$ and decides how much of each good he or she would want to buy at those prices.

One warning is in order here. If there are really only two people involved in the transaction, then it doesn't make much sense for them to behave in a competitive manner. Instead they would probably attempt to bargain over the terms of trade. One way around this difficulty is to think of the Edgeworth box as depicting the average demands in an economy with only two *types* of consumers, but with many consumers of each type. Another way to deal with this is to point out that the behavior is implausible in the two-person case, but it makes perfect sense in the many-person case, which is what we are really concerned with.

Either way, we know how to analyze the consumer-choice problem in this framework—it is just the standard consumer-choice problem we described in Chapter 5. In Figure 32.3 we illustrate the two demanded bundles of the two agents. (Note that the situation depicted in Figure 32.3 is not an equilibrium configuration since the demand by one agent is not equal to the supply of the other agent.)

As in Chapter 9 there are two relevant concepts of "demand" in this framework. The **gross demand** of agent A for good 1, say, is the total amount of good 1 that he wants at the going prices. The **net demand** of agent A for good 1 is the difference between this total demand and the initial endowment of good 1 that agent A holds. In the context of general equilibrium analysis, net demands are sometimes called **excess demands**. We will denote the excess demand of agent A for good 1 by $e_A^1$. By definition, if A's gross demand is $x_A^1$, and his endowment is $w_A^1$, we have

$$e_A^1 = x_A^1 - w_A^1.$$

The concept of excess demand is probably more natural, but the concept of gross demand is generally more useful. We will typically use the word "demand" to mean gross demand and specifically say "net demand" or "excess demand" if that is what we mean.

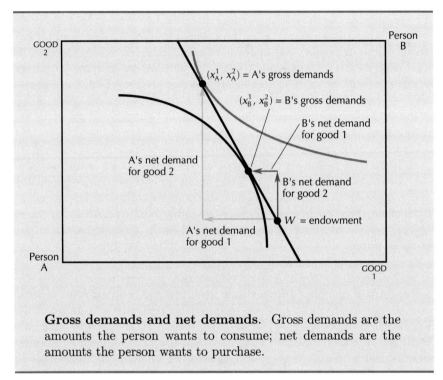

Person B

GOOD 2

$(x_A^1, x_A^2)$ = A's gross demands

$(x_B^1, x_B^2)$ = B's gross demands

B's net demand for good 1

A's net demand for good 2

B's net demand for good 2

W = endowment

A's net demand for good 1

Person A

GOOD 1

Figure 32.3

**Gross demands and net demands.** Gross demands are the amounts the person wants to consume; net demands are the amounts the person wants to purchase.

For arbitrary prices $(p_1, p_2)$ there is no guarantee that supply will equal demand—in either sense of demand. In terms of net demand, this means that the amount that A wants to buy (or sell) will not necessarily equal the amount that B wants to sell (or buy). In terms of gross demand, this means that the total amount that the two agents want hold of the goods is not equal to the total amount of that goods available. Indeed, this is true in the example depicted in Figure 32.3. In this example the agents will not be able to complete their desired transactions: the markets will not clear.

We say that in this case the market is in **disequilibrium**. In such a situation, it is natural to suppose that the auctioneer will change the prices of the goods. If there is excess demand for one of the goods, the auctioneer will raise the price of that good, and if there is excess supply for one of the goods, the auctioneer will lower its price.

Suppose that this adjustment process continues until the demand for each of the goods equals the supply. What will the final configuration look like?

The answer is given in Figure 32.4. Here the amount that A wants to buy of good 1 just equals the amount that B wants to sell of good 1, and similarly for good 2. Said another way, the total amount that each person wants to buy of each good at the current prices is equal to the total amount available. We say that the market is in **equilibrium**. More precisely, this is called a **market equilibrium**, a **competitive equilibrium**, or a **Walrasian equilibrium**.[2] Each of these terms refers to the same thing: a set of prices such that each consumer is choosing his or her most-preferred affordable bundle, and all consumers' choices are compatible in the sense that demand equals supply in every market.

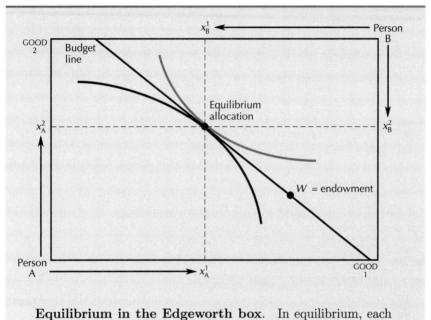

**Equilibrium in the Edgeworth box.**   In equilibrium, each person is choosing the most-preferred bundle in his budget set, and the choices exhaust the available supply.

Figure 32.4

We know that if each agent is choosing the best bundle that he can afford, then his marginal rate of substitution between the two goods must be equal to the ratio of the prices. But if all consumers are facing the same prices, then all consumers will have to have the *same* marginal rate of substitution between each of the two goods. In terms of Figure 32.4, an equilibrium has the property that each agent's indifference curve is tangent to his budget line. But since each agent's budget line has the slope $-p_1/p_2$, this means that the two agents' indifference curves must be tangent to each other.

## 32.5 The Algebra of Equilibrium

[2]  Leon Walras (1834–1910) was a French economist at Lausanne who was an early investigator of general equilibrium theory.

If we let $x_A^1(p_1, p_2)$ be agent A's demand function for good 1 and $x_B^1(p_1, p_2)$ be agent B's demand function for good 1, and define the analogous expressions for good 2, we can describe this equilibrium as a set of prices $(p_1^*, p_2^*)$ such that

$$x_A^1(p_1^*, p_2^*) + x_B^1(p_1^*, p_2^*) = w_A^1 + w_B^1$$
$$x_A^2(p_1^*, p_2^*) + x_B^2(p_1^*, p_2^*) = w_A^2 + w_B^2.$$

These equations say that in equilibrium the total demand for each good should be equal to the total supply.

Another way to describe the equilibrium is to rearrange these two equations to get

$$[x_A^1(p_1^*, p_2^*) - w_A^1] + [x_B^1(p_1^*, p_2^*) - w_B^1] = 0$$
$$[x_A^2(p_1^*, p_2^*) - w_A^2] + [x_B^2(p_1^*, p_2^*) - w_B^2] = 0.$$

These equations say that the sum of *net demands* of each agent for each good should be zero. Or, in other words, the net amount that A chooses to demand (or supply) must be equal to the net amount that B chooses to supply (or demand).

Yet another formulation of these equilibrium equations comes from the concept of the **aggregate excess demand function**. Let us denote the net demand function for good 1 by agent A by

$$e_A^1(p_1, p_2) = x_A^1(p_1, p_2) - w_A^1$$

and define $e_B^1(p_1, p_2)$ in a similar manner.

The function $e_A^1(p_1, p_2)$ measures agent A's **net demand** or his **excess demand**—the difference between what she wants to consume of good 1 and what she initially has of good 1. Now let us add together agent A's net demand for good 1 and agent B's net demand for good 1. We get

$$z_1(p_1, p_2) = e_A^1(p_1, p_2) + e_B^1(p_1, p_2)$$
$$= x_A^1(p_1, p_2) + x_B^1(p_1, p_2) - w_A^1 - w_B^1,$$

which we call the **aggregate excess demand** for good 1. There is a similar aggregate excess demand for good 2, which we denote by $z_2(p_1, p_2)$.

Then we can describe an equilibrium $(p_1^*, p_2^*)$ by saying that the aggregate excess demand for each good is zero:

$$z_1(p_1^*, p_2^*) = 0$$
$$z_2(p_1^*, p_2^*) = 0.$$

Actually, this definition is stronger than necessary. It turns out that if the aggregate excess demand for good 1 is zero, then the aggregate excess demand for good 2 must necessarily be zero. In order to prove this, it is convenient to first establish a property of the aggregate excess demand function known as **Walras' law**.

## 32.6 Walras' Law

Using the notation established above, Walras' law states that

$$p_1 z_1(p_1, p_2) + p_2 z_2(p_1, p_2) \equiv 0.$$

That is, *the value of aggregate excess demand is identically zero.* To say that the value of aggregate demand is identically zero means that it is zero for *all* possible choices of prices, not just equilibrium prices.

The proof of this follows from adding up the two agents' budget constraints. Consider first agent A. Since her demand for each good satisfies her budget constraint, we have

$$p_1 x_A^1(p_1, p_2) + p_2 x_A^2(p_1, p_2) \equiv p_1 w_A^1 + p_2 w_A^2$$

or

$$p_1[x_A^1(p_1, p_2) - w_A^1] + p_2[x_A^2(p_1, p_2) - w_A^2] \equiv 0$$
$$p_1 e_A^1(p_1, p_2) + p_2 e_A^2(p_1, p_2) \equiv 0.$$

This equation says that the *value of agent A's net demand is zero.* That is, the value of how much A wants to buy of good 1 plus the value of how much she wants to buy of good 2 must equal zero. (Of course the amount that she wants to buy of *one* of the goods must be negative—that is, she intends to sell some of one of the goods to buy more of the other.)

We have a similar equation for agent B:

$$p_1[x_B^1(p_1, p_2) - w_B^1] + p_2[x_B^2(p_1, p_2) - w_B^2] \equiv 0$$
$$p_1 e_B^1(p_1, p_2) + p_2 e_B^2(p_1, p_2) \equiv 0.$$

Adding the equations for agent A and agent B together and using the definition of aggregate excess demand, $z_1(p_1, p_2)$ and $z_2(p_1, p_2)$, we have

$$p_1[e_A^1(p_1, p_2) + e_B^1(p_1, p_2)] + p_2[e_A^2(p_1, p_2) + e_B^2(p_1, p_2)] \equiv 0$$
$$p_1 z_1(p_1, p_2) + p_2 z_2(p_1, p_2) \equiv 0.$$

Now we can see where Walras' law comes from: since the value of each agent's excess demand equals zero, the value of the sum of the agents' excess demands must equal zero.

We can now demonstrate that if demand equals supply in one market, demand must also equal supply in the other market. Note that Walras' law must hold for all prices, since each agent must satisfy his or her budget constraint for all prices. Since Walras' law holds for all prices, in particular, it holds for a set of prices where the excess demand for good 1 is zero:

$$z_1(p_1^*, p_2^*) = 0.$$

According to Walras' law it must also be true that

$$p_1^* z_1(p_1^*, p_2^*) + p_2^* z_2(p_1^*, p_2^*) = 0.$$

It easily follows from these two equations that if $p_2 > 0$, then we must have

$$z_2(p_1^*, p_2^*) = 0.$$

Thus, as asserted above, if we find a set of prices $(p_1^*, p_2^*)$ where the demand for good 1 equals the supply of good 1, we are guaranteed that the demand for good 2 must equal the supply of good 2. Alternatively, if we find a set of prices where the demand for good 2 equals the supply of good 2, we are guaranteed that market 1 will be in equilibrium.

In general, if there are markets for $k$ goods, then we only need to find a set of prices where $k - 1$ of the markets are in equilibrium. Walras' law then implies that the market for good $k$ will automatically have demand equal to supply.

## 32.7 Relative Prices

As we've seen above, Walras' law implies that there are only $k - 1$ independent equations in a $k$-good general equilibrium model: if demand equals supply in $k - 1$ markets, demand must equal supply in the final market. But if there are $k$ goods, there will be $k$ prices to be determined. How can you solve for $k$ prices with only $k - 1$ equations?

The answer is that there are really only $k - 1$ *independent* prices. We saw in Chapter 2 that if we multiplied all prices and income by a positive number $t$, then the budget set wouldn't change, and thus the demanded bundle wouldn't change either. In the general equilibrium model, each consumer's income is just the value of his or her endowment at the market prices. If we multiply all prices by $t > 0$, we will automatically multiply each consumer's income by $t$. Thus, if we find some equilibrium set of prices $(p_1^*, p_2^*)$, then $(tp_1^*, tp_2^*)$ are equilibrium prices as well, for any $t > 0$.

This means that we are free to choose one of the prices and set it equal to a constant. In particular it is often convenient to set one of the prices equal to 1 so that all of the other prices can be interpreted as being measured relative to it. As we saw in Chapter 2, such a price is called a **numeraire** price. If we choose the first price as the numeraire price, then it is just like multiplying all prices by the constant $t = 1/p_1$.

The requirement that demand equal supply in every market can only be expected to determine the equilibrium relative prices, since multiplying all prices by a positive number will not change anybody's demand and supply behavior.

## EXAMPLE: An Algebraic Example of Equilibrium

The Cobb-Douglas utility function described in Chapter 6 has the form $u_A(x_A^1, x_A^2) = (x_A^1)^a (x_A^2)^{1-a}$ for person A, and a similar form for person B. We saw there that this utility function gave rise to the following demand functions:

$$x_A^1(p_1, p_2, m_A) = a\frac{m_A}{p_1}$$

$$x_A^2(p_1, p_2, m_A) = (1-a)\frac{m_A}{p_2}$$

$$x_B^1(p_1, p_2, m_B) = b\frac{m_B}{p_1}$$

$$x_B^2(p_1, p_2, m_B) = (1-b)\frac{m_B}{p_2},$$

where $a$ and $b$ are the parameters of the two consumers' utility functions.

We know that in equilibrium, the money income of each individual is given by the value of his or her endowment:

$$m_A = p_1 w_A^1 + p_2 w_A^2$$

$$m_B = p_1 w_B^1 + p_2 w_B^2.$$

Thus the aggregate excess demands for the two goods are

$$z_1(p_1, p_2) = a\frac{m_A}{p_1} + b\frac{m_B}{p_1} - w_A^1 - w_B^1$$

$$= a\frac{p_1 w_A^1 + p_2 w_A^2}{p_1} + b\frac{p_1 w_B^1 + p_2 w_B^2}{p_1} - w_A^1 - w_B^1$$

and

$$z_2(p_1, p_2) = (1-a)\frac{m_A}{p_2} + (1-b)\frac{m_B}{p_2} - w_A^2 - w_B^2$$

$$= (1-a)\frac{p_1 w_A^1 + p_2 w_A^2}{p_2} + (1-b)\frac{p_1 w_B^1 + p_2 w_B^2}{p_2} - w_A^2 - w_B^2.$$

You should verify that these aggregate demand functions satisfy Walras' law.

Let us choose $p_2$ as the numeraire price, so that these equations become

$$z_1(p_1, 1) = a\frac{p_1 w_A^1 + w_A^2}{p_1} + b\frac{p_1 w_B^1 + w_B^2}{p_1} - w_A^1 - w_B^1$$

$$z_2(p_1, 1) = (1-a)(p_1 w_A^1 + w_A^2) + (1-b)(p_1 w_B^1 + w_B^2) - w_A^2 - w_B^2.$$

All we've done here is set $p_2 = 1$.

We now have an equation for the excess demand for good 1, $z_1(p_1, 1)$, and an equation for the excess demand for good 2, $z_2(p_1, 1)$, with each equation expressed as a function of the relative price of good 1, $p_1$. In order to find the *equilibrium* price, we set either of these equations equal to zero and solve for $p_1$. According to Walras' law, we should get the same equilibrium price, no matter which equation we solve.

The equilibrium price turns out to be

$$p_1^* = \frac{a\omega_A^2 + b\omega_B^2}{(1-a)\omega_A^1 + (1-b)\omega_B^1}.$$

(Skeptics may want to insert this value of $p_1$ into the demand equals supply equations to verify that the equations are satisfied.)

## 32.8 The Existence of Equilibrium

In the example given above, we had specific equations for each consumer's demand function and we could explicitly solve for the equilibrium prices. But in general, we don't have explicit algebraic formulas for each consumer's demands. We might well ask how do we know that there is *any* set of prices such that demand equals supply in every market? This is known as the question of the **existence of a competitive equilibrium**.

The existence of a competitive equilibrium is important insofar as it serves as a "consistency check" for the various models that we have examined in previous chapters. What use would it be to build up elaborate theories of the workings of a competitive equilibrium if such an equilibrium commonly did not exist?

Early economists noted that in a market with $k$ goods there were $k - 1$ relative prices to be determined, and there were $k - 1$ equilibrium equations stating that demand should equal supply in each market. Since the number of equations equaled the number of unknowns, they asserted that there would be a solution where all of the equations were satisfied.

Economists soon discovered that such arguments were fallacious. Merely counting the number of equations and unknowns is not sufficient to prove that an equilibrium solution will exist. However, there are mathematical tools that can be used to establish the existence of a competitive equilibrium. The crucial assumption turns out to be that the aggregate excess demand function is a **continuous function**. This means, roughly speaking, that small changes in prices should result in only small changes in aggregate demand: a small change in prices should not result in a big jump in the quantity demanded.

Under what conditions will the aggregate demand functions be continuous? Essentially there are two kinds of conditions that will guarantee continuity. One is that each individual's demand function be continuous—that small changes in prices will lead to only small changes in demand. This turns out to require that each consumer have convex preferences, which we discussed in Chapter 3. The other condition is more general. Even if consumers themselves have discontinuous demand behavior, as long as all consumers are small relative to the size of the market, the aggregate demand function will be continuous.

This latter condition is quite nice. After all, the assumption of competitive behavior only makes sense when there are a lot of consumers who are small relative to the size of the market. This is exactly the condition that we need in order to get the aggregate demand functions to be continuous. And continuity is just the ticket to ensure that a competitive equilibrium exists. Thus the very assumptions that make the postulated behavior reasonable will ensure that the equilibrium theory will have content.

## 32.9 Equilibrium and Efficiency

We have now analyzed market trade in a pure exchange model. This gives us a specific model of trade that we can compare to the general model of trade that we discussed in the beginning of this chapter. One question that might arise about the use of a competitive market is whether this mechanism can really exhaust all of the gains from trade. After we have traded to a competitive equilibrium where demand equals supply in every market, will there be any more trades that people will desire to carry out? This is just another way to ask whether the market equilibrium is Pareto efficient: will the agents desire to make any more trades after they have traded at the competitive prices?

We can see the answer by inspecting Figure 32.4: it turns out that the market equilibrium allocation *is* Pareto efficient. The proof is this: an allocation in the Edgeworth box is Pareto efficient if the set of bundles that A prefers doesn't intersect the set of bundles that B prefers. But at the market equilibrium, the set of bundles preferred by A must lie above her budget set, and the same thing holds for B, where "above" means "above from B's point of view." Thus the two sets of preferred allocations can't intersect. This means that there are no allocations that both agents prefer to the equilibrium allocation, so the equilibrium is Pareto efficient. Every competitive equilibrium has to satisfy conditions like those in equations (32.3) and (32.4).

## 32.10 The Algebra of Efficiency

We can also show this algebraically. Suppose that we have a market equilibrium that is *not* Pareto efficient. We will show that this assumption leads to a logical contradiction.

To say that the market equilibrium is not Pareto efficient means that there is some other feasible allocation $(y_A^1, y_A^2, y_B^1, y_B^2)$ such that

$$y_A^1 + y_B^1 = \omega_A^1 + \omega_B^1 \tag{32.5}$$

$$y_A^2 + y_B^2 = \omega_A^2 + \omega_B^2 \tag{32.6}$$

and

$$(y_A^1, y_A^2) \succ_A (x_A^1, x_A^2) \tag{32.7}$$

$$(y_B^1, y_B^2) \succ_B (x_B^1, x_B^2). \tag{32.8}$$

The first two equations say that the $y$–allocation is feasible, and the next two equations say that it is preferred by each agent to the $x$–allocation. (The symbols $\succ_A$ and $\succ_B$ refer to the preferences of agents $A$ and $B$.)

But by hypothesis, we have a market equilibrium where each agent is purchasing the best bundle he or she can afford. If $(y_A^1, y_A^2)$ is better than the bundle that A is choosing, then it must cost more than A can afford, and similarly for B:

$$p_1 y_A^1 + p_2 y_A^2 > p_1 \omega_A^1 + p_2 \omega_A^2$$

$$p_1 y_B^1 + p_2 y_B^2 > p_1 \omega_B^1 + p_2 \omega_B^2.$$

Now add these two equations together to get

$$p_1(y_A^1 + y_B^1) + p_2(y_A^2 + y_B^2) > p_1(\omega_A^1 + \omega_B^1) + p_2(\omega_A^2 + \omega_B^2).$$

Substitute from equations (32.5) and (32.6) to get

$$p_1(\omega_A^1 + \omega_B^1) + p_2(\omega_A^2 + \omega_B^2) > p_1(\omega_A^1 + \omega_B^1) + p_2(\omega_A^2 + \omega_B^2),$$

which is clearly a contradiction, since the left-hand side and the right-hand side are the same.

We derived this contradiction by assuming that the market equilibrium was not Pareto efficient. Therefore, this assumption must be wrong. It follows that all market equilibria are Pareto efficient: a result known as the **First Theorem of Welfare Economics**.

The First Welfare Theorem guarantees that a competitive market will exhaust all of the gains from trade: an equilibrium allocation achieved by a set of competitive markets will necessarily be Pareto efficient. Such an allocation may not have any other desirable properties, but it will necessarily be efficient.

In particular, the First Welfare Theorem says nothing about the distribution of economic benefits. The market equilibrium might not be a "just" allocation—if person A owned everything to begin with, then she would own everything after trade. That would be efficient, but it would probably not be very fair. But, after all, efficiency does count for something, and it is reassuring to know that a simple market mechanism like the one we have described is capable of achieving an efficient allocation.

## EXAMPLE: Monopoly in the Edgeworth Box

In order to understand the First Welfare Theorem better, it is useful to consider another resource allocation mechanism that does not lead to efficient outcomes. A nice example of this occurs when one consumer attempts to behave as a monopolist. Suppose now that there is no auctioneer and that instead, agent A is going to quote prices to agent B, and agent B will decide how much he wants to trade at the quoted prices. Suppose further that A knows B's "demand curve" and will attempt to choose the set of prices that makes A as well-off as possible, given the demand behavior of B.

In order to examine the equilibrium in this process, it is appropriate to recall the definition of a consumer's **price offer curve**. The price offer curve, which we discussed in Chapter 6, represents all of the optimal choices of the consumer at different prices. B's offer curve represents the bundles that he will purchase at different prices; that is, it describes B's demand behavior. If we draw a budget line for B, then the point where that budget line intersects his offer curve represents B's optimal consumption.

Thus, if agent A wants to choose the prices to offer to B that make A as well-off as possible, she should find that point on B's offer curve where A has the highest utility. Such a choice is depicted in Figure 32.5.

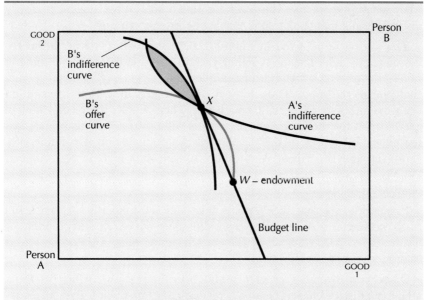

**Monopoly in the Edgeworth box.**  A chooses the point on B's offer curve that gives her the highest utility.

Figure
32.5

This optimal choice will be characterized by a tangency condition as usual: A's indifference curve will be tangent to B's offer curve. If B's offer curve cut A's indifference curve, there would be some point on B's offer curve that A preferred—so we couldn't be at the optimal point for A.

Once we have identified this point—denoted by $X$ in Figure 32.5—we just draw a budget line to that point from the endowment. At the prices that generate this budget line, B will choose the bundle $X$, and A will be as well-off as possible.

Is this allocation Pareto efficient? In general the answer is no. To see this simply note that A's indifference curve will not be tangent to the budget line at $X$, and therefore A's indifference curve will not be tangent to B's indifference curve. A's indifference curve is tangent to B's *offer curve*, but it cannot then be tangent to B's indifference curve. The monopoly allocation is Pareto inefficient.

In fact, it is Pareto inefficient in exactly the same way as described in the discussion of monopoly in Chapter 25. At the margin A would like to sell more at the equilibrium prices, but she can only do so by lowering the price at which she sells—and this will lower her income received from all her inframarginal sales.

We saw in Chapter 26 that a perfectly discriminating monopolist would end up producing an efficient level of output. Recall that a discriminating monopolist was one who was able to sell each unit of a good to the person who was willing to pay the most for that unit. What does a perfectly discriminating monopolist look like in the Edgeworth box?

The answer is depicted in Figure 32.6. Let us start at the initial endowment, $W$, and imagine A selling each unit of good 1 to B at a different price—the price at which B is just indifferent between buying or not buying that unit of the good. Thus, after A sells the first unit, B will remain on the same indifference curve through $W$. Then A sells the second unit of good 1 to B for the maximum price he is willing to pay. This means that the allocation moves further to the left, but remains on B's indifference curve through $W$. Agent A continues to sell units to B in this manner, thereby moving up B's indifference curve to find her—A's—most preferred point, denoted by an $X$ in Figure 32.6.

It is easy to see that such a point must be Pareto efficient. Agent A will be as well-off as possible given B's indifference curve. At such a point, A has managed to extract all of B's consumer's surplus: B is no better off than he was at his endowment.

These two examples provide useful benchmarks with which to think about the First Welfare Theorem. The ordinary monopolist gives an example of a resource allocation mechanism that results in inefficient equilibria, and the discriminating monopolist gives another example of a mechanism that results in efficient equilibria.

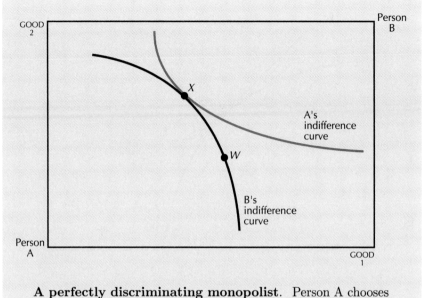

**A perfectly discriminating monopolist.** Person A chooses the point $X$ on person B's indifference curve through the endowment that gives her the highest utility. Such a point must be Pareto efficient.

Figure
32.6

## 32.11 Efficiency and Equilibrium

The First Welfare Theorem says that the equilibrium in a set of competitive markets is Pareto efficient. What about the other way around? Given a Pareto efficient allocation, can we find prices such that it is a market equilibrium? It turns out that the answer is yes, under certain conditions. The argument is illustrated in Figure 32.7.

Let us pick a Pareto efficient allocation. Then we know that the set of allocations that A prefers to her current assignment is disjoint from the set that B prefers. This implies of course that the two indifference curves are tangent at the Pareto efficient allocation. So let us draw in the straight line that is their common tangent, as in Figure 32.7.

Suppose that the straight line represents the agents' budget sets. Then if each agent chooses the best bundle on his or her budget set, the resulting equilibrium will be the original Pareto efficient allocation.

Thus the fact that the original allocation is efficient automatically determines the equilibrium prices. The endowments can be any bundles that give rise to the appropriate budget set—that is, bundles that lie somewhere on the constructed budget line.

Can the construction of such a budget line always be carried out? Un-

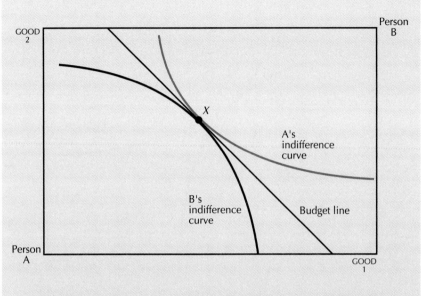

Figure
32.7

**The Second Theorem of Welfare Economics**. When preferences are convex, a Pareto efficient allocation is an equilibrium for some set of prices.

fortunately, the answer is no. Figure 32.8 gives an example. Here the illustrated point $X$ is Pareto efficient, but there are no prices at which A and B will want to consume at point $X$. The most obvious candidate is drawn in the diagram, but the optimal demands of agents A and B don't coincide for that budget. Agent A wants to demand the bundle $Y$, but agent B wants the bundle $X$—demand does not equal supply at these prices.

The difference between Figure 32.7 and Figure 32.8 is that the preferences in Figure 32.7 are convex while the ones in Figure 32.8 are not. If the preferences of both agents are convex, then the common tangent will not intersect either indifference curve more than once, and everything will work out fine. This observation gives us the **Second Theorem of Welfare Economics**: if all agents have convex preferences, then there will always be a set of prices such that each Pareto efficient allocation is a market equilibrium for an appropriate assignment of endowments.

The proof is essentially the geometric argument we gave above. At a Pareto efficient allocation, the bundles preferred by agent A and by agent B must be disjoint. Thus if both agents have convex preferences we can draw a straight line between the two sets of preferred bundles that separates one from the other. The slope of this line gives us the relative prices, and any endowment that puts the two agents on this line will lead to the final market equilibrium being the original Pareto efficient allocation.

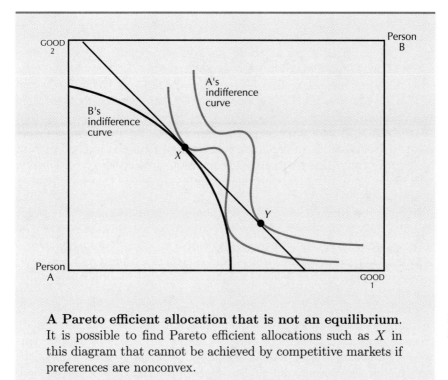

**A Pareto efficient allocation that is not an equilibrium.** It is possible to find Pareto efficient allocations such as $X$ in this diagram that cannot be achieved by competitive markets if preferences are nonconvex.

Figure
32.8

## 32.12 Implications of the First Welfare Theorem

The two theorems of welfare economics are among the most fundamental results in economics. We have demonstrated the theorems only in the simple Edgeworth box case, but they are true for much more complex models with arbitrary numbers of consumers and goods. The welfare theorems have profound implications for the design of ways to allocate resources.

Let us consider the First Welfare Theorem. This says that any competitive equilibrium is Pareto efficient. There are hardly any explicit assumptions in this theorem—it follows almost entirely from the definitions. But there are some implicit assumptions. One major assumption is that agents only care about their own consumption of goods, and not about what other agents consume. If one agent does care about another agent's consumption, we say that there is a **consumption externality**. We shall see that when consumption externalities are present, a competitive equilibrium need not be Pareto efficient.

To take a simple example, suppose that agent A cares about agent B's consumption of cigars. Then there is no particular reason why each agent choosing his or her own consumption bundle at the market prices will result in a Pareto efficient allocation. After each person has purchased the best bundle he or she can afford, there may still be ways to make both of them better off—such as A paying B to smoke fewer cigars. We will discuss externalities in more detail in Chapter 35.

Another important implicit assumption in the First Welfare Theorem is that agents actually behave competitively. If there really were only two agents, as in the Edgeworth box example, then it is unlikely that they would each take price as given. Instead, the agents would probably recognize their market power and would attempt to use their market power to improve their own positions. The concept of competitive equilibrium only makes sense when there are enough agents to ensure that each behaves competitively.

Finally, the First Welfare Theorem is only of interest if a competitive equilibrium actually exists. As we have argued above, this will be the case if the consumers are sufficiently small relative to the size of the market.

Given these provisos, the First Welfare Theorem is a pretty strong result: a private market, with each agent seeking to maximize his or her own utility, will result in an allocation that achieves Pareto efficiency.

The importance of the First Welfare Theorem is that it gives a general mechanism—the competitive market—that we can use to ensure Pareto efficient outcomes. If there are only two agents involved, this doesn't matter very much; it is easy for two people to get together and examine the possibilities for mutual trades. But if there are thousands, or even millions, of people involved there must be some kind of structure imposed on the trading process. The First Welfare Theorem shows that the particular structure of competitive markets has the desirable property of achieving a Pareto efficient allocation.

If we are dealing with a resource problem involving many people, it is important to note that the use of competitive markets economizes on the information that any one agent needs to possess. The only things that a consumer needs to know to make his consumption decisions are the prices of the goods he is considering consuming. Consumers don't need to know anything about how the goods are produced, or who owns what goods, or where the goods come from in a competitive market. If each consumer knows only the prices of the goods, he can determine his demands, and if the market functions well enough to determine the competitive prices, we are guaranteed an efficient outcome. The fact that competitive markets economize on information in this way is a strong argument in favor of their use as a way to allocate resources.

## 32.13 Implications of the Second Welfare Theorem

The Second Theorem of Welfare Economics asserts that under certain conditions, every Pareto efficient allocation can be achieved as a competitive equilibrium.

What is the meaning of this result? The Second Welfare Theorem implies that the problems of distribution and efficiency can be separated. Whatever Pareto efficient allocation you want can be supported by the market mechanism. The market mechanism is distributionally neutral; whatever your criteria for a good or a just distribution of welfare, you can use competitive markets to achieve it.

Prices play two roles in the market system: an *allocative* role and a *distributive* role. The allocative role of prices is to indicate relative scarcity; the distributive role is to determine how much of different goods different agents can purchase. The Second Welfare Theorem says that these two roles can be separated: we can redistribute endowments of goods to determine how much wealth agents have, and then use prices to indicate relative scarcity.

Policy discussions often become confused on this point. One often hears arguments for intervening in pricing decisions on grounds of distributional equity. However, such intervention is typically misguided. As we have seen above, a convenient way to achieve efficient allocations is for each agent to face the true social costs of his or her actions and to make choices that reflect those costs. Thus in a perfectly competitive market the marginal decision of whether to consume more or less of some good will depend on the price—which measures how everyone else values this good on the margin. The considerations of efficiency are inherently marginal decisions—each person should face the correct marginal tradeoff in making his or her consumption decisions.

The decision about *how much* different agents should consume is a totally different issue. In a competitive market this is determined by the value of the resources that a person has to sell. From the viewpoint of the pure theory, there is no reason why the state can't transfer purchasing power—endowments—among consumers in any way that is seen fit.

In fact the state doesn't need to transfer the physical endowments themselves. All that is necessary is to transfer the purchasing power of the endowment. The state could tax one consumer on the basis of the value of his endowment and transfer this money to another. As long as the taxes are based on the value of the consumer's *endowment* of goods there will be no loss of efficiency. It is only when taxes depend on the *choices* that a consumer makes that inefficiencies result, since in this case, the taxes will affect the consumer's marginal choices.

It is true that a tax on endowments will generally change people's behavior. But, according to the First Welfare Theorem, trade from any initial endowments will result in a Pareto efficient allocation. Thus no matter how one redistributes endowments, the equilibrium allocation as determined by market forces will still be Pareto efficient.

However, there are practical matters involved. It would be easy to have a lump-sum tax on consumers. We could tax all consumers with blue eyes, and redistribute the proceeds to consumers with brown eyes. As long as eye color can't be changed, there would be no loss in efficiency. Or we could tax consumers with high IQs and redistribute the funds to consumers with low IQs. Again, as long as IQ can be measured, there is no efficiency loss in this kind of tax.

But there's the problem. How do we measure people's endowment of goods? For most people, the bulk of their endowment consists of their own labor power. People's endowments of labor consist of the labor that they *could* consider selling, not the amount of labor that they actually end up selling. Taxing labor that people decide to sell to the market is a **distortionary tax**. If the sale of labor is taxed, the labor supply decision of consumers will be distorted—they will likely supply less labor than they would have supplied in the absence of a tax. Taxing the potential value of labor—the endowment of labor—is not distortionary. The potential value of labor is, by definition, something that is not changed by taxation. Taxing the value of the endowment sounds easy until we realize that it involves identifying and taxing something that *might* be sold, rather than taxing something that is sold.

We could *imagine* a mechanism for levying this kind of tax. Suppose that we considered a society where each consumer was required to give the money earned in 10 hours of his labor time to the state each week. This kind of tax would be independent of how much the person actually worked—it would only depend on the endowment of labor, not on how much was actually sold. Such a tax is basically transferring some part of each consumer's endowment of labor time to the state. The state could then use these funds to provide various goods, or it could simply transfer these funds to other agents.

According to the Second Welfare Theorem, this kind of lump-sum taxation would be nondistortionary. Essentially any Pareto efficient allocation could be achieved by such lump-sum redistribution.

However, no one is advocating such a radical restructuring of the tax system. Most people's labor supply decisions are relatively insensitive to variations in the wage rate, so the efficiency loss from taxing labor may not be too large anyway. But the message of the Second Welfare Theorem is important. Prices should be used to reflect scarcity. Lump-sum transfers of wealth should be used to adjust for distributional goals. To a large degree, these two policy decisions can be separated.

People's concern about the distribution of welfare can lead them to advocate various forms of manipulation of prices. It has been argued, for example, that senior citizens should have access to less expensive telephone service, or that small users of electricity should pay lower rates than large users. These are basically attempts to redistribute income through the price system by offering some people lower prices than others.

When you think about it this is a terribly inefficient way to redistribute income. If you want to redistribute income, why don't you simply redistribute income? If you give a person an extra dollar to spend, then he can choose to consume more of any of the goods that he wants to consume—not necessarily just the good being subsidized.

## Summary

1. General equilibrium refers to the study of how the economy can adjust to have demand equal supply in all markets at the same time.

2. The Edgeworth box is a graphical tool to examine such a general equilibrium with 2 consumers and 2 goods.

3. A Pareto efficient allocation is one in which there is no feasible reallocation of the goods that would make all consumers at least as well-off and at least one consumer strictly better off.

4. Walras' law states that the value of aggregate excess demand is zero for all prices.

5. A general equilibrium allocation is one in which each agent chooses a most preferred bundle of goods from the set of goods that he or she can afford.

6. Only relative prices are determined in a general equilibrium system.

7. If the demand for each good varies continuously as prices vary, then there will always be some set of prices where demand equals supply in every market; that is, a competitive equilibrium.

8. The First Theorem of Welfare Economics states that a competitive equilibrium is Pareto efficient.

9. The Second Theorem of Welfare Economics states that as long as preferences are convex, then every Pareto efficient allocation can be supported as a competitive equilibrium.

## REVIEW QUESTIONS

1. Is it possible to have a Pareto efficient allocation where someone is worse off than he is at an allocation that is not Pareto efficient?

2. Is it possible to have a Pareto efficient allocation where everyone is worse off than they are at an allocation that is not Pareto efficient?

3. True or false? If we know the contract curve, then we know the outcome of any trading.

4. Can some individual be made better off if we are at a Pareto efficient allocation?

5. If the value of excess demand in 8 out of 10 markets is equal to zero, what must be true about the remaining two markets?

# CHAPTER 33

# PRODUCTION

In the last chapter we described a general equilibrium model of a pure exchange economy and discussed issues of resource allocation when a fixed amount of each good was available. In this chapter we want to describe how production fits into the general equilibrium framework. When production is possible, the amounts of the goods are not fixed but will respond to market prices.

If you thought the two-consumer two-good assumption was a restrictive framework in which to examine trade, imagine what production is going to look like! The minimal set of players that we can have to make an interesting problem is one consumer, one firm, and two goods. The traditional name for this economic model is the **Robinson Crusoe economy**, after Defoe's shipwrecked hero.

## 33.1 The Robinson Crusoe Economy

In this economy Robinson Crusoe plays a dual role: he is both a consumer and a producer. Robinson can spend his time loafing on the beach thereby consuming leisure, or he can spend time gathering coconuts. The more coconuts he gathers the more he has to eat, but the less time he has to improve his tan.

Robinson's preferences for coconuts and leisure are depicted in Figure 33.1. They are just like the preferences for leisure and consumption depicted in Chapter 9, except we are measuring labor on the horizontal axis rather than leisure. So far nothing new has been added.

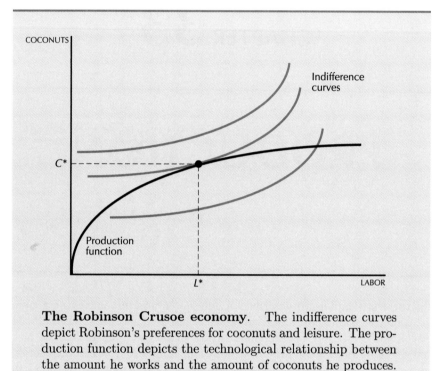

Figure 33.1

**The Robinson Crusoe economy.** The indifference curves depict Robinson's preferences for coconuts and leisure. The production function depicts the technological relationship between the amount he works and the amount of coconuts he produces.

Now let's draw in the **production function**, the function that illustrates the relationship between how much Robinson works and how many coconuts he gets. This will typically have the shape depicted in Figure 33.1. The more Robinson works, the more coconuts he will get; but, due to diminishing returns to labor, the marginal product of his labor declines: the number of extra coconuts that he gets from an extra hour's labor decreases as the hours of labor increase.

How much does Robinson work and how much does he consume? To answer these questions, look for the highest indifference curve that just touches the production set. This will give the most-preferred combination of labor and consumption that Robinson can get, given the technology for gathering coconuts that he is using.

At this point, the slope of the indifference curve must equal the slope of the production function by the standard argument: if they crossed, there would be some other feasible point that was preferred. This means that the marginal product of an extra hour of labor must equal the marginal rate of substitution between leisure and coconuts. If the marginal product were greater than the marginal rate of substitution, it would pay for Robinson to give up a little leisure in order to get the extra coconuts. If the marginal product were less than the marginal rate of substitution, it would pay for Robinson to work a little less.

## 33.2 Crusoe, Inc.

So far this story is only a slight extension of models we have already seen. But now let's add a new feature. Suppose that Robinson is tired of simultaneously being a producer and consumer and that he decides to alternate roles. One day he will behave entirely as a producer, and the next day he will behave entirely as a consumer. In order to coordinate these activities, he decides to set up a labor market and a coconut market.

He also sets up a firm, Crusoe, Inc., and becomes its sole shareholder. The firm is going to look at the prices for labor and coconuts and decide how much labor to hire and how many coconuts to produce, guided by the principle of profit maximization. Robinson, in his role as a worker, is going to collect income from working at the firm; in his role as shareholder in the firm he will collect profits; and, in his role as consumer he will decide how much to purchase of the firm's output. (No doubt this sounds peculiar, but there really isn't that much else to do on a desert island.)

In order to keep track of his transactions, Robinson invents a currency he calls "dollars," and he chooses, somewhat arbitrarily, to set the price of coconuts at one dollar apiece. Thus coconuts are the numeraire good for this economy; as we've seen in Chapter 2, a numeraire good is one whose price has been set to one. Since the price of coconuts is normalized at one, we have only to determine the wage rate. What should his wage rate be in order to make this market work?

We're going to think about this problem first from the viewpoint of Crusoe, Inc., and then from the viewpoint of Robinson, the consumer. The discussion is a little schizophrenic at times, but that's what you have to put up with if you want to have an economy with only one person. We're going to look at the economy after it has been running along for some time, and everything is in equilibrium. In equilibrium, the demand for coconuts will equal the supply of coconuts and the demand for labor will equal the supply of labor. Both Crusoe, Inc. and Robinson the consumer will be making optimal choices given the constraints they face.

## 33.3 The Firm

Each evening, Crusoe, Inc. decides how much labor it wants to hire the next day, and how many coconuts it wants to produce. Given a price of coconuts of 1 and a wage rate of labor of $w$, we can solve the firm's profit-maximization problem in Figure 33.2. We first consider all combinations of coconuts and labor that yield a constant level of profits, $\pi$. This means that

$$\pi = C - wL.$$

Solving for $C$, we have

$$C = \pi + wL.$$

Just as in Chapter 20, this formula describes the isoprofit lines—all combinations of labor and coconuts that yield profits of $\pi$. Crusoe, Inc. will choose a point where the profits are maximized. As usual, this implies a tangency condition: the slope of the production function—the marginal product of labor—must equal $w$, as illustrated in Figure 33.2.

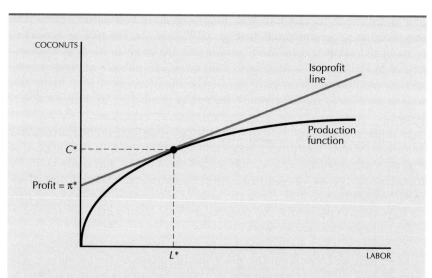

Figure
33.2

**Profit maximization.** Crusoe, Inc. chooses a production plan that maximizes profits. At the optimal point the production function must be tangent to an isoprofit line.

Thus the vertical intercept of the isoprofit line measures the maximal level of profits measured in units of coconuts: if Robinson generates $\pi^*$ dollars of profit, this money can buy $\pi^*$ coconuts, since the price of coconuts has been chosen to be 1. There we have it. Crusoe, Inc. has done its job. Given the wage $w$, it has determined how much labor it wants to hire, how many coconuts it wants to produce, and what profits it will generate by following this plan. So Crusoe, Inc. declares a stock dividend of $\pi^*$ dollars and mails it off to its sole shareholder, Robinson.

## 33.4 Robinson's Problem

The next day Robinson wakes up and receives his dividend of $\pi^*$ dollars. While eating his coconut breakfast, he contemplates how much he wants to work and consume. He may consider just consuming his endowment— spend his profits on $\pi^*$ coconuts and consume his endowment of leisure. But listening to his stomach growl is not so pleasant, and it might make sense to work for a few hours instead. So Robinson trudges down to Crusoe, Inc. and starts to gather coconuts, just as he has done every other day.

We can describe Robinson's labor-consumption choice using standard indifference curve analysis. Plotting labor on the horizontal axis and coconuts on the vertical axis, we can draw in an indifference curve as illustrated in Figure 33.3.

Since labor is a bad, by assumption, and coconuts are a good, the indifference curve has a positive slope as shown in the diagram. If we indicate the maximum amount of labor by $\overline{L}$, then the distance from $\overline{L}$ to the chosen supply of labor gives Robinson's demand for leisure. This is just like the supply of labor model examined in Chapter 9, except we have reversed the origin on the horizontal axis.

Robinson's budget line is also illustrated in Figure 33.3. It has a slope of $w$ and passes through his endowment point $(\pi^*, 0)$. (Robinson has a zero endowment of labor and a $\pi^*$ endowment of coconuts since that would be his bundle if he engaged in no market transactions.) Given the wage rate, Robinson chooses optimally how much he wants to work and how many coconuts he wants to consume. At his optimal consumption, the marginal rate of substitution between consumption and leisure must equal the wage rate, just as in a standard consumer choice problem.

## 33.5 Putting Them Together

Now we superimpose Figures 33.2 and 33.3 to get Figure 33.4. Look at what has happened! Robinson's bizarre behavior has worked out all right after all. He ends up consuming at exactly the same point as he would have if he had made all the decisions at once. Using the market system

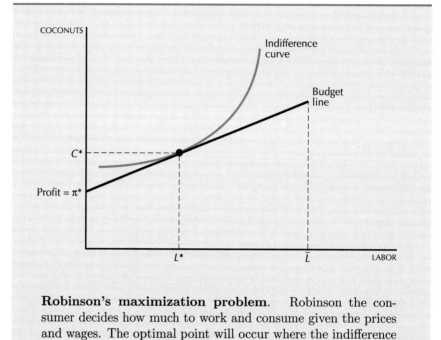

Figure
33.3

**Robinson's maximization problem.**    Robinson the consumer decides how much to work and consume given the prices
and wages. The optimal point will occur where the indifference
curve is tangent to the budget line.

results in the same outcome as choosing the consumption and production
plans directly.

Since the marginal rate of substitution between leisure and consumption equals the wage, and the marginal product of labor equals the wage,
we are assured that the marginal rate of substitution between labor and
consumption equals the marginal product—that is, that the slopes of the
indifference curve and the production set are the same.

In the case of a one-person economy, using the market is pretty silly. Why
should Robinson bother to break up his decision into two pieces? But in an
economy with many people, breaking up decisions no longer seems so odd.
If there are many firms, then questioning each person about how much they
want of each good is simply impractical. In a market economy the firms
simply have to look at the prices of goods in order to make their production
decisions. For the prices of goods measure how much the consumers value
*extra* units of consumption. And the decision that the firms face, for the
most part, is whether they should produce more or less output.

The market prices reflect the marginal values of the goods that the firms
use as inputs and outputs. If firms use the change in profits as a guide
to production, where the profits are measured at market prices, then their
decisions will reflect the marginal values that consumers place on the goods.

**Equilibrium in both consumption and production.** The amount of coconuts demanded by the consumer Robinson equals the amount of coconuts supplied by Crusoe, Inc.

Figure
33.4

## 33.6 Different Technologies

In the above discussion we have assumed that the technology available to Robinson exhibited diminishing returns to labor. Since labor was the only input to production, this was equivalent to decreasing returns to scale. (This is not necessarily true if there is more than one input!)

It is useful to consider some other possibilities. Suppose, for example, that the technology exhibited constant returns to scale. Recall that constant returns to scale means that using twice as much of all inputs produces twice as much output. In the case of a one-input production function, this means that the production function must be a straight line through the origin as depicted in Figure 33.5.

Since the technology has constant returns to scale, the argument in Chapter 20 implies that the only reasonable operating position for a competitive firm is at zero profits. This is because if the profits were ever greater than zero, it would pay for the firm to expand output indefinitely, and if profits were ever less than zero, it would pay the firm to produce zero output.

Thus Robinson's endowment involves zero profits and $\overline{L}$, his initial endowment of labor time. His budget set coincides with the production set, and the story is much the same as before.

The situation is somewhat different with an increasing returns to scale

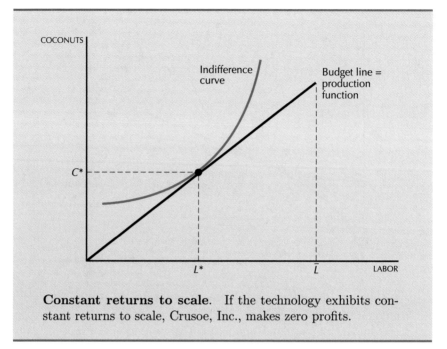

COCONUTS

Indifference curve

Budget line = production function

$C^*$

$L^*$    $\bar{L}$    LABOR

Figure
33.5

**Constant returns to scale.** If the technology exhibits constant returns to scale, Crusoe, Inc., makes zero profits.

technology, as depicted in Figure 33.6. There is no difficulty in this simple example in exhibiting the optimal choice of consumption and leisure for Robinson. The indifference curve will be tangent to the production set as usual. The problem arises in trying to support this point as a profit-maximizing point. For if the firm were faced with the prices given by Robinson's marginal rate of substitution, it would want to produce more output than Robinson would demand.

If the firm exhibits increasing returns to scale at the optimal choice, then the average costs of production will exceed the marginal costs of production—and that means that the firm will be making negative profits. The goal of profit maximization would lead the firm to want to increase its output—but this would be incompatible with the demands for output and the supplies of inputs from the consumers. In the case depicted, there is *no* price at which the utility-maximizing demand by the consumer will equal the profit-maximizing supply from the firm.

Increasing returns to scale is an example of a **nonconvexity**. In this case the production set—the set of coconuts and labor that are feasible for the economy—is not a convex set. Thus the common tangent to the indifference curve and the production function at the point $(L^*, C^*)$ in Figure 33.6 will not separate the preferred points from the feasible points as it does in Figure 33.4.

Nonconvexities such as this pose grave difficulties for the functioning of competitive markets. In a competitive market consumers and firms look

**Increasing returns to scale.** The production set exhibits increasing returns to scale and the Pareto efficient allocation cannot be achieved by a competitive market.

Figure
33.6

at just one set of numbers—the market prices—to determine their consumption and production decisions. If the technology and the preferences are convex, then the only things that the economic agents need to know to make efficient decisions are the relationship between the prices and the marginal rates of substitution near the points where the economy is currently producing: the prices tell the agents everything that is necessary in order to determine an efficient allocation of resources.

But if the technology and/or the preferences are nonconvex, then the prices do not convey all the information necessary in order to choose an efficient allocation. Information about the slopes of the production function and indifference curves far away from the current operating position is also necessary.

However, these observations apply only when the returns to scale are large relative to the size of the market. Small regions of increasing returns to scale do not pose undue difficulties for a competitive market.

## 33.7 Production and the First Welfare Theorem

Recall that in the case of a pure exchange economy, a competitive equilibrium is Pareto efficient. This fact is known as the First Theorem of Welfare Economics. Does the same result hold in an economy with production? The diagrammatic approach used above is not adequate to answer this question, but a generalization of the algebraic argument we provided in Chapter 32 does nicely. It turns out that the answer is yes: if all firms act as competitive profit maximizers, then a competitive equilibrium will be Pareto efficient.

This result has the usual caveats. First, it has nothing to do with distribution. Profit maximization only ensures efficiency, not justice! Second, this result only makes sense when a competitive equilibrium actually exists. In particular, this will rule out large areas of increasing returns to scale. Third, the theorem implicitly assumes that the choices of any one firm do not affect the production possibilities of other firms. That is, it rules out the possibility of **production externalities**. Similarly, the theorem requires that firms' production decisions do not directly affect the consumption possibilities of consumers; that is, that there are no **consumption externalities**. More precise definitions of externalities will be given in Chapter 35, where we will examine their effect on efficient allocations in more detail.

## 33.8 Production and the Second Welfare Theorem

In the case of a pure exchange economy, every Pareto efficient allocation is a possible competitive equilibrium, as long as consumers exhibit convex preferences. In the case of an economy involving production, the same result is true, but now we require not only that consumers' preferences are convex, but also that firms' production sets are convex. As discussed above, this requirement effectively rules out the possibility of increasing returns to scale: if firms have increasing returns to scale at the equilibrium level of production, they would want to produce more output at the competitive prices.

However, with constant or decreasing returns to scale, the Second Welfare Theorem works fine. Any Pareto efficient allocation can be achieved through the use of competitive markets. Of course in general it will be necessary to redistribute endowments among the consumers to support different Pareto efficient allocations. In particular, both the income from endowments of labor and ownership shares of the firm will have to be redistributed. As indicated in the last chapter, there may be significant practical difficulties involved with this sort of redistribution.

## 33.9 Production Possibilities

We have now seen how production and consumption decisions can be made in a one-input, one-output economy. In this section we want to explore how this model can be generalized to an economy with several inputs and outputs. Although we will deal only with the two-good case, the concepts will generalize naturally to many goods.

So let us suppose that there is some other good that Robinson might produce—say fish. He can devote his time to gathering coconuts or to fishing. In Figure 33.7 we have depicted the various combinations of coconuts and fish that Robinson can produce from devoting different amounts of time to each activity. This set is known as a **production possibilities set**. The boundary of the production possibilities set is called the **production possibilities frontier**. This should be contrasted with the production function discussed earlier that depicts the relationship between the input good and the output good; the production possibilities set depicts only the set of *output* goods that is feasible. (In more advanced treatments, both inputs and outputs can be considered part of the production possibilities set, but these treatments cannot easily be handled with two-dimensional diagrams.)

**A production possibilities set.** The production possibili-          Figure
ties set measures the set of outputs that are feasible given the        33.7
technology and the amounts of inputs.

The shape of the production possibilities set will depend on the nature of the underlying technologies. If the technologies for producing coconuts and fish exhibit constant returns to scale the production possibilities set will take an especially simple form. Since by assumption there is only one input to production—Robinson's labor—the production functions for fish and coconuts will be simply *linear* functions of labor.

For example, suppose that Robinson can produce 10 pounds of fish per hour or 20 pounds of coconuts per hour. Then if he devotes $L_f$ hours to fish production and $L_c$ hours to coconut production, he will produce $10L_f$ pounds of fish and $20L_c$ pounds of coconuts. Suppose that Robinson decides to work 10 hours a day. Then the production possibilities set will consist of all combinations of coconuts, $C$, and fish, $F$, such that

$$F = 10L_f$$
$$C = 20L_c$$
$$L_c + L_f = 10.$$

The first two equations measure the production relationships, and the third measures the resource constraint. To determine the production possibilities frontier solve the first two equations for $L_f$ and $L_c$ to get

$$L_f = \frac{F}{10}$$
$$L_c = \frac{C}{20}.$$

Now add these two equations together, and use the fact that $L_f + L_c = 10$ to find

$$\frac{F}{10} + \frac{C}{20} = 10.$$

This equation gives us all the combinations of fish and coconuts that Robinson can produce if he works 10 hours a day. It is depicted in Figure 33.8A.

The slope of this production possibilities set measures the **marginal rate of transformation**—how much of one good Robinson can get if he decides to sacrifice some of the other good. If Robinson gives up enough labor to produce 1 less pound of fish, he will be able to get 2 more pounds of coconuts. Think about it: if Robinson works one hour less on fish production, he will get 10 pounds less fish. But then if he devotes that time to coconuts, he will get 20 pounds more coconuts. The tradeoff is at a ratio of 2 to 1.

## 33.10 Comparative Advantage

The construction of the production possibilities set given above was quite simple since there was only one way to produce fish and one way to produce coconuts. What if there is more than one way to produce each good? Suppose that we add another worker to our island economy, who has different skills in producing fish and coconuts.

To be specific, let us call the new worker Friday, and suppose that he can produce 20 pounds of fish per hour, or 10 pounds of coconuts per hour.

Thus if Friday works for 10 hours, his production possibilities set will be determined by

$$F = 20L_f$$
$$C = 10L_c$$
$$L_c + L_f = 10.$$

Doing the same sort of calculations as we did for Robinson, Friday's production possibilities set is given by

$$\frac{F}{20} + \frac{C}{10} = 10.$$

This is depicted in Figure 33.8B. Note that the marginal rate of transformation between coconuts and fish for Friday is $\Delta C / \Delta F = -1/2$, whereas for Robinson the marginal rate of transformation is $-2$. For every pound of coconuts that Friday gives up, he can get two pounds of fish; for every pound of fish that Robinson gives up, he can get two pounds of coconuts. In this circumstance we say that Friday has a **comparative advantage** in fish production, and Robinson has a comparative advantage in coconut production. In Figure 33.8 we have depicted three production possibilities sets: Panel A shows Robinson's, panel B shows Friday's, and panel C depicts the joint production possibilities set—how much of each good could be produced in total by both people.

**Joint production possibilities.** Robinson's and Friday's production possibilities sets and the joint production possibilities set.

Figure 33.8

The joint production possibilities set combines the best of both workers. If both workers are used entirely to produce coconuts, we will get 300 coconuts—100 from Friday and 200 from Robinson. If we want to get more fish, it makes sense to shift the person who is most productive at fish—Friday—out of coconut production and into fish production. For each pound of coconuts that Friday doesn't produce we get 2 pounds of fish; thus the slope of the joint production possibilities set is $-1/2$—which is exactly Friday's marginal rate of transformation.

When Friday is producing 200 pounds of fish, he is fully occupied. If we want even more fish, we have to switch to using Robinson. From this point on the joint production possibilities set will have a slope of $-2$, since we will be operating along Robinson's production possibilities set. Finally, if we want to produce as much fish as possible, both Robinson and Friday concentrate on fish production and we get 300 pounds of fish, 200 from Friday, and 100 from Robinson.

Since the workers each have a comparative advantage in different goods, the joint production possibilities set will have a "kink," as shown in Figure 33.8C. There is only one kink in this example since there are just two different ways to produce output—Crusoe's way and Friday's way. If there are many different ways to produce output, the production possibilities set will have the more typical "rounded" structure, as depicted in Figure 33.7.

## 33.11 Pareto Efficiency

In the last two sections we saw how to construct the production possibilities set, the set that describes the feasible consumption bundles for the economy as a whole. Here we consider Pareto efficient ways to choose among the feasible consumption bundles.

We will indicate aggregate consumption bundles by $(X^1, X^2)$. This indicates that there are $X^1$ units of good 1 and $X^2$ units of good 2 that are available for consumption. In the Crusoe/Friday economy, the two goods are coconuts and fish, but we will use the $(X^1, X^2)$ notation in order to emphasize the similarities with the analysis in Chapter 32. Once we know the total amount of each good, we can draw an Edgeworth box as in Figure 33.9.

Given $(X^1, X^2)$, the set of Pareto efficient consumption bundles will be the same sort as those examined in the last chapter: the Pareto efficient consumption levels will lie along the Pareto set—the line of mutual tangencies of the indifference curves, as illustrated in Figure 33.9. These are the allocations in which each consumer's marginal rate of substitution—the rate at which he or she is just willing to trade—equals that of the other.

These allocations are Pareto efficient as far as the consumption decisions are concerned. If people can simply trade one good for another, the Pareto set describes the set of bundles that exhausts the gains from trade. But in an economy with production, there is another way to "exchange" one good for another—namely, to produce less of one good and more of another.

**Production and the Edgeworth box.** At each point on the production possibilities frontier, we can draw an Edgeworth box to illustrate the possible consumption allocations.

Figure
33.9

The Pareto set describes the set of Pareto efficient bundles *given* the amounts of goods 1 and 2 available, but in an economy with production those amounts can themselves be chosen out of the production possibilities set. Which choices from the production possibilities set will be Pareto efficient choices?

Let us think about the logic underlying the marginal rate of substitution condition. We argued that in a Pareto efficient allocation, the MRS of consumer A had to be equal to the MRS of consumer B: the rate at which consumer A would just be willing to trade one good for the other should be equal to the rate at which consumer B would just be willing to trade one good for the other. If this were not true, then there would be some trade that would make both consumers better off.

Recall that the marginal rate of transformation (MRT) measures the rate at which one good can be "transformed" into the other. Of course, one good really isn't being literally *transformed* into the other. Rather the factors of production are being moved around so as to produce less of one good and more of the other.

Suppose that the economy were operating at a position where the marginal rate of substitution of one of the consumers was not equal to the marginal rate of transformation between the two goods. Then such a position cannot be Pareto efficient. Why? Because at this point, the rate at which the consumer is willing to trade good 1 for good 2 is different from the rate at which good 1 can be transformed into good 2—there is a way to make the consumer better off by rearranging the pattern of production.

Suppose, for example, that the consumer's MRS is 1; the consumer is just willing to substitute good 1 for good 2 on a one-to-one basis. Suppose that the MRT is 2, which means that giving up one unit of good 1 will allow society to produce two units of good 2. Then clearly it makes sense to reduce the production of good 1 by one unit; this will generate two extra units of good 2. Since the consumer was just indifferent between giving up one unit of good 1 and getting one unit of the other good in exchange, he or she will now certainly be better off by getting *two* extra units of good 2.

The same argument can be made whenever one of the consumers has a MRS that is different from the MRT—there will always be a rearrangement of consumption and production that will make that consumer better off. We have already seen that for Pareto efficiency each consumer's MRS should be the same, and the argument given above implies that each consumer's MRS should in fact be equal to the MRT.

Figure 33.9 illustrates a Pareto efficient allocation. The MRSs of each consumer are the same, since their indifference curves are tangent in the Edgeworth box. And each consumer's MRS is equal to the MRT—the slope of the production possibilities set.

Let us derive the calculus conditions for Pareto efficiency in an economy with production. The first thing we need is a convenient way to describe the production possibilities frontier—all the combinations of $X^1$ and $X^2$ that are technologically feasible. The most useful way to do this for our purposes is by use of the **transformation function**. This is a function of the aggregate amounts of the two goods $T(X^1, X^2)$, such that the combination $(X^1, X^2)$ is on the production possibilities frontier (the boundary of the production possibilities set) if and only if

$$T(X^1, X^2) = 0.$$

Once we have described the technology, we can calculate the marginal rate of transformation: the rate at which we have to sacrifice good 2 in order to produce more of good 1. The marginal rate of transformation is just the slope of the production possibilities set, which we denote by $dX^2/dX^1$.

Consider a small change in production $(dX^1, dX^2)$ that remains feasible. Thus we have

$$\frac{\partial T(X^1, X^2)}{\partial X^1} dX^1 + \frac{\partial T(X^1, X^2)}{\partial X^2} dX^2 = 0.$$

Solving for the marginal rate of transformation:

$$\frac{dX^2}{dX^1} = -\frac{\partial T/\partial X^1}{\partial T/\partial X^2}.$$

We'll use this formula in a moment.

A Pareto efficient allocation is one that maximizes any one person's utility, given the level of the other people's utility. In the two-person case, we can write this maximization problem as

$$\max_{x_A^1, x_A^2, x_B^1, x_B^2} u_A(x_A^1, x_A^2)$$

$$\text{such that } u_B(x_B^1, x_B^2) = \bar{u}$$

$$T(X^1, X^2) = 0.$$

The Lagrangian for this problem is

$$L = u_A(x_A^1, x_A^2) - \lambda(u_B(x_B^1, x_B^2) - \bar{u})$$
$$- \mu(T(X_1, X_2) - 0),$$

and the first-order conditions are

$$\frac{\partial L}{\partial x_A^1} = \frac{\partial u_A}{\partial x_A^1} - \mu \frac{\partial T}{\partial X^1} = 0$$

$$\frac{\partial L}{\partial x_A^2} = \frac{\partial u_A}{\partial x_A^2} - \mu \frac{\partial T}{\partial X^2} = 0$$

$$\frac{\partial L}{\partial x_B^1} = -\lambda \frac{\partial u_B}{\partial x_B^1} - \mu \frac{\partial T}{\partial X^1} = 0$$

$$\frac{\partial L}{\partial x_B^2} = -\lambda \frac{\partial u_B}{\partial x_B^2} - \mu \frac{\partial T}{\partial X^2} = 0.$$

Rearranging and dividing the first equation by the second gives

$$\frac{\partial u_A/\partial x_A^1}{\partial u_A/\partial x_A^2} = \frac{\partial T/\partial X^1}{\partial T/\partial X^2}.$$

Performing the same operation on the third and fourth equations gives

$$\frac{\partial u_B/\partial x_B^1}{\partial u_B/\partial x_B^2} = \frac{\partial T/\partial X^1}{\partial T/\partial X^2}.$$

The left-hand sides of these equations are our old friends, the marginal rates of substitution. The right-hand side is the marginal rate of transformation. Thus the equations require that each person's marginal rate of substitution between the goods must equal the marginal rate of transformation: the rate at which each person is just willing to substitute one good for the other must be the same as the rate at which it is technologically feasible to transform one good into the other.

The intuition behind this result is straightforward. Suppose that the MRS for some individual was not equal to the MRT. Then the rate at which the individual would be willing to sacrifice one good to get more of the other would be different than the rate that was technologically feasible—but this means that there would be some way to increase that individual's utility while not affecting anyone else's consumption.

## 33.12 Castaways, Inc.

In the last section we derived the necessary conditions for Pareto efficiency: the MRS of each consumer must equal the MRT. Any way of distributing resources that results in Pareto efficiency must satisfy this condition. Earlier in this chapter, we claimed that a competitive economy with profit-maximizing firms and utility-maximizing consumers would result in a Pareto efficient allocation. In this section we explore the details of how this works.

Our economy now contains two individuals, Robinson and Friday. There are four goods: two factors of production (Robinson's labor and Friday's labor) and two output goods (coconuts and fish). Let us suppose that Robinson and Friday are both shareholders of the firm, which we will now refer to as Castaways, Inc. Of course, they are also the sole employees and customers, but as usual we shall examine each role in turn, and not allow the participants to see the wider picture. After all, the object of the analysis is to understand how a *decentralized* resource allocation system works—one in which each person only has to determine his or her own decisions, without regard for the functioning of the economy as a whole.

Start first with Castaways, Inc., and consider the profit-maximization problem. Castaways, Inc., produces two outputs, coconuts ($C$) and fish ($F$), and it uses two kinds of labor, Crusoe's labor ($L_C$) and Friday's labor ($L_F$). Given the price of coconuts ($p_C$), the price of fish ($p_F$), and the wage rates of Crusoe and Friday ($w_C$ and $w_F$), the profit-maximization problem is

$$\max_{C,F,L_F,L_C} p_C C + p_F F - w_C L_C - w_F L_F$$

subject to the technological constraints described by the production possibilities set.

Let us suppose that the firm finds it optimal in equilibrium to hire $L_F^*$ units of Friday's labor and $L_C^*$ units of Crusoe's labor. The question we want to focus on here is how profit maximization determines the pattern of output to produce. Let $L^* = w_C L_C^* + w_F L_F^*$ represent the labor costs of production, and write the profits of the firm, $\pi$, as

$$\pi = p_C C + p_F F - L^*.$$

Rearranging this equation, we have

$$C = \frac{\pi + L^*}{p_C} - \frac{p_F F}{p_C}.$$

This equation describes the **isoprofit lines** of the firm, as depicted in Figure 33.10, with a slope of $-p_F/p_C$ and a vertical intercept of $(\pi + L^*)/p_C$.

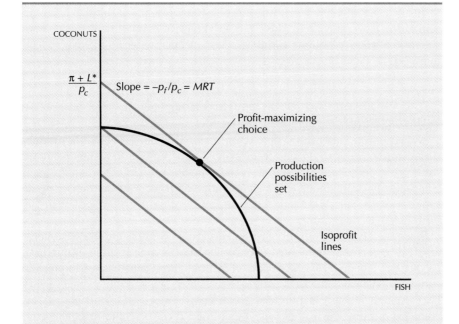

COCONUTS

$\frac{\pi + L^*}{p_C}$  Slope $= -p_f/p_c = MRT$

Profit-maximizing
choice

Production
possibilities
set

Isoprofit
lines

FISH

**Profit maximization.**  At the point yielding maximum profits, the marginal rate of transformation must equal the slope of the isoprofit line, $-p_F/p_C$.

Figure
33.10

Since $L^*$ is fixed by assumption, higher profits will be associated with isoprofit lines that have higher vertical intercepts.

If the firm wants to maximize its profits, it will choose a point on the production possibilities set such that the isoprofit line through that point has the highest possible vertical intercept. By this stage, it should be clear that this implies that the isoprofit line must be tangent to the production possibilities set; that is, that the slope of the production possibilities set (the MRT) should be equal to the slope of the isoprofit line, $-p_F/p_C$:

$$\text{MRT} = -\frac{p_F}{p_C}.$$

We've described this profit-maximization problem in the case of one firm, but it holds for an arbitrary number of firms: each firm that chooses the most profitable way to produce coconuts and fish will operate where the marginal rate of transformation between any two goods equals the price ratio between those two goods. This holds true even if the firms have quite different production possibilities sets, as long as they face the same prices for the two goods.

This means that in equilibrium the prices of the two goods will measure the marginal rate of transformation—the opportunity cost of one good in terms of the other. If you want more coconuts, you will have to give up some fish. How much fish? Just look at the price ratio of fish to coconuts: the ratio of these economic variables tells us what the technological tradeoff must be.

## 33.13 Robinson and Friday as Consumers

We've seen how Castaways, Inc., determines its profit-maximizing production plan. In order to do this, it must hire some labor and it may generate some profits. When it hires labor, it pays wages to the labor; when it makes profits, it pays dividends to its shareholders. Either way the money made by Castaways, Inc., gets paid back to Robinson and Friday, either in the form of wages or profits.

Since the firm pays out all of its receipts to its workers and its shareholders, this means that they must necessarily have enough income to purchase its output. This is just a variation on Walras' law discussed in Chapter 32: people get their income from selling their endowments, so they must always have enough income to purchase those endowments. Here people get income from selling their endowments and also receive profits from the firm. But since money never disappears from or is added to the system, people will always have exactly enough money to purchase what is produced.

What do the consumers do with the money from the firm? As usual, they use the money to purchase consumption goods. Each person chooses the best bundle of goods that he can afford at the prices $p_F$ and $p_C$. As we've seen earlier, the optimal consumption bundle for each consumer must satisfy the condition that the marginal rate of substitution between the two goods must be equal to the common price ratio. But this price ratio is also equal to the marginal rate of transformation, due to profit maximization by the firm. Thus the necessary conditions for Pareto efficiency are met: the MRS of each consumer equals the MRT.

In this economy, the prices of the goods serve as a signal of relative scarcity. They indicate the technological scarcity—how much the production of one good must be reduced in order to produce more of the other; and they indicate the consumption scarcity—how much people are willing to reduce their consumption of one good in order to acquire some of the other good.

## 33.14 Decentralized Resource Allocation

The Crusoe-Friday economy is a drastically simplified picture. In order to make a start on a larger model of the functioning of an economy, one needs to use substantially more elaborate mathematics. However, even this simple model contains some useful insights.

The most important of these is the relationship between individuals' *private* goals of utility maximization and the *social* goals of efficient use of resources. Under certain conditions, the individuals' pursuit of private goals will result in an allocation that is Pareto efficient overall. Furthermore, any Pareto efficient allocation can be supported as an outcome of a competitive market, if initial endowments—including the ownership of firms—can be suitably redistributed.

The great virtue of a competitive market is that each individual and each firm only has to worry about its own maximization problem. The only facts that need to be communicated among the firms and the consumers are the prices of the goods. Given these signals of relative scarcity, consumers and firms have enough information to make decisions that achieve an efficient allocation of resources. In this sense, the social problems involved in efficiently utilizing resources can be decentralized, and solved at the individual level.

Each individual can solve his or her own problem of what to consume. The firms face the prices of the goods the consumers consume and decide how much to produce of each of them. In making this decision, they are guided by profit signals. In this context, profits serve as exactly the right guide. To say that a production plan is profitable is to say that people are willing to pay more for some good than it costs to produce it—so it is natural to expand the production of such goods. If all firms pursue a competitive profit-maximizing policy, and all consumers choose consumption bundles to maximize their own utility, then resulting competitive equilibrium must be a Pareto efficient allocation.

## Summary

1. The general equilibrium framework can be extended by allowing competitive, profit-maximizing firms to produce goods destined for exchange in the economy.

2. Under certain conditions there exists a set of prices for all of the input and output goods in the economy such that the profit-maximizing actions of firms along with the utility-maximizing behavior of individuals results in the demand for each good equaling the supply in all markets—that is, a competitive equilibrium exists.

3. Under certain conditions the resulting competitive equilibrium will be Pareto efficient: the First Welfare Theorem holds in an economy with production.

4. With the addition of convex production sets, the Second Welfare Theorem also holds in the case of production.

5. When goods are being produced as efficiently as possible, the marginal rate of transformation between two goods indicates the number of units of one good the economy must give up to obtain additional units of the other good.

6. Pareto efficiency requires that each individual's marginal rate of substitution be equal to the marginal rate of transformation.

7. The virtue of competitive markets is that they provide a way to achieve an efficient allocation of resources by decentralizing production and consumption decisions.

## REVIEW QUESTIONS

1. The competitive price of coconuts is $6 per pound and the price of fish is $3 per pound. If society were to give up 1 pound of coconuts, how many more pounds of fish could be produced?

2. What would happen if the firm depicted in Figure 33.2 decided to pay a higher wage?

3. In what sense is a competitive equilibrium a good or bad thing for a given economy?

4. If Robinson's marginal rate of substitution between coconuts and fish is −2 and the marginal rate of transformation between the two goods is −1, what should he do if he wants to increase his utility?

5. Suppose that Robinson and Friday both want 60 pounds of fish and 60 pounds of coconuts per day. Using the production rates given in the chapter, how many hours must Robinson and Friday work per day if they don't help each other? Suppose they decide to work together in the most efficient manner possible. Now how many hours each day do they have to work? What is the economic explanation for the reduction in hours?

# CHAPTER **34**

# WELFARE

Up until now we have focused on considerations of Pareto efficiency in evaluating economic allocations. But there are other important considerations. It must be remembered that Pareto efficiency has nothing to say about the distribution of welfare across people; giving everything to one person will typically be Pareto efficient. But the rest of us might not consider this a reasonable allocation. In this chapter we will investigate some techniques that can be used to formalize ideas related to the distribution of welfare.

Pareto efficiency is in itself a desirable goal—if there is some way to make some group of people better off without hurting other people, why not do it? But there will usually be many Pareto efficient allocations; how can society choose among them?

The major focus of this chapter will be the idea of a **welfare function**, which provides a way to "add together" different consumers' utilities. More generally, a welfare function provides a way to rank different distributions of utility among consumers. Before we investigate the implications of this concept, it is worthwhile considering just how one might go about "adding together" the individual consumers' preferences to construct some kind of "social preferences."

## 34.1 Aggregation of Preferences

Let us return to our early discussion of consumer preferences. As usual, we will assume that these preferences are transitive. Originally, we thought of a consumer's preferences as being defined over his own bundle of goods, but now we want to expand on that concept and think of each consumer as having preferences over the entire allocation of goods among the consumers. Of course, this includes the possibility that the consumer might not care about what other people have, just as we had originally assumed.

Let us use the symbol $\mathbf{x}$ to denote a particular allocation—a description of what every individual gets of every good. Then given two allocations, $\mathbf{x}$ and $\mathbf{y}$, each individual $i$ can say whether or not he or she prefers $\mathbf{x}$ to $\mathbf{y}$.

Given the preferences of all the agents, we would like to have a way to "aggregate" them into one **social preference**. That is, if we know how all the individuals rank various allocations, we would like to be able to use this information to develop a social ranking of the various allocations. This is the problem of social decision making at its most general level. Let's consider a few examples.

One way to aggregate individual preferences is to use some kind of voting. We could agree that $\mathbf{x}$ is "socially preferred" to $\mathbf{y}$ if a majority of the individuals prefer $\mathbf{x}$ to $\mathbf{y}$. However, there is a problem with this method— it may not generate a transitive social preference ordering. Consider, for example, the case illustrated in Table 34.1.

**Preferences that lead to intransitive voting.**    Table 34.1

| Person A | Person B | Person C |
|:--------:|:--------:|:--------:|
| x | y | z |
| y | z | x |
| z | x | y |

Here we have listed the rankings for three alternatives, $\mathbf{x}$, $\mathbf{y}$, and $\mathbf{z}$, by three people. Note that a majority of the people prefer $\mathbf{x}$ to $\mathbf{y}$, a majority prefer $\mathbf{y}$ to $\mathbf{z}$, and a majority prefer $\mathbf{z}$ to $\mathbf{x}$. Thus aggregating individual preferences by majority vote won't work since, in general, the social preferences resulting from majority voting aren't well-behaved preferences, since they are not transitive. Since the preferences aren't transitive, there will be no "best" alternative from the set of alternatives $(\mathbf{x}, \mathbf{y}, \mathbf{z})$. Which outcome society chooses will depend on the order in which the vote is taken.

To see this suppose that the three people depicted in Table 34.1 decide to vote first on **x** versus **y**, and then vote on the winner of this contest versus **z**. Since a majority prefer **x** to **y**, the second contest will be between **x** and **z**, which means that **z** will be the outcome.

But what if they decide to vote on **z** versus **x** and then pit the winner of this vote against **y**? Now **z** wins the first vote, but **y** beats **z** in the second vote. Which outcome is the overall winner depends crucially on the order in which the alternatives are presented to the voters.

Another kind of voting mechanism that we might consider is rank-order voting. Here each person ranks the goods according to his preferences and assigns a number that indicates its rank in his ordering: for example, a 1 for the best alternative, 2 for the second best, and so on. Then we sum up the scores of each alternative across the people to determine an aggregate score for each alternative and say that one outcome is socially preferred to another if it has a lower score.

In Table 34.2 we have illustrated a possible preference ordering for three allocations **x**, **y**, and **z** by two people. Suppose first that only alternatives **x** and **y** were available. Then in this example **x** would be given a rank of 1 by person A and 2 by person B. The alternative **y** would be given just the reverse ranking. Thus the outcome of the voting would be a tie with each alternative having an aggregate rank of 3.

Table
34.2

**The choice between x and y depends on z.**

| Person A | Person B |
|:---:|:---:|
| x | y |
| y | z |
| z | x |

But now suppose that **z** is introduced to the ballot. Person A would give **x** a score of 1, **y** a score of 2, and **z** a rank of 3. Person B would give **y** a score of 1, **z** a score of 2, and **x** a score of 3. This means that **x** would now have an aggregate rank of 4, and **y** would have an aggregate rank of 3. In this case **y** would be preferred to **x** by rank-order voting.

The problem with both majority voting and rank-order voting is that their outcomes can be manipulated by astute agents. Majority voting can be manipulated by changing the order on which things are voted so as to yield the desired outcome. Rank-order voting can be manipulated by introducing new alternatives that change the final ranks of the relevant alternatives.

The question naturally arises as to whether there are social decision mechanisms—ways of aggregating preferences—that are immune to this kind of manipulation? Are there ways to "add up" preferences that don't have the undesirable properties described above?

Let's list some things that we would want our social decision mechanism to do:

1. Given any set of complete, reflexive, and transitive individual preferences, the social decision mechanism should result in social preferences that satisfy the same properties.

2. If everybody prefers alternative **x** to alternative **y**, then the social preferences should rank **x** ahead of **y**.

3. The preferences between **x** and **y** should depend only on how people rank **x** versus **y**, and not on how they rank other alternatives.

All three of these requirements seem eminently plausible. Yet it can be quite difficult to find a mechanism that satisfies all of them. In fact, Kenneth Arrow has proved the following remarkable result:[1]

**Arrow's Impossibility Theorem.**   *If a social decision mechanism satisfies properties 1, 2, and 3, then it must be a dictatorship: all social rankings are the rankings of one individual.*

Arrow's Impossibility Theorem is quite surprising. It shows that three very plausible and desirable features of a social decision mechanism are inconsistent with democracy: there is no "perfect" way to make social decisions. There is no perfect way to "aggregate" individual preferences to make one social preference. If we want to find a way to aggregate individual preferences to form social preferences, we will have to give up one of the properties of a social decision mechanism described in Arrow's theorem.

## 34.2 Social Welfare Functions

If we were to drop any of the desired features of a social welfare function described above, it would probably be property 3—that the social preference between two alternatives only depends on the ranking of those two alternatives. If we do that, certain kinds of rank-order voting become possibilities.

---

[1] See Kenneth Arrow, *Social Choice and Individual Values* (New York: Wiley, 1963). Arrow, a professor at Stanford University, was awarded the Nobel Prize in economics for his work in this area.

Given the preferences of each individual $i$ over the allocations, we can construct utility functions, $u_i(\mathbf{x})$, that summarize the individuals' value judgments: person $i$ prefers $\mathbf{x}$ to $\mathbf{y}$ if and only if $u_i(\mathbf{x}) > u_i(\mathbf{y})$. Of course, these are just like all utility functions—they can be scaled in any way that preserves the underlying preference ordering. There is no *unique* utility representation.

But let us pick some utility representation and stick with it. Then one way of getting social preferences from individuals' preferences is to add up the individual utilities and use the resulting number as a kind of social utility. That is, we will say that allocation $\mathbf{x}$ is socially preferred to allocation $\mathbf{y}$ if

$$\sum_{i=1}^{n} u_i(\mathbf{x}) > \sum_{i=1}^{n} u_i(\mathbf{y}),$$

where $n$ is the number of individuals in the society.

This works—but of course it is totally arbitrary, since our choice of utility representation is totally arbitrary. The choice of using the sum is also arbitrary. Why not use a weighted sum of utilities? Why not use the product of utilities, or the sum of the squares of utilities?

One reasonable restriction that we might place on the "aggregating function" is that it be increasing in each individual's utility. That way we are assured that if everybody prefers $\mathbf{x}$ to $\mathbf{y}$, then the social preferences will prefer $\mathbf{x}$ to $\mathbf{y}$.

There is a name for this kind of aggregating function; it is called a **social welfare function**. A social welfare function is just some function of the individual utility functions: $W(u_1(\mathbf{x}), \ldots, u_n(\mathbf{x}))$. It gives a way to rank different allocations that depends only on the individual preferences, and it is an increasing function of each individual's utility.

Let's look at some examples. One special case mentioned above is the *sum* of the individual utility functions

$$W(u_1, \ldots, u_n) = \sum_{i=1}^{n} u_i.$$

This is sometimes referred to as a **classical utilitarian** or **Benthamite** welfare function.[2] A slight generalization of this form is the **weighted-sum-of-utilities welfare function**:

$$W(u_1, \ldots, u_n) = \sum_{i=1}^{n} a_i u_i.$$

---

[2] Jeremy Bentham (1748–1832) was the founder of the utilitarian school of moral philosophy, a school that considers the highest good to be the greatest happiness for the greatest number.

Here the weights, $a_1, \ldots, a_n$, are supposed to be numbers indicating how important each agent's utility is to the overall social welfare. It is natural to take each $a_i$ as being positive.

Another interesting welfare function is the **minimax** or **Rawlsian** social welfare function:

$$W(u_1, \ldots, u_n) = \min\{u_1, \ldots, u_n\}.$$

This welfare function says that the social welfare of an allocation depends only on the welfare of the worst off agent—the person with the minimal utility.[3]

Each of these is a possible way to compare individual utility functions. Each of them represents different ethical judgments about the comparison between different agents' welfares. About the only restriction that we will place on the structure of the welfare function at this point is that it be increasing in each consumer's utility.

## 34.3 Welfare Maximization

Once we have a welfare function we can examine the problem of welfare maximization. Let us use the notation $x_i^j$ to indicate how much individual $i$ has of good $j$, and suppose that there are $n$ consumers and $k$ goods. Then the allocation $\mathbf{x}$ consists of the list of how much each of the agents has of each of the goods.

If we have a total amount $X^1, \ldots, X^k$ of goods $1, \ldots, k$ to distribute among the consumers, we can pose the welfare maximization problem:

$$\max \ W(u_1(\mathbf{x}), \ldots, u_n(\mathbf{x}))$$

$$\text{such that } \sum_{i=1}^{n} x_i^1 = X^1$$

$$\vdots$$

$$\sum_{i=1}^{n} x_i^k = X^k.$$

Thus we are trying to find the feasible allocation that maximizes social welfare. What properties does such an allocation have?

The first thing that we should note is that a maximal welfare allocation must be a Pareto efficient allocation. The proof is easy: suppose that

---

[3] John Rawls (1931–2002) was a philosopher at Harvard who has argued for this principle of justice.

it were not. Then there would be some other feasible allocation that gave everyone at least as large a utility, and someone strictly greater utility. But the welfare function is an increasing function of each agent's utility. Thus this new allocation would have to have higher welfare, which contradicts the assumption that we originally had a welfare maximum.

We can illustrate this situation in Figure 34.1, where the set $U$ indicates the set of possible utilities in the case of two individuals. This set is known as the **utility possibilities set**. The boundary of this set—the **utility possibilities frontier**—is the set of utility levels associated with Pareto efficient allocations. If an allocation is on the boundary of the utility possibilities set, then there are no other feasible allocations that yield higher utilities for both agents.

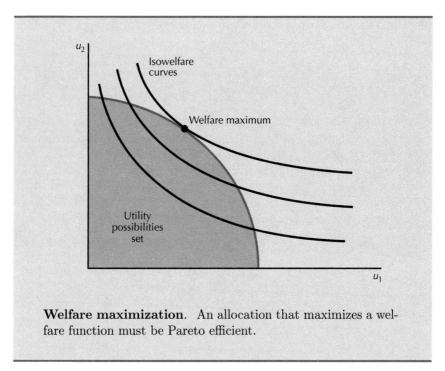

Figure
34.1

**Welfare maximization.** An allocation that maximizes a welfare function must be Pareto efficient.

The "indifference curves" in this diagram are called **isowelfare curves** since they depict those distributions of utility that have constant welfare. As usual, the optimal point is characterized by a tangency condition. But for our purposes, the notable thing about this maximal welfare point is that it is Pareto efficient—it must occur on the boundary of the utility possibilities set.

The next observation we can make from this diagram is that *any* Pareto efficient allocation must be a welfare maximum for some welfare function.

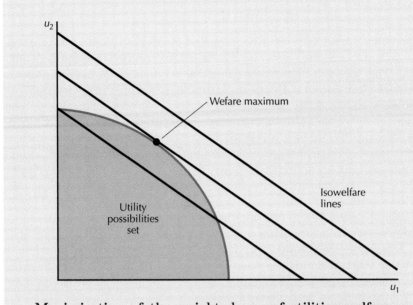

**Maximization of the weighted-sum-of-utilities welfare function.** If the utility possibility set is convex, then every Pareto efficient point is a maximum for a weighted-sum-of-utilities welfare function.

Figure 34.2

An example is given in Figure 34.2.

In Figure 34.2 we have picked a Pareto efficient allocation and found a set of isowelfare curves for which it yields maximal welfare. Actually, we can say a bit more than this. If the set of possible utility distributions is a convex set, as illustrated, then every point on its frontier is a welfare maximum for a weighted-sum-of-utilities welfare function, as illustrated in Figure 34.2. The welfare function thus provides a way to single out Pareto efficient allocations: every welfare maximum is a Pareto efficient allocation, and every Pareto efficient allocation is a welfare maximum.

## 34.4 Individualistic Social Welfare Functions

Up until now we have been thinking of individual preferences as being defined over entire allocations rather than over each individual's bundle of goods. But, as we remarked earlier, individuals might only care about their own bundles. In this case, we can use $x_i$ to denote individual $i's$ consumption bundle, and let $u_i(x_i)$ be individual $i's$ utility level using some fixed representation of utility. Then a social welfare function will have the form

$$W = W(u_1(x_1), \ldots, u_n(x_n)).$$

The welfare function is directly a function of the individuals' utility levels, but it is indirectly a function of the individual agents' consumption bundles. This special form of welfare function is known as an **individualistic welfare function** or a **Bergson-Samuelson welfare function**.[4]

If each agent's utility depends only on his or her own consumption, then there are no consumption externalities. Thus the standard results of Chapter 32 apply and we have an intimate relationship between Pareto efficient allocations and market equilibria: all competitive equilibria are Pareto efficient, and, under appropriate convexity assumptions, all Pareto efficient allocations are competitive equilibria.

Now we can carry this categorization one step further. Given the relationship between Pareto efficiency and welfare maxima described above, we can conclude that all welfare maxima are competitive equilibria and that all competitive equilibria are welfare maxima for some welfare function.

Using the transformation function described in Chapter 33 to describe the production possibilities frontier, we write the problem of welfare maximization using an individualistic welfare function as

$$\max_{x_A^1, x_A^2, x_B^1, x_B^2} W(u_A(x_A^1, x_A^2), u_B(x_B^1, x_B^2))$$

$$\text{such that } T(X^1, X^2) = 0,$$

where we use $X^1$ and $X^2$ to denote the total amount of good 1 and good 2 produced and consumed.

The Lagrangian for this problem is

$$L = W(u_A(x_A^1, x_A^2), u_B(x_B^1, x_B^2)) - \lambda(T(X^1, X^2) - 0).$$

Differentiating with respect to each of the choice variables gives us the first-order conditions

$$\frac{\partial L}{\partial x_A^1} = \frac{\partial W}{\partial u_A} \frac{\partial u_A(x_A^1, x_A^2)}{\partial x_A^1} - \lambda \frac{\partial T(X^1, X^2)}{\partial X^1} = 0$$

$$\frac{\partial L}{\partial x_A^2} = \frac{\partial W}{\partial u_A} \frac{\partial u_A(x_A^1, x_A^2)}{\partial x_A^2} - \lambda \frac{\partial T(X^1, X^2)}{\partial X^2} = 0$$

$$\frac{\partial L}{\partial x_B^1} = \frac{\partial W}{\partial u_B} \frac{\partial u_B(x_B^1, x_B^2)}{\partial x_B^1} - \lambda \frac{\partial T(X^1, X^2)}{\partial X^1} = 0$$

$$\frac{\partial L}{\partial x_B^2} = \frac{\partial W}{\partial u_B} \frac{\partial u_B(x_B^1, x_B^2)}{\partial x_B^2} - \lambda \frac{\partial T(X^1, X^2)}{\partial X^2} = 0.$$

[4] Abram Bergson (1914–2002) and Paul Samuelson (1915–2009) were economists who investigated properties of this kind of welfare function in the early 1940s. Samuelson was awarded a Nobel Prize in economics for his many contributions.

Rearranging and dividing the first equation by the second, and the third by the fourth, we have

$$\frac{\partial u_A/\partial x_A^1}{\partial u_A/\partial x_A^2} = \frac{\partial T/\partial X^1}{\partial T/\partial X^2}$$

$$\frac{\partial u_B/\partial x_B^1}{\partial u_B/\partial x_B^2} = \frac{\partial T/\partial X^1}{\partial T/\partial X^2}.$$

Note that these are exactly the same equations that we encountered in Chapter 33. Thus the welfare maximization problem gives us the same first-order conditions as the Pareto efficiency problem.

This is obviously no accident. The allocation resulting from the maximization of a Bergson-Samuelson welfare function is Pareto efficient, and every Pareto efficient allocation maximizes some welfare function. Thus welfare maxima and Pareto efficient allocations have to satisfy the same first-order conditions.

## 34.5 Fair Allocations

The welfare function approach is a very general way to describe social welfare. But because it is so general it can be used to summarize the properties of many kinds of moral judgments. On the other hand, it isn't much use in deciding what kinds of ethical judgments might be reasonable ones.

Another approach is to start with some specific moral judgments and then examine their implications for economic distribution. This is the approach taken in the study of **fair allocations**. We start with a definition of what might be considered a fair way to divide a bundle of goods, and then use our understanding of economic analysis to investigate its implications.

Suppose that you were given some goods to divide fairly among $n$ equally deserving people. How would you do it? It is probably safe to say that in this problem most people would divide the goods equally among the $n$ agents. Given that they are by hypothesis equally deserving, what else could you do?

What is appealing about this idea of equal division? One appealing feature is that it is *symmetric*. Each agent has the same bundle of goods; no agent prefers any other agent's bundle of goods to his or her own, since they all have exactly the same thing.

Unfortunately, an equal division will not necessarily be Pareto efficient. If agents have different tastes they will generally desire to trade away from equal division. Let us suppose that this trade takes place and that it moves us to a Pareto efficient allocation.

The question arises: is this Pareto efficient allocation still fair in any sense? Does trade from equal division inherit any of the symmetry of the starting point?

The answer is: not necessarily. Consider the following example. We have three people, A, B, and C. A and B have the same tastes, and C has different tastes. We start from an equal division and suppose that A and C get together and trade. Then they will typically both be made better off. Now B, who didn't have the opportunity to trade with C, will **envy** A—that is, he would prefer A's bundle to his own. Even though A and B started with the same allocation, A was luckier in her trading, and this destroyed the symmetry of the original allocation.

This means that arbitrary trading from an equal division will not necessarily preserve the symmetry of the starting point of equal division. We might well ask if there is any allocation that preserves this symmetry? Is there any way to get an allocation that is both Pareto efficient and equitable at the same time?

## 34.6 Envy and Equity

Let us now try to formalize some of these ideas. What do we mean by "symmetric" or "equitable" anyway? One possible set of definitions is as follows.

We say an allocation is **equitable** if no agent prefers any other agent's bundle of goods to his or her own. If some agent $i$ does prefer some other agent $j's$ bundle of goods, we say that $i$ **envies** $j$. Finally, if an allocation is both equitable and Pareto efficient, we will say that it is a **fair** allocation.

These are ways of formalizing the idea of symmetry alluded to above. An equal division allocation has the property that no agent envies any other agent—but there are many other allocations that have this same property.

Consider Figure 34.3. To determine whether any allocation is equitable or not, just look at the allocation that results if the two agents swap bundles. If this swapped allocation lies "below" each agent's indifference curve through the original allocation, then the original allocation is an equitable allocation. (Here "below" means below from the point of view of each agent; from our point of view the swapped allocation must lie between the two indifference curves.)

Note also that the allocation in Figure 34.3 is also Pareto efficient. Thus it is not only equitable, in the sense that we defined the term, but it is also efficient. By our definition, it is a fair allocation. Is this kind of allocation a fluke, or will fair allocations typically exist?

It turns out that fair allocations *will* generally exist, and there is an easy way to see that this is so. We start as we did in the last section, where we had an equal division allocation and considered trading to a Pareto efficient allocation. Instead of using just any old way to trade, let us use the special mechanism of the competitive market. This will move us to a new allocation where each agent is choosing the best bundle of goods he or

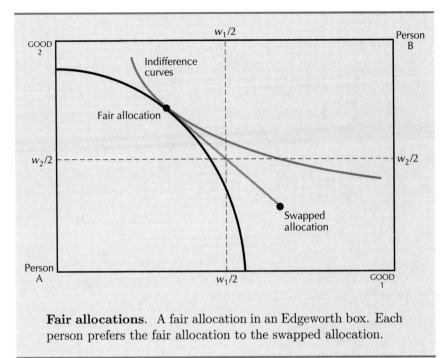

**Fair allocations.** A fair allocation in an Edgeworth box. Each person prefers the fair allocation to the swapped allocation.

Figure
34.3

she can afford at the equilibrium prices $(p_1, p_2)$, and we know from Chapter 32 that such an allocation must be Pareto efficient.

But is it still equitable? Well, suppose not. Suppose that one of the consumers, say consumer A, envies consumer B. This means that A prefers what B has to her own bundle. In symbols:

$$(x_A^1, x_A^2) \prec_A (x_B^1, x_B^2).$$

But, if A prefers B's bundle to her own, and if her own bundle is the best bundle she can afford at the prices $(p_1, p_2)$, this means that B's bundle must cost more than A can afford. In symbols:

$$p_1 \omega_A^1 + p_2 \omega_A^2 < p_1 x_B^1 + p_2 x_B^2.$$

But this is a contradiction! For by hypothesis, A and B started with exactly the same bundle, since they started from an equal division. If A can't afford B's bundle, then B can't afford it either.

Thus we can conclude that it is impossible for A to envy B in these circumstances. A competitive equilibrium from equal division must be a fair allocation. Thus the market mechanism will preserve certain kinds of equity: if the original allocation is equally divided, the final allocation must be fair.

## Summary

1. Arrow's Impossibility Theorem shows that there is no ideal way to aggregate individual preferences into social preferences.

2. Nevertheless, economists often use welfare functions of one sort or another to represent distributional judgments about allocations.

3. As long as the welfare function is increasing in each individual's utility, a welfare maximum will be Pareto efficient. Furthermore, every Pareto efficient allocation can be thought of as maximizing some welfare function.

4. The idea of fair allocations provides an alternative way to make distributional judgments. This idea emphasizes the idea of symmetric treatment.

5. Even when the initial allocation is symmetric, arbitrary methods of trade will not necessarily produce a fair allocation. However, it turns out that the market mechanism will provide a fair allocation.

## REVIEW QUESTIONS

1. Suppose that we say that an allocation **x** is socially preferred to an allocation **y** only if *everyone* prefers **x** to **y**. (This is sometimes called the Pareto ordering, since it is closely related to the idea of Pareto efficiency.) What shortcoming does this have as a rule for making social decisions?

2. A Rawlsian welfare function counts only the welfare of the worst off agent. The opposite of the Rawlsian welfare function might be called the "Nietzschean" welfare function—a welfare function that says the value of an allocation depends only on the welfare of the *best off* agent. What mathematical form would the Nietzschean welfare function take?

3. Suppose that the utility possibilities set is a convex set and that consumers care only about their own consumption. What kind of allocations represent welfare maxima of the Nietzschean welfare function?

4. Suppose that an allocation is Pareto efficient, and that each individual only cares about his own consumption. Prove that there must be some individual that envies no one, in the sense described in the text. (This puzzle requires some thought, but it is worth it.)

5. The ability to set the voting agenda can often be a powerful asset. Assuming that social preferences are decided by pair-wise majority voting and that the preferences given in Table 34.1 hold, demonstrate this fact by

producing a voting agenda that results in allocation **y** winning. Find an agenda that has **z** as the winner. What property of the social preferences is responsible for this agenda-setting power?

# CHAPTER **35**

# EXTERNALITIES

We say that an economic situation involves a **consumption externality** if one consumer cares directly about another agent's production or consumption. For example, I have definite preferences about my neighbor playing loud music at 3 in the morning, or the person next to me in a restaurant smoking a cheap cigar, or the amount of pollution produced by local automobiles. These are all examples of *negative* consumption externalities. On the other hand, I may get pleasure from observing my neighbor's flower garden—this is an example of a *positive* consumption externality.

Similarly, a **production externality** arises when the production possibilities of one firm are influenced by the choices of another firm or consumer. A classic example is that of an apple orchard located next to a beekeeper, where there are mutual positive production externalities—each firm's production positively affects the production possibilities of the other firm. Similarly, a fishery cares about the amount of pollutants dumped into its fishing area, since this will negatively influence its catch.

The crucial feature of externalities is that there are goods people care about that are not sold on markets. There is no market for loud music at 3 in the morning, or drifting smoke from cheap cigars, or a neighbor who keeps a beautiful flower garden. It is this lack of markets for externalities that causes problems.

Up until now we have implicitly assumed that each agent could make consumption or production decisions without worrying about what other agents were doing. All interactions between consumers and producers took place via the market, so that all the economic agents needed to know were the market prices and their own consumption or production possibilities. In this chapter we will relax this assumption and examine the economic consequences of externalities.

In earlier chapters we saw that the market mechanism was capable of achieving Pareto efficient allocations when externalities were *not* present. If externalities are present, the market will not necessarily result in a Pareto efficient provision of resources. However, there are other social institutions such as the legal system, or government intervention, that can "mimic" the market mechanism to some degree and thereby achieve Pareto efficiency. In this chapter we'll see how these institutions work.

## 35.1 Smokers and Nonsmokers

It is convenient to start with an example to illustrate some of the main considerations. We'll imagine two roommates, A and B, who have preferences over "money" and "smoke." We suppose that both consumers like money, but that A likes to smoke and B likes clean air.

We can depict the consumption possibilities for the two consumers in an Edgeworth box. The length of the horizontal axis will represent the total amount of money the two agents have, and the height of the vertical axis will represent the total amount of smoke that can be generated. The preferences of agent A are increasing in both money and smoke, while agent B's preferences are increasing in money and clean air—the absence of smoke. We'll measure smoke on a scale from 0 to 1, where 0 is no smoke at all, and 1 is the proverbial smoke-filled room.

This setup gives us a diagram like that depicted in Figure 35.1. Note that the picture looks very much like the standard Edgeworth box, but the interpretation is quite different. The amount of smoke is a good for A and a bad for B, so that B is moved to a more preferred position as A consumes less smoke. Be sure to note the difference in the way things are measured on the horizontal and vertical axes. We measure A's money horizontally from the lower left-hand corner of the box, and B's money horizontally from the upper right-hand corner. But the total amount of smoke is measured vertically from the lower left-hand corner. The difference occurs because money can be divided between the two consumers, so there will always be two amounts of money to measure, but there is only one amount of smoke that they must both consume.

In the ordinary Edgeworth box diagram B is made better off when A reduces his consumption of good 2—but that is because B then gets to consume more of good 2. In the Edgeworth box in Figure 35.1 B is also better off when A reduces his consumption of good 2 (smoke), but for a very different reason. In this example, B is better off when A reduces his consumption of smoke since both agents must consume the same amount of smoke and smoke is a bad for agent B.

We've now illustrated the consumption possibilities of the two roommates and their preferences. What about their endowments? Let's assume that they both have the same amount of money, say $100 apiece, so that their endowments will lie somewhere on the vertical line $EE'$ in Figure 35.1. In order to determine exactly where on this line the endowments lie, we must determine the initial "endowment" of smoke/clean air.

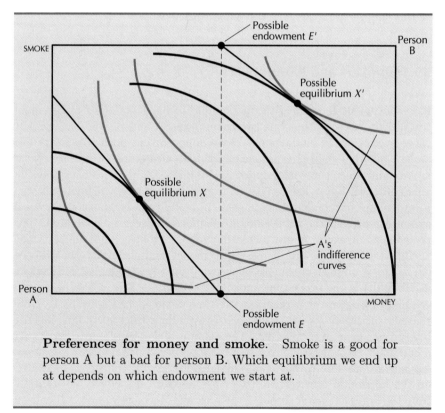

**Figure 35.1**    **Preferences for money and smoke.**    Smoke is a good for person A but a bad for person B. Which equilibrium we end up at depends on which endowment we start at.

The answer to this question depends on the legal rights of smokers and nonsmokers. It may be that A has a right to smoke as much as he wants, and B just has to put up with it. Or, it could be that B has a right to clean air. Or the legal right to smoke and clean air could be somewhere between these two extremes.

The initial endowment of smoke depends on the legal system. This is not so different from the initial endowment of ordinary sorts of goods. To say that A has an initial endowment of $100 means that A can decide to consume the $100 himself, or he can give it away or trade it to any other individual. There is a legal definition of property involved in saying that a person "owns" or "has a right to" $100. Similarly if a person has a property right to clean air, it means that he can consume clean air if he wants to, or he can give it away or sell that right to someone else. In this way, having a property right to clean air is no different from having a property right to $100.

Let's start by considering a legal situation where person B has a legal right to clean air. Then the initial endowment in Figure 35.1 is labeled $E$; it is where A has $(100,0)$ and B has $(100,0)$. This means that both A and B have $100, and that the initial endowment—what there would be in the absence of trade—is clean air.

Just as before, in the case with no externalities, there is no reason why the initial endowment is Pareto efficient. One of the aspects of having a property right to clean air is having the right to trade some of it away for other desirable goods—in this case, for money. It can easily happen that B would prefer to trade some of his right to clean air for some more money. The point labeled $X$ in Figure 35.1 is an example of such a case.

As before, a Pareto efficient allocation is one where neither consumer can be made better off without the other being made worse off. Such an allocation will be characterized by the usual tangency condition that the marginal rates of substitution between smoke and money should be the same between the two agents, as illustrated in Figure 35.1. It is easy to imagine A and B trading to such a Pareto efficient point. In effect, B has the right to clean air, but he can allow himself to be "bribed" to consume some of A's smoke.

Of course, other assignments of property rights are possible. We could imagine a legal system where A had a right to smoke as much as he wanted, and B would have to bribe A to reduce his consumption of smoke. This would correspond to the endowment labeled $E'$ in Figure 35.1. Just as before, this would typically not be Pareto efficient, so we could imagine the agents trading to a mutually preferred point such as the one labeled $X'$.

Both $X$ and $X'$ are Pareto efficient allocations; they just come from different initial endowments. Certainly the smoker, A, is better off at $X'$ than at $X$, and the nonsmoker, B, is better off at $X$ than at $X'$. The two points have different distributional consequences, but on grounds of efficiency they are equally satisfactory.

In fact, there is no reason to limit ourselves to just these two efficient points. As usual there will be a whole contract curve of Pareto efficient allocations of smoke and money. If agents are free to trade both of these goods, we know that they will end up somewhere on this contract curve. The exact position will depend on their property rights involving smoke and money and on the precise mechanism that they use to trade.

One mechanism that they could use to trade is the price mechanism. Just as before we could imagine an auctioneer calling out prices and asking how much each agent would be willing to buy at those prices. If the initial endowment point gave A the property rights to smoke, he could consider selling some of his smoking rights to B in exchange for B's money. Similarly, if the property rights for clean air were given to B, he could sell some of his clean air to A.

When the auctioneer manages to find a set of prices where supply equals demand everything is fine: we have a nice Pareto efficient outcome. If there is a market for smoke, a competitive equilibrium will be Pareto efficient. Furthermore, the competitive prices will measure the marginal rate of substitution between the two goods, just as in the standard case.

This is just like the usual Edgeworth box analysis, but described in a slightly different framework. As long as we have well-defined property rights in the good involving the externality—no matter who holds the property rights—the agents can trade from their initial endowment to a Pareto efficient allocation. If we want to set up a market in the externality to encourage trade, that will work as well.

The only problem arises if the property rights are *not* well defined. If A believes that he has the right to smoke and B believes that he has the right to clean air, we have difficulties. *The practical problems with externalities generally arise because of poorly defined property rights.*

My neighbor may believe that he has the right to play his trumpet at 3 in the morning, and I may believe that I have the right to silence. A firm may believe that it has the right to dump pollutants into the atmosphere that I breathe, while I may believe that it doesn't. Cases where property rights are poorly defined can lead to an inefficient production of externalities—which means that there would be ways to make both parties involved better off by changing the production of externalities. If property rights are well defined, and mechanisms are in place to allow for negotiation between people, then people can trade their rights to produce externalities in the same way that they trade rights to produce and consume ordinary goods.

## 35.2 Quasilinear Preferences and the Coase Theorem

We argued above that as long as property rights were well defined, trade between agents would result in an efficient allocation of the externality. In general, the amount of the externality that will be generated in the efficient solution will depend on the assignment of property rights. In the case of the two roommates, the amount of smoke generated will depend on whether the smoker has the property rights or the nonsmoker has them.

But there is a special case where the outcome of the externality is independent of the assignment of property rights. If the agents' preferences are **quasilinear**, then every efficient solution must have the same amount of the externality.

This case is illustrated in Figure 35.2 for the Edgeworth box case of the smoker versus the nonsmoker. Since the indifference curves are all horizontal translates of each other, the locus of mutual tangencies—the set of Pareto efficient allocations—will be a horizontal line. This means that the amount of smoke is the same in every Pareto efficient allocation; only the dollar amounts held by the agents differ across the efficient allocations.

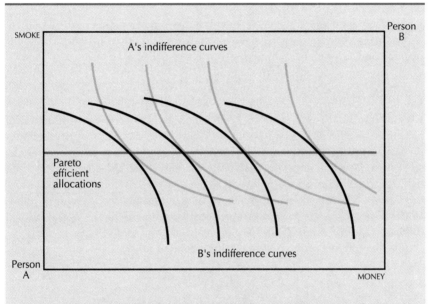

**Quasilinear preferences and the Coase theorem.** If each consumer's preferences are quasilinear, so that they are all horizontal translates of each other, the set of Pareto efficient allocations will be a horizontal line. Thus there will be a unique amount of the externality, in this case smoke, at each Pareto efficient allocation.

Figure 35.2

The result that under certain conditions the efficient amount of the good involved in the externality is independent of the distribution of property rights is sometimes known as the **Coase Theorem**. However, it should be emphasized just how special these conditions are. The quasilinear preference assumption implies that the demands for the good causing the exter-

nality doesn't depend on the distribution of income. Therefore a reallocation of endowments doesn't affect the efficient amount of the externalities.
This is sometimes expressed by saying that the Coase theorem is valid if
there are no "income effects."[1]

In this case, the Pareto efficient allocations will involve a unique amount
of the externality being generated. The different Pareto efficient allocations
will involve different amounts of money being held by the consumers; but
the amount of the externality—the amount of smoke—will be independent
of the distribution of wealth.

## 35.3 Production Externalities

Let us now consider a situation involving production externalities. Firm
S produces some amount of steel, $s$, and also produces a certain amount
of pollution, $x$, which it dumps into a river. Firm F, a fishery, is located
downstream and is adversely affected by S's pollution.

Suppose that firm S's cost function is given by $c_s(s, x)$, where $s$ is the
amount of steel produced and $x$ is the amount of pollution produced. Firm
F's cost function is given by $c_f(f, x)$, where $f$ indicates the production of
fish and $x$ is the amount of pollution. Note that F's costs of producing a
given amount of fish depend on the amount of pollution produced by the
steel firm. We will suppose that pollution increases the cost of providing
fish $\partial c_f / \partial x > 0$, and that pollution *decreases* the cost of steel production,
$\partial c_s / \partial x \leq 0$. This last assumption says that increasing the amount of pollution will decrease the cost of producing steel—that reducing pollution will
increase the cost of steel production, at least over some range.

The steel firm's profit-maximization problem is

$$\max_{s,x} \; p_s s - c_s(s, x)$$

and the fishery's profit-maximization problem is

$$\max_{f} \; p_f f - c_f(f, x).$$

Note that the steel mill gets to choose the amount of pollution that it
generates, but the fishery must take the level of pollution as outside of its
control.

---

[1] Ronald Coase is an emeritus professor at the University of Chicago Law School. His
famous paper, "The Problem of Social Costs," *The Journal of Law & Economics*, 3
(October 1960), has been given a variety of interpretations. Some authors suggest
that Coase only asserted that costless bargaining over externalities achieves a Pareto
efficient outcome, not that the outcome will be independent of the assignment of
property rights. Coase received the 1991 Nobel Prize in Economics for this work.

The conditions characterizing profit maximization will be

$$p_s = \frac{\partial c_s(s^*, x^*)}{\partial s}$$

$$0 = \frac{\partial c_s(s^*, x^*)}{\partial x}$$

for the steel firm and

$$p_f = \frac{\partial c_f(f^*, x^*)}{\partial f}$$

for the fishery. These conditions say that at the profit-maximizing point, the price of each good—steel and pollution—should equal its marginal cost. In the case of the steel firm, one of its products is pollution, which, by assumption, has a zero price. So the condition determining the profit-maximizing supply of pollution says to produce pollution until the cost of an extra unit is zero.

It is not hard to see the externality here: the fishery cares about the production of pollution but has no control over it. The steel firm looks only at the cost of producing steel when it makes its profit-maximizing calculation; it doesn't consider the cost it imposes on the fishery. The increase in the cost of fishing associated with an increase in pollution is part of the **social cost** of steel production, and it is being ignored by the steel firm. In general, we expect that the steel firm will produce too much pollution from a social point of view since it ignores the impact of that pollution on the fishery.

What does a Pareto efficient production plan for steel and fish look like? There is an easy way to see what it should be. Suppose that the fishery and the steel firm merged and formed one firm that produced both fish and steel (and possibly pollution). Then there is no externality! For a production externality only arises when one firm's actions affect another firm's production possibilities. If there is only one firm, then it will take the interactions between its different "divisions" into account when it chooses the profit-maximizing production plan. We say that the externality has been **internalized** by this reassignment of property rights. Before the merger, each firm had the right to produce whatever amount of steel or fish or pollution that it wanted, regardless of what the other firm did. After the merger, the combined firm has the right to control the production of both the steel mill and the fishery.

The merged firm's profit-maximization problem is

$$\max_{s,f,x} \; p_s s + p_f f - c_s(s, x) - c_f(f, x),$$

which yields optimality conditions of

$$p_s = \frac{\partial c_s(\hat{s}, \hat{x})}{\partial s}$$

$$p_f = \frac{\partial c_f(\hat{f}, \hat{x})}{\partial f}$$

$$0 = \frac{\partial c_s(\hat{s}, \hat{x})}{\partial x} + \frac{\partial c_f(\hat{f}, \hat{x})}{\partial x}.$$

The crucial term is the last one. This shows that the merged firm will take into account the effect of pollution on the marginal costs of both the steel firm and the fishery. When the steel division decides how much pollution to produce, it considers the effect of this action on the profits of the fish division; that is, it takes the social cost of its production plan into account.

What does this imply about the amount of pollution produced? When the steel firm acted independently, the amount of pollution was determined by the condition

$$\frac{\partial c_s(s^*, x^*)}{\partial x} = 0. \tag{35.1}$$

That is, the steel mill produced pollution until the marginal cost was zero:

$$MC_S(s^*, x^*) = 0.$$

In the merged firm, the amount of pollution is determined by the condition

$$\frac{\partial c_s(\hat{s}, \hat{x})}{\partial x} + \frac{\partial c_f(\hat{f}, \hat{x})}{\partial x} = 0. \tag{35.2}$$

That is, the merged firm produces pollution until the *sum* of the marginal cost to the steel mill and the marginal cost to the fishery is zero. This condition can also be written as

$$-\frac{\partial c_s(\hat{s}, \hat{x})}{\partial x} = \frac{\partial c_f(\hat{f}, \hat{x})}{\partial x} > 0 \tag{35.3}$$

or

$$-MC_S(\hat{s}, \hat{x}) = MC_F(\hat{f}, \hat{x}).$$

In this latter expression $MC_F(\hat{f}, \hat{x})$ is positive, since more pollution increases the cost of producing a given amount of fish. Hence the merged firm will want to produce where $-MC_S(\hat{s}, \hat{x})$ is positive; that is, it will want to produce *less* pollution than the independent steel firm. When the true social cost of the externality involved in the steel production is taken into account, the optimal production of pollution will be reduced.

When the steel firm considers minimizing its **private costs** of producing steel, it produces where the marginal cost of extra pollution equals zero;

but the Pareto efficient level of pollution requires minimizing the **social costs** of the pollution. At the Pareto efficient level of pollution, the *sum* of the two firm's marginal costs of pollution must be equal to zero.

This argument is illustrated in Figure 35.3. In this diagram $-MC_S$ measures the marginal cost to the steel firm from producing more pollution. The curve labeled $MC_F$ measures the marginal cost to the fishery of more pollution. The profit-maximizing steel firm produces pollution up to the point where its marginal cost from generating more pollution equals zero.

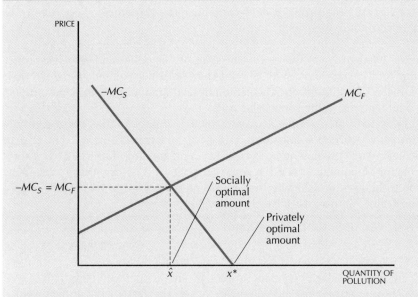

**Social cost and private cost.** The steel firm produces pollution up to the point where the marginal cost of extra pollution equals zero. But the Pareto efficient production of pollution is at the point where price equals marginal social cost, which includes the cost of pollution borne by the fishery.

Figure 35.3

But at the Pareto efficient level of pollution, the steel firm pollutes up to the point where the effect of a marginal increase in pollution is equal to the marginal social cost, which counts the impact of pollution on the costs of both firms. At the efficient level of pollution production, the amount that the steel firm is willing to pay for an extra unit of pollution should equal the social costs generated by that extra pollution—which include the costs it imposes on the fishery.

This is perfectly consistent with the efficiency arguments given in earlier chapters. There we assumed that there were no externalities, so that private costs and social costs coincided. In this case the free market will determine a Pareto efficient amount of output of each good. But if the private costs and the social costs diverge, the market alone may not be sufficient to achieve Pareto efficiency.

## EXAMPLE: Pollution Vouchers

Everyone wants a clean environment ... as long as someone else pays for it. Even if we reach a consensus on how much we should reduce pollution, there is still the problem of determining the most cost-effective way to achieve the targeted reduction.

Take the case of nitrogen oxide emissions. One emitter may find it relatively inexpensive to reduce its emissions of this pollutant, whereas another may find it very expensive. Should they both be required to reduce their emission of pollutants by the same physical amount, by the same proportional amount, or by some other rule?

Let's look at a simple economic model. Suppose that there are only two firms. Firm 1's emission quota is $x_1$ and firm 2's is $x_2$. The cost of achieving an emission quota $x_1$ is $c_1(x_1)$ and similarly for firm 2. The total amount of emission is fixed at some target level $X$. If we want to minimize the total costs of achieving the emissions target, subject to the aggregate constraint, we need to solve the following problem:

$$\min_{x_1, x_2} \; c_1(x_1) + c_2(x_2)$$

$$\text{such that } x_1 + x_2 = X.$$

A by now standard economic argument shows that the marginal cost of emission control must be equalized across the firms. If one firm had a higher marginal cost of emission control than the other, then we could lower total costs by reducing its quota and increasing the quota of the other firm.

How can we achieve this outcome? If the government regulators had information on the cost of emissions for all firms, they could calculate the appropriate pattern of production and impose it on all the relevant parties. But the cost of gathering all this information, and keeping it up-to-date, is staggering. It is much easier to characterize the optimal solution than to actually implement it!

Many economists have argued that the best way to implement the efficient solution to the emission control problem is to use a market. It appears that such a market based emissions control system will soon be put into effect in Southern California. Here is how the California plan works.[2]

---

[2] See Richard Stevenson, "Trying a Market Approach to Smog," *New York Times*, March 25, 1992, C1.

Each of the 2700 largest polluters in Southern California is assigned a quota for their emissions of nitrogen oxide. This quota is initially set to be 8 percent less than their previous year's emission. If the firm exactly meets its emissions quota it faces no fines or penalties. However, if it reduces its emissions by *more* than its emissions quota, it can sell the extra "right to emit" on the open market.

Suppose that a firm's quota is 95 tons of nitrogen oxide emissions per year. If it manages to produce only 90 tons in a given year, then it can sell the right to emit 5 tons of nitrogen oxide to some other firm. Each firm can compare the market price of an emission credit to the cost of reducing its emissions and decide whether it was more cost-effective to reduce emissions further or purchase emission credits from other firms.

Firms that find it easy to reduce emissions will sell credits to firms that find it costly to reduce emissions. In equilibrium, the market price of the right to emit one ton of pollution should just equal the marginal cost of reducing emissions by one ton. But this is exactly the condition characterizing the optimal pattern of emissions! The market for emission permits produces the efficient pattern of emissions automatically.

## 35.4 Interpretation of the Conditions

There are several useful interpretations of the conditions for Pareto efficiency derived above. Each of these interpretations suggests a scheme to correct the efficiency loss created by the production externality.

The first interpretation is that the steel firm faces the wrong price for pollution. As far as the steel firm is concerned, its production of pollution costs it nothing. But that neglects the costs that the pollution imposes on the fishery. According to this view, the situation can be rectified by making sure that the polluter faces the correct social cost of its actions.

One way to do this is to place a tax on the pollution generated by the steel firm. Suppose that we put a tax of $t$ dollars per unit of pollution generated by the steel firm. Then the profit-maximization problem of the steel firm becomes

$$\max_{s,x} p_s s - c_s(s, x) - tx.$$

The profit-maximization conditions for this problem will be

$$p_s - \frac{\partial c_s(s, x)}{\partial s} = 0$$

$$-\frac{\partial c_s(s, x)}{\partial x} - t = 0.$$

Comparing these conditions to equation (35.3), we see that setting

$$t = \frac{\partial c_f(\hat{f}, \hat{x})}{\partial x}$$

will make these conditions the same as the conditions characterizing the Pareto efficient level of pollution.

This kind of a tax is known as a **Pigouvian tax**.[3] The problem with Pigouvian taxes is that we need to know the optimal level of pollution in order to impose the tax. But if we knew the optimal level of pollution we could just tell the steel firm to produce exactly that much and not have to mess with this taxation scheme at all.

Another interpretation of the problem is that there is a missing market— the market for the pollutant. The externality problem arises because the polluter faces a zero price for an output good that it produces, even though people would be willing to pay money to have that output level reduced. From a social point of view, the output of pollution should have a *negative* price.

We could imagine a world where the fishery had the right to clean water, but could sell the right to allow pollution. Let $q$ be the price per unit of pollution, and let $x$ be the amount of pollution that the steel mill produces. Then the steel mill's profit-maximization problem is

$$\max_{s,x} \; p_s s - qx - c_s(s, x),$$

and the fishery's profit-maximization problem is

$$\max_{f,x} \; p_f f + qx - c_f(f, x).$$

The term $qx$ enters with a negative sign in the profit expression for the steel firm since it represents a cost—the steel firm must buy the right to generate $x$ units of pollution. But it enters with a positive sign in the expression for the profits of the fishery, since the fishery gets revenue from selling this right.

The profit-maximization conditions are

$$p_s = \frac{\partial c_s(s, x)}{\partial s} \tag{35.4}$$

$$q = -\frac{\partial c_s(s, x)}{\partial x} \tag{35.5}$$

$$p_f = \frac{\partial c_f(f, x)}{\partial f} \tag{35.6}$$

$$q = \frac{\partial c_f(f, x)}{\partial x}. \tag{35.7}$$

---

[3] Arthur Pigou (1877–1959), an economist at Cambridge University, suggested such taxes in his influential book *The Economics of Welfare*.

Thus each firm is facing the social marginal cost of each of its actions when it chooses how much pollution to buy or sell. If the price of pollution is adjusted until the demand for pollution equals the supply of pollution, we will have an efficient equilibrium, just as with any other good.

Note that at the optimal solution, equations (35.5) and (35.7) imply that

$$-\frac{\partial c_s(s, x)}{\partial x} = \frac{\partial c_f(f, x)}{\partial x}.$$

This says that the marginal cost to the steel firm of reducing pollution should equal the marginal benefit to the fishery of that pollution reduction. If this condition were not satisfied, we couldn't have the optimal level of pollution. This is, of course, the same condition we encountered in equation (35.3).

In analyzing this problem we have stated that the fishery had a right to clean water and that the steel mill had to purchase the right to pollute. But we could have assigned the property rights in the opposite way: the steel mill could have the right to pollute and the fishery would have to pay to induce the steel mill to pollute less. Just as in the case of the smoker and nonsmoker, this would also give an efficient outcome. In fact, it would give precisely the *same* outcome, since exactly the same equations would have to be satisfied.

To see this, we now suppose that the steel mill has the right to pollute up to some amount $\bar{x}$, say, but the fishery is willing to pay it to reduce its pollution. The profit-maximization problem for the steel mill is then

$$\max_{s,x} \; p_s s + q(\bar{x} - x) - c_s(s, x).$$

Now the steel mill has two sources of income: it can sell steel, and it can sell pollution relief. The price equals marginal cost conditions become

$$p_s - \frac{\partial c_s(s, x)}{\partial s} = 0 \qquad (35.8)$$

$$-q - \frac{\partial c_s(s, x)}{\partial x} = 0. \qquad (35.9)$$

The fishery's maximization problem is now

$$\max_{f,x} \; p_f f - q(\bar{x} - x) - c_f(f, x),$$

which has optimality conditions

$$p_f - \frac{\partial c_f(f, x)}{\partial f} = 0 \qquad (35.10)$$

$$q - \frac{\partial c_f(f, x)}{\partial x} = 0. \qquad (35.11)$$

Now observe: the four equations (35.8)–(35.11) are precisely the same as the four equations (35.4)–(35.7). In the case of production externalities, the optimal pattern of production is independent of the assignment of property rights. Of course, the distribution of profits will generally depend on the assignment of property rights. Even though the social outcome will be independent of the distribution of property rights, the owners of the firms in question may have strong views about what is an appropriate distribution.

## 35.5 Market Signals

Finally we turn to the third interpretation of externalities, which in some respects is the most profound. In the case of the steel mill and the fishery there is no problem if both firms merge—so why don't they merge? In fact, when you think about it, there is a definite incentive for the two firms to merge: if the actions of one affect the other, then they can make higher profits together by coordinating their behavior than by each going alone. *The objective of profit maximization itself should encourage the internalization of production externalities.*

Said another way: if the joint profits of the firms with coordination exceed the sum of the profits without coordination, then the current owners could each be bought out for an amount equal to the present value of the stream of profits for their firm, the two firms could be coordinated, and the buyer could retain the excess profits. The new buyer could be either of the old firms, or anybody else for that matter.

The market itself provides a signal to internalize production externalities, which is one reason this kind of production externality is rarely observed. Most firms have *already* internalized the externalities between units that affect each other's production. The case of the apple orchard and the beekeeper mentioned earlier is a case in point. Here there *would* be an externality if the two firms ignored their interaction ... but why would they be so foolish as to do so? It is more likely that one or both of the firms would realize that more profits could be made by coordinating their activities, either by mutual agreement or by the sale of one of the firms to the other. Indeed, it is very common for apple orchards to keep honey bees for the purpose of fertilizing the trees. That particular externality is easily internalized.

## EXAMPLE: Bees and Almonds

Many varieties of fruit and nut trees need bees to pollinate their blossoms, thereby allowing the trees to produce crops.

According to the Carl Hayden Bee Research Center in Tucson, Arizona, honeybees pollinate about one-third of the human diet and more than 50 different agricultural crops valued at more than \$20 billion a year in the United States.[4]

Some owners of orchards keep their own bees; some rely on their neighbors' bees or wild bees. However, as the theory of externalities suggests, the most natural solution to the problem of inadequate bee supply is a market for bee services.

Consider, for example, the California almond market. There are 530,000 acres of almond trees in California, and every year, more than 1 million honeybee hives are needed to pollinate the trees. But California only has 440,000 resident bee hives. There aren't enough California bees to pollinate all those almond trees!

The solution is to import bees from other nearby states. There is, in fact, a ready market for such services, with beekeepers bringing hives from North Dakota, Washington, and Colorado to supplement the native California bees. The almond growers pay well for these services: in 2004, bee pollination services sold for \$54 per hive.

## 35.6 The Tragedy of the Commons

We have argued above that if property rights are well defined, there will be no problem with production externalities. But if property rights are not well defined, the outcome of the economic interactions will undoubtedly involve inefficiencies.

In this section we will examine a particularly well-known inefficiency called "the tragedy of the commons."[5] We will pose this problem in the original context of a common grazing land, although there are many other possible illustrations.

Consider an agricultural village in which the villagers graze their cows on a common field. We want to compare two allocation mechanisms: the first is the private ownership solution where someone owns the field and decides how many cows should graze there; the second is the solution where the field is owned in common by the villagers and access to it is free and unrestricted

Suppose that it costs $a$ dollars to buy a cow. How much milk the cow produces will depend on how many other cows are grazed on the common land. We'll let $f(c)$ be the value of the milk produced if there are $c$ cows grazed on the common. Thus the value of the milk per cow is just the average product, $f(c)/c$.

---

[4] Anna Oberthur, "Almond Growers Face Need for Bees," Associated Press, February 29, 2004.

[5] See G. Hardin, "The Tragedy of the Commons," *Science*, 1968, 1243–47.

How many cows would be grazed on the common if we wanted to maximize the total wealth of the village? In order to maximize the total amount of wealth, we set up the following problem:

$$\max_{c} \ f(c) - ac.$$

It should be clear by now that the maximal production will occur when the marginal product of a cow equals its cost, $a$:

$$MP(c^*) = a.$$

If the marginal product of a cow were greater than $a$, it would pay to put another cow on the commons; and if it were less than $a$, it would pay to take one off.

If the common grazing ground were owned by someone who could restrict access to it, this is indeed the solution that would result. For in this case, the owner of the grazing grounds would purchase just the right amount of cows to maximize his profits.

Now what would happen if the individual villagers decided whether or not to use the common field? Each villager has a choice of grazing a cow or not grazing one, and it will be profitable to graze a cow as long as the output generated by the cow is greater than the cost of a cow. Suppose that there are $c$ cows currently being grazed, so that the current output per cow is $f(c)/c$. When a villager contemplates adding a cow, the total output will be $f(c+1)$, and the total number of cows will be $c+1$. Thus the revenue that the cow generates for the villager will be $f(c+1)/(c+1)$. He must compare this revenue to the cost of the cow, $a$. If $f(c+1)/(c+1) > a$, it is profitable to add the cow since the value of the output exceeds the cost. Hence the villagers will choose to graze cows until the average product of a cow is driven to $a$. It follows that the total number of cows grazed will be $\hat{c}$, where

$$\frac{f(\hat{c})}{\hat{c}} = a.$$

Another way to derive this result is to appeal to free entry. If it is profitable to graze a cow on the common field, villagers will purchase cows. They will stop adding cows to the common only when the profits have been driven to zero, that is, when

$$f(\hat{c}) - a\hat{c} = 0,$$

which is just a rearrangement of the condition in the last paragraph.

When an individual decides whether or not to purchase a cow, he looks at the extra value he will get $f(c)/c$ and compares this to the cost of the cow, $a$. This is fine for him, but what has been left out of this calculation is the fact that his extra cow will reduce the output of milk from all the *other* cows. Since he is ignoring this **social cost** of his purchase, too many cows will be grazed on the common ground. (We assume that each individual has a number of cows that is negligible relative to the total number grazed on the common.)

This argument is illustrated in Figure 35.4. Here we have depicted a falling average product curve, since it is reasonable to suppose that the output per cow declines as more and more cows are grazed on the common land.

**The tragedy of the commons.** If the grazing area is privately owned, the number of cows will be chosen so that the marginal product of a cow equals its cost. But if grazing area is common property, cows will be grazed until the profits are driven to zero; thus the area will be overgrazed.

Figure 35.4

Since the average product is falling, it must be that the marginal product curve always lies below the average product curve. Thus the number of cows where the marginal product equals $a$ must be less than where the average product equals $a$. The field will be overgrazed in the absence of a mechanism to restrict use.

Private property provides such a mechanism. Indeed, we have seen that if everything that people care about is owned by someone who can control its use and, in particular, can exclude others from overusing it, then there are by definition no externalities. The market solution leads to a Pareto efficient outcome. Inefficiencies can only result from situations where there is no way to exclude others from using something, a topic that we will investigate in the next chapter.

Of course, private property is not the only social institution that can encourage efficient use of resources. For example, rules could be formulated about how many cows can be grazed on the village common. If there is a legal system to enforce those rules, this may be a cost-effective solution to providing an efficient use of the common resource. However, in situations where the law is ambiguous or nonexistent, the tragedy of the commons can easily arise. Overfishing in international waters and the extermination of several species of animals due to overhunting are sobering examples of this phenomenon.

## EXAMPLE: Overfishing

According to a report in the *New York Times, "*... overfishing has decimated the stocks of cod, haddock and flounder that have sustained New Englanders for centuries."[6]  According to one expert, fishermen in New England are taking 50 to 70 percent of the available stock, over twice the sustainable amount.

This overfishing is a prime example of the problem of the commons: each fisherman has a negligible impact on the total stock of fish, but the accumulated efforts of thousands of fishermen results in serious depletion. The New England Fisheries Management Council is attempting to alleviate the problem by banning new entry to the industry, requiring fishermen to limit their days at sea, and increasing the mesh size of their nets.

It appears that the supplies of fish could be restocked in as little as 5 years if conservation measures were undertaken. The present value of profits to the industry as a whole would be larger with regulation to prevent overfishing. However, such measures would almost certainly imply a substantial reduction in the number of fishing boats in the industry, which is highly unpopular with the small fishermen, who would likely be forced to leave the industry.

## EXAMPLE: New England Lobsters

Some fishing industries have already applied stringent rules to avoid overfishing. For example, lobster fishermen work under carefully designed rules to ensure that they do not fish themselves out of a livelihood. For example, they are required to toss back any female lobster bearing eggs, any lobster

---

[6] "Plenty of Fish in the Sea? Not Anymore," *New York Times,* March 25, 1992, A15.

shorter than a minimum size, and any lobsters bigger than a maximum size.

The "eggers" give birth to more lobsters and the small "tiddlers" grow up to mate. But why throw back the big lobsters? According to marine biologists, large lobsters produce more offspring and larger offspring. If fishermen always took the largest lobsters, the remaining small lobsters would pass their genes onto their progeny, resulting in smaller and smaller lobsters in each generation.

With lobsters there is good news and bad news. First the good news. The 2003 Maine lobster harvest was 5.4 million pounds, more than 2.5 times the 1945–85 average. This suggests that the careful husbandry practiced by the industry has yielded a significant growth in the lobster population.

However, it appears that conservation isn't the only factor. There have also been considerable changes in the population of other species of marine life off the Maine coast, such as sea urchins, and some observers believe that these changes are the primary driver of change in the lobster population.[7]

This leads to the bad news. Further south, in Massachusetts and New York, the lobster catch has fallen dramatically. No one is quite sure why one region is doing so well and the other so poorly. Ironically, Maine may be doing well due to increased harvesting of finned fish and of sea urchins, both of which eat young lobsters. Massachusetts' problems may be due to specific factors, such as a large oil spill and a disfiguring shell disease. Another culprit is warming water: Narragansett Bay temperatures have risen almost two degrees Celsius in the last 20 years.

Ecologies can be very complex and can change rapidly. The efforts to avoid overfishing are to be applauded, but they are only part of the story.

## 35.7 Automobile Pollution

As suggested above, pollution is a prime example of an economic externality. The activity of one consumer operating an automobile will typically lower the quality of the air that other consumers breathe. It seems unlikely that an unregulated free market would generate the optimal amount of pollution; more likely, if the consumer bears no cost in generating pollution, too much pollution would be produced.

One approach to controlling the amount of automobile pollution is to require that automobiles meet certain standards in the amount of pollution that they generate. This has been the basic thrust of U.S. antipollution policy since the Clean Air Act of 1963. That act, or, more properly, the subsequent amendments, set automobile emission standards for the manufacturers of vehicles in the United States.

---

[7] See *The Economist*, "Claws!" August 19, 2004, and Cornelia Dean, "Lobster Boom and Bust," *New York Times*, August 9, 2004.

Lawrence White has examined the benefits and costs of this program; most of the following discussion is drawn from this work.[8]

White estimates that the cost of emission control equipment is about $600 per car, the extra maintenance costs are about $180 per car, and the costs of the reduced gasoline mileage and the necessity for unleaded gasoline come to about $670 per car. Thus the total cost per car of the emission control standards is about $1450 over the lifetime of the car. (All figures are in 1981 dollars.)

He argues that there are several problems with the current approach to the regulation of automobile emissions. First, it requires that all automobiles meet the same standards. (California is the only state with different standards for emission control.) This means that *everyone* who buys a car must pay an extra $1450 whether they live in a high pollution area or not. A 1974 National Academy of Sciences study concluded that 63 percent of all U.S. cars did not require the stringent standards now in effect. According to White, "almost two-thirds of car buyers are spending ... substantial sums for unnecessary systems."

Secondly, most of the responsibility for meeting the standards falls on the manufacturer, and little falls on the user. Owners of cars have little incentive to keep their pollution control equipment in working order unless they live in a state with required inspections.

More significantly, motorists have no incentive to economize on their driving. In cities such as Los Angeles, where pollution is a significant hazard, it makes good economic sense to encourage people to drive less. Under the current system, people who drive 2000 miles a year in North Dakota pay exactly the same amount for pollution control as people who drive 50,000 miles a year in Los Angeles.

An alternative solution to pollution would be *effluent fees*. As described by White, effluent fees would require an annual inspection of all vehicles along with an odometer reading and tests that would estimate the likely emissions of the vehicle during the past year. Different communities could then levy fees based on the estimated amount of pollution that had actually been generated by the operation of the vehicle. This method would ensure that people would face the true cost of generating pollution and would encourage them to choose to generate the socially optimal amount of pollution.

Such a system of effluent fees would encourage the vehicle owners themselves to find low-cost ways of reducing their emissions—investing in pollution control equipment, changing their driving habits, and changing the kinds of vehicles that they operate. A system of effluent fees could impose even higher standards than are now in effect in communities where pollution is a serious problem. Any desired level of pollution control can

---

[8] See Lawrence White, *The Regulation of Air Pollutant Emissions from Motor Vehicles* (Washington, D.C.: American Enterprise Institute for Public Policy Research, 1982).

be achieved by appropriate effluent fees ... and it can be achieved at a substantially lower cost than the current system of mandated standards.

Of course, there is no reason why there might not also be some federally mandated standards for the two-thirds of the vehicles that are operated in localities where pollution is not a serious problem. If it is cheaper to impose standards than to require inspections, then by all means that should be the proper choice. The appropriate method of pollution control for automobiles should depend on a rational analysis of benefits and costs—as should all social policies of this nature.

## Summary

1. The First Theorem of Welfare Economics shows that a free, competitive market will provide an efficient outcome in the absence of externalities.

2. However, if externalities are present, the outcome of a competitive market is unlikely to be Pareto efficient.

3. However, in this case, the state can sometimes "mimic" the role of the market by using prices to provide correct signals about the social cost of individual actions.

4. More importantly, the legal system can ensure that property rights are well defined, so that efficiency-enhancing trades can be made.

5. If preferences are quasilinear, the efficient amount of a consumption externality will be independent of the assignment of property rights.

6. Cures for production externalities include the use of Pigouvian taxes, setting up a market for the externality, simply allowing firms to merge, or transferring property rights in other ways.

7. The tragedy of the commons refers to the tendency for common property to be overused. This is a particularly prevalent form of externality.

## REVIEW QUESTIONS

1. True or false? An explicit delineation of property rights usually eliminates the problem of externalities.

2. True or false?  The distributional consequences of the delineation of property rights are eliminated when preferences are quasilinear.

3. List some other examples of positive and negative consumption and production externalities.

4. Suppose that the government wants to control the use of the commons, what methods exist for achieving the efficient level of use?

# CHAPTER 36

# INFORMATION TECHNOLOGY

One of the most radical changes in the economy in the last 15 years has been the emergence of the **information economy**. The popular press is filled with stories about advances in computer technology, the Internet, and new software. Not surprisingly, many of these stories are on the business pages of the newspaper, for this *technological* revolution is also an *economic* revolution.

Some observers have gone so far as to put the Information Revolution on a par with the Industrial Revolution. Just as the Industrial Revolution transformed the way *goods* were produced, distributed, and consumed, the Information Revolution is transforming the way *information* is produced, distributed, and consumed.

It has been claimed that these dramatically new technologies will require a fundamentally different form of economics. Bits, it is argued, are fundamentally different than atoms. Bits can be reproduced costlessly and distributed around the world at the speed of light, and they never deteriorate. Material goods, made of atoms, have none of these properties: they are costly to produce and transport, and they inevitably deteriorate.

It is true that the unusual properties of bits require new economic analysis, but I would argue that they do not require a new *kind* of economic analysis. After all, economics is primarily about *people* not *goods*. The models we have analyzed in this book have had to do with how people make choices and interact with each other. We have rarely had occasion to refer to the specific goods that were involved in the transactions. The fundamental concerns were the tastes of the individuals, the technology of production, and the structure of the market, and *these* same factors will determine how markets for information will work ... or not work.

In this chapter we will investigate a few economic models relevant to the information revolution. The first has to do with the economics of networks, the second with switching costs, and the third with rights management for information goods. These examples will illustrate how the fundamental tools of economic analysis can help us to understand the world of bits as well as the world of atoms.

## 36.1 Systems Competition

Information technology is generally used in *systems*. Such systems involve several components, often provided by different firms, that only have value if they work together. Hardware is useless without software, a DVD player is useless without DVD disks, an operating system is worthless without applications, and a web browser is useless without web servers. All of these are examples of **complements**: goods where the value of one component is significantly enhanced by the presence of another component.

In our discussion of consumer theory, we described left shoes and right shoes as complements. The cases above are equally extreme: the best computer hardware in the world can't function unless there is software written for it. But unlike shoes, the more software that is available for it, the more valuable it becomes.

Competition among the providers of these components often have to worry just as much about their "complementors" as their competitors. A key part of Apple's competitive strategy has to involve their relations with software developers. This gives competitive strategy in information technology (IT) industries a different flavor than strategy in traditional industries.[1]

## 36.2 The Problem of Complements

To illustrate these points, let us consider the case of a Central Processing Unit (CPU) and an Operating System (OS). A CPU is an integrated

---

[1] See Shapiro, Carl and Hal R. Varian, *Information Rules: A Strategic Guide to the Network Economy*, Harvard Business School Press, 1998, for a guide to competitive strategy in IT industries.

circuit that is the "brain" of a computer. Two familiar manufacturers of CPUs are Intel and Motorola. An OS is the software that allows users and applications to access the functions of the CPU. Apple and Microsoft both make operating systems. Normally, a special version of an operating system has to be created for each CPU.

From the viewpoint of the end user, the CPU can only be used if there is a compatible operating system. The CPU and the OS are complements, just as left shoes and right shoes are complements.

The most popular CPUs and OSs in the world today are made by Intel and Microsoft, respectively. These are, of course, two separate companies that set the prices of their products independently. The PowerPC, another popular CPU, was designed by a consortium consisting of IBM, Motorola, and Apple. Two commercial operating systems for the PowerPC are the Apple OS and IBM's AIX. In addition to these commercial operating systems, there are free systems like BSD and GNU-Linux that are provided by groups of programmers working on a volunteer basis.

Let us consider the pricing problem facing sellers of complementary products. The critical feature is that the demand for *either* product depends on the price of *both* products. If $p_1$ is the price of the CPU and $p_2$ is the price of the OS, the cost to the end user depends on $p_1 + p_2$. Of course, you need more than just a CPU and an OS to make a useful system, but that just adds more prices to the sum; we'll keep things simple by sticking with two components.

The demand for CPUs depends on the price of the total system, so we write $D(p_1+p_2)$. If we let $c_1$ be the marginal cost of a CPU and $F$ the fixed cost, the profit-maximization problem of the CPU maker can be written

$$\max_{p_1} \ (p_1 - c_1)D(p_1 + p_2) - F_1.$$

Similarly, the profit-maximization problem of the OS maker can be written

$$\max_{p_2} \ (p_2 - c_2)D(p_1 + p_2) - F_2.$$

In order to analyze this problem, let us assume that the demand function has the linear form

$$D(p) = a - bp.$$

Let us also assume, for simplicity, that the marginal costs are so small that they can be ignored. Then the CPU profit-maximization problem becomes

$$\max_{p_1} \ p_1[a - b(p_1 + p_2)] - F_1,$$

or

$$\max_{p_1} \ ap_1 - bp_1^2 - bp_1p_2 - F_1.$$

The first-order condition for profit maximization implies that the change in revenue from an increase in $p_1$ must be zero:

$$a - 2bp_1 - bp_2 = 0.$$

Solving this equation we have

$$p_1 = \frac{a - bp_2}{2b}.$$

In exactly the same way, we can solve for the profit-maximizing choice of the OS price:

$$p_2 = \frac{a - bp_1}{2b}.$$

Note that the optimal choice of each firm's price depends on what it expects the other firm to charge for its component. As usual, we are interested in a **Nash equilibrium**, where each firm's expectations about the other's behavior are satisfied.

Solving the system of two equations in two unknowns, we have

$$p_1 = p_2 = \frac{a}{3b}.$$

This gives us the profit-maximizing prices if each firm unilaterally and independently sets the price of its component of the system. The price of the total system is

$$p_1 + p_2 = \frac{2a}{3b}.$$

Now let us consider the following experiment. Suppose that the two firms merge to form an integrated firm. Instead of setting the prices of the components, the integrated firm sets the price of the final system, which we denote by $p$. Its profit-maximization problem is therefore

$$\max_{p} \; p(a - bp).$$

The marginal revenue from increasing the system price by $\Delta p$ is

$$(a - 2bp)\,\Delta p.$$

Setting this equal to zero and solving, we find that the price that the integrated firm will set for the final system is

$$p = \frac{a}{2b}.$$

Note the following interesting fact: the profit-maximizing price set by the integrated firm is *less* than the profit-maximizing price set by the two independent firms. Since the price of the system is lower, consumers will buy more of them and be better off. Furthermore, the profits of the integrated firm are larger than the sum of the equilibrium profits of the two independent firms. Everyone has been made better off by coordinating the pricing decision!

This turns out to be true in general: a merger of two monopolies that produce complementary products results in lower prices and higher profits than if the two firms set their prices independently.[2]

The intuition is not hard to see. When firm 1 contemplates a price decrease for the CPU, it will increase demand for CPUs *and* OSs. But it only takes into account the impact on its own profit from cutting price, ignoring the profits that will accrue to the other firm. This leads it to cut prices less than it would if it were interested in maximizing joint profit. The same analysis applies to firm 2, leading to prices that are "too high" from the viewpoint of both profit-maximization and consumer surplus.

## Relationships among Complementors

The "merger of complementors" analysis is provocative, but we shouldn't immediately leap to the conclusion that mergers of OS and CPU manufacturers are a good idea. What the result says is that *independent* price setting will lead to prices that are too high from the viewpoint of joint profitability, but there are lots of intermediate cases between totally independent and fully integrated.

For example, one of the firms can negotiate prices for components and then sell an integrated bundle. This is, more or less, what Apple does. They buy PowerPC CPUs in bulk from Motorola, build them into computers, and then bundle the operating system and computers together for sale to the end customers.

Another model for dealing with the systems pricing problem is to use revenue sharing. Boeing builds airplane bodies and GE builds airplane engines. The end user generally wants both a body and an engine. If GE and Boeing each set their prices independently, they could decide to set their prices too high. So what they do instead is to negotiate a deal in which GE will receive a fraction of the revenue from the sale of the assembled aircraft. Then GE is happy to have Boeing negotiate to get as high a price as possible for the package, confident that it will receive its specified share.

There are other mechanisms that work in different industries. Consider, for example, the DVD industry mentioned in the introduction. This has

---

[2]  This rather remarkable fact was discovered by Augustin Cournot, whom we previously met in Chapter 27.

been a very successful new product, but making it work was tricky. Consumer electronics firms didn't want to produce players unless they were assured that there would be plenty of content available, and content providers didn't want to produce content unless they were sure that would be lots of DVD players out there.

On top of this, both the consumer electronics firms and the content producers would have to worry about the pricing of complements problem: if there were only a few providers of players and only a few providers of content, then they would each want to price their products "too high," reducing the total profit available in the industry and making consumers worse off.

Sony and Philips, who held the basic patents on the DVD technology, helped solve this problem by licensing the technology widely at attractive prices. They also realized that there had to be a lot of competition to keep the prices down and kick start the industry. They recognized that it was much better to have a small share of a large, successful industry than to have a large share of a nonexistent industry.

Yet another model for relationships among complementors might be called "commoditize the complement." Look back at firm 1's profit maximization problem:

$$\max_{p_1} p_1 D(p_1 + p_2) - F_1.$$

At any given configuration of prices, reducing $p_1$ may or may not increase firm 1's revenues, depending on the demand elasticity. But lowering $p_2$ will *always* increase firm 1's revenue. The challenge facing firm 1 is then: how can I get firm 2 to cut its price?

One way is to try to make competition for firm 2 more intense. Various strategies are possible here, depending on the nature of the industry. In technology-intensive industries, standardization becomes an important tool. An OS producer, for example, would want to encourage standardized hardware. This not only makes its job easier, but it also ensures that the hardware industry will be highly competitive. This will ensure that competitive forces push down the price of hardware and reduce the total system price to end users, thereby increasing the demand for operating systems.[3]

## EXAMPLE: Apple's iPod and iTunes

Apple's iPod music player is hugely popular. As of February 2010, Apple had sold 10 billion songs, accounting for an estimated 70% of online music sales and an 88% market share in the United States.

---

[3] See Brandenburger, Adam and Barry Nalebuff, *Co-opetition*, Doubleday, 1997 for further analysis of strategy for complementors.

There is an obvious complementary relationship between the music player and the music. The classic business model for complements comes from Gillette: "Give away the razor and sell the blades." But in this case the model is reversed: most of Apple's profit comes from selling the iPod, with only a small fraction coming from selling the music.

This is primarily due to the fact that Apple does not own the music, so the revenue from music sold on iTunes must be shared between the producers of the music and Apple. Since Apple makes most of its money from the player, it wants to have cheap music. Since the studios make most of their money from the songs, they want to have expensive music. This has led to some conflicts between Apple and the music studios.

Originally, all songs on iTunes sold for 99 cents. Some music publishers felt that prices should be higher for new releases. After much back and forth, Apple announced a new policy in March of 2009, where some new releases would sell for $1.29. This is a form of differential pricing, or "versioning," which is common in media markets. Those who are enthused and impatient pay the higher price, while those who are more patient can wait for the price reduction.

## EXAMPLE: Who Makes an iPod?

Hint: it's not Apple. In fact, iPods are assembled in a number of Asian countries, by a variety of assemblers, including Asustek, Inventec Appliances, and Foxconn.

But that's not the end of the story. These companies merely assemble the parts that are purchased from other companies. In 2009, some economists tried to track down the origin of the 451 parts that go into an iPod.[4]

The retail value of the 30-gigabyte video iPod that the authors examined was $299. The most expensive component in it was the hard drive, which was manufactured by Toshiba and costs about $73. The next most costly components were the display module (about $20), the video/multimedia processor chip ($8), and the controller chip ($5). They estimated that the final assembly, done in China, cost only about $4 a unit.

The authors of the report tried to track down where the major parts were manufactured and how much value was added at each stage of the production process. The researchers estimated that $163 of the iPod's $299 retail value in the United States was captured by American companies and workers, breaking it down to $75 for distribution and retail costs, $80 to Apple, and $8 to various domestic component makers. Japan contributed

---

[4] Greg Linden, Kenneth L. Kraemer, and Jason Dedrick, "Who Captures Value in a Global Innovation Network," *Communications of the ACM*, 52 (3), March 2009, 140–144.

about \$26 to the value added (mostly via the Toshiba disk drive), while Korea contributed less than \$1.

Ideally, each component was purchased from the lowest-cost provider, and to a large extent these decisions reflected the comparative advantage of the different providers.

Even though the assembly in China only contributed about 1% of the value of the iPod, each imported iPod contributed about \$150 of the bilateral trade deficit between China and the United States. What this shows is that the bilateral trade deficit makes no sense. Most of the high-value parts in the iPod were in fact imported into China from other countries in the first place. The highest-value component of the iPod—the design and engineering that went into it—came from the United States.

## EXAMPLE: AdWords and AdSense

Two of Google's advertising programs are AdWords, which shows ads targeted to search queries, and AdSense, which shows ads based on the contents of a web page. AdWords shows "search targeted ads" and AdSense shows "contextually targeted ads."

When a user clicks on a contextually targeted ad on a particular site, the advertiser pays a price per click determined by an auction, similar to that described in Chapter 18. The revenue from this ad click is divided between the publisher and Google according to a revenue-sharing formula. Hence the AdSense program provides a simple way for a publisher to generate advertising revenue without having to manage an advertising program on its own.

There is a strong **complementarity** between the AdWords and AdSense programs. By providing a way for publishers to make money from their content, AdSense encourages the production of content. This means that there is more useful information available on the web and therefore content for Google to index and search. By creating a business model for content creation, Google makes its search service more valuable.

## 36.3 Lock-In

Since IT components often work together as systems, switching any one component often involves switching others as well. This means that the **switching costs** associated with one component in IT industries may be quite substantial. For example, switching from a Macintosh to a Windows-based PC involves not only the hardware costs of the computer itself, but also involves purchasing of a whole new library of software, and, even more importantly, learning how to use a brand new system.

When switching costs are very high, users may find themselves experiencing **lock-in**, a situation where the cost of changing to a different system is so high that switching is virtually inconceivable. This is bad for the consumers, but is, of course, quite attractive for the seller of the components that make up the system in question. Since the locked-in user has a very *inelastic* demand, the seller(s) can jack up the prices of their components to extract consumer surplus from the user.

Of course, wary consumers will try to avoid such lock-in, or, at the very least, bargain hard to be compensated for being locked in. Even if the consumers themselves are poor at bargaining, competition among sellers of systems will force prices down for the *initial* purchase, since the locked-in consumers can provide them with a steady revenue stream afterwords.

Consider, for example, choosing an Internet service provider (ISP). Once you have committed to such a choice, it may be inconvenient to switch due to the cost of notifying all of your correspondents about your new e-mail address, reconfiguring your Internet access programs, and so on. The monopoly power due to these switching costs means that the ISP can charge more than the marginal cost of providing service, once it has acquired you as a customer. But the flip side of this effect is that the stream of profits of the locked-in customers is a valuable asset, and ISPs will compete up front to acquire such customers by offering discounts and other inducements to sign up with them.

## A Model of Competition with Switching Costs

Let's examine a model of this phenomenon. We assume that the cost of providing a customer with Internet access is $c$ per month. We also assume a perfectly competitive market, with many identical firms, so that in the absence of any switching costs, the price of Internet service would simply be $p = c$.

But now suppose that there is a cost $s$ of switching ISPs and that ISPs can offer a discount of size $d$ for the first month to attract new customers. At the start of a given month, a consumer contemplates switching to a new ISP. If he does so, he only has to pay the discounted price, $p - d$, but he also has to endure the switching costs $s$. If he stays with his old provider, he has to pay the price $p$ forever. After the first month, we assume that both providers continue to charge the same price $p$ forever.

The consumer will switch if the present value of the payments to the new provider plus the switching cost is less than the present value of the payments to the original ISP. Letting $r$ be the (monthly) interest rate, the consumer will switch if

$$(p - d) + \frac{p}{r} + s < p + \frac{p}{r}.$$

Competition between providers ensures that the consumer is indifferent between switching or not switching, which implies

$$(p - d) + s = p.$$

It follows that $d = s$, which means the discount offered just covers the switching cost of the consumer.

On the producer side, we suppose that competition forces the present value of profits to be zero. The present value of profit associated with a single customer is the price minus the initial discount, plus the present value of the profits in future months. Letting $r$ be the (monthly) interest rate, and using the fact that $d = s$, the zero-profit condition can be written as

$$(p - s) - c + \frac{p - c}{r} = 0. \tag{36.1}$$

Rearranging this equation gives us two equivalent ways to describe the equilibrium price:

$$p - c + \frac{p - c}{r} = s, \tag{36.2}$$

or

$$p = c + \frac{r}{1 + r} s. \tag{36.3}$$

Equation (36.2) says that the present value of the future profits from the consumer must just equal the consumer's switching cost. Equation (36.3) says that the price of service is a markup on marginal cost, where the amount of the markup is proportional to the switching costs.

Adding switching costs to the model raises the *monthly* price of service above cost, but competition for this profit flow forces the *initial* price down. Effectively, the producer is investing in the discount $d = s$ in order to acquire the flow of markups in the future.

In reality many ISPs have other sources of revenue than just the monthly income from their customers. America Online, for example, derives a substantial part of its operating revenue from advertising. It makes sense for them to offer large up-front discounts, in order to capture advertising revenue, even if they have to provide Internet connections at rates at or below cost.

We can easily add this effect to the model. If $a$ is the advertising revenue generated by the consumer each month, the zero-profit condition requires

$$(p - s) + a - c + \frac{p + a - c}{r} = 0. \tag{36.4}$$

Solving for $p$ we have

$$p = c - a + \frac{r}{1 + r} s.$$

This equation shows that what is relevant is the *net* cost of servicing the customer, $c - a$, which involves both the service cost and the advertising revenues.

## EXAMPLE: Online Bill Payment

Many banks offer low-cost or even free bill payment services. Some banks will even pay customers who start using their online bill payment services.

Why the big rush to pay bills online? The answer is that banks have found that once a customer goes to the trouble of setting up the bill-paying service, he or she is much less likely to switch banks. According to a Bank of America study, the frequency of switching goes down by 80 percent for such customers.[5]

It's true that once you get online bill payment up and running, it's hard to give it up. Switching to another bank to get an extra tenth of a percent of interest on your checking account doesn't seem very attractive. As in the analysis of lock-in presented above, investing in services that create switching costs can be very profitable for businesses.

## EXAMPLE: Number Portability on Cell Phones

At one time, cell phone providers prevented individuals from transferring their phone numbers when they switched carriers. This prohibition increases individual switching costs significantly, since anyone who switched would have to notify all of his or her friends about the new number.

As the model presented in this chapter describes, the fact that customers could be charged more when they faced high switching costs meant that the phone providers would compete even more aggressively to sign up such highly profitable customers. This competition took the form of providing low-cost or even free phones, along with offers of "free minutes," "rollover plans," "cell-to-cell discounts," and other marketing gimmicks.

The cell phone industry was united in its efforts to block number portability and lobbied regulatory agencies and Congress to maintain the status quo.

Slowly but surely, the tide started to turn against the cell phone industry as consumers demanded number portability. The Federal Communications Commission, which regulates the telephone business, started dropping hints that cell phone providers should consider ways in which they could implement number portability.

In June 2003, Verizon Wireless said it would drop opposition to number portability. Their decision appeared to rest on two considerations. First, it was becoming clear that they were fighting a losing battle: eventually cell-number portability would win out. Perhaps more significantly, several recent consumer surveys showed that Verizon led the industry in terms of

---

[5] Michelle Higgins, "Banks Use Online Bill Payment In Effort to Lock In Customers," *Wall Street Journal*, September 4, 2002.

customer satisfaction. It appeared quite possible that Verizon would gain more customers than it lost if switching costs were reduced. Indeed, it appears that ultimately Verizon benefited from number portability.

This episode provides a good lesson in business strategy: tactics to increase customer switching costs may be valuable for a while. But ultimately service quality plays a decisive role in attracting and retaining customers.

## 36.4 Network Externalities

We have already examined the idea of **externalities** in Chapter 35. Recall that economists use this term to describe situations in which one person's consumption directly influences another person's utility. **Network externalities** are a special kind of externalities in which one person's utility for a good depends on the *number* of other people who consume this good.[6]

Take for example a consumer's demand for a fax machine. People want fax machines so they can communicate with each other. If no one else has a fax machine, it certainly isn't worthwhile for you to buy one. Modems have a similar property: a modem is only useful if there is another modem somewhere that you can communicate with.

Another more indirect effect for network externalities arises with complementary goods. There is no reason for a video store to locate in a community where no one owns a video player; but then again, there is little reason to buy a video player unless you have access to pre-recorded video tapes to play in the machine. In this case the demand for video tapes depends on the number of VCRs, and the demand for VCRs depends on the number of video tapes available, resulting in a slightly more general form of network externalities.

## 36.5 Markets with Network Externalities

Let us try to model network externalities using a simple demand and supply model. Suppose that there are 1000 people in a market for some good and we index the people by $v = 1, \ldots, 1000$. Think of $v$ as measuring the **reservation price** for the good by person $v$. Then if the price of the good is $p$, the number of people who think that the good is worth at least $p$ is $1000 - p$. For example, if the price of the good is \$200, then there are 800 people who are willing to pay at least \$200 for the good, so the total number of units sold would be 800. This structure generates a standard, downward-sloping demand curve.

---

[6] More generally, a person's utility could depend on the *identity* of other users; it is easy to add this to the analysis.

But now let's add a twist to the model. Suppose that the good we are examining exhibits network externalities, like a fax machine or a telephone. For simplicity, let us suppose that the value of the good to person $v$ is $vn$, where $n$ is the number of people who consume the good—the number of people who are connected to the network. The more people there are who consume the good, the more *each* person is willing to pay to acquire it.[7] What does the demand function look like for this model?

If the price is $p$, there is someone who is just indifferent between buying the good and not buying it. Let $\hat{v}$ denote the index of this marginal individual. By definition, he is just indifferent to purchasing the good, so his willingness to pay for the good equals its price:

$$p = \hat{v}n. \tag{36.5}$$

Since this "marginal person" is indifferent, everyone with a *higher* value of $v$ than $\hat{v}$ must definitely want to buy. This means that the number of people who want to buy the good is

$$n = 1000 - \hat{v}. \tag{36.6}$$

Putting equations (36.5) and (36.6) together, we have a condition that characterizes equilibrium in this market:

$$p = n(1000 - n).$$

This equation gives us a relationship between the price of the good and the number of users. In this sense, it is a kind of demand curve; if there are $n$ people who purchase the good, then the willingness to pay of the marginal individual is given by the height of the curve.

However, if we look at the plot of this curve in Figure 36.1, we see that it has quite a different shape than a standard demand curve! If the number of people who connect is low, then the willingness to pay of the marginal individual is low, because there aren't many other people out there that he can communicate with. If there are a large number of people connected, then the willingness to pay of the marginal individual is low, because everyone else who valued it more highly has already connected. These two forces lead to the humped shape depicted in Figure 36.1.

Now that we understand the demand side of the market, let's look at the supply side. To keep things simple, let us suppose that the good can be provided by a constant returns to scale technology. As we've seen, this means that the supply curve is a flat line at price equals average cost.

Note that there are three possible intersections of the demand and supply curve. There is a low-level equilibrium where $n^* = 0$. This is where no one

---

[7] We should really interpret $n$ as the number of people who are *expected* to consume the good, but this distinction won't be very important for what follows.

Figure
36.1

**Network externalities.** The demand is given by the curved hump, the supply by the horizontal line. Note that there are three intersections where demand equals supply.

consumes the good (connects to the network), so no one is willing to pay anything to consume the good. This might be referred to as a "pessimistic expectations" equilibrium.

The middle equilibrium with a positive but small number of consumers is one where people don't think the network will be very big, so they aren't willing to pay that much to connect to it—and therefore the network isn't very big.

Finally the last equilibrium has a large number of people, $n_H$. Here the price is small because the marginal person who purchases the good doesn't value it very highly, even though the market is very large.

## 36.6 Market Dynamics

Which of the three equilibria will we see occur? So far the model gives us no reason to choose among them. At each of these equilibria, demand equals supply. However, we can add a dynamic adjustment process to help us decide which equilibrium is more likely to occur.

It is plausible to assume that when people are willing to pay more than the cost of the good, the size of the market expands and, when they are willing to pay less, the market contracts. Geometrically this is saying that when the demand curve is above the supply curve, the quantity goes up and, when it is beneath the supply curve, the quantity goes down. The arrows in Figure 36.1 illustrate this adjustment process.

These dynamics give us a little more information. It is now evident that the low-level equilibrium, where no one connects, and the high-level equilibrium, where many people connect, are stable whereas the middle equilibrium is unstable. Hence it is unlikely that the final resting point of the system will be the middle equilibrium.

We are now left with two possible stable equilibria; how can we tell which is likely to occur? One idea is to think about how costs might change over time. For the kinds of examples we have discussed—faxes, VCRs, computer networks, and so on—it is natural to suppose that the cost of the good starts out high and then decreases over time due to technological progress. This process is illustrated in Figure 36.2. At a high unit cost there is only one stable equilibrium—where demand equals zero. When the cost decreases sufficiently, there are two stable equilibria.

**Cost adjustment and network externalities**. When the cost is high, the only equilibrium implies a market of size zero. As the cost goes down, other equilibria become possible.

Figure
36.2

Now add some noise to the system. Think of perturbing the number of people connected to the network around the equilibrium point of $n^* = 0$. These perturbations could be random, or they could be part of business strategies such as initial discounts or other promotions. As the cost gets smaller and smaller, it becomes increasingly likely that one of these perturbations will kick the system up *past* the unstable equilibrium. When this happens, the dynamic adjustment will push the system up to the high-level equilibrium.

A possible path for the number of consumers of the good is depicted in Figure 36.3.

It starts out at essentially zero, with a few small perturbations over time. The cost decreases, and at some point we reach a critical mass that kicks us up past the low-level equilibrium and the system then zooms up to the high-level equilibrium.

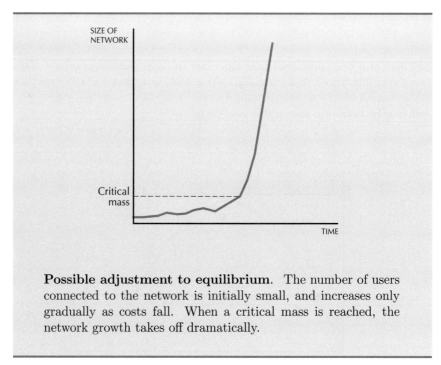

Figure
36.3

**Possible adjustment to equilibrium.** The number of users connected to the network is initially small, and increases only gradually as costs fall. When a critical mass is reached, the network growth takes off dramatically.

A real-life example of this kind of adjustment is the market for fax machines. Figure 36.4 illustrates the price and number of fax machines shipped over a period of 12 years.[8]

## EXAMPLE: Network Externalities in Computer Software

Network externalities arise naturally in the provision of computer software. It is very convenient to be able to exchange data files and tips with other

---

[8] This diagram is taken from "Critical Mass and Network Size with Applications to the US Fax Market," by Nicholas Economides and Charles Himmelberg (Discussion Paper no. EC-95-11, Stern School of Business, N.Y.U., 1995). See also Michael L. Katz and Carl Shapiro, "Systems Competition and Network Effects," *Journal of Economic Perspectives*, 8 (1994), 93–116, for a nice overview of network externalities and their implications.

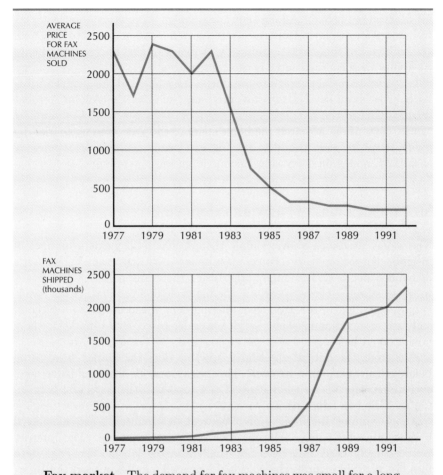

**Fax market**. The demand for fax machines was small for a long time since so few people used them. During the mid-eighties the price fell significantly and the demand suddenly exploded.

Figure
36.4

users of the same software. This gives a significant advantage to the largest seller in a given market and leads software producers to invest heavily in acquiring market share.

Examples of this abound. Adobe Systems for example, invested heavily in developing a "page description language" called PostScript for desktop publishing. Adobe realized clearly that no one would invest the time and resources necessary to learn PostScript unless it was the clear "industry standard." So the firm deliberately allowed competitors to "clone" its language in order to create a competitive market in PostScript interpreters. Adobe's strategy paid off: several competitors emerged (including one that gave its product away) and PostScript became a widely used standard for desktop publishing. Adobe kept a few things proprietary—for instance, techniques for displaying fonts at low resolution—and managed to dominate the high end of the market. Ironically, Adobe's market success was due to its ability to encourage entry by its competitors!

In recent years, many software producers have followed this model. Adobe itself gives away several software products, such as the Adobe Acrobat reader. One of the hot new stock issues of 1995, Netscape Communications Corporation, acquired the lion's share of the Web browser market by giving away its main product, making it a prime example of a company that "lost money on every sale, but made up for it in volume."

## 36.7 Implications of Network Externalities

The model described above, simple though it is, still yields a number of insights. For example, the critical mass issue is very important: if one user's demand depends on how many other users there are, it is very important to try to stimulate growth early in the life cycle of a product. Nowadays it is quite common to see producers offering very cheap access to a piece of software or a communications service in order to "create a market" where none existed before.

Of course, the critical question is how big does the market have to be before it can take off on its own? Theory can provide little guidance here; everything depends on the nature of the good and the costs and benefits the users face in adopting it.

Another important implication of network externalities is the role played by governmental policy. The Internet is a prime example. The Internet was originally used only by a few small research labs to exchange data files. In the mid-eighties the National Science Foundation used the Internet technology to connect several large universities to 12 supercomputers deployed at various locations. The original vision was that researchers at the universities would send data back and forth to the supercomputers. But a fundamental property of communications networks is that if you are all connected to the same thing, you are all connected to each other. This allowed researchers to send email to each other that had nothing to do with the supercomputers. Once a critical mass of users had been connected to the Internet, its value to new users increased dramatically. Most of these new users had no interest in the supercomputer centers, even though this was the original motivation for providing the network.

### EXAMPLE: The Yellow Pages

The familiar local yellow pages phone directories are a $14 billion business.

Ten years ago, it was dominated by telephone companies, who had about 95 percent of the market. Nowadays, they have only 85 percent.

The difference is due to competition. Several small upstarts entered the market in recent years, taking business away from the local phone companies. This is no easy task, as the local business directories exhibit a classic form of network effects: it used to be that consumers all used the yellow page directory provided by their local phone companies, so local merchants were forced to advertise in them.

One upstart, Yellow Book, managed to overcome the network effects by using clever business strategies, such as dramatically undercutting the phone companies' ad rates and distributing its directory just before the local phone company's directory came out. The incumbent providers, thinking that their market was secure, dismissed the threat of aggressive newcomers until it was nearly too late. In the last few years, competition has heated up in this industry. This example goes to show that even industries with strong network effects aren't immune to competitive forces, particularly when the incumbents become overconfident.

## EXAMPLE: Radio Ads

The "killer app" for radio in 1910 was ship-to-shore communication. Unfortunately, radio conversations were not private since they were broadcast to anyone who tuned into the right frequency. At some point David Sarnoff recognized that this bug might be a feature and offered a "radio music box" that sent music over the airwaves. His colleagues were skeptical, saying, "The wireless music box has no imaginable commercial value. Who would pay for a message sent to nobody in particular?"

They had a point. Even though people found broadcast radio attractive, the industry did not have a business model. How would they make money?

The magazine *Wireless World* held a contest in which it proposed 5 business models for broadcast radio and people voted for their favorite. The business models were:

- support from general taxation;

- donations from the public;

- radio hardware makers subsidized the production of radio content;

- advertising-supported radio;

- vacuum tube tax used to support content production.

The winner was the last model: a tax on vacuum tubes. Some of the other models are still used today. BBC Radio and TV is supported by a tax on TVs, and National Public Radio in the United States is supported by donations from the public at large. However, in most countries advertising has become the most popular business model.

In 1922, 30 radio stations were in operation in the United States, and a hundred thousand radios were sold. By the next year there were 556 stations with half-a-million receivers being sold. Radio was on its way.

## 36.8 Two-sided Markets

A **two-sided market** is a special kind of network effect. Think about the case of a new technology, like Blu-ray DVDs. I don't really care what sort of DVD player other people have, so there is no direct network effect. But there is a kind of *indirect* network effect: the more Blu-ray players that are sold, the more disks that will become available, and the more disks there are available, the more attractive it will be to buy a Blu-ray player.

One can think of many other examples. Consider a new credit card: the more merchants accept the credit card, the more attractive the credit card will be to consumers. But the more consumers who adopt the card, the more attractive it will be to merchants.

Or think about Adobe's PDF platform. The more users who have the PDF-viewing software (Acrobat Reader) the more graphics designers will want to distribute content in this format, and the more demand there will be for the Acrobat Distiller, the software used to create PDF files.

This last example illustrates an important point: it may pay Adobe to give away one product (Reader) in order to encourage demand for another product (Distiller). This is as old as "giving away the razor to sell the blades," but since the combination of digital goods and the Internet has made distribution so cheap, the strategy has become very common.

Apple, for example, sells the popular iPod music player. They also distribute music for the iPod on their iTunes store. According to industry reports, Apple makes very little money on the music—most of the profits go to the music studios. However, from Apple's point of view it makes sense to give away the blades (songs) to sell the razors (iPods).

### A Model of Two-sided Markets

Let us generalize the model used in section 34.5 to apply to two-sided markets.

Suppose now that there are two goods. The reservation price for good 1 is $v_1$ and it takes on values $v_1 = 1, \ldots, 1000$. Similarly the reservation price for good 2 takes on values $v_2 = 1, \ldots, 1000$.

The total value for good 1 depends on how many people adopt good 2, and the total value for good 2 depends on how many people adopt good 1, so we write $U_1 = v_1 n_2$ and $U_2 = v_2 n_1$. Finally, there are some exogenous prices for supplying good 1 and good 2, which we denote by $p_1$ and $p_2$. (You can think of these as costs from a constant-returns to scale production process.)

The marginal adopters for goods 1 and 2 are determined by $\hat{v}_1 n_2 = p_1$ and $\hat{v}_2 n_1 = p_2$. Everybody who has a value higher than $\hat{v}_1$ will purchase good 1, so $n_1 = 1000 - \hat{v}_1$. Similarly, $n_2 = 1000 - \hat{v}_2$.

Putting all these equations together we have

$$\hat{v}_1 n_2 = p_1$$
$$\hat{v}_2 n_1 = p_2$$
$$n_1 = 1000 - \hat{v}_1$$
$$n_2 = 1000 - \hat{v}_2$$

Substituting from equations (3) and (4) into (1) and (2) we find

$$(1000 - n_1)n_2 = p_1$$
$$(1000 - n_2)n_1 = p_2$$

The first thing we observe is that there is always an equilibrium at $n_1 = n_2 = 0$. If no one purchases good 1, the value of good 2 will be zero and vice versa. To find the other solutions, we plot the two functions. As you might guess, generally there will be two solutions as depicted in the example in Figure 36.5. There is a low-level equilibrium where little is sold of either good and a high-level equilibrium where there are substantial sales of both goods.

The challenge facing a supplier is how to get to the high-level equilibrium. One strategy, mentioned above, is to subsidize the production of one of the goods. Selling one good below cost can make sense if it leads to a larger market and more profits for other goods you sell.

## 36.9 Rights Management

There is much interest these days in new business models for intellectual property (IP). IP transactions take a variety of forms: books are sold outright and also borrowed from libraries. Videos can either be sold or rented. Some software is licensed for particular uses; other software is sold outright. Shareware is a form of software in which payment is voluntary.

Choosing the terms and conditions under which a piece of intellectual property is offered is a critical business decision. Should you use copy protection? Should you encourage users to share a news item with a friend? Should you sell to individuals or use site license?

Some simple economics helps to understand the relevant issues. Let's consider a purely digital good, such as an online newspaper, so we don't

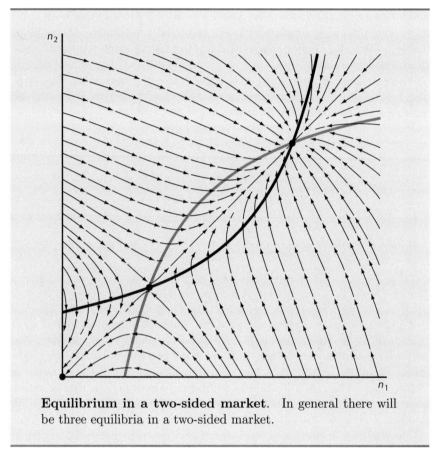

Figure
36.5

**Equilibrium in a two-sided market.** In general there will
be three equilibria in a two-sided market.

have to worry about marginal cost of production. First let us consider
behavior under some default set of terms and conditions. The owner of the
digital good will choose a price and, implicitly, a quantity to sell so as to
maximize profit:

$$\max_{y} \; p(y)y \qquad (36.7)$$

This yields some optimal $(p^*, y^*)$.

Now the seller of the good contemplates liberalizing terms and conditions:
let's say extending a trial period of free use from 1 week to 1 month. This
has two effects on the demand curve. First, it increases the value of the
product to each of the potential users, shifting the demand curve up. But
it also may easily result in less of the item being sold, since some users will
find the longer trial period enough to meet their needs.

Let us model this by defining the new amount consumed by $Y = by$,
where $b > 1$, and the new demand curve by $P(Y) = ap(Y)$, where $a > 1$.

The new profit-maximization problem now becomes

$$\max_{Y} \; P(Y)y.$$

Note that we multiply price times the amount sold, $y$, not the amount consumed, $Y$.

Applying the definitions $Y = by$ and $P(Y) = ap(Y)$, we can write this as

$$\max_{Y} \; ap(Y)\frac{Y}{b} = \max_{Y} \; \frac{a}{b}p(Y)Y.$$

This maximization problem looks like problem (36.7) except for the constant $a/b$ in front of the max. This will not affect the optimal choice, so we can conclude that $Y^* = y^*$.

This simple analysis allows us to make several conclusions:

- The amount of the good consumed, $Y^*$, is independent of the terms and conditions.

- The amount of the good produced is $y^*/b$ which is less than $y^*$.

- The profits could go up or down depending on whether $a/b$ is greater or less than 1. Profits go up if the increase in value to the consumers who buy the product compensates for the reduced number of buyers.

## EXAMPLE: Video Rental

Video stores can choose the terms and conditions under which they rent videos. The longer you can keep the video, the more valuable it is to you, since you have a longer period of time during which you can watch it. But the longer you keep the video, the less profit the store makes from it, since it is unable to rent it to someone else. The optimal choice for the rental period involves trading off these two effects.

In practice, this has tended to lead to a form of product differentiation. New releases are rented for short periods, since the the the profits from other renters being excluded are very substantial. Older videos are rented for longer periods, since there is less cost to the store from the video being unavailable.

## 36.10 Sharing Intellectual Property

Intellectual property is often shared. Libraries, for example, facilitate the sharing of books. Video stores help people to "share" videos—and charge a price for doing so. Interlibrary loan helps libraries share books among themselves. Even textbooks—such as the one you are holding—are shared among students from one term to the next via the resale market.

There is considerable debate in the publishing and library communities about the proper role of sharing. Librarians have established an informal "rule of five" for interlibrary loan: an item may be loaned out up to five times before additional royalty payments should be made to the publisher. Publishers and authors have traditionally been unenthusiastic about the resale market for books.

The advent of digital information has made this situation even more acute. Digital information can be perfectly reproduced, and "sharing" can be taken to new extremes. Recently, a well-known country music singer engaged in a vociferous public relations campaign against stores selling used CDs. The problem was that CDs do not deteriorate with replay and it is possible to buy a CD, tape it, and then sell the CD to the used-CD store.

Let us try to construct a model of this sort of sharing phenomenon. We begin with the baseline case in which there is no sharing. In this case a video maker chooses to produce $y$ copies of a video to maximize profit:

$$\max_{y} \ p(y)y - cy - F. \tag{36.8}$$

As usual, $p(y)$ is the inverse demand function, $c$ is the (constant) marginal cost, and $F$ is the fixed cost. Let the profit maximizing output be denoted by $y_n$, where the $n$ stands for "no sharing."

Now suppose that a video rental market is allowed. In this case the number of videos *viewed* will be distinct from the number of copies produced. If $y$ is the number of videos produced and each video is shared among $k$ viewers, then the number of viewings will be $x = ky$. (For simplicity we are assuming that *all* copies of the video are rented in this case.)

We need to specify how the consumers sort themselves into the "clubs" that share the videos. The simplest assumption is that the consumers with high values associate with each other, and the consumers with low-values associate with each other. That is, one club consists of consumers with the $k$ highest values, another club consists of the consumers with the next $k$ highest values, and so on. (Other assumptions could be used, but this one gives a very simple analysis.)

If $y$ copies of the video are produced, $x = ky$ copies will be viewed, so the willingness to pay of the marginal individual will be $p(x) = p(ky)$. However, it is clearly the case that there is some inconvenience cost to renting a video rather than owning it yourself. Let us denote this "transactions cost" by $t$, so that the willingness to pay of the marginal individual becomes $p(x) - t$.

Recall that we have assumed that all copies of the video are shared among $k$ users. Therefore the willingness to pay of a *video store* will just be $k$ times the willingness to pay of the marginal individual. That is, if $y$

copies are produced, the willingness to pay of the video store will be

$$P(y) = k[p(ky) - t].  \tag{36.9}$$

Equation (36.9) contains the two key effects that arise from sharing: the willingness to pay goes *down* since more videos are viewed than are produced; but the willingness to pay also goes *up* since the cost of a single video is shared among several individuals.

The profit maximization problem of the producer now becomes

$$\max_{y} \ P(y)y - cy - F,$$

which can be written as

$$\max_{y} \ k[p(ky) - t]y - cy - F,$$

or

$$\max_{y} \ p(ky)ky - \left(\frac{c}{k} + t\right)ky - F.$$

Recalling that the number of viewings, $x$, is related to the number produced, $y$, via $x = ky$, we can also write the maximization problem as

$$\max_{x} \ p(x)x - \left(\frac{c}{k} + t\right)x - F.$$

Note that this problem is identical to problem (36.8), with the exception that the marginal cost is now $(c/k + t)$ rather than $c$.

The close relationship between the two problems is very useful since it allows us to make the following observation: *profits will be larger when rental is possible than when it is not if and only if*

$$\frac{c}{k} + t < c.$$

Rearranging this condition, we have

$$\left(\frac{k}{k+1}\right)t < c.$$

For large $k$, the fraction on the left is about 1. Hence the critical issue is the relationship between the marginal cost of production, $c$, and the transactions cost of renting, $t$.

If the cost of production is large and the cost of renting is small, then the most profitable thing for a producer to do is to produce a few copies, sell them at a high price, and let the consumers rent. On the other hand, if the transactions cost of renting is larger than the cost of production, it is more profitable for a producer to have renting prohibited: since renting is so inconvenient for the consumers, video stores aren't willing to pay much more for the "shared" videos, and so the producer is better off selling.

## EXAMPLE: Online Two-sided Markets

There are several examples of two-sided markets on the Internet. For example, eBay serves as a meeting place for those who wish to buy and sell collectibles. If you are selling rare coins, for example, you want to offer them on a market where there are many potential buyers. Similarly, if you are a buyer, you want to go to a market where there are several competing sellers. This two-sided network effect tends to lead to a single meeting place. In the last several years, eBay has expanded beyond collectibles and now sells a variety of merchandise.

Another set of interesting examples are social networking sites, such as Facebook, MySpace, LinkedIn, and others. Participants want to register on sites where their friends have registered. This again leads to a network effect—the largest network attracts the most new participants.

Facebook has seen particularly rapid growth. It was launched in February of 2004 and by December of that year had 1 million active users. In September of 2009, Facebook had over 300 million active users worldwide, according to statistics from its website.

## Summary

1. Because information technology works together in systems, it is costly to consumers to switch any one component.

2. If two monopoly providers of complementary products coordinate their price setting, then they will both set their prices lower than they would than if they set them independently.

3. This will increase profit for the two monopolists *and* make consumers better off.

4. There are many ways to achieve this coordination, including merger, negotiation, revenue sharing, and commoditization.

5. In a lock-in equilibrium the discount offered first period is paid for by increased prices in future periods.

6. Network externalities arise when one person's willingness to pay for a good depends on the number of other users of that good.

7. Models with network externalities typically exhibit multiple equilibria. The ultimate outcome often depends on the history of the industry.

8. Rights management involves a tradeoff between increased value and prices versus reduced sales.

9. Information goods like books and videos are often rented or shared as well as purchased. Rental or purchase can be more profitable depending on how transactions costs compare with production costs.

## REVIEW QUESTIONS

1. If the cost to a customer from switching long-distance carriers is on the order of $50, how much should a long-distance carrier be willing to pay to acquire a new customer?

2. Describe how the demand for a word processing package might exhibit network externalities.

3. Suppose that the marginal cost of producing an extra video is zero and the transactions cost of renting a video is zero. Does a producer make more money by selling the video or by renting it?

# CHAPTER 37

# PUBLIC GOODS

In Chapter 35 we argued that for certain kinds of externalities, it was not difficult to eliminate the inefficiencies. In the case of a consumption externality between two people, for example, all one had to do was to ensure that initial property rights were clearly specified. People could then trade the right to generate the externality in the normal way. In the case of production externalities, the market itself provided profit signals to sort out the property rights in the most efficient way. In the case of common property, assigning property rights to someone would eliminate the inefficiency.

Unfortunately, not all externalities can be handled in that manner. As soon as there are more than two economic agents involved things become much more difficult. Suppose, for example, that instead of the two roommates examined in the last chapter, we had *three* roommates—one smoker and two nonsmokers. Then the amount of smoke would be a negative externality for both of the nonsmokers.

Let's suppose that property rights are well defined—say the nonsmokers have the right to demand clean air. Just as before, although they have the *right* to clean air, they also have the right to trade some of that clean air away in return for appropriate compensation. But now there is a problem involved—the nonsmokers have to agree among themselves how much smoke should be allowed and what the compensation should be.

Perhaps one of the nonsmokers is much more sensitive than the other, or one of them is much richer than the other. They may have very different preferences and resources, and yet they both have to reach some kind of agreement to allow for an efficient allocation of smoke.

Instead of roommates, we can think of inhabitants of a whole country. How much pollution should be allowed in the country? If you think that reaching an agreement is difficult with only three roommates, imagine what it is like with millions of people!

The smoke externality with three people is an example of a **public good**—a good that must be provided in the same amount to all the affected consumers. In this case the amount of smoke generated will be the same for all consumers—each person may value it differently, but they all have to face the same amount.

Many public goods are provided by the government. For example, streets and sidewalks are provided by local municipalities. There are a certain number and quality of streets in a town, and everyone has that number available to use. National defense is another good example; there is one level of national defense provided for all the inhabitants of a country. Each citizen may value it differently—some may want more, some may want less—but they are all provided with the same amount.

Public goods are an example of a particular kind of consumption externality: everyone must consume the same amount of the good. They are a particularly troublesome kind of externality, for the decentralized market solutions that economists are fond of don't work very well in allocating public goods. People can't purchase different amounts of public defense; somehow they have to decide on a common amount.

The first issue to examine is what the ideal amount of the public good should be. Then we'll discuss some ways that might be used to make social decisions about public goods.

## 37.1 When to Provide a Public Good?

Let us start with a simple example. Suppose that there are two roommates, 1 and 2. They are trying to decide whether or not to purchase a TV. Given the size of their apartment, the TV will necessarily go in the living room, and both roommates will be able to watch it. Thus it will be a public good, rather than a private good. The question is, is it worth it for them to acquire the TV?

Let's use $w_1$ and $w_2$ to denote each person's initial wealth, $g_1$ and $g_2$ to denote each person's contribution to the TV, and $x_1$ and $x_2$ to denote each person's money left over to spend on private consumption. The budget constraints are given by

$$x_1 + g_1 = w_1$$
$$x_2 + g_2 = w_2.$$

We also suppose that the TV costs $c$ dollars, so that in order to purchase it, the sum of the two contributions must be at least $c$:

$$g_1 + g_2 \geq c.$$

This equation summarizes the technology available to provide the public good: the roommates can acquire one TV if together they pay the cost $c$.

The utility function of person 1 will depend on his or her private consumption, $x_1$, and the availability of the TV—the public good. We'll write person 1's utility function as $u_1(x_1, G)$, where $G$ will either be 0, indicating no TV, or 1, indicating that a TV is present. Person 2 will have utility function $u_2(x_2, G)$. Each person's private consumption has a subscript to indicate that the good is consumed by person 1 or person 2, but the public good has no subscript. It is "consumed" by both people. Of course, it isn't really consumed in the sense of being "used up"; rather, it is the *services* of the TV that are consumed by the two roommates.

The roommates may value the services of the TV quite differently. We can measure the value that each person places on the TV by asking how much each person would be willing to pay to have the TV available. To do this, we'll use the concept of the **reservation price**, introduced in Chapter 15.

The reservation price of person 1 is the maximum amount that person 1 would be willing to pay to have the TV present. That is, it is that price, $r_1$, such that person 1 is just indifferent between paying $r_1$ and having the TV available, and not having the TV at all. If person 1 pays the reservation price and gets the TV, he will have $w_1 - r_1$ available for private consumption. If he doesn't get the TV, he will have $w_1$ available for private consumption. If he is to be just indifferent between these two alternatives, we must have

$$u_1(w_1 - r_1, 1) = u_1(w_1, 0).$$

This equation defines the reservation price for person 1—the maximum amount that he would be willing to pay to have the TV present. A similar equation defines the reservation price for person 2. Note that in general the reservation price of each person will depend on that person's wealth: the maximum amount that an individual will be *willing* to pay will depend to some degree on how much that individual is *able* to pay.

Recall that an allocation is Pareto efficient if there is no way to make both people better off. An allocation is Pareto *inefficient* if there *is* some way to make both people better off; in this case, we say that a **Pareto improvement** is possible. In the TV problem there are only two sorts of allocations that are of interest. One is an allocation where the TV is not provided. This allocation takes the simple form $(w_1, w_2, 0)$; that is, each person spends his wealth only on his private consumption.

The other kind of allocation is the one where the public good is provided. This will be an allocation of the form $(x_1, x_2, 1)$, where

$$x_1 = w_1 - g_1$$

$$x_2 = w_2 - g_2.$$

These two equations come from rewriting the budget constraints. They say that each individual's private consumption is determined by the wealth that he has left over after making his contribution to the public good.

Under what conditions should the TV be provided? That is, when is there a payment scheme $(g_1, g_2)$ such that both people will be better off having the TV and paying their share than not having the TV? In the language of economics, when will it be a Pareto improvement to provide the TV?

It will be a Pareto improvement to provide the allocation $(x_1, x_2, 1)$ if both people would be better off having the TV provided than not having it provided. This means

$$u_1(w_1, 0) < u_1(x_1, 1)$$
$$u_2(w_2, 0) < u_2(x_2, 1).$$

Now use the definition of the reservation prices $r_1$ and $r_2$ and the budget constraint to write

$$u_1(w_1 - r_1, 1) = u_1(w_1, 0) < u_1(x_1, 1) = u_1(w_1 - g_1, 1)$$
$$u_2(w_2 - r_2, 1) = u_2(w_2, 0) < u_2(x_2, 1) = u_2(w_2 - g_2, 1).$$

Looking at the left- and the right-hand sides of these inequalities, and remembering that more private consumption must increase utility, we can conclude that

$$w_1 - r_1 < w_1 - g_1$$
$$w_2 - r_2 < w_2 - g_2,$$

which in turn implies

$$r_1 > g_1$$
$$r_2 > g_2.$$

This is a condition that must be satisfied if an allocation $(w_1, w_2, 0)$ is Pareto inefficient: it must be that the contribution that each person is making to the TV is less than his willingness to pay for the TV. If a consumer can acquire the good for less than the maximum that he would be willing to pay, then the acquisition would be to his benefit. Thus the condition that the reservation price exceeds the cost share simply says that a Pareto improvement will result when each roommate can acquire the services of the TV for less than the maximum that he would be willing to pay for it. This is clearly a *necessary* condition for purchase of the TV to be a Pareto improvement.

If each roommate's willingness to pay exceeds his cost share, then the *sum* of the willingnesses to pay must be greater than the cost of the TV:

$$r_1 + r_2 > g_1 + g_2 = c. \tag{37.1}$$

This condition is a *sufficient* condition for it to be a Pareto improvement to provide the TV. If the condition is satisfied, then there will be some payment plan such that both people will be made better off by providing the public good. If $r_1 + r_2 \geq c$, then the total amount that the roommates will be willing to pay is at least as large as the cost of purchase, so they can easily find a payment plan $(g_1, g_2)$ such that $r_1 \geq g_1$, $r_2 \geq g_2$, and $g_1 + g_2 = c$. This condition is so simple that you might wonder why we went through all the detail in deriving it. Well, there are a few subtleties involved.

First, it is important to note that the condition describing when provision of the public good will be a Pareto improvement only depends on each agent's *willingness* to pay and on the total cost. If the sum of the reservation prices exceeds the cost of the TV, then there will always *exist* a payment scheme such that both people will be better off having the public good than not having it.

Second, whether or not it is Pareto efficient to provide the public good will, in general, depend on the initial distribution of wealth $(w_1, w_2)$. This is true because, in general, the reservation prices $r_1$ and $r_2$ will depend on the distribution of wealth. It perfectly possible that for some distributions of wealth $r_1 + r_2 > c$, and for other distributions of wealth $r_1 + r_2 < c$.

To see how this can be, imagine a situation where one roommate really loves the TV and the other roommate is nearly indifferent about acquiring it. Then if the TV-loving roommate had all of the wealth, he would be willing to pay more than the cost of the TV all by himself. Thus it would be a Pareto improvement to provide the TV. But if the indifferent roommate had all of the wealth, then the TV lover wouldn't have much money to contribute toward the TV, and it would be Pareto efficient *not* to provide the TV.

Thus, in general, whether or not the public good should be provided will depend on the distribution of wealth. But in specific cases the provision of the public good may be independent of the distribution of wealth. For example, suppose that the preferences of the two roommates were quasilinear. This means that the utility functions take the form

$$u_1(x_1, G) = x_1 + v_1(G)$$
$$u_2(x_2, G) = x_2 + v_2(G),$$

where $G$ will be 0 or 1, depending on whether or not the public good is available. For simplicity, suppose that $v_1(0) = v_2(0) = 0$. This says that no TV provides zero utility from watching TV.[1]

In this case the definitions of the reservation prices become

$$u_1(w_1 - r_1, 1) = w_1 - r_1 + v_1(1) = u_1(w_1, 0) = w_1$$
$$u_2(w_2 - r_2, 1) = w_2 - r_2 + v_2(1) = u_2(w_2, 0) = w_2,$$

[1] Perhaps watching TV should be assigned a negative utility.

which implies that the reservation prices are given by

$$r_1 = v_1(1)$$
$$r_2 = v_2(1).$$

Thus the reservation prices are independent of the amount of wealth, and hence the optimal provision of the public good will be independent of wealth, at least over some range of wealths.[2]

## 37.2 Private Provision of the Public Good

We have seen above that acquiring the TV will be Pareto efficient for the two roommates if the sum of their willingnesses to pay exceeds the cost of providing the public good. This answers the question about efficient allocation of the good, but it does not necessarily follow that they will actually decide to acquire the TV. Whether they actually decide to acquire the TV depends on the particular method they adopt to make joint decisions.

If the two roommates cooperate and truthfully reveal how much they value the TV, then it should not be difficult for them to agree on whether or not they should buy the TV. But under some circumstances, they may not have incentives to tell the truth about their values.

For example, suppose that each person valued the TV equally, and that each person's reservation price was greater than the cost, so that $r_1 > c$ and $r_2 > c$. Then person 1 might think that if he said he had 0 value for the TV, the other person would acquire it anyway. But person 2 could reason the same way! One can imagine other situations where both people would refuse to contribute in the hopes that the other person would go out and unilaterally purchase the TV.

In this kind of situation, economists say that the people are attempting to **free ride** on each other: each person hopes that the other person will purchase the public good on his own. Since each person will have full use of the services of the TV if it is acquired, each person has an incentive to try to pay as little as possible toward the provision of the TV.

## 37.3 Free Riding

Free riding is similar, but not identical, to the prisoner's dilemma that we examined in Chapter 29. To see this, let us construct a numerical example of the TV problem described above. Suppose that each person has a wealth of $500, that each person values the TV at $100, and that the cost of the

---

[2] Even this will only be true for some ranges of wealth, since we must always require that $r_1 \leq w_1$ and $r_2 \leq w_2$—i.e., the willingness to pay is less than the ability to pay.

TV is $150. Since the sum of the reservation prices exceeds the cost, it is Pareto efficient to buy the TV.

Let us suppose that there is no way for one of the roommates to exclude the other one from watching the TV and that each roommate will decide independently whether or not to buy the TV. Consider the decision of one of the roommates, Player A. If he buys the TV, he gets benefits of $100 and pays a cost of $150, leaving him with net benefits of −50. However, if Player A buys the TV, Player B gets to watch it for free, which gives B a benefit of $100. The payoffs to the game are depicted in Table 37.1.

<table>
<tr><td rowspan="2">Table 37.1</td><td colspan="3">Free riding game matrix.</td></tr>
</table>

|  |  | Player B | |
|---|---|---|---|
|  |  | Buy | Don't buy |
| **Player A** | Buy | −50, −50 | −50, 100 |
|  | Don't buy | 100, −50 | 0, 0 |

The dominant strategy equilibrium for this game is for neither player to buy the TV. If player A decides to buy the TV, then it is in player B's interest to free ride: to watch the TV but not contribute anything to paying for it. If player A decides not to buy, then it is in player B's interest not to buy the TV either. This is similar to the prisoners' dilemma, but not exactly the same. In the prisoners' dilemma, the strategy that maximizes the sum of the players' utilities is for each player to make the *same* choice. Here the strategy that maximizes the sum of the utilities is for just one of the players to buy the TV (and both players to watch it).

If Player A buys the TV and both players watch it, we can construct a Pareto improvement simply by having Player B make a "sidepayment" to Player A. For example, if Player B gives Player A $51, then both players will be made better off when Player A buys the TV. More generally, any payment between $50 and $100 will result in a Pareto improvement for this example.

In fact, this is probably what would happen in practice: each player would contribute some fraction of the cost of the TV. This public goods problem is relatively easy to solve, but more difficult free riding problems can arise in the sharing of other household public goods. For example, what about cleaning the living room? Each person may prefer to see the living room clean and is willing to do his part. But each may also be tempted to free ride on the other—so that neither one ends up cleaning the room, with the usual untidy results.

The situation becomes even worse if there are more than just two people involved—since there are more people on whom to free ride! Letting the other guy do it may be optimal from an *individual* point of view, but it is Pareto inefficient from the viewpoint of society as a whole.

## 37.4 Different Levels of the Public Good

In the above example, we had an either/or decision: either provide the TV or not. But the same kind of phenomena occurs when there is a choice of *how much* of the public good to provide. Suppose, for example, that the two roommates have to decide how much money to spend on the TV. The more money they decide to spend, the better the TV they can get.

As before we'll let $x_1$ and $x_2$ measure the private consumption of each person and $g_1$ and $g_2$ be their contributions to the TV. Let $G$ now measure the "quality" of the TV they buy, and let the cost function for quality be given by $c(G)$. This means that if the two roommates want to purchase a TV of quality $G$, they have to spend $c(G)$ dollars to do so.

The constraint facing the roommates is that the total amount that they spend on their public and private consumption has to add up to how much money they have:

$$x_1 + x_2 + c(G) = w_1 + w_2.$$

A Pareto efficient allocation is one where consumer 1 is as well-off as possible given consumer 2's level of utility. If we fix the utility of consumer 2 at $\bar{u}_2$, we can write this problem as

$$\max_{x_1,x_2,G} u_1(x_1,G)$$

$$\text{such that } u_2(x_2,G) = \bar{u}_2$$

$$x_1 + x_2 + c(G) = w_1 + w_2.$$

To solve this maximization problem, we set up the Lagrangian:

$$L = u_1(x_1,G) - \lambda[u_2(x_2,G) - \bar{u}_2] - \mu[x_1 + x_2 + c(G) - w_1 - w_2]$$

and differentiate with respect to $x_1$, $x_2$, and $G$ to get

$$\frac{\partial L}{\partial x_1} = \frac{\partial u_1(x_1,G)}{\partial x_1} - \mu = 0$$

$$\frac{\partial L}{\partial x_2} = -\lambda \frac{\partial u_2(x_2,G)}{\partial x_2} - \mu = 0$$

$$\frac{\partial L}{\partial G} = \frac{\partial u_1(x_1,G)}{\partial G} - \lambda \frac{\partial u_2(x_2,G)}{\partial G} - \mu \frac{\partial c(G)}{\partial G} = 0.$$

If we divide the third equation by $\mu$ and rearrange, we get

$$\frac{1}{\mu}\frac{\partial u_1(x_1,G)}{\partial G} - \frac{\lambda}{\mu}\frac{\partial u_2(x_2,G)}{\partial G} = \frac{\partial c(G)}{\partial G}. \qquad (37.2)$$

Now solve the first equation for $\mu$ to get

$$\mu = \frac{\partial u_1(x_1,G)}{\partial x_1},$$

and solve the second equation for $\mu/\lambda$ to get

$$\frac{\mu}{\lambda} = -\frac{\partial u_2(x_2,G)}{\partial x_2}.$$

Substitute these two equations into equation (37.2) to find

$$\frac{\partial u_1(x_1,G)/\partial G}{\partial u_1(x_1,G)/\partial x_1} + \frac{\partial u_2(x_2,G)/\partial G}{\partial u_2(x_2,G)/\partial x_2} = \frac{\partial c(G)}{\partial G},$$

which implies that the appropriate optimality condition for this problem is that the *sum* of the absolute values of the marginal rates of substitution between the private good and the public good for the two consumers equals the marginal cost of providing an extra unit of the public good:

$$|MRS_1| + |MRS_2| = MC(G).$$

In order to see why this must be the right efficiency condition, let us apply the usual trick and think about what would be the case if it were violated. Suppose, for example, that the sum of the marginal rates of substitution were less than the marginal cost: say $MC = 1$, $|MRS_1| = 1/4$, and $|MRS_2| = 1/2$. We need to show that there is some way to make both people better off.

Given his marginal rate of substitution, we know that person 1 would be willing to accept $1/4$ more dollars of the private good for the loss of 1 dollar of the public good (since both goods cost \$1 per unit). Similarly, person 2 would accept $1/2$ more dollars of the private good for a 1-dollar decrease in the public good. Suppose we reduce the amount of the public good and offer to compensate both individuals. When we reduce the public good by one unit we save a dollar. After we pay each individual the amount he requires to allow this change ($3/4 = 1/4 + 1/2$), we find that we still have $1/4$ of a dollar left over. This remaining money could be shared between the two individuals, thereby making them both better off.

Similarly, if the sum of the marginal rates of substitution were greater than 1, we could increase the amount of the public good to make them both better off. If $|MRS_1| = 2/3$ and $|MRS_2| = 1/2$, say, this means that person 1 would give up 2/3 of a dollar of private consumption to get 1 unit more of the public good and person 2 would give up 1/2 of a dollar of private consumption to get 1 unit more of the public good. But if person 1 gave up his 2/3 units, and person 2 gave up his 1/2 unit, we would have more than enough to produce the extra unit of the public good, since the marginal cost of providing the public good is 1. Thus we could give the left-over amount back to both people, thereby making them both better off.

What does the condition for Pareto efficiency mean? One way to interpret it is to think of the marginal rate of substitution as measuring the *marginal* willingness to pay for an extra unit of the public good. Then the efficiency condition just says that the *sum* of the marginal willingnesses to pay must equal the marginal cost of providing an extra unit of the public good.

In the case of a discrete good that was either provided or not provided, we said that the efficiency condition was that the sum of the willingnesses to pay should be at least as large as the cost. In the case we're considering here, where the public good can be provided at different levels, the efficiency condition is that the sum of the *marginal* willingnesses to pay should *equal* the marginal cost at the optimal amount of the public good. For whenever the sum of the marginal willingnesses to pay for the public good exceeds the marginal cost, it is appropriate to provide more of the public good.

It is worthwhile comparing the efficiency condition for a public good to the efficiency condition for a private good. For a private good, each person's marginal rate of substitution must equal the marginal cost; for a public good, the *sum* of the marginal rates of substitution must equal the marginal cost. In the case of a private good, each person can consume a different amount of the private good, but they all must value it the same at the margin—otherwise they would want to trade. In the case of a public good, each person must consume the same amount of the public good, but they can all value it differently at the margin.

We can illustrate the public good efficiency condition in Figure 37.1. We simply draw each person's MRS curve and then add them vertically to get the sum of the MRS curves. The efficient allocation of the public good will occur where the sum of the MRSs equals the marginal cost, as illustrated in Figure 37.1.

## 37.5 Quasilinear Preferences and Public Goods

In general, the optimal amount of the public good will be different at different allocations of the private good. But if the consumers have quasilinear preferences it turns out that there will be a unique amount of the public good supplied at every efficient allocation. The easiest way to see this is to think about the kind of utility function that represents quasilinear preferences.

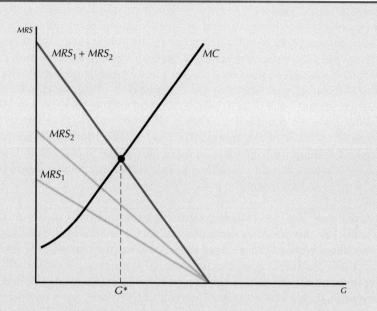

Figure
37.1
**Determining the efficient amount of a public good.** The sum of the marginal rates of substitution must equal the marginal cost.

As we saw in Chapter 4, quasilinear preferences have a utility representation of the form: $u_i(x_i, G) = x_i + v_i(G)$. This means that the marginal utility of the private good is always 1, and thus the marginal rate of substitution between the private and the public good—the ratio of the marginal utilities—will depend only on $G$. In particular:

$$|MRS_1| = \frac{\partial u_1(x_1, G)/\partial G}{\partial u_1/\partial x_1} = \frac{\delta v_1(G)}{\delta G}$$

$$|MRS_2| = \frac{\partial u_2(x_2, G)/\partial G}{\partial u_2/\partial x_2} = \frac{\delta v_2(G)}{\delta G}.$$

We already know that a Pareto efficient level of the public good must satisfy the condition

$$|MRS_1| + |MRS_2| = MC(G).$$

Using the special form of the MRSs in the case of quasilinear utility, we can write this condition as

$$\frac{\delta v_1(G)}{\delta G} + \frac{\delta v_2(G)}{\delta G} = MC(G).$$

Note that this equation determines $G$ without any reference to $x_1$ or $x_2$. Thus there is a unique efficient level of provision of the public good.

Another way to see this is to think about the behavior of the indifference curves. In the case of quasilinear preferences, all of the indifference curves are just shifted versions of each other. This means, in particular, that the slope of the indifference curves—the marginal rate of substitution—doesn't change as we change the amount of the private good. Suppose that we find one efficient allocation of the public and private goods, where the sum of the absolute value of the MRSs equals $MC(G)$. Now if we take some amount of the private good away from one person and give it to another, the slopes of both indifference curves stay the same, so the sum of the absolute value of the MRSs is still equal to $MC(G)$ and we have another Pareto efficient allocation.

In the case of quasilinear preferences, all Pareto efficient allocations are found by just redistributing the private good. The amount of the public good stays fixed at the efficient level.

## EXAMPLE: Pollution Revisited

Recall the model of the steel firm and the fishery described in Chapter 35. There we argued that the efficient provision of pollution was one which internalized the pollution costs borne by the steel firm and the fishery. Suppose now that there are two fisheries, and that the amount of pollution produced by the steel firm is a public good. (Or, perhaps more appropriately, is a public bad!)

Then the efficient provision of pollution will involve maximizing the sum of the profits of all three firms—that is, minimizing the total social cost of the pollution. Formally, let $c_s(s, x)$ be the cost to the steel firm of producing $s$ units of steel and $x$ units of pollution, and write $c_f^1(f_1, x)$ for the costs for firm 1 to catch $f_1$ fish when the pollution level is $x$, and $c_f^2(f_2, x)$ as the analogous expression for firm 2. Then to compute the Pareto efficient amount of pollution, we maximize the sum of the three firms' profits:

$$\max_{s, f_1, f_2, x} p_s s + p_f f_1 + p_f f_2 - c_s(s, x) - c_f^1(f_1, x) - c_f^2(f_2, x).$$

The interesting effect for our purposes is the effect on aggregate profits of increasing pollution. Increasing pollution lowers the cost of producing steel but raises the costs of producing fish for each of the fisheries. The appropriate optimality condition from the profit-maximization problem is

$$\frac{\Delta c_s(\hat{s}, \hat{x})}{\Delta x} + \frac{\Delta c_f^1(\hat{f}_1, \hat{x})}{\Delta x} + \frac{\Delta c_f^2(\hat{f}_2, \hat{x})}{\Delta x} = 0,$$

which simply says that the *sum* of the marginal costs of pollution over the three firms should equal zero. Just as in the case of a public consumption good, it is the *sum* of the marginal benefits or costs over the economic agents that is relevant for determining the Pareto efficient provision of a public good.

## 37.6 The Free Rider Problem

Now that we know what the Pareto efficient allocations of public goods are, we can turn our attention to asking how to get there. In the case of private goods with no externalities we saw that the market mechanism will generate an efficient allocation. Will the market work in the case of public goods?

We can think of each person as having some endowment of a private good, $w_i$. Each person can spend some fraction of this private good on his own private consumption, or he or she can contribute some of it to purchase the public good. Let's use $x_1$ for 1's private consumption, and let $g_1$ denote the amount of the public good he buys, and similarly for person 2. Suppose for simplicity that $c(G) \equiv G$, which implies that the marginal cost of providing a unit of the public good is constant at 1. The total amount of the public good provided will be $G = g_1 + g_2$. Since each person cares about the *total* amount of the public good provided, the utility function of person $i$ will have the form $u_i(x_i, g_1 + g_2) = u_i(x_i, G)$.

In order for person 1 to decide how much he should contribute to the public good, he has to have some forecast of how much person 2 will contribute. The simplest thing to do here is to adopt the Nash equilibrium model described in Chapter 29, and suppose that person 2 will make some contribution $\bar{g}_2$. We assume that person 2 also makes a guess about person 1's contribution, and we look for an equilibrium where each person is making an optimal contribution given the other person's behavior.

Thus person 1's maximization problem takes the form

$$\max_{x_1, g_1} u_1(x_1, g_1 + \bar{g}_2)$$

such that $x_1 + g_1 = w_1$.

This is just like an ordinary consumer maximization problem. The optimization condition is therefore the same: if both people purchase both goods the marginal rate of substitution between the public and the private goods should be 1 for each consumer:

$$|MRS_1| = 1$$

$$|MRS_2| = 1.$$

However, we have to be careful here. It is true that if person 2 purchases any amount of the public good at all, he will purchase it until the marginal rate of substitution equals one. But it can easily happen that person 2 decides that the amount already contributed by person 1 is sufficient and that it would therefore be unnecessary for him to contribute anything toward the public good at all.

Formally, we are assuming that the individuals can only make positive contributions to the public good—they can put money into the collection plate, but they can't take money out. Thus there is an extra constraint on each person's contributions, namely, that $g_1 \geq 0$ and $g_2 \geq 0$. Each person can only decide whether or not he wants to *increase* the amount of the public good. But then it may well be that one person decides that the amount provided by the other is just fine and would prefer to make no contribution at all.

A case like this is depicted in Figure 37.2. Here we have illustrated each person's private consumption on the horizontal axis and his or her public consumption on the vertical axis. The "endowment" of each person consists of his or her wealth, $w_i$, along with the amount of the public good contribution of the *other* person—since this is how much of the public good will be available if the person in question decides not to contribute. Figure 37.2A shows a case where person 1 is the only contributor to the public good, so that $g_1 = G$. If person 1 contributes $G$ units to the public good, then person 2's endowment will consist of her private wealth, $w_2$, and the amount of the public good $G$—since person 2 gets to consume the public good whether or not she contributes to it. Since person 2 cannot reduce the amount of the public good, but can only increase it, her budget constraint is the bold line in Figure 37.2B. Given the shape of 2's indifference curve, it is optimal from her point of view to free ride on 1's contribution and simply consume her endowment, as depicted.

This is an example where person 2 is free riding on person 1's contribution to the public good. Since a public good is a good that everyone must consume in the same amount, the provision of a public good by any one person will tend to reduce the other peoples' provision. Thus in general there will be too little of the public good supplied in a voluntary equilibrium, relative to an efficient provision of the public good.

## 37.7 Comparison to Private Goods

In our discussion of private goods, we were able to show that a particular social institution—the competitive market—was capable of achieving a Pareto efficient allocation of private goods. Each consumer deciding for himself or herself how much to purchase of various goods would result in a pattern of consumption that was Pareto efficient. A major assumption in this analysis was that an individual's consumption did not affect other people's utility—that is, that there were no consumption externalities. Thus

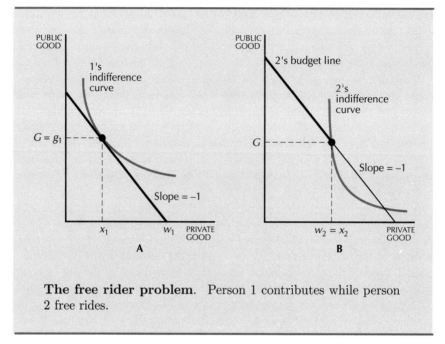

Figure
37.2

**The free rider problem.** Person 1 contributes while person
2 free rides.

each person optimizing with respect to his or her own consumption was
sufficient to achieve a kind of social optimum.

The situation is radically different with respect to public goods. In this
case, the utilities of the individuals are inexorably linked since everyone
is required to consume the same amount of the public good. In this case
the market provision of *public* goods would be very unlikely to result in a
Pareto efficient provision.

Indeed, for the most part we use *different* social institutions to determine
the provision of public goods. Sometimes people use a **command mechanism**, where one person or small group of people determines the amount
of various public goods that will be provided by the populace. Other times
people use a **voting system** where individuals vote on the provision of
public goods. One can well ask the same sorts of questions about voting,
or other social mechanisms for decision making, that we asked about the
private market: are they capable of achieving a Pareto efficient allocation
of public goods? Can any Pareto efficient allocation of public goods be
achieved by such mechanisms? A complete analysis of these questions is
beyond the scope of this book, but we will be able to shed a little light on
how some methods work below.

## 37.8 Voting

Private provision of a public good doesn't work very well, but there are several other mechanisms for social choice. One of the most common mechanisms in democratic countries is **voting**. Let's examine how well it works for the provision of public goods.

Voting isn't very interesting in the case of two consumers, so we will suppose that we have $n$ consumers. Furthermore, so as not to worry about ties, we'll suppose that $n$ is an odd number. Let's imagine that the consumers are voting about the size of some public good—say the magnitude of expenditures on public defense. Each consumer has a most-preferred level of expenditure, and his valuation of other levels of expenditure depends on how close they are to his preferred level of expenditure.

The first problem with voting as a way of determining social outcomes has already been examined in Chapter 34. Suppose that we are considering three levels of expenditure, A, B, and C. It is perfectly possible that there is a majority of the consumers who prefer A to B, a majority who prefer B to C ... and a majority who prefer C to A!

Using the terminology of Chapter 34, the social preferences generated by these consumers are not transitive. This means that the outcome of voting on the level of public good may not be well defined—there is always a level of expenditure that beats every expenditure. If a society is allowed to vote many times on an issue, this means that it may "cycle" around various choices. Or if a society votes only once on an issue, the outcome depends on the order in which the choices are presented.

If first you vote on A versus B and then on A versus C, C will be the outcome. But if you vote on C versus A and then C versus B, B will be the outcome. You can get any of the three outcomes by choosing how the alternatives are presented!

The "paradox of voting" described above is disturbing. One natural thing to do is to ask what restrictions on preferences will allow us to rule it out; that is, what form must preferences have so as to ensure that the kinds of cycles described above cannot happen?

Let us depict the preferences of consumer $i$ by a graph like those in Figure 37.3, where the height of the graph illustrates the value or the net utility for different levels of the expenditure on the public good. The term "net utility" is appropriate since each person cares both about the level of the public good, and the amount that he has to contribute to it. Higher levels of expenditure mean more public goods but also higher taxes in order to pay for those public goods. Thus it is reasonable to assume that the net utility of expenditure on the public good rises at first due to the benefits of the public good but then eventually falls, due to the costs of providing it.

One restriction on preferences of this sort is that they be **single-peaked**. This means that preferences must have the shape depicted in Figure 37.3A rather than that depicted in Figure 37.3B. With single-peaked preferences, the net utility of different levels of expenditure rises until the most-preferred point and then falls, as it does in Figure 37.3A; it never goes up, down, and then up again, as it does in Figure 37.3B, an example of multi-peaked preferences.

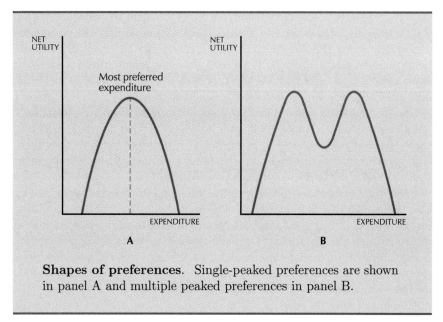

**Figure 37.3**    **Shapes of preferences.**  Single-peaked preferences are shown in panel A and multiple peaked preferences in panel B.

If each individual has single-peaked preferences, then it can be shown that the social preferences revealed by majority vote will never exhibit the kind of intransitivity we described above. Accepting this result for the moment, we can ask which level of expenditure will be chosen if everyone has single-peaked preferences. The answer turns out to be the **median expenditure**—that expenditure such that one-half of the population wants to spend more, and one-half wants to spend less. This result is reasonably intuitive: if more than one-half wanted more expenditure on the public good, they would vote for more, so the only possible equilibrium voting outcome is when the votes for increasing and decreasing expenditure on the public good are just balanced.

Will this be an efficient level of the public good? In general, the answer is no. The median outcome just means that half the population wants more and half wants less; it doesn't say anything about *how much more* they want of the public good. Since efficiency takes this kind of information into account, voting will not in general lead to an efficient outcome.

Furthermore, even if peoples' true preferences are single-peaked, so that voting may lead to a reasonable outcome, individuals may choose to misrepresent their true preferences when they vote. Thus people will have an incentive to vote differently than their true preferences would indicate in order to manipulate the final outcome.

## EXAMPLE: Agenda Manipulation

We have seen that the outcome of a sequence of votes may depend on the order in which the votes are taken. Experienced politicians are well aware of this possibility. In the U.S. Congress, amendments to a bill must be voted on before the bill itself, and this provides a commonly used way to influence the legislative process.

In 1956 the House of Representatives considered a bill calling for Federal aid to school construction. One representative offered an amendment requiring that the bill would only provide Federal aid to states with integrated schools. There were three more-or-less equally sized groups of representatives with strongly held views on this issue.

• Republicans. They were opposed to Federal aid to education, but preferred the amended bill to the original. Their ranking of the alternatives was no bill, amended bill, original bill.

• Northern Democrats. They wanted Federal aid to education and supported integrated schools, so they ranked the alternatives amended bill, original bill, no bill.

• Southern Democrats. This group wanted Federal aid to education, but would not get any aid under the amended bill due to the segregated schools in the South. Their ranking was original bill, no bill, amended bill.

In the vote on the amendment, the Republicans and the Northern Democrats were in the majority, thereby substituting the amended bill for the original. In the vote on the amended bill, the Republicans and the Southern Democrats were in the majority, and the amended bill was defeated. However, before being amended the original bill had a majority of the votes!

## 37.9 The Vickrey-Clarke-Groves Mechanism

Let us think about the public good problem in a very general framework. The goal is to choose some outcome (for example, whether or not to provide a streetlight) so as to maximize the sum of utilities of the agents involved. The challenge is to determine just what those individual utility functions are, since consumers may not have good incentives to report true values.

In the simplest case the choice might be a zero-one decision: if $x = 1$ the streetlight is built, if $x = 0$ it is not. In a more general case, the choice might be how much of something to provide—how many streetlights, or how bright they are, or where they are located. We will use $x$ to represent the possible choices, whatever they may be. We suppose that there are $n$ agents, and let $u_i(x)$ be the utility of agent $i$. The goal is to choose $x$ to maximize the sum of the agents' utility, $\sum_i u_i(x)$.

This would be easy if the decision maker knew the utility functions. Unfortunately, in any realistic situation, the decision maker won't know this. And, as we've seen, the agents may well have an incentive to misrepresent their true utility functions.

Somewhat surprisingly, there is a clever way to get the agents to tell the truth and achieve an efficient outcome. This **economic mechanism** is known as the **Vickrey-Clarke-Groves mechanism**, or **VCG mechanism**.

## Groves Mechanism

We will describe the VCG mechanism in two stages. First, we describe what is known as a **Groves mechanism**.

1. The center asks each agent $i$ to report how much he is willing to pay to have $x$ units of the public good provided. We denote this reported utility for $x$ units of the public good by $r_i(x)$.

2. The center chooses the level of the public good $x^*$ that maximizes the sum of the reported utilities, $R = \sum_{i=1}^{n} r_i(x)$.

3. Each agent $i$ receives a sidepayment which is the sum of the reported utilities of everyone else, evaluated at the level of $x$ determined in step 2. Denote this sidepayment by $R_i = \sum_{j \neq i} r_j(x^*)$.

It turns out that in this mechanism it is a **dominant strategy** for each agent to report his true utility function. To see why, consider the total payoff to agent $i$, which is his utility plus his sidepayment

$$u_i(x) + \sum_{j \neq i} r_j(x).$$

Note that agent $i$ cares about his *true* utility function but his sidepayment depends on the sum of the others' *reported* utility functions.

Agent $i$ recognizes that the decision maker will maximize the sum of utilities using his *reported* utility,

$$r_i(x) + \sum_{j \neq i} r_j(x).$$

However, agent $i$ wants the decision maker to maximize his own true utility plus sidepayment,

$$u_i(x) + \sum_{j \neq i} r_j(x).$$

Agent $i$ can ensure that the decision maker makes a choice that will maximize this expression by reporting his true utility; that is, by setting $r_i(x) = u_i(x)$.

The Groves mechanism essentially "internalizes the externality" among the agents. It makes each agent face the costs and benefits that his report imposes on the other agents. Each agent wants to report his true utility, since that is what he wants to be maximized.

## The VCG Mechanism

The trouble with the Groves mechanism alone is it is potentially very costly: the center has to pay every agent an amount equal to the sum of the others' reported utilities. How can the magnitude of the sidepayments be reduced?

One important observation is that we can impose a "tax" on each agent as long as this tax is independent of the agent's choice. If the tax is independent of $i$'s choice, then it can't affect his decision.[3] We will choose the tax in a way that guarantees that the net payments the center will receive are either positive or zero. Thus the center will always have at least as much money as necessary to pay for the public good.

A particularly convenient tax is to charge agent $i$ an amount equal to the *maximum* sum of reported utilities excluding agent $i$. That is, we charge each agent the sum of the reported utilities that would occur if he were not present. The net tax imposed on agent $i$ is then

$$W_i - R_i = \sum_{j \neq i} r_j(x) - \max_z \sum_{j \neq i} r_j(z).$$

Note that this number is either positive or zero. Why? Because the *maximum* sum of the $n - 1$ reported utilities has to be larger than any other value for that sum.

What we are computing here is the difference between what would happen with agent $i$ present, and what would happen with him absent. Thus it measures the net cost that agent $i$ imposes on the other agents. As long as $i$ faces the cost that he imposes on the other agents, he will have appropriate incentives to report his true utility.

Now we can complete the description of the VCG mechanism. We use steps 1 and 2 above, but then substitute the following steps for step 3 above.

---

[3] This is where the quasilinear assumption about utility is important.

3. The center also calculates the outcome that maximizes the sum of the $n-1$ reported utilities if agent $1, 2, \ldots, n$ were not present. Let $W_i$ be the maximum sum of reported utilities that results without agent $i$.

4. Each agent $i$ pays a tax equal to $W_i - R_i$.

## 37.10 Examples of VCG

The discussion in the last section was admittedly abstract, so it is helpful to examine some specific cases.

### Vickrey Auction

The first case we look at is the **Vickrey auction**, as described in Chapter 18. Here the outcome is simple: which person should get the item being auctioned. Let $v_1 > v_2$ be the true values of two bidders and $r_1 > r_2$ be the reported values.

If agent 1 is present, he gets a utility of $v_1$. If he is absent, the item is awarded to the other agent so agent 1's total payoff is $v_1 - r_2$. Agent 2 gets a payoff of zero no matter what. Each agent has an incentive to report its true value, so we end up with the optimal outcome.

### Clarke-Groves Mechanism

The next example is a public goods problem along the lines of the TV-buying game described in Table 37.1. As in that example, suppose that there are two roommates who are trying to decide whether they will buy a TV. Let $c_i$ be how much agent $i$ will pay if the TV is purchased. Since the total cost of the TV is \$150, we must have $c_1 + c_2 = 150$.

According to the VCG mechanism, each agent reports a value for the TV, denoted by $r_i$. If $r_1 + r_2 > 150$ the TV will be purchased and the agents will make the payments according to the mechanism. Let $x = 1$ if the TV is purchased and $x = 0$ if it is not.

Before we look at the VCG mechanism, let us think about what would happen if we followed a naive mechanism: ask each agent to report his value and then acquire the TV if the sum of the reported values exceeds the cost of the TV.

Suppose person 1's value exceeds his cost share, so that $v_1 - c_1 > 0$. Then person 1 may as well report a million dollars; this will ensure the TV get purchased, which is what he wants to see. On the other hand if $v_1 < c_1$ person 1 may as well report a negative million dollars.

The problem is that each agent, acting independently, has no reason to take into account the other agent's values. The agents have a strong incentive to exaggerate their reported values one way or the other.

Let's see how the VCG mechanism solves this problem. The payoff to agent 1 is

$$(v_1 - c_1)x + (r_2 - c_2)x - max_y(r_2 - c_2)y.$$

The first term is his net utility from the TV: the value to him minus the cost he has to pay. The second term is the reported net utility to his roommate. The last term is the maximum utility his roommate would get if agent 1 were not present. Since agent 1 can't influence this, we can just ignore it for now.

Rearranging the first 2 terms we have agent's payoff as

$$[(v_1 + r_2) - (c_1 + c_2)]x.$$

If this is positive then he can ensure the TV is purchased if he reports $r_1 = v_1$, since then the sum of the *reported* values will exceed the total cost. If this is negative he can ensure that the TV is not purchased by reporting $r_1 = v_1$. Either way, it is optimal to report the true value. The same thing is true for agent 2. If both report the truth, the TV will be purchased only when $v_1 + v_2 > 150$, which is the optimal thing to do.

Note that agent $i$ will have to make a payment only if he changes the social decision. In this case we say agent $i$ is **pivotal**. The amount of the payment a pivotal agent makes is simply the cost that he imposes on the other agents.

## 37.11 Problems with the VCG

The VCG mechanism leads to truthtelling and leads to the optimal level of the public good. However, it is not without problems.

The first problem is that it only works with quasilinear preferences. This is because we can't have the amount that you have to pay influence your demand for the public good. It is important that there is a unique optimal level of the public good.

The second problem is that the VCG mechanism doesn't really generate a Pareto efficient outcome. The level of the public good will be optimal, but the private consumption could be greater. This is because of the tax collection. Remember that in order to have the correct incentives, the pivotal people must actually pay some taxes that reflect the harm that they do to the other people. And these taxes cannot go to anybody else involved in the decision process, since that might affect their decisions. The taxes have to disappear from the system. And that's the problem—if the taxes actually have to be paid, the private consumption will end up being lower than it could be otherwise, and therefore be Pareto inefficient.

However, the taxes only have to be paid if someone is pivotal. If there are many people involved in the decision, the probability that any one person is pivotal may not be very large; thus the tax collections might typically be expected to be rather small.

A third problem with VCG is that it is susceptible to collusion. Consider, for example, the public goods problem described above. Suppose that there are 3 roommates participating in the TV auction, but two of them collude. The colluders agree to each state $1 million as their net benefit from the TV. This ensures that the TV will be purchased but since neither of the agents is pivotal (i.e., neither of the colluding agents changed the decision) then neither one has to pay the tax.

The final problem concerns the equity and efficiency tradeoff inherent in the VCG mechanism. Since the payment scheme must be fixed in advance, there will generally be situations where some people will be made worse off by providing the public good, even though the Pareto efficient *amount* of the public good will be provided. To say that it is Pareto efficient to provide the public good is to say that there is *some* payment scheme under which everyone is better off having the public good provided than not having it. But this doesn't mean that for an *arbitrary* payment scheme everyone will be better off. The VCG mechanism ensures that if everyone *could* be better off having the good provided, then it will be provided. But that doesn't imply that everyone will actually be better off.

It would be nice if there were a scheme that determined not only whether or not to provide the public good, but also a Pareto efficient way to pay for it—that is, a payment plan that makes everyone better off. However, it does not appear that such a general plan is available.

## Summary

1. Public goods are goods for which everyone must "consume" the same amount, such as national defense, air pollution, and so on.

2. If a public good is to be provided in some fixed amount or not provided at all, then a necessary and sufficient condition for provision to be Pareto efficient is that the sum of the willingnesses to pay (the reservation prices) exceeds the cost of the public good.

3. If a public good can be provided in a variable amount, then the necessary condition for a given amount to be Pareto efficient is that the sum of the marginal willingnesses to pay (the marginal rates of substitution) should equal the marginal cost.

4. The free rider problem refers to the temptation of individuals to let others provide the public goods. In general, purely individualistic mechanisms

will not generate the optimal amount of a public good because of the free rider problem.

5. Various collective decision methods have been proposed to determine the supply of a public good. Such methods include the command mechanism, voting, and the VCG mechanism.

## REVIEW QUESTIONS

1. Suppose that 10 people live on a street and that each of them is willing to pay $2 for each extra streetlight, regardless of the number of streetlights provided. If the cost of providing $x$ streetlights is given by $c(x) = x^2$, what is the Pareto efficient number of streetlights to provide?

# CHAPTER 38

# ASYMMETRIC INFORMATION

So far in our study of markets we have not examined the problems raised by differences in information: by assumption buyers and sellers were both perfectly informed about the quality of the goods being sold in the market. This assumption can be defended if it is easy to verify the quality of an item. If it is not costly to tell which goods are high-quality goods and which are low-quality goods, then the prices of the goods will simply adjust to reflect the quality differences.

But if information about quality is costly to obtain, then it is no longer plausible that buyers and sellers have the same information about goods involved in transactions. There are certainly many markets in the real world in which it may be very costly or even impossible to gain accurate information about the quality of the goods being sold.

One obvious example is the labor market. In the simple models described earlier, labor was a homogeneous product—everyone had the same "kind" of labor and supplied the same amount of effort per hour worked. This is clearly a drastic simplification! In reality, it may be very difficult for a firm to determine how productive its employees are.

Costly information is not just a problem with labor markets. Similar problems arise in markets for consumer products. When a consumer buys a used car it may be very difficult for him to determine whether or not it is a good car or a lemon. By contrast, the seller of the used car probably has a pretty good idea of the quality of the car. We will see that this **asymmetric information** may cause significant problems with the efficient functioning of a market.

## 38.1 The Market for Lemons

Let us look at a model of a market where the demanders and suppliers have different information about the qualities of the goods being sold.[1]

Consider a market with 100 people who want to sell their used cars and 100 people who want to buy a used car. Everyone knows that 50 of the cars are "plums" and 50 are "lemons."[2] The current owner of each car knows its quality, but the prospective purchasers don't know whether any given car is a plum or a lemon.

The owner of a lemon is willing to part with it for $1000 and the owner of a plum is willing to part with it for $2000. The buyers of the car are willing to pay $2400 for a plum and $1200 for a lemon.

If it is easy to verify the quality of the cars there will be no problems in this market. The lemons will sell at some price between $1000 and $1200 and the plums will sell at some price between $2000 and $2400. But what happens to the market if the buyers *can't* observe the quality of the car?

In this case the buyers have to guess about how much each car is worth. We'll make a simple assumption about the form that this guess takes: we assume that if a car is equally likely to be a plum as a lemon, then a typical buyer would be willing to pay the expected value of the car. Using the numbers described above this means that the buyer would be willing to pay $\frac{1}{2}1200 + \frac{1}{2}2400 = \$1800$.

But who would be willing to sell their car at that price? The owners of the lemons certainly would, but the owners of the plums wouldn't be willing to sell their cars—by assumption they need at least $2000 to part with their cars. The price that the buyers are willing to pay for an "average" car is less than the price that the sellers of the plums want in order to part with their cars. At a price of $1800 only lemons would be offered for sale.

But if the buyer was certain that he would get a lemon, then he wouldn't be willing to pay $1800 for it! In fact, the equilibrium price in this market would have to be somewhere between $1000 and $1200. For a price in this range only owners of lemons would offer their cars for sale, and buyers

---

[1] The first paper to point out some of the difficulties in markets of this sort was George Akerlof, "The Market for Lemons: Quality Uncertainty and the Market Mechanism," *The Quarterly Journal of Economics*, 84, 1970, pp. 488-500. He was awarded the 2001 Nobel Prize in economics for this work.

[2] A "plum" is slang for a good car; a "lemon" is slang for a bad car.

would therefore (correctly) expect to get a lemon. In this market, none of the plums ever get sold! Even though the price at which buyers are willing to buy plums exceeds the price at which sellers are willing to sell them, no such transactions will take place.

It is worth contemplating the source of this market failure. The problem is that there is an externality between the sellers of good cars and bad cars; when an individual decides to try to sell a bad car, he affects the purchasers' perceptions of the quality of the average car on the market. This lowers the price that they are willing to pay for the average car, and thus hurts the people who are trying to sell good cars. It is this externality that creates the market failure.

The cars that are most likely to be offered for sale are the ones that people want most to get rid of. The very act of offering to sell something sends a signal to the prospective buyer about its quality. If too many low-quality items are offered for sale it makes it difficult for the owners of high-quality items to sell their products.

## 38.2 Quality Choice

In the lemons model there were a fixed number of cars of each quality. Here we consider a variation on that model where quality may be determined by the producers. We will show how the equilibrium quality is determined in this simple market.

Suppose that each consumer wants to buy a single umbrella and that there are two different qualities available. Consumers value high-quality umbrellas at $14 and low-quality umbrellas at $8. It is impossible to tell the quality of the umbrellas in the store; this can only be determined after a few rainstorms.

Suppose that some manufacturers produce high-quality umbrellas and some produce low-quality umbrellas. Suppose further that both high-quality and low-quality umbrellas cost $11.50 to manufacture and that the industry is perfectly competitive. What would we expect to be the equilibrium quality of umbrellas produced?

We suppose that consumers judge the quality of the umbrellas available in the market by the *average* quality sold, just as in the case of the lemons market. If the fraction of high-quality umbrellas is $q$, then the consumer would be willing to pay $p = 14q + 8(1 - q)$ for an umbrella.

There are three cases to consider.

*Only low-quality manufacturers produce.* In this case then the consumers would be willing to pay only $8 for an average umbrella. But it costs $11.50 to produce an umbrella, so none would be sold.

*Only high-quality manufacturers produce.* In this case the producers would compete the price of an umbrella down to marginal cost, $11.50. The consumers are willing to pay \$14 for an umbrella, so they would get some consumers' surplus.

*Both qualities are produced.* In this case competition ensures that the price will be \$11.50. The average quality available must therefore have a value to the consumer of at least \$11.50. This means that we must have

$$14q + 8(1 - q) \geq 11.50.$$

The lowest value of $q$ that satisfies this inequality is $q = 7/12$. This means that if 7/12 of the suppliers are high-quality the consumers are just willing to pay \$11.50 for an umbrella.

The determination of the equilibrium ratio of high-quality producers is depicted in Figure 38.1. The horizontal axis measures $q$, the fraction of high-quality producers. The vertical axis measures the consumers' willingness to pay for an umbrella if the fraction of high-quality umbrellas offered is $q$. Producers are willing to supply either quality of umbrella at a price of \$11.50, so the supply conditions are summarized by the colored horizontal line at \$11.50.

Consumers are willing to purchase umbrellas only if $14q+8(1-q) \geq 11.50$; the boundary of this region is illustrated by the dashed line. Any value of $q$ between 7/12 and 1 is an equilibrium.

In this market the equilibrium price is \$11.50, but the value of the average umbrella to a consumer can be anywhere between \$11.50 and \$14, depending on the fraction of high-quality producers. Any value of $q$ between 1 and 7/12 is an equilibrium.

However, all of these equilibria are not equivalent from the social point of view. The producers get zero producer surplus in all the equilibria, due to the assumption of pure competition and constant marginal cost, so we only have to examine the consumers' surplus. Here it is easy to see that the higher the average quality, the better off the consumers are. The best equilibrium from the viewpoint of the consumers is the one in which only the high-quality goods are produced.

## Choosing the Quality

Now let us change the model a bit. Suppose that each producer can choose the quality of umbrella that he produces and that it costs \$11.50 to produce a high-quality umbrella and \$11 to produce a low-quality umbrella. What will happen in this case?

Suppose that the fraction of producers who choose high-quality umbrellas is $q$, where $0 < q < 1$. Consider one of these producers. If it behaves competitively and believes that it has only a negligible effect on the market

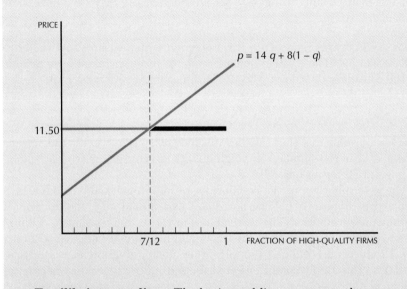

**Figure
38.1**

**Equilibrium quality.** The horizontal line represents the supply conditions: the market is willing to supply any quality of
umbrella for $11.50. The slanted line represents the demand
conditions: consumers are willing to pay more if the average
quality is higher. The market is in equilibrium if the fraction of
high-quality producers is at least 7/12.

price *and* quality, then it would always want to produce only low-quality
umbrellas. Since this producer is by assumption only a small part of the
market, it neglects its influence on the market price and therefore chooses
to produce the more profitable product.

But every producer will reason the same way and only low-quality umbrellas will be produced. But consumers are only willing to pay $8 for a
low-quality umbrella, so there is no equilibrium. Or, if you will, the only
equilibrium involves zero production of *either* quality of umbrella! The pos-
siblity of low-quality production has destroyed the market for *both* qualities
of the good!

## 38.3 Adverse Selection

The phenomenon described in the last section is an example of **adverse
selection**. In the model we just examined the low-quality items crowded
out the high-quality items because of the high cost of acquiring information.
As we just saw, this adverse selection problem may be so severe that it can

completely destroy the market. Let's consider a few other examples of adverse selection.

Consider first an example from the insurance industry. Suppose that an insurance company wants to offer insurance for bicycle theft. They do a careful market survey and find that the incident of theft varies widely across communities. In some areas there is a high probability that a bicycle will be stolen, and in other areas thefts are quite rare. Suppose that the insurance company decides to offer the insurance based on the *average* theft rate. What do you think will happen?

Answer: the insurance company is likely to go broke quickly! Think about it. Who is going to buy the insurance at the average rate? Not the people in the safe communities—they don't need much insurance anyway. Instead the people in the communities with a high incidence of theft will want the insurance—they're the ones who need it.

But this means that the insurance claims will mostly be made by the consumers who live in the high-risk areas. Rates based on the *average* probability of theft will be a misleading indication of the actual experience of claims filed with the insurance company. The insurance company will not get an unbiased selection of customers; rather they will get an *adverse* selection. In fact the term "adverse selection" was first used in the insurance industry to describe just this sort of problem.

It follows that in order to break even the insurance company must base their rates on the "worst-case" forecasts and that consumers with a low, but not negligible, risk of bicycle theft will be unwilling to purchase the resulting high-priced insurance.

A similar problem arises with health insurance—insurance companies can't base their rates on the *average* incidence of health problems in the population. They can only base their rates on the average incidence of health problems in the group of potential purchasers. But the people who want to purchase health insurance the most are the ones who are likely to need it the most and thus the rates must reflect this disparity.

In such a situation it is possible that everyone can be made better off by *requiring* the purchase of insurance that reflects the average risk in the population. The high-risk people are better off because they can purchase insurance at rates that are lower than the actual risk they face and the low-risk people can purchase insurance that is more favorable to them than the insurance offered if *only* high-risk people purchased it.

A situation like this, where the market equilibrium is dominated by a compulsary purchase plan, is quite surprising to most economists. We usually think that "more choice is better," so it is peculiar that restricting choice can result in a Pareto improvement. But it should be emphasized that this paradoxical result is due to the externality between the low-risk and high-risk people.

In fact there are social institutions that help to solve this market inefficiency. It is commonly the case that employers offer health plans to their employees as part of the package of fringe benefits. The insurance company can base its rates on the averages over the set of employees and is assured that *all* employees must participate in the program, thus eliminating the adverse selection.

## 38.4 Moral Hazard

Another interesting problem that arises in the insurance industry is known as the **moral hazard** problem. The term is somewhat peculiar, but the phenomenon is not hard to describe. Consider the bicycle-theft insurance market again and suppose for simplicity that all of the consumers live in areas with identical probabilities of theft, so that there is no problem of adverse selection. On the other hand, the probability of theft may be affected by the *actions* taken by the bicycle owners.

For example, if the bicycle owners don't bother to lock their bikes or use only a flimsy lock, the bicycle is much more likely to be stolen than if they use a secure lock. Similar examples arise in other sorts of insurance. In the case of health insurance, for example, the consumers are less likely to need the insurance if they take actions associated with a healthy lifestyle. We will refer to actions that affect the probability that some event occurs as *taking care*.

When it sets its rates the insurance company has to take into account the incentives that the consumers have to take an appropriate amount of care. If no insurance is available consumers have an incentive to take the maximum possible amount of care. If it is impossible to buy bicycle-theft insurance, then all bicyclists would use large expensive locks. In this case the individual bears the full cost of his actions and accordingly he wants to "invest" in taking care until the marginal benefit from more care just equals the marginal cost of doing so.

But if a consumer can purchase bicycle insurance, then the cost inflicted on the individual of having his bicycle stolen is much less. After all, if the bicycle is stolen then the person simply has to report it to the insurance company and he will get insurance money to replace it. In the extreme case, where the insurance company completely reimburses the individual for the theft of his bicycle, the individual has no incentive to take care at all. This lack of incentive to take care is called **moral hazard**.

Note the tradeoff involved: too little insurance means that people bear a lot of risk, too much insurance means that people will take inadequate care.

If the amount of care is observable, then there is no problem. The insurance company can base its rates on the amount of care taken. In real life it is common for insurance companies to give different rates to businesses that have a fire sprinkler system in their building, or to charge smokers different rates than nonsmokers for health insurance. In these cases the insurance firm attempts to discriminate among users depending on the choices they have made that influence the probability of damage.

But insurance companies can't observe all the relevant actions of those they insure. Therefore we will have the tradeoff described above: full insurance means too little care will be undertaken because the individuals don't face the full costs of their actions.

What does this imply about the types of insurance contracts that will be offered? In general, the insurance companies will not want to offer the consumers "complete" insurance. They will always want the consumer to face some part of the risk. This is why most insurance policies include a "deductible," an amount that the insured party has to pay in any claim. By making the consumers pay part of a claim, the insurance companies can make sure that the consumer always has an incentive to take *some* amount of care. Even though the insurance company would be willing to insure a consumer completely if they could verify the amount of care taken, the fact that the consumer can *choose* the amount of care he takes implies that the insurance company will not allow the consumer to purchase as much insurance as he wants if the company cannot observe the level of care.

This is also a paradoxical result when compared with the standard market analysis. Typically the amount of a good traded in a competitive market is determined by the condition that demand equals supply—the marginal willingness to pay equals the marginal willingness to sell. In the case of moral hazard, a market equilibrium has the property that each consumer would like to buy more insurance, and the insurance companies would be willing to provide more insurance if the consumers continued to take the same amount of care ... but this trade won't occur because if the consumers were able to purchase more insurance they would rationally choose to take less care!

## 38.5 Moral Hazard and Adverse Selection

Moral hazard refers to situations where one side of the market can't observe the actions of the other. For this reason it is sometimes called a **hidden action** problem.

Adverse selection refers to situations where one side of the market can't observe the "type" or quality of the goods on other side of the market. For this reason it is sometimes called a **hidden information** problem.

Equilibrium in a market involving hidden action typically involves some form of rationing—firms would like to provide more than they do, but they are unwilling to do so since it will change the incentives of their customers. Equilibrium in a market involving hidden information will typically involve too little trade taking place because of the externality between the "good" and "bad" types.

Equilibrium outcomes in this market appear to be inefficient, but one has to be careful in making such a claim. The question to ask is "inefficient relative to what?" The equilibrium will always be inefficient relative to the equilibrium with full information. But this is of little help in making policy decisions: if the firms in the industry find it too costly to collect more information the government would probably find it too costly as well.

The real question to ask is whether some sort of governmental intervention in the market could improve efficiency even if the government had the same information problems as the firms.

In the case of hidden action considered above, the answer is usually "no." If the government can't observe the care taken by the consumers, then it can do no better than the insurance companies. Of course the government might have other tools at its disposal that are not available to the insurance company—it could compel a particular level of care, and it could set criminal punishments for those who did not take due care. But if the government can only set prices and quantities, then it can do no better than the private market can do.

Similar issues arise in the case of hidden information. We have already seen that if the government can *compel* people of all risk classes to purchase insurance, it is possible for everyone to be made better off. This is, on the face of it, a good case for intervention. On the other hand, there are costs to government intervention as well; economic decisions made by governmental decree may not be as cost-effective as those made by private firms. Just because there are governmental actions that *can* improve social welfare doesn't mean that these actions will be taken!

Furthermore, there may be purely private solutions to the adverse selection problems. For example, we have already seen how providing health insurance as a fringe benefit can help to eliminate the adverse selection problem.

## 38.6 Signaling

Recall our model of the used-car market: the owners of the used cars knew the quality, but the purchasers had to guess at the quality. We saw that this asymmetric information could cause problems in the market; in some cases, the adverse selection problem would result in too few transactions being made.

However, the story doesn't end there. The owners of the good used cars have an incentive to try to convey the fact that they have a good car to the potential purchasers. They would like to choose actions that **signal** the quality of their car to those who might buy it.

One sensible signal in this context would be for the owner of a good used car to offer a **warranty**. This would be a promise to pay the purchaser some agreed upon amount if the car turned out to be a lemon. Owners of the good used cars can afford to offer such a warranty while the owners of the lemons can't afford this. This is a way for the owners of the good used cars to signal that they have good cars.

In this case signaling helps to make the market perform better. By offering the warranty—the signal—the sellers of the good cars can distinguish themselves from the sellers of the bad used cars. But there are other cases where signaling can make a market perform less well.

Let's consider a very simplified model of the education market first examined by Michael Spence.[3] Suppose that we have two types of workers, able and unable. The able workers have a marginal product of $a_2$, and the unable workers have a marginal product of $a_1$, where $a_2 > a_1$. Suppose that a fraction $b$ of the workers are able and $1 - b$ of them are unable.

For simplicity we assume a linear production function so that the total output produced by $L_2$ able workers and $L_1$ unable workers is $a_1 L_1 + a_2 L_2$. We also assume a competitive labor market.

If worker quality is easily observable, then firms would just offer a wage of $w_2 = a_2$ to the able workers and of $w_1 = a_1$ to the unable workers. That is, each worker would be paid his marginal product and we would have an efficient equilibrium.

But what if the firm can't observe the marginal products? If a firm can't distinguish the types of workers, then the best that it can do is to offer the average wage, which is $w = (1-b)a_1 + ba_2$. As long as the good and the bad workers both agree to work at this wage there is no problem with adverse selection. And, given our assumption about the production function, the firm produces just as much output and makes just as much profit as it would if it could perfectly observe the type of the worker.

However, suppose now that there is some signal that the workers can acquire that will distinguish the two types. For example, suppose that the workers can acquire education. Let $e_1$ be the amount of education attained by the type 1 workers and $e_2$ the amount attained by the type 2 workers. Suppose that the workers have different costs of acquiring education, so that the total cost of education for the able workers is $c_2 e_2$ and the total cost of education for the unable workers is $c_1 e_1$. These costs are meant to include not only the dollar costs of attending school, but also includes the opportunity costs, the costs of the effort required, and so on.

Now we have two decisions to consider. The workers have to decide how much education to acquire and the firms have to decide how much to pay workers with different amounts of education. Let us make the extreme assumption that the education doesn't affect worker productivity at all. Of course this isn't true in real life—especially for economics courses—but it helps to keep the model simple.

---

[3] Michael Spence, *Market Signaling* (Cambridge, Mass: Harvard University Press, 1974).

It turns out that the nature of the equilibrium in this model depends crucially on the cost of acquiring education. Suppose that $c_2 < c_1$. This says that the marginal cost of acquiring education is less for the able workers than the unable workers. Let $e^*$ be an education level that satisfies the following inequalities:

$$\frac{a_2 - a_1}{c_1} < e^* < \frac{a_2 - a_1}{c_2}.$$

Given our assumption that $a_2 > a_1$ and that $c_2 < c_1$ there must be such an $e^*$.

Now consider the following set of choices: the able workers all acquire education level $e^*$ and the unable workers all acquire education level 0, and the firm pays workers with education level $e^*$ a wage of $a_2$ and workers with less education than this a wage of $a_1$. Note that the choice of the education level of a worker perfectly signals his type.

But is this an equilibrium? Does anyone have an incentive to change his or her behavior? Each firm is paying each worker his or her marginal product, so the firms have no incentive to do anything differently. The only question is whether the workers are behaving rationally given the wage schedule they face.

Would it be in the interest of an unable worker to purchase education level $e^*$? The benefit to the worker would be the increase in wages $a_2 - a_1$. The cost to the unable worker would be $c_1 e^*$. The benefits are less than the costs if

$$a_2 - a_1 < c_1 e^*.$$

But we are guaranteed that this condition holds by the choice of $e^*$. Hence the unable workers find it optimal to choose a zero educational level.

Is it actually in the interest of the able workers to acquire the level of education $e^*$? The condition for the benefits to exceed the costs is

$$a_2 - a_1 > c_2 e^*,$$

and this condition also holds due to the choice of $e^*$.

Hence this pattern of wages is indeed an equilibrium: if each able worker chooses education level $e^*$ and each unable worker chooses a zero educational level, then no worker has any reason to change his or her behavior. Due to our assumption about the cost differences, the education level of a worker can, in equilibrium, serve as a signal of the different productivities. This type of signaling equilibrium is sometimes called a **separating equilibrium** since the equilibrium involves each type of worker making a choice that allows him to separate himself from the other type.

Another possibility is a **pooling equilibrium**, in which each type of worker makes the *same* choice. For example, suppose that $c_2 > c_1$, so that the able workers have a higher cost of acquiring education than the unable workers. In this case it can be shown that the only equilibrium involves the workers all getting paid a wage based on their average ability, and so no signaling occurs.

The separating equilibrium is especially interesting since it is inefficient from a social point of view. Each able worker finds it in his interest to pay for acquiring the signal, even though it doesn't change his productivity at all. The able workers want to acquire the signal not because it makes them any more productive, but just because it distinguishes them from the unable workers. Exactly the same amount of output is produced in the (separating) signaling equilibrium as would be if there were no signaling at all. In this model the acquisition of the signal is a total waste from the social point of view.

It is worth thinking about the nature of this inefficiency. As before, it arises because of an externality. If both able and unable workers were paid their *average* product, the wage of the able workers would be depressed because of the presence of the unable workers. Thus they would have an incentive to invest in signals that will distinguish them from the less able. This investment offers a private benefit but no social benefit.

Of course signaling doesn't always lead to inefficiencies. Some types of signals, such as the used-car warranties described above, help to facilitate trade. In that case the equilibrium with signals is preferred to the equilibrium without signals. So signaling can make things better or worse; each case has to be examined on its own merits.

## EXAMPLE: The Sheepskin Effect

In the extreme form of the educational signaling model described above education has no effect on productivity: the years spent in school serve only to signal the fixed ability of an individual. This is obviously an exaggeration: a student with 11 years of schooling almost certainly is more productive than one with 10 years of schooling due to the fact that he has acquired more useful skills during the additional year. Presumably part of the returns to schooling are due to signaling, and part are due to the acquisition of useful skills while in school. How can we separate these two factors?

Labor economists who have studied the returns to education have observed the following suggestive fact: the earnings of people who have graduated from high school are much higher than the incomes of people who have only completed 3 years of high school. One study found that graduating from high school increases earnings by 5 to 6 times as much as does completing a year in high school that does not result in graduation. The same discontinuous jump occurs for people who graduate from college. According to one estimate, the economic return to the 16th year of schooling are about three times as high as the return to the 15th year of schooling.[4]

If education imparts productive skills, we might well expect that people with 11 years of education are paid more than people with 10 years of education. What is surprising is that there is a huge jump in earnings associated with high school graduation. Economists have termed this the **sheepskin effect**, in reference to the fact that diplomas were often written on sheepskins. Presumably, graduation from high school is some kind of signal. But what is it a signal of? In the educational signaling model described earlier, educational attainment was a signal of ability. Is that what high school graduation signals? Or is it something else?

Andrew Weiss, a Boston University economist, attempted to answer these questions.[5] He looked at a set of data describing how workers assembled equipment and was able to obtain a measure of how much output they produced in their first month on the job. He found that there was a very small effect of education on output: each year of secondary education increased a worker's output by about 1.3 percent. Furthermore, high school graduates produced essentially the same amount of output as nongraduates. Apparently education contributed only a small amount to the initial productivity of these workers.

Weiss then looked at another data set that described various characteristics of workers in a variety of occupations. He found that high school graduates had significantly lower quit and absentee rates than nongraduates. It seems that high school graduates receive higher wages because they are more productive—but the reason that they are more productive is because they stay with the firm longer and have fewer absences. This suggests that the signaling model does give us insight into real-world labor markets. However, the actual signal sent by educational attainment is considerably more complex than the simplest version of the signaling model suggests.

## 38.7 Incentives

We turn now to a slightly different topic, the study of **incentive systems**. As it turns out, our investigation of this topic will naturally involve asymmetric information. But it is useful to start with the case of full information.

The central question in the design of incentive systems is "How can I get someone to do something for me?" Let's pose this question in a specific

---

[4] See Thomas Hungerford and Gary Solon, "Sheepskin Effects in the Returns to Education," *Review of Economics and Statistics*, 69, 1987, 175–77.

[5] "High School Graduation, Performance and Wages," *Journal of Political Economy*, 96, 4, 1988, 785–820.

context. Suppose that you own a plot of land but you are unable to work on the land yourself. So you try to hire someone to do the farming for you. What sort of compensation system should you set up?

One plan might involve paying the worker a lump-sum fee independent of how much he produces. But then he would have little incentive to work. In general a good incentive plan will make the payment of the worker depend in some way on the output he produces. The problem of incentive design is to determine exactly how sensitive the payment should be to the produced output.

Let $x$ be the amount of "effort" that the worker expends, and let $y = f(x)$ be the amount of output produced; for simplicity we suppose that the price of output is 1 so that $y$ also measures the value of the output. Let $s(y)$ be the amount that you pay the worker if he produces $y$ dollars worth of output. Presumably you would like to choose the function $s(y)$ to maximize your profits $y - s(y)$.

What are the constraints that you face? In order to answer this question we have to look at things from the worker's perspective.

We assume that the worker finds effort costly, and write $c(x)$ for the cost of effort $x$. We assume that this cost function has the usual shape: both total and marginal costs increase as effort increases. The utility of the worker who chooses effort level $x$ is then simply $s(y)-c(x) = s(f(x))-c(x)$. The worker may have other alternatives available that give him some utility $\bar{u}$. This could come from working at other jobs or from not working at all. All that is relevant for the design of the incentive scheme is that the utility that the worker gets from this job must be at least as great as the utility he could get elsewhere. This gives us the **participation constraint**:

$$s(f(x)) - c(x) \geq \bar{u}.$$

Given this constraint we can determine how much output we can get from the worker. You want to induce the worker to choose an effort level $x$ that yields you the greatest surplus given the constraint that the worker is willing to work for you:

$$\max_{x} f(x) - s(f(x))$$

$$\text{such that } s(f(x)) - c(x) \geq \bar{u}.$$

In general, you will want the worker to choose $x$ to just satisfy the constraint so that $s(f(x)) - c(x) = \bar{u}$. Substituting this into the objective function we have the unconstrained maximization problem

$$\max_{x} f(x) - c(x) - \bar{u}.$$

But it is easy to solve this problem! Just choose $x^*$ so that the marginal product equals the marginal cost:

$$MP(x^*) = MC(x^*).$$

Any choice of $x^*$ where the marginal benefit is not equal to the marginal cost cannot maximize profits.

This tells us what level of effort the owner wants to achieve; now we have to ask what he has to pay the worker to achieve that effort. That is, what does the function $s(y)$ have to look like to induce the worker to choose to make $x^*$ the optimal choice?

Suppose that you decide that you want to induce the worker to put in $x^*$ amount of effort. Then you must make it in his interest to do so; that is, you must design your incentive scheme $s(y)$ so that the utility from choosing to work $x^*$ is larger than the utility of worker any other amount $x$. This gives us the constraint

$$s(f(x^*)) - c(x^*) \geq s(f(x)) - c(x) \quad \text{for all } x.$$

This constraint is called the **incentive compatibility constraint**. It simply says that the utility to the worker from choosing $x^*$ must be greater than the utility of any other choice of effort.

So we have two conditions that the incentive scheme must satisfy: first, it must give total utility to the worker of $\bar{u}$, and second, it must make the marginal product of effort equal to the marginal cost of effort at the effort level $x^*$. There are several ways to do this.

*Rent.* The landowner could simply rent the land to the worker for some price $R$, so that the worker gets all the output he produces after he pays the owner $R$. For this scheme

$$s(f(x)) = f(x) - R.$$

If the worker maximizes $s(f(x)) - c(x) = f(x) - R - c(x)$, he will choose the effort level where $MP(x^*) = MC(x^*)$, which is exactly what the owner wants. The rental rate $R$ is determined from the participation condition. Since the total utility to the worker must be $\bar{u}$ we have

$$f(x^*) - c(x^*) - R = \bar{u},$$

which says $R = f(x^*) - c(x^*) - \bar{u}$.

*Wage labor.* In this scheme the landowner pays the worker a constant wage per unit of effort along with a lump sum $K$. This means that the incentive payment takes the form

$$s(x) = wx + K.$$

The wage rate $w$ is equal to the marginal product of the worker at the optimal choice $x^*$, $MP(x^*)$. The constant $K$ is chosen to just make the worker indifferent between working for the landowner and working elsewhere; that is, it is chosen to satisfy the participation constraint.

The problem of maximizing $s(f(x)) - c(x)$ then becomes

$$\max_{x} \ wx + K - c(x),$$

which means that the worker will choose $x$ so as to set his marginal cost equal to the wage: $w = MC(x)$. Since the wage is $MP(x^*)$, this means that the *optimal* choice of the worker will be $x^*$ such that $MP(x^*) = MC(x^*)$ which is just what the firm wants.

*Take-it-or-leave-it.* In this scheme the landowner pays the worker $B^*$ if he works $x^*$ and zero otherwise. The amount $B^*$ is determined by the participation constraint $B^* - c(x^*) = \bar{u}$, so $B^* = \bar{u} + c(x^*)$. If the worker chooses any level of effort $x \neq x^*$, he gets a utility of $-c(x)$. If he chooses $x^*$, he gets a utility of $\bar{u}$. Hence the optimal choice for the worker is to set $x = x^*$.

Each of these schemes is equivalent as far as the analysis goes: each one gives the worker a utility of $\bar{u}$, and each one gives the worker an incentive to work the optimal amount $x^*$. At this level of generality there is no reason to choose between them.

If all of these schemes are optimal, what could a nonoptimal scheme look like? Here is an example.

*Sharecropping.* In sharecropping the worker and the landowner each get some fixed percentage of the output. Suppose that the worker's share takes the form $s(x) = \alpha f(x) + F$, where $F$ is some constant and $\alpha < 1$. This is *not* an efficient scheme for the problem under consideration. It is easy to see why. The worker's maximization problem is

$$\max_{x} \ \alpha f(x) + F - c(x),$$

which means that he would choose a level of effort $\hat{x}$ where

$$\alpha MP(\hat{x}) = MC(\hat{x}).$$

Such an effort level clearly cannot satisfy the efficiency condition that $MP(x) = MC(x)$.

Here is a way to summarize this analysis. In order to design an efficient incentive scheme it is necessary to ensure that the person who makes the effort decision is the **residual claimant** to the output. The way the owner can make himself as well off as possible is to make sure that he gets the worker to produce the optimal amount of output. This is the output level where the marginal product of the worker's extra effort equals the marginal cost of putting forth that effort. It follows that the incentive scheme must provide a marginal benefit to the worker equal to his marginal product.

## EXAMPLE: Voting Rights in the Corporation

Normally shareholders in a corporation have the right to vote on various issues related to the management of the corporation while bondholders do not. Why is this? The answer comes from looking at the structure of payoffs to stockholders and bondholders. If a corporation produces $X$ dollars of profit in a given years, the bondholders have first claim on these profits, while the amount that is left over goes to the stockholders. If the total claim by the bondholders is $B$, then the amount that goes to the stockholders is $X - B$. This makes the stockholders the residual claimants—so they have an incentive to make $X$ as large as possible. The bondholders on the other hand only have an incentive to make sure that $X$ is at least $B$, since that is the most that they are entitled to. Hence giving the stockholders the right to make decisions will generally result in larger profits.

## EXAMPLE: Chinese Economic Reforms

Prior to 1979 Chinese rural communes were organized along orthodox Marxist lines. Workers were paid according to a rough estimate of how much they contributed to the commune income. Five percent of the commune's land was set aside for private plots, but peasants were not allowed to travel to cities to sell the output from their private farms. All trade had to take place through a highly regulated government market.

At the end of 1978 the Chinese central government instituted a major reform in the structure of agriculture, known as the "responsibility system." In the responsibility system, any production in excess of a fixed quota was kept by the household and could be sold on private markets. The government removed restrictions on private plots and increased the amount of land devoted to private farming. By the end of 1984, 97 percent of the farmers operated under this responsibility system.

Note that the structure of the system is very much like the optimal incentive mechanism described above: each household makes a lump-sum payment to the commune but can keep anything in excess of this quota. Hence the *marginal* incentives for household production are the economically appropriate ones.

The effect of this new system on agricultural output was phenomenal: between 1978 and 1984, the output of Chinese agriculture increased by over 61 percent! However, not all of this increase is due to better incentives; at the same time these reforms were going on, the Chinese government also changed the controlled prices of agricultural goods, and even allowed some of these prices to be determined on private markets.

Three economists attempted to divide the increase in output into the part due to better incentives and the part due to the change in prices.[6] They found that over three-fourths of the increase was due to the improvement in incentives, and only one-fourth was due to the price reforms.

## 38.8 Asymmetric Information

The above analysis provides some insights about the use of different sorts of incentive schemes. For example, it shows that renting the land to a worker is better than sharecropping. But this really proves too much. If our analysis is a good description of the world, then we would expect to see rental or wage labor used in agriculture and never see sharecropping used, except by mistake.

Clearly this isn't right. Sharecropping has been used for thousands of years in some parts of the world, so it is likely that it fulfills some kind of need. What have we left out of our model?

Given the title of this section it is not hard to guess the answer: we've left out problems involving imperfect information. We assumed that the owner of the firm could perfectly observe the effort of the worker. In many situations of interest it may be impossible to observe the effort. At best the owner may observe some *signal* of the effort such as the resulting production of output. The amount of output produced by a farmer may depend in part on his effort, but it may also depend on the weather, the quality of the inputs, and many other factors. Because of this kind of "noise," a payment from the owner to the worker based on output will not in general be equivalent to a payment based on effort alone.

This is essentially a problem of asymmetric information: the worker can choose his effort level, but the owner cannot perfectly observe it. The owner has to guess the effort from the observed output, and the design of the optimal incentive scheme has to reflect this inference problem.

Consider the four incentive schemes described above. What goes wrong if effort is not perfectly correlated with output?

*Rent.* If the firm rents the technology to the worker, then the worker can get all of the output that remains after paying the fixed rental fee. If output has a random component, this means that the worker will have to bear all the risk from the random factors. If the worker is more risk averse than the owner—which is the likely case—this will be inefficient. In general, the worker would be willing to give up some of the residual profits in order to have a less risky income stream.

---

[6] J. McMillan, J. Whalley, and L. Zhu, "The Impact of China's Economic Reforms on Agricultural Productivity Growth," *Journal of Political Economy,* 97, 4, 1989, 781–807.

*Wage labor.* The problem with wage labor is that it requires observation of the *amount* of labor input. The wage has to be based on the effort put in to production, not just the hours spent in the firm. If the owner can't observe the amount of labor input, then it will be impossible to implement this kind of incentive scheme.

*Take-it-or-leave-it.* If the incentive payment is based on the labor input, then we have the same problem with this scheme as with wage labor. If the payment is based on *output,* then the scheme involves the worker bearing all the risk. Even missing the "target output" by a small amount results in a zero payment.

*Sharecropping.* This is something of a happy medium. The payment to the worker depends in part on observed output, but the worker and the owner share the risk of output fluctuations. This gives the worker an incentive to produce output but it doesn't leave him bearing all the risk.

The introduction of asymmetric information has made a drastic change in our evaluation of the incentive methods. If the owner can't observe effort, then wage labor is infeasible. Rent and the take-it-or-leave-it scheme leave the worker bearing too much risk. Sharecropping is a compromise between the two extremes: it gives the worker some incentive to produce, but it doesn't leave him with all the risk.

## EXAMPLE: Monitoring Costs

It is not always easy to observe the amount of effort an employee puts into his or her job. Consider, for example, a job as a clerk in a 24-hour convenience store. How can the manager observe the employees' performance when the manager isn't around? Even if there are ways to observe the physical output of the employee (shelves stocked, sales rung up) it is much harder to observe things like politeness to customers.

There is little doubt that some of the worst service in the world was provided in the formerly Communist countries in Eastern Europe: once you managed to attract the attention of a clerk, you were more likely to be greeted by a scowl than a smile. Nevertheless, a Hungarian entrepreneur, Gabor Varszegi, has made millions by providing high-quality service in his photo developing shops in Budapest.[7]

Varszegi says that he got his start as a businessman in the mid-sixties by playing bass guitar and managing a rock group. "Back then," he says, "the only private businessmen in Eastern Europe were rock musicians."

---

[7] See Steven Greenhouse, "A New Formula in Hungary: Speed Service and Grow Rich," *New York Times,* June 5, 1990, A1.

He introduced one-hour film developing to Hungary in 1985; the next best alternative to his one-hour developing shops was the state-run agency that took one month.

Varszegi follows two rules in labor relations: he never hires anyone who worked under Communism, and he pays his workers four times the market wage. This makes perfect sense in light of the above remarks about monitoring costs: there are very few employees per store and monitoring their behavior is very costly. If there were only a small penalty to being fired, there would be great temptation to slack off. By paying the workers much more than they could get elsewhere, Varszegi makes it very costly for them to be fired—and reduces his monitoring costs significantly.

## EXAMPLE: The Grameen Bank

A village moneylender in Bangladesh charges over 150 percent interest a year. Any American banker would love a return of that size: why isn't Citibank installing money machines in Bangladesh? To ask the question is to answer it: Citibank would probably not do as well as the moneylender. The village moneylender has a comparative advantage in these small-scale loans for several reasons.

• The village moneylender can deal more effectively with the small scale of lending involved;

• The moneylender has better access to information about who are good and bad credit risks than an outsider does.

• The moneylender is in a better position to monitor the progress of the loan payments to insure repayment.

These three problems—returns to scale, adverse selection and moral hazard—allow the village moneylender to maintain a local monopoly in the credit market.

Such a local monopoly is especially pernicious in an underdeveloped country such as Bangladesh. At an interest rate of 150 percent there are many profitable projects that are not being undertaken by the peasants. Improved access to credit could lead to a major increase in investment, and a corresponding increase in the standards of living.

Muhammad Yunus, an American-trained economist from Bangladesh, has developed an ingenious institution known as the Grameen Bank (village bank) to address some of these problems. In the Grameen plan, entrepreneurs with separate projects get together and apply for a loan as a group. If the loan is approved, two members of the group get their loan and commence their investment activity. If they are successful in meeting the repayment schedule, two more members get loans. If they are also successful the last member, the group leader, will get a loan.

The Grameen bank addresses each of the three problems described above. Since the quality of the group influences whether or not individual members will get loans, potential members are highly selective about who they will join with. Since members of the group can only get loans if other members succeed in their investments, there are strong incentives to help each other out and share expertise. Finally, these activities of choosing candidates for loans and monitoring the progress of the repayments are all done by the peasants themselves, not directly by the loan officers at the bank.

The Grameen bank has been very successful. It makes about 475,000 loans a month with an average size of $70. Their loan-recovery rate is about 98 percent, while conventional lenders in Bangladesh achieve a loan-recovery rate of about 30 to 40 percent. The success of the group responsibility program in encouraging investment has led to its adoption in a number of other poverty-stricken areas in North and South America.

## Summary

1. Imperfect and asymmetric information can lead to drastic differences in the nature of market equilbrium.

2. Adverse selection refers to situations where the type of the agents is not observable so that one side of the market has to guess the type or quality of a product based on the behavior of the other side of the market.

3. In markets involving adverse selection too little trade may take place. In this case it is possible that everyone can be made better off by forcing them to transact.

4. Moral hazard refers to a situation where one side of the market can't observe the actions of the other side.

5. Signaling refers to the fact that when adverse selection or moral hazard are present some agents will want to invest in signals that will differentiate them from other agents.

6. Investment in signals may be privately beneficial but publically wasteful. On the other hand, investment in signals may help to solve problems due to asymmetric information.

7. Efficient incentive schemes (with perfect observability of effort) leave the worker as the residual claimant. This means that the worker will equate marginal benefits and marginal costs.

8. But if information is imperfect this is no longer true. In general, an incentive scheme that shares risks as well as providing incentives will be appropriate.

## REVIEW QUESTIONS

1. Consider the model of the used-car market presented in this chapter. What is the maximum amount of consumers' surplus that is created by trade in the market equilibrium?

2. In the same model, how much consumers' surplus would be created by *randomly* assigning buyers to sellers? Which method gives the larger surplus?

3. A worker can produce $x$ units of output at a cost of $c(x) = x^2/2$. He can achieve a utility level of $\bar{u} = 0$ working elsewhere. What is the optimal wage-labor incentive scheme $s(x)$ for this worker?

4. Given the setup of the previous problem, what would the worker be willing to pay to rent the production technology?

5. How would your answer to the last problem change if the worker's alternative employment gave him $\bar{u} = 1$?

# MATHEMATICAL APPENDIX

In this Appendix we will provide a brief review of some of the mathematical concepts that are used in the text. This material is meant to serve as a reminder of the definitions of various terms used in the text. It is emphatically not a tutorial in mathematics. The definitions given will generally be the simplest, not the most rigorous.

## A.1 Functions

A **function** is a rule that describes a relationship between numbers. For each number $x$, a function assigns a *unique* number $y$ according to some rule. Thus a function can be indicated by describing the rule, as "take a number and square it," or "take a number and multiply it by 2," and so on. We write these particular functions as $y = x^2$, $y = 2x$. Functions are sometimes referred to as **transformations**.

Often we want to indicate that some variable $y$ depends on some other variable $x$, but we don't know the specific algebraic relationship between the two variables. In this case we write $y = f(x)$, which should be interpreted as saying that the variable $y$ depends on $x$ according to the rule $f$.

Given a function $y = f(x)$, the number $x$ is often called the **independent variable**, and the number $y$ is often called the **dependent variable**.

The idea is that $x$ varies independently, but the value of $y$ *depends* on the value of $x$.

Often some variable $y$ depends on several other variables $x_1$, $x_2$, and so on, so we write $y = f(x_1, x_2)$ to indicate that both variables together determine the value of $y$.

## A.2 Graphs

A **graph** of a function depicts the behavior of a function pictorially. Figure A.1 shows two graphs of functions. In mathematics the independent variable is usually depicted on the horizontal axis, and the dependent variable is depicted on the vertical axis. The graph then indicates the relationship between the independent and the dependent variables.

However, in economics it is common to graph functions with the independent variable on the vertical axis and the dependent variable on the horizontal axis. Demand functions, for example, are usually depicted with the price on the vertical axis and the amount demanded on the horizontal axis.

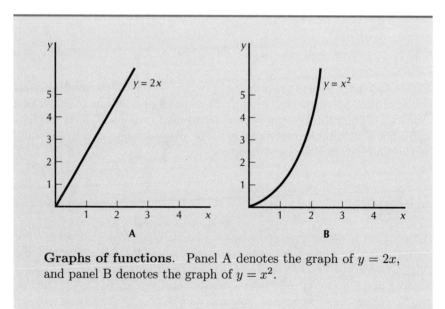

Figure
A.1

**Graphs of functions.** Panel A denotes the graph of $y = 2x$, and panel B denotes the graph of $y = x^2$.

## A.3 Properties of Functions

A **continuous function** is one that can be drawn without lifting a pencil from the paper: there are no jumps in a continuous function. A **smooth**

**function** is one that has no "kinks" or corners. A **monotonic** function is one that always increases or always decreases; a **positive monotonic function** always increases as $x$ increases, while a **negative monotonic function** always decreases as $x$ increases.

## A.4 Inverse Functions

Recall that a function has the property that for each value of $x$ there is a unique value of $y$ associated with it and that a monotonic function is one that is always increasing or always decreasing. This implies that for a monotonic function there will be a unique value of $x$ associated with each value of $y$.

We call the function that relates $x$ to $y$ in this way an **inverse function**. If you are given $y$ as a function of $x$, you can calculate the inverse function just by solving for $x$ as a function of $y$. If $y = 2x$, then the inverse function is $x = y/2$. If $y = x^2$, then there is no inverse function; given any $y$, both $x = +\sqrt{y}$ and $x = -\sqrt{y}$ have the property that their square is equal to $y$. Thus there is not a *unique* value of $x$ associated with each value of $y$, as is required by the definition of a function.

## A.5 Equations and Identities

An **equation** asks when a function is equal to some particular number. Examples of equations are

$$2x = 8$$
$$x^2 = 9$$
$$f(x) = 0.$$

The **solution** to an equation is a value of $x$ that satisfies the equation. The first equation has a solution of $x = 4$. The second equation has two solutions, $x = 3$ and $x = -3$. The third equation is just a general equation. We don't know its solution until we know the actual rule that $f$ stands for, but we can denote its solution by $x^*$. This simply means that $x^*$ is a number such that $f(x^*) = 0$. We say that $x^*$ **satisfies** the equation $f(x) = 0$.

An **identity** is a relationship between variables that holds for *all* values of the variables. Here are some examples of identities:

$$(x + y)^2 \equiv x^2 + 2xy + y^2$$
$$2(x + 1) \equiv 2x + 2.$$

The special symbol $\equiv$ means that the left-hand side and the right-hand side are equal for *all* values of the variables. An equation only holds for some values of the variables, whereas an identity is true for all values of the variables. Often an identity is true by the definition of the terms involved.

## A.6 Linear Functions

A **linear function** is a function of the form

$$y = ax + b,$$

where $a$ and $b$ are constants. Examples of linear functions are

$$y = 2x + 3$$
$$y = x - 99.$$

Strictly speaking, a function of the form $y = ax + b$ should be called an **affine function**, and only functions of the form $y = ax$ should be called linear functions. However, we will not insist on this distinction.

Linear functions can also be expressed implicitly in forms like $ax + by = c$. In such a case, we often like to solve for $y$ as a function of $x$ to convert this to the "standard" form:

$$y = \frac{c}{b} - \frac{a}{b}x.$$

## A.7 Changes and Rates of Change

The notation $\Delta x$ is read as "the change in $x$." It does *not* mean $\Delta$ times $x$. If $x$ changes from $x^*$ to $x^{**}$, then the change in $x$ is just

$$\Delta x = x^{**} - x^*.$$

We can also write

$$x^{**} = x^* + \Delta x$$

to indicate that $x^{**}$ is $x^*$ plus a change in $x$.

Typically $\Delta x$ will refer to a *small* change in $x$. We sometimes express this by saying that $\Delta x$ represents a **marginal change**.

A **rate of change** is the ratio of two changes. If $y$ is a function of $x$ given by $y = f(x)$, then the rate of change of $y$ with respect to $x$ is denoted by

$$\frac{\Delta y}{\Delta x} = \frac{f(x + \Delta x) - f(x)}{\Delta x}.$$

The rate of change measures how $y$ changes as $x$ changes.

A linear function has the property that the rate of change of $y$ with respect to $x$ is constant. To prove this, note that if $y = a + bx$, then

$$\frac{\Delta y}{\Delta x} = \frac{a + b(x + \Delta x) - a - bx}{\Delta x} = \frac{b\Delta x}{\Delta x} = b.$$

For nonlinear functions, the rate of change of the function will depend on the value of $x$. Consider, for example, the function $y = x^2$. For this function

$$\frac{\Delta y}{\Delta x} = \frac{(x + \Delta x)^2 - x^2}{\Delta x} = \frac{x^2 + 2x\Delta x + (\Delta x)^2 - x^2}{\Delta x} = 2x + \Delta x.$$

Here the rate of change from $x$ to $x + \Delta x$ depends on the value of $x$ and on the size of the change, $\Delta x$. But if we consider very small changes in $x$, $\Delta x$ will be nearly zero, so the rate of change of $y$ with respect to $x$ will be approximately $2x$.

## A.8 Slopes and Intercepts

The rate of change of a function can be interpreted graphically as the **slope** of the function. In Figure A.2A we have depicted a linear function $y = -2x + 4$. The **vertical intercept** of this function is the value of $y$ when $x = 0$, which is $y = 4$. The **horizontal intercept** is the value of $x$ when $y = 0$, which is $x = 2$. The slope of the function is the rate of change of $y$ as $x$ changes. In this case, the slope of the function is $-2$.

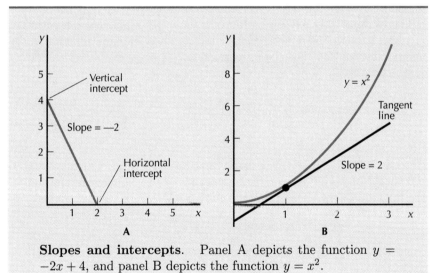

**Slopes and intercepts.** Panel A depicts the function $y = -2x + 4$, and panel B depicts the function $y = x^2$.

Figure A.2

In general, if a linear function has the form $y = ax + b$, the vertical intercept will be $y^* = b$ and the horizontal intercept will be $x^* = -b/a$. If a linear function is expressed in the form

$$a_1 x_1 + a_2 x_2 = c,$$

then the horizontal intercept will be the value of $x_1$ when $x_2 = 0$, which is $x_1^* = c/a_1$, and the vertical intercept will occur when $x_1 = 0$, which means $x_2^* = c/a_2$. The slope of this function is $-a_1/a_2$.

A nonlinear function has the property that its slope changes as $x$ changes. A **tangent** to a function at some point $x$ is a linear function that has the same slope. In Figure A.2B we have depicted the function $x^2$ and the tangent line at $x = 1$.

If $y$ increases whenever $x$ increases, then $\Delta y$ will always have the same sign as $\Delta x$, so that the slope of the function will be positive. If on the other hand $y$ decreases when $x$ increases, or $y$ increases when $x$ decreases, $\Delta y$ and $\Delta x$ will have opposite signs, so that the slope of the function will be negative.

## A.9 Absolute Values and Logarithms

The **absolute value** of a number is a function $f(x)$ defined by the following rule:

$$f(x) = \begin{cases} x & \text{if } x \geq 0 \\ -x & \text{if } x < 0. \end{cases}$$

Thus the absolute value of a number can be found by dropping the sign of the number. The absolute value function is usually written as $|x|$.

The (natural) **logarithm** or **log** of $x$ describes a particular function of $x$, which we write as $y = \ln x$ or $y = \ln(x)$. The logarithm function is the unique function that has the properties

$$\ln(xy) = \ln(x) + \ln(y)$$

for all positive numbers $x$ and $y$ and

$$\ln(e) = 1.$$

(In this last equation, $e$ is the base of natural logarithms which is equal to $2.7183\ldots$) In words, the log of the product of two numbers is the sum of the individual logs. This property implies another important property of logarithms:

$$\ln(x^y) = y\ln(x),$$

which says that the log of $x$ raised to the power $y$ is equal to $y$ times the log of $x$.

## A.10 Derivatives

The **derivative** of a function $y = f(x)$ is defined to be

$$\frac{df(x)}{dx} = \lim_{\Delta x \to 0} \frac{f(x + \Delta x) - f(x)}{\Delta x}.$$

In words, the derivative is the limit of the rate of change of $y$ with respect to $x$ as the change in $x$ goes to zero. The derivative gives precise meaning to the phrase "the rate of change of $y$ with respect to $x$ for small changes in $x$." The derivative of $f(x)$ with respect to $x$ is also denoted by $f'(x)$.

We have already seen that the rate of change of a linear function $y = ax + b$ is constant. Thus for this linear function

$$\frac{df(x)}{dx} = a.$$

For a nonlinear function the rate of change of $y$ with respect to $x$ will usually depend on $x$. We saw that in the case of $f(x) = x^2$, we had $\Delta y/\Delta x = 2x + \Delta x$. Applying the definition of the derivative

$$\frac{df(x)}{dx} = \lim_{\Delta x \to 0} 2x + \Delta x = 2x.$$

Thus the derivative of $x^2$ with respect to $x$ is $2x$.

It can be shown by more advanced methods that if $y = \ln x$, then

$$\frac{df(x)}{dx} = \frac{1}{x}.$$

## A.11 Second Derivatives

The **second derivative** of a function is the derivative of the derivative of that function. If $y = f(x)$, the second derivative of $f(x)$ with respect to $x$ is written as $d^2 f(x)/dx^2$ or $f''(x)$. We know that

$$\frac{d(2x)}{dx} = 2$$

$$\frac{d(x^2)}{dx} = 2x.$$

Thus

$$\frac{d^2(2x)}{dx^2} = \frac{d(2)}{dx} = 0$$

$$\frac{d^2(x^2)}{dx^2} = \frac{d(2x)}{dx} = 2.$$

The second derivative measures the curvature of a function. A function with a negative second derivative at some point is concave near that point; its slope is decreasing. A function with a positive second derivative at a point is convex near that point; its slope is increasing. A function with a zero second derivative at a point is flat near that point.

## A.12 The Product Rule and the Chain Rule

Suppose that $g(x)$ and $h(x)$ are both functions of $x$. We can define the function $f(x)$ that represents their product by $f(x) = g(x)h(x)$. Then the derivative of $f(x)$ is given by

$$\frac{df(x)}{dx} = g(x)\frac{dh(x)}{dx} + h(x)\frac{dg(x)}{dx}.$$

Given two functions $y = g(x)$ and $z = h(y)$, the **composite function** is

$$f(x) = h(g(x)).$$

For example, if $g(x) = x^2$ and $h(y) = 2y + 3$, then the composite function is

$$f(x) = 2x^2 + 3.$$

The **chain rule** says that the derivative of a composite function, $f(x)$, with respect to $x$ is given by

$$\frac{df(x)}{dx} = \frac{dh(y)}{dy}\frac{dg(x)}{dx}.$$

In our example, $dh(y)/dy = 2$, and $dg(x)/dx = 2x$, so the chain rule says that $df(x)/dx = 2 \times 2x = 4x$. Direct calculation verifies that this is the derivative of the function $f(x) = 2x^2 + 3$.

## A.13 Partial Derivatives

Suppose that $y$ depends on both $x_1$ and $x_2$, so that $y = f(x_1, x_2)$. Then the **partial derivative** of $f(x_1, x_2)$ with respect to $x_1$ is defined by

$$\frac{\partial f(x_1, x_2)}{\partial x_1} = \lim_{\Delta x_1 \to 0} \frac{f(x_1 + \Delta x_1, x_2) - f(x_1, x_2)}{\Delta x_1}.$$

The partial derivative of $f(x_1, x_2)$ with respect to $x_1$ is just the derivative of the function with respect to $x_1$, *holding $x_2$ fixed*. Similarly, the partial derivative with respect to $x_2$ is

$$\frac{\partial f(x_1, x_2)}{\partial x_2} = \lim_{\Delta x_2 \to 0} \frac{f(x_1, x_2 + \Delta x_2) - f(x_1, x_2)}{\Delta x_2}.$$

Partial derivatives have exactly the same properties as ordinary derivatives; only the name has been changed to protect the innocent (that is, people who haven't seen the $\partial$ symbol).

In particular, partial derivatives obey the chain rule, but with an extra twist. Suppose that $x_1$ and $x_2$ both depend on some variable $t$ and that we define the function $g(t)$ by

$$g(t) = f(x_1(t), x_2(t)).$$

Then the derivative of $g(t)$ with respect to $t$ is given by

$$\frac{dg(t)}{dt} = \frac{\partial f(x_1, x_2)}{\partial x_1} \frac{dx_1(t)}{dt} + \frac{\partial f(x_1, x_2)}{\partial x_2} \frac{dx_2(t)}{dt}.$$

When $t$ changes, it affects both $x_1(t)$ and $x_2(t)$. Therefore, we need to calculate the derivative of $f(x_1, x_2)$ with respect to each of those changes.

## A.14 Optimization

If $y = f(x)$, then $f(x)$ achieves a **maximum** at $x^*$ if $f(x^*) \geq f(x)$ for all $x$. It can be shown that if $f(x)$ is a smooth function that achieves its maximum value at $x^*$, then

$$\frac{df(x^*)}{dx} = 0$$

$$\frac{d^2 f(x^*)}{dx^2} \leq 0.$$

These expressions are referred to as the **first-order condition** and the **second-order condition** for a maximum. The first-order condition says that the function is flat at $x^*$, while the second-order condition says that the function is concave near $x^*$. Clearly both of these properties have to hold if $x^*$ is indeed a maximum.

We say that $f(x)$ achieves its **minimum** value at $x^*$ if $f(x^*) \leq f(x)$ for all $x$. If $f(x)$ is a smooth function that achieves its minimum at $x^*$, then

$$\frac{df(x^*)}{dx} = 0$$

$$\frac{d^2 f(x^*)}{dx^2} \geq 0.$$

The first-order condition again says that the function is flat at $x^*$, while the second-order condition now says that the function is convex near $x^*$.

If $y = f(x_1, x_2)$ is a smooth function that achieves its maximum or minimum at some point $(x_1^*, x_2^*)$, then we must satisfy

$$\frac{\partial f(x_1^*, x_2^*)}{\partial x_1} = 0$$

$$\frac{\partial f(x_1^*, x_2^*)}{\partial x_2} = 0.$$

These are referred to as the **first-order conditions**. There are also second-order conditions for this problem, but they are more difficult to describe.

## A.15 Constrained Optimization

Often we want to consider the maximum or minimum of some function over some restricted values of $(x_1, x_2)$. The notation

$$\max_{x_1, x_2} f(x_1, x_2)$$

$$\text{such that } g(x_1, x_2) = c.$$

means

find $x_1^*$ and $x_2^*$ such that $f(x_1^*, x_2^*) \geq f(x_1, x_2)$ for all values of $x_1$ and $x_2$ that satisfy the equation $g(x_1, x_2) = c$.

The function $f(x_1, x_2)$ is called the **objective function**, and the equation $g(x_1, x_2) = c$ is called the **constraint**. Methods for solving this kind of constrained maximization problem are described in the Appendix to Chapter 5.

# ANSWERS

## 1 The Market

1.1. It would be constant at $500 for 25 apartments and then drop to $200.

1.2. In the first case, $500, and in the second case, $200. In the third case, the equilibrium price would be any price between $200 and $500.

1.3. Because if we want to rent one more apartment, we have to offer a lower price. The number of people who have reservation prices greater than $p$ must always increase as $p$ decreases.

1.4. The price of apartments in the inner ring would go up since demand for apartments would not change but supply would decrease.

1.5. The price of apartments in the inner ring would rise.

1.6. A tax would undoubtedly reduce the number of apartments supplied in the long run.

1.7. He would set a price of 25 and rent 50 apartments. In the second case he would rent all 40 apartments at the maximum price the market would bear. This would be given by the solution to $D(p) = 100 - 2p = 40$, which is $p^* = 30$.

1.8. Everyone who had a reservation price higher than the equilibrium price in the competitive market, so that the final outcome would be Pareto efficient. (Of course in the long run there would probably be fewer new apartments built, which would lead to another kind of inefficiency.)

## 2 Budget Constraint

2.1. The new budget line is given by $2p_1x_1 + 8p_2x_2 = 4m$.

2.2. The vertical intercept ($x_2$ axis) decreases and the horizontal intercept ($x_1$ axis) stays the same. Thus the budget line becomes flatter.

2.3. Flatter. The slope is $-2p_1/3p_2$.

2.4. A good whose price has been set to 1; all other goods' prices are measured relative to the numeraire good's price.

2.5. A tax of 8 cents a gallon.

2.6. $(p_1 + t)x_1 + (p_2 - s)x_2 = m - u$.

2.7. Yes, since all of the bundles the consumer could afford before are affordable at the new prices and income.


## 3 Preferences

3.1. No. It might be that the consumer was indifferent between the two bundles. All we are justified in concluding is that $(x_1, x_2) \succeq (y_1, y_2)$.

3.2. Yes to both.

3.3. It is transitive, but it is not complete—two people might be the same height. It is not reflexive since it is false that a person is strictly taller than himself.

3.4. It is transitive, but not complete. What if A were bigger but slower than B? Which one would he prefer?

3.5. Yes. An indifference curve can cross itself, it just can't cross another distinct indifference curve.

3.6. No, because there are bundles on the indifference curve that have strictly more of both goods than other bundles on the (alleged) indifference curve.

3.7. A negative slope. If you give the consumer more anchovies, you've made him worse off, so you have to take away some pepperoni to get him back on his indifference curve. In this case the direction of increasing utility is *toward* the origin.

3.8. Because the consumer weakly prefers the weighted average of two bundles to either bundle.

3.9. If you give up one $5 bill, how many $1 bills do you need to compensate you? Five $1 bills will do nicely. Hence the answer is $-5$ or $-1/5$, depending on which good you put on the horizontal axis.

3.10. Zero—if you take away some of good 1, the consumer needs zero units of good 2 to compensate him for his loss.

3.11. Anchovies and peanut butter, scotch and Kool Aid, and other similar repulsive combinations.

## 4 Utility

4.1. The function $f(u) = u^2$ is a monotonic transformation for positive $u$, but not for negative $u$.

4.2. (1) Yes. (2) No (works for $v$ positive). (3) No (works for $v$ negative). (4) Yes (only defined for $v$ positive). (5) Yes. (6) No. (7) Yes. (8) No.

4.3. Suppose that the diagonal intersected a given indifference curve at two points, say $(x, x)$ and $(y, y)$. Then either $x > y$ or $y > x$, which means that one of the bundles has more of *both* goods. But if preferences are monotonic, then one of the bundles would have to be preferred to the other.

4.4. Both represent perfect substitutes.

4.5. Quasilinear preferences. Yes.

4.6. The utility function represents Cobb-Douglas preferences. No. Yes.

4.7. Because the MRS is measured *along* an indifference curve, and utility remains constant along an indifference curve.

## 5 Choice

5.1. $x_2 = 0$ when $p_2 > p_1$, $x_2 = m/p_2$ when $p_2 < p_1$, and anything between 0 and $m/p_2$ when $p_1 = p_2$.

5.2. The optimal choices will be $x_1 = m/p_1$ and $x_2 = 0$ if $p_1/p_2 < b$, $x_1 = 0$ and $x_2 = m/p_2$ if $p_1/p_2 > b$, and any amount on the budget line if $p_1/p_2 = b$.

5.3. Let $z$ be the number of cups of coffee the consumer buys. Then we know that $2z$ is the number of teaspoons of sugar he or she buys. We must satisfy the budget constraint

$$2p_1 z + p_2 z = m.$$

Solving for $z$ we have

$$z = \frac{m}{2p_1 + p_2}.$$

5.4. We know that you'll either consume all ice cream or all olives. Thus the two choices for the optimal consumption bundles will be $x_1 = m/p_1$, $x_2 = 0$, or $x_1 = 0$, $x_2 = m/p_2$.

5.5. This is a Cobb-Douglas utility function, so she will spend $4/(1+4) = 4/5$ of her income on good 2.

5.6. For kinked preferences, such as perfect complements, where the change in price doesn't induce any change in demand.

## 6 Demand

6.1. No. If her income increases, and she spends it all, she must be purchasing more of at least one good.

6.2. The utility function for perfect substitutes is $u(x_1, x_2) = x_1 + x_2$. Thus if $u(x_1, x_2) > u(y_1, y_2)$, we have $x_1 + x_2 > y_1 + y_2$. It follows that $tx_1 + tx_2 > ty_1 + ty_2$, so that $u(tx_1, tx_2) > u(ty_1, ty_2)$.

6.3. The Cobb-Douglas utility function has the property that

$$u(tx_1, tx_2) = (tx_1)^a (tx_2)^{1-a} = t^a t^{1-a} x_1^a x_2^{1-a} = tx_1^a x_2^{1-a} = tu(x_1, x_2).$$

Thus if $u(x_1, x_2) > u(y_1, y_2)$, we know that $u(tx_1, tx_2) > u(ty_1, ty_2)$, so that Cobb-Douglas preferences are indeed homothetic.

6.4. The demand curve.

6.5. No. Concave preferences can only give rise to optimal consumption bundles that involve zero consumption of one of the goods.

6.6. Normally they would be complements, at least for non-vegetarians.

6.7. We know that $x_1 = m/(p_1 + p_2)$. Solving for $p_1$ as a function of the other variables, we have

$$p_1 = \frac{m}{x_1} - p_2.$$

6.8. False.

## 7 Revealed Preference

7.1. No. This consumer violates the Weak Axiom of Revealed Preference since when he bought $(x_1, x_2)$ he could have bought $(y_1, y_2)$ and vice versa. In symbols:

$$p_1 x_1 + p_2 x_2 = 1 \times 1 + 2 \times 2 = 5 > 4 = 1 \times 2 + 2 \times 1 = p_1 y_1 + p_2 y_2$$

and

$$q_1y_1 + q_2y_2 = 2 \times 2 + 1 \times 1 = 5 > 4 = 2 \times 1 + 1 \times 2 = q_1x_1 + q_2x_2.$$

7.2. Yes. No violations of WARP are present, since the y-bundle is not affordable when the x-bundle was purchased and vice versa.

7.3. Since the y-bundle was more expensive than the x-bundle when the x-bundle was purchased and vice versa, there is no way to tell which bundle is preferred.

7.4. If both prices changed by the same amount. Then the base-year bundle would still be optimal.

7.5. Perfect complements.

## 8 Slutsky Equation

8.1. Yes. To see this, use our favorite example of red pencils and blue pencils. Suppose red pencils cost 10 cents a piece, and blue pencils cost 5 cents a piece, and the consumer spends $1 on pencils. She would then consume 20 blue pencils. If the price of blue pencils falls to 4 cents a piece, she would consume 25 blue pencils, a change which is entirely due to the income effect in this case.

8.2. Yes.

8.3. Then the income effect would cancel out. All that would be left would be the pure substitution effect, which would automatically be negative.

8.4. They are receiving $tx'$ in revenues and paying out $tx$, so they are losing money.

8.5. Since their old consumption is affordable, the consumers would have to be at least as well-off. This happens because the government is giving them back *more* money than they are losing due to the higher price of gasoline.

## 9 Buying and Selling

9.1. Her gross demands are $(9, 1)$.

9.2. The bundle $(y_1, y_2) = (3, 5)$ costs more than the bundle $(4, 4)$ at the current prices. The consumer will not necessarily prefer consuming this bundle, but would certainly prefer to own it, since she could sell it and purchase a bundle that she would prefer.

9.3. Sure. It depends on whether she was a net buyer or a net seller of the good that became more expensive.

9.4. Yes, but only if the U.S. switched to being a net exporter of oil.

9.5. The new budget line would shift outward and remain parallel to the old one, since the increase in the number of hours in the day is a pure endowment effect.

9.6. The slope will be positive.

# 10 Intertemporal Choice

10.1. According to Table 10.1, $1 20 years from now is worth 3 cents today at a 20 percent interest rate. Thus $1 million is worth $.03 \times 1,000,000 = $30,000$ today.

10.2. The slope of the intertemporal budget constraint is equal to $-(1+r)$. Thus as $r$ increases the slope becomes more negative (steeper).

10.3. If goods are perfect substitutes, then consumers will only purchase the cheaper good. In the case of intertemporal food purchases, this implies that consumers only buy food in one period, which may not be very realistic.

10.4. In order to remain a lender after the change in interest rates, the consumer must be choosing a point that he could have chosen under the old interest rates, but decided not to. Thus the consumer must be worse off. If the consumer becomes a borrower after the change, then he is choosing a previously unavailable point that cannot be compared to the initial point (since the initial point is no longer available under the new budget constraint), and therefore the change in the consumer's welfare is unknown.

10.5. At an interest rate of 10%, the present value of $100 is $90.91. At a rate of 5% the present value is $95.24.

# 11 Asset Markets

11.1. Asset A must be selling for $11/(1 + .10) = $10$.

11.2. The rate of return is equal to $(10,000 + 10,000)/100,000 = 20\%$.

11.3. We know that the rate of return on the nontaxable bonds, $r$, must be such that $(1 - t)r_t = r$, therefore $(1 - .40).10 = .06 = r$.

11.4. The price today must be $40/(1 + .10)^{10} = \$15.42$.

## 12 Uncertainty

12.1. We need a way to reduce consumption in the bad state and increase consumption in the good state. To do this you would have to *sell* insurance against the loss rather than buy it.

12.2. Functions (a) and (c) have the expected utility property (they are affine transformations of the functions discussed in the chapter), while (b) does not.

12.3. Since he is risk-averse, he prefers the expected value of the gamble, $325, to the gamble itself, and therefore he would take the payment.

12.4. If the payment is $320 the decision will depend on the form of the utility function; we can't say anything in general.

12.5. Your picture should show a function that is initially convex, but then becomes concave.

12.6. In order to self-insure, the risks must be independent. However, this does not hold in the case of flood damage. If one house in the neighborhood is damaged by a flood it is likely that all of the houses will be damaged.

## 13 Risky Assets

13.1. To achieve a standard deviation of 2% you will need to invest $x = \sigma_x/\sigma_m = 2/3$ of your wealth in the risky asset. This will result in a rate of return equal to $(2/3).09 + (1 - 2/3).06 = 8\%$.

13.2. The price of risk is equal to $(r_m - r_f)/\sigma_m = (9 - 6)/3 = 1$. That is, for every additional percent of standard deviation you can gain 1% of return.

13.3. According to the CAPM pricing equation, the stock should offer an expected rate of return of $r_f + \beta(r_m - r_f) = .05 + 1.5(.10 - .05) = .125$ or 12.5%. The stock should be selling for its expected present value, which is equal to $100/1.125 = \$88.89$.

## 14 Consumer's Surplus

14.1. The equilibrium price is $10 and the quantity sold is 100 units. If the tax is imposed, the price rises to $11, but 100 units of the good will still be sold, so there is no deadweight loss.

14.2. We want to compute the area under the demand curve to the left of the quantity 6. Break this up into the area of a triangle with a base of 6 and a height of 6 and a rectangle with base 6 and height 4. Applying the formulas from high school geometry, the triangle has area 18 and the rectangle has area 24. Thus gross benefit is 42.

14.3. When the price is 4, the consumer's surplus is given by the area of a triangle with a base of 6 and a height of 6; i.e., the consumer's surplus is 18. When the price is 6, the triangle has a base of 4 and a height of 4, giving an area of 8. Thus the price change has reduced consumer's surplus by $10.

14.4. Ten dollars. Since the demand for the discrete good hasn't changed, all that has happend is that the consumer has had to reduce his expenditure on other goods by ten dollars.

## 15 Market Demand

15.1. The inverse demand curve is $P(q) = 200 - 2q$.

15.2. The decision about whether to consume the drug at all could well be price sensitive, so the adjustment of market demand on the extensive margin would contribute to the elasticity of the market demand.

15.3. Revenue is $R(p) = 12p - 2p^2$, which is maximized at $p = 3$.

15.4. Revenue is $pD(p) = 100$, regardless of the price, so all prices maximize revenue.

15.5. True. The weighted average of the income elasticities must be 1, so if one good has a *negative* income elasticity, the other good must have an elasticity *greater* than 1 to get the average to be 1.

## 16 Equilibrium

16.1. The entire subsidy gets passed along to the consumers if the supply curve is flat, but the subsidy is totally received by the producers when the supply curve is vertical.

16.2. The consumer.

16.3. In this case the demand curve for red pencils is horizontal at the price $p_b$, since that is the most that they would be willing to pay for a red pencil. Thus, if a tax is imposed on red pencils, consumers will end up paying $p_b$ for them, so the entire amount of the tax will end up being borne by the producers (if any red pencils are sold at all—it could be that the tax would induce the producer to get out of the red pencil business).

16.4. Here the supply curve of foreign oil is flat at $25. Thus the price to the consumers must rise by the $5 amount of the tax, so that the net price to the consumers becomes $30. Since foreign oil and domestic oil are perfect substitutes as far as the consumers are concerned, the domestic producers will sell their oil for $30 as well and get a windfall gain of $5 per barrel.

16.5. Zero. The deadweight loss measures the value of lost output. Since the same amount is supplied before and after the tax, there is no deadweight loss. Put another way: the suppliers are paying the entire amount of the tax, and everything they pay goes to the government. The amount that the suppliers would pay to avoid the tax is simply the tax revenue the government receives, so there is no excess burden of the tax.

16.6. Zero revenue.

16.7. It raises negative revenue, since in this case we have a net subsidy of borrowing.

## 17 Measurement

17.1. This is an example of Simpson's paradox.

17.2. If the coin is fair, then it has a probability $1/2$ of coming up heads the first time, $1/2$ of coming up heads the second time, and so on. The probability of coming up heads 5 times in a row would be $1/2^5 - 1/32 \approx$ .03.

17.3. If you take the natural log of each side, you see that $\log(x) = c + bp$ which is a semi-log demand function.

## 18 Auctions

18.1. Since the collectors likely have their own values for the quilts, and don't particularly care about the other bidders' values, it is a private-value auction.

18.2. Following the analysis in the text, there are four equally likely configurations of bidders: (8,8), (8,10), (10,8), and (10,10). With zero reservation price, the optimal bids will be (8,9,9,10), resulting in expected profit of $9. The only candidate for a reservation price is $10, which yields expected profit of $30/4 = \$7.50$. Hence zero is a profit-maximizing reservation price in this auction.

18.3. Have each person write down a value, then award the two books to the students with the two highest values, but just charge them the bid of the third highest student.

18.4. It was efficient in the sense that it awarded the license to the firm that valued it most highly. But it took a year for this to happen, which is inefficient. A Vickrey auction or an English auction would have achieved the same result more quickly.

18.5. This is a common-value auction since the value of the prize is the same to all bidders. Normally, the winning bidder overestimates the number of pennies in the jar, illustrating the winner's curse.

## 19 Technology

19.1. Increasing returns to scale.

19.2. Decreasing returns to scale.

19.3. If $a + b = 1$, we have constant returns to scale, $a + b < 1$ gives decreasing returns to scale, and $a + b > 1$ gives increasing returns to scale.

19.4. $4 \times 3 = 12$ units.

19.5. True.

19.6. Yes.

## 20 Profit Maximization

20.1. Profits will decrease.

20.2. Profit would increase, since output would go up more than the cost of the inputs.

20.3. If the firm really had decreasing returns to scale, dividing the scale of all inputs by 2 would produce more than half as much output. Thus the subdivided firm would make more profits than the big firm. This is one argument why having everywhere decreasing returns to scale is implausible.

20.4. The gardener has ignored opportunity costs. In order to accurately account for the true costs, the gardener must include the cost of her own time used in the production of the crop, even if no explicit wage was paid.

20.5. Not in general. For example, consider the case of uncertainty.

20.6. Increase.

20.7. The use of $x_1$ does not change, and profits will increase.

20.8. May not.

## 21 Cost Minimization

21.1. Since profit is equal to total revenue minus total costs, if a firm is not minimizing costs then there exists a way for the firm to increase profits; however, this contradicts the fact that the firm is a profit maximizer.

21.2. Increase the use of factor 1 and decrease the use of factor 2.

21.3. Since the inputs are identically priced perfect substitutes, the firm will be indifferent between which of the inputs it uses. Thus the firm will use any amounts of the two inputs such that $x_1 + x_2 = y$.

21.4. The demand for paper either goes down or stays constant.

21.5. It implies that $\sum_{i=1}^{n} \Delta w_i \Delta x_i \leq 0$, where $\Delta w_i = w_i^t - w_i^s$ and $\Delta x_i = x_i^t - x_i^s$.

## 22 Cost Curves

22.1. True, true, false.

22.2. By simultaneously producing more output at the second plant and reducing production at the first plant, the firm can reduce costs.

22.3. False.

## 23 Firm Supply

23.1. The inverse supply curve is $p = 20y$, so the supply curve is $y = p/20$.

23.2. Set $AC = MC$ to find $10y + 1000/y = 20y$. Solve to get $y^* = 10$.

23.3. Solve for $p$ to get $P_s(y) = (y - 100)/20$.

23.4. At 10 the supply is 40 and at 20 the supply is 80. The producer's surplus is composed of a rectangle of area $10 \times 40$ plus a triangle of area $\frac{1}{2} \times 10 \times 40$, which gives a total change in producer's surplus of 600. This is the same as the change in profits, since the fixed costs don't change.

23.5. The supply curve is given by $y = p/2$ for all $p \geq 2$, and $y = 0$ for all $p \leq 2$. At $p = 2$ the firm is indifferent between supplying 1 unit of output or not supplying it.

23.6. Mostly technical (in more advanced models this could be market), market, could be either market or technical, technical.

23.7. That all firms in the industry take the market price as given.

23.8. The market price. A profit-maximizing firm will set its output such that the marginal cost of producing the last unit of output is equal to its marginal revenue, which in the case of pure competition is equal to the market price.

23.9. The firm should produce zero output (with or without fixed costs).

23.10. In the short run, if the market price is greater than the average variable cost, a firm should produce some output even though it is losing money. This is true because the firm would have lost more had it not produced since it must still pay fixed costs. However, in the long run there are no fixed costs, and therefore any firm that is losing money can produce zero output and lose a maximum of zero dollars.

23.11. The market price must be equal to the marginal cost of production for all firms in the industry.

## 24 Industry Supply

24.1. The inverse supply curves are $P_1(y_1) = 10 + y_1$ and $P_2(y_2) = 15 + y_2$. When the price is below 10 neither firm supplies output. When the price is 15 firm 2 will enter the market, and at any price above 15, both firms are in the market. Thus the kink occurs at a price of 15.

24.2. In the short run, the consumers pay the entire amount of the tax. In the long run it is paid by the producers.

24.3. False. A better statement would be: convenience stores can charge high prices because they are near the campus. Because of the high prices the stores are able to charge, the landowners can in turn charge high rents for the use of the convenient location.

24.4. True.

24.5. The profits or losses of the firms that are currently operating in the industry.

24.6. Flatter.

24.7. No, it does not violate the model. In accounting for the costs we failed to value the rent on the license.


## 25 Monopoly

25.1. No. A profit-maximizing monopolist would never operate where the demand for its product was inelastic.

25.2. First solve for the inverse demand curve to get $p(y) = 50 - y/2$. Thus the marginal revenue is given by $MR(y) = 50 - y$. Set this equal to marginal cost of 2, and solve to get $y = 48$. To determine the price, substitute into the inverse demand function, $p(48) = 50 - 48/2 = 26$.

25.3. The demand curve has a constant elasticity of $-3$. Using the formula $p[1 + 1/\epsilon] = MC$, we substitute to get $p[1 - 1/3] = 2$. Solving, we get $p = 3$. Substitute back into the demand function to get the quantity produced: $D(3) = 10 \times 3^{-3}$.

25.4. The demand curve has a constant elasticity of $-1$. Thus marginal revenue is zero for all levels of output. Hence it can never be equal to marginal cost.

25.5. For a linear demand curve the price rises by half the change in cost. In this case, the answer is $3.

25.6. In this case $p = kMC$, where $k = 1/(1 - 1/3) = 3/2$. Thus the price rises by $9.

25.7. Price will be two times marginal cost.

25.8. A subsidy of 50 percent, so the marginal costs facing the monopolist are half the actual marginal costs. This will ensure that price equals marginal cost at the monopolist's choice of output.

25.9. A monopolist operates where $p(y) + y\delta p/\delta y = MC(y)$. Rearranging, we have $p(y) = MC(y) - y\delta p/\delta y$. Since demand curves have a negative slope, we know that $\delta p/\delta y < 0$, which proves that $p(y) > MC(y)$.

25.10. False. Imposing a tax on a monopolist may cause the market price to rise more than, the same as, or less than the amount of the tax.

25.11. A number of problems arise, including: determining the true marginal costs for the firm, making sure that all customers will be served, and ensuring that the monopolist will not make a loss at the new price and output level.

25.12. Some appropriate conditions are: large fixed costs and small marginal costs, large minimum efficient scale relative to the market, ease of collusion, etc.

## 26 Monopoly Behavior

26.1. Yes, if it can perfectly price discriminate.

26.2. $p_i = \epsilon_i c/(1 + \epsilon_i)$ for $i = 1, 2$.

26.3. If he can perfectly price discriminate, he can extract the entire consumers' surplus; if he can charge for admission, he can do the same. Hence, the monopolist does equally well under either pricing policy. (In practice, it is much easier to charge for admission than to charge a different price for every ride.)

26.4. This is third-degree price discrimination. Apparently the Disneyland administrators believe that residents of Southern California have more elastic demands than other visitors to their park.

## 27 Factor Markets

27.1. Sure. A monopsonist can produce at any level of supply elasticity.

27.2. Since the supply of labor would exceed the demand for labor at such a wage, we would presumably see unemployment.

27.3. We find the equilibrium prices by substituting into the demand functions. Since $p = a - by$, we can use the solution for $y$ to find

$$p = \frac{3a + c}{4}.$$

Since $k = a - 2bx$, we can use the solution for $x$ to find

$$k = \frac{a + c}{2}.$$

## 28 Oligopoly

28.1. In equilibrium each firm will produce $(a - c)/3b$, so the total industry output is $2(a - c)/3b$.

28.2. Nothing. Since all firms have the same marginal cost, it doesn't matter which of them produces the output.

28.3. No, because one of the choices open to the Stackelberg leader is to choose the level of output it would have in the Cournot equilibrium. So it always has to be able to do at least this well.

28.4. We know from the text that we must have $p[1 - 1/n|\epsilon|] = MC$. Since $MC > 0$, and $p > 0$, we must have $1 - 1/n|\epsilon| > 0$. Rearranging this inequality gives the result.

28.5. Make $f_2(y_1)$ steeper than $f_1(y_2)$.

28.6. In general, no. Only in the case of the Bertrand solution does price equal the marginal cost.

## 29 Game Theory

29.1. The second player will defect in response to the first player's (mistaken) defection. But then the first player will defect in response to that, and each player will continue to defect in response to the other's defection! This example shows that tit-for-tat may not be a very good strategy when players can make mistakes in either their actions or their perceptions of the other player's actions.

29.2. Yes and no. A player prefers to play a dominant strategy regardless of the strategy of the opponent (even if the opponent plays her own dominant strategy). Thus, if all of the players are using dominant strategies then it is the case that they are all playing a strategy that is optimal given the strategy of their opponents, and therefore a Nash equilibrium exists. However, not all Nash equilibria are dominant strategy equilibria; for example, see Table 29.2.

29.3. Not necessarily. We know that your Nash equilibrium strategy is the best thing for you to do as long as your opponent is playing her Nash equilibrium strategy, but if she is not then perhaps there is a better strategy for you to pursue.

29.4. Formally, if the prisoners are allowed to retaliate the payoffs in the game may change. This could result in a Pareto efficient outcome for the game (for example, think of the case where the prisoners both agree that they will kill anyone who confesses, and assume death has a very low utility).

29.5. The dominant Nash equilibrium strategy is to defect in every round. This strategy is derived via the same backward induction process that was used to derive the finite 10-round case. The experimental evidence using much smaller time periods seems to indicate that players rarely use this strategy.

29.6. The equilibrium has player B choosing left and player A choosing top. Player B prefers to move first since that results in a payoff of 9 versus a payoff of 1. (Note, however, that moving first is not always advantageous in a sequential game. Can you think of an example?)

## 30 Game Applications

30.1. In a Nash equilibrium, each player is making a best response to the other player's best response. In a dominant strategy equilibrium, each player's choice is a best response to any choice the other player makes.

30.2. No, because when $r = 1/3$ there is an infinity of best responses, not a single one, as is required for the mathematical definition of a function.

30.3. Not necessarily; it depends on the payoffs of the game. In chicken if both choose to drive straight they receive the worst payoff.

30.4. It is row's expected payoff in the equilibrium strategy of kicking to the left with probability .7, while column jumps to the left with probability .6. We have to sum the payoffs to row over four events: the probability row kicks left and column defends left × row's payoff in this case + probability row kicks right and column defends left × row's payoff in this case, and so on. The numbers are $(.7)(.6)50 + (.7)(.4)80 + (.3)(.6)90 + (.3)(.4)20 = 62$.

30.5. He means that he will bid low in order to get the contract, but then charge high prices subsequently for any changes. The client has to go along, since it is costly for him to switch in the middle of a job.

## 31 Behavioral Economics

31.1. The first group is more likely to buy, due to the "framing effect."

31.2. The "bracketing effect" makes it likely that the meals chosen by Mary will have more variety.

31.3. From the viewpoint of classical consumer theory, more choice is better. But it is certainly possible that too much choice could confuse the employees, so 10 might be a safer choice. If you did decide to offer 50 mutual funds, it would be a good idea to group them into a relatively small number of categories.

31.4. The probability of heads coming up 3 times in a row is $\frac{1}{2} \times \frac{1}{2} \times \frac{1}{2} = \frac{1}{8} = .125$. The probability of tails coming up in a row is also $.125$, so the probability of a run of 3 heads or tails is .25.

31.5. It is called "time inconsistency."

## 32 Exchange

32.1. Yes. For example, consider the allocation where one person has everything. Then the other person is worse off at this allocation than he would be at an allocation where he had something.

32.2. No. For this would mean that at the allegedly Pareto efficient allocation there is some way to make everyone better off, contradicting the assumption of Pareto efficiency.

32.3. If we know the contract curve, then any trading should end up somewhere on the curve; however, we don't know where.

32.4. Yes, but not without making someone else worse off.

32.5. The value of excess demand in the remaining two markets must sum to zero.

## 33 Production

33.1. Giving up 1 coconut frees up $6 worth of resources that could be used to produce 2 pounds (equals $6 worth) of fish.

33.2. A higher wage would produce a steeper isoprofit line, implying that the profit maximizing level for the firm would occur at a point to the left of the current equilibrium, entailing a lower level of labor demand. However, under this new budget constraint Robinson will want to supply more than the required level of labor (why?) and therefore the labor market will not be in equilibrium.

33.3. Given a few assumptions, an economy that is in competitive equilibrium is Pareto efficient. It is generally recognized that this is a good thing for a society since it implies that there are no opportunities to make any individual in the economy better off without hurting someone else. However, it may be that the society would prefer a different distribution of welfare; that is, it may be that society prefers making one group better off at the expense of another group.

33.4. He should produce more fish. His marginal rate of substitution indicates that he is willing to give up two coconuts for an additional fish. The marginal rate of transformation implies that he only has to give up one coconut to get an additional fish. Therefore, by giving up a single coconut (even though he would have been willing to give up two) he can have an additional fish.

33.5. Both would have to work 9 hours per day. If they both work for 6 hours per day (Robinson producing coconuts, and Friday catching fish) and give half of their total production to the other, they can produce the same output. The reduction in the hours of work from 9 to 6 hours per day is due to rearranging production based on each individual's comparative advantage.

## 34 Welfare

34.1. The major shortcoming is that there are many allocations that cannot be compared—there is no way to decide between any two Pareto efficient allocations.

34.2. It would have the form: $W(u_1, \ldots, u_n) = \max\{u_1, \ldots, u_n\}$.

34.3. Since the Nietzschean welfare function cares only about the best off individual, welfare maxima for this allocation would typically involve one person getting everything.

34.4. Suppose that this is not the case. Then each individual envies someone else. Let's construct a list of who envies whom. Person A envies someone—call him person B. Person B in turn envies someone—say person C. And so on. But eventually we will find someone who envies someone who came earlier in the list. Suppose the cycle is "C envies D envies E envies C." Then consider the following swap: C gets what D has, D gets what E has, and E gets what C has. Each person in the cycle gets a bundle that he prefers, and thus each person is made better off. But then the original allocation couldn't have been Pareto efficient!

34.5. First vote between $x$ and $z$, and then vote between the winner ($z$) and $y$. First pair $x$ and $y$, and then vote between the winner ($x$) and $z$. The fact that the social preferences are intransitive is responsible for this agenda-setting power.

## 35 Externalities

35.1. True. Usually, efficiency problems can be eliminated by the delineation of property rights. However, when we impose property rights we are also imposing an endowment, which may have important distributional consequences.

35.2. False.

35.3. Come on, your roommates aren't all bad ...

35.4. The government could just give away the optimal number of grazing rights. Another alternative would be to sell the grazing rights. (Question: how much would these rights sell for? Hint: think about rents.) The government could also impose a tax, $t$ per cow, such that $f(c^*)/c^* + t = a$.

## 36 Information Technology

36.1. They should be willing to pay up to \$50, since this is the present value of the profit they can hope to get from that customer in the long run.

36.2. Users would gravitate toward packages with the most users, since that would make it more convenient for them to exchange files and information about how to use the program.

36.3. In this case the profit maximization conditions are identical. If two people share a video, the producer would just double the price and make exactly the same profits.

## 37 Public Goods

37.1. We want the sum of the marginal rates of substitution to equal the marginal cost of providing the public good. The sum of the MRSs is 20 ($= 10 \times 2$), and the marginal cost is $2x$. Thus we have the equation $2x = 20$, which implies that $x = 10$. So the Pareto efficient number of streetlights is 10.

## 38 Asymmetric Information

38.1. Since only the low-quality cars get exchanged in equilibrium and there is a surplus of $200 per transaction, the total surplus created is $50 \times 200 =$ $10,000$.

38.2. If the cars were assigned randomly, the average surplus per transaction would be the average willingness to pay, $1800, minus the average willingness to sell, $1500. This gives an average surplus of $300 per transaction and there are 100 transactions, so we get a total surplus of $30,000, which is much better than the market solution.

38.3. We know from the text that the optimal incentive plan takes the form $s(x) = wx + K$. The wage $w$ must equal the marginal product of the worker, which in this case is 1. The constant $K$ is chosen so that the worker's utility at the optimal choice is $\bar{u} = 0$. The optimal choice of $x$ occurs where price, 1, equals marginal cost, $x$, so $x^* = 1$. At this point the worker gets a utility of $x^* + K - c(x^*) = 1 + K - 1/2 = 1/2 + K$. Since the worker's utility must equal 0, it follows that $K = -1/2$.

38.4. We saw in the last answer that the profits at the optimal level of production are $1/2$. Since $\bar{u} = 0$, the worker would be willing to pay $1/2$ to rent the technology.

38.5. If the worker is to achieve a utility level of 1, the firm would have to give the worker a lump-sum payment of $1/2$.

# INDEX